COPYRIGHT FOR THE NINETIES

CONTEMPORARY
LEGAL EDUCATION SERIES

Copyright for the Nineties

CASES AND MATERIALS

Fourth Edition

ROBERT A. GORMAN
Kenneth W. Gemmill
   Professor of Law
University of Pennsylvania

JANE C. GINSBURG
Morton L. Janklow Professor of Literary
   and Artistic Property Law
Columbia University

THE MICHIE COMPANY
Law Publishers
CHARLOTTESVILLE, VIRGINIA

Library of Congress Catalog Card No. 93-80499
ISBN 1-55834-110-2

To

George, Paul and Clara

and to

Caryl, Mark, Andrew and Jeffrey

Preface

In the four years since the third edition was published, there has been an exponential growth in the attention being paid to Copyright — by courts (especially the Supreme Court), by Congress, by owners of intellectual property, and by the public. The law of Copyright determines the extent of ownership rights in all manner of creative products — embodied in books, plays, theatrical and television films, recordings, computer software, and other forms of expression. This is a period in which these creations of the mind have vastly increased in value, in the United States and abroad, as the public seems to have developed an unlimited appetite for them, in an increasing number of media. We are never very far from our television screen, or our portable compact disc or cassette player, or our video rental store, or our notebook computer.

Along with this enhanced appetite has come an equally enhanced capacity to replicate these works without the authority of their owners. Photocopy machines have become faster and more versatile; home taping equipment permits copying musical recordings with a fidelity essentially as high as the original's; computer software can be copied instantaneously; and the computer has become perhaps our most powerful device for making copies (and potentially for creating derivative works based thereon), through disk-to-disk reproduction, or by downloading from an electronic data base, or by scanning hard-copy texts.

Little wonder that as copyrights have become more valuable, and as the means of unauthorized use and exploitation have multiplied (by persons and in settings often difficult to detect and monitor), litigation and demands for legislative reform have increased. So, too, has the interest in international and foreign copyright law. The Founders of the Nation appreciated that books traveled easily across state boundaries and were not likely to be satisfactorily regulated by the individual states. Today, copyrighted properties are being distributed and exploited in ever greater dimensions across national boundaries; hence, the growing importance of international treaties and conflict of laws.

This fourth edition of *Copyright for the Nineties* reflects these rapid, complex and important developments. The Supreme Court, whose slow but steady diet of copyright cases had been at the rate of perhaps one case per half-century, has decided three major cases in the past four years — dealing with fundamental issues of authorship and the protection of compilations, ownership of copyright under the "work made for hire" doctrine, and the extent of licensed "derivative" rights during the renewal term of an underlying copyrighted work — and at this writing has two more cases on its docket.

The lower courts have also been busily elaborating upon the copyright statute, particularly as to such relatively new — and highly valuable — media as computer software. Major decisions have been rendered concerning the scope of copyright protection for "nonliteral" elements of a computer program (sometimes referred to as "structure, sequence and organization"), the proper analysis of infringement in a software case, the extent of protection of "user interface" (such as screen menus and icons and keystroke sequences), and the application of the fair use doctrine to "reverse engineering." So too, courts have with increasing frequency had to interpret the language of grants made half a century ago, to determine whether those grants embrace such unforeseen uses as videocassette distribution. The courts have also been asked to decide, in two highly visible cases, whether photocopying of copyrighted materials falls within the fair use exception — when a commercial copy center prepares packets of copied material for university classroom use, and when researchers working for a profitmaking company make single copies of journal articles for personal convenience on the job.

Since the third edition of this casebook, the Copyright Act — which had just then been amended in the most fundamental respects (with respect to copyright notice) so as to permit accession of the U.S. to the Berne Convention — has been amended and re-amended several times over.

These statutory changes, some of profound significance, have eliminated registration as a prerequisite for suing to enforce some copyrights; granted automatic renewal for works first published from 1964 to 1977 (for which the format of an initial 28-year term still applies); granted visual artists "moral rights," familiar to Europe and Latin America, of integrity and attribution; granted protection to architectural works against their unauthorized construction; clarified that home audiotaping is not an infringement, while creating a fund (from the sales of tapes and tape machines) for songwriters and publishers, and for performers and recording companies; clarified the status of unpublished copyrighted works under the doctrine of fair use; banned the commercial rental of computer software; and made states subject to copyright infringement liability.

Even as this book goes to press, there are hard-fought efforts underway to change the statute even further — most significantly by eliminating altogether the need for registration in order to sue and to secure enhanced damages; and by eliminating the Copyright Royalty Tribunal (created by the 1976 Act to administer the several compulsory-license funds), and replacing it with ad hoc arbitration royalty panels. Users of this fourth edition should thus be alert for imminent judicial and legislative developments — and the authors will surely reflect them in the inevitable periodic supplements.

When we began revising *Copyright For the Nineties* for this fourth edition, we requested suggestions from copyright teachers who had adopted the book for classroom use. We received an encouragingly large number of helpful suggestions, many of which we have incorporated; we would especially like to thank Professors Benjamin Kaplan, Shira Perlmutter, Leo J. Raskind, Pamela Samuelson, and Alfred C. Yen. We also express our gratitude to Paul Smith, Columbia Law School class of 1993, and Judy Polachek, Columbia Law School class of 1994, for general research assistance, and to Ariel Reich, Columbia Law School class of 1993, for revisions of the materials on copyright protection for computer programs.

Robert A. Gorman   Jane C. Ginsburg

October 1993

Summary Table of Contents

Table of Contents

Page

Anno Octavo

Annæ Reginæ.

An Act for the Encouragement of Learning, by Vesting the Copies of Printed Books in the Authors or Purchasers of such Copies, during the Times therein mentioned.

Whereas Printers, Booksellers, and other Persons have of late frequently taken the Liberty of Printing, Reprinting, and Publishing, or causing to be Printed, Reprinted, and Published Books, and other Writings, without the Consent of the Authors or Proprietors of such Books and Writings, to their very great Detriment, and too often to the Ruin of them and their Families: For Preventing therefore such Practices for the future, and for the Encouragement of Learned Men to Compose and Write useful Books; May it please Your Majesty, that it may be Enacted, and be it Enacted by the Queens most Excellent Majesty, by and with the Advice and Consent of the Lords Spiritual and Temporal, and Commons in this present Parliament Assembled, and by the Authority of the same, That from and after the Tenth Day of April, One thousand seven hundred and ten, the Author of any Book or Books already Printed, who hath not Transferred to any other the Copy or Copies of such Book or Books, Share or Shares thereof, or the Bookseller or Booksellers, Printer or Printers, or other Person or Persons, who hath or have Purchased or Acquired the Copy or Copies of any Book or Books, in order to Print or Reprint the same, shall have the sole Right and Liberty of Printing such Book and Books for the Term of One and twenty Years, to Commence from the said Tenth Day of April, and no longer; and that the Author of any Book or Books already Composed and not Printed and Published, or that shall hereafter be Composed, and his Assignee, or Assigns, shall have the sole Liberty of Printing and Reprinting such Book and Books for the Term of Four-

6   Ttt 2   teen

Chapter 1

THE CONCEPT OF COPYRIGHT

A. HISTORICAL PERSPECTIVE

1. ENGLAND AND THE STATUTE OF ANNE

Our whole law relating to literary and artistic property is essentially an inheritance from England. It seems that from the time "whereof the memory of man runneth not to the contrary," the author's right to his or her manuscript was recognized on principles of natural justice, being the product of intellectual labor and as much the author's own property as the substance on which it was written. Blackstone, 2 Commentaries 405, associates it with the Law of Occupancy, which involves personal labor and results in "property," something peculiarly one's own (as implied by the Latin root "proprius"). But ages before Blackstone, an Irish king had enunciated the same principle in settling the question of property rights in a manuscript: "To every cow her calf."

When printing from type was invented and works could be reproduced in quantities for circulation, however, it seems that the author was without protection as soon as the work got into print.

In 1556, the Stationers' Company, made up of the leading publishers of London, was established by royal decree for the primary purpose of checking the spread of the Protestant Reformation by concentrating the whole printing business in the hands of the members of that company. Printing was subject to the orders of the Star Chamber so that the Government and the Church could exercise effective censorship and prevent seditious or heretical works from getting into print. Hallam, 1 Constitutional History 238. This was essentially a means of controlling the press and in no sense afforded protection to authors.

Under this decree all published works had to be entered in the register of the Stationers' Company and in the name of some member of that company. By virtue of this entry, and supported by the Star Chamber, the stationer successfully claimed the sole right to print and publish the work for himself, his heirs, and assigns forever. In the course of time, and especially after the last of the old Licensing Acts expired in 1694, the ban against unlicensed printing was lifted and independent printers began to spring up and invade the sacred domain of the Stationers' Company. As a result, the company applied to Parliament for a law to protect its alleged rights in perpetuity against these pirates. As the event turned out, the stationers got much less than they had reckoned on, for Parliament, instead of recognizing their perpetual rights, proceeded to pass a law limiting the exclusive right of publication to a paltry term of years. Drone, Law of Property in Intellectual Productions 69 (1879).

This law was the celebrated Statute of Anne (8 Anne c. 19, 1710), the first statute of all time specifically to recognize the rights of authors and the foundation of all subsequent legislation on the subject of copyright both here and abroad. *See* Ransom, The First Copyright Statute (1956). Because of its historical importance in relation to the study of our own copyright laws, it is well to note some of its provisions.

Title.

"An Act for the Encouragement of Learning, by Vesting the Copies of Printed Books in the Authors or Purchasers of such Copies, during the Times therein mentioned."

Preamble.

"Whereas Printers, Booksellers and other Persons have of late frequently taken the Liberty of Printing, Reprinting, and Publishing ... Books and other Writings without the Consent of the Authors or Proprietors ... to their very great Detriment, and too often to the Ruin of them and their Families:

For Preventing therefore such Practices for the future, and for the Encouragement of Learned Men to Compose and write useful Books; May it please your Majesty that it may be Enacted ...."

Key Provisions.

1. Exclusive right of author of new work to print book for fourteen years;
2. Renewal period of fourteen years if author living;
3. Registration requirement
   a. register title at Stationers' Hall
   b. deposit nine copies at official libraries;
4. "... if any other Bookseller, Printer, or other Person whatsoever, ... shall Print, Reprint or Import ... any such Book or Books without the Consent of the Proprietor ... then such Offender or Offenders shall forfeit such Book or Books to the Proprietor or Proprietors of the Copy thereof, who shall forthwith Damask and make Waste Paper of them; and further, that every such Offender or Offenders shall forfeit one Penny for every Sheet which shall be found in his, her, or their Custody."

Interesting Sidelights.

1. "Provided, That nothing in this Act contained do extend, or shall be construed to extend, to Prohibit the Importation, Vending, or Selling of any Books in Greek, Latin, or any other Foreign Language Printed beyond the Seas; Any thing in this Act contained to the contrary notwithstanding."
2. It was further provided that if any printer or bookseller shall sell any book "at such a Price or Rate as shall be Conceived by any Person or Persons to be High and Unreasonable;" then such person may "make Complaint thereof to the Lord Archbishop of Canterbury for the time being; the Lord Chancellor, or Lord Keeper of the Great Seal of Great Britain for the time being; the Lord Bishop of London for the time being;

[or other judges or Government or academic officials] who ... shall and have hereby full Power and Authority from time to time, to Send for, Summon, or Call before him or them such Bookseller or Booksellers, Printer or Printers, and to Examine and Enquire of the reason of the Dearness and Inhauncement of the Price or Value of such Book or Books by him or them so Sold or Exposed to Sale; and if upon such Enquiry and Examination it shall be found, that the Price of such Book or Books is Inhaunced, or any wise too High or Unreasonable, Then and in such case the said [official shall] have hereby full Power and Authority to Reform and Redress the same, and to Limit and Settle the Price of every such Printed Book and Books, from time to time, according to the best of their Judgments, and as to them shall seem Just and Reasonable; ....

In such case the offending bookseller or printer had to pay costs and give public notice of the new, limited price. Any bookseller or printer selling in excess of such price

shall Forfeit the Sum of Five Pounds for every such Book so by him, her, or them Sold or Exposed to Sale, One Moiety thereof to the Queens most Excellent Majesty, Her Heirs and Successors, and the other Moiety to any Person or Persons that shall Sue for the Same, to be Recovered, with Costs of Suit, in any of Her Majesties Courts of Record at Westminster, by Action of Debt, Bill, Plaint or Information, in which no Wager of Law, Essoign, Privilege or Protection, or more than one Imparlance shall be allowed.

So far as existing works were concerned, the statute provided that the "authors or their assigns" should have the sole right of publication for twenty-one years, but it will be noted that for new works the right was to run for fourteen years, and the author, if living at the expiration of such term, was granted the privilege of renewal for fourteen more years. Suitable penalties were provided for violation of the Act, but conditioned always upon entry of the title of the work in the Register books of the Stationers' Hall as evidence of ownership and deposit of copies of the work itself in certain designated libraries of the Kingdom. Somewhat later, as a further security to the general public so that "none may offend through ignorance of the copyright," the provision for notice of such entry was required to appear on every copy of the published work.

While the statute seemed plain enough, the stationers nevertheless still contended that their perpetual rights were not taken away but that the purpose of the Act was merely to enable them to obtain speedier relief against piracy, this being the only thing they had sought from Parliament in the first place. For more than half a century the lower courts sustained them in this view by granting many injunctions, even after the expiration of the term fixed by the statute. But in the famous case of *Donaldson v. Becket*, 4 Burr. (4th ed.) 2408, 2417, 98 Eng. Rep. 257, 262 (H.L. 1774), the House of Lords overruled a case decided only five years earlier by the King's Bench, *Millar v. Taylor*, 4 Burr. (4th ed.) 2303, 98 Eng. Rep. 201 (K.B. 1769), and determined that copyright (i.e., the exclusive right to publish and sell copies) had never existed as a right at common law. The full House of Lords thus rejected the divided decision of the judicial branch of the House of Lords, which had ruled that copyright had existed at common law; that prior to adoption of the Statute of Anne, common-law copyright existed in perpetuity even after publication of the work; but that (according to some reports of the decision) the Statute of Anne substituted a limited term of statutory protection with regard to published works. (Other reports of the decision indicate that a bare majority of the judges determined that the Statute of Anne did not in any way limit common-law copyright.) The various opinions of the judges of the House of Lords and the decision of the full House in *Donaldson v. Becket* are meticulously examined in Abrams, *The Historic Foundation of American Copyright Law: Exploding the Myth of Common Law Copyright,* 29 Wayne L. Rev. 1119, 1156-71, 1188-91 (1983).

The Statute of Anne expressly sanctioned the importation of books in foreign languages without the recognition of any rights on the part of the foreign authors; but it said nothing about importation of books in English printed or reprinted abroad. Such a contingency seemed out of the question, as the printing business had not as yet become a flourishing institution in the Colonies. But later on, had Benjamin Franklin chosen to enlarge his printing plant, it is conceivable that books rather than tea might well have become the bone of contention leading to the Revolution.

The Statute of Anne has long been treated as a startling result of the parliamentary process. Perhaps the most significant shift in English law was its recognition of the rights of authors, and not merely those of printers and booksellers. Equally dramatic, but less frequently noted, is its reflection of consumerism, eighteenth century style. Thus, one finds the inclusion of a provision for judicial rate-making in the very first Anglo-American copyright law, triggered by the copyright proprietor's sales of books at "High and Unreasonable" prices.

Although this pro-consumer approach in England was repealed in 1739, supposedly as ineffective (see Ransom, The First Copyright Statute 107 n.13 (1956)), it was followed in the last quarter of the eighteenth century by several colonial statutes in America. Indeed the statutes of New York, Connecticut and Georgia provided for a remedy not only for unreasonably high prices, but for insufficient editions as well. (These remarkable provisions might be viewed as early examples of a "compulsory license," see pp. 45-46 *infra.*) For other provisions of the colonial statutes, see Crawford, *Pre-Constitutional Copyright Statutes,* 23 Bull. Copyright Soc'y 11 (1975).

2. THE COLONIES AND THE CONSTITUTION

After the close of the Revolution, all of the Colonies except Delaware passed laws to afford a measure of protection to authors, pursuant to a recommendation of the Continental Congress, 24 Journals, Continental Congress 326 (1783), and the entreaties of Noah Webster. While many states patterned their statutes after the Statute of Anne, many others mingled natural rights rhetoric with the more utilitarian inspiration of the English model. See Massachusetts, Act of March 17, 1783, the preamble to which states:

> Whereas the improvement of knowledge, the progress of civilization, the public weal of the community, and the advancement of human happiness, greatly depend on the efforts of learned and ingenious persons in the various arts and sciences: As the principal encouragement such persons can have to make great and beneficial exertions of this nature, must exist in the legal security of the fruits of their study and industry to themselves; and as such security is one of the natural rights of all men, there being no property more peculiarly a man's own than that which is procured by the labor of his mind.

Reprinted in Solberg ed., Copyright Enactments of the United States 14 (1906). Connecticut, New Hampshire, Rhode Island, North Carolina, Georgia, and New York also enacted copyright laws combining natural rights and public-benefit rationales. *See* Solberg at 11, 18, 19, 25, 27, and 29.

But whatever the state copyright statute's philosophy, these laws were limited in their operation to the boundaries of each state. Hence, if an author in one state wished to secure protection for his work throughout the other states, he was obliged to comply with a multitude of laws. *See Hudson & Goodwin v. Patten,* 1 Root 133 (Conn. 1789), for a clash of interests between the assignees of copyright in different states. The same situation prevailed at that time in Europe, but on this side of the Atlantic, where all spoke the same language and read the same books, a uniform national law soon became imperative.

The framers of the Constitution, therefore, embodied in that immortal instrument a simple and direct clause empowering Congress "to promote the progress of science and useful arts, by securing for limited times to authors and inventors the exclusive right to their respective writings and discoveries." U.S. Const., art. I, sec. 8, cl. 8. *See* Fenning, *The Origin of the Patent and Copyright Clause of the Constitution,* 17 Geo. L.J. 109 (1929). It should be noted that this clause does not use the terms "copyrights" and "patents," but nevertheless covers both forms of property. The selection of the "writings" of "authors" terminology for copyrights was made by the committee on detail or style and the clause was adopted by the Constitutional Convention without debate.

Some contemporaneous light on the clause is often sought from the succinct, if not enigmatic, comment of Madison in The Federalist, No. 43 at 279 (Mod. Lib. ed. 1941):

> The utility of this power will scarcely be questioned. The copyright of authors has been solemnly adjudged, in Great Britain, to be a right of common law. The right to useful inventions seems with equal reason to belong to the inventors. The public good fully coincides in both cases with the claims of individuals. The States cannot separately make effectual provision for either of the cases, and most of them have anticipated the decision of this point, by laws passed at the instance of Congress.

3. THE FIRST UNITED STATES COPYRIGHT STATUTE

There is no committee report on the first federal Copyright Act of May 31, 1790, 1 Stat. 124, and the Act itself must be looked to for enlightenment as to its purpose and policy. Congress adopted the system of formalities and restrictions inaugurated by the old Statute of Anne, which, as we saw earlier, had been enacted purely as a municipal measure to replace the Licensing Acts and, incidentally, curb the pretentious claims to perpetual copyright on the part of the members of the Stationers' Company.

The Act of 1790 assured protection to the author or his assigns of any "map, chart or book " for fourteen years upon:

> (1) recording the title, prior to publication, in the register book of the clerk's office of the district court where the author or proprietor resided;
> (2) publishing a copy of the record so made in one or more newspapers for four weeks; and
> (3) depositing a copy of the work itself in the office of the Secretary of State within six months after publication.

The privilege of renewal of the copyright for fourteen more years was granted to the author or his assigns on condition of again entering the title and publishing the record. The renewal term, as in the Statute of Anne, was dependent on the survival of the author throughout the first term. By subsequent Act, 2 Stat. 171 (1802), the notice of entry, including the date thereof, was required to be inserted in every copy of the published work. Suitable penalties were provided in the case of infringement.

There was also a provision against the unauthorized use of an author's manuscript, thus recognizing the old common-law right before publication, without requiring the proprietor to observe any formality. With respect to published works, however, Congress seemed extremely solicitous to safeguard the public in general from offending against the Act and incurring the penalties through ignorance of the copyright claim. It is not clear why it was deemed necessary to shift the burden from those who might want to use the work to those who created it, but presumably it was because copyright is in the nature of a monopoly and, therefore, "odious in the eye of the law." Likewise, the courts at the beginning construed the Act very strictly and hence the author was obliged to proceed with the utmost caution along the tortuous copyright route lest any slip prove his undoing.

Wheaton v. Peters, 33 U.S. (8 Pet.) 591 (1834), like *Donaldson v. Becket* in England, posed the questions whether common-law copyright existed in the United States, and, if it did, whether and to what extent the enactment of the federal Copyright Act abrogated common-law copyright. Plaintiff Wheaton was a former Reporter for the United States Supreme Court. Defendant Peters, Wheaton's successor as Reporter, sought to publish "Consolidated Reports" of Supreme Court decisions. Peters' work included decisions previously reported in published volumes by Wheaton. Wheaton alleged infringement of his federal statutory and common-law copyrights in the reports.

The Supreme Court observed that while an author had the right at common law to prevent another from depriving him of his manuscript, and to prevent the unlawful publication of an unpublished work, the case raised the different question whether, once the work was published, the common law recognized a copyright in the form of "a perpetual and exclusive property in the future publication of the work."

The Court held there was no federal common-law copyright. Rather, the question would be resolved under the law of the state where Wheaton's work was published, Pennsylvania. In determining whether Pennsylvania recognized common-law copyright, the Court held that two matters must be addressed: First, did England recognize common-law copyright? Second, even if it did, did Pennsylvania adopt that aspect of the English common law or, alternatively, develop its own common-law copyright? Reviewing *Donaldson v. Becket*, the Supreme Court determined that the existence and scope of common-law copyright in England was "a question by no means free from doubt." The Court then ruled that, regardless of the state of common-law copyright in England, the concept had not been adopted in any form in England until after Pennsylvania had developed its own common law. The Court concluded that English common-law copyright was not part of the common law of Pennsylvania, and that Pennsylvania had not developed a common-law copyright of its own.

The Court went on to state its view that common-law copyright in published works had not existed in any state. Rather, the right to copy and sell published works was entirely a creation of Congress. Wheaton's sole recourse, then, was to federal statutory copyright. But Wheaton's federal statutory claim also failed because, upon publication of his work, Wheaton had not complied strictly with all the requirements of the Copyright Act. (The Court also observed, in passing, that no one was entitled to a copyright in the text of the Court's decisions.)

The Court's decision in *Wheaton v. Peters* thus did not address the question whether the federal Copyright Act would preempt state common-law copyright in published works. (Peters' counsel had argued that no preemption question was posed, because there was no state common-law copyright to interfere with the federal Copyright Act. Alternatively, he argued that the constitutional copyright clause vested in Congress the sole power to grant copyrights.) The subsistence and survival of state law rights in certain published works was upheld almost a century and a half later by the Supreme Court, in a five-to-four decision; without even citing *Wheaton v. Peters*, the Court introduced a limitation upon the preemptive effect of the federal statute. *Goldstein v. California*, 412 U.S. 546, 178 U.S.P.Q. 129 (1973), *infra*.

4. STATUTORY REVISION

Step by step after the 1790 statute, new subjects were added, and the scope and term of protection enlarged. In 1802, prints were added (2 Stat. 171); in 1831, musical compositions (4 Stat. 436), but not the right of public performance (this right came for the first time in 1897, Rev. Stat. § 4966). At the same time (1831), the first term was extended to twenty-eight years with the privilege of renewal for fourteen years solely to the author or his widow and children. In 1856, dramatic compositions, with the right of public performance thereof, were added (11 Stat. 138); in 1865, photographs (13 Stat. 540); in 1870, paintings, drawings, sculpture, and models or designs for works of the fine arts. This Act of 1870 (16 Stat. 212, Rev. Stat. § 4948-71) facilitated the whole process by centralizing the copyright business in the Library of Congress, then located in the Capitol Building.

It was about this time that the general movement for international copyright began to gather momentum and there was much agitation for it in this country as well as abroad. The result in the United States was the so-called International Copyright Act of 1891 (26 Stat. 1106), by the terms of which the copyright privilege was for the first time made available to foreigners — but only on the hard condition of their complying with the age-old requirements of entry of title, notice, and deposit, as well as that of American manufacture of "any book, photograph, chromo or lithograph." Thus it was essentially a national rather than an international measure, maintaining a good part of the century-old pattern of "encouraging learning" by granting incentives to *American* authors, while permitting pirating of most foreign works. There may have been some cultural, if not ethical, justification for allowing freebooters to offer inexpensive foreign reprints at a time when it could be said that no one "in the four quarters of the globe ... reads an American book." (Statement of Sidney Smith in 1820, quoted in *United Dictionary Co. v. Merriam Co.,* 208 U.S. 260, 264 (1908).) But toward the end of the nineteenth century it seemed to many, especially those abroad, that more than a token international protection was needed.

The result was the Berne Convention, which established an International Copyright Union in 1886. Under this Convention, as subsequently amended, protection was made automatic throughout all the countries acceding to it on behalf of the authors and artists of every country in the world, whether inside or outside of the Union, and without the need to comply with any formalities whatever, the sole condition being publication of the work in any Union country not later than the date of publication elsewhere. The protection of unpublished works under the Convention was and still is limited to citizens or residents of a Union country. Beginning with a membership of only ten countries, by January 1, 1993, 95 countries had adhered to the Berne Union, among them almost all of the leading countries of the world, including the United States and the People's Republic of China. Russia, however, remains outside the Berne Union. Periodic revisions of the Convention have taken place at Paris (1896), Berlin (1908), Rome (1928), Brussels (1948), Stockholm (1967), and Paris (1971). Discussions are now under way to draft a Protocol to the Berne Convention that may address a variety of problems spawned by new technology, as well as the neighboring rights of producers and performers.

5. THE 1909 ACT

The Copyright Act of 1909 — which, with minor amendments, was the law in force for the next sixty-eight years — was the outcome of several years of painstaking labor and extensive discussion on the part of every interest involved, including eminent members of the bar. Care was taken to use in the text, as far as possible, words and phrases that had already received judicial construction. In its final form, however, the Act was very largely a compromise measure, being a composite of several tentative bills and proposals embodying different points of view and interests. Changes appear to have often been made in one place without the necessary corresponding changes in other places. This process resulted in a lack of clarity and coherence in certain sections that caused no little perplexity in the practical administration of the Act, not to speak of disturbance in the mind of the interested public.

Moreover, the subsequent development of the motion picture, the phonograph, radio, television, and other techniques of aural and visual recording, together with changes in business methods and practices, created new factors to be considered. While the courts found the terms of the Act fairly adaptable to meet the situation, there was a lack of uniformity in their application to particular cases. However, some notable improvements over the old law were achieved in 1909, among which may be mentioned:

> (1) making the subject matter of copyright include "all the writings of an author" (this also caused problems);
> (2) exempting books of foreign origin in foreign languages from the requirement that they be reprinted in the United States (this being the greatest advance from the international standpoint);
> (3) in the case of published works, making copyright date from publication with the notice, instead of from the date of filing the title, which often took place long before the work was ready for publication;
> (4) making statutory copyright available for unpublished works designed for exhibition, performance, or oral delivery;
> (5) extending the renewal term of protection by fourteen years, to bring the possible maximum term of protection up to fifty-six years;
> (6) making the certificate of registration prima facie evidence of the facts recorded in relation to any work.

Nevertheless, this substantial progress fell far short of meeting the fundamental requisites of the Berne Convention, because the formalities of notice, deposit, and registration were retained, as well as the requirement of American manufacture of books and periodicals in the English language even though of foreign origin.

6. THE UNIVERSAL COPYRIGHT CONVENTION

Most of the attempted comprehensive revisions of our law after 1909 were motivated by an interest in United States membership in the Berne Union. *See* Goldman, *The History of U.S.A. Copyright Law Revision From 1901 to 1954*, 2 Studies on Copyright 1106 (Arthur Fisher mem. ed. 1963). The last unsuccessful attempt was the so-called "Shotwell Committee" bill of 1940. When activity was resumed after World War II, a new approach toward international copyright was taken. It was apparently recognized that comprehensive revision of the United States law to conform with the Berne Convention was then as unlikely as modification of the Convention to permit United States adherence. The formation of the United Nations and the establishment of UNESCO offered a new international organ through which some compromise might be reached. In 1952 success was achieved with the signing of the Universal Copyright Convention.

This multilateral treaty, which did not alter the obligations of the Berne Convention as among its adherents, offered a new route for international protection. Works by a national of a member nation, as well as works first published within its borders, were protected in every other member nation. Domestic formalities were excused if all published copies of the work bore a prescribed notice, or if the work remained unpublished. Although a member nation could not discriminate against protected foreigners, it could impose additional requirements with respect to works written by its own nationals or first published within its territory.

The United States in 1954 was one of the first nations to ratify this Convention, amending its domestic law slightly more than necessary to comply with its treaty obligations. Public Law 743, 83d Cong., 68 Stat. 1030 (1954). The Convention became effective in 1955. As of January 1, 1993, 89 nations had ratified the Universal Copyright Convention.

7. THE 1976 ACT

Notwithstanding the 1954 amendments, the American system under the 1909 Act contrasted sharply with most foreign copyright regimes; the latter have largely dispensed with formalities as a prerequisite to protection, as a result of which everything published therein is automatically protected against unauthorized copying. In the United States, however, in only a small percentage of the total number of literary, informational, musical, and artistic works published has the creator or his assigns been sufficiently interested to seek and perfect by registration the privileges of a statutory monopoly. The percentage varies with different classes of works, and music has constituted the largest class of all.

Despite the lingering argument by some that the American system had on the whole proved eminently suited to American needs, it had long been accepted that an intensive and objective examination of our law, with a view to its general revision, was overdue. *See, e.g.,* Note, *Revision of the Copyright Law,* 51 Harv. L. Rev. 906 (1938).

A comprehensive project along these lines was authorized by Congress in 1955. Under this authorization, the Copyright Office prepared a number of legal and factual studies of the major substantive problems inherent in any revision of the law. Distribution of these studies gave rise to the healthy interchange of ideas, comments, and suggestions necessary for the development of an improved law. (In addition, they serve as valuable research tools irrespective of their original purpose and have accordingly been published in an Arthur Fisher Memorial Edition in honor of the Register of Copyrights who launched the project.) In July 1961, Register Kaminstein submitted to Congress a detailed report of his tentative recommendations for revision with a view to the introduction, after further public comment, of a new proposed law. *Report of the Register of Copyrights on the General Revision of the U.S. Copyright Law, Report to House Committee on the Judiciary,* 87th Cong., 1st Sess. (1961) (hereinafter cited as *Register's Report of 1961*). (A 1965 *Supple-*

mentary Report and 1975 *Draft Second Supplementary Report* were later issued by the Register.)

During the next three years, a tentative draft and resulting comments led to the development and introduction in 1964 of H.R. 11947 and S. 3008, 88th Cong., 2d Sess. In 1965 and 1966 unusually extensive hearings followed, culminating in H.R. Rep. No. 83, 90th Cong., 1st Sess. (1967). In 1967, the House, but not the Senate, passed a revision bill, H.R. 2512, 90th Cong., 1st Sess. After a delay occasioned by political and technological issues, such as cable television and educational and library uses, the Senate passed S. 1361, 93d Cong., in 1974, and the substantially similar S. 22, 94th Cong., in February 1976. An important piece of legislative history is embodied in S. Rep. No. 94-473, 94th Cong., 1st Sess. (1975), which preceded the 1976 vote.

Another set of extensive hearings produced a House-passed version of S. 22 supported by another comprehensive Judiciary Committee report, H.R. Rep. No. 94-1476, 94th Cong., 2d Sess. (1976), which recapitulated significant segments of the tortuous legislative history. The differences between the chambers were resolved in a conference report, H.R. Rep. No. 94-1733, 94th Cong., 2d Sess. (1976), accepted by both houses, and the President approved Public Law 94-553, 90 Stat. 2541, on October 19, 1976.

The 1976 Act marked a significant philosophical departure from the centuries-old traditions reflected in the Statute of Anne, the first U.S. statute in 1790, and the 1909 statute. At the same time, much of the substance of the 1909 Act will remain with us, either directly or indirectly, well into the twenty-first century, if not indefinitely.

The key provisions of the new law included the following:

(1) A single federal system of protection for all "original works of authorship," published or unpublished, from the moment they are fixed in a tangible medium of expression. (Pertinent state law is expressly preempted.)

(2) A single term of protection generally measured by the life of the author(s) plus fifty years after his or her death, with a term based on publication (or creation, in the case of unpublished works) reserved only for special situations, such as works made for hire.

(3) A provision for an inalienable option in individual authors generally permitting termination of any transfer after thirty-five years, but with the transferee still permitted to exploit derivative works produced under the transfer before it was terminated.

(4) A provision for notice on visually perceptible copies distributed to the public, with some flexibility as to the form and position of the notice, curative provisions for notice deficiencies, and incentives for use of a proper notice, as well as for prompt registration.

(5) Recognition of a fair use limitation on exclusive rights (with an indication of the criteria for its applicability) as well as other limitations in favor of nonprofit, library, educational, and public broadcasting uses.

(6) Imposition of copyright liability on cable television systems and jukeboxes that use copyrighted material, but subject to compulsory license provisions and other limitations.

(7) Establishment of a Copyright Royalty Tribunal to review or establish rates under compulsory licenses and to provide for certain distributions to claimants under such licenses.

(8) Protection of unpublished works regardless of the nationality of the author, as well as contraction and scheduled deletion of the requirement of domestic manufacture of books.

(9) Provisions implementing divisibility of copyright ownership.

During the long progress of the revision effort, three significant matters were resolved by separate legislative action. First, beginning on September 19, 1962, terms of renewal copyrights that would otherwise have expired were extended so as to bring these copyrights under the protection of the new Act. Second, in 1971 and 1974, limited federal copyright protection was extended to recorded performances insofar as duplication of recordings was concerned, but not as to independently recorded imitation of sound or as to the performance of the recordings. Third, a National Commission on New Technological Uses of Copyrighted Works (CONTU) was established to study new technology, such as computers and reprography, for recommendation to Congress of detailed provisions to replace the stopgap provisions in the 1976 Act governing these fast-moving areas. In this connection, the frustrating history of decades of attempts to revise the 1909 Act seems to have convinced Congress to provide machinery for the amendment of the 1976 Act before it had even become effective. Several amendments were recommended by CONTU in its Final Report of July 31, 1978 and were adopted by Congress on December 12, 1980. Pub. L. 96-517. *See* Chapter 7, Subchapter A, *infra*. Several other amendments, narrow in scope, have been enacted since 1976, and will be discussed below.

8. THE 1988 AMENDMENTS IMPLEMENTING UNITED STATES ADHERENCE TO THE BERNE CONVENTION

In October 1988, the United States at last ratified the Berne Convention. Changes in our internal copyright law accompanied the ratification. Congress determined that the Berne Convention's substantive provisions were not self-executing; i.e., that the Convention's mandates were not directly incorporated into domestic law, but must be implemented by domestic legislation. As a result, Congress amended the copyright law to remove those inconsistencies with Berne standards which still persisted under the 1976 Act.

The most significant of these amendments include modification of the provision on notice of copyright to make notice optional rather than mandatory; elimination of the need, as a prerequisite to suit, to record transfers of rights; and initial substitution of negotiated licenses for the previous "compulsory license" publicly to perform musical compositions on jukeboxes (the compulsory license remained as a residual measure in the event private negotiations fail). The legislation also modifies the registration provisions of the Act but only with respect to Berne works of foreign origin. Claimants in these works need no longer register as a prerequisite to suit (fulfillment of these formalities remains necessary, however, to obtain certain enhanced remedies). Presuit registration remains required for works of U.S. origin.

9. SUBSEQUENT AMENDMENTS TO THE 1976 COPYRIGHT ACT

In 1990, and again in 1992, Congress made further substantial changes in the copyright law. In 1990, Congress enacted the Visual Artists Rights Act, the Architectural Works Copyright Protection Act, and the Computer Software Rental Amendment. The Visual Artists Rights Act affords authors of certain pictorial, sculptural and photographic works limited rights of attribution and integrity in the original physical copies of their works. The Architectural Works Copyright Protection Act grants protection to completed architectural structures as well as plans and models. The Computer Software Rental Amendment, which closely follows the 1984 Record Rental Amendment, grants to copyright owners of computer programs the exclusive right to authorize (or to refuse to authorize) rentals of copies, even after their first sale.

In 1992, Congress provided for automatic renewal of the copyright terms of pre-1978 Act works then in their first term of copyright. Congress also modified the fair use exception to make clear that a work's unpublished status does not preclude successful invocation of the fair use defense. Moreover, for the first time, Congress directly, albeit only partially, addressed the problem of private copying in the Audio Home Recording Act of 1992. This law imposed a surcharge on digital audio tape (DAT) recorders and recording media, to be distributed among song writers and publishers, and performers and producers of sound recordings. The law also obliges manufacturers of DAT machines to include a "serial copy management system," to prevent recording subsequent-generation tapes from the initial tape copy. The law does not, however, impose levies or other restrictions concerning analogue audio recording devices or media; indeed, it explicitly exempts private analogue audio copying from liability for copyright infringement.

Legislation under consideration in 1993 would abolish the Copyright Royalty Tribunal and replace it with ad hoc royalty arbitration panels, which would have the powers both to adjust statutory compulsory-license royalty rates and to distribute collected royalties among claimants.

B. GENERAL PRINCIPLES

UNITED STATES CONSTITUTION

Article I, Section 8, Clause 8

The Congress shall have power ... To promote the Progress of Science and useful Arts, by securing for limited Times to Authors and Inventors the exclusive Right to their respective Writings and Discoveries.

REPORT OF THE REGISTER OF COPYRIGHTS ON THE GENERAL REVISION OF THE U.S. COPYRIGHT LAW 3-6 (1961)

B. The Nature of Copyright

1. In General

In essence, copyright is the right of an author to control the reproduction of his intellectual creation. As long as he keeps his work in his sole possession, the author's absolute control is a physical fact. When he discloses the work to others, however, he makes it possible for them to reproduce it. Copyright is a legal device to give him the right to control its reproduction after it has been disclosed.

Copyright does not preclude others from using the ideas or information revealed by the author's work. It pertains to the literary, musical, graphic, or artistic form in which the author expresses intellectual concepts. It enables him to prevent others from reproducing his individual expression without his consent. But anyone is free to create his own expression of the same concepts, or to make practical use of them, as long as he does not copy the author's form of expression.

2. Copyright as Property

Copyright is generally regarded as a form of property, but it is property of a unique kind. It is intangible and incorporeal. The thing to which the property right attaches — the author's intellectual work — is incapable of possession except as it is embodied in a tangible article such as a manuscript, book, record, or film. The tangible articles containing the work may be in the possession of many persons other than the copyright owner, and they may use the work for their own enjoyment, but copyright restrains them from reproducing the work without the owner's consent.

Justice Holmes, in his famous concurring opinion in *White-Smith Music Publishing Co. v. Apollo Co.* (209 U.S. 1 (1908)), gave a classic definition of the special characteristics of copyright as property:

> The notion of property starts, I suppose, from confirmed possession of a tangible object and consists in the right to exclude other[s] from interference with the more or less free doing with it as one wills. But in copyright property has reached a more abstract expression. The right to exclude is not directed to an object in possession or owned, but is now in vacuo, so to speak. It restrains the spontaneity of men where, but for it, there would be nothing of any kind to hinder their doing as they saw fit. It is a prohibition of conduct remote from the persons or tangibles of the party having the right. It may be infringed a thousand miles from the owner and without his ever becoming aware of the wrong.

3. Copyright as a Personal Right

a. Generally

Some commentators, particularly in European countries, have characterized copyright as a personal right of the author, or as a combination of personal and property rights. It is true that an author's intellectual creation has the stamp of his personality and is identified with him. But insofar as his rights can be assigned to other persons and survive after his death, they are a unique kind of personal rights.

....

4. Copyright as a Monopoly

Copyright has sometimes been said to be a monopoly. This is true in the sense that the copyright owner is given exclusive control over the market for his work. And if his control were unlimited, it could become an undue restraint on the dissemination of the work.

On the other hand, any one work will ordinarily be competing in the market with many others. And copyright, by preventing mere duplication, tends to encourage the independent creation of competitive works. The real danger of monopoly might arise when many works of the same kind are pooled and controlled together.

C. The Purposes of Copyright

1. Constitutional Basis of the Copyright Law

... As reflected in the Constitution, the ultimate purpose of copyright legislation is to foster the growth of learning and culture for the public welfare, and the grant of exclusive rights to authors for a limited time is a means to that end. A fuller statement of these principles was contained in the legislative report (H. Rep. No. 2222, 60th Cong., 2d Sess.) on the Copyright Act of 1909:

> The enactment of copyright legislation by Congress under the terms of the Constitution is not based upon any natural right that the author has in his writings, for the Supreme Court has held that such rights as he has are purely statutory rights, but upon the ground that the welfare of the public will be served and progress of science and useful arts will be promoted by securing to authors for limited periods the exclusive rights to their writings. The Constitution does not establish copyrights, but provides that Congress shall have the power to grant such rights if it thinks best. Not primarily for the benefit of the author, but primarily for the benefit of the public, such rights are given. Not that any particular class of citizens, however worthy, may benefit, but because the policy is believed to be for the benefit of the great body of people, in that it will stimulate writing and invention to give some bonus to authors and inventors.
>
> In enacting a copyright law Congress must consider ... two questions: First, how much will the legislation stimulate the producer and so benefit the public, and, second, how much will the monopoly granted be detrimental to the public? The granting of such exclusive rights, under the proper terms and conditions, confers a benefit upon the public that outweighs the evils of the temporary monopoly.

2. The Rights of Authors and the Public Interest

a. In General

Although the primary purpose of the copyright law is to foster the creation and dissemination of intellectual works for the public welfare, it also has an important secondary purpose: To give authors the reward due them for their contribution to society.

These two purposes are closely related. Many authors could not devote themselves to creative work without the prospect of remuneration. By giving authors a means of securing the economic reward afforded by the market, copyright stimulates their creation and dissemination of intellectual works. Similarly, copyright protection enables publishers and other distributors to invest their resources in bringing those works to the public.

b. Limitations on Author's Rights

Within reasonable limits, the interests of authors coincide with those of the public. Both will usually benefit from the widest possible dissemination of the author's works. But it is often cumbersome for would-be users to seek out the copyright owner and get his permission. There are many situations in which copyright restrictions would inhibit dissemination, with little or no benefit to the author. And the interests of authors must yield to the public welfare where they conflict.

Accordingly, the U.S. copyright law has imposed certain limitations and conditions on copyright protection:

The rights of the copyright owner do not extend to certain uses of the work. (See ch. III of this report.)

The term of copyright is limited, as required by the Constitution. (See ch. V.)

A notice of copyright in published works has been required. (See ch. VI.) The large mass of published material for which the authors do not wish copyright is thus left free of restrictions.

The registration of copyrights and the recordation of transfers of ownership have been required. (See chs. VII and VIII.) The public is thus given the means of determining the status and ownership of copyright claims.

c. The Author's Reward

While some limitations and conditions on copyright are essential in the public interest, they should not be so burdensome and strict as to deprive authors of their just reward. Authors wishing copyright protection should be able to secure it readily and simply. And their rights should be broad enough to give them a fair share of the revenue to be derived from the market for their works.

CHAFEE, REFLECTIONS ON THE LAW OF COPYRIGHT,
45 Columbia Law Review 503, 506-11 (1945)

We should start by reminding ourselves that copyright is a monopoly. Like other monopolies, it is open to many objections; it burdens both competitors and the public. Unlike most other monopolies, the law permits and even encourages it because of its peculiar great advantages. Still, remembering that it is a monopoly, we must be sure that the burdens do not outweigh the benefits. So it becomes desirable for us to examine who is benefited and how much and at whose expense.

The primary purpose of copyright is, of course, to benefit the author.

> ... [I]ntellectual property is, after all, the only absolute possession in the world.... The man who brings out of nothingness some child of his thought has rights therein which cannot belong to any other sort of property....

As Macaulay said in his first speech on the bill which led to the English Act of 1842:[9]

> It is desirable that we should have a supply of good books: we cannot have such a supply unless men of letters are liberally remunerated; and the least objectionable way of remunerating them is by means of copyright.

We do not expect that much of the literature and art which we desire can be produced by men who possess independent means or who derive their living from other occupations and make literature a by-product of their leisure hours. Support by the government or by patrons on which authors used to depend, is today no good substitute for royalties. So we resort to a monopoly, in spite of the plain disadvantage which Macaulay forcibly points out:[10]

> The principle of copyright is this. It is a tax on readers for the purpose of giving a bounty to writers. The tax is an exceedingly bad one; it is a tax on one of the most innocent and most salutary of human pleasures....

Here, as in the case of patents, the Constitution takes the unusual course of expressly sanctioning a gain by private persons. Authors, musicians, painters are among the greatest benefactors of the race. So we incline to protect them. Yet the very effect of protecting them is to make the enjoyment of their creations more costly and hence to limit the possibility of that enjoyment especially by persons of slender purses. Moreover, a monopoly, here as always, makes it possible for the wares to be kept off the market altogether. Therefore, we must be sure that a particular provision of the Copyright Act really helps the author — that it does not impose a burden on the public substantially greater than the benefit it gives to the author.

If we were dealing with only authors and readers, this adjustment of conflicting interests would be fairly simple. But the problem is greatly complicated by the intervention of two other groups who may also be heavily benefited by copyright.

There is the author's surviving family. It often happens that the author does not receive the full benefit of a copyright because he dies before it expires. The benefit and the monopoly may then pass to his widow and children, or to more remote relatives. So far as the widow and minor children go, we all recognize this result as eminently desirable. It goes against the conscience of society that destitution should seize on the family of a man who has made possible

---

[9] Macaulay, Copyright (1841 speech in House of Commons), in 8 Works (Trevelyan ed. 1879) 195, 197.
[10] *Id.* at 201.

great public good. Furthermore, the wish to provide for one's widow and children is one of the strongest incentives to work for all human beings. Erskine, after his maiden argument at the bar, was asked how he had the courage to stand up so boldly before Lord Mansfield, and answered: "I could feel my little children tugging at my gown."[11] ... [But] the benefit becomes dubious when it is conferred on the author's remote relatives; then the tax on the public is less justifiable.

Still another possible beneficiary of copyright has to be considered. Often neither the author nor his family owns the copyright. It belongs to the publisher. (I use the word to include other marketing agencies such as motion-picture companies.) Historically, it was not authors who got the Statute of Anne, but publishers — the London booksellers of those days. A publisher may own the copyright free and clear, and take all the gross income; or he may pay royalties, and take most of the gross income. Either way, he usually gets more from a copyrighted book than when he is subject to open competition. Therefore, much of the tax which the Copyright Act imposes on readers goes directly to publishers.

Then is not the talk of helping authors just a pretense? A vigorous attack of this sort has been widely made on the patent system. Most patents are not owned by the inventors, but by manufacturers, who are often very big corporations. Consequently, it is said that we are betraying the purpose of the Constitution, which was to secure to "Inventors the exclusive Right to their ... Discoveries." Big business is hiding behind the inventor's skirts. This reasoning seems to me unsound. After the inventor makes his invention *work,* an immense expenditure of money is usually necessary to make it *sell.* The inventor is rarely in a position to finance this great development expense himself.... Consequently, the inventor is indirectly benefited by the assignability of his patent.

Similar reasoning applies to copyrights. Although the development expense is not so huge for a book as for a machine or a process, it does cost a good deal to print a book and to attract buyers. Even if an author could afford to publish his own book, he would not do the job well. And if the publishers did not get the benefit of the copyright monopoly, it would be hard for an author to find a publisher to bring out the book. Once the book was launched and became a success, any authorized competitor would eagerly jump into the market because his advertising would be low. He could reap where he had not sown. Both authors and readers would be helpless without publishers. As the poet Wither quaintly said of the good publisher:[12]

> He is the caterer that gathers together provision to satisfy the curious appetite of the soule....

One reason, therefore, for protecting the copyright in the hands of the publisher is to give an indirect benefit to authors by enabling them to get royalties or to sell the manuscript outright for a higher price. A second reason is, that it is only equitable that the publisher should obtain a return on his

---

[11] 6 Campbell, Lives of the Lord Chancellors (1848), c. CLXXVII.
[12] Wither, The Scholler's Purgatory (1624), quoted in Birrell, Seven Lectures on the Law and History of Copyright in Books (1899) 84.

investment. No doubt the return to a publisher from a particular book which becomes a bestseller may be far above the customary six per cent. But we mustn't concentrate our gaze on this one book. Publishing is close to gambling. Many of the same publisher's books never pay back his original outlay. Only an occasional killing makes it possible for us to read a number of less popular but perhaps more valuable books. If we look at the rate of return on *all* books published by any firm, it does not seem excessive. Few publishers become millionaires. Thus copyright is necessary to make good publishers possible....

Mazer v. Stein, 347 U.S. 201 (1954): "The copyright law, like the patent statutes, makes reward to the owner a secondary consideration." *United States v. Paramount Pictures,* 334 U.S. 131, 158. However, it is "intended definitely to grant valuable enforceable rights to authors, publishers, etc., without burdensome requirements; 'to afford greater encouragement to the production of literary [or artistic] works of lasting benefit to the world.'" *Washingtonian Pub. Co. v. Pearson,* 306 U.S. 30.

"The economic philosophy behind the clause empowering Congress to grant patents and copyrights is the conviction that encouragement of individual effort by personal gain is the best way to advance public welfare through the talents of authors and inventors in "Science and useful Arts." Sacrificial days devoted to such creative activities deserve rewards commensurate with the services rendered."

Twentieth Century Music Corp. v. Aiken, 422 U.S. 151 (1975): "The limited scope of the copyright holder's statutory monopoly, like the limited copyright duration required by the Constitution, reflects a balance of competing claims upon the public interest: Creative work is to be encouraged and rewarded, but private motivation must ultimately serve the cause of promoting broad public availability of literature, music, and the other arts.... When technological change has rendered its literal terms ambiguous, the Copyright Act must be construed in light of this basic purpose."

Sony Corp. of America v. Universal City Studios, 464 U.S. 417 (1984): "The monopoly privileges that Congress may authorize are neither unlimited nor primarily designed to provide a special private benefit. Rather, the limited grant is a means by which an important public purpose may be achieved. It is intended to motivate the creative activity of authors and inventors by the provision of a special reward, and to allow the public access to the products of their genius after the limited period of exclusive control has expired.
    ....

As the text of the Constitution makes plain, it is Congress that has been assigned the task of defining the scope of the limited monopoly that should be granted to authors or to inventors in order to give the public appropriate access to their work product. Because this task involves a difficult balance between the interest of authors and inventors in the control and exploitation of their writings and discoveries on the one hand, and society's competing interest in the free flow of ideas, information, and commerce on the other hand, our patent and copyright statutes have been amended repeatedly...."

American Geophysical Union v. Texaco, Inc., 802 F. Supp. 1 (S.D.N.Y. 1992): "[The] attempt to deprecate the interest of the copyright owner by reason of profits it has realized through its copyrights is directly contrary to the theory on which the copyright law is premised. The copyright law *celebrates* the profit motive, recognizing that the incentive to profit from the exploitation of copyrights will redound to the public benefit by resulting in the proliferation of knowledge. Again quoting Madison, 'The public good fully coincides ... with the claims of individuals.' The Federalist, No. 43 at 186. The profit motive is the engine that ensures the progress of science."

ECONOMIC ANALYSIS OF COPYRIGHT DOCTRINE

The economic analysis of law, which has become an influential school of thinking about legal doctrine and institutions, found its way relatively early into the area of copyright. One would think that the fields of intellectual property generally, and copyright in particular, would lend themselves to economic analysis, because they have at their foundation the assumption that economic incentives for creative activity will contribute to society's welfare (i.e., will "promote the progress of science and the useful arts"). In a sense, the drafters of the constitutional patent and copyright clause were engaging in a bit of armchair economic analysis.

Some sixty years ago, scholars interested in law and economics began to question whether it was indeed necessary to provide to prospective authors a monopoly over the distribution and derivative exploitation of their writings in order to coax them to produce works of literature, art and music that would enrich society. A number of scholarly writers asserted that authors have a variety of incentives to write, apart from royalties, and that adequate royalties can in any event be obtained — with publishers quite willing to publish — by virtue of the "headstart" (accompanied by prestige and by some degree of economic leverage) that comes from a publisher's being first to print and distribute a book. *See* A. Plant, *The Economic Aspects of Copyright in Books,* 1 Economica (n.s.) 167 (1934); R. Hurt & R. Schuchman, *The Economic Rationale of Copyright,* 56 Am. Econ. Rev. Papers & Proc. 42 (1966); S. Breyer, *The Uneasy Case for Copyright: A Study of Copyright in Books, Photocopies, and Computer Programs,* 84 Harv. L. Rev. 281 (1970).

Hurt and Schuchman, for example, conjectured that copyright might well provide unnecessary and excessive incentives for persons whose energies might otherwise be put to use in more socially beneficial ways: "We can intuitively discern books which are less meritorious than given alternative products under any conventional value standard. Even if literature is an intrinsically superior product, it still does not follow that copyright protection is the best device for inducing the optimal number of books." (56 Am. Econ. Rev. Papers & Proc. at 429.) They acknowledge that "some works with high costs of creation, as well as literary creation induced by the expectation of incremental income from subsidiary and reprint rights" might not be produced without "some device to assist authors in receiving compensation for their services," but they suggest that this might be done more aptly and timely (i.e., during the period of creative production) "through private patronage by tax-exempt foundations, universities, and the like, or even by government support for desired literary creation." (*Id.* at 426.)

Professor Breyer (now Associate Justice of the United States Supreme Court) also argued that "copyright is not the only way to resolve the conflict between revenues high enough to secure adequate production and prices low enough not to interfere with widespread dissemination." (84 Harv. L. Rev. at 282.) After examining some data and patterns in book publishing and speculating on alternatives to copyright, he concluded that "the case for copyright rests not on proven need, but rather upon uncertainty as to what would happen if protection were removed." (*Id.* at 322.)

These not altogether charitable assessments of the need for and wisdom of copyright were promptly rebutted; particular attacks were leveled at the assumption that a "headstart" in the publishing marketplace could promise adequate economic rewards to induce publication of most new works. *See* 56 Am. Econ. Rev. Papers & Proc. 435-38 (1966) (Frase rebuttal to Hurd & Schuchman); B. Tyerman, *The Economic Rationale for Copyright Protection for Published Books: A Reply to Professor Breyer,* 18 UCLA L. Rev. 1100 (1971); Breyer, *Copyright: A Rejoinder,* 20 UCLA L. Rev. (1972).

The student should consider both the proposed alternatives to copyright protection (and others you might imagine) and particularly the tenability of the "headstart" proposition (especially in a world of electronic access and downloading, optical scanning, and desktop publishing, and the vast increase in subsidiary markets such as foreign distribution and translation, along with derivative media, character and merchandising rights, and the like). The student should also consider the argument often made by copyright proponents (particularly book publishers and motion picture producers) that exclusive rights must be of a duration more than momentary, not only so that subsidiary markets may be exploited, turning losses into profits for many works, but also so that profitable works can be made as profitable as possible, thus subsidizing the creation and distribution of works whose success is more speculative and whose market is narrower, and whose publication will in fact not be profitable; many of the latter works can make a particularly worthwhile contribution to our fund of knowledge, culture and entertainment, and would otherwise go undisseminated.

The literature exploring the economic underpinnings of copyright — and of a wide array of copyright doctrines — has markedly expanded in the past decade. *See, e.g., Symposium on the Law and Economics of Intellectual Property,* 78 Va. L. Rev. 1-419 (1992). The doctrine of fair use has been especially well scrutinized through the use of economic analysis. The seminal work was W. Gordon, *Fair Use as Market Failure: A Structural and Economic Analysis of the Betamax Case and Its Predecessors,* 82 Colum. L. Rev. 1600 (1982). *See also* W. Fisher, *Reconstructing the Fair Use Doctrine,* 101 Harv. L. Rev. 1659 (1988); R. Posner, *When Is Parody Fair Use?,* 21 J. Legal Stud. 67 (1992); W. Landes, *Copyright Protection of Letters, Diaries, and Other Unpublished Works: An Economic Approach,* 21 J. Legal Stud. 79 (1992).

Perhaps the most comprehensive application of economic analysis to a variety of copyright doctrines — and to the principle of copyright itself — is by Professor William M. Landes and Judge-Professor Richard A. Posner. The following excerpts are from that article, *An Economic Analysis of Copyright Law,* 18 J. Legal Stud. 325 (1989). *See also* R. Posner, Law and Literature, 338-52 (1988).

LANDES & POSNER, AN ECONOMIC ANALYSIS OF COPYRIGHT, 18 J. Legal Stud. 325-33, 344-46 (1989)

... [N]o article examines the field of copyright as a whole, discussing the evolution and major doctrines in the law from an economic standpoint. This article, which is in the spirit of our recent articles on the economics of trademark law, tries to fill this gap — although the field is so vast that our analysis cannot be exhaustive. As in most of our work, we are particularly interested in positive analysis, and specifically in the question to what extent copyright law can be explained as a means for promoting efficient allocation of resources.

A distinguishing characteristic of intellectual property is its "public good" aspect. While the cost of creating a work subject to copyright protection — for example, a book, movie, song, ballet, lithograph, map, business directory, or computer software program — is often high, the cost of reproducing the work, whether by the creator or by those to whom he has made it available, is often low. And once copies are available to others, it is often inexpensive for these users to make additional copies. If the copies made by the creator of the work are priced at or close to marginal cost, others may be discouraged from making copies, but the creator's total revenues may not be sufficient to cover the cost of creating the work. Copyright protection — the right of the copyright's owner to prevent others from making copies — trades off the costs of limiting access to a work against the benefits of providing the incentives to create the work in the first place. Striking the correct balance between access and incentives is the central problem in copyright law. For copyright law to promote economic efficiency, its principal legal doctrines must, at least approximately, maximize the benefits from creating additional works minus both the losses from limiting access and the costs of administering copyright protection....

I. The Basic Economics of Copyright

A. *Number of Works as a Function of Copyright and Other Factors*

1. General Considerations

The cost of producing a book or other copyrightable work (we start by talking just about books and later branch out to other forms of expression) has two components. The first is the cost of creating the work. We assume that it does not vary with the number of copies produced or sold, since it consists primarily of the author's time and effort plus the cost to the publisher of soliciting and editing the manuscript and setting it in type. Consistent with copyright usage we call the sum of these costs the "cost of expression."

To simplify the analysis, we ignore any distinction between costs incurred by authors and by publishers, and therefore use the term "author" (or "creator") to mean both author and publisher....

The second component of the cost of producing a work increases with the number of copies produced, for it is the cost of printing, binding, and distributing individual copies. The cost of expression does not enter into the making of copies because, once the work is created, the author's efforts can be incorporated into another copy virtually without cost.

For a new work to be created, the expected return — typically, and we shall assume exclusively, from the sales of copies — must exceed the expected cost. . . . Since the decision to create the work must be made before the demand for copies is known, the work will be created only if the difference between expected revenues and the cost of making copies equals or exceeds the cost of expression. . . .

This description of the market for copies and the number of works created assumes the existence of copyright protection. In its absence anyone can buy a copy of the book when it first appears and make and sell copies of it. The market price of the book will eventually be bid down to the marginal cost of copying, with the unfortunate result that the book probably will not be produced in the first place, because the author and publisher will not be able to recover their costs of creating the work. The problem is magnified by the fact that the author's cost of creating the work, and many publishing costs (for example, editing costs), are incurred before it is known what the demand for the work will be. Uncertainty about demand is a particularly serious problem with respect to artistic works, such as books, plays, movies, and recordings. Even with copyright protection, sales may be insufficient to cover the cost of expression and may not even cover the variable cost of making copies. Thus, the difference between the price and marginal cost of the successful work must not only cover the cost of expression but also compensate for the risk of failure. If a copier can defer making copies until he knows whether the work is a success, the potential gains from free riding on expression will be even greater, because the difference between the price and marginal cost of the original work will rise to compensate for the uncertainty of demand, thus creating a bigger profit potential for copies. So uncertainty generates an additional disincentive to create works in the absence of copyright protection.

Practical obstacles limit copying the original works of others even in the absence of any copyright protection. But these obstacles, while serious in some cases, can easily be exaggerated. When fully analyzed, they not do make a persuasive case for eliminating copyright protection.

1. *The copy may be of inferior quality, and hence not a perfect substitute for the original.* In the case of books and other printed matter, the copier may not be able to match the quality of paper or binding of the original or the crispness of the printing, and there may be errors in transcription. None of these is an important impediment to good copies any longer, but in the case of works of art — such as a painting by a famous artist — a copy, however accurate, may be such a poor substitute in the market that it will have no negative effects on the price of the artist's work. Indeed, the copy may have a positive effect on that price, by serving as advertising for his works. On the other hand, it may also deprive him of income from selling derivative works — the copies of his paintings — himself. (More on derivative works shortly.) To generalize, when either the cost of making equivalent copies is higher for the copier than for the

creator or the copier's product is a poor substitute for the original, the originator will be able to charge a price greater than his marginal cost, even without
legal protection. And obviously, the greater the difference in the costs of
making copies and in the quality of copies between creator and copier (assuming the latter's cost is higher or quality lower), the less need there is for
copyright protection.

2. *Copying may involve some original expression — as when the copy is not a
literal copy but involves paraphrasing, deletions, marginal notes, and so on —
and so a positive cost of expression.* The copier may incur fixed costs as well,
for example costs of rekeying the words from the copy he bought or of photographing them. Still, we would expect the copier's average cost to be lower
than the creator's because it will not include the author's time or the cost of
soliciting and editing the original manuscript. Nevertheless, when the copier
cannot take a complete free ride on the creator's investment in expression and
his other fixed costs, the need for copyright protection is reduced....

3. *Copying takes time, so there will be an interval during which the original
publisher will not face competition.* This point, which is related to the first
because generally the cost of production is inverse to time, has two implications for the analysis of copyright law. First, because modern technology has
reduced the time it takes to make copies as well as enabled more perfect copies
to be made at low cost, the need for copyright protection has increased over
time. Second, for works that are faddish — where demand is initially strong
but falls sharply after a brief period — copyright protection may not be as
necessary in order to give the creator of the work a fully compensatory return.

4. *There are contractual alternatives to copyright protection for limiting
copying.* One is licensing the original work on condition that the licensee not
make copies of it or disclose it to others in a way that would enable them to
make copies. But contractual prohibitions on copying may, like trade secrets,
be costly to enforce and feasible only if there are few licensees. Where widespread distribution is necessary to generate an adequate return to the author
or where the work is resold or publicly performed, contractual prohibitions
may not prevent widespread copying. Thus, the greater the potential market
for a work, the greater the need for copyright protection. The development of
radio, television, and the phonograph has expanded the market for copies and
thereby increased the value of copyright protection.

5. *Since a copier normally must have access to a copy in order to make copies,
the creator may be able to capture some of the value of copies made by charging
a high price for the copies he makes and sells.* For example, a publisher of
academic journals may be able to capture part of the value that individuals
obtain from copying articles by charging a higher price for the journal —
especially to libraries; or a record company may be able to charge a higher
price because of home taping. Although this possibility limits the need for
copyright protection, it does not eliminate it. If one can make many copies of
the first copy, and many copies of subsequent copies, the price of copies will be
driven down to marginal cost and the creator will not be able to charge a
sufficiently higher price for his copy to capture its value in allowing others to
make more copies; no one (except the first copier and the most impatient
readers) will buy from him rather than from a copier.

6. *Many authors derive substantial benefits from publication that are over and beyond any royalties.* This is true not only in terms of prestige and other nonpecuniary income but also pecuniary income in such forms as a higher salary for a professor who publishes than for one who does not, or greater consulting income. Publishing is an effective method of self-advertisement and self-promotion. The norms against plagiarism (that is, against copying without giving the author credit) reinforce the conferral of prestige by publishing; to the extent that those norms are effective, they ensure that the author will obtain recognition, if not always royalties, from the works he publishes.

Such points have convinced some students of copyright law that there is no need for copyright protection. Legal rights are costly to enforce — rights in intangibles especially so — and the costs may outweigh the social gains in particular settings. Perhaps copyright in books is one of them. After all, the first copyright law in England dates from 1710 (and gave much less protection than modern copyright law), yet publishing had flourished for hundreds of years in England despite censorship and widespread illiteracy. The point is a little misleading, however. In the old days, the costs of making copies were a higher fraction of total cost than they are today, so the problem of appropriability was less acute. Also, there were alternative institutions for internalizing the benefits of expression. And before freedom of expression became generally applauded, publishing was often believed to impose negative externalities — so there was less, sometimes no, desire to encourage it. Finally, while it may be difficult to determine whether, on balance, copyright is a good thing, it is easy to note particular distortions that a copyright law corrects. Without copyright protection, authors, publishers, and copiers would have inefficient incentives with regard to the timing of various decisions. Publishers, to lengthen their head start, would have a disincentive to engage in prepublication advertising and even to announce publication dates in advance, and copiers would have an incentive to install excessively speedy production lines. There would be increased incentives to create faddish, ephemeral, and otherwise transitory works because the gains from being first in the market for such works would be likely to exceed the losses from absence of copyright protection. There would be a shift toward the production of works that are difficult to copy; authors would be more likely to circulate their works privately rather than widely, to lessen the risk of copying; and contractual restrictions on copying would multiply.

A neglected consideration — one that shows not that copyright protection may be unnecessary but that beyond some level copyright protection may actually be counterproductive by raising the cost of expression — will play an important role both in our model and in our efforts to explain the salient features of copyright law. Creating a new work typically involves borrowing or building on material from a prior body of works, as well as adding original expression to it. A new work of fiction, for example, will contain the author's expressive contribution but also characters, situations, plot details, and so on, invented by previous authors. Similarly, a new work of music may borrow tempo changes and chord progressions from earlier works. The less extensive copyright protection is, the more an author, composer, or other creator can borrow from previous works without infringing copyright and the lower, therefore, the costs of creating a new work. Of course, even if copyright protection effectively prevented all unauthorized copying from a copyrighted work, authors would still copy. But they would copy works whose copyright protection had run out, or they would disguise their copying, engage in costly searches to avoid copying protected works, or incur licensing and other transaction costs to obtain permission to copy such works. The effect would be to raise the cost of creating new works — the cost of expression, broadly defined — and thus, paradoxically, perhaps lower the number of works created.

Copyright holders might, therefore, find it in their self-interest, ex ante, to limit copyright protection. To the extent that a later author is free to borrow material from an earlier one, the later author's cost of expression is reduced; and, from an ex ante viewpoint, every author is both an earlier author from whom a later author might want to borrow material and the later author himself. In the former role, he desires maximum copyright protection for works he creates; in the latter, he prefers minimum protection for works created earlier by others. In principle, there is a level of copyright protection that balances these two competing interests optimally — although notice that the first generation of authors, having no one to borrow from, will have less incentive to strike the optimal balance than later ones. We shall see in Section II that various doctrines of copyright law, such as the distinction between idea and expression and the fair use doctrine, can be understood as attempts to promote economic efficiency by balancing the effect of greater copyright protection — in encouraging the creation of new works by reducing copying — against the effect of less protection — in encouraging the creation of new works by reducing the cost of creating them.

....

II. Applications

A. The Nature of Copyright Protection

... We begin with the nature of the protection that a copyright gives its owner. In contrast to a patent, a copyright merely gives protection against copying; independent (that is, accidental) duplication of the copyrighted work is not actionable as such. In speaking of "independent [accidental, inadvertent] duplication" we are addressing only the problem of an independent recreation of the original copyrighted work. The accidental use of someone else's work might be thought of as duplication, but in that context liability for infringement is strict, much as it is for the trespass on a neighbor's land made by a person who thinks that he owns it.

The more difficult question is to explain why duplication in the sense of independent recreation is not actionable. Our analysis suggests two possible explanations. The first is the added cost to the author of checking countless numbers of copyrighted works to avoid inadvertent duplication. The costs (if actually incurred — a qualification whose significance will become apparent shortly) would ... lower social welfare because both net welfare per work ... and the number of works created would fall. True, the author's gross revenues might rise if the reduction in the amount of accidental duplication raised the demand for copies or made the demand less elastic. But since accidental duplication of copyrighted works is rare (except in the area of popular music, discussed below), the net effect of making it unlawful would be to lower social welfare.

In contrast to copyright, accidental infringements of patents are actionable, and the difference makes economic sense. A patent is issued only after a search by the applicant and by the Patent Office of prior patented inventions. This procedure is feasible because it is possible to describe an invention compactly and to establish relatively small classes of related inventions beyond which the searchers need to go. The procedure makes it relatively easy for an inventor to avoid accidentally duplicating an existing patent.

No effort is made by the Copyright Office to search copyrighted works before issuing a copyright, so copyright is not issued but is simply asserted by the author or publisher. There are billions of pages of copyrighted material, any one page of which might contain a sentence or paragraph that a later writer might, by pure coincidence, duplicate so closely that he would be considered an infringer if he had actually copied the words in question or if copying were not required for liability. What is infeasible for the Copyright Office is also infeasible for the author. He cannot read all the copyrighted literature in existence (in all languages, and including unpublished works!) in order to make sure that he has not accidentally duplicated some copyrighted material.

The cost of preventing accidental duplication would be so great, and the benefits in terms of higher revenues (and so the amount of damages if such duplication were actionable) so slight because such duplication is rare, that even if it were actionable no writer or publisher would make much effort to avoid accidental duplication, so the increase in the cost of expression would probably be slight. But social welfare would be reduced somewhat. At best we would have a system of strict liability that had no significant allocative effect; and as explained in the literature on negligence and strict liability in tort law, the costs of enforcing such a regime are socially wasted because their only product is an occasional redistribution of wealth (here that would be from the accidental "infringer" to the first author or publisher of the material duplicated).

The second reason we expect accidental duplication not to be made unlawful derives from the economic rationale for copyright protection, which is to prevent free-riding on the author's expression. Accidental duplication does not involve free-riding. Since the second work is independently created, its author incurs the full cost of expression. If the works are completely identical — a remote possibility, to say the least[30] — competition between the two works could drive the price of copies down to marginal cost and prevent either au-

[30] Recall Learned Hand's remark in Sheldon v. Metro-Goldwyn Pictures, 81 F.2d 49 (2d Cir. 1936), that "if by some magic a man who had never known it were to compose anew Keats' Ode on a Grecian Urn, he would be an author, and if he copyrighted it, others might not copy that poem, though they might of course copy Keats." Hand, of course, though such accidental duplication a remote possibility. The probability of accidental duplication of Keats' poem word for word is too small to justify courts in treating it as a litigable question, that is, one fairly open to doubt.

thor from recovering his cost of creating the work. It is more likely that significant differences between the two works will remain, so that both authors may be able to earn enough to cover their respective costs of expression — particularly if neither author is the marginal author, whose gross revenues would just cover the cost of expression in the absence of accidental duplication.

Although for simplicity our analysis focuses on copyright protection for literature and other written works, it is applicable, *mutatis mutandis*, to other forms of expression as well. A significant difference between literary and musical copyright is that courts hold that accidental duplication may infringe a songwriter's copyright if his song has been widely performed.[31] Since most popular songs have simple melodies and the number of melodic variations is limited, the possibility of accidental duplication of several bars is significant. Widespread playing of these songs on the radio makes it likely that the second composer will have had access to the original work, which both increases the likelihood of accidental duplication and reduces the costs of avoiding it. If proof of intentional duplication were required for infringement, composers of popular songs would have little copyright protection and social welfare would fall....

David Ladd, the Register of Copyrights from 1980 through January 1985, has taken issue with the characterization of copyright as a "monopoly" begrudgingly tolerated only to the extent necessary to induce authors to produce works that will enrich human knowledge. He has also disputed the perceived tension between copyright and society's interest in full dissemination of ideas and information. Mr. Ladd criticizes those who would limit copyright protection to cases in which competitive economic harm has been suffered by the author. He states that "the notion of economic 'harm' as a prerequisite for copyright protection is mischievous because it disserves the basic constitutional design which embraces both copyright and the First Amendment." Excerpts from his article follow.

LADD, THE HARM OF THE CONCEPT OF HARM IN COPYRIGHT, 30 Journal of the Copyright Society 421 (1983)

The twenty-seven words in Art. I, § 8, which give Congress the power to legislate copyrights and patents are plain and straightforward (and, incidentally, contain the only use of the word "right" in the entire main body of the Constitution) ....

---

[31] For example, in ABKO Music, Inc. v. Harrisongs Music, Ltd., 722 F.2d 988, 998-99 (2d Cir. 1983), the court found that George Harrison's "My Sweet Lord" had infringed "He's So Fine," recorded by the Chiffons. "He's So Fine" had been one of the most popular songs in the United States and England during the same year that Harrison (a former member of the Beatles) composed "My Sweet Lord." The court found an infringement even though it also found that Harrison had copied the Chiffons' song unconsciously rather than deliberately.

Proponents of the harm argument insist that a showing of harm is virtually required as a constitutional limitation: if there is no harm to the copyright owner, there is no demonstrated need for rewards under copyright to motivate the creation and dissemination of the work, and thus "to promote the progress of science." The argument is not only unhistoric, but specious. It paves the way for government interference with information, speech, and discourse which, however indirect, is quite as unlovely as prior restraint....

The framers of the Constitution were men to whom the right to hold property was enormously important. They were not far removed from Locke. His ideas pervaded their debates and decision. Property was seen not as opposed to liberty, but indispensable to it; for men with property would be independent of the power of the State, in that rough-and-tumble roiling of opinion and power which marks freedom.

....

That rights of the author are thus of a special kind, rooted both in utility and felt justice, has long been recognized in our country. This has rarely been recalled with greater eloquence than in a statement by Professor Nathaniel Shaler of Harvard, presented to Congress in 1936 by Thorvald Solberg, one of my predecessors in this office:

> When we come to weigh the rights of the several sorts of property which can be held by man, and in this judgment take into consideration only the absolute question of justice, leaving out the limitations of expediency and prejudice, it will be clearly seen that intellectual property is, after all, the only absolute possession in the world.... The man who brings out of the nothingness some child of his thought has rights therein which cannot belong to any other sort of property.... The inventor of a book or other contrivance of thought holds his property, as a god holds it, by right of creation.... Whatever tends to lower the protection given to intellectual property is so much taken from the forces which have been active in securing the advances of society during the last centuries.

....

The purpose of copyright is to reward authors as a matter of justice, yes; but only as a beginning. Copyright also is intended to support a system, a macrocosm, in which authors and publishers complete for the attention and favor of the public, independent of the political will of the majority, the powerful, and above all the government, no matter how unorthodox, disturbing, or revolutionary their experience, views, or visions.

The argument for copyright here, to be sure, is an argument of utility — but not mere economic utility. Utility is found in the fostering of a pluralism of opinion, experience, vision, and utterance within the world of authors.... [O]ur freedom depends not only on freedom for a few, but also on variety, regardless of the ultimate commingling of truth and error. Copyright fosters that variety.

The marketplace of ideas which the First Amendment nurtures is, then, and must be more widely understood to be, essentially a *copyright* marketplace.... Just as we are best served by many visions and visionaries speaking from and to the breadth of human experience, so also do we require a vibrant, heterogeneous, and dissonant community of publishers. The greater their number and variety, the more likely is any author to find a publisher. And while this is of special importance in the areas of thought and political opinion, it is likewise crucial in the fine arts. Joyce and Proust, Beethoven and Stravinsky were all at one time scorned for works for which they later became immortal, but each found the publisher he needed. Those who pioneer, and thereby often disturb, cannot be silenced by anyone if publishers are numerous and the mail delivers the royalty checks.

. . . .

By limiting potential rewards in the copyright market — whether by capping them with a compulsory license, or barring them with a complete exemption, or refusing to extend copyright to new uses, or curtailing them in any way under arguments of "harm" — the entrepreneurial calculus which precedes risk-taking in authorship and publishing is shifted in the direction of not taking a chance, *i.e.*, not writing or publishing a "risky" work, whether ideologically or economically risky. Every limitation on copyright is a kind of rate-setting. And however high-minded, every person who thus sets rates applies a value-judgment: how much the author or publisher should receive. Whoever makes this judgment regulates — *i.e.*, controls — how successful a class of authors, works, or publishers shall be. This control of idea-laden copyrighted works is more wisely left with the people than vested in a government tribunal, a statutory license fee, or even a sincere judge searching a record for undefined harm....

[The Supreme Court has echoed Register Ladd's evocation of the beneficial interdependence of copyright and the First Amendment. In *Harper & Row Publishers, Inc. v. Nation Enters.*, 471 U.S. 539 (1985), Justice O'Connor emphasized, "it should not be forgotten that the Framers intended copyright itself to be the engine of free expression. By establishing a marketable right to the use of one's expression, copyright supplies the economic incentive to create and disseminate ideas."]

BURROW-GILES LITHOGRAPHIC CO. v. SARONY

111 U.S. 53 (1884)

Mr. Justice Miller delivered the opinion of the court.

This is a writ of error to the Circuit Court for the Southern District of New York.

Plaintiff is a lithographer and defendant a photographer, with large business in those lines in the city of New York.

The suit was commenced by an action at law in which Sarony was plaintiff and the lithographic company was defendant, the plaintiff charging the defendant with violating his copyright in regard to a photograph, the title of which is "Oscar Wilde No. 18." A jury being waived, the court made a finding of facts on which a judgment in favor of the plaintiff was rendered for the sum of $600 for the plates and 85,000 copies sold and exposed to sale, and $10 for copies found in his possession, as penalties under section 4965 of the Revised Statutes.

Among the findings of fact made by the court the following presents the principal question raised by the assignment of errors in the case:

"3. That the plaintiff about the month of January, 1882, under an agreement with Oscar Wilde, became and was the author, inventor, designer, and proprietor of the photograph in suit, the title of which is 'Oscar Wilde No. 18,' being the number used to designate this particular photograph and of the negative thereof; that the same is a useful, new, harmonious, characteristic, and graceful picture, and that said plaintiff made the same at his place of business in said city of New York, and within the United States, entirely from his own original mental conception, to which he gave visible form by posing the said Oscar Wilde in front of the camera, selecting and arranging the costume, draperies, and other various accessories in said photograph, arranging the subject so as to present graceful outlines, arranging and disposing the light and shade, suggesting and evoking the desired expression, and from such disposition, arrangement, or representation, made entirely by the plaintiff, he produced the picture in suit, Exhibit A, April 14th, 1882, and that the terms 'author,' 'inventor,' and 'designer,' as used in the art of photography and in the complaint, mean the person who so produced the photograph."

Other findings leave no doubt that plaintiff had taken all the steps required by the act of Congress to obtain copyright of this photograph; and section 4952 names photographs among other things for which the author, inventor, or designer may obtain copyright, which is to secure him the sole privilege of reprinting, publishing, copying and vending the same. That defendant is liable under that section and section 4965 there can be no question, if those sections are valid as they relate to photographs.

Accordingly, the two assignments of error in this court by plaintiff in error, are:

1. That the court below decided that Congress had and has the constitutional right to protect photographs and negatives thereof by copyright.

The second assignment related to the sufficiency of the words "Copyright, 1882, by N. Sarony," in the photographs, as a notice of the copyright of Napoleon Sarony under the act of Congress on that subject.

. . . .

The constitutional question is not free from difficulty.

The eighth section of the first article of the Constitution is the great repository of the powers of Congress, and by the eighth clause of that section Congress is authorized:

"To promote the progress of science and useful arts, by securing, for limited times to authors and inventors, the exclusive right to their respective writings and discoveries."

The argument here is, that a photograph is not a writing nor the production of an author. Under the acts of Congress designed to give effect to this section, the persons who are to be benefited are divided into two classes, authors and inventors. The monopoly which is granted to the former is called a copyright, that given to the latter, letters patent, or, in the familiar language of the present day, *patent right*.

We have, then, copyright and patent right, and it is the first of these under which plaintiff asserts a claim for relief.

It is insisted in argument, that a photograph being a reproduction on paper of the exact features of some natural object or of some person, is not a writing of which the producer is the author.

Section 4952 of the Revised Statutes places photographs in the same class as things which may be copyrighted with "books, maps, charts, dramatic or musical compositions, engravings, cuts, prints, paintings, drawings, statues, statuary, and models or designs intended to be perfected as works of the fine arts." "According to the practice of legislation in England and America," says Judge Bouvier, 2 Law Dictionary, 363, "the copyright is confined to the exclusive right secured to the author or proprietor of a writing or drawing which may be multiplied by the arts of printing in any of its branches."

The first Congress of the United States, sitting immediately after the formation of the Constitution, enacted that the "author or authors of any map, chart, book or books, being a citizen or resident of the United States, shall have the sole right and liberty of printing, reprinting, publishing and vending the same for the period of fourteen years from the recording of the title thereof in the clerk's office, as afterwards directed." 1 Stat. 124, 1.

This statute not only makes maps and charts subjects of copyright, but mentions them before books in the order of designation. The second section of an act to amend this act, approved April 29, 1802, 2 Stat. 171, enacts that from the first day of January thereafter, he who shall invent and design, engrave, etch or work, or from his own works shall cause to be designed and engraved, etched or worked, any historical or other print or prints shall have the same exclusive right for the term of fourteen years from recording the title thereof as prescribed by law.

By the first section of the act of February 3d, 1831, 4 Stat. 436, entitled an act to amend the several acts respecting copyright, musical compositions and cuts, in connection with prints and engravings, are added, and the period of protection is extended to twenty-eight years. The caption or title of this act uses the word copyright for the first time in the legislation of Congress.

The construction placed upon the Constitution by the first act of 1790, and the act of 1802, by the men who were contemporary with its formation, many of whom were members of the convention which framed it, is of itself entitled to very great weight, and when it is remembered that the rights thus established have not been disputed during a period of nearly a century, it is almost conclusive.

Unless, therefore, photographs can be distinguished in the classification on this point from the maps, charts, designs, engravings, etchings, cuts, and other prints, it is difficult to see why Congress cannot make them the subject of copyright as well as the others.

These statutes certainly answer the objection that books only, or writing in the limited sense of a book and its author, are within the constitutional provision. Both these words are susceptible of a more enlarged definition than this. An author in that sense is "he to whom anything owes its origin; originator; maker; one who completes a work of science or literature." Worcester. So, also, no one would now claim that the word writing in this clause of the Constitution, though the only word used as to subjects in regard to which authors are to be secured, is limited to the actual script of the author, and excludes books and all other printed matter. By writings in that clause is meant the literary productions of those authors, and Congress very properly has declared these to include all forms of writing, printing, engraving, etching, & c., by which the ideas in the mind of the author are given visible expression. The only reason why photographs were not included in the extended list in the act of 1802 is probably that they did not exist, as photography as an art was then unknown, and the scientific principle on which it rests, and the chemicals and machinery by which it is operated, have all been discovered long since that statute was enacted.

Nor is it to be supposed that the framers of the Constitution did not understand the nature of copyright and the objects to which it was commonly applied, for copyright, as the exclusive right of a man to the production of his own genius or intellect, existed in England at that time....

We entertain no doubt that the Constitution is broad enough to cover an act authorizing copyright of photographs, so far as they are representatives of original intellectual conceptions of the author.

But it is said that an engraving, a painting, a print, does embody the intellectual conception of its author, in which there is novelty, invention, originality, and therefore comes within the purpose of the Constitution in securing its exclusive use or sale to its author, while the photograph is the mere mechanical reproduction of the physical features or outlines of some object animate or inanimate, and involves no originality of thought or any novelty in the intellectual operation connected with its visible reproduction in shape of a picture. That while the effect of light on the prepared plate may have been a discovery in the production of these pictures, and patents could properly be obtained for the combination of the chemicals, for their application to the paper or other surface, for all the machinery by which the light reflected from the object was thrown on the prepared plate, and for all the improvements in this machinery, and in the materials, the remainder of the process is merely mechanical, with no place for novelty, invention or originality. It is simply the manual operation, by the use of these instruments and preparations, of transferring to the plate the visible representation of some existing object, the accuracy of this representation being its highest merit.

This may be true in regard to the ordinary production of a photograph, and, further, that in such case a copyright is no protection. On the question as thus stated we decide nothing.

In regard, however, to the kindred subject of patents for invention, they cannot by law be issued to the inventor until the novelty, the utility, and the actual discovery or invention by the claimant have been established by proof before the Commissioner of Patents; and when he has secured such a patent, and undertakes to obtain redress for a violation of his right in a court of law, the question of invention, of novelty, of originality, is always open to examination. Our copyright system has no such provision for previous examination by a proper tribunal as to the originality of the book, map, or other matter offered for copyright. A deposit of two copies of the article or work with the Librarian of Congress, with the name of the author and its title page, is all that is necessary to secure a copyright. It is, therefore, much more important that when the supposed author sues for a violation of his copyright, the existence of those facts of originality, of intellectual production, of thought, and conception on the part of the author should be proved, than in the case of a patent right.

In the case before us we think this has been done.

The third finding of facts says, in regard to the photograph in question, that it is a "useful, new, harmonious, characteristic, and graceful picture, and that plaintiff made the same ... entirely from his own original mental conception, to which he gave visible form by posing the said Oscar Wilde in front of the camera, selecting and arranging the costume, draperies, and other various accessories in said photograph, arranging the subject so as to present graceful outlines, arranging and disposing the light and shade, suggesting and evoking the desired expression, and from such disposition, arrangement, or representation, made entirely by plaintiff, he produced the picture in suit."

These findings, we think, show this photograph to be an original work of art, the product of plaintiff's intellectual invention, of which plaintiff is the author, and of a class of inventions for which the Constitution intended that

Congress should secure to him the exclusive right to use, publish and sell, as it has done by section 4952 of the Revised Statutes.

....

The judgment of the Circuit Court is accordingly affirmed.

BLEISTEIN v. DONALDSON LITHOGRAPHING CO.

188 U.S. 239 (1903)

MR. JUSTICE HOLMES delivered the opinion of the court.

... The alleged infringements consisted in the copying in reduced form of three chromolithographs prepared by employes of the plaintiffs for advertisements of a circus owned by one Wallace. Each of the three contained a portrait of Wallace in the corner and lettering bearing some slight relation to the scheme of decoration, indicating the subject of the design and the fact that the reality was to be seen at the circus. One of the designs was of an ordinary ballet, one of a number of men and women, described as the Stirk family, performing on bicycles, and one of groups of men and women whitened to represent statues. The Circuit Court directed a verdict for the defendant on the ground that the chromolithographs were not within the protection of the copyright law, and this ruling was sustained by the Circuit Court of Appeals. *Courier Lithographing Co. v. Donaldson Lithographing Co.,* 104 Fed. Rep. 993.

....

We shall do no more than mention the suggestion that painting and engraving unless for a mechanical end are not among the useful arts, the progress of which Congress is empowered by the Constitution to promote. The Constitu-

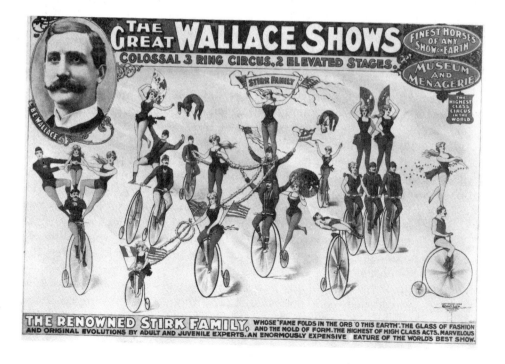

tion does not limit the useful to that which satisfies immediate bodily needs. *Burrow-Giles Lithographic Co. v. Sarony,* 111 U.S. 53. It is obvious also that the plaintiffs' case is not affected by the fact, if it be one, that the pictures represent actual groups — visible things. They seem from the testimony to have been composed from hints or description, not from sight of a performance. But even if they had been drawn from the life, that fact would not deprive them of protection. The opposite proposition would mean that a portrait by Velasquez or Whistler was common property because others might try their hand on the same face. Others are free to copy the original. They are not free to copy the copy. *Blunt v. Patten,* 2 Paine, 397, 400. See *Kelly v. Morris,* L. R. 1 Eq. 697; *Morris v. Wright,* L. R. 5 Ch. 279. The copy is the personal reaction of an individual upon nature. Personality always contains something unique. It expresses its singularity even in handwriting, and a very modest grade of art has in it something irreducible, which is one man's alone. That something he may copyright unless there is a restriction in the words of the act.

If there is a restriction it is not to be found in the limited pretensions of these particular works. The least pretentious picture has more originality in it than directories and the like, which may be copyrighted. Drone, Copyright, 153. See *Henderson v. Tomkins,* 60 Fed. Rep. 758, 765. The amount of training required for humbler efforts than those before us is well indicated by Ruskin. "If any young person, after being taught what is, in polite circles, called 'drawing,' will try to copy the commonest piece of real *work,* — suppose a lithograph on the title page of a new opera air, or a woodcut in the cheapest illustrated newspaper of the day — they will find themselves entirely beaten." Elements of Drawing, 1st ed. 3. There is no reason to doubt that these prints in their *ensemble* and in all their details, in their design and particular combinations of figures, lines and colors, are the original work of the plaintiffs' designer. If it be necessary, there is express testimony to that effect. It would be pressing the defendant's right to the verge, if not beyond, to leave the question of originality to the jury upon the evidence in this case, as was done in *Hegeman v. Springer,* 110 Fed. Rep. 374.

We assume that the construction of Rev. Stat. § 4952, allowing a copyright to the "author, inventor, designer, or proprietor ... of any engraving, cut, print ... [or] chromo" is affected by the act of 1874, c. 301, § 3, 18 Stat. 78, 79. That section provides that "in the construction of this act the words 'engraving,' 'cut' and 'print' shall be applied only to pictorial illustrations or works connected with the fine arts." We see no reason for taking the words "connected with the fine arts" as qualifying anything except the word "works," but it would not change our decision if we should assume further that they also qualified "pictorial illustrations," as the defendant contends.

These chromolithographs are "pictorial illustrations." The word "illustrations" does not mean that they must illustrate the text of a book, and that the etchings of Rembrandt or Steinla's engraving of the Madonna di San Sisto could not be protected today if any man were able to produce them. Again, the act however construed, does not mean that ordinary posters are not good enough to be considered within its scope. The antithesis to "illustrations or works connected with the fine arts" is not works of little merit or of humble degree, or illustrations addressed to the less educated classes; it is "prints or labels designed to be used for any other articles of manufacture." Certainly works are not the less connected with the fine arts because their pictorial quality attracts the crowd and therefore gives them a real use — if use means to increase trade and to help to make money. A picture is none the less a picture and none the less a subject of copyright that it is used for an advertisement. And if pictures may be used to advertise soap, or the theatre, or monthly magazines, as they are, they may be used to advertise a circus. Of course, the ballet is as legitimate a subject for illustration as any other. A rule cannot be laid down that would excommunicate the paintings of Degas.

Finally, the special adaptation of these pictures to the advertisement of the Wallace shows does not prevent a copyright. That may be a circumstance for the jury to consider in determining the extent of Mr. Wallace's rights, but it is not a bar. Moreover, on the evidence, such prints are used by less pretentious exhibitions when those for whom they were prepared have given them up.

It would be a dangerous undertaking for persons trained only to the law to constitute themselves final judges of the worth of pictorial illustrations, outside of the narrowest and most obvious limits. At the one extreme some works of genius would be sure to miss appreciation. Their very novelty would make them repulsive until the public had learned the new language in which their author spoke. It may be more than doubted, for instance, whether the etchings of Goya or the paintings of Manet would have been sure of protection when seen for the first time. At the other end, copyright would be denied to pictures which appealed to a public less educated than the judge. Yet if they command the interest of any public, they have a commercial value — it would be bold to say that they have not an aesthetic and educational value — and the taste of any public is not to be treated with contempt. It is an ultimate fact for the moment, whatever may be our hopes for a change. That these pictures had their worth and their success is sufficiently shown by the desire to reproduce them without regard to the plaintiffs' rights. See *Henderson v. Tomkins*, 60 Fed. Rep. 758, 765. We are of opinion that there was evidence that the plaintiffs have rights entitled to the protection of the law.

The judgment of the Circuit Court of Appeals is reversed; the judgment of the Circuit Court is also reversed and the cause remanded to that court with directions to set aside the verdict and grant a new trial.

MR. JUSTICE HARLAN, with whom concurred MR. JUSTICE McKENNA, dissenting.

Judges Lurton, Day and Severens, of the Circuit Court of Appeals, concurred in affirming the judgment of the District Court. Their views were thus expressed in an opinion delivered by Judge Lurton: "What we hold is this: That if a chromo, lithograph, or other print, engraving, or picture has no other use than that of a mere advertisement, and no value aside from this function, it would not be promotive of the useful arts, within the meaning of the constitutional provision, to protect the 'author' in the exclusive use thereof, and the copyright statute should not be construed as including such a publication, if any other construction is admissible. If a mere label simply designating or describing an article to which it is attached, and which has no value separated from the article, does not come within the constitutional clause upon the subject of copyright, it must follow that a pictorial illustration designed and useful only as an advertisement, and having no intrinsic value other than its function as an advertisement, must be equally without the obvious meaning of the Constitution. It must have some connection with the fine arts to give it intrinsic value, and that it shall have is the meaning which we attach to the act of June 18, 1874, amending the provisions of the copyright law. We are unable to discover anything useful or meritorious in the design copyrighted by the plaintiffs in error other than as an advertisement of acts to be done or exhibited to the public in Wallace's show. No evidence, aside from the deductions which are to be drawn from the prints themselves, was offered to show that these designs had any original artistic qualities. The jury could not reasonably have found merit or value aside from the purely business object of advertising a show, and the instruction to find for the defendant was not error...."

I entirely concur in these views, and therefore dissent from the opinion and judgment of this court. The clause of the Constitution giving Congress power to promote the progress of science and useful arts, by securing for limited terms to authors and inventors the exclusive right to their respective works and discoveries, does not, as I think, embrace a mere advertisement of a circus.

MR. JUSTICE MCKENNA authorizes me to say that he also dissents.

QUESTIONS

Consider the following issues in connection with the copyright clause of the United States Constitution:

1. Why, in establishing a new federal government, did the founding fathers repose this power in the central government, rather than in the separate states? More generally, why give this power to *any* government unit? More specifically, would state copyright control be effectual, and would it be constitutional after the adoption of the copyright clause?

2. Does the copyright monopoly promote "the Progress of Science" or does it promote "the useful Arts"? *How* does such an exclusive right promote one or the other? Can a specific copyright be struck down because it does *not* promote science or the useful arts? Who would so decide? Is a comic strip constitutionally subject to copyright protection? A design for a flag? A pornographic work? An unpublished work kept in a desk drawer? Does the purpose of promoting progress make for broader or narrower protection in particular cases?

3. Could Congress extend the period of copyright protection to 1000 years? Ninety-nine years? Life of the author plus fifty years? Why is the "property" interest in works of literature, music and art limited in time, when the "property" interest in real and personal property is typically of indefinite duration? Could a *state* grant perpetual copyright protection?

4. Does the reference in the copyright clause to "Authors" have substantive import regarding the nature and amount of work necessary to secure valid copyright protection? Can Congress give such protection to one who copies the work of another? To one who, although not copying, "originates" a work

exactly identical to one already written? Or is there a requirement, such as in the patent law, that the work in order to secure copyright protection must be "novel"? If an "Author" is necessary, can Congress extend copyright protection to music, photographs and sculpture?

5. Can Congress constitutionally provide that under certain circumstances, all persons are free, without the prior consent of the copyright owner, to make copies of a copyrighted work upon the payment of a statutorily specified royalty?

6. Is the definition of "Writings" to be limited to the conventional understanding, or to the understanding in 1789? In either case, may Congress constitutionally grant copyright protection of a map, a painting, a photograph, a motion picture, a choreographed dance, a puppet, a sculpture, a Frank Lloyd Wright building? Can a work which is reduced to form only in a phonograph record or a tape be given copyright protection? A computer program? A completely unrecorded work, such as a conversation or an improvised "live" performance? If a work is treated as a "non-writing," may the states grant copyright protection?

C. OVERVIEW OF COPYRIGHT LAW

1. NATURE OF COPYRIGHT

A copyright is essentially a set of exclusive rights in literary, musical, choreographic, dramatic and artistic works. The rights under copyright pertain to the reproduction, adaptation, public distribution, and public display or performance of the work. The copyright owner's exclusive rights, however, are limited in several important respects. There are three basic limitations:

(a) Because a copyright protects only against copying (or paraphrasing or "colorable alterations" of) the copyrighted work, a copyright does not prohibit another author from *independently* producing the same or a similar work. (Thus, to use a familiar simian example, if one hundred monkeys sat down at one hundred typewriters, and one of them eventually produced *Hamlet*, this remarkable result could not be copyright infringement.)

(b) Anyone may copy the *ideas* from a copyrighted work; copyright protects only the particular express of ideas. Frequently, however, this "idea/expression dichotomy" is easier to state than to apply. The often hair-splitting, and even hair-rending, exercise of separating ideas from their protected expression will be the subject of considerable attention in later chapters of the casebook. For the moment, an example may suffice to illustrate the difference. The idea that remorse may overwhelm the subconscious is not protectible; Lady Macbeth's sleepwalking scene (to stick with Shakespeare) is a particular expression of that idea, and would be subject to protection, were Shakespeare's works not already in the public domain (i.e., copyrights in such works have expired).

(c) A copyright extends neither to systems explained in a work, nor to discrete facts contained within a work. Like the idea/expression dichotomy, the distinction between facts and their expression can be elusive. By way of example, consider the copyrightability of this Overview. The overall presentation of the topic and the specific words chosen would be protectible, but the facts the reader learns are not. Thus there is no copyright protection for the *fact* that the Copyright Act covers choreographic works, even though the reader may have ascertained this only by perusing this discussion.

2. SUBJECT MATTER OF COPYRIGHT

Copyright is available for "original works of authorship fixed in any tangible medium of expression, now known or later developed from which they can be perceived, reproduced or otherwise communicated, either directly or with the aid of a machine or device." 17 U.S.C. § 102(a). This formulation includes several ingredients. First, in accordance with the provision in art. I, sec. 8, cl. 8 of the Constitution, which grants authors the exclusive right to their "writings," fixation in a tangible medium is a prerequisite. For example, an extemporaneous speech or a completely improvised dramatic or musical performance would not be covered. It should be noted, however, that such creations might be protected under other legal theories, such as "common-law copyright," "unfair competition," or "right of publicity."

In addition to being "fixed," a protected work must reflect "originality" and "authorship." These requirements also follow the constitutional provision for protection for the "writings" of "authors." The legislative history of the 1976 Copyright Act makes clear that the standards for satisfying these requirements are intended to be pretty much what they have been throughout the years. These standards have not been high. An author need not have made an objective contribution to society. (Such a contribution *would* be required of an inventor in order to earn a patent.) Similarly, an author need not produce a work of recognized intellectual or artistic merit. It suffices if the author refrains from copying from prior works and contributes more than a minimal amount of creativity. Courts have often stated that neither judges nor administrators may appropriately act as the arbiters of merit. Rather, a *system* of protection will promote knowledge even if particular works do not.

Although works copied from other works do not qualify for protection, many works are consciously based on earlier works. They may incorporate part of the earlier work but significantly add to it. Examples would be translations, revisions, or adaptations. These are called "derivative works." They can be protected, but only to the extent of the new material that is added. The same principle applies to a "compilation," which is defined as "a work formed by the collection and assembling of preexisting materials or of data that are selected, coordinated, or arranged in such a way that the resulting work as a whole constitutes an original work of authorship." Thus a compilation ranges from a collection of unadorned facts, such as the names and addresses in a college alumni directory, to subjective listings, such as a food critic's choice of the ten best restaurants in New York City, to highly elaborated works, such as an anthology of poetry with accompanying critical essays. It would also include, in this electronic era, computerized data bases. Copyright protection for the compilation extends only to the material newly contributed by the compiler, particularly the selection and arrangement of the component elements; it will not, for example in the last illustration, affect the copyright status — or the public-domain status — of the poetry incorporated in the compilation.

3. DURATION, OWNERSHIP, AND FORMALITIES

a. Duration of Copyright

When copyright protection begins and ends depends on when the work was created. As to works created today or in the future, copyright attaches automatically as soon as the work is put down on paper or tape or some other tangible medium. 17 U.S.C. § 102(a). Its duration depends on whether its author was one individual; more than one individual; or someone creating the work in the employ of or at the direction of some other person or organization. The last situation may result in a so-called "work made for hire." To take, at this time, only the example of a literary, musical or artistic work created by an individual after January 1, 1978, copyright lasts for a period of 50 years from the death of the author. This contrasts with the two-term format that has characterized our copyright law since its beginnings and that was in place under the 1909 Act — an initial term of 28 years, starting typically with the work's publication with copyright notice, followed by a 28-year renewal term if timely application were made to the Copyright Office.

The period of copyright protection for a work that was created before the present law became effective on January 1, 1978, depends on a number of factors: whether it was "published" (a term of art that was elaborated under the prior statutes) and whether it was on January 1, 1978 protected in its initial or renewal term of copyright under the 1909 Act. The elaborate provisions of the present statute will be explored below. It suffices to say that, for the most part, unpublished works (e.g., manuscripts and personal letters) will be protected until at least 2002 (or, if later, 50 years after the author's death), and that works published before 1978 may be protected for 75 years. Works published more than 75 years ago are in the public domain.

b. Ownership

The Copyright Act gives initial copyright ownership to the author (or authors who jointly create a work). 17 U.S.C. § 201(a). In the case of "works made for hire" — a work prepared by an employee within the scope of his employment and certain works commissioned from independent contractors — the employer is considered the author. As "intangible property," a copyright can be transferred from the author to another, *inter vivos* or by will or by intestate succession, in whole or in part. To be an effective transfer, a grant of "exclusive" rights must be in writing and signed by the grantor; a "non-exclusive" grant may be valid even though oral. The grant may cover the entire scope of copyright, or be limited to a particular time period or territory (e.g., a one-year license to perform a copyrighted play in New York City) or medium of expression (e.g., only the right to print a novel but not the right to serialize it in a magazine or prepare a screenplay based on it). A grant need not be recorded in the U.S. Copyright Office, but there are significant advantages in doing so.

In addition to the considerable flexibility afforded the copyright owner to subdivide his or her copyright and otherwise exploit it, the 1976 Act confers a special protective privilege on author-transferors and their families. Because of the highly speculative value of literary, artistic and musical works — at least shortly after they are created — an author who grants an interest in a copyright, after January 1, 1978, may terminate that grant, upon complying with certain procedures, effective 35 years after the grant was made. (There is also a termination right with respect to a narrow category of copyright transfers made prior to January 1, 1978.) This termination option cannot be contracted away or waived in advance.

Finally, one should note the distinction between ownership of a copyright, or of any of the exclusive rights under a copyright, and ownership of "any material object in which the work is embodied." Suppose an artist paints a work, and sells the finished canvas. Unless the artist has made specific provision otherwise, he or she retains all exploitation rights in the work. Thus the artist would have the sole right to create postcards — a derivative work — based on the painting. But the artist cannot prevent the buyer from selling, renting, or making certain public displays (for example, in an art gallery) of the physical object — the canvas — which the buyer now owns. *See* 17 U.S.C. §§ 109, 202.

c. Notice and Registration of Copyright

The role of the copyright notice has been sharply reduced since United States adherence to the Berne Convention, which forbids conditioning the enjoyment of copyright upon compliance with formalities. Nonetheless, because adherence does not affect the status of works published before the effective date of the ratification, familiarity with pre-Berne notice requirements remains important. These requirements, in turn, differ depending on whether the work is governed by the 1976 Act or by its predecessor the 1909 Act.

Before January 1, 1978, in order to enjoy a copyright, published works had to bear a copyright notice, which would follow a prescribed form. If the notice was not properly affixed upon publication, the work went into the public domain. These rules remain important even after 1978 if a pre-1978 work is at issue.

The 1976 Act liberalized the notice rules for works published on or after January 1, 1978. As originally written, the 1976 Act continued to prescribe the use of a copyright notice on all copies and phonorecords publicly distributed (anywhere in the world) under authority of the copyright owner. The notice consisted of the three familiar elements — a copyright word or symbol, the name of the copyright owner, and the year of first publication. But the formal requirements were made more flexible, both with respect to location of the notice and the consequences of error in, or total lack of, notice.

Most recently, after 200 years of requiring some form of notice as a condition of a valid copyright, our law was changed effective March 1, 1989. Notice is no longer necessary on copies and phonorecords publicly distributed after that date. Nonetheless, copyright notice continues to be routinely used; there are modest statutory incentives to do so, and in any event the notice is an effective and inexpensive way for the copyright owner to call its claim to the attention of potential users.

A common misunderstanding is that registration with the Copyright Office is a condition to a valid copyright. In fact, registration of claims to copyright is optional. But the advantages of registration are very significant. Among other things, it is generally a prerequisite to an action for infringement; and it provides a number of advantages in proving a case and securing remedies. *See* 17 U.S.C. §§ 408-12. Accordingly, it is most advisable to register promptly in the case of any work of significance. (Legislation pending as this book goes to press would repeal the requirement of pre-suit registration and would eliminate preferential remedies for those who promptly register.)

The registration procedure is relatively simple. A short application form states the required information regarding authorship, year in which the work was created, and the like — and is to be accompanied by deposit of one or two copies of the work (as prescribed by regulation) and a $20 fee. The Copyright Office examines the application and deposit copies to see that they are generally in proper form. The Office does not compare the deposit copies to earlier material or judge their worth.

4. SCOPE OF EXCLUSIVE RIGHTS UNDER COPYRIGHT

a. Exclusive Rights

Among the exclusive rights comprised within a copyright, the **reproduction** right, or right to produce copies, is the most basic of all. The right protects against verbatim copying and against paraphrasing. But the right prohibits only actual use of the copyright owner's work as a model, either directly or indirectly; it does not cover coincidental similarities in a work created independently and without reference to the first. Moreover, the second author must have copied protected material. As explained earlier, a second author may freely copy a copyrighted work's ideas and discrete facts, so long as he or she does not also copy the expression or particular manner in which the first author set forth these ideas and facts. In addition, to violate the exclusive right of reproduction, the second author's copying must be "substantial." No set rule or formula can determine when the defendant's copying has been substantial; even a small extract from a larger work may be found to infringe, depending on the nature of the copyrighted work and of the portion copied.

The adaptation right, or right to make **derivative works**, overlaps somewhat with the reproduction right. Thus, a poster containing a photograph of a copyrighted painting is in a sense a "copy." But, whether or not a translation or a motion picture version of a copyrighted novel is comfortably thought of as a "copy," they too will infringe if unauthorized — for they are "derivative works." A derivative work "is a work based upon one or more pre-existing works," and includes "any ... form in which a work may be recast, transformed, or adapted."

The copyright owner also has the exclusive right to **distribute** the work to the public "by sale or other transfer of ownership, or by rental, lease, or lending." The right clearly prohibits sales of unlawfully produced copies of a work. Whether the right also protects the copyright owner against sale of licensed copies at a time or place or under circumstances that the copyright owner did not authorize depends principally on whether the accused act was the first or a subsequent distribution of the copy involved. The copyright owner has the right to control only the *first* public distribution of a particular copy of the work, whether by rental or sale. After first distribution, it is not infringement (although it may be breach of contract) for the owner of particular copies within the United States to rent or sell them without authority of the copyright owner. An important exception to this so-called "first sale doctrine" is the unauthorized rental for profit of phonograph records or computer programs — even though those records or programs were lawfully manufactured and lawfully purchased by the commercial renter; the purpose of course is to inhibit those who would make a profit inducing retail patrons to engage in home copying.

The rights of **public performance and display** are of great importance to dramatic, musical, and audiovisual works. This last category includes both conventional works such as motion pictures, and works in newer media such as computer-generated videogames. The display right also covers pictorial, graphic, and sculptural works, although the copyright proprietor may not, absent an appropriate contractual provision, prevent the owner of a particular copy (including the original) from displaying it in a museum, art gallery, or other public place.

The statute defines a public performance or display as one presented at a place open to the public or where a substantial number of persons outside of a normal circle of a family or its social acquaintances is gathered, or presented by a transmission, such as a radio or television broadcast. Thus, absent the consent of the copyright owner, reading a copyrighted lecture or poem aloud in a public auditorium, or showing a painting or sculpture on a television program (or a computer network), will constitute respectively an infringing public performance and public display.

How can the copyright owner of, say, a popular song monitor all of the possible infringements of his or her musical work through public performances in nightclubs, concert halls, and radio and television broadcasts? That is the task of the so-called performing rights societies, most notably the American Society of Composers, Authors and Publishers (ASCAP) and Broadcast Music Incorporated (BMI). These societies license the performance rights in nondramatic musical compositions, pursue unlicensed users, and distribute royalties to their composer, lyricist, and publisher members. Performing rights societies are the most well-established examples of collective licensing entities in the United States — and are serving as a model for licensing arrangements for the photocopying of books and periodicals. By representing the interests of large numbers of copyright holders, the performing rights societies are able to secure better enforcement and compensation than could individual claimants. The collective nature of the licensing also benefits users: rather than seek out individual authors, a party wishing to perform quantities of copyrighted music may obtain all the requisite authorizations from one or two sources.

b. Copyright Litigation

28 U.S.C. § 1338(a) vests exclusive jurisdiction over copyright (and patent) claims in the federal courts. A party seeking to prove the infringement of exclusive rights under copyright, and particularly of the reproduction and derivative works rights, must make out the following **elements of a claim**: (1) *Ownership* of a valid copyright (or of an exclusive right under copyright). If registration occurs within five years of first publication of the work, the certificate of registration serves as *prima facie* evidence of the validity of the copyright. (2) *Copying* of plaintiff's work by the defendant. Because copyright protects against reproduction, but not against independent generation of the same or similar work, there can be no copyright infringement unless defendant came into contact with and in fact copied plaintiff's work. Copying is ordinarily proved through circumstantial evidence: did the defendant have access to the plaintiff's work and are there similarities of expression (i.e., the sequence of words or notes) that are probative of copying rather than independent origination. The copying need not have been intentional: subconscious or unconscious copying of a work can constitute infringing copying. The kind of similarity that permits an inference of copying is called *probative similarity*. (3) As a result of the copying, defendant's work is *substantially similar* to plaintiff's. Substantial similarity may be determined with respect to either the quantity or the quality of the copying. Copying a small, but central, portion of plaintiff's original work can constitute substantial and infringing copying.

If plaintiff succeeds in the above demonstration, it has made out a *prima facie* case of copyright infringement. The burden now shifts to the defendant to justify its conduct, if it can, by application of a relevant statutory exception to copyright infringement (discussed immediately below).

If the copyright owner prevails, the available **remedies** include preliminary and permanent injunctions against further infringements, impoundment and destruction of infringing articles, and damages. Damages can either be actual, as determined by the plaintiff's actual damages and the defendant's profits, or can take the form of what is known as "statutory damages"; the latter measure, with a largely deterrent objective, is to be determined by the judge under the circumstances of the case, and typically fits within a minimum of $500 and a maximum of $20,000 for each work infringed (with a possible assessment as high as $100,000 where the infringement is willful). The court also has discretion to award the prevailing party its attorney's fees.

5. LIMITATIONS ON THE EXCLUSIVE RIGHTS UNDER COPYRIGHT

a. Exemptions and Compulsory Licenses

The exclusive rights of copyright proprietors to reproduce, adapt, distribute, perform, or display their works encounter manifold and complicated statutory limitations. For example, the Copyright Act permits many classroom, religious, and charitable performances and displays of copyrighted works. The statute exempts most live classroom uses, including the performance of copyrighted dramatic works. Songs may be sung, and other musical compositions played, in most school settings — and also in a number of other noncommercial settings. Instructional broadcasts are also exempted from copyright liability if they meet statutory requirements. The Act also provides that a public performance or display of a work through a transmission on a "home-type receiving apparatus" is not an infringement, if there is no direct charge to see or hear the transmission, and if there is no further public transmission. Essentially, this provision concerns the use by small commercial establishments of a radio to provide background music.

In other instances, the Act removes certain reproductions, performances, and displays from the copyright owner's exclusive control and substitutes a "compulsory licensing" scheme. This compromise provision permits certain uses of the copyrighted work without the copyright owner's consent, but requires the user to adhere to statutory formalities, and to pay specified fees to the copyright owner. The most important and longstanding example of the compulsory license — incorporated in our law since the 1909 Act — relates to making recordings of nondramatic musical works. The current statute provides that once the copyright owner of a nondramatic musical composition has authorized distribution to the public in the United States of a "phonorecord" embodying the composition, another producer may make and distribute phonorecords of the composition to the public. The compulsory licensee may not, without authorization, simply duplicate a preexisting recording; it must produce an independent sound recording with its own musical performers and arrangement. Therefore, the statute permits the compulsory licensee some leeway to arrange the music (technically, the making of a derivative work).

The 1976 Act, as originally written, extended the compulsory-license format to other situations as well: performances of music in jukeboxes, certain retransmissions of television programs by cable services, and certain uses of music and art by public broadcasting stations. The jukebox compulsory license has since been displaced by negotiated arrangements between jukebox operators and performing rights societies, so as to comply with the pertinent provisions of the Berne Convention. The cable compulsory license — since extended to television retransmissions effected by satellite technology — is coming under reconsideration in Congress, as the cable industry has become an economic giant among the communications media and is thought by many no longer to need the boost given by the compulsory-license provisions of the Copyright Act.

b. Fair Use

Perhaps the best known, most important, and most elusive exception to the exclusive rights of the copyright owner is embodied in the doctrine known as fair use. The doctrine, a feature of our copyright law since the middle of the nineteenth century through judicial creation and elaboration, was developed in order to allow unauthorized uses that the courts thought were reasonable and that did not unduly deprive the plaintiff's work of a market. Fair use is now expressly incorporated in the statute for the first time, in Section 107.

That section lists several kinds of illustrative uses subject to the defense, including criticism, comment, news reporting, teaching, scholarship, and research. Nonetheless, a defendant who has reproduced, adapted, or publicly distributed, performed, or displayed a copyrighted work without authorization must do more than invoke one of the above socially beneficent purposes. The statute also enumerates four factors to be reviewed in the disposition of the defense. These factors are: the nature of the defendant's use; the nature of the copyrighted work; the amount and substantiality of the portions taken from the copyrighted work; and the effect of the taking upon the potential market for the copyrighted work. These four factors are not exhaustive. Because the fair-use doctrine is still "an equitable rule of reason," courts are free to consider other factors, or to give greater weight to some factors than to others, depending on the given case. A defendant invoking the fair-use defense must establish that the balance of the statutory and any additional judicial criteria weighs in his or her favor.

Fair use has been characteristically invoked as a defense in cases involving historical and biographical works that have quoted from or paraphrased earlier such works or original source materials still in copyright. It has also been invoked by parodists who have borrowed from an earlier work, to poke fun either at that work or at some extrinsic social or political phenomenon. Among the most perplexing applications of the fair use doctrine has been to the relatively new copying technologies, such as audiotaping, videotaping, and photocopying. The Supreme Court has held, for example, that home videotaping of copyrighted television programs, to facilitate later viewing, is a fair use. Lower courts continue to wrestle with the question of photocopying for a variety of purposes, both commercial and nonprofit. A factor that some courts have considered in assessing the fairness of certain photocopying practices is the existence of the Copyright Clearance Center, a consortium of publishers of scientific and technical books and journals, which undertakes collective licensing efforts, much as ASCAP and BMI do for music copyright holders. Fair use questions in connection with the duplication and use of copyrighted computer programs are also arising with increasing frequency.

When the photocopying is by a library — whether for internal purposes such as the preservation of archival material or the replacement of a lost copy, or for service to library users engaged in research — the Copyright Act does not rely on the elusive and generalized treatment of fair use in § 107. Rather, one must turn to the much more detailed provisions in § 108. This section, reflecting a hard-fought adjustment of interests between libraries and researchers on the one hand and authors and publishers on the other, allows the making of single photocopies of certain kinds of works under certain stipulated circumstances. It does not govern the "systematic" making of multiple photocopies that in effect substitute for subscriptions or purchases; nor does it exempt photocopying done by library users at photocopy machines made available by the library for their convenience.

Several commentators have contended that the First Amendment affords a privilege, separate from statutory exemptions or limitations, to make otherwise infringing reproductions, adaptations, performances, or displays of a copyrighted work. Courts, however, have generally declined to recognize a

First Amendment-copyright conflict. The Supreme Court, in fact, has held that two features inherent in copyright law amply secure protection of free speech interests. First, copyright does not prevent the free dissemination of the author's facts and ideas. Second, even "expression" may be copied, by virtue of the fair-use doctrine, in many instances in which there is a compelling societal justification for doing so.

6. STRUCTURE AND OPERATIONS OF THE COPYRIGHT OFFICE

The Copyright Office, a department of the Library of Congress, has for a century been charged with the registration of claims to copyright and with related duties. The copies of works that have been deposited in conjunction with such registration have been used to enrich the holdings of the Library. Beyond that most important day-to-day task, the Office also exercises the power to promulgate regulations (as is true of federal administrative agencies generally). Section 702 of the Copyright Act provides: "The Register of Copyrights is authorized to establish regulations not inconsistent with law for the administration of the functions and duties made the responsibility of the Register under this title. All regulations established by the Register under this title are subject to the approval of the Librarian of Congress." Excerpts from the regulations of the Copyright Office are set forth in Appendix C to this casebook. These regulations cover a variety of subjects, from the kinds of works that are ineligible for registration to the details of copyright notice and of registration and deposit. Because these regulations reflect the Register's interpretation of the statute, they are always subject to challenge in a court for their consistency with the Act (as provided in § 702).

In addition to its power to issue regulations, the Copyright Office has also with increasing frequency — both at congressional direction and on its own initiative — prepared a variety of reports on significant policy issues relating to copyright. In addition, throughout the various copyright reform efforts since the turn of the century, the Register of Copyrights — the head of the Copyright Office — has been a major voice for change and improvement of our copyright law.

While registration has important procedural, and even substantive ramifications, it must be emphasized that the Copyright Office does not grant copyrights; copyright subsists in a work as soon as that work is "created," i.e., "fixed in a copy or phonorecord for the first time." (Even under the 1909 Act, copyright attached to a work when it was publicly disseminated with an appropriate notice; registration could follow later. Copyright is to be distinguished in this respect from the functions of the Patent and Trademark Office, in the Department of Commerce, which issues patents (the effectiveness of which dates only from the date of issuance, the claim of "patent pending" to the contrary notwithstanding). See 35 U.S.C. § 131. Compare § 7(a) of the Lanham Trademark Act, 15 U.S.C. § 1057(a) (registration of trademarks).

When an application for copyright registration is filed, however, the function of the Examining Division, though modest, is not altogether nonexistent. It has commonly been assumed that the Register of Copyrights has the power to decline to register a work, a power of some significance since registration — while not a condition of copyright itself — has long been a condition to suing for infringement. Registration has been denied for works deemed by the Register to lack sufficient originality, or to be solely utilitarian in design, or to be covered by an existing design patent, or to be obscene. (*But see Mitchell Bros. Film Group v. Cinema Adult Theater, infra.*) This power to deny registration has been controversial and has been exercised sparingly; the Register, in fact, adheres to a policy that, in cases of doubt, dictates registration. (This policy was, for example, employed beginning in 1964 to explain the Register's willingness to register computer programs.) If registration is denied, and a copyright claimant wishes to sue for infringement, he or she is not barred from doing so; but the plaintiff must give notice of the lawsuit to the Register, who is empowered to intervene with respect to the issue of registrability. Recordation of assignments, mortgages and other transactions involving copyright has long complemented the basic examining and registration function of the office.

The Copyright Office has a number of divisions which carry out the various functions necessary to implement the statute. Among those divisions are: the Deposits and Acquisitions Division, which establishes controls over the collections of the Library of Congress through implementation of the statute's deposit requirements; the Examining Division, which examines all applications and material presented to the Copyright Office for registration of original and renewal copyright claims and which determines whether the material deposited constitutes copyrightable subject matter and whether the other legal and formal requirements of the statute have been met; and the Information and Reference Division, which, among other things, educates staff and the public on the copyright law, issues and distributes informational materials, responds to reference requests regarding copyright matters, and prepares search reports based upon copyright records. The interested student can obtain on-line access to copyright registration records dating from 1978.

D. DISTINCTIONS: PATENTS

PATENT STATUTE

35 U.S.C. 101-03, 112, 154, 171, 173, 271

§ 101. *Inventions patentable*

Whoever invents or discovers any new and useful process, machine, manufacture, or composition of matter, or any new and useful improvement thereof, may obtain a patent therefor, subject to the conditions and requirements of this title.

§ 102. *Conditions for patentability; novelty and loss of right to patent*

A person shall be entitled to a patent unless

(a) the invention was known or used by others in this country, or patented or described in a printed publication in this or a foreign country, before the invention thereof by the applicant for patent, or

(b) the invention was patented or described in a printed publication in this or a foreign country or in public use or on sale in this country, more than one year prior to the date of the application for patent in the United States, or

(c) he has abandoned the invention, or

(d) the invention was first patented or caused to be patented, or was the subject of an inventor's certificate, by the applicant or his legal representatives or assigns in a foreign country prior to the date of the application for patent in this country on an application for patent or inventor's certificate filed more than twelve months before the filing of the application in the United States, or

(e) the invention was described in a patent granted on an application for patent by another filed in the United States before the invention thereof by the applicant for patent, or on an international application by another who has fulfilled the requirements of paragraphs (1), (2), and (4) of section 371(c) of this title before the invention thereof by the applicant for patent, or

(f) he did not himself invent the subject matter sought to be patented, or

(g) before the applicant's invention thereof the invention was made in this country by another who had not abandoned, suppressed, or concealed it. In determining priority of invention there shall be considered not only the respective dates of conception and reduction to practice of the invention, but also the reasonable diligence of one who was first to conceive and last to reduce to practice, from a time prior to conception by the other.

§ 103. Conditions for patentability; non-obvious subject matter

A patent may not be obtained though the invention is not identically disclosed or described as set forth in section 102 of this title, if the differences between the subject matter sought to be patented and the prior art are such that the subject matter as a whole would have been obvious at the time the invention was made to a person having ordinary skill in the art to which said subject matter pertains. Patentability shall not be negatived by the manner in which the invention was made.

§ 112. Specification

The specification shall contain a written description of the invention, and of the manner and process of making and using it, in such full, clear, concise, and exact terms as to enable any person skilled in the art to which it pertains, or with which it is most nearly connected, to make and use the same, and shall set forth the best mode contemplated by the inventor of carrying out his invention.

The specification shall conclude with one or more claims particularly pointing out and distinctly claiming the subject matter which the applicant regards as his invention....

§ 154. Contents and term of patent

Every patent shall contain a short title of the invention and a grant to the patentee, his heirs or assigns, for the term of seventeen years, subject to the payment of fees as provided for in this title, of the right to exclude others from making, using, or selling the invention throughout the United States, referring to the specification for the particulars thereof. A copy of the specification and drawings shall be annexed to the patent and be a part thereof.

§ 171. Patents for designs

Whoever invents any new, original and ornamental design for an article of manufacture may obtain a patent therefor, subject to the conditions and requirements of this title.

The provisions of this title relating to patents for inventions shall apply to patents for designs, except as otherwise provided.

§ 173. Term of design patent

Patents for designs shall be granted for the term of fourteen years.

§ 271. Infringement of patent

(a) Except as otherwise provided in this title, whoever without authority makes, uses or sells any patented invention, within the United States during the term of the patent therefor, infringes the patent.

(b) Whoever actively induces infringement of a patent shall be liable as an infringer.

(c) Whoever sells a component of a patented machine, manufacture, combination or composition, or a material or apparatus for use in practicing a patented process, constituting a material part of the invention, knowing the same to be especially made or especially adapted for use in an infringement of such patent, and not a staple article or commodity of commerce suitable for substantial noninfringing use, shall be liable as a contributory infringer.

GRAHAM v. JOHN DEERE CO.

383 U.S. 1 (1965)

MR. JUSTICE CLARK delivered the opinion of the Court.

After a lapse of 15 years, the Court again focuses its attention on the patentability of inventions under the standard of Art. I, § 8, cl. 8, of the Constitution and under the conditions prescribed by the laws of the United States. Since our last expression on patent validity, *A. & P. Tea Co. v. Super-market Corp.*, 340 U.S. 147 (1950), the Congress has for the first time expressly added a third statutory dimension to the two requirements of novelty and utility that had been the sole statutory test since the Patent Act of 1793. This is the test of obviousness, *i.e.*, whether "the subject matter sought to be patented and the prior art are such that the subject matter as a whole would have been obvious at the time the invention was made to a person having ordinary skill in the art to which said subject matter pertains. Patentability shall not be negatived by the manner in which the invention was made." § 103 of the Patent Act of 1952, 35 U.S.C. § 103 (1964 ed.).

The questions, involved in each of the companion cases before us, are what effect the 1952 Act had upon traditional statutory and judicial tests of patentability and what definitive tests are now required. We have concluded that the 1952 Act was intended to codify judicial precedents embracing the principle long ago announced by this Court in *Hotchkiss v. Greenwood,* 11

How. 248 (1851), and that, while the clear language of § 103 places emphasis on an inquiry into obviousness, the general level of innovation necessary to sustain patentability remains the same.

   . . . .

II

At the outset it must be remembered that the federal patent power stems from a specific constitutional provision which authorizes the Congress "To promote the Progress of ... useful Arts, by securing for limited Times to ... Inventors the exclusive Right to their ... Discoveries." Art. I, § 8, cl. 8. The clause is both a grant of power and a limitation. This qualified authority, unlike the power often exercised in the sixteenth and seventeenth centuries by the English Crown, is limited to the promotion of advances in the "useful arts." It was written against the backdrop of the practices — eventually curtailed by the Statute of Monopolies — of the Crown in granting monopolies to court favorites in goods or businesses which had long before been enjoyed by the public. The Congress in the exercise of the patent power may not overreach the restraints imposed by the stated constitutional purpose. Nor may it enlarge the patent monopoly without regard to the innovation, advancement or social benefit gained thereby. Moreover, Congress may not authorize the issuance of patents whose effects are to remove existent knowledge from the public domain, or to restrict free access to materials already available. Innovation, advancement, and things which add to the sum of useful knowledge are inherent requisites in a patent system which by constitutional command must "promote the Progress of ... useful Arts." This is the *standard* expressed in the Constitution and it may not be ignored. And it is in this light that patent validity "requires reference to a standard written into the Constitution." *A. & P. Tea Co. v. Supermarket Corp., supra,* at 154 (concurring opinion).

Within the limits of the constitutional grant, the Congress may, of course, implement the stated purpose of the Framers by selecting the policy which in its judgment best effectuates the constitutional aim. This is but a corollary to the grant to Congress of any Article I power. Within the scope established by the Constitution, Congress may set out conditions and tests for patentability. It is the duty of the Commissioner of Patents and of the courts in the administration of the patent system to give effect to the constitutional standard by appropriate application, in each case, of the statutory scheme of the Congress.

Congress quickly responded to the bidding of the Constitution by enacting the Patent Act of 1790 during the second session of the First Congress. It created an agency in the Department of State headed by the Secretary of State, the Secretary of the Department of War and the Attorney General, any two of whom could issue a patent for a period not exceeding 14 years to any petitioner that "hath ... invented or discovered any useful art, manufacture, ... or device, or any improvement therein not before known or used" if the board found that "the invention or discovery [was] sufficiently useful and important ...." 1 Stat. 110. This group, whose members administered the patent system along with their other public duties, was known by its own designation as "Commissioners for the Promotion of Useful Arts."

Thomas Jefferson, who as Secretary of State was a member of the group, was its moving spirit and might well be called the "first administrator of our patent system." See Federico, Operation of the Patent Act of 1790, 18 J. Pat. Off. Soc. 237, 238 (1936). He was not only an administrator of the patent system under the 1790 Act, but was also the author of the 1793 Patent Act. In addition, Jefferson was himself an inventor of great note. His unpatented improvements on plows, to mention but one line of his inventions, won acclaim and recognition on both sides of the Atlantic. Because of his active interest and influence in the early development of the patent system, Jefferson's views on the general nature of the limited patent monopoly under the Constitution, as well as his conclusions as to conditions for patentability under the statutory scheme, are worthy of note.

Jefferson, like other Americans, had an instinctive aversion to monopolies. It was a monopoly on tea that sparked the Revolution and Jefferson certainly did not favor an equivalent form of monopoly under the new government. His abhorrence of monopoly extended initially to patents as well. From France, he wrote to Madison (July 1788) urging a Bill of Rights provision restricting monopoly, and as against the argument that limited monopoly might serve to incite "ingenuity," he argued forcefully that "the benefit even of limited monopolies is too doubtful to be opposed to that of their general suppression," V Writings of Thomas Jefferson, at 47 (Ford ed., 1895).

His views ripened, however, and in another letter to Madison (Aug. 1789) after the drafting of the Bill of Rights, Jefferson stated that he would have been pleased by an express provision in this form:

> Art 9. Monopolies may be allowed to persons for their own productions in literature & their own inventions in the arts, for a term not exceeding — years but for no longer term & no other purpose. *Id.*, at 113....

... He rejected a natural-rights theory in intellectual property rights and clearly recognized the social and economic rationale of the patent system. The patent monopoly was not designed to secure to the inventor his natural right in his discoveries. Rather, it was a reward, an inducement, to bring forth new knowledge. The grant of an exclusive right to an invention was the creation of society — at odds with the inherent free nature of disclosed ideas — and was not to be freely given. Only inventions and discoveries which furthered human knowledge, and were new and useful, justified the special inducement of a limited private monopoly. Jefferson did not believe in granting patents for small details, obvious improvements, or frivolous devices. His writings evidence his insistence upon a high level of patentability.

As a member of the patent board for several years, Jefferson saw clearly the difficulty in "drawing a line between the things which are worth to the public the embarrassment of an exclusive patent, and those which are not." The board on which he served sought to draw such a line and formulated several rules which are preserved in Jefferson's correspondence. Despite the board's efforts, Jefferson saw "with what slow progress a system of general rules could be matured." Because of the "abundance" of cases and the fact that the investigations occupied "more time of the members of the board than they could spare from higher duties, the whole was turned over to the judiciary, to be matured into a system, under which every one might know when his actions were safe and lawful." Apparently Congress agreed with Jefferson and the board that the courts should develop additional conditions for patentability. Although the Patent Act was amended, revised or codified some 50 times between 1790 and 1950, Congress steered clear of a statutory set of requirements other than the bare novelty and utility tests reformulated in Jefferson's draft of the 1793 Patent Act.

III

The difficulty of formulating conditions for patentability was heightened by the generality of the constitutional grant and the statutes implementing it, together with the underlying policy of the patent system that "the things which are worth to the public the embarrassment of an exclusive patent," as Jefferson put it, must outweigh the restrictive effect of the limited patent monopoly. The inherent problem was to develop some means of weeding out those inventions which would not be disclosed or devised but for the inducement of a patent.

This Court formulated a general condition of patentability in 1851 in *Hotchkiss v. Greenwood,* 11 How. 248. The patent involved a mere substitution of materials — porcelain or clay for wood or metal in doorknobs — and the Court condemned it, holding:

> [U]nless more ingenuity and skill ... were required ... than were possessed by an ordinary mechanic acquainted with the business, there was an absence of that degree of skill and ingenuity which constitute essential elements of every invention. In other words, the improvement is the work of the skilful mechanic, not that of the inventor.
> At p. 267.

Hotchkiss, by positing the condition that a patentable invention evidence more ingenuity and skill than that possessed by an ordinary mechanic acquainted with the business, merely distinguished between new and useful innovations that were capable of sustaining a patent and those that were not. The *Hotchkiss* test laid the cornerstone of the judicial evolution suggested by Jefferson and left to the courts by Congress. The language in the case, and in those which followed, gave birth to "invention" as a word of legal art signifying patentable inventions. Yet, as this Court has observed, "[t]he truth is the word ['invention'] cannot be defined in such manner as to afford any substantial aid in determining whether a particular device involves an exercise of the inventive faculty or not." *McClain v. Ortmayer,* 141 U.S. 419, 427 (1891); *A. & P. Tea Co. v. Supermarket Corp., supra,* at 151. Its use as a label brought about a large variety of opinions as to its meaning both in the Patent Office, in the courts, and at the bar. The *Hotchkiss* formulation, however, lies not in any label, but in its functional approach to questions of patentability. In practice, *Hotchkiss* has required a comparison between the subject matter of the patent, or patent application, and the background skill of the calling. It has been from this comparison that patentability was in each case determined.

IV. *The 1952 Patent Act*

The Act sets out the conditions of patentability in three sections. An analysis of the structure of these three sections indicates that patentability is dependent upon three explicit conditions: novelty and utility as articulated and defined in § 101 and § 102, and nonobviousness, the new statutory formulation, as set out in § 103. The first two sections, which trace closely the 1874 codification, express the "new and useful" tests which have always existed in the statutory scheme and, for our purposes here, need no clarification. The pivotal section around which the present controversy centers is § 103. It provides:

> § 103. *Conditions for patentability; non-obvious subject matter*
>
> A patent may not be obtained though the invention is not identically disclosed or described as set forth in section 102 of this title, if the differences between the subject matter sought to be patented and the prior art are such that the subject matter as a whole would have been obvious at the time the invention was made to a person having ordinary skill in the art to which said subject matter pertains. Patentability shall not be negatived by the manner in which the invention was made.

The section is cast in relatively unambiguous terms. Patentability is to depend, in addition to novelty and utility, upon the "non-obvious" nature of the "subject matter sought to be patented" to a person having ordinary skill in the pertinent art.

The first sentence of this section is strongly reminiscent of the language in *Hotchkiss*. Both formulations place emphasis on the pertinent art existing at the time the invention was made and both are implicitly tied to advances in that art. The major distinction is that Congress has emphasized "non-obviousness" as the operative test of the section, rather than the less definite "invention" language of *Hotchkiss* that Congress thought had led to "a large variety" of expressions in decisions and writings....

It is undisputed that this section was, for the first time, a statutory expression of an additional requirement for patentability, originally expressed in *Hotchkiss*. It also seems apparent that Congress intended by the last sentence of § 103 to abolish the test it believed this Court announced in the controversial phrase "flash of creative genius," used in *Cuno Corp. v. Automatic Devices Corp.*, 314 U.S. 84 (1941).

It is contended, however, by some of the parties and by several of the *amici* that the first sentence of § 103 was intended to sweep away judicial precedents and to lower the level of patentability. Others contend that the Congress intended to codify the essential purpose reflected in existing judicial precedents — the rejection of insignificant variations and innovations of a commonplace sort — and also to focus inquiries under § 103 upon nonobviousness, rather than upon "invention," as a means of achieving more stability and predictability in determining patentability and validity.

The Reviser's Note to this section, with apparent reference to *Hotchkiss*, recognizes that judicial requirements as to "lack of patentable novelty [have] been followed since at least as early as 1850." The note indicates that the section was inserted because it "may have some stabilizing effect, and also to serve as a basis for the addition at a later time of some criteria which may be worked out." To this same effect are the reports of both Houses, *supra,* which state that the first sentence of the section "paraphrases language which has often been used in decisions of the courts, and the section is added to the statute for uniformity and definiteness."

We believe that this legislative history, as well as other sources, shows that the revision was not intended by Congress to change the general level of patentable invention. We conclude that the section was intended merely as a codification of judicial precedents embracing the *Hotchkiss* condition, with congressional directions that inquiries into the obviousness of the subject matter sought to be patented are a prerequisite to patentability.

V

Approached in this light, the § 103 additional condition, when followed realistically, will permit a more practical test of patentability. The emphasis on nonobviousness is one of inquiry, not quality, and, as such, comports with the constitutional strictures.

While the ultimate question of patent validity is one of law, the § 103 condition, which is but one of three conditions, each of which must be satisfied, lends itself to several basic factual inquiries. Under § 103, the scope and content of the prior art are to be determined; differences between the prior art and the claims at issue are to be ascertained; and the level of ordinary skill in the pertinent art resolved. Against this background, the obviousness or nonobviousness of the subject matter is determined. Such secondary considerations as commercial success, long felt but unsolved needs, failure of others, etc., might be utilized to give light to the circumstances surrounding the origin of the subject matter sought to be patented. As indicia of obviousness or nonobviousness, these inquiries may have relevancy....

QUESTIONS

1. The *John Deere* case shows that the philosophical tension between the "natural rights" and "inducement" theories is found in the law of patent as well as in the law of copyright. Is there any reason to believe that the Founding Fathers would have resolved that tension by opting for one theory in patent and another in copyright? Phrased differently, does the same "instinctive aversion to monopolies" come into play as much for works of literature, art, and music as it does for inventions?

2. The administration of the patent statute involves a fairly rigorous examination of patent applications by a government official, and a comparison with the prior art. Are there significant differences in the field of copyright so as to explain why there is no comparable examining system? There is, as noted previously, an Examining Division within the Copyright Office. What do you suppose it does?

3. Note that § 171 of the Patent Act extends the entire patent regime — novelty, nonobviousness, examining system, etc. — to ornamental designs for manufactured articles. How would the standard of nonobviousness be applied

to determine whether a design patent should be granted, for example, to an attractively shaped dress or piece of furniture? Should the examiner, or court, consider the reaction of the skilled dress or furniture designer, or of the average consumer?

4. Would it be constitutional for Congress to accord protection to dress and furniture designs under the law of copyright? That is, are they "writings"? Does the availability of design patent protection — with strict standards of patentability and a relatively short period of protection — indicate that Congress intends to exclude these designs from the scope of copyright? (These issues will be explored in greater detail in Chapter 2, Subchapter E, *infra*.)

ALFRED BELL & CO. v. CATALDA FINE ARTS, INC.

191 F.2d 99 (2d Cir. 1951)

[Plaintiff sought protection for certain reproductions of public-domain paintings by the old masters. These were produced by plaintiff through a tedious and exacting form of engraving known as the "mezzotint method." Among its detailed findings, the district court stated: "The work of the engraver upon the plate requires the individual conception, judgment and execution by the engraver on the depth and shape of the depressions in the plate to be made by the scraping process in order to produce in this other medium the engraver's concept of the effect of the oil painting. No two engravers can produce identical interpretations of the same oil painting."]

FRANK, CIRCUIT JUDGE. 1. Congressional power to authorize both patents and copyrights is contained in Article 1, § 8 of the Constitution. In passing on the validity of patents, the Supreme Court recurrently insists that this constitutional provision governs. On this basis, pointing to the Supreme Court's consequent requirement that, to be valid, a patent must disclose a high degree of uniqueness, ingenuity and inventiveness, the defendants assert that the same requirement constitutionally governs copyrights. As several sections of the Copyright Act — *e.g.*, those authorizing copyrights of "reproductions of works of art," maps, and compilations — plainly dispense with any such high standard, defendants are, in effect, attacking the constitutionality of those sections. But the very language of the Constitution differentiates (a) "authors" and their "writings" from (b) "inventors" and their "discoveries." Those who penned the Constitution,[2] of course, knew the difference. The pre-revolutionary English statutes had made the distinction.[3] In 1783, the Continental

---

[2]Many of them were themselves authors.

[3]The Act of Anne 8, c. 10, was entitled "An Act for the encouraging of learning, by vesting of the copies of printed books in the authors or purchasers of such copies, during the times therein mentioned."

The previous history shows the source of the word "copyright." See 1 Laddas, The International Protection of Literary and Artistic Property (1938) 15:

"In England, the royal grants of privilege to print certain books were not copyrights. They were not granted to encourage learning or for the benefit of authors; they were commercial monopolies, licenses to tradesmen to follow their calling. As gradually monopolies became unpopular, the printers sought to base their claims on other grounds, and called the 'right of copy' not a monopoly, but a property right. The

Congress had passed a resolution recommending that the several states enact legislation to "secure" to authors the "copyright" of their books. Twelve of the thirteen states (in 1783-1786) enacted such statutes. Those of Connecticut and North Carolina covered books, pamphlets, maps, and charts.

Moreover, in 1790, in the year after the adoption of the Constitution, the first Congress enacted two statutes, separately dealing with patents and copyrights. The patent statute, enacted April 10, 1790, 1 Stat. 109, provided that patents should issue only if the Secretary of State, Secretary of War and the Attorney General, or any two of them "shall deem the invention or discovery sufficiently useful and important"; the applicant for a patent was obliged to file a specification "so particular" as "to distinguish the invention or discovery from other things before known and used ..."; the patent was to constitute *prima facie* evidence that the patentee was "the first and true inventor or ... discoverer ... of the thing so specified." The Copyright Act, enacted May 31, 1790, 1 Stat. 124, covered "maps, charts, and books." A printed copy of the title of any map, chart or book was to be recorded in the Clerk's office of the District Court, and a copy of the map, chart or book was to be delivered to the Secretary of State within six months after publication. Twelve years later, Congress in 1802, 2 Stat. 171, added, to matters that might be copyrighted, engravings, etchings and prints.

Thus legislators peculiarly familiar with the purpose of the Constitutional grant, by statute, imposed far less exacting standards in the case of copyrights. They authorized the copyrighting of a mere map which, patently, calls for no considerable uniqueness. They exacted far more from an inventor. And, while they demanded that an official should be satisfied as to the character of an invention before a patent issued, they made no such demand in respect of a copyright. In 1884, in *Burrow-Giles Lithographic Co. v. Sarony,* 111 U.S. 53, 57, the Supreme Court, adverting to these facts said: "The construction placed upon the constitution by the first act of 1790 and the act of 1802, by the men who were contemporary with its formation, many of whom were members of the convention which framed it, is of itself entitled to very great weight, and when it is remembered that the rights thus established have not been disputed during a period of nearly a century, it is almost conclusive." Accordingly, the Constitution, as so interpreted, recognizes that the standards for patents and copyrights are basically different.

The defendants' contention apparently results from the ambiguity of the word "original." It may mean startling, novel or unusual, a marked departure from the past. Obviously this is not what is meant when one speaks of "the original package," or the "original bill," or (in connection with the "best evi-

---

Stationers Company had a register in which its members entered the titles of the works they were privileged to print. A custom developed by which members refrained from printing the books which stood on the register in the name of another. Thus members respected each other's 'copy,' as it was called, and there grew up a trade recognition of 'the right of copy' or copyright. This right was subsequently embodied in a by-law of the Stationers Company. The entry in the register was regarded as a record of the rights of the individual named, and it was assumed that possession of a manuscript carried with it the right to print copies." See also Sheavyn, The Literary Profession in the Elizabethan Age (1909) 52-53, 64-65, 70-71, 76-80.

dence" rule) an "original" document; none of those things is highly unusual in creativeness. "Original" in reference to a copyrighted work means that the particular work "owes its origin" to the "author." No large measure of novelty is necessary. Said the Supreme Court in *Baker v. Selden,* 101 U.S. 99, 102-103: "The copyright of the book, if not pirated from other works, would be valid without regard to the novelty, or want of novelty, of its subject-matter. The novelty of the art or thing described or explained has nothing to do with the validity of the copyright. To give to the author of the book an exclusive property in the art described therein, when no examination of its novelty has ever been officially made, would be a surprise and a fraud upon the public. That is the province of letters-patent, not of copyright. The claim to an invention or discovery of an art or manufacture must be subjected to the examination of the Patent Office before an exclusive right therein can be obtained; and it can only be secured by a patent from the government. The difference between the two things, letters-patent and copyright, may be illustrated by reference to the subjects just enumerated. Take the case of medicines. Certain mixtures are found to be of great value in the healing art. If the discoverer writes and publishes a book on the subject (as regular physicians generally do), he gains no exclusive right to the manufacture and sale of the medicine; he gives that to the public. If he desires to acquire such exclusive right, he must obtain a patent for the mixture as a new art, manufacture, or composition of matter. He may copyright his book, if he pleases; but that only secures to him the exclusive right of printing and publishing his book. So of all other inventions or discoveries."

In *Bleistein v. Donaldson Lithographing Co.,* 183 U.S. 239, 250, 252, the Supreme Court cited with approval *Henderson v. Tompkins, C.C.,* 60 F. 758, where it was said, 60 F. at page 764: "There is a *very broad distinction between what is implied in the word 'author,' found in the constitution, and the word 'inventor.' The latter carries an implication which excludes the results of only ordinary skill, while nothing of this is necessarily involved in the former.* Indeed, the statutes themselves make broad distinctions on this point. So much as relates to copyrights … is expressed, so far as this particular is concerned, by the mere words, 'author, inventor, designer or proprietor,' with such aid as may be derived from the words 'written, composed or made,' …. But a *multitude of books rest safely under copyright, which show only ordinary skill and diligence in their preparation.* Compilations are noticeable examples of this fact. With reference to this subject, the courts have not undertaken to assume the functions of critics, or to measure carefully the degree of originality, or literary skill or training involved."

It is clear, then, that nothing in the Constitution commands that copyrighted matter be strikingly unique or novel. Accordingly, we were not ignoring the Constitution when we stated that a "copy of something in the public domain" will support a copyright if it is a "distinguishable variation"; or when we rejected the contention that "like a patent, a copyrighted work must be not only original, but new," adding, "That is not … the law as is obvious in the case of maps or compendia, where later works will necessarily be anticipated." All that is needed to satisfy both the Constitution and the statute is that the "author" contributed something more than a "merely trivial" variation, something recognizably "his own." Originality in this context "means little more than a prohibition of actual copying."[13] No matter how poor artistically the "author's" addition, it is enough if it be his own. *Bleistein v. Donaldson Lithographing Co.,* 188 U.S. 239, 47 L. Ed. 460.

On that account, we have often distinguished between the limited protection accorded a copyright owner and the extensive protection granted a patent owner. So we have held that "independent reproduction of a copyrighted ... work is not infringement," whereas it is *vis à vis* a patent. Correlative with the greater immunity of a patentee is the doctrine of anticipation which does not apply to copyrights: The alleged inventor is chargeable with full knowledge of all the prior art, although in fact he may be utterly ignorant of it. The "author" is entitled to a copyright if he independently contrived a work completely identical with what went before; similarly, although he obtains a valid copyright, he has no right to prevent another from publishing a work identical with his, if not copied from his. A patentee, unlike a copyrightee, must not merely produce something "original"; he must also be "the first inventor or discoverer." "Hence it is possible to have a plurality of valid copyrights directed to closely identical or even identical works. Moreover, none of them, if independently arrived at without copying, will constitute an infringement of the copyright of the others."[16]

    ....

---

[13] Hoague-Sprague Corp. v. Frank C. Meyer, Inc., D.C.N.Y., 31 F.2d 583, 586. See also as to photographs Judge Learned Hand in Jewelers Circular Publishing Co. v. Keystone Pub. Co., D.C.N.Y., 274 F. 932, 934.
    The English doctrine is the same. See Copinger, The Law of Copyrights (7th ed. 1936) 40-44: "Neither original thought nor original research is essential"; he quotes the English courts to the effect that the statute "does not require that the expression must be in an original or novel form, but that the work must not be copied from another work — that it should originate from the author," but only that "though it may be neither novel or ingenious, [it] is the claimant's original work in that it originates from him, and is not copied."
    [16] *Id.* See Lawrence v. Dana, 15 Fed. Cas. 26, 60 No. 8,136: "Persons making, using or vending to others to be used, the patented article are guilty of infringing the letters-patent, even though they may have subsequently invented the same thing without any knowledge of the existence of the letters-patent; but the recomposition of the same book without copying, though not likely to occur, would not be an infringement." See also Fred Fisher, Inc. v. Dillingham, D.C.N.Y., 298 F. 145, 147.
    The English doctrine is the same. See Copinger, The Law of Copyrights (7th ed. 1936) 2: "It is not infrequently urged as an objection to granting copyright protection for a long term, that the effect is to create a monopoly, but at least, it is not a monopoly of knowledge. The grant of a patent does prevent full use being made of knowledge, but the reader of a book is not by the copyright laws prevented from making full use of any information he may acquire from his reading. He is only prohibited from disseminating that information or knowledge by multiplying copies of the book or of material portions of it: or, possibly, by reading the book aloud in public. Copyright is, in fact, only a negative right to prevent the appropriation of the labours of an author by another. If it could be shown that two precisely similar works were in fact produced wholly independently of one another, the author of the work that was published first would have no right to restrain the publication by the other author of that author's independent and original work. A patentee, on the other hand, has the right to prevent another from using his invention if it in fact infringes the former's patent, notwithstanding that the latter's invention was the subject of independent investigation on his part."

2. We consider untenable defendants' suggestion that plaintiff's mezzotints could not validly be copyrighted because they are reproductions of works in the public domain. Not only does the Act include "Reproductions of a work of art," but — while prohibiting a copyright of "the original text of any work ... in the public domain" — it explicitly provides for the copyrighting of "translations, or other versions of works in the public domain." The mezzotints were such "versions." They "originated" with those who made them, and — on the trial judge's findings well supported by the evidence — amply met the standards imposed by the Constitution and the statute.[22] There is evidence that they were not intended to, and did not, imitate the paintings they reproduced. But even if their substantial departures from the paintings were inadvertent, the copyrights would be valid.[23] A copyist's bad eyesight or defective musculature, or a shock caused by a clap of thunder, may yield sufficiently distinguishable variations. Having hit upon such a variation unintentionally, the "author" may adopt it as his and copyright it.[25]

....

QUESTIONS

1. How is the "progress of science and the useful arts" advanced by sustaining copyright in a work that is the same, although unknowingly and independently created, as an earlier work? How is it advanced by a knowing adaptation of an earlier work, such as an engraving of an old master, or a translation of a great novel?

2. If the plaintiff's engraving in the *Catalda* case had been based not on an old master but on a copyrighted painting, should it be eligible for copyright? Is it eligible for copyright under the 1976 Copyright Act?

---

[22] See Copinger, The Law of Copyrights (7th ed. 1936) 46: "Again, an engraver is almost invariably a copyist, but although his work may infringe copyright in the original painting if made without the consent of the owner of the copyright therein, his work may still be original in the sense that he has employed skill and judgment in its production. He produces the resemblance he is desirous of obtaining by means very different from those employed by the painter or draughtsman from whom he copies; means which require great labour and talent. The engraver produces his effects by the management of light and shade, or, as the term of his art expresses it, the *chiarooscuro*. The due degrees of light and shade are produced by different lines and dots; he who is the engraver must decide on the choice of the different lines or dots for himself, and on his choice depends the success of his print."

[23] See Kallen, Art and Freedom (1942) 977 to the effect that "the beauty of the human singing voice, as the western convention of music hears it, depends upon a physiological dysfunction of the vocal cords...."

Plutarch tells this story: A painter, enraged because he could not depict the foam that filled a horse's mouth from champing at the bit, threw a sponge at his painting; the sponge splashed against the wall — and achieved the desired result.

[25] Consider inadvertent errors in a translation. Compare cases holding that a patentable invention may stem from an accidental discovery. See, e.g., Radiator Specialty Co. v. Buhot, 3 Cir., 39 F.2d 373, 376; Nichols v. Minnesota Mining & Mfg. Co., 4 Cir., 109 F.2d 162, 165; New Wrinkle v. Fritz, D.C.W.D.N.Y., 45 F. Supp. 108, 117; Byerley v. Sun Co., 3 Cir., 184 F. 455, 456-457.

Many great scientific discoveries have resulted from accidents, e.g., the galvanic circuit and the x-ray.

3. Do you agree that a stroke of the pen resulting from "bad eyesight or defective musculature" is copyrightable? Can you distinguish from such a situation the results of "a shock caused by a clap of thunder"? How would dropping globs of paint from a ladder be treated by the *Catalda* court?

4. When Judge Frank quotes from an earlier opinion that notes that "originality in this context means little more than a prohibition of actual copying," what does he mean by "little more"?

5. Three standards (at least) might be applied to determine eligibility for copyright: (a) *Originality,* in the sense of independent origination or non-copying; (b) *Creativity,* in the sense of some modest level of imagination or "escape from the commonplace"; or (c) *Novelty and Invention,* in the sense (like a patent) of a "leap" beyond the "prior art," which would represent a major development in that art (and one that would not be obvious to a person skilled in that art). What are the arguments for and against the application of one or more of these standards? Which standard would Judge Frank apply on the basis of the *Catalda* case?

E. DISTINCTIONS: TRADEMARKS

TRADE-MARK CASES

100 U.S. 82 (1879)

MR. JUSTICE MILLER delivered the opinion of the court.

The three cases whose titles stand at the head of this opinion are criminal prosecutions for violations of what is known as the trade-mark legislation of Congress. The first two are indictments in the southern district of New York, and the last is an information in the southern district of Ohio. In all of them the judges of the circuit courts in which they are pending have certified to a difference of opinion on what is substantially the same question; namely, are the acts of Congress on the subject of trade-marks founded on any rightful authority in the Constitution of the United States?

The entire legislation of Congress in regard to trade-marks is of very recent origin. It is first seen in sects. 77 to 84, inclusive, of the act of July 8, 1870, entitled "An Act to revise, consolidate, and amend the statutes relating to patents and copyrights." 16 Stat. 198. The part of this act relating to trade-marks is embodied in chap. 2, tit. 60, sects. 4937 to 4947, of the Revised Statutes.

It is sufficient at present to say that they provide for the registration in the Patent Office of any device in the nature of a trade-mark to which any person has by usage established an exclusive right, or which the person so registering intends to appropriate by that act to his exclusive use; and they make the wrongful use of a trade-mark, so registered, by any other person, without the owner's permission, a cause of action in a civil suit for damages. Six years later we have the act of Aug. 14, 1876 (19 Stat. 141), punishing by fine and imprisonment the fraudulent use, sale, and counterfeiting of trade-marks registered in pursuance of the statutes of the United States, on which the informations and indictments are founded in the cases before us.

The right to adopt and use a symbol or a device to distinguish the goods or property made or sold by the person whose mark it is, to the exclusion of use by all other persons, has been long recognized by the common law and the chancery courts of England and of this country, and by the statutes of some of the States. It is a property right for the violation of which damages may be recovered in an action at law, and the continued violation of it will be enjoined by a court of equity, with compensation for past infringement. This exclusive right was not created by the act of Congress, and does not now depend upon it for its enforcement. The whole system of trade-mark property and the civil remedies for its protection existed long anterior to that act, and have remained in full force since its passage.

These propositions are so well understood as to require neither the citation of authorities nor an elaborate argument to prove them.

As the property in trade-marks and the right to their exclusive use rest on the laws of the States, and, like the great body of the rights of person and of property, depend on them for security and protection, the power of Congress to legislate on the subject, to establish the conditions on which these rights shall be enjoyed and exercised, the period of their duration, and the legal remedies for their enforcement, if such power exist at all, must be found in the Constitution of the United States, which is the source of all the powers that Congress can lawfully exercise.

In the argument of these cases this seems to be conceded, and the advocates for the validity of the acts of Congress on this subject point to two clauses of the Constitution, in one or in both of which, as they assert, sufficient warrant may be found for this legislation.

The first of these is the eighth clause of sect. 8 of the first article. That section, manifestly intended to be an enumeration of the powers expressly granted to Congress, and closing with the declaration of a rule for the ascertainment of such powers as are necessary by way of implication to carry into efficient operation those expressly given, authorizes Congress, by the clause referred to, "to promote the progress of science and useful arts, by securing for limited times, to authors and inventors, the exclusive right to their respective writings and discoveries."

As the first and only attempt by Congress to regulate the *right of trademarks* is to be found in the act of July 8, 1870, to which we have referred, entitled "An Act to revise, consolidate and amend the statutes relating to *patents and copyrights*," terms which have long since become technical, as referring, the one to inventions and the other to the writings of authors, it is a reasonable inference that this part of the statute also was, in the opinion of Congress, an exercise of the power found in that clause of the Constitution. It may also be safely assumed that until a critical examination of the subject in the courts became necessary, it was mainly if not wholly to this clause that the advocates of the law looked for its support.

Any attempt, however, to identify the essential characteristics of a trademark with inventions and discoveries in the arts and sciences, or with the writings of authors, will show that the effort is surrounded with insurmountable difficulties.

The ordinary trade-mark has no necessary relation to invention or discovery. The trade-mark recognized by the common law is generally the growth of a considerable period of use, rather than a sudden invention. It is often the result of accident rather than design, and when under the act of Congress it is sought to establish it by registration, neither originality, invention, discovery, science, nor art is any way essential to the right conferred by that act. If we should endeavor to classify it under the head of writings of authors, the objections are equally strong. In this, as in regard to inventions, originality is required. And while the word *writings* may be liberally construed, as it has been, to include original designs for engravings, prints, &c., it is only such as are *original,* and are founded in the creative powers of the mind. The writings which are to be protected are *the fruits of intellectual labor,* embodied in the form of books, prints, engravings, and the like. The trade-mark may be, and generally is, the adoption of something already in existence as the distinctive symbol of the party using it. At common law the exclusive right to it grows out of its *use,* and not its mere adoption. By the act of Congress this exclusive right attaches upon registration. But in neither case does it depend upon novelty, invention, discovery, or any work of the brain. It requires no fancy or imagination, no genius, no laborious thought. It is simply founded on priority of appropriation. We look in vain in the statute for any other qualification or condition. If the symbol, however plain, simple, old, or well-known, has been first appropriated by the claimant as his distinctive trade-mark, he may by registration secure the right to its exclusive use. While such legislation may be a judicious aid to the common law on the subject of trade-marks, and may be within the competency of legislatures whose general powers embrace that class of subjects, we are unable to see any such power in the constitutional provision concerning authors and inventors, and their writings and discoveries.

The other clause of the Constitution supposed to confer the requisite authority on Congress is the third of the same section, which, read in connection with the granting clause, is as follows: "The Congress shall have power to regulate commerce with foreign nations, and among the several States, and with the Indian tribes."

The argument is that the use of a trade-mark — that which alone gives it any value — is to identify a particular class or quality of goods as the manufacture, produce, or property of the person who puts them in the general market for sale; that the sale of the article so distinguished is commerce; that the trade-mark is, therefore, a useful and valuable aid or instrument of commerce, and its regulation by virtue of the clause belongs to Congress, and that the act in question is a lawful exercise of this power.

Every species of property which is the subject of commerce, or which is used or even essential in commerce, is not brought by this clause within the control of Congress. The barrels and casks, the bottles and boxes in which alone certain articles of commerce are kept for safety and by which their contents are transferred from the seller to the buyer, do not thereby become subjects of congressional legislation more than other property. *Nathan v. Louisiana,* 8 How. 73....

[The Court found that the statutes in question were not limited to interstate transactions and were accordingly invalid. The Court expressly left undecided the question "whether the trade-mark bears such a relation to commerce in general terms as to bring it within congressional control, when used or applied to classes of commerce which fall within that control."]

QUESTIONS

1. Are there weaknesses in the Court's distinction of trademark and patent? Are there any additional weaknesses in its distinction of trademark and copyright?

2. Does this case hold that trademarks are per se not copyrightable?

3. Can the title of a book or song be protected by copyright?

4. Why couldn't the trademarks in question have been subject to congressional regulation under the commerce clause? Does the procedural setting of the case affect the answer? If Congress enacted a copyright law pursuant to the commerce clause, what additional restrictions on its power would be imposed? What restrictions would be lifted?

TRADEMARKS AND THE LANHAM ACT

When used in connection with goods or services, certain words, phrases, designs or pictures come to identify in the mind of the public the source of those goods or services. The word "Ivory," for example, when used in marketing soap or soap-related products will normally be understood by the purchasing public to stand for a specific manufacturer (even though the purchasing public may not be aware of the identity of the manufacturer, i.e., Procter & Gamble). The same is true for the use of a small knit alligator in connection with sportswear, or a tiger in connection with breakfast cereals or automotive fuel. When such a word or picture identifies the source of goods or services, rather than merely the goods or services themselves, it is said to function as a trademark or a service mark. It is a symbol that represents the reputation or goodwill of the manufacturer or provider, and signifies the quality of its goods or services. The mark provides useful information for the consumer and aids in marketplace competition.

The law has long recognized the commercial value of the trademark (or service mark) and has protected it against unauthorized confusing use by others. Another person who improperly uses, say, the word "Ivory" in the merchandising of skin cream will surely be found to have created the misleading impression that its cream was manufactured by the same company that produces the well-known soap. An injunction will protect Procter & Gamble against the possible sullying of its reputation, and will protect the consumer against being misled about source and quality. The common law of the various states has traditionally afforded protection against "unfair competition" that takes the form of the unauthorized "passing off" of the defendant's product under the guise of another's mark. The two key elements of the claim for passing off are that the copied word, phrase, design or picture identify the plaintiff as source (i.e., that it have "secondary meaning"), and that the defendant's use will cause confusion among a substantial number of persons in the marketplace. To help "warn off" persons from making potentially confusing uses of such marks, states have supplemented their common-law remedies with systems for the registration and publication of such marks.

Obviously, in a national economy in which goods and services routinely cross state lines, the protection of trademarks and service marks would be significantly encumbered by the need to register and enforce claims on a state-by-state basis. The Trade-Mark Cases show that Congress enacted federal trademark-registration legislation in 1870. The present-day version of that legislation is known as the Lanham Act of 1946. It provides for the registration of distinctive marks (i.e., those with secondary meaning) on a Principal Register, and the protection of registered marks by actions in federal court against unauthorized confusing uses. The basic substantive doctrines and protections under the Lanham Act are essentially congruent to those afforded by the states (and do not purport to preempt state unfair competition laws). Registration under the federal act provides certain additional substantive and procedural rights not necessarily available under state law. In the very important § 43(a) of the Lanham Act, Congress has gone beyond the protection of registered marks to afford federal relief against more general kinds of false representations in interstate commerce.

The most significant provisions of the Lanham Act follow.

LANHAM ACT

15 U.S.C. §§ 1051, 1052, 1114, 1125, 1127

Sec. 1 (15 U.S.C. § 1051). Registration; application ....

(a) The owner of a trademark used in commerce may register his trademark under this Chapter on the principal register hereby established:

(1) By filing in the Patent and Trademark Office —

(A) a written application, in such form as may be prescribed by the Commissioner, verified by the applicant, or by a member of the firm or an officer of the corporation or association applying, specifying applicant's domicile and citizenship, the date of applicant's first use of the mark, the date of applicant's first use of the mark in commerce, the goods in connection with which the mark is used and the mode or manner in which the mark is used in connection with such goods,...

(B) a drawing of the mark; and

(C) such number of specimens or facsimiles of the mark as actually used as may be required by the Commissioner.

....

Sec. 2 (15 U.S.C. § 1052). Trademarks registrable on the principal register; concurrent registration

No trademark by which the goods of the applicant may be distinguished from the goods of others shall be refused registration on the principal register on account of its nature unless it —

(a) consists of or comprises immoral, deceptive, or scandalous matter; or matter which may disparage or falsely suggest a connection with persons, living or dead, institutions, beliefs, or national symbols, or bring them into contempt, or disrepute;

(b) consists of or comprises the flag or coat of arms or other insignia of the United States, or of any State or municipality, or of any foreign nation, or any simulation thereof;

(c) consists of or comprises a name, portrait, or signature identifying a particular living individual except by his written consent, or the name, signature, or portrait of a deceased President of the United States during the life of his widow, if any, except by the written consent of the widow;

(d) consists of or comprises a mark which so resembles a mark registered in the Patent Office or a mark or trade name previously used in the United States by another and not abandoned, as to be likely, when applied to the goods of the applicant, to cause confusion, or to cause mistake, or to deceive ... [subject to a proviso which specifies the circumstances under which the same mark may be registered concurrently by different persons].

(e) consists of a mark which, (1) when applied to the goods of the applicant is merely descriptive or deceptively misdescriptive of them, or (2) when applied to the goods of the applicant is primarily geographically descriptive or deceptively misdescriptive of them, except as indications of regional origin may be registrable under section 4 hereof, or (3) is primarily merely a surname;

(f) except as expressly excluded in paragraphs (a), (b), (c) and (d) of this section, nothing herein shall prevent the registration of a mark used by the applicant which has become distinctive of the applicant's goods in commerce. The Commissioner may accept as prima facie evidence that the mark has become distinctive, as applied to the applicant's goods in commerce, proof of substantially exclusive and continuous use thereof as a mark by the applicant in commerce for the five years before the date on which the claim of distinctiveness is made.

Sec. 32(1) (15 U.S.C. § 1114(1)). Remedies; infringement ...

Any person who shall, without the consent of the registrant —

(a) use in commerce any reproduction, counterfeit, copy, or colorable imitation of a registered mark in connection with the sale, offering for sale, distribution, or advertising of any goods or services on or in connection with which such use is likely to cause confusion, or to cause mistake, or to deceive; or

(b) reproduce, counterfeit, copy or colorably imitate a registered mark and apply such reproduction, counterfeit, copy, or colorable imitation to labels, signs, prints, packages, wrappers, receptacles or advertisements intended to be used in commerce upon or in connection with the sale, offering for sale, distribution, or advertising of goods or services on or in connection with which such use is likely to cause confusion, or to cause mistake, or to deceive;

shall be liable in a civil action by the registrant for the remedies hereinafter provided. Under subsection (b) of this section, the registrant shall not be entitled to recover profits or damages unless the acts have been committed with knowledge that such imitation is intended to be used to cause confusion, or to cause mistake, or to deceive.

Sec. 43 (15 U.S.C. § 1125). False designations of origin and false descriptions forbidden

(a) Any person who, on or in connection with any goods or services, or any container for goods, uses in commerce any word, term, name, symbol, or device, or any combination thereof, or any false designation of origin, false or misleading description of fact, or false or misleading representation of fact, which —

(1) is likely to cause confusion, or to cause mistake, or to deceive as to the affiliation, connection, or association of such person with another person, or as to the origin, sponsorship, or approval of his or her goods, services, or commercial activities by another person, or

(2) in commercial advertising or promotion, misrepresents the nature, characteristics, qualities, or geographic origin of his or her or another person's goods, services, or commercial activities,

shall be liable in a civil action by any person who believes that he or she is or is likely to be damaged by such act.

Sec. 45 (15 U.S.C. § 1127). Construction and definitions; intent of chapter

In the construction of this Act, unless the contrary is plainly apparent from the context:

....

The word "commerce" means all commerce which may lawfully be regulated by Congress.

....

The term "trademark" includes any word, name, symbol, or device, or any combination thereof —

(1) used by a person, or

(2) which a person has a bona fide intention to use in commerce and applies to register on the principal register established by this Act,

to identify and distinguish his or her goods, including a unique product, from those manufactured or sold by others and to indicate the source of the goods, even if that source is unknown.

The term "service mark" means any word, name, symbol, or device, or any combination thereof —

> (1) used by a person, or
> (2) which a person has a bona fide intention to use in commerce and applies to register on the principal register established by this Act,

to identify and distinguish the services of one person, including a unique service, from the services of others and to indicate the source of the services, even if that source is unknown. Titles, character names, and other distinctive features of radio or television programs may be registered as service marks notwithstanding that they, or the programs, may advertise the goods of the sponsor.

. . . .

The term "mark" includes any trademark, service mark, collective mark, or certification mark.

The term "use in commerce" means the bona fide use of a mark in the ordinary course of trade, and not made merely to reserve a right in a mark. For purposes of this Act, a mark shall be deemed to be in use in commerce —

> (1) on goods when —
> (A) it is placed in any manner on the goods or their containers or the displays associated therewith or on the tags or labels affixed thereto, or if the nature of the goods makes such placement impracticable, then on documents associated with the goods or their sale, and
> (B) the goods are sold or transported in commerce, and
> (2) on services when it is used or displayed in the sale or advertising of services and the services are rendered in commerce, or the services are rendered in more than one State or in the United States and a foreign country and the person rendering the services is engaged in commerce in connection with the services.

A mark shall be deemed to be "abandoned" when either of the following occurs:

> (1) When its use has been discontinued with intent not to resume such use. Intent not to resume may be inferred from circumstances. Nonuse for two consecutive years shall be prima facie evidence of abandonment. 'Use' of a mark means the bona fide use of that mark made in the ordinary course of trade, and not made merely to reserve a right in a mark.
> (2) When any course of conduct of the owner, including acts of omission as well as commission, causes the mark to become the generic name for the goods or services on or in connection with which it is used or otherwise to lose its significance as a mark. Purchaser motivation shall not be a test for determining abandonment under this paragraph.

QUESTIONS

1. Could an author secure a trademark for a character name in a popular story or series of stories (e.g., James Bond or Sam Spade)? Could an author secure a trademark for a character apart from the name, e.g., the physical appearance of a character or the personality traits of a character? What would be the scope of protection afforded by trademark for such a name or character?

2. Could a copyright be secured for such a name or character? (Consider both the Constitution and the Copyright Act.) What would be the scope of copyright protection?

TITLES IN THE LAW OF UNFAIR COMPETITION

The law of unfair competition protects the title of a copyrightable work against potentially confusing usage by another, much as it does with respect to other designations of goods, services, persons, or organizations. Under this branch of the law, the test is whether the public will assume some connection between the works designated by the same or confusingly similar titles. However, this principle must also accommodate copyright public domain policies. In the ordinary case, when a work has fallen into the public domain, the title goes with it and may be freely used. *Clemens v. Belford,* 14 F. 728 (N.D. Ill. 1883); *Chamberlain v. Columbia Pictures Corp.,* 186 F.2d 923, 89 U.S.P.Q. 7 (9th Cir. 1951). *See* Kurtz, *Protection for Titles of Literary Works in the Public Domain,* 37 RUTGERS L. REV. 53 (1984). In *G. & C. Merriam Co. v. Ogilvie,* 159 F. 638 (1st Cir. 1908), the defendant was held entitled to use the title "Webster's Dictionary," but was required to print in large type on the title page of the public domain reprint a statement clearly differentiating it from earlier copyrighted editions by the plaintiff, whose name had been associated with the famous dictionary from the beginning.

The public-confusion test in the context of titles relating to the public domain is illustrated by a pair of cases involving, respectively, "Alice in Wonderland" and "Wyatt Earp." When two motion pictures using the former title were released at about the same time, the producer of the more costly and widely advertised picture was denied a preliminary injunction because the title had not become riveted in the public mind to plaintiff's picture (as distinct from the Lewis Carroll story). *Walt Disney Productions, Inc. v. Souvaine Selective Pictures, Inc.,* 98 F. Supp. 774, 90 U.S.P.Q. 138 (S.D.N.Y.), *aff'd,* 192 F.2d 856, 91 U.S.P.Q. 313 (2d Cir. 1951). On the other hand, the obscure historical basis for a U.S. marshal in the early West named "Wyatt Earp" did not permit a manufacturer to use the name, which was likely to be connected by the public with the television series responsible for injecting this little-known U.S. marshal into the public's consciousness. *Wyatt Earp Enterprises, Inc. v. Sackman, Inc.,* 157 F. Supp. 621, 116 U.S.P.Q. 122 (S.D.N.Y. 1958).

The problems become even more complicated when a title is used to designate a *series* of works, one or more of which is in the public domain. Reprinting the public domain work under its title (but perhaps with a disclaimer) is permissible under the cases discussed above. But what of an adaptation or other derivative work? The right to produce such works is part of an author's rights under copyright that, by definition, is no longer subsisting; the value of having a public domain is to facilitate public exercise of those rights that have expired. On the other hand, a new version of a mystery novel or a cartoon character by someone unconnected with the original creator is likely to confuse the public. These questions arise with respect not only to titles but to character names. *See* Waldheim, *Characters — May They Be Kidnapped?*, 12 Bull. Copyright Soc'y 210 (1965).

The law of unfair competition is constantly changing. Thus, even with respect to the use of titles, we find courts tending to be less concerned with actual competition between the media involved than with the unfairness of the use. *Compare Atlas Mfg. Co. v. Street & Smith*, 204 F. 398 (8th Cir. 1913), *with Golenpaul v. Rosett*, 174 Misc. 114, 18 N.Y.S.2d 889, 45 U.S.P.Q. 45 (N.Y. Sup. Ct. 1940), and *Children's Television Workshop v. Sesame Nursery Centers, Inc.*, 171 U.S.P.Q. 105 (N.Y. Sup. Ct. 1970), *aff'd*, 319 N.Y.S.2d 589 (1st Dep't 1971). These developments may account for a conservative attitude on the part of large users of literary and musical material, who may pay substantial amounts for titles. *See* Tannenbaum, *Uses of Titles for Copyright and Public Domain Works*, 6 Bull. Copyright Soc'y 64 (1958).

It also appears that titles or names may in some cases qualify for registration as trademarks, especially as applied to periodicals or a series of cartoons or other works, but without thereby extending the term of copyright in the work itself. *See* Shapiro, *The Validity of Registered Trademarks for Titles and Characters After Expiration of Copyright on the Underlying Work*, 31 Copyr. L. Symp. 69 (ASCAP) (1984). So also an arbitrary designation applied to a set or series of books may constitute a valid trademark, such as "Dr. Eliot's five-foot shelf of books." *Collier v. Jones*, 66 Misc. 97, 120 N.Y.S. 991 (N.Y. Sup. Ct. 1910). But if the title is merely the name of one of the books in the series, it is regarded as "merely descriptive" and therefore not subject to trademark protection. *In re Page Co.*, 47 App. D.C. 195 (D.C. Cir. 1917); *In re Cooper*, 254 F.2d 611, 117 U.S.P.Q. 396 (C.C.P.A.), *cert. denied*, 358 U.S. 840, 119 U.S.P.Q. 501 (1958).

QUESTIONS

1. A motion picture called "Best Man Wins" was based upon the Mark Twain short story "The Celebrated Jumping Frog of Calaveras County," which was in the public domain. The film was advertised as "A Story Only Mark Twain Could Tell," "Mark Twain's Favorite Story," etc. If Mark Twain did not write (or otherwise endorse) the screenplay of the motion picture, and if that motion picture was "corny" and inferior to Twain's "Jumping Frog" story, would Mark Twain's literary executor have a cause of action for trademark infringement or unfair competition in the form of "passing off"? *See Chamberlain v. Columbia Pictures Corp.*, 186 F.2d 923 (9th Cir. 1951).

2. Had a film company used the title "The Celebrated Jumping Frog of Calaveras County" on a motion picture depicting a completely different story, having no incidents in common with the Twain story, would that have constituted infringement of copyright? Would it have constituted trademark infringement?

3. The famous children's book author Dr. Seuss created a number of cartoons for Liberty Magazine in 1932. The copyrights were owned by Liberty. More than thirty years later, Liberty authorized Don Poynter to make three-dimensional dolls based on these cartoons. Dr. Seuss, finding these dolls to be "tasteless, unattractive and of an inferior quality," sought to enjoin the use of his name and to recover damages therefor. Should he succeed with respect to the following hang-tag?

See Geisel v. Poynter Products, Inc., 283 F. Supp. 261 (S.D.N.Y. 1968). Does the following tag call for a different answer (*see* 295 F. Supp. 331 (S.D.N.Y. 1968))?

FREDERICK WARNE & CO. v. BOOK SALES, INC.

481 F. Supp. 1191 (S.D.N.Y. 1979)

SOFAER, DISTRICT JUDGE. Frederick Warne & Co., Inc. ("Warne"), brings this trademark infringement action against Book Sales, Inc. ("BSI") under Sections 32(1) and 43(a) of the Lanham Act, 15 U.S.C. § 1114(1) and § 1125(a) respectively, as well as under the New York Anti-Dilution Statute, General

Business Law § 368-d. The case is before the court on cross motions for summary judgment filed pursuant to Rule 56 of the Federal Rules of Civil Procedure.

[Plaintiff Warne has, since 1902, been the publisher of the "Original Peter Rabbit Books," a well-known series of children's books written and illustrated by Beatrix Potter. Seven books in the series are no longer, or never were, covered by United States copyright, and several new editions of Miss Potter's works have been marketed in competition with the Warne editions. Although Warne concedes that the seven works are in the public domain, it claims exclusive rights in the cover illustrations (and character marks derived therefrom) originally created by Miss Potter; it also claims exclusive trademark rights in a "sitting rabbit" illustration that appeared within the text of *The Tale of Peter Rabbit*. Warne registered three of the covers under the Lanham Act as book trademarks, and also claims protection for the unregistered marks under § 43(a) of that Act, which permits proof of validity of a trademark even without the benefit of the presumption of validity that registration confers. Warne has used, and licensed others to use, the eight illustrations on a variety of commercial products, including book packaging, other original Warne publications (including a cookbook and coloring book), and toys and clothing; licensed products have generated sales of $5 million per year, with royalties to Warne in the amount of $250,000.

[The defendant has since 1977 marketed copies of the seven Potter stories now in the public domain, bound as a single colorful volume. It has photographically reproduced the original Potter text illustrations; it also has redrawn the Potter cover illustrations, and the "sitting rabbit," and relocated them at the beginning and end of the appropriate stories, and has placed photographic reproductions of the original Warne covers as corner ornaments on most of the pages of the seven stories.

[Warne contends that BSI's use of all eight illustrations constitutes trademark infringement, and seeks injunctive relief as well as damages and an accounting. Both parties moved for summary judgment, which the court denied because of genuine issues of material fact.]

I. Plaintiff's Claim to Trademark Protection

To succeed in this action, plaintiff must first establish that it has valid trademark rights in the eight character illustrations as used on its books and other products. Section 45 of the Lanham Act defines a trademark as any "word, name, symbol, or device ... adopted and used by a manufacturer or merchant to identify his goods and distinguish them from those manufactured or sold by others." 15 U.S.C. § 1127. Although the illustrations here are *capable* of distinguishing Warne's books from those of others, it cannot be said that they are so arbitrary, unique, and non-descriptive as to constitute "technical trademarks," which are presumed valid as soon as they are affixed to the goods and the goods are sold. *Blisscraft of Hollywood v. United Plastics Co.,* 294 F.2d 694 (2d Cir. 1961). Accordingly, plaintiff has the burden of establishing that these illustrations have acquired secondary meaning, defined as "[t]he power of a name or other configuration to symbolize a particular business, product or company." *Dallas Cowboys Cheerleaders, Inc. v. Pussycat Cinema, Ltd.*, 604 F.2d 200, 203, n. 5 (2d Cir. 1979), *quoting Ideal Toy Corp. v. Kenner Products Division of General Mills Fun Group, Inc.*, 443 F. Supp. 291, 305 n. 14 (S.D.N.Y. 1977).

In the instant case, it would not be enough that the illustrations in question have come to signify Beatrix Potter as author of the books; plaintiff must show that they have come to represent its goodwill and reputation as *publisher* of those books. Whether or not the illustrations have acquired that kind of secondary meaning is a question of fact, *Speed Products Co. v. Tinnerman Products, Inc.*, 222 F.2d 61 (2d Cir. 1955); *Turner v. HMH Publishing Co.*, 380 F.2d 224 (5th Cir.), *cert. denied*, 389 U.S. 1006 (1967); *see generally* McCarthy, *Trademarks and Unfair Competition* § 5:10, which may be proven by either direct or circumstantial evidence. As to those marks registered under the Lanham Act, the registration constitutes prima facie evidence of trademark validity. *See* Section 33(a), 15 U.S.C. § 1115(a); *see generally* McCarthy, *supra*, § 11:16, § 15:12.

In addition, plaintiff must establish that defendant's use of the eight illustrations is trademark infringement. Under Section 32(1) of the Act, a cause of action for infringement of a registered mark exists where a person uses the mark "in connection with the sale ... or advertising of any goods ... [where] such use is likely to cause confusion, or to cause mistake, or to deceive." 15 U.S.C. § 1114(1). With respect to the unregistered illustrations, plaintiff may succeed under Section 43(a), a broadly worded provision which creates a federal cause of action for false designation of origin or false representation of goods or services. *Boston Professional Hockey Association, Inc. v. Dallas Cap & Emblem Manufacturing, Inc.*, 510 F.2d 1004, 1010 (5th Cir.), *cert. denied*, 423 U.S. 868 (1975); *Joshua Meier Co. v. Albany Novelty Manufacturing Co.*, 236 F.2d 144, 147 (2d Cir. 1956). As a general rule, the same facts which support an action for trademark infringement — facts indicating likelihood of confusion — will support an action for unfair competition under Section 43(a). *Dallas Cap, supra*, 510 F.2d at 1010; *see American Footwear Corp. v. General Footwear Co., Ltd.*, 609 F.2d 655, 665 (2d Cir. 1979). Likelihood of confusion is a factual inquiry, depending on a host of factors, no one of which is controlling. *E.g., Mushroom Makers, Inc. v. R. G. Barry Corporation*, 580 F.2d 44 (2d Cir. 1978), *cert. denied*, 439 U.S. 1116 (1979).

Contrary to what the parties suggested in their motion papers, and even though some of plaintiff's illustrations have been registered under the Lanham Act, defendant is unwilling to concede that any of the illustrations in issue are valid trademarks. Nor is defendant prepared to admit that there would be a likelihood of confusion arising from its use of those illustrations and marks in connection with its own Peter Rabbit publication. Because the present record does not permit a finding that the necessary elements of trademark infringement — secondary meaning and likelihood of confusion — exist, the plaintiff's motion for summary judgment must be denied. *See, e.g., Syntex Laboratories, Inc. v. Norwich Pharmacal Co.*, 315 F. Supp. 45 (S.D.N.Y. 1970) (granting plaintiff's motion for preliminary injunction but denying plaintiff's motion for summary judgment), *aff'd*, 437 F.2d 556 (2d Cir. 1971) (affirming injunctive relief); *National Color Laboratories, Inc. v. Philip's Foto Co.*, 273 F. Supp. 1002 (S.D.N.Y. 1967); *see generally* McCarthy, *supra*, § 32:36.

II. *Defendant's Claim to Publish Freely*

Defendant contends that the disputed questions of fact requiring denial of plaintiff's motion need not be reached to find in defendant's favor. Defendant argues that its use of the illustrations and marks is legally protected because they are part of copyrightable works now in the public domain. This argument is not persuasive. The fact that a copyrightable character or design has fallen into the public domain should not preclude protection under the trademark laws so long as it is shown to have acquired independent trademark significance, identifying in some way the source or sponsorship of the goods. *See Wyatt Earp Enterprises v. Sackman, Inc.*, 157 F. Supp. 621 (S.D.N.Y. 1958). Because the nature of the property right conferred by copyright is significantly different from that of trademark, trademark protection should be able to co-exist, and possibly to overlap, with copyright protection without posing preemption difficulties. As the Fifth Circuit persuasively reasoned in *Boston Professional Hockey Association, Inc. v. Dallas Cap & Emblem Manufacturing, Inc.*, 510 F.2d 1004, 1014 (5th Cir.), *cert. denied*, 423 U.S. 868 (1975):

> A trademark is a property right which is acquired by use. *Trade-Mark Cases*, 100 U.S. 82 (1879). It differs substantially from a copyright, in both its legal genesis and its scope of federal protection. The legal cornerstone for the protection of copyrights is Article I, section 8, clause 8 of the Constitution. In the case of a copyright, an individual creates a unique design and, because the Constitutional fathers saw fit to encourage creativity, he can secure a copyright for his creation for a [limited period of time]. After the expiration of the copyright, his creation becomes part of the public domain. In the case of a trademark, however, the process is reversed. An individual selects a word or design that might otherwise be in the public domain to represent his business or product. If that word or design comes to symbolize his product or business in the public mind, the individual acquires a property right in the mark. The acquisition of such a right through use represents the passage of a word or design out of the public domain into the protective ambits of trademark law. Under the provisions of the Lanham Act, the owner of a mark acquires a protectable [sic] property interest in his mark through registration and use.

Dual protection under copyright and trademark laws is particularly appropriate for graphic representations of characters. A character deemed an artistic creation deserving copyright protection, *see Walt Disney Productions v. Air Pirates*, 581 F.2d 751 (9th Cir. 1978), *cert. denied*, 439 U.S. 1132 (1979), may also serve to identify the creator, thus meriting protection under theories of trademark or unfair competition, *see Edgar Rice Burroughs, Inc. v. Manns Theaters*, 195 U.S.P.Q. 159 (C.D. Cal. 1976); *Patten v. Superior Talking Pictures*, 8 F. Supp. 196 (S.D.N.Y. 1934); *see generally* Waldheim, *Characters — May They Be Kidnapped?*, 55 T.M.R. 1022 (1965). Indeed, because of their special value in distinguishing goods and services, names and pictorial representations of characters are often registered as trademarks under the Lanham Act. 5 U.S.C. §§ 1052 & 1053; *see* Brylawski, *Protection of Characters — Sam Spade Revisited,* 22 Bull. Soc. Cr. 77 (1974); Adams, *Superman, Mickey Mouse and Gerontology,* 64 T.M.R. 183 (1974).[3]

Plaintiff correctly admits that, under *G. Ricordi v. Haendler,* 194 F.2d 914 (2d Cir. 1952) (L. Hand, J.), defendant is entitled to reproduce the contents of the seven public domain works as they were originally published. But as Judge Hand also acknowledged in *G. Ricordi,* the reproduction of a public domain work may result in unfair competition if the party goes beyond mere copying. The defendant in *G. Ricordi* had made an exact photographic reproduction of the book in question. Here, defendant assembled a new book consisting of multiple stories, and embellished the cover and interior with plaintiff's character illustrations in a way in which those illustrations were never used in the public domain books. If any of these illustrations, including the "sitting rabbit" design, has come to identify Warne publications, defendant's use of it may lead the public to believe that defendant's different, and allegedly inferior, publication has been published by or is somehow associated with plaintiff. This kind of danger of misrepresentation as to the source of copied public domain material may establish a claim for unfair competition. *See Desclee & Cie, S. A. v. Nemmers,* 190 F. Supp. 381, 390 (E.D. Wis. 1961).

Defendant argues, however, that it has the right to copy the covers as well as the contents of the original books. Relying on *Triangle Publications, Inc. v. Knight-Ridder Newspapers, Inc.,* 445 F. Supp. 875 (S.D. Fla. 1978), and *Nimmer on Copyright,* defendant contends that a book cover should be deemed a copyrightable component of the copyrighted book. Once copyright protection ends, it contends, the entire book should be free to copy.

In principle, defendant seems correct. Covers of books as well as their contents may be entitled to copyright protection. But defendant exaggerates the significance of its logic. None of the authorities it relies upon suggests that trademark and copyright protection are mutually exclusive or that the fate of a book cover is necessarily wedded to the fate of the underlying work. Professor Nimmer suggests only that, where a cover is sufficiently original to merit copyright protection, the copyright applicable to the underlying work should *extend* to the cover. Thus, for example, a separate copyright registration should be unnecessary for the cover of a periodical. M. Nimmer, 1 *Nimmer on Copyright* § 2.04[D], at 2-50....

Furthermore, the rule urged by defendant — that copyrightable book covers may not obtain trademark or unfair competition protection — would permit incongruous results: a book cover lacking sufficient originality to warrant copyright protection could be protected for a potentially unlimited duration under the trademark laws, while covers revealing great artistry or ingenuity would be limited to the duration of the copyright. The better rule would protect all book covers according to the same standards that govern tradi-

---

[3]Some commentators have suggested that trademark and unfair competition theories might serve to protect a character beyond the term of copyright applicable to the underlying work. This provocative question need not be reached, since plaintiff does not seek to establish exclusive trademark rights in the characters themselves but only to protect its limited right to use specific illustrations of those characters.

tional trade dress or packaging cases. *See Sub-Contractors Register, Inc. v. McGovern's Contractors & Builders Manual, Inc.*, 69 F. Supp. 507, 511 (S.D.N.Y. 1946), *citing with approval, E. P. Dutton & Co. v. Cupples*, 117 App. Div. 172, 102 N.Y.S. 309 (1st Dept. 1907). Thus, the proper factual inquiry in this case is not whether the cover illustrations were once copyrightable and have fallen into the public domain, but whether they have acquired secondary meaning, identifying Warne as the publisher or sponsor of goods bearing those illustrations, and if so, whether defendant's use of these illustrations in "packaging" or "dressing" its editions is likely to cause confusion. Summary judgment is an inappropriate vehicle for determining these questions.

Defendant's "fair use" defense based on Section 33(b)(4) of the Lanham Act, 15 U.S.C. § 1115(b)(4), is also unpersuasive.[4] ... [It is not] clear that defendant's use of these illustrations is necessary to the full and effective exploitation of the public domain works. Defendant twice changed the cover of its Peter Rabbit book, suggesting that the "sitting rabbit" — which has been abandoned — was never necessary for its cover. With respect to the seven original cover illustrations, the fact that other publishers have reproduced Miss Potter's stories without copying the covers suggests they may not be crucial to the successful exploitation of the works. And, contrary to what defendant contends, the cover illustrations are not analogous to titles of public domain works, which, Professor Nimmer suggests, may be essential to effective distribution of the works. 1 Nimmer on Copyright § 2.16. A title is generally the primary identifier of a literary work; the cover illustrations are not. Of course, as noted at the outset, if the illustrations merely identify Miss Potter and her works, plaintiff will have no claim to trademark protection. If, however, plaintiff can establish a specialized secondary meaning — that the illustrations represent Warne's goodwill and reputation as the source of children's books and other products — it will have a protectible trademark interest, except to the extent that the covers contain material necessary to identify the book itself. Resolution of these questions must await trial.

The foregoing should not be construed to suggest that plaintiff will have an easy task at trial. Because the claimed marks are derived from or are similar in appearance to the illustrations in the text of the books, they may well prove to be "weak" marks. As a general rule, weak or descriptive marks are accorded less protection than inherently distinctive marks. *See generally* McCarthy, *supra*, § 11.24. Plaintiff must, however, be given an opportunity to meet this relatively greater burden by producing evidence of consumer recognition and likelihood of confusion with respect to each of the marks in dispute.

The motions for summary judgment are denied. The parties will complete discovery within ninety days of this order, at which time the case will be set down for trial.

So ordered.

---

[4] Section 33(b)(4) provides a defense to a charge of infringement if the use is "otherwise than as a trade or service mark ... of a term or device which is descriptive of and used fairly and in good faith only to describe to users the goods or services of such party, or their geographic origin." 15 U.S.C. § 1115(b)(4).

F. DISTINCTIONS: CHATTELS

FORWARD v. THOROGOOD

985 F.2d 604 (1st Cir. 1993)

BOUDIN, CIRCUIT JUDGE.

This is an appeal from a final judgment determining the copyright ownership of certain unpublished tape recordings of the musical group George Thorogood and the Destroyers (the "Band"). The district court ruled that the Band held the copyright to the tapes and enjoined appellant John Forward from making commercial use of the recordings. We affirm.

The basic facts can be briefly stated. Forward is a music aficionado and record collector with a special interest in blues and country music. In 1975, Forward was working as a bus driver when he first met Thorogood at a Boston nightclub where the Band was performing. Forward was immediately taken with the Band's act and struck up a friendship with Thorogood. Thorogood and his fellow band members, a drummer and a guitar player, had been playing together at East Coast colleges and clubs since 1973. Upon learning that the Band had yet to release its first album, Forward began a campaign to persuade his friends at Rounder Records to sign the Band to a recording contract. Rounder Records is a small, Boston based record company specializing in blues and folk music. As part of this effort, Forward arranged and paid for two recording sessions for the Band in 1976. The purpose of the sessions was to create a "demo" tape that would capture Rounder Records' interest. At Forward's invitation, one of the principals of Rounder Records attended the Band's second recording session. Other than requesting specific songs to be recorded, Forward's contribution to the sessions was limited to arranging and paying for them.

Rounder Records was impressed by what it heard; the day after the second session, it arranged to sign the Band to a contract. The Band agreed that Forward could keep the tapes for his own enjoyment, and they have remained in his possession ever since. In 1977, the Band's first album was released under the Rounder Records label. Forward was singled out for "special thanks" in the album's acknowledgements. Since then, Thorogood and the Destroyers have released a number of records and gone on to achieve success as a blues/rock band.

The dispute between the parties arose in early 1988, when Forward told the Band that he intended to sell the 1976 tapes to a record company for commercial release. The Band objected, fearing that release of the tapes would harm its reputation; they were, the district court found, of "relatively primitive quality" compared to the Band's published work. On July 5, 1988, Forward filed suit in the district court, seeking a declaratory judgment that he held the common law copyright to the tapes. Determination of copyright ownership is governed by the common law of copyright because the tapes are unpublished and were recorded in 1976, prior to the January 1, 1978, effective date of the

Copyright Act of 1976, 17 U.S.C. § 101 et seq.[1] The Band responded with a counterclaim for declaratory and injunctive relief.

In the district court, Forward advanced a number of theories in support of his claim to copyright ownership. After a five-day bench trial, the district court filed its findings of fact and conclusions of law, ruling that Forward did not hold the copyright under any of the theories he advanced. *Forward v. Thorogood,* 758 F. Supp. 782 (D. Mass. 1991). The court entered judgment for the Band, declaring Thorogood and other Band members to be the copyright owners and permanently enjoining Forward from commercially exploiting the tapes. Forward now appeals.

On this appeal, Forward's first theory in support of his claim of copyright ownership is based on his ownership and possession of the tapes. According to Forward, ownership of a copyrightable work carries with it ownership of the copyright. Alternatively, he argues that the evidence mandated a finding that the copyright was implicitly transferred to him along with the demo tapes. We find no merit in either claim.

The creator of a work is, at least presumptively, its author and the owner of the copyright, *Community for Creative Non-Violence v. Reid,* 490 U.S. 730, 737, 109 S. Ct. 2166, 2171, 104 L. Ed. 2d 811 (1989). The performer of a musical work is the author, as it were, of the performance. 1 Nimmer, § 2.10[A](2)(a), at 2-149. The courts, in applying the common law of copyright, did in a number of cases infer from an unconditional sale of a manuscript or painting an intent to transfer the copyright. 3 Nimmer § 10.09[B], at 10-76.1. This doctrine, often criticized and subject to various judicial and statutory exclusions, *id.,* is the source of Forward's principal claim. The difficulty for Forward is that even under the doctrine this physical transfer merely created a presumption and the ultimate question was one of intent. *Id.*

In this case, the district court found that "[n]either the band nor any of its members ever conveyed, or agreed to convey, their copyright interest in the tapes to Forward." 758 F. Supp. at 784. Rather the Band allowed Forward to keep the tapes solely for his personal enjoyment. *Id.* Forward's disregard of this central finding is premised on a highly artificial attempt to claim "constructive possession" of the tapes from the outset and then to argue that any reservation by the Band at the end of the sessions was an invalid attempt to reconvey or qualify his copyright. The reality is that the Band never surrendered the copyright in the first place and the transfer of the tapes' ownership to Forward was not a sharply defined event distinct from the reservation of the Band's rights....

---

[1]*See* M. Nimmer & D. Nimmer, 1 Nimmer on Copyright, § 2.10[A] n.18, at 2-147 (1992) ("Nimmer"). *See also* Roth v. Pritikin, 710 F.2d 934, 938 (2d Cir.) (1976 Act, which preempts the common law of copyright as of January 1, 1978, determines the rights but not the identity of the copyright owners of works created prior to that date), *cert. denied,* 464 U.S. 961, 104 S. Ct. 394, 78 L. Ed. 2d 337 (1983).

§ 202. Ownership of copyright as distinct from ownership of material object*

Ownership of a copyright, or of any of the exclusive rights under a copyright, is distinct from ownership of any material object in which the work is embodied. Transfer of ownership of any material object, including the copy or phonorecord in which the work is first fixed, does not of itself convey any rights in the copyrighted work embodied in the object; nor, in the absence of an agreement, does transfer of ownership of a copyright or of any exclusive rights under a copyright convey property rights in any material object.

QUESTIONS

1. The court in the *Forward* case referred to "common law copyright." Throughout our copyright history, until 1978, the right to make copies of an unpublished work was governed typically by state law, known as common-law copyright (whether or not the state copyright law was manifested in court opinions or in a statute). Common-law copyright was potentially perpetual in duration; it lasted until the work was first "published" with the author's consent. As stated in *Forward*, it was generally understood that an author who unconditionally transferred ownership of the chattel embodying the creative work was presumed to have transferred the right of first publication as well. This was often referred to as the "*Pushman* presumption," based on *Pushman v. New York Graphic Soc'y*, 287 N.Y. 302 (1942), in which New York's highest court held that an artist who had sold a painting to the University of Illinois — with no mention of copyright — could not prevent the University from authorizing another to make copies of it.

The *Forward* court observes that the *Pushman* presumption was often criticized. What would you assume was the basis for the presumption? (Does it likely reflect the intentions of the parties? Does it reflect a broader social policy?) What would you assume were the criticisms?

2. If, in your historical researches, you were to unearth a letter written by Miles Standish to Priscilla Alden, would you feel free to publish it without concern for copyright infringement? (You would have to ascertain, first, whether such an old letter was still protected by copyright. Is it?) If not, how would you go about securing legal immunity for your publication? (You would have to ascertain whether Miles' transfer of the letter to Priscilla was governed by the *Pushman* presumption. Do you think it was?)

3. The present Copyright Act became effective on January 1, 1978 — after the recording session in the *Forward* case but before the litigation. Consult § 202 of the Act. What impact does it have upon the *Pushman* presumption? Would you have supported it had you been in the 1976 Congress that enacted the statute? Can it be applied retroactively to transactions that preceded its effective date, such as that in *Forward*? Had it been applied, would the result or reasoning have been changed? (The student can begin to appreciate the

---

*Material in this format, unless otherwise indicated, will comprise sections of the 1976 Act, Pub. L. 94-553, 94th Cong., title 17, U.S.C.

current importance of understanding the law that developed under the 1909 Copyright Act, in addition to the provisions of the 1976 Copyright Act.)

4. Under § 202 of the 1976 Act, transfer of the object does not "of itself" transfer the copyright. Transfer of the copyright does not transfer the object "in the absence of an agreement." What is the difference, if any, between "of itself" and "in the absence of an agreement"? That is, can there ever be circumstances when, even in the absence of an agreement, the transfer of ownership in the physical object would be deemed also to transfer ownership of the copyright? Could, for example, the purchaser of a canvas prove that, although nothing was said about copyright at the time of the transfer of the canvas, the right to reproduce the painting was also conveyed, because that was the unwritten understanding pursuant to a trade custom among local art dealers? (Would such a custom, in any event, become part of "an agreement" between buyer and seller, or does that phrase contemplate a writing?)

5. In *Dowling v. United States,* 473 U.S. 207 (1985), the Supreme Court dealt with the question whether the shipment across state lines of "bootleg records" — i.e., unauthorized recordings of musical compositions from concert performances, motion picture soundtracks, television appearances, and the like — were criminal acts in violation of the National Stolen Property Act, 18 U.S.C. § 2314. That statute imposes criminal penalties, including up to ten years' imprisonment, for one who "transports in interstate or foreign commerce any goods, wares, merchandise, securities or money, of the value of $5,000 or more, knowing the same to have been stolen, converted or taken by fraud." The government contended that the bootleg records shipped in large quantities from Los Angeles to Maryland and to Florida were "stolen" because they embodied infringing performances of musical compositions. What arguments could you make for the accused? How should the Supreme Court rule?

Compare United States v. Brown, 925 F.2d 1301 (10th Cir. 1991) (Court dismisses indictment for violation of National Stolen Property Act for unauthorized theft of computer program embodied in notebooks and hard disk: "We hold that the computer program itself is an intangible intellectual property, and as such, it alone cannot constitute goods, wares, merchandise, securities or moneys which have been stolen, converted, or taken within the meaning of § 2314 or 2315 [of the NSPA]."), *with Advents Sys., Ltd. v. Unisys Corp.,* 925 F.2d 670 (3d Cir. 1991) (Court holds computer software to be a "good" under Uniform Commercial Code: "That a computer program may be copyrightable as intellectual property does not alter the fact that once in the form of a floppy disc or other medium, the program is tangible, movable and available in the market place.").

---

§ 109. Limitations on exclusive rights: Effect of transfer of particular copy or phonorecord

(a) Notwithstanding the provisions of section 106(3), the owner of a particular copy or phonorecord lawfully made under this title, or any person authorized by such owner, is entitled, without the authority of the copyright owner, to sell or otherwise dispose of the possession of that copy or phonorecord.

Section 109(a) confirms the traditional understanding that, in view of the difference in ownership rights in the copyright and in the physical object in which a work is embodied, the owner of the object is free to transfer it or even to destroy it. (§ 202 provides, of course, that such a transfer will not of itself transfer the right to copy the incorporated literary, artistic or musical work.) Destruction of the object, however — particularly a work of art — will typically destroy the right to make copies as well. As a result, should the copyright law impose on the chattel owner the duty to preserve it and indeed to make it available to the person entitled to make copies? Although copyright is ordinarily viewed as the "negative" right to prevent others from making copies, it might well also be viewed as providing a correlative "affirmative" right to derive economic benefits from copying and other such uses.

In *Community for Creative Non-Violence v. Reid*, 1992 CCH Copyr. L. Dec. ¶ 26,860 (D.D.C. 1991), a case that had reached the Supreme Court and been remanded (see Chapter 3A1), there was a dispute about copyright ownership of a sculpture that was commissioned from sculptor Reid by an advocacy group for the homeless. As a result of a settlement agreement, CCNV was given ownership of the physical sculpture, Reid was given the exclusive right to make three-dimensional reproductions, and both were to share joint ownership in two-dimensional reproductions. Reid sought temporary possession of the original sculpture, held by CCNV, in order to make a mold of the sculpture, but the organization refused access. Reid set forth a unique infringement claim — prevention, rather than unauthorized reproduction.

The court ruled for Reid. It concluded that it had jurisdiction to issue an order relating to the disposition of the chattel, and that "defendant is not required to re-create an original work of art to enable him to avail himself of his copyright solely by reason of CCNV's assertion of its possessory property right in the sculpture. Reid is entitled to a limited possessory right of his own, in the nature of an implied easement of necessity, to cause a master mold to be made of the sculpture, whereupon it shall be returned promptly to CCNV." The court stipulated that Reid was to have the master mold completed within thirty days of delivery and was to return the sculpture to CCNV ten days after the mold was completed.

QUESTIONS

1. Was the lower court in *CCNV* correct in its conclusion that copyright affords the author an affirmative right to have reasonable access to the physical embodiment of his artistic work in order to reproduce it? Or, rather, should copyright be properly conceived as no more than the "negative" right to prevent *others* from making reproductions (or the right to demand compensation in exchange for a license)? *See Baker v. Libbie*, 210 Mass. 599 (1912).

2. Should copyright, or some other body of law, provide — perhaps in the interest of preserving our cultural and aesthetic heritage — that *all* works of art must be preserved, and must not physically be mutilated or altered, or destroyed? As a result of amendments to the Copyright Act in 1990, a "work of visual art" can in fact be afforded such protection. *See* Sections 101 and 106A of the Act, and Chapter 6B, *infra.*

Chapter 2
COPYRIGHTABLE SUBJECT MATTER

A. IN GENERAL

§ 102. Subject matter of copyright: In general

(a) Copyright protection subsists, in accordance with this title, in original works of authorship fixed in any tangible medium of expression, now known or later developed, from which they can be perceived, reproduced, or otherwise communicated, either directly or with the aid of a machine or device. Works of authorship include the following categories:

(1) literary works;
(2) musical works, including any accompanying words;
(3) dramatic works, including any accompanying music;
(4) pantomimes and choreographic works;
(5) pictorial, graphic, and sculptural works;
(6) motion pictures and other audiovisual works;
(7) sound recordings; and
(8) architectural works.

1. ORIGINAL WORKS OF AUTHORSHIP

HOUSE REPORT

H.R. Rep. No. 94-1476, 94th Cong., 2d Sess. 51-52 (1976)

The two fundamental criteria of copyright protection — originality and fixation in tangible form — are restated in the first sentence of this cornerstone provision. The phrase "original works of authorship," which is purposely left undefined, is intended to incorporate without change the standard of originality established by the courts under the present copyright statute. This standard does not include requirements of novelty, ingenuity, or esthetic merit, and there is no intention to enlarge the standard of copyright protection to require them....

The history of copyright law has been one of gradual expansion in the types of works accorded protection, and the subject matter affected by this expansion has fallen into two general categories. In the first, scientific discoveries and technological developments have made possible new forms of creative expression that never existed before. In some of these cases the new expressive forms — electronic music, film-strips, and computer programs, for example — could be regarded as an extension of copyrightable subject matter Congress had already intended to protect, and were thus considered copyrightable from the outset without the need of new legislation. In other cases, such as photographs, sound recordings, and motion pictures, statutory enactment was deemed necessary to give them full recognition as copyrightable works.

Authors are continually finding new ways of expressing themselves, but it is impossible to foresee the forms that these new expressive methods will take. The bill does not intend either to freeze the scope of copyrightable technology or to allow unlimited expansion into areas completely outside the present congressional intent. Section 102 implies neither that that subject matter is unlimited nor that new forms of expression within that general area of subject matter would necessarily be unprotected.

The historic expansion of copyright has also applied to forms of expression which, although in existence for generations or centuries, have only gradually come to be recognized as creative and worthy of protection. The first copyright statute in this country, enacted in 1790, designated only "maps, charts, and books"; major forms of expression such as music, drama, and works of art achieved specific statutory recognition only in later enactments. Although the coverage of the present statute is very broad, and would be broadened further by the explicit recognition of all forms of choreography, there are unquestionably other areas of existing subject matter that this bill does not propose to protect but that future Congresses may want to.

Feist Publications, Inc. v. Rural Telephone Service, 499 U.S. 340, 111 S. Ct. 1282, 113 L. Ed. 358 (1991): "The *sine qua non* of copyright is originality. To qualify for copyright protection, a work must be original to the author.... Original, as the term is used in copyright, means only that the work was independently created by the author (as opposed to copied from other works), and that it possesses at least some minimal degree of creativity.... To be sure, the requisite level of creativity is extremely low; even a slight amount will suffice. The vast majority of works make the grade quite easily, as they possess some creative spark, 'no matter how crude, humble or obvious' it might be. [Nimmer on Copyright § 1.08[C][1].] Originality does not signify novelty; a work may be original even though it closely resembles other works so long as the similarity is fortuitous, not the result of copying. To illustrate, assume that two poets, each ignorant of the other, compose identical poems. Neither work is novel, yet both are original and, hence, copyrightable.... Originality is a constitutional requirement."

MAGIC MARKETING v. MAILING SERVICES OF PITTSBURGH

634 F. Supp. 769 (W.D. Pa. 1986)

ZIEGLER, DISTRICT JUDGE.

[Defendant] American Paper now moves for summary judgment on the issue of copyrightability. We hold that the envelopes allegedly manufactured by American Paper cannot be accorded copyright protection. We will grant the motion for summary judgment in part.

I. Facts

Plaintiff, Magic Marketing, Inc., designs and markets mass mailing advertising campaigns for businesses. In December 1983, plaintiff and defendant,

Mailing Services of Pittsburgh, Inc., entered into a contract whereby Mailing Services agreed to supply certain letters, forms and envelopes to plaintiff. Mailing Services subcontracted a portion of the printing work to American Paper. American Paper admits that it supplied envelopes pursuant to orders dated December 11, 1983, May 4, 1984 and June 6, 1984. Affidavit of John E. Gill dated February 13, 1986. However, it denies supplying any forms or letters. *Id.*

Plaintiff alleges that it holds a valid copyright in the relevant letters, forms and envelopes pursuant to an application filed July 23, 1985. According to plaintiff, Mailing Services infringed its copyright by selling copies of the materials to other customers. Plaintiff complains that American Paper manufactured and supplied infringing copies of the letters, forms and envelopes with knowledge of plaintiff's copyright.

Copies of the envelopes in question are contained in Exhibits A and F. *See* Complaint at Exhibits A, F. Both envelopes are conventional in size and contain standard instructions to the postmaster printed on the front. A solid black stripe runs horizontally across the middle of one envelope. Complaint at Exhibit A. The words "PRIORITY MESSAGE: CONTENTS REQUIRE IMMEDIATE ATTENTION" are printed in large white letters within the stripe. A shorter black stripe encasing the word "TELEGRAM" lies at the bottom right corner of the envelope. The other envelope has no stripe. Complaint at Exhibit F. Printed in bold-faced letters just above the window are the words "GIFT CHECK ENCLOSED." The copyright mark, "© 1984 Magic Marketing Inc." is imprinted on the backs of both envelopes.

II. Copyrightability of the Envelopes

A. Resolution by Summary Judgment

American Paper contends that the envelopes lack the level of originality to warrant copyright protection. We agree. Since a copyright infringement action cannot be maintained without a valid copyright, American Paper's attack is lethal to plaintiff's claim that the envelopes infringe its copyright. *Towle Manufacturing Co. v. Godinger Silver Art Co.*, 612 F. Supp. 986, 992 (S.D.N.Y. 1985).

The issue of copyrightability is typically resolved by a motion for summary judgment. *See, e.g., Carol Barnhart Inc. v. Economy Cover Corp.*, 773 F.2d 411 (2d Cir. 1985); *Norris Industries, Inc. v. International Telephone and Telegraph Corp.*, 696 F.2d 918 (11th Cir.), *cert. denied*, 464 U.S. 818, 104 S. Ct. 78, 78 L. Ed. 2d 89 (1983); *Kieselstein-Cord v. Accessories by Pearl, Inc.*, 632 F.2d 989 (2d Cir. 1980). Very often no issues of material fact are in dispute and the only task for the court is to analyze the allegedly copyrightable item in light of applicable copyright law. Of course, as in any case, summary judgement may only be granted if, viewing the evidence in a light most favorable to the non-moving party, there is no genuine issue of material fact and the movant is entitled to judgment as a matter of law. *Lang v. New York Life Insurance Co.*, 721 F.2d 118, 119 (3d Cir. 1983). For purposes of this motion, we will assume that American Paper manufactured both envelopes even though it admits printing only the envelope marked "PRIORITY MESSAGE: CONTENTS REQUIRE IMMEDIATE ATTENTION."

B. Originality

Section 102 of the Copyright Act provides that copyright protection subsists in "original works of authorship." 17 U.S.C. § 102. Originality is the "one pervading element" essential for copyright protection regardless of the form of the work. *L. Batlin & Sons, Inc. v. Snyder,* 536 F.2d 486, 489-90 (2d Cir.), *cert. denied,* 429 U.S. 857, 97 S. Ct. 156, 50 L. Ed. 2d 135 (1976); 1 Nimmer on Copyright § 2.01 (1985). Originality is distinct from novelty. To be original, a work must be the product of independent creation. *L. Batlin,* 536 F.2d at 490. While the test for originality is a "low threshold," the "author" must contribute more than a trivial variation of a previous work, i.e., the work must be recognizably "his own." *Id.* There is a narrow class of cases where even admittedly independent efforts may be deemed too trivial or insignificant to support copyright protection. 1 Nimmer on Copyright § 2.01[B] at 2-13.

This class is illustrated by case authority denying copyright protection to "fragmentary words and phrases" and to "forms of expression dictated solely by functional considerations." 1 Nimmer on Copyright § 2.01[B] at 2-13-14. Such material does not exhibit the minimal level of creativity necessary to warrant copyright protection. Indeed, regulations promulgated pursuant to the Copyright Act list the following works as not subject to copyright:

> Words and short phrases such as names, titles, and slogans; familiar symbols or designs; mere variations of typographic ornamentation, lettering or coloring; mere listing of ingredients or contents.

37 C.F.R. § 202.1(a) (1985). Moreover, clichéd language and expressions communicating an idea which may only be conveyed in a more or less stereotyped manner are not copyrightable. *Merritt Forbes & Co. v. Newman Investment Securities, Inc.,* 604 F. Supp. 943, 951 (S.D.N.Y. 1985); *Perma Greetings, Inc. v. Russ Berrie & Co.,* 598 F. Supp. 445, 448 (E.D. Mo. 1984).

We hold that the envelopes do not exhibit a sufficient degree of creativity to be copyrightable. The terse phrases on the envelopes describe their contents: "TELEGRAM," "GIFT CHECK," and "PRIORITY MESSAGE." The listing of the contents of an envelope or package, like a listing of ingredients, is not protected under the copyright regulations. 37 C.F.R. § 202.1(a). We note that even more colorful descriptions, such as advertising slogans, are not accorded copyright protection. For example, the phrase "most personal sort of deodorant" on a feminine hygiene product is not copyrightable. *Alberto-Culver Co. v. Andrea Dumon, Inc.,* 466 F.2d 705, 711 (7th Cir. 1972).

The phrase "CONTENTS REQUIRE IMMEDIATE ATTENTION" merely exhorts the recipient to open the envelope immediately upon delivery. It is nothing more than a direction or instruction for use. As such, it is unprotected. More complex directions, such as the serving directions on a frozen dessert package, are not copyrightable. *Kitchens of Sara Lee, Inc. v. Nifty Foods Corp.,* 266 F.2d 541 (2d Cir. 1959). *See also* 1 Nimmer on Copyright § 2.08[G] at 2-117. In sum, the phrases printed on the envelopes are generic in nature and lack the minimal degree of creativity necessary for copyright protection.

C. "Pictorial, graphic or sculptural" works

The protection accorded "pictorial, graphic or sculptural" works under the Copyright Act is inapplicable....

Initially we note that the envelopes cannot be considered a "pictorial, graphic or sculptural" work if they fail to embody a minimal level of creativity. 37 C.F.R. § 202.10(c). We held above that the envelopes lack this requisite level of creativity.

Furthermore, no part of the envelope constitutes a "pictorial, graphic or sculptural" work. No pictures or designs are imprinted on the face of the envelopes except the solid black stripe. Solid black stripes are not copyrightable. The printing within the stripe is nothing more than a distinctive typeface, which is not protected. 37 C.F.R. § 202.1(a); *Alberto-Culver, supra,* 466 F.2d at 711....

. . . .

IT IS ORDERED that the motion of defendant, American Paper Products Company, for summary judgment be and hereby is granted on the issue of the copyrightability of the allegedly infringing envelopes.

Sebastian Int'l, Inc. v. Consumer Contacts (PTY) Ltd., 664 F. Supp. 909 (D.N.J. 1987), *rev'd on other grounds,* 847 F.2d 1093 (3d Cir. 1988). The plaintiff manufactures and markets beauty products including shampoos, conditioners and hair sprays, which are available in the United States only in professional hair care salons. The plaintiff shipped certain of its products to a purchaser in South Africa, who promptly re-shipped them to the United States for public sale here. An action was brought to prevent disposing of the products here, relying on theories of contract, trademark infringement, and copyright infringement. In considering the issuance of a preliminary injunction, the court rejected the defendants' claim that the labels on the plaintiff's products (including a product known as WET 4) were not copyrightable. The court of appeals reversed the injunction issued by the district court, see p. 496 *infra,* but did not address the correctness of that court's conclusion that the labels were indeed copyrightable. The lower court's analysis follows.

"It is well established that labels are subject to copyright protection, see *Kitchens of Sara Lee, Inc. v. Nifty Foods Corp.,* 266 F.2d 541 (2d Cir. 1959), if the label manifests the necessary modicum of creativity. *See, e.g., Drop Dead Co. v. S.C. Johnson & Son, Inc.,* 326 F.2d 87 (9th Cir. 1963) (copyright in PLEDGE label is valid); *Abli Inc. v. Standard Brands Paint Co.,* 323 F. Supp. 1400 (C.D. Cal. 1970) (label was copyrightable when it contained such phrases as "Cut to desired length ... Will not run ... Simply slide top bead into rod as illustrated"). Catch phrases, mottos, slogans and short advertising expressions are not copyrightable. *See, e.g., Perma Greetings Inc. v. Russ Berrie & Co., Inc.,* 598 F. Supp. 445 (E.D. Mo. 1984) (expressions such as "hang in there" and "along the way take time to smell the flowers" not copyrightable).

But, of course, the length of a sentence is not dispositive of whether it is subject to protection. *Rockford Map Publishers, Inc. v. Directory Service Co. of Colorado, Inc.,* 768 F.2d 145, 148 (7th Cir. 1985).

"The following, taken from a WET 4 container is an example of text being challenged in this case.

> Hair stays wet-looking as long as you like. Brushes out to full-bodied dry look. WET 4 is one step-four choice (finishing) in Sebastian's four step program for a healthy scalp and head of hair. WET is not oily, won't flake and keeps hair wet-looking for hours, allowing you to sculpture, contour, wave or curl. It stays looking wet until it's brushed out. When brushed, hair looks and feels thicker, extra full. Try brushing partly, leaving some parts wet for a different look.

This language is more than simply a list of ingredients, directions, or a catchy phrase. No one can seriously dispute that if plaintiff were to discover that a competitor's package utilized the exact language as above with the exception of the product's name, plaintiff would be entitled to protection. While this text tries the limits of the modicum of creativity necessary for a work to be copyrightable, I find that taken as a whole it comes within the purview of the Copyright Act."

B. KAPLAN, AN UNHURRIED VIEW OF COPYRIGHT 45-46 (1967)

Are there compositions which though original are too small to qualify for copyright or to figure as the subjects of actionable infringement? Some of Holmes's language suggests that any emanation of personality, however slight, any uncopied collocation, however slim, should be protected, and his abnegation of judicial responsibility for passing on the merit of intellectual productions points in the same direction.[25] So also does the appearance in the statute of so mean a category as "prints or labels used for articles of merchandise"[26] — though we must always beware of a false development of copyright law by a process of treating extreme applications as being normal, thus inviting applications even more extreme.[27] There are, on the other hand, definite indications of some rule *de minimis.*

Some have thought it inherent in the very notion of "personality," of spontaneity, that a copyright claimant must exceed the utterly stilted or trite, must satisfy some threshold requirement of "creativity."[28] And though Judge Frank pushed hard in the *Alfred Bell* case to show the theoretical protectibility of any original production, he still admitted that a variation, say, on a public domain work must be more than "trivial" to support copy-

---

[25]*See* Bleistein v. Donaldson Lithographing Co., 188 U.S. 239 (1903)....

[26]17 U.S.C. § 5(k).

[27]*Cf.* Lord Robertson's remarks, dissenting in Walter v. Lane, [1900] A.C. 539, 561.

[28]*See* Register of Copyrights, Copyright Law Revision: Report on the General Revision of the U.S. Copyright Law, printed for the use of the House Comm. on the Judiciary, 87th Cong., 1st Sess., at 9 (Comm. Print 1961). *But see* Supplementary Report, Copyright Law Revision, Pt. 6, at 3 (Comm. Print 1965) (89th Cong., 1st Sess.), where an express requirement of "creativity" is abandoned.

right.[29] Judge Hand wrote to similar effect in the *National Comics* case.[30] Courts are disinclined to permit copyright to attach to short word sequences or to find plagiarism in the copying of such sequences; this lies close to the slogan that "titles" are not protected through copyright.[31] More generally it has been said that only substantial takings are actionable: Judge Hand would apply this to the appropriation of a separate scene or part of the dialogue of a play, and thought the same question of substantiality arose in adjudging infringement of any work.[32] We can, I think, conclude that to make the copyright turnstile revolve, the author should have to deposit more than a penny in the box, and some like measure ought to apply to infringement. Surely there is danger in trying to fence off small quanta of words or other collocations; these pass quickly into the idiom; to allow them copyright, particularly if aided by a doctrine of "unconscious" plagiarism, could set up untoward barriers to expression.

QUESTIONS

Are the following works copyrightable under the Copyright Act of 1976?

(a) A design of a cross (with arms of equal length) inside a circle.

(b) The rearrangement of the three color bars upon a flag.

(c) A slogan "Things Go Better with Glurp" (Glurp being a carbonated beverage).

(d) A drawing of the University Law School (to be used for display in the law building or in an advertising brochure for applicants).

(e) A snapshot of the Law School on a cloudy day.

(f) The Zapruder films of the assassination of President Kennedy.

(g) A Picasso "re-treatment" of a Velasquez painting of the members of the royal family in Spain.

(h) A three-dimensional replica, as statues, of the Velasquez painting.

(i) A black-and-white photocopy of the Velasquez painting.

(j) A printing of a long-lost play by Shakespeare (published and performed in Shakespeare's time but only recently discovered after years of search and analysis by Professor Falstaff of the University's English Department).

(k) A translation of a Moliere play.

(*l*) A telephone book, derived by original gathering and collection of names, addresses and telephone numbers.

(m) A chart containing, in headings and columns, information about Latin American countries (e.g., capital, population, principal products, square miles), gathered from one encyclopedia.

---

[29] Alfred Bell & Co., Ltd. v. Catalda Fine Arts, Inc., 191 F.2d 99, 103 (2d Cir. 1951).

[30] National Comics Pub., Inc. v. Fawcett Pub., Inc., 191 F.2d 594, 600 (2d Cir. 1951).

[31] *Cf.* Regulations of the Copyright Office, 37 C.F.R., ch. II, § 202.1(a) (1959). *See also* Nimmer, Copyright § 34 (1965). *But cf.* Heim v. Universal Pictures Co., Inc., 154 F.2d 480, 487 n.8 (2d Cir. 1946); Life Music, Inc. v. Wonderland Music Co., 241 F. Supp. 653, 656 (S.D.N.Y. 1965).

[32] Nichols v. Universal Pictures Corp., 45 F.2d 119, 121 (2d Cir. 1930), *cert. denied*, 282 U.S. 902 (1931).

(n) A map, derived from original exploration (or derived from collating several public domain maps of different age and size).

(o) An article in *Time* magazine about a current news event, derived from original investigation (or derived from other published news reports).

HOUSE REPORT

H.R. Rep. No. 94-1476, 94th Cong., 2d Sess. 53-56 (1976)

Categories of copyrightable works

The second sentence of section 102 lists seven broad categories which the concept of "works of authorship" is said to "include." The use of the word "include," as defined in section 101, makes clear that the listing is "illustrative and not limitative," and that the seven categories do not necessarily exhaust the scope of "original works of authorship" that the bill is intended to protect.... Of the seven items listed, four are defined in section 101. The three undefined categories — "musical works," "dramatic works," and "pantomimes and choreographic works" — have fairly settled meanings. There is no need, for example, to specify the copyrightability of electronic or concrete music in the statute since the form of a work would no longer be of any importance, nor is it necessary to specify that "choreographic works" do not include social dance steps and simple routines.

The four items defined in section 101 are "literary works," "pictorial, graphic, and sculptural works," "motion pictures and audiovisual works," and "sound recordings." In each of these cases, definitions are needed not only because the meaning of the term itself is unsettled but also because the distinction between "work" and "material object" requires clarification. The term "literary works" does not connote any criterion of literary merit or qualitative value: it includes catalogs, directories, similar factual, reference, or instructional works and compilations of data. It also includes computer data bases, and computer programs to the extent that they incorporate authorship in the programmer's expression of original ideas, as distinguished from the ideas themselves.

....

Enactment of Public Law 92-140 in 1971 marked the first recognition in American copyright law of sound recordings as copyrightable works. As defined in section 101, copyrightable "sound recordings" are original works of authorship comprising an aggregate of musical, spoken, or other sounds that have been fixed in tangible form. The copyrightable work comprises the aggregation of sounds and not the tangible medium of fixation. Thus, "sound recordings" as copyrightable subject matter are distinguished from "phonorecords," the latter being physical objects in which sounds are fixed. They are also distinguished from any copyrighted literary, dramatic, or musical works that may be reproduced on a "phonorecord."

As a class of subject matter, sound recordings are clearly within the scope of the "writings of an author" capable of protection under the Constitution, and the extension of limited statutory protection to them was too long delayed. Aside from cases in which sounds are fixed by some purely mechanical means without originality of any kind, the copyright protection that would prevent the reproduction and distribution of unauthorized phonorecords of sound recordings is clearly justified.

The copyrightable elements in a sound recording will usually, though not always, involve "authorship" both on the part of the performers whose performance is captured and on the part of the record producer responsible for setting up the recording session, capturing and electronically processing the sounds, and compiling and editing them to make the final sound recording. There may, however, be cases where the record producer's contribution is so minimal that the performance is the only copyrightable element in the work, and there may be cases (for example, recordings of bird calls, sounds of racing cars, et cetera) where only the record producer's contribution is copyrightable.

Sound tracks of motion pictures, long a nebulous area in American copyright law, are specifically included in the definition of "motion pictures," and excluded in the definition of "sound recordings.".... [T]he bill equates audiovisual materials such as filmstrips, slide sets, and sets of transparencies with "motion pictures" rather than with "pictorial, graphic, and sculptural works." Their sequential showing is closer to a "performance" than to a "display," and the definition of "audiovisual works," which applies also to "motion pictures," embraces works consisting of a series of related images that are by their nature, intended for showing by means of projectors or other devices.

QUESTION

Are the categories in § 102(a) discrete or overlapping? Can you think of creative endeavors that do not fall within the § 102(a) categories? Watch for the substantive significance of these categories as you proceed through your study of the statute.

2. FIXATION IN TANGIBLE FORM

HOUSE REPORT

H.R. Rep. No. 94-1476, 94th Cong., 2d Sess. 52-53 (1976)

As a basic condition of copyright protection, the bill perpetuates the existing requirement that a work be fixed in a "tangible medium of expression," and adds that this medium may be one "now known or later developed," and that the fixation is sufficient if the work "can be perceived, reproduced, or otherwise communicated, either directly or with the aid of a machine or device." This broad language is intended to avoid the artificial and largely unjustifiable distinctions, derived from cases such as *White-Smith Publishing Co. v. Apollo Co.,* 209 U.S. 1 (1908), under which statutory copyrightability in certain cases has been made to depend upon the form or medium in which the work is fixed. Under the bill it makes no difference what the form, manner, or medium of fixation may be — whether it is in words, numbers, notes, sounds, pictures, or any other graphic or symbolic indicia, whether embodied in a physical object in written, printed, photographic, sculptural, punched, magnetic, or any other stable form, and whether it is capable of perception directly or by means of any machine or device "now known or later developed."

Under the bill, the concept of fixation is important since it not only determines whether the provisions of the statute apply to a work, but it also represents the dividing line between common law and statutory protection. As will be noted in more detail in connection with section 301, an unfixed work of authorship, such as an improvisation or an unrecorded choreographic work, performance, or broadcast, would continue to be subject to protection under State common law or statute, but would not be eligible for Federal statutory protection under section 102.

The bill seeks to resolve, through the definition of "fixation" in section 101, the status of live broadcasts — sports, news coverage, live performances of music, etc. — that are reaching the public in unfixed form but that are simultaneously being recorded. When a football game is being covered by four television cameras, with a director guiding the activities of the four cameramen and choosing which of their electronic images are sent out to the public and in what order, there is little doubt that what the cameramen and the director are doing constitutes "authorship." The further question to be considered is whether there has been a fixation.... [T]he content of a live transmission should be accorded statutory protection if it is being recorded simultaneously with its transmission. On the other hand, the definition of "fixation" would exclude from the concept purely evanescent or transient reproductions such as those projected briefly on a screen, shown electronically on a television or other cathode ray tube, or captured momentarily in the "memory" of a computer.

Under the first sentence of the definition of "fixed" in section 101, a work would be considered "fixed in a tangible medium of expression" if there has been an authorized embodiment in a copy or phonorecord and if that embodiment "is sufficiently permanent or stable" to permit the work "to be perceived, reproduced, or otherwise communicated for a period of more than transitory duration." The second sentence makes clear that, in the case of "a work consisting of sounds, images, or both, that are being transmitted," the work is regarded as "fixed" if a fixation is being made at the same time as the transmission.

Under this definition "copies" and "phonorecords" together will comprise all of the material objects in which copyrightable works are capable of being fixed. The definitions of these terms in section 101, together with their usage in section 102 and throughout the bill, reflect a fundamental distinction between the "original work" which is the product of "authorship" and the multitude of material objects in which it can be embodied. Thus, in the sense of the bill, a "book" is not a work of authorship, but is a particular kind of "copy." Instead, the author may write a "literary work," which in turn can be embodied in a wide range of "copies" and "phonorecords," including books, periodicals, computer punch cards, microfilm, tape recordings, and so forth. It is possible to have an "original work of authorship" without having a "copy" or "phonorecord" embodying it, and it is also possible to have a "copy" or "phonorecord" embodying something that does not qualify as an "original work of authorship." The two essential elements — original work and tangible object — must merge through fixation in order to produce subject matter copyrightable under the statute.

VIDEO GAMES AND THE "FIXATION" REQUIREMENT

The "fixation" requirement figured conspicuously in several cases involving claimed infringement of copyrighted videogames. The visual images and synthesized sounds that make up these now familiar action games are generated by computer programs that are stored in different kinds of memory devices; the patterns of sights and sounds are repetitive in the so-called "attract mode" (when the game is not being played but the customer is being enticed to do so) and are subject to variation during the "play mode" by virtue of human intervention. Relying upon some of the language in the House Report set forth above, defendants in a number of cases claimed that they were free to copy the plaintiffs' games, classified as "audiovisual works," because they were not fixed in a tangible medium of expression but were rather merely ephemeral projections of sight and sound on a cathode ray tube. It was also argued that the inevitable variations in the appearance and sound of the games that result from the differing skill and judgment of the persons playing them prevent any kind of consistent pattern necessary for a "fixation."

These contentions have been uniformly rejected. *See, e.g., M. Kramer Mfg. Co. v. Andrews,* 783 F.2d 421 (4th Cir. 1986). In *Stern Elecs., Inc. v. Kaufman,* 669 F.2d 852 (2d Cir. 1982), it was held that the audiovisual game was "permanently embodied in a material object, the memory devices, from which it can be perceived with the aid of the other components of the game." And in *Midway Mfg. Co. v. Dirkschneider,* 543 F. Supp. 466 (D. Neb. 1981), the court concluded that "The printed circuit boards are tangible objects from which the audiovisual works may be perceived for a period of time more than transitory. The fact that the audiovisual works cannot be viewed without a machine does not mean the works are not fixed." As to the claim that the player's participation prevents the fixing of particular audiovisual patterns, the court in *Williams Elecs., Inc. v. Artic Int'l, Inc.,* 685 F.2d 870 (3d Cir. 1982), concluded:

> Although there is player interaction with the machine during the play mode which causes the audiovisual presentation to change in some respects from one game to the next in response to the player's varying participation, there is always a repetitive sequence of a substantial portion of the sights and sounds of the game, and many aspects of the display remain constant from game to game regardless of how the player operates the controls.... Furthermore, there is no player participation in the attract mode which is displayed repetitively without change.

QUESTIONS

1. Is a live performance of music in a coffee house, simultaneously being tape recorded by the performer, within the coverage of the federal Copyright Act? As to the possibility of protection under common-law copyright, compare *Estate of Hemingway v. Random House,* 23 N.Y.2d 341, 244 N.E.2d 250, 296 N.Y.S.2d 771 (1968) with *Falwell v. Penthouse Int'l,* 521 F. Supp. 1204 (W.D. Va. 1981).

2. Is a lecture in a law school classroom protected under the federal Act? What if it is being tape recorded without the consent of the instructor? What if students are taking copious (but not verbatim) written notes?

3. Event Designers, Inc. (EDI) is in the business of planning, organizing and promoting events such as holiday parades. One of its major projects each year is a Thanksgiving Day parade in Chicago, which includes more than 100 participating units, including decorative floats, horse troops, marching bands, bagpipe groups, tumblers and dancers, large helium-filled balloons, novelty acts, political figures and entertainers. EDI, among other things, determines the sequence in which the parade units will march, and a number of the decorative floats are of its own design and manufacture. EDI has sold the exclusive Chicago-area television broadcast rights in the parade to the American Broadcasting Company and its local station WLS-TV, and it has sold broadcasting rights in other parts of the country to other television stations. WLS-TV will make a tape of its telecast simultaneously as its program is broadcast. Another Chicago television station, WGN-TV, has announced that it intends to use its own equipment, camera personnel and director to broadcast live images of the EDI parade; it does not intend in any way to tape or to retransmit the images shown over WLS-TV. EDI and WLS-TV have brought an action in a federal court seeking an injunction against the WGN-TV broadcast. How should the court decide? *See Production Contractors, Inc. v. WGN Continental Broadcasting Co.,* 622 F. Supp. 1500 (N.D. Ill. 1985).

4. Study the definitions of "copy" and "phonorecord" and "fixed" in § 101. What is the difference between a copy and a phonorecord? Can a copyrightable work be embodied in a material object other than these two formats?

B. THE "IDEA/EXPRESSION DICHOTOMY"

§ 102. Subject matter of copyright: In general

. . . .

(b) In no case does copyright protection for an original work of authorship extend to any idea, procedure, process, system, method of operation, concept, principle, or discovery, regardless of the form in which it is described, explained, illustrated, or embodied in such work.

HOUSE REPORT

H.R. Rep. No. 94-1476, 94th Cong., 2d Sess. 56-57 (1976)

Copyright does not preclude others from using the ideas or information revealed by the author's work. It pertains to the literary, musical, graphic, or artistic form in which the author expressed intellectual concepts.... Some concern has been expressed lest copyright in computer programs should extend protection to the methodology or processes adopted by the programmer, rather than merely to the "writing" expressing his ideas. Section 102 (b) is intended, among other things, to make clear that the expression adopted by the programmer is the copyrightable element in a computer program, and that the actual processes or methods embodied in the program are not within the scope of the copyright law.

Section 102 (b) in no way enlarges or contracts the scope of copyright protection under the present law. Its purpose is to restate, in the context of the new single Federal system of copyright, that the basic dichotomy between expression and idea remains unchanged.

BAKER v. SELDEN

101 U.S. 99 (1879)

Mr. Justice Bradley delivered the opinion of the court.

Charles Selden, the testator of the complainant in this case, in the year 1859 took the requisite steps for obtaining the copyright of a book, entitled "Selden's Condensed Ledger, or Bookkeeping Simplified," the object of which was to exhibit and explain a peculiar system of book-keeping. In 1860 and 1861, he took the copyright of several other books, containing additions to and improvements upon the said system. The bill of complaint was filed against the defendant, Baker, for an alleged infringement of these copyrights. The latter, in his answer, denied that Selden was the author or designer of the books, and denied the infringement charged, and contends on the argument that the matter alleged to be infringed is not a lawful subject of copyright.

The parties went into proofs, and the various books of the complainant, as well as those sold and used by the defendant, were exhibited before the examiner, and witnesses were examined on both sides. A decree was rendered for the complainant, and the defendant appealed.

The book or series of books of which the complainant claims the copyright consists of an introductory essay explaining the system of book-keeping referred to, to which are annexed certain forms or blanks, consisting of ruled lines, and headings, illustrating the system and showing how it is to be used and carried out in practice. This system effects the same results as book-keeping by double entry; but, by a peculiar arrangement of columns and headings, presents the entire operation, of a day, a week, or a month, on a single page, or on two pages facing each other, in an account-book. The defendant uses a similar plan so far as results are concerned; but makes a different arrangement of the columns, and uses different headings. If the complainant's testator had the exclusive right to the use of the system explained in his book, it would be difficult to contend that the defendant does not infringe it, notwithstanding the difference in his form of arrangement; but if it be assumed that the system is open to public use, it seems to be equally difficult to contend that the books made and sold by the defendant are a violation of the copyright of the complainant's book considered merely as a book explanatory of the system. Where the truths of a science or the methods of an art are the common property of the whole world, any author has the right to express the one, or explain and use the other, in his own way. As an author, Selden explained the system in a particular way. It may be conceded that Baker makes and uses account-books arranged on substantially the same system; but the proof fails to show that he has violated the copyright of Selden's book, regarding the latter merely as an explanatory work; or that he has infringed Selden's right in any way, unless the latter became entitled to an exclusive right in the system.

CONDENSED LEDGER.

Bro't Forw'd.		ON TIME.		DATE:		SUNDRIES to SUNDRIES.	DISTRIBU-TION.		TOTAL.		BALANCE.	
DR.	CR.	DR.	CR.	DR.	CR.		DR.	CR.	DR.	CR.	DR.	CR.

CASH.

DR.	CR.
$	$

Carried Forward....

The account book ledger design in which
Selden claimed a copyright

The evidence of the complainant is principally directed to the object of showing that Baker uses the same system as that which is explained and illustrated in Selden's books. It becomes important, therefore, to determine whether, in obtaining the copyright of his books, he secured the exclusive right to the use of the system or method of book-keeping which the said books are intended to illustrate and explain. It is contended that he has secured such exclusive right, because no one can use the system without using substantially the same ruled lines and headings which he has appended to his books in illustration of it. In other words, it is contended that the ruled lines and headings, given to illustrate the system, are a part of the book, and, as such, are secured by the copyright; and that no one can make or use similar ruled lines and headings, or ruled lines and headings made and arranged on substantially the same system, without violating the copyright. And this is really the question to be decided in this case. Stated in another form, the question is, whether the exclusive property in a system of book-keeping can be claimed, under the law of copyright, by means of a book in which that system is explained? The complainant's bill, and the case made under it, are based on the hypothesis that it can be.

It cannot be pretended, and indeed it is not seriously urged, that the ruled lines of the complainant's account-book can be claimed under any special class of objects, other than books, named in the law of copyright existing in 1859. The law then in force was that of 1831, and specified only books, maps, charts, musical compositions, prints, and engravings. An account-book, consisting of ruled lines and blank columns, cannot be called by any of these names unless by that of a book.

There is no doubt that a work on the subject of book-keeping, though only explanatory of well-known systems, may be the subject of a copyright; but, then, it is claimed only as a book. Such a book may be explanatory either of old systems, or of an entirely new system; and, considered as a book, as the work of an author, conveying information on the subject of book-keeping, and containing detailed explanations of the art, it may be a very valuable acquisition to the practical knowledge of the community. But there is a clear distinction between the book, as such, and the art which it is intended to illustrate. The mere statement of the proposition is so evident, that it requires hardly any argument to support it. The same distinction may be predicated of every other art as well as that of book-keeping. A treatise on the composition and use of medicines, be they old or new; on the construction and use of ploughs, or watches, or churns; or on the mixture and application of colors for painting or dyeing; or on the mode of drawing lines to produce the effect of perspective, — would be the subject of copyright; but no one would contend that the copyright of the treatise would give the exclusive right to the art or manufacture described therein. The copyright of the book, if not pirated from other works, would be valid without regard to the novelty, or want of novelty, of its subject-matter. The novelty of the art or thing described or explained has nothing to do with the validity of the copyright. To give to the author of the book an exclusive property in the art described therein, when no examination of its novelty has ever been officially made, would be a surprise and a fraud upon the public. That is the province of letters-patent, not of copyright. The claim to an invention or discovery of an art or manufacture must be subjected to the examination of the Patent Office before an exclusive right therein can be obtained; and it can only be secured by a patent from the government.

The difference between the two things, letters-patent and copyright, may be illustrated by reference to the subjects just enumerated. Take the case of medicines. Certain mixtures are found to be of great value in the healing art. If the discoverer writes and publishes a book on the subject (as regular physicians generally do), he gains no exclusive right to the manufacture and sale of the medicine; he gives that to the public. If he desires to acquire such exclusive right, he must obtain a patent for the mixture as a new art, manufacture, or composition of matter. He may copyright his book, if he pleases; but that only secures to him the exclusive right of printing and publishing his book. So of all other inventions or discoveries.

The copyright of a book on perspective, no matter how many drawings and illustrations it may contain, gives no exclusive right to the modes of drawing described, though they may never have been known or used before. By publishing the book, without getting a patent for the art, the latter is given to the public. The fact that the art [is] described in the book by illustrations of lines and figures which are reproduced in practice in the application of the art, makes no difference. Those illustrations are the mere language employed by the author to convey his ideas more clearly. Had he used words of description instead of diagrams (which merely stand in the place of words), there could not be the slightest doubt that others, applying the art to practical use, might lawfully draw the lines and diagrams which were in the author's mind, and which he thus described by words in his book.

The copyright of a work on mathematical science cannot give to the author an exclusive right to the methods of operation which he propounds, or to the diagrams which he employs to explain them, so as to prevent an engineer from using them whenever occasion requires. The very object of publishing a book on science or the useful arts is to communicate to the world the useful knowledge which it contains. But this object would be frustrated if the knowledge could not be used without incurring the guilt of piracy of the book. And where the art it teaches cannot be used without employing the methods and diagrams used to illustrate the book, or such as are similar to them, such methods and diagrams are to be considered as necessary incidents to the art, and given therewith to the public; not given for the purpose of publication in other works explanatory of the art, but for the purpose of practical application.

Of course, these observations are not intended to apply to ornamental designs, or pictorial illustrations addressed to the taste. Of these it may be said, that their form is their essence, and their object, the production of pleasure in their contemplation. This is their final end. They are as much the product of genius and the result of composition, as are the lines of the poet or the historian's periods. On the other hand, the teachings of science and the rules and methods of useful art have their final end in application and use; and this application and use are what the public derive from the publication of a book which teaches them. But as embodied and taught in a literary composition or book, their essence consists only in their statement. This alone is what is secured by the copyright. The use by another of the same methods of statement, whether in words or illustrations, in a book published for teaching the art, would undoubtedly be an infringement of the copyright.

Recurring to the case before us, we observe that Charles Selden, by his books, explained and described a peculiar system of book-keeping, and illustrated his method by means of ruled lines and blank columns, with proper headings on a page, or on successive pages. Now, whilst no one has a right to print or publish his book, or any material part thereof, as a book intended to convey instruction in the art, any person may practice and use the art itself which he has described and illustrated therein. The use of the art is a totally different thing from a publication of the book explaining it. The copyright of a book on book-keeping cannot secure the exclusive right to make, sell, and use account-books prepared upon the plan set forth in such book. Whether the art might or might not have been patented, is a question which is not before us. It was not patented, and is open and free to the use of the public. And, of course, in using the art, the ruled lines and headings of accounts must necessarily be used as incident to it.

The plausibility of the claim put forward by the complainant in this case arises from a confusion of ideas produced by the peculiar nature of the art described in the books which have been made the subject of copyright. In describing the art, the illustrations and diagrams employed happen to correspond more closely than usual with the actual work performed by the operator who uses the art. Those illustrations and diagrams consist of ruled lines and headings of accounts; and it is similar ruled lines and headings of accounts which, in the application of the art, the book-keeper makes with his pen, or the stationer with his press; whilst in most other cases the diagrams and illustrations can only be represented in concrete forms of wood, metal, stone, or some other physical embodiment. But the principle is the same in all. The description of the art in a book, though entitled to the benefit of copyright, lays no foundation for an exclusive claim to the art itself. The object of the one is explanation; the object of the other is use. The former may be secured by copyright. The latter can only be secured, if it can be secured at all, by letters-patent.

....

The conclusion to which we have come is, that blank account-books are not the subject of copyright; and that the mere copyright of Selden's book did not confer upon him the exclusive right to make and use account-books, ruled and arranged as designated by him and described and illustrated in said book.

The decree of the Circuit Court must be reversed, and the cause remanded with instructions to dismiss the complainant's bill; and it is

So ordered.

QUESTIONS

1. What is the precise holding of this case: that the accounting forms were copyrightable (and copyrighted) but that such copyright was not infringed? Or that the accounting forms were not eligible for copyright?

2. Could the Court simply have ruled for the defendant on the ground that his form did not substantially copy the plaintiff's? Wouldn't such an approach avoid the question whether copyright extended to the accounting system described in the plaintiff's book?

3. Professor Nimmer has argued that had the defendant's forms been identical copies of the plaintiff's there should have been a finding of infringement. *See* 1 Nimmer on Copyright § 2.18(C)(2). Do you agree?

4. What would be the proper analysis of the case if the defendant had been an accountant and had photocopied (assuming that was possible at the time the case arose) the plaintiff's forms? What if the defendant, instead, was in the printing business, and had printed thousands of copies of the forms, which he then sold in a retail store to accountants (along with ledger pads, electronic calculators, accounting magazines, and the like)?

5. If the defendant had written a book describing, in his own words, plaintiff's accounting system, would that be an infringement of copyright? If, in that book, the defendant had included exact copies of the plaintiff's forms in an appendix for the purpose of illustrating the system described in the book, would that be an infringement? If the former question is answered no, doesn't that compel the same answer to the latter question?

MORRISSEY v. PROCTER & GAMBLE CO.

379 F.2d 675 (1st Cir. 1967)

ALDRICH, CHIEF JUDGE. This is an appeal from a summary judgment for the defendant. The plaintiff, Morrissey, is the copyright owner of a set of rules for a sales promotional contest of the "sweepstakes" type involving the social security numbers of the participants. Plaintiff alleges that the defendant, Procter & Gamble Company, infringed, by copying, almost precisely, Rule 1. In its motion for summary judgment, based upon affidavits and depositions, defendant denies that plaintiff's Rule 1 is copyrightable material, and denies access. The district court held for the defendant on both grounds.

[The court found an issue of fact as to access precluding summary judgment.]

The second aspect of the case raises a more difficult question. Before discussing it we recite plaintiff's Rule 1, and defendant's Rule 1, the italicizing in the latter being ours to note the defendant's variations or changes.

>   1. Entrants should print name, address and social security number on a boxtop, or a plain paper. Entries must be accompanied by ... boxtop or by plainpaper on which the name ... is copied from any source. Official rules are explained on ... packages or leaflets obtained from dealer. If you do not have a social security number you may use the name and number of any member of your immediate family living with you. Only the person named on the entry will be deemed an entrant and may qualify for prize.

Use the correct social security number belonging to the person named on entry ... wrong numbers will be disqualified.

(Plaintiff's Rule)

1. Entrants should print name, address and Social Security number on a Tide boxtop, or *on* [a] plain paper. Entries must be accompanied by Tide boxtop *(any size)* or by plain paper on which the name 'Tide' is copied from any source. Official rules are *available* on Tide Sweepstakes packages, or *on* leaflets *at* Tide dealers, *or you can send a stamped, self-addressed envelope to:* Tide "Shopping Fling" Sweepstakes, P.O. Box 4459, Chicago 77, Illinois.

If you do not have a Social Security number, you may use the name and number of any member of your immediate family living with you. Only the person named on the entry will be deemed an entrant and may qualify for a prize.

Use the correct Social Security number, belonging to the person named on *the* entry — wrong numbers will be disqualified.

(Defendant's Rule)

The district court, following an earlier decision, *Gaye v. Gillis,* D. Mass., 1958, 167 F. Supp. 416, took the position that since the substance of the contest was not copyrightable, which is unquestionably correct, *Baker v. Selden,* 1879, 101 U.S. 99; *Affiliated Enterprises v. Gruber,* 1 Cir., 1936, 86 F.2d 958; *Chamberlin v. Uris Sales Corp.,* 2 Cir., 1945, 150 F.2d 512, and the substance was relatively simple, it must follow that plaintiff's rule sprung directly from the substance and "contains no original creative authorship." 262 F. Supp. at 738. This does not follow. Copyright attaches to form of expression, and defendant's own proof, introduced to deluge the court on the issue of access, itself established that there was more than one way of expressing even this simple substance. Nor, in view of the almost precise similarity of the two rules, could defendant successfully invoke the principle of a stringent standard for showing infringement which some courts apply when the subject matter involved admits of little variation in form of expression. E.g., *Dorsey v. Old Surety Life Ins. Co.,* 10 Cir., 1938, 98 F.2d 872, 874, 119 A.L.R. 1250 ("a showing of appropriation in the exact form or substantially so."); *Continental Casualty Co. v. Beardsley,* 2 Cir., 1958, 253 F.2d 702, 705, cert. denied, 358 U.S. 816 ("a stiff standard for proof of infringement.").

Nonetheless, we must hold for the defendant. When the uncopyrightable subject matter is very narrow, so that "the topic necessarily requires," *Sampson & Murdock Co. v. Seaver-Radford Co.,* 1 Cir., 1905, 140 F. 539, 541; cf. Kaplan, An Unhurried View of Copyright, 64-65 (1967), if not only one form of expression, at best only a limited number, to permit copyrighting would mean that a party or parties, by copyrighting a mere handful of forms, could exhaust all possibilities of future use of the substance. In such circumstances it does not seem accurate to say that any particular form of expression comes from the subject matter. However, it is necessary to say that the subject matter would be appropriated by permitting the copyrighting of its expression. We cannot recognize copyright as a game of chess in which the public can be checkmated. Cf. *Baker v. Selden, supra.*

Upon examination the matters embraced in Rule 1 are so straightforward and simple that we find this limiting principle to be applicable. Furthermore, its operation need not await an attempt to copyright all possible forms. It cannot be only the last form of expression which is to be condemned, as completing defendant's exclusion from the substance. Rather, in these circumstances, we hold that copyright does not extend to the subject matter at all, and plaintiff cannot complain even if his particular expression was deliberately adopted.

Affirmed.

BIBBERO SYSTEMS, INC. v. COLWELL SYSTEMS, INC.

893 F.2d 1104 (9th Cir. 1990)

GOODWIN, CHIEF JUDGE:

This case requires us to examine the scope of the blank forms rule, 37 C.F.R. § 202.1(c) (1982), which provides that blank forms are not copyrightable. Plaintiff Bibbero Systems, Inc. (Bibbero) contends that Colwell Systems, Inc. (Colwell) infringed upon its copyright by duplicating its medical insurance claim form. The district court granted summary judgment to Colwell, finding that the billing form was an uncopyrightable blank form designed for recording information. On cross-appeal, Colwell argues that the district court erroneously denied its request for attorney's fees. We have jurisdiction under 28 U.S.C. § 1291, and we affirm.

Bibbero designs and markets blank forms known as "superbills" which doctors use to obtain reimbursement from insurance companies. Each superbill contains simple instructions to the patient for filing insurance claims; boxes for patient information; simple clauses assigning insurance benefits to the doctor and authorizing release of patient information; and two lengthy checklists for the doctor to indicate the diagnosis and any services performed, as well as the applicable fee. All entries on the checklists are categories specified by the American Medical Association (AMA) or government publications, as are the code numbers accompanying each entry. The superbills differ according to specialty, to reflect the illnesses and treatments most relevant to the individual doctor.

The forms are personalized to include the doctor's name and address, the nature of the doctor's practice, and the hospitals or clinics at which services may be performed. Doctors may use either the checklists provided on the sample form, or may create their own checklists of the most relevant diagnoses, treatments and procedures. Bibbero encourages doctors to create their own checklists, which most doctors choose to do.

Bibbero includes approximately 25 or 30 sample superbills in its catalog. Bibbero claims a copyright in each of these forms, as well as in the forms designed by its customers. Bibbero has supplied the family practice superbill at issue in this case since 1984. The superbill contains a notice of copyright. In its fall 1987 catalog, Colwell featured a superbill which was nearly identical to Bibbero's superbill, except for slightly different typefaces and shading, as

JOHN R. JOHNNSON, M.D.
Type of Practice or Specialty
1000 MAIN STREET, SUITE 10
SOME PLACE, USA 70000

STATE LIC. # 123456789
SOC. SEC. # 000-11-0000

TELEPHONE: (123) 234-5678

□PRIVATE □BLUE CROSS □BLUE SHIELD □IND. □MEDICAID □MEDICARE □GOV'T.

Family Practice

well as a different sample doctor's name and address. Bibbero saw Colwell's superbill in Colwell's catalog. Bibbero then submitted an application to register its superbill with the Copyright Office, and a certificate of copyright was issued effective October 13, 1987. Upon the issuance of the certificate, Bibbero demanded that Colwell cease infringing upon its copyright in the superbill. Colwell refused to comply with Bibbero's demand, and Bibbero brought suit in district court. Bibbero moved for a preliminary injunction to prevent Colwell from distributing its fall 1987 catalog or future catalogs containing the infringing superbill, and from selling superbills which infringe upon Bibbero's copyright.

After taking the deposition of Bibbero's president, Michael Buckley, Colwell moved for summary judgment on the basis that Bibbero's superbill was not copyrightable because the work was a "blank form" among other reasons.

The district court granted summary judgment to Colwell, denied Bibbero's motion for a preliminary injunction, and dismissed Bibbero's complaint. The district court held that Bibbero's superbill is a blank form which, under the doctrine of *Baker v. Selden,* 101 U.S. 99, 25 L. Ed. 841 (1879), now codified at 37 C.F.R. § 202.1(c) (1982), is not copyrightable.

1. *Is Bibbero's Blank Form "Superbill" Copyrightable?*

Bibbero contends that the district court erroneously granted summary judgment to Colwell because the superbill is not an uncopyrightable blank form, but instead a form which conveys information. Specifically, Bibbero contends that the superbill contains concise descriptions of medical procedures and diagnoses to ensure fair and accurate billing, provisions for assignment of claims and release of information, and instructions for completion.

Bibbero obtained a certificate of registration for its superbill from the Copyright Office. In judicial proceedings, a certificate of copyright registration constitutes prima facie evidence of copyrightability and shifts the burden to the defendant to demonstrate why the copyright is not valid. 17 U.S.C. § 410(c).

It is well-established that blank forms which do not convey information are not copyrightable. *John H. Harland Co. v. Clarke Checks, Inc.,* 711 F.2d 966, 971 (11th Cir. 1983). The blank forms rule, first articulated in *Baker v. Selden,* 101 U.S. 99, is codified at 37 C.F.R. § 202.1(c) (1982):

> The following are examples of works not subject to copyright:
> * * *
>
> (c) Blank forms, such as time cards, graph paper, account books, diaries, bank checks, scorecards, address books, report forms, order forms and the like, which are designed for recording information and do not in themselves convey information.

Although blank forms are generally not copyrightable, there is a well-established exception where text is integrated with blank forms. Where a work consists of text integrated with blank forms, the forms have explanatory force because of the accompanying copyrightable textual material. *See Edwin K. Williams & Co. v. Edwin K. Williams & Co. — East,* 542 F.2d 1053, 1061 (9th Cir. 1976) (combination of instruction book and blank forms constituting an integrated work held to be copyrightable), *cert. denied,* 433 U.S. 908, 97 S. Ct. 2973, 53 L. Ed. 2d 1092 (1977); *Continental Casualty Co. v. Beardsley,* 253 F.2d 702, 704 (2d Cir.) (form with inseparable instructions copyrightable), *cert. denied,* 358 U.S. 816, 79 S. Ct. 25, 3 L. Ed. 2d 58 (1958); *Januz Marketing Communications, Inc. v. Doubleday & Co.,* 569 F. Supp. 76, 79 (S.D.N.Y. 1982) (same).

We agree with the district court that cases interpreting the blank forms rule do not yield a consistent line of reasoning. In support of its contention that the superbill is copyrightable, Bibbero relies on *Norton Printing Co. v. Augustana Hospital,* 155 U.S.P.Q. 133 (N.D.Ill. 1967), in which the court found copyrightable a medical laboratory test form containing a checklist of possible laboratory tests. The court determined that "the format and arrangement used, together with the different boxes and terms, can ... serve to convey information as to the type of tests to be conducted and the information which is deemed important." Bibbero also relies on *Harcourt Brace & World, Inc. v. Graphic Controls Corp.,* 329 F. Supp. 517 (S.D.N.Y. 1971) which held that test answer sheets were copyrightable because the sheets were "designed to guide the student in recording his answer" and thus conveyed information. *Id.* at 524. Bibbero similarly claims that its superbill conveys information.

Norton cannot be distinguished from this case. We agree with Colwell, however, that it should be disapproved. *Norton* indicates a dislike for the blank forms rule, asserting that the rule "has been strongly criticized and would appear to be without foundation." 155 U.S.P.Q. at 134. *Harcourt Brace* is arguably distinguishable because the answer sheets at issue in that case contained unique symbols to guide students in recording their answers and explanations and answers appeared on some of the answer sheets. *Id.* at 524. To the extent that *Harcourt Brace* contravenes the principles established in *Baker,* however, we decline to follow it.

The Copyright Office recently reaffirmed *Baker v. Selden,* decided not to revise the blank forms regulation, and cited *John H. Harland Co. v. Clarke Checks,* 207 U.S.P.Q. 664 (N.D. Ga. 1980) (declining to follow *Harcourt Brace*), *aff'd,* 711 F.2d 966, 972 n.8 (11th Cir. 1983) (agreeing that *Harcourt Brace* should not be followed), as a proper interpretation of the regulation. *See* Notice of Termination of Inquiry Regarding Blank Forms, 45 Fed. Reg. 63297-63300 (September 24, 1980). Despite extensive comments from blank-form suppliers favoring revision of the blank forms rule, the Copyright Office found "no persuasive arguments against the validity of regulation 37 C.F.R. § 202.1(c)." *Id.* at 63299.

We agree with the Eleventh Circuit's "bright-line" approach to the blank forms rule in *Clarke Checks. Norton*'s holding that a medical laboratory test form "conveyed information" because it contained some of the possible categories of information but not others, thus indicating which information was important, is potentially limitless. All forms seek only certain information, and, by their selection, convey that the information sought is important. This cannot be what the Copyright Office intended by the statement "convey information" in 37 C.F.R. § 202.1(c). The purpose of Bibbero's superbill is to record information. Until the superbill is filled out, it conveys no information about the patient, the patient's diagnosis, or the patient's treatment. Doctors do not look to Bibbero's superbill in diagnosing or treating patients. The superbill is simply a blank form which gives doctors a convenient method for recording services performed. The fact that there is a great deal of printing on the face of the form — because there are many possible diagnoses and treatments — does not make the form any less blank.

We also find that the "text with forms" exception to the blank forms rule is inapplicable here. It is true, as Bibbero notes, that the superbill includes some simple instructions to the patient on how to file an insurance claim using the form, such as "complete upper portion of this form."[2] These instructions are far too simple to be copyrightable as text in and of themselves, unlike the instructions in other "text with forms" cases. *See, e.g., Williams,* 542 F.2d at 1060-61 (account books with several pages of instructions on the use of the forms and advice on the successful management of a service station conveyed information and were therefore copyrightable). We therefore affirm the district court's holding that Bibbero's superbill is not copyrightable.[3] ...

Continental Casualty Co. v. Beardsley, 253 F.2d 702 (2d Cir.), *cert. denied,* 358 U.S. 816 (1958). The copyright owner (Beardsley) developed a new kind of insurance, covering lost securities. He published a pamphlet describing the policy and including forms (bond, affidavit of loss, indemnity agreement, instruction letter and board resolutions). A competitor (Continental) copied the forms, but not the description. The court rejected Continental's contention that principles derived from *Baker v. Selden* forbade a copyright in the forms. Unlike the essentially blank forms in *Baker,* Beardsley's forms contained prose that was "explanatory" of his insurance plan. The court also found that nothing in the Constitution barred such copyright.

The difficult question for the Second Circuit was not the *existence* of copyright, but its *scope.* The court recognized that

> in the fields of insurance and commerce the use of specific language in forms and documents may be so essential to accomplish a desired result and so integrated with the use of a legal or commercial conception that the proper standard of infringement is one which will protect as far as possible the copyrighted language and yet allow free use of the thought beneath the language.

The court concluded, in effect, that the copyright on the forms may protect against only the exact rendition of the precise wording employed by the copy-

---

[2]The complete instructions read as follows: 1. Complete upper portion of this form. 2. Sign and date. 3. Mail this form directly to your insurance company. You may attach your own insurance company's form if you wish, although it is not necessary.

[3]Bibbero also contends that its superbill is copyrightable as a compilation. Our holding that the superbill falls within the blank forms rule precludes it from being copyrightable as a compilation. A "compilation" is a work formed by the collection and assembling of preexisting materials or data that are selected, coordinated or arranged in such a way that the work as a whole constitutes an original work of authorship, and may consist entirely of uncopyrightable elements. 17 U.S.C. § 101; *Harper House, Inc. v. Thomas Nelson, Inc.,* 889 F.2d 197, 204 (9th Cir. 1989). For example, a collection of common property and blank forms, although not individually copyrightable, may be selected, coordinated or arranged in such a way that they are copyrightable as a compilation. *Harper House,* 204-07. Here, however, the superbill consists in its entirety of one uncopyrightable blank form and hence cannot be copyrightable as a compilation.

right owner. (This is commonly referred to as a "thin" copyright.) It acknowledged that its ruling "comes near to invalidating the copyright," but concluded that this was necessary in order to make available the "practical use of the art." To require a second-comer in such cases to generate different words and phrases which mean the same thing "borders on the preposterous."

The court found the evidence to support the conclusion that the language of Beardsley's forms was being used by Continental "only as incidental to its use of the underlying idea," and thus that the valid copyright was not infringed.

QUESTIONS

1. Note that the court begins its opinion by stating that it is required to interpret Copyright Office Regulation 202.1(c), which announces the so-called blank form rule. *Is* the court so required? Isn't it rather obliged to interpret § 102(a) of the Copyright Act, or *Baker v. Selden* and its statutory counterpart in § 102(b)? Recall that the regulations of the Copyright Office are simply the Register's best effort to interpret the statute, and that their consistency with the Act (see § 702) is definitively to be determined by the federal courts. (Is it not odd that the court, in attempting to apply the blank form rule as fashioned by the Copyright Office, did not make very much of the fact that the Office had accepted the *Bibbero* form for registration?!)

2. Is, indeed, the blank form rule a proper reading of § 102(a), and of *Baker v. Selden? See Januz Mktg. Commun., Inc. v. Doubleday & Co.,* 569 F. Supp. 76 (S.D.N.Y. 1982). Why should it be necessary, to secure copyright, that the words or graphic images on a form be designed to communicate information rather than to record it? And, even assuming the form is "blank" rather than explanatory, does the court in *Bibbero* properly dispose of the plaintiff's "compilation" claim?

3. Are the findings of copyrightability in *Sebastian* (see p. 89 *supra*) and noncopyrightability in *Morrissey* compatible? Are the findings of copyrightability in *Continental v. Beardsley* and noncopyrightability in *Bibbero* compatible? Are there sufficiently marked differences on such issues as original authorship, minimal creativity, tangible expression, and separability of form and function?

4. The *Beardsley* case involved business and legal forms. Because such forms must frequently be drafted to conform to the "terms of art" that have been held by courts to be essentially necessary to implement certain legal transactions, the opportunities for fanciful variation in authoring such forms are quite limited. Using the analysis of the court in *Morrissey,* would that not likely compel the conclusion that such business and legal forms are ineligible for copyright? (Indeed, should not legal forms be far less susceptible to copyright protection than contest rules?) *See Donald v. Zack Meyer's T.V. Sales & Serv.,* 426 F.2d 1027 (5th Cir. 1970), *cert. denied,* 400 U.S. 992 (1971); *Financial Control Assocs. v. Equity Bldrs. Inc.,* 799 F. Supp. 1103 (D. Kan. 1992).

5. Is there any practical difference between allowing copying because (as in *Morrissey*) the forms are not copyrightable and allowing copying because (as in *Beardsley*) the copyrightable forms were not infringed? For example, if a legal publisher prints a compendium of forms for various business transactions, does copyright on the formbook protect only the compilation (i.e., the selection and arrangement) or does it also protect the text of individual forms? Would it infringe to make an unauthorized copy of: (a) the entire formbook? (b) individual forms for purposes of servicing clients? (c) individual forms in order to sell them to attorneys for a profit?

C. FACTS AND COMPILATIONS

§ 101. Definitions

A "compilation" is a work formed by the collection and assembling of preexisting materials or of data that are selected, coordinated, or arranged in such a way that the resulting work as a whole constitutes an original work of authorship. The term "compilation" includes collective works.

§ 103. Subject matter of copyright: Compilations and derivative works

(a) The subject matter of copyright as specified by section 102 includes compilations and derivative works, but protection for a work employing preexisting material in which copyright subsists does not extend to any part of the work in which such material has been used unlawfully.

(b) The copyright in a compilation or derivative work extends only to the material contributed by the author of such work, as distinguished from the preexisting material employed in the work, and does not imply any exclusive right in the preexisting material. The copyright in such work is independent of, and does not affect or enlarge the scope, duration, ownership, or subsistence of, any copyright protection in the preexisting material.

HOUSE REPORT

H.R. Rep. No. 94-1476, 94th Cong., 2d Sess. 57-58 (1976)

Between them the terms "compilations" and "derivative works" which are defined in section 101, comprehend every copyrightable work that employs preexisting material or data of any kind. There is necessarily some overlapping between the two, but they basically represent different concepts. A "compilation" results from a process of selecting, bringing together, organizing, and arranging previously existing material of all kinds, regardless of whether the individual items in the material have been or ever could have been subject to copyright. A "derivative work," on the other hand, requires a process of recasting, transforming, or adapting "one or more preexisting works"; the "preexisting work" must come within the general subject matter of copyright set forth in section 102, regardless of whether it is or was ever copyrighted....

... [T]he criteria of copyrightable subject matter stated in section 102 apply with full force to works that are entirely original and to those containing preexisting material.... The most important point [made in § 103(b)] is one that is commonly misunderstood today: copyright in a "new version" covers only the material added by the later author, and has no effect one way or the other on the copyright or public domain status of the preexisting material....

FEIST PUBLICATIONS, INC. v. RURAL TELEPHONE SERVICE

499 U.S. 340, 111 S. Ct. 1282, 113 L. Ed. 2d 358 (1991)

JUSTICE O'CONNOR delivered the opinion of the Court.

This case requires us to clarify the extent of copyright protection available to telephone directory white pages.

I

Rural Telephone Service Company is a certified public utility that provides telephone service to several communities in northwest Kansas. It is subject to a state regulation that requires all telephone companies operating in Kansas to issue annually an updated telephone directory. Accordingly, as a condition of its monopoly franchise, Rural publishes a typical telephone directory, consisting of white pages and yellow pages. The white pages list in alphabetical order the names of Rural's subscribers, together with their towns and telephone numbers. The yellow pages list Rural's business subscribers alphabetically by category and feature classified advertisements of various sizes. Rural distributes its directory free of charge to its subscribers, but earns revenue by selling yellow pages advertisements.

Feist Publications, Inc., is a publishing company that specializes in area-wide telephone directories. Unlike a typical directory, which covers only a particular calling area, Feist's area-wide directories cover a much larger geographical range, reducing the need to call directory assistance or consult multiple directories. The Feist directory that is the subject of this litigation covers 11 different telephone service areas in 15 counties and contains 46,878 white pages listings — compared to Rural's approximately 7,700 listings. Like Rural's directory, Feist's is distributed free of charge and includes both white pages and yellow pages. Feist and Rural compete vigorously for yellow pages advertising.

As the sole provider of telephone service in its service area, Rural obtains subscriber information quite easily. Persons desiring telephone service must apply to Rural and provide their names and addresses; Rural then assigns them a telephone number. Feist is not a telephone company, let alone one with monopoly status, and therefore lacks independent access to any subscriber information. To obtain white pages listings for its area-wide directory, Feist approached each of the 11 telephone companies operating in northwest Kansas and offered to pay for the right to use its white pages listings.

Of the 11 telephone companies, only Rural refused to license its listings to Feist. Rural's refusal created a problem for Feist, as omitting these listings would have left a gaping hole in its area-wide directory, rendering it less attractive to potential yellow pages advertisers. In a decision subsequent to that which we review here, the District Court determined that this was precisely the reason Rural refused to license its listings. The refusal was motivated by an unlawful purpose "to extend its monopoly in telephone service to a monopoly in yellow pages advertising." *Rural Telephone Service Co. v. Feist Publications, Inc.*, 737 F. Supp. 610, 622 (Kan. 1990).

Unable to license Rural's white pages listings, Feist used them without Rural's consent. Feist began by removing several thousand listings that fell outside the geographic range of its area-wide directory, then hired personnel to investigate the 4,935 that remained. These employees verified the data reported by Rural and sought to obtain additional information. As a result, a typical Feist listing includes the individual's street address; most of Rural's listings do not. Notwithstanding these additions, however, 1,309 of the 46,878 listings in Feist's 1983 directory were identical to listings in Rural's 1982-1983 white pages. App. 54 (para. 15-16), 57. Four of these were fictitious listings that Rural had inserted into its directory to detect copying.

Rural sued for copyright infringement in the District Court for the District of Kansas taking the position that Feist, in compiling its own directory, could not use the information contained in Rural's white pages. Rural asserted that Feist's employees were obliged to travel door-to-door or conduct a telephone survey to discover the same information for themselves. Feist responded that such efforts were economically impractical and, in any event, unnecessary because the information copied was beyond the scope of copyright protection. The District Court granted summary judgment to Rural, explaining that "courts have consistently held that telephone directories are copyrightable" and citing a string of lower court decisions. 663 F. Supp. 214, 218 (1987). In an unpublished opinion, the Court of Appeals for the Tenth Circuit affirmed "for substantially the reasons given by the district court." App. to Pet. for Cert. 4a, judgt. order reported at 916 F.2d 718 (1990). We granted certiorari, 498 U.S. __ (1990), to determine whether the copyright in Rural's directory protects the names, towns, and telephone numbers copied by Feist.

II

A

This case concerns the interaction of two well-established propositions. The first is that facts are not copyrightable; the other, that compilations of facts generally are. Each of these propositions possesses an impeccable pedigree. That there can be no valid copyright in facts is universally understood. The most fundamental axiom of copyright law is that "no author may copyright his ideas or the facts he narrates." *Harper & Row, Publishers, Inc. v. Nation Enterprises,* 471 U.S. 539, 556 (1985). Rural wisely concedes this point, noting in its brief that "facts and discoveries, of course, are not themselves subject to copyright protection." Brief for Respondent 24. At the same time, however, it is beyond dispute that compilations of facts are within the subject matter of copyright. Compilations were expressly mentioned in the Copyright Act of 1909, and again in the Copyright Act of 1976.

There is an undeniable tension between these two propositions. Many compilations consist of nothing but raw data — i.e., wholly factual information not accompanied by any original written expression. On what basis may one claim a copyright in such a work? Common sense tells us that 100 uncopyrightable facts do not magically change their status when gathered together in one place. Yet copyright law seems to contemplate that compilations that consist exclusively of facts are potentially within its scope.

The key to resolving the tension lies in understanding why facts are not copyrightable. The *sine qua non* of copyright is originality. To qualify for copyright protection, a work must be original to the author. *See Harper & Row, supra,* at 547-549. Original, as the term is used in copyright, means only that the work was independently created by the author (as opposed to copied from other works), and that it possesses at least some minimal degree of creativity. 1 M. Nimmer & D. Nimmer, Copyright §§ 2.01[A], [B] (1990) (hereinafter Nimmer). To be sure, the requisite level of creativity is extremely low; even a slight amount will suffice. The vast majority of works make the grade quite easily, as they possess some creative spark, "no matter how crude, humble or obvious" it might be. *Id.,* § 1.08[C][1]. Originality does not signify novelty; a work may be original even though it closely resembles other works so long as the similarity is fortuitous, not the result of copying. To illustrate, assume that two poets, each ignorant of the other, compose identical poems. Neither work is novel, yet both are original and, hence, copyrightable. *See Sheldon v. Metro-Goldwyn Pictures Corp.,* 81 F.2d 49, 54 (CA2 1936).

Originality is a constitutional requirement. The source of Congress' power to enact copyright laws is Article I, § 8, cl. 8, of the Constitution, which authorizes Congress to "secure for limited Times to Authors ... the exclusive Right to their respective Writings." In two decisions from the late 19th Century — *The Trade-Mark Cases,* 100 U.S. 82 (1879); and *Burrow-Giles Lithographic Co. v. Sarony,* 111 U.S. 53 (1884) — this Court defined the crucial terms "authors" and "writings." In so doing, the Court made it unmistakably clear that these terms presuppose a degree of originality.... Leading scholars agree on this point. As one pair of commentators succinctly puts it: "The originality requirement is *constitutionally mandated* for all works." Patterson & Joyce, *Monopolizing the Law: The Scope of Copyright Protection for Law Reports and Statutory Compilations,* 36 UCLA L. Rev. 719, 763, n. 155 (1989) (emphasis in original) (hereinafter Patterson & Joyce). *Accord id.,* at 759-760, and n. 140; Nimmer § 1.06[A] ("originality is a statutory as well as a constitutional requirement"); *id.,* § 1.08[C][1] ("a modicum of intellectual labor ... clearly constitutes an essential constitutional element").

It is this bedrock principle of copyright that mandates the law's seemingly disparate treatment of facts and factual compilations. "No one may claim originality as to facts." *Id.,* § 2.11[A], p. 2-157. This is because facts do not owe their origin to an act of authorship. The distinction is one between creation and discovery: the first person to find and report a particular fact has not created the fact; he or she has merely discovered its existence. To borrow from *Burrow-Giles,* one who discovers a fact is not its "maker" or "originator." 111 U.S., at 58. "The discoverer merely finds and records." Nimmer § 2.03[E]. Census-takers, for example, do not "create" the population figures that emerge from their efforts; in a sense, they copy these figures from the world around them. Denicola, *Copyright in Collections of Facts: A Theory for the Protection of Nonfiction Literary Works,* 81 Colum. L. Rev. 516, 525 (1981) (hereinafter Denicola). Census data therefore do not trigger copyright because these data are not "original" in the constitutional sense. Nimmer § 2.03[E]. The same is true of all facts — scientific, historical, biographical, and news of the day. "They may not be copyrighted and are part of the public domain available to every person." Miller, *supra,* at 1369.

Factual compilations, on the other hand, may possess the requisite original-ity. The compilation author typically chooses which facts to include, in what order to place them, and how to arrange the collected data so that they may be used effectively by readers. These choices as to selection and arrangement, so long as they are made independently by the compiler and entail a minimal degree of creativity, are sufficiently original that Congress may protect such compilations through the copyright laws. Nimmer §§ 2.11[D], 3.03; Denicola 523, n. 38. Thus, even a directory that contains absolutely no protectible written expression, only facts, meets the constitutional minimum for copy-right protection if it features an original selection or arrangement. *See Harper & Row,* 471 U.S., at 547. *Accord* Nimmer § 3.03.

This protection is subject to an important limitation. The mere fact that a work is copyrighted does not mean that every element of the work may be protected. Originality remains the *sine qua non* of copyright; accordingly, copyright protection may extend only to those components of a work that are original to the author. Patterson & Joyce 800-802; Ginsburg, *Creation and Commercial Value: Copyright Protection of Works of Information,* 90 Colum. L. Rev. 1865, 1868, and n.12 (1990) (hereinafter Ginsburg). Thus, if the compila-tion author clothes facts with an original collocation of words, he or she may be able to claim a copyright in this written expression. Others may copy the underlying facts from the publication, but not the precise words used to present them. In *Harper & Row,* for example, we explained that President Ford could not prevent others from copying bare historical facts from his autobiography, see 471 U.S., at 556-557, but that he could prevent others from copying his "subjective descriptions and portraits of public figures." *Id.,* at 563. Where the compilation author adds no written expression but rather lets the facts speak for themselves, the expressive element is more elusive. The only conceivable expression is the manner in which the compiler has selected and arranged the facts. Thus, if the selection and arrangement are original, these elements of the work are eligible for copyright protection. *See* Patry, *Copyright in Compilations of Facts (or Why the "White Pages" Are Not Copyrightable),* 12 Com. & Law 37, 64 (Dec. 1990) (hereinafter Patry). No matter how original the format, however, the facts themselves do not become original through association. *See* Patterson & Joyce 776.

This inevitably means that the copyright in a factual compilation is thin. Notwithstanding a valid copyright, a subsequent compiler remains free to use the facts contained in another's publication to aid in preparing a competing work, so long as the competing work does not feature the same selection and arrangement. As one commentator explains it: "No matter how much original authorship the work displays, the facts and ideas it exposes are free for the taking .... The very same facts and ideas may be divorced from the context imposed by the author, and restated or reshuffled by second comers, even if the author was the first to discover the facts or to propose the ideas." Ginsburg 1868.

It may seem unfair that much of the fruit of the compiler's labor may be used by others without compensation. As Justice Brennan has correctly ob-served, however, this is not "some unforeseen byproduct of a statutory scheme." *Harper & Row,* 471 U.S., at 589 (dissenting opinion). It is, rather, "the essence of copyright," *ibid.*, and a constitutional requirement. The primary objective of copyright is not to reward the labor of authors, but "to promote the Progress of Science and useful Arts." Art. I, § 8, cl. 8. *Accord Twentieth Century Music Corp. v. Aiken,* 422 U.S. 151, 156 (1975). To this end, copyright assures authors the right to their original expression, but encourages others to build freely upon the ideas and information conveyed by a work. *Harper & Row, supra,* at 556-557. This principle, known as the idea/expression or fact/expression dichotomy, applies to all works of authorship. As applied to a factual compilation, assuming the absence of original written expression, only the compiler's selection and arrangement may be protected; the raw facts may be copied at will. This result is neither unfair nor unfortunate. It is the means by which copyright advances the progress of science and art....

This, then, resolves the doctrinal tension: Copyright treats facts and factual compilations in a wholly consistent manner. Facts, whether alone or as part of a compilation, are not original and therefore may not be copyrighted. A factual compilation is eligible for copyright if it features an original selection or arrangement of facts, but the copyright is limited to the particular selection or arrangement. In no event may copyright extend to the facts themselves.

B

As we have explained, originality is a constitutionally mandated prerequisite for copyright protection. The Court's decisions announcing this rule predate the Copyright Act of 1909, but ambiguous language in the 1909 Act caused some lower courts temporarily to lose sight of this requirement.

The 1909 Act embodied the originality requirement, but not as clearly as it might have. *See* Nimmer § 2.01. The subject matter of copyright was set out in § 3 and § 4 of the Act. Section 4 stated that copyright was available to "all the writings of an author." 35 Stat. 1076. By using the words "writings" and "author" — the same words used in Article I, § 8 of the Constitution and defined by the Court in *The Trade-Mark Cases* and *Burrow-Giles* — the statute necessarily incorporated the originality requirement articulated in the Court's decisions. It did so implicitly, however, thereby leaving room for error.

Section 3 was similarly ambiguous. It stated that the copyright in a work protected only "the copyrightable component parts of the work." It thus stated an important copyright principle, but failed to identify the specific characteristic — originality — that determined which component parts of a work were copyrightable and which were not.

Most courts construed the 1909 Act correctly, notwithstanding the less-than-perfect statutory language. They understood from this Court's decisions that there could be no copyright without originality....

But some courts misunderstood the statute. *See, e.g., Leon v. Pacific Telephone & Telegraph Co.,* 91 F.2d 484 (CA9 1937); *Jeweler's Circular Publishing Co. v. Keystone Publishing Co.,* 281 F. 83 (CA2 1922). These courts ignored § 3 and § 4, focusing their attention instead on § 5 of the Act. Section 5, however, was purely technical in nature: it provided that a person seeking to register a work should indicate on the application the type of work, and it listed 14 categories under which the work might fall. One of these categories was "books, including composite and cyclopedic works, directories, gazetteers, and other compilations." § 5(a). Section 5 did not purport to say that all compilations were automatically copyrightable. Indeed, it expressly disclaimed any such function, pointing out that "the subject-matter of copyright is defined in section four." Nevertheless, the fact that factual compilations were mentioned specifically in § 5 led some courts to infer erroneously that directories and the like were copyrightable *per se*, "without any further or precise showing of original — personal — authorship." Ginsburg 1895.

Making matters worse, these courts developed a new theory to justify the protection of factual compilations. Known alternatively as "sweat of the brow" or "industrious collection," the underlying notion was that copyright was a reward for the hard work that went into compiling facts. The classic formulation of the doctrine appeared in *Jeweler's Circular Publishing Co.*, 281 F., at 88:

> "The right to copyright a book upon which one has expended labor in its preparation does not depend upon whether the materials which he has collected consist or not of matters which are *publici juris,* or whether such materials show literary skill *or originality,* either in thought or in language, or anything more than industrious collection. The man who goes through the streets of a town and puts down the names of each of the inhabitants, with their occupations and their street number, acquires material of which he is the author" (emphasis added).

The "sweat of the brow" doctrine had numerous flaws, the most glaring being that it extended copyright protection in a compilation beyond selection and arrangement — the compiler's original contributions — to the facts themselves. Under the doctrine, the only defense to infringement was independent creation. A subsequent compiler was "not entitled to take one word of information previously published," but rather had to "independently work out the matter for himself, so as to arrive at the same result from the same common sources of information." *Id.,* at 88-89 (internal quotations omitted). "Sweat of the brow" courts thereby eschewed the most fundamental axiom of copyright law — that no one may copyright facts or ideas....

Decisions of this Court applying the 1909 Act make clear that the statute did not permit the "sweat of the brow" approach. The best example is *International News Service v. Associated Press,* 248 U.S. 215 (1918). In that decision, the Court stated unambiguously that the 1909 Act conferred copyright protection only on those elements of a work that were original to the author. Associated Press had conceded taking news reported by International News Service and publishing it in its own newspapers. Recognizing that § 5 of the Act specifically mentioned "periodicals, including newspapers," § 5(b), the Court acknowledged that news articles were copyrightable. *Id.,* at 234. It flatly rejected, however, the notion that the copyright in an article extended to the factual information it contained: "The news element — the information respecting current events contained in the literary production — is not the creation of the writer, but is a report of matters that ordinarily are *publici juris;* it is the history of the day." *Ibid.*[*]

Without a doubt, the "sweat of the brow" doctrine flouted basic copyright principles. Throughout history, copyright law has "recognized a greater need to disseminate factual works than works of fiction or fantasy." *Harper & Row,* 471 U.S., at 563. *Accord* Gorman, *Fact or Fancy: The Implications for Copyright,* 29 J. Copyright Soc. 560, 563 (1982). But "sweat of the brow" courts took a contrary view; they handed out proprietary interests in facts and declared that authors are absolutely precluded from saving time and effort by relying upon the facts contained in prior works. In truth, "it is just such wasted effort that the proscription against the copyright of ideas and facts ... [is] designed to prevent." *Rosemont Enterprises, Inc. v. Random House, Inc.,* 366 F.2d 303, 310 (CA2 1966), *cert. denied,* 385 U.S. 1009 (1967). "Protection for the fruits of such research ... may in certain circumstances be available under a theory of unfair competition. But to accord copyright protection on this basis alone distorts basic copyright principles in that it creates a monopoly in public domain materials without the necessary justification of protecting and encouraging the creation of 'writings' by 'authors.'" Nimmer § 3.04, p. 3-23 (footnote omitted).

C

... In enacting the Copyright Act of 1976, Congress dropped the reference to "all the writings of an author" and replaced it with the phrase "original works of authorship." 17 U.S.C. § 102(a). In making explicit the originality requirement, Congress announced that it was merely clarifying existing law: "The two fundamental criteria of copyright protection [are] originality and fixation in tangible form .... The phrase 'original works of authorship,' which is purposely left undefined, is intended to incorporate without change *the standard of originality established by the courts under the present [1909] copyright statute.*" H.R. Rep. No. 94-1476, p. 51 (1976) (emphasis added) (hereinafter H.R. Rep.); S. Rep. No. 94-473, p. 50 (1975) (emphasis added) (hereinafter S. Rep.). This sentiment was echoed by the Copyright Office: "Our intention here is to maintain the *established standards* of originality ...." Supplementary Report of the Register of Copyrights on the General Revision of U.S. Copyright Law, 89th Cong., 1st Sess., Part 6, p. 3 (H. Judiciary Comm. Print 1965) (emphasis added).

To ensure that the mistakes of the "sweat of the brow" courts would not be repeated, Congress took additional measures. For example, § 3 of the 1909 Act had stated that copyright protected only the "copyrightable component parts" of a work, but had not identified originality as the basis for distinguishing those component parts that were copyrightable from those that were not. The 1976 Act deleted this section and replaced it with § 102(b), which identifies specifically those elements of a work for which copyright is not available: "In no case does copyright protection for an original work of authorship extend to any idea, procedure, process, system, method of operation, concept, principle,

---

[*]The Court ultimately rendered judgment for International News Service on noncopyright grounds that are not relevant here. *See* 248 U.S., at 235, 241-242.

or discovery, regardless of the form in which it is described, explained, illustrated, or embodied in such work." § 102(b) is universally understood to prohibit any copyright in facts. *Harper & Row, supra,* at 547, 556. *Accord* Nimmer § 2.03[E] (equating facts with "discoveries"). As with § 102(a), Congress emphasized that § 102(b) did not change the law, but merely clarified it: "Section 102(b) in no way enlarges or contracts the scope of copyright protection under the present law. Its purpose is to restate ... that the basic dichotomy between expression and idea remains unchanged." H.R. Rep., at 57; S. Rep., at 54.

Congress took another step to minimize confusion by deleting the specific mention of "directories ... and other compilations" in § 5 of the 1909 Act. As mentioned, this section had led some courts to conclude that directories were copyrightable *per se* and that every element of a directory was protected. In its place, Congress enacted two new provisions. First, to make clear that compilations were not copyrightable per se, Congress provided a definition of the term "compilation." Second, to make clear that the copyright in a compilation did not extend to the facts themselves, Congress enacted 17 U.S.C. § 103.

The definition of "compilation" is found in § 101 of the 1976 Act. It defines a "compilation" in the copyright sense as "a work formed by the collection and assembly of preexisting materials or of data *that* are selected, coordinated, or arranged *in such a way that* the resulting work as a whole constitutes an original work of authorship" (emphasis added).

The purpose of the statutory definition is to emphasize that collections of facts are not copyrightable *per se*. It conveys this message through its tripartite structure, as emphasized above by the italics. The statute identifies three distinct elements and requires each to be met for a work to qualify as a copyrightable compilation: (1) the collection and assembly of pre-existing material, facts, or data; (2) the selection, coordination, or arrangement of those materials; and (3) the creation, by virtue of the particular selection, coordination, or arrangement, of an "original" work of authorship. "This tripartite conjunctive structure is self-evident, and should be assumed to 'accurately express the legislative purpose.'" Patry 51, quoting *Mills Music,* 469 U.S., at 164.

At first glance, the first requirement does not seem to tell us much. It merely describes what one normally thinks of as a compilation — a collection of pre-existing material, facts, or data. What makes it significant is that it is not the *sole* requirement. It is not enough for copyright purposes that an author collects and assembles facts. To satisfy the statutory definition, the work must get over two additional hurdles. In this way, the plain language indicates that not every collection of facts receives copyright protection. Otherwise, there would be a period after "data."

The third requirement is also illuminating. It emphasizes that a compilation, like any other work, is copyrightable only if it satisfies the originality requirement ("an *original* work of authorship"). Although § 102 states plainly that the originality requirement applies to all works, the point was emphasized with regard to compilations to ensure that courts would not repeat the mistake of the "sweat of the brow" courts by concluding that fact-based works are treated differently and measured by some other standard. As Congress explained it, the goal was to "make plain that the criteria of copyrightable subject matter stated in section 102 apply with full force to works ... containing preexisting material." H.R. Rep., at 57; S. Rep., at 55.

The key to the statutory definition is the second requirement. It instructs courts that, in determining whether a fact-based work is an original work of authorship, they should focus on the manner in which the collected facts have been selected, coordinated, and arranged. This is a straightforward application of the originality requirement. Facts are never original, so the compilation author can claim originality, if at all, only in the way the facts are presented. To that end, the statute dictates that the principal focus should be on whether the selection, coordination, and arrangement are sufficiently original to merit protection.

Not every selection, coordination, or arrangement will pass muster. This is plain from the statute. It states that, to merit protection, the facts must be selected, coordinated, or arranged "in such a way" as to render the work as a whole original. This implies that some "ways" will trigger copyright, but that others will not. See Patry 57, and n. 76. Otherwise, the phrase "in such a way" is meaningless and Congress should have defined "compilation" simply as "a work formed by the collection and assembly of preexisting materials or data that are selected, coordinated, or arranged." That Congress did not do so is dispositive. In accordance with "the established principle that a court should give effect, if possible, to every clause and word of a statute," *Moskal v. United States*, 498 U.S. __, __ (1990) (slip op., at 5) (internal quotations omitted), we conclude that the statute envisions that there will be some fact-based works in which the selection, coordination, and arrangement are not sufficiently original to trigger copyright protection.

As discussed earlier, however, the originality requirement is not particularly stringent. A compiler may settle upon a selection or arrangement that others have used; novelty is not required. Originality requires only that the author make the selection or arrangement independently (i.e., without copying that selection or arrangement from another work), and that it display some minimal level of creativity. Presumably, the vast majority of compilations will pass this test, but not all will. There remains a narrow category of works in which the creative spark is utterly lacking or so trivial as to be virtually nonexistent. *See generally Bleistein v. Donaldson Lithographing Co.*, 188 U.S. 239, 251 (1903) (referring to "the narrowest and most obvious limits"). Such works are incapable of sustaining a valid copyright. Nimmer § 2.01[B].

Even if a work qualifies as a copyrightable compilation, it receives only limited protection. This is the point of § 103 of the Act. Section 103 explains that "the subject matter of copyright ... includes compilations," § 103(a), but that copyright protects only the author's original contributions — not the facts or information conveyed:

> "The copyright in a compilation ... extends only to the material contributed by the author of such work, as distinguished from the preexisting material employed in the work, and does not imply any exclusive right in the preexisting material." § 103(b).

As § 103 makes clear, copyright is not a tool by which a compilation author may keep others from using the facts or data he or she has collected. "The most important point here is one that is commonly misunderstood today: copyright ... has no effect one way or the other on the copyright or public domain status of the preexisting material." H.R. Rep., at 57; S. Rep., at 55. The 1909 Act did not require, as "sweat of the brow" courts mistakenly assumed, that each subsequent compiler must start from scratch and is precluded from relying on research undertaken by another. *See, e.g., Jeweler's Circular Publishing Co.,* 281 F., at 88-89. Rather, the facts contained in existing works may be freely copied because copyright protects only the elements that owe their origin to the compiler — the selection, coordination, and arrangement of facts.

In summary, the 1976 revisions to the Copyright Act leave no doubt that originality, not "sweat of the brow," is the touchstone of copyright protection in directories and other fact-based works. Nor is there any doubt that the same was true under the 1909 Act. The 1976 revisions were a direct response to the Copyright Office's concern that many lower courts had misconstrued this basic principle, and Congress emphasized repeatedly that the purpose of the revisions was to clarify, not change, existing law. The revisions explain with painstaking clarity that copyright requires originality, § 102(a); that facts are never original, § 102(b); that the copyright in a compilation does not extend to the facts it contains, § 103(b); and that a compilation is copyrightable only to the extent that it features an original selection, coordination, or arrangement, § 101.

The 1976 revisions have proven largely successful in steering courts in the right direction....

                                        III

There is no doubt that Feist took from the white pages of Rural's directory a substantial amount of factual information. At a minimum, Feist copied the names, towns, and telephone numbers of 1,309 of Rural's subscribers. Not all copying, however, is copyright infringement. To establish infringement, two elements must be proven: (1) ownership of a valid copyright, and (2) copying of constituent elements of the work that are original. *See Harper & Row,* 471 U.S., at 548. The first element is not at issue here; Feist appears to concede that Rural's directory, considered as a whole, is subject to a valid copyright because it contains some foreword text, as well as original material in its yellow pages advertisements. *See* Brief for Petitioner 18; Pet. for Cert. 9.

The question is whether Rural has proved the second element. In other words, did Feist, by taking 1,309 names, towns, and telephone numbers from Rural's white pages, copy anything that was "original" to Rural? Certainly, the raw data does not satisfy the originality requirement. Rural may have been the first to discover and report the names, towns, and telephone numbers of its subscribers, but this data does not "'owe its origin'" to Rural. *Burrow-Giles,* 111 U.S., at 58. Rather, these bits of information are uncopyrightable facts; they existed before Rural reported them and would have continued to exist if Rural had never published a telephone directory. The originality requirement "rules out protecting ... names, addresses, and telephone numbers of which the plaintiff by no stretch of the imagination could be called the author." Patterson & Joyce 776.

Rural essentially concedes the point by referring to the names, towns, and telephone numbers as "preexisting material." Brief for Respondent 17. Section 103(b) states explicitly that the copyright in a compilation does not extend to "the preexisting material employed in the work."

The question that remains is whether Rural selected, coordinated, or arranged these uncopyrightable facts in an original way. As mentioned, originality is not a stringent standard; it does not require that facts be presented in an innovative or surprising way. It is equally true, however, that the selection and arrangement of facts cannot be so mechanical or routine as to require no creativity whatsoever. The standard of originality is low, but it does exist....

The selection, coordination, and arrangement of Rural's white pages do not satisfy the minimum constitutional standards for copyright protection. As mentioned at the outset, Rural's white pages are entirely typical. Persons desiring telephone service in Rural's service area fill out an application and Rural issues them a telephone number. In preparing its white pages, Rural simply takes the data provided by its subscribers and lists it alphabetically by surname. The end product is a garden-variety white pages directory, devoid of even the slightest trace of creativity.

Rural's selection of listings could not be more obvious: it publishes the most basic information — name, town, and telephone number — about each person who applies to it for telephone service. This is "selection" of a sort, but it lacks the modicum of creativity necessary to transform mere selection into copyrightable expression. Rural expended sufficient effort to make the white pages directory useful, but insufficient creativity to make it original.

We note in passing that the selection featured in Rural's white pages may also fail the originality requirement for another reason. Feist points out that Rural did not truly "select" to publish the names and telephone numbers of its subscribers; rather, it was required to do so by the Kansas Corporation Commission as part of its monopoly franchise. See 737 F. Supp., at 612. Accordingly, one could plausibly conclude that this selection was dictated by state law, not by Rural.

Nor can Rural claim originality in its coordination and arrangement of facts. The white pages do nothing more than list Rural's subscribers in alphabetical order. This arrangement may, technically speaking, owe its origin to Rural; no one disputes that Rural undertook the task of alphabetizing the names itself. But there is nothing remotely creative about arranging names alphabetically in a white pages directory. It is an age-old practice, firmly rooted in tradition and so commonplace that it has come to be expected as a matter of course. See Brief for Information Industry Association et al. as Amici Curiae 10 (alphabetical arrangement "is universally observed in directories published by local exchange telephone companies"). It is not only unoriginal, it is practically inevitable. This time-honored tradition does not possess the minimal creative spark required by the Copyright Act and the Constitution.

We conclude that the names, towns, and telephone numbers copied by Feist were not original to Rural and therefore were not protected by the copyright in Rural's combined white and yellow pages directory. As a constitutional matter, copyright protects only those constituent elements of a work that possess more than a *de minimis* quantum of creativity. Rural's white pages, limited to basic subscriber information and arranged alphabetically, fall short of the mark. As a statutory matter, 17 U.S.C. § 101 does not afford protection from copying to a collection of facts that are selected, coordinated, and arranged in a way that utterly lacks originality. Given that some works must fail, we cannot imagine a more likely candidate. Indeed, were we to hold that Rural's white pages pass muster, it is hard to believe that any collection of facts could fail.

Because Rural's white pages lack the requisite originality, Feist's use of the listings cannot constitute infringement. This decision should not be construed as demeaning Rural's efforts in compiling its directory, but rather as making clear that copyright rewards originality, not effort. As this Court noted more than a century ago, "'great praise may be due to the plaintiffs for their industry and enterprise in publishing this paper, yet the law does not contemplate their being rewarded in this way.'" *Baker v. Selden,* 101 U.S., at 105.

The judgment of the Court of Appeals is

Reversed.

Justice Blackmun concurs in the judgment.

QUESTIONS

1. If the *Feist* Court has now told us what is not original in a compilation of information, it has failed to tell us what is. How far beyond the "obvious" and "commonplace" must a compilation's selection and arrangement stretch to be "original"? If, for example, a telephone directory publisher includes unusual information — such as marital status, religion, and educational level — do the listings thereby become copyrightable? If, by contrast, a compiler seeking to make the work as comprehensive as possible eschews "selection," is the compilation then by definition not original? (Does this accord with the "incentive" rationale for copyright?)

2. Consider the directory of name, address, marital status, religion, etc., envisioned in Question 1. Even if the unusual category-selections manifested in the directory were to render it copyrightable as a whole, the component facts remain unoriginal. Under the terms of the Supreme Court's decision, the copyright would not forbid a second-comer from extracting the "obvious" information concerning names and telephone numbers. But would the copyright protect the unobvious information (either separately or in conjunction)? Or, because the unusual facts (and their conjunction) are still "facts," does it not follow that they too may be copied?

3. In light of the decision in *Feist* and its rationale, could a state prohibit copying a white-page directory? Could Congress do so through the enactment of some federal law other than the Copyright Act?

The *Feist* court made clear that the expenditure of "sweat" alone no longer justifies copyright protection of the fruits of labor; there must be a "modicum of creativity." But even if "sweat" is no longer a *sufficient* condition, is it nonetheless a *necessary* condition — i.e., together with minimal creativity must the author also have demonstrated minimal effort or enterprise? Consider the following:

Rockford Map Publishers, Inc. v. Directory Service Co., 768 F.2d 145 (7th Cir. 1985), *cert. denied,* 474 U.S. 1061. Defendant challenged copyright protection for plaintiff's map, which was drawn principally from numerical information in public land-title record books; the defense was that plaintiff expended little time and effort in compiling the map that defendant copied. Judge Easterbrook rejected defendant's theory:

> The copyright laws protect the work, not the amount of effort expended. A person who produces a short new work or makes a small improvement in a few hours gets a copyright for that contribution fully as effective as that on a novel written as a life's work. Perhaps the smaller the effort the smaller the contribution; if so, the copyright simply bestows fewer rights. Others can expend the same effort to the same end. Copyright covers, after all, only the incremental contribution and not the underlying information. *Mazer v. Stein,* 347 U.S. 201, 74 S. Ct. 460, 98 L. Ed. 2d 630 (1954).
>
> The input of time is irrelevant. A photograph may be copyrighted, although it is the work of an instant and its significance may be accidental. *Burrow-Giles Lithographic Co. v. Sarony,* 111 U.S. 53, 4 S. Ct. 279, 28 L. Ed. 349 (1884); *Bleistein v. Donaldson Lithographing Co.,* 188 U.S. 239, 23 S. Ct. 298, 47 L. Ed. 460 (1903); *Time, Inc. v. Bernard Geis Assoc.,* 293 F. Supp. 130 (S.D.N.Y. 1968) (Zapruder film of Kennedy assassination). In 14 hours Mozart could write a piano concerto, J.S. Bach a cantata, or Dickens a week's installment of *Bleak House.* The Laffer Curve, an economic graph prominent in political debates, appeared on the back of a napkin after dinner, the work of a minute. All of these are copyrightable.[1]
>
> Dickens did not need to complete *Bleak House* before receiving a copyright; every chapter — indeed every sentence — could be protected standing alone. Rockford Map updates and republishes maps on more than 140 counties every year. If it put out one large book with every map, even Directory Service would concede that the book was based on a great deal of "industry." Rockford Map, like Dickens, loses none of its rights by publishing copyrightable matter in smaller units.

---

[1] In principle, Mozart's work is in the public domain and anyway was work for hire. The Archbishop of Salzburg probably held the rights. There were no copyright laws in seventeenth-century Germany, and Bach had no way to protect his rights. Dickens was at the mercy of his publishers. Only Laffer's napkin, and not the idea represented by the graph, may be copyrighted. But the principle's the thing.

1. FACTUAL NARRATIVES

NASH v. CBS

899 F.2d 1537 (7th Cir. 1990)

EASTERBROOK, CIRCUIT JUDGE.

John Dillinger, Public Enemy No. 1, died on July 22, 1934, at the Biograph Theater in Chicago. He emerged from the air conditioned movie palace into a sweltering evening accompanied by two women, one wearing a bright red dress. The "lady in red," Anna Sage, had agreed to betray his presence for $10,000. Agents of the FBI were waiting. Alerted by Polly Hamilton, the other woman, Dillinger wheeled to fire, but it was too late. A hail of bullets cut him down, his .45 automatic unused. William C. Sullivan, The Bureau 30-33 (1979). Now a national historic site, the Biograph bears a plaque commemorating the event. It still shows movies, and the air conditioning is no better now than in 1934.

Jay Robert Nash believes that Dillinger did not die at the Biograph. In *Dillinger: Dead or Alive?* (1970), and *The Dillinger Dossier* (1983), Nash maintains that Dillinger learned about the trap and dispatched Jimmy Lawrence, a small-time hoodlum who looked like him, in his stead. The FBI, mortified that its set-up had no sting, kept the switch quiet. Nash points to discrepancies between Dillinger's physical characteristics and those of the corpse: Dillinger had a scar on his upper lip and the corpse did not; Dillinger lacked a tooth that the corpse possessed; Dillinger had blue eyes, the corpse brown eyes; Dillinger's eyebrows were thicker than those of the corpse. Although Dillinger's sister identified the dead man, Nash finds the circumstances suspicious, and he is struck by the decision of Dillinger's father to encase the corpse in concrete before burial. As part of the cover-up, according to Nash, the FBI planted Dillinger's fingerprints in the morgue. After interviewing many persons connected with Dillinger's gang and the FBI's pursuit of it, Nash tracked Dillinger to the west coast, where Dillinger married and lay low. Nash believes that he survived at least until 1979. The *Dillinger Dossier* contains pictures of a middle-aged couple and then an elderly man who, Nash believes, is Dillinger in dotage. Nash provides capsule versions of his conclusions in his *Bloodletters and Badmen: A Narrative Encyclopedia of American Criminals from the Pilgrims to the Present* (1973), and his expose *Citizen Hoover* (1972).

Nash's reconstruction of the Dillinger story has not won adherents among historians — or the FBI. Someone in Hollywood must have read *The Dillinger Dossier*, however, because in 1984 CBS broadcast an episode of its Simon and Simon series entitled The Dillinger Print. Simon and Simon featured brothers Rick and A.J. Simon, private detectives in San Diego. [The challenged episode was full of plot intricacies and twists, involving a murdered retired FBI agent (who before his death was heard to speculate that Dillinger was not shot dead at the Biograph), a mysterious bank robber wearing clothing from the 1930s and using a gun once belonging to Dillinger and bearing a fresh fingerprint of his, the suggestion by A.J. Simon that Dillinger is alive (relying upon several physical discrepancies between Dillinger and the corpse described in the 1934 autopsy, as did Nash in his book), a shooting by the 1930s-style gangster directed at A.J. while he is playing racquetball, a police tip that Dillinger is living in the home of a San Diego dentist, other intimations that Dillinger lives, another shooting in a closed-down movie theater, a solution of the crime against the retired FBI agent that began the show, and an assertion by Rick Simon that Dillinger is probably alive and well in Oregon.]

Nash filed this suit seeking damages on the theory that The Dillinger Print violates his copyrights in the four books setting out his version of Dillinger's escape from death and new life on the west coast. The district court determined that the books' copyrighted material consists in Nash's presentation and exposition, not in any of the historical events. 691 F. Supp. 140 (N.D. Ill. 1988). CBS then moved for summary judgment, conceding for this purpose both access to Nash's books and copying of the books' factual material. The court granted this motion, 704 F. Supp. 823, holding that The Dillinger Print did not appropriate any of the material protected by Nash's copyrights.

CBS's concession removes from this case two questions that bedevil copyright litigation. See Selle v. Gibb, 741 F.2d 896, 901-02 (7th Cir. 1984). It leaves the questions whether the copier used matter that the copyright law protects and, if so, whether it took "too much."...

Learned Hand, whose opinions still dominate this corner of the law, observed in Nichols v. Universal Pictures Corp., 45 F.2d 119, 121 (2d Cir. 1930), that all depends on the level of abstraction at which the court conceives the interest protected by the copyright. If the court chooses a low level (say, only the words the first author employed), then a copier may take the plot, exposition, and all other original material, even though these may be the most important ingredients of the first author's contribution. As a practical matter this would mean that anyone could produce the work in a new medium without compensating the original author, despite the statute's grant to the author of the privilege to make "derivative works." If on the other hand the court should select a high level of abstraction, the first author may claim protection for whole genres of work ("the romantic novel" or, more modestly, any story involving doomed young lovers from warring clans, so that a copyright on Romeo and Juliet would cover West Side Story too). Even a less sweeping degree of abstraction creates a risk of giving copyright protection to "the idea" although the statute protects only "expression."...

Sometimes called the "abstractions test," Hand's insight is not a "test" at all. It is a clever way to pose the difficulties that require courts to avoid either extreme of the continuum of generality. It does little to help resolve a given case ... [or] answer the essential question: at what level of generality? After 200 years of wrestling with copyright questions, it is unlikely that courts will come up with the answer any time soon, if indeed there is "an" answer, which we doubt.

Hand returned again and again to the opposing forces that make the formulation of a single approach so difficult. Intellectual (and artistic) progress is possible only if each author builds on the work of others. No one invents even a tiny fraction of the ideas that make up our cultural heritage. Once a work has been written and published, any rule requiring people to compensate the author slows progress in literature and art, making useful expressions "too expensive" forcing authors to re-invent the wheel, and so on. Every work uses scraps of thought from thousands of predecessors, far too many to compensate even if the legal system were frictionless, which it isn't. Because any new work depends on others even if unconsciously, broad protection of intellectual property also creates a distinct possibility that the cost of litigation — old authors trying to get a "piece of the action" from current successes — will prevent or penalize the production of new works, even though the claims be rebuffed. Authors as a group therefore might prefer limited protection for their writings — they gain in the ability to use others' works more than they lose in potential royalties. *See* William M. Landes & Richard A. Posner, *An Economic Analysis of Copyright Law*, 18 J. Legal Studies 325, 332-33, 349-59 (1989).

Yet to deny authors all reward for the value their labors contribute to the works of others also will lead to inefficiently little writing, just as surely as excessively broad rights will do. The prospect of reward is an important stimulus for thinking and writing, especially for persons such as Nash who are full-time authors. Before the first work is published, broad protection of intellectual property seems best; after it is published, narrow protection seems best. At each instant some new works are in progress, and every author is simultaneously a creator in part and a borrower in part. In these roles, the same person has different objectives. Yet only one rule can be in force. This single rule must achieve as much as possible of these inconsistent demands. Neither Congress nor the courts has the information that would allow it to determine which is best. Both institutions must muddle through, using not a fixed rule but a sense of the consequences of moving dramatically in either direction.

If Nash had written a novel that another had translated into a screenplay, this would be a difficult case. Although The Dillinger Print is substantially original, it does not matter that almost all of the second author's expression is new. "[N]o plagiarist can excuse the wrong by showing how much of his work he did not pirate." *Sheldon v. Metro-Goldwyn Pictures Corp.*, 81 F.2d 49, 56 (2d Cir. 1936) (L. Hand, J.). The TV drama took from Nash's works the idea that Dillinger survived and retired to the west coast, and employed many of the ingredients that Nash used to demonstrate that the man in the Cook County morgue was not Dillinger....

Nash does not portray *The Dillinger Dossier* and its companion works as fiction, however, which makes all the difference. The inventor of Sherlock Holmes controls that character's fate while the copyright lasts; the first person to conclude that Dillinger survived does not get dibs on history. If Dillinger survived, that fact is available to all. Nash's rights lie in his expression: in his words, in his arrangement of facts (his deployment of narration interspersed with interviews, for example), but not in the naked "truth." The Dillinger Print does not use any words from *The Dillinger Dossier* or Nash's other books; it does not take over any of Nash's presentation but instead employs a setting of its own invention with new exposition and development. Physical differences between Dillinger and the corpse, planted fingerprints, photographs of Dillinger and other gangsters in the 1930s, these and all the rest are facts as Nash depicts them....

The cases closest to ours are not plays translated to the movie screen (as in *Sheldon*) but movies made from speculative works representing themselves as fact. For example, Universal made a motion picture based on the premise that an idealistic crewman planted a bomb that destroyed the dirigible Hindenberg on May 6, 1937. The theory came straight from A.A. Hoehling's *Who Destroyed the Hindenberg?* (1962), a monograph based on exhaustive research. The motion picture added sub-plots and development, but the thesis and the evidence adduced in support of it could be traced to Hoehling. Nonetheless, the Second Circuit concluded that this did not infringe Hoehling's rights, because the book placed the facts (as opposed to Hoehling's exposition) in the public domain. *Hoehling v. Universal City Studios, Inc.*, 618 F.2d 972 (1980). *See also Miller v. Universal City Studios* (facts about a notorious kidnapping are not protected by copyright)....

Hoehling suggested that "[t]o avoid a chilling effect on authors who contemplate tackling an historical issue or event, broad latitude must be granted to subsequent authors who make use of historical subject matter, including theories or plots." 618 F.2d at 978. As our opinion in *Toksvig* [*v. Bruce Publishing Co.*, 181 F.2d 664 (7th Cir. 1950)] shows, we are not willing to say that "anything goes" as long as the first work is about history. *Toksvig* held that the author of a biography of Hans Christian Andersen infringed the copyright of the author of an earlier biography by using portions of Andersen's letters as well as some of the themes and structure. *Hoehling* rejected *Toksvig*, see 618 F.2d at 979, concluding that "[k]nowledge is expanded ... by granting new authors of historical works a relatively free hand to build upon the work of their predecessors." *Id.* at 980 (footnote omitted). With respect for our colleagues of the east, we think this goes to the extreme of looking at incentives only *ex post*. The authors in *Hoehling* and *Toksvig* spent years tracking down leads. If all of their work, right down to their words, may be used without compensation, there will be too few original investigations, and facts will not be available on which to build.

In *Toksvig* the first author, who knew Danish, spent three years learning about Andersen's life; the second author, who knew no Danish, wrote her biography in less than a year by copying out of the first book scenes and letters that the original author discovered or translated. Reducing the return on such effort, by allowing unhindered use, would make the initial leg-work less attractive and so less frequent. Copyright law does not protect hard work (divorced from expression), and hard work is not an essential ingredient of copyrightable expression (see *Rockford Map*); to the extent *Toksvig* confuses work or ideas with expression, it has been justly criticized.... We need not revisit *Toksvig* on its own facts to know that it is a mistake to hitch up at either pole of the continuum between granting the first author a right to forbid all similar treatments of history and granting the second author a right to use anything he pleases of the first's work....

... Long before the 1976 revision of the statute [including § 102(b)], courts had decided that historical facts are among the "ideas" and "discoveries" that the statute does not cover. *International News Service v. Associated Press*, 248 U.S. 215, 234 (1918). This is not a natural law; Congress could have made copyright broader (as patent law is). But it is law, which will come as no surprise to Nash. His own books are largely fresh expositions of facts looked up in other people's books. Consider the introduction to the bibliography in

Murder, America: Homicide in the United States from the Revolution to the Present 447 (1980): The research for this book was done in libraries and archives throughout the United States, in addition to interviews and lengthy correspondence. The author's own files, exceeding more than a quarter of a million separate entries and a personal crime library of more than 25,000 volumes, were heavily employed. The producers of Simon and Simon used Nash's work as Nash has used others': as a source of facts and ideas, to which they added their distinctive overlay. As the district court found, CBS did no more than § 102(b) permits. Because The Dillinger Print uses Nash's analysis of history but none of his expression, the judgment is

Affirmed.

Wainwright Securities v. Wall Street Transcript Corp., 558 F.2d 91 (2d Cir. 1977), *cert. denied,* 434 U.S. 1014 (1978). Plaintiff, in the institutional research and brokerage business, prepares in-depth analytical reports on industrial, financial, utility and railroad corporations. These reports, which may run as many as forty pages in length, are used by nearly 1,000 Wainwright clients, including major banks, insurance companies and mutual funds. The Wainwright analysts examine a company's financial characteristics, trends in an industry, major developments at a company, growth prospects, and profit expectations, and highlight both corporate strengths and weaknesses. The defendant publishes the Wall Street Transcript, a weekly newspaper — available by subscription and at some newsstands — concerned with economic, business, and financial news. One of the Transcript's major features is the "Wall Street Roundup," a column consisting almost exclusively of abstracts of institutional research reports; advertisements for the Transcript expressly promise its readers "a fast-reading, pinpointed account of heavyweight reports from the top institutional research firms." The following is a typical abstract by the defendant of a Wainwright report:

> W.D. Williams of H.C. Wainwright & Co. says in a Special Report (April 13 — 7 pp) on FMC CORP. that 1976 prospects are strengthened by the magnitude of the increase in industrial and agricultural chemical earnings in last year's recessionary environment. And second, he says that likely to aid comparisons this year was the surprisingly limited extent to which the Fiber Division's losses shrank last year.
>
> His estimated earnings for 1976 is [sic] $3.76 per share compared with earnings of $3.24 per share in 1975.
>
> According to Williams, one of the most hopeful developments in recent years was the decision by management last year to attempt to negotiate sale of the Fiber Division. He says the company could wind up with possibly $100 million, plus a tax writeoff and a sizable one-time charge against earnings. And, concerning the tanker situation, he writes that the company is now far enough along on the learning curve that additional cost overruns, if any, will be small, the major incremental financial cost to FMC will lie in the determination of what share of the present unreserved overrun is the company's responsibility.

Despite protests from Wainwright, Transcript continued to publish these abstracts, contending among other things that the Wainwright reports were essentially news events and that the Transcript's abstracts were simply financial news coverage. The Court of Appeals for the Second Circuit rejected these contentions.

> It is, of course, axiomatic that "news events" may not be copyrighted.... But in considering the copyright protections due a report of news events or factual developments, it is important to differentiate between the substance of the information contained in the report, i.e., the event itself, and "the particular form or collocation of words in which the writer has communicated it."... What is protected is the manner of expression, the author's analysis or interpretation of events, the way he structures his material and marshals facts, his choice of words, and the emphasis he gives to particular developments....
>
> Here, the appellants did not bother to distinguish between the events contained in the reports and the manner of expression used by the Wainwright analysts.... Rather, the Transcript appropriated almost verbatim the most creative and original aspects of the reports, the financial analyses and predictions, which represent a substantial investment of time, money and labor....

The court pointed out a number of side-by-side paraphrases, the defendant's recurrent use of the Wainwright reports, and its apparent efforts to fulfill the demand for the original work, and concluded that "This was not legitimate coverage of a news event; instead it was, and there is no other way to describe it, chiseling for personal profit."

QUESTIONS

1. Should the "facts" as they are comprehensively recounted in an historical narrative be entitled, in whole or in part, to copyright protection? The Supreme Court decision in the *Feist* case may explain why single discrete facts are unprotectible because of their preexistence and the absence of human authorship. But in the writing of a comprehensive history, does not the historian "select, coordinate and arrange" from among a potentially unlimited number of such "facts" so as to create a compilation that should not lawfully be recounted by another, even in freshly generated sentences?

2. In *Hoehling v. Universal City Studios, Inc.*, discussed in *Nash*, the defendant's film incorporated from the plaintiff's historical account of the explosion of the German dirigible Hindenberg his speculation that the Hindenberg had been deliberately sabotaged by a member of its crew to embarrass the Nazi regime. The Court of Appeals for the Second Circuit held that such "explanatory hypotheses" (i.e., speculative historical reconstructions regarding unknowable occurrences and motivations) are just as much in the public domain as are "documented facts." To what extent does the *Nash* court disagree? Did it mean to suggest that the scenes from Hans Christian Andersen's life, uncovered by plaintiff Toksvig after arduous research, were subject to copy-

right protection? (It disclaims the "sweat of the brow" theory, but how else could such protection be justified?) Which court is correct?

If the *Nash* and *Wainwright Securities* decisions are correct, would that mean that copyright protection should be accorded to such historical theories as that of Marx regarding the economic underpinning of politics, or of Turner regarding the impact of the western frontier on the history of the United States — so that (if the works of Marx and Turner were still in copyright) no other person could reiterate these "explanations" in her own language, and indeed presumably could not even apply them in historical writing about nations different from those discussed by Marx and Turner?

3. The court in *Hoehling* also denied copyright protection to certain sequences of events, such as pre-voyage scenes of the Hindenberg crew in a German beer hall, the singing of songs such as the German national anthem, and the mandatory "Heil Hitler" exchange of greetings. These, the court referred to as *scenes a faire,* i.e., "incidents, characters or settings which are as a practical matter indispensable, or at least standard, in the treatment of a given topic." The court concluded: "Because it is virtually impossible to write about a particular historical era or fictional theme without employing certain 'stock' or standard literary devices, we have held that *scenes a faire* are not copyrightable as a matter of law." Do you see any difficulty with the court's analysis?

4. In *Harper & Row, Inc. v. Nation Enters.,* 723 F.2d 195 (2d Cir. 1983), *rev'd on other grounds,* 471 U.S. 539 (1984), a case involving the autobiography of Gerald R. Ford, the author of the *Hoehling* opinion, speaking for the court majority, stated that in works of history and biography "courts have carefully confined that troublesome concept 'expression' to its barest elements — the ordering and choice of the words themselves. *See Hoehling v. Universal City Studios.*" In light of this statement, what difference, if any, is there between the scope of protection accorded works of history or biography and that which is accorded to insurance and legal forms, test answer sheets, and the like? Should they be treated alike?

For discussions of the concept of "expression" in works of history and of the *Hoehling* decision, compare Gorman, *Fact or Fancy: The Implications for Copyright,* 29 J. Copyright Soc'y 560 (1982), with Ginsburg, *Sabotaging and Reconstructing History: A Comment on the Scope of Copyright Protection in Works of History After Hoehling v. Universal City Studios,* 29 J. Copyright Soc'y 647 (1982).

5. Not too long ago, a journalist on the staff of the Washington Post wrote a lengthy story about the travails of a young black boy growing up in an urban ghetto. After she was awarded the Pulitzer Prize for news reporting, it gradually became clear that the journalist's story was totally fabricated; she ultimately admitted so, to the consternation of her newspaper (which accepted her resignation) and the Pulitzer panel (to which the prize was relinquished). If, believing the news story to be truthful, a screen writer prepared a motion picture script based on the life of the youngster as depicted in detail in the Washington Post, and a television or theatrical film were produced and widely exhibited, would the Post (assuming it to be the copyright owner in the underlying article) have a successful claim for infringement? Would it have such a claim if the motion picture were produced *after* the exposure of the hoax? *Compare Houts v. Universal City Studios, Inc.*, 603 F. Supp. 26 (C.D. Cal. 1984), *and Huie v. National Broadcasting Co.*, 184 F. Supp. 198 (S.D.N.Y. 1960) *with De Acosta v. Brown*, 146 F.2d 408 (2d Cir. 1944), *cert. denied*, 325 U.S. 862 (1945), *and Belcher v. Tarbox*, 486 F.2d 1087 (9th Cir. 1973).

2. COMPILATIONS

Roth Greeting Cards v. United Card Co., 429 F.2d 1106 (9th Cir. 1970). The plaintiff, designer and distributor of greeting cards, claimed infringement on seven cards. These cards consisted of a simple drawing (e.g., a cute moppet suppressing a smile or a forlorn boy sitting on a curb) on the cover and a prosaic phrase on the inside. The trial court found that the artwork, although copyrightable, was not copied by the defendant, and that the text was prosaic and not protectable.

A divided appeals court accepted these conclusions but nonetheless found that the copyright on the card had been infringed. All the judges agreed that the text was indeed too commonplace to be copyrighted, and could have been freely copied alone. The majority stated: "However, proper analysis of the problem requires that all elements of each card, including text, arrangement of text, art work, and association between art work and text, be considered as a whole. Considering all of these elements together, the Roth cards are, in our opinion, both original and copyrightable." To prove infringement, a plaintiff must show that the defendant copied protectable material (a factual conclusion that the appeals court found to be compelled by the record) to the extent that the works in question are substantially similar. "It appears to us that in total concept and feel the cards of United are the same as the copyrighted cards of Roth. [T]he characters depicted in the art work, the mood they portrayed, the combination of art work conveying a particular mood with a particular message, and the arrangement of the words on the greeting card are substantially the same as in Roth's cards. In several instances the lettering is also very similar." Although in each case, the defendant's art work was "somewhat different" from the plaintiff's, the overall cards would be recognizable by an ordinary observer as having been taken from the copyrighted works. (One example given by the court was the plaintiff's card showing a weeping boy, with "I miss you already" on the front of the card, and "and You Haven't even Left" on the inside, and the defendant's card with the same text showing a weeping man.)

The dissenting judge stated: "I cannot ... follow the logic of the majority in holding that the uncopyrightable words and the imitated, but not copied art work, constitutes such total composition as to be subject to protection under the copyright laws. The majority concludes that in the overall arrangement of the text, the art work and the association of the art work to the text, the cards were copyrightable and the copyright infringed. This conclusion, as I view it, results in the whole becoming substantially greater than the sum total of its parts. With this conclusion, of course, I cannot agree.... Feeling, as I do, that the copyright act is a grant of limited monopoly to the authors of creative literature and art, I do not think that we should extend a 56-year monopoly in a situation where neither infringement of text, nor infringement of art work can be found. On these facts, we should adhere to our historic philosophy requiring freedom of competition."

Sem-Torq, Inc. v. K Mart Corp., 936 F.2d 851 (6th Cir. 1991). The plaintiff designed placards with simple phrases on both sides, such as "For Rent" and "For Sale." It decided on the phrases, their pairing, and the lettering and coloring. It marketed such signs in sets of five to stores such as K-Mart, the defendant, which placed them in slotted display stands in its stores; customers could buy single signs apart from the set. The plaintiff learned that a competitor was copying the sets, at K-Mart's suggestion, and was also selling them at K-Mart. Although the plaintiff acknowledged that its individual signs could not be separately copyrighted, it forwarded the set of signs to the Copyright Office for registration as a group; its registration application claimed authorship in selection and arrangement. The Copyright Office registered the copyright, but only after informing the plaintiff that the matter was a close one and that it was relying on its "rule of doubt."

The district court found that the set did not qualify as a compilation; the set of signs "is not an independent work; it is incapable of existing separately from its components. Rather, the plaintiff has created five individual works for which the copyright laws provide no protection." The court of appeals agreed. "Because [a] compilation is protected, while its individual components may not be, '[t]he whole of a compilation is thus greater than the sum of its parts.'... The set here, however, is no greater than the sum of its individual unprotected parts. The five double-sided signs comprising the set are not sold as a set .... In contrast, copyrightable compilations usually involve a work whose value to consumers is in the combination of its individual parts: a baseball card price guide ... a daily organizer ... and a gardening directory .... The signs are displayed together as a set, but there is no value to the consuming public in this arrangement.... The resulting work, then, is the individual unprotected signs, not the set."

BELLSOUTH ADVERTISING & PUBLISHING CORP. v. DONNELLEY INFORMATION PUBLISHING, INC.

999 F.2d 1436 (11th Cir. *en banc* 1993)

BIRCH, CIRCUIT JUDGE:

I. *Introduction*

In this appeal, we must decide whether acts of copying infringed the compilation copyright registered in a "yellow pages" classified business directory. The parties have stipulated that the directory, which is a typical yellow pages directory, qualifies for compilation copyright protection. Thus, we are called upon to apply *Feist Publications, Inc. v. Rural Tel. Serv. Co.*, __ U.S. __, 111 S. Ct. 1282, 113 L. Ed. 2d 358 (1991), which addressed copyright protection for a "white pages" telephone directory, to resolve the infringement claims presented to us concerning a directory of a different color.

The pivotal issue in this case is whether that which was copied by the alleged infringer was protected by the registered claim of compilation copyright. The parties agree that the only elements of a work entitled to compilation copyright protection are the selection, arrangement or coordination as they appear in the work as a whole. The parties dispute what elements of a classified directory constitute such selection, arrangement or coordination. Mindful that the protection afforded to a whole work by a compilation copyright is "thin," the determination as to whether an infringement of a compilation copyright has occurred is particularly difficult where less than the entire work is copied.

II. *Background*

BellSouth Advertising & Publishing Corporation ("BAPCO") is a wholly owned subsidiary of BellSouth Corporation ("BellSouth") created for the purpose of preparing, publishing and distributing telephone directories. Using telephone listing information supplied by Southern Bell Telephone and Telegraph Company ("Southern Bell"), another wholly owned subsidiary of BellSouth, BAPCO publishes a classified, "yellow pages," advertising directory for the Greater Miami area. The BAPCO directory is organized into an alphabetical list of business classifications. Each business-rate telephone service subscriber is listed in alphabetical order under one appropriate heading without charge. A subscriber may purchase cross listings under different business classifications or advertisements to appear along with its business listing.

After BAPCO published its 1984 directory for the Greater Miami area, Donnelley Information Publishing, Inc. and Reuben H. Donnelley Corp. (collectively "Donnelley") began promoting and selling classified advertisements to be placed in a competitive classified directory for the Greater Miami area. To generate a list of business telephone subscribers to be solicited for placement in its directory, Donnelley gave copies of BAPCO's directory to Appalachian Computer Services, Inc. ("ACS"), a data entry company. Donnelley first marked each listing in the BAPCO directory with one alphanumeric code indicating the size and type of advertisement purchased by the subscriber[2] and a similar code indicating the type of business represented by the BAPCO heading under which the listing appeared. For each listing appearing in the BAPCO directory: ACS created a computer data base containing the name, address, and telephone number of the subscriber, as well as the codes corresponding to business type and unit of advertising. From this data base, Donnelley printed sales lead sheets, listing this information for each subscriber, to be used to contact business telephone subscribers to sell advertisements and listings in the Donnelley directory. Relying on this information

---

[2] The code corresponding to the type of advertising appearing in the BAPCO directory indicated only the unit of advertising purchased. Donnelley did not record, nor was alleged to have recorded, information regarding the graphic appearance or page location of the advertising material, nor did it copy facts concerning individual businesses, such as product lines, services, hours of operation, contained in the advertisements themselves.

copied from the BAPCO directory, Donnelley ultimately prepared its own competitive directory for the Greater Miami area.

BAPCO sued Donnelley for alleged copyright infringement, trademark infringement, and unfair competition. After the district court denied BAPCO's motion for a preliminary injunction, Donnelley answered and counterclaimed against BAPCO, Southern Bell and BellSouth, for alleged violations of federal antitrust law. On the copyright infringement claim, the district court granted summary judgment to BAPCO and denied Donnelley's motion seeking partial summary judgment in its favor, *BellSouth Advertising & Publishing Corp. v. Donnelly Info. Publishing, Inc.*, 719 F. Supp. 1551 (S.D. Fla. 1988).

The district court found, and Donnelley admitted, that BAPCO owned a valid compilation copyright in its classified directory. Donnelley stipulated that, in preparing its data base and sales lead sheets, it obtained from each listing in the BAPCO directory, the telephone number, name, address, kind of business, and unit of advertising for the listed subscriber. As further evidence of copying, the district court relied on affidavits and deposition testimony from Donnelley's representatives and the presence of a number of erroneous listings common to the BAPCO and Donnelley directories. From the process by which Donnelley prepared its competitive yellow pages directory, the district court identified three acts of copying: (1) the entry of subscriber information into the computer data base by ACS; (2) the printout of sales lead sheets from this data base; and (3) the publication of Donnelley's directory. Based on these acts of copying, the court granted BAPCO's motion for summary judgment on its copyright infringement claims. Donnelley appealed the district court's resolution of the parties' motions on the copyright claim.[6]

III. *Discussion*

....

B. *BAPCO's Claim of Infringement*

....

The district court found that BAPCO engaged in a number of acts of selection in compiling its listings. For example, BAPCO determined the geographic scope of its directory and the closing date after which no changes in listings would be included. *BellSouth*, 719 F. Supp. at 1557-58. The district court erred, however, in implicitly determining that these selective acts were sufficiently original to merit copyright protection. Rural obviously established a geographic scope and a closing date for its white pages, which were held uncopyrightable as a matter of law in *Feist*. The district court's analysis would protect such factual elements of every compilation; any collection of facts "fixed in any tangible medium of expression" will by necessity have a closing date and, where applicable, a geographic limit selected by the compiler. The district court found that BAPCO "selected" its listings by requiring its yellow

---

[6]The judgment of the district court was affirmed by a panel of this court, but was subsequently vacated by a grant of rehearing en banc. *BellSouth Adv. & Pub. Corp. v. Donnelley Info. Pub., Inc.*, 933 F.2d 952 (11th Cir. 1991), vacated and reh'g en banc granted, 977 F.2d 1435 (11th Cir. 1992).

pages subscribers to use a business telephone service. *Id.* at 1557. The district court also focused on a number of marketing techniques employed by BAPCO to generate its listings, such as the determination of the number of free listings offered to each subscriber, the selection of which customers to contact by an on-premise visit from sales personnel, the selection of the date of commencement of its advertisement sales campaign, and the procedure used to recommend the purchase of listings under multiple headings. *Id.* at 1557. The district court again failed to consider whether these "acts of selection" met the level of originality required to extend the protection of copyright to BAPCO's selection.

More fundamental, these acts are not acts of authorship, but techniques for the discovery of facts. In *Feist*, the Court emphasized the distinction "between creation and discovery: the first person to find and report a particular fact has not created the fact; he or she has merely discovered its existence." ___ U.S. at ___, 111 S. Ct. at 1288. By employing its sales strategies, BAPCO discovered that certain subscribers describe their businesses in a particular fashion and were willing to pay for a certain number of listings under certain available business descriptions. To be sure, BAPCO employed a set of strategies or techniques for discovering this data. Any useful collection of facts, however, will be structured by a number of decisions regarding the optimal manner in which to collect the pertinent data in the most efficient and accurate manner. If this were sufficient, then the protection of copyright would extend to census data, cited in *Feist* as a paradigmatic example of a work that lacks the requisite originality. ___ U.S. at ___, 111 S. Ct. at 1288. Just as the Copyright Act does not protect "industrious collection," it affords no shelter to the resourceful, efficient, or creative collector. See *Miller v. Universal City Studios, Inc.*, 650 F.2d 1365, 1372 (5th Cir. July 1981) ("The valuable distinction in copyright law between facts and the expression of facts cannot be maintained if research is held to be copyrightable."). The protection of copyright must inhere in a creatively original selection of facts to be reported and not in the creative means used to discover those facts. See 17 U.S.C. § 102(b) ("In no case does copyright protection ... extend to any idea, procedure, process, system, method of operation, concept, principle, or discovery, regardless of the form in which it is described, explained, illustrated, or embodied in such work."). Ultimately, the district court erred by extending copyright protection to the collection of facts in the BAPCO directory based on the uncopyrightable formative acts used to generate those listings.

In addition to these acts of selection, the district court found that BAPCO engaged in feats of coordination and arrangement to generate its yellow pages directory. The court explains that BAPCO arranged its directory in an alphabetized list of business types, with individual businesses listed in alphabetical order under the applicable headings. The Copyright Act protects "original works of authorship." 17 U.S.C. § 102(a). BAPCO's arrangement and coordination is "entirely typical" for a business directory. *Feist*, ___ U.S. at ___, 111 S. Ct. at 1296.[13] With respect to business telephone directories, such an ar-

---

[13] While the listings in BAPCO's yellow pages required somewhat more organization and arrangement than the white pages directory considered in *Feist*, BAPCO's

rangement "is not only unoriginal, it is practically inevitable." __ U.S. at __, 111 S. Ct. at 1297.

BAPCO's claim of copyright in the arrangement of its directory also does not survive application of the "merger" doctrine. Under the merger doctrine, "expression is not protected in those instances where there is only one or so few ways of expressing an idea that protection of the expression would effectively accord protection to the idea itself." *Kregos v. Associated Press*, 937 F.2d 700, 705 (2d Cir. 1991). See also *Baker v. Selden*, 101 U.S. (11 Otto) 99, 25 L. Ed. 841 (1879). Because this is the one way to construct a useful business directory, the arrangement has "merged" with the idea of a business directory, and thus is uncopyrightable.[15]

The district court's suggestion that BAPCO could have arranged its headings according to the number of advertisers or to list its subscribers under

---

claim of "originality" must be resolved by comparison to other business telephone directories. BAPCO did not deviate from the arrangement of the typical business directory, which employs an alphabetical list of headings to describe the various types of businesses and then alphabetizes the listings under the appropriate headings.

Applying *Feist*, the Second Circuit declined to extend copyright protection to the selection and arrangement of certain charts displaying the results of horse racing. *Victor Lalli Enters. v. Big Red Apple, Inc.*, 936 F.2d 671, 673-74 (2d Cir. 1991). "The format of the charts is a convention: Lalli exercises neither selectivity in what he reports nor creativity in how he reports it." *Id.* at 673. Similarly, the Ninth Circuit rejected a claim that two automobile catalogs listing replacement radiators and associated parts were substantially similar. *Cooling Sys. & Flexibles, Inc. v. Stuart Radiator*, 777 F.2d 485, 491 (9th Cir. 1985). Although both works were arranged into three sections (an illustrations section, an original equipment manufacturer section, and an applications section), the court found that this arrangement was obligatory for a useful radiator parts catalog. "The fewer the methods of expressing an idea, the more the allegedly infringing work must resemble the copyrighted work in order to establish substantial similarity." *Id.* A subsequent collector is not required to arrange its compilation in a fashion not usable by those for whom it is intended. *Id.* at 492. The format of a typical business telephone directory is even more obvious and well established than the radiator catalogs at issue in *Cooling Systems*.

[15] In *Matthew Bender & Co. v. Kluwer Law Book Publishers, Inc.*, 672 F. Supp. 107 (S.D.N.Y. 1987), the court considered the application of the merger doctrine to a claim of copyright in a system of charts displaying information regarding the amount of recovery in previous personal injury cases. Both the plaintiff's work and that of the alleged infringer divided the cases into chapters corresponding to the part of the body injured and further divided the cases within each chapter based on whether the recovery was a result of a settlement, or an "adequate," "inadequate," or "excessive" award. 672 F. Supp. at 108. Each work listed the cases according to forum state, arranging awards from the same state from largest to smallest amount. In both collections, information regarding each case was organized into categories for amount, case name, plaintiff, event, injury, and further relevant data. The court rejected the plaintiff's claim of copyright, concluding that the plaintiff's work employed one of the few practical and useful means of organizing data regarding personal injury awards. The idea and the expression of such a work thus "merged." *Id.* at 109-10. Further, the information selected for display about each case was obvious and did not demonstrate the original selection, arrangement or coordination required for copyright protection. *Id.* at 112; see also *Coates-Freeman Assocs., Inc. v. Polaroid Corp.*, 792 F. Supp. 879, 883-84 (D. Mass. 1992) (Placement of decisionmaking steps on chart purporting to categorize leadership styles was not a copyrightable feature where selection of those particular steps out of a universe of very limited options resulted in merger of any creativity into the basic idea of the chart).

each heading according to the length of time for which that subscriber had appeared under that heading misapprehends the question. The relevant inquiry is not whether there is some imaginable, although manifestly less useful, method of arranging business telephone listings. In *Feist*, Rural could have published multiple directories for its service area or listed its numbers in numerical order, by age, or by neighborhood within a single directory. The pertinent inquiry is whether the compiler has demonstrated originality, the "sine qua non" of copyright, in its arrangement or coordination. The arrangement of BAPCO's yellow pages, like that of Rural's white pages, is "entirely typical" of its respective type.

The district court also identified acts of coordination and arrangement in the particular system of headings used in the BAPCO directory. The district court appears to find that, when Donnelley entered the listing information from the BAPCO directory, it also copied the particular heading under which that listing appeared in the BAPCO directory. 719 F. Supp. at 1558-59. BAPCO, however, failed to introduce evidence sufficient to establish a genuine dispute of material fact as to whether Donnelley copied the particular heading structure employed by BAPCO. Donnelley stipulated that it obtained the "business type" for each listing from the BAPCO directory. R1-8. The evidence submitted to the district court in the form of affidavit, deposition, and witness testimony reveals that Donnelley established its own system of headings and that, in constructing its data base, Donnelley entered an alphanumeric code that corresponded to the Donnelley heading with each BAPCO listing, 5SR2 at 183-85; 1SR-434 at 76-77, 143-44; 1SR-435 at 253-54 and Ex. 278; Deposition of John Notestein at 10, 12, 14-15, 22. Further, the sales lead sheets generated by Donnelley from its database and pages of the respective directories submitted to the district court illustrate that Donnelley selected a somewhat different category of headings to describe the listings originally appearing in the BAPCO directory. Considering the extent to which the heading structure of a classified business directory is dictated by functional considerations and common industry practice, the differences apparent in the glossary of headings employed by Donnelley are sufficient to rebut any inference of copying that otherwise might be drawn from those terms that are common to both directories. In sum, the evidence before the district court requires the conclusion that, by determining the type of business of each subscriber by observation of the BAPCO directory and translating that business type into an encoded heading of its own creation, Donnelley extracted uncopyrightable information regarding the business activities of BAPCO's subscribers without appropriating any arguably original, protectable expressive element in the BAPCO glossary of headings.

Additionally, BAPCO failed to present evidence that, even if copied, its heading structure constitutes original expression warranting copyright protection. Initially, many of the selected headings, for example "Attorneys" or "Banks," represent such an obvious label for the entities appearing under these headings as to lack the requisite originality for copyright protection. BAPCO can claim no copyright in the idea of dividing churches by denomination or attorneys by area of specialty. Further, any expressive act in including a category such as "Banks" or in dividing "Attorneys" into categories such as

"Bankruptcy" or "Criminal Law" would lose copyright protection because it would merge with the idea of listing such entities as a class of businesses in a business directory. The evidence submitted by Donnelley also establishes that many of BAPCO's headings result from certain standard industry practices, such as the recommendations of the National Yellow Pages Sales Association, with regard to the selection and phrasing of headings in business directories. Finally, as established by the testimony of BAPCO's representatives, the ultimate appearance of a particular subscriber under a certain heading is determined by the subscriber's willingness to purchase those listings in the BAPCO directory. While BAPCO may select the headings that are offered to the subscriber, it is the subscriber who selects from those alternatives the headings under which the subscriber will appear in the copyrighted directory. The headings that actually appear in the directory thus do not owe their origin to BAPCO and BAPCO has claimed no copyright in the larger universe of headings that are offered to subscribers. Thus, the elements of selection, coordination and arrangement identified by the district court, and purportedly copied by Donnelley, as a matter of law, do not display the originality required to merit copyright protection.

Although purporting to consider whether Donnelley copied the original elements of selection, arrangement or coordination from the BAPCO directory, the opinion of the district court rests, at least in part, on a comparison of the appearance of corresponding pages from both directories.[21] For example, the court concluded that "Donnelley used a format nearly identical to that used by BAPCO" and that "although Donnelley's directory is not identical to BAPCO's directory, the material was copied and used to produce a directory substantially similar in both content and format." 719 F. Supp. at 1559. The district court erred, however, by failing to consider the degree to which the similarity between the two directories was because of Donnelley's use of the uncopyrightable facts, such as name, number, address, and business type, from the BAPCO directory. Further, to the extent that this similarity of format resulted from was due [sic] to the common arrangement and coordination of the two directories into alphabetized business classifications, with alphabetized listings under each classification, the district court erred by extending the scope of BAPCO's copyright to capture the system of organization common to all classified directories in the public domain. Moreover, the other elements of format common to the two directories, such as the organization of listings into four columns, are also manifestly typical, obvious and unoriginal.

By comparing the overall appearance of the two directories through its comparison of the corresponding pages, the district court effectively failed to

---

[21] A comparison of corresponding pages from the two directories ... reveals several obvious differences in type face and graphic layout. Donnelley included different advertisements, not only in content, but also in number and design. BAPCO underlines its headings while Donnelley marks its headings with a sideways triangle. Donnelley uses a different type face. Whatever original authorship is represented by these types of presentation choices was clearly not copied by Donnelley. Further, the sales lead sheets produced from the ACS data base are obviously not similar in appearance or arrangement to BAPCO's directory, in which its claim of copyright was registered.

consider whether Donnelley copied the "constituent elements of the work that are original." *Feist*, ___ U.S. at ___, 111 S. Ct. at 1296. In the case of a factual compilation, a comparison of the copyright holder's work with that of the alleged infringer must distinguish similarities attributable to ideas, which are unprotected per se, or to expression not owned by the copyright holder, from those similarities resulting from the copying of the compiler's original elements.[22] We consider this conclusion to be compelled by section 103(b) of the Copyright Act, which directs that "the copyright in a compilation or derivative work extends only to the material contributed by the author of such work, as distinguished from the preexisting material employed in the work, and does not imply any exclusive right in the preexisting material." 17 U.S.C. § 103(b).

We note that Donnelley did not copy, nor was alleged to have copied, the text or graphic material from the advertisements in the BAPCO directory, the positioning of these advertisements, the typeface, or the textual material included by BAPCO to assist the user. Unlike the infringer in *Southern Bell Tel. & Tel. Co. v. Associated Tel. Directory Publishers*, 756 F.2d 801 (11th Cir. 1985), Donnelley did not photocopy, or reproduce by any equivalent means, the page by page arrangement or appearance of its competitor's directory in the process of creating its own work. Although the amount of material taken from the BAPCO directory was substantial in a purely quantitative sense, Donnelley did not, by this process, appropriate whatever original elements might arguably inhere in the BAPCO directory. Given that the copyright protection of a factual compilation is "thin," a competitor's taking the bulk of the factual material from a preexisting compilation without infringement of the author's copyright is not surprising.

IV. *Conclusion*

By copying the name, address, telephone number, business type, and unit of advertisement purchased for each listing in the BAPCO directory,[23]

---

[22] The Second Circuit has observed:

> Although the test for infringement of original works and compilations is one of "substantial similarity," the appropriate inquiry is narrowed in the case of a compilation. As noted, the components of a compilation are generally in the public domain, and a finding of substantial similarity or even absolute identity as to matters in the public domain will not suffice to prove infringement. What must be shown is substantial similarity between those elements, and only those elements, that provide copyrightability to the allegedly infringed compilation.

Key Publications, Inc. v. Chinatown Today Publishing Enters., Inc., 945 F.2d 509, 514 (2d Cir. 1991) (citations omitted); see also *Cooling Sys.*, 777 F.2d at 492-93 ("What is important is not whether there is substantial similarity in the total concept and feel of the works, but whether the very small amount of protectable expression in Cooling Systems' catalog is substantially similar to the equivalent portions of Stuart's catalog.") (citation omitted).

[23] The common errors in the BAPCO and Donnelley listings prove only that Donnelley admittedly copied the name, number, address, and type of business from every BAPCO listing. The presence of common errors is not probative of whether the portions of the BAPCO directory copied by Donnelley included the copyrightable elements of original selection, coordination and arrangement. In *Feist*, the alleged in-

Donnelley copied no original element of selection, coordination or arrangement; Donnelley thus was entitled to summary judgment on BAPCO's claim of copyright infringement.[24] We REVERSE the judgment of the district court granting summary judgment to BAPCO on its claim of copyright infringement and enter judgment in favor of Donnelley on this claim.

HATCHETT, CIRCUIT JUDGE, dissenting:

The majority's holding establishes a rule of law that transforms the multibillion dollar classified publishing industry from a business requiring the production of a useful directory based on multiple layers of creative decision-making, into a business requiring no more than a successful race to a data processing agency to copy another publisher's copyrighted work-product. In reaching this incredible result, the majority forsakes thoughtful analysis of the evidence under the governing principles articulated in *Feist*, and leaps to a conclusion based on nothing more than its collective judgment of what ought to be copyrightable.

....

DISCUSSION

....

I. *Copyrightability of Compilations*

... [T]his court must first determine what particular elements of BAPCO's selection, coordination, and arrangement of preexisting facts in the 1984 Yellow Pages are sufficiently original to merit copyright protection.

II. *Original Selection, Coordination, or Arrangement*

... Donnelley is correct to assert that the holding in *Feist* precludes this court from concluding that BAPCO satisfied the originality requirement based on the mere alphabetizing of business listings and classified headings, or based on the mere coordination of the name, address, and telephone number of a particular business into one complete business listing. See *Feist*, ___ U.S. at ___, 111 S. Ct. at 1297, 113 L. Ed. 2d at 380-81 (holding that a tele-

---

fringer copied every listing from the compilers' white pages, including four erroneous listings. ___ U.S. at ___, 111 S. Ct. at 1287. Because Rural copied only uncopyrightable facts, however, the presence of common errors was not relevant. See also Shira Perlmutter, *The Scope of Copyright in Telephone Directories: Keeping Listing Information in the Public Domain*, 38 J. Copyright Society 1, 5-6 (Fall 1990) ("Where, as in *Feist*, the defendant has admitted copying, such evidence is simply irrelevant. Copying of erroneous or fictitious entries has no bearing on the question of whether material admittedly copied is protected by the plaintiff's copyright, and if so, whether the taking is substantial."); Alan Latman, *Probative Similarity as Proof of Copying: Toward Dispelling Some Myths in Copyright Infringement*, 90 Columbia L. Rev. 1187, 1204-06 (1990) (distinguishing use of common errors as proof of copying from use as proof of substantial similarity of protected material).

[24] Summary judgment in favor of the defendant in an infringement action is appropriate where the similarity between the two works concerns only uncopyrightable elements of the plaintiff's work. *Arica Inst., Inc. v. Palmer*, 970 F.2d 1067, 1072 (2d Cir. 1992); *Warner Bros., Inc. v. American Broadcasting Cos.*, 720 F.2d 231, 240 (2d Cir. 1983).

phone company's white pages lack the requisite originality for copyright protection where the telephone company merely published basic subscriber information — name, town, and telephone number — and arranged it alphabetically based on surnames).

Donnelley is also correct to assert that the district court erred in characterizing BAPCO's decision to offer one free listing and decisions on the dates and procedures for soliciting advertisements as original acts of "selection." "Selection implies the exercise of judgment in choosing which facts from a given body of data to include in a compilation." *Key Publications v. Chinatown Today Publishing Enterprises, Inc.*, 945 F.2d 509, 513 (2d Cir. 1991) (citations omitted). BAPCO's decisions regarding a free listing and solicitation procedures did not entail the exercise of judgment in choosing among facts to be included in its directories. "Selection" is not an appropriate term to describe the choices to include all of the data in a given body of data, on a given date. Instead of acts of selection, these BAPCO's decisions are more closely analogous to ideas or procedures for reliably and profitably collecting facts. As ideas or procedures, BAPCO's decision to offer a free listing and its decisions regarding soliciting advertisements, are not copyrightable. See 17 U.S.C. § 102(b) (providing that no copyright protection for an original work of authorship extends to any "idea, procedure, process, system, method of operation, concept, principle, or discovery, regardless of the form in which it is described, explained, illustrated, or embodied in such work").

However, even ignoring these erroneously identified acts of selection, coordination, or arrangement, BAPCO's other acts of selection and arrangement in compiling the 1984 Yellow Pages were sufficiently original to merit copyright protection under *Feist*.

A. *Selection of Classified Headings*

The clearest example of BAPCO's original selection is its choice of the classified headings that would be included in the 1984 Yellow Pages. Accord *Key Publications*, 945 F.2d at 514 (holding that a publisher's selection of 260 different categories, even if including particular categories that have been used in other directories, involved sufficient creativity to contribute to the overall originality of a classified directory). BAPCO selected the approximate 7,000 classified headings in the 1984 Yellow Pages from the 4,700 primary headings and approximately 34,000 related headings in the BAPCO headings book. BAPCO presented the undisputed testimony of Gerald Brown that the BAPCO headings book is not standardized to coincide with the menu of classified headings used in National Yellow Page Sales Association (NYPSA) publications. Moreover, even if BAPCO's selection of classified headings is similar to other NYPSA publications, it would still be copyrightable under *Feist* so long as BAPCO selected independently. See *Feist*, __ U.S. at __, 111 S. Ct. at 1287, 113 L. Ed. 2d at 369 (holding that "originality does not signify novelty; a work may be original even though it closely resembles other works so long as the similarity is fortuitous, not the result of copying").

In addition, the testimony of Donnelley's own witness supports the district court's conclusion that BAPCO's selection of headings constituted an original act of selection. Donnelley's corporate representative, Jon Notestein, responded to a question about whether Donnelley created its headings especially for the Donnelley Miami directory, with the following statement: "What we have learned in this business after 99 years is that individual markets may have local terminology that reflect differently in different parts of the country. So, yes, I'm sure we have created some headings, classifications to represent types of business that we didn't normally use in Donnelley in the Mid-west, for example." See Deposition of Jon Notestein, p. 50. In further describing the process of particularizing headings for a specific directory, Notestein explained that Donnelley maintains a list of over 7,000 headings that are generally applied across the country, but "in the end the type of business [that] appears in our directory is a reflection of the marketing and needs of the market and users of the product. It is an ongoing process changing every day." See Deposition of Jon Notestein, p. 51 (also stating that Donnelley probably selected its headings for Miami from "looking at" the 1984 Yellow Pages).

On appeal, Donnelley appears to concede that copyright protection extends to a publisher's selection of which headings to include in a particular classified directory, arguing instead that it did not copy BAPCO's selection of classified headings. Donnelley asserts that its 1985 Miami North directory contains approximately 4,000 headings and that its 1985 Miami South directory contains approximately 4,300 headings, as compared to the 7,000 headings in BAPCO's 1984 Yellow Pages. Even though more relevant to the separate issue of substantial copying, Donnelley's assertion that it independently selected a substantially smaller and distinct "universe" of classified headings underscores the originality, and thus copyrightability of BAPCO's selection of headings.

B. *Categorizing Businesses Under Classified Headings*

The originality of BAPCO's arrangement of business listings under a particular classified heading is also clear under the standard definition of "arrangement" in the copyright laws. "Arrangement 'refers to the ordering or grouping of data into lists or categories that go beyond the mere mechanical grouping of data as such, for example, the alphabetical, chronological, or sequential listings of data.'" *Key Publications*, 945 F.2d at 513-14 (quoting Copyright Office, Guidelines for Registration of Fact-Based Compilations 1 (Rev. Oct. 11, 1989)). In this case, BAPCO presented the undisputed affidavit testimony of its General Manager-Publishing, Bob Johnson, regarding BAPCO's grouping of listings under a particular classified heading. See Exhibit A to Donnelley's En Banc Brief (copy of Affidavit of Bob Johnson). Because most business subscribers offer multiple product lines, goods, and services, Johnson testified that BAPCO sales representatives were responsible for itemizing the products or services of a business subscriber, determining the degree of importance or profitability to the business, and recommending an appropriate classified heading for listing the business in the 1984 Yellow Pages. Johnson further testified that BAPCO annually updates and publishes its heading book in order to provide sales representatives with a quick-reference of the approximately 34,000 authorized BAPCO "related headings" for making recommendations to businesses about additional listings.

... BAPCO presented the district court with conclusive evidence concerning the originality of its groupings of business listings under classified headings. BAPCO attached to Johnson's affidavit a sample page from its heading book, which includes the primary heading of "Bakers-Retail" and related headings including "Biscuits," "Cakes," "Pastries," "Bagels," "Candy & Confectionery," "Caterers," "Cookies & Crackers," "Delicatessens," "Donuts," "Food Products," "Foods-Carry Out," "Grocers-Retail," "Health & Diet Food Products-Retail," "Pies," "Pretzels," "Restaurants," "Sandwiches," "Snack Products," "Wedding Supplies & Services." Although some primary entries on the sample page contain less related headings than the "Bakers-Retail" example, other primary headings contain more related heading options. Hence, the "Bakers-Retail" example provides a representative illustration of the wide-ranging choices that BAPCO sales representatives made in categorizing the 32,559 businesses under the appropriate related headings from the approximately 34,000 options in the heading book. With so many related headings to describe a business principally known as a bakery, BAPCO's arrangement of the listing of a particular bakery under one, two, three, four, or more headings is neither "obvious" nor "practically inevitable" as defined in *Feist*. See *Feist*, ___ U.S. at ___, 111 S. Ct. at 1297, 113 L. Ed. 2d at 380. Accordingly, the evidence is clear that BAPCO's arrangement was in no sense mechanical. On the contrary, the 1984 Yellow Pages reflects several layers of BAPCO choices on grouping 106,398 business listings under approximately 7,000 classified headings, which BAPCO selected from a heading book containing 4,700 primary entries and 34,000 related headings. Accord *Key Publications*, 945 F.2d at 514 (holding that a classified publisher's grouping of over 9,000 listings into approximately 260 different categories constituted original arrangement entitled to copyright protection).

Donnelley challenges BAPCO's evidence of an original arrangement with repeated assertions that the businesses themselves, not BAPCO, selected the appropriate classified heading or headings with which to describe their businesses. In its reply brief to the panel, Donnelley conceded that if BAPCO supported its "belated allegation that BAPCO selects the headings, there would result a material issue of fact, making summary judgment improper on the issue of infringement." Donnelley Panel Reply Brief at p. 13. The evidence before the district court not only supports BAPCO's so-called "belated allegation," but the only evidence presented to the district court conclusively establishes that BAPCO makes the final decisions on whether to list a business under a particular classified heading.

... Donnelley's argument completely ignores the undisputed evidence that BAPCO presented on the editorial role of its Heading Committee in arranging business listings under a particular classified heading. In addition to discussing the role of a BAPCO sales representative in recommending related headings to businesses, Gerald Brown testified via deposition that BAPCO's Heading Committee had the final responsibility for deciding whether a requested classified heading was appropriate for inclusion in the 1984 Yellow Pages. Brown further testified that a business's willingness to pay for a listing under a particular classified heading did not influence the Heading Committee's decision on whether to approve the proposed new heading....

C. Selection of Only Businesses with Business Telephone Service

BAPCO's selection of only businesses with business telephone service, as opposed to residential service, is also an act of selection contributing to the originality of the 1984 Yellow Pages. As noted earlier, selection involves "the exercise of judgment in choosing which facts from a given body of data to include in a compilation." See *Key Publications*, 945 F.2d at 513. BAPCO exercised such judgment in choosing only business service subscribers from the body of data including both business and residential subscribers for inclusion in the 1984 Yellow Pages. The originality in BAPCO's choice is amply demonstrated in the fact that Donnelley, unlike BAPCO, would accept listings and advertising from residential telephone service subscribers in addition to business telephone service subscribers. For example, the Assistant Vice-President and General Manager of the Southeast Operation of Donnelley Information Publishing, Louis Sudholz, testified about the disparate treatment of a hypothetical prospective customer, "John, the painter."...

D. Selection of a Geographic Area to Be Covered Comprehensively

Although a closer question, BAPCO's geographic scoping also represents an original act of selection. BAPCO asserts that its selection of a geographic scope refers to a choice about what geographic region would be covered comprehensively in the 1984 Yellow Pages. BAPCO argues that its selection of a geographic area is not determined simply based on the scope of a white-page directory for the same community, but is instead selected based on BAPCO's evaluation of the shopping habits and desired shopping areas of consumers within a white-pages community. Donnelley responds that geographic scoping merely refers to BAPCO's decision about the geographic area for free distribution of copies of its 1984 Yellow Pages. Donnelley further asserts that BAPCO did not, in fact, limit advertisements in its directory to businesses in a particular area. Based on Bob Johnson's affidavit testimony that the 1984 Yellow Pages contains advertisements from 1,772 businesses in nearby cities and from 2,215 national businesses, the evidence supports Donnelley's assertion that BAPCO did not limit classified listings to only businesses in a certain geographic area....

The evidence before the district court also compels a conclusion that the geographic scoping of a classified directory is not an "obvious" act of selection. See *Feist*, __ U.S. at __, 111 S. Ct. at 1297, 113 L. Ed. 2d at 380 (describing a white-page publisher's selection of basic information—name, town, and telephone number — as "obvious" and lacking sufficient creativity to make it original). On this point, BAPCO presented "Donnelley Directory Publishing Start-Up Business Plan October 21, 1984," which discussed Donnelley's own geographic scoping decisions as being based on "extensive research [leading Donnelley] to scope differently from its competitors." See 6SR12-34, Volume IV — Appendix to Summary Memorandum of Bellsouth Advertising & Publishing Corporation, p.DM207045 (stating that Donnelley generally will scope to cover areas of two or more telco directories, and stating that "more logical scoping is intended to be a key selling point for [Donnelley]"). Therefore, even though Donnelley now argues that geographic scoping represents an obvious decision lacking a modicum of creativity, the evidence before the district court was uncontroverted that geographic scoping results from thoughtful analysis of research on shopping habits and analysis of how to distinguish one directory from its competitors. Such thoughtful selection is sufficient under *Feist* to contribute to the originality of the 1984 Yellow Pages. See *Feist*, __ U.S. at __, 111 S. Ct. at 1294, 113 L. Ed. 2d at 377 (explaining that "the originality requirement is not particularly stringent").

In sum, the record on this case demonstrates that BAPCO performed at least four original acts of selection and arrangement: (1) the selection of 7,000 classified headings; (2) the arrangement of 106,398 business listings, from 32,559 businesses under the 7,000 classified headings; (3) the selection of only businesses with business telephone service, as opposed to businesses having either business service or residential service; and (4) the selection of a geographic area to be covered comprehensively in the 1984 Yellow Pages. Accordingly, I would hold that BAPCO performed four acts of selection or arrangement which are sufficiently original to merit copyright protection. The analysis of BAPCO's infringement claim, however, does not end with a finding of originality. This court must next determine whether Donnelley copied those constituent elements of selection and arrangement which are copyrightable.

III. *Substantial Copying of BAPCO's Original Selection or Arrangement*

Because the copyright in a factual compilation is "thin," a plaintiff must prove "substantial similarity" between the defendant's compilation and the original elements of the plaintiff's compilation.... Based on the previous discussion identifying those elements of selection or arrangement that are copyrightable, BAPCO must prove that Donnelley substantially appropriated BAPCO's selection of classified headings, arrangement of business listings under classified headings, selection of only businesses with business telephone service, or selection of a geographic area to be covered comprehensively.

A proper analysis of whether Donnelley substantially appropriated BAPCO's original selection or arrangement requires this court to analyze separately each of the three acts of copying at issue in this case. The district court concluded that Donnelley engaged in the following three acts of copying: (1) hiring Appalachian Computer Services, Inc. (Appalachian), a data entry company in London, Kentucky, to key BAPCO's compilation into a computer database; (2) using the computer database to print out sales lead sheets that represented a reproduction of substantially the entire 1984 Yellow Pages in inverted or crisscross form; and (3) publishing the 1985 Miami North and 1985 Miami South directories based on the information copied into the computer database and onto the sales lead sheets. See *BellSouth*, 719 F. Supp. at 1558-59. Similarly, this court should evaluate each alleged act of copying separately.

A. *Computer Database*

Donnelley does not dispute that it obtained copies of the 1984 Yellow Pages, separated and mounted each sheet individually, and assigned a classified heading code, advertising code, and directory code for every business listing. It is also undisputed that Appalachian keyed the following information into a computer database: name, address, telephone number, code corresponding to a classified heading, code corresponding to the unit of advertising, and a code for the directory from which the listing came. Appalachian stored this information on magnetic tape and sent it to Donnelley for reproduction in the form of sales lead sheets. The only factual dispute concerning the creation of the computer database derives from Donnelley's assertion that Appalachian entered a code corresponding to a previously chosen Donnelley classified heading, as opposed to a code corresponding to the BAPCO heading directly next to each code....

Therefore, even resolving the alleged factual dispute regarding Appalachian's coding of headings in favor of Donnelley's version, Johnson's and Notestein's testimony makes it clear that Donnelley did not previously select a universe of headings for particular use in its Miami directories. Instead, Donnelley copied BAPCO's selection of headings with what can only be described as a high-tech copying process. Donnelley's high-tech copying involved Appalachian keying codes rather than the words of BAPCO headings into a database, from which the wording of the BAPCO headings could be reconstructed later using the Donnelley heading book as a decoder....

Although the keying of each code in isolation would amount to the lawful copying of facts, Appalachian's grouping of the business listing with an associated heading code and a directory code amounts to the appropriation of virtually all of BAPCO's original acts of selection and arrangement. That is, Donnelley copied BAPCO's selection of headings based on Appalachian's keying of a heading code, even if it corresponded to headings in Donnelley's own heading book, for virtually every heading used in the 1984 Yellow Pages. Donnelley copied BAPCO's arrangement of business listings under a particular classified heading based on Appalachian's grouping of the business listing data with a heading code that corresponded to a heading like or similar to BAPCO's. Donnelley copied BAPCO's selection of only businesses with business telephone service based on Appalachian's keying of every business listed in the 1984 Yellow Pages. In addition, Donnelley copied BAPCO's selection of a geographic area based on Appalachian's grouping of the business listing data and the code indicating the directory source.

Because the keyed information was stored in or on some material object until later printed on the sales lead sheets, Donnelley's creation of the computer database represents an act of "copying" as defined in the Copyright Act. See 17 U.S.C. § 101 (defining a copy as a material object "in which a work is fixed by any method now known or later developed, and from which the work can be perceived, reproduced, or otherwise communicated, either directly or with the aid of a machine or device"). Accordingly, I would hold that Donnelley's substantial appropriation of BAPCO's original acts of selection or arrangement in creating the computer database, represented an act of copyright infringement.

B. *Sales Lead Sheets*

Donnelley's substantial appropriation of BAPCO's original act of selection or arrangement is also apparent in the printed sales lead sheets.... Because it is uncontroverted that the sales lead sheets represented merely a printed version of the same information that Appalachian keyed into the computer database, the previous analysis of how Donnelley substantially appropriated BAPCO's original selection or arrangement in creating the database applies equally to its printing of the sales lead sheets. Hence, I would also hold that Donnelley's printing sales lead sheets using the information already copied into the computer database, represented a second act of copyright infringement....

C. *The Donnelley Directories*

... [N]one of the references in the district court's opinion provide a basis for this court to engage in side-by-side comparisons of all pages in the 1984 Yellow Pages with those in the 1985 Miami North and 1985 Miami South directories. It is only possible to conclude that the district court examined the pages of the directories that BAPCO attached to the Second Affidavit of Barbara J. Wiggs. Because Donnelley failed to present its own comparative analysis of pages from the actual directories and also failed to place physical copies of the directories in the record until January, 1993, this court is required to limit its determination on the substantial similarity of the directories to those pages attached to the Second Affidavit of Barbara J. Wiggs, and only to the extent of Wiggs's comparative analysis.

The district court relied on Wiggs's analysis of pages from the directories as support for the following conclusion: "Although Donnelley's directory is not identical to BAPCO's directory, the material was copied and used to produce a directory substantially similar in both content and format."... [T]he presence of the common errors in the published directories is [also] significant evidence that Donnelley substantially appropriated BAPCO's original arrangement of business listings under particular classified headings....

... Wiggs found a high (averaging seventy-five percent) statistical correlation of listings under particular headings when comparing the 1984 Yellow Pages with the Donnelley directories. Donnelley did not respond with its own correlation analysis, and thus, Wiggs's findings represent further undisputed evidence that Donnelley's published directories contain a substantially similar arrangement of business listings under particular classified headings....

I would affirm the district court's conclusion that Donnelley substantially appropriated BAPCO's original acts of selection and arrangement when publishing the 1985 Miami North and 1985 Miami South directories.

QUESTIONS

1. How should the following cases be decided? (What additional facts, if any, do you need to know in order to decide?) *See* J. Ginsburg, *No "Sweat"? Copyright and Other Protection of Works of Information After Feist v. Rural Telephone,* 92 Colum. L. Rev. 338 (1992); R. Gorman, *The Feist Case: Reflections on a Pathbreaking Copyright Decision,* 18 Rutgers Computer & Tech. L.J. 731 (1992).

(a) The plaintiff has written a book about protecting the assets of the elderly so that Medicaid can be used to cover the costs of nursing-home care. Because Medicaid rules vary from state to state, he has prepared tables, alphabetically organized by state, containing categories of information about the applicable rules for Medicaid eligibility. His tables are based upon the text and upon even more exhaustive tables found in a public-domain report prepared by a commission of state governors. The defendant has copied the plaintiff's tables in her book on the same subject matter. *See Budish v. Gordon,* 784 F. Supp. 1320 (N.D. Ohio 1992).

(b) The National Automobile Dealers Association publishes a well-known and frequently used compendium of prices for used automobiles and trucks. The NADA Guide purports to represent the trade-in or wholesale value and the retail value of some 7,200 models of used cars and trucks for the seven years preceding the publication year. The NADA staff collects sales information from auction houses, car dealers, and newspapers and periodicals, then combines statistical data, analysis of the economy, and market trends and conditions, and then factors in its own judgment to generate the final prices. The defendant publishes another guide that uses an altogether different tabular arrangement but that incorporates the dollar values for the cars and trucks as set forth in the NADA Guide. *See NADA Servs. Corp. v. CCC Info. Servs. Inc.,* 1991 WL 287961 (N.D. Ill. Nov. 15, 1991).

(c) The plaintiff, a publisher of a sports newspaper, compiles and publishes charts during the baseball season that set forth nine categories of past-performance statistics for the day's starting pitchers (e.g., their earned run average against the same opposing team at the same site previously that season), to assist the reader in making judgments about the likely outcome of scheduled baseball games. There are, of course, a large possible number of such categories of pitching information; of the plaintiff's nine, three such categories have been commonly incorporated in widely published baseball statistical charts. The defendant reproduced the plaintiff's charts in its own newspaper. (Would it matter if the defendant copied only six of the plaintiff's categories, and which six were copied? Would it matter if the plaintiff suggested assigning various weights to each of the nine categories so as to permit a near-scientific prediction of the likely winner of the games?) *See Kregos v. Associated Press,* 937 F.2d 700 (2d Cir. 1991).

(d) The plaintiff compiled a reference guidebook of information designed for companies that own and operate pay telephones. Of its 160 pages, 51 (one for each state and one for the District of Columbia) summarized state tariffs regulating the fees payable to telephone utilities; the plaintiff employed several attorneys to comb the state tariffs and "collapse" them into a simple and readable format. The defendant has copied the 51 pages into its own book on the same subject. *See U.S. Payphone, Inc. v. Executives Unlimited,* 18 U.S.P.Q.2d 2049 (4th Cir. 1991).

(e) A law school publishes an alumni directory containing three parts. In the first, the names of alumni (along with their home and business addresses and telephone numbers) are organized alphabetically; in the second, they are organized by graduating classes (and alphabetically within those); and, in the third, they are organized by city and state (and alphabetically within those). You have been asked whether the directory is copyrightable. Are there any additional elements of "authorship" that the law school might contribute in order to provide greater assurance of copyrightability?

(f) The Dow Jones Industrial Index. This index is based upon 30 selected stocks, representing a variety of major business corporations, whose collective performance, in the belief of the compilers of the Index, affords a good indication of stock market trends. *See Dow Jones & Co. v. Board of Trade,* 546 F. Supp. 113 (S.D.N.Y. 1982).

(g) The text of an advertisement with these phrases (in different size and type of print): "Why are we giving away SOLEX Electric Toothbrush Sets for Only $3?" "This is NOT a misprint." "Hard to believe, but true." The defendant uses the same format and text for its own product advertisements, but gives a different product description, price, picture, and mailing directions. *See Raffoler, Ltd. v. Peabody & Wright, Ltd.,* 671 F. Supp. 947 (E.D.N.Y. 1987). Would protection for such an advertisement be compatible with the decisions in *Magic Marketing* and *Bibbero, supra* pp. 86 and 104?

2. Some manufacturers of phonograph records have concluded that the uninterrupted radio play of an entire record album (or record side) is an invitation to unauthorized home tape recording, which substitutes for the purchase of the album itself. As will be discussed below, at Chapter 6, Subchapter D5c, the typical radio broadcast of a single musical composition is not a copyright infringement, either of the composition (which is typically covered by a license granted by a performing rights society, such as ASCAP or BMI) or of the recorded performance (which is not protected against unauthorized playing). The record manufacturers mentioned above have argued that their *sequencing* of recorded performances on a phonograph record constitutes a separate copyrightable compilation, the public performance of which on the radio, without authorization from the manufacturer, is an infringement under § 106(4). Does the selection and sequencing of the songs on a long-playing album amount to "originality" and "authorship," and does the end-product constitute a "compilation"?

WEST PUBLISHING CO. v. MEAD DATA CENTRAL, INC.

799 F.2d 1219 (8th Cir. 1986), *cert. denied,* 479 U.S. 1070 (1987)

Arnold, Circuit Judge.

Mead Data Central, Inc. (MDC) appeals from a preliminary injunction issued by the District Court for the District of Minnesota in a copyright-infringement action brought by West Publishing Company (West). West's claim is based upon MDC's proposed introduction of "star pagination," keyed to

West's case reports, into the LEXIS system of computer-assisted legal research.

For more than a century, West has been compiling and reporting opinions of state and federal courts. West publishes these opinions in a series of books known as the "National Reporter System." Before it publishes an opinion, West checks the accuracy of case and statutory citations in the opinion and adds parallel citations, prepares headnotes and a synopsis for the opinion, and arranges the opinion in West's style and format. West then assigns its report of each opinion to one of the individual series in the National Reporter System, such as *Federal Reporter, Second Series* or *Bankruptcy Reporter;* this assignment is based on the court and/or the subject matter of the opinion. Next, West assigns the case to a volume in the series, further categorizes and arranges the cases within the volume, and prepares additional materials, such as indices and tables of cases, for each volume. Volumes and pages are numbered sequentially to facilitate precise reference to West reports; citing the proper volume number, series name, and page number communicates the exact location of a West report, or a portion thereof, within the National Reporter System. West represents that upon completion of each volume, it registers a copyright claim with the Register of Copyrights and receives a Certificate of Registration for the volume.

MDC developed, owns, and operates LEXIS, a computer-assisted, on-line legal-research service first marketed in 1973. LEXIS, like West's National Reporter System, reports the decisions of state and federal courts. Since LEXIS's inception, MDC has included on the first computer screen of each LEXIS case report the citation to the first page of West's report of the opinion. West concedes that citation to the first page of its report is a noninfringing "fair use" under 17 U.S.C. § 107, so these citations are not at issue here.

On June 24, 1985, MDC announced that it planned to add "star pagination" to the text of opinions stored in the LEXIS database. This new service, named the LEXIS Star Pagination Feature, was to be available to LEXIS users by September or October of 1985. This feature would insert page numbers from West's National Reporter System publications into the body of LEXIS reports, providing "jump" or "pinpoint" citations to the location in West's reporter of the material viewed on LEXIS. Thus, with the LEXIS Star Pagination Feature, LEXIS users would be able to determine the West page number corresponding to the portion of an opinion viewed on LEXIS without ever physically referring to the West publication in which the opinion appears.

In response to MDC's announcement, West brought this action, claiming, *inter alia,* that the LEXIS Star Pagination Feature is an appropriation of West's comprehensive arrangement of case reports in violation of the Copyright Act of 1976, 17 U.S.C. §§ 101-810. West sought, and was granted, a preliminary injunction. *West Publishing Co. v. Mead Data Central, Inc.,* 616 F. Supp. 1571 (D. Minn. 1985). The District Court held that there is a substantial likelihood that West's arrangements of case reports are protected by copyright law, that MDC's copying of West's pagination constitutes copyright infringement, and that MDC's star pagination is not a fair use of West's copyrighted works. 616 F. Supp. at 1575-1581. The Court further held that the balance of the harms to West and to MDC involved in granting or denying a preliminary injunction weighed in favor of granting an injunction, and that the public interest also favored preliminary injunctive relief. 616 F. Supp. 1581-1583. We affirm.

ANALYSIS

....

I

MDC's principal contention here is that there is no likelihood that West will succeed on the merits of its copyright claim. MDC readily concedes that portions of West's National Reporter System publications that are not at issue here, such as headnotes prepared by West, merit copyright protection.[2] Yet, MDC maintains that any aspects of West's reporters affected by the LEXIS Star Pagination Feature are not copyrightable. The dominant chord of MDC's argument is that West claims copyright in mere page numbers. MDC adds that in any event, whether West claims copyright in its case arrangement or simply in its pagination, West's claim must fail because neither case arrangement nor pagination can ever qualify as the original work of an author. Even were this possible, MDC goes on, West's case arrangement and pagination do not in fact meet this standard. Finally, MDC contends that even were West's arrangement of cases protected by copyright, the proposed use of West's page numbers in LEXIS reports would not constitute infringement.

We do not agree with MDC that West's claim here is simply one for copyright in its page numbers. Instead, we concur in the District Court's conclusion that West's arrangement is a copyrightable aspect of its compilation of cases, that the pagination of West's volumes reflects and expresses West's arrangement, and that MDC's intended use of West's page numbers infringes West's copyright in the arrangement.

A. Copyright Protection

The Copyright Act provides copyright protection for "original works of authorship fixed in any tangible medium of expression." 17 U.S.C. § 102(a). The standard for "originality" is minimal. It is not necessary that the work be novel or unique, but only that the work have its origin with the author — that it be independently created. *Hutchinson Telephone Co. v. Fronteer Directory Co.,* 770 F.2d 128, 131 (8th Cir. 1985). Little more is involved in this requirement than "a prohibition of actual copying." *Alfred Bell & Co. v. Catalda Fine Arts,* 191 F.2d 99, 102-103 (2d Cir. 1951); *see also* M. Nimmer, 1 Nimmer on Copyright § 2.01 (1985).

....

MDC argues that case arrangement is *per se* uncopyrightable because it cannot meet these standards. However, it is apparent on the face of the Copyright Act that it is possible for an arrangement of pre-existing materials to be an independently produced work of intellectual creation. Section 103 of the

---

[2]West does not and could not claim any copyright in the judicial opinions themselves. *See Wheaton v. Peters,* 8 Pet. 591, 668, 33 U.S. 591, 8 L. Ed. 1055 (1834) ("no reporter ... can have any copyright in the written opinions delivered by this court").

Act, 17 U.S.C. § 103, establishes that "the subject matter of copyright ... includes compilations and derivative works." A "compilation" is defined in the Act as

> a work formed by the collection and assembling of preexisting materials or of data that are selected, coordinated, or arranged in such a way that the resulting work as a whole constitutes an original work of authorship.

17 U.S.C. § 101. An arrangement of opinions in a case reporter, no less than a compilation and arrangement of Shakespeare's sonnets, can qualify for copyright protection.

We find support for this view in *Callaghan v. Myers,* 128 U.S. 617, 9 S. Ct. 177, 32 L. Ed. 547 (1888), which indicates that an original arrangement of opinions is copyrightable whenever it is the product of labor, talent or judgment....

As MDC points out, the treatment of case arrangement and pagination in *Callaghan* was not crucial to the Court's decision, since the defendants had also made use of other portions of Myers' volumes, such as headnotes and statements of facts. Nonetheless, we find *Callaghan*'s discussion of the copyrightability of case arrangements instructive. The Supreme Court noted that while the reporter could claim no copyright in the opinions themselves, 128 U.S. at 649, 9 S. Ct. at 185, *citing Wheaton v. Peters,* 8 Pet. 591, 668, 33 U.S. 591, 668, 8 L. Ed. 1055 (1834), he could copyright other portions of his reports. Mr. Justice Blatchford wrote that, in addition to headnotes, statements of facts, arguments of counsel, case tables, and indices,

> [s]uch work of the reporter, which may be the lawful subject of copyright, comprehends ... the order of arrangement of the cases, the division of the reports into volumes, the numbering *and paging* of the volumes, the table of the cases cited in the opinions, (where such table is made,) and the subdivision of the index into appropriate, condensed titles, involving the distribution of the subjects of the various head-notes, and cross-references, where such exist.

Callaghan, 128 U.S at 649, 9 S. Ct. at 185 (emphasis ours).

Later in its opinion, however, when considering several volumes that Myers claimed the defendants had infringed by copying their case arrangement and pagination, the Court quoted with approval the opinion of the Circuit Court, which stated:

> Undoubtedly, in some cases, where are involved labor, talent, judgment, the classification and disposition of subjects in a book entitle it to a copyright. But the arrangement of law cases and the paging of the book may depend simply on the will of the printer, of the reporter, or publisher, or the order in which the cases have been decided, or upon other accidental circumstances.

128 U.S. at 662, 9 S. Ct. at 190 .... The teaching of *Callaghan* with respect to the issues before us does not come through with unmistakable clarity. But as we read it, *Callaghan* establishes at least that there is no *per se* rule excluding case arrangement from copyright protection, and that instead, in each case

the arrangement must be evaluated in light of the originality and intellectual-creation standards.

For the proposition that case arrangement and pagination cannot, as a
matter of law, meet originality and intellectual-creation requirements, MDC
relies heavily upon *Banks Law Publishing Co. v. Lawyer's Co-Operative Publishing Co.,* 169 Fed. 386 (2d Cir. 1909) (per curiam), *appeal dismissed by
stipulation,* 223 U.S. 738, 32 S. Ct. 530, 56 L. Ed. 636 (1911). The plaintiff in
Banks was the successor to the copyrights of an official reporter of the United
States Supreme Court in published volumes of opinions compiled by the reporter. The defendant published a competing edition of the Supreme Court's
decisions. The plaintiff claimed copyright infringement based on the defendant's reproduction of the plaintiff's arrangement of cases and on the defendant's star pagination to the plaintiff's reports. The trial court rejected the
plaintiff's claim that its case arrangement and pagination merited copyright
protection; the Second Circuit, in a per curiam opinion, reproduced the trial
court's opinion in full, adopting the opinion as its own.

In our view, *Banks* does not support MDC's claim that case arrangement is
uncopyrightable *per se;* we agree with the District Court that instead, the
denial of copyright protection in *Banks* was based upon the official status of
the reporter ....

... We conclude that the ultimate rationale for the *Banks* decision was that
while under *Callaghan* the official reporter could copyright any material that
was the product of his intellectual labor, because the reporter's statutory
duties required case arrangement and pagination, these should not be considered the product of the reporter's intellectual labor.

....

MDC argues, citing, e.g., Order of June 7, 1978, Minnesota Supreme Court
(unreported), that West is the "official reporter" for some states, and that,
therefore, even a narrow reading of *Banks* supports its position. We are inclined to think that the term "official reporter" in orders discontinuing, for
example, the *Minnesota Reports,* and providing that the *Northwestern Reporter* should henceforth be the "official reporter" for the opinions of the Supreme Court of Minnesota, means something quite different from the title
"official reporter" held by Messrs. Wheaton and Peters. We do not believe that
West is employed by any State, with a salary and duties fixed by statute, and
with the details of its work controlled by statute or rule. But even if it is, the
facts of this case, as found on the present record by the District Court, convince us that West has used sufficient talent and industry in compiling and
arranging cases to entitle it to copyright protection under the 1976 Act as
construed by the more recent cases.

Having determined that there is no *per se* rule that case arrangements are
not copyrightable, we turn to examine the District Court's findings that
West's arrangements in fact meet originality and intellectual-creation requirements.

West publishes opinions not from just one court, but from every state and
all the federal courts in the United States. As it collects these opinions, West
separates the decisions of state courts from federal-court decisions. West further divides the federal opinions and the state opinions and then assigns them

to the appropriate West reporter series. State court decisions are divided by geographic region and assigned to West's corresponding regional reporter. Federal decisions are first divided by the level of the court they come from into district court decisions, court of appeals decisions, and Supreme Court decisions; Court of Claims and military court decisions are also separated out. Before being assigned to a reporter, district court decisions are subdivided according to subject matter into bankruptcy decisions, federal rules decisions, and decisions on other topics. After an opinion is assigned to a reporter, it is assigned to a volume of the reporter and then arranged within the volume. Federal court of appeals decisions, for example, are arranged according to circuit within each volume of West's *Federal Reporter, Second Series*, though there may be more than one group of each circuit's opinions in each volume.

We conclude, as did the District Court, that the arrangement West produces through this process is the result of considerable labor, talent, and judgment. As discussed above, *supra* pp. 1223-1224, to meet intellectual-creation requirements a work need only be the product of a modicum of intellectual labor; West's case arrangements easily meet this standard. Further, since there is no allegation that West copies its case arrangements from some other source, the requirement of originality poses no obstacle to copyrighting the arrangements. In the end, MDC's position must stand or fall on its insistence that all West seeks to protect is numbers on pages. If this is a correct characterization, MDC wins: two always comes after one, and no one can copyright the mere sequence of Arabic numbers. As MDC points out, the specific goal of this suit is to protect some of West's page numbers, those occurring within the body of individual court opinions. But protection for the numbers is not sought for their own sake. It is sought, rather, because access to these particular numbers — the "jump cites" — would give users of LEXIS a large part of what West has spent so much labor and industry in compiling, and would *pro tanto* reduce anyone's need to buy West's books. The key to this case, then, is not whether numbers are copyrightable, but whether the copyright on the books as a whole is infringed by the unauthorized appropriation of these particular numbers. On the record before us (and subject to reconsideration if materially new evidence comes in at the plenary trial on the merits), the District Court's findings of fact relevant to this issue are supportable. We therefore hold (again subject to reexamination after the record has closed) that West's case arrangements, an important part of which is internal page citations, are original works of authorship entitled to copyright protection.

B. Infringement

We further hold (with a similar qualification) that MDC's proposed use of West page numbers will infringe West's copyright in the arrangement. The LEXIS Star Pagination Feature, when used in conjunction with another LEXIS feature called "LEXSEE," will permit LEXIS users to view the arrangement of cases in every volume of West's National Reporter System. LEXSEE enables the LEXIS user to have his or her terminal display a case by "inputting" the citation to the first page of West's report of the case. With the LEXIS Star Pagination Feature, a LEXIS user could summon up the first case in a West Volume, page through it until he or she reaches the end of the case, and discern from the "jump cite" for the final page of the case the citation for the first page of the next case in the volume. The LEXIS user could then use LEXSEE to call up the next case. By repeating this procedure, the LEXIS user would be able to page through each succeeding case in the West reporter. MDC conceded at oral argument that this operation would be possible, but argued that LEXIS users would be unlikely to perform it because of the cost involved in doing repeated LEXSEE searches. However, MDC has cited no authority, nor do we see any persuasive argument, for the proposition that because consumers may find an infringing work uneconomical, the work is not an infringement. An author's rights in a copyrighted work protect the author not only against infringing works less expensive than the original, but against more expensive infringements as well. Further, though this use of LEXIS may presently be uneconomical, changes in technology and other market conditions could well alter the situation.

Even if the LEXIS Star Pagination Feature did not make it possible to use LEXIS to page through cases as they are arranged in West volumes, we would still hold that MDC's use of West's page numbers infringes West's copyright in the arrangement. Jump cites to West volumes within a case on LEXIS are infringing because they enable LEXIS users to discern the precise location in West's arrangement of the portion of the opinion being viewed....

With MDC's star pagination, consumers would no longer need to purchase West's reporters to get every aspect of West's arrangement. Since knowledge of the location of opinions and parts of opinions within West's arrangement is a large part of the reason one would purchase West's volumes, the LEXIS star pagination feature would adversely affect West's market position. "[A] use that supplants any part of the normal market for a copyrighted work would ordinarily be considered an infringement." S. Rep. No. 473, 94th Cong., 1st Sess. 65 (1975), *quoted in Harper & Row Publishers v. Nation Enterprises,* 471 U.S. 539, 105 S. Ct. 2218, 2235, 85 L. Ed. 2d 588 (1985).

MDC asserts that enjoining its use of West page numbers is tantamount to giving West a copyright in the Arabic numbering system. West cannot, MDC argues, claim that its use of the numbering system is an original work of authorship. It is true that some uses of a numbering system cannot meet originality requirements for copyright. *See Toro Co. v. R & R Products Co.,* 787 F.2d 1208 (8th Cir. 1986) (arbitrary assignment of random numbers to replacement parts did not qualify for copyright protection). However, as already noted, the copyright we recognize here is in West's arrangement, not in its numbering system; MDC's use of West's page numbers is problematic because it infringes West's copyrighted arrangement, not because the numbers themselves are copyrighted.

MDC also argues that the LEXIS Star Pagination Feature does not infringe West's copyright because its citations to page numbers in West reporters are merely statements of pure fact. The flaw in this argument is that it does not distinguish between isolated use of the factual aspects of a compilation or arrangement and wholesale appropriation of the arrangement. "Isolated instances of minor infringements, when multiplied many times, become in the aggregate a major inroad on copyright that must be prevented." S. Rep. No.

473, 94th Cong., 1st Sess. 65 (1975), *quoted in Harper & Row,* 105 S. Ct. at 2235. The names, addresses, and phone numbers in a telephone directory are "facts"; though isolated use of these facts is not copyright infringement, copying each and every listing is an infringement. See *Hutchinson Telephone v. Fronteer Directory,* 770 F.2d 128 (8th Cir. 1985). Similarly, MDC's wholesale appropriation of West's arrangement and pagination for a competitive, commercial purpose is an infringement.[3]

We hold that West's arrangement of cases in its National Reporter System publications is entitled to copyright protection and that the LEXIS Star Pagination Feature infringes West's copyright in the arrangement. On the basis of the present record, it is probable that West will succeed on the merits at trial.

II

MDC also contends that the District Court did not accurately assess and weigh the three remaining *Dataphase* factors: the threat of irreparable harm to West, the relative harm to MDC, and the public interest. We disagree.

....

We conclude that the District Court correctly assessed the various *Dataphase* factors and that it did not abuse its discretion in determining that the balance of equities in this case favors issuing a preliminary injunction.

....

[In dissent, Judge Oliver contended that West had not demonstrated any "originality." To him, the record disclosed no evidence that West's "arrangement" resulted from anything other than random receipt of decisions from the various courts on which West reports.]

Toro Co. v. R & R Products Co., 787 F.2d 1208 (8th Cir. 1986). Plaintiff manufactures and sells lawn-care equipment, as well as replacement parts to which it assigns hyphenated five- or six-digit numbers for reference and reordering purposes. The defendant manufactures replacement parts designed to fit a number of brands of lawn-care machines, plaintiff's among them; because it can limit its production to the most frequently needed parts, the defendant's prices are significantly lower than those charged by the original manufacturers. The defendant's principal sales tool is a catalog which contains illustrations of machinery and parts, as well as lists of various original manufacturers' replacement parts indexed according to the original manufacturer part name and number. Thus, for Toro replacement parts, the defendant's catalog

---

[3]In the District Court MDC also argued that its star pagination, like its citation to the first page of West's report of a case, is "fair use" of copyrighted material under 17 U.S.C. § 107. The District Court rejected this contention, noting that MDC's use is commercial, that MDC is appropriating the whole of West's arrangement, and that MDC's use will supersede a substantial use of West's volumes. 616 F. Supp. at 1580-1581. *See Sony Corp. of America v. University City Studios, Inc.,* 464 U.S. 417, 451, 104 S. Ct. 774, 793, 78 L. Ed. 2d 574 (1984); *Harper & Row,* 105 S. Ct. at 2226, 2235. MDC did not raise this issue in its brief or its argument on appeal, and we find the reasoning of the District Court persuasive.

lists the Toro part numbers, the defendant's corresponding part numbers (which are identical to the Toro numbers but are preceded with the letter R), and the defendant's prices. Plaintiff brought an action, among other things, for copyright infringement of its parts-numbers.

The district court dismissed this claim, holding that Toro's numbering system fell outside the protection of copyright by virtue of § 102(b). The court of appeals affirmed, but relied on different reasons. Although § 102(b) might prevent the plaintiff from copyrighting the idea of using numbers to designate replacement parts, that section would not in itself preclude protection for the plaintiff's particular expression of that idea. That particular expression, however, was found by the court of appeals not to be an original work of authorship. The plaintiff arbitrarily assigned its five- or six-digit numbers to particular parts in a random fashion. "There was no evidence that a particular series or configuration of numbers denoted a certain type or category of parts or that the numbers used encoded any kind of information at all. In short, numbers were assigned to a part without rhyme or reason." The "public domain numbers" showed no variation "other than the trivial hyphen," and exhibited no "effort or judgment" in their selection or composition. The plaintiff "simply has not added enough to its parts numbers to make them original and remove them from the public domain." The court distinguished the telephone directory cases, in which the plaintiffs — by gathering, collating and updating data — create an original work.

QUESTIONS

1. What does the court believe to be original about West's arrangement of cases? Is it the allocation of categories of cases among different reporter series? Is it the sequencing of cases within reporter volumes? Are these sufficiently original to warrant copyright protection, individually or in combination? (The student might examine a West advance sheet or bound volume, perhaps of the *Federal Second Reporter* or *Federal Supplement*. Is the sequencing principle discernible, and is it original under the law of copyright?) How are your answers to these questions affected, if at all, by the Supreme Court decision in the *Feist* case?

2. Should originality regarding the arrangement of cases in the West reporters turn — as urged by the defendant, but rejected by the court — on whether the West Publishing Company is the "official reporter" in some states? Might this factor be more relevant on the issue whether, even if West's compilations are copyrightable, Mead ought to be permitted by law to reproduce the arrangement in copies? (Consider this question again after studying the materials on fair use.)

3. If Mead had photocopied West's reporters — while eliminating from the photocopy all text copyrightable by West (such as the headnotes, syllabi, tables, etc.) — and had marketed the resulting volume, would Mead infringe West's copyright? Should the outcome be different when Mead, by star pagination in its computer data base, enables a LEXIS subscriber to generate a similar hard copy printout or screen display?

4. Is the *Toro* decision, rendered by the same court the previous year, so easily distinguishable? In any event, is the *Toro* decision sound to the extent it bases authorship on the subjective process of generating parts numbers? Is there any way that a person preparing a parts catalog can prevent others from copying its parts numbers?

5. Would copyright protection in the *Toro* case unfairly inhibit competition in the marketing of replacement parts? Does copyright protection for West unfairly inhibit competition in the development of computerized legal research services? (Which company *is* dominant in the pertinent market?) Is not any such inhibition necessarily contemplated whenever copyright is afforded?

6. If West is claiming copyright protection for its compilation and sequencing of cases, is that not already replicated by Mead when the full citation referring to the first page of the opinion is incorporated in the LEXIS data base? Why, as a practical matter, does West not complain about LEXIS reference to the first page of the case, but only about reference to the so-called jump pages that follow? How, analytically, can it justify such a distinction?

MASON v. MONTGOMERY DATA, INC.

967 F.2d 135 (5th Cir. 1992)

REAVLEY, CIRCUIT JUDGE:

Hodge E. Mason, Hodge Mason Maps, Inc., and Hodge Mason Engineers, Inc. (collectively Mason) sued Montgomery Data, Inc. (MDI), Landata, Inc. of Houston (Landata), and Conroe Title & Abstract Co. (Conroe Title), claiming that the defendants infringed Mason's copyrights on 233 real estate ownership maps of Montgomery County, Texas. The district court initially held that Mason cannot recover statutory damages or attorney's fees for any infringement of 232 of the copyrights. The court later held that Mason's maps are not copyrightable under the idea/expression merger doctrine, and granted summary judgment for the defendants. We agree with Mason that the maps are copyrightable, so we reverse the district court's judgment and remand the case. But we agree with the district court that, if Mason proves that the defendants infringed his copyrights, he can only recover statutory damages and attorney's fees for the infringements of one of the 233 maps.

I. BACKGROUND

Between August 1967 and July 1969, Mason created and published 118 real estate ownership maps that, together, cover all of Montgomery County. The maps, which display copyright notices, pictorially portray the location, size, and shape of surveys, land grants, tracts, and various topographical features within the county. Numbers and words on the maps identify deeds, abstract numbers, acreage, and the owners of the various tracts. Mason obtained the information that he included on the maps from a variety of sources.[3] Relying

---

[3]These sources included tax, deed, and survey records from Montgomery County; data provided by the San Jacinto River Authority; survey records, maps, and abstracts

on these sources, Mason initially determined the location and dimensions of each survey in the county, and then drew the corners and lines of the surveys onto topographical maps of the county that were published by the United States Geological Survey (USGS).[4] He then determined the location of the property lines of the real estate tracts within each survey and drew them on the USGS maps. Finally, Mason traced the survey and tract lines onto transparent overlays, enlarged clean USGS maps and the overlays, added names and other information to the overlays, and combined the maps and overlays to print the final maps. Mason testified that he used substantial judgment and discretion to reconcile inconsistencies among the various sources, to select which features to include in the final map sheets, and to portray the information in a manner that would be useful to the public. From 1970 to 1980, Mason revised the original maps and eventually published 115 new maps with copyright notices, for a total of 233 maps. Mason sold copies of his maps individually and in sets.

Mason's infringement claims are based on the defendants' use of his maps as part of a geographical indexing system that Landata created to continuously organize and store ever-changing title information on each tract in Montgomery County. [Landata used Mason's maps, in a re-configured format, to prepare its own overlays and other copies, on which it recorded continuously updated information about land grants; it keyed these copies to landtitle data that it stored in its computers. Landata, by contractual arrangements with a company known as MDI, made these copies and data available to several title-insurance companies, which had jointly incorporated MDI. Landata had asked Mason for permission to use his maps as part of its system, but when Mason denied the request because Landata refused to pay a licensing fee, Landata used the Mason maps anyway. Landata prepared updated overlays and copies, using the Mason maps, between 1982 and 1989.]

[Mason registered the copyright for one of the original 118 maps in October 1968. After learning of Landata's use of his maps, Mason registered the copyrights for the remaining 117 original maps and the 115 revised maps between October and December 1987. On motions for summary judgment, the district court dismissed Mason's claims, finding that his maps were uncopyrightable, because the "idea" embodied in them was inseparable from the maps' "expression" of that idea.]

---

of land titles from the Texas General Land Office; title data and subdivision information provided by Conroe Title; a map from the City of Conroe, Texas; and maps from the United States Coast and Geodetic Survey.

[4]The USGS has mapped much of the United States, including Montgomery County. Most private mapmakers, like Mason, use USGS topographical maps as starting points for their own maps. *See* David B. Wolf, *Is There Any Copyright Protection for Maps after Feist?*, 39 J. Copyright Soc'y USA 224, 226 (1992).

II. DISCUSSION

A. *The Copyrightability of Mason's Maps*

1. *The Idea/Expression Merger Doctrine*

The Copyright Act extends copyright protection to "original works of authorship fixed in any tangible medium of expression." 17 U.S.C. § 102(a). The scope of that protection, however, is not unlimited. "In no case does copyright protection for an original work of authorship extend to any *idea*, ... regardless of the form in which it is described, explained, illustrated, or embodied in such work." *Id.* § 102(b) (emphasis added). Thus, while a copyright bars others from copying an author's original expression of an idea, it does not bar them from using the idea itself. "Others are free to utilize the 'idea' so long as they do not plagiarize its 'expression.'" *Herbert Rosenthal Jewelry Corp. v. Kalpakian*, 446 F.2d 738, 741 (9th Cir. 1971). In some cases, however, it is so difficult to distinguish between an idea and its expression that the two are said to merge. Thus, when there is essentially only one way to express an idea, "copying the 'expression' will not be barred, since protecting the 'expression' in such circumstances would confer a monopoly of the 'idea' upon the copyright owner free of the conditions and limitations imposed by the patent law." *Id.* at 742. By denying protection to an expression that is merged with its underlying idea, we "prevent an author from monopolizing an idea merely by copyrighting a few expressions of it." *Toro Co. v. R & R Products Co.*, 787 F.2d 1208, 1212 (8th Cir. 1986).[5]

The district court applied these principles to the present case and concluded that "the problem with the Hodge Mason maps is ... that [they] express the only pictorial presentation which could result from a correct interpretation of the legal description and other factual information relied upon by the plaintiffs in producing the maps." *Mason*, 765 F. Supp. at 355.... The court thus concluded that "the plaintiffs' idea to create the maps, based on legal and factual public information, is inseparable from its expression embodied within the maps, and hence not subject to copyright protection." *Id.*

We agree with Mason that the district court erred in applying the merger doctrine in this case. To determine whether the doctrine is applicable in any case, the court must "focus on whether the idea is capable of various modes of expression." *Apple Computer*, 714 F.2d at 1253. Thus, the court must first identify the idea that the work expresses, and then attempt to distinguish that idea from the author's expression of it. If the court concludes that the idea

---

[5]Mason argues that application of the merger doctrine does not render a work uncopyrightable, but rather prevents a finding of infringement of an otherwise copyrightable work. See *Kregos v. Associated Press*, 937 F.2d 700, 705 (2d Cir. 1991) (Second Circuit "has considered this so-called 'merger' doctrine in determining whether actionable infringement has occurred, rather than whether a copyright is valid"). But this court has applied the merger doctrine to the question of copyrightability. See *Kern River Gas Transmission Co. v. Coastal Corp.*, 899 F.2d 1458, 1460 (5th Cir.) (because the idea and its expression embodied in plaintiff's maps are inseparable, "the maps at issue are not copyrightable"), *cert. denied*, __ U.S. __, 111 S. Ct. 374, 112 L. Ed. 2d 336 (1990). In any event, because we find the merger doctrine inapplicable in this case, the effect of its application is irrelevant.

and its expression are inseparable, then the merger doctrine applies and the expression will not be protected. Conversely, if the court can distinguish the idea from its expression, then the expression will be protected because the fact that one author has copyrighted one expression of that idea will not prevent other authors from creating and copyrighting their own expressions of the same idea. In all cases, "[t]he guiding consideration in drawing the line is the preservation of the balance between competition and protection reflected in the patent and copyright laws." *Herbert Rosenthal Jewelry,* 446 F.2d at 742.

The district court determined that Mason's idea, "which includes drawing the abstract and tract boundaries, indicating the ownership name, the tract size, and the other factual information" on a map of Montgomery County, was "to create the maps, based on legal and factual public information." *Mason,* 765 F. Supp. at 356. Mason argues that the court clearly erred in finding that this idea can be expressed in only one or a limited number of ways. We agree. The record in this case contains copies of maps created by Mason's competitors that prove beyond dispute that the idea embodied in Mason's maps is capable of a variety of expressions. Although the competitors' maps and Mason's maps embody the same idea, they differ in the placement, size, and dimensions of numerous surveys, tracts, and other features. The record also contains affidavits in which licensed surveyors and experienced mapmakers explain that the differences between Mason's maps and those of his competitors are the natural result of each mapmaker's selection of sources, interpretation of those sources, discretion in reconciling inconsistencies among the sources, and skill and judgment in depicting the information.[6]

MDI argues that this evidence is irrelevant because there is no proof that Mason and his competitors obtained their information from the same sources. But the fact that different mapmakers with the same idea could reach different conclusions by relying on different sources only supports our result. Whether Mason and his competitors relied on different sources, or interpreted the same sources and resolved inconsistencies among them differently, or

---

[6] One of the experts, Pliny M. Gale, examined Mason's maps and the competitors' maps and concluded that: the assembly, graphic representation, and positioning of various records and features involves considerable skill, judgment and originality.... The differences I note between the Mason maps and the other maps which I have examined are to be expected because of the numerous interpretations of records, individual judgments, and map base selection which must be taken into account when producing an ownership map based on a large number of instruments spanning over 100 years of development.... In my inspection of the maps, I found that the Mason map includes many features which are unique to the graphic representations selected by Mason, and which do not appear in any public record information. Gale Aff. at 2-4. Another mapmaker, Milton R. Hanks, stated: In compiling a map as detailed and complex as the Mason maps of Montgomery County, the mapmaker will necessarily make many individual judgments in placing various features from various sets of records onto a single map.... When the Mason map is overlaid with the Tobin map at the same scale ..., many differences in placement of various features and surveys are readily observed. The differences between the two maps are exactly the sort of differences that I would expect to observe between two independently produced maps based on the same ancient records. The reason for the differences is that a large number of independent judgments must be made in any large-scale mapping project of this type. Hanks Aff. at 2, 5.

made different judgments as to how to best depict the information from those sources, the differences in their maps confirm the fact that the idea embodied in Mason's maps can be expressed in a variety of ways. By selecting different sources, or by resolving inconsistencies among the same sources differently, or by coordinating, arranging, or even drawing the information differently, other mapmakers may create — and indeed have created — expressions of Mason's idea that differ from those that Mason created.

. . . .

We focus in this case on an earlier point in the mapping process, a point prior to the selection of information and decisions where to locate tract lines. The idea here was to bring together the available information on boundaries, landmarks, and ownership, and to choose locations and an effective pictorial expression of those locations. That idea and its final expression are separated by Mason's efforts and creativity that are entitled to protection from competitors. . . . Extending protection to that expression will not grant Mason a monopoly over the idea, because other mapmakers can express the same idea differently. The protection that each map receives extends only to its original expression, and neither the facts nor the idea embodied in the maps is protected. "[T]he facts and ideas . . . are free for the taking. . . . [T]he very same facts and ideas may be divorced from the context imposed by the author, and restated or reshuffled by second comers, even if the author was the first to discover the facts or to propose the ideas." *Feist*, 111 S. Ct. at 1289 (quoting Jane C. Ginsburg, *Creation and Commercial Value: Copyright Protection of Works of Information*, 90 Colum. L. Rev. 1865, 1868 (1990)).

For these reasons, we conclude that the district court erred by applying the merger doctrine in this case. Because the idea embodied in Mason's maps can be expressed in a variety of ways, the merger doctrine does not render Mason's expression of that idea uncopyrightable.

2. The "Originality" Requirement

Landata contends that, even if the merger doctrine does not apply, Mason's maps are uncopyrightable because they are not "original" under *Feist*. Although the district court applied the merger doctrine to hold that Mason's maps are not copyrightable, it found that "the problem with the Hodge Mason maps is not a lack of originality." *Mason*, 765 F. Supp. at 355. We agree that Mason's maps are original. Originality does not require "novelty, ingenuity, or aesthetic merit." H.R. Rep. No. 1476, 94th Cong., 2d Sess. 51 (1976), reprinted in 1976 U.S.C.C.A.N. 5659, 5664; *see also Feist*, 111 S. Ct. at 1287. Instead, originality "means only that the work was independently created by the author (as opposed to copied from other works), and that it possesses at least some minimal degree of creativity." *Feist*, 111 S. Ct. at 1287 (citing 1 M. Nimmer & D. Nimmer, Copyright § 2.01[A]-[B] (1990)). The parties do not dispute Mason's claim that he independently created his maps, but Landata contends that they do not possess the degree of creativity necessary to qualify them as original under *Feist*.

. . . .

[T]he evidence in this case demonstrates that Mason exercised sufficient creativity when he created his maps. In his deposition and affidavit, Mason explained the choices that he independently made to select information from numerous and sometimes conflicting sources, and to depict that information on his maps. Mason's compilation of the information on his maps involved creativity that far exceeds the required minimum level.

Mason's maps also possess sufficient creativity to merit copyright protection as pictorial and graphic works of authorship. Historically, most courts have treated maps solely as compilations of facts. *See* Wolf, *supra* note 4, at 227. The Copyright Act, however, categorizes maps not as factual compilations but as "pictorial, graphic, and sculptural works" — a category that includes photographs and architectural plans. 17 U.S.C.A. § 101 (West Supp. 1992). Some courts have recognized that maps, unlike telephone directories and other factual compilations, have an inherent pictorial or photographic nature that merits copyright protection. *See, e.g., Rockford Map Publishers, Inc. v. Directory Service Co.,* 768 F.2d 145, 149 (7th Cir. 1985) ("Teasing pictures from the debris left by conveyancers is a substantial change in the form of the information. The result is copyrightable...."), *cert. denied,* 474 U.S. 1061, 106 S. Ct. 806, 88 L. Ed. 2d 781 (1986); *United States v. Hamilton,* 583 F.2d 448, 451 (9th Cir. 1978) ("Expression in cartography is not so different from other artistic forms seeking to touch upon external realities that unique rules are needed to judge whether the authorship is original."). We agree with these courts. As Wolf explains in his article:

> It is true that maps are factual compilations insofar as their subject matter is concerned. Admittedly, most maps present information about geographic relationships, and the "accuracy" of this presentation, with its utilitarian aspects, is the reason most maps are made and sold. Unlike most other factual compilations, however, maps translate this subject-matter into pictorial or graphic form.... Since it is this pictorial or graphic form, and not the map's subject matter, that is relevant to copyright protection, maps must be distinguished from non-pictorial fact compilations.... A map does not present objective reality; just as a photograph's pictorial form is central to its nature, so a map transforms reality into a unique pictorial form central to its nature.

Wolf, *supra* note 4, at 239-40.

The level of creativity required to make a work of authorship original "is extremely low; even a slight amount will suffice." *Feist,* 111 S. Ct. at 1287. We think that the process by which Mason, using his own skill and judgment, pictorially portrayed his understanding of the reality in Montgomery County by drawing lines and symbols in particular relation to one another easily exceeds that level.

Because Mason's maps possess sufficient creativity in both the selection, coordination, and arrangement of the facts that they depict, and the pictorial, graphic nature of the way that they do so, we find no error in the district court's determination that Mason's maps are original.

QUESTIONS

1. Are you convinced that the plaintiff's claim is not fatally undermined by the *Feist* case, which finds a lack of authorship in works that are commonplace, time-honored, garden-variety, and practically inevitable? On the other hand, would reference by the plaintiff to the 1790 Copyright Act, protecting "maps, charts [nautical maps], and books," be altogether conclusive in his favor?

2. Would a person using Mason's maps infringe — i.e., would it be copying copyrightable material — if it used his painstakingly detailed information about land boundaries to devise a chart with columns, names and numbers, repeating in tabular form the data that Mason had inscribed in pictorial form? *Compare Rand McNally & Co. v. Fleet Mgt. Sys.*, 634 F. Supp. 604 (N.D. Ill. 1986).

3. Would Landata have infringed had it taken Mason's maps to the land-title record office and verified all of the detailed information depicted on the maps, and only then made the overlays and copies that it did in the case above? In other words, should verification of the material in a compilation be a defense to a claim of unauthorized copying?

Atari Games Corp. v. Oman, 979 F.2d 242 (D.C. Cir. 1992). The Register of Copyrights had previously declined to register as an audiovisual work the videogame called Breakout, and the court of appeals had remanded so that the Register could articulate the standard he had used in finding the game uncopyrightable. Although the district court found that the Register's reiterated denial of registration was not an abuse of discretion, the court of appeals reversed (again), noting the *Feist* Court's statement that "the requisite level of creativity [for copyrightability] is extremely low."

Breakout involves competitive play using paddles to strike a ball against and through a wall, composed of strips of colored rectangular bricks (red, amber, green, yellow), with the paddle changing size, the ball changing speed, and four musical tones sounding. In his second refusal to register Breakout, the Register characterized the representations of the wall, ball, and paddle as "simple geometric shapes and coloring" which "per se are not copyrightable." Even viewing the game "as a whole," the Register found "no original authorship in either the selection or arrangement of the images or their components." He explained: "If the Copyright Office were to examine a painting consisting entirely of rectangles and find it copyrightable, it is important to understand that this decision would be based on creative elements such as depth, perspective, shading, texture of brushstroke, etc. and not on the geometric shapes per se."

The court, however, stated that "[r]ecalling the creativity of the work of Mondrian and Malevich, for example, we note that arrangement itself may be indicative of authorship." Invoking the statutory definitions of a compilation and of an audiovisual work (requiring, among other things, "a series of related images"), the court stated that even if the individual graphic elements of each screen are not copyrightable, "[e]ven so, Breakout would be copyrightable if the requisite level of creativity is met by either the individual screens or the relationship of each screen to the other and/or the accompanying sound effects." The court noted the Register's apparent failure to assess "the flow of the game as a whole," "the entire effect of the game as it appears and sounds," "the sequential aspect of the work." Among the elements that contributed to the "creativity" of the audiovisual elements of the game, the court mentioned the square ball, the rectangular shrinking paddles, "the choice of colors (not the solid red, brown, or white of most brick walls), the placement and design of the scores, the changes in speed, the use of sounds, and the synchronized graphics and sounds which accompany the ball's bounces behind the wall."

The court reversed, for a second time, the summary judgment for the Register, and remanded so that the Register, for a third time, could consider Atari's registration application in a manner consistent with the court's opinion.

Consider the image below: is it a compilation? Is it copyrightable?

Swimmer of Liberty, postcard collage by Michael Langenstein

© Michael Langenstein 1977

D. DERIVATIVE WORKS

KUDDLE TOY, INC. v. PUSSYCAT-TOY, INC.

183 U.S.P.Q. 642 (E.D.N.Y. 1974)

[In the course of considering the copyrightability of a stuffed teddy bear, Judge Dooling was faced with the broad dicta in *Alfred Bell & Co. v. Catalda Fine Arts, Inc., supra.* Before finding that the bear in question had "[n]o touch of fresh authorship," he analyzed the *Bell* dicta as follows:]

Against this background Judge Frank's later opinion in *Alfred Bell & Co. v. Catalda Fine Arts, Inc., supra,* 191 F.2d 99, 90 USPQ 153, falls into place. Plaintiff had obtained copyrights on mezzotint engravings of eight paintings of the late 18th and early 19th centuries which were in the public domain. The laborious and highly skilled process of preparing mezzotint engravings is described in the proceeding below (74 F. Supp. 973, 75 USPQ 66); the very idea of the mezzotint is to reproduce as precisely as the craftsman can manage the impression of the original public-domain paintings. The Court below noted (74 F. Supp. at 975, 75 USPQ at 67-68) that, since the engraver had to use an individual engraving conception and exercise judgment, no two engravers could produce identical interpretations of the same oil painting and a color-photographically exact reproduction of the painting could not be produced by the method in question. What the Court considered that it had to decide in *Bell v. Catalda* was really whether such difficult and elevated copying was itself sufficiently an exercise of authorship — an originality in copying — to be independently the subject of a copyright. Such engravings might fall under Section 5(h) as "Reproductions of a work of art," and certainly they were within the idea of so much of Section 7 as treated as "new works subject to copyright" "versions of works in the public domain ...." Section 7 continued, "... but the publication of any such new works shall not ... be construed to imply an exclusive right to such use of the original works ...." The Court in *Bell v. Catalda* concluded, as had the Court below, that the mezzotint craftsmen were the authors of what it was that they brought to the art of making excellently veracious copies, and so much they could copyright. It was just that that defendant purloined, using the plaintiff's plates, which carried plaintiff's notice of copyright. Defendant photographed the plates with continuous tone negatives, used color filters, etc., to prepare printing plates, and, simply, printed plaintiff's mezzotint etchings by the familiar color printing process. Nothing of mistaken or inadequate copying of old oil paintings was involved in *Bell v. Catalda.* The more nearly the mezzotints approached perfection of copying, the more brilliantly "original" within their own special art of copying they were: the "authorship" lay in the very art of the copying, and it was that artfulness of copying that the case protected, not any interest of any kind in the eight underlying oil paintings or in the mezzotints of them as copyrightable variants of the paintings and thus, as new works of art copyrightable as colored works of art. The mezzotint was a transformation of the original oil painting into a different medium of artistic presentation and of that transformation only the copyright owner was the author. The paintings remained wholly in the public domain completely accessible to other craftsmen who could produce other mezzotint engravings or color prints of the original paintings. The only thing protected was what was original with the plaintiffs, the mezzotint engravings as such.

When *Bell v. Catalda* is subdued to its facts, it is seen that it has nothing to do with limited "originality"; every line of the mezzotint was "original" with the engravers. It has nothing to do with imperfect or variant copying; it was a copy and the plaintiffs were the authors of an independently copyrightable copy where copying itself required new and genuine "authorship." It was not a tracing of an old map. It was not a copy of an old text, with advertent or inadvertent blunders. And *Bell v. Catalda* had nothing to do with modesty of originality or meanness of conception. It had to do only with whether an honest copy made in a new medium by a laborious process could be protected against color reprinting. The Court held that it was protected.

QUESTION

Why should a reproduction of a public domain work be eligible for copyright? Consider, on the one hand, a color postcard embodying a Picasso painting, and on the other hand, a newly typeset edition of a play by Shakespeare.

L. BATLIN & SON v. SNYDER

536 F.2d 486 (2d Cir. *en banc* 1976)

OAKES, CIRCUIT JUDGE: Appellants Jeffrey Snyder and Etna Products Co., Inc., his licensee, appeal from a preliminary injunction granted L. Batlin & Son, Inc. (Batlin), compelling appellants to cancel a recordation of a copyright with the United States Customs Service and restraining them from enforcing that copyright. The district court held, 394 F. Supp. 1389 (S.D.N.Y. 1975), as it had previously in *Etna Products Co. v. E. Mishan & Sons,* 75 Civ. 428 (S.D.N.Y. Feb. 13, 1975), that there was "little probability" that appellants' copyright "will be found valid in the trial on the merits" on the basis that any variations between appellants' copyrighted plastic bank and a cast iron bank in the public domain were merely "trivial," and hence appellants' bank insufficiently "original" to support a copyright. 394 F. Supp. at 1390, *citing Alfred Bell & Co. v. Catalda Fine Arts, Inc.,* 191 F.2d 99 (2d Cir. 1951). We agree with the district court and therefore affirm the judgment granting the preliminary injunction.

Uncle Sam mechanical banks have been on the American scene at least since June 8, 1886, when Design Patent No. 16,723, issued on a toy savings bank of its type. The basic delightful design has long since been in the public domain. The banks are well documented in collectors' books and known to the average person interested in Americana. A description of the bank is that Uncle Sam, dressed in his usual stove pipe hat, blue full dress coat, starred vest and red and white striped trousers, and leaning on his umbrella, stands on a four or five-inch wide base, on which sits his carpetbag. A coin may be placed in Uncle Sam's extended hand. When a lever is pressed, the arm lowers, and the coin falls into the bag, while Uncle Sam's whiskers move up and down. The base has an embossed American eagle on it with the words "Uncle Sam" on streamers above it, as well as the word "Bank" on each side. Such a bank is listed in a number of collectors' books, the most recent of which may be F. H. Griffith, Mechanical Banks (1972 ed.) where it was listed as No. 280, and is said to be not particularly rare.

Appellant Jeffrey Snyder doing business as "J.S.N.Y." obtained a registration of copyright on a plastic "Uncle Sam bank" in Class G ("Works of Art") as "sculpture" on January 23, 1975. According to Snyder's affidavit, in January, 1974, he had seen a cast metal antique Uncle Sam bank with an overall height of the figure and base of 11 inches. In April, 1974, he flew to Hong Kong to arrange for the design and eventual manufacture of replicas of the

Original Cast Iron Bank   Snyder Plastic Bank

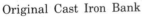

bank as Bicentennial items, taking the cast metal Uncle Sam bank with him.
His Hong Kong buying agent selected a firm, "Unitoy," to make the plastic
"prototype" because of its price and the quality of its work. Snyder wanted his
bank to be made of plastic and to be shorter than the cast metal sample "in
order to fit into the required price range and quality and quantity of material
to be used." The figure of Uncle Sam was thus shortened from 11 to nine
inches, and the base shortened and narrowed. It was also decided, Snyder
averred, to change the shape of the carpetbag and to include the umbrella in a
one-piece mold for the Uncle Sam figure, "so as not to have a problem with a
loose umbrella or a separate molding process." The Unitoy representative
made his sketches while looking at the cast metal bank. After a "clay model"
was made, a plastic "prototype" was approved by Snyder and his order placed
in May, 1974. The plastic bank carried the legend "© Copyright J.S.N.Y." and
was assertedly first "published" on October 15, 1974, before being filed with
the Register of Copyrights in January, 1975.

   Appellee Batlin is also in the novelty business and as early as August 9,
1974, ordered 30 cartons of cast iron Uncle Sam mechanical banks from Taiwan where its president had seen the bank made. When he became aware of
the existence of a plastic bank, which he considered "an almost identical copy"
of the cast iron bank, Batlin's trading company in Hong Kong procured a
manufacturer and the president of Batlin ordered plastic copies also. Begin-

ning in April, 1975, Batlin was notified by the United States Customs Service that the plastic banks it was receiving were covered by appellants' copyright. In addition the Customs Service was also refusing entry to cast iron banks previously ordered, according to the Batlin affidavit. Thus Batlin instituted suit for a judgment declaring appellants' copyright void and for damages for unfair competition and restraint of trade. The sole question on this appeal is whether Judge Metzner abused his discretion in granting Batlin a preliminary injunction. We find that he did not.

This court has examined both the appellants' plastic Uncle Sam bank made under Snyder's copyright and the uncopyrighted model cast iron mechanical bank which is itself a reproduction of the original public domain Uncle Sam bank. Appellant Snyder claims differences not only of size but also in a number of other very minute details: the carpetbag shape of the plastic bank is smooth, the iron bank rough; the metal bank bag is fatter at its base; the eagle on the front of the platform in the metal bank is holding arrows in his talons while in the plastic bank he clutches leaves, this change concededly having been made, however, because "the arrows did not reproduce well in plastic on a smaller size." The shape of Uncle Sam's face is supposedly different, as is the shape and texture of the hats, according to the Snyder affidavit. In the metal version the umbrella is hanging loose while in the plastic item it is included in the single mold. The texture of the clothing, the hairline, shape of the bow tie and of the shirt collar and left arm as well as the flag carrying the name on the base of the statue are all claimed to be different, along with the shape and texture of the eagles on the side. Many of these differences are not perceptible to the casual observer. Appellants make no claim for any difference based on the plastic mold lines in the Uncle Sam figure which are perceptible.

Our examination of the banks results in the same conclusion as that of Judge Metzner in *Etna Products,* the earlier case enjoining Snyder's copyright, that the Snyder bank is "extremely similar to the cast iron bank, save in size and material" with the only other differences, such as the shape of the satchel and the leaves in the eagle's talons being "by all appearances, minor." Similarities include, more importantly, the appearance and number of stripes on the trousers; buttons on the coat, and stars on the vest and hat, the attire and pose of Uncle Sam, the decor on his base and bag, the overall color scheme, the method of carpetbag opening, to name but a few. [The court below saw the banks and heard] conflicting testimony from opposing expert witnesses as to the substantiality or triviality of the variations and as to the skill necessary to make the plastic model ....

... The substance of appellee's expert's testimony on which the district judge evidently relied was that the variations found in appellants' plastic bank were merely "trivial" and that it was a reproduction of the metal bank made as simply as possible for the purposes of manufacture. In other words, there were no elements of difference that amounted to significant alteration or that had any purpose other than the functional one of making a more suitable (and probably less expensive) figure in the plastic medium.

... It has been the law of this circuit for at least 30 years that in order to obtain a copyright upon a reproduction of a work of art under 17 U.S.C. § 5(h)

that the work "contain some substantial, not merely trivial originality ...."
Chamberlin v. Uris Sales Corp., supra, 150 F.2d at 513.

Originality is, however, distinguished from novelty; there must be independent creation, but it need not be invention in the sense of striking uniqueness, ingeniousness, or novelty, since the Constitution differentiates "authors" and their "writings" from "inventors" and their "discoveries." *Alfred Bell & Co. v. Cataldo Fine Arts, Inc., supra,* 191 F.2d at 100; *Runge v. Lee,* 441 F.2d 579, 581 (9th Cir.), *cert. denied,* 404 U.S. 887 (1971). Originality means that the work owes its creation to the author and this in turn means that the work must not consist of actual copying. *Alfred Bell & Co. v. Cataldo Fine Arts, Inc., supra,* 191 F.2d at 102-03; *Sheldon v. Metro-Goldwyn Pictures Corp.,* 81 F.2d 49, 54 (2d Cir. 1936), *aff'd,* 309 U.S. 390 (1940).[3]

....

[We] follow the school of cases in this circuit and elsewhere supporting the proposition that to support a copyright there must be at least some substantial variation, not merely a trivial variation such as might occur in the translation to a different medium.

Nor can the requirement of originality be satisfied simply by the demonstration of "physical skill" or "special training" which, to be sure, Judge Metzner found was required for the production of the plastic molds that furnished the basis for appellants' plastic bank. A considerably *higher* degree of skill is required, true artistic skill, to make the reproduction copyrightable. Thus in *Alfred Bell & Co. v. Cataldo Fine Arts, Inc., supra,* 191 F.2d at 104-05 n.22, Judge Frank pointed out that the mezzotint engraver's art there concerned required "great labour and talent" to effectuate the "management of light and shade ... produced by different lines and ...," means "very different from those employed by the painter or draughtsman from whom he copies...." *See also Millworth Converting Corp. v. Slifka, supra* (fabric designer required one month of work to give three-dimensional color effect to flat surface). Here on the basis of appellants' own expert's testimony it took the Unitoy representative "[a]bout a day and a half, two days work" to produce the plastic mold sculpture from the metal Uncle Sam bank. If there be a point in the copyright law pertaining to reproductions at which sheer artistic skill and effort can act as a substitute for the requirement of substantial variation, it was not reached here.

Appellants rely heavily upon *Alva Studios, Inc. v. Winninger* [177 F. Supp. 265 (S.D.N.Y. 1959)] the "Hand of God" case, where the court held that "great skill and originality [were required] to produce a scale reduction of a great

---

[3] The only case that appears to be an exception to this rule is the "Hand of God" case. *Alva Studios, Inc. v. Winninger,* 177 F. Supp. 265 (S.D.N.Y. 1959) (exact scale artistic reproduction of highly complicated statue made with great precision was "original" as requiring "great skill and originality"). This case is discussed in the text *infra.*

The test of originality is concededly one with a low threshold in that "[a]ll that is needed ... is that the 'author' contributed something more than a 'merely trivial' variation, something recognizably 'his own.'" *Alfred Bell & Co. v. Cataldo Fine Arts, Inc.,* 191 F.2d at 103. But as this court said many years ago, "[w]hile a copy of something in the public domain will not, if it be merely a copy, support a copyright, a distinguishable variation will...." *Gerlach-Barklow Co. v. Morris & Bendien, Inc.,* 23 F.2d 159, 161 (2d Cir. 1927).

work with exactitude." 177 F. Supp. at 267. There, the original sculpture was, "one of the most intricate pieces of sculpture ever created" with "[i]nnumerable planes, lines and geometric patterns ... interdependent in [a] multidimensional work." *Id.* Originality was found by the district court to consist primarily in the fact that "[i]t takes 'an extremely skilled sculptor' many hours working directly in front of the original" to effectuate a scale reduction. *Id.* at 266. The court, indeed, found the exact replica to be so original, distinct, and creative as to constitute a work of art in itself. The complexity and exactitude there involved distinguishes that case amply from the one at bar. As appellants themselves have pointed out, there are a number of trivial differences or deviations from the original public domain cast iron bank in their plastic reproduction. Thus concededly the plastic version is not, and was scarcely meticulously produced to be, an exactly faithful reproduction. Nor is the creativity in the underlying work of art of the same order of magnitude as in the case of the "Hand of God." Rodin's sculpture is, furthermore, so unique and rare, and adequate public access to it such a problem that a significant public benefit accrues from its precise, artistic reproduction. No such benefit can be imagined to accrue here from the "knock-off" reproduction of the cast iron Uncle Sam bank. Thus appellants' plastic bank is neither in the category of exactitude required by *Alva Studios* nor in a category of substantial originality; it falls within what has been suggested by the amicus curiae is a copyright no-man's land.

Absent a genuine difference between the underlying work of art and the copy of it for which protection is sought, the public interest in promoting progress in the arts — indeed, the constitutional demand, *Chamberlin v. Uris Sales Corp., supra* — could hardly be served. To extend copyrightability to minuscule variations would simply put a weapon for harassment in the hands of mischievous copiers intent on appropriating and monopolizing public domain work....

Judgment affirmed.

MESKILL, CIRCUIT JUDGE (dissenting) (with whom TIMBERS and VAN GRAAFEILAND, CIRCUIT JUDGES, concur): I respectfully dissent.

In the instant case the author has contributed substantially more than a merely trivial variation. "Any 'distinguishable variation' of a prior work will constitute sufficient originality to support a copyright if such variation is the product of the author's independent efforts, and is more than merely trivial." 1 Nimmer on Copyright § 10.1 at 34.2. In accord with the purposes of the copyright law to promote progress by encouraging individual effort through copyright protection, we should require only minimal variations to find copyrightability. The independent sculpting of the mold for the plastic bank and the aggregated differences in size and conformation of the figurine should satisfy this standard.

The plastic bank in question admittedly is based on a work now in the public domain. This does not render it uncopyrightable since "[i]t is hornbook [law] that a new and original plan or combination of existing materials in the public domain is sufficiently original to come within the copyright protection ...." *Alva Studios, Inc. v. Winninger,* 177 F. Supp. 265, 267 (S.D.N.Y.

1959). The courts have repeatedly emphasized that only a modest level of originality is necessary to be eligible for a copyright.... *Dan Kasoff, Inc. v. Novelty Jewelry Co., Inc.,* 309 F.2d 745, 746 (2d Cir. 1962), where this Court required only a "faint trace of originality" to support a copyright.

Looking first to copyright cases involving sculptures, in *Puddu v. Buonamici Statuary, Inc.,* 450 F.2d 401, 402 (2d Cir. 1971), this Court found that where plaintiff's employee had sculpted statuettes from scratch, even though there was a "strong family resemblance between the copyrighted and the uncopyrighted models, the differences suffice to satisfy the modest requirement of originality.... Originality sufficient for copyright protection exists if the 'author' has introduced any element of novelty as contrasted with the material previously known to him." ... The fabric cases likewise have found designs copyrightable with only a "very modest grade of originality." *Peter Pan Fabrics, Inc. v. Dan River Mills, Inc.,* 295 F. Supp. 1366, 1368 (S.D.N.Y. 1969). In the latter case, the embellishment and expansion of purchased designs before being rolled onto fabric constituted the "slight addition" sufficient to qualify as originality. Finally, there are also cases where *no* changes were required because the process of reproduction itself required great skill....

Turning to the case at bar, Judge Metzner made a factual finding that the plastic bank embodied only trivial variations from the bank in the public domain.... I make no claim that the process of sculpting involved here is as complex as in *Alva Studios* (scaled version of Rodin sculpture) or in *Alfred Bell* (mezzotint engravings of art classics). However, those cases depended solely on difficulty of process to establish originality, since there was no attempt to alter or improve upon the underlying work.

The most obvious differences between the two exhibits in this case are size and medium. While these factors alone may not be sufficient to render a work copyrightable, they surely may be considered along with the other variations. On the other hand, the author's reasons for making changes should be irrelevant to a determination of whether the differences are trivial. As noted in *Alfred Bell, supra,* 191 F.2d at 105, even an inadvertent variation can form the basis of a valid copyright. After the fact speculation as to whether Snyder made changes for aesthetic or functional reasons should not be the basis of decision.

The primary variations between the two banks involve height; medium; anatomical proportions of the Uncle Sam figure, including shape and expression of face; design of the clothing (hat, tie, shirt, collar, trousers); detail around the eagle figure on the platform; placement of the umbrella; and the shape and texture of the satchel. Granting Snyder a copyright protecting these variations would ensure only that no one could copy his particular version of the bank now in the public domain, i.e., protection from someone using Snyder's figurine to slavishly copy and make a mold. In *Alva Studios, supra,* 177 F. Supp. at 267, where the author produced no distinctive variations of his own in reproducing the Rodin sculpture, the court still found that the reproduction was copyrightable and that infringement was possible; although mere resemblance would not justify a finding of infringement where the principal elements of a design were taken from the public domain, evidence of actual copying would support such a finding.

This approach seems quite in accord with the purpose of the copyright statute — to promote progress by encouraging individual effort through copyright protection. The relatively low standard of originality required for copyrightability is derived from this purpose. The objective is to progress first and, if necessary, litigate the question of infringement later. In the meantime, the public culture benefits from progress; the issue of who is entitled to the profits should not induce rigidity and slowness in industries and fields naturally subject to great flux.

Accordingly, I would reverse the district court decision.

ORIGINALITY IN DERIVATIVE WORKS

The *Batlin* case endorses a standard of "originality" for authorized derivative works that is arguably stiffer than that which obtains for copyrightable works generally. It cannot be said with confidence that *Batlin* announces the prevailing view regarding derivative works, and the decisions even within the Second Circuit are somewhat difficult to reconcile with one another. That court reaffirmed the *Batlin* approach in *Durham Indus., Inc. v. Tomy Corp.*, 630 F.2d 905 (2d Cir. 1980), involving Tomy's authorized wind-up plastic figures based upon the Disney characters Mickey Mouse, Donald Duck, and Pluto Dog; those figures were admittedly copied by Durham without consent. The court found that "the three Tomy figures are instantly identifiable as embodiments of the Disney characters in yet another form," and rejected the contention "that the originality requirement of copyrightability can be satisfied by the mere reproduction of a work of art in a different medium, or by the demonstration of some 'physical' as opposed to 'artistic' skill." The court found "no independent creation, no distinguishable variation from preexisting works, nothing recognizably the author's own contribution that sets Tomy's figures apart from the prototypical Mickey, Donald, and Pluto." The court observed that persons whom Disney licensed to copy its characters might otherwise, in order to avoid lawsuits by prior licensees, have to make substantial changes in the Disney characters; "In theory, of course, there would be no infringement of Tomy's rights if Durham copied Disney's characters and not Tomy's figures, ... but because proof of access plus substantial similarity can support a finding of infringement, Durham would at the very least be vulnerable to harassment. Yet any significant changes made by Durham to avoid liability would carry it away from the original Disney characters, in which Tomy concededly has no copyrights, and Disney's right to copy (or to permit others to copy) its own creations would, in effect, be circumscribed."

The same court, however, in *Eden Toys, Inc. v. Florelee Undergarment Co.*, 697 F.2d 27 (2d Cir. 1982), purporting to apply *Batlin* and *Durham*, reversed a finding of insufficient originality for the plaintiff's drawing of Paddington Bear that was an authorized derivation of an earlier copyrighted illustration. The underlying work is illustration A below, the plaintiff's work is illustration B, and the defendant's drawing (held by the court to be an infringement) is illustration C. The court of appeals concluded that the district court had

Illustration A   Illustration B   Illustration C
(underlying work)   (authorized derivation   (infringing copy of B)
                          from A)

applied an improperly stiff standard of originality, and that it had mistakenly
concluded that similarities of appearance in derivative pictorial works sufficient to justify an infringement finding must necessarily undermine a
copyrightability finding. Even a work having the "same aesthetic appeal" as
an underlying work such as to constitute an infringement if unauthorized,
might incorporate "non-trivial contributions" to the underlying work and thus
be copyrightable if authorized. The court found the plaintiff's illustration B to
incorporate "original and substantial" variations upon illustration A, citing
"the changed proportions of the hat, the elimination of individualized fingers
and toes, the overall smoothing of lines" that provided a "different, cleaner"
look than the illustration on which it was based. For a similar favorable
treatment of Raggedy Ann and Raggedy Andy dolls, on the defendant's motion for summary judgment, see *Knickerbocker Toy Co. v. Winterbrook Corp.*,
554 F. Supp. 1309 (D.N.H. 1982).

The Paddington Bear case was distinguished in *Sherry Mfg. Co. v. Towel
King of Florida, Inc.*, 753 F.2d 1565 (11th Cir. 1985). There the plaintiff had
marketed without copyright notice towels bearing the design of palm trees at
the water's edge; it later changed the design slightly, affixed copyright notice,
and brought an action for infringement of the design. The trial court noted the
differences between the public domain design and the revised design: the
surface of the seawater was painted differently; the amount of sand was increased so as to make the land look more like a beach than merely an island;
the palm leaves "are sharper and more lifelike"; the clouds were shaped differently; the effect of the wind is diminished; the water level was lowered so that
the drooping palm leaves no longer touch the water; and the palm leaves of
the small tree to the right are shortened. The court of appeals held, however
— stating that the "clearly erroneous" standard of review was not appropriate
when the reviewing court has the opportunity to view the same tangible
exhibits as did the trial court — that "the majority of those distinguishing

Sherry's original design   Sherry's corrected new design

details are so minor that they are virtually unnoticeable upon a cursory comparison of the two towels." The court stated that a cursory side-by-side comparison of the pertinent Paddington Bear drawings, however, showed immediately discernible differences. It also pointed out that "the primary purpose of making the changes [in the towel design] was to make the work copyrightable, and not to make it more aesthetically appealing." (Do you regard this as a pertinent observation?)

The concern of the *Batlin* court regarding potential harassment by claimants of derivative-work copyrights was exalted into the very rationale for the originality requirement by another court of appeals in *Gracen v. Bradford Exch.*, 698 F.2d 300 (7th Cir. 1983). There, the plaintiff had prepared an authorized painting of Judy Garland portraying Dorothy in the motion picture "The Wizard of Oz"; this was done in connection with a contest that was intended to lead to the production by the defendant Bradford of a series of collectors' plates based on the film. Although Gracen's painting was selected as the one that best captured the "essence" of the Dorothy character, she could not come to terms with Bradford, and the task of creating designs for the plates was given to one Auckland, who proceeded to copy Ms. Gracen's painting. The court found that her painting — reproduced below as illustration 1, and based upon "stills" from the motion picture (illustrations 2 and 3) —

lacked sufficient originality for copyright. The court viewed the originality standard as designed, especially as applied to derivative works, to prevent overlapping claims; it gave as an example an artist who makes immaterial modifications in a reproduction of the Mona Lisa and who then sues another artist who copied from the da Vinci original. "[I]f the difference between the original and A's reproduction is slight, the difference between A's and B's reproduction will also be slight, so that if B had access to A's reproductions the trier of fact will be hard-pressed to decide whether B was copying A or copying the Mona Lisa itself." The court concluded that the painting of the Dorothy character as superimposed upon a rendition of the movie set of Oz was insufficiently original, "always bearing in mind that the purpose of the term in copyright law is not to guide aesthetic judgments but to assure a sufficiently

Illustration 1 — Gracen's painting

Illustration 2 — film still Gracen followed for figure

Illustration 3 — film still Gracen followed for background

gross difference between the underlying and the derivative work to avoid entangling subsequent artists depicting the underlying work in copyright problems"; were originality construed too broadly "it would paradoxically inhibit rather than promote the creation of such works."

QUESTIONS

1. In the field of art reproductions, presumably the aesthetic and educational value of the work derives from its being as exact a reproduction as possible. Is it therefore proper — either under the Constitution or the statute — for a court to deny copyright to such a reproduction unless there is a substantial variation from the original? Would it run afoul of the Supreme Court decision in *Feist* to extend copyright protection to art reproductions that are painstakingly exact?

2. Would a photograph of the public domain cast-iron bank (in the *Batlin* case) be a proper subject of copyright? If so, then why is not Snyder's rendition in plastic?

3. Is there a constitutional or philosophical justification for the court's suggestion that copyright may be used to protect reproductions when the underlying work is "unique and rare" and not readily accessible to the public? Does copyright make works more or less accessible to the public?

4. Had the Snyder plastic bank been granted copyright, would that effectively remove the cast-iron original from the public domain so that others would be forbidden to copy it?

5. Consider the reasoning in the *Gracen* case. First, do you agree that the principal function of the "originality" requirement in copyright generally, and in derivative works in particular, is to eliminate harassing litigation? Second, was it consistent for the court to strike down Ms. Gracen's claim for that reason while concluding — on the basis of Auckland's admission that Bradford had given him Ms. Gracen's painting with directions to "clean it up" and Bradford's failure to attach a copy of Auckland's painting to its motion for summary judgment — that Auckland had indeed copied directly from Ms. Gracen? Third, does the court's approach really provide incentives to *B* to make reproductions of the Mona Lisa? Consider whether *B* will have any recourse when a new hypothetical reproducer, *C,* comes on the scene and makes a direct copy of *B*'s reproduction. Fourth, although the court concluded that the superimposition of the Dorothy figure on the Oz background lacked sufficient originality, couldn't it be argued that a copyrightable compilation was created under the reasoning of *Roth Greeting Cards*? Fifth, assuming the court's analysis to be applicable to pictorial, graphic and sculptural works, does it apply with equal vigor to musical and literary works (e.g., to a case in which the plaintiff has prepared an authorized dramatic script based upon a copyrighted or public domain novel)?

6. What, if anything, is copyrightable in a painting consisting of a faithful reproduction of the Mona Lisa, with the addition of a moustache? Could someone freely copy the reproduction while omitting the moustache? *See Millworth Converting Corp. v. Slifka,* 276 F.2d 443 (2d Cir. 1960).

E. PICTORIAL, GRAPHIC AND SCULPTURAL WORKS

JOHN MULLER & CO. v. NEW YORK ARROWS SOCCER TEAM

802 F.2d 989 (8th Cir. 1986)

PER CURIAM.

John Muller & Company, Inc. appeals from a district court judgment in favor of the New York Arrows and the Register of Copyrights. The district court granted partial summary judgment for defendants, finding that plaintiff's logo for the New York Arrows was not copyrightable, and dismissed plaintiff's pendent state law claims. For reversal, appellant argues that its logo did show the degree of creativity required to make a work of art copyrightable, and that it was error for the district court to use an abuse of discretion standard to review the Register of Copyright's refusal to register the logo. We affirm on the basis of the district court's opinion. *See* 8th Cir. R. 14.

John Muller & Company, Inc. (Muller) contracted with Dr. David Schoenstadt, owner of the New York Arrows soccer team, to do advertising work, including the design of a logo for the team. A dispute over fees arose, and Muller attempted to copyright the team logo. The Register of Copyrights twice refused to register the logo, saying that it lacked the minimal creativity necessary to support a copyright. Muller sued Schoenstadt in district court on grounds of copyright infringement, breach of contract and other state claims. The Register of Copyrights was served notice of the suit and chose to intervene to support its position that the logo is not copyrightable. The logo consists of four angled lines which form an arrow and the word "Arrows" in cursive script below the arrow (*See* Appendix A, District Court Opinion).

The parties agree that there are no disputed issues of material fact, and that the copyrightability of the logo may be decided as a matter of law. In order to be copyrightable, a work must show certain minimal levels of creativity and originality. *Donald v. Uarco Business Forms,* 478 F.2d 764, 765 (8th

Cir. 1973) (per curiam). The district court correctly noted that the issue here is creativity, not originality, although appellant's argument tends to confuse the two. If, as here, the creator seeks to register the item as a "work of art" or "pictorial, graphic or sculptural work, then the work must embody some creative authorship in its delineation or form." 37 C.F.R. § 202.10(a) (1985); *Gardenia Flowers, Inc. v. Joseph Markovits, Inc.,* 280 F. Supp. 776, 781 (S.D.N.Y. 1968); 1 M. Nimmer, *Nimmer on Copyright,* § 2.08[B][1] (1985). There is no simple way to draw the line between "some creative authorship" and not enough creative authorship, and there are no cases involving "works" exactly like this one.[3] The district court considered the cases cited by appellant, but distinguished them and held that the Register had not abused his discretion in finding the appellant's logo lacked the level of creativity needed for copyrightability.

The Register's decisions are subject to judicial review, but only on an abuse of discretion standard. 17 U.S.C. § 701 (1982); 5 U.S.C. § 706(2)(A) (1982). *See also Norris Industries v. International Telephone and Telegraph Corp.,* 696 F.2d 918, 922 (11th Cir.), *cert. denied,* 464 U.S. 818, 104 S. Ct. 78, 78 L. Ed. 2d 89 (1983); *Esquire, Inc. v. Ringer,* 591 F.2d 796, 806 & n. 28 (D.C. Cir. 1978), *cert. denied,* 440 U.S. 908, 99 S. Ct. 1217, 59 L. Ed. 2d 456 (1979). Appellant cites no cases to support his argument that the wrong standard of review was used.

We conclude that the district court's opinion is correct and well-reasoned, and we affirm on the basis of that opinion. *See* 8th Cir. R. 14.

Kitchens of Sara Lee, Inc. v. Nifty Foods Corp., 266 F.2d 541 (2d Cir. 1957). Both plaintiff and defendant bake and sell to the public frozen bakery products. On the plaintiff's cardboard covering over the aluminum foil pans in which it sells its chocolate cake, cream cheesecake and pound cake are realistic color drawings of those cakes, as a part of the Sara Lee label.

According to the court, "visual inspection plus the testimony and exhibits more than justify the district court's conclusion that the [defendant's] drawings or pictures of the chocolate cake, cheesecake and pound cake were copied from plaintiff's labels." The plaintiff had copyrighted its labels under the 1909 Act, which permitted registration of "prints and labels published in connection with the sale or advertisement of articles of merchandise." The court, acknowledging that a commercial label to be copyrightable must contain "an appreciable amount of original text or pictorial material," concluded that the Sara Lee drawings, despite their prosaic subject matter and their accurate depiction, were copyrightable. "Plaintiff's artists and lithographers have achieved most realistic pictures of cakes which resemble all well-baked cakes of similar type including those baked by fondly remembered grandmothers. A

---

[3]One case decided after the district court opinion was filed is perhaps closer than any cited by either party. In *Magic Marketing, Inc. v. Mailing Services of Pittsburgh, Inc.,* 634 F. Supp. 769 (W.D. Pa. 1986), the court held that envelopes printed with solid black stripes and a few words such as "Priority Message" or "Gift Check" did not exhibit the minimal level of creativity necessary for copyright registration.

fanciful, imaginary or unique representation of such standard commodities might well not serve its desired purpose to attract the American appetite .... [D]espite the force of arguments questioning the copyrightability of pictures of these homely and domestic articles of food, such obvious copying as here occurred is not to be encouraged. Plaintiff has put time, some creative thought and money into its pictorial representations of its cakes and for the copying it is entitled to damages.... The pictures of the cakes used by plaintiff on its labels although possibly not achieving the quality of a Leonardo 'Still Life' nevertheless have sufficient commercial artistry to entitle them to protection against obvious copying." The court concluded, however, that the plaintiff could not use copyright to prevent the copying of such uncopyrightable features of the label as the circular, rectangular or octagonal shape, or the ingredients or serving directions. The court also reversed the conclusion of the trial court that the defendant had engaged in unfair competition under New York law; the lower court had erred in finding that customers would be confused by the defendants' cake labels into believing that its products were in fact baked by Sara Lee.

QUESTIONS

1. Does the court's decision in the *John Muller* case violate the principles articulated by Justice Holmes in *Bleistein, supra*? Is it compatible with the decision in *Roth Greeting Cards, supra*? With the decision in *Sara Lee*? Does the *Sara Lee* decision represent the present view of the Court of Appeals for the Second Circuit, in light of the en banc decision of that court in *L. Batlin & Son v. Snyder, supra*?

2. One reason for attacking the plaintiff's case in *Sara Lee* is that the cake drawings are commonplace depictions of commonplace objects; this was rejected by the court. Couldn't the defendant use the same claim to show that it had not copied the plaintiff's drawings? How *could* the plaintiff prove copying in *Sara Lee,* absent direct admissions by the defendant's artists?

3. Could the defendant argue that even if it did copy from the Sara Lee drawings, the copying should be allowed as de minimis? Could the defendant argue that even if it did copy, it was copying only the "idea" embodied in the plaintiff's cake drawings rather than the "expression"? Compare the *Morrissey* case, *supra,* and the *Kalpakian* case, *infra* Chapter 6, regarding the limited number of ways in which the contest or bee-pin "idea" can be "expressed."

4. Note the emphasis placed by the *Sara Lee* court upon the time, thought and money invested by the plaintiff in designing and executing its cake labels. Note too that the court appeared to reinforce its finding of copyrightability by its condemnation of the defendant's "obvious copying." Apart from the circularity of its latter reasoning, are these conclusions any longer tenable after the *Feist* decision? Does not *Feist* celebrate rather than condemn the copying of unprotected material no matter how much effort and expense went into its creation?

DRAFT, SECOND SUPPLEMENTARY REPORT OF THE REGISTER OF COPYRIGHTS ON THE GENERAL REVISION OF THE U.S. COPYRIGHT LAW, CHAPTER VII, 4-13 (1975)

Legislative History of Section 113 and Title II

Until 1954 it had been widely assumed that the only statutory protection for the designs of utilitarian articles was that available under the design patent law, which dated back to 1842. That patents have proved inadequate as a practical form of protection for designs is something on which most people will agree. The main arguments usually advanced against the patent law as a means of protecting designs are:

   1) *Inappropriateness.* Patentable designs must be more than "original" (created independently without copying); they must also be "novel" (new in the absolute sense of never having existed before anywhere) and "non-obvious" (the product of a creative act going beyond mere talent or artistry). A patented design that meets these extraordinarily high standards gets more than rights against copying; a design patent consists of a complete monopoly over the use of the design in any manner.

   2) *Judicial hostility.* Because the standards of protection are so high and the scope of protection is so broad, the mortality rate of those design patents that have been tested in the courts has been extremely high.

   3) *Cost.* Obtaining a design patent is expensive, in some cases prohibitively so. Nearly all applicants are required to retain an attorney, and the substantial costs of filing and pursuing an application through the searching process often operate as a deterrent, especially since the chances of issuance are problematical. An applicant with several new

designs has no way of knowing which will be popular, but in most cases cannot afford to apply for design patents on all of them.

4) *Delay.* The patent examining process consists of searching the "prior art" to determine novelty in an absolute sense. Whatever realistically may be the effectiveness of prior-art searching in the case of designs, the process is inevitably a slow one. In the design patent area, the Patent and Trademark Office now has a backlog of about 7 months, and the average time lag between filing and issuance for a design patent is about 21 months. It must be emphasized that protection under a patent starts only upon issuance, so that a design may be vulnerable to copying during the time a patent application is pending.

Beginning around 1914, the growth and economic impact of design piracy, and the nearly total failure of the patent law as a method to combat it, led to a variety of alternative efforts to protect original designs. The attempts to stop design piracy by industry self-regulation ... combined with a form of boycott, were quite effective for a time during the 1930's, but were eventually struck down by the courts. Judicial actions aimed at getting the courts to declare design piracy illegal on any one of a number of theories — Federal copyright, State common law copyright, Federal and State trademarks, unfair competition (including claims of "passing off" and "misappropriation"), fraud and breach of confidence, implied contract, etc. — were almost entirely unsuccessful.

During this period there were constant and frequently intense efforts to obtain Congressional enactment of separate design legislation. Between 1914 and 1957 nearly 50 design protection bills were introduced, and a number of hearings were held. Some of the bills were closer to copyright than patent; some leaned the other way; most of them took the form of special protection based on copyright principles but considerably more limited in scope and duration than traditional copyright. Several of the bills came close to enactment, but none made it all the way through both Houses.

In 1952, a successful program for the general revision of the patent laws resulted in comprehensive new patent legislation in which the design patent provisions were deliberately left untouched. The basic reason for leaving the design provisions alone was an agreement among the sponsors of the legislation that the patent law was not the place to deal with design protection.... [Soon after, the Copyright Office joined with the Patent Office and other patent experts in the development and drafting of a design-protection bill that became, in the early 1960s, a proposed Title II to the comprehensive copyright revision bill.[4]]...

---

[4]*Editors' footnote.* As it turned out, the Senate passed the Design Bill as title II of the bill that ultimately became the Copyright Act of 1976. S. 22, 94th Cong., 2d Sess. (Feb. 1976). Title II, however, was stricken in its entirety by the House Judiciary Committee and was not restored by the conference committee after the bill passed the full House. Since that time, almost every Congress has seen the introduction of design-protection bills. The most recent bill was the Design Innovation and Technology Act of 1991, H.R. 1790, introduced by Richard A. Gephardt, D-Mo. It was not enacted. The 1991 bill, like its predecessor, contained these key provisions:

A radical change in the legal status of original designs in the United States occurred on March 8, 1954. On that date the United States Supreme Court, by a seven-to-two majority in *Mazer v. Stein*, 347 U.S. 201, upheld the copyrightability of "works of art" that had been incorporated as the designs of useful articles. The Court strongly endorsed a Copyright Office Regulation accepting as copyrightable "works of artistic craftsmanship, in so far as their form but not their mechanical or utilitarian aspects are concerned, such as artistic jewelry, enamels, glassware, and tapestries, as well as all works belonging to the fine arts, such as paintings, drawings and sculpture...."

The *Mazer* case involved identical copies of lamp bases in the form of statuettes representing human figures. The figurines had been registered for copyright as "works of art." The majority of the Court, with Justices Douglas and Black dissenting, held that works of art are copyrightable as the "writings of an author," that original works of art do not cease to be copyrightable, as works of art, when they are embodied in useful articles, and that for this purpose the following factors make no difference whatever:

1) the potential availability of design patent protection for the same subject matter; on this point Justice Reed said:

> We ... hold that the patentability of the statuettes, fitted as lamps or unfitted, does not bar copyright as works of art. Neither the Copyright Statute nor any other says that because a thing is patentable it may not be copyrighted. We should not so hold.... The dichotomy of protection for the aesthetic is not beauty and utility but art for the copyright and the invention of original and ornamental design for design patents. We find nothing in the copyright statute to support the argument that the intended use or use in industry of an article eligible for copyright bars or invalidates its registration. We do not read such a limitation into the copyright law.

---

(1) The design of a useful article can be protected if it is the original creation of its author (i.e., not copied), regardless whether it is novel or non-obvious; it cannot, however, be "staple or commonplace" or be "dictated solely by a utilitarian function of the article that embodies it."

(2) The original designer is protected only against the unauthorized copying of the substance of the design; independent creation of a similar design will not infringe.

(3) Protection begins when the design is "made public" by public exhibition, sale or offering, and continues for a term of ten years.

(4) A claim to protection must be registered in a Government office within one year after the design is made public, or else protection is lost. The Government official undertakes no search or comparison with earlier designs, but must register the design if it "on its face appears to be subject to protection" under the bill. Proceedings may be initiated by third parties to cancel the registration of a design not subject to protection.

(5) There are flexible requirements for placing notice on the design; failure to comply does not forfeit protection but may sharply limit remedies against infringers.

(6) Major remedies are injunctions and compensatory damages (which the court in its discretion may increase to $1.00 per copy or $50,000, whichever is greater).

(7) Certain accommodations are made with the Copyright Act, the Design Patent Act, and state common law.

The Balinese Dancer statuette (and lamp base)
at issue in *Mazer v. Stein*

2) the intention of the artist as to commercial application and mass production of the design.

3) the aesthetic value of the design, or its total lack thereof; the majority opinion on this point states:

> The successive acts, the legislative history of the 1909 Act and the practice of the Copyright Office unite to show that "works of art" and "reproductions of works of art" are terms that were intended by Congress to include the authority to copyright these statuettes. Individual perception of the beautiful is too varied a power to permit a narrow or rigid concept of art.... They must be original, that is, the author's tangible expression of his ideas.... Such expression, whether meticulously delineating the model or mental image or conveying the meaning by modernistic form or color, is copyrightable.

4) the fact that the design, in its useful embodiment, was mass-produced and merchandised commercially on a nation-wide scale....

The revolutionary impact of the *Mazer* decision upon design protection took some time to sink in. Its reach clearly went beyond lamp base designs, but did it go so far as to cover all original industrial designs (machinery, automobiles, refrigerators, etc.)?

[Editor's note: The issue raised by the Register at this point in her Report was initially addressed, soon after the *Mazer* decision, by detailed regulations of the Copyright Office. These regulations were incorporated, with little change, in the 1976 Act; the principal sections are 101 and 113.]

---

§ 101. Definitions

"Pictorial, graphic, and sculptural works" include two-dimensional and three-dimensional works of fine, graphic, and applied art, photographs, prints and art reproductions, maps, globes, charts, diagrams, models, and technical drawings, including architectural plans. Such works shall include works of artistic craftsmanship insofar as their form but not their mechanical or utilitarian aspects are concerned; the design of a useful article, as defined in this section, shall be considered a pictorial, graphic, or sculptural work only if, and only to the extent that, such design incorporates pictorial, graphic, or sculptural features that can be identified separately from, and are capable of existing independently of, the utilitarian aspects of the article.

§ 113. Scope of exclusive rights in pictorial, graphic, and sculptural works

(a) Subject to the provisions of subsections (b) and (c) of this section, the exclusive right to reproduce a copyrighted pictorial, graphic, or sculptural work in copies under section 106 includes the right to reproduce the work in or on any kind of article, whether useful or otherwise.

(b) This title does not afford, to the owner of copyright in a work that portrays a useful article as such, any greater or lesser rights with respect to the making, distribution, or display of the useful article so portrayed than those afforded to such works under the law, whether title 17 or the common law or statutes of a State, in effect on December 31, 1977, as held applicable and construed by a court in an action brought under this title.

(c) In the case of a work lawfully reproduced in useful articles that have been offered for sale or other distribution to the public, copyright does not include any right to prevent the making, distribution, or display of pictures or photographs of such articles in connection with advertisements or commentaries related to the distribution or display of such articles, or in connection with news reports.

HOUSE REPORT

H.R. Rep. No. 94-1476, 94th Cong., 2d Sess. 105 (1976)

Section 113 deals with the extent of copyright protection in "works of applied art." The section takes as its starting point the Supreme Court's decision in *Mazer v. Stein,* 347 U.S. 201 (1954), and the first sentence of subsection (a) restates the basic principle established by that decision. The rule of *Mazer,* as affirmed by the bill, is that copyright in a pictorial, graphic or sculptural work will not be affected if the work is employed as the design of a useful article, and will afford protection to the copyright owner against the unauthorized reproduction of his work in useful as well as nonuseful articles. The terms "pictorial, graphic, and sculptural works" and "useful article" are defined in section 101 ....

The broad language of section 106(1) and of subsection (a) of section 113 raises questions as to the extent of copyright protection for a pictorial, graphic, or sculptural work that portrays, depicts, or represents an image of a useful article in such a way that the utilitarian nature of the article can be seen. To take the example usually cited, would copyright in a drawing or model of an automobile give the artist the exclusive right to make automobiles of the same design?

The 1961 Report of the Register of Copyrights stated, on the basis of judicial precedent, that "copyright in a pictorial, graphic, or sculptural work, portraying a useful article as such, does not extend to the manufacture of the useful article itself," and recommended specifically that "the distinctions drawn in this area by existing court decisions" not be altered by the statute. The Register's Supplementary Report, at page 48, cited a number of these decisions, and explained the insuperable difficulty of finding "any statutory formulation that would express the distinction satisfactorily." Section 113(b) reflects the Register's conclusion that "the real need is to make clear that there is no intention to change the present law with respect to the scope of protection in a work portraying a useful article as such."

WHAT IS A "USEFUL ARTICLE"?

§ 101. Definitions

A "useful article" is an article having an intrinsic utilitarian function that is not merely to portray the appearance of the article or to convey information. An article that is normally part of a useful article is considered a "useful article."

Masquerade Novelty Inc. v. Unique Industries, 912 F.2d 663 (3d Cir. 1990). The Third Circuit reversed the trial court's holding that masks designed to resemble the noses of a pig, an elephant, or a parrot, were unprotectable "useful articles." The appellate court found that "the only utilitarian function of the nose masks is in their portrayal of animal noses.... [N]ose masks have no utility that does not derive from their appearance."

> That nose masks are meant to be worn by humans to evoke laughter does not distinguish them from clearly copyrightable works of art like paintings. When worn by a human being, a nose mask may evoke chuckles and guffaws from onlookers. When hung on a wall, a painting may evoke a myriad of human emotions, but we would not say that the painting is not copyrightable because its artistic elements could not be

separated from the emotional effect its creator hoped it would have on persons viewing it. The utilitarian nature of an animal nose mask or a painting of the crucifixion of Jesus Christ inheres solely in its appearance, regardless of the fact that the nose mask's appearance is intended to evoke mirth and the painting's appearance a feeling of religious reverence. Thus, [plaintiff's] nose masks are not "useful articles" ....

What if Masquerade's nose masks could also serve to keep the wearer's nose warm in winter? Should this additional, albeit improbable, utility recast the article as "useful" in the sense of the copyright statute? What about theatrical costumes, or Halloween disguises? Should these items be considered merely "depictive" or should they also be considered articles of clothing? For example, in *Whimsicality, Inc. v. Rubie's Costume Co.,* 891 F.2d 452 (2d Cir. 1989), the court rejected plaintiff's characterization of Halloween costumes as "soft sculptures," finding them to be uncopyrightable clothing.

Subsequently, the Copyright Office issued a Policy Decision on the Registrability of Costume Designs, 56 FR 56530 (November 5, 1991), stating: "Under the adopted practices, masks will be registrable on the basis of pictorial and/or sculptural authorship. Costumes will be treated as useful articles, and will be registrable only upon a finding of separable artistic authorship." The Copyright Office determined that "Since masks generally portray their own appearance, this subject matter appears to fall outside of the definition of 'useful article.'" By contrast, according to the Copyright Office, "Costumes serve a dual purpose of clothing the body and portraying their appearance. Since clothing the body serves as a useful function, costumes fall within the literal definition of useful article."

Does this make sense? If a costume does "clothe the body," it does so in order to permit the wearer to "portray the appearance" of the character depicted by the costume. Although a costume may also be worn for warmth or modesty, those are generally not its purposes. On the other hand, the statute defines a "useful article" as one having "*an* intrinsic utilitarian function." Thus, a subsidiary utilitarian purpose, such as keeping the trick-or-treater warm as well as looking like a dinosaur, might suffice to characterize a Halloween Stegosaurus costume as "useful," no matter how unlikely it is to be used to "clothe the body" at times other than those at which the wearer seeks to portray the extinct reptile. (Of course, under the Policy Decision, the Stegosaurus mask, not being "useful," would be protectable, leaving the determination of the copyrightability of the decapitated remainder of the costume to assessment under the "separability" test, discussed *infra*.)

Is the application of copyright to the design of useful articles consistent with the Constitution, which grants Congress the power to protect "writings" and "authors"? In a concurring opinion in *Mazer v. Stein,* Justice Douglas observed:

> The Copyright Office has supplied us with a long list of such articles which have been copyrighted — statuettes, book ends, clocks, lamps, door

knockers, candlesticks, inkstands, chandeliers, piggy banks, sundials, salt and pepper shakers, fish bowls, casseroles, and ash trays. Perhaps these are all "writings" in the constitutional sense. But to me, at least, they are not obviously so. It is time that we came to the problem full face.

In *Goldstein v. California,* 412 U.S. 546 (1973), involving the question whether states could bar the duplication of musical performances from phonograph records, the Court noted that the terms in the copyright clause of the Constitution "have not been construed in their narrow literal sense but, rather, with the reach necessary to reflect the broad scope of constitutional principles"; it interpreted the word "writings" to "include any physical rendering of the fruits of creative intellectual or aesthetic labor."

KIESELSTEIN-CORD v. ACCESSORIES BY PEARL, INC.

632 F.2d 989 (2d Cir. 1980)

OAKES, CIRCUIT JUDGE: This case is on a razor's edge of copyright law. It involves belt buckles, utilitarian objects which as such are not copyrightable. But these are not ordinary buckles; they are sculptured designs cast in precious metals — decorative in nature and used as jewelry is, principally for ornamentation. We say "on a razor's edge" because the case requires us to draw a fine line under applicable copyright law and regulations. Drawing the line in favor of the appellant designer, we uphold the copyrights granted to him by the Copyright Office and reverse the district court's grant of summary judgment, 489 F. Supp. 732, in favor of the appellee, the copier of appellant's designs.

Facts

Appellant Barry Kieselstein-Cord designs, manufactures exclusively by handcraftsmanship, and sells fashion accessories. To produce the two buckles in issue here, the "Winchester" and the "Vaquero," he worked from original renderings which he had conceived and sketched. He then carved by hand a waxen prototype of each of the works from which molds were made for casting the objects in gold and silver. Difficult to describe, the buckles are solid sculptured designs, in the words of district court Judge Goettel, "with rounded corners, a sculpted surface, ... a rectangular cut-out at one end for the belt attachment," and "several surface levels." The Vaquero gives the appearance of two curved grooves running diagonally across one corner of a modified rectangle and a third groove running across the opposite corner. On the Winchester buckle two parallel grooves cut horizontally across the center of a more tapered form, making a curving ridge which is completed by the tongue of the buckle. A smaller single curved groove flows diagonally across the corner above the tongue.

The Vaquero buckle, created in 1978, was part of a series of works that the designer testified was inspired by a book on design of the art nouveau school and the subsequent viewing of related architecture on a trip to Spain. The buckle was registered with the Copyright Office by appellant's counsel on March 3, 1980, with a publication date of June 1, 1978, as "jewelry," although

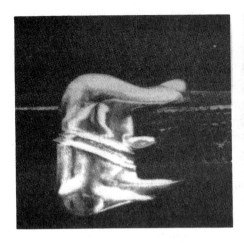 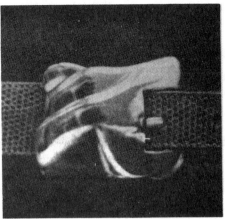

Winchester   Vaquero

the appellant's contribution was listed on the certificate as "original sculpture and design." Explaining why he named the earlier buckle design "Winchester," the designer said that he saw "in [his] mind's eye a correlation between the art nouveau period and the butt of an antique Winchester rifle" and then "pulled these elements together graphically." The registration, which is recorded on a form used for works of art, or models or designs for works of art, specifically describes the nature of the work as "sculpture."

The Winchester buckle in particular has had great success in the marketplace: more than 4,000 belts with Winchester buckles were sold from 1976 to early 1980, and in 1979 sales of the belts amounted to 95% of appellant's more than $300,000 in jewelry sales. A small women's size in silver with "double truncated triangle belt loops" sold, at the time this lawsuit commenced, at wholesale for $147.50 and a larger silver version for men sold at wholesale with loops for $662 and without loops for $465. Lighter-weight men's versions in silver wholesaled for $450 and $295, with and without loops respectively. The gold versions sold at wholesale from $1,200 to $6,000. A shortened version of the belt with the small Winchester buckle is sometimes worn around the neck or elsewhere on the body rather than around the waist. Sales of both buckles were made primarily in high fashion stores and jewelry stores, bringing recognition to appellant as a "designer." This recognition included a 1979 Coty American Fashion Critics' Award for his work in jewelry design as well as election in 1978 to the Council of Fashion Designers of America. Both the Winchester and the Vaquero buckles, donated by appellant after this lawsuit was commenced, have been accepted by the Metropolitan Museum of Art for its permanent collection.

As the court below found, appellee's buckles "appear to be line-for-line copies but are made of common metal rather than" precious metal. Appellee admitted to copying the Vaquero and selling its imitations, and to selling copies of the Winchester. Indeed some of the order blanks of appellee's customers specifically referred to "Barry K Copy," "BK copy," and even "Barry Kieselstein Knock-off.".. [1]

We ... only reach the question whether the buckles may be copyrighted.

Discussion

We commence our discussion by noting that no claim has been made that the appellant's work here in question lacks originality or creativity, elements necessary for copyrighting works of art. *See L. Batlin & Son, Inc. v. Snyder,* 536 F.2d 486 (2d Cir.), *cert. denied,* 429 U.S. 857 (1976); *Alfred Bell & Co. v. Catalda Fine Arts, Inc.,* 191 F.2d 99 (2d Cir. 1951); 1 *Nimmer on Copyright* §§ 2.01, 2.08[B] (1980). The thrust of appellee's argument, as well as of the court's decision below, is that appellant's buckles are not copyrightable because they are "useful articles" with no "pictorial, graphic, or sculptural features that can be identified separately from, and are capable of existing independently of, the utilitarian aspects" of the buckles. The 1976 copyright statute does not provide for the copyrighting of useful articles except to the extent that their designs incorporate artistic features that can be identified separately from the functional elements of the articles. *See* 17 U.S.C. §§ 101, 102. With respect to this question, the law adopts the language of the longstanding Copyright Office regulations, 37 C.F.R. § 202.10(c) (1977) (revoked Jan. 5, 1978, 43 Fed. Reg. 965, 966 (1978)). The regulations in turn were adopted in the mid-1950's, under the 1909 Act, in an effort to implement the Supreme Court's decision in *Mazer v. Stein,* 347 U.S. 201 (1954)....

Ultimately, as Professor Nimmer concludes, none of the authorities — the *Mazer* opinion, the old regulations, or the statute — offer any "ready answer to the line-drawing problem inherent in delineating the extent of copyright protection available for works of applied art." *Id.* at 2-89....

Appellee argues that the belt buckles are merely useful objects, which include decorative features that serve an aesthetic as well as a utilitarian purpose. And the copyright laws, appellee points out, were never intended to nor would the Constitution permit them to protect monopolies on useful articles. But appellee goes too far by further arguing that "copyrightability cannot adhere in the 'conceptual' separation of an artistic element." Brief for Defendant-Appellee at 17. This assertion flies in the face of the legislative intent as expressed in the House Report, which specifically refers to elements that "physically or conceptually, can be identified as separable from the utilitarian aspects of" a useful article. *House Report* at 55, [1976] U.S. Code Cong. & Admin. News at 5668.

We see in appellant's belt buckles conceptually separable sculptural elements, as apparently have the buckles' wearers who have used them as ornamentation for parts of the body other than the waist. The primary ornamental aspect of the Vaquero and Winchester buckles is conceptually separable from their subsidiary utilitarian function. This conclusion is not at variance with the expressed congressional intent to distinguish copyrightable applied art and uncopyrightable industrial design. *House Report* at 55, [1976] U.S. Code

---

[1] The Winchester buckle was registered before the January 1, 1978, effective date of the Copyright Act of 1976.

Cong. & Admin. News at 5668. Pieces of applied art, these buckles may be considered jewelry, the form of which is subject to copyright protection....

Appellant's designs are not, as the appellee suggests in an affidavit, mere variations of "the well-known western buckle." As both the expert witnesses for appellant testified and the Copyright Office's action implied, the buckles rise to the level of creative art.

....

We reverse the grant of summary judgment to the appellee and remand the case for consideration of whether appellant has satisfied the copyright notice requirements.

WEINSTEIN, DISTRICT JUDGE (dissenting): The trial judge was correct on both the law and the facts for the reasons given in his excellent opinion holding that plaintiff was not entitled to copyright protection. *Kieselstein-Cord v. Accessories by Pearl, Inc.*, 489 F. Supp. 732 (S.D.N.Y. 1980). The works sued on are, while admirable aesthetically pleasing examples of modern design, indubitably belt buckles and nothing else; their innovations of form are inseparable from the important function they serve — helping to keep the tops of trousers at waist level.

The conclusion that affirmance is required is reached reluctantly. The result does deny protection to designers who use modern three-dimensional abstract works artfully incorporated into a functional object as an inseparable aspect of the article while granting it to those who attach their independent representational art, or even their trite gimmickry, to a useful object for purposes of enhancement. Moreover, this result enables the commercial pirates of the marketplace to appropriate for their own profit, without any cost to themselves, the works of talented designers who enrich our lives with their intuition and skill. The crass are rewarded, the artist who creates beauty is not. All of us are offended by the flagrant copying of another's work. This is regrettable, but it is not for this court to twist the law in order to achieve a result Congress has denied.

....

The statute follows the decision of the Supreme Court in *Mazer v. Stein*, 347 U.S. 201, *rehearing denied*, 347 U.S. 949 (1954). In *Mazer*, the Court held that independent works of art may be copyrighted even if they are incorporated into useful articles — "nothing in the copyright statute ... support[s] the argument that the intended use or use in industry of an article eligible for copyright bars or invalidates its registration." *Id.* at 218. But the copyright protection covered only that aspect of the article that was a separately identifiable work of art independent of the useful article, in that instance a statuette used as part of a lamp.

Among recent decisions making this same distinction is *Esquire v. Ringer*, 591 F.2d 796 (D.C. Cir.), *cert. denied*, 440 U.S. 908, *rehearing denied*, 441 U.S. 917 (1979). *Esquire* denied copyright protection to the overall shape of a lighting fixture because of its integration of the functional aspects of the entire lighting assembly. The "overall design or configuration of a utilitarian object, even if it is determined by aesthetic as well as functional considerations, is not eligible for copyright." *Id.* at 804.

While the distinction is not precise, the courts, both before and after *Mazer*, have tried to follow the principle of the copyright act permitting copyright to extend only to ornamental or superfluous designs contained within useful objects while denying it to artistically designed functional components of useful objects. Generally they have favored representational art as opposed to non-representation[al] artistic forms which are embodied in, and part of the structure of, a useful article. *Compare, e.g., Ted Arnold Ltd. v. Silvercraft Co.*, 259 F. Supp. 733 (S.D.N.Y. 1966) (antique telephone used to encase a pencil sharpener copyrightable); *Royalty Designs Inc. v. Thrifticheck Service Corp.*, 204 F. Supp. 702 (S.D.N.Y. 1962) (toy banks in shape of dogs copyrightable); *Scarves by Vera, Inc. v. United Merchants and Mfrs., Inc.*, 173 F. Supp. 625 (S.D.N.Y. 1959) (designs printed upon scarves copyrightable); *Syracuse China Corp. v. Stanley Roberts, Inc.*, 180 F. Supp. 527 (S.D.N.Y. 1960) (designs on dinnerware copyrightable) *with Esquire v. Ringer*, 591 F.2d 796 (D.C. Cir.), cert. denied, 440 U.S. 908, *rehearing denied*, 441 U.S. 917 (1979) (copyright denied to overall design of lighting fixture); *SCOA Industries, Inc. v. Famolare, Inc.*, 192 U.S.P.Q. 216 (S.D.N.Y. 1976) (wavy lines on soles of shoes not copyrightable); *Vacheron & Constantin-Le Coultre Watches, Inc. v. Benrus Watch Co.*, 155 F. Supp. 932 (S.D.N.Y. 1957), *affirmed in part, reversed on other grounds*, 260 F.2d 637 (2d Cir. 1958) (artistically designed non-representational watchface not copyrightable); *Russell v. Trimfit, Inc.*, 428 F. Supp. 91 (E.D. Pa. 1977), *affirmed*, 568 F.2d 770 (3d Cir. 1978) (designs of "toe socks" not copyrightable); *Jack Adelman, Inc. v. Sonners & Gordon, Inc.*, 112 F. Supp. 187 (S.D.N.Y. 1934) (picture of a dress may be copyrighted but the dress itself may not be). The relative certainty that has developed in this area of the law should not be disturbed absent some compelling development — and none has thus far been presented.

Interpretation and application of the copyright statute is facilitated by House Report No. 94-1476, U.S. Code Cong. & Admin. News 1976, p. 5658, by the Committee on the Judiciary. It explicitly indicated that the rule of *Mazer* was incorporated.

> In accordance with the Supreme Court's decision in *Mazer v. Stein*, 347 U.S. 201, 74 S. Ct. 460, 98 L. Ed. 630 (1954), works of "applied art" encompass all original pictorial, graphic, and sculptural works that are intended to be or have been embodied in useful articles, regardless of factors such as mass production, commercial exploitation, and the potential availability of design patent protection ....

> The Committee has added language to the definition of "pictorial, graphic, and sculptural works" in an effort to make clearer the distinction between works of applied art protectable under the bill and industrial designs not subject to copyright protection. The declaration that "pictorial, graphic, and sculptural works" include "works of artistic craftsmanship insofar as their form but not their mechanical or utilitarian aspects are concerned" is classic language: it is drawn from Copyright Office regulations promulgated in the 1940's and expressly endorsed by the Supreme Court in the *Mazer* case.

>   ....

In adopting this amendatory language, the Committee is seeking to draw as clear a line as possible between copyrightable works of applied art and uncopyrighted works of industrial design. A two-dimensional painting, drawing, or graphic work is still capable of being identified as such when it is printed on or applied to utilitarian articles such as textile fabrics, wallpaper, containers, and the like. The same is true when a statue or carving is used to embellish an industrial product or, as in the *Mazer* case, is incorporated into a product without losing its ability to exist independently as a work of art. On the other hand, *although the shape of an industrial product may be aesthetically satisfying and valuable, the Committee's intention is not to offer it copyright protection under the bill.* Unless the shape of an automobile, airplane, ladies' dress, food processor, television set, or any other industrial product contains some element that, physically or conceptually, can be identified as separable from the utilitarian aspects of that article, the design would not be copyrighted under the bill. The test of separability and independence from "the utilitarian aspects of the article" does not depend upon the nature of the design — that is, even if the appearance of an article is determined by aesthetic (as opposed to functional) considerations, only elements, if any, which can be identified separately from the useful article as such are copyrightable. *And, even if the three-dimensional design contains some such element (for example, a carving on the back of a chair or a floral relief design on silver flatware), copyright protection would extend only to that element, and would not cover the overall configuration of the utilitarian article as such.*

1976 U.S. Code Cong. & Admin. News, pp. 5667-5668. (Emphasis supplied.)
Congress considered and declined to enact legislation that would have extended copyright protection to "[t]he 'design of a useful article' ... including its two-dimensional or three-dimensional features of shape and surface, which make up the appearance of the article." H.R. 2223, Title II, § 201(b)(2), 94th Cong., 1st Sess. (January 28, 1975). Passage of this provision was recommended by the Register of Copyrights, ... and the United States Department of Commerce.... It was opposed by the Department of Justice on policy grounds.... The Justice Department noted the important substantive objections to the proposal — primarily it would charge the public a fee for the use of improved and pleasing new designs and styles in useful articles.

....

While the protection period as proposed for the new type of ornamental design protection is only a maximum of 10 years as compared with the maximum of 14 years available for a design patent, it is granted without the need of meeting the novelty and unobviousness requirements of the patent statute. A threshold consideration before finding that the needs are such that this new type of protection should be available *is whether the benefits to the public of such protection outweigh the burdens. We believe that insufficient need has been shown to date to justify removing from the public domain and possible use by others of the rights and benefits proposed under the present bill for such ornamental designs. We be-*

lieve that design patents, as are granted today, are as far as the public should go to grant exclusive rights for ornamental designs of useful articles in the absence of an adequate showing that the new protection will provide substantial benefits to the general public which outweigh removing such designs from free public use.

While it has been said that the examination procedure in the Patent Office results in serious delays in the issuance of a design patent so as to be a significant problem and damaging to "inventors" of ornamental designs of useful articles, *the desirable free use of designs which do not rise to patentable invention of ornamental designs of useful articles are believed* to be paramount.

If the contribution made to the public by the creation of an ornamental design of a useful article is insufficient to rise to patentable novelty, the design should not be protected by the law. The Department of Justice has consistently opposed legislation of this character.

To omit Federal statutory protection for the form of a useful object is not to deny the originator of that form any remedy whatsoever. If he can prove that competitors are passing their goods as the originator's by copying the product's design, he may bring an unfair competition action against such copyists.

Id. at 139-140. (Emphasis supplied.)

No additional testimony was received with respect to this aspect of the House bill. The Joint Senate-House Conference Committee deleted the design protection section to give further consideration to its administrative difficulties and to the benefits and burdens created by limiting the free public domain. 1976 U.S. Code Cong. & Admin. News, pp. 5663, 5832. The attempt to gain protection was again mounted when Representative Thomas F. Railsback introduced H.R. 4530 on June 19, 1979 to amend the Copyright Act of 1976. H.R. 4530's section 902 contains protections for the design of useful objects identical to those omitted from the 1976 Copyright Act. It was not adopted by Congress.

Interestingly, even if the design protection section proposed by the Department of Commerce and Representative Railsback had been passed, appellant's buckles might still have been excluded under the following subsection excluding three-dimensional features of apparel:

Designs Not Subject to Protection

§ 202. *Protection under this title shall not be available for a design that is —*

   . . .

   (e) *composed of three-dimensional features of shape and surface with respect to men's, women's and children's apparel,* including undergarments and outerwear.

(Emphasis supplied.) *See also* proposed § 202(b) (shape which has become common); § 202(c) (variants).

The distinctions between copyrightable "pictorial, graphic and sculptural works" and noncopyrightable industrial "designs" reflect serious concerns about the promotion of competition, the widespread availability of quality products and the advancement of technology through copying and modification. *See, e.g.,* G. Nelson, Design, 170 (1979) (experience suggests that free copying results in more rapid development)....

Important policies are obviously at stake. Should we encourage the artist and increase the compensation to the creative? Or should we allow cheap reproductions which will permit our less affluent to afford beautiful artifacts? Appellant sold the original for $600.00 and up. Defendant's version went for one-fiftieth of that sum.

Thus far Congress and the Supreme Court have answered in favor of commerce and the masses rather than the artists, designers and the well-to-do. Any change must be left to those higher authorities. The choices are legislative not judicial.

QUESTIONS

1. Was the ornamental belt buckle in the principal case also protectible, as an initial matter, under the design patent laws? Now that the court has held that it is protectible under copyright, must Kieselstein-Cord opt for protection under one or the other statute, or may he claim protection under both? Can you formulate any argument, based upon the Constitution or otherwise, that would in effect require "preemption" as between the copyright and patent laws? *See Application of Yardley,* 493 F.2d 1389 (C.C.P.A. 1974); 37 C.F.R. § 202.10(b), reproduced at Appendix C to Casebook.

2. In the *Esquire* case (discussed in the principal case), the claimant of copyright in the street-light design, reproduced just below, argued that, for

the better part of the day, the fixture had no utilitarian function at all but was in fact exclusively a publicly displayed work of sculpture. If you agree, does this not make *Esquire* an even more appealing case for copyright protection than *Kieselstein-Cord* (despite their opposite results)?

3. It has been argued that the view of the dissenting judge in the *Kieselstein-Cord* case would work an impermissible discrimination against designs that emphasize line and shape rather than the ornate, thus ignoring the admonition of Justice Holmes in *Bleistein v. Donaldson Lithographing Co.*, at Chapter 1, Subchapter B, *supra* that judges must not sit as arbiters of national taste. Do you agree?

4. On the other hand, do you agree with the claim of the Register of Copyrights (set forth by the Court of Appeals for the District of Columbia Circuit in *Esquire, Inc. v. Ringer*) that protection of such designs as those in the principal case would mean that "the whole realm of consumer products — garments, toasters, refrigerators, furniture, bathtubs, automobiles, etc. — and industrial products designed to have aesthetic appeal — subway cars, computers, photocopying machines, typewriters, adding machines, etc." would also qualify for copyright protection?

CAROL BARNHART INC. v. ECONOMY COVER CORP.

773 F.2d 411 (2d Cir. 1985)

MANSFIELD, CIRCUIT JUDGE:

Carol Barnhart Inc. ("Barnhart"), which sells display forms to department stores, distributors, and small retail stores, appeals from a judgment of the Eastern District of New York, Leonard D. Wexler, Judge, granting a motion for summary judgment made by defendant Economy Cover Corporation ("Economy"), which sells a wide variety of display products primarily to jobbers and distributors. Barnhart's complaint alleges that Economy has infringed its copyright and engaged in unfair competition by offering for sale display forms copied from four original "sculptural forms" to which Barnhart holds the copyright. Judge Wexler granted Economy's motion for summary judgment on the ground that plaintiff's mannequins of partial human torsos used to display articles of clothing are utilitarian articles not containing separable works of art, and thus are not copyrightable. We affirm.

The bones of contention are four human torso forms designed by Barnhart, each of which is life-size, without neck, arms, or a back, and made of expandable white styrene. Plaintiff's president created the forms in 1982 by using clay, buttons, and fabric to develop an initial mold, which she then used to build an aluminum mold into which the polystyrene is poured to manufacture the sculptural display form. There are two male and two female upper torsos. One each of the male and female torsos is unclad for the purpose of displaying shirts and sweaters, while the other two are sculpted with shirts for displaying sweaters and jackets. All the forms, which are otherwise life-like and anatomically accurate, have hollow backs designed to hold excess fabric when the garment is fitted onto the form. Barnhart's advertising stresses the forms' uses to display items such as sweaters, blouses, and dress shirts, and states that they come "[p]ackaged in UPS-size boxes for easy shipping and [are] sold in multiples of twelve.". . .

Since the four Barnhart forms are concededly useful articles, the crucial issue in determining their copyrightability is whether they possess artistic or aesthetic features that are physically or conceptually separable from their utilitarian dimension. . . .

[The court reviewed the legislative history, since 1909, of protection for pictorial and sculptural works and traced the development of the "separability" principle.]

The legislative history thus confirms that, while copyright protection has increasingly been extended to cover articles having a utilitarian dimension, Congress has explicitly refused copyright protection for works of applied art or industrial design which have aesthetic or artistic features that cannot be identified separately from the useful article. Such works are not copyrightable regardless of the fact that they may be "aesthetically satisfying and valuable." H.R. Rep. No. 1476, *supra,* at 55, 1976 U.S. Code Cong. & Admin. News at 5668.

Applying these principles, we are persuaded that since the aesthetic and artistic features of the Barnhart forms are inseparable from the forms' use as utilitarian articles the forms are not copyrightable. Appellant emphasizes that clay sculpting, often used in traditional sculpture, was used in making the molds for the forms. It also stresses that the forms have been responded to as sculptural forms, and have been used for purposes other than modeling clothes, e.g., as decorating props and signs without any clothing or accessories. While this may indicate that the forms are "aesthetically satisfying and valuable," it is insufficient to show that the forms possess aesthetic or artistic features that are physically or conceptually separable from the forms' use as utilitarian objects to display clothes. On the contrary, to the extent the forms possess aesthetically pleasing features, even when these features are considered in the aggregate, they cannot be conceptualized as existing independently of their utilitarian function.

Appellant seeks to rebut this conclusion by arguing that the four forms represent a concrete expression of a particular idea, e.g., the idea of a woman's blouse, and that the form involved, a human torso, is traditionally copyrightable. Appellant suggests that since the Barnhart forms fall within the traditional category of sculpture of the human body, they should be subjected to a lower level of scrutiny in determining [their] copyrightability. We disagree. We find no support in the statutory language or legislative history for the claim that merely because a utilitarian article falls within a traditional art form it is entitled to a lower level of scrutiny in determining its copyrightability. Recognition of such a claim would in any event conflict with the anti-discrimination principle Justice Holmes enunciated in *Bleistein v. Donaldson Lithographing Co., supra,* 188 U.S. at 251-52, 23 S. Ct. at 300.

Nor do we agree that copyrightability here is dictated by our decision in *Kieselstein-Cord v. Accessories by Pearl, Inc.,* 632 F.2d 989 (2d Cir. 1980) . . . .

What distinguishes those buckles from the Barnhart forms is that the ornamented surfaces of the buckles were not in any respect required by their utilitarian functions; the artistic and aesthetic features could thus be conceived of as having been added to, or superimposed upon, an otherwise utilitarian article. The unique artistic design was wholly unnecessary to performance of the utilitarian function. In the case of the Barnhart forms, on the other hand, the features claimed to be aesthetic or artistic, e.g., the life-size configuration of the breasts and the width of the shoulders, are inextricably intertwined with the utilitarian feature, the display of clothes. Whereas a model of a human torso, in order to serve its utilitarian function, must have some configuration of the chest and some width of shoulders, a belt buckle can serve its function satisfactorily without any ornamentation of the type that renders the *Kieselstein-Cord* buckles distinctive.[5]

The judgment of the district court is affirmed.

JON O. NEWMAN, CIRCUIT JUDGE, dissenting:

This case concerns the interesting though esoteric issue of "conceptual separability" under the Copyright Act of 1976. Because I believe the majority has

---

[5] Our learned colleague, Judge Newman, would have copyrightability of a utilitarian article turn on "whether visual inspection of the article and consideration of all pertinent evidence would engender in the [ordinary] observer's mind a separate non-utilitarian concept that can displace, at least temporarily, the utilitarian aspect." (Dissenting Op. p. 423). The difficulty with this proposal is that it uses as its yardstick a standard so ethereal as to amount to a "non-test" that would be extremely difficult, if not impossible, to administer or apply. Whether a utilitarian object could temporarily be conceived of as a work of art would require a judicial investigation into the ways in which it might on occasion have been displayed and the extent of the displays. It might involve expert testimony and some kind of survey evidence, as distinguished from reliance upon the judge as an ordinary observer.

Almost any utilitarian article may be viewed by some separately as art, depending on how it is displayed (e.g., a can of Campbell Soup or a pair of ornate scissors affixed to the wall of a museum of modern art). But it is the object, not the form of display, for which copyright protection is sought. Congress has made it reasonably clear that copyrightability of the object should turn on its ordinary use as viewed by the average observer, not by a temporary flight of fancy that could attach to any utilitarian object, including an automobile engine, depending on how it is displayed.

The illusory nature of the standard suggested by Judge Newman is confirmed by his suggestion that under it some mannequins might qualify as copyrightable sculptures whereas others might not, depending on numerous factors, including the material used, the angular configuration of the limbs, the facial figures and the hair. Indeed, his uncertainty as to whether the styrene mannequin chests clothed with a shirt or blouse could be viewed by the ordinary observer as art only serves to underscore the bottomless pit that would be created by such a vague test. However, regardless of which standard is applied we disagree with the proposition that the mannequins here, when viewed as hollowed-out three-dimensional forms (as presented for copyright) as distinguished from two-dimensional photographs, could be viewed by the ordinary observer as anything other than objects having a utilitarian function as mannequins. It would only be by concealing the open, hollowed-out rear half of the object, which is obviously designed to facilitate pinning or tucking in of garments, that an illusion of a sculpture can be created. In that case (as with the photos relied on by the dissent) the subject would not be the same as that presented for copyright.

either misunderstood the nature of this issue or applied an incorrect standard in resolving the issue in this case, I respectfully dissent from the judgment affirming the District Court's grant of summary judgment for the defendant. I would grant summary judgment to the plaintiff as to two of the objects in question and remand for trial of disputed issues of fact as to the other two objects in question.

... Each of the four forms in this case is indisputably a "useful article" as that term is defined in section 101 of the Act, 17 U.S.C. § 101 (1982), since each has the "intrinsic utilitarian function" of serving as a means of displaying clothing and accessories to customers of retail stores. Thus, the issue becomes whether the designs of these useful articles have "sculptural features that can be identified separately from, and are capable of existing independently of, the utilitarian aspects" of the forms.

This elusive standard was somewhat clarified by the House Report accompanying the bill that became the 1976 Act. The Report states that the article must contain "some element that, *physically or conceptually,* can be identified as separable from the utilitarian aspects of that article." H.R. Rep. No. 1476, 94th Cong., 2d Sess. 55, reprinted in 1976 U.S. Code Cong. & Admin. News 5668 (emphasis added). In this Circuit it is settled, and the majority does not dispute, that "conceptual separability" is distinct from "physical separability" and, when present, entitles the creator of a useful article to a copyright on its design....

What must be carefully considered is the meaning and application of the principle of "conceptual separability." Initially, it may be helpful to make the obvious point that this principle must mean something other than "physical separability." That latter principle is illustrated by the numerous familiar examples of useful objects ornamented by a drawing, a carving, a sculpted figure, or any other decorative embellishment that could physically appear apart from the useful article. Professor Nimmer offers the example of the sculptured jaguar that adorns the hood of and provides the name for the well-known British automobile. *See* 1 Nimmer on Copyright § 2.08[B] at 2-96.1 (1985). With all of the utilitarian elements of the automobile physically removed, the concept, indeed the embodiment, of the artistic creation of the jaguar would remain. Since "conceptual separability" is not the same as "physical separability," it should also be obvious that a design feature can be "conceptually separable" from the utilitarian aspect of a useful article even if it cannot be separated physically.

There are several possible ways in which "conceptual separability" might be understood. One concerns usage. An article used primarily to serve its utilitarian function might be regarded as lacking "conceptually separable" design elements even though those design elements rendered it usable secondarily solely as an artistic work. There is danger in this approach in that it would deny copyright protection to designs of works of art displayed by a minority because they are also used by a majority as useful articles. The copyrightable design of a life-size sculpture of the human body should not lose its copyright protection simply because mannequin manufacturers copy it, replicate it in cheap materials, and sell it in large quantities to department stores to display clothing.

A somewhat related approach, suggested by a sentence in Judge Oakes' opinion in *Kieselstein-Cord,* is to uphold the copyright whenever the decorative or aesthetically pleasing aspect of the article can be said to be "primary" and the utilitarian function can be said to be "subsidiary." 632 F.2d at 993. This approach apparently does not focus on frequency of utilitarian and non-utilitarian usage since the belt buckles in that case were frequently used to fasten belts and less frequently used as pieces of ornamental jewelry displayed at various locations other than the waist. The difficulty with this approach is that it offers little guidance to the trier of fact, or the judge endeavoring to determine whether a triable issue of fact exists, as to what is being measured by the classifications "primary" and "subsidiary."

Another approach, also related to the first, is suggested by Professor Nimmer, who argues that "conceptual separability exists where there is any substantial likelihood that even if the article had no utilitarian use it would still be marketable to some significant segment of the community simply because of its aesthetic qualities." 1 Nimmer, *supra,* § 2.08[B] at 2-96.2 (footnote omitted). This "market" approach risks allowing a copyright only to designs of forms within the domain of popular art, a hazard Professor Nimmer acknowledges. *See id.* at 2-96.3. However, various sculpted forms would be recognized as works of art by many, even though those willing to purchase them for display in their homes might be few in number and not a "significant segment of the community."

Some might suggest that "conceptual separability" exists whenever the design of a form has sufficient aesthetic appeal to be appreciated for its artistic qualities. That approach has plainly been rejected by Congress. The House Report makes clear that, if the artistic features cannot be identified separately, the work is not copyrightable even though such features are "aesthetically satisfying and valuable." H.R. Rep. No. 1476, *supra,* at 55, 1976 U.S. Code Cong. & Admin. News at 5668. A chair may be so artistically designed as to merit display in a museum, but that fact alone cannot satisfy the test of "conceptual separateness." The viewer in the museum sees and apprehends a well-designed chair, not a work of art with a design that is conceptually separate from the functional purposes of an object on which people sit.

How, then, is "conceptual separateness" to be determined? In my view, the answer derives from the word "conceptual." For the design features to be "conceptually separate" from the utilitarian aspects of the useful article that embodies the design, the article must stimulate in the mind of the beholder a concept that is separate from the concept evoked by its utilitarian function. The test turns on what may reasonably be understood to be occurring in the mind of the beholder or, as some might say, in the "mind's eye" of the beholder. This formulation requires consideration of who the beholder is and when a concept may be considered "separate."

... [Judge Newman concluded that the "relevant beholder must be that most useful legal personage — the ordinary, reasonable observer."] The "separateness" of the utilitarian and non-utilitarian concepts engendered by an article's design is itself a perplexing concept. I think the requisite "separateness" exists whenever the design creates in the mind of the ordinary observer two different concepts that are not inevitably entertained simultaneously. Again, the example of the artistically designed chair displayed in a museum may be helpful. The ordinary observer can be expected to apprehend the design of a chair whenever the object is viewed. He may, in addition, entertain the concept of a work of art, but, if this second concept is engendered in the observer's mind simultaneously with the concept of the article's utilitarian function, the requisite "separateness" does not exist. The test is not whether the observer fails to recognize the object as a chair but only whether the concept of the utilitarian function can be displaced in the mind by some other concept. That does not occur, at least for the ordinary observer, when viewing even the most artistically designed chair. It may occur, however, when viewing some other object if the utilitarian function of the object is not perceived at all; it may also occur, even when the utilitarian function is perceived by observation, perhaps aided by explanation, if the concept of the utilitarian function can be displaced in the observer's mind while he entertains the separate concept of some non-utilitarian function. The separate concept will normally be that of a work of art.

Some might think that the requisite separability of concepts exists whenever the design of a form engenders in the mind of the ordinary observer any concept that is distinct from the concept of the form's utilitarian function. Under this approach, the design of an artistically designed chair would receive copyright protection if the ordinary observer viewing it would entertain the concept of a work of art in addition to the concept of a chair. That approach, I fear, would subvert the Congressional effort to deny copyright protection to designs of useful articles that are aesthetically pleasing....

In endeavoring to draw the line between the design of an aesthetically pleasing useful article, which is not copyrightable, and the copyrightable design of a useful article that engenders a concept separate from the concept of its utilitarian function, courts will inevitably be drawn into some minimal inquiry as to the nature of art. The need for the inquiry is regrettable, since courts must not become the arbiters of taste in art or any other aspect of aesthetics. However, as long as "conceptual separability" determines whether the design of a useful article is copyrightable, some threshold assessment of art is inevitable since the separate concept that will satisfy the test of "conceptual separability" will often be the concept of a work of art. Of course, courts must not assess the *quality* of art, but a determination of whether a design engenders the concept of a work of art, separate from the concept of an article's utilitarian function, necessarily requires some consideration of whether the object *is* a work of art.

... Our case involving the four styrene chest forms seems to me a much easier case than *Kieselstein-Cord*. An ordinary observer, indeed, an ordinary reader of this opinion who views the two unclothed forms depicted in figures 1 and 2 below, would be most unlikely even to entertain, from visual inspection alone, the concept of a mannequin with the utilitarian function of displaying a shirt or a blouse. The initial concept in the observer's mind, I believe, would be of an art object, an entirely understandable mental impression based on previous viewing of unclad torsos displayed as artistic sculptures. Even after learning that these two forms are used to display clothing in retail stores, the only reasonable conclusion that an ordinary viewer would reach is that the

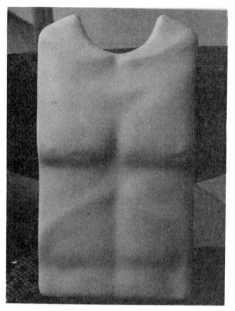

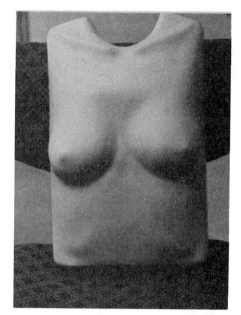

Figure 1   Figure 2

forms have both a utilitarian function and an entirely separate function of serving as a work of art. I am confident that the ordinary observer could reasonably conclude only that these two forms are not simply mannequins that happen to have sufficient aesthetic appeal to qualify as works of art, but that the conception in the mind is that of a work of art *in addition to and capable of being entertained separately from* the concept of a mannequin, if the latter concept is entertained at all. As appellant contends, with pardonable hyperbole, the design of Michelangelo's "David" would not cease to be copyrightable simply because cheap copies of it were used by a retail store to display clothing.

This is not to suggest that the design of every form intended for use as a mannequin automatically qualifies for copyright protection whenever it is deemed to have artistic merit. Many mannequins, perhaps most, by virtue of the combination of the material used, the angular configuration of the limbs, the facial features, and the representation of hair create the visual impression that they are mannequins and not anything else. The fact that in some instances a mannequin of that sort is displayed in a store as an eye-catching item apart from its function of enhancing the appearance of clothes, in a living room as a conversation piece, or even in a museum as an interesting example of contemporary industrial design does not mean that it engenders a concept separate from the concept of a mannequin. The two forms depicted in figures 1 and 2, however, if perceived as mannequins at all, clearly engender an entirely separable concept of an art object, one that can be entertained in the mind without simultaneously perceiving the forms as mannequins at all.

....

Of course, appellant's entitlement to a copyright on the design of the un-clothed forms would give it only limited, though apparently valuable, protection. The copyright would not bar imitators from designing human chests. It would only bar them from copying the precise design embodied in appellant's forms.

As for the two forms, depicted in figures 3 and 4 below, of chests clothed with a shirt or a blouse, I am uncertain what concept or concepts would be engendered in the mind of an ordinary observer.

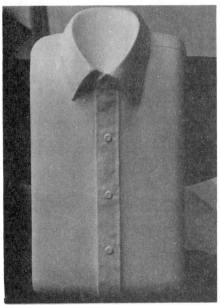

Figure 3　　　　　　　　　　　　　　　　Figure 4

I think it is likely that these forms too would engender the separately entertained concept of an art object whether or not they also engendered the concept of a mannequin. But this is not the only conclusion a reasonable trier could reach as to the perception of an ordinary observer. That observer might always perceive them as mannequins or perhaps as devices advertising for sale the particular style of shirt or blouse sculpted on each form. I think a reasonable trier could conclude either way on the issue of "conceptual separability" as to the clothed forms. That issue is therefore not amenable to summary judgment and should, in my view, be remanded for trial. In any event, I do not agree that the only reasonable conclusion a trier of fact could reach is that the clothed forms create no concept separable from the concept of their utilitarian function.

I would grant summary judgment to the copyright proprietor as to the design of the two nude forms and remand for trial with respect to the two clothed forms.

The Second Circuit has continued to struggle with conceptual separability. Judge Oakes, *Kieselstein-Cord*'s majority author, attempted to harmonize that decision with *Carol Barnhart* in a controversy concerning the copyrightability of a bicycle rack (see photograph below). In *Brandir Int'l v. Cascade Pac. Lumber Co.*, 834 F.2d 1142 (2d Cir. 1987), the panel majority held the form of an undulating tubed bicycle rack inseparable from its function. According to the majority, if functional concerns influenced the work's aesthetically pleasing appearance, the sculptural features would be deemed inseparable under § 101. (The court gave credit to Denicola, *Applied Art and Industrial Design: A Suggested Approach to Copyright in Useful Articles,* 67 Minn. L. Rev. 707 (1983), for devising the test.) The majority indicated that the inquiry into whether form follows function in the work under scrutiny would relieve judges of the improper burden of evaluating the aesthetic merits of nonfunctional art. In dissent, Judge Winter contended that the majority's approach virtually eliminated "conceptual separability." Worse, rather than protecting judges from art criticism, the majority's emphasis on the influence of utilitarian concerns in the design process would in fact require too much inquiry into the creative processes.

Reproduced with permission
Photograph by Joanne Gere

Although the Second Circuit affirmed the denial of copyright protection to plaintiff's bicycle rack, it reversed the district court's holding that the rack also failed to qualify for trademark protection. The appellate court emphasized that

> the principle of conceptual separability of functional design elements in copyright law is different from the somewhat similar principle of functionality as developed in trademark law.... [As a matter of trademark law] the fact that a design feature performs a function does not make it essential to the performance of that function; it is instead the absence of alternative constructions performing the same function that renders the feature functional.

The court remanded for a determination whether the particular form of plaintiff's bicycle rack passed this more forgiving standard.

QUESTIONS

1. The *Brandir* case, like *Frederick Warne & Co. v. Book Sales, supra,* provides an example of the overlapping of copyright and trademark law. In both instances, trademark law afforded potential relief to the claimant when copyright protection failed. In *Warne,* trademark protection may have been available even though the copyrights on the Peter Rabbit drawings had expired. In *Brandir,* trademark protection may have applied despite the copyright policy barring protection for nonseparable useful objects. Why should a claimant be able to achieve through trademark doctrines a result which the copyright law forecloses?

2. Suppose copyright protection is sought for an abstract horizontal shape embodied in plaster and entitled "Repose." Would embodiment of this shape in a bed or other piece of furniture disqualify the design as the kind of "overall shape or configuration of a utilitarian article" excluded from protection under the language of the House Report, or would it still be protectible?

3. For each of the following objects, determine first whether it is a "useful article" and second, if it is, whether it is eligible for copyright protection:

(a) A toy/model airplane, see *Gay Toys, Inc. v. Buddy L Corp.,* 703 F.2d 970 (6th Cir. 1983);

(b) A wire-spoked automobile wheel cover (see next page) that simulates an old-fashioned wire wheel, see *Norris Indus., Inc. v. International Tel. & Tel. Corp.,* 696 F.2d 918 (11th Cir.), *cert. denied,* 464 U.S. 818 (1983);

(c) A display case for eyeglasses, shaped like a box containing a curving "free form sculpture" which creates a scalloped effect, see *Trans-World Mfg. v. Al Nyman & Sons,* 95 F.R.D. 95 (D. Del. 1982).

4. Which of the following pictured works, if any, are copyrightable? *

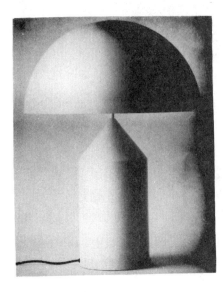

---

*All of the works in the photographs on this page and page 209 were displayed in the exhibition "Design Since 1945" at the Philadelphia Museum of Art, from October 1983 to January 1984. The designer, title, and date of each work is as follows: *This page*. Top left: P. McCobb, "Planner Group" components (1949). Top right: H.T. Baumann, "Brasilia" coffee and tea service (1975). Bottom left: V. Magistretti, "Atollo" table lamp (1977). Bottom right: S. Yanagi, "Butterfly" stool (1956). *Page 209*. Top: DePas, D'Urbino, Lomazzi, "Joe" chair (1970). Bottom: F.O. Gehry, "Easy Edges" rocking chair (1972). These works are reproduced with the permission of the Philadelphia Museum of Art (and, for the "Joe" chair, the permission of Stendig, Inc.).

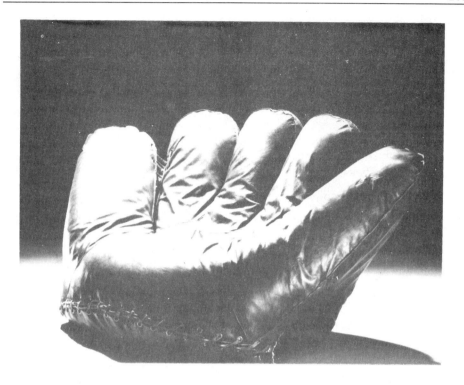

COPYRIGHTABILITY OF TYPEFACE DESIGNS

A troubling issue of design protection that was raised in the debates leading to the enactment of the 1976 Copyright Act concerned typeface design. The House Report (at page 55) included the following passage:

> The Committee has considered, but chosen to defer, the possibility of protecting the design of typefaces. A "typeface" can be defined as a set of letters, numbers, or other symbolic characters, whose forms are related by repeating design elements consistently applied in a notational system and are intended to be embodied in articles whose intrinsic utilitarian function is for use in composing text or other cognizable combinations of characters. The Committee does not regard the design of typeface, as thus defined, to be a copyrightable "pictorial, graphic, or sculptural work" within the meaning of this bill and the application of the dividing line in section 101.

The issue of typeface protection had become particularly heated by the early 1970's, as a result of the development of new photocomposition techniques that made it possible readily to make unauthorized copies of typeface designs. Register Barbara Ringer, on November 6, 1974, held the first rulemaking hearing in the history of the Copyright Office, for the purpose of determining whether to modify an existing Office regulation that was generally understood to bar copyright for typeface designs. Proponents of protection contended — at the Copyright Office hearing and at concurrent congressional hearings on the pending revision bill — that original designs for fonts of type are "writings of an author" under both the Constitution and the 1909 statute, that caselaw was not inconsistent with such protection, that registration would impose no burden on authors and reprinters, and that protection should be made available under both copyright and the projected new design legislation (at that time, title II of the copyright bill, ultimately deleted before passage). Opponents claimed, among other things, that design protection would simply invite the major typeface manufacturers to engage in behavior violative of the antitrust laws and would lead to suits to enjoin publication of printed matter. The Copyright Office chose ultimately to decline registration for typeface designs, and a mandamus action was brought to compel such registration. In *Eltra Corp. v. Ringer*, 579 F.2d 294 (4th Cir. 1978), mandamus was denied, the court concluding that typeface was not a "work of art" within the subject matter covered by the 1909 Act. Should that result be controlling today? How dispositive is the pertinent passage from the House Report quoted above? While considering these questions, study the typeface samples reproduced (lawfully?) below.

Lightline LIGHTLINE
LINCOLN GOTHIC
Lubalin Graph LUBALI
Lubalin Graph LUBAI
Lubalin Graph LUB
Lubalin Graph LUI
Lubalin Graph LUI
Lubalin Graph LUI
Lucifer LUCIFER
Lys Calligraph L
Macbeth MACBETH macbi
MACHINE
MACHINE
MADISON MADISON
Madisonian MADISO
Manchester MANCHE!
MANDARIN
Mandate MANDATE
Manhattan MANHATT
MANUSCRIPT INITIAI
MARBLEHEART

Marten Roman MARI
Mastodon MASTOD(
Maxie MAXIE
Melior MELIOR
Melior MELIOR
Melior MELIOR
MICHELANGELO
MICROGRAMMA
MICROGRAMM
MICROGRAMI
Milano Roman MILAN
Mistral MISTRAL
Modern No 20 MODE
Modernique MODI
Modernique MODI
Moonshadow MOONSHA
MOORE COMPUTER
MOORE LIBERTY
Musketeer MUSKETEER
Musketeer MUSKETEE
Musketeer MUSKETEE

ROBERT MERGES, OVERVIEW OF DESIGN PATENTS*

Due to a lengthy processing time, high application cost, strict and wavering standards, and a long history of judicial hostility, the design patent system has been criticized as ineffective and in need of reform. J.H. Reichman, *Design Protection and the New Technologies: The United States Experience in a Transnational Perspective*, 19 U. BALT. L. REV. 6, 23 (1991). As the courts have recently become more receptive to design patents, interest has been renewed in this form of intellectual property protection. This section provides a basic introduction to the design patent system.

A design may consist of surface ornamentation, configuration, or both. The Design Patent Act was codified under the Patent Act of 1954 in 35 U.S.C.

---

*The following materials are reprinted from *Patent Law and Policy, Cases and Materials* (1992), by Robert P. Merges. The editors wish to thank Professor Merges for authorizing the inclusion of this excerpt from his book.

§ 171, which allows a design patent to be obtained for "any new, original and ornamental design for an article of manufacture ..." and provides that all provisions relating to patents for inventions also apply to design patents. Design patents are issued for a fourteen-year term.

I. *Requirements for Patentability*

A design is patentable if it meets the usual requirements for patentability (novelty, nonobviousness, etc.) and, in addition, is ornamental and not dictated by functional considerations. The Patent and Trademark Office defines a design as "the visual characteristics or aspects displayed by the object. It is the appearance presented by the object which creates a visual impact upon the mind of the observer." U.S. Patent and Trademark Office, *Manual of Patent Examining Procedure* § 1502 (5th ed. rev. 8, 1988).

The statute provides that the design must appear on an "article of manufacture." This includes silverware, *Gorham Mfg. Co. v. White*, 81 U.S. (14 Wall.) 511 (1871); cement mixers, *In re Koehring,* 37 F.2d 241 (C.C.P.A. 1930); furniture, *In re Rosen*, 673 F.2d 388 (C.C.P.A. 1982); and containers for liquids, *Unette Corp. v. Unit Pack Co.*, 785 F.2d 1026 (Fed. Cir. 1986).

A. *Novelty*

Novelty is established if no prior art shows exactly the same design. A design is novel if the "ordinary observer," viewing the new design as a whole, would consider it to be different from, rather than a modification of, an already existing design. *See, e.g., Clark Equip. Co. v. Keller*, 570 F.2d 778, 799 (8th Cir. 1978). Although the § 102(b) statutory bars apply, i.e., there is a one-year grace period, there is no "experimental use" exception for design patents. *See Tone Bros. v. Sysco*, 23 U.S.P.Q. (BNA) 1184 (S.D. Iowa 1992).

B. *Nonobviousness*

Because Section 171 provides that the provisions of Title 35 relating to utility patents also apply to design patents, a design must be nonobvious, which requires the "exercise of the inventive or originative faculty." *Smith v. Whitman*, 148 U.S. 674, 679 (1893).

Prior to the adoption of a uniform standard to determine nonobviousness in design patents, the courts were in conflict over whether to use an "ordinary designer" standard or that of an "ordinary intelligent man" when applying the *Graham* test. *See In re Laverne*, 356 F.2d 1003 (C.C.P.A. 1966). Determining the nonobviousness of a design patent, as opposed to a utility patent, is unpredictable, as it is an inherently subjective inquiry, depending largely on personal taste. In evaluating nonobviousness of utility patents, judges can measure the distance between the prior art and a new invention on the basis of uniform scientific criteria and technical data, while the evaluation of the distance between an appearance design and its predecessors necessarily involves "value judgments that are hard to quantify and unreliable at best." Reichman, *supra*, at 33 n.164. *See In re Bartlett*, 300 F.2d 942, 944 (C.C.P.A. 1962) (noting that the determination of patentability in design cases depends on the subjective conclusion of each judge). The requirement of nonobviousness has been cited as a primary factor in limiting the availability of design protection in the United States from the 1920's on. Reichman, *supra*, at

24. The Federal Circuit's liberalization of the nonobviousness requirement has lowered the invalidation rate of design patents from seventy-five to one hundred percent only a few years ago, to thirty-eight percent today. *Id.* at 37.

In 1981, the Court of Customs and Patent Appeals held that the *Graham* test applies to design patents, and that nonobviousness should be measured in terms of a "designer of ordinary capability who designs articles of the type presented in the application." *In re Nalbandian*, 661 F.2d 1214, 1216 (C.C.P.A. 1981). The new standard allows for objective evidence of expert testimony from designers in the field to be used to prove nonobviousness. *Id.* at 1217. The Federal Circuit subsequently adopted this standard. While this approach appears more evenhanded and has led to more patents being upheld as valid, it may not solve the problem of unpredictability, because the opinions of different designers can vary considerably. William T. Fryer, III, *Industrial Design Protection in the United States of America — Present Situation and Plans for Revision*, 70 J. Pat. & Trademark Off. Soc'y 821, 829 (1988).

The Federal Circuit emphasized the presumptive validity of a design patent and placed the burden on the challenger to come forward with clear and convincing proof of nonobviousness. *See, e.g., Trans-World Mfg. Corp. v. Al Nyman & Sons*, 750 F.2d 1552, 1559-60 (Fed. Cir. 1984); *Avia Group Int'l v. L.A. Gear Cal.*, 853 F.2d 1557, 1562 (Fed. Cir. 1988). The court also upheld the notion that, to find obviousness, reference must be made to prior art with the same overall appearance of the patented design rather than referring to a combination of features from several references. *Litton Sys., Inc. v. Whirlpool Corp.*, 728 F.2d 1423, 1443 (Fed. Cir. 1984). Most significantly, the Federal Circuit held that objective secondary considerations, such as commercial success and copying, which apply to utility patents, are relevant to determining nonobviousness of design patents. *See, e.g., Litton*, 728 F.2d at 1441; *Avia*, 853 F.2d at 1564. The theory supporting the consideration of commercial success is that the purpose of a design patent is to increase salability, so if a design has been a success it "must have been sufficiently novel and superior to attract attention." *Robert W. Brown & Co. v. De Bell*, 243 F.2d 200, 202 (9th Cir. 1957); *see also* 1 Donald S. Chisum, Patents § 1.04[2][f], at 1-208 (1992). Evidence of commercial success must be related to the patented design rather than to factors such as functional improvement or advertising. *See, e.g., Litton*, 728 F.2d at 1443; *Avia*, 853 F.2d at 1564.

C. Ornamentality

A patentable design must be ornamental — it must create a pleasing appearance. To satisfy the requirement of ornamentality, a design "must be the product of aesthetic skill and artistic conception." *Blisscraft of Hollywood v. United Plastics Co.*, 294 F.2d 694, 696 (2d Cir. 1964). This requirement has been met by articles which are outside the realm of traditional "art." *See In re Koehring*, 37 F.2d 421, 422 (C.C.P.A. 1930) (determining a design for a cement mixer to be ornamental because it "possessed more grace and pleasing appearance" than prior art). A number of cases have denied patentability to designs which are concealed during the normal use of an object on the basis that ornamentality requires the design to be visible while the object is in its normal and intended use. *See* Chisum, *supra*, § 1.04[2][c], at 1-190—91.

D. *Functionality*

If a design is "primarily functional rather than ornamental," or is "dictated by functional considerations," it is not patentable. *Power Controls Corp. v. Hybrinetics, Inc.*, 806 F.2d 234, 238 (Fed. Cir. 1986). The functionality rule furthers the purpose of the design patent statute, which is to promote the decorative arts. In addition, the rule prevents granting in essence a monopoly to functional features that do not meet the requirements of a utility patent. Recognizing that strict application of the functionality rule would invalidate the majority of modern designs, the Federal Circuit validated designs with a higher functionality factor than had been tolerated by the courts previously. Reichman, *supra*, at 40. This is evidenced in cases upholding design patents for an eyeglass display rack, *Trans-World Mfg. Corp. v. Al Nyman & Sons*, 750 F.2d 1552 (Fed. Cir. 1984); fiberglass camper shells, *Fiberglass in Motion, Inc. v. Hindelang*, No. 83-1266 (Fed. Cir., Apr. 19, 1984) (LEXIS, Genfed library, USApp file); and containers for dispensing liquids, *Unette Corp. v. Unit Pack Co.*, 785 F.2d 1026 (Fed. Cir. 1986). The Federal Circuit has held that a design may have functional components as long as the design does not embody a function that is necessary to compete in the market. *Avia*, 853 F.2d at 1563. If the functional aspect of a design may be achieved by other design techniques, then it is not primarily functional. *Id.* This more flexible approach reflects a recognition by the court that the majority of valuable industrial designs that should be granted protection in order to stimulate economic growth are a combination of functional and aesthetic features.

II. *Claim Requirements and Procedure*

Two major criticisms of the design patent system in the United States are that it is too expensive and that protection takes too long to obtain. *See* Fryer, *supra*, at 834; Reichman, *supra*, at 24 (procedural requirements make design protection in the United States much "slower and costlier to obtain" than in other countries); Perry J. Saidman, *Design Patents — the Whipping Boy Bites Back*, 73 J. Pat. & Trademark Off. Soc'y 859 (1991) (defending these criticisms).

In 1988, the cost of a design patent application was estimated at $1,000. Fryer, *supra*, at 835. A large part of this cost is the expense of preparing the drawings which constitute the claim. The drawings "must contain a sufficient number of views to constitute a complete disclosure of the appearance of the article." 37 C.F.R. § 1.152. All that is required in writing is a very brief description of the drawings. The adequate disclosure and definiteness of the claim required by Section 112 are accomplished by the drawings. No more than one claim may be included in a design application. An application may illustrate more than one embodiment of a design only if the embodiments involve a "single inventive concept" and can be protected by a single claim. *In re Rubenfield*, 270 F.2d 391, 396 (C.C.P.A. 1959).

Design patents normally issue two to three years after filing. Saidman, *supra*, at 861. This leaves a design patent applicant without any protection from copiers during this long waiting period, as opposed to copyright protection which requires no initial procedural requirement and takes only a few months for registration to be issued. Fryer, *supra*, at 840, 835. It has been noted that the current system is "unsuited to the fast-moving but short-lived product cycle characteristic of today's market for mass-produced consumer goods." Reichman, *supra*, at 24. While there is general agreement that a new form of protection for industrial design is needed, Congress has yet to adopt any of the proposed legislation. An example of proposed legislation that would afford better protection for designs is Design Copyright Protection, which employs a modifed copyright form of protection as an alternative to the design patent. *See* Fryer, *supra*, at 839-46. Alternatively, proposed legislation would protect functional industrial designs, including those that are neither aesthetically nor technically innovative. Reichman, *supra*, at 121-22.

III. *Infringement*

The standard for finding infringement of a design patent was defined in *Gorham Mfg. Co. v. White*, where the Supreme Court held that "if in the eye of an ordinary observer, giving such attention as a purchaser usually gives, two designs are substantially the same, if the resemblance is such as to deceive such an observer, inducing him to purchase one supposing it to be the other, the first one patented is infringed by the other." 81 U.S. (14 Wall.) 511, 528 (1872).

The "eye of the ordinary observer" standard continues to be the rule. *See Oakley, Inc. v. International Tropic-Cal, Inc.*, 923 F.2d 167, 169 (Fed. Cir. 1991). The ordinary observer is one who has "reasonable familiarity" with the object in question and is capable of making a comparison to other objects which have preceded it. *Applied Arts Corp. v. Grand Rapids Metalcraft Corp.*, 67 F.2d 428, 430 (6th Cir. 1933). The key factor is similarity, rather than consumer confusion. *Unette*, 785 F.2d at 1029 (holding that "likelihood of confusion as to the source of goods is not a necessary or appropriate factor for determining infringement of a design patent.").

The second prong of the infringement analysis is the "point of novelty" test, which is distinct from the issue of similarity. Under the "point of novelty" test, the similarity found by the ordinary observer must be attributable to the novel elements of the patented design which distinguish it from prior art. *Litton*, 728 F.2d at 1444; *Avia*, 853 F.2d at 1565; *FMC Corp. v. Hennessy Indus., Inc.*, 836 F.2d 521, 527 (Fed. Cir. 1987). Unless the accused design appropriates the novel features of the patented design, there has been no infringement. *Avia*, 853 F.2d at 1565. The scope of the patented claim, and its points of novelty, are determined by examining the field of the prior art. *See Litton*, 728 F.2d at 1444 (holding that where the field of prior art is "crowded," the scope of a claim will be construed narrowly).

After determining the scope of the patented claim, the infringement inquiry focuses only on the protectable aesthetic components of a patented design. *See Lee v. Dayton-Hudson Corp.*, 838 F.2d 1186, 1188 (Fed. Cir. 1988) (holding that "it is the non-functional, design aspects that are pertinent to determinations of infringement"). Thus, this test permits strong similarities to be excused if the defendant can prove that she borrowed "only commonplace or generic ideas, functional features, or other nonprotectable matter" while adding sufficient variation to protectable elements of the design. Reichman, *supra*, at 44.

Whether a design is infringed when it is used on an entirely different type of article than the patented one has not been settled. CHISUM, *supra*, § 1.04[4], at 1-225. In *Avia Group Int'l v. L.A. Gear Cal.*, where the patented design was for an adult athletic shoe and the accused design was for a children's shoe, the court found infringement, and held that even in a situation where the patent holder has not put out a product, or where the patented design is embodied in a product that does not compete with the patent holder's product, a finding of infringement is not precluded. 853 F.2d at 1565. This decision indicates that the Federal Circuit is willing to extend design patent protection beyond "literal infringement" and protect the design concept itself. Reichman, *supra*, at 53.

F. ARCHITECTURAL WORKS

One of the creative art forms that we encounter daily, and that has historically had an ill-defined coverage by our copyright laws, is architecture. As was recently stated in a congressional committee report accompanying proposed legislation (which ultimately became the Architectural Works Copyright Protection Act of 1990) that was designed to expand the scope of copyright protection for architectural works:

> ... All copyright legislation is premised on Article I, section 8, clause 8 of the Constitution, which grants Congress the power to protect the "writings" of authors in order to "promote the progress of science." The proposed legislation must (and the Committee believes does) further this constitutional goal. Architecture plays a central role in our daily lives, not only as a form of shelter or as an investment, but also as a work of art. It is an art form that performs a very public, social purpose. As Winston Churchill is reputed to have once remarked: "We shape our buildings and our buildings shape us." We rarely appreciate works of architecture alone, but instead typically view them in conjunction with other structures and the environment at large, where, at their best, they serve to express the goals and aspirations of the entire community. Frank Lloyd Wright aptly observed: "buildings will always remain the most valuable aspect in a people's environment, the one most capable of cultural reaction."

> ... [T]he Committee concluded that the design of a work of architecture is a "writing" under the Constitution and fully deserves protection under the Copyright Act. Protection for works of architecture should stimulate excellence in design, thereby enriching our public environment in keeping with the constitutional goal.

(H.R. Rep. No. 101-735, 101st Cong. 2d Sess. 12-13 (1990).)

PROTECTION UNDER THE 1976 COPYRIGHT ACT

In the 1976 Copyright Act, as originally enacted, architecture could be protected, if at all, as a "pictorial, graphic, or sculptural work," which, as defined in § 101, included "technical drawings, diagrams, and models"; as a gesture toward greater protection for architecture, but with uncertain implications, the definition was altered in 1988 to include "diagrams, models, and technical drawings, including architectural plans." Of course, most architecture would also fall within the definition in § 101 of a "useful article," i.e., "an article having an intrinsic utilitarian function." As such, copyright protection for a work of architecture would be subject to the usual limitations for PGS works generally — it would extend only to features "that can be identified separately from, and are capable of existing independently of, the utilitarian aspects of the article." Thus, detachable decorative features such as friezes or caryatids would most likely have been protectible by copyright; the building as a whole would probably not. Indeed, the less exuberant the architecture, the less likely the building would be to meet the definition in the 1976 Act. This was, of course, the fate of all useful articles, be they furniture, street lighting fixtures or automobiles. Despite the cryptic notion of "conceptual separability" articulated in the House Report, it was generally understood that the overall shape of a residential or office building was not likely to be protectible by copyright; "eyeballing" a building while constructing its likeness across the street, although generally thought worthy of professional and moral condemnation, would probably not have given rise to a substantial copyright infringement claim.

A similar limitation under the original 1976 Act affected copyrighted architectural plans and drawings. These were not "useful articles," because their purpose was "merely to portray the appearance of the article or to convey information" (§ 101); no "separability" limitation was pertinent. But there was another obstacle. Unauthorized copying of the two-dimensional plan would infringe, but would constructing a three-dimensional building based on those plans? Courts almost uniformly found that the unauthorized construction was not an infringement of the plans. It was held either that the plagiarizing structure embodied merely the "ideas" of the plan rather than the "expression" (was that likely so?) — or, more tenably, that *Baker v. Selden* barred a copyright claim for converting the plan into its functional counterpart, a building. Perhaps the most thorough exploration of the issue is to be found in the following case.

Demetriades v. Kaufmann, 690 F. Supp. 658 (S.D.N.Y. 1988). In somewhat simplified terms, the plaintiff designed the plans for an expensive "one of a kind" residence in Scarsdale; the defendant couple secured unauthorized access to the plans, had their architect *trace* the plaintiff's plans, and began to build essentially the same house — a few doors down the street! The plaintiff sought an injunction against the completion of the house, claiming copyright infringement of his architectural plans. He conceded that, had the defendants based their construction on photographs or drawings that they had made of his house, they would not have infringed; he argued, however, that basing their house directly on his copyrighted plans did. The court disagreed.

The court found that the traced plans infringed; but it held that the construction of the offending residence did not. Invoking § 113(b) of the 1976 Act, which "froze" the law as it was in 1977 with respect to the "making" of a useful article depicted in a drawing, the court found the key element of that earlier law to be the Supreme Court decision in *Baker v. Selden*. The court read that decision to hold that although copyright protection extends to the particular *explanation* of an art or work, it does not protect *use* of the art or work described by the copyrighted document. Thus, "although an owner of copyrighted architectural plans is granted the right to prevent the unauthorized copying of those plans, that individual, without benefit of a design patent, does not obtain a protectible interest in the useful article depicted by those plans."

The *Demetriades* court also relied upon an often-discussed case, *Muller v. Triborough Bridge Auth.*, 43 F. Supp. 298 (S.D.N.Y. 1942), in which the owner of copyright in plans depicting an approach to the Cross Bay Parkway Bridge alleged that the defendant had infringed by constructing a similar approach to its bridge; the court had concluded that the plantiff's copyrighted drawing, "showing a novel bridge approach to unsnarl traffic congestion, does not prevent any one from using and applying the system of traffic separation therein set forth."

The preliminary relief ultimately issued by the *Demetriades* court, however, gave the plaintiff essentially what he had sought. The court enjoined the defendants from any further unauthorized copying of the architectural plans, and "from relying on any infringing copies of those plans" in constructing their house; it also ordered that all infringing copies within the defendants' control be impounded.

As will be noted immediately below, the Copyright Act has been recently amended so as to extend protection to "architectural works" that goes beyond the protection accorded by the 1976 Act in its original form. However, the amendments do not apply to buildings constructed before the effective date of the legislation, December 1, 1990. Therefore it is necessary to be familiar with the pre-1990 law just recounted, for it applies to most of the buildings we see around us (regardless of the date on which any alleged infringement might take place).

Given the economic-incentive rationale underlying the law of copyright, is it justifiable to give the architect protection only against unauthorized two-dimensional copies of his or her plan, while freely allowing the unauthorized construction of the depicted building? Which is the exclusive right that truly has economic value to the architect? Is it sensible to make infringement turn upon whether the defendant, in constructing the building, photocopies the plaintiff's plans (which would infringe) or steals them (which would not)?

THE ARCHITECTURAL WORKS COPYRIGHT PROTECTION ACT OF 1990

A principal incentive for expanding copyright protection for architectural works is the Berne Convention, which the United States ratified in October 1988. Article 2.1 of the Convention includes "works of architecture" among copyrightable subject matter which member countries must protect. The 1990 amendments to the 1976 Copyright Act — signed by President Bush on December 1, 1990 and immediately effective — added "architectural works" as protectible subject matter under § 102(a), defined that term in § 101, and set forth certain limitations on protection in § 120. The importance of creating a separate category for architectural works, apart from pictorial, graphic and sculptural works, is that the "separability" requirement that applies to the latter works does not apply to the former. The new provisions cover any architectural work created on or after December 1, 1990, and any such work that on that date "is unconstructed and embodied in unpublished plans or drawings" (with protection to terminate on December 31, 2002 unless the work is constructed by that date).

During the formulation of regulations by the Copyright Office, a question arose as to whether an architectural plan or drawing was "published" when it was filed with a public record office, or when copies were given to construction subcontractors. Although the Copyright Office conceded that the limited case law supported the proposition that these acts did not "publish" the plans, its final regulations took no explicit stand on the matter. See Regs. § 202.11(c)(5).

The following are some relevant sections of the 1990 Act:

§ 101. Definitions

An "architectural work" is the design of a building as embodied in any tangible medium of expression, including a building, architectural plans, or drawings. The work includes the overall form as well as the arrangement and composition of spaces and elements in the design, but does not include individual standard features.

§ 120. Scope of exclusive rights in architectural works

(a) *Pictorial Representations Permitted* — The copyright in an architectural work that has been constructed does not include the right to prevent the making, distributing, or public display of pictures, paintings, photographs, or other pictorial representations of the work, if the building in which the work is embodied is located in or ordinarily visible from a public place.

(b) *Alteration to and Destruction of Buildings* — Notwithstanding the provisions of section 106(2), the owners of a building embodying an architectural work may, without the consent of the author or copyright owner of the architectural work, make or authorize the making of alterations of such building, and destroy or authorize the destruction of such building.

HOUSE REPORT

H.R. Rep. No. 101-735, 101st Cong. 2d Sess. 18-21, 24 (1990)

Definitions

... The protected work is the design of a building. The term "design" includes the overall form as well as the arrangement and composition of spaces and elements in the design. The phrase "arrangement and composition of spaces and elements," recognizes that: (1) creativity in architecture frequently takes the form of a selection, coordination, or arrangement of unprotectible elements into an original, protectible whole; (2) an architect may incorporate new, protectible design elements into otherwise standard, unprotectible building features; and (3) interior architecture may be protected.

Consistent with other provisions of the Copyright Act and Copyright Office regulations, the definition makes clear that protection does not extend to individual standard features, such as common windows, doors, and other staple building components. A grant of exclusive rights in such features would impede, rather than promote, the progress of architectural innovation. The provision is not, however, intended to exclude from the copyright in the architectural work any individual features that reflect the architect's creativity.

....

The Subcommittee made a second amendment in the definition of architectural work: the deletion of the phrase "or three-dimensional structure." This phrase was included in [an earlier bill] to cover cases where architectural works are embodied in innovative structures that defy easy classification. Unfortunately, the phrase also could be interpreted as covering interstate highway bridges, cloverleafs, canals, dams, and pedestrian walkways. The Subcommittee examined protection for these works, some of which form important elements of this nation's transportation system, and determined that copyright protection is not necessary to stimulate creativity or prohibit unauthorized reproduction.

The sole purpose of legislating at this time is to place the United States unequivocally in compliance with its Berne Convention obligations. Protection for bridges and related nonhabitable three-dimensional structures is not required by the Berne Convention. Accordingly, the question of copyright protection for these works can be deferred to another day. As a consequence, the phrase "or other three-dimensional structures" was deleted from the definition of architectural work and from all other places in the bill.

This deletion, though, raises more sharply the question of what is meant by the term "building." Obviously, the term encompasses habitable structures such as houses and office buildings. It also covers structures that are used, but not inhabited, by human beings; such as churches, pergolas, gazebos, and garden pavilions.

....

Subject Matter of Copyright

This provision amends section 102, title 17, United States Code, to create a new category of protected subject matter: "architectural works." By creating a new category of protectible subject matter in new section 102(a)(8), and, therefore, by deliberately not encompassing architectural works as pictorial, graphic, or sculptural works in existing section 102(a)(5), the copyrightability of architectural works shall not be evaluated under the separability test applicable to pictorial, graphic, or sculptural works embodied in useful articles. There is considerable scholarly and judicial disagreement over how to apply the separability test, and the principal reason for not treating architectural works as pictorial, graphic, or sculptural works is to avoid entangling architectural works in this disagreement.

The Committee does not suggest, though, that in evaluating the copyrightability or scope of protection for architectural works, the Copyright

Office or the courts should ignore functionality. A two-step analysis is envisioned. First, an architectural work should be examined to determine whether there are original design elements present, including overall shape and interior architecture. If such design elements are present, a second step is reached to examine whether the design elements are functionally required. If the design elements are not functionally required, the work is protectible without regard to physical or conceptual separability. As a consequence, contrary to the Committee's report accompanying the 1976 Copyright Act with respect to industrial products, the aesthetically pleasing overall shape of an architectural work would be protected under this bill.

QUESTIONS

1. Think of a strikingly designed architectural work with which you are familiar — a residence, an office building, a place of worship, or a museum. Can you identify features that are "physically or conceptually separable" and are therefore copyrightable under the pre-December 1990 tests? Is the overall shape of the building copyrightable?

Articulate the differences between the functionality limitation on the copyrightability of works of architecture (discussed in the House Report, *supra*), and the various statements of the "conceptual separability" standard for the copyrightability of pictorial, graphic and sculptural works.

2. Is the structure depicted below copyrightable under the 1990 Amendments? Would it have been protectible as a "pictorial, graphic or sculptural work" before the 1990 amendments?

Reproduced with permission of
Dennis A. Rocha

3. Is there an aesthetic, economic or pragmatic reason — as distinguished from the desire to comply with the Berne Convention — for extending copyright protection to the overall shape of architectural works, but denying such protection to other forms of useful sculptural works such as furniture, dresses, automobiles, silverware, vacuum cleaners, and the like? Can designers of buildings make a convincing distinctive claim for protection?

4. What reasons can you advance for § 120(a), *supra*, which excludes pictorial representations of a building from the scope of the architect's copyright? Note that the statute's exemption from protection applies to two-dimensional, but not to three-dimensional, representations of buildings. As a result, the architect's copyright entitlement to compensation for and control over reproductions and derivative exploitations of her work would reach such three-dimensional exploitations as pencil sharpeners in the form of miniature Chrysler Buildings, or tiny U.S. Capitol Buildings in liquid-filled plastic bubbles which, when shaken, give the illusion of falling snow, but her copyright would not extend to unlicensed posters, T-shirts, shower curtains, etc. Is there a good reason for this?

G. CHARACTERS

Nichols v. Universal Pictures Corp., 45 F.2d 119, 121 (2d Cir. 1930) (L. Hand, J.): "[W]e do not doubt that two plays may correspond in plot closely enough for infringement. How far that correspondence must go is another matter. Nor need we hold that the same may not be true as to the characters, quite independently of the 'plot' proper, though, as far as we know, such a case has never arisen. If Twelfth Night were copyrighted, it is quite possible that a second comer might so closely imitate Sir Toby Belch or Malvolio as to infringe, but it would not be enough that for one of his characters he cast a riotous knight who kept wassail to the discomfort of the household, or a vain and foppish steward who became amorous of his mistress. These would be no more than Shakespeare's 'ideas' in the play, as little capable of monopoly as Einstein's Doctrine of Relativity, or Darwin's theory of the Origin of Species. It follows that the less developed the characters, the less they can be copyrighted; that is the penalty an author must bear for marking them too indistinctly."

[Editors' Note: The Court of Appeals for the Second Circuit has indicated, without elaboration, that the Hopalong Cassidy and Amos & Andy characters, in their textual description, meet Judge Hand's test. See *Filmvideo Releasing Corp. v. Hastings,* 668 F.2d 91 (2d Cir. 1981); *Silverman v. CBS Inc.,* 870 F.2d 40 (2d Cir.), *cert. denied,* 492 U.S. 907 (1989)].

Warner Bros., Inc. v. Columbia Broadcasting System, 216 F.2d 945 (9th Cir. 1954), *cert. denied*, 348 U.S. 971 (1955). [Long before litigation about rights to use characters in films and on television became routine, this case was the preeminent one in the genre; its influence has been somewhat narrowed by later events, to be explored below.] The well-known mystery-detective story, "The Maltese Falcon," was written by Dashiell Hammett, and was published serially in a magazine and then in a book by the publisher Knopf, which held the copyright. In 1930, Hammett and Knopf conveyed to Warner Brothers, for $8,500, certain defined exclusive rights (along with a copyright assignment) to the use of The Maltese Falcon in moving pictures, radio, and television. Warner's highly successful motion picture, starring Humphrey Bogart as the detective protagonist Sam Spade, was released in 1941 (it was a new version of a Warner Brothers film made in 1931). In 1946, Hammett granted to CBS the right to use the Sam Spade character and name, along with the names and characters of others in The Maltese Falcon, on radio programs — except their use in the Falcon story; CBS broadcast weekly half-hour Sam Spade radio programs from 1946 to 1950. Warner sued CBS, Hammett, and Knopf, claiming that the programs infringed its rights to the Falcon story and characters under copyright and unfair competition law.

The court interpreted the 1930 grants to Warner and held that they could not properly be read to have conveyed rights to the characters outside of the Falcon story. The court pointed out that Warner was a "large, experienced moving picture producer," that ambiguities in the contract should be construed against it, that rights to characters and their names were nowhere expressly mentioned in the agreement, and that these — given their value particularly in detective sequels, as was customary in the genre (citing among others Sir Arthur Conan Doyle) — should not be interpreted as falling within the general grants made to Warner. The court also noted that Warner had not objected to Hammett's publication in 1932 of three stories using the Falcon characters, nor to the use by CBS of those characters in a radio program, "The Kandy Tooth," after negotiations between CBS and Warner for the Falcon had broken down. The court also observed that Warner's purchase price of $8,500 "would seem inadequate compensation for the complete surrender of the characters made famous" in the Falcon book. It concluded that the intention of the parties was not to deprive Hammett of using, and licensing others to use, the Falcon characters in other stories.

Having in effect fully decided the case, the court went on, however, "to consider whether it was ever intended by the copyright statute that characters with their names should be under its protection."

> ... If Congress had intended that the sale of the right to publish a copyrighted story would foreclose the author's use of its characters in subsequent works for the life of the copyright, it would seem Congress would have made specific provision therefor. Authors work for the love of their art no more than other professional people work in other lines of work for the love of it. There is the financial motive as well. The characters of an author's imagination and the art of his descriptive talent, like a painter's or like a person with his penmanship, are always limited and

always fall into limited patterns. The restriction argued for is unreasonable, and would effect the very opposite of the statute's purpose which is to encourage the production of the arts....

It is conceivable that the character really constitutes the story being told, but if the character is only the chessman in the game of telling the story he is not within the area of the protection afforded by the copyright.... We conclude that even if the owners assigned their complete rights in the copyright to the Falcon, such assignment did not prevent the author from using the characters used therein, in other stories. The characters were vehicles for the story told, and the vehicles did not go with the sale of the story.

On the question whether "The Kandy Tooth" infringed the copyright in "The Maltese Falcon" motion picture, the court found no clear error in the trial court's conclusion that the similarities in the former were not such as to constitute "practically the same story"; what they had in common was a "long complicated search for a lost article of fabulous value," along with "complications, fatalities, and moral delinquencies by characters" and some similar action. "There is no textual copying; the mystery of the Tooth and the suspense to the reader would not be dulled through his having read the Falcon. In a phrase, they are different stories though of the same general nature." The court found no unfair competition by means of degrading or cheapening of the Falcon characters or deceiving the public into believing that they were seeing the Falcon rather than the defendants' other stories.

ANDERSON v. STALLONE

11 U.S.P.Q.2D 1161 (C.D. Cal. 1989)

WILLIAM D. KELLER, UNITED STATES DISTRICT JUDGE.

....

FACTUAL BACKGROUND

The movies Rocky I, II, and III were extremely successful motion pictures. Sylvester Stallone wrote each script and played the role of Rocky Balboa, the dominant character in each of the movies. In May of 1982, while on a promotional tour for the movie Rocky III, Stallone informed members of the press of his ideas for Rocky IV. Although Stallone's description of his ideas would vary slightly in each of the press conferences, he would generally describe his ideas as follows:

> I'd do it [Rocky IV] if Rocky himself could step out a bit. Maybe tackle world problems. So what would happen, say, if Russia allowed her boxers to enter the professional ranks? Say Rocky is the United States' representative and the White House wants him to fight with the Russians before the Olympics. It's in Russia with everything against him. It's a giant stadium in Moscow and everything is Russian Red. It's a fight of astounding proportions with 50 monitors sent to 50 countries. It's the World Cup — a war between 2 countries.

Waco Tribune Herald, May 28, 1982; Section D, pg. 1 (EX 168). In June of 1982, after viewing the movie Rocky III, Timothy Anderson wrote a thirty-one page treatment entitled "Rocky IV" that he hoped would be used by Stallone and MGM/UA Communications Co. (hereinafter "MGM") as a sequel to Rocky III. The treatment incorporated the characters created by Stallone in his prior movies and cited Stallone as a co-author.

In October of 1982, Mr. Anderson met with Art Linkletter, who was a member of MGM's board of directors. Mr. Linkletter set up a meeting on October 11, 1982, between Mr. Anderson and Mr. Fields, who was president of MGM at the time. Mr. Linkletter was also present at this October 11, 1982 meeting. During the meeting, the parties discussed the possibility that plaintiff's treatment would be used by defendants as the script for Rocky IV. At the suggestion of Mr. Fields, the plaintiff, who is a lawyer and was accompanied by a lawyer at the meeting, signed a release that purported to relieve MGM from liability stemming from use of the treatment. Plaintiff alleges that Mr. Fields told him and his attorney that "if they [MGM & Stallone] use his stuff [Anderson's treatment] it will be big money, big bucks for Tim."

On April 22, 1984, Anderson's attorney wrote MGM requesting compensation for the alleged use of his treatment in the forthcoming Rocky IV movie. On July 12, 1984, Stallone described his plans for the Rocky IV script on the Today Show before a national television audience. Anderson, in his deposition, states that his parents and friends called him to tell him that Stallone was telling "his story" on television. In a diary entry of July 12, 1984, Anderson noted that Stallone "explained my story" on national television.

Stallone completed his Rocky IV script in October of 1984. Rocky IV was released in November of 1985. The complaint in this action was filed on January 29, 1987.

CONCLUSIONS OF LAW

[The court first held that Anderson's claim for breach of confidence, under state law, was barred by the statute of limitations; and that his state-law claims for unjust enrichment and unfair competition were equivalent to copyright infringement and were thus preempted by the federal Copyright Act as provided in § 301. The court also held that Stallone and his co-defendants were entitled to summary judgment on Anderson's copyright infringement claim, because Anderson's film treatment was not copyrightable. To reach that conclusion, the court found that the "Rocky characters developed in Rocky I, II and III constitute expression protected by copyright independent from the story in which they are contained"; that Anderson's treatment was an infringing derivative work based on those copyrightable characters; and that the unlawful use of those characters forfeited the plaintiff's copyright by virtue of § 103(a) of the Copyright Act. In holding the Rocky characters copyrightable, the court found them to meet both the "specificity" test of Learned Hand and the "story being told" test in the *Sam Spade* (Warner Brothers) case. Finally, the court held that the story elements in the Rocky IV film were not substantially similar to those in the plaintiff's treatment. What follows is the court's discussion of the copyrightability of the Rocky characters.]

. . . .

The Rocky characters are one of the most highly delineated groups of characters in modern American cinema. The physical and emotional characteristics of Rocky Balboa and the other characters were set forth in tremendous detail in the three Rocky movies before Anderson appropriated the characters for his treatment. The interrelationships and development of Rocky, Adrian, Apollo Creed, Clubber Lang, and Paulie are central to all three movies. Rocky Balboa is such a highly delineated character that his name is the title of all four of the Rocky movies and his character has become identified with specific character traits ranging from his speaking mannerisms to his physical characteristics. This Court has no difficulty ruling as a matter of law that the Rocky characters are delineated so extensively that they are protected from bodily appropriation when taken as a group and transposed into a sequel by another author. Plaintiff has not and cannot put before this Court any evidence to rebut the defendants' showing that the Rocky characters are so highly delineated that they warrant copyright protection.

Plaintiff's unsupported assertions that Rocky is merely a stock character, made in the face of voluminous evidence that the Rocky characters are copyrightable, do not bar this Court from granting summary judgment on this issue. If any group of movie characters is protected by copyright, surely the Rocky characters are protected from bodily appropriation into a sequel which merely builds on the relationships and characteristics which these characters developed in the first three Rocky movies. No reasonable jury could find otherwise.

This Court need not and does not reach the issue of whether any single character alone, apart from Rocky, is delineated with enough specificity so as to garner copyright protection. Nor does the Court reach the issue of whether these characters are protected from less than bodily appropriation. *See* I M. Nimmer, § 2.12, pg. 2-171 (copyrightability of characters is "more properly framed as relating to the degree of substantial similarity required to constitute infringement rather than in terms of copyrightability per se").

This Court also finds that the Rocky characters were so highly developed and central to the three movies made before Anderson's treatment that they "constituted the story being told." All three Rocky movies focused on the development and relationships of the various characters. The movies did not revolve around intricate plots or story lines. Instead, the focus of these movies was the development of the Rocky characters. The same evidence which supports the finding of delineation above is so extensive that it also warrants a finding that the Rocky characters — Rocky, Adrian, Apollo Creed, Clubber Lang, and Paulie — "constituted the story being told" in the first three Rocky movies. . . .

QUESTIONS

1. Articulate the features that make each of the "Rocky" characters sufficiently well developed to meet Judge Hand's standard. For example, how would you delineate in detail the character attributes of Rocky's wife Adrian? (Be sure to separate her character attributes from the details of plot in which

she is involved. Is that possible?) And would it infringe to prepare an unauthorized film for television featuring a shy monosyllabic underdog amateur prizefighter (wrestler? chess player? karate kid?) who trains in the gyms and on the streets of Baltimore or Boston? Does each of the Rocky characters — even Rocky himself — satisfy the "story being told" test? Are Rocky and Adrian more fully developed than the "chessmen" Sam Spade and Brigid O'Shaughnessey from *The Maltese Falcon*? Which of the two tests is the easier to satisfy?

2. Did the *Stallone* court find infringement not of the individual Rocky characters but of the several of them as a group? (If so, is that really character protection, or story protection?)

3. "The Amos 'n Andy Show" was a popular radio comedy program that was broadcast from 1928 to 1955, depicting a number of black characters. It also became a network television program from 1951 to 1953 and was shown in non-network syndication until 1966. Your client is interested in adapting some of the old radio programs for use in a Broadway-style musical comedy. You have ascertained that all of the pertinent radio scripts are now in the public domain. Your client asks whether, even assuming he can use the text of those scripts in his show, he is free without the consent of the Columbia Broadcasting System (the owner of copyright in the television programs) to use the characters of Amos, Andy, and others portrayed on the television programs, and particularly whether his performers can be chosen so as to resemble those on the programs. What advice do you give? *See Silverman v. CBS Inc.*, 870 F.2d 40 (2d Cir.), *cert. denied*, 492 U.S. 907 (1989).

WINCOR, BOOK REVIEW OF KAPLAN, AN UNHURRIED VIEW OF COPYRIGHT, 76 Yale Law Journal 1473, 1478-83 (1967)*

How far should the bounds of protection extend? *An Unhurried View of Copyright* sets out many of the standards used in measuring traditional copyrights. Professor Kaplan relies on existing case law, which is a reasonable road for a lawyer to travel. But it is not the way life is lived in the communications industries.

There a dynamic world is making ground rules for current contracts and future laws. If the genius of the common law is its ability to catch up with the market place, it had better look twice at the communications field. As suggested earlier, "copyright" is the wrong word — wrong chiefly in being incomplete — for describing the exotic new plants that grow in this surrealist garden.

Consider the following passage, introduced less in the hope of affording readers innocent amusement than of bringing out a point:

> Florienbad was burning. The world's espionage capital, on the outskirts of Bucharest, was half destroyed. Among the ruins strolled tall, indifferent Secret Agent Leverett Lowell (Harvard, '42) wearing as always his Black Belt, Fifth Degree for Kiaijutsu (Zen combat by Screaming), puffing casually on a consciousness-expanding cigarette and followed by Alec,

---

*Reprinted by permission of the Yale Law Journal Co. and Fred B. Rothman & Co.

his lame ocelot who had figured so gallantly in the Tower of London Demolition Case. Lowell was flanked, as always, by two of his luscious Eurasian girl bodyguards.

A small man disguised as a passerby stood by a burning building, watching the flames with satisfaction. Lowell recognized him as Q 50, a medium-ranking agent of the dreaded ACL, Arson Consultants, Ltd. Q 50's eyes glistened as he turned from the conflagration and addressed Lowell.

"That's one for the insurance company, mate," observed Q 50.

"Touché," Lowell replied indifferently.

That deeply affecting passage, by this reviewer, appears in Vol. IV, *Television Quarterly,* Fall, 1965. Its want of literary excellence makes it thoroughly part of a tradition in copyright cases.

Leverett Lowell and his bizarre entourage may actually constitute property. Taken together, they are a sort of compound of elements that the public values. Taken separately, each element may have value in its own right, even in a different setting. As things actually happen, especially in television, one of the girl bodyguards, with or without the lame ocelot, may be extracted from a series about Leverett Lowell and star in her own series without Lowell next season.

Television is the most voracious consumer of literary property on a repeating basis. It serves, accordingly, as the ideal subject for the study of new theories, new forms of legal life, new property concepts. Snobbishness has no place in such studies. Judge Learned Hand's concern was not confined to *Twelfth Night.*

In television the Leverett Lowell extract might be the subject of protracted negotiation and sale. Probably but not inevitably the character would in fact have been more fully developed in successive episodes without appreciable enrichment. Be that as it may, Lowell and his entourage might be dealt with as a commodity.

They might originate in a spy novel, or a film, or a series "presentation" designed specifically for television. Typically an independent production company acquires an option, sometimes on the text of Leverett Lowell stories, sometimes merely on the character himself and his attendant props. The most elaborate negotiations accompany such acquisitions. Does one remember to secure rights to Mrs. Hudson besides Holmes and Watson? How much does the original owner receive per new program episode if the series is one hour, how much if the series is half-hour? To what extent does he share in proceeds from a sound track album, or Leverett Lowell figurines, or theatrical exhibition of two program segments stuck together as a feature film? Does he share "spin-off" proceeds when one of the minor characters goes into a different series? All of it sounds fantastic, but it happens.

The J. R. R. Tolkien mythology affords even more vivid illustration of the kinds of intangibles which may be sold in the market place of incorporeal property these days. This author creates a fictitious world filled with imaginary people, imaginary races, imaginary eras, languages, curses, treasures — all of it, each element in the compound, at least partly original and potentially valuable on its own. H. P. Lovecraft did the same thing, and a devoted reader-ship kept buying his macabre fancies.

Television thrives on this sort of traffic. *Honey West* was telecast weekly as a spin-off from *Burke's Law*. For each spin-off that gets on, there are hundreds that occupy serious men and women in tortured negotiation for months at a time, but never appear. The spin-off concept is crucial. It means the trans-plant of one or more fictitious elements into new settings. It describes extrac-tion in business terms, and it comes up in nearly all contracts for the acquisi-tion of television rights. There is no use pretending it will all go away if we ignore it.

Professor Kaplan and others who decry excessive protection may have a plausible rebuttal to the argument that real life has outrun their law. They may suggest that purchasers in this field merely buy quit-claims to avoid lawsuits. Sometimes that will be true; television moves quickly, and there is no time for test cases. Some of the fictitious elements that command royalties probably are nothing but ideas with names, and belong in the public domain. Certainly a slight shift in presentation, a change of name, a different occupa-tion or nationality is sufficient to avoid legal trouble in many instances of copying. Still, there is more to it. Once in a long time we find fictitious ele-ments such as characters that are both original and valuable, even under a different name, even snipped off and planted in a new garden. The point is that conceptually protection for elements such as these is all quite possible.

If trade custom means anything, the broadcasting industry has created standards that the common law must consider. Industry-wide collective bar-gaining agreements between management and the Writers Guild of America contain royalty provisions for the use of characters. Some day they may en-compass additional elements, at least in general language.

Nevertheless trade custom is not everything, and Professor Kaplan is enti-tled to legal analysis in support of our new heresies.

In supplying it, one comes back to the question of names again. Fictitious characters are not "copyrights." Neither are fictitious eras, languages or bat-tles. If Shakespeare were under copyright today, another's piracy of Falstaff might be a crucial factor in determining copyright infringement of particular plays, but Sir John is no copyright. He is something else, something without a name.

And yet not entirely without a name. The right name is "literary service mark protected against dilution." It lacks grace, but perhaps we shall coin something better after examining what lies behind it.

The trademark, sibling concept to the service mark, began as a liability and became an asset. In this happy course it ran parallel to the copyright. One originated as a device for policing measures and standards in the medieval guilds. The other began (in England, at any rate) as a device to record hereti-cal authors and publishers. Then the trademark became a sales badge identi-fying the source of products, and the copyright turned into an economic *res,* a legal claim to rights in a work of art.

The two doctrines have different rules. Trademark is of uncertain duration; its geography is not fixed, and there are sometimes restrictions on its transfer so as to avoid deceiving the public. It depends largely on facts postulated at a given moment. Such and such a name is well known in Hawaii this year as a device for identifying pineapples, but not in Bonn, where it was famous a decade ago as a name for bicycles. Copyright is quite different. The owner has the security of fixed time periods, and his protection is national, often international, in scope. Trademark is the more flexible, copyright the more certain. The trouble with copyright is that it leaves off too soon, and fails to protect characters and related imaginings by Lovecraft and Tolkien.

Here trademark is a useful supplement — or service mark to be more exact about it, since the author's creations identify his services. These services are literary, hence the term "literary service mark." Dilution in turn is a German doctrine, adopted by several states including New York and Massachusetts, that protects marks against "whittling away" by use on disparate products, even where there is no likelihood of public confusion. In this doctrine the medieval mark ripens fully into an asset without any of the old hurdles in the way of protection. Rolls-Royce shoes, theoretically, would be enjoined under the dilution doctrine. With this concept we round out the translation of that awkward phrase for Sir John Falstaff: "literary service mark protected against dilution." Today that is what Falstaff would be in law.

....

An Unhurried View of Copyright is a way of looking at things in terms of franchises and grants from the sovereign. It has on its side American copyright history, with its concern for the public interest in free or cheap communications and its unconcern for authors. At least it has American history on its side as far as it goes.

Against this Kaplanesque view is a different way of looking at things, more as writers and publishers and producers do. A good statement of this second view is what G. K. Chesterton wrote in *Charles Dickens* (Methuen, 1906) at p. 81:

> Ordinary men would understand you if you referred currently to Sherlock Holmes. Sir Arthur Conan Doyle would no doubt be justified in rearing his head to the stars, remembering that Sherlock Holmes is the only really familiar figure in modern fiction. But let him droop that head again with a gentle sadness, remembering that if Sherlock Holmes is the only familiar figure in modern fiction, Sherlock Holmes is also the only familiar figure in the Sherlock Holmes Tales. Not many people could say offhand what was the name of the owner of Silver Blaze, or whether Mrs. Hudson was dark or fair. But if Dickens had written the Sherlock Holmes stories, every character in them would have been equally arresting and memorable. A Sherlock Holmes would have cooked the dinner for Sherlock Holmes; a Sherlock Holmes would have driven his cab. If Dickens brought in a man merely to carry a letter, he had time for a touch or two, and made him a giant.

The touch that creates giants, there perhaps is the point Professor Kaplan forgets. It appears only occasionally, and not even the most avid protectionist wants to dignify stock characters and mere ideas with property attributes. By all means enlarge the public domain with unworthy artifice, but recognize too that there are magicians among us.

Walt Disney Productions v. Air Pirates, 581 F.2d 751 (9th Cir. 1978). The defendants (ironically named) published two cartoon magazines which depicted several Disney cartoon characters (including Mickey and Minnie Mouse, Donald Duck, the Big Bad Wolf, the Three Little Pigs, and Goofy), with their names, engaging in bawdy, promiscuous, and drug-ingesting behavior. Disney sued for copyright infringement, and asserted other federal and state claims. As to copyright, the defendants claimed that the Disney characters were not copyrightable and that in any event their admitted copying was protected by the fair use doctrine and the first amendment; the court of appeals upheld summary judgment for Disney. At the outset, relying on comic-strip cases dating back to 1914, the court rejected the contention that characters are never copyrightable. The court's analysis focused upon its earlier decision in the *Sam Spade* case, *supra.* (Its reasons for rejecting the fair use contention are set forth at Chapter 6, Subchapter E.2, *infra.*)

It is true that this Court's opinion in *Warner Brothers Pictures v. Columbia Broadcasting System,* 216 F.2d 945 (9th Cir. 1954), *certiorari denied,* 348 U.S. 971, lends some support to the position that characters ordinarily are not copyrightable.... Judge Stephens' opinion considered "whether it was ever intended by the copyright statute that characters with their names should be under its protection." In that context he concluded that such a restriction on Hammett's future use of a character was unreasonable, at least when the characters were merely vehicles for the story and did not "really constitute" the story being told. Judge Stephens' reasons for that conclusion provide an important indication of the applicability of that conclusion to comic book characters as opposed to literary characters. In reasoning that characters "are always limited and always fall into limited patterns," Judge Stephens recognized that it is difficult to delineate distinctively a literary character. Cf. *Nichols v. Universal Pictures Corp.,* 45 F.2d 119 (2d Cir. 1930), *certiorari denied,* 282 U.S. 902. When the author can add a visual image, however, the difficulty is reduced. See generally 1 *Nimmer on Copyright* § 30. Put another way, while many literary characters may embody little more than an unprotected idea (see *Sid & Marty Krofft Television v. McDonald's Corp.,* 562 F.2d 1157 (9th Cir. 1977)), a comic book character, which has physical as well as conceptual qualities, is more likely to contain some unique elements of expression. Because comic book characters therefore are distinguishable from literary characters, the *Warner Brothers* language does not preclude protection of Disney's characters.

The court added in a footnote:

Because this conclusion is sufficient to justify protection of the characters, we need not endorse the district court's conclusion that Disney's characters fell within the *Warner Brothers* exception for characters who "really constitute" the story. The district judge did not state which Disney stories were the basis of the protection for any character, nor did [he] state which characters were so protected. Apart from failing to recognize that this exception seems to be limited to a "story devoid of plot" (1 Nimmer on Copyright § 30), the district court's conclusion may have been based on the incorrect assumption that Disney's characters could be protected if together they constitute a whole story. Obviously the larger the group of characters that is selected, the easier it is to say that they "constitute" the entire story, particularly when only a general abstraction and not a particular story is analyzed.

King Features Syndicates v. Fleischer, 299 F.2d 533 (2d Cir. 1924). The plaintiff was engaged in the creation and syndication to daily newspapers of a copyrighted comic strip known as "Barney Google and Spark Plug." "Spark Plug" (sometimes referred to as "Sparky") was, in the court's language, "a new grotesque and comic race horse." The defendant manufactured and sold a toy which was an exact reproduction of "Sparky." The district court denied a preliminary injunction, but the court of appeals reversed. The court concluded that, even though the defendant had not plagiarized all of the comic strip or all of its principal characters, it had infringed by copying "Sparky": "We do not think it avoids the infringement of the copyright to take the substance or idea, and produce it through a different medium.... Differences which relate merely to size and material are not important." [The court's language was surely broader than it had to be?] "The concept of beauty expressed in the materials of statuary or drawing, is the thing which is copyrighted. That is what the infringer copies. The Copyright Act was intended to prohibit the taking of this conception. The Copyright Act protects the conception of humor which a cartoonist may produce, as well as the conception of genius which an artist or sculptor may use.... The artist's concept of humor ... cannot be copied, by manufacturing a toy or doll as the [defendant] did, without taking the copyrightable form of that concept, and without at the same time taking the commercial value — the fruits of the cartoonist's genius which consisted in his capacity to entertain and amuse."

Detective Comics, Inc. v. Bruns Publishing, Inc., 111 F.2d 432 (2d Cir. 1940). Plaintiff owned the copyright in the comic book "Action Comics," which portrayed "Superman," while the defendants published and distributed a "Wonderman" comic book. The court affirmed the conclusion of the district court that the defendants had infringed plaintiff's copyright by copying the pictures in "Action Comics." Both Superman and Wonderman are men "of miraculous strength and speed"; their "attributes and antics ... are closely similar"; each sheds his ordinary clothing to stand "revealed in full panoply in a skin-tight acrobatic costume," the only real difference being that Superman's is blue and Wonderman's is red; each can crush a gun in his powerful hands and can deflect bullets without injury; Superman is shown leaping over buildings while Wonderman leaps from roof to roof, and each is described as being the strongest man in the world and an enemy of evil and injustice. The court rejected the defendant's argument that Superman's attributes were general and unoriginal, with prototypes among heroes of literature and mythology. "[I]f the author of 'Superman' has portrayed a comic

Hercules, yet if his production involves more than the presentation of a general type he may copyright it and say of it 'A poor thing but mine own.' Perhaps the periodicals of the complainant are foolish rather than comic, but they embody an original arrangement of incidents and a pictorial and literary form which preclude the contention that Bruns was not copying the antics of 'Superman' portrayed in 'Action Comics.' We think it plain that the defendants have used more than general types and ideas and have appropriated the pictorial and literary details embodied in the complainant's copyrights." Although plaintiff is not entitled to a monopoly "of the mere character of a 'Superman' who is a blessing to mankind," it may invoke copyright protection to the extent its work embodies "an arrangement of incidents and literary expressions original with the author." The court's injunction forbade, among other things, printing or distributing any cartoon or book "portraying any of the feats of strength or powers performed by 'Superman' or closely imitating his costume or appearance in any feat whatever."

QUESTIONS

1. Doesn't the injunction in the "Wonderman" case overreach the breadth of the court's analysis and of the defendant's infringement? Has the court properly limited itself to protecting the plaintiff's "expression" rather than its "idea"?

2. If the defendant in the "Wonderman" case were subsequently to publish a prose book, without pictures, describing Wonderman engaging in the same heroic feats that it had depicted in its comic books, would it be in contempt of court? Should it be?

If a literary character were sufficiently well-delineated to qualify for copyright protection, would unauthorized pictorial representations of the character infringe the copyright?

3. Is a chair in the shape of Mickey Mouse, manufactured by Disney, copyrightable? Does this situation differ from that presented by the abstract shape entitled "Repose" mentioned above? On what basis? Do you now understand what led the drafters of the 1976 Act to throw up their hands, thereby producing § 113(b)? Note in this connection the following observation: "For some reason which is not entirely clear, cartoons, whether still or animated, are the most advantageous form in which to embody anything designed for copyright." Umbreit, *A Consideration of Copyright*, 87 U. Pa. L. Rev. 932, 936 (1939).

H. GOVERNMENT WORKS AND OTHER PUBLIC POLICY ISSUES

§ 105. Subject matter of copyright: United States Government works

Copyright protection under this title is not available for any work of the United States Government, but the United States Government is not precluded from receiving and holding copyrights transferred to it by assignment, bequest, or otherwise.

HOUSE REPORT

H.R. Rep. No. 94-1476, 94th Cong., 2d Sess. 58-59 (1976)

Scope of the prohibition

The general prohibition against copyright in section 105 applies to "any work of the United States Government," which is defined in section 101 as "a work prepared by an officer or employee of the United States Government as part of that person's official duties." Under this definition a Government official or employee would not be prevented from securing copyright in a work written at that person's own volition and outside his or her duties, even though the subject matter involves the Government work or professional field of the official or employee. Although the wording of the definition of "work of the United States Government" differs somewhat from that of the definition of "work made for hire," the concepts are intended to be construed in the same way.

A more difficult and far-reaching problem is whether the definition should be broadened to prohibit copyright in works prepared under U.S. Government contract or grant. As the bill is written, the Government agency concerned could determine in each case whether to allow an independent contractor or grantee to secure copyright in works prepared in whole or in part with the use of Government funds. The argument that has been made against allowing copyright in this situation is that the public should not be required to pay a "double subsidy," and that it is inconsistent to prohibit copyright in works by Government employees while permitting private copyrights in a growing body of works created by persons who are paid with Government funds. Those arguing in favor of potential copyright protection have stressed the importance of copyright as an incentive to creation and dissemination in this situation and the basically different policy considerations applicable to works written by Government employees and those applicable to works prepared by private organizations with the use of Federal funds.

The bill deliberately avoids making any sort of outright, unqualified prohibition against copyright in works prepared under Government contract or grant. There may well be cases where it would be in the public interest to deny copyright in the writings generated by Government research contracts and the like; it can be assumed that, where a Government agency commissions a work for its own use merely as an alternative to having one of its own employees prepare the work the right to secure a private copyright would be withheld. However, there are almost certainly many other cases where the denial of copyright protection would be unfair or would hamper the production and publication of important works. Where, under the particular circumstances, Congress or the agency involved finds that the need to have work freely available outweighs the need of the private author to secure copyright, the problem can be dealt with by specific legislation, agency regulations, or contractual restrictions.

QUESTIONS

1. Examine the official reports of the United States Supreme Court and the volumes in the Federal Second series. What parts of these volumes, if any, are eligible for copyright?

2. Are state statutes and court decisions eligible for federal copyright? Are there compelling reasons to afford copyright protection to such primary legal sources (e.g., the need to assure that others do not distort or misquote)? Are there compelling reasons to deny such protection (e.g., possible issues of due process of law)? *See Georgia v. Harrison Co.,* 548 F. Supp. 110 (N.D. Ga. 1982), *vacated upon settlement,* 559 F. Supp. 37 (N.D. Ga. 1983).

3. Is the case for copyright protection for state statutes strengthened if they have been based on model laws created and copyrighted by private organizations with a view toward legislative adoption? *See Building Officials & Code Admin. v. Code Technology, Inc.,* 628 F.2d 730 (1st Cir. 1980).

4. Is the *Scott Stamp Catalogue* — which reproduces all United States stamps and lists such accompanying information as perforations, watermarks and value new and used — an infringement of copyright? Can United States stamps be freely reproduced as part of a fabric design for curtains or clothing? The House Report states (at page 60) that § 105 "does not apply to works created by employees of the United States Postal Service" because of its separate status under the 1970 Postal Reorganization Act. The Postal Service "could, if it chooses, use the copyright law to prevent the reproduction of postage stamp designs for private or commercial non-postal services (for example, in philatelic publications and catalogs, in general advertising, in art reproductions, in textile designs, and so forth)." Is this exclusion from § 105 tenable?

5. The Administrative Office of the United States Courts entered into a contract with a public television station to "produce for the Judicial Conference of the United States five films about the Supreme Court entitled 'Equal Justice Under the Law.'" The station was to copyright the films and thereafter assign the copyright to the Government. The films have been produced starring professional actors in the role of Supreme Court Justices and depicting the background of five major cases in Supreme Court history. They have been exhibited on public television through the Public Broadcasting Service. Copyright has been registered for each film in the name of the station. A journalist has commenced an action for declaratory and injunctive relief (with the Director of the Administrative Office, the Register of Copyrights, the producing television station, PBS and one of its exhibiting stations as named defendants) seeking a determination that the copyrights are invalid. What ruling should the court make? *See Schnapper v. Foley,* 667 F.2d 102 (D.C. Cir. 1981), *cert. denied,* 455 U.S. 948 (1982).

6. Hyman Rickover was Vice Admiral in the Navy Department as Assistant Chief of the Bureau of Ships for Nuclear Propulsion. During his tenure in that position, Admiral Rickover prepared a number of speeches on a wide range of subjects, such as "Nuclear Power and the Navy," "Engineering and Scientific Education," "The Education of Our Talented Children," "Nuclear Power — Challenge to Industry," "Energy Resources and Our Future," "Revolution at Sea," and "European Secondary Schools." These speeches were delivered at such places as chambers of commerce, the Minnesota State Medical Association, the Detroit Engineering Society, the Nuclear Power Training School, and the Columbia University Forum. In all instances, the locations were near places where Rickover had duties of supervision and inspection, so that no transportation costs were borne by him; he made the speeches in free or off-duty hours. The final drafts of the speeches were typed by his Navy secretary on his office typewriter, and copies were made with Navy photocopy machines on the paper stock used for press releases by the Department of Defense. (Assume that all copies bore a copyright notice in the name of Admiral Rickover.) An educational publishing company has compiled many of the Rickover speeches and is about to publish them in hard-cover form. Rickover has brought an action to enjoin this publication, but the publishing company has asserted that his speeches are in the public domain. Should the injunction be granted? *See Public Affairs Assocs. v. Rickover*, 177 F. Supp. 601 (D.D.C. 1959), *rev'd and remanded*, 284 F.2d 262 (D.C. Cir. 1960), *vacated for further proceedings*, 369 U.S. 111 (1962), *on remand*, 268 F. Supp. 444 (D.D.C. 1967).

MITCHELL BROTHERS FILM GROUP v. CINEMA ADULT THEATER

604 F.2d 852 (5th Cir. 1979)

GODBOLD, CIRCUIT JUDGE: This is a copyright infringement suit, arising under the now-superseded Copyright Act of 1909. But it is more than the usual commercial contest between copyright holder and alleged infringer. The infringers asserted as an affirmative defense that the copyrighted material — a movie — was obscene, and that, therefore, under the equitable rubric of "unclean hands" plaintiffs were barred from relief. After viewing the film the court found it obscene, adopted the unclean hands rationale, and denied relief to the copyright owners. Review of this holding requires us to consider the constitutional limits upon the power granted to Congress to issue copyrights, the manner in which Congress has chosen to exercise that power, and the applicability of the unclean hands doctrine.

Plaintiffs-appellants owned a properly registered copyright on a motion picture titled "Behind the Green Door," issued under the 1909 Act, 17 U.S.C. § 34 (1970) (repealed). Two groups of defendants, each group consisting of a theater and several individuals, obtained copies of the movie without plaintiffs' permission and infringed the copyright by exhibiting the film at the theaters....

We hold that the district court erred in permitting the assertion of obscenity as an affirmative defense to the claim of infringement, and, accordingly, reverse without reaching the question whether the film is obscene.

I. *The Statutory Language*

The statutory provision that controls in this case reads:

> The works for which copyright may be secured under this title shall include all the writings of an author.

17 U.S.C. § 4 (1970) (repealed). Motion pictures are unquestionably "writings" under the Copyright Act.

The district court did not base its decision on standards found within the Act, which it described as "silent as to works which are subject to registration and copyright." The Act is not "silent." Rather, the statutory language "all the writings of an author" is facially all-inclusive, within itself admitting of no exceptions. There is not even a hint in the language of § 4 that the obscene nature of a work renders it any less a copyrightable "writing." There is no other statutory language from which it can be inferred that Congress intended that obscene materials could not be copyrighted.

Moreover, there is good reason not to read an implied exception for obscenity into the copyright statutes. The history of content-based restrictions on copyrights, trademarks, and patents suggests that the absence of such limitations in the Copyright Act of 1909 is the result of an intentional policy choice and not simply an omission. *See generally* 74 Colum. L. Rev. 1351, 1354 n.27 (1974). From the first copyright act in 1790, Congress has seldom added restrictions on copyright based on the subject matter of the work, and in each instance has later removed the content restriction. These congressional additions and subsequent deletions, though certainly not conclusive, suggest that Congress has been hostile to content-based restrictions on copyrightability. In contrast Congress has placed explicit content-related restrictions in the current statutes governing the related areas of trademarks and patents. The Lanham Act prohibits registration of any trademark that "[c]onsists of or comprises immoral, deceptive, or scandalous matter," 15 U.S.C. § 1052(a), and inventions must be shown to be "useful" before a patent is issued. *See* 35 U.S.C. § 101.

The legislative history of the 1976 Act reveals that Congress intends to continue the policy of the 1909 Act of avoiding content restrictions on copyrightability. In recommending passage of the 1976 Act, the House Judiciary Committee stated:

> The phrase "original works of authorship," [§ 102] which is purposely left undefined, is intended to incorporate without change the standard of originality established by the courts under the present copyright statute. This standard does not include requirements of novelty, ingenuity, or *esthetic merit,* and there is no intention to enlarge the standard of copyright protection to require them.

H.R. Rep. No. 1476, 94th Cong., 2d Sess., 51, *reprinted in* [1976] U.S. Code Cong. & Admin. News pp. 5659, 5664 (emphasis added).

It appears to us that Congress has concluded that the constitutional purpose of its copyright power, "[t]o promote the Progress of Science and useful Arts," U.S. Const. art. I, § 8, cl. 8, is best served by allowing all creative works (in a copyrightable format) to be accorded copyright protection regardless of subject matter or content, trusting to the public taste to reward creators of useful works and to deny creators of useless works any reward....

[The Ninth Circuit recently rejected the defense of fraudulent content in copyright infringement actions, saying]:

> There is nothing in the Copyright Act to suggest that the courts are to pass upon the truth or falsity, the soundness or unsoundness, of the views embodied in a copyrighted work. The gravity and immensity of the problems, theological, philosophical, economic and scientific, that would confront a court if this view were adopted are staggering to contemplate. It is surely not a task lightly to be assumed, and we decline the invitation to assume it.

Belcher v. Tarbox, 486 F.2d 1087, 1088 (CA9, 1973).

In our view, the absence of content restrictions on copyrightability indicates that Congress has decided that the constitutional goal of encouraging creativity would not be best served if an author had to concern himself not only with the marketability of his work but also with the judgment of government officials regarding the worth of the work.

Further, if Congress were receptive to subject matter restrictions on copyright, there are many reasons why it would be unlikely to choose obscenity as one of those restrictions. Obscenity law is a concept not adapted for use as a means for ascertaining whether creative works may be copyrighted. Obscenity as a constitutional doctrine has developed as an effort to create a tolerable compromise between First Amendment considerations and police power. It is an awkward, barely acceptable concept that continues to dog our judicial system and society at large. The purpose underlying the constitutional grant of power to Congress to protect writings is the promotion of original writings, an invitation to creativity. This is an expansive purpose with no stated limitations of taste or governmental acceptability. Such restraints, if imposed, would be antithetical to promotion of creativity. The pursuit of creativity requires freedom to explore into the gray areas, to the cutting edge, and even beyond. Obscenity, on the other hand, is a limiting doctrine constricting the scope of acceptability of the written word.

....

Denying copyright protection to works adjudged obscene by the standards of one era would frequently result in lack of copyright protection (and thus lack of financial incentive to create) for works that later generations might consider to be not only non-obscene but even of great literary merit. *See* Phillips, *Copyright in Obscene Works: Some British and American Problems,* 6 Anglo-Am. L. Rev. 138, 168-69 (1977). Many works that are today held in high regard have been adjudged obscene in previous eras....

Further, Congress in not enacting an obscenity exception to copyrightability avoids substantial practical difficulties and delicate First Amendment issues. Since what is obscene in one local community may be non-obscene protected speech in another, *see Miller v. California,* 413 U.S. 15 (1973), and the copyright statute does not in other respects vary in its applicability from locality to locality, Congress in enacting an obscenity exception would create the dilemma of choosing between using community standards that would (arguably unconstitutionally) fragment the uniform national standards of the copyright system and venturing into the uncharted waters of a national obscenity standard. *See* Phillips, *Copyright in Obscene Works: Some British and American Problems,* 6 Anglo-Am. L. Rev. 138, 170-71 (1977); Schneider, *supra* note 3, at 715; Comment, *Constitutional Protection of Obscene Material Against Censorship as Correlated with Copyright Protection of Obscene Material Against Infringement,* 31 S. Cal. L. Rev. 301, 306 (1958); 46 Fordham L. Rev. 1037, 1043-47 (1978). We can only conclude that we must read the facially all-inclusive 1909 copyright statute as containing no explicit or implicit bar to the copyrighting of obscene materials, and as therefore providing for the copyright of all creative works, obscene or non-obscene, that otherwise meet the requirements of the Copyright Act.[12]

II. *Constitutionality of the Copyright Statute*

The conclusion that the 1909 Act was all-inclusive[13] and did not provide an exception for obscenity does not end our inquiry, however. We must consider whether the statute, in allowing copyright of obscene material, was constitutional and whether despite congressional intent the courts should take it upon themselves to permit the defense of obscenity in copyright infringement cases. We first turn to the question of constitutionality.

The Copyright and Patent Clause of the Constitution provides that "The Congress shall have Power ... To promote the Progress of Science and useful Arts, by securing for limited Times to Authors and Inventors the exclusive Right to their respective Writings and Discoveries ...." U.S. Const. art. I, § 8, cl. 8. The district court construed this clause to limit the congressional power to grant copyrights solely to works that promote the sciences and useful arts. If one carries the district court's reasoning to its necessary conclusion, Congress acted unconstitutionally in enacting an all-inclusive statute that allows copyrighting of non-useful works (such as, arguably, obscenity) as well as useful works. Several lower courts and commentators have agreed with this construction of the Copyright and Patent Clause. Other commentators disagree, however, and argue that Congress has power to grant copyrights even for individual works that cannot be shown to promote the useful arts so long as Congress in its exercise of its copyright power generally promotes the constitutional goal. In our view the district court's reading of the Copyright and Patent Clause is unduly restrictive of Congress' power and is inconsistent

[12] Of course, Congress does not approve of obscenity and has enacted several measures aimed at reducing the distribution of obscene materials. *See, e.g.,* 18 U.S.C. § 1461 (crime to mail obscene materials); 18 U.S.C. § 1462 (crime to ship obscene materials interstate by common carrier); 18 U.S.C. § 1465 (crime to ship obscene materials interstate for purposes of sale or distribution). However, the existence of such statutes does not indicate that Congress intends obscene material to be uncopyrightable. Rendering obscene material uncopyrightable would add little to the existing arsenal of weapons against pornography and would have many undesirable consequences, as discussed in the text.

[13] The 1976 Act substitutes the equally-inclusive phrase "original works of authorship" for the phrase "all the writings of an author" in the 1909 Act. *See* 17 U.S.C. § 102 (1976, App.).

with the Supreme Court's broad view of the congressional powers granted by this Clause. As one commentator has pointed out,

> The words of the copyright clause of the constitution do not require that *writings* shall promote science or useful arts: they require that *Congress* shall promote those ends. It could well be argued that by passing general laws to protect all works, Congress better fulfills its designated ends than it would by denying protection to all books the contents of which were open to real or imagined objection.

Phillips, *op. cit. supra* note 15, at 165-66 (emphasis original).

... The courts will not find that Congress has exceeded its power so long as the means adopted by Congress for achieving a constitutional end are "appropriate" and "plainly adapted" to achieving that end. *McCulloch v. Maryland,* 17 U.S. (4 Wheat.) 316, 421 (1819). It is by the lenient standard of *McCulloch* that we must judge whether Congress has exceeded its constitutional powers in enacting an all-inclusive copyright statute.

Judging by this standard, it is obvious that although Congress could require that each copyrighted work be shown to promote the useful arts (as it has with patents), it need not do so. As discussed in the previous section, Congress could reasonably conclude that the best way to promote creativity is not to impose any governmental restrictions on the subject matter of copyrightable works. By making this choice Congress removes the chilling effect of governmental judgments on potential authors and avoids the strong possibility that governmental officials (including judges) will err in separating the useful from the non-useful. Moreover, unlike patents, the grant of a copyright to a non-useful work impedes the progress of the sciences and the useful arts only very slightly, if at all, for the possessor of a copyright does not have any right to block further dissemination or use of the ideas contained in his works.[20] *See Baker v. Selden,* 101 U.S. 99 (1879).

The all-inclusive nature of the 1909 Act reflects the policy judgment that encouraging the production of wheat also requires the protection of a good deal of chaff. We cannot say this judgment was so unreasonable as to exceed congressional power. We conclude that the protection of all writings, without regard to their content, is a constitutionally permissible means of promoting science and the useful arts.

III. *Judicially-Created Defenses to Infringement Actions Involving Immoral or Obscene Works*

Some courts have denied legal redress in infringement suits to holders of copyrights on immoral or obscene works by applying judicially-created doctrines....

....

---

[20]This is not true in the patent area, where an inventor has the right to prevent others from using his discovery. Thus Congress and the courts have been careful to require that each patented invention advance the useful arts in some way. *See generally Brenner v. Manson*, 383 U.S. 519 (1966); *Alfred Bell & Co. v. Catalda Fine Arts, Inc.*, 191 F.2d 99 (CA2, 1951).

Assuming for the moment that the equitable doctrine of unclean hands has any field of application in this case, it should not be used as a conduit for asserting obscenity as a limit upon copyright protection. Creating a defense of obscenity — in the name of unclean hands or through any other vehicle — adds a defense not authorized by Congress that may, as discussed above, actually frustrate the congressional purpose underlying an all-inclusive copyright statute. It will discourage creativity by freighting it with a requirement of judicial approval. Requiring authors of controversial, unpopular, or new material to go through judicial proceedings to validate the content of their writings is antithetical to the aim of copyrights. If the copyright holder cannot obtain financial protection for his work because of actual or possible judicial objections to the subject matter, the pro-creativity purpose of the copyright laws will be undercut.

. . . .

The effectiveness of controlling obscenity by denying copyright protection is open to question. The district court thought that on the whole the long-term discouragement of the creation of obscene works would outweigh the short-term increase in the dissemination of obscene works caused by the refusal of an injunction. This theory, reached without empirical evidence or expert opinion, is at least doubtful. Many commentators disagree and are of the view that denial of injunctions against infringers of obscene materials will only increase the distribution of such works. The existence of this difference of view, which we need not resolve, makes clear that the question of how to deal with the relationship between copyrights and obscenity is not best suited for case-by-case judicial resolution but is instead most appropriately resolved by legislatures. Congress has not chosen to refuse copyrights on obscene materials, and we should be cautious in overriding the legislative judgment on this issue.

Reversed and remanded.

QUESTION

The *Mitchell Bros.* court rejects the argument that each work must individually promote the progress of knowledge. Should courts adopt a similar position with respect to another feature of the constitutional copyright clause: while copyright is conceived as an incentive to the production of works of authorship, must it be demonstrated in each case that it was copyright protection that spurred each author to create the work at issue? *Compare Hutchinson Tel. Co. v. Fronteer Directory Co.*, 770 F.2d 128 (8th Cir. 1985), with *Feist Pubs., Inc. v. Rural Tel. Serv.*, Chapter 2A, *supra*: in both cases, the obligation to publish a telephone directory in order to secure the telephone service franchise afforded a significant incentive to creation of the compilation; the *Hutchinson* court found that this fact did not compromise plaintiff's copyright, while the *Feist* court observed that plaintiff had other incentives than copyright to create its directory.

The *Mitchell Bros.* decision seems consistent with the longstanding copyright policy of refraining from assessing the aesthetic merit of the work. *See Bleistein v. Donaldson Lithographing Co., supra*. Would avoidance of inquiry into specific economic incentives be as well-founded? *Should* a court attempt to discern what role the prospect of copyright protection played in the creation or elaboration of the work? What problems do you see with such an inquiry?

Chapter 3

OWNERSHIP

A. INITIAL OWNERSHIP

1. AUTHORSHIP STATUS

ANDRIEN v. SOUTHERN OCEAN COUNTY CHAMBER OF COMMERCE

927 F.2d 132 (3d Cir. 1991)

WEIS, CIRCUIT JUDGE.

The district court held that the plaintiff who assembled a series of maps and turned them over to a printing firm to prepare a composite was not the author for copyright purposes. Accepting the plaintiff's version of events for summary judgment purposes, we conclude that the record does not support depriving plaintiff of his status as author. Accordingly, we will reverse the summary judgment in favor of defendants and remand for further proceedings.

Plaintiff James Andrien was a real estate agent on Long Beach Island, New Jersey. In 1980, he received a copyright registration from the Copyright Office for a map of Long Beach Island. The certificate described a copyright for a compilation of pre-existing maps, street names, street lines and other information assembled and created from a personal survey of the island. Andrien engaged the A & H Company to print the map....

Andrien decided to prepare a map of the area when he found the sketch distributed by defendant Chamber of Commerce incomplete and difficult to read. He collected available maps of local taxing bodies and a divers' map locating shipwrecks in the area. In a personal survey Andrien noted civic landmarks, fishing sites and previously unlisted street names. He determined the scale to be used on the finished map by driving his automobile between intersecting streets and measuring the distance on the odometer.

The collection of maps that Andrien took to A & H Printers used varied scales and almost illegible street names. To prepare the new map for printing, A & H assigned Carolyn Haines to do the "art work." This included coordinating the scales, relettering the street names and adding designations for the diving sites as well as for local points of interest. Haines photographed the various maps to synchronize the scales and typed individual labels for the street names. After a large paste-up working map was completed, it was reduced to a commercially useable size and printed.

In his deposition Andrien testified that Haines performed these assignments at his direction, "with me at her elbow practically." Almost daily he spent about an hour at the print shop over a three week period....

The district court concluded that Andrien was not the author because, although he had closely supervised the project, "he did none of the actual layout

[and] was not always present when Haines worked on the map." The judge believed that Andrien had not translated his idea into a fixed, tangible expression but that had been done by A & H Printing, "or more specifically, Carolyn Haines." The judge also rejected joint authorship, "I think since Andrien supplied information and ideas from which A & H and Haines created the map, Andrien cannot even claim to be a joint author with A & H Printing.".…

On appeal, Andrien contends that whether he is the author is the subject of a genuine factual dispute and therefore summary judgment was inappropriate.…

As a general rule copyright protection is available for maps, 17 U.S.C. § 102(a)(5), or a compilation of existing maps. 17 U.S.C. § 103. *See Rockford Map Publishers, Inc. v. Directory Service Co.,* 768 F.2d 145 (7th Cir. 1985), *cert. denied,* 474 U.S. 1061 (1986); *United States v. Hamilton,* 583 F.2d 448 (9th Cir. 1978); *Amsterdam v. Triangle Publications, Inc.,* 189 F.2d 104 (3d Cir. 1951).[1] *See generally* 1 M. Nimmer & D. Nimmer, Nimmer on Copyright § 2.08[A] (1990). Accepting the copyright statute's application to the map under consideration, the parties present us with a narrow issue: the controversy over Andrien's status as an author.

Copyright is available only for the expression of a work of authorship, not for a mere idea.…

The Supreme Court has stated that "as a general rule, the author is the party who actually creates the work, that is, the person who translates an idea into a fixed, tangible expression entitled to copyright protection." *Community for Creative Non-Violence,* 109 S. Ct. at 2171. The Copyright Act defines a work as "fixed" in a tangible medium of expression when "its embodiment in a copy … by or under the authority of the author, is sufficiently permanent … to permit it to be … reproduced." 17 U.S.C. § 101.

The critical phrase is "by or under the authority of the author." That statutory language and the Supreme Court's guidance produce a definition of an author as the party who actually creates the work, that is, the person who translates an idea into an expression that is embodied in a copy by himself or herself, or who authorizes another to embody the expression in a copy. The definition, however, has limits. When one authorizes embodiment, that process must be rote or mechanical transcription that does not require intellectual modification or highly technical enhancement such as occurred in *M.G.B. Homes, Inc. v. Ameron Homes, Inc.,* 903 F.2d 1486 (11th Cir. 1990) (architectural drawings), *Geshwind v. Garrick,* 734 F. Supp. 644 (S.D.N.Y. 1990) (computer animated film), and *Whelan Associates, Inc. v. Jaslow Dental Laboratory, Inc.,* 609 F. Supp. 1307 (E.D. Pa. 1985) (computer program), *aff'd,* 797 F.2d 1222 (3d Cir. 1986), *cert. denied,* 479 U.S. 1031 (1987).

Poets, essayists, novelists, and the like may have copyrights even if they do not run the printing presses or process the photographic plates necessary to fix the writings into book form. These writers are entitled to copyright protec-

---

[1]Professor Nimmer questions whether the direct observation rule articulated in *Amsterdam* survives the 1976 Act. 1 M. Nimmer & D. Nimmer, Nimmer on Copyright § 2.08[A][b] at 2-80 (1990). We need not decide that point because the map under consideration here meets the more stringent *Amsterdam* criteria.

tion even if they do not perform with their own hands the mechanical tasks of putting the material into the form distributed to the public.

There is a "fundamental distinction" between an "original work" of authorship and "the multitude of material objects in which it can be embodied." H.R. Rep. No. 1476, 94th Cong., 2d Sess. 53, reprinted in 1976 U.S. Code Cong. & Admin. News 5659, 5666. As the House Report explained:

> Thus, in the sense of the bill, a "book" is not a work of authorship, but is a particular kind of "copy." Instead, the author may write a "literary work," which in turn can be embodied in a wide range of "copies" and "phonorecords," including books, periodicals, computer punch cards, microfilm, tape recordings, and so forth.

Id.

The Copyright Act does not specifically define the relationship between writer and printer, but does address a somewhat analogous, albeit more ambiguous, situation. Some forms of sound recordings are protected under 17 U.S.C. § 102(a)(7). According to the House Report, these recordings "are clearly within the scope of the 'writings of an author' capable of protection." H.R. Rep. No. 1476, 94th Cong., 2d Sess. 56, reprinted in 1976 U.S. Code Cong. & Admin. News 5659, 5669. The Report considered authorship to apply not only to the performer, but also to the producer responsible for setting up the recording session, processing the sounds and compiling and editing them to make a final sound recording. In some cases, however, the record producer's contribution could be so minimal that the performance is the only copyrightable element in the work.

In questioning the House Report, Professor Nimmer remarks that the solitary act of "setting up the recording session" is "ill-based" for claiming authorship on behalf of the record producer. 1 M. Nimmer & D. Nimmer, Nimmer on Copyright § 2.10[A][b] at 2-146 (1990). Indeed, "this is no more an act of 'authorship' than is the act of one who makes available to a writer a room, a stenographer, a typewriter, and paper." *Id.*

Mechanically transposing an author's expressions or compilations is somewhat analogous to producing a sound recording, although the latter process may require more technical choice and artistic discretion. Significant to the case at hand is Nimmer's comment emphasizing that a party can be considered an author when his or her expression of an idea is transposed by mechanical or rote transcription into tangible form under the authority of the party.

Andrien testified that he expressly directed the copy's preparation in specific detail. His compilation needed only simple transcription to achieve final tangible form. From his description, Carolyn Haines acted as his amanuensis just as does a stenographer in typing material dictated by another person.

On this record none of Haines' activities in any way intellectually modified or technically enhanced the concept articulated by Andrien other than to arrange it in a form that could be photographed as part of the embodiment process. Moreover, when A & H employees printed the maps they did not change the substance of Andrien's original expression. Based on the statute, its legislative history, caselaw and academic commentary, we conclude that the activities to which Andrien testified qualified him as an author within the copyright statute's requirements. In the present procedural posture of this case, it was therefore inappropriate to enter summary judgment....

WHAT IS AUTHORSHIP?

The *Andrien* decision elects between two competing concepts of authorship: one based on conception, the other based on execution. (As we shall see, there are yet other concepts of authorship relevant to the copyright regime.) While arguments supporting execution failed to persuade the *Andrien* court, the notion that the "author" and copyright owner is the person who causes the work to come into physical being (in modern terminology, "fixes" the work) enjoys at least historical authority. In *Walter v. Lane,* [1900] A.C. 539, the House of Lords held that a London *Times* reporter's verbatim transcription of after-dinner speeches composed and pronounced by Lord Rosebury, a renowned Victorian post-prandial wit, met the statutory requirements of "authorship." It sufficed that the reporter "brought [the speeches] into existence in the form of a writing" (Lord Davey), even though the reports "present[ed] the speaker's thoughts untinctured by the slightest trace or colour of the reporter's mind" (Lord Robertson, dissenting). Thus, defendant's compilation of a book of Rosebery's speeches from the *Times* reports (with Rosebery's apparent permission) infringed the newspaper's copyright.

The *Andrien* court's view, certainly today the dominant one, prefers the intellectual to the muscular contribution to creation. But it would be an overstatement to claim that U.S. copyright today rests entirely on an intellectual characterization of authorship. There is another competing concept of authorship in our copyright law, an economic one. Under this conception, the "author" is the person or entity who finances the work's creation and dissemination, including covering the cost of the persons actually creating the work. This person's or entity's assumption of all economic risks entitles it to be treated as the "author." This is the concept sustaining the "works made for hire" rule of U.S. copyright law. As you review the following materials, consider the differences in philosophy and result between the various concepts of authorship.

2. AUTHORSHIP AS AN ECONOMIC CONCEPT: WORKS MADE FOR HIRE

The Constitution authorizes Congress to "secur[e] to *Authors* ... the exclusive Right to their ... Writings," Art. I, § 1, cl. 8 (emphasis added). In determining who is an "author" for constitutional purposes, one might conclude that the text reserves to the actual creators of works the initial entitlement to copyright. However, the United States copyright statute does not limit authorship status to human beings. The Copyright Act permits corporate entities to claim the "author" title: the "work made for hire" doctrine (*see infra,* part a) designates as "authors" employers and certain commissioning parties.

Is conferring authorship status on corporations and on other persons who did not create the work (certain commissioning parties) any more than a formalistic, but substantively inadequate, compliance with the language of the Constitutional copyright clause? What kinds of efforts make one an "author" in the Constitutional sense? Doesn't the Constitutional text imply a closer connection between "Author" and "Writing" (money may talk, but it doesn't write)? On the other hand, if the United States conception of copyright, as expressed in the copyright clause, is primarily economic, is it not consonant with the Constitution to award the limited monopoly to the person or entity who finances the work's creation and takes the risk of bringing it to market? If "Author" signifies not one who is merely a payor, but one "to whom anything owes its origin; originator; maker; one who completes a work of science or literature," *Burrow-Giles v. Sarony, supra* Chapter 1, does Congress' recognition of any other person or entity as an "author" contravene the Constitution?

§ 101. Definitions

As used in this title, the following terms and their variant forms mean the following:

A "work made for hire" is —

(1) a work prepared by an employee within the scope of his or her employment; or

(2) a work specially ordered or commissioned for use as a contribution to a collective work, as a part of a motion picture or other audiovisual work, as a translation, as a supplementary work, as a compilation, as an instructional text, as a test, as answer material for a test, or as an atlas, if the parties expressly agree in a written instrument signed by them that the work shall be considered a work made for hire. For the purpose of the foregoing sentence, a "supplementary work" is a work prepared for publication as a secondary adjunct to a work by another author for the purpose of introducing, concluding, illustrating, explaining, revising, commenting upon, or assisting in the use of the other works, such as forewords, afterwords, pictorial illustrations, maps, charts, tables, editorial notes, musical arrangements, answer material for tests, bibliographies, appendixes, and indexes, and an "instructional text" is a literary, pictorial, or graphic work prepared for publication with the purpose of use in systematic instructional activities.

§ 201. Ownership of copyright

. . . .

(b) *Works Made For Hire* — In the case of a work made for hire, the employer or other person for whom the work was prepared is considered the author for purposes of this title, and, unless the parties have expressly agreed otherwise in a written instrument signed by them, owns all of the rights comprised in the copyright.

QUESTION

Why should employees and commissioned persons who create works for hire be deprived of the status of an "author" by virtue of § 201(b)? Why should the hiring party be deemed the initial owner of copyright? Why should the "life plus fifty years" period of protection not apply to works made for hire? Why should the power given to an "author" to terminate certain long-term grants of copyright (to be studied below) not also apply to creators of works made for hire?

COMMUNITY FOR CREATIVE NON-VIOLENCE v. REID

490 U.S. 730, 109 S. Ct. 2166, 104 L. Ed. 2d 811 (1989)

JUSTICE MARSHALL delivered the opinion of the Court.

In this case, an artist and the organization that hired him to produce a sculpture contest the ownership of the copyright in that work. To resolve this dispute, we must construe the "work made for hire" provisions of the Copyright Act of 1976 (Act or 1976 Act), 17 U.S.C. §§ 101 and 201(b), and in particular, the provision in § 101, which defines as a "work made for hire" a "work prepared by an employee within the scope of his or her employment" (hereinafter § 101(1)).

I

Petitioners are the Community for Creative Non-Violence (CCNV), a non-profit unincorporated association dedicated to eliminating homelessness in America, and Mitch Snyder, a member and trustee of CCNV. In the fall of 1985, CCNV decided to participate in the annual Christmastime Pageant of Peace in Washington, D.C., by sponsoring a display to dramatize the plight of the homeless. As the District Court recounted:

> "Snyder and fellow CCNV members conceived the idea for the nature of the display: a sculpture of a modern Nativity scene in which, in lieu of the traditional Holy Family, the two adult figures and the infant would appear as contemporary homeless people huddled on a streetside steam grate. The family was to be black (most of the homeless in Washington being black); the figures were to be life-sized, and the steam grate would be positioned atop a platform 'pedestal,' or base, within which special-effects equipment would be enclosed to emit simulated 'steam' through the grid to swirl about the figures. They also settled upon a title for the work — 'Third World America' — and a legend for the pedestal: 'and still there is no room at the inn.'" 652 F. Supp. 1453, 1454 (DC 1987).

Snyder made inquiries to locate an artist to produce the sculpture. He was referred to respondent James Earl Reid, a Baltimore, Maryland, sculptor. In the course of two telephone calls, Reid agreed to sculpt the three human figures. CCNV agreed to make the steam grate and pedestal for the statue. Reid proposed that the work be cast in bronze, at a total cost of approximately $100,000 and taking six to eight months to complete. Snyder rejected that

AND STILL THERE IS NO ROOM AT THE INN

Reproduced with permission of James Earl Reid

proposal because CCNV did not have sufficient funds, and because the statue had to be completed by December 12 to be included in the pageant. Reid then suggested, and Snyder agreed, that the sculpture would be made of a material known as "Design Cast 62," a synthetic substance that could meet CCNV's monetary and time constraints, could be tinted to resemble bronze, and could withstand the elements. The parties agreed that the project would cost no more than $15,000, not including Reid's services, which he offered to donate. The parties did not sign a written agreement. Neither party mentioned copyright.

After Reid received an advance of $3,000, he made several sketches of figures in various poses. At Snyder's request, Reid sent CCNV a sketch of a proposed sculpture showing the family in a crechelike setting: the mother seated, cradling a baby in her lap; the father standing behind her, bending over her shoulder to touch the baby's foot. Reid testified that Snyder asked for the sketch to use in raising funds for the sculpture. Snyder testified that it was also for his approval. Reid sought a black family to serve as a model for the sculpture. Upon Snyder's suggestion, Reid visited a family living at CCNV's Washington shelter but decided that only their newly born child was a suitable model. While Reid was in Washington, Snyder took him to see homeless people living on the streets. Snyder pointed out that they tended to recline on steam grates, rather than sit or stand, in order to warm their bodies. From that time on, Reid's sketches contained only reclining figures.

Throughout November and the first two weeks of December 1985, Reid worked exclusively on the statue, assisted at various times by a dozen different people who were paid with funds provided in installments by CCNV. On a number of occasions, CCNV members visited Reid to check on his progress and to coordinate CCNV's construction of the base. CCNV rejected Reid's proposal to use suitcases or shopping bags to hold the family's personal belongings, insisting instead on a shopping cart. Reid and CCNV members did not discuss copyright ownership on any of these visits.

On December 24, 1985, 12 days after the agreed-upon date, Reid delivered the completed statue to Washington. There it was joined to the steam grate and pedestal prepared by CCNV and placed on display near the site of the pageant.

Snyder paid Reid the final installment of the $15,000. The statue remained on display for a month. In late January 1986, CCNV members returned it to Reid's studio in Baltimore for minor repairs. Several weeks later, Snyder began making plans to take the statue on a tour of several cities to raise money for the homeless. Reid objected, contending that the Design Cast 62 material was not strong enough to withstand the ambitious itinerary. He urged CCNV to cast the statue in bronze at a cost of $35,000, or to create a master mold at a cost of $5,000. Snyder declined to spend more of CCNV's money on the project.

In March 1986, Snyder asked Reid to return the sculpture. Reid refused. He then filed a certificate of copyright registration for "Third World America" in his name and announced plans to take the sculpture on a more modest tour than the one CCNV had proposed. Snyder, acting in his capacity as CCNV's trustee, immediately filed a competing certificate of copyright registration.

Snyder and CCNV then commenced this action against Reid and his photographer, Ronald Purtee,[1] seeking return of the sculpture and a determination of copyright ownership. The District Court granted a preliminary injunction, ordering the sculpture's return. After a 2-day bench trial, the District Court declared that "Third World America" was a "work made for hire" under § 101 of the Copyright Act and that Snyder, as trustee for CCNV, was the exclusive owner of the copyright in the sculpture. 652 F. Supp., at 1457. The court reasoned that Reid had been an "employee" of CCNV within the meaning of § 101(1) because CCNV was the motivating force in the statue's production. Snyder and other CCNV members, the court explained, "conceived the idea of a contemporary Nativity scene to contrast with the national celebration of the season," and "directed enough of [Reid's] effort to assure that, in the end, he had produced what they, not he, wanted." Id., at 1456.

The Court of Appeals for the District of Columbia Circuit reversed and remanded, holding that Reid owned the copyright because "Third World America" was not a work for hire. 270 U.S. App. D.C. 26, 35, 846 F.2d 1485, 1494 (1988). Adopting what it termed the "literal interpretation" of the Act as

---

[1]Purtee was named as a defendant but never appeared or claimed any interest in the statue.

articulated by the Fifth Circuit in *Easter Seal Society for Crippled Children and Adults of Louisiana, Inc. v. Playboy Enterprises,* 815 F.2d 323, 329 (1987), *cert. denied,* 485 U.S. 981 (1988), the court read § 101 as creating "a simple dichotomy in fact between employees and independent contractors." 270 U.S. App. D.C., at 33, 846 F.2d, at 1492. Because, under agency law, Reid was an independent contractor, the court concluded that the work was not "prepared by an employee" under § 101(1). *Id.,* at 35, 846 F.2d, at 1494. Nor was the sculpture a "work made for hire" under the second subsection of § 101 (hereinafter § 101(2)): sculpture is not one of the nine categories of works enumerated in that subsection, and the parties had not agreed in writing that the sculpture would be a work for hire. *Ibid.* The court suggested that the sculpture nevertheless may have been jointly authored by CCNV and Reid, *id.,* at 36, 846 F.2d, at 1495, and remanded for a determination whether the sculpture is indeed a joint work under the Act, *id.,* at 39-40, 846 F.2d, at 1498-1499.

We granted certiorari to resolve a conflict among the Courts of Appeals over the proper construction of the "work made for hire" provisions of the Act. 488 U.S. 940 (1988). We now affirm.

II

A

The Copyright Act of 1976 provides that copyright ownership "vests initially in the author or authors of the work." 17 U.S.C. § 201(a). As a general rule, the author is the party who actually creates the work, that is, the person who translates an idea into a fixed, tangible expression entitled to copyright protection. § 102. The Act carves out an important exception, however, for "works made for hire." If the work is for hire, "the employer or other person for whom the work was prepared is considered the author" and owns the copyright, unless there is a written agreement to the contrary. § 201(b). Classifying a work as "made for hire" determines not only the initial ownership of its copyright, but also the copyright's duration, § 302(c), and the owners' renewal rights, § 304(a), termination rights, § 203(a), and right to import certain goods bearing the copyright, § 601(b)(1). *See* 1 M. Nimmer & D. Nimmer, Nimmer on Copyright § 5.03[A], pp. 5-10 (1988). The contours of the work for hire doctrine therefore carry profound significance for freelance creators — including artists, writers, photographers, designers, composers, and computer programmers — and for the publishing, advertising, music, and other industries which commission their works.[4]

... The petitioners do not claim that the statue satisfies the terms of § 101(2). Quite clearly, it does not. Sculpture does not fit within any of the nine categories of "specially ordered or commissioned" works enumerated in

---

[4] As of 1955, approximately 40 percent of all copyright registrations were for works for hire, according to a Copyright Office study. *See* Varmer, *Works Made for Hire and On Commission,* in Studies Prepared for the Subcommittee on Patents, Trademarks, and Copyrights of the Senate Committee on the Judiciary, Study No. 13, 86th Cong., 2d Sess. 139, n. 49 (Comm. Print, 1960) (hereinafter Varmer, *Works Made for Hire*). The Copyright Office does not keep more recent statistics on the number of work for hire registrations.

that subsection, and no written agreement between the parties establishes "Third World America" as a work for hire.

The dispositive inquiry in this case therefore is whether "Third World America" is "a work prepared by an employee within the scope of his or her employment" under § 101(1). The Act does not define these terms. In the absence of such guidance, four interpretations have emerged. The first holds that a work is prepared by an employee whenever the hiring party retains the right to control the product. *See Peregrine v. Lauren Corp.,* 601 F. Supp. 828, 829 (Colo. 1985); *Clarkstown v. Reeder,* 566 F. Supp. 137, 142 (SDNY 1983). Petitioners take this view. Brief for Petitioners 15; Tr. of Oral Arg. 12. A second, and closely related, view is that a work is prepared by an employee under § 101(1) when the hiring party has actually wielded control with respect to the creation of a particular work. This approach was formulated by the Court of Appeals for the Second Circuit, *Aldon Accessories Ltd. v. Spiegel, Inc.,* 738 F.2d 548, *cert. denied,* 469 U.S. 982, 105 S. Ct. 387, 83 L. Ed. 2d 321 (1984), and adopted by the Fourth Circuit, *Brunswick Beacon, Inc. v. Schock-Hopchas Publishing Co.,* 810 F.2d 410 (1987), the Seventh Circuit, *Evans Newton, Inc. v. Chicago Systems Software,* 793 F.2d 889, *cert. denied,* 479 U.S. 949, 107 S. Ct. 434, 93 L. Ed. 2d 383 (1986), and, at times, by petitioners, Brief for Petitioners 17. A third view is that the term "employee" within § 101(1) carries its common law agency law meaning. This view was endorsed by the Fifth Circuit in *Easter Seal Society for Crippled Children and Adults of Louisiana, Inc. v. Playboy Enterprises,* 815 F.2d 323 (1987), and by the Court of Appeals below. Finally, respondent and numerous *amici curiae* contend that the term "employee" only refers to "formal, salaried" employees. See, e.g., Brief for Respondents 23-24; Brief for Register of Copyrights as *Amicus Curiae* 7. The Court of Appeals for the Ninth Circuit recently adopted this view. *See Dumas v. Gommerman,* 865 F.2d 1093 (1989).

The starting point for our interpretation of a statute is always its language. *Consumer Product Safety Comm'n v. GTE Sylvania, Inc.,* 447 U.S. 102, 108, 100 S. Ct. 2051, 2056, 64 L. Ed. 2d 766 (1980). The Act nowhere defines the terms "employee" or "scope of employment." It is, however, well established that "[w]here Congress uses terms that have accumulated settled meaning under ... the common law, a court must infer, unless the statute otherwise dictates, that Congress means to incorporate the established meaning of these terms." *NLRB v. Amax Coal Co.,* 453 U.S. 322, 329, 101 S. Ct. 2789, 2794, 69 L. Ed. 2d 672 (1981); *see also Perrin v. United States,* 444 U.S. 37, 42, 100 S. Ct. 311, 314, 62 L. Ed. 2d 199 (1979). In the past, when Congress has used the term "employee" without defining it, we have concluded that Congress intended to describe the conventional master-servant relationship as understood by common law agency doctrine.... Nothing in the text of the work for hire provisions indicates that Congress used the words "employee" and "employment" to describe anything other than "'the conventional relation of employer and employee.'"... On the contrary, Congress' intent to incorporate the agency law definition is suggested by § 101(1)'s use of the term, "scope of employment," a widely used term of art in agency law. *See* Restatement (Second) of Agency § 228 (1958) (hereinafter Restatement).

In past cases of statutory interpretation, when we have concluded that Congress intended terms such as "employee," "employer," and "scope of employment" to be understood in light of agency law, we have relied on the general common law of agency, rather than on the law of any particular State, to give meaning to these terms.... This practice reflects the fact that "federal statutes are generally intended to have uniform nationwide application." *Mississippi Band of Choctaw Indians v. Holyfield,* 490 U.S. —, —, 109 S. Ct. 1597, 1605, 104 L. Ed. 2d 29 (1989). Establishment of a federal rule of agency, rather than reliance on state agency law, is particularly appropriate here given the Act's express objective of creating national uniform copyright law by broadly pre-empting state statutory and common-law copyright regulation. *See* 17 U.S.C. § 301(a). We thus agree with the Court of Appeals that the term "employee" should be understood in light of the general common law of agency.

In contrast, neither test proposed by petitioners is consistent with the text of the Act. The exclusive focus of the right to control the product test on the relationship between the hiring party and the product clashes with the language of § 101(1), which focuses on the relationship between the hired and hiring parties. The right to control the product test also would distort the meaning of the ensuing subsection, § 101(2). Section 101 plainly creates two distinct ways in which a work can be deemed for hire: one for works prepared by employees, the other for those specially ordered or commissioned works which fall within one of the nine enumerated categories and are the subject of a written agreement. The right to control the product test ignores this dichotomy by transforming into a work for hire under § 101(1) any "specially ordered or commissioned" work that is subject to the supervision and control of the hiring party. Because a party who hires a "specially ordered or commissioned" work by definition has a right to specify the characteristics of the product desired, at the time the commission is accepted, and frequently until it is completed, the right to control the product test would mean that many works that could satisfy § 101(2) would already have been deemed works for hire under § 101(1). Petitioners' interpretation is particularly hard to square with § 101(2)'s enumeration of the nine specific categories of specially ordered or commissioned works eligible to be works for hire, e.g., "a contribution to a collective work," "a part of a motion picture," and "answer material for a test." The unifying feature of these works is that they are usually prepared at the instance, direction, and risk of a publisher or producer. By their very nature, therefore, these types of works would be works by an employee under petitioners' right to control the product test.

The actual control test, articulated by the Second Circuit in *Aldon Accessories,* fares only marginally better when measured against the language and structure of § 101. Under this test, independent contractors who are so controlled and supervised in the creation of a particular work are deemed "employees" under § 101(1). Thus work for hire status under § 101(1) depends on a hiring party's *actual* control, rather than *right to* control, of the product. *Aldon Accessories,* 738 F.2d, at 552. Under the actual control test, a work for hire could arise under § 101(2), but not under § 101(1), where a party commissions, but does not actually control, a product which falls into one of the nine enumerated categories. Nonetheless, we agree with the Fifth Circuit Court of Appeals that "[t]here is simply no way to milk the 'actual control' test of *Aldon Accessories* from the language of the statute." *Easter Seal Society*, 815 F.2d, at 334. Section 101 clearly delineates between works prepared by an employee and commissioned works. Sound though other distinctions might be as a matter of copyright policy, there is no statutory support for an additional dichotomy between commissioned works that are actually controlled and supervised by the hiring party and those that are not.

We therefore conclude that the language and structure of § 101 of the Act do not support either the right to control the product or the actual control approaches.[8] The structure of § 101 indicates that a work for hire can arise through one of two mutually exclusive means, one for employees and one for independent contractors, and ordinary canons of statutory interpretation indicate that the classification of a particular hired party should be made with reference to agency law.

This reading of the undefined statutory terms finds considerable support in the Act's legislative history. *Cf. Diamond v. Chakrabarty*, 447 U.S. 303, 315, 100 S. Ct. 2204, 2210-11, 65 L. Ed. 2d 144 (1980). The Act, which almost completely revised existing copyright law, was the product of two decades of negotiation by representatives of creators and copyright-using industries, supervised by the Copyright Office and, to a lesser extent, by Congress. *See Mills Music, Inc. v. Snyder*, 469 U.S. 153, 159, 105 S. Ct. 638, 642-43, 83 L. Ed. 2d 556 (1985); Litman, *Copyright, Compromise, and Legislative History*, 72 Cornell L. Rev. 857, 862 (1987). Despite the lengthy history of negotiation and compromise which ultimately produced the Act, two things remained constant. First, interested parties and Congress at all times viewed works by employees and commissioned works by independent contractors as separate entities. Second, in using the term "employee," the parties and Congress meant to refer to a hired party in a conventional employment relationship. These factors militate in favor of the reading we have found appropriate.

In 1955, when Congress decided to overhaul copyright law, the existing work for hire provision was § 62 of the 1909 Copyright Act, 17 U.S.C. § 26 (1976 ed.) (1909 Act). It provided that "the word 'author' shall include an employer in the case of works made for hire." Because the 1909 Act did not define "employer" or "works made for hire," the task of shaping these terms

---

[8] We also reject the suggestion of respondent and *amici* that the § 101(1) term "employee" refers only to formal, salaried employees. While there is some support for such a definition in the legislative history, see Varmer, Works Made for Hire 130; *infra* at n. 11, the language of § 101(1) cannot support it. The Act does not say "formal" or "salaried" employee, but simply "employee." Moreover, the respondent and those *amici* who endorse a formal, salaried employee test do not agree upon the content of this test. Compare, e.g., Brief for Respondent 37 (hired party who is on payroll is an employee within § 101(1)) with Tr. of Oral Arg. 31 (hired party who receives a salary or commissions regularly is an employee within § 101(1)); and Brief for Volunteer Lawyers for the Arts Inc. et al. as *Amici Curiae* 4 (hired party who receives a salary *and* is treated as an employee for Social Security and tax purposes is an employee within § 101(1)). Even the one Court of Appeals to adopt what it termed a formal, salaried employee test in fact embraced an approach incorporating numerous factors drawn from the agency law definition of employee which we endorse. *See Dumas*, 865 F.2d, at 1104.

fell to the courts. They concluded that the work for hire doctrine codified in § 62 referred only to works made by employees in the regular course of their employment. As for commissioned works, the courts generally presumed that the commissioned party had impliedly agreed to convey the copyright, along with the work itself, to the hiring party....

In 1961, the Copyright Office's first legislative proposal retained the distinction between works by employees and works by independent contractors. See Report of the Register of Copyrights on the General Revision of the U.S. Copyright Law, 87th Cong., 1st Sess., Copyright Law Revision 86-87 (H. Judiciary Comm. Print 1961). After numerous meetings with representatives of the affected parties, the Copyright Office issued a preliminary draft bill in 1963. Adopting the Register's recommendation, it defined "work made for hire" as "a work prepared by an employee within the scope of the duties of his employment, but not including a work made on special order or commission." Preliminary Draft for Revised U.S. Copyright Law and Discussions and Comments on the Draft, 88th Cong., 2d Sess., Copyright Law Revision, Part 3, p. 15, n. 11 (H. Judiciary Comm. Print 1964) (hereinafter Preliminary Draft).

In response to objections by book publishers that the preliminary draft bill limited the work for hire doctrine to "employees," the 1964 revision bill expanded the scope of the work for hire classification to reach, for the first time, commissioned works. The bill's language, proposed initially by representatives of the publishing industry, retained the definition of work for hire insofar as it referred to "employees," but added a separate clause covering commissioned works, without regard to the subject matter, "if the parties so agree in writing." S. 3008, H.R. 11947, H.R. 1254, 88th Cong., 2d Sess., § 54 (1964) reproduced in 1964 Revision Bill with Discussions and Comments, 89th Cong., 1st Sess., Copyright Law Revision, Part 5, p. 31 (H. Judiciary Comm. Print 1965). Those representing authors objected that the added provision would allow publishers to use their superior bargaining position to force authors to sign work for hire agreements, thereby relinquishing all copyright rights as a condition of getting their books published. See Supplementary Report, at 67.

In 1965, the competing interests reached an historic compromise which was embodied in a joint memorandum submitted to Congress and the Copyright Office, incorporated into the 1965 revision bill, and ultimately enacted in the same form and nearly the same terms 11 years later, as § 101 of the 1976 Act. The compromise retained as subsection (1) the language referring to "a work prepared by an employee within the scope of this employment." However, in exchange for concessions from publishers on provisions relating to the termination of transfer rights, the authors consented to a second subsection which classified four categories of commissioned works as works for hire if the parties expressly so agreed in writing: works for use "as a contribution to a collective work, as a part of a motion picture, as a translation, or as supplementary work." S. 1006, H.R. 4347, H.R. 5680, H.R. 6835, 89th Cong., 1st Sess., § 101 (1965). The interested parties selected these categories because they concluded that these commissioned works, although not prepared by employees and thus not covered by the first subsection, nevertheless should be treated as works for hire because they were ordinarily prepared "at the instance, direction, and risk of a publisher or producer." Supplementary Report, at 67. The Supplementary Report emphasized that only the "four special cases specifically mentioned" could qualify as works made for hire; "[o]ther works made on special order or commission would not come within the definition." *Id.*, at 67-68.

In 1966, the House Committee on the Judiciary endorsed this compromise in the first legislative report on the revision bills. *See* H.R. Rep. No. 2237, 89th Cong., 2d Sess., 114, 116 (1966). Retaining the distinction between works by employees and commissioned works, the House Committee focused instead on "how to draw a statutory line between those works written on special order or commission that should be considered as works made for hire, and those that should not." *Id.*, at 115. The House Committee added four other enumerated categories of commissioned works that could be treated as works for hire: compilations, instructional texts, tests, and atlases. *Id.*, at 116. With the single addition of "answer material for a test," the 1976 Act, as enacted, contained the same definition of works made for hire as did the 1966 revision bill, and had the same structure and nearly the same terms as the 1966 bill.[13] Indeed, much of the language of the 1976 House and Senate Reports was borrowed from the Reports accompanying the earlier drafts. *See, e.g.,* H.R. Rep. No. 94-1476, p. 121 (1976); S. Rep. No. 94-473, p. 105 (1975), U.S. Code Cong. & Admin. News 1976, p. 5659.

Thus, the legislative history of the Act is significant for several reasons. First, the enactment of the 1965 compromise with only minor modifications demonstrates that Congress intended to provide two mutually exclusive ways for works to acquire work for hire status: one for employees and the other for independent contractors. Second, the legislative history underscores the clear import of the statutory language: only enumerated categories of commissioned works may be accorded work for hire status. The hiring party's right to control the product simply is not determinative. *See* Note, *The Creative Commissioner: Commissioned Works Under the Copyright Act of 1976,* 62 N.Y.U. L. Rev. 373, 388 (1987). Indeed, importing a test based on a hiring party's right to control or actual control of a product would unravel the "'carefully worked out compromise aimed at balancing legitimate interests on both sides.'" H.R. Rep. No. 2237, *supra,* at 114, quoting Supplemental Report, at 66.

We do not find convincing petitioners' contrary interpretation of the history of the Act. They contend that Congress, in enacting the Act, meant to incorporate a line of cases decided under the 1909 Act holding that an employment

---

[13] An attempt to add "photographic or other portrait[s]," S. Rep. No. 94-473, p. 4 (1975), to the list of commissioned works eligible for work for hire status failed after the Register of Copyrights objected:

> The addition of portraits to the list of commissioned works that can be made into "works made for hire" by agreement of the parties is difficult to justify. Artists and photographers are among the most vulnerable and poorly protected of all the beneficiaries of the copyright law, and it seems clear that, like serious composers and choreographers, they were not intended to be treated as "employees" under the carefully negotiated definition in section 101.

Second Supplementary Report of the Register of Copyrights on the General Revision of the U.S. Copyright Law: 1975 Revision Bill, Chapter XI, pp. 12-13.

relationship exists sufficient to give the hiring party copyright ownership whenever that party has the right to control or supervise the artist's work. *See, e.g., Siegel v. National Periodical Publications, Inc.,* 508 F.2d 909, 914 (CA2 1974); *Picture Music, Inc. v. Bourne, Inc.,* 457 F.2d 1213, 1216 (CA2), *cert. denied,* 409 U.S. 997, 93 S. Ct. 320, 34 L. Ed. 2d 262 (1972); *Scherr v. Universal Match Corp.,* 417 F.2d 497, 500 (CA2 1969), *cert. denied,* 397 U.S. 936, 90 S. Ct. 945, 25 L. Ed. 2d 116 (1970); *Brattleboro Publishing Co. v. Winmill Publishing Corp.,* 369 F.2d 565, 567-568 (CA2 1966). In support of this position, petitioners note: "[n]owhere in the 1976 Act or in the Act's legislative history does Congress state that it intended to jettison the control standard or otherwise to reject the pre-Act judicial approach to identifying a work for hire employment relationship." Brief for Petitioners 20, citing *Aldon Accessories,* 738 F.2d, at 552.

We are unpersuaded. Ordinarily, "Congress' silence is just that — silence." *Alaska Airlines, Inc. v. Brock,* 480 U.S. 678, 686, 107 S. Ct. 1476, 1481, 94 L. Ed. 2d 661 (1987). Petitioners' reliance on legislative silence is particularly misplaced here because the text and structure of § 101 counsel otherwise. *See Bourjaily v. United States,* 483 U.S. 171, 178, 107 S. Ct. 2775, 2780, 97 L. Ed. 2d 144 (1987); *Harrison v. PPG Industries Inc.,* 446 U.S. 578, 592, 100 S. Ct. 1889, 1897, 64 L. Ed. 2d 525 (1980). Furthermore, the structure of the work for hire provisions was fully developed in 1965 and the text was agreed upon in essentially final form by 1966. At that time, however, the courts had applied the work for hire doctrine under the 1909 Act exclusively to traditional employees. Indeed, it was not until after the 1965 compromise was forged and adopted by Congress that a federal court for the first time applied the work for hire doctrine to commissioned works. *See, e.g., Brattleboro Publishing Co., supra,* at 567-568. Congress certainly could not have "jettisoned" a line of cases that had not yet been decided.

Finally, petitioners' construction of the work for hire provisions would impede Congress' paramount goal in revising the 1976 Act of enhancing predictability and certainty of copyright ownership. *See* H.R. Rep. No. 94-1476, *supra,* at 129. In a "copyright marketplace," the parties negotiate with an expectation that one of them will own the copyright in the completed work. *Dumas,* 865 F.2d, at 1104-1105, n. 18. With that expectation, the parties at the outset can settle on relevant contractual terms, such as the price for the work and the ownership of reproduction rights.

To the extent that petitioners endorse an actual control test, CCNV's construction of the work for hire provisions prevents such planning. Because that test turns on whether the hiring party has closely monitored the production process, the parties would not know until late in the process, if not until the work is completed, whether a work will ultimately fall within § 101(1). Under petitioners' approach, therefore, parties would have to predict in advance whether the hiring party will sufficiently control a given work to make it the author. "If they guess incorrectly, their reliance on 'work for hire' or an assignment may give them a copyright interest that they did not bargain for." *Easter Seal Society,* 815 F.2d, at 333; *accord Dumas,* 865 F.2d, at 1103. This understanding of the work for hire provisions clearly thwarts Congress' goal of ensuring predictability through advance planning. Moreover, petitioners' interpretation "leaves the door open for hiring parties, who have failed to get a full assignment of copyright rights from independent contractors falling outside the subdivision (2) guidelines, to unilaterally obtain work-made-for-hire rights years after the work has been completed as long as they directed or supervised the work, a standard that is hard not to meet when one is a hiring party." Hamilton, *Commissioned Works as Works Made for Hire Under the 1976 Copyright Act: Misinterpretation and Injustice,* 135 U. Pa. L. Rev. 1281, 1304 (1987).

In sum, we must reject petitioners' argument. Transforming a commissioned work into a work by an employee on the basis of the hiring party's right to control, or actual control of, the work is inconsistent with the language, structure, and legislative history of the work for hire provisions. To determine whether a work is for hire under the Act, a court first should ascertain, using principles of general common law of agency, whether the work was prepared by an employee or an independent contractor. After making this determination, the court can apply the appropriate subsection of § 101.

B

We turn, finally, to an application of § 101 to Reid's production of "Third World America." In determining whether a hired party is an employee under the general common law of agency, we consider the hiring party's right to control the manner and means by which the product is accomplished. Among the other factors relevant to this inquiry are the skill required; the source of the instrumentalities and tools; the location of the work; the duration of the relationship between the parties; whether the hiring party has the right to assign additional projects to the hired party; the extent of the hired party's discretion over when and how long to work; the method of payment; the hired party's role in hiring and paying assistants; whether the work is part of the regular business of the hiring party; whether the hiring party is in business; the provision of employee benefits; and the tax treatment of the hired party. *See* Restatement § 220(2) (setting forth a non-exhaustive list of factors relevant to determining whether a hired party is an employee). No one of these factors is determinative. *See Ward,* 362 U.S., at 400, 80 S. Ct., at 792; *Hilton Int'l Co. v. NLRB,* 690 F.2d 318, 321 (CA2 1982).

Examining the circumstances of this case in light of these factors, we agree with the Court of Appeals that Reid was not an employee of CCNV but an independent contractor. 270 U.S. App. D.C., at 35, n. 11, 846 F.2d, at 1494, n. 11. True, CCNV members directed enough of Reid's work to ensure that he produced a sculpture that met their specifications. 652 F. Supp., at 1456. But the extent of control the hiring party exercises over the details of the product is not dispositive. Indeed, all the other circumstances weigh heavily against finding an employment relationship. Reid is a sculptor, a skilled occupation. Reid supplied his own tools. He worked in his own studio in Baltimore, making daily supervision of his activities from Washington practicably impossible. Reid was retained for less than two months, a relatively short period of time. During and after this time, CCNV had no right to assign additional projects to Reid. Apart from the deadline for completing the sculpture, Reid had absolute freedom to decide when and how long to work. CCNV paid Reid $15,000, a sum dependent on "completion of a specific job, a method by which independent contractors are often compensated." *Holt v. Winpisinger,* 258 U.S. App. D.C. 343, 351, 811 F.2d 1532, 1540 (1987). Reid had total discretion in hiring and paying assistants. "Creating sculptures was hardly 'regular business' for CCNV." 270 U.S. App. D.C., at 35, n. 11, 846 F.2d, at 1494, n. 11. Indeed, CCNV is not a business at all. Finally, CCNV did not pay payroll or social security taxes, provide any employee benefits, or contribute to unemployment insurance or workers' compensation funds.

Because Reid was an independent contractor, whether "Third World America" is a work for hire depends on whether it satisfies the terms of § 101(2). This petitioners concede it cannot do. Thus CCNV is not the author of "Third World America" by virtue of the work for hire provisions of the Act. However, as the Court of Appeals made clear, CCNV nevertheless may be a joint author of the sculpture if, on remand, the District Court so determines that CCNV and Reid prepared the work "with the intention that their contributions be merged into inseparable or interdependent parts of a unitary whole." 17 U.S.C. § 101. In that case, CCNV and Reid would be co-owners of the copyright in the work. *See* § 201(a).

For the aforestated reasons, we affirm the judgment of the Court of Appeals for the District of Columbia.

It is so ordered.

Taking the case on remand on the issue of joint authorship, the district court persuaded both CCNV and Reid to submit that issue to mediation. The mediation resulted in a mutually satisfactory resolution which was reflected in a consent judgment entered on January 7, 1991. Under the terms of that agreement, CCNV is awarded sole ownership of the original sculpture (i.e., the physical chattel) while Reid is to be recognized as the sole "author" of the work. Reid is to have the exclusive right to make three-dimensional reproductions of the statue. Both CCNV and Reid are given the right to make two-dimensional reproductions of the statue: but Reid is to omit the base and inscription in the reproductions he makes, and CCNV is to give credit to Reid as sculptor in its reproductions. Each party is to be sole owner of any income derived from exercising its own reproduction rights.

The agreement was apparently silent about the issue of Reid's access to the original statue. That issue came to a head when Reid sought possession of that statue in order to make a master mold so that he could in fact make three-dimensional reproductions as contemplated by the mediated agreement, but CCNV refused. The district court ruled that "Reid is entitled to a limited possessory right of his own, in the nature of an implied easement of necessity, to cause a master mold to be made of the sculpture, whereupon it shall be returned promptly to CCNV." 1992 CCH Copyr. Dec. ¶ 26,860 (D.D.C. 1991).

QUESTIONS

1. Articulate the difference between the rejected "right to supervise and control" test of employment and the approved agency test of "right to control the manner and means by which the product is accomplished."

2. Dan's Department Store decided to place an advertisement in one of the local newspapers, The Brunswick Beacon. Because Dan's had no advertising layout to supply to The Beacon — other than Dan's slogan — original advertising copy was prepared by The Beacon's staff, which designed both text and graphic work. Shortly after the advertisement was paid for and run in The Beacon, several competing local newspapers ran the same ad; Dan's had authorized them to do so. The Beacon has brought an action against Dan's Department Store and the other newspapers. Decide the case. Deal, in particular, with the defendant's contention that it would be absurd to hold that The Beacon is copyright owner, because then advertisers like Dan's would be forbidden to make use of the advertisement — which is obviously useful only to them — in any other media. *Compare Brunswick Beacon, Inc. v. Schock-Hopchas Pub. Co.,* 810 F.2d 410 (4th Cir. 1987), *with Canfield v. The Ponchatoula Times,* 759 F.2d 493 (5th Cir. 1985).

3. Note that even if, in cases like *Brunswick* and *CCNV,* the relationship between a person doing work for another and the person requesting the work is that of independent contract (and not of conventional employment), the latter person is not at a loss for theories to justify copyright ownership. As noted in W. Patry, The Copyright Law 124-25 (1986):

> If, as in *Aldon,* the hiring party contributes significant artistic effort, that party is a joint author along with the independent contractor. Where the hiring party has contributed all of the expression and the independent contractor acts as a mere amenuensis, the hiring party should be considered the sole author. Where, however, the hiring party contributes only ideas or generalized expression incapable of copyright protection, copyright vests in the independent contractor regardless of "whether the alleged employer has the right to direct and supervise the manner in which the writer performs his work." Yet the hiring party under such circumstances may still obtain a transfer of all rights from the independent contractor as a condition to the creation of the work.

In light of these ways to protect the commissioning party, are you convinced of the need to place *any* commissioned works within the definition of works made for hire, as in § 101(2)? Do you see the justification behind each of the nine categories of works listed in that definition?

4. Various groups representing creative free-lance authors — particularly photographers and graphic artists — have supported proposed legislation that would drastically constrict the "work for hire" definitions presently in § 101. Among the proposed changes would be the requirement, in order to make out an "employment" relationship under § 101(1), that federal income taxes be withheld from the compensation of the putative employee; and a reduction of the categories of works in § 101(2) to only one, the motion picture. *See* S. 1223,

100th Cong., 1st Sess. (1987). Would you support such legislation? Does the following decision affect your determination?

MARCO v. ACCENT PUBLISHING CO.

969 F.2d 1547 (3d Cir. 1992)

MANSMANN, CIRCUIT JUDGE.

We focus here on the application of agency law in the context of the "work for hire" provision of the Copyright Act of 1976. 17 U.S.C. § 101(1). We find that the district court misapplied agency principles to the facts in holding that a freelance photographer was the employee of a publisher. Because the district court premised the denial of a preliminary injunction on this erroneous conclusion of law, we will vacate the district court's judgment and remand for further consideration.

....

II

Most of the salient facts are not in dispute. In 1990, the appellant, Ed Marco, photographed jewelry for Accent Magazine, a monthly trade journal for the costume jewelry industry. Accent Publishing Co., Inc. had engaged Marco on the basis of his portfolio, without a written contract and without negotiation concerning copyright or licensing. Accent supplied the jewelry and the props, sketched the shots, and retained the right to have Marco reshoot unsatisfactory photographs. Accent did not name Marco on the magazine's masthead.

Marco, who has ten years' experience and who earned a Bachelor of Fine Arts degree in photography at the Philadelphia College of Art, made images for about six consecutive issues of the magazine and then for one or two later issues. He thus worked during every month except one over the course of his business with Accent.

Marco shot the pictures in his own studio on his own time, subject to Accent's deadlines. For the most part, he worked on still-lifes, without anyone from Accent present. On a few occasions, however, Accent provided live models; Accent's Art Director, Kevin Myers, would pose the models.

The exact scope of Myers' control at the live sessions remains in dispute. Marco challenges as clearly erroneous the district court's finding that Myers "directed, supervised, and provided artistic contribution to the photographic work." Testimony supports this finding. Myers generally concerned himself with the way models and jewelry looked in the photographs. Myers also would instruct Marco, in very general terms, to use more light. Myers candidly admitted, however, that he did not become involved in the technical aspects of the photographs. For example, Myers described matters such as color balance and light meter readings to be beyond his ken and to be within the purview of a professional photographer.

Marco did not receive an hourly wage or periodic salary. The district court's finding, that "Marco was paid at the rate of approximately $150 per photograph used in advertisements, and $450 per month for all photographs used in connection with articles," must be read as shorthand for the facts that Marco received about $450 per issue, that issues appeared monthly, and that Marco invoiced about one job each month. Insofar as the finding implies that Marco received a salary of $450 per month, the finding is clearly erroneous.

Accent thus paid Marco by the job. Accent also reimbursed Marco's film and processing expenses. Accent did not withhold taxes or pay employee benefits.

Marco claims to have authored the photographs and therefore to own the copyrights to the images. He moved for a preliminary injunction to prevent their unlicensed republication. After a hearing, the district court considered Marco's likelihood of success on the merits, and, reasoning that the photographs were works for hire, determined that Marco could not prevail on the merits of a copyright claim. Given its determination that Marco had little chance of success on the merits, the district court found Marco's evidence of irreparable injury to be insufficient, and the district court denied the preliminary injunction.

III

The photographs in dispute would be classified as "made for hire" if they were "prepared by an employee within the scope of his or her employment ...." 17 U.S.C.A. § 101(1) (definition). The district court thus premised its judgment on the conclusion that Marco was Accent's employee, as determined by reference to principles of the general common law of agency. *Community for Creative Non-Violence v. Reid,* 490 U.S. 730, 750-51, 104 L. Ed. 2d 811, 109 S. Ct. 2166 (1989) ("*CCNV*"); *see also* Restatement (Second) of Agency § 220 (1957) (definition of master-servant relation) (cited in *CCNV*).

....

B

Application of the *CCNV* and the Restatement factors demonstrates that the district court erred in concluding that Marco was Accent's employee. Under the common law of agency, Marco was an independent contractor.

In its application of agency law to the facts, the district court recognized only two factors that indicated independent contractor status: Marco used his own equipment and paid his own taxes. The district court did not discuss four more factors that indicate independent contractor status: Marco supplied his own studio, did not receive employee benefits, works in a distinct occupation, and was paid by the job. We need not further develop these six factors, which all indicate that Marco was an independent contractor.

In addition, the district court did not properly recognize that Marco had discretion over his work hours; he could work on any day, at any hour, and for any stretch of time he chose. The district court did consider Accent's imposition of deadlines in this context, but deadlines do not alter an independent contractor's discretion over work hours. We note that in *CCNV*, the charity had imposed a strict deadline for completion, yet the Court did not weigh that deadline against a determination of independent contractor status.

Nor did the district court recognize that Accent's absence of a right to assign more work indicates Marco's independent contractor status. Although the district court considered Accent's right to require Marco to reshoot unsatisfactory images, this right was merely a right to final approval, which differs from the right to assign more work. The record does not suggest that Accent could assign any more than one issue's worth of photographs to Marco during any particular period. Accent could not, for example, require Marco to photograph its employee of the month.

Another factor, the skill required of a magazine photographer, indicates Marco's independent contractor status, although the district court held otherwise. The district court wrote: "Marco was not a skilled worker. The position of staff photographer did not have an educational requirement or [require] more than a minimal knowledge of photography." *Marco,* No. 91-2057 at 15. In this age of Polaroids and Handicams, the photography profession might not demand the expertise once required to create an image. Nonetheless, something beyond owning a camera is necessary to make photographs suitable for a trade journal. Accent, after all, did not hire Marco off the street; Accent hired him after seeing his portfolio. Accent's own Art Director testified that "[Marco is] the person that makes the shot work technically.... That's why I hire a photographer, I'm not a professional photographer, I'm an art director."

Photographers, moreover, fall along a spectrum in their skills. Near one end fall the likes of Ansel Adams, recording the American landscape with an 8 × 10 view camera. Near the other falls an untrained clerk, snapping mug shots with an instamatic. Marco, with a degree in photography and ten years' experience, falls somewhere in between. As a factual matter, Marco may not be skilled in the sense that Ansel Adams was skilled. From a legal perspective, however, Marco is certainly skilled in the sense that Reid, the sculptor in the *CCNV* case, was skilled.

As regards another factor, the length of the relationship, Marco produced photographs for Accent for six months, but without a regular schedule or regular hours. Although the district court considered that the continuing nature of the relationship indicated employee status, the duration of a relationship indicates an employment relationship when the work is scheduled and periodic, or full-time. *See* Restatement § 220 cmt. h (factors indicating employment relationship include "employment over a considerable period of time with *regular hours*" (emphasis added)); *compare CCNV,* 490 U.S. at 734 (Reid worked on charity's sculpture exclusively). Thus, the duration of this relationship provides only weak evidence, if any, of an employment relationship.

Indeed, of all the factors that the district court considered, only three would weigh in favor of a determination that an employment relationship existed. First, Accent is in business, which increases the possibility that it would employ people. Second, Accent regularly publishes photographs of its own conception. As between Accent and a charity that does not regularly produce sculptures, it is more plausible that Accent would engage an artist as an employee, but Accent might easily accomplish its regular business by using independent contractors rather than employees.

Third, Accent exercised control over the details of the work. Specifically, Accent supplied jewelry, props, models, sketches intended to describe the exact composition of the photographs, and, at some sessions, an Art Director. This factor is not dispositive. *CCNV*, 490 U.S. at 752. Indeed, courts should keep this factor in perspective, since it resembles the "control of the product" test rejected by the Supreme Court in *CCNV*. *See* 490 U.S. at 737-51.

Moreover, Accent controlled only the subject matter and composition of the images. Accent did not control most aspects of the work, which include the choice of light sources, filters, lenses, camera, film, perspective, aperture setting, shutter speed, and processing techniques. It should be recalled that Art Director Myers attended only the live sessions and that his direction there was limited to composing the subjects and to commenting on the "feel" of the work. In his own words, "I am directing [Marco] on the composition of a photograph, I am directing him on the mood of the lighting, the emotion within a given scenario." This testimony illuminates the district court's finding that Myers "supervised" some of the sessions; even that supervision was limited to subject matter, composition, and "mood."

Accent's control of the product was thus no greater than the control exercised by the charity in *CCNV*, who articulated the subject and composition, who supplied models, who occasionally supervised the work, who constructed part of the sculpture, and who was still not an employer. Although the district court was correct to consider this factor, it appears to have given it disproportionate consideration. The only significant difference between this case and *CCNV* is that here the hiring party is in the business of regularly publishing photographs in connection with advertisements and articles. That distinction does not give rise to an employment relationship.

We note that the remaining three factors are indeterminate in this case. First, the record before the district court was barren of evidence of custom, so we will not address that factor. Second, the district court did not make any findings as to the parties' beliefs regarding the assumption of control by Accent and submission to control by Marco. *See* Restatement § 220 cmt. m (only parties' beliefs about assumption of control are dispositive). It appears, however, that the parties here did not hold a common belief. Third, there were no photography assistants, only models and stylists. Accent paid the models; Marco, the stylists. Even if Accent had paid both, Accent did no more than supply the models as subjects for the photographs. Supplying a subject represents some facet of control of the product, a factor already counted in favor of a determination that an employment relationship existed. Mischaracterizing a human subject as an "assistant," however, resulted in an improper double-counting of factors by the district court.

In summary, a magazine publisher's regular practice of commissioning photographs of its own conception does not create an employment relationship with an experienced photographer who uses his own equipment; who works at his own studio, on days and times of his choosing, without photography assistants hired by the publisher; and who receives payment without income tax withheld, without employee benefits, for discrete assignments rather than for hourly or periodic work.

Aymes v. Bonelli, 980 F.2d 857 (2d Cir. 1992):

"We begin our analysis by noting that the *Reid* test can be easily misapplied, since it consists merely of a list of possible considerations that may or may not be relevant in a given case. *Reid* established that no one factor was dispositive, but gave no direction concerning how the factors were to be weighed. It does not necessarily follow that because no one factor is dispositive all factors are equally important, or indeed that all factors will have relevance in every case. The factors should not merely be tallied but should be weighed according to their significance in the case....

"Some factors will often have little or no significance in determining whether a party is an independent contractor or an employee. In contrast, there are some factors that will be significant in virtually every situation. These include: (1) the hiring party's right to control the manner and means of creation; (2) the skill required; (3) the provision of employee benefits; (4) the tax treatment of the hired party; and (5) whether the hiring party has the right to assign additional projects to the hired party. These factors will almost always be relevant and should be given more weight in the analysis, because they will usually be highly probative of the true nature of the employment relationship."

"Although the *Reid* test has not yet received widespread application, other courts that have interpreted the test have in effect adopted this weighted approach by only addressing those factors found to be significant in the individual case. *See, e.g., Marco v. Accent Publishing Co.,* 969 F.2d 1547 (3d Cir. 1992) (holding that photographer was an independent contractor while ignoring some factors and noting that some were "indeterminate" and should not be considered); *MacLean Assocs., Inc. v. Wm. M. Mercer-Meidinger-Hansen, Inc.,* 952 F.2d 769 (3d Cir. 1991) (in appeal from a directed verdict for hiring party, holding that a computer programmer could be an independent contractor without addressing several of the *Reid* factors); *M.G.B. Homes, Inc. v. Ameron Homes, Inc.,* 903 F.2d 1486 (11th Cir. 1990) (finding that a drafting service operated as an independent contractor to a builder based on only eight factors, ignoring others); *Johannsen v. Brown,* 797 F. Supp. 835 (D. Or. 1992) (finding that artist/printer is a graphic designer based on several factors, ignoring others); *Kunycia v. Melville Realty Co.,* 755 F. Supp. 566 (S.D.N.Y. 1990) (finding an architect to be an independent contractor on the basis of only four factors, ignoring others); *Kelstall-Whitney v. Mahar,* No. 89 Civ. 4684, 1990 U.S. Dist. LEXIS 6186 (E.D. Pa. May 23, 1990) (finding that computer programmer was independent contractor based on only a few factors, ignoring others)...."

"The importance of the [employee benefits and tax treatment] factors is underscored by the fact that every case since *Reid* that has applied the test has found the hired party to be an independent contractor where the hiring party failed to extend benefits or pay social security taxes...."

QUESTION

If the Second Circuit is correct that the most important *Reid* factors are provision of employee benefits and tax treatment, is there any difference between a Restatement of Agency "employee" and a "formal, salaried" employee?

IF A WORK IS "SPECIALLY ORDERED OR COMMISSIONED" WITHIN § 101(2), AT WHAT POINT IN THE PARTIES' RELATIONSHIP MUST A CONTRACT MAKING IT A "WORK FOR HIRE" BE EXECUTED?

In providing for certain kinds of contractually created commissioned works for hire, § 101(2) mandates that "the parties expressly agree in a written instrument signed by them" that the specially ordered or commissioned work shall be a work for hire. But § 101(2) does not say *when* the parties must so agree. At the outset of the commission? In the course of the work's creation? When the work is delivered to the commissioning party? When the commissioning party pays the creator? One might anticipate that a hiring party could compensate for a failure to negotiate the authorship status of the work at the outset of the commission, were it to make subsequent receipt of payment conditional upon signing a work for hire agreement. One might also imagine that such a scheme, capitalizing on the absence of a specific provision, takes advantage of the letter (or its lack), but clashes with the spirit of the work for hire provision, particularly as interpreted by the Supreme Court in *CCNV*.

A recent decision by Judge Posner reaches a similar conclusion. In *Schiller & Schmidt, Inc. v. Nordisco Corp.*, 969 F.2d 410 (7th Cir. 1992), the publisher of a catalogue claimed to be the employer for hire of a photographer whose work appeared in the catalogue. Judge Posner wrote:

> Bertel [the photographer] made the 18 photos, but Schiller [the catalogue publisher] owned the copyrights in them if they were "works for hire," or if Bertel assigned the copyrights to Schiller. 17 U.S.C. §§ 101(1), (2), 201(b), (d). Since no one could suppose after *Community for Creative Non-Violence v. Reid* that Bertel was an employee of Schiller, they were works for hire only if they fell in one or more of the categories of intellectual property enumerated in section 101(2), as they did, and were specially commissioned by Schiller, as they were, and the parties had signed a statement to that effect — which they had not. What is true is that in 1988, long after this suit had begun, Bertel obligingly signed a statement in which he "agreed that Schiller and Schmidt has owned the copyright [in the photos], and I hereby assign any remaining copyright which I may own in any photographs which I took for Schiller and Schmidt, and any right to maintain actions, now or hereafter existing, for alleged infringement thereof" to Schiller. The statement was not signed by Schiller, however, as the statute required if the photos were to be works for hire. The statutory language is "signed by them," that is, by both parties, and it means what it says.
>
> The statement also came too late. The requirement of a written statement regarding the copyright on a specially commissioned work is not merely a statute of frauds, although that is the purpose emphasized by the cases [citations omitted]. That is, it is not only designed to protect people against false claims of oral agreements. If it were, then it might

not matter when the statement had been made or signed, although there is authority that it must be signed before suit is brought. *Watson v. McCabe*, 527 F.2d 286, 289 (6th Cir. 1975); E. Allan Farnsworth, Contracts § 6.7, at p. 428 and n. 19 (2d ed. 1990). This is an esoteric question, since ordinarily the absence of the requisite statement will lead to the dismissal of the suit before it can be tendered. We need not try to resolve the question here. For the signed-statement requirement in section 101(2) has a second purpose — to make the ownership of property rights in intellectual property clear and definite, so that such property will be readily marketable. The creator of the property is the owner, unless he is an employee creating the property within the scope of his employment or the parties have agreed in a writing signed by both that the person who commissioned the creation of the property is the owner. The writing must precede the creation of the property in order to serve its purpose of identifying the (noncreator) owner unequivocally. It did not precede it here.

WORK FOR HIRE UNDER THE 1976 ACT AND THE "TEACHER EXCEPTION"

Two decisions from the Seventh Circuit, *Weinstein v. University of Illinois*, 811 F.2d 1091 (7th Cir. 1987), and *Hays v. Sony Corp. of Am.*, 847 F.2d 412 (7th Cir. 1988), authored by two former law professors, Judges Easterbrook and Posner, considered whether, under the 1976 Act, academic writings were works made for hire whose copyrights belonged to the schools and universities employing the teacher or professor writers.

Addressing a written university policy which purported to claim copyright ownership of works created pursuant to a university "requirement or duty," Judge Easterbrook concluded that the academic writing at issue was not produced under the kind of compulsion implicit in a work for hire employment relationship.

> A University "requires" all of its scholars to write. Its demands — especially the demands of departments deciding whether to award tenure — will be "the motivating factor in the preparation of" many a scholarly work. When [plaintiff's dean] told [plaintiff] to publish or perish he was not simultaneously claiming for the University a copyright on the ground that the work had become a "requirement or duty" within the meaning of [the university policy]. The University concedes in this court that a professor of mathematics who proves a new theorem in the course of his employment will own the copyright to his article containing that proof. This has been the academic tradition since copyright law began.

The tradition Judge Easterbrook cited is indeed venerable — proponents of the doctrine that professors own the copyright in their works include great figures in the common law. According to Lord Eldon, Sir William Blackstone owned the copyright in his lectures on law; this precedent warranted Eldon's recognition of the litigant's claim to ownership of his lectures on medicine. *See Abernethy v. Hutchinson*, 3 L.J. 209, 214-15 (Ch.) (1825). A slim, but apparently unanimous, common-law copyright caselaw in the United States follows the English tradition. *See, e.g., C.O. Sherrill v. L.C. Grieves,* 57 Wash. L. Rep. 286, 20 C.O. Bull. 675 (1929) ("the court does not know of any authority holding that a professor is obliged to reduce his lectures to writing or if he does so they become the property of the institution employing him"); *Williams v. Weisser,* 78 Cal. Rptr. 542 (Cal. App. 1969) (lectures delivered in class are the professor's common-law copyright property). *Compare Manasa v. University of Miami,* 320 So. 2d 467 (Fla. App. 1975) (university owns copyright in funding proposal written by administrative officer).

For Judge Posner in the *Hays* case, this tradition deserved deference, despite possibly contradictory statutory language in the 1976 Act:

> Until 1976, the statutory term "work made for hire" was not defined, and some courts had adopted a "teacher exception" whereby academic writing was presumed not to be work made for hire. *See* Dreyfuss, *The Creative Employee and the Copyright Act of 1976,* 54 U. Chi. L. Rev. 590, 597-98 (1987). The authority for this conclusion was in fact scanty, as explained in Simon, *Faculty Writings: Are They "Works for Hire" Under the 1976 Copyright Act?,* 9 J. College & University L. 485, 495-99 (1982) — but it was scanty not because the merit of the exception was doubted, but because, on the contrary, virtually no one questioned that the academic author was entitled to copyright his writings. Although college and university teachers do academic writing as a part of their employment responsibilities and use their employer's paper, copier, secretarial staff, and (often) computer facilities in that writing, the universal assumption and practice was that (in the absence of an explicit agreement as to who had the right to copyright) the right to copyright such writing belonged to the teacher rather than to the college or university. There were good reasons for the assumption. A college or university does not supervise its faculty in the preparation of academic books and articles, and is poorly equipped to exploit their writings, whether through publication or otherwise; we may set to one side cases where a school directs a teacher to prepare teaching materials and then directs its other teachers to use the materials too.
>
> The reasons for a presumption against finding academic writings to be work made for hire are as forceful today as they ever were. Nevertheless it is widely believed that the 1976 Act abolished the teacher exception, *see* Dreyfuss, *supra,* at 598-600; Simon, *supra,* at 502-09; *Weinstein v. University of Illinois,* 811 F.2d 1091, 1093-94 (7th Cir. 1987) — though, if so, probably inadvertently, for there is no discussion of the issue in the legislative history, and no political or other reasons come to mind as to why Congress might have wanted to abolish the exception. To a literalist of statutory interpretation, the conclusion that the Act abolished the exception may seem inescapable. The argument would be that academic writing, being within the scope of academic employment, is work made for hire, per se; so, in the absence of an express written and signed waiver of the academic employer's rights, the copyright in such writing must belong to the employer. But considering the havoc that such a conclusion would wreak in the settled practices of academic institutions, the lack of

fit between the policy of the work-for-hire doctrine and the conditions of academic production, and the absence of any indication that Congress meant to abolish the teacher exception, we might, if forced to decide the issue, conclude that the exception had survived the enactment of the 1976 Act....

Judge Posner's decision also indicated a further reason academic writings may not be works for hire: while they may have been "prepared by an employee within the scope of his employment," § 101, they may not have been prepared *"for"* the educational institution. *See* § 201(b). That is, while professors are expected to produce scholarly works, it does not follow that these works have been created at the school's or university's behest for its own use. The proposition that academics do not write *"for"* their institutions rests on two premises: academic freedom, and a sense of personal independence recalling the medieval model of the professor as autonomous, even itinerant, scholar; *see, e.g.,* Abelard, *History of My Troubles* (describing Peter Abelard's glorious, but brief, association with the University of Paris); *NLRB v. Yeshiva Univ.,* 444 U.S. 672, 680 (1980) ("guilds of scholars were responsible only to themselves").

QUESTIONS

1. Is the "teacher exception" limited to teachers? What of scholars employed at think tanks, such as the Brookings Institution, or research corporations, such as Bell Labs? What about leaders of religious congregations who regularly deliver sermons? If these persons exercise unfettered discretion in research and writing, do they benefit from the exception as well? Should they? Is there a good rationale for a specific "teacher" exception, apart from tradition (and, perhaps, self-interest on the part of former academics now on the bench)?

2. Judge Posner suggested that one basis of the teacher exception was that the academic institution "is poorly equipped to exploit [professorial] writings." Is this persuasive? Should certain academic writings be deemed works for hire if certain universities develop the capacity to exploit faculty writings? Isn't it true that if universities have been "poorly equipped," that it is because academic copyrights have traditionally yielded an economic return insufficiently large to make university exploitation worthwhile? Put another way, does the teacher exception exist simply because it doesn't cost universities very much? Might analysis of the exception change if the kinds of works at issue, for example, computer software, could be exploited to produce substantial rewards?

3. If the university is indeed deemed to be the author and copyright owner of works prepared by its faculty, what would you advise a faculty member — who has prepared her lecture notes while an assistant professor at University A — about freely using and updating them for her lecture notes at University B, where she has just begun to teach as an associate professor?

4. Assuming the "work for hire" definition does apply, at least *prima facie,* does the existence of a printed university faculty handbook recognizing professorial ownership of copyright in noncompulsory writings suffice to establish such ownership?

OWNERSHIP DEFINITIONS AND RETROACTIVITY

An interesting and important question posed in a number of cases dealing with works for hire is whether, when a current litigation involves a work created pursuant to a particular relationship formed, or transaction undertaken, prior to 1978, the governing definitions regarding ownership are to be those under the 1909 Act or those provided under the 1976 Act. This issue of retroactive application of the 1976 Act will of course be presented in any number of future litigations, for allegedly infringing conduct can take place many years after a work is created and ownership interests allocated. The issue is important not only in connection with works made for hire — which were given broader scope under the 1909 Act than under the present law — but also in connection with "joint works," which was also defined more broadly under the 1909 Act. (A related question is whether, when a canvas, sculpture or other physical embodiment of a work was transferred outright prior to 1978, this should be treated as having conveyed the copyright as well; the usual answer under the 1909 Act was that it did, but that conclusion has been otherwise since implementation of § 202 of the 1976 Act.)

In *Meltzer v. Zoller,* 520 F. Supp. 847 (D.N.J. 1981), an architect prepared designs for a house, at the behest of the prospective homeowner and his builder, in 1977; the alleged infringement, the architect's use of essentially the same plans to build a house for a neighbor, took place in 1978, and the lawsuit was brought in 1981. The court examined § 301(a) (which the student should also study at this point), and concluded that because the alleged cause of action for the infringement of the architectural plans arose after January 1, 1978, the new act was necessarily to apply, including its definition of works made for hire. (The court adverted to possible "due process concerns" that would result from the retroactive application of the new law; but it concluded that such concerns were valid only if the cause of action had accrued prior to 1978, which was not the situation before it.)

In *Roth v. Pritikin,* 710 F.2d 934 (2d Cir.), *cert. denied,* 464 U.S. 961 (1983), recipes for the defendants' diet book were prepared by the plaintiff pursuant to a contract made in 1977; the extremely successful book was published in 1979, and the plaintiff claimed that the more restrictive "work for hire" definitions of the new Copyright Act should be applied so that she, rather than the commissioning diet-book writers, would be regarded as the "author" of the recipes. The court of appeals firmly rejected the contention that the "work for hire" definitions of the Act that became effective on January 1, 1978 should be applied to the 1977 arrangement between Ms. Roth and the book's authors for whom she prepared the recipes. The court construed § 301(a) to mean that the exclusive rights now set forth in the statute may be asserted by the present copyright owner for acts of infringement taking place after January 1, 1978, even regarding works created before 1978; but that the section did not purport to have the new statutory provisions determine *who* the copyright owner in fact was by virtue of pre-1978 transactions. The court stated that retroactive application of the new "work for hire" definitions — which would have the effect, for example, of divesting in 1978 the "authorship" status (and related copyright ownership rights) held by the book authors since mid-1977 regarding the Roth recipes — would raise the most serious constitutional problems as possible takings of property without compensation and without due process of law. For that reason alone, the court felt obliged to construe the statute so that the "work for hire" definitions apply only to transactions effected after January 1, 1978.

The position of the court in *Roth* has been recently adopted by the Court of Appeals for the First Circuit in *Forward v. Thorogood*, 985 F.2d 604 (1st Cir. 1993), in which the plaintiff claimed that he was entitled to copyright in a recording made by the defendant band members; the plaintiff in 1976 had suggested that the band make a "demo tape" and he had arranged and paid for two recording sessions. As a result of a dispute in 1988 over his right to sell the 1976 tapes for commercial release, the plaintiff sought a declaratory judgment that, among other things, the recording was a work made for hire and that he was thus the author and copyright owner. The court observed that the scope of commissioned works that could have been "works made for hire" in 1976 was greater than under the act that became effective in 1978 (and which requires a signed writing and limited subject-matter categories). The court held that the present act determines the rights of the copyright owner, who is the person who held the copyright on the date the act became effective, a matter that was of course determined by the law in effect at the time of the transaction — but that even under that broader definition of "work made for hire" the plaintiff fell short.

Is the *Meltzer* or the *Roth-Forward* reading of § 301(a), and application of the principles of retroactivity, more convincing?

3. AUTHORSHIP AS AN INTELLECTUAL CONCEPT: JOINT WORKS

§ 101. Definitions

A joint work is a work prepared by two or more authors with the intention that their contributions be merged into inseparable or interdependent parts of a unitary whole.

CHILDRESS v. TAYLOR

945 F.2d 500 (2d Cir. 1991):

NEWMAN, CIRCUIT JUDGE.

This appeal requires consideration of the standards for determining when a contributor to a copyrighted work is entitled to be regarded as a joint author. The work in question is a play about the legendary Black comedienne Jackie "Moms" Mabley. The plaintiff-appellee Alice Childress claims to be the sole author of the play. Her claim is disputed by defendant-appellant Clarice Taylor, who asserts that she is a joint author of the play. Taylor appeals from the judgment, on motion for summary judgment, that Childress is the sole author. We affirm.

Facts

Defendant Clarice Taylor has been an actress for over forty years, performing on stage, radio, television, and in film. After portraying "Moms" Mabley in a skit in an off-off-Broadway production ten years ago, Taylor became interested in developing a play based on Mabley's life. Taylor began to assemble material about "Moms" Mabley, interviewing her friends and family, collecting her jokes, and reviewing library resources.

In 1986, Taylor contacted the plaintiff, playwright Alice Childress, about writing a play based on "Moms" Mabley. Childress had written many plays, for one of which she won an "Obie" award. Taylor had known Childress since the 1940s when they were both associated with the American Negro Theatre in Harlem and had previously acted in a number of Childress's plays.

Taylor turned over all of her research material to Childress, and later did further research at Childress's request. It is undisputed that Childress wrote the play, entitled "Moms: A Praise Play for a Black Comedienne." However, Taylor, in addition to providing the research material, which according to her involved a process of sifting through facts and selecting pivotal and key elements to include in a play on "Moms" Mabley's life, also discussed with Childress the inclusion of certain general scenes and characters in the play. Additionally, Childress and Taylor spoke on a regular basis about the progress of the play.

Taylor identifies the following as her major contributions to the play: (1) she learned through interviews that "Moms" Mabley called all of her piano players "Luther," so Taylor suggested that the play include such a character; (2) Taylor and Childress together interviewed Carey Jordan, "Moms" Mabley's housekeeper, and upon leaving the interview they came to the conclusion that she would be a good character for the play, but Taylor could not recall whether she or Childress suggested it; (3) Taylor informed Childress that "Moms" Mabley made a weekly trip to Harlem to do ethnic food shopping; (4) Taylor suggested a street scene in Harlem with speakers because she recalled having seen or listened to such a scene many times; (5) the idea of using a minstrel scene came out of Taylor's research; (6) the idea of a card game scene also came out of Taylor's research, although Taylor could not recall who specifically suggested the scene; (7) some of the jokes used in the play came from Taylor's research; and (8) the characteristics of "Moms" Mabley's personality portrayed in the play emerged from Taylor's research. Essentially, Taylor contributed facts and details about "Moms" Mabley's life and discussed some of them with Childress. However, Childress was responsible for the actual structure of the play and the dialogue.

Childress completed the script. Childress filed for and received a copyright for the play in her name. Taylor produced the play at the Green Plays Theatre in Lexington, New York, during the 1986 summer season and played the title role. After the play's run at the Green Plays Theatre, Taylor planned a second production of the play at the Hudson Guild Theatre in New York City.

At the time Childress agreed to the project, she did not have any firm arrangements with Taylor, although Taylor had paid her $2,500 before the play was produced. On May 9, 1986, Taylor's agent, Scott Yoselow, wrote to Childress's agent, Flora Roberts, stating:

> Per our telephone conversation, this letter will bring us up-to-date on the current status of our negotiation for the above mentioned project:
>
> 1. CLARICE TAYLOR will pay ALICE CHILDRESS for her playwriting services on the MOMS MABLEY PROJECT the sum of $5,000.00, which will also serve as an advance against any future royalties.
> 2. The finished play shall be equally owned and be the property of both CLARICE TAYLOR and ALICE CHILDRESS.
>
> It is my understanding that Alice has commenced writing the project. I am awaiting a response from you regarding any additional points we have yet to discuss.

Flora Roberts responded to Yoselow in a letter dated June 16, 1986:

> As per our recent telephone conversation, I have told Alice Childress that we are using your letter to me of May 9, 1986 as a partial memo preparatory to our future good faith negotiations for a contract. There are two points which I include herewith to complete your two points in the May 9th letter, i.e.:
>
> 1) The $5,000 advance against any future royalties being paid by Clarice Taylor to Alice Childress shall be paid as follows. Since $1,000 has already been paid, $1,500 upon your receipt of this letter and the final $2,500 to be paid upon submission of the First Draft, but in no event later than July 7, 1986.
> 2) It is to be understood that pending the proper warranty clauses to be included in the contract, Miss Childress is claiming originality for her words only in said script.

After the Green Plays Theatre production, Taylor and Childress attempted to formalize their relationship. Draft contracts were exchanged between Taylor's attorney, Jay Kramer, and Childress's agent, Roberts. During this period, early 1987, the play was produced at the Hudson Guild Theatre with the consent of both Taylor and Childress. Childress filed for and received a copyright for the new material added to the play produced at the Hudson Guild Theatre.

In March 1987, Childress rejected the draft agreement proposed by Taylor, and the parties' relationship deteriorated. Taylor decided to mount another production of the play without Childress. Taylor hired Ben Caldwell to write another play featuring "Moms" Mabley; Taylor gave Caldwell a copy of the Childress script and advised him of elements that should be changed.

The "Moms" Mabley play that Caldwell wrote was produced at the Astor Place Theatre in August 1987. No reference to Childress was made with respect to this production. However, a casting notice in the trade paper "Back

Stage" reported the production of Caldwell's play and noted that it had been "presented earlier this season under an Equity LOA at the Hudson Guild Theatre."

Childress sued Taylor and other defendants alleging violations of the Copyright Act. Taylor contended that she was a joint author with Childress, and therefore shared the rights to the play. Childress moved for summary judgment, which the District Court granted. The Court concluded that Taylor was not a joint author of Childress's play and that Caldwell's play was substantially similar to and infringed Childress's play. In rejecting Taylor's claim of joint authorship, Judge Haight ruled (a) that a work qualifies as a "joint work" under the definition section of the Copyright Act only when both authors intended, at the time the work was created, "that their contributions be merged into inseparable or interdependent parts of a unitary whole," and (b) that there was insufficient evidence to permit a reasonable trier to find that Childress had the requisite intent. The Court further ruled that copyright law requires the contributions of both authors to be independently copyrightable, and that Taylor's contributions, which consisted of ideas and research, were not copyrightable.

Discussion

In common with many issues arising in the domain of copyrights, the determination of whether to recognize joint authorship in a particular case requires a sensitive accommodation of competing demands advanced by at least two persons, both of whom have normally contributed in some way to the creation of a work of value. Care must be taken to ensure that true collaborators in the creative process are accorded the perquisites of co-authorship and to guard against the risk that a sole author is denied exclusive authorship status simply because another person rendered some form of assistance. Copyright law best serves the interests of creativity when it carefully draws the bounds of "joint authorship" so as to protect the legitimate claims of both sole authors and co-authors....

Some aspects of the statutory definition of joint authorship are fairly straightforward. Parts of a unitary whole are "inseparable" when they have little or no independent meaning standing alone. That would often be true of a work of written text, such as the play that is the subject of the pending litigation. By contrast, parts of a unitary whole are "interdependent" when they have some meaning standing alone but achieve their primary significance because of their combined effect, as in the case of the words and music of a song. Indeed, a novel and a song are among the examples offered by the legislative committee reports on the 1976 Copyright Act to illustrate the difference between "inseparable" and "interdependent" parts. *See* H.R. Rep. No. 1476, 94th Cong., 2d Sess. 120 (1976) (*"House Report"*).

The legislative history also clarifies other aspects of the statutory definition, but leaves some matters in doubt. Endeavoring to flesh out the definition, the committee reports state:

> [A] work is "joint" if the authors collaborated with each other, or if *each* of the authors prepared his or her contribution with the knowledge and

intention that it would be merged with the contributions of other authors as "inseparable or interdependent parts of a unitary whole." The touchstone here is the *intention, at the time the writing is done*, that the parts be absorbed or combined into an integrated unit ....

House Report at 120 (emphasis added). This passage appears to state two alternative criteria — one focusing on the act of collaboration and the other on the parties' intent. However, it is hard to imagine activity that would constitute meaningful "collaboration" unaccompanied by the requisite intent on the part of both participants that their contributions be merged into a unitary whole, and the case law has read the statutory language literally so that the intent requirement applies to all works of joint authorship. *See, e.g., Weissmann v. Freeman*, 868 F.2d 1313, 1317-19 (2d Cir. 1989); *Eckert v. Hurley Chicago Co., Inc.*, 638 F. Supp. 699, 702-03 (N.D. Ill. 1986).

A more substantial issue arising under the statutory definition of "joint work" is whether the contribution of each joint author must be copyrightable or only the combined result of their joint efforts must be copyrightable. The Nimmer treatise argues against a requirement of copyrightability of each author's contribution, see 1 Nimmer on Copyright § 6.07; Professor Goldstein takes the contrary view, see 1 Paul Goldstein, Copyright: Principles, Law and Practice § 4.2.1.2 (1989), with the apparent agreement of the Latman treatise, see William F. Patry, Latman's The Copyright Law 116 (6th ed. 1986) (hereinafter "Latman"). The case law supports a requirement of copyrightability of each contribution. The Register of Copyrights strongly supports this view, arguing that it is required by the statutory standard of "authorship" and perhaps by the Constitution. *See* Moral Rights in Our Copyright Laws: Hearings on S. 1198 and S. 1253 Before the Subcomm. on Patents, Copyrights and Trademarks of the Senate Comm. on the Judiciary, 101st Cong., 1st Sess. 210-11 (1989) (statement of Ralph Oman).

The issue, apparently open in this Circuit, is troublesome. If the focus is solely on the objective of copyright law to encourage the production of creative works, it is difficult to see why the contributions of all joint authors need be copyrightable. An individual creates a copyrightable work by combining a non-copyrightable idea with a copyrightable form of expression; the resulting work is no less a valuable result of the creative process simply because the idea and the expression came from two different individuals. Indeed, it is not unimaginable that there exists a skilled writer who might never have produced a significant work until some other person supplied the idea. The textual argument from the statute is not convincing. The Act surely does not say that each contribution to a joint work must be copyrightable, and the specification that there be "authors" does not necessarily require a copyrightable contribution. "Author" is not defined in the Act and appears to be used only in its ordinary sense of an originator. The "author" of an uncopyrightable idea is nonetheless its author even though, for entirely valid reasons, the law properly denies him a copyright on the result of his creativity. And the Register's tentative constitutional argument seems questionable. It has not been supposed that the statutory grant of "authorship" status to the employer of a work made for hire exceeds the Constitution, though the employer has shown skill only in selecting employees, not in creating protectable expression.

Nevertheless, we are persuaded to side with the position taken by the case law and endorsed by the agency administering the Copyright Act. The insistence on copyrightable contributions by all putative joint authors might serve to prevent some spurious claims by those who might otherwise try to share the fruits of the efforts of a sole author of a copyrightable work, even though a claim of having contributed copyrightable material could be asserted by those so inclined. More important, the prevailing view strikes an appropriate balance in the domains of both copyright and contract law. In the absence of contract, the copyright remains with the one or more persons who created copyrightable material. Contract law enables a person to hire another to create a copyrightable work, and the copyright law will recognize the employer as "author." 17 U.S.C. § 201(b). Similarly, the person with non-copyrightable material who proposes to join forces with a skilled writer to produce a copyrightable work is free to make a contract to disclose his or her material in return for assignment of part ownership of the resulting copyright. *Id.* § 201(d). And, as with all contract matters, the parties may minimize subsequent disputes by formalizing their agreement in a written contract. *Cf.* 17 U.S.C. § 101 ("work made for hire" definition of "specially ordered" or "commissioned" work includes requirement of written agreement). It seems more consistent with the spirit of copyright law to oblige all joint authors to make copyrightable contributions, leaving those with non-copyrightable contributions to protect their rights through contract.

There remains for consideration the crucial aspect of joint authorship — the nature of the intent that must be entertained by each putative joint author at the time the contribution of each was created. The wording of the statutory definition appears to make relevant only the state of mind regarding the unitary nature of the finished work — an intention "that their contributions be merged into inseparable or interdependent parts of a unitary whole." However, an inquiry so limited would extend joint author status to many persons who are not likely to have been within the contemplation of Congress. For example, a writer frequently works with an editor who makes numerous useful revisions to the first draft, some of which will consist of additions of copyrightable expression. Both intend their contributions to be merged into inseparable parts of a unitary whole, yet very few editors and even fewer writers would expect the editor to be accorded the status of joint author, enjoying an undivided half interest in the copyright in the published work. Similarly, research assistants may on occasion contribute to an author some protectable expression or merely a sufficiently original selection of factual material as would be entitled to a copyright, yet not be entitled to be regarded as a joint author of the work in which the contributed material appears. What distinguishes the writer-editor relationship and the writer-researcher relationship from the true joint author relationship is the lack of intent of both participants in the venture to regard themselves as joint authors.

Focusing on whether the putative joint authors regarded themselves as joint authors is especially important in circumstances, such as the instant case, where one person (Childress) is indisputably the dominant author of the work and the only issue is whether that person is the sole author or she and another (Taylor) are joint authors. *See Fisher v. Klein*, 16 U.S.P.Q.2D (BNA) 1795, 1798 (S.D.N.Y. 1990); *Picture Music, Inc. v. Bourne, Inc.*, 314 F. Supp. 640, 647 (S.D.N.Y. 1970), *aff'd on other grounds*, 457 F.2d 1213 (2d Cir.), *cert. denied*, 409 U.S. 997 (1972). This concern requires less exacting consideration in the context of traditional forms of collaboration, such as between the creators of the words and music of a song.

In this case, appellant contends that Judge Haight's observation that "Childress never shared Taylor's notion that they were co-authors of the play" misapplies the statutory standard by focusing on whether Childress "intended the legal consequences which flowed from her prior acts." We do not think Judge Haight went so far. He did not inquire whether Childress intended that she and Taylor would hold equal undivided interests in the play. But he properly insisted that they entertain in their minds the concept of joint authorship, whether or not they understood precisely the legal consequences of that relationship. Though joint authorship does not require an understanding by the co-authors of the legal consequences of their relationship, obviously some distinguishing characteristic of the relationship must be understood in order for it to be the subject of their intent. In many instances, a useful test will be whether, in the absence of contractual agreements concerning listed authorship, each participant intended that all would be identified as co-authors. Though "billing" or "credit" is not decisive in all cases and joint authorship can exist without any explicit discussion of this topic by the parties,[7] consideration of the topic helpfully serves to focus the fact-finder's attention on how the parties implicitly regarded their undertaking.

An inquiry into how the putative joint authors regarded themselves in relation to the work has previously been part of our approach in ascertaining the existence of joint authorship. In *Gilliam v. American Broadcasting Companies, Inc.*, 538 F.2d 14 (2d Cir. 1976), we examined the parties' written agreements and noted that their provisions indicated "that the parties *did not consider themselves joint authors* of a single work." *Id.* at 22. This same thought is evident in Judge Leval's observation that "it is only where the dominant author *intends to be sharing authorship* that joint authorship will result." *Fisher v. Klein*, 16 U.S.P.Q.2d at 1798. And it echoes the approach taken by then-District Judge Learned Hand when he determined that the facts showed that two authors "*agreed to a joint authorship in the piece*, and that they accepted whatever the law implied as to the rights and obligations which arose from such an undertaking." *Maurel v. Smith*, 220 F. at 198. *See also Weissmann v. Freeman*, 868 F.2d at 1318 (each of those claiming to be joint authors "must intend to contribute to a joint work."). Judge Haight was entirely correct to inquire whether Childress ever shared Taylor's "notion that they were co-authors of the Play."

Examination of whether the putative co-authors ever shared an intent to be co-authors serves the valuable purpose of appropriately confining the bounds

---

[7]Obviously, consideration of whether the parties contemplated listed co-authorship (or would have accepted such billing had they thought about it) is not a helpful inquiry for works written by an uncredited "ghost writer," either as a sole author, as a joint author, or as an employee preparing a work for hire.

of joint authorship arising by operation of copyright law, while leaving those not in a true joint authorship relationship with an author free to bargain for an arrangement that will be recognized as a matter of both copyright and contract law. Joint authorship entitles the co-authors to equal undivided interests in the work, see 17 U.S.C. § 201(a); *Community for Creative Non-Violence v. Reid*, 846 F.2d 1485, 1498 (D.C. Cir. 1988), *aff'd without consideration of this point*, 490 U.S. 730 (1989). That equal sharing of rights should be reserved for relationships in which all participants fully intend to be joint authors. The sharing of benefits in other relationships involving assistance in the creation of a copyrightable work can be more precisely calibrated by the participants in their contract negotiations regarding division of royalties or assignment of shares of ownership of the copyright, see 17 U.S.C. § 201(d).

In this case, the issue is not only whether Judge Haight applied the correct standard for determining joint authorship but also whether he was entitled to conclude that the record warranted a summary judgment in favor of Childress. We are satisfied that Judge Haight was correct as to both issues. We need not determine whether we agree with his conclusion that Taylor's contributions were not independently copyrightable since, even if they were protectable as expression or as an original selection of facts, we agree that there is no evidence from which a trier could infer that Childress had the state of mind required for joint authorship. As Judge Haight observed, whatever thought of co-authorship might have existed in Taylor's mind "was emphatically not shared by the purported co-author." There is no evidence that Childress ever contemplated, much less would have accepted, crediting the play as "written by Alice Childress and Clarice Taylor."

Childress was asked to write a play about "Moms" Mabley and did so. To facilitate her writing task, she accepted the assistance that Taylor provided, which consisted largely of furnishing the results of research concerning the life of "Moms" Mabley. As the actress expected to portray the leading role, Taylor also made some incidental suggestions, contributing ideas about the presentation of the play's subject and possibly some minor bits of expression. But there is no evidence that these aspects of Taylor's role ever evolved into more than the helpful advice that might come from the cast, the directors, or the producers of any play. A playwright does not so easily acquire a co-author.

Judge Haight was fully entitled to bolster his decision by reliance on the contract negotiations that followed completion of the script. Though his primary basis for summary judgment was the absence of any evidence supporting an inference that Childress shared "Taylor's notion that they were co-authors," he properly pointed to the emphatic rejection by Childress of the attempts by Taylor's agent to negotiate a co-ownership agreement and Taylor's acquiescence in that rejection. Intent "at the time the writing is done" remains the "touchstone," House Report at 120, but subsequent conduct is normally probative of a prior state of mind....

[The matter of damages was subsequently decided by the district court. The court rejected Childress's claim for actual damages based upon an asserted six percent royalty from the gross box office sales realized by the infringing production and also upon a supposed non-refundable advance that Childress might have been paid against income from future stock and amateur productions. The court did award statutory damages, in the amount of $30,000, for willful infringement; and Taylor's (and a co-author's) profits in the form of royalties they received for the infringing play. 798 F. Supp. 981 (S.D.N.Y. 1992).]

QUESTIONS

1. Recall the court's reference to the suggestion in the Nimmer treatise that one can become a joint author although one's contribution, if viewed separately, does not manifest sufficient originality and authorship to be protected by copyright. Is such a suggestion sound, as a matter of copyright theory or practical application? Would it affect your judgment that both parties *intended* to collaborate?

2. The court concluded that ownership rights in works of authorship are better distributed by requiring contributors of non-copyright material to contract for ownership interests in the work, rather than claiming co-authorship status. Do you see any problems with this approach?

3. John Q. Homeowner has consulted and retained an architect to prepare plans to be used in the construction of a house. Homeowner has informed Architect that he wishes to have a two-story colonial with four bedrooms and two bathrooms upstairs, and a kitchen, family room (with fireplace), library, laundry room and bathroom downstairs. He also provided Architect with a rough pencil sketch of the layout he had been inspired to draw by examining several floor plans reproduced in home-decorating magazines. Architect prepared her first sketches and showed them to Homeowner, who made several suggestions about the shape (to accommodate certain items of furniture) and dimensions of the rooms; he also suggested changes in the angles of roof and windows. These suggestions were then incorporated by Architect in a final set of detailed plans, which Homeowner approved. Homeowner paid Architect $5,000 for her services and had the house built for $100,000. Nothing was said either orally or in writing between Homeowner and Architect about the ownership of the architectural plans. Homeowner has just learned that Architect has used essentially the same plans in designing a house to be built across town. He has consulted you and wishes to know whether he may stop Architect from doing so. What is your advice? *See Joseph J. Legat Architects, P.C. v. United States Dev. Corp.*, 625 F. Supp. 293 (N.D. Ill. 1985); *Meltzer v. Zoller*, 520 F. Supp. 847 (D.N.J. 1981); *M.G.B. Homes, Inc. v. Ameron Homes, Inc.*, 903 F.2d 1486 (11th Cir. 1990).

4. Alfonse and Gaston have collaborated on several editions of a manual of proper deportment, originally titled *Etiquette for the Eighties,* and now titled *Etiquette for the Nineties.* Following a falling-out with Gaston, Alfonse is preparing the update, *Etiquette for the Millennium,* on his own. *Etiquette for the Millennium* will include new material by Alfonse, but will also incorporate substantial portions of the prior co-authored editions. Is *Etiquette for the Millennium* a joint work? *See Weissmann v. Freeman*, 868 F.2d 1313 (2d Cir.), *cert. denied*, 493 U.S. 883 (1989).

The concept of joint works, particularly as articulated in the Second Circuit, seems to presume collaboration. A work will not be deemed "joint" unless its creators together intended to elaborate a work containing their contributions. Moreover, at least by implication, the parties should express this intent, together, at the same time. This is not the only conceivable model of co-authorship. For example, a composer might write a melody, hoping and intending that, at some later date, a lyricist would come along and supply the words. In this instance, although the authors did not work together toward their goal (indeed, the authors may never have met or corresponded), both sought to create a work that would combine words and music. Here, there is intent, but it is not simultaneously expressed. Or suppose the composer has no intent regarding the pairing of her tune with words, but a subsequent lyricist nonetheless joins the text to the tune. The lyricist certainly intends to create a work that is "joint" in the sense that he has bound the words and music together. The Second Circuit, in a much-criticized decision under the 1909 Act, held that the intent of the subsequent author sufficed to qualify the combined work as "joint." *See Shapiro, Bernstein & Co. v. Jerry Vogel Music Co.,* 221 F.2d 569 (2d Cir.), *modified on rehearing,* 223 F.2d 252 (2d Cir. 1955) (the *"Twelfth Street Rag"* case).

The 1976 Act clearly intended to reject the expanded concept of "joint works" in the "Twelfth Street Rag" case by its emphasis on the intent of the *authors* at the time their respective contributions were made. *See* S. Rep. No. 94-473, 94th Cong., 1st Sess. 103 (1975); H.R. Rep. No. 94-1476, 94th Cong., 2d Sess. 120 (1976). The expansion of the concept of joint works within the Second Circuit was probably motivated by a desire to avoid characterization of the works as "composite," with attendant renewal ownership by the proprietor rather than the author. A third alternative is to consider the contributions separable and owned separately by their respective authors. *See Harris v. Coca Cola Co.,* 73 F.2d 370, 23 U.S.P.Q. 182 (5th Cir. 1934). The result of expansion of the joint works concept was a confusing and potentially unfair array of renewal interests, particularly where derivative works were involved. For example, would the author of a play necessarily be deemed co-author of a motion picture later using his dramatic material? Although an affirmative answer might well be beyond even the extreme holding in the "Twelfth Street Rag" case, such an approach was expressly rejected in the congressional explanation of joint works. S. Rep. No. 94-473, *supra,* at 104; H.R. Rep. No. 94-1476, *supra,* at 120.

But, if the 1976 Act requires *both* authors to intend to create a joint work, one may still inquire whether that intent must be simultaneously expressed. As the *Childress* court noted, the House Report envisions two situations giving rise to a joint work: (1) "the authors collaborated with each other," or (2) "each of the authors prepared his or her contribution with the knowledge and intention that it would be merged with the contributions of other authors as 'inseparable or interdependent parts of a unitary whole.'" While a collaboration implies simultaneity of intent, the House Report's other example, of contributions created with the intent that they be merged, arguably accommodates the hypothetical composer awaiting a lyricist. Nonetheless, the more likely interpretation of Congress' design in defining joint works would be that, while the authors need not actually meet and work together, they must not only intend, but must also be aware of, each other's contributions. Hence the House Report's requirement of "*knowledge* and intention" (emphasis added). The hypothetical composer does not meet this standard: while she anticipates and hopes that someday her lyricist will come along, she does not *know* that this will happen. For there to be not only an "intention at the time the writing is done" to combine the parts, but also the knowledge that the contributions will be merged, it would seem that the intent must be joined in time. The actual composition or combination of the parts may be staggered over time (one co-author may require more time than the other needs to create her contribution), but the contributors should know, before either begins, that their efforts will form "inseparable or interdependent parts of a unitary whole."

Because a work's "joint" status depends on the authors' mutual intent to create a unitary work, the question arises whether a claim of co-authorship and co-ownership of a "joint" work presents an issue of state or federal law. Just as claims alleging co-ownership of copyright through assignments or licenses have been held to arise under state contract law, see, e.g., *T.B. Harms v. Eliscu,* 339 F.2d 823 (2d Cir. 1964), *cert. denied,* 381 U.S. 915 (1965), one might contend that construction of the parties' intent to create a joint work also poses a question of state contract law.

This position is probably incorrect. The test for whether a claim arises under the Copyright Act, or under state law, is whether the claim asserts a remedy expressly granted by the Act, or requires construction of the Act, or at least implicates federal copyright policy. *See T.B. Harms, supra.* A claim of co-authorship of a joint work requires construction and application of the statutory definition of a joint work, and seeks the remedy of a declaration of an undivided one-half interest in the work, as contemplated in 17 U.S.C. § 201(a). *See Lieberman v. Estate of Chayefsky,* 535 F. Supp. 90 (S.D.N.Y. 1982). *Compare Royal v. Leading Edge Prods., Inc.,* 833 F.2d 1 (1st Cir. 1987). In effect, the Act's requirement of a demonstration of intent to create a joint work may result in articulation of a federal law definition of the requisite intent.

A joint owner may generally use or license the use of the work without the consent of his or her co-owners, *Werbungs und Commerz Union Austalt v. LeShufy,* 6 U.S.P.Q.2d 1153 (S.D.N.Y. 1987), but must account to them for their share of profits derived from such license of a third party, *Jerry Vogel Music Co. v. Miller Music, Inc.,* 272 App. Div. 571, 74 N.Y.S.2d 425, 75 U.S.P.Q. 205 (1st Dep't 1947), *aff'd,* 299 N.Y. 782, 82 U.S.P.Q. 458 (1949), and presumably even for his or her own use. *See Oddo v. Ries,* 743 F.2d 630 (9th Cir. 1984). This applies not only to ownership of joint works but also to co-ownership in other situations, e.g., where rights of a single owner are transferred to several who own an undivided interest.

B. TRANSFER OF COPYRIGHT OWNERSHIP

1. DIVISIBILITY AND FORMAL REQUIREMENTS

DIVISIBILITY

The 1976 Act contains "the first explicit statutory recognition of the principle of divisibility of copyright in our law." H.R. Rep. No. 94-1476 at 123. Repudiation of the concept of indivisibility, a concept of long standing in the prior law, was long an important objective of authors and other groups.

The indivisibility concept mandated a single owner or proprietor of copyright at any one time; all others having an interest under the copyright were deemed licensees. The ramifications of indivisibility reached such questions as notice, ownership, recordation of transfers, standing to sue, and taxes. For example, under the 1909 Act the name of the copyright "proprietor" was to be placed in the notice inscribed upon all publicly distributed copies; the failure to do so would usually thrust the work into the public domain. Thus, the indivisibility doctrine made it advisable for contributing authors and periodicals to structure their arrangement so that a complete transfer or "assignment" to the magazine was effected. A single notice in the name of the magazine would thus secure copyright. *Cf. Kaplan v. Fox Film Corp.,* 19 F. Supp. 780 (S.D.N.Y. 1937). The author would frequently accompany the assignment with a provision for a future reconveyance of the copyright in his or her contribution. *See Geisel v. Poynter Prods., Inc.,* 295 F. Supp. 331, 337-42 (S.D.N.Y. 1968).

The 1976 Act expressly contemplates a divisible copyright by providing: "'Copyright owner', with respect to any one of the exclusive rights comprised in a copyright, refers to the owner of that particular right." § 101. This definition underlies § 201(d)(2), which provides that "[a]ny of the exclusive rights comprised in a copyright, including any subdivision of any of the rights specified by section 106 [the provision enumerating protected rights], may be transferred ... and owned separately." In line with the definition quoted immediately above, this subsection then provides that "[t]he owner of any particular exclusive right is entitled, to the extent of that right, to all of the protection and remedies accorded to the copyright owner by this title."

The committee reports indicate that this provision may be taken literally. The House Report states:

> It is thus clear, for example, that a local broadcasting station holding an exclusive license to transmit a particular work within a particular geographic area and for a particular period of time, could sue, in its own name as copyright owner, someone who infringed that particular exclusive right.

H.R. Rep. No. 94-1476, *supra* at 123. *Cf.* S. Rep. No. 94-473, *supra* at 107.

One of the rights that can be exercised by an exclusive licensee is the right to bring an action for copyright infringement. Thus § 501(b) provides: "The legal or beneficial owner of an exclusive right under a copyright is entitled ... to institute an action for any infringement of that particular right committed while he or she is the owner of it." It follows that a person holding a nonexclusive license to one or more of the rights in § 106 may not properly sue for infringement.

This principle was applied in *Broadcast Music, Inc. v. CBS Inc.*, 421 F. Supp. 592 (S.D.N.Y. 1983), rather startlingly a case of first impression as applied to the plaintiff, one of the two major performing-rights societies for musical compositions (the other being the American Society of Composers, Authors and Publishers). BMI and ASCAP are given nonexclusive licenses by copyright owners of popular music (some being composers and some being music publishers) to license others, such as radio and television broadcasters, publicly to perform that music. BMI and ASCAP have an elaborate system of granting permissions to broadcasters, night clubs, restaurants, and the like, and of policing those who publicly perform copyrighted music without permission, and of collecting and distributing royalties to the copyright owners. In *BMI v. CBS*, the defendant — apparently for the first time in the history of the many lawsuits brought by BMI and ASCAP — pressed to decision the question of BMI's capacity to sue for infringement of the public-performance right. The court held that, because BMI was only a nonexclusive licensee, it had no standing to sue. Nonetheless, recognizing that joining a large number of publishers when many different songs are at issue may be burdensome for BMI, the court suggested that BMI might seek to have the publishers declared a plaintiff class under Fed. R. Civ. P. 23(b).

---

§ 201. Ownership of copyright

. . . .

(d) *Transfer of Ownership.* —
(1) The ownership of a copyright may be transferred in whole or in part by any means of conveyance or by operation of law, and may be bequeathed by will or pass as personal property by the applicable laws of intestate succession.

(2) Any of the exclusive rights comprised in a copyright, including any subdivision of any of the rights specified by section 106, may be transferred as provided by clause (1) and owned separately. The owner of any particular exclusive right is entitled, to the extent of that right, to all of the protection and remedies accorded to the copyright owner by this title.

§ 204. Execution of transfers of copyright ownership

(a) A transfer of copyright ownership, other than by operation of law, is not valid unless an instrument of conveyance, or a note or memorandum of the transfer, is in writing and signed by the owner of the rights conveyed or such owner's duly authorized agent.

Friedman v. Stacey Data Processing Services, 17 U.S.P.Q.2d 1858 (N.D. Ill. 1990). Friedman, a collection attorney, hired the defendant Stacey, a provider of computer services, to furnish debt-collection software according to

Friedman's specifications. The parties orally agreed in 1977 that the resulting programs would belong entirely to Friedman and that Stacey would not sell the programs or copies of them to anyone else; this understanding was reduced to writing in 1978. Stacey retained an independent contractor to design and write the programs, with some guidance from Friedman, and the programmer turned over all of his ownership rights to Stacey. When the programs were completed, Stacey in turn gave them to Friedman, but also began actively marketing them to other collection attorneys.

In 1985, Stacey's president sent letters to Friedman stating that the programs are "your property" and that Stacey had not and would not sell them to any other person. In 1989, Friedman brought an action against Stacey for copyright infringement. Stacey moved to dismiss, arguing that all that it had conveyed to Friedman was the physical property in the computer programs, but that it, Stacey, had retained the copyright.

The court considered the application of § 204(a), the statute of frauds of the Copyright Act. The court suggested that had the writings signed by Stacey made no mention of the transfer of any property in the programs, § 204(a) would have rendered any alleged copyright transfer invalid, and Stacey would have prevailed. However, because there was reference in the 1978 and 1985 writings to "property" — which was ambiguous, because it could refer either to "simple ownership rights to the programs themselves, or … those rights plus the copyright" — it was appropriate under conventional contract doctrine (i.e., the parol evidence rule) to admit extrinsic evidence of the parties' intention. Such extrinsic evidence would include not only the plaintiff's subjective intent but also the course of the relationship between the parties and other documents signed by the defendant. "The court does not rule that the contract sufficed to assign the copyright; it merely holds that extrinsic evidence of the type generally allowed with respect to ambiguous contracts shall be relevant in determining whether the contract assigned the copyright." Accordingly, it denied Stacey's motion to dismiss.

What is the purpose underlying § 204(a)? Is that purpose arguably frustrated by the court's willingness to hear parol evidence that the parties intended the word "property" to include copyright as well as the physical programs?

EFFECTS ASSOCIATES v. COHEN

908 F.2d 555 (9th Cir. 1990), *cert. denied,*
498 U.S. 1103 (1991)

KOZINSKI, CIRCUIT JUDGE.

What we have here is a failure to compensate. Larry Cohen, a low-budget horror movie mogul, paid less than the agreed price for special effects footage he had commissioned from Effects Associates. Cohen then used this footage without first obtaining a written license or assignment of the copyright; Effects sued for copyright infringement. We consider whether a transfer of copyright without a written agreement, an arrangement apparently not uncommon in the motion picture industry, conforms with the requirements of the Copyright Act.

Facts

This started out as a run-of-the-mill Hollywood squabble. Defendant Larry Cohen wrote, directed and executive produced "The Stuff," a horror movie with a dash of social satire: Earth is invaded by an alien life form that looks (and tastes) like frozen yogurt but, alas, has some unfortunate side effects — it's addictive and takes over the mind of anyone who eats it. Marketed by an unscrupulous entrepreneur, the Stuff becomes a big hit. An industrial spy hired by ice cream manufacturers eventually uncovers the terrible truth; he alerts the American people and blows up the yogurt factory, making the world safe once again for lovers of frozen confections.

In cooking up this gustatory melodrama, Cohen asked Effects Associates, a small special effects company, to create footage to enhance certain action sequences in the film. In a short letter dated October 29, 1984, Effects offered to prepare seven shots, the most dramatic of which would depict the climactic explosion of the Stuff factory. Cohen agreed to the deal orally, but no one said anything about who would own the copyright in the footage.

Cohen was unhappy with the factory explosion Effects created, and he expressed his dissatisfaction by paying Effects only half the promised amount for that shot. Effects made several demands for the rest of the money (a little over $8,000), but Cohen refused. Nevertheless, Cohen incorporated Effects's footage into the film and turned it over to New World Entertainment for distribution. Effects then brought this copyright infringement action, claiming that Cohen (along with his production company and New World) had no right to use the special effects footage unless he paid Effects the full contract price. Effects also brought pendent state law claims for fraud and conspiracy to infringe copyright.

The district court initially dismissed the suit, holding that it was primarily a contract dispute and, as such, did not arise under federal law. In an opinion remarkable for its lucidity, we reversed and remanded, concluding that plaintiff was "master of his claim" and could opt to pursue the copyright infringement action instead of suing on the contract. *Effects Assocs., Inc. v. Cohen,* 817 F.2d 72, 73 (9th Cir. 1987). We recognized that the issue on remand would be whether Effects had transferred to Cohen the right to use the footage. *Id.* at 73 & n. 1, 74.

On remand, the district court granted summary judgment to Cohen on the infringement claim, holding that Effects had granted Cohen an implied license to use the shots. Accordingly, the court dismissed the remaining state law claims, allowing Effects to pursue them in state court. We review the district court's grant of summary judgment de novo.

Discussion

A. *Transfer of Copyright Ownership*

The law couldn't be clearer: The copyright owner of "a motion picture or other audiovisual work" has the exclusive rights to copy, distribute or display the copyrighted work publicly. 17 U.S.C. § 106 (1988). While the copyright owner can sell or license his rights to someone else, section 204 of the Copyright Act invalidates a purported transfer of ownership unless it is in writing. 17 U.S.C. § 204(a) (1988).[2] Here, no one disputes that Effects is the copyright owner of the special effects footage used in "The Stuff,"[3] and that defendants copied, distributed and publicly displayed this footage without written authorization.

Cohen suggests that section 204's writing requirement does not apply to this situation, advancing an argument that might be summarized, tongue in cheek, as: Moviemakers do lunch, not contracts. Cohen concedes that "in the best of all possible legal worlds" parties would obey the writing requirement, but contends that moviemakers are too absorbed in developing "joint creative endeavors" to "focus upon the legal niceties of copyright licenses." Appellees' Brief at 16, 18. Thus, Cohen suggests that we hold section 204's writing requirement inapplicable here because "it is customary in the motion picture industry ... not to have written licenses." *Id.* at 18. To the extent that Cohen's argument amounts to a plea to exempt moviemakers from the normal operation of section 204 by making implied transfers of copyrights "the rule, not the exception," *id.,* we reject his argument.

Common sense tells us that agreements should routinely be put in writing. This simple practice prevents misunderstandings by spelling out the terms of a deal in black and white, forces parties to clarify their thinking and consider problems that could potentially arise, and encourages them to take their promises seriously because it's harder to backtrack on a written contract than on an oral one. Copyright law dovetails nicely with common sense by requiring that a transfer of copyright ownership be in writing. Section 204 ensures that the creator of a work will not give away his copyright inadvertently and forces a party who wants to use the copyrighted work to negotiate with the creator to determine precisely what rights are being transferred and at what price. Cf. *Community for Creative Non-Violence v. Reid,* 109 S. Ct. 2166, 2177-78 (1989) (describing purpose of writing requirement for works made for hire). Most importantly, section 204 enhances predictability and certainty of copyright ownership — "Congress' paramount goal" when it revised the Act in 1976. *Community for Creative Non-Violence,* 109 S. Ct. at 2177; see also *Dumas v. Gommerman,* 865 F.2d 1093, 1103-04 (9th Cir. 1989). Rather than look to the courts every time they disagree as to whether a particular use of the work violates their mutual understanding, parties need only look to the writing that sets out their respective rights.

Section 204's writing requirement is not unduly burdensome; it necessitates neither protracted negotiations nor substantial expense. The rule is really quite simple: If the copyright holder agrees to transfer ownership to another party, that party must get the copyright holder to sign a piece of paper saying

---

[2]The Copyright Act defines "transfer of copyright ownership" as an "assignment, mortgage, exclusive license, or any other conveyance, alienation, or hypothecation of a copyright or of any of the exclusive rights comprised in a copyright ... but not including a nonexclusive license." 17 U.S.C. § 101.

[3]Cohen concedes that he licensed Effects to prepare the footage as a derivative work incorporating other shots from "The Stuff," and that Effects has a valid copyright in this footage. Appellees' Brief at 25 n. 3.

so. It doesn't have to be the Magna Charta; a one-line pro forma statement will do.

Cohen's attempt to exempt moviemakers from the requirements of the Copyright Act is largely precluded by recent Supreme Court and circuit authority construing the work-for-hire doctrine.[4] ... [W]here a non-employee contributes to a book or movie, as Effects did here, the exclusive rights of copyright ownership vest in the creator of the contribution, unless there is a written agreement to the contrary....

Thus, section 101 specifically addresses the movie and book publishing industries, affording moviemakers a simple, straightforward way of obtaining ownership of the copyright in a creative contribution — namely, a written agreement. The Supreme Court and this circuit, while recognizing the custom and practice in the industry, have refused to permit moviemakers to sidestep section 204's writing requirement. Accordingly, we find unpersuasive Cohen's contention that section 204's writing requirement, which singles out no particular group, somehow doesn't apply to him. As section 204 makes no special allowances for the movie industry, neither do we.

B. *Nonexclusive Licenses*

Although we reject any suggestion that moviemakers are immune to section 204, we note that there is a narrow exception to the writing requirement that may apply here. Section 204 provides that all transfers of copyright ownership must be in writing; section 101 defines transfers of ownership broadly, but expressly removes from the scope of section 204 a "nonexclusive license." See note 2 *supra*. The sole issue that remains, then, is whether Cohen had a nonexclusive license to use plaintiff's special effects footage.

The leading treatise on copyright law states that "[a] nonexclusive license may be granted orally, or may even be implied from conduct." 3 M. Nimmer & D. Nimmer, Nimmer on Copyright § 10.03[A], at 10-36 (1989). Cohen relies on the latter proposition; he insists that, although Effects never gave him a written or oral license, Effects's conduct created an implied license to use the footage in "The Stuff."

Cohen relies largely on our decision in *Oddo v. Ries*, 743 F.2d 630 (9th Cir. 1984). There, we held that Oddo, the author of a series of articles on how to restore Ford F-100 pickup trucks, had impliedly granted a limited non-exclusive license to Ries, a publisher, to use plaintiff's articles in a book on the same topic. We relied on the fact that Oddo and Ries had formed a partnership to create and publish the book, with Oddo writing and Ries providing capital. *Id.* at 632 & n. 1. Oddo prepared a manuscript consisting partly of material taken from his prior articles and submitted it to Ries. *Id.* at 632. Because the manuscript incorporated pre-existing material, it was a derivative work; by publishing it, Ries would have necessarily infringed the copyright in Oddo's articles, unless Oddo had granted him a license. *Id.* at 634. We concluded that, in preparing and handing over to Ries a manuscript intended for publication

---

[4] Because Effects is not an employee and there is no written agreement stating that plaintiff's footage is a work made for hire, Cohen can't take advantage of this doctrine....

that, if published, would infringe Oddo's copyright, Oddo "impliedly gave the partnership a license to use the articles insofar as they were incorporated in the manuscript, for without such a license, Oddo's contribution to the partnership venture would have been of minimal value." *Id.*[5]

The district court agreed with Cohen, and we agree with the district court: *Oddo* controls here. Like the plaintiff in *Oddo,* Effects created a work at defendant's request and handed it over, intending that defendant copy and distribute it. To hold that Effects did not at the same time convey a license to use the footage in "The Stuff" would mean that plaintiff's contribution to the film was "of minimal value," a conclusion that can't be squared with the fact that Cohen paid Effects almost $56,000 for this footage. Accordingly, we conclude that Effects impliedly granted nonexclusive licenses to Cohen and his production company to incorporate the special effects footage into "The Stuff" and to New World Entertainment to distribute the film.

Conclusion

We affirm the district court's grant of summary judgment in favor of Cohen and the other defendants. We note, however, that plaintiff doesn't leave this court empty-handed. Copyright ownership is comprised of a bundle of rights; in granting a nonexclusive license to Cohen, Effects has given up only one stick from that bundle — the right to sue Cohen for copyright infringement. It retains the right to sue him in state court on a variety of other grounds, including breach of contract. Additionally, Effects may license, sell or give away for nothing its remaining rights in the special effects footage. Those rights may not be particularly valuable, of course: "The Stuff" was something less than a blockbuster, and it remains to be seen whether there's a market for shots featuring great gobs of alien yogurt oozing out of a defunct factory. On the other hand, the shots may have much potential for use in music videos. See generally Kozinski & Banner, *Who's Afraid of Commercial Speech?,* 76 Va. L. Rev. 627, 641 (1990). In any event, whatever Effects chooses to do with the footage, Cohen will have no basis for complaining. And that's an important lesson that licensees of more versatile film properties may want to take to heart.

QUESTIONS

1. Why heed the court's cautionary tale about the § 204(a) requirement of a writing if a course of conduct will imply a license anyway?

2. Medical Publications, Inc., publishes and owns the copyright to a best-selling home medical book, *Heal Thyself.* Last year, it orally agreed with Book Placement Company (BPC) that BPC would have the right to place the book in all bookstores not then being supplied by Medical Publications. Within a

---

[5]Oddo did nevertheless prevail, but on other grounds. Ries was unhappy with Oddo's manuscript and hired another writer to do the job right. This writer added much new material, but also used large chunks of Oddo's manuscript, thereby incorporating portions of Oddo's pre-existing articles. 743 F.2d at 632. By publishing the other writer's book, Ries exceeded the scope of his implied license to use Oddo's articles and was liable for copyright infringement. *Id.* at 634.

matter of months, however, Medical Publications began to distribute *Heal Thyself* to the nationwide Dalton chain of bookstores, a new account. BPC has brought an action against Medical Publications for breach of contract. The defendant has moved for summary judgment, claiming that the oral exclusive license is void because not in writing. BPC, however, claims that its license was not an exclusive license, because Medical Publications retained the right to distribute *Heal Thyself* to its old accounts. Rule on the defendant's motion. *See Library Pubs., Inc. v. Medical Economics Co.,* 548 F. Supp. 1231 (E.D. Pa. 1982), *aff'd without opinion,* 714 F.2d 173 (3d Cir. 1983).

3. Paddington & Company in 1980 licensed Eden Company to make certain exclusive uses of the famous Paddington Bear cartoon figure on such items as stuffed animals, children's furniture, and children's clothing; the written license agreement made no mention of adults' clothing. In 1982, an informal understanding developed between Paddington & Company and Eden, whereby Eden was given the exclusive license to produce any Paddington Bear product (including adults' clothing) except books and phonograph records. In 1984, Florelee marketed adult pajamas bearing the Paddington Bear figure. In 1985, Paddington & Company reduced to writing the transfer of exclusive rights that had been informally granted Eden since 1982. Eden has brought an action against Florelee for the 1984 pajama infringement.

Florelee has moved for summary judgment on the ground that Eden is not the proper plaintiff; it points to § 204(a), as well as § 501(b) which in pertinent part provides: "The legal or beneficial owner of an exclusive right under a copyright is entitled ... to institute an action for any infringement of that particular right committed while he or she is the owner of it." Eden contends, however, that the purpose of § 204(a) is to protect copyright holders (such as Paddington & Company) from persons (such as Eden) who might mistakenly or fraudulently claim an oral license; thus, the "note or memorandum of the transfer" required in § 204(a) may be a later writing that confirms an earlier oral understanding, because this shows no dispute between Paddington and Eden. Eden claims, in short, that a third-party infringer cannot invoke § 204(a) against the licensee.

Which party has the more persuasive argument? *See Eden Toys, Inc. v. Florelee Undergarment Co.,* 697 F.2d 27 (2d Cir. 1982).

RECORDATION OF TRANSFERS AND OTHER DOCUMENTS

"The recording and priority provisions of section 205 [of the 1976 Act] are intended to clear up a number of uncertainties arising from sections 30 and 31 of the present [1909] law and to make them more effective and practical in operation." S. Rep. No. 94-473, *supra* at 112; H.R. Rep. No. 94-1476, *supra* at 128.

The recordation system established by the 1976 Act expressly provides that, in addition to transfers of copyright ownership, any signed document pertaining to a copyright — for example, a will or a mortgage — may be recorded (§ 205(a)). Its operation as constructive notice is also expressly provided, subject to two conditions: (1) specific identification of the work and (2) registration of a claim to copyright in the work (§ 205(c)).

Such recordation of a transfer affords the transferee priority over any subsequent transfer later so recorded. The first transferee is also granted a one-month grace period (two months, if the transfer was executed abroad) in which he or she will in any event prevail. Even without observing these time limits, the first transferee may prevail if the subsequent transferee had notice of the earlier transfer or otherwise was not in good faith or had not taken his or her transfer "for valuable consideration or on the basis of a binding promise to pay royalties." (§ 205(e).)

The 1976 Act also tackles the difficult problem of priority between conflicting transfers and nonexclusive licenses. It will be recalled that such licenses, being excluded from the definition of a "transfer of copyright ownership," need not even be in writing much less recorded. (Of course, they *may* be recorded.) But written, signed nonexclusive licenses, whether or not recorded, prevail over conflicting transfers if the license was taken either before the transfer or in good faith before recordation of the transfer and without notice of it. § 205(f).

In a case of first instance, it was decided in *National Peregrine Inc. v. Capitol Fed. Sav. & Loan Ass'n,* 116 Bankr. Rptr. 194, 16 U.S.P.Q.2d 1017 (C.D. Cal. 1990) (Kozinski, Circuit Judge, sitting by designation), that § 205 of the Copyright Act, providing for recordation of transfers in the Copyright Office and a priority for timely recorders over conflicting claimants, preempts state laws (i.e., the Uniform Commercial Code) providing for recording of security interests in various state offices. In that case, the plaintiff, NPI, was a debtor-in-possession in a bankruptcy proceeding, and it sought to preserve for the benefit of the bankruptcy estate some 145 copyrighted films and the licensing income therefrom. NPI's predecessor had earlier obtained a $6 million loan from the defendant Capitol Federal Savings, and that bank took the film library and future income as security or collateral for the loan. Capitol filed a UCC-1 financing statement in three states, pursuant to their respective state laws, but it did not record the transfer of the security interest in the Copyright Office.

The district court stated the question for decision to be: "Is a security interest in a copyright perfected by an appropriate filing with the Copyright Office or by a UCC-1 financing statement with the relevant secretary of state?" and concluded that the former was the correct answer. It held that the transfer of the copyright as collateral for a loan is a "transfer" of the copyright (as defined in § 101) that may be recorded in the Copyright Office under § 205(a). The court went on to conclude that the comprehensive scope of the recording provisions of the Act, along with the unique federal interests implicated, supports the view that federal law preempts state methods of perfecting security interests in copyrights and related accounts receivable. If state methods of perfection were valid, lenders would be forced to search for security interests in a variety of states, leading to expense and delay; this "could hinder the purchase and sale of copyrights, frustrating Congress's policy that copyrights be readily transferable in commerce." The court also found that Article 9 of the UCC itself had a "step back" provision which displaced the state recording system in the face of a federal recording system such as that provided under the Copyright Act.

Because under the Bankruptcy Act, NPI was to be treated as a "hypothetical lien creditor" taking its interest in good faith for valuable consideration and without notice — and also treated as recording its interest with the Copyright Office in a timely manner — the priority provisions of § 205(d) of the Copyright Act thus entitled NPI to avoid Capitol Federal's interest and capture the disputed copyright interests for the benefit of the bankruptcy estate.

An apparent consequence of the court's decision is that a person, typically a bank, taking a transfer of a security interest in the copyrights in many works — for example, the 145 films involved in the case itself — will in order to protect its interest have to record separately in the Copyright Office the transfers to each of those 145 films. Moreover, under § 205(c)(2), the bank would have to take steps to assure that the copyright in each work is registered. A filing under the UCC instead, in the name of the borrower and showing a security interest in "a library of 145 copyrighted films," accompanied by a list of the names of the films, would of course be much more conveniently done by the bank.

Proposed legislation introduced in early 1993 (S. 373 and H.R. 897) would, among other things, overturn the *Peregrine* decision and a later decision of a bankruptcy court reaching the same conclusion. One of the bill's sponsors, Congressmen Hughes, had this to say: "These decisions have turned a relatively simple business transaction into a nightmare for businesses and lenders. Moreover, given that a number of lenders have, in the past, only made UCC filings, there is considerable uncertainty about past transactions. This uncertainty is heightened by lenders' inability to register the work. Congress' intent in enacting the relevant provisions in section 205 was to provide a system for ordering the priority between conflicting transfers, not to preempt state procedures for ensuring that a secured creditor's rights are protected. There is no reason the Federal and State systems cannot coexist in this area."

The bill would achieve this objective quite simply — by amending § 301(b) so as to add state laws dealing with "perfecting security interests" to the list of state-based rights and remedies that are not preempted by the federal Copyright Act. Would you endorse such legislation? Would such legislation promote development of a comprehensive and reliable copyright recordation system?

2. SCOPE OF GRANT

BARTSCH v. METRO-GOLDWYN-MAYER, INC.

391 F.2d 150 (2d Cir. 1968)

FRIENDLY, CIRCUIT JUDGE: This appeal from a judgment of the District Court for the Southern District of New York raises the question whether, on the facts here appearing, an assignee of motion picture rights to a musical play is entitled to authorize the telecasting of its copyrighted film. We affirm the judgment dismissing the complaint of the copyright owner.

In January 1930, the authors, composers, and publishers of and owners of certain other interests in a German musical play "Wie Einst im Mai," which had been produced in this country as "Maytime" with a changed libretto and score, assigned to Hans Bartsch [all of their motion picture rights in the musical play for the whole world, and for the full period of any applicable copyrights.] In May of that year Bartsch assigned to Warner Bros. Pictures, Inc.

> the motion picture rights throughout the world, in and to a certain musical play entitled "Wie Einst im Mai," libretto and lyrics by Rudolf Schanzer and Rudolph Bernauer, music by Walter Kollo and Willy Bredschneider, for the full period of all copyrights and any renewed and extended terms thereof, together with the sole and exclusive right to use, adapt, translate, add to, subtract from, interpolate in and change said musical play, and the title thereof (subject so far as the right to use said title is concerned to Paragraph 7 hereof), in the making of motion picture photoplays and to project, transmit and otherwise reproduce the said musical play or any adaptation or version thereof visually or audibly by the art of cinematography or any process analogous thereto, and to copyright, vend, license and exhibit such motion picture photoplays throughout the world, together with the further sole and exclusive right by mechanical and/or electrical means to record, reproduce and transmit sound, including spoken words, dialogue, songs and music, and to change such dialogue, if extracted from said musical play, and at his own expense and responsibility to interpolate and use other dialogue, songs and music in or in connection with or as part of said motion picture photoplays, and the exhibition, reproduction and transmission thereof, and to make, use, license, import, vend and copyright any and all records or other devices made or required or desired for any such purposes.

By another clause Bartsch reserved the right to exercise for himself the rights generally granted to Warner Brothers insofar as these concerned German language motion pictures in certain countries and subject to specified restrictions:

> but it is expressly understood ánd agreed that nothing herein contained shall in any way limit or restrict the absolute right of Purchaser to produce, release, distribute and/or exhibit the photoplay or photoplays produced hereunder based in whole or in part on "Wie Einst im Mai" and/or "Maytime," in all countries of the world, including the territory mentioned in this paragraph, at any time, and regardless of the right herein reserved to the Owner.

A further clause recited

> The rights which the Purchaser obtains from the Owner in "Wie Einst im Mai" and/or "Maytime" are specifically limited to those granted herein. All other rights now in existence or which may hereafter come into existence shall always be reserved to the Owner and for his sole benefit, but nothing herein contained shall in any way limit or restrict the rights which Purchaser has acquired or shall hereafter acquire from any other

person, firm or corporation in and to "Wie Einst im Mai" and/or "Maytime."

Warner Brothers transferred its rights to defendant Metro-Goldwyn-Mayer, Inc. early in 1935, which made, distributed and exhibited a highly successful motion picture "Maytime." The co-authors of the German libretto, one in 1935 and the other in 1938, transferred all their copyright interests and renewal rights to Bartsch, whose rights in turn have devolved to the plaintiff, his widow. The controversy stems from MGM's licensing its motion picture for television, beginning in 1958.

. . . .

As we read the instruments, defendant's rights [turn on] the broad grant, in the assignments to and from Bartsch, of "the motion picture rights throughout the world," which were spelled out to include the right "to copyright, vend, license and exhibit such motion picture photoplays throughout the world.". . . [D]ecision turns on whether a broad assignment of the right "to copyright, vend, license and exhibit such motion picture photoplays throughout the world" includes the right to "license" a broadcaster to "exhibit" the copyrighted motion picture by a telecast without a further grant by the copyright owner.

A threshold issue is whether this question should be determined under state or federal law. The seventeenth paragraph of Bartsch's assignment says, somewhat unhelpfully, that "Each and every term of this agreement shall be construed in accordance with the laws of the United States of America *and* of the State of New York." [Emphasis supplied.] We hold that New York law governs. The development of a "federal common law" of contracts is justified only when required by a distinctive national policy and, as we found in *T.B. Harms v. Eliscu*, 339 F.2d 823, 828 (2 Cir. 1964), citing many cases, "the general interest that copyrights, like all other forms of property, should be enjoyed by their true owner is not enough to meet this . . . test.". . . The fact that plaintiff is seeking a remedy granted by Congress to copyright owners removes any problem of federal jurisdiction but does not mean that federal principles must govern the disposition of every aspect of her claim. Cf. *DeSylva v. Ballentine*, 351 U.S. 570 (1956).

Unfortunately, when we turn to state law, we find that it offers little assistance. Two other situations must be distinguished. This is not a case like *Manners v. Morosco*, 252 U.S. 317 (1920), cited with approval, *Underhill v. Schenck*, 238 N.Y. 7, 143 N.E. 773, 33 A.L.R. 303 (1924), in which an all encompassing grant found in one provision must be limited by the context created by other terms of the agreement indicating that the use of the copyrighted material in only one medium was contemplated. The words of Bartsch's assignment . . . were well designed to give the assignee the broadest rights with respect to *its* copyrighted property, to wit, the photoplay. "Exhibit" means to "display" or to "show" by any method, and nothing in the rest of the grant sufficiently reveals a contrary intention.[1] Nor is this case like *Kirke La*

---

[1]The plaintiff points to paragraph 13 of the agreement, reproduced in the text, as indicating an intention to exclude television rights. The provision limits the rights of

Shelle Co. v. Paul Armstrong Co., 263 N.Y. 79, 188 N.E. 163 (1938), in which the new medium was completely unknown at the time when the contract was written. Rather, the trial court correctly found that, "During 1930 the future possibilities of television were recognized by knowledgeable people in the entertainment and motion picture industries," though surely not in the scope it has attained. While *Kirke La Shelle* teaches that New York will not charge a grantor with the duty of expressly saving television rights when he could not know of the invention's existence, we have found no case holding that an experienced businessman like Bartsch is not bound by the natural implications of the language he accepted when he had reason to know of the new medium's potential.[2]

Plaintiff, naturally enough, would not frame the issue in precisely this way. Instead, she argues that even in 1930 Warner Brothers often attempted to obtain an express grant of television rights and that its failure to succeed in Bartsch's case should persuade us that, despite the broad language, only established forms of exhibition were contemplated. She buttresses this argument by producing a number of 1930 assignments to Warner Brothers, some of which specifically granted the right to televise motion pictures and others of which granted full television rights, and by adducing testimony of the Warner Brothers lawyer who had approved the assignment from Bartsch that on many occasions Warner Brothers attempted to secure an express grant of such rights but did not always succeed.

However, this is not enough to show that the Bartsch assignments were a case of that sort. For all that appears Warner Brothers may have decided that, in dealing with Bartsch, it would be better tactics to rely on general words that were sufficiently broad rather than seek an express inclusion and perhaps end up with the opposite, or may have used a form regular in the industry without thinking very precisely about television, or — perhaps most likely — may simply have parroted the language in the grant from Bartsch's assignors to him on the theory it would thus be getting all he had, whatever that might be. Indeed, it is really the assignment to Bartsch rather than the one from him that must control. While plaintiff suggests that Warner Brothers may have furnished Bartsch the forms to be used with his assignors, this is sheer speculation. There is no showing that the form was unique to Warner Brothers; indeed the contrary appears.

With Bartsch dead, his grantors apparently so, and the Warner Brothers lawyer understandably having no recollection of the negotiation, any effort to reconstruct what the parties actually intended nearly forty years ago is

---

the assignee to those "specifically ... granted herein," and saves to Bartsch "all other rights now in existence or which may hereafter come into existence." We cannot read this as standing for more than the truism that whatever Bartsch had not granted, he had retained.

[2]In Ettore v. Philco Television Broadcasting Corp., 229 F.2d 481, *cert. denied,* 351 U.S. 926 (1956), the Third Circuit, applying Pennsylvania law, held that a 1935 contract granting moving picture rights did not permit the grantee to televise the film. However, unlike Bartsch, the grantor, Ettore, was not an experienced businessman but a prize fighter, and the Court relied heavily on his lack of sophistication in determining whether it was fair to charge him with knowledge of the new medium. *Id.* at 491, n. 14.

doomed to failure. In the end, decision must turn, as Professor Nimmer has suggested, The Law of Copyright § 125.3 (1964), on a choice between two basic approaches more than on an attempt to distill decisive meaning out of language that very likely had none. As between an approach that "a license of rights in a given medium (e.g., 'motion picture rights') includes only such uses as fall within the unambiguous core meaning of the term (e.g., exhibition of motion picture film in motion picture theaters) and exclude any uses which lie within the ambiguous penumbra (e.g., exhibition of motion picture film on television)" and another whereby "the licensee may properly pursue any uses which may reasonably be said to fall within the medium as described in the license," he prefers the latter. So do we. But see Warner, Radio and Television Rights § 52 (1953). If the words are broad enough to cover the new use, it seems fairer that the burden of framing and negotiating an exception should fall on the grantor; if Bartsch or his assignors had desired to limit "exhibition" of the motion picture to the conventional method where light is carried from a projector to a screen directly beheld by the viewer, they could have said so. A further reason favoring the broader view in a case like this is that it provides a single person who can make the copyrighted work available to the public over the penumbral medium, whereas the narrower one involves the risk that a deadlock between the grantor and the grantee might prevent the work's being shown over the new medium at all. Quite apart from the probable impracticality, the assignments are broad enough even on plaintiff's view to prevent the copyright owners from licensing anyone else to make a photoplay for telecasting. The risk that some May might find the nation's television screens bereft of the annual display of "Maytime," interlarded with the usual liberal diet of commercials, is not one a court can take lightly.

Affirmed.

QUESTIONS

1. Note the presumption by the court, near the end of its opinion, that a grant of rights to exploit a work should be construed in a reasonably all-embracing manner. In § 202 of the Copyright Act, in a not dissimilar setting, Congress adopted a different presumption with regard to transfers of a material object, which are to be treated as not transferring the copyright as well, even though that might limit the reproduction and exploitation of the work and generate conflicts between the owners of the two different rights. Does this suggest that the court's presumption in *Bartsch* is unsound?

2. Suppose an author grants "the exclusive, complete and entire motion picture rights" in a novel, licensing not only the production and theatrical exhibition of a "photoplay" based on the novel, but also "the right to broadcast and transmit any photoplay produced hereunder by the process of television." Does this grant cover a television *series* of photoplays? *See Goodis v. United Artists T.V.,* 425 F.2d 397 (2d Cir. 1970). Does it cover the filming of a sequel, using the same characters, after the making of an initial successful film? *See Trust Co. Bank v. MGM/UA Entertainment Co.,* 593 F. Supp. 580 (N.D. Ga. 1984).

3. Does a grant of "all book rights" include paperback books? Translations? Microform? Computer-readable disk? *Cf. Dolch v. Garrard Pub'g Co.,* 289 F. Supp. 687 (S.D.N.Y. 1968).

COHEN v. PARAMOUNT PICTURES CORP.

845 F.2d 851 (9th Cir. 1988)

Hug, Circuit Judge.

This case involves a novel issue of copyright law: whether a license conferring the right to exhibit a film "by means of television" includes the right to distribute videocassettes of the film. We hold it does not.

Facts

Herbert Cohen is the owner of the copyright in a musical composition entitled "Merry-Go-Round" (hereinafter "the composition"). On May 12, 1969, Cohen granted H&J Pictures, Inc., a "synchronization" license, which gave H&J the right to use the composition in a film called "Medium Cool" and to exhibit the film in theatres and on television. Subsequently, H&J assigned to Paramount Pictures all of its rights, title, and interest in the movie "Medium Cool," including all of the rights and interests created by the 1969 license from Cohen to H&J. Sometime later, Paramount furnished a negative of the film to a videocassette manufacturer, who made copies of the film — including a recording of the composition — and supplied these copies to Paramount. Paramount, in turn, sold approximately 2,725 videocassettes of the film, receiving a gross revenue of $69,024.26 from the sales.

On February 20, 1985, Cohen filed suit against Paramount in federal district court alleging copyright infringement. Cohen contended that the license granted to H&J did not confer the right to use the composition in a videocassette reproduction of the film. The parties stipulated to the facts and both filed motions for summary judgment. The district court entered judgment in favor of Paramount, and Cohen appeals....

. . . .

To resolve this case, we must examine the terms of the license, in order to determine whether the license conveyed the right to use the composition in videocassette reproductions of "Medium Cool." The document begins by granting the licensee the "authority ... to record, in any manner, medium, form or language, the words and music of the musical composition ... with ['Medium Cool'], *all in accordance* with the terms, conditions, and limitations hereinafter set forth ...." (Emphasis added.) Paragraph 4 states, "The ... license herein granted to perform ... said musical composition is granted for: (a) The exhibition of said motion picture ... to audiences in motion picture theatres .... (b) The exhibition of said motion picture ... *by means of television* ..., including 'pay television', 'subscription television' and 'closed circuit into homes' television...." (Emphasis added.) Finally, paragraph 6 of the license reserves to the grantor "all rights and uses in and to said musical composition, except those herein granted to the Licensee ...."

Notably, the license does not expressly grant rights to use the composition in connection with a videocassette reproduction of "Medium Cool." Paramount argues that this right is conferred by the language granting the licensee the authority to record "in any manner, medium, form or language" the composition with the film. This seemingly broad grant, however, is expressly subject to the limitations set forth thereafter. The authority to present the composition as part of the film is found in paragraph 4, and that paragraph expressly limits such presentation to two mediums: theatre and television. Unless videocassette production falls into either of those categories, the license does not authorize Paramount's actions, because paragraph 6 expressly reserves to the licensor all rights not granted by the terms of the license.

Not surprisingly, Paramount argues that videocassette display is the equivalent of "exhibition ... by means of television." We cannot agree. Though videocassettes may be displayed by using a television monitor, it does not follow that, for copyright purposes, videocassettes constitute "exhibition by television." Exhibition of a film on television differs fundamentally from exhibition by means of a videocassette recorder ("VCR"). Television requires an intermediary network, station, or cable to send the television signals into consumers' homes. The menu of entertainment appearing on television is controlled entirely by the intermediary and, thus, the consumer's selection is limited to what is available on various channels. Moreover, equipped merely with a conventional television set, a consumer has no means of capturing any part of the television display; when the program is over it vanishes, and the consumer is powerless to replay it. Because they originate outside the home, television signals are ephemeral and beyond the viewer's grasp.

Videocassettes, of course, allow viewing of a markedly different nature. Videocassette entertainment is controlled within the home, at the viewer's complete discretion. A consumer may view exactly what he or she wants (assuming availability in the marketplace) at whatever time he or she chooses. The viewer may even "fast forward" the tape so as to quickly pass over parts of the program he or she does not wish to view. By their very essence, then, videocassettes liberate viewers from the constraints otherwise inherent in television, and eliminate the involvement of an intermediary, such as a network.

Television and videocassette display thus have very little in common besides the fact that a conventional monitor of a television set may be used both to receive television signals and to display a videocassette. It is in light of this fact that Paramount argues that VCRs are equivalent to "exhibition by means of television." Yet, even that assertion is flawed. Playing a videocassette on a VCR does not require a standard television set capable of receiving television signals by cable or by broadcast; it is only necessary to have a monitor capable of displaying the material on the magnetized tape.

Perhaps the primary reason why the words "exhibition by means of television" in the license cannot be construed as including videocassette reproduction is that, although in use by the networks, VCRs for home use were not invented or known in 1969, when the license was executed. The parties both acknowledge this fact and it is noted in the order of the district judge. Thus, in 1969 — long before the market for videocassettes burgeoned — Cohen could not have assumed that the public would have free and virtually unlimited access to the film in which the composition was played; instead, he must have assumed that viewer access to the film "Medium Cool" would be largely controlled by theatres and networks. By the same token, the original licensee could not have bargained for, or paid for, the rights associated with videocassette reproduction. *See* Comment, Past Copyright Licenses and the New Video Software Medium, 29 U.C.L.A. L. Rev. 1160, 1184 (1982). The holder of the license should not now "reap the entire windfall" associated with the new medium. *See id.* As noted above, the license reserved to the grantor "all rights and uses in and to said musical composition, except those herein granted to the licensee ...." This language operates to preclude uses not then known to, or contemplated by the parties.

Moreover, the license must be construed in accordance with the purpose underlying federal copyright law. Courts have repeatedly stated that the Copyright Act was "intended definitively to grant valuable, enforceable rights to authors, publishers, etc., ... 'to afford greater encouragement to the production of literary works of lasting benefit to the world.'"... We would frustrate the purposes of the Act were we to construe this license — with its limiting language — as granting a right in a medium that had not been introduced to the domestic market at the time the parties entered into the agreement.

Paramount directs our attention to two district court cases, which, it contends, compel the opposite result. Both, however, involve licenses that contain language markedly different from the language in the license at hand.

Platinum Record Company, Inc. v. Lucasfilm, Ltd., 566 F. Supp. 226 (D.N.J. 1983), involved an agreement executed in 1973 in which plaintiff's predecessor in interest granted Lucasfilm, a film producer, the right to use four popular songs on the soundtrack of the motion picture *American Graffiti.* The agreement expressly conferred the right to "exhibit, distribute, exploit, market and perform said motion picture, its air, screen and television trailers, perpetually throughout the world *by any means or methods now or hereafter known.*" *Id.* at 227 (emphasis added). Lucasfilm produced *American Graffiti* under a contract with Universal. *Id.* The film was shown in theatres and on cable, network, and local television. In 1980, a Universal affiliate released the film for sale and rental to the public on videocassettes. *Id.* Plaintiffs brought suit against Universal and its affiliate, alleging that the agreement did not give them the right to distribute the film on videocassettes.

The district court granted summary judgment in favor of the defendants. *Id.* at 226. It reasoned that the language in the agreement conferring the right to exhibit the film "'by any means or methods now or hereafter known'" was "extremely broad and completely unambiguous, and precludes any need in the Agreement for an exhaustive list of specific potential uses of the film .... It is obvious that the contract in question may 'fairly be read' as including newly developed media, and the absence of any specific mention in the Agreement of videotapes and video cassettes is thus insignificant." *Id.* at 227.

Similarly, the district court in *Rooney v. Columbia Pictures Industries, Inc.,* 538 F. Supp. 211 (S.D.N.Y. 1982), *aff'd,* 714 F.2d 117 (2d Cir. 1982), *cert. denied,* 460 U.S. 1084 (1983) found that the contracts in question, which granted rights to exhibit certain films, also gave defendants the right to sell videocassettes of the films. *Id.* at 228. Like the contract in *Platinum,* the contracts in *Rooney* contained sweeping language, granting, for example, the right to exhibit the films "by any present or *future* methods or means," and by "any other means *now known or unknown.*" *Id.* at 223 (emphasis added). The court stated, "The contracts in question gave defendants extremely broad rights in the distribution and exhibition of [the films], plainly intending that such rights would be without limitation unless otherwise specified and further indicating that future technological advances in methods of reproduction, transmission, and exhibition would inure to the benefit of defendants." *Id.* at 228.

In contrast to the contracts in *Platinum* and *Rooney,* the license in this case lacks such broad language. The contracts in those cases expressly conferred the right to exhibit the films by methods yet to be invented. Not only is this language missing in the license at hand, but the license also expressly reserves to the copyright holder all rights not expressly granted. We fail to find the *Rooney* and *Platinum* decisions persuasive.[3]

Conclusion

We hold that the license did not give Paramount the right to use the composition in connection with videocassette production and distribution of the film "Medium Cool." The district court's award of summary judgment in favor of Paramount is reversed.

Reversed and remanded.

Tele-Pac, Inc. v. Grainger, 168 A.D.2d 11 (N.Y. App. Div., 1st Dep't 1991). The Supreme Court of New York, Appellate Division, ruled that a 1964 agreement that granted the right to distribute certain motion pictures "for broadcasting by television or any other similar device now known or hereafter to be made known" did not encompass the videocassette and videodisc rights to the subject motion pictures.

> The clause at issue does not itself expressly require transmission of sound and images from a point outside the home for reception by the general public — the definition of "broadcasting" which [the grantor] urges us to adopt. Nevertheless, we believe that such a transmission is implicit in the concept of "broadcasting by television." Conversely, while one may speak of "playing," "showing," "displaying" or even perhaps "exhibiting" a videotape, we are unaware of any usage of the term "broadcasting" in that context. The term must be construed in accordance with its plain and ordinary meaning. Even if we agree that videocassettes are "broadcast," the "broadcasting" device is a VCR or videocassette player, an entirely different device involving an entirely different concept and technology from that involved in a television broadcast.

---

[3] Paramount argues that those courts did not rest their holdings entirely on the broad language of the contracts, but that they also found, as a general proposition, that exhibition by means of a home videocassette player is equivalent to television exhibition. *See Rooney,* 538 F. Supp. at 228 ("As defendants point out, whether the exhibition apparatus is a home videocassette player or a television station's broadcast transmitter, the films are 'exhibited' as images on home television screens.") *See also Platinum,* 566 F. Supp. at 227-28. To the extent those courts may have equated exhibition by means of television with home video display, we reject their conclusions.

The New York court rejected attempts to distinguish the Ninth Circuit's decision in *Cohen*:

> *Cohen* cannot be distinguished on the ground that the 1964 grant involved herein does not, in contrast to the license in *Cohen*, explicitly reserve "all rights and uses in and to [the work in issue] except those herein granted." The right to "distribute films for broadcasting by television or any other similar device" is, by its own terms, sufficiently limited so that no express reservation of rights is required. [Grantee] points out that in *Cohen* the court found it significant that the parties "acknowledge[d]" that VCRs for home use were not invented or known in 1969 when the license therein was executed, while here, in contrast, [Grantee] argued before the court that such devices were well known in the entertainment business in 1964 and referred to contemporaneous news articles which announced the marketing of home video recorders (see, e.g., Oct. 1963 Popular Mechanics; Dec. 16, 1963 and July 15, 1964 Wall Street Journal). In *Cohen*, the parties' lack of knowledge was significant because of the grant's qualifying clause, which, since it reserved to the grantor all rights and uses "except those herein granted," was thus held to preclude all uses not then known to the parties. However, where, as here, the grant was limited by its own terms, the parties' knowledge or lack thereof of the new technology is of little significance.

QUESTIONS

1. Are *Bartsch* and *Cohen v. Paramount Pictures* consistent? Do the different results depend on the terms of the respective contracts? On the respectively then-applicable copyright laws? On the state of the pertinent technologies when the contracts were made?

2. Viewed through the lens of the copyright law, the Cohen-Paramount agreement explicitly conveyed two exclusive rights: one, the right to reproduce the copyrighted song in copies, by synchronization with the action of a film on its sound track; the other, the right of public performance, by exhibition in motion picture theaters and over television. Paramount needed the latter right so that it in turn could license theater owners and television stations to show the film containing the plaintiff's music. The dispute in the case arose because Paramount was exercising yet another exclusive right under the copyright law, i.e., the right to distribute copies of the song to the public by sale. Were the court's energies therefore misdirected in construing those provisions in the license agreement that dealt with the exhibition (i.e., public performance) right?

3. If you were contracting for a transfer of copyright interests, how, in light of *Bartsch*, *Cohen*, and *Tele-Pac*, would you draft the document to insure that you (the grantee) received the right to unknown future uses? If you were the grantor, how would you draft the contract to preserve your rights to future modes of exploitation?

"ARISING UNDER" COPYRIGHT OR CONTRACT LAW?

In *Bartsch,* according to Judge Friendly, the federal court had subject matter jurisdiction over Ms. Bartsch's claim of alleged copyright infringement. Nonetheless, defendant's contention that plaintiff did not own a copyright to be infringed raised a question which federal law did not govern. The *Bartsch* court ruled that state contract law governed the designation of the copyright owner of television exhibition rights to the motion picture at issue because construction of the contract would determine ownership of the disputed rights.

While state law may play an important, indeed potentially dispositive, role in a copyright infringement case in which ownership of the copyright may be placed at issue, so long as the complaint alleges infringement and seeks remedies under the federal Copyright Act, the controversy arises under federal copyright law. The Ninth Circuit has reaffirmed the application of the "well-pleaded complaint rule" to copyright cases. The court stated:

> The fact that [plaintiff] claims ownership of the copyrights through a contested contract governed by state law is not fatal to federal jurisdiction.... In fact, ownership will almost always be a threshold issue in a copyright infringement action. [Defendant's] intention to contest [plaintiff's] alleged ownership as part of its defense, regardless of any potential for success, does not affect jurisdiction.

Vestron, Inc. v. Home Box Office, Inc., 839 F.2d 1380 (9th Cir. 1988).

Recent Second Circuit decisions, however, cast doubt on the "well-pleaded complaint" rule, or at least narrow the class of grantors that will have standing to assert a copyright infringement claim as well as, or in lieu of, a contract claim. In *U.S. Naval Inst. v. Charter Commun., Inc.,* 936 F.2d 692 (2d Cir. 1991), the court held that the licensor of the exclusive right to distribute the work *The Hunt for Red October* could bring a claim for breach of contract, but not for copyright infringement, when the licensee distributed the work early in violation of the contract. The court determined that the licensor, having transferred an exclusive right, was no longer the copyright owner of that right, and therefore had no pertinent copyright to infringe. The court stated:

> Copyright "infringement is the violation of an owner's copyright interest by a non-owner.... It is elementary that the lawful owner of a copyright is incapable of infringing a copyright interest that is owned by him." *Cortner v. Israel,* 732 F.2d 267, 271 (2d Cir. 1984). Hence, an exclusive licensee of any of the rights comprised in the copyright, though it is capable of breaching the contractual obligations imposed on it by the license, cannot be liable for infringing the copyright rights conveyed to it. *See Fantastic Fakes, Inc. v. Pickwick International, Inc.,* 661 F.2d 479, 483-84 (5th Cir. Unit B 1981) ("mere breach of covenant may support a claim of damages for breach of contract but will not disturb the remaining rights and obligations under the license including the authority to use the copyrighted material"); *see also* 3 M. Nimmer & D. Nimmer, Nimmer on Copyright, § 12.02 at 12-29 (1990) ("Once the copyright owner grants an exclusive license of particular rights, only the exclusive licensee and not his grantor may sue for later occurring infringements of such rights.

Indeed, the licensor may be liable to the exclusive licensee for copyright infringement if the licensor exercises rights which have theretofore been exclusively licensed." (Footnote omitted.)).

On the other hand, the court also indicated that where the grantee has committed a material breach, the grantor may sue for rescission of the contract. Logically, if the contract is rescinded, the exclusive right under copyright returns to the grantor, and the grantor does have standing to allege copyright infringement. The court made this logic clear in *Schoenberg v. Shapolsky Pubs., Inc.*, 971 F.2d 926 (2d Cir. 1992), while adding yet another element to the analysis. The court distinguished between conditions and covenants: if a condition is breached, the contract fails, and the district court has subject matter jurisdiction over a copyright infringement claim. However, if the alleged breach is "merely" of a covenant, then "the court must next determine whether the breach is so material as to create a right of rescission in the grantor. If the breach would create a right of rescission, then the asserted claim arises under the Copyright Act."

Even under the Ninth Circuit's "well pleaded complaint" rule, the federal copyright infringement claim must be genuine. It must seek "statutory relief under federal copyright law, which, by virtue of [the federal courts'] exclusive jurisdiction, only a federal court can administer." *Vestron*. When the complaint is "couched in terms of copyright but ... in fact seek[s] to vindicate rights created under state law, e.g., contractual rights to ownership or royalties ... the suit should be dismissed for lack of subject matter jurisdiction." *Id*. Similarly, courts in the Second Circuit have also found federal jurisdiction wanting in actions to recover royalties from copyright grantees; such claims essentially seek enforcement of the contract, not relief under the Copyright Act. *See, e.g., Kelley v. April Music,* 1988 CCH Copyright L. Dec. ¶ 26,237 (S.D.N.Y. 1988). Note, however, that when the complaint seeks statutorily created royalties, such as those pursuant to a compulsory license, the federal courts have exclusive jurisdiction. *See, e.g., NBC, Inc. v. Copyright Royalty Tribunal,* 848 F.2d 1289, 1295 n.4 (D.C. Cir. 1988).

COPYRIGHT TRANSFER "BY OPERATION OF LAW"

What does a transfer of ownership "by operation of law," as contemplated in §§ 201(d) and 204(a), encompass? Can a copyright be the subject of an exercise of eminent domain? Section 201(e) would appear to preclude that result. On the other hand, that same section explicitly contemplates transfers of copyright as part of a bankruptcy sale or reorganization. Section 201(d) explicitly accommodates transfers of the decedent's copyright under state intestacy rules. What, if any, role in designating copyright ownership may state law play when the initial copyright holder is alive? May state community property laws step in to enforce a sharing of the copyright, or would application of such laws contravene § 201(e)?

A California appellate court, in deciding *In re Marriage of Susan M. & Frederick L. Worth,* 241 Cal. Rptr. 135, 195 Cal. App. 3d 768 (1st Dist. 1987), held that copyrights in works written during the marriage are community property; that § 201(d)(1) accommodates transfer of the copyright "by operation of law" from the husband, in whom the copyright initially vested, to the community; and that the federal copyright act does not preempt the application of state community property laws. The consequences of this result may be quite broad. If copyrights are community property, then a former (or, indeed, a present) spouse is entitled not merely to half of any royalties the community's copyrighted works may earn; the spouse is also, as a joint owner, as fully entitled as is the author to license or assign rights in the work, without first securing the author's agreement to the alienation of the rights under copyright. While the licensing spouse must account to the other co-owner (i.e., the author) for sums earned through the grant of rights, absent written agreement to the contrary the author has no independent right to veto or control the terms of the grant. Is it arguable that this result is inconsistent with the economic-incentive rationale of the Copyright Act, and the provisions in § 201(a) allocating initial ownership of copyright? *See* M. Nimmer & D. Nimmer, Nimmer on Copyright § 6:13; Patry, *Copyright and Community Property: The Question of Preemption,* 28 Bull. Copyright Soc'y 237 (1981).

---

§ 201. Ownership of copyright

. . . .

(c) *Contributions to Collective Works.* — Copyright in each separate contribution to a collective work is distinct from copyright in the collective work as a whole, and vests initially in the author of the contribution. In the absence of an express transfer of the copyright or of any rights under it, the owner of copyright in the collective work is presumed to have acquired only the privilege of reproducing and distributing the contribution as part of that particular collective work, any revision of that collective work, and any later collective work in the same series.

QUESTIONS

1. The above-quoted provision has induced many student-edited law reviews to prepare, and to proffer to authors of articles accepted for publication, contract forms containing a grant by the author of the copyright and all exclusive rights thereunder. If such a form contract were proffered to you for your signature, would you sign it? If not, what modifications to such a sweeping copyright grant would you in turn proffer to the law review?

2. If, on the other hand, you represented the law review, would you be content, in dealing with the authors of your articles, to forgo a formal written contract and to rely instead upon the allocation set forth in § 201(c)? (In the House Report, at page 123, for example, it states: "Under the language of [§ 201(c)] a publishing company could reprint a contribution from one issue in a later issue of its magazine, and could reprint an article from a 1980 edition of an encyclopedia in a 1990 revision of it; the publisher could not revise the contribution itself or include it in a new anthology or an entirely different magazine or other collective work.")

3. BENEFICIAL OWNERSHIP

Although a transfer of copyright divests the transferor of what might be called legal title, situations have arisen in which the transferor claims to continue to have "beneficial ownership." The 1976 Copyright Act, in § 501(b), gives explicit recognition to the concept of beneficial ownership, and gives such owner the right to sue for infringement: "The legal or beneficial owner of an exclusive right under a copyright is entitled ... to institute an action for any infringement of that particular right committed while he or she is the owner of it." The following case illustrates the most common kind of beneficial ownership; how far the concept goes beyond this core example is difficult to say.

FANTASY, INC. v. FOGERTY

654 F. Supp. 1129 (N.D. Cal. 1987)

CONTI, DISTRICT JUDGE.

Plaintiff brings this action against defendants John C. Fogerty and Wenaha Music Co., (collectively "Fogerty") and Fogerty's licensees, defendants WEA International, Inc. and Warner Bros. Records, Inc. (collectively "Warner") for copyright infringement.

In 1970, Fogerty wrote the song "Run Through the Jungle" ("Jungle"). Later, Fogerty granted the exclusive rights in the Jungle copyright to plaintiff's predecessors, Cireco Music and Galaxy Records. In return, Fogerty was to receive a sales percentage and other royalties derived from the plaintiff's exploitation of Jungle. In 1984, Fogerty wrote the song "The Old Man Down the Road" ("Old Man"). Fogerty registered a copyright to Old Man and then authorized Warner to distribute copies of Fogerty's performance of Old Man. Plaintiff claims Old Man is Jungle with new words and has sued for infringement.

This matter is presently before the court on Warner's motion for summary judgment on plaintiff's claim for copyright infringement. Warner argues that since co-owners of a copyright can not infringe that copyright, neither can a beneficial owner of that copyright. Warner contends that Fogerty is the beneficial owner of the Jungle copyright. Warner concludes that as the beneficial owner's authorized licensee, Warner also can not infringe upon plaintiff's interest in the Jungle copyright. Fogerty joins Warner's motion.

. . . .

17 U.S.C. § 101 defines a "copyright owner" as the holder of any one of the exclusive rights comprised in a copyright. The exclusive rights under a copyright include reproduction, preparation of derivative works, public performance or presentation, and distribution and sale. *See* 17 U.S.C. § 106. These exclusive rights can be transferred and owned separately. 17 U.S.C. § 201(d). A copyright owner can sue to protect any of these exclusive rights from infringement. 17 U.S.C. § 501(b). Note, a copyright owner can not infringe upon the particular interest owned by him; nor can a joint copyright owner sue his co-owner for infringement. *Cortner v. Israel,* 732 F.2d 267, 271 (2nd Cir. 1984); *Oddo v. Ries,* 743 F.2d 630, 633 (9th Cir. 1984). For the purposes of this

motion, Warner admits that plaintiff is the legal owner of the Jungle copyright. Memorandum in Support of Warner's Motion for Summary Judgment, p. 2.

A "beneficial owner" is defined as including "an author who had parted with legal title to the copyright in exchange for percentage royalties based on sales or license fees." *Cortner,* 732 F.2d at 271, *quoting,* H.R. Rep. No. 1476, 94th Cong., 2d Sess. 159, *reprinted in* 1976 U.S. Code Cong. & Ad. News 5659, 5775. A beneficial owner may bring an infringement action to protect his economic interest in the copyright from being diluted by a wrongdoer's infringement. 17 U.S.C. § 501(b); *Cortner,* 732 F.2d at 271. For the purposes of this motion, both Warner and plaintiff agree that Fogerty falls within the definition of a "beneficial owner" of the Jungle copyright. Memorandum in Support of Warner's Motion for Summary Judgment, p. 2; Memorandum in Opposition to Warner's Motion for Summary Judgment, p. 2.

Warner argues that the prohibition against infringement suits between co-owners of a copyright also prohibits an infringement suit by the legal owner of the copyright against the beneficial owner. Warner cites no authority for this proposition. Instead, Warner's authority supports the propositions (1) that a copyright owner or a joint copyright owner cannot infringe upon the particular copyright interest owned by them, *Oddo,* 743 F.2d at 632-33; *Cortner,* 732 F.2d at 271; *Richmond v. Weiner,* 353 F.2d 41, 46 (9th Cir. 1965), *cert. denied,* 384 U.S. 928, 86 S. Ct. 1447, 16 L. Ed. 2d 531 (1966); *Meredith v. Smith,* 145 F.2d 620, 621 (9th Cir. 1944); *Donna v. Dodd, Mead & Co.,* 374 F. Supp. 429, 430 (S.D.N.Y. 1974); and (2) that a beneficial owner has standing to bring an infringement suit to protect his economic interest in the copyright. 17 U.S.C. 501(b); *Kamakazi Corp. v. Robbins Music Corp.,* 534 F. Supp. 69, 73-74 (S.D.N.Y. 1982). Warner infers from this authority that since the beneficial owner has a "property interest" in the copyright and can enforce that interest through an infringement suit, prohibitions against infringement suits between copyright co-owners should also apply to suits between a copyright's legal owner and its beneficial owner. Defendant Warner's Reply Memorandum in Support of Motion for Summary Judgment, p. 3-8.

Warner's argument ignores the elementary rationale behind prohibiting infringement suits between copyright co-owners. As joint owners of such exclusive rights as reproduction, preparation of derivative works, public performance, and distribution and sale, each co-owner has "an independent right to use or license the use of the copyright." *Oddo,* 743 F.2d at 633. Thus, the prohibition against infringement suits between copyright co-owners is an outgrowth of the axiom that a copyright owner cannot infringe upon his own copyright. *See Richard,* 353 F.2d at 46.

On the other hand, "beneficial owners" do not have an independent right to use or license the use of the copyright. "Beneficial owners" are described as individuals who have given up these exclusive "use" rights in exchange for a sales percentage or royalties derived from the exploitation of the copyright. *See Cortner,* 732 F.2d at 271, *quoting,* H.R. Rep. No. 1476, 94th Cong., 2d Sess. 159, *reprinted in* 1976 U.S. Code Cong. & Ad. News 5659, 5775. A beneficial owner then has only an *economic interest* in the copyright. This economic interest extends merely to the proceeds derived from *the use of the copyright by its legal owner.*

Since a beneficial owner has no independent right to use or license the copyright, the beneficial owner can infringe upon the legal owner's exclusive rights. A copyright owner can infringe upon any exclusive right which he transfers or grants to another. *See Dodd, Mead & Co., Inc. v. Lilienthal,* 514 F. Supp. 105, 108 (S.D.N.Y. 1981) (publisher granted exclusive right to print, publish and sell book can sue author/grantor for infringement when author/grantor attempted to print and sell book). A beneficial owner has transferred his exclusive rights over the copyright's use in exchange for an economic interest in proceeds derived from that use. Therefore, if the beneficial owner attempts to exercise the exclusive "use" rights he has transferred, the legal owner of those exclusive rights may seek an action for infringement.

In the present case, Fogerty's beneficial interest in the Jungle copyright does not immunize him from an infringement suit brought by plaintiff. Fogerty conveyed all rights in the Jungle copyright to plaintiff's predecessors-in-interest in exchange for the right to receive royalties and a sales percentage. Declaration of Malcolm Burnstein, Exs. A & B. This transfer placed all exclusive rights concerning the use of the Jungle copyright under the plaintiff's sole ownership. *Id.* Therefore, if Fogerty's Old Man is a derivative work of Jungle, then Fogerty has exercised one of the exclusive rights that he previously granted to plaintiff. Under these facts, plaintiff could sue Fogerty for copyright infringement. Fogerty's status as a beneficial owner of the Jungle copyright does not change this conclusion.

Since plaintiff can bring an infringement action against Fogerty, Warner, as Fogerty's licensee, may also be liable to plaintiff for infringement. *See* 17 U.S.C. 501(a). Therefore, the court denies Warner's motion for summary judgment on plaintiff's first claim for relief.

In accordance with the foregoing, it is hereby ordered that: Warner's motion for summary judgment on plaintiff's first claim for relief is denied.

QUESTIONS

1. Author writes a scientific text in 1980, and in that year he assigns the copyright to Publisher in exchange for the payment of $10,000 (paid in two installments six months apart). In the publishing agreement, Publisher promises to reconvey the copyright to Author in the event all copies of the book are sold and Publisher decides not to reprint. (As the student will learn shortly, the 1980 transfer of copyright will be terminable by Author effective in 2015.) If Author learns today that the Pirate Publishing Company is making unauthorized copies of his book, may he bring a copyright infringement action as "beneficial owner"? *See Hearn v. Meyer,* 664 F. Supp. 832 (S.D.N.Y. 1987).

2. Author assigns copyright to Publisher in exchange for payment of royalties. Publisher, in need of a substantial loan, assigns the copyright (and Publisher's anticipated income therefrom) as security to Bank. It has been discovered that unauthorized copies of the book are being made and distributed. Who may sue for infringement? *See Hearst Corp. v. Stark,* 639 F. Supp. 970 (N.D. Cal. 1986).

Chapter 4

DURATION AND RENEWAL AND TERMINATION OF TRANSFERS

A. DURATION AND RENEWAL

1. THE POLICY DEBATE

CHAFEE, REFLECTIONS ON THE LAW OF COPYRIGHT, 45 Columbia Law Review 719-21, 725-27, 729-30 (1945)

a. *A long or a short monopoly?* Recall that our primary purpose is to benefit the author.* One's first impression is, that the longer the monopoly, the better for him. How far this is from being true was pointed out by Macaulay in 1841:[1]

> [T]he evil effects of the monopoly are proportioned to the length of its duration. But the good effects for the sake of which we bear with the evil effects are by no means proportioned to the length of its duration. A monopoly of sixty years produces twice as much evil as a monopoly of thirty years, and thrice as much evil as a monopoly of twenty years. But it is by no means the fact that a posthumous monopoly of sixty years gives to an author thrice as much pleasure and thrice as strong a motive as a posthumous monopoly of twenty years. On the contrary, the difference is so small as to be hardly perceptible. We all know how faintly we are affected by the prospect of very distant advantages, even when they are advantages which we may reasonably hope that we shall ourselves enjoy. But an advantage that is to be enjoyed more than half a century after we are dead, by somebody, we know not by whom, perhaps by somebody unborn, by somebody utterly unconnected with us, is really no motive at all to action.... Considered as a boon to [authors, long posthumous duration of the copyright monopoly] is a mere nullity; but, considered as an impost on the public, it is no nullity, but a very serious and pernicious reality. I will take an example. Dr. Johnson died fifty-six years ago. If the law [prolonged the copyright for sixty years after the author's death], somebody would now have the monopoly of Dr. Johnson's works. Who that somebody would be it is impossible to say; but we may venture to guess. I guess, then, that it would have been some bookseller, who was the assign of another bookseller, who was the grandson of a third bookseller, who had bought the copyright from Black Frank, the Doctor's servant and residuary legatee, in 1785 or 1786. Now, would the knowl-

---

But see the excerpts at pp. 19-20, *supra*. — Eds.
[1] 8 Macaulay, Works (Trevelyan ed. 1879) 199-201 (hereafter cited as Works).

edge that this copyright would exist in 1841 have been a source of gratification to Johnson? Would it have stimulated his exertions? Would it have once drawn him out of his bed before noon? Would it have once cheered him under a fit of the spleen? Would it have induced him to give us one more allegory, one more life of a poet, one more imitation of Juvenal? I firmly believe not. I firmly believe that a hundred years ago, when he was writing our debates for the Gentleman's Magazine, he would very much rather have had twopence to buy a plate of shin of beef at a cook's shop underground. Considered as a reward to him, the difference between a twenty years' term and a sixty years' term of posthumous copyright would have been nothing or next to nothing. But is the difference nothing to us? I can buy Rasselas for sixpence; I might have had to give five shillings for it. I can buy the Dictionary, the entire genuine Dictionary, for two guineas, perhaps for less; I might have had to give five or six guineas for it. Do I grudge this to a man like Dr. Johnson? Not at all. Show me that the prospect of this boon roused him to any vigorous effort, or sustained his spirits under depressing circumstances, and I am quite willing to pay the price of such an object, heavy as that price is. But what I do complain of is that my circumstances are to be worse, and Johnson's none the better; that I am to give five pounds for what to him was not worth a farthing.

Johnson was a childless widower, and it may be supposed that an author with a widow and progeny would care more about a prolonged monopoly. Yet Macaulay tells us[2] that in the middle of the eighteenth century when the common law copyright on Milton's Works was supposed to be perpetual, Milton's grand-daughter had to be relieved from abject poverty by a benefit performance of *Comus* at the very time that the publisher who owned Milton's Works was enjoining a pirate in Chancery. Milton had sold his perpetual rights to the booksellers for cash down, and whatever happened after that was of no use to him or his family.

Plainly the kind of pecuniary bargain which the author makes with his publisher is a vital fact in determining whether a long monopoly is of value to the author or not. If the author makes a royalty agreement for the life of the copyright, then he and his family will gain, the longer it is. But if the author sells his rights for a lump sum, the only value to him from length depends on whether it enhances the price which the publisher pays. Given the speculative nature of publishing, the price is not likely to be affected by the difference between fifty-six years, let us say, and life plus fifty years. How much more would any publisher pay for the right to monopolize after fifty-six years a book brought out in 1945? As Birrell says,[3] "The money market takes short views." A businessman remarked to J. M. Maguire that for him "fifteen years was eternity."[4] The publisher must have always shaped his lump-sum offer

---

[2]*Id.* at 203.

[3]Birrell, Seven Lectures on the Law and History of Copyright in Books (1899) 25. The whole passage, 23-26, is excellent.

[4]Maguire, Capitalization of Periodical Payments by Gift (1920) 34 Harv. L. Rev. 20, 40.

according to his expectation of sales within the first few years of the copyright. That is when he makes his killing. This is probably truer today than ever, because of the rapid waning of most books and songs. Where are the Hit Parades of yesteryear? Leave out classics and lawbooks — how many books published before 1940 did lawyers read during 1944? Good publishing accounting writes off all books within three years after publication as no longer an asset. Rudy Vallee keeps *The Maine Stein Song* alive and the current motion picture *To The Victor* is drawn from a dog-story of 1898, but such resurrections are too problematical to raise the lump-sum price for a new book or song. Royalties, however, reflect the ups-and-downs of sales....

Therefore, the last part of a long copyright does no good to the author who sells all his rights at once. It really taxes the readers for the benefit of the publisher. He gets a windfall for which he paid practically nothing. A long term is desirable only if the author and his family are sure to get the benefit of the latter years. The law can accomplish this in various ways. It can require a royalty contract, at least for the latter years; or it can make rights in those years revert to the author and limit the effect of an outright sale to the early part of the copyright. The Act of 1909 attempts to use the second method, how successfully we shall now ask.

....

c. *Should all the incidents of the author's monopoly pass to his surviving family?* Insofar as copyright yields pecuniary benefits to the author, these should pass to his family on his death. Copyright, however, involves several non-pecuniary rights which are much more useful in the hands of the author than in the hands of those who did not create the work.

The author has the power to keep a copyrighted work off the market entirely. It is right for him to decide whether what he has created shall be published or not. Thus when Southey in his flaming youth entrusted the manuscript of a revolutionary poem on Wat Tyler to a bookseller, who after years of inaction proposed to publish it when Southey had become a sedate poet laureate, it was harsh on him to lose his injunction on the ground that a revolutionary author did not come into equity with clean hands.[11] Yet the veto power of the copyright owner loses most of its desirability on the author's death and may become a nuisance when it passes to his descendants.

... Yet the 1909 Act gives a posthumous veto power to the surviving relatives, perhaps for decades. They have the same control of his unpublished works under the common law of literary property. The letters of James McNeill Whistler are lost to the world because his crabbed niece would not allow his chosen biographers to print them.[14] Suppose that the manuscript of a new poem by Poe should be discovered tomorrow. His descendants could keep it hidden if they so desired, and according to judicial *dicta* they could do so forever. The British statute avoids this dog-in-the-manger situation. It gives copyright for life plus fifty years; but after the author has been dead twenty-five years, anybody can publish his work on paying a 10 per cent

---

[11]Southey v. Sherwood, 2 Mer. 435, 35 Eng. Rep. 1006 (1817).
[14]Phillip v. Pennell, [1907] 2 Ch. 577; 1 Pennell, Life of James McNeill Whistler (1908) xxiv.

royalty to the copyright owner. This not only prevents the family from bury-
ing the book, but also keeps a single publisher from controlling it exclusively
and charging high prices. And even during the first twenty-five years, if the
copyright-owner has let a book go out of print or refused to allow the public
performance of a play, a compulsory license may be ordered on terms fixed by
the Judicial Committee of the Privy Council.[15]

... (In) order to protect the public from the evil of garbled editions of the
books of a dead author, a distinguished novelist and essayist desires to prolong copyright far beyond the English period of 50 years after death, and even
make it perpetual. In *The House of Macmillan*, Charles Morgan writes:

> That the public interest is, in fact, served by throwing a great writer's
> work to the wolves and depriving his representatives of control of it is a
> delusion.... The only plausible argument for the present system rests
> upon the notion that, if an author's heirs are deprived of copyright, his
> books will be more easily and cheaply available to the public, and this
> notion is false....
>
> [B]y depriving an author's work of copyright within a few decades of his
> death ... there is nothing to prevent its being garbled or bowdlerized,
> nothing to induce any publisher with a long view to nurse a work of art or
> scholarship during the periods when it is out of fashion, and, since reduc-
> tion of the price of a book depends much more upon one publisher's assur-
> ance of a steady market than upon a sacrifice of the author's royalty,
> there is a tendency to raise prices against the public rather than to lower
> them.... Apart from any financial consideration, it is to the public advan-
> tage that works of literature should be protected from those whose habit
> is to mutilate or misapply them, and that the author's representative and
> one publisher should have power and interest to do so.[23]

Morgan's attitude is the opposite of Macaulay's. Macaulay wants a short
copyright period because he is afraid that the owner after an author's death
will be a dog in the manger. Morgan wants a long period because he is sure
that the surviving owner will be a watch dog. I think that it is just a matter of
chance what kind of a dog you get. If all publishers were as fond of "a steady,
long-term and consistent enterprise" as the founders of the House of Macmillan, perhaps we could safely entrust to them the supervision of an author's
works forever. Unfortunately, many publishers are disposed to sleep on their
rights when the author is no longer able to write letters demanding a new
edition. Thus Henry James is one of the greatest of American novelists and
constantly the object of attention; and yet the owners of his remaining copyrights have shown little interest in making his books accessible to the public
in cheap editions or indeed any editions at all. His publishers are probably too
busy with authors of a later vintage. Who believes that a perpetual copyright

---

[15]Copyright Act, 1911, 1 & 2 Geo. V, c. 46, §§ 3, 4. This device of compulsory licenses
originated in the early seventies with Sir Thomas Henry Farrer, a distinguished civil
servant. See Supplement I, 2 Dict. Nat. Biog. 201. Birrell, *op. cit. supra* note 3, at 207,
calls it "This preposterous scheme ... knocked on the head by Mr. Herbert Spencer...."
But it became law twelve years after Birrell wrote.

[23]Morgan, The House of Macmillan (1944) 174-177.

would spur them into activity? The best prospect for popular reprints of Henry James lies in the fact that everything he wrote will soon be in the public domain....

Therefore, I conclude that the copyright period after an author's death should be roughly limited by the lives of his children, subject perhaps to compulsory licensing in order to prevent them from keeping his books off the market. The evil of garbled editions is not sufficiently serious to justify the imposition of a possible tax on readers for the benefit of his remote descendants and a monopolizing publisher. Simpler remedies for this evil are the production of adequate new editions by good publishers, and the alertness of book-reviewers and scholars, who ought to denounce vigorously any publisher of a mangled edition.

Another question at issue in the copyright duration debate concerns the choice between fixed terms measured from publication of each work, or a single indefinite term calculated with respect to the author's life/death. The 1909 Act opted for fixed terms of twenty-eight years. Under this system, each work received protection for the same period of time (assuming timely renewals). By the same token, the *corpus* of an author's work would not fall into the public domain at one single date; protection expired in staggered fashion, following the successive publications of each work. Measuring copyright duration from the author's death thus provides the convenience of a uniform public domain date for all of an author's writings (subject to transitional provisions regarding pre-1978 unpublished works). On the other hand, while the author is still alive, this kind of term is indefinite. Lord Macaulay found a further kind of fault with copyright terms whose expiration is calculated from the author's death. In a Speech to the House of Commons, April 6, 1842, Macaulay objected to a bill which would have extended copyright protection till twenty-five years following the author's death. Beginning from the premise that "the protection which we give to books ought to be distributed as evenly as possible, that every book should have a fair share of that protection, and no book more than a fair share," Macaulay complained that granting copyright protection to all of an author's works until twenty-five years after death would be worse than a lottery in which the periods of protection for different works were determined by chance. He suggested that the proposed bill would in fact have the effect of protecting the least valuable of an author's works, the fruits of youth, longer than the outstanding works of his mature years. *See* 1 T.B. Macaulay, *Speeches, Poems & Miscellaneous Writings* 677, 681, 683-85 (Longmans 1898).

HOUSE REPORT

H.R. Rep. No. 94-1476, 94th Cong., 2d Sess. 133-36 (1976)

The debate over how long a copyright should last is as old as the oldest copyright statute and will doubtless continue as long as there is a copyright law. With certain exceptions, there appears to be strong support for the principle, as embodied in the bill, of a copyright term consisting of the life of the author and 50 years after his death. In particular, the authors and their representatives stressed that the adoption of a life-plus-50 term was by far their most important legislative goal in copyright law revision. The Register of Copyrights now regards a life-plus-50 term as the foundation of the entire bill.

Under the present law statutory copyright protection begins on the date of publication (or on the date of registration in unpublished form) and continues for 28 years from that date; it may be renewed for a second 28 years, making a total potential term of 56 years in all cases.[1] The principal elements of this system — a definite number of years, computed from either publication or registration, with a renewal feature — have been a part of the U.S. copyright law since the first statute in 1790. The arguments for changing this system to one based on the life of the author can be summarized as follows:

1. The present 56-year term is not long enough to insure an author and his dependents the fair economic benefits from his works. Life expectancy has increased substantially, and more and more authors are seeing their works fall into the public domain during their lifetimes, forcing later works to compete with their own early works in which copyright has expired.

2. The tremendous growth in communications media has substantially lengthened the commercial life of a great many works. A short term is particularly discriminatory against serious works of music, literature, and art, whose value may not be recognized until after many years.

3. Although limitations on the term of copyright are obviously necessary, too short a term harms the author without giving any substantial benefit to the public. The public frequently pays the same for works in the public domain as it does for copyrighted works, and the only result is a commercial windfall to certain users at the author's expense. In some cases the lack of copyright protection actually restrains dissemination of the work, since publishers and other users cannot risk investing in the work unless assured of exclusive rights.

4. A system based on the life of the author would go a long way toward clearing up the confusion and uncertainty involved in the vague concept of "publication," and would provide a much simpler, clearer method for computing the term. The death of the author is a definite, determinable event, and it would be the only date that a potential user would have to worry about. All of a particular author's works, including successive revisions of them, would fall into the public domain at the same time, thus avoiding the present problems of determining a multitude of publication dates and of distinguishing "old" and "new" matter in later editions. The bill answers the problems of determining when relatively obscure authors

---

[1]Under Public Laws 87-668, 89-142, 90-141, 90-416, 91-147, 91-555, 92-170, 92-566, and 93-573, copyrights that were subsisting in their renewal term on September 19, 1962, and that were scheduled to expire before Dec. 31, 1976, have been extended to that later date, in anticipation that general revision legislation extending their terms still further will be enacted by then.

died, by establishing a registry of death dates and a system of presumptions.

5. One of the worst features of the present copyright law is the provision for renewal of copyright. A substantial burden and expense, this unclear and highly technical requirement results in incalculable amounts of unproductive work. In a number of cases it is the cause of inadvertent and unjust loss of copyright. Under a life-plus-50 system the renewal device would be inappropriate and unnecessary.

6. Under the preemption provisions of section 301 and the single Federal system they would establish, authors will be giving up perpetual, unlimited exclusive common law rights in their unpublished works, including works that have been widely disseminated by means other than publication. A statutory term of life-plus-50 years is no more than a fair recompense for the loss of these perpetual rights.

7. A very large majority of the world's countries have adopted a copyright term of the life of the author and 50 years after the author's death. Since American authors are frequently protected longer in foreign countries than in the United States, the disparity in the duration of copyright has provoked considerable resentment and some proposals for retaliatory legislation. Copyrighted works move across national borders faster and more easily than virtually any other economic commodity, and with the techniques now in common use this movement has in many cases become instantaneous and effortless. The need to conform the duration of U.S. copyright to that prevalent throughout the rest of the world is increasingly pressing in order to provide certainty and simplicity in international business dealings. Even more important, a change in the basis of our copyright term would place the United States in the forefront of the international copyright community. Without this change, the possibility of future United States adherence to the Berne Copyright Union would evaporate, but with it would come a great and immediate improvement in our copyright relations. All of these benefits would accrue directly to American and foreign authors alike.

The need for a longer total term of copyright has been conclusively demonstrated....

No country in the world has provisions on the duration of copyright like ours. Virtually every other copyright law in the world bases the term of protection for works by natural persons on the life of the author, and a substantial majority of these accord protection for 50 years after the author's death. This term is required for adherence to the Berne Convention. It is worth noting that the 1965 revision of the copyright law of the Federal Republic of Germany adopted a term of life plus 70 years.

A point that has concerned some educational groups arose from the possibility that, since a large majority (now about 85 percent) of all copyrighted works are not renewed, a life-plus-50 year term would tie up a substantial body of material that is probably of no commercial interest but that would be more readily available for scholarly use if free of copyright restrictions. A statistical study of renewal registrations made by the Copyright Office in 1966 supports the generalization that most material which is considered to be of continuing or potential commercial value is renewed. Of the remainder, a certain proportion is of practically no value to anyone, but there are a large number of unrenewed works that have scholarly value to historians, archivists, and specialists in a variety of fields. This consideration lay behind the proposals for retaining the renewal device or for limiting the term for unpublished or unregistered works.

It is true that today's ephemera represent tomorrow's social history, and that works of scholarly value, which are now falling into the public domain after 29 [sic] years, would be protected much longer under the bill. Balanced against this are the burdens and expenses of renewals, the near impossibility of distinguishing between types of works in fixing a statutory term, and the extremely strong case in favor of a life-plus-50 system. Moreover, it is important to realize that the bill would not restrain scholars from using any work as source material or from making "fair use" of it; the restrictions would extend only to the unauthorized reproduction or distribution of copies of the work, its public performance, or some other use that would actually infringe the copyright owner's exclusive rights. The advantages of a basic term of copyright enduring for the life of the author and for 50 years after the author's death outweigh any possible disadvantages.

2. COPYRIGHT DURATION UNDER THE 1976 ACT

a. Works Created or Unpublished After 1977

§ 302. Duration of copyright: Works created on or after January 1, 1978

(a) *In General* — Copyright in a work created on or after January 1, 1978, subsists from its creation and, except as provided by the following subsections, endures for a term consisting of the life of the author and fifty years after the author's death.

(b) *Joint Works* — In the case of a joint work prepared by two or more authors who did not work for hire, the copyright endures for a term consisting of the life of the last surviving author and fifty years after such last surviving author's death.

(c) *Anonymous Works, Pseudonymous Works, and Works Made for Hire* — In the case of an anonymous work, a pseudonymous work, or a work made for hire, the copyright endures for a term of seventy-five years from the year of its first publication, or a term of one hundred years from the year of its creation, whichever expires first....

(d) *Records Relating to Death of Authors* — Any person having an interest in a copyright may at any time record in the Copyright Office a statement of the date of death of the author of the copyrighted work, or a statement that the author is still living on a particular date....

(e) *Presumption as to Author's Death* — After a period of seventy-five years from the year of first publication of a work, or a period of one hundred years from the year of its creation, whichever expires first, any person who obtains from the Copyright Office a certified report that the records provided by subsection (d) disclose nothing to indicate that the author of the work is living, or died less than fifty years before, is entitled to the benefit of a presumption that the author has been dead for at least fifty years. Reliance in good faith upon this presumption shall be a complete defense to any action for infringement under this title.

HOUSE REPORT

H.R. Rep. No. 94-1476, 94th Cong., 2d Sess. 136-38 (1976)

Basic copyright term

Under subsection (a) of section 302, a work "created" on or after the effective date of the revised statute would be protected by statutory copyright "from its creation" and, with exceptions to be noted below, "endures for a term consisting of the life of the author and 50 years after the author's death."...

Anonymous works, pseudonymous works, and works made for hire

Computing the term from the author's death also requires special provisions to deal with cases where the authorship is not revealed or where the "author" is not an individual. Section 302(c) therefore provides a special term for anonymous works, pseudonymous works, and works made for hire: 75 years from publication or 100 years from creation, whichever is shorter.... [These alternative terms] are necessary to set a time limit on protection of unpublished material. For example, copyright in a work created in 1978 and published in 1988 would expire in 2063 (75 years from publication). A question arises as to when the copyright should expire if the work is never published. Both the Constitution and the underlying purposes of the bill require the establishment of an alternative term for unpublished works and the only practicable basis for this alternative is "creation." Under the bill a work created in 1980 but not published until after 2005 (or never published) would fall into the public domain in 2080 (100 years after creation).

The definition in section 101 provides that "creation" takes place when a work "is fixed in a copy or phonorecord for the first time." Although the concept of "creation" is inherently lacking in precision, its adoption in the bill would, for example, enable a scholar to use an unpublished manuscript written anonymously, pseudonymously, or for hire, if he determines on the basis of internal or external evidence that the manuscript is at least 100 years old. In the case of works written over a period of time or in successive revised versions, the definition provides that the portion of the work "that has been fixed at any particular time constitutes the work as of that time," and that, "where the work has been prepared in different versions, each version constitutes a separate work." Thus, a scholar or other user, in attempting to determine whether a particular work is in the public domain, needs to look no further than the particular version he wishes to use.

Although "publication" would no longer play the central role assigned to it under the present law, the concept would still have substantial significance under provisions throughout the bill, including those on Federal preemption and duration. Under the definition in section 101, a work is "published" if one or more copies or phonorecords embodying it are distributed to the public —

that is, generally to persons under no explicit or implicit restrictions with respect to disclosure of its contents — without regard to the manner in which the copies or phonorecords changed hands. The definition clears up the question of whether the sale of phonorecords constitutes publication, and it also makes plain that any form of dissemination in which a material object does not change hands — performances or displays on television, for example — is not a publication no matter how many people are exposed to the work. On the other hand, the definition also makes clear that, when copies or phonorecords are offered to a group of wholesalers, broadcasters, motion picture theaters, etc., publication takes place if the purpose is "further distribution, public performance, or public display."...

QUESTIONS

1. Would it be feasible to have different periods of copyright protection for different classes of works (e.g., artistic designs of useful articles, news photographs, compilations of public domain data)? A number of foreign nations so provide. Why has Congress chosen not to do so?

2. What are the benefits and detriments of having the copyrights in all of an author's works terminate at the same time? What are the reasons for having the copyright of some works measured by the author's life and the copyright of other works measured from the creation or publication of those works?

3. Will the "limited times" feature of the law of copyright be substantially frustrated by collaborations between an author and much younger joint authors?

4. By virtue of the renewal format under the 1909 Act, a great many copyrights terminated a mere twenty-eight years after publication. Indeed, it was probably a contemplated benefit in the public interest thus to shorten the copyright term. Has Congress, then, provided adequate justification for extending copyright protection for almost all works created after January 1, 1978 to the life of the author plus fifty years?

5. In light of the European Community's recent adoption of a Life-Plus-70 copyright term, the U.S. Copyright Office is holding hearings on a proposal similarly to extend the U.S. term. (The standard copyright term in Brazil and Spain, for example, is life plus 60 years; and in Austria and Germany it is life plus 70 years.) Apart from considerations of international trade and reciprocity, is there any good reason for the U.S. Copyright Office and Congress to support such an extension of copyright duration?

----

§ 303. Duration of copyright: Works created but not published or copyrighted before January 1, 1978

Copyright in a work created before January 1, 1978, but not theretofore in the public domain or copyrighted, subsists from January 1, 1978, and endures for the term provided by section 302. In no case, however, shall the term of copyright in such a work expire before December 31, 2002; and, if the work is published on or before December 31, 2002, the term of copyright shall not expire before December 31, 2027.

HOUSE REPORT

H.R. Rep. No. 94-1476, 94th Cong., 2d Sess. 138-39 (1976)

Theoretically, at least, the legal impact of section 303 would be far reaching. Under it, every "original work of authorship" fixed in tangible form that is in existence would be given statutory copyright protection as long as the work is not in the public domain in this country. The vast majority of these works consist of private material that no one is interested in protecting or infringing, but section 303 would still have practical effects for a prodigious body of material already in existence.

Looked at another way, however, section 303 would have a genuinely restrictive effect. Its basic purpose is to substitute statutory for common law copyright for everything now protected at common law, and to substitute reasonable time limits for the perpetual protection now available. In general, the substituted time limits are those applicable to works created after the effective date of the law; for example, an unpublished work written in 1945 whose author dies in 1980 would be protected under the statute from the effective date through 2030 (50 years after the author's death).

A special problem under this provision is what to do with works whose ordinary statutory terms will have expired or will be nearing expiration on the effective date. The committee believes that a provision taking away subsisting common law rights and substituting statutory rights for a reasonable period is fully in harmony with the constitutional requirements of due process, but it is necessary to fix a "reasonable period" for this purpose. Section 303 provides that under no circumstances would copyright protection expire before December 31, 2002, and also attempts to encourage publication by providing 25 years more protection (through 2027) if the work were published before the end of 2002.

Unlike the 1909 Act, which dated its 28-year and 56-year periods from the precise date of publication (and, in connection with certain unpublished works, the date of registration in the Copyright Office) — including the day and month — the 1976 Act provides, in Section 305: "All terms of copyright provided by sections 302 through 304 run to the end of the calendar year in which they would otherwise expire." The purpose, as stated in the House Report, was to "make the duration of copyright much easier to compute." This was a matter of particular pertinence in determining when an application for renewal of copyright had to be filed with the Copyright Office; it is considerably less significant today, for reasons that will appear below, but it still remains of some importance.

b. 1976 Act Treatment of Works First Published Under the 1909 Act

RENEWAL

A distinctive feature of our copyright law since its inception until 1978 was the renewal term, which the copyright owner could secure after a relatively short initial term upon timely re-registration. The Statute of Anne of 1710 provided, for works to be published thereafter, an initial term of fourteen years and a renewal term of equal length. Initial and renewal terms of fourteen years were also featured in the first United States Copyright Act of 1790. In both that statute and its British antecedent, renewal was not available unless the author survived through the first copyright term. In 1831, the initial term was expanded to twenty-eight years, and under the 1909 Act both the initial and renewal terms ran for twenty-eight years. To secure the benefit of the renewal term, an application had to be filed within the last year of the initial term. The purposes of the renewal format will be explored presently, but it should be noted here that its effect, because of the significant proportion of copyrighted works for which renewal was not sought, was a rather short period of copyright protection for many works. While almost all copyright laws in the world were adopting a lengthy period of protection, usually measured by the life of the author plus fifty years, the United States, all but alone, retained the renewal format until 1978.

Under the 1909 Act, it was provided that the renewal term could be claimed by the author if he or she survived the initial term (or at least until the date in the twenty-eighth year when renewal was sought; the statute was altogether silent about such details). If the author had died, then the right to claim the renewal passed successively to three other statutory beneficiaries — the surviving spouse or children, or for lack of those the author's executor, or in the absence of a will the author's next of kin. Exceptions to this statutory sequence were provided for a limited number of categories of works. The details, purposes and implications of these provisions are discussed in the following study prepared in connection with the revision of the 1909 Act.

Although that act was in almost all significant respects superseded by the 1976 Act, renewal of copyright for pre-1978 works — in precisely the manner, and by precisely the same person, as provided by § 24 of the 1909 Act — remained a central feature of the 1976 Act, in § 304(a) as originally enacted. The 28-year duration of the renewal term was, however, increased to 47 years, so that timely renewal would lead to copyright protection for 75 years rather than 56. As was true under the 1909 Act, the renewal term came into being only if an application for renewal registration was filed with the Copyright Office. That feature of the law was, however, significantly changed in 1992, when Congress provided for automatic renewal of works whose first terms would expire following passage of the amendment. Thus, renewal at the initiative of a copyright claimant is no longer required for pre-1978 works published in or after 1964 (but, as we shall see, *infra*, whether the renewal is automatic or voluntary still carries important consequences for, inter alia, ownership of renewal term rights).

RINGER, RENEWAL OF COPYRIGHT, in STUDIES ON COPYRIGHT (Fisher mem. ed. 1960) (Study No. 31)

. . . .

The Nature and Theoretical Basis of Renewal Copyright

The renewal copyright established in the Act of 1831 and elaborated in the Act of 1909 is a unique form of property whose nature and theoretical basis are still unclear. The courts and the commentators have repeatedly characterized a renewal as a "new estate" or a "new grant" rather than a mere continuation or extension. Renewals are said to be separate from and independent of the original copyright, to be "free and clear of any rights, interests, or licenses attached to the copyright for the initial term," and to have "absolutely all of the attributes of a new work copyrighted at the time the renewal is effected." The right of renewal is considered a personal right given directly to certain named beneficiaries; it "does not follow the author's estate but ... is derived directly from the statute."

These generalizations, though mostly true, have suffered from too much uncritical repetition. To get at what renewals really are, one must look closely at what Congress wanted to do, what it said in the statute, and what the courts have said the statute means.

The legislative history shows that, in retaining the reversionary aspect of renewals, Congress was trying to accomplish two things:

1) If the author were still living, Congress wanted to give him an opportunity to benefit from the success of his work and to renegotiate disadvantageous bargains. It has often been said that the renewal provision was based on "the familiar imprudence of authors in commercial matters." While superficially logical, there is nothing in the legislative history to support this supposition. There is more evidence of a Congressional recognition that author-publisher contracts must frequently be made at a time when the value of the work is unknown or conjectural and the author (regardless of his business ability) is necessarily in a poor bargaining position.[128]

2) If the author were dead, Congress wanted to insure that his "dependent relatives"[129] would receive the benefits of the renewal, regardless of any agreements the author had entered into.

To attain these results Congress had to depart from ordinary concepts of property in two important respects:

1) *Reversion.* The statute had to break the continuity of title at the end of the first term and provide for a reversion of ownership to the author, if living.

2) *Statutory designation of beneficiaries.* To make sure that the renewal benefits went to "those naturally dependent upon the deceased author's bounty," something more than a reversion to the author's "executors, administrators, or heirs" had to be provided. If the renewal reverted to the author's estate, it was entirely possible that legatees and creditors might gain the

---

[128]See H.R. Rep. No. 2222, 60th Cong., 2d Sess. 15 (1909); Comment, 33 N.Y.U.L. Rev. 1027, 1029 n.20 (1958); 6 U. Det. L.J. 79, 83-84 (1943)....

[129]S. Rep. No. 6187, 59th Cong., 2d Sess. 8 (Pt. I, 1907).

benefits at the expense of the author's family and dependents. Apparently in a deliberate effort to avoid this result, Congress set up a schedule of successive classes of persons who were entitled to take the renewal as "a new personal grant of a right."

These features made renewals so unusual that, immediately after the 1909 Act came into effect, there was uncertainty whether this could really be what Congress intended. Within a few years, however, it had been firmly established that a proprietor or assignee, as such, had no right in a renewal copyright, that the right was a personal one, and that a renewal is not "really and truly an extension to the author, his assigns, executors, and administrators, but a new grant to the author or others enumerated."

Acceptance of these basic principles still left open some important questions:

1) *Is a future copyright assignable?* Assuming that assignment of the first term does not carry with it the renewal copyright, can the author or any other statutory beneficiary make a valid separate assignment of his potential renewal copyright before he has secured it? This turned out to be a very close question, which the Supreme Court finally settled in favor of alienability.[135]

2) *Whom does the executor represent?* The executor is different from the author's widow, children, and next of kin, since he obviously cannot take the renewal for his own personal benefit. Does he take it as representative of (1) the author, (2) the corpus of the author's estate, or (3) the legatees? The cases have now established that the executor represents neither the author[136] nor the author's estate,[137] but that he takes the renewal as personal representative or trustee of the author's legatees; since the renewal does not become part of the author's estate, an assignment by the author of his renewal rights would be invalidated at the author's death, and the executor would take the renewal for the benefit of the author's legatees rather than his assignees. The decisions, culminating in a recent 5-4 holding by the Supreme Court, thus indicate a most unusual role for the executor....

Rights of Statutory Renewal Beneficiaries

It is now well-established that, even though the author can assign away his own renewal expectancy, he cannot cut off, defeat, or diminish the independent statutory renewal rights of his widow and children or next of kin. And, as we have seen, the Supreme Court has now settled that executors take the renewal for the direct benefit of the author's legatees, without regard to any assignment of renewal rights the author may have made before he died. At one time there was some feeling that, if the author parted absolutely with all of his rights in a work, both he and his family would be estopped from claiming rights under the renewal term, but this theory is now completely discredited. It is clear that the rights of the author's assignees are dependent on his survival and fail if he dies before the renewal year.

---

[135]Fred Fisher Music Co. v. M. Witmark & Sons, 318 U.S. 643 (1943).

[136]Fox Film Corp. v. Knowles, 261 U.S. 326 (1923).

[137]Miller Music Corp. v. Charles N. Daniels, Inc., 158 F. Supp. 188 (1957), *aff'd mem.*, 265 F.2d 925 (1959), *aff'd*, 362 U.S. 373, 125 U.S.P.Q. 147 (1960).

At the same time it is settled that the widow, children, and next of kin can also assign their own rights in the renewal expectancy, no matter how contingent or fragmentary. They can join the author in his assignment or execute an independent transfer, although in either case a separate consideration for each assignor would probably be needed for validity.

Rights of Assignees and Licensees Under a Binding Transfer

The renewal assignee stands in the shoes of his assignor, and takes the renewal only if the assignor is the beneficiary entitled under the statute....

THE STATUTORY RENEWAL PROVISIONS

As originally drafted in the 1976 Copyright Act, § 304(a) provided that the copyright in a work which was in its initial term of protection on January 1, 1978 would last for only 28 years, unless an application for renewal was made to and registered by the Copyright Office in the twenty-eighth year. This was true under the 1909 Act as well; the only change from the earlier law, and it was quite significant, was that if renewal was secured in a timely manner, the renewal term was to last not for 28 years but for 47 years. The same categories of persons entitled to own the renewal under the 1909 Act were so entitled under the 1976 Act.

Section 304(b) as originally enacted provided, simply, that works already in their renewal term in 1977 would have that term automatically extended from 28 years to 47 years. (Beginning in 1962, Congress — in anticipation of imminent copyright reform that would predictably extend the term of copyright — in a series of "interim renewal extension" laws prolonged the life of renewal copyrights that would have otherwise expired; thus, when the new law came into effect in 1978, a work copyrighted in 1906 and renewed in 1934 would still have been in its renewal term, so that its new overall 75-year copyright would last through 1981.)

In the House Report that accompanied the original §§ 304(a) and (b), it was stated: "The arguments in favor of lengthening the duration of copyright apply to subsisting as well as future copyrights. The bill's basic approach is to increase the present 56-year term to 75 years in the case of copyrights subsisting in both their first and their renewal terms." Do you agree with the proposition stated in the first quoted sentence? If Congress was intent on extending the life of existing copyrights, why did it choose not to apply the "life plus 50" measure to such works rather than retain the cumbersome and unique renewal format?

For all of their importance and complexity, the renewal provisions of both the 1909 and 1976 Acts have been the subject of infrequent judicial interpretation. Among the most significant decisions, already mentioned in the Ringer study, *supra*, was *Fred Fisher Music Co. v. M. Witmark & Sons*, 318 U.S. 643 (1943), in which the Supreme Court held — despite the obvious purpose of the renewal format to protect the author against unremunerative copyright transfers during the initial term — that an author could validly assign in the initial term of copyright his or her interest in the renewal term. (The student should consider how much money the author would likely receive for assignment of the renewal interest, as distinguished from payment by the assignee for the right to market the work for the balance of the initial 28-year term, particularly when the assignment is made early in the initial term.)

In a recent case, the Court of Appeals for the Second Circuit was confronted with the question whether the songwriter of the popular song, "Desafinado," which contributed to the initial popularity of the bossa nova in the United States, had effectively assigned his renewal interest in the song. In 1958 and 1960, Antonio Carlos Jobim — in a contract written in Portuguese in Brazil — assigned to a music publisher (Arapua) the United States copyright in five songs, one of which was "Desafinado." Through successive assignments from Arapua, the copyright came into the hands of Hollis (and its affiliate Songways). In 1987 and 1988, apparently believing that he was entitled to the renewal copyright in the U.S., Jobim purported to assign the renewal to Corcovado. Because Hollis continued to collect royalties and claim copyright at the start of the renewal term, Corcovado brought an action for copyright infringement. *Corcovado Music Corp. v. Hollis Music, Inc.*, 981 F.2d 679 (2d Cir. 1993).

The court of appeals concluded that despite the 1958 Desafinado contract's specification that all litigation thereunder should be in Brazil, this was a copyright infringement action rather than one for breach of contract, all of the parties to the action were in New York so that New York was a proper forum, and that U.S. law rather than the law of Brazil should be used in construing Jobim's grant of copyright in order to determine whether it embraced the renewal term. There were slight differences in the parties' translation of the Portuguese; the defendant's interpretation was: "The Authors assign and transfer to the Publisher, the full property, for the exercise of the corresponding rights in all the countries of the world, of their ownership rights in the musical composition ... in the form, scope and application which they hold by virtue of the laws and treaties in force and those which become effective hereinafter."

The Court of Appeals for the Second Circuit, after reciting the author-protective purposes of the renewal provisions of the 1909 Copyright Act, stated that "there is a strong presumption against the conveyance of renewal rights: 'In the absence of language which expressly grants rights in "renewals of copyright" or "extensions of copyright" the courts are hesitant to conclude that a transfer of copyright (even if it includes a grant of "all right, title and interest") is intended to include a transfer with respect to the renewal expectancy.'" The court noted that in *Fisher v. Witmark*, the Supreme Court had held that "an assignment by the author of his 'copyright' in general terms did not include conveyance of his renewal interest." The court of appeals concluded: "The presumption against conveyance of renewal rights serves the congressional purpose of protecting authors' entitlement to receive new rights in the 28th year of the original term. In the present case, Jobim's 1958 and 1960 contracts with Arapua were silent as to renewal rights. Accordingly, under federal copyright law Jobim retained renewal rights to the Five Songs and could validly assign them to Corcovado." The court distinguished an earlier case in which the author had agreed to convey his "exclusive right ... forever," and not to convey it "at any time hereafter."

Of course, an author who purports to assign the renewal term can assign only the interest that he himself possesses — which is a right to own the renewal interest only if the author survives until the renewal term vests (at some unspecified point in the twenty-eighth year of the initial term.) Absent such survival, the 1909 Act provided for succession to renewal ownership by the surviving spouse and children — who would take in preference to the assignee, who took only a conditional interest.

In a case decided under section 304(a) as originally written in the 1976 Copyright Act, *Saroyan v. William Saroyan Found.*, 675 F. Supp. 843 (S.D.N.Y. 1987), it was held that the author's children, who would otherwise be entitled to succeed to the renewal term, would not be foreclosed from doing so by virtue of their long-term estrangement from their author-father. The noted author William Saroyan wrote and copyrighted in 1958 a play titled The Cave Dwellers. On his death in 1981, he left a will which purported to give "all copyrights" to the William Saroyan Foundation, which was to maintain his writings and disburse the income therefrom to charitable and educational entities. The court found in the statute a "non-discretionary order of renewal rights" that gave priority to the surviving children over persons named in an author's will, and it rejected the defendant's argument that its charitable purposes should prevail over the private interests of the children (especially in view of their "stormy relationship" with their father). It quoted from earlier authorities to the effect that "[e]ach of these named classes is separated in the statute by a condition precedent to the passing of renewal rights, namely, that the persons named in the preceding class be deceased," and that "[a]n author in effect is required by statutory mandate to leave the right to obtain renewals to his widow and children if he has any." The court concluded that "the bequest of renewal rights to the Foundation was without effect because the renewal rights never became part of the estate ... This result is fortified by court decisions holding that widows who re-marry and illegitimate children meet the statutory definition, thereby precluding executors' renewal rights."

Two decisions — rendered very late in the day under the unchanged phrases of the 1909 renewal provisions as carried forward into the 1976 Act — flatly disagreed on the question whether an author who assigned the renewal term had to live *through* the twenty-eighth year of the initial term in order to vest the renewal interest of the author's assignee. In both *Marascalco v. Fantasy Inc.*, 953 F.2d 469 (9th Cir. 1991), *cert. denied*, 112 S. Ct. 1997, 118 L. Ed. 2d 592 (1992), and *Frederick Music Co. v. Sickler*, 708 F. Supp. 587 (S.D.N.Y. 1989), the authors registered the renewal claim with the Copyright Office during the last year of the first term, but died before the commencement of the second term of copyright. While the *Frederick Music* court held that the author need not have remained alive through the end of the first term to vest the renewal interest of his assignee, so long as the author was alive to file the renewal registration, the *Marascalco* court held that the grantee's expectancy interest did not vest unless the grantor survived the first copyright term.

Which is the sounder interpretation of the 1909 Act and section 304(a) of the 1976 Act as originally written? (That text is set forth in Appendix A to the casebook.) Is the answer compelled by a careful reading of the "shall be entitled"/"when" phrasing? If the language is ambiguous, and resort to underlying statutory policy is appropriate, should a court give greater weight to the policy of "author primacy" (i.e., implementing the intention of the author to convey ownership of the renewal term) or the "second chance policy" embodied in the renewal term (i.e., to provide the author and the statutory successors with a new opportunity to enjoy the benefits of a creative work that proves successful)?

These are no longer perplexing issues with respect to works first published between 1964 and 1977, and which are thus eligible for renewal between 1992 and 2005. Section 304(a) as amended in 1992, as noted above, provides not only for automatic renewal as an alternative to voluntary renewal, but also expressly for the vesting, in the twenty-eighth year of the initial term, of the future right to enjoy the renewal interest; that depends on whether the renewal is voluntary, in which case ownership of the renewal copyright vests in the assignee if the author is alive at the time the renewal application is made, or whether it is automatic, in which case the renewal interest vests in the assignee only if the author lives to the end of the twenty-eighth year of the initial term.

Finally, one must take note of the somewhat odd segment of the renewal provisions that departs from the standard four-tier allocation of renewal rights (i.e., author if alive, then widow, widower or children, etc.) in connection with a limited number of works, the most important being works made for hire and posthumous works. (As was usual with the 1909 Act, neither of those important terms was defined.) As to those works, the renewal term is owned by the then copyright owner, and not by the author's family, legatee, or next of kin. These provisions were interpreted in two 1975 decisions of the United States Court of Appeals for the Second Circuit.

In *Epoch Producing Corp. v. Killiam Shows, Inc.*, 522 F.2d 737 (2d Cir. 1975), the court resolved a dispute regarding D.W. Griffith's 1915 silent film classic "The Birth of a Nation." Although plaintiff Epoch had applied for, and received, a renewal certificate claiming that it was the "author" of the film as an employer (in a work-for-hire situation) and still the copyright owner, the court of appeals held as a matter of law that it was not. The court found that neither Epoch nor its predecessor in interest had employed Griffith, or paid him any salary, or supervised or controlled him in making the motion picture, or had done anything more than finance the production. The court also held that Epoch could not claim the renewal term through an assignment of that term from the party who originally secured copyright (DWG Corp., controlled by Griffith). Because no person other than Epoch had applied for the renewal copyright, the effect of the court's decision was that "The Birth of a Nation" passed into the public domain in 1943, after the initial twenty-eight-year term.

In *Bartok v. Boosey & Hawkes, Inc.*, 523 F.2d 941 (2d Cir. 1975), the court was confronted with the question whether Bela Bartok's well-known Concerto for Orchestra was a "posthumous work" under § 24 of the 1909 Act. If it was, then Bartok's copyright assignee, the music publisher Boosey & Hawkes, would own the renewal term (and by contract would have been obliged to pay Bartok's share of the royalties to his widow, until her death, and only then to Bartok's two sons); if it was not a "posthumous work," then the usual four-tier sequence would have applied, and the renewal term would have been owned jointly — one-third each — by Bartok's widow and sons. Because the Concerto was printed and copyrighted by Boosey six months after Bartok's death, the trial court had concluded, using standard dictionary definitions, that the work was posthumous.

A divided court of appeals reversed. The majority stated: "[W]here the legislative purpose of the statute is to extend protection to an author and his family, it makes better sense to read the 'posthumous work' exception as a withholding of unncessary protection where the family can protect itself.... In this case, however, where the copyright contract was executed before the author's death, the family has no means of protection other than the statutory renewal right; this is equally true whether the work is available in print or not." Not only had Bartok assigned the copyright before his death to Boosey, but he had also heard the completed Concerto performed by an orchestra, as had the public, and he had corrected printer's proofs of the score. The court also cautioned that a definition of "posthumous" that would turn on whether a work was published after the author's death "carries with it the implicit problem what is publication as well as the implicit danger that an unscrupulous publisher could purposely delay publication in order to obtain renewal rights."

The present § 304(a) carries over from § 24 of the 1909 Act the provision for renewal of "posthumous works" by the then copyright owner, but the act continues to have no definition of that phrase. The pertinent legislative history, however, indicates that the *Bartok* decision has been given the drafters' blessing. See H.R. Rep. No. 94-1476, 94th Cong., 2d Sess. 139-40 (1976): "[T]he Committee intends that the reference to a 'posthumous work' in this section has the meaning given to it in [the Bartok case] — one as to which no copyright assignment or other contract for exploitation of the work has occurred during an author's lifetime, rather than one which is simply first published after the author's death." (If Congress had meant to provide such a controlling definition, why did it not do so in § 101 of the 1976 Act? Is it sound legislative process to amend the law by way of an obscure passage in a committee report?)

The student may appropriately wonder why Congress chose to make several exceptions — including works for hire and posthumous works — to the generally prevailing principle of "author renewal." The sad truth is that the exceptions were a product of nothing more than inadvertent and mangled draftsmanship in the shaping of the 1909 Act, and offer up no plausible rationale. The four categories had initially been grouped in a proposed section that dealt with the duration of copyright; the proposal assumed the use of an author's life as the yardstick for copyright protection (and these excepted categories were thought ill-fitting), and that the renewal format would be abandoned altogether. At the eleventh hour, Congress reversed the tide for the "life plus" formula, retained the renewal format, and inadvertently retained and incorporated these categories — pertinent to duration — into the provision that assigned renewal-term ownership rights. The depressing tale is recounted in Ringer, *Renewal of Copyright,* in Studies on Copyright (Study No. 31, 1960).

QUESTIONS

1. Assuming that works were first published and copyrighted in the following years, when did or will copyright terminate? 1910, 1950, 1970, 1978. What further facts, if any, would you have to know to answer this question?

2. Author writes a novel in 1975, and in 1976 he assigns "all of my copyright interest" to Publisher for $10,000. Publisher prints and distributes the book and secures copyright in its own name, in 1976. In the year 2004, both Author and Publisher apply for renewal of the copyright. Whose claim should prevail? (Note that under the 1992 amendments to § 304, it will not be necessary for either the Author or the Publisher to take the initiative to apply for renewal; renewal will be automatic. But the issue of ownership will remain.)

3. Assume instead that Author had in 1976 conveyed "both the initial and renewal terms of copyright" to Publisher, which published and copyrighted the work that year. If Author is alive throughout the year 2004, who is entitled to the enjoyment of the renewal term? If Author dies before the year 2004, leaving a widow and two children (who are alive in 2004), who is entitled to the enjoyment of the renewal term? Assume the widow and children take; what are their respective shares? (Could Publisher in 1976 have fully protected itself against the eventuality of Author's early death, by taking assignments of the renewal term not only from him but also from his wife and children?)

AUTOMATIC RENEWAL OF PRE-1978 WORKS NOW IN THEIR FIRST TERM

At the time of U.S. adherence to the Berne Convention in 1989, Congress took no steps to amend the 1976 Act to remove the formalities of an initial and renewal registration as prerequisites to the second term of copyright, despite the probable inconsistency between the renewal requirement and Berne's prohibition upon formalities. Persistence of the renewal obligation has, through the years, been a trap for all authors (even large corporate copyrightholders have neglected to renew works), but especially so for foreign authors whose own copyright laws contain no similar requirement.

This concern was finally addressed (after 200 years) through an amendment of the Copyright Act, enacted in June 1992, that provides for the automatic renewal of pre-1978 works then in their first term of copyright. The law, Pub. L. 102-307, 106 Stat. 264, substitutes a single 75-year term for the prior dual terms, by making the second term (28 plus 19 years) vest without filing for renewal. This means that pre-1978 works then in their first term of copyright, i.e., works first published between 1964 and 1977 (inclusive), will enjoy the full 75-year copyright term, without having to register and then to renew the registration during the 28th year following publication.

However, the law includes certain incentives to renewal registration. A registration issuing from an application made within one year before expiration of the first term will "constitute prima facie evidence as to the validity of the copyright during its renewal and extended term and of the facts stated in the certificate." § 304(a)(4)(B). This benefit may be most significant to copyright owners of works that never were registered during the first term of copyright. The law as passed does not require a first term registration as a prerequisite to automatic vesting of the renewal term.

The automatic renewal amendment also resolves an issue that had divided the courts: When must the deceased author have died to prevent vesting of the expectancy of the renewal term in the author's grantee? Assume that in the initial term of copyright A assigns the renewal term to B, and that renewal is applied for early in the 28th year but that A dies before the end of the year, leaving a widow. B claims that its renewal interest vested on the date of renewal registration (to be enjoyed beginning with the 29th year), while the widow claims that vesting does not occur unless and until A survives to the end of the 28th year, so that she takes the renewal term rather than the assignee. Courts reached different conclusions. *Compare Marascalco v. Fantasy Inc.*, 953 F.2d 469 (9th Cir. 1991), *with Frederick Music Co. v. Sickler*, 708 F. Supp. 587 (S.D.N.Y. 1989).

This confusion is now resolved by the amended § 304(a)(2)(B). If renewal is secured by "voluntary" application and registration in the 28th year, then ownership of the renewal vests at that time (to be enjoyed in the 29th year and thereafter); in the hypothetical above, B will enjoy the renewal. If, however, the renewal is effected not voluntarily but "automatically" by virtue of the statutory amendment, then rights to the renewal term will not vest until the last day of the 28th year, and the spouse will take.

For the effect of the "automatic renewal" amendment upon derivative works created by an assignee during the initial term of the underlying work, see page 342 *infra*.

REMARKS OF REP. HUGHES

138 Cong. Rec. H4133 (June 4, 1992)

[The Copyright Renewal Act] reforms the archaic renewal system presently in place for copyrighted works published before January 1, 1978, by providing for their automatic renewal. Currently, authors of works first published between 1964 and 1977 must file a timely renewal application with the Copyright Office during the 28th year after the first publication. Failure to file such an application results in loss of a second, 47-year term of protection, called the renewal term. The renewal requirements are highly technical and have resulted in the unintended loss of valuable copyrights. In addition to countless individuals who do not have knowledge of the requirements, even famous directors such as Frank Capra have fallen victim. Capra's "It's a Wonderful Life," starring Jimmy Stewart and Donna Reed, went into the public domain when the film production company that owned the copyright went bankrupt and no one was around to file the renewal application.

[The Act] will prevent such losses. At the same time, the [Act] recognizes that public records containing information about the creation and ownership of copyrighted works are desirable. In order to encourage — but not require —

copyright owners to provide such information, the [Act] contains incentives for copyright owners to continue to file renewal applications.

---

§ 304. Duration of copyright: Subsisting copyrights

(a) *Copyrights in Their First Term on January 1, 1978.*

(1)(A) Any copyright, the first term of which is subsisting on January 1, 1978, shall endure for 28 years from the date it was originally secured.

(B) In the case of —

(i) any posthumous work or ...

(ii) any work copyrighted ... by an employer for whom such work is made for hire,

the proprietor of such copyright shall be entitled to a renewal and extension of the copyright in such work for the further term of 47 years.

(C) In the case of any other copyrighted work, including a contribution by an individual author to a periodical or to a cyclopedic or other composite work —

(i) the author of such work, if the author is still living,

(ii) the widow, widower, or children of the author, if the author is not living,

(iii) the author's executors, if such author, widow, widower, or children are not living, or

(iv) the author's next of kin, in the absence of a will of the author,

shall be entitled to a renewal and extension of the copyright in such work for a further term of 47 years.

(2) ... (B) At the expiration of the original term of copyright in a work specified in paragraph (1)(C) of this subsection, the copyright shall endure for a renewed and extended further term of 47 years, which —

(i) if an application to register a claim to such further term has been made to the Copyright Office within 1 year before the expiration of the original term of copyright, and the claim is registered, shall vest, upon the beginning of such further term, in any person who is entitled under paragraph (1)(C) to the renewal and extension of the copyright at the time the application is made; or

(ii) if no such application is made or the claim pursuant to such application is not registered, shall vest, upon the beginning of such further term, in any person entitled under paragraph (1)(C), as of the last day of the original term of copyright, to the renewal and extension of the copyright.

(3)(A) An application to register a claim to the renewed and extended term of copyright in a work may be made to the Copyright Office —

    (i) within 1 year before the expiration of the original term of copyright by any person entitled under paragraph (1)(B) or (C) to such further term of 47 years; and

    (ii) at any time during the renewed and extended term by any person in whom such further term vested, under paragraph (2)(A) or (B) ....

(B) Such an application is not a condition of the renewal and extension of the copyright in a work for a further term of 47 years.

(4) ... (B) If an application to register a claim to the renewed and extended term of copyright in a work is made within 1 year before its expiration, and the claim is registered, the certificate of such registration shall constitute prima facie evidence as to the validity of the copyright during its renewed and extended term and of the facts stated in the certificate....

(b) *Copyrights in Their Renewal Term or Registered for Renewal Before January 1, 1978.*

The duration of any copyright, the renewal term of which is subsisting at any time between December 31, 1976, and December 31, 1977, inclusive, or for which renewal registration is made between December 31, 1976, and December 31, 1977, inclusive, is extended to endure for a term of seventy-five years from the date copyright was originally secured.

WORKS IN THE PUBLIC DOMAIN PRIOR TO JANUARY 1, 1978 (AND THEREAFTER)

None of the statutory sections treated above deals with the duration of copyright protection for works that were already in the public domain when the Copyright Act became effective on January 1, 1978. As the student might assume, Congress intended to leave all such works in the public domain, available for copying and other forms of use by anyone interested in doing so. Congress enacted a number of "transitional and supplementary provisions" in addition to the substantive provisions of the 1976 Act, and T & S § 103 provides, in pertinent part: "This Act does not provide copyright protection for any work that goes into the public domain before January 1, 1978."

The question of recapture of works from the public domain remains a lively one, however. As the student is already aware, among the world's copyright regimes, the U.S. 28-year term was peculiarly short. As the student will learn in Chapter 5, another peculiarity of U.S. copyright, the notice requirement, also could cause a work's early demise into the public domain. As a result, pressure has been brought from time to time to revive the copyrights in foreign works that fell prey to the draconian features of the U.S. copyright system. For example, under article 18 of the Berne Convention, which the U.S. ratified in 1989, new member nations upon accession are to protect all works from other member countries whose copyrights have not yet expired in their countries of origin. Nonetheless, the U.S. acceded to Berne without providing for protection of foreign Berne Union works whose U.S. copyrights had lapsed. The 1992 North American Free Trade Agreement would obligate the

U.S. to revive the copyrights in Mexican motion pictures that had fallen into the public domain in the U.S. through failure to comply with the 1976 Act notice requirement. No legislation has yet been enacted to implement this portion of NAFTA.

Does Congress have power to reanimate dead copyrights? Arguably, retrieval of works from the public domain would violate the constitutional restriction of copyright to "limited Times." On the other hand, one might contend that the Constitution merely forbids *perpetual* copyright protection; as long as the duration is limited, there is no requirement that the period of protection be single and uninterrupted. Indeed, Congress has in the past authorized the President to issue proclamations reinstating lapsed copyrights. The Act of Dec. 18, 1919, 41 Stat. 368, and the Act of Sept. 25, 1941, subsequently codified in section 9 of the 1909 Copyright Act, provided for the revival of copyrights of foreign works that would have fallen into the public domain due to the authors' inability (due principally to the world wars) to comply with U.S. formalities. A more significant, but not insuperable, problem may concern a different constitutional provision, the "takings" clause. Revival of copyright may prejudice the interests of those who exploit the work in reliance on its public domain status. The World War I and II copyright extension laws both exculpated unauthorized exploitations occurring before the extension laws' enactment. Moreover, the World War II extension law also permitted unauthorized users whose exploitation predated the extension legislation to continue their exploitation during one year from the date on which the then-lawful unauthorized exploitation commenced. Similar compromises between the interests of the exploiters and the authors may be necessary for enactment of a constitutionally compatible law to revive fallen copyrights.

THE TRANSITION FROM 1909 TO 1976 ACT AND ITS AMENDMENTS

The following table may help the student review the applicable duration periods.

Date of Work	When Protection Attaches	First Term	Renewal Term
Created in 1978 or later	Upon being fixed in a tangible medium		Unitary term of life + 50 (or, if anonymous or pseudonymous work, or work for hire, 75 years from publication, or 100 years from creation, whichever is first)
Published 1964-1977	Upon Publication with Notice	28 years	47 years, second term now commences automatically; renewal registration optional

Date of Work	When Protection Attaches	First Term	Renewal Term
Published between 75 years ago and 1963	Upon Publication with Notice	28 years	47 years, if renewal was sought, otherwise these works are in the public domain (note that even as to works whose first terms expired after 1977, it remained necessary to effect a renewal registration)*
Published more than 75 years ago	The work is now in the public domain		
Created, but not published, before 1978	On 1/1/1978, when federal copyright displaced state copyright		Unitary term of at least life + 50, earliest expiration dates 12/31/2002 (if work remains unpublished) or 12/31/2027 (if work is published by the end of 2002)

*Note that despite expiration of the former 56-year copyright term before enactment of the 1976 Act, Congress, beginning in 1962, anticipated an extension of copyright duration, and therefore regularly extended the renewal terms of works whose copyrights were about to expire. The works benefitting from such interim extensions were those published from 1906 through 1921.

B. RENEWALS AND DERIVATIVE WORKS

A number of vexing issues generated by the renewal format in the 1909 Act, and still with us, concern the ownership and use of derivative works after the end of the initial copyright term on the underlying work. For example, assume that *A*, the author of a copyrighted novel, conveys to *B* during the initial term of copyright in the novel the exclusive right to produce a play or motion picture based upon the novel. *B* produces such a play or motion picture and secures copyright for it. Twenty-eight years after the publication and copyrighting of the underlying novel, *A* (or *A*'s statutory successor) renews the copyright. What are the respective rights of *A* and *B*?

A number of possible situations come to mind.

(1) Is *A* free to perform *B*'s play or publicly exhibit *B*'s motion picture without *B*'s consent? That would surely be an infringement of *B*'s copyright to the extent *B* has contributed as an "author" some "original" elements in the play or motion picture.

(2) Is A free to grant to a third person, C, the right to produce an altogether new play or motion picture based on A's underlying novel? At least to that extent, the renewal term has been said to create a "new estate" in A (or A's statutory successor) that is not encumbered by A's promise during the initial term of the underlying copyright not to grant such derivative rights to persons other than B. After all, the principal purpose of the renewal format was to permit A to benefit, through the right to make new grants and licenses, from the unanticipated popularity of his underlying novel.

(3) Is B free (assuming A's initial grant to have made no mention of the renewal term) to make an altogether new version of a play or motion picture based on A's novel? Here, too, it has been generally assumed that A's renewal, and the "new estate" created thereby, empowers A to prevent B from indefinitely exploiting A's underlying novel, during its renewal term, in the form of wholly new plays and motion pictures. To the extent such plays and films borrow from A's novel without A's consent, this would be an infringement of the renewal copyright.

(4) Is B free, however, to continue to perform B's own play, or exhibit B's own motion picture, exactly as written by him, during the renewal term of A's underlying novel, without A's consent? Strict application of the "new estate" theory might suggest that A takes the renewal free and clear of all licenses granted earlier, all of which terminate and revert to A, so that A can renegotiate the license with B and thus directly benefit from the success of A's underlying novel (as a component in B's play or motion picture). If so, B would infringe. B's equities in this situation are, however, weighty, especially if the grant of derivative rights and the preparation of his derivative work came late in the initial copyright term of the underlying work, and particularly if the success of the play or motion picture is largely attributable to the literary or artistic contributions of B (and if B is indeed making no changes in the derivative work he has previously been performing or exhibiting).

This fourth variation is the issue that is presented in the Supreme Court's recent decision in *Stewart v. Abend*, which is featured immediately below.

(5) Assume that not only does the initial copyright term of the underlying work expire, and that a renewal is secured, but also that the initial copyright term of the derivative play or motion picture expires — and that it is *not* renewed. Is a third person free to publish, publicly perform, or publicly exhibit the derivative play or motion picture? Is A free to do so? Strict application of copyright theory would suggest that because B's copyright protects only those elements he authored in the play or motion picture, only those discrete elements fall into the public domain when no renewal copyright is secured for the derivative work; the publication, performance, or exhibition of the derivative work would therefore infringe the elements of A's underlying novel that are still being protected by A's renewal copyright. Thus a third person so using B's work would infringe A's. A, however, would be free so to use B's work. One difficulty with such a conclusion is that it appears to undermine the public-domain policy of the Copyright Act, for it would prevent all persons (except A) from exploiting B's work despite the termination of its copyright; and it places in jeopardy those third persons who exploit B's work in reliance on the apparent expiration of protection.

This dilemma is raised and explored in *Russell v. Price, infra.*

STEWART v. ABEND

495 U.S. 207, 110 S. Ct. 1750, 109 L. Ed. 2d 184 (1990)

JUSTICE O'CONNOR delivered the opinion of the Court.

The author of a pre-existing work may assign to another the right to use it in a derivative work. In this case the author of a pre-existing work agreed to assign the rights in his renewal copyright term to the owner of a derivative work, but died before the commencement of the renewal period. The question presented is whether the owner of the derivative work infringed the rights of the successor owner of the pre-existing work by continued distribution and publication of the derivative work during the renewal term of the pre-existing work.

I

Cornell Woolrich authored the story "It Had to Be Murder," which was first published in February 1942 in Dime Detective Magazine. The magazine's publisher, Popular Publications, Inc., obtained the rights to magazine publication of the story and Woolrich retained all other rights. Popular Publications obtained a blanket copyright for the issue of Dime Detective Magazine in which "It Had to Be Murder" was published.

The Copyright Act of 1909, 35 Stat. 1075, 17 U.S.C. § 1 *et seq.* (1976 ed.) (1909 Act), provided authors a 28-year initial term of copyright protection plus a 28-year renewal term. See 17 U.S.C. § 24 (1976 ed.). In 1945, Woolrich agreed to assign the rights to make motion picture versions of six of his stories, including "It Had to Be Murder," to B. G. De Sylva Productions for $9,250. He also agreed to renew the copyrights in the stories at the appropriate time and to assign the same motion picture rights to De Sylva Productions for the 28-year renewal term. In 1953, actor Jimmy Stewart and director Alfred Hitchcock formed a production company, Patron, Inc., which obtained the motion picture rights in "It Had to Be Murder" from De Sylva's successors in interest for $10,000.

In 1954, Patron, Inc., along with Paramount Pictures, produced and distributed, "Rear Window," the motion picture version of Woolrich's story "It Had to Be Murder." Woolrich died in 1968 before he could obtain the rights in the renewal term for petitioners as promised and without a surviving spouse or child. He left his property to a trust administered by his executor, Chase Manhattan Bank, for the benefit of Columbia University. On December 29, 1969, Chase Manhattan Bank renewed the copyright in the "It Had to Be Murder" story pursuant to 17 U.S.C. § 24 (1976 ed.). Chase Manhattan assigned the renewal rights to respondent Abend for $650 plus 10% of all proceeds from exploitation of the story.

"Rear Window" was broadcast on the ABC television network in 1971. Respondent then notified petitioners Hitchcock (now represented by co-trustees of his will), Stewart, and MCA Inc., the owners of the "Rear Window" motion picture and renewal rights in the motion picture, that he owned the renewal rights in the copyright and that their distribution of the motion picture without permission infringed his copyright in the story. Hitchcock, Stewart, and MCA nonetheless entered into a second license with ABC to rebroadcast the motion picture. In 1974, respondent filed suit against these same petitioners, and others, in the United States District Court for the Southern District of New York, alleging copyright infringement. Respondent dismissed his complaint in return for $25,000.

Three years later, the United States Court of Appeals for the Second Circuit decided *Rohauer v. Killiam Shows, Inc.,* 551 F.2d 484, *cert. denied,* 431 U.S. 949 (1977), in which it held that the owner of the copyright in a derivative work may continue to use the existing derivative work according to the original grant from the author of the pre-existing work even if the grant of rights in the pre-existing work lapsed. 551 F.2d, at 494. Several years later, apparently in reliance on *Rohauer,* petitioners re-released the motion picture in a variety of media, including new 35 and 16 millimeter prints for theatrical exhibition in the United States, videocassettes, and videodiscs. They also publicly exhibited the motion picture in theaters, over cable television, and through videodisc and videocassette rentals and sales.

Respondent then brought the instant suit in the United States District Court for the Central District of California against Hitchcock, Stewart, MCA, and Universal Film Exchanges, a subsidiary of MCA and the distributor of the motion picture. Respondent's complaint alleges that the re-release of the motion picture infringes his copyright in the story because petitioners' right to use the story during the renewal term lapsed when Woolrich died before he could register for the renewal term and transfer his renewal rights to them. Respondent also contends that petitioners have interfered with his rights in the renewal term of the story in other ways. He alleges that he sought to contract with Home Box Office (HBO) to produce a play and television version of the story, but that petitioners wrote to him and HBO stating that neither he nor HBO could use either the title, "Rear Window" or "It Had to Be Murder." Respondent also alleges that petitioners further interfered with the renewal copyright in the story by attempting to sell the right to make a television sequel and that the re-release of the original motion picture itself interfered with his ability to produce other derivative works.

Petitioners filed motions for summary judgment, one based on the decision in *Rohauer, supra,* and the other based on alleged defects in the story's copyright. Respondent moved for summary judgment on the ground that petitioners' use of the motion picture constituted copyright infringement. Petitioners responded with a third motion for summary judgment based on a "fair use" defense. The District Court granted petitioners' motions for summary judgment based on *Rohauer* and the fair use defense, and denied respondent's motion for summary judgment, as well as petitioners' motion for summary judgment alleging defects in the story's copyright. Respondent appealed to the United States Court of Appeals for the Ninth Circuit and petitioners cross-appealed.

The Court of Appeals reversed, holding that respondent's copyright in the renewal term of the story was not defective. 863 F.2d 1465, 1472 (1988). The issue before the court, therefore, was whether petitioners were entitled to distribute and exhibit the motion picture without respondent's permission despite respondent's valid copyright in the pre-existing story.... The Court of Appeals in the instant case [concluded] that even if the pre-existing work had been incorporated into a derivative work, use of the pre-existing work was infringing unless the owner of the derivative work held a valid grant of rights in the renewal term.

The court relied on *Miller Music Corp. v. Charles N. Daniels, Inc.*, 362 U.S. 373 (1960), in which we held that assignment of renewal rights by an author before the time for renewal arrives cannot defeat the right of the author's statutory successor to the renewal rights if the author dies before the right to renewal accrues.... Finding further support in the legislative history of the 1909 Act and rejecting the *Rohauer* court's reliance on the equities and the termination provisions of the 1976 Act, 17 U.S.C. §§ 203(b)(1), 304(c)(6)(A) (1988 ed.), the Court of Appeals concluded that petitioners received from Woolrich only an expectancy in the renewal rights that never matured; upon Woolrich's death, Woolrich's statutory successor, Chase Manhattan Bank, became "entitled to a renewal and extension of the copyright," which Chase Manhattan secured "within one year prior to the expiration of the original term of copyright." 17 U.S.C. § 24 (1976 ed.). Chase Manhattan then assigned the existing rights in the copyright to respondent.

The Court of Appeals also addressed at length the proper remedy, an issue not relevant to the issue on which we granted certiorari. We granted certiorari to resolve the conflict between the decision in *Rohauer, supra,* and the decision below. 493 U.S. (1989). Petitioners do not challenge the Court of Appeals' determination that respondent's copyright in the renewal term is valid and we express no opinion regarding the Court of Appeals' decision on this point.

II

A

Petitioners would have us read into the Copyright Act a limitation on the statutorily created rights of the owner of an underlying work. They argue in essence that the rights of the owner of the copyright in the derivative use of the pre-existing work are extinguished once it is incorporated into the derivative work, assuming the author of the pre-existing work has agreed to assign his renewal rights. Because we find no support for such a curtailment of rights in either the 1909 Act, the 1976 Act, or the legislative history of either, we affirm the judgment of the Court of Appeals.

....

The right of renewal found in § 24 [of the 1909 Act] provides authors a second opportunity to obtain remuneration for their works....

Since the earliest copyright statute in this country, the copyright term of ownership has been split between an original term and a renewal term. Originally, the renewal was intended merely to serve as an extension of the original term; at the end of the original term, the renewal could be effected and claimed by the author, if living, or by the author's executors, administrators or assigns. See Copyright Act of May 31, 1790, ch. XV, § 1, 1 Stat. 124. In 1831, Congress altered the provision so that the author could assign his contingent interest in the renewal term, but could not, through his assignment, divest the rights of his widow or children in the renewal term. See Copyright Act of February 3, 1831, ch. XVI, 4 Stat. 436; see also G. Curtis, Law of Copyright 235 (1847). The 1831 renewal provisions created "an entirely new policy, completely dissevering the title, breaking up the continuance ... and vesting an absolutely new title eo nomine in the persons designated." *White-Smith Music Publishing Co. v. Goff,* 187 F. 247, 250 (CA1 1911). In this way, Congress attempted to give the author a second chance to control and benefit from his work. Congress also intended to secure to the author's family the opportunity to exploit the work if the author died before he could register for the renewal term. See Bricker, *Renewal and Extension of Copyright,* 29 S. Cal. L. Rev. 23, 27 (1955) ("The renewal term of copyright is the law's second chance to the author and his family to profit from his mental labors"). "The evident purpose of [the renewal provision] is to provide for the family of the author after his death. Since the author cannot assign his family's renewal rights, [it] takes the form of a compulsory bequest of the copyright to the designated persons." *De Sylva v. Ballentine,* 351 U.S. 570, 582 (1956). See *Fred Fisher Music Co. v. M. Witmark & Sons,* 318 U.S. 643, 651 (1943) (if at the end of the original copyright period, the author is not living, "his family stand[s] in more need of the only means of subsistence ordinarily left to them" (citation omitted)).

In its debates leading up to the Copyright Act of 1909, Congress elaborated upon the policy underlying a system comprised of an original term and a completely separate renewal term. See *G. Ricordi & Co. v. Paramount Pictures, Inc.,* 189 F.2d 469, 471 (CA2) (the renewal right "creates a new estate, and the ... cases which have dealt with the subject assert that the new estate is clear of all rights, interests or licenses granted under the original copyright"), *cert. denied,* 342 U.S. 849 (1951). "It not infrequently happens that the author sells his copyright outright to a publisher for a comparatively small sum." H.R. Rep. No. 2222, 60th Cong. 2d Sess., 14 (1909). The renewal term permits the author, originally in a poor bargaining position, to renegotiate the terms of the grant once the value of the work has been tested. "[U]nlike real property and other forms of personal property, [a copyright] is by its very nature incapable of accurate monetary evaluation prior to its exploitation." 2 M. Nimmer & D. Nimmer, Nimmer on Copyright, § 9.02, p. 9-23 (1989) (hereinafter Nimmer). "If the work proves to be a great success and lives beyond the term of twenty-eight years, ... it should be the exclusive right of the author to take the renewal term, and the law should be framed ... so that [the author] could not be deprived of that right." H.R. Rep. No. 2222, *supra,* at 14. With these purposes in mind, Congress enacted the renewal provision of the Copyright Act of 1909, 17 U.S.C. § 24 (1976 ed.). With respect to works in their original or renewal term as of January 1, 1978, Congress retained the two-term system of copyright protection in the 1976 Act. See 17 U.S.C. §§ 304(a) and (b) (1988 ed.) (incorporating language of 17 U.S.C. § 24 (1976 ed.)).

Applying these principles in *Miller Music Corp. v. Charles N. Daniels, Inc.,* 362 U.S. 373 (1960), this Court held that when an author dies before the renewal period arrives, his executor is entitled to the renewal rights, even though the author previously assigned his renewal rights to another party. "An assignment by an author of his renewal rights made before the original copyright expires is valid against the world, if the author is alive at the commencement of the renewal period. *[Fred] Fisher Co. v. Witmark & Sons,* 318 U.S. 643, so holds." *Id.,* at 375. If the author dies before that time, the "next of kin obtain the renewal copyright free of any claim founded upon an assignment made by the author in his lifetime. These results follow not because the author's assignment is invalid but because he had only an expectancy to assign; and his death, prior to the renewal period, terminates his interest in the renewal which by § 24 vests in the named classes." *Ibid.* The legislative history of the 1909 Act echoes this view: "The right of renewal is contingent. It does not vest until the end [of the original term]. If [the author] is alive at the time of renewal, then the original contract may pass it, but his widow or children or other persons entitled would not be bound by the contract." 5 Legislative History of the 1909 Copyright Act, part K, p. 77 (E. Brylawski & A. Goldman eds. 1976) (statement of Mr. Hale).[2] Thus, the renewal provisions were intended to give the author a second chance to obtain fair remuneration for his creative efforts and to provide the author's family a "new estate" if the author died before the renewal period arrived.

An author holds a bundle of exclusive rights in the copyrighted work, among them the right to copy and the right to incorporate the work into derivative works. By assigning the renewal copyright in the work without limitation, as in *Miller Music,* the author assigns all of these rights. After *Miller Music,* if the author dies before the commencement of the renewal period, the assignee holds nothing. If the assignee of all of the renewal rights holds nothing upon the death of the assignor before arrival of the renewal period, then *a fortiori,* the assignee of a portion of the renewal rights, *e.g.,* the right to produce a derivative work, must also hold nothing. See also Brief for Register of Copyrights as *Amicus Curiae* 22 ("[A]ny assignment of renewal rights made during the original term is void if the author dies before the renewal period"). Therefore, if the author dies before the renewal period, then the assignee may continue to use the original work only if the author's successor transfers the renewal rights to the assignee. This is the rule adopted by the Court of Appeals below and advocated by the Register of Copyrights. See 863 F.2d, at 1478; Brief for Register of Copyrights as Amicus Curiae 22. Application of this rule to this case should end the inquiry. Woolrich died before the commencement of the renewal period in the story, and, therefore, petitioners hold only an unfulfilled expectancy. Petitioners have been "deprived of nothing. Like all purchasers of contingent interests, [they took] subject to the possibility that the contingency may not occur." *Miller Music, supra,* at 378.

---

[2] Neither *Miller Music* nor *Fred Fisher* decided the question of when the renewal rights vest, *i.e.,* whether the renewal rights vest upon commencement of the registration period, registration, or the date on which the original term expires and the renewal term begins. We have no occasion to address the issue here.

B

The reason that our inquiry does not end here, and that we granted certio-rari, is that the Court of Appeals for the Second Circuit reached a contrary result in *Rohauer v. Killiam Shows, Inc.,* 551 F.2d 484 (1977). Petitioners' theory is drawn largely from *Rohauer.* The Court of Appeals in *Rohauer* attempted to craft a "proper reconciliation" between the owner of the pre-existing work, who held the right to the work pursuant to *Miller Music,* and the owner of the derivative work, who had a great deal to lose if the work could not be published or distributed. 551 F.2d, at 490. Addressing a case factually similar to this case, the court concluded that even if the death of the author caused the renewal rights in the pre-existing work to revert to the statutory successor, the owner of the derivative work could continue to exploit that work. The court reasoned that the 1976 Act and the relevant precedents did not preclude such a result and that it was necessitated by a balancing of the equities:

> "[T]he equities lie preponderantly in favor of the proprietor of the deriva-tive copyright. In contrast to the situation where an assignee or licensee has done nothing more than print, publicize and distribute a copyrighted story or novel, a person who with the consent of the author has created an opera or a motion picture film will often have made contributions liter-ary, musical and economic, as great as or greater than the original au-thor.... [T]he purchaser of derivative rights has no truly effective way to protect himself against the eventuality of the author's death before the renewal period since there is no way of telling who will be the surviving widow, children or next of kin or the executor until that date arrives." 551 F.2d, at 493.

The Court of Appeals for the Second Circuit thereby shifted the focus from the right to use the pre-existing work in a derivative work to a right inhering in the created derivative work itself. By rendering the renewal right to use the original work irrelevant, the court created an exception to our ruling in *Miller Music* and, as petitioners concede, created an "intrusion" on the statutorily created rights of the owner of the pre-existing work in the renewal term.

Though petitioners do not, indeed could not, argue that its language ex-pressly supports the theory they draw from *Rohauer,* they implicitly rely on § 6 of the Act, 17 U.S.C. § 7 (1976 ed.), which states that "dramatizations ... of copyrighted works when produced with the consent of the proprietor of the copyright in such works ... shall be regarded as new works subject to copy-right under the provisions of this title." Petitioners maintain that the creation of the "new," i.e., derivative, work extinguishes any right the owner of rights in the pre-existing work might have had to sue for infringement that occurs during the renewal term.

We think, as stated in Nimmer on Copyright, that "[t]his conclusion is neither warranted by any express provision of the Copyright Act, nor by the rationale as to the scope of protection achieved in a derivative work. It is moreover contrary to the axiomatic copyright principle that a person may exploit only such copyrighted literary material as he either owns or is licensed to use." 1 Nimmer § 3.07[A], pp. 3-23 to 3-24 (footnotes omitted). The aspects of a derivative work added by the derivative author are that author's property, but the element drawn from the pre-existing work remains on grant from the owner of the pre-existing work. See *Russell v. Price,* 612 F.2d 1123, 1128 (CA9 1979) (reaffirming "well-established doctrine that a derivative copyright protects only the new material contained in the derivative work, not the matter derived from the underlying work"), cert. denied, 446 U.S. 952 (1980) .... So long as the pre-existing work remains out of the public domain, its use is infringing if one who employs the work does not have a valid license or assignment for use of the pre-existing work. *Russell v. Price, supra,* at 1128 .... It is irrelevant whether the pre-existing work is inseparably intertwined with the derivative work.... Indeed, the plain language of § 7 supports the view that the full force of the copyright in the pre-existing work is preserved despite incorporation into the derivative work. See 17 U.S.C. § 7 (1976 ed.) (publication of the derivative work "shall not affect the force or validity of any subsisting copyright upon the matter employed"); see also 17 U.S.C. § 3 (1976 ed.) (copyright protection of a work extends to "all matter therein in which copyright is already subsisting, but without extending the duration or scope of such copyright"). This well-settled rule also was made explicit in the 1976 Act:

> "The copyright in a compilation or derivative work extends only to the material contributed by the author of such work, as distinguished from the preexisting material employed in the work, and does not imply any exclusive right in the preexisting material. The copyright in such work is independent of, and does not affect or enlarge the scope, duration, ownership, or subsistence of, any copyright protection in the pre-existing material." 17 U.S.C. § 103(b).

See also B. Ringer, Renewal of Copyright (1960), reprinted as Copyright Law Revision Study No. 31, prepared for the Senate Committee on the Judiciary, 86th Cong., 2d. Sess., 169-170 (1961) ("[O]n the basis of judicial authority, legislative history, and the opinions of the commentators, ... someone cannot avoid his obligations to the owner of a renewal copyright merely because he created and copyrighted a 'new version' under a license or assignment which terminated at the end of the first term") (footnotes omitted)....

[W]e conclude that neither the 1909 Act nor the 1976 Act provides support for the theory set forth in *Rohauer.* And even if the theory found some support in the statute or the legislative history, the approach set forth in *Rohauer* is problematic. Petitioners characterize the result in *Rohauer* as a bright-line "rule." The Court of Appeals in *Rohauer,* however, expressly implemented policy considerations as a means of reconciling what it viewed as the competing interests in that case. See 551 F.2d, at 493-494. While the result in *Rohauer* might make some sense in some contexts, it makes no sense in others. In the case of a condensed book, for example, the contribution by the derivative author may be little, while the contribution by the original author is great. Yet, under the *Rohauer* "rule," publication of the condensed book would not infringe the pre-existing work even though the derivative author has no license or valid grant of rights in the pre-existing work.... Thus, even if the *Rohauer* "rule" made sense in terms of policy in that case, it makes little sense when it is applied across the derivative works spectrum. Indeed, in the view of the commentators, *Rohauer* did not announce a "rule," but rather an "interest-balancing approach." See Jaszi, *When Works Collide: Derivative Motion Pictures, Underlying Rights, and the Public Interest*, 28 UCLA L. Rev. 715, 758-761 (1981); Note, *Derivative Copyright and the 1909 Act — New Clarity or Confusion?*, 44 Brooklyn L. Rev. 905, 926-927 (1978).

Finally, petitioners urge us to consider the policies underlying the Copyright Act. They argue that the rule announced by the Court of Appeals will undermine one of the policies of the Act — the dissemination of creative works — by leading to many fewer works reaching the public. Amicus Columbia Pictures asserts that "[s]ome owners of underlying work renewal copyrights may refuse to negotiate, preferring instead to retire their copyrighted works, and all derivative works based thereon, from public use. Others may make demands — like respondent's demand for 50% of petitioners' future gross proceeds in excess of advertising expenses ... — which are so exorbitant that a negotiated economic accommodation will be impossible." Brief for Columbia Pictures et al. as Amicus Curiae 21. These arguments are better addressed by Congress than the courts.

In any event, the complaint that the respondent's monetary request in this case is so high as to preclude agreement fails to acknowledge that an initially high asking price does not preclude bargaining. Presumably, respondent is asking for a share in the proceeds because he wants to profit from the distribution of the work, not because he seeks suppression of it.

Moreover, although dissemination of creative works is a goal of the Copyright Act, the Copyright Act creates a balance between the artist's right to control the work during the term of the copyright protection and the public's need for access to creative works. The copyright term is limited so that the public will not be permanently deprived of the fruits of an artist's labors.... But nothing in the copyright statutes would prevent an author from hoarding all of his works during the term of the copyright. In fact, this Court has held that a copyright owner has the capacity arbitrarily to refuse to license one who seeks to exploit the work. See *Fox Film Corp. v. Doyal*, 286 U.S. 123, 127 (1932).

The limited monopoly granted to the artist is intended to provide the necessary bargaining capital to garner a fair price for the value of the works passing into public use.... When an author produces a work which later commands a higher price in the market than the original bargain provided, the copyright statute is designed to provide the author the power to negotiate for the realized value of the work. That is how the separate renewal term was intended to operate.... At heart, petitioners' true complaint is that they will have to pay more for the use of works they have employed in creating their own works. But such a result was contemplated by Congress and is consistent with the goals of the Copyright Act.

With the Copyright Act of 1790, Congress provided an initial term of protection plus a renewal term that did not survive the author. In the Copyright Act of 1831, Congress devised a completely separate renewal term that survived the death of the author so as to create a "new estate" and to benefit the author's family, and, with the passage of the 1909 Act, his executors. The

1976 Copyright Act provides a single, fixed term, but provides an inalienable termination right. See 17 U.S.C. §§ 203, 302. The evolution of the duration of copyright protection tellingly illustrates the difficulties Congress faces in attempting to "secur[e] for limited Times to Authors ... the exclusive Right to their respective Writings." U.S. Const., Art. I, § 8, cl. 8. Absent an explicit statement of congressional intent that the rights in the renewal term of an owner of a pre-existing work are extinguished upon incorporation of his work into another work, it is not our role to alter the delicate balance Congress has labored to achieve.

. . . .

III

Petitioners assert that even if their use of "It Had to Be Murder" is unauthorized, it is a fair use and, therefore, not infringing. . . .

The Court of Appeals determined that the use of Woolrich's story in the petitioners' motion picture was not fair use. We agree. The motion picture neither falls into any of the categories enumerated in § 107 nor meets the four criteria set forth in § 107. "[E]very [unauthorized] commercial use of copyrighted material is presumptively an unfair exploitation of the monopoly privilege that belongs to the owner of the copyright." *Sony Corp. of America v. Universal Studios, Inc.,* [464 U.S. 417 (1984)] at 451. Petitioners received $12 million from the re-release of the motion picture during the renewal term. 863 F.2d, at 1468. Petitioners asserted before the Court of Appeals that their use was educational rather than commercial. The Court of Appeals found nothing in the record to support this assertion, nor do we.

Applying the second factor, the Court of Appeals pointed out that "[a] use is less likely to be deemed fair when the copyrighted work is a creative product." 863 F.2d, at 1481 (citing *Brewer v. Hustler Magazine, Inc.,* 749 F.2d 527, 529 (CA9 1984)). In general, fair use is more likely to be found in factual works than in fictional works. . . .

Examining the third factor, the Court of Appeals determined that the story was a substantial portion of the motion picture. See *Harper & Row,* 471 U.S., at 564-565 (finding unfair use where quotation from book "'took what was essentially the heart of the book'"). The motion picture expressly uses the story's unique setting, characters, plot, and sequence of events. Petitioners argue that the story comprised only 20% of the motion picture's story line, Brief for Petitioners 40, n. 69, but that does not mean that a substantial portion of the story was not used in the motion picture. "[A] taking may not be excused merely because it is insubstantial with respect to the infringing work." *Harper & Row, supra,* at 565.

The fourth factor is the "most important, and indeed, central fair use factor." 3 Nimmer § 13.05[A], p. 13-81. The record supports the Court of Appeals' conclusion that re-release of the film impinged on the ability to market new versions of the story. Common sense would yield the same conclusion. Thus, all four factors point to unfair use. "This case presents a classic example of an unfair use: a commercial use of a fictional story that adversely affects the story owner's adaptation rights." 863 F.2d, at 1482.

For the foregoing reasons, the judgment of the Court of Appeals is affirmed and the case is remanded for further proceedings consistent with this opinion.

It is so ordered.

[The concurring opinion of Justice White and the dissent of Justice Stevens are omitted.]

QUESTIONS

1. Didn't the Supreme Court avoid the thorniest issue regarding renewals and derivative works: apportionment of control and/or compensation when the immense success of the derivative work owes much to the "new matter"? How would you resolve the question?

2. If you were the owner of copyright in a motion picture that had been based on a previously published (or unpublished) story, must you stop exhibiting and distributing it to the public? What information would you need in order to decide that question, and how would you go about securing such information?

3. If you were the owner of copyright in a motion picture that had been based on a completely original screenplay but that incorporates a three-minute song written by a well-known songwriter (who had assigned copyright in the song to the motion picture producer), must you stop exhibiting and distributing the film to the public?

The recent amendment to § 304(a), which provides for automatic renewal of copyrighted works published between 1964 and 1977 (see pp. 326-27, *supra*), would partly limit the effect of the *Rear Window* decision. If a renewal registration is filed, the author's heirs would take a "new estate" despite the author's grant, as in *Rear Window*. But, under § 304(a)(4)(A) of the new law, if no filing is made, and renewal simply occurs by operation of law, then even if the author has died before the renewal term vested, "a derivative work prepared under authority of a grant or transfer or license of copyright that is made before the expiration of the original term of copyright may continue to be used during the renewed and extended term of copyright without infringing the copyright, except that such use does not extend to the preparation during such renewed and extended term of other derivative works based upon the copyrighted work covered by such grant." *Cf.* 17 U.S.C. § 203(b)(1) (implementing a similar solution for derivative works prepared under the authority of a terminated grant).

RUSSELL v. PRICE

612 F.2d 1123 (9th Cir. 1979)

Goodwin, Circuit Judge: Defendants distributed copies of the film "Pygmalion," the copyright for which had expired. They were sued by the owners of the renewal copyright in the George Bernard Shaw play upon which the film was based. Defendants appeal the resulting judgment for damages and attorney fees.

Plaintiffs cross appeal, claiming that the court erred in not awarding them statutory "in lieu" damages. We affirm.

In 1913 Shaw registered a copyright on his stage play "Pygmalion." The renewal copyright on the play, obtained in 1941 and originally scheduled to expire in 1969, was extended by Congressional action to the year 1988. Shaw died in 1950 and the plaintiffs, except for Janus Films, are current proprietors of the copyright. Janus Films is a licensee.

In 1938 a derivative version of the play, a motion picture also entitled "Pygmalion," was produced under a license from Shaw; neither the terms nor the licensee's identity appear in the record. The film was produced by Gabriel Pascal, copyrighted by Loew's, and distributed by Metro-Goldwyn-Mayer ("MGM"). For undisclosed reasons, the film's copyright was allowed to expire in 1966. When and if the original film rights agreement expired is also not disclosed.

In 1971 the play's copyright proprietors licensed Janus Films to be the exclusive distributor of the film "Pygmalion." Shortly after discovering in 1972 that Budget Films was renting out copies of the 1938 film, Janus brought an action against Budget in a California state court, alleging state causes of action — in particular, unfair competition. That case ended in Budget's favor upon a determination that the action was essentially one for copyright infringement over which the state court lacked jurisdiction. The English copyright proprietors then executed a power of attorney in favor of their licensee Janus, and Janus promptly brought this action in federal district court in May 1975.

. . . .

II. *Infringement*

Defendants' main contention on the primary issue in this litigation is simply stated: Because the film copyright on "Pygmalion" has expired, that film is in the public domain, and, consequently, prints of that film[9] may be used freely by anyone. Thus, they argue that their renting out of the film does not infringe the statutory copyright on Shaw's play.

Defendants rely almost entirely on the recent opinion of Judge Friendly in *Rohauer v. Killiam Shows, Inc.*, 551 F.2d 484 (2d Cir.), *cert. denied*, 431 U.S. 949 (1977). However, in so relying, they ignore or fail to appreciate the significant differences between that case and this one. [The court discussed and distinguished *Rohauer*.]

[W]hen the independent copyright on the derivative work has been allowed to expire, ... there is no longer a conflict between two copyrights, each apparently granting "their proprietors overlapping 'exclusive' rights to use whatever underlying material ... had been incorporated into the derivative film." Thus, the persons who might have had standing to raise the *Rohauer* claim

---

[9]Defendants admit that any new motion picture or other derivative work produced without the permission of the proprietors of the copyright on Shaw's play would infringe that underlying copyright.

here could, consistently with that case, be held to have forfeited it by their failure to renew the derivative copyright. Defendants here could never have laid claim to the right recognized in *Rohauer,* and we perceive no reason to award it to them at the expense of the holders of the renewal copyright which still covers the Shaw play.

Thus, we reaffirm, without finding it necessary to repeat the rationale, the well-established doctrine that a derivative copyright protects only the new material contained in the derivative work, not the matter derived from the underlying work. 1 Nimmer on Copyright § 3.04 (1979). Thus, although the derivative work may enter the public domain, the matter contained therein which derives from a work still covered by statutory copyright is not dedicated to the public. [Citations omitted.] The established doctrine prevents unauthorized copying or other infringing use of the underlying work or any part of that work contained in the derivative product so long as the underlying work itself remains copyrighted. Therefore, since exhibition of the film "Pygmalion" necessarily involves exhibition of parts of Shaw's play, which is still copyrighted, plaintiffs here may prevent defendants from renting the film for exhibition without their authorization.

Defendants seek finally to avoid this result by citing *Classic Film Museum, Inc. v. Warner Bros., Inc.,* 597 F.2d 13 (1st Cir. 1979), *aff'g* 453 F. Supp. 852 (D. Me. 1978). That decision concerned "the legal effect of an expired statutory copyright on work derived from an underlying work in which there exists a common-law copyright." 597 F.2d at 13. Although defendants would have us ignore the major difference between an underlying common-law copyright and an underlying statutory copyright (the former extending in perpetuity,[17] the latter restricted in length) that difference is the linchpin of the court's holding in *Classic Film* that a person could exhibit the motion picture "A Star is Born," on which the film copyright had expired, without infringing the common-law copyright in the unpublished screenplay and musical score from which the film was derived. The court found the [new estate] doctrine inapplicable for the following reason:

> [A]ny protection offered by the [new estate] doctrine was limited to the fixed life of the underlying copyright (28 years plus the renewal period). The [new estate] doctrine is not equally applicable where there is an underlying common-law copyright which might extend indefinitely. Such unending protection of the derivative work would allow the [new estate] exception to swallow the rule of limited monopoly found in the constitution and copyright statutes.

597 F.2d at 14. The underlying statutory copyright in the instant case will expire in 1988. After that time Budget may freely distribute its copies of the 1938 film. The result we reach here does not conflict with the limited monop-

---

[17] A common-law copyright, which exists from the time the original work is created, was lost only upon the proprietor's publication of the matter protected. 1 Nimmer on Copyright § 2.02 at 2.16 (1979). Common-law copyright is no longer recognized under the new Act, 17 U.S.C. § 301 (1978), although one existing prior to January 1, 1978 may continue to receive lengthy protection. 17 U.S.C. §§ 303, 302 (1978). *See, e.g.,* Classic Film Museum, Inc. v. Warner Bros., Inc., 453 F. Supp. at 856 n.4.

oly policy rooted in the Copyrights Clause of the constitution and advanced in the congressional acts.

For the foregoing reasons, we conclude that defendants' activities here infringed the subsisting copyright in Shaw's play and were properly enjoined.
....

Affirmed.

Filmvideo Releasing Corp. v. Hastings, 668 F.2d 91 (2d Cir. 1981). In a case presenting issues similar to those confronted in *Russell v. Price,* the Second Circuit upheld the copyright infringement claim of the estate of the author of the Hopalong Cassidy books against a party seeking, without authorization from the author or his estate, to sell television exhibition rights in early motion pictures based on the books. The copyrights in the motion pictures, which had been created under license from the author, had expired through non-renewal. The books were still in their renewal term. The party seeking to sell television exhibition rights had argued in the district court that the author, having sold film rights, had no claim with respect to exhibition of the films on television. The district court held that although the author had parted with theatrical motion picture exhibition rights, the author had specifically reserved all television, broadcasting and radio rights.

On appeal, the Second Circuit stated that it agreed with the Ninth Circuit's *Russell v. Price* decision that the expiration of the copyright in a film that incorporates portions of an underlying copyrighted work does not cast the incorporated portions of the underlying work into the public domain along with the film. The Second Circuit also observed that the Hopalong Cassidy author had retained television rights when he licensed the production of the films which subsequently fell into the public domain. (In *Russell v. Price,* the terms of George Bernard Shaw's contract with the film company that produced the movie version of *Pygmalion* were not of record.)

QUESTION

In 1945, Augustus Author published a memoir of his school days, *Class After Class.* That same year, in return for a lump sum, he assigned all motion picture and television rights in the first and renewal terms to Film Company. In 1947, Film Company created and registered the movie *Endless Class* for copyright. In 1973 Author, still living, renewed the copyright in *Class After Class.* In 1975, *Endless Class* "fell into the public domain" through Film Company's failure to renew the copyright in the motion picture. In 1992, WOOP-TV, without having secured a license from anybody, broadcasts *Endless Class.* Author sues WOOP-TV on the basis of the subsisting copyright in *Class After Class.* What arguments would you raise in WOOP's defense?

C. TERMINATION OF TRANSFERS

Under the 1909 Copyright Act and its predecessors, the principal purpose of the renewal format was to assure that a transferred copyright, when the transfer was made in the initial term, could be recaptured by the author (or his surviving family, or legatee, or next of kin) after a reasonable time. The economic rewards during the renewal term could thus be fully enjoyed by the author, unencumbered by any rights, interests, or licenses previously contracted away. The author, or her statutory successors, was to have a "new estate," a second chance to license or assign for a new consideration.

Once Congress decided to abandon the two-part renewal format and to endorse a single term of copyright — beginning with the work's creation and ending fifty years after the author's death — it had to determine whether, and how, to structure a "right of recapture" of the copyright comparable to that provided under the earlier statutes. This was not only an issue with respect to works created after January 1, 1978, to which the "life plus 50" yardstick applied. It was even more of an issue for works that were already in copyright under the 1909 Act, as to which the author (or statutory successor) had conveyed the renewal term — at a time (prior to January 1, 1978) when that term was understood by the parties to last for only 28 years. In such a case, who should benefit from the 19 years that Congress added to the renewal term subsequent to the grant, the author or the assignee? — and if the former, how should the recapture be effected?

In these two situations, Congress provided for a termination of copyright transfer. Section 203 governs transfers made after the effective date of the 1976 Act, and section 304(c) governs transfers of renewal interests made before that date.

HOUSE REPORT

H.R. Rep. No. 94-1476, 94th Cong., 2d Sess. 124-28 (1976)

The problem in general

The provisions of section 203 are based on the premise that the reversionary provisions of the present section on copyright renewal (17 U.S.C. sec. 24) should be eliminated, and that the proposed law should substitute for them a provision safeguarding authors against unremunerative transfers. A provision of this sort is needed because of the unequal bargaining position of authors, resulting in part from the impossibility of determining a work's value until it has been exploited. Section 203 reflects a practical compromise that will further the objectives of the copyright law while recognizing the problems and legitimate needs of all interests involved.

Scope of the provision

Instead of being automatic, as is theoretically the case under the present renewal provision, the termination of a transfer or license under section 203 would require the serving of an advance notice within specified time limits and under specified conditions. However, although affirmative action is needed to effect a termination, the right to take this action cannot be waived in advance or contracted away. Under section 203(a) the right of termination would apply only to transfers and licenses executed after the effective date of the new statute, and would have no retroactive effect.

The right of termination would be confined to inter vivos transfers or licenses executed by the author, and would not apply to transfers by the author's successors in interest or to the author's own bequests. The scope of the right would extend not only to any "transfer of copyright ownership," as defined in section 101, but also to nonexclusive licenses. The right of termination would not apply to "works made for hire," which is one of the principal reasons the definition of that term assumed importance in the development of the bill.

Who can terminate a grant

Two issues emerged from the disputes over section 203 as to the persons empowered to terminate a grant: (1) the specific classes of beneficiaries in the case of joint works; and (2) whether anything less than unanimous consent of all those entitled to terminate should be required to make a termination effective. The bill to some extent reflects a compromise on these points, including a recognition of the dangers of one or more beneficiaries being induced to "hold out" and of unknown children or grandchildren being discovered later. The provision can be summarized as follows:

1. In the case of a work of joint authorship, where the grant was signed by two or more of the authors, majority action by those who signed the grant, or by their interests, would be required to terminate it.

2. There are three different situations in which the shares of joint authors, or of a dead author's widow or widower, children, and grandchildren, must be divided under the statute: (1) The right to effect a termination; (2) the ownership of the terminated rights; and (3) the right to make further grants of reverted rights. The respective shares of the authors, and of a dead author's widow or widower, children, and grandchildren, would be divided in exactly the same way in each of these situations. The terms "widow," "widower," and "children" are defined in section 101 in an effort to avoid problems and uncertainties that have arisen under the present renewal section.

3. The principle of per stirpes representation would also be applied in exactly the same way in all three situations. Take for example, a case where a dead author left a widow, two living children, and three grandchildren by a third child who is dead. The widow will own half of the reverted interests, the two children will each own $16\frac{2}{3}$ percent, and the three grandchildren will each own a share of roughly $5\frac{1}{2}$ percent. But who can exercise the right of termination? Obviously, since she owns 50 percent, the widow is an essential party, but suppose neither of the two surviving children is willing to join her in the termination; is it enough that she gets one of the children of the dead child to join, or can the dead child's interest be exercised only by the action of a majority of his children? Consistent with the per stirpes principle, the interest of a dead child can be exercised only as a unit by majority action of his surviving children. Thus, even though the widow and one grandchild would own $55\frac{1}{2}$ percent of the reverted copyright, they would have to be joined by another child or grandchild in order to effect a termination or a further

transfer of reverted rights. This principle also applies where, for example, two joint authors executed a grant and one of them is dead; in order to effect a termination, the living author must be joined by a per stirpes majority of the dead author's beneficiaries. The notice of termination may be signed by the specified owners of termination interests or by "their duly authorized agents," which would include the legally appointed guardians or committees of persons incompetent to sign because of age or mental disability.

When a grant can be terminated

Section 203 draws a distinction between the date when a termination becomes effective and the earlier date when the advance notice of termination is served. With respect to the ultimate effective date, section 203(a)(3) provides, as a general rule, that a grant may be terminated during the 5 years following the expiration of a period of 35 years from the execution of the grant. As an exception to this basic 35-year rule, the bill also provides that "if the grant covers the right of publication of the work, the period begins at the end of 35 years from the date of publication of the work under the grant or at the end of 40 years from the date of execution of the grant, whichever term ends earlier." This alternative method of computation is intended to cover cases where years elapse between the signing of a publication contract and the eventual publication of the work.

The effective date of termination, which must be stated in the advance notice, is required to fall within the 5 years following the end of the applicable 35- or 40-year period, but the advance notice itself must be served earlier. Under section 203(a)(4)(A), the notice must be served "not less than two or more than ten years' before the effective date stated in it.

As an example of how these time-limit requirements would operate in practice, we suggest two typical contract situations:

Case 1: Contract for theatrical production signed on September 2, 1987. Termination of grant can be made to take effect between September 2, 2022 (35 years from execution) and September 1, 2027 (end of 5 year termination period). Assuming that the author decides to terminate on September 1, 2022 (the earliest possible date) the advance notice must be filed between September 1, 2012 and September 1, 2020.

Case 2: Contract for book publication executed on April 10, 1980; book finally published on August 23, 1987. Since contract covers the right of publication, the 5-year termination period would begin on April 10, 2020 (40 years from execution) rather than April 10, 2015 (35 years from execution) or August 23, 2022 (35 years from publication). Assuming that the author decides to make the termination effective on January 1, 2024, the advance notice would have to be served between January 1, 2014, and January 1, 2022.

Effect of termination

Section 203(b) makes clear that, unless effectively terminated within the applicable 5-year period, all rights covered by an existing grant will continue unchanged, and that rights under other Federal, State, or foreign laws are unaffected. However, assuming that a copyright transfer or license is terminated under section 203, who are bound by the termination and how are they affected?

Under the bill, termination means that ownership of the rights covered by the terminated grant reverts to everyone who owns termination interests on the date the notice of termination was served, whether they joined in signing the notice or not. In other words, if a person could have signed the notice, that person is bound by the action of the majority who did; the termination of the grant will be effective as to that person, and a proportionate share of the reverted rights automatically vests in that person. Ownership is divided proportionately on the same per stirpes basis as that provided for the right to effect termination under section 203(a) and, since the reverted rights vest on the date notice is served, the heirs of a dead beneficiary would inherit his or her share.

Under clause (3) of subsection (b), majority action is required to make a further grant of reverted rights. A problem here, of course, is that years may have passed between the time the reverted rights vested and the time the new owners want to make a further transfer; people may have died and children may have been born in the interim. To deal with this problem, the bill looks back to the date of vesting; out of the group in whom rights vested on that date, it requires the further transfer or license to be signed by "the same number and proportion of the owners" (though not necessarily the same individuals) as were then required to terminate the grant under subsection (a). If some of those in whom the rights originally vested have died, their "legal representatives, legatees, or heirs at law" may represent them for this purpose and, as in the case of the termination itself, any one of the minority who does not join in the further grant is nevertheless bound by it.

An important limitation on the rights of a copyright owner under a terminated grant is specified in section 203(b)(1). This clause provides that, notwithstanding a termination, a derivative work prepared earlier may "continue to be utilized" under the conditions of the terminated grant; the clause adds, however, that this privilege is not broad enough to permit the preparation of other derivative works. In other words, a film made from a play could continue to be licensed for performance after the motion picture contract had been terminated but any remake rights covered by the contract would be cut off. For this purpose, a motion picture would be considered as a "derivative work" with respect to every "preexisting work" incorporated in it, whether the preexisting work was created independently or was prepared expressly for the motion picture.

Section 203 would not prevent the parties to a transfer or license from voluntarily agreeing at any time to terminate an existing grant and negotiating a new one, thereby causing another 35-year period to start running. However, the bill seeks to avoid the situation that has arisen under the present renewal provision, in which third parties have bought up contingent future interests as a form of speculation. Section 203(b)(4) would make a further grant of rights that revert under a terminated grant valid "only if it is made after the effective date of the termination." An exception, in the nature of a right of "first refusal," would permit the original grantee or a successor of such grantee to negotiate a new agreement with the persons effecting the termination at any time after the notice of termination has been served.

Nothing contained in this section or elsewhere in this legislation is intended to extend the duration of any license, transfer or assignment made for a period of less than thirty-five years. If, for example, an agreement provides an earlier termination date or lesser duration, or if it allows the author the right of cancelling or terminating the agreement under certain circumstances, the duration is governed by the agreement. Likewise, nothing in this section or legislation is intended to change the existing state of the law of contracts concerning the circumstances in which an author may cancel or terminate a license, transfer, or assignment.

Section 203(b)(6) provides that, unless and until termination is effected under this section, the grant, "if it does not provide otherwise," continues for the term of copyright. This section means that, if the agreement does not contain provisions specifying its term or duration, and the author has not terminated the agreement under this section, the agreement continues for the term of the copyright, subject to any right of termination under circumstances which may be specified therein. If, however, an agreement does contain provisions governing its duration — for example, a term of fifty years — and the author has not exercised his or her right of termination under the statute, the agreement will continue according to its terms — in this example, for only fifty years. The quoted language is not to be construed as requiring agreements to reserve the right of termination.

SUMMARY OF TERMINATION PROVISIONS UNDER § 203

1. *Grants covered*

(a) transfers *or* licenses of *any* rights under copyright — exclusive or non-exclusive
(b) executed *on or after* January 1, 1978
(c) by an author
(d) as to *any* work — i.e., created before or after January 1, 1978 and whether, on that date, work was subject to common law (§ 303), statutory first term (§ 304(a)), renewal (§ 304(b)), life-plus-fifty (§ 302(a)) or alternative fixed term (§ 302(c)) protection
(e) except as to:

(i) works made for hire
(ii) dispositions by will

2. *Persons who may exercise right*

(a) the author or a majority of the authors who made grant
(b) if an author is dead, his or her right may be exercised by (or if he or she was one of joint authors, his or her interest may be "voted" by) majority action of the owners of more than one-half of author's termination interest, such interest being owned as follows:

(i) by surviving spouse (if no children or grandchildren)

(ii) by children and surviving children of deceased child (if no surviving spouse) or

(iii) shared, one-half by widow and one-half by children and deceased child's children (per stirpes and by majority action)

3. *Effective date of termination*

(a) designated time during 36th through 40th year after grant or

(b) if grant covers right of publication, designated time during five-year period beginning on the earlier of the following dates:

(i) 35 years after publication

(ii) 40 years after grant

(c) Upon 2-10 years notice

4. *Manner of terminating*

(a) written and signed notice by required persons to "grantee or grantee's successor in title"

(b) specification of effective date, within above limits

(c) form, content and manner of service in accordance with Copyright Office regulation

(d) recordation in Copyright Office before effective date

(e) termination right may not be waived or contracted away in advance

(f) interests under termination vest on service of notice

5. *Effect of termination*

reversion to author, authors or others owning author's termination interest (including those who did not join in signing termination notice) in proportionate shares

6. *Exceptions to termination*

(a) utilization of derivative work made under grant prior to termination (but no right to make a new derivative work)

(b) rights outside federal copyright statute

7. *Further grants of terminated rights*

(a) must be made by same number and proportion of owners required for termination, then binds all

(b) must be made after termination, except, as to original grantee or successor in title, agreement may be made after service of notice of termination

SUMMARY OF TERMINATION PROVISIONS UNDER § 304(c)

As discussed above in this chapter, § 304(a) extended the twenty-eight year length of the renewal term that was provided under the 1909 Act. Under the 1976 Act, if works in their initial term of copyright on January 1, 1978 were made the subject of a proper renewal application, the renewal term would last forty-seven years. Works already in their renewal term on that date would automatically have that term extended to forty-seven years. With Congress having decided to permit the termination after thirty-five years of copyright transfers made after January 1, 1978, the case was all the more compelling to provide for a similar termination power regarding renewal-term transfers that were effected prior to that date, when the nineteen-year extension of the renewal term was obviously not made part of the bargain. As stated in the House Report (at page 140), "the extended term represents a completely new property right, and there are strong reasons for giving the author, who is the fundamental beneficiary of copyright under the Constitution, an opportunity to share in it." Thus, for pre-1978 transfers, the nineteen-year extension of the renewal term may be recaptured by the transferor, but only by complying with the notification provisions of § 304(c), which substantially parallel those of § 203.

1. *Grants covered*

    (a) transfers *or* licenses of *renewal* rights — exclusive or nonexclusive
    (b) executed *before* January 1, 1978
    (c) by a person designated by section 304(a)(1)(C)
    (d) where statutory copyright — first or renewal term — is subsisting on January 1, 1978 (common-law copyrights are not covered)
    (e) except as to

        (i) works made for hire
        (ii) dispositions by will

2. *Persons who may exercise right*

    (a) as to grants by author(s):

        (i) the author(s) to extent of such author(s)' interest
        (ii) if an author is dead, by owners of more than one-half of author's termination interest, such interest being owned as follows:
        (A) By surviving spouse (if no children or grandchildren)
        (B) By children and surviving children of dead child (if no surviving spouse) or
        (C) shared, one-half by widow and one-half by children and deceased's child's children (per stirpes and by majority action)

    (b) as to grants by others — *all* surviving grantors

3. *Effective date of termination*

    (a) Designated time during five-year period beginning on *later* of following dates:

        (i) end of 56th year of copyright *or*
        (ii) January 1, 1978

    (b) Upon 2-10 years' notice

4. *Manner of terminating*

(a) written and signed notice by required persons or agents to grantee or grantee's "successor in title"

(b) specification of effective date, within above limits

(c) form, content and manner of service in accordance with Copyright Office regulations (These have now been issued. 37 CFR § 201.10).

(d) recordation in Copyright Office before effective date

(e) termination right may not be waived or contracted away in advance

(f) interests under termination vest on service of notice

5. *Effect of a termination*

(a) of grant by author

    (i) reversion to that author or, if dead, those owning author's termination interest (including those who did not join in signing termination notice) in proportionate shares

(b) of grant by others — reversion to all entitled to terminate

(c) in either case, future rights to revert vest upon proper service of notice of termination

6. *Exceptions to termination*

(a) utilization of derivative work prepared under grant prior to termination (no right to make another derivative work)

(b) rights outside federal copyright statute

7. *Further grants of terminated rights*

(a) each owner is tenant in common except that a further grant by owners of particular dead author's rights must be made by same number and proportion of his beneficiaries as required to terminate, but then binds them all, including non-signers, as to such rights

(b) must be made after termination, except that, as to original grantee or successor in title, agreement may be after *notice* of termination

COMPARISON OF TERMINATION PROVISIONS

The key distinctions between termination rights under § 304(c) and § 203 may be summarized as follows:

1. Grants Covered

§ 304(c)	§ 203
(a) before Jan. 1, 1978	(a) on or after Jan. 1, 1978
(b) by author or other person designated by § 304(a)(1)(C)	(b) by author
(c) of renewal right in statutory copyright	(c) of any right under any copyright

2. Persons Who May Exercise

Author or majority interest of his statutory beneficiaries (*per stirpes*) to the extent of that author's share	Author or majority of granting authors or majority of their respective beneficiaries, voting as a unit for each author and per stirpes

or

in case of grant by others, *all* surviving grantors

3. Beginning of Five-Year Termination Period

End of 56 years of copyright or January 1, 1978, whichever is later	End of 35 years from grant, or if covering publication right, either 35 years from publication or 40 years from grant whichever is earlier

4. Further Grants

Generally tenants in common with right to deal separately, except where dead author's rights are shared, then majority action (per stirpes) as to that author's share	Requires same number and proportion as required for termination

---

QUESTIONS

1. Songwriter, in 1965, near the end of the initial term of copyright in his song, assigned the renewal term (which was to begin in 1970) to Music Publisher. You, as counsel for Author, had him serve in 1990 a notice of termination of that transfer, the termination to become effective in 1998. The song is currently in the midst of a lucrative revival, and you believe that Topp Publisher will be willing to pay a great deal more for a transfer of the copyright in 1999. However, Music Publisher has written to your client, insisting that: (a) Songwriter has a statutory obligation to negotiate with Music Publisher between now and 1998, and (b) If Songwriter wishes to convey after 1998 any rights to the song, he has a statutory obligation to give Music Publisher a "right of first refusal" to match the offer made by any other interested publisher. Music Publisher rests its claims upon an interpretation of § 304(c)(6)(D). Are those claims meritorious? *See Bourne Co. v. MPL Commun., Inc.*, 675 F. Supp. 859 (S.D.N.Y. 1987).

2. Songwriter, in 1965, near the end of the initial term of copyright in his song, assigned the renewal term (which was to begin in 1970) to Music Publisher, in exchange for royalties. Songwriter died in 1980, and in his will he bequeathed "all of the income from my copyrights, including renewals," to his widow and his mistress in equal shares; Music Publisher has been making royalty payments to the two women. You represent the widow. On her behalf, you have served Music Publisher with notice of termination of the renewal grant, effective at the end of 1998. Counsel for the mistress, however, has claimed that the grant is not terminable, and therefore that the widow will have to continue to share the royalty payments made by Music Publisher until the copyright ends in December 2017. In making this claim, she asserts that § 304(c) does not provide for termination, because it applies only to renewal grants "otherwise than by will," and because Songwriter's widow has a copyright interest in the song only by virtue of the bequest in his will. Is this a convincing interpretation of the quoted phrase in § 304? *See Larry Spier, Inc. v. Bourne Co.,* 953 F.2d 774 (2d Cir. 1992).

TRANSFERS, RENEWALS AND TERMINATIONS

1. Work is created, published and copyrighted in 1960. In 1960, Author (hereinafter *A*) assigns the initial and renewal terms to *B*. If *A* lives through 1988, the assignment to *B* is effective and *A* will take the renewal on behalf of *B*. If *A* dies before 1988, leaving Surviving Spouse (hereinafter *S*), *S* is entitled to claim the renewal, and *B* will have no rights in the renewal term. (These results flow from § 304(a), as embellished (in its earlier form as § 24 of the 1909 Act) by *Fred Fisher Music Co. v. M. Witmark & Sons,* 318 U.S. 643 (1943).)

However, the additional nineteen years added to the renewal term by the 1976 Act can be recaptured by the giving of timely notice to *B*. If, when notice is given, *A* is alive, then it is *A* who is entitled to give the notice. If, when notice is given, *A* is dead and *S* is alive, then it is *S* who is entitled to give the notice. The right to give this notice and recapture the added nineteen years of the renewal term cannot be waived or assigned in advance by either *A* or *S*. (These results flow from § 304(c).)

2. Work is created (and therefore automatically copyrighted) by *A* in 1980. *A* transfers inter vivos the copyright (which will last for *A*'s life plus fifty years) to *B* the same year. That transfer may be terminated effective thirty-five to forty years thereafter (i.e., beginning in 2015) by timely notice. If, when notice of termination is given, *A* is alive, then it is *A* who is entitled to give the notice and claim the "reversion." If, when notice is given, *A* is dead and *S* is alive, then it is *S* who is entitled to give the notice and claim the "reversion." Neither *A* nor *S* can waive or assign in advance that power to terminate. (These results flow from § 203(a).)

3. As in case 2, work is created by *A* in 1980, but *A* transfers the copyright to *B* by a will upon *A*'s death in 1980, rather than inter vivos. The transfer may *not* be terminated and the copyright may *not* be recaptured by *S*, at any date in the future. (*See* § 203(a).) Is there any sense to the different outcomes in case 2 and case 3?

4. Work is created, published, and copyrighted in 1960 by *A*. In 1980, *A* assigns the initial and renewal terms to *B*.

If *A* lives into 1988, the assignment to *B* of the renewal term will be effective: Under *Fisher v. Witmark, A* will apply for the renewal but *B* will really own it. *A* will not be able to recapture the added nineteen years of the renewal term pursuant to § 304(c), since that section governs only transfers executed prior to January 1, 1978, and this transfer was made by *A* in 1980. Therefore,

B will be entitled to ownership of the renewal term throughout its duration, 1988 through 2035.

However, § 203 *will* govern, since the transfer by *A* to *B* was executed after January 1, 1978. Therefore, *A* may "recapture" the copyright thirty-five years after the 1980 transfer, or in 2015, even though at that time there are still twenty years remaining in *B*'s renewal term. And, if *A* dies between 1988 when the copyright was renewed and 2015, then *S* can exercise the termination right under § 203. In short, although *S* cannot oust *B* of *B*'s right to claim the renewal under these facts, *S* can shorten the renewal term enjoyed by *B*, simply by a timely termination.

5. As in case 4, the work is created, published and copyrighted by *A* in 1960, and the initial and renewal terms are assigned by *A* to *B* in 1980. However, *A* dies before 1988. By § 304(a), the assignment of the renewal term is ineffective, and *S* will be entitled to secure the renewal term, to the exclusion of *B*.

6. Finally, as in the above two cases, the work is created, published, and copyrighted by *A* in 1960. *A* dies in 1980, and by will transfers the initial and renewal terms to *B*. *S* will not be able to terminate that transfer in 2015, pursuant to § 203, because the transfer by *A* was not inter vivos. But do not anguish for *S* just yet. Although *A* can, in 1980, assign the remaining eight years of the initial term — either inter vivos or by will — *A*'s death before 1988 makes *S* the proper claimant of the renewal term, to the exclusion of *B*.

QUESTIONS

1. Author secures copyright in her novel in 1950, and in 1970 she executes a will in which she purports to devise the initial and renewal terms of the copyright to Princeton University. In 1978 she applies for and secures a renewal of the copyright. Author dies in 1980, leaving three daughters. In the year 2006 (fifty-six years from the date of the initial copyright, and twenty-eight years from the beginning of the renewal term) the daughters seek to join together to terminate the transfer of the renewal term in order to enjoy the remaining nineteen years of that term. May they do so under the 1976 Copyright Act? If not, why not?

2. Author creates and publishes a work in 1979, and transfers his copyright to Publisher by a will upon his death in 1980. At his death, Author leaves a widow, a son, and a daughter. In the year 2015, thirty-five years from the date of the transfer of the copyright to Publisher, Author's widow, son, and daughter are still living and wish to terminate the transfer in order to enjoy the remaining fifteen years of the copyright term. May they do so under the 1976 Copyright Act? If not, why not?

3. Section 203(a)(5) explicitly seeks to assure that the termination right will not be bargained away by the author and his family at the same time (or later) as they transfer their interest in the copyright itself. As attorney for the transferee of the copyright, is there a contract provision you can draft that would permit you, in effect, to prolong the transfer for more than thirty-five years? For example, would it be effective to provide that the grant shall terminate in thirty years and that the author (and any spouse and children

making the initial grant) shall be obligated to re-transfer the copyright for an additional thirty years at a stipulated price? (Even assuming some such provision to comply technically with the statute, would you as counsel conclude that this so frustrates the spirit of § 203(a)(5) that it would be improper for you to insert this in the contract of transfer?)

4. Is a termination right available in the following situations: (a) Work is created, published, and copyrighted in 1975. In 1980, *both* the author and his wife assign original and renewal copyrights to *B*. *A* dies in 1985 and *W* renews in 2003. (b) In 1974, *A* enters into a contract with Publisher *P* assigning to *P* the copyright in a future book, which *A* completes in 1976. The work is published in 1978.

5. Author creates a musical composition and assigns the copyright in the composition to Publishing Company in 1980. Publishing Company subsequently licenses Record Company to create a sound recording of the composition, and Record Company makes and distributes the sound recording. Effective 2015, Author terminates the assignment to Publishing Company. Is Record Company's license also terminated by the termination of the assignment to Publishing Company? If the rights of Record Company are not terminated, should Record Company pay royalties for continued distribution of the sound recording to Publishing Company, or to Author? *See Mills Music, Inc. v. Snyder,* 469 U.S. 153 (1985).

PROBLEM

Hundreds of manuscripts of songs, many of them previously unknown, by popular American composers, including George Gershwin, Jerome Kern, Cole Porter, Richard Rodgers, and Victor Herbert, have recently been discovered in a Warner Brothers warehouse in Secaucus, New Jersey. Many of these songs were never included in the depression-era movie musicals, such as *Showboat*, for which they had been composed.

Following national news coverage of the find, many claimants of rights in the songs are expected to come forward. You are counsel to Warner Brothers. What issues do you see regarding ownership of rights in the songs, and how would you resolve them?

Chapter 5

FORMALITIES

Perhaps no feature of United States copyright law has been more controversial than our requirement that, as a condition of protection, a work that has been "published" must contain a notice of copyright. Nor has any feature of our law been as subject to as rapid statutory change in the past twenty years. A notice requirement had been a feature of every United States copyright statute since the original Act of 1790. Although the placing of notice on published copies can serve as a warning to the unauthorized user, and can provide useful information, there is no *a priori* reason why the inclusion of a copyright notice need be required as a condition of protection. Indeed, for more than a century most of the major publishing nations of the world — with the principal exception of the United States — have had no notice requirements. This liberal approach toward the grant of copyright protection has been in large measure fostered by the dominant international copyright convention, the Berne Convention. Article 5(2) of Berne states that "the enjoyment and the exercise of [copyright] shall not be subject to any formality." Nonetheless, the United States throughout the twentieth century, even in the 1976 amendments effective on January 1, 1978, continued strictly to impose a notice requirement and thereby rendered itself ineligible for participation in the Berne Convention.

As will be noted below, the 1909 Act — although it failed to define the term "publication," the very significant behavior that gave rise to the notice requirement — provided detailed rules regarding the form and placement of the copyright notice. Failure of the copyright owner to comply with the notice requirements of the 1909 Act generally caused the work to fall into the public domain. Careless or inadvertent oversights thus resulted in many cases of loss of copyright. These consequences, and the desire to bring United States law closer to that contemplated by the Berne Convention, induced Congress in 1976 to make its first significant liberalization of the notice requirement. As will be noted further below, placement of notice on all copies of published works was still required, but omission was no longer fatal; most significantly, it could be cured by registration of the copyright and other action by the copyright owner within five years after publication.

Because the uncured failure to meet the statutory notice requirements continued even after January 1, 1978 to result in the loss of copyright protection, our law still failed to comport with Article 5(2) of the Berne Convention. A vigorous campaign in and out of Congress to amend our law to make it Berne-compatible resulted in the enactment of the Berne Convention Implementation Act of 1988, which became effective on March 1, 1989. For the first time in our history, notice on published copies and phonorecords is now no longer a condition of copyright protection. It remains, however, an option that is afforded to the copyright owner, an option that Congress continues to seek to promote.

What must be emphasized is that the recent changes in our law regarding copyright notice give no reason to the student to ignore the more strict requirements that prevailed under the 1909 Act or during the pre-Berne years of the 1976 Act (i.e., between January 1, 1978 and February 28, 1989). The statutory rules regarding copyright notice that were in effect at the time of the first publication of a work determine the copyright status of that work; failure to comply with those rules would thrust the work into the public domain, and no liberalizing amendments to the law thereafter can retrieve such work from the public domain. Because litigation well into the twenty-first century will involve works allegedly "published" while the 1909 Act was in effect, it is essential that the student be familiar with the pertinent formalities under that Act, and even more so with the formalities that were in effect during the first ten years of operation of the 1976 Act.

A. PUBLICATION AND NOTICE BEFORE THE 1976 ACT

The pivot of the 1909 law was the concept of "publication." This event was generally the dividing line between common-law protection on the one hand and either statutory or no protection on the other. Thus the traditional litany was that publication with the prescribed copyright notice secured statutory copyright, while publication without such notice placed a work in the public domain.

This rule was anchored in the text of § 10 of the 1909 Act, which provided: "Any person entitled thereto by this title *may* secure copyright for his work by *publication* thereof with the notice of copyright required by this title." (Emphasis added.) (For certain categories of works, however, the 1909 Act did allow, in § 12, for securing statutory protection through registration even in the absence of publication.) Publication, as the traditional requirement for statutory protection in this country, results from the legendary bargain between the public and the author reflected in a statutory system of copyright as construed by *Donaldson v. Becket*, 4 Burrows 2303, 98 Eng. Rep. 257 (1774). In order to induce the author to disclose his work to the public notwithstanding the resulting loss of his common-law protection, the statute substitutes new rights, albeit limited in time. As a corollary, the term of copyright was measured from "the date of first publication" according to § 24 of the statute.

The concept of "publication" as utilized in § 10 developed into a rather technical construct; it is not always coterminous with the general notion of "making public," nor even with the act that divests the author of common-law rights.

Definition of "Publication." The 1909 Act did not expressly define "publication." This omission was apparently based on the assumption that a general definition of this concept was too difficult. *Hearings on S. 6330 and H.R. 19853 Before Committee on Patents*, 59th Cong., 1st Sess. 71 (June 1906). In § 26, however, we are told that in the case of a work "of which copies are reproduced for sale or distribution," "the 'date of publication' shall ... be held to be the earliest date when copies of the first authorized edition were placed on sale, sold or publicly distributed by the proprietor of the copyright or under his authority." As noted by the court in *Cardinal Film Co. v. Beck,* 248 F. 368 (S.D.N.Y. 1918), the section was evidently intended to fix the date from which the term of copyright should begin to run for such a work, rather than to provide a general definition of what should constitute publication in all cases. The importance of the actual date of publication — the day, month, and year — arose because, in the case of every work copyrighted in the first instance by publication with notice, the first term of 28 years began to run from that date; hence any error on the part of the applicant could have had serious consequences, especially in connection with applications for renewals of copyright, which had to be made "within one year prior to the expiration of the original term of copyright." (This problem is avoided in the 1976 Act by the calendar-year ending of all terms, including those with renewals.)

Despite how crucial it was to have a clear understanding of the concept of "publication" under the 1909 Act, a number of rather arbitrary distinctions emerged in giving content to that term. Among the most well known, and most important, was the generally accepted rule that the public performance of a spoken drama did not constitute publication. This rule was established under the pre-1909 law. *Ferris v. Frohman,* 223 U.S. 424 (1912). The *Ferris* rule was applied by analogy to the exhibition of a motion picture, *DeMille v. Casey,* 12 Misc. 78 (N.Y. Sup. Ct. 1923); the public performance of a musical composition, whether for profit or not, *McCarthy v. White,* 259 F. 364 (S.D.N.Y. 1919); and the oral delivery of a lecture or address, *Nutt v. National Institute, Inc.,* 31 F.2d 236 (2d Cir. 1929), all irrespective of the methods employed, including radio broadcasting. *Uproar Co. v. National Broadcasting Co.,* 81 F.2d 373 (1st Cir. 1936). Thus, the oral delivery of the Martin Luther King speech before 200,000 people over radio and television did not amount to a divestive publication. *King v. Mister Maestro, Inc.,* 224 F. Supp. 101 (S.D.N.Y. 1963).

There was considerable uncertainty whether, under the 1909 Act, the general distribution of phonograph records of a musical or a literary work constituted a publication that forfeited common-law protection and required use of a copyright notice in order to secure statutory protection. A key influence in contributing to this uncertainty was a Supreme Court decision, under the pre-1909 law, which held that a perforated "pianola" music roll was not a "copy" of a musical composition and therefore did not infringe the copyright in the composition. *White-Smith Music Pub'g Co. v. Apollo Co.,* 209 U.S. 1 (1908). While Congress directly remedied this situation in 1909 by giving the copyright owner control in § 1(e) over mechanical reproduction of music, it did so without equating mechanical reproduction with "copy."

Accordingly, for many years, it was generally accepted in a number of contexts that a recording is not a "copy" of the work recorded, and in particular that the sale of records of a song did not oust common-law copyright and did not require the use of a copyright notice. The contrary view was stated by a few scholars and jurists, who thought that fully exploited works should not be entitled to perpetual common-law protection. It was stated in dictum, for example, in *Shapiro, Bernstein & Co. v. Miracle Record Co.*, 91 F. Supp. 473, 475 (N.D. Ill. 1950):

> It seems to me that production and sale of a phonograph record is fully as much a publication as production and sale of sheet music.

But it was later held in an influential appellate decision that under New York law the sale of records did not forfeit the performer's common-law right in his recorded performance. *Capitol Records, Inc. v. Mercury Records Corp.*, 221 F.2d 657 (2d Cir. 1955). The most detailed treatment of the problem was in *Rosette v. Rainbo Record Mfg. Corp.*, 354 F. Supp. 1183 (S.D.N.Y. 1973), *aff'd per curiam*, 546 F.2d 461 (2d Cir. 1976).

Moreover, considerable uncertainty was created as to the effect of publication of a derivative work — such as a reproduction of a work of art, or the motion picture based on a novel — on the status of the underlying work on which it is based. *Compare Rushton v. Vitale*, 218 F.2d 434 (2d Cir. 1955), *with Leigh v. Gerber*, 86 F. Supp. 320 (S.D.N.Y. 1949). This question has been most troublesome in connection with notice requirements. Presumably the answer in this context depends on whether the derivative work should be considered a "copy" of the underlying work within the meaning of the notice provisions.

Limited Publication. It should be apparent from the above discussion that disclosure or communication of a work to another person does not always amount to "publication" under the copyright law. Restricted communication of the contents of a work was generally held not to be a publication of the work. Distribution with limitation by the proprietor of the persons to whom the work is communicated and of the purpose of the disclosure was long known as "limited," "restricted," or "private" publication, but is, more accurately, no publication at all. *See White v. Kimmell*, 193 F.2d 774 (9th Cir.), *cert. denied*, 343 U.S. 957 (1952).

The absence of any effort to limit distribution or use of copies of speeches by a public official could result in a finding of publication with divestive effect. In *Public Affairs Assocs. v. Rickover*, 284 F.2d 262 (D.C. Cir. 1960), *judgment vacated*, 369 U.S. 111 (1962), *on remand*, 268 F. Supp. 444 (D.D.C. 1967), Justice Reed (sitting by designation) stated:

> Certainly when all of Admiral Rickover's acts of distribution are considered together — performance, distribution to the press, the copies sent to individuals at the recipient's request and those sent unsolicited, the copies sent in batches of 50 for distribution by the sponsors of speeches — it is difficult to avoid the conclusion that these acts, in their totality, constitute publication of the speeches and their dedication to the public domain.

284 F.2d at 271. The court remanded for further hearing, but its judgment was vacated by the Supreme Court for a more adequate record.

The *Rickover* case was distinguished in *King v. Mister Maestro, Inc.*, 224 F. Supp. 101 (S.D.N.Y. 1963), in which distribution in a press kit of "advance copies" of Rev. Martin Luther King Jr.'s famous "I Have a Dream" speech was held to be a limited publication because the copies were not offered *to the public*.

It is noteworthy that despite the stricter approach of the court of appeals in *Rickover,* that court nevertheless had recognized that limited distribution is easier to find in the case where divestiture, rather than securing copyright, is in issue. Thus the significance of "divestive" versus "investive" publication cannot be overlooked in this area. Because a "divestive" publication had the serious consequence of forfeiting common-law copyright and thrusting a work into the public domain if copies were distributed without copyright notice, a judicial trend developed, relatively late in the day, to demand a more convincing showing of extensive and unrestricted distribution for loss of copyright than would be required of an author who has affixed a notice to copies of his work and seeks to invoke federal copyright under § 10.

For example, it has been held that distribution of no less than two thousand copies of sheet music for "plugging" purposes did not divest copyright. *Hirshon v. United Artists Corp.,* 243 F.2d 640 (D.C. Cir. 1957) (§ 12 copyright preserved). On the other hand, unsupervised distribution of approximately two hundred copies of a book at a convention of persons potentially interested in using it was held to be a "publication" of the book within the meaning of § 10. *American Visuals Corp. v. Holland,* 239 F.2d 740. *Cf. Atlantic Monthly Co. v. Post Pub'g Co.,* 27 F.2d 556 (D. Mass. 1928) (sale of proof copy of magazine to publisher's treasurer held investive publication "insofar as the statutory formalities are concerned").

The Notice Requirement. Once a determination was made that a work was "published," the 1909 Act — as did most of its forebears — required the placement of a copyright notice in a specified location. This requirement was rooted in § 10: "Any person entitled thereto by this title may secure copyright for his work by publication thereof with the notice of copyright required by this title; and such notice shall be affixed to each copy thereof published or offered for sale in the United States by authority of the copyright proprietor." The required form of notice was set forth in § 19, which (with some minor exceptions) provided for the word "copyright" (or abbreviation) or the familiar copyright symbol, the name of the copyright proprietor and the year of publication. That section also mandated the location of the notice — for a book, "upon its title page or the page immediately following"; for a periodical, "either upon the title page or upon the first page of text of each separate number or under the title heading"; and for a musical work "either upon its title page or the first page of music."

Some courts were prepared to overlook minor departures from the form and location requirements of the 1909 Act, provided there was substantial compliance. This was particularly true if a technically inaccurate corporate or partnership name was used, but it was close enough to the name of the true copyright proprietor (e.g., a company with identical officers) such that no one could reasonably claim to have been misled. But other courts were more punctilious, operating on the theory that the copyright was a special legislative privilege that could be secured only through full compliance with formalities. Although a notice accompanying the masthead of a periodical (typically on the editorial page of a newspaper) was commonly regarded as satisfactory, it was, for example, held that it was improper to place the copyright notice on the back cover of a twenty-eight page pamphlet; such a defect was regarded as fatal, and the work was thrust into the public domain. *J.A. Richards, Inc. v. New York Post, Inc.,* 23 F. Supp. 619 (S.D.N.Y. 1938).

Inaccuracies in the year date placed in the notice could also be fatal to the copyright. The general rule that developed, through judicial decisions and Copyright Office regulations, was that an inaccurately *early* date was not fatal, but the beginning of the statutory term would be reckoned from that year (so as to shorten the term of protection, for the benefit of the public); while a notice that was *postdated* by more than one year (thus allowing for end-of-the-year slippage in publication schedules) was regarded as fatally defective.

Of course, if the required notice was altogether omitted, that too was fatal. The statute itself, however, in § 21, allowed of one exception: when the copyright owner had "sought to comply" with the notice provisions but "by accident or mistake" had omitted the notice "from a particular copy or copies." That oversight would not invalidate the copyright, but would "prevent the recovery of damages against an innocent infringer who has been misled by the omission of the notice." This statutory exception, however, was held not to apply if the omission of notice was through "neglect or oversight," *Sieff v. Continental Auto Supply, Inc.,* 39 F. Supp. 683 (D. Minn. 1941), or through a mistake of law, *Wildman v. New York Times Co.,* 42 F. Supp. 412 (S.D.N.Y. 1941).

THE CONTINUING IMPORTANCE OF "PUBLICATION" UNDER THE 1909 ACT

The adoption of a single federal statutory copyright from creation, instead of a dual system with publication as its line of bifurcation, has been considered to "accomplish a fundamental and significant change" in copyright law. S. Rep. No. 94-473, 94th Cong., 1st Sess. 112 (1975); H.R. Rep. No. 94-1476, 94th Cong., 2d Sess. 129 (1976). But the significance of publication under the 1909 law remains with us, both directly and indirectly. Its indirect significance is its precedential value in filling the interstices of the 1976 Act definition. Its direct significance is based on the underlying principle that the new law "does not provide copyright protection for any work that goes into the public domain before January 1, 1978." Trans. & Suppl. § 103 (90 Stat. 2599). Thus it seems inescapable that a court reviewing an alleged infringement committed in 1995, with respect to a work arguably first "published" in 1975 (or in 1935), will examine the statutory conditions of protection in 1975 to determine whether or not the work was in the public domain on January 1, 1978. *See* Nimmer, *Preface — The Old Copyright Act as a Part of the New Act,* 22 N.Y. L. Sch. L. Rev. 471 (1977). Among these will be the question whether "publication" has taken place at all and, if so, whether publication occurred with or without a notice proper under the 1909 Act. It is thus not accurate to say that the provisions of the 1909 Copyright Act concerning publication, and the many court decisions interpreting those provisions, were "displaced" on January 1, 1978.

ACADEMY OF MOTION PICTURE ARTS AND SCIENCES
v. CREATIVE HOUSE PROMOTIONS, INC.

944 F.2d 1446 (9th Cir. 1991)

PREGERSON, J.

....

The Academy was established by film industry leaders in 1927 to promote cultural, educational, and technological progress in general, and to advance motion picture arts and sciences in particular. In 1929, the Academy began its annual awards ceremony, in which it recognizes industry artists for outstanding achievement in their fields and bestows upon them the coveted "Oscar" statuette. The awards ceremony has been televised annually since 1953, and is seen across the United States and throughout the world. Pictures of the Oscar have been featured in the media since 1929.

From 1929 through 1941, the Academy claimed common law copyright protection for the Oscar as an unpublished work of art. Each of the 158 Oscars awarded during that time bore its winner's name, but did not display any statutory copyright notice. In 1941, the Academy registered the Oscar with the United States Copyright Office as an unpublished work of art not reproduced for sale. All Oscars awarded since that time contained statutory copyright notices. In 1968, the statutory copyright was renewed.

After securing the original copyright registration in 1941, the Academy restricted the manner in which winners could advertise their Oscars. Specifically, any advertisements featuring the Oscar had to identify the year and category in which the recipient won the award. The Academy also required recipients to give the Academy rights of first refusal on any intended sale of their Oscar. Before this time, the Academy had not placed any express restrictions on the use or disposal of the award.

In 1950, the estate of post-mortem Oscar recipient Sid Grauman offered Grauman's Oscar for sale at a public auction. No Oscar had previously been offered for sale. An Academy representative ultimately purchased the award.

In 1976, Creative House, a manufacturer and distributor of advertising specialty items, commissioned a trophy sculptor to design a striking figure holding a star in its hand. The finished product was a naked, muscular male figure closely resembling the Oscar, known as the "Star Award." Both the Star Award and the Oscar are solid metal with a shiny gold finish and stand on a circular gold cap mounted on a round base. The district court found only two significant differences between the two: the Star Award is two inches shorter than the Oscar, and holds a star rather than a sword.

Although Creative House initially produced the Star Award to honor its advertising agency client's "star" salespeople, it later sold the award to other corporate buyers. In the Chicago area, Creative House marketed the award directly to various corporate buyers through the Star Award incentive program. Under the program, corporate sales personnel who reached the highest level of achievement would receive the Star Award. In other areas of the country, the award was advertised in catalogs and single-page "cut sheets" and marketed through distributors. Most customers were corporate buyers who purchased the awards for employees as gifts.

In 1983, the Academy demanded that Creative House discontinue or significantly change the Star Award. Creative House refused. After negotiations between the parties broke down, the Academy filed suit for copyright infringement ....

After a bench trial, the district court ruled, in a published opinion that the Oscar was not entitled to copyright protection because a divesting, general publication of the Oscar occurred before the 1976 Copyright Act's effective date of January 1, 1978, which triggered a loss of the pre-1941, common law copyright. In concluding that the Oscar had "entered the public domain" through a general publication, the court rejected the Academy's argument that publication of the Oscar had been limited to a select group of persons for a limited purpose.

DISCUSSION

I. Copyright Validity

Under the Copyright Act of 1976 ("the 1976 Act"), 17 U.S.C. §§ 101-810, a copyrighted work is entitled to protection if it has not become part of the public domain prior to the Act's effective date of January 1, 1978. The district court ruled that the Oscar was not entitled to protection under the 1976 Act because it had entered the public domain through a general publication before it was protected by statutory copyright in 1941. The Academy attacks that ruling by arguing that the district court (1) failed to recognize and apply a presumption that the Oscar was a protected, unpublished work in light of its 1941 copyright registration certificate; and (2) erred in finding that a general publication of the Oscar occurred before January 1, 1987.

A. *Statutory Presumption*

The Academy maintains that the Oscar's 1941 copyright registration as a work "not reproduced for sale" under § 11 of the 1909 Copyright Act raised a statutory presumption of copyright validity that the district court ignored. Essentially, the Academy argues that if the Oscar had been "published" (i.e., made available to the general public in a manner that resulted in a "general publication" — see Section IB, *infra*) before 1941, it would not have been eligible for copyright under § 11; conversely, the fact the copyright was granted establishes that the Oscar had not been published before that date.

We agree that the district court erred in failing to afford the Academy's 1941 copyright a presumption of validity. Section 209 of the 1909 Act provides that a certificate of registration shall be prima facie evidence "of the facts stated therein." Although the "facts" stated in a certificate of registration are limited to the date, name and description of the work, and name of the registration holder, a majority of courts have held that § 209 creates a rebuttable presumption that the certificate holder has met all the requirements for copyright validity. *See Gaste v. Kaiserman*, 863 F.2d 1061, 1064-65 (2d Cir. 1988); *see also* H.R. No. 94-1476, 94th Cong., 2d Sess. at 157 (1976) ("The principle that a certificate represents prima facie evidence of copyright validity has been established in a long line of court decisions, and it is a sound one."). In this case, the certificate of registration creates a rebuttable presumption that the Oscar was an unpublished work in 1941. As a result, Creative House bore the burden of showing that the Oscar entered the public domain before 1941.

B. *General v. Limited Publication*

Under the common law, the creator of an artistic work has the right to copy and profit from the work, and can distribute or show it to a limited class of persons for a limited purpose without losing that common law copyright. *Burke v. National Broadcasting Co., Inc.*, 598 F.2d 688, 691 (1st Cir.), *cert. denied*, 444 U.S. 869 (1979). This sort of limited distribution is known as a "limited publication." If the creator exceeds the scope of a limited publication and allows the work to pass into the public domain, a "general publication" of the work occurs. At that point, unless the creator has obtained a statutory copyright, anyone can copy, distribute or sell the work. *Id.* Although an artistic work may be exposed to the public by exhibition, by limited publication, or by general publication, only general publication triggers the loss of the creator's common law copyright. *Id.* The distinction between general and limited publication reflects an attempt by courts to mitigate the harsh forfeiture effects of a divesting general publication. *American Vitagraph, Inc. v. Levy*, 659 F.2d 1023, 1027 (9th Cir. 1981). As a result, "it takes more in the way of publication to invalidate any copyright, whether statutory or common law, than to validate it." *Id., quoting Hirshon v. United Artists Corp.*, 100 App. D.C. 217, 243 F.2d 640, 645 (D.C. Cir. 1957).

The district court correctly determined that the Oscar did not become part of the public domain merely by being publicly displayed or presented at the award ceremonies. In general under the common law, mere performance or exhibition of an artistic work does not amount to a publication. *Ferris v. Frohman*, 223 U.S. 424 (1912); *Burke*, 598 F.2d at 691; *cf. Letter Edged in Black Press, Inc. v. Public Bldg. Comm'n of Chicago*, 320 F. Supp. 1303, 1309 (N.D. Ill. 1970). Moreover, publishing pictures of the Oscar in books, newspapers, and magazines did not thrust the award into the public domain, because publishing two-dimensional pictures does not constitute a divesting publication of three-dimensional objects. *See Kamar Intern, Inc. v. Russ Berrie and Co.*, 657 F.2d 1059, 1061-62 (9th Cir. 1981).

Although merely displaying the Oscar to the public does not divest the award of common law copyright protection, Creative House argues that the Academy's distribution of the Oscar to 158 recipients between 1929 and 1941 without any express restriction on the use or sale of the award amounted to a divesting, general publication of the work. The Academy maintains that the Oscar's distribution was merely a limited publication.

A general publication occurs when a work is made available to members of the public regardless of who they are or what they will do with it. *Burke*, 598 F.2d at 691. In contrast, a publication is "limited" — and does not trigger the loss of a common law copyright — when tangible copies of the work are distributed both (1) to a "definitely selected group," and (2) for a limited purpose, without the right of further reproduction, distribution or sale. *White v. Kimmell*, 193 F.2d 744, 746-47 (9th Cir.), *cert. denied*, 343 U.S. 957 (1952).

We consider each element of *White* 's two-part "limited publication" test separately.

1. Selected group

As the district court concluded, "There is no question that the Academy has awarded the Oscar only to a select group of persons." The Academy distributes the coveted Oscar to performers and members of the motion picture industry selected for outstanding achievement. At the 63rd Annual Academy Awards held this year, for example, the film "Dances With Wolves" was chosen among hundreds as the best film of 1990; its director, Kevin Costner, was selected from a field of five distinguished directors as "Best Director" of the year.

The majority of performers in the industry will never receive an Oscar. More importantly, the Academy has never sold or distributed the award to the general public.

2. Limited purpose

To meet the "limited purpose" prong of the *White* test, the Academy must show both (a) that the purpose of distributing the Oscar was limited; and (b) that Oscar recipients had no right of sale or further distribution — i.e., that their right of distribution was expressly or impliedly limited. *See White*, 193 F.2d at 746-47; *Brown v. Tabb*, 714 F.2d 1088, 1091 (11th Cir. 1983) ("under the *White* test the requirement that there be no right of sale or distribution is separate from and in addition to the requirement that there be a limited purpose"). The district court found that the Academy's purpose was not sufficiently limited, and did not reach the second issue regarding distribution restrictions. We examine both requirements.

(a) *Limited purpose*

The district court ruled that the Academy's purpose in presenting the Oscar at its annual awards gala was not just to honor the distinguished recipients, but also to promote the film industry. The court noted that the Academy spends over $800,000 annually to promote the awards ceremony, and that recipients are allowed to advertise their Oscars, with certain limitations. Relying on *Brown v. Tabb*, 714 F.2d 1088 (11th Cir. 1983), the court concluded that the Academy's purpose was not sufficiently limited because the Academy "exploited the Oscar" to promote the movie industry. We disagree.

The Eleventh Circuit decision in *Brown* involved a copyright infringement action brought by a composer who had sold several customized advertising jingles to car dealers. When a former dealership manager used the jingle to promote his own new dealership, Brown sued. The district court entered judgment for the defendant, ruling that the work was not entitled to protection under the 1976 Act because it had already entered the public domain. The court of appeals affirmed, holding that the distribution was not limited because Brown sold the jingle to any dealer willing to pay for it, and because each dealer was free to broadcast the jingle as broadly as he wished. *Id.* at 1092.

In the case now before us, the district court concluded that just as Brown exploited his jingle for pecuniary gain, the Academy exploited the Oscar to promote the movie industry. The district court's reliance on *Brown*, however, was misplaced. In *Brown*, the composer sold his jingle to anyone who paid for it, thereby enjoying "'the more worldly rewards that come with exploitation of his work.'" *Id., quoting* 1 Nimmer § 4.03 at 15-16. The Academy, in contrast, has never sold the Oscar to anyone. In addition, while Brown widely distributed actual copies of his work, the Academy has never distributed the Oscar to anyone other than the recipients. The fact that Oscar winners are permitted to advertise the *fact* they won their award, or display pictures of it, does not amount to a distribution. *See Kamar*, 657 F.2d at 1062; *American Vitagraph*, 659 F.2d at 1027-28.

Moreover, unlike Brown, the Academy does not promote the Oscar for its own commercial benefit. While the film industry may benefit incidentally from the Oscar's promotion, indirect commercial benefits do not necessarily transform a limited distribution into a general publication where no direct sales of the work are involved. *See, e.g., Brewer v. Hustler Magazine, Inc.*, 749 F.2d 527, 529 (9th Cir. 1984) (business cards featuring a reproduced photograph distributed for employment purposes amounted to a limited publication); *Hirshon*, 243 F.2d at 645-46 (distribution of 2000 copies of song to broadcasting stations and musicians for "plugging" purposes was a limited publication); *American Vitagraph*, 659 F.2d at 1027 (screening movie to gauge audience reaction found to be a limited publication although small admission fee was charged). We therefore find that the Academy's purpose of advancing the motion picture arts and sciences is a limited one.

(b) *Right of further distribution*

Before 1941, the Academy did not expressly prohibit recipients from selling or disposing of their Oscars. After 1941, the Academy required recipients to give the Academy a right of first refusal on any sale of their award, and imposed various restrictions on advertising.

Although no express restrictions on recipients' use or distribution of the Oscar existed before 1941, we conclude that restrictions on further distribution were implied. We find support for our conclusion in the District of Columbia Circuit's decision in *Hirshon v. United Artists Corp.*, 243 F.2d 640 (D.C. Cir. 1957). In *Hirshon*, the D.C. Circuit held that distributing copies of a song to radio stations for promotional purposes was a limited publication even though further distribution was not expressly restricted. The court noted that not a single copy of the song was ever sold, that no one had been given permission to use the song, and that nothing had been done to give any recipient the impression that he could use the song without first obtaining a license. *Id.* at 645.

Similarly here, neither the Academy nor any living Oscar recipient has ever offered to transfer an Oscar to the general public. Each Oscar trophy is personalized with the name of the individual winner, reflecting the Academy's expectation that the trophy will belong to the recipient alone. Although the Academy has given Oscar recipients permission to advertise their awards, it has never given them permission to sell or distribute their Oscars. Finally, the Academy has done nothing to suggest that recipients are free to make copies of the Oscars and distribute them. *Cf. Brewer*, 749 F.2d at 529 (distribution of business cards deemed a limited publication even though recipients were free to further distribute the cards); *King v. Mister Maestro, Inc.*, 224 F. Supp. 101, 107 (S.D.N.Y. 1963) (oral delivery of King's "I Have a Dream" speech to vast audience found to be a limited publication even though press was given copies of speech for reprinting).

From 1929 until the end of the Oscar's common law copyright protection in 1941, the Academy distributed personalized Oscar statuettes to a select group of distinguished artists. The Academy did not sell or directly profit from the award, nor did it encourage its further distribution. Under the *White* test, the Academy's actions constituted a limited publication that did not divest the Oscar of its common law protection. We therefore reverse the district court's contrary ruling, and remand to allow the Academy to present evidence of copyright infringement....

QUESTIONS

1. What was the policy that underlay the divestiture of perpetual common-law copyright once a work was "published"? Is that policy not frustrated when it is held that the delivery of a speech before 200,000 people (plus all of the news media) is not divestive? Would your analysis be the same with regard to a Broadway play that runs for three years before capacity audiences but which is not yet marketed in book form? A painting exhibited indefinitely in a public museum?

2. Was the court in the *Martin Luther King* case correct in finding no divestive publication when Reverend King gave advance copies of the text of his speech to the press to assist them in covering and reporting the event (without being offered to the public at large)? And was the court in *Hirshon* correct in finding no divestive publication when 2000 copies of a song were distributed to broadcasting stations to induce them to "plug" the song over the air?

3. The Ninth Circuit held that publication of a two-dimensional representation of a three-dimensional work — for example, distribution of photographs of a sculpture — does not publish the three-dimensional work. Why is that so? Under the court's analysis, would the Academy's marketing of three-dimensional miniature Oscar statuettes divest common-law copyright? Is that not just as much a "derivative work" of the original statue as is a photograph? (If you *wished* to "publish" a sculpture, how would you do it?)

Would the court find that common-law copyright in a two-dimensional painting is lost when the artist distributes two-dimensional representations? If not, is the court wrong?

4. In order to facilitate broadcasting of copyrighted television programs, videotapes are disseminated pursuant to contract to many local television broadcasting stations; the typical contract forbids copying or turning over possession of the tapes to other persons. Under the 1909 Act, would this have been regarded as a "general publication" so that insertion of copyright notice would have been required? *See Silverman v. CBS, Inc.,* 632 F. Supp. 1344 (S.D.N.Y. 1986), *rev'd on other grounds,* 870 F.2d 40 (2d Cir.), *cert. denied,* 492 U.S. 907 (1989); *Paramount Pictures v. Rabinowitz,* 217 U.S.P.Q. 48 (E.D.N.Y. 1981).

B. 1976 ACT SOLUTIONS AS TO PUBLICATION AND NOTICE

1. "PUBLICATION": DEFINITION AND CONTEXTS

Section 101 defines publication as:

> the distribution of copies or phonorecords of a work to the public by sale or other transfer of ownership, or by rental, lease, or lending. The offering to distribute copies or phonorecords to a group of persons for purposes of further distribution, public performance, or public display, constitutes publication. A public performance or display of a work does not itself constitute publication.

This definition resolves many of the problems that arose by virtue of the definitional vacuum in the 1909 Act, particularly by providing that a public performance or display of a work is not a "publication" that bears upon the use of a copyright notice; but that the public distribution of phonograph records does constitute publication of the recorded work (as well as of the sound recording).

Not all confusion or uncertainty is dispelled, however. For example, almost seventy years after *White-Smith Music Pub'g Co. v. Apollo Co.,* 209 U.S. 1 (1908), Congress still declined to equate recordings with copies. Thus, in this definition and throughout the statute, one notes the refrain "copies or phono-records." And, as will be noted below, there is no provision for use of a © copyright notice on phonorecords pertaining to the underlying recorded work. (There *is* a provision for a ℗ notice pertaining to the recorded *performance* under § 402.) And, while the statute uses "copies" and "phonorecords" in the plural, the committee reports state that under this definition "a work is 'published' if *one or more* copies or phonorecords embodying it are distributed to the public." (Emphasis added.) S. Rep. No. 94-473 at 121; H.R. Rep. No. 94-1476 at 138. But Chairman Kastenmeier of the House subcommittee stated on the House Floor that "in the case of a work of art, such as a painting or statue, that exists in only one copy ... [i]t is not the committee's intention that such a work should be regarded as 'published' when the single existing copy is sold or offered for sale in the traditional way — for example, through an art dealer, gallery, or auction house." 122 Cong. Rec. H10875 (Sept. 22, 1976).

When one hears the overstatement that the 1976 Act "does away with" publication, one should consider at least the following contexts in which the concept of publication is significant:

§ 104 — *national origin:* Unpublished works are protected irrespective of the nationality of the author, while with respect to *published* works such nationality at the time of first publication is relevant.

§ 107 — *fair use:* The Supreme Court has held (although the text of § 107 is silent on the matter) that "the scope of fair use is narrower with respect to unpublished works," *Harper & Row Pub'rs, Inc. v. Nation Enters.*, 471 U.S. 539, 564 (1985). Following a series of Second Circuit decisions that, to some, seemed unduly to insulate unpublished works from fair use, Congress in 1992 amended § 107 to provide that a work's unpublished status is not dispositive of the fair use defense; nonetheless it presumably remains an important element of a work's "nature" under § 107(2).

§ 108 — *library photocopying:* Archival reproduction of *unpublished* works is permitted under subsection (b), while other privileges restricted to *published* works are provided in subsection (c).

§ 302(c) and (e) — *duration:* Duration of protection for anonymous and pseudonymous works and works made for hire, and presumptions regarding the date of an author's death, are measured from *publication* or creation under the formula already discussed.

§ 303 — *unpublished works:* As noted above, the thrust of this section is to provide for the duration of protection for *unpublished* material protected by the common law or state statutory law. Moreover, *publication* can extend such duration for twenty-five years.

§ 407 — deposit: Deposit for Library of Congress purposes is mandatory for *published* works.

Over and above the foregoing, publication was most integrally connected under the 1976 Act before Berne adherence (as it was under the 1909 Act) with the question of *notice* covered in Chapter 4 of the Act.

QUESTIONS

Which of the following acts amount to "publication" under the 1976 Copyright Act:

1. A professor distributes outlines and questions to her students.

2. An architect distributes blueprints to a municipal agency and subcontractors. *See Kunycia v. Melville Realty Co.*, 755 F. Supp. 566 (S.D.N.Y. 1990).

3. An author, or her agent, offers copies of a manuscript to five publishers for their consideration.

4. A producer of computer hardware and software leases programs, encoded on magnetic tape, under a restrictive licensing agreement to purchasers of the producer's hardware. *See Hubco Data Prods. Corp. v. Management Assistance, Inc.*, 219 U.S.P.Q. 450 (D. Idaho 1983).

5. An artist produces five signed prints from a master and offers them to an association of nonprofit museums and schools for distribution to appropriate association members.

6. An artist produces five signed prints from a master and offers them to five museums for exhibition.

7. An artist offers an original oil painting to a museum for exhibition.

8. A record company distributes a "single" of a song; the song has not yet been sold as sheet music or otherwise distributed. *See, e.g., Greenwich Film Prods. v. DRG Records, Inc.*, 25 U.S.P.Q.2d 1435 (S.D.N.Y. 1992).

2. THE NOTICE REQUIREMENT: 1978 TO MARCH 1989

Among the issues that were hotly debated during the comprehensive revision of the 1909 Copyright Act was the continued imposition of a requirement to place copyright notice on "published" works and the sanction for a failure to do so. Congress decided to retain the notice requirement but to make less draconian the consequences of an error or omission. The reasons are set forth in the House Report.

HOUSE REPORT

H.R. Rep. No. 94-1476, 94th Cong., 2d Sess. 143-44 (1976)

A requirement that the public be given formal notice of every work in which copyright is claimed was a part of the first U.S. copyright statute enacted in 1790, and since 1802 our copyright laws have always provided that the published copies of copyrighted works must bear a specified notice as a condition of protection. Under the present law the copyright notice serves four principal functions:

    (1) It has the effect of placing in the public domain a substantial body of published material that no one is interested in copyrighting;

    (2) It informs the public as to whether a particular work is copyrighted;

    (3) It identifies the copyright owner; and

    (4) It shows the date of publication.

Ranged against these values of a notice requirement are its burdens and unfairness to copyright owners. One of the strongest arguments for revision of the present statute has been the need to avoid the arbitrary and unjust forfeitures now resulting from unintentional or relatively unimportant omissions or errors in the copyright notice. It has been contended that the disadvantages of the notice requirement outweigh its values and that it should therefore be eliminated or substantially liberalized.

The fundamental principle underlying the notice provisions of the bill is that the copyright notice has real values which should be preserved, and that this should be done by inducing use of notice without causing outright forfeiture for errors or omissions. Subject to certain safeguards for innocent infringers, protection would not be lost by the complete omission of copyright notice from large numbers of copies or from a whole edition, if registration for the work is made before or within 5 years after publication. Errors in the name or date in the notice could be corrected without forfeiture of copyright.

The notice requirements were set forth in Sections 401 and 402 of the 1976 Act. Section 401 applied to "copies" of published works, and Section 402 to "phonorecords." The text of Section 401 follows as originally written. (The principal change in its current text, as a result of an amendment in 1989, is that the word "shall" in the first sentence of § 401(a) has been replaced by the word "may.")

§ 401. Notice of copyright: Visually perceptible copies

(a) *General Requirement.* — Whenever a work protected under this title is published in the United States or elsewhere by authority of the copyright owner, a notice of copyright as provided by this section shall be placed on all publicly distributed copies from which the work can be visually perceived, either directly or with the aid of a machine or device.

(b) *Form of Notice.* — The notice appearing on the copies shall consist of the following three elements:

> (1) the symbol © (the letter C in a circle), or the word "Copyright," or the abbreviation "Copr."; and
>
> (2) the year of first publication of the work; in the case of compilations or derivative works incorporating previously published material, the year date of first publication of the compilation or derivative work is sufficient. The year date may be omitted where a pictorial, graphic, or sculptural work, with accompanying text matter, if any, is reproduced in or on greeting cards, postcards, stationery, jewelry, dolls, toys, or any useful articles; and
>
> (3) the name of the owner of copyright in the work, or an abbreviation by which the name can be recognized, or a generally known alternative designation of the owner.

(c) *Position of Notice.* — The notice shall be affixed to the copies in such manner and location as to give reasonable notice of the claim of copyright. The Register of Copyrights shall prescribe by regulation, as examples, specific methods of affixation and positions of the notice on various types of works that will satisfy this requirement, but these specifications shall not be considered exhaustive.

NOTICE FOR SOUND RECORDINGS, GOVERNMENT WORKS, AND COLLECTIVE WORKS

In § 402 as enacted in 1976 (and effective January 1, 1978), Congress provided for a different notice for sound recordings that were embodied in publicly distributed phonorecords. Congress thought it appropriate to afford a means for signaling a claim of copyright in the sound recording, as distinct from a claim of copyright in the literary or musical work that is performed in the sound recording.

Because the phonorecord (i.e., the vinyl or compact disc, or the audiotape) in which a song is embodied is not a "copy" of that song under § 101 of the Copyright Act, no © notice was required under § 401 in order to protect copyright in the song. But to protect copyright in the sound recording — so that it would be an infringement to make an unauthorized duplication of the recorded sounds — the 1976 Act required that a ℗ notice be placed on each phonorecord publicly distributed "in the United States or elsewhere by authority of the copyright owner." The form of notice was, in all respects, similar to the form of the © notice; and "the notice shall be placed on the surface of the phonorecord, or on the phonorecord label or container, in such manner and location as to give reasonable notice of the claim of copyright." (These provisions apply today as well, but on a permissive rather than required basis.) The use of the ℗ notice for the sound recording not only permits a clear claim of copyright to the sound recording as distinguished from the underlying literary or musical work; it also effects a distinction from the claim of any copyright in the printed text or art work appearing on the record label, album cover, or liner notes on the record jacket or tape container.

Section 403 dealt with a work, published in copies or phonorecords, that consisted "preponderantly of one or more works of the United States Government." For such works, the notice under § 401 or 402 was to include "a statement identifying, either affirmatively or negatively, those portions of the copies or phonorecords embodying any work or works protected under this title." Congress thereby expected those who, for example, marketed commercially a public-domain government report or federal judicial opinions — and merely added an introduction or illustrations or commentary — to include a copyright notice that would avoid misleading the public into believing that the entire work was protected by the publisher's copyright and thus could not be copied. (You might wish to consult volumes of the West reporter system published between 1978 and 1989, to see whether they contained a proper copyright notice.) Apart from this provision in § 403, there is nothing in the Copyright Act that requires or encourages a copyright claimant to clearly identify those parts of its publication that are in the public domain and thus free for others to copy. Should there be?

Finally, § 404 of the 1976 Act drew a distinction between the copyright notice for a collective work and the distinct notice for separate articles or other contributions included therein. It provided that a separate contribution could bear its own notice, but also that the notice requirements of the statute for that contribution could be satisfied by using a single notice that was applicable to the collective work as a whole, even though the copyright owners of the collective work and the individual contribution were not the same. Because of the possible resulting confusion that might flow, Congress provided that a person misled by such a confusion — and who dealt with the wrong person in seeking permission to use an individual contribution — could have the defenses set forth in § 406(a), which deals with mistakes in the name placed in a copyright notice.

QUESTIONS

1. Your client had a short story published in 1985 in *Science Fiction Magazine*. What copyright notice should be affixed, and where? (What significant information will the notice give the reader, and what will be omitted?)

2. Assume that it is 1986, and your client wishes to reprint her story, as written, in a paperback edition. Must she secure the consent of the magazine? When reprinted, what notice should the story bear? (What is the consequence of the notice bearing the date 1976? What is the consequence of the notice bearing the date 1990?)

3. If the story mentioned above is reprinted not alone, but with an unpublished short story written by your client in 1968, what should the copy-

right notice be? (What significant information about the copyright status of the two works will not be disclosed?)

4. *A,* an author, grants book rights to *B,* a publisher, which in turn grants paperback rights to *C.* Whose name should appear in the notice on the paperback edition?

5. You represent Pineapple Records, Inc., a manufacturer of phonograph records and tapes. A song composed by Alan Robert in 1985 is recorded by your client in 1986. The recording is released in 1987. (a) What copyright notice should be affixed and where? (b) Would your answer be any different if there were original artwork on the labels and jacket and textual notes on the jacket? (c) Sheet music embodying this song is distributed in 1988. What copyright notice should be affixed? Is this answer affected by the identity or lack of identity of the material embodied on the recording and on the sheet music? (d) Would "A. Robert" be a sufficient element of the copyright notice? "A. R."? "Pineapple Records"? "Pineapple"?

---

§ 405. Notice of copyright: Omission of notice

(a) *Effect of Omission on Copyright.* — The omission of the copyright notice prescribed by sections 401 through 403 from copies or phonorecords publicly distributed by authority of the copyright owner does not invalidate the copyright in a work if —

> (1) the notice has been omitted from no more than a relatively small number of copies or phonorecords distributed to the public; or
>
> (2) registration for the work has been made before or is made within five years after the publication without notice, and a reasonable effort is made to add notice to all copies or phonorecords that are distributed to the public in the United States after the omission has been discovered; or
>
> (3) the notice has been omitted in violation of an express requirement in writing that, as a condition of the copyright owner's authorization of the public distribution of copies or phonorecords, they bear the prescribed notice.

(b) *Effect of Omission on Innocent Infringers.* — Any person who innocently infringes a copyright, in reliance upon an authorized copy or phonorecord from which the copyright notice has been omitted, incurs no liability for actual or statutory damages under section 504 for any infringing acts committed before receiving actual notice that registration for the work has been made under section 408, if such person proves that he or she was misled by the omission of notice. In a suit for infringement in such a case the court may allow or disallow recovery of any of the infringer's profits attributable to the infringement, and may enjoin the continuation of the infringing undertaking or may require, as a condition of permitting the continuation of the infringing undertaking, that the infringer pay the copyright owner a reasonable license fee in an amount and on terms fixed by the court.

(c) *Removal of Notice.* — Protection under this title is not affected by the removal, destruction, or obliteration of the notice, without the authorization of the copyright owner, from any publicly distributed copies or phonorecords.

HOUSE REPORT

H.R. Rep. No. 94-1476, 94th Cong., 2d Sess. 146-48 (1976)

Effect of omission on copyright protection

The provisions of section 405(a) make clear that the notice requirements of sections 401, 402, and 403 are not absolute and that, unlike the law now in effect, the outright omission of a copyright notice does not automatically forfeit protection and throw the work into the public domain. This not only represents a major change in the theoretical framework of American copyright law, but it also seems certain to have immediate practical consequences in a great many individual cases. Under the proposed law a work published without any copyright notice will still be subject to statutory protection for at least 5 years, whether the omission was partial or total, unintentional or deliberate.

....

Effect of omission on innocent infringers

In addition to the possibility that copyright protection will be forfeited under section 405(a) (2) if the notice is omitted, a second major inducement to use of the notice is found in subsection (b) of section 405. That provision, which limits the rights of a copyright owner against innocent infringers under certain circumstances, would be applicable whether the notice has been omitted from a large number or from a "relatively small number" of copies. The general postulates underlying the provision are that a person acting in good faith and with no reason to think otherwise should ordinarily be able to assume that a work is in the public domain if there is no notice on an authorized copy or phonorecord and that, if he relies on this assumption, he should be shielded from unreasonable liability.

Under section 405(b) an innocent infringer who acts "in reliance upon an authorized copy or phonorecord from which the copyright notice has been omitted," and who proves that he was misled by the omission, is shielded from liability for actual or statutory damages with respect to "any infringing acts committed before receiving actual notice" of registration. Thus, where the infringement is completed before actual notice has been served — as would be the usual case with respect to relatively minor infringements by teachers, librarians, journalists, and the like — liability, if any, would be limited to the profits the infringer realized from the act of infringement. On the other hand, where the infringing enterprise is one running over a period of time, the copyright owner would be able to seek an injunction against continuation of the infringement, and to obtain full monetary recovery for all infringing acts committed after he had served notice of registration. Persons who undertake major enterprises of this sort should check the Copyright Office registration records before starting, even where copies have been published without notice.

....

Hasbro Bradley, Inc. v. Sparkle Toys, Inc., 780 F.2d 189 (2d Cir. 1985). Takara, a Japanese company, designed and manufactured in Japan certain toys — robotic action figures — but neglected to place any copyright notice on them. This was apparently because such toys are not covered by Japanese copyright law (but rather by its Design Act) and because Takara was unaware of any requirement of notice under the copyright law of the U.S. (which along with Japan was a signatory of the Universal Copyright Convention). 213,000 such figures, without copyright notice, were sold in Japan in early 1984; and in June 1984, Takara assigned to Hasbro its U.S. copyrights and the right to import and sell the toys in the U.S. All of the toys sold thereafter by Hasbro in the U.S. bore a copyright notice. Defendant Sparkle copied its toy designs from those sold by Takara in Asia, and sought to market them in the U.S. The district court issued a preliminary injunction, despite Sparkle's claim that the toy designs were in the public domain in the U.S., and the court of appeals affirmed.

The court of appeals stated that, because the toys were authored by a Japanese national and first sold in Japan, they enjoyed copyright protection under U.S. law from the moment they were created (by virtue of both the U.C.C. and § 104(b) of our Copyright Act); despite Japanese law to the contrary, the toys were pictorial and sculptural works covered by the U.S. statute. Their sale without copyright notice — even in Japan — was found to violate § 401(a): "Whenever a work protected under this title is published in the United States *or elsewhere* by authority of the copyright owner, a notice of copyright as provided by this section shall be placed on all publicly distributed copies ...." This omission could, however, be excused or cured, the court held, "under certain circumstances, in which case the copyright is valid from the moment the work was created, just as if no omission had occurred.... In effect, § 405(a)(2) allows a person who publishes a copyrightable work without notice to hold a kind of incipient copyright in the work for five years thereafter: if the omission is cured in that time through registration and the exercise of 'a reasonable effort ... to add notice to all copies ... that are distributed to the public in the United States after the omission has been discovered,' the copyright is perfected and valid retroactively for the entire period after cure; if the omission is not cured in that time, the incipient copyright never achieves enforceability." The court held that Takara was the relevant "copyright owner" for purposes of the notice requirement of § 401(a), such that the sale of the toys without notice in Japan by its authorization placed the copyright in jeopardy. Takara's assignment in June 1984 gave Hasbro only an incipient copyright, subject to cure.

Sparkle argued that Hasbro had no power to cure under § 405(a)(2) because that section allows cure only when the omission is inadvertent and Takara's omission of notice was deliberate. The court rejected that reading of the section, and held that cure could be effected even when the initial omission of notice was deliberate. It relied, among other things, upon a statement in the House Report that "under the proposed law a work published without any copyright notice will still be subject to statutory protection for at least 5 years, whether the omission was partial or total, unintentional or deliberate," and a contemporaneous statement by the Register of Copyrights that "we concluded that questions involving the subjective state of mind of one or more persons and their ignorance or knowledge of the law should be avoided if at all possible ... we decided that the bill should drop any distinction between 'deliberate' and 'inadvertent' or 'unintentional' omission and, subject to certain conditions, should preserve the copyright in all cases."

The court held that its conclusion was not inconsistent with the requirement in the cure provisions of § 405(a)(2) that there be reasonable efforts made to add the notice to all copies distributed to the public in the U.S. "after the omission has been discovered." The court explained: "No violence is done to the statutory language by saying that the omission, though deliberate on the part of the assignor or licensor, was 'discovered' by the person later attempting to cure it. Similarly, a deliberate omission at a lower level of a corporate hierarchy might well be 'discovered,' in all realistic terms, by someone at a higher level. Instances like these at least indicate that the 'discovered' language does not reveal a plain intent to exclude all deliberate omissions."

Hasbro had in fact registered its copyrights in the Takara designs within five years of publication of the unmarked toys. The court left for resolution at trial in connection with the permanent injunction the two other significant issues — whether reasonable efforts were made by Hasbro to add notice to toys later sold in the U.S. and whether Sparkle was an innocent infringer under § 405(b).

---

§ 406. Notice of copyright: Error in name or date

(a) *Error in Name.* — Where the person named in the copyright notice on copies or phonorecords publicly distributed by authority of the copyright owner is not the owner of copyright, the validity and ownership of the copyright are not affected. In such a case, however, any person who innocently begins an undertaking that infringes the copyright has a complete defense to any action for such infringement if such person proves that he or she was misled by the notice and began the undertaking in good faith under a purported transfer or license from the person named therein, unless before the undertaking was begun —

(1) registration for the work had been made in the name of the owner of copyright; or

(2) a document executed by the person named in the notice and showing the ownership of the copyright had been recorded.

The person named in the notice is liable to account to the copyright owner for all receipts from transfers or licenses purportedly made under the copyright by the person named in the notice.

(b) *Error in Date.* — When the year date in the notice on copies or phonorecords distributed by authority of the copyright owner is earlier than the year in which publication first occurred, any period computed from the year of first publication under section 302 is to be computed from the year in the notice.

Where the year date is more than one year later than the year in which publication first occurred, the work is considered to have been published without any notice and is governed by the provisions of section 405.

(c) *Omission of Name or Date.* — Where copies or phonorecords publicly distributed by authority of the copyright owner contain no name or no date that could reasonably be considered a part of the notice, the work is considered to have been published without any notice and is governed by the provisions of section 405.

QUESTIONS

1. Recall the publication of your client's short story in *Science Fiction Magazine* in 1985. Assume that the issue in which your client's story appears lacks any copyright notice, either on the masthead or on the story itself. Are there any steps your client could have taken (by what date?) to prevent copyright from being forfeited? Would a motion picture producer who saw the story in 1989 be free to base a script on it and produce a film?

2. Recall (yet again) the publication of your client's short story in *Science Fiction Magazine.* Assume that the only copyright notice in *Science Fiction* when your client's story was printed was the "masthead notice" in the name of *Science Fiction.* Assume, too, that a motion picture producer buys the motion picture rights to the story from *Science Fiction* for $20,000; that one month later, he hires a scriptwriter; that two months later, he hires stars; that five months later, he begins production; and that the movie, when released, quickly nets $5 million. When your client learns of this, what are her rights (if any) against *Science Fiction* and the producer?

When Author brings an action against Magazine for the unauthorized (indeed fraudulent) transfer of copyright to Movie Producer, will Author's recovery be limited to $20,000? If the last sentence of § 406(a) sets forth a limitation on recovery rather than a "floor," why should that be so? Is the House Report a reliable source when it states that the apparent limitation in § 406(a) does not apply to willful and knowing transfers by Magazine?

What steps would you recommend that your client have taken at the outset to avoid this problem? What steps should the producer have taken?

3. OPTIONAL NOTICE UNDER THE BERNE-IMPLEMENTATION ACT

As noted above, the major change required in the 1976 Act in order to permit United States adherence to the Berne Convention has been the elimination of the copyright notice as a precondition to copyright protection (even allowing for the five-year grace period for registration as a cure for omission of notice). In part because it is difficult to break with such a longstanding practice as the use of copyright notice, and in part because Congress and the Copyright Office continue to believe that notice serves useful purposes in warning unauthorized users and in conveying information, the Berne-Implementation amendments to the 1976 Act continue to provide incentives to the copyright owner to avail himself of what is now — since March 1, 1989 — merely a discretionary option to use the notice on published works.

For works first published on or after March 1, 1989 — and also for copies or phonorecords distributed after that date of works that had been published previously — sections 401(a) and 402(a) no longer require placement of notice on publicly distributed copies and phonorecords, but instead provide that the © notice "may" be placed on copies and the ℗ notice "may" be placed on phonorecords of sound recordings. The form and placement of the optional notice are as they were previously when the notice was mandated. The incentive provided for use of the notice is set forth in a new subsection (d) to §§ 401 and 402. Section 401(d) now provides:

> *Evidentiary Weight of Notice.* — If a notice of copyright in the form specified by this section appears on the published copy or copies to which a defendant in a copyright infringement suit had access, then no weight shall be given to such a defendant's interposition of a defense based on innocent infringement in mitigation of actual or statutory damages, except as provided in the last sentence of section 504(c)(2).

The student should consult § 504(c)(2), and should note how the use of optional notice will protect the copyright owner against the reduction to $200 of an award of statutory damages which has a normal floor of $500.

Will that be a sufficient inducement to use the now optional copyright notice? Will there be any other inducements to do so, other than inertia? *See* H.R. Rep. No. 100-609, 100th Cong., 2d Sess. 26-67 (1988): "It is entirely possible that elimination of the notice formality may not in the end curtail its use. Old habits die hard; it remains useful under the Universal Copyright Convention; and, it is, in all probability, the cheapest deterrent to infringement which a copyright holder may take." Compare the inducements that have since 1978 been in effect for registering the copyright (and depositing copies or phonorecords) with the Copyright Office, an issue to be discussed immediately below.

Other amendments were made to the notice provisions of the 1976 Act to take account of the now optional copyright notice. In particular, the provisions in sections 405 and 406 dealing with exceptions to the notice requirement, cure for omissions of notice, the protection of innocent infringers when notice is omitted or there is an error in name, and the inclusion of an incorrect date, are all limited so as to apply only to copies and phonorecords that were distributed between January 1, 1978 and the effective date of the Berne-implementation amendments.

C. DEPOSIT AND REGISTRATION

Sections 407 through 412 of the 1976 Act enact a modernized administrative scheme with the dual purpose of enriching the resources of the Library of Congress and securing a comprehensive record of copyright claims. The former is achieved in § 407, which prescribes a mandatory system of deposit as to published works for Library purposes with administrative flexibility as to implementation and realistic sanctions for noncompliance under § 407(d) (not including forfeiture of copyright). The latter is embodied in what is consistently described as a "permissive" registration provision, § 408.

Although the Berne Convention Implementation Act of 1988 has as one of its objectives the elimination of the need to comply with statutory formalities, its principal focus is upon the elimination of the notice requirement for published works; it makes few changes in the sections on deposit and registration as they were written in the 1976 Act. The major change in this respect is that registration of copyright is no longer a prerequisite to an action for infringement of copyright "in Berne Convention works whose country of origin is not the United States." Most pertinently, this means that registration remains a prerequisite for an infringement action when the copyrighted work is first published in the United States or when the work, if unpublished, is by a United States author. The 1988 Act thus creates what is known as a two-tier registration system, with works of U.S. origin being on the "lower" tier for purposes of litigation. Legislation proposed in 1993 would eliminate the two-tier system; U.S. works would no longer be subject to a pre-suit registration requirement. See H.R. 897, S. 373 (103d Cong., 1st Sess.).

The Library deposit under § 407 may do double duty as the deposit required for registration under § 408. Moreover, the incentives for registration are quite strong. Accordingly, the dichotomy between these two deposit provisions may not be quite as sharp as initially thought.

1. DEPOSIT FOR LIBRARY OF CONGRESS

The § 407 deposit, which "shall" be made by "the owner of copyright or of the exclusive right of publication" within three months after publication in the United States, is to consist of "two complete copies of the best edition" or, if the work is a sound recording, two complete phonorecords of the best edition, together with all accompanying printed material. The term "best edition" is defined in § 101 as "the edition, published in the United States at any time before the date of deposit, that the Library of Congress determines to be most suitable for its purposes." The Library has issued a policy statement on what constitutes such a "best edition," and this is now referred to in the implementing Copyright Office regulations. See 37 C.F.R. § 202.19(b)(1).

The material for use or disposition of the Library of Congress under § 407(b) of the 1976 Act is to be deposited in the Copyright Office. The Register of Copyrights is given authority to issue regulations exempting categories of material from the deposit requirements of this section, reducing the required copies or phonorecords to one, or, in the case of certain pictorial, graphic, or sculptural works, providing for exemptions or alternative forms of deposit. § 407(c). The Register is also empowered, under § 408(c), to specify classes of works for purposes of deposit and to permit the deposit of "identifying material instead of copies or phonorecords." Acting pursuant to this provision, the Copyright Office has promulgated what is known as a "secure test" regulation, 37 C.F.R. § 202.20, which covers such examinations as the SAT, the LSAT, and the Multistate Bar Examination. The regulation permits the Copyright Office, after examining such a test, to determine that it is copyrightable and to return the test to the copyright applicant while retaining only "sufficient portions, description, or the like ... so as to constitute a sufficient archival record of the deposit." In *National Conf. of Bar Exmrs. v. Multistate Legal*

Studies, 692 F.2d 478 (7th Cir. 1982), *cert. denied,* 464 U.S. 814 (1983), the defendant — proprietor of a bar review course — challenged this regulation as inconsistent with a federal policy, anchored in the copyright clause of the Constitution, favoring full disclosure of works for which copyright is claimed. The court rejected the defendant's contention, pointing out several instances in which the Library of Congress is allowed to distribute or to destroy works in its collection.

Precisely the opposite contention was made in *Ladd v. Law & Technology Press,* 762 F.2d 809 (9th Cir. 1985), *cert. denied,* 475 U.S. 1045 (1986), in which the defendant (The Press), the copyright claimant, argued that the deposit requirement was *forbidden* by the United States Constitution. When The Press failed to deposit two copies of its periodical, The Scott Report, with the Library of Congress, Register of Copyrights Ladd sent a demand notice under § 407. The Press refused to comply, suggesting that if the Library wanted The Scott Report, it should become a paid subscriber. Ladd brought an action to recover the statutory fine of $250 for each issue not deposited, and the retail price of two copies of each issue. The Press challenged the constitutionality of the deposit requirement in § 407 on three grounds, each of which was rejected by the court of appeals, which affirmed a grant of summary judgment for Register Ladd.

The Press first argued that the deposit requirement was not "necessary and proper" to carry out Congress's power under the Copyright Clause of the Constitution. The court concluded that the primary purpose of that clause is to promote the arts and sciences, that the necessary and proper clause should be broadly construed, and that a "provision of the Copyright Act which sustains a national library for the public use is necessary and proper." The Press then argued that the requirement that a copyright owner give two copies of its work to the Library of Congress is "a taking of private property for public use without just compensation and violates the fifth amendment." The court, however, adopted the Register's contention that the deposit rule is not a taking but is rather a "condition which Congress may legitimately attach to the grant of a benefit," i.e., copyright protection which The Press voluntarily sought. The court held that "Congress indubitably can place conditions on the grant of a statutory benefit."

The court also rejected The Press's argument that the deposit requirement is equivalent to a tax that imposes a burden on works that are protected by the first amendment. The court held that the first amendment protects the expression and dissemination of ideas, which in themselves do not trigger the deposit requirement. Deposit "comes into play only if the publisher voluntarily seeks the statutory benefit of copyright. The first amendment does not protect the right to copyright, and therefore a condition placed on copyright protection does not implicate first amendment rights."

2. REGISTRATION

a. Procedure

If the Library deposit under § 407 is accompanied by a prescribed application for registration along with a fee (currently $20 for most works), it may be used to satisfy the deposit requirements of registration. It should be noted that the registration provision permits a deposit of one copy or phonorecord, rather than two, in the case of unpublished works, works published abroad, and contributions to a collective work (where a copy of the collective work is required).

Registration under § 408 contrasts with the Library deposit provision under § 407 in the following respects: (1) it may be made by not only the owner of copyright but also the owner of any exclusive right thereunder rather than by the owner of the exclusive right of publication; (2) it applies to unpublished as well as published works; (3) it includes works published abroad; (4) it may be made "at any time" during the subsistence of copyright.

The purpose of the registration fee is to defray the expenses of operating the Copyright Office. The income from registration fees represents roughly one-half of the budget of the Copyright Office, with Government appropriations constituting the other half.

The TX form, for nondramatic literary works, is shown on the following two pages.

The application for registration includes various items of information potentially required for computation of duration, e.g., dates of death, year of creation, and year of publication if any, as well as the basis of ownership for persons other than authors and a brief, general statement of preexisting and added material used in any derivative work or compilation. § 409.

b. Register's Authority and Effect of Registration

The 1976 Act, in § 410(b), expressly provides that the Register may refuse registration upon his or her determination that a claim is invalid. Under the 1909 Act, actual registration, rather than merely application for registration, was required as a prerequisite for an infringement action. But this result has been reversed by § 411(a), which permits an infringement suit even where registration has been refused, provided that the deposit, application, and fee are in proper form *and* notice is given to the Register who is given the right to intervene. *See Nova Stylings, Inc. v. Ladd,* 695 F.2d 1179 (9th Cir. 1983) (mandamus no longer available to compel registration).

Even this more lenient approach to pre-suit registration presupposes a deposit of plaintiff's work with the Copyright Office. But what if the would-be plaintiff no longer possesses a copy of the infringed-upon work? This situation may arise, for example, in the case of a manuscript, see, e.g., *Dodd v. Fort Smith Special Sch. Dist. No. 100,* 666 F. Supp. 1278 (W.D. Ark. 1987), or of photographic negatives. Does another's (often the defendant's) possession of the author's copy of the work frustrate the author's ability to seek judicial redress for the alleged infringement? Despite the *Dodd* court's affirmative response, this result appears entirely inequitable. Indeed, recognizing the potential inequities, the Copyright Office has devised practical solutions to the problem. Under the Copyright Office's power to grant special relief, 37 C.F.R. § 202.20(d), the Office may accept a deposit either of a copy of the defendant's work, or even of a description of the author's work, with an appropriate accompanying affidavit. *See, e.g., Pacific & S. Co. v. Duncan,* 744 F.2d 1490 (11th Cir. 1984), *cert. denied,* 471 U.S. 1004 (1985) (plaintiff television

FORM TX
For a Literary Work
UNITED STATES COPYRIGHT OFFICE

REGISTRATION NUMBER

_____

TX _____ TXU

EFFECTIVE DATE OF REGISTRATION

_____

Month _____ Day _____ Year

DO NOT WRITE ABOVE THIS LINE. IF YOU NEED MORE SPACE, USE A SEPARATE CONTINUATION SHEET.

1

TITLE OF THIS WORK ▼

PREVIOUS OR ALTERNATIVE TITLES ▼

PUBLICATION AS A CONTRIBUTION If this work was published as a contribution to a periodical, serial, or collection, give information about the collective work in which the contribution appeared. **Title of Collective Work ▼**

If published in a periodical or serial give: **Volume ▼**   **Number ▼**   **Issue Date ▼**   **On Pages ▼**

2
a

NAME OF AUTHOR ▼

DATES OF BIRTH AND DEATH
Year Born ▼   Year Died ▼

Was this contribution to the work a "work made for hire"?
☐ Yes
☐ No

AUTHOR'S NATIONALITY OR DOMICILE
Name of Country
OR { Citizen of ▶ _____
Domiciled in ▶ _____

WAS THIS AUTHOR'S CONTRIBUTION TO THE WORK
Anonymous?   ☐ Yes ☐ No
Pseudonymous? ☐ Yes ☐ No
If the answer to either of these questions is "Yes," see detailed instructions.

NATURE OF AUTHORSHIP Briefly describe nature of material created by this author in which copyright is claimed. ▼

NOTE

Under the law, the "author" of a "work made for hire" is generally the employer, not the employee (see instructions). For any part of this work that was "made for hire" check "Yes" in the space provided, give the employer (or other person for whom the work was prepared) as "Author" of that part, and leave the space for dates of birth and death blank.

b

NAME OF AUTHOR ▼

DATES OF BIRTH AND DEATH
Year Born ▼   Year Died ▼

Was this contribution to the work a "work made for hire"?
☐ Yes
☐ No

AUTHOR'S NATIONALITY OR DOMICILE
Name of Country
OR { Citizen of ▶ _____
Domiciled in ▶ _____

WAS THIS AUTHOR'S CONTRIBUTION TO THE WORK
Anonymous?   ☐ Yes ☐ No
Pseudonymous? ☐ Yes ☐ No
If the answer to either of these questions is "Yes," see detailed instructions.

NATURE OF AUTHORSHIP Briefly describe nature of material created by this author in which copyright is claimed. ▼

c

NAME OF AUTHOR ▼

DATES OF BIRTH AND DEATH
Year Born ▼   Year Died ▼

Was this contribution to the work a "work made for hire"?
☐ Yes
☐ No

AUTHOR'S NATIONALITY OR DOMICILE
Name of Country
OR { Citizen of ▶ _____
Domiciled in ▶ _____

WAS THIS AUTHOR'S CONTRIBUTION TO THE WORK
Anonymous?   ☐ Yes ☐ No
Pseudonymous? ☐ Yes ☐ No
If the answer to either of these questions is "Yes," see detailed instructions.

NATURE OF AUTHORSHIP Briefly describe nature of material created by this author in which copyright is claimed. ▼

3
a **YEAR IN WHICH CREATION OF THIS WORK WAS COMPLETED** This information must be given ◀ Year in all cases.
b **DATE AND NATION OF FIRST PUBLICATION OF THIS PARTICULAR WORK** Complete this information ONLY if this work has been published. Month ▶ _____ Day ▶ _____ Year ▶ _____ ◀ Nation

4

See instructions before completing this space.

COPYRIGHT CLAIMANT(S) Name and address must be given even if the claimant is the same as the author given in space 2. ▼

TRANSFER If the claimant(s) named here in space 4 is (are) different from the author(s) named in space 2, give a brief statement of how the claimant(s) obtained ownership of the copyright. ▼

DO NOT WRITE HERE OFFICE USE ONLY

APPLICATION RECEIVED

ONE DEPOSIT RECEIVED

TWO DEPOSITS RECEIVED

FUNDS RECEIVED

MORE ON BACK ▶ • Complete all applicable spaces (numbers 5-11) on the reverse side of this page.
• See detailed instructions.   • Sign the form at line 10.

DO NOT WRITE HERE
Page 1 of _____ pages

EXAMINED BY	FORM TX
CHECKED BY	
☐ CORRESPONDENCE Yes	FOR COPYRIGHT OFFICE USE ONLY

DO NOT WRITE ABOVE THIS LINE. IF YOU NEED MORE SPACE, USE A SEPARATE CONTINUATION SHEET.

PREVIOUS REGISTRATION Has registration for this work, or for an earlier version of this work, already been made in the Copyright Office?
☐ Yes ☐ No If your answer is "Yes," why is another registration being sought? (Check appropriate box) ▼
a. ☐ This is the first published edition of a work previously registered in unpublished form.
b. ☐ This is the first application submitted by this author as copyright claimant.
c. ☐ This is a changed version of the work, as shown by space 6 on this application.
If your answer is "Yes." give: **Previous Registration Number ▼**   **Year of Registration ▼**

5

DERIVATIVE WORK OR COMPILATION Complete both space 6a and 6b for a derivative work; complete only 6b for a compilation.
a. Preexisting Material Identify any preexisting work or works that this work is based on or incorporates. ▼

b. Material Added to This Work Give a brief, general statement of the material that has been added to this work and in which copyright is claimed. ▼

6

See instructions
before completing
this space.

—space deleted—

7

REPRODUCTION FOR USE OF BLIND OR PHYSICALLY HANDICAPPED INDIVIDUALS A signature on this form at space 10 and a check in one of the boxes here in space 8 constitutes a non-exclusive grant of permission to the Library of Congress to reproduce and distribute solely for the blind and physically handicapped and under the conditions and limitations prescribed by the regulations of the Copyright Office: (1) copies of the work identified in space 1 of this application in Braille (or similar tactile symbols); or (2) phonorecords embodying a fixation of a reading of that work; or (3) both.

     a ☐ Copies and Phonorecords   b ☐ Copies Only   c ☐ Phonorecords Only

8

See instructions.

DEPOSIT ACCOUNT If the registration fee is to be charged to a Deposit Account established in the Copyright Office, give name and number of Account.
Name ▼   **Account Number ▼**

9

CORRESPONDENCE Give name and address to which correspondence about this application should be sent. Name/Address/Apt/City/State/ZIP ▼

Be sure to
give your
daytime phone
◀ number

Area Code and Telephone Number ▶

CERTIFICATION* I, the undersigned, hereby certify that I am the
Check only one ▶
☐ author
☐ other copyright claimant
☐ owner of exclusive right(s)
☐ authorized agent of _____
         Name of author or other copyright claimant, or owner of exclusive right(s) ▲
of the work identified in this application and that the statements made
by me in this application are correct to the best of my knowledge.

10

Typed or printed name and date ▼ If this application gives a date of publication in space 3, do not sign and submit it before that date.

_____ date ▶ _____

 Handwritten signature (X) ▼

MAIL CERTIFI-CATE TO		**YOU MUST:** • Complete all necessary spaces • Sign your application in space 10	**11**
	Name ▼	**SEND ALL 3 ELEMENTS IN THE SAME PACKAGE:**	
	Number/Street/Apartment Number ▼	1. Application form 2. Nonrefundable $20 filing fee in check or money order payable to *Register of Copyrights* 3. Deposit material	The Copyright Office has the authority to adjust fees at 5-year intervals, based on changes in the Consumer Price Index. The next adjustment is due in 1996. Please contact the Copyright Office after July 1995 to determine the actual fee schedule.
Certificate will be mailed in window envelope	City/State/ZIP ▼	**MAIL TO:** Register of Copyrights Library of Congress Washington, D.C. 20559-6000	

station, having erased its copy of a broadcast which plaintiff subsequently learned had been copied without authorization, obtained from defendant's customer a tape containing the unauthorized copy of the broadcast, and registered that tape with the Copyright Office).

Registration as a prerequisite to suit — a formality to which domestic works at present remain subject even after ratification of the Berne Convention — poses other problems. If a copyright owner seeks prospective relief against future infringements, pre-suit registration may be impossible either because the potentially infringed-on titles are unknown, or indeed, have not yet been created. Seeking to avoid potential stalemate, "[c]ourts have not hesitated to enjoin the infringement of future registered works when equity has required." *Association of Am. Med. Colleges v. Carey,* 482 F. Supp. 1358, 1364 n.15 (N.D.N.Y. 1980) (citing decisions).

Although registration of copyright is "permissive," the statute has provided the following incentives for timely registration: (1) Early registration will ensure prima facie proof of validity of the copyright (§ 410(c)); (2) for works of United States origin, registration is a prerequisite to an infringement action (§ 411(a)); (3) statutory damages and attorney's fees may be awarded only if registration is made prior to the commencement of the infringement (§ 412, which makes these remedies available even as to infringements before registration if the latter is made within three months after first publication). Among copyright litigators, the last-mentioned incentive is regarded as particularly important.

The § 412 three-month grace period is of significance, however, only for works infringed shortly following publication. Congress expressed concern to "take care of newsworthy or suddenly popular works which may be infringed almost as soon as they are published, before the copyright owner has had a reasonable opportunity to register his claim." H.R. Rep. No. 94-1476, 94th Cong., 2d Sess. at 158 (1976). Ironically, § 412 appears to preclude an award of attorney's fees when the work is so popular that it is infringed before its publication. *See Harper & Row Pub'rs, Inc. v. Nation Enters.,* 557 F. Supp. 1067 (S.D.N.Y. 1980), *rev'd on other grounds,* 723 F.2d 195 (2d Cir. 1983), *rev'd,* 471 U.S. 539 (1985). This ruling might at first seem to disadvantage authors of works which are "unpublished," but publicly accessible, for example, works of the visual arts. The reader should recall, however, that § 408(a) provides for registration of unpublished works.

Pending legislation would repeal the § 412 bar to statutory damages and attorney's fees. Various author groups — particularly photographers, graphic artists, and foreign copyright owners — have argued that the registration requirements are unduly onerous and unfairly inhibit meaningful access to judicial relief.

QUESTIONS

1. What are the purposes of the registration system? Would those purposes be significantly frustrated if Congress were to eliminate the incentives found in §§ 411(a) and 412? Even assuming that such elimination would result in diminished registration (and accompanying deposit): (a) Would that be a reasonable loss to bear in light of the alleged unfairness of the present registration regime? and (b) Would there be alternative measures that you would propose in order to promote registrations?

2. Making reference to other sections of the Act, what are the reasons for requiring that each of the items listed in § 409 be included in the application for copyright registration?

FORMALITIES UNDER 1909 ACT AND UNDER 1976 ACT BEFORE AND AFTER THE BERNE CONVENTION IMPLEMENTATION ACT

The following chart may assist the student in determining whether and which formalities may be applicable:

	Work published Before 1978	*1978-Feb. 1989*	*After Feb. 1989*
Notice	Federal copyright arose upon publication with notice; if no notice, work fell into public domain.	Affixation of notice perfected protection; five years to cure omissions, otherwise work fell into public domain.	Optional: incentive — unavailability of innocent infringer defense.
Registration	Optional until last year of first term; mandatory for renewal of works first published before 1964; prerequisite to initiation of infringement suit during *both* terms of copyright.	Optional, *but* prerequisite to initiation of suit. Incentives: statutory damages and attorneys fees not available unless work was registered before infringement commenced*	Optional for non-U.S. Berne works; remains prerequisite to suit for U.S. and other foreign works. Same incentives apply.
Deposit	Prerequisite to suit; in addition, fines may be imposed for failure to deposit copies with Library of Congress.	Same.	No longer a prerequisite to suit for non-U.S. Berne works; *but* fines may still be imposed.

*Or unless the work is infringed within the first three months of publication, and registration is made before the third month elapses.

	Work published Before 1978	*1978-Feb. 1989*	*After Feb. 1989*
Recordation of Transfers	Unrecorded transfer void against subsequent bona fide purchaser for value.	Same, *plus* a prerequisite to suit.	No longer a prerequisite to suit; unrecorded transfers still void against subsequent b.f.p.v.'s.

Chapter 6
RIGHTS, LIMITATIONS AND REMEDIES

A. THE RIGHT TO REPRODUCE THE WORK IN COPIES AND PHONORECORDS UNDER § 106(1)

§ 106. Exclusive rights in copyrighted works

Subject to sections 107 through 120, the owner of copyright under this title has the exclusive rights to do and to authorize any of the following:

 (1) to reproduce the copyrighted work in copies or phonorecords;

 (2) to prepare derivative works based upon the copyrighted work;

 (3) to distribute copies or phonorecords of the copyrighted work to the public by the sale or other transfer of ownership, or by rental, lease, or lending;

 (4) in the case of literary, musical, dramatic, and choreographic works, pantomimes, and motion pictures and other audiovisual works, to perform the copyrighted work publicly; and

 (5) in the case of literary, musical, dramatic, and choreographic works, pantomimes, and pictorial, graphic, or sculptural works, including the individual images of a motion picture or other audiovisual work, to display the copyrighted work publicly.

HOUSE REPORT

H.R. Rep. No. 94-1476, 94th Cong., 2d Sess. 61-62 (1976)

Rights of reproduction, adaptation, and publication

The first three clauses of section 106, which cover all rights under a copyright except those of performance and display, extend to every kind of copyrighted work. The exclusive rights encompassed by these clauses, though closely related, are independent; they can generally be characterized as rights of copying, recording, adaptation, and publishing. A single act of infringement may violate all of these rights at once, as where a publisher reproduces, adapts, and sells copies of a person's copyrighted work as part of a publishing venture. Infringement takes place when any one of the rights is violated: where, for example, a printer reproduces copies without selling them or a retailer sells copies without having anything to do with their reproduction. The references to "copies or phonorecords," although in the plural, are intended here and throughout the bill to include the singular (1 U.S.C. § 1).

Reproduction. — Read together with the relevant definitions in section 101, the right "to reproduce the copyrighted work in copies or phonorecords" means the right to produce a material object in which the work is duplicated, transcribed, imitated, or simulated in a fixed form from which it can be "perceived, reproduced, or otherwise communicated, either directly or with the aid of a machine or device." As under the present law, a copyrighted work would be infringed by reproducing it in whole or in any substantial part, and by duplicating it exactly or by imitation or simulation. Wide departures or variations from the copyrighted works would still be an infringement as long as the author's "expression" rather than merely the author's "ideas" are taken....

"Reproduction" under clause (1) of section 106 is to be distinguished from "display" under clause (5). For a work to be "reproduced," its fixation in tangible form must be "sufficiently permanent or stable to permit it to be perceived, reproduced, or otherwise communicated for a period of more than transitory duration." Thus, the showing of images on a screen or tube would not be a violation of clause (1), although it might come within the scope of clause (5).

1. THE RIGHT TO MAKE COPIES

ARNSTEIN v. PORTER

154 F.2d 464 (2d Cir. 1946), *cert. denied*, 330 U.S. 851 (1947)

Plaintiff, a citizen and resident of New York, brought this suit, charging infringement by defendant, a citizen and resident of New York, of plaintiff's copyrights to several musical compositions, infringement of his rights to other uncopyrighted musical compositions, and wrongful use of the titles of others. Plaintiff, when filing his complaint, demanded a jury trial. Plaintiff took the deposition of defendant, and defendant, the deposition of plaintiff. Defendant then moved for an order striking out plaintiff's jury demand, and for summary judgment. Attached to defendant's motion papers were the depositions, phonograph records of piano renditions of the plaintiff's compositions and defendant's alleged infringing compositions, and the court records of five previous copyright infringement suits brought by plaintiff in the court below against other persons, in which judgments had been entered, after trials, against plaintiff. Defendant also moved for dismissal of the action on the ground of "vexatiousness."

Plaintiff alleged that defendant's "Begin the Beguine" is a plagiarism from plaintiff's "The Lord Is My Shepherd" and "A Mother's Prayer." Plaintiff testified, on deposition, that "The Lord Is My Shepherd" had been published and about 2,000 copies sold, that "A Mother's Prayer" had been published, over a million copies having been sold. In his depositions, he gave no direct evidence that defendant saw or heard these compositions. He also alleged that defendant's "My Heart Belongs to Daddy" had been plagiarized from plaintiff's "A Mother's Prayer."

Plaintiff also alleged that defendant's "I Love You" is a plagiarism from plaintiff's composition "La Priere," stating in his deposition that the latter composition had been sold. He gave no direct proof that defendant knew of this composition.

He also alleged that defendant's song "Night and Day" is a plagiarism of plaintiff's song "I Love You Madly," which he testified had not been published but had once been publicly performed over the radio, copies having been sent to divers radio stations but none to defendant; a copy of this song, plaintiff testified, had been stolen from his room. He also alleged that "I Love You

Madly" was in part plagiarized from "La Priere." He further alleged that defendant's "You'd Be So Nice To Come Home To" is plagiarized from plaintiff's "Sadness Overwhelms My Soul." He testified that this song had never been published or publicly performed but that copies had been sent to a movie producer and to several publishers. He also alleged that defendant's "Don't Fence Me In" is a plagiarism of plaintiff's song "A Modern Messiah" which has not been published or publicly performed; in his deposition he said that about a hundred copies had been sent to divers radio stations and band leaders but that he sent no copy to defendant. Plaintiff said that defendant "had stooges right along to follow me, watch me, and live in the same apartment with me," and that plaintiff's room had been ransacked on several occasions. Asked how he knew that defendant had anything to do with any of these "burglaries," plaintiff said, "I don't know that he had to do with it, but I only know that he could have." He also said "... many of my compositions had been published. No one had to break in to steal them. They were sung publicly."

Defendant in his deposition categorically denied that he had ever seen or heard any of plaintiff's compositions or had had any acquaintance with any persons said to have stolen any of them.

The prayer of plaintiff's original complaint asked "at least one million dollars out of the millions the defendant has earned and is earning out of all the plagiarism." In his amended complaint the prayer is "for judgment against the defendant in the sum of $1,000,000 as damages sustained by the plagiarism of all the compositions named in the complaint." Plaintiff, not a lawyer, appeared pro se below and on this appeal.

FRANK, CIRCUIT JUDGE. 1. Plaintiff with his complaint filed a jury demand which defendant moved to strike out. Defendant urges that the relief prayed in the complaint renders a jury trial inappropriate. We do not agree. Plaintiff did not ask for an injunction but solely for damages. Such a suit is an action at "law." That it is founded solely on a statute does not deprive either party of a right to a trial by jury; an action for treble damages under the Sherman Act is likewise purely statutory, but it is triable at "law" and by a jury as of right.

2. The principal question on this appeal is whether the lower court, under Rule 56, properly deprived plaintiff of a trial of his copyright infringement action. The answer depends on whether "there is the slightest doubt about the facts." [Citations omitted.] In applying that standard here, it is important to avoid confusing two separate elements essential to a plaintiff's case in such a suit: (a) that defendant copied from plaintiff's copyrighted work and (b) that the copying (assuming it to be proved) went so far as to constitute improper appropriation.

As to the first — copying — the evidence may consist (a) of defendant's admission that he copied or (b) of circumstantial evidence — usually evidence of access — from which the trier of the facts may reasonably infer copying. Of course, if there are no similarities, no amount of evidence of access will suffice to prove copying. If there is evidence of access and similarities exist, then the trier of the facts must determine whether the similarities are sufficient to prove copying. On this issue, analysis ("dissection") is relevant, and the testimony of experts may be received to aid the trier of the facts. If evidence of access is absent, the similarities must be so striking as to preclude the possibility that plaintiff and defendant independently arrived at the same result.

If copying is established, then only does there arise the second issue, that of illicit copying (unlawful appropriation). On that issue (as noted more in detail below) the test is the response of the ordinary lay hearer; accordingly, on that issue, "dissection" and expert testimony are irrelevant.

In some cases, the similarities between the plaintiff's and defendant's work are so extensive and striking as, without more, both to justify an inference of copying and to prove improper appropriation. But such double-purpose evidence is not required; that is, if copying is otherwise shown, proof of improper appropriation need not consist of similarities which, standing alone, would support an inference of copying.

Each of these two issues — copying and improper appropriation — is an issue of fact. If there is a trial, the conclusions on those issues of the trier of the facts — of the judge if he sat without a jury, or of the jury if there was a jury trial — binds this court on appeal, provided the evidence supports those findings, regardless of whether we would ourselves have reached the same conclusions. But a case could occur in which the similarities are so striking that we would reverse a finding of no access, despite weak evidence of access (or no evidence thereof other than the similarities); and similarly as to a finding of no illicit appropriation.

3. We turn first to the issue of copying. After listening to the compositions as played in the phonograph recordings submitted by defendant, we find similarities; but we hold that unquestionably, standing alone, they do not compel the conclusion, or permit the inference, that defendant copied. The similarities, however, are sufficient so that, if there is enough evidence of access to permit the case to go to the jury, the jury may properly infer that the similarities did not result from coincidence.

Summary judgment was, then, proper if indubitably defendant did not have access to plaintiff's compositions. Plainly that presents an issue of fact. On that issue, the district judge, who heard no oral testimony, had before him the depositions of plaintiff and defendant. The judge characterized plaintiff's story as "fantastic"; and, in the light of the references in his opinion to defendant's deposition, the judge obviously accepted defendant's denial of access and copying. Although part of plaintiff's testimony on deposition (as to "stooges" and the like) does seem "fantastic," yet plaintiff's credibility, even as to those improbabilities, should be left to the jury. If evidence "is of a kind that greatly taxes the credulity of the judge, he can say so, or, if he totally disbelieves it, he may announce that fact, leaving the jury free to believe it or not." If, said Winslow J., "evidence is always to be disbelieved because the story told seems remarkable or impossible, then a party whose rights depend on the proof of some facts out of the usual course of events will always be denied justice simply because his story is improbable." We should not overlook the shrewd proverbial admonition that sometimes truth is stranger than fiction.

But even if we were to disregard the improbable aspects of plaintiff's story, there remains parts by no means "fantastic." On the record now before us, more than a million copies of one of his compositions were sold; copies of others were sold in smaller quantities or distributed to radio stations or band leaders or publishers, or the pieces were publicly performed. If, after hearing both parties testify, the jury disbelieves defendant's denials, it can, from such facts, reasonably infer access. It follows that, as credibility is unavoidably involved, a genuine issue of material fact presents itself. With credibility a vital factor, plaintiff is entitled to a trial where the jury can observe the witnesses while testifying. Plaintiff must not be deprived of the invaluable privilege of cross-examining the defendant — the "crucial test of credibility" — in the presence of the jury. Plaintiff, or a lawyer on his behalf, on such examination may elicit damaging admissions from defendant; more important, plaintiff may persuade the jury, observing defendant's manner when testifying, that defendant is unworthy of belief.

. . . .

With all that in mind, we cannot now say — as we think we must say to sustain a summary judgment — that at the close of a trial the judge could properly direct a verdict.

. . . .

We do not believe that, in a case in which the decision must turn on the reliability of witnesses, the Supreme Court, by authorizing summary judgments, intended to permit a "trial by affidavits," if either party objects. That procedure which, so the historians tell us, began to be outmoded at common law in the 16th century, would, if now revived, often favor unduly the party with the more ingenious and better paid lawyer. Grave injustice might easily result.

. . . .

4. Assuming that adequate proof is made of copying, that is not enough; for there can be "permissible copying," copying which is not illicit. Whether (if he copied) defendant unlawfully appropriated presents, too, an issue of fact. The proper criterion on that issue is not an analytic or other comparison of the respective musical compositions as they appear on paper or in the judgment of trained musicians.[19] The plaintiff's legally protected interest is not, as such, his reputation as a musician but his interest in the potential financial returns from his compositions which derive from the lay public's approbation of his efforts. The question, therefore, is whether defendant took from plaintiff's works so much of what is pleasing to the ears of lay listeners, who comprise the audience for whom such popular music is composed, that defendant wrongfully appropriated something which belongs to the plaintiff.

Surely, then, we have an issue of fact which a jury is peculiarly fitted to determine.[22] Indeed, even if there were to be a trial before a judge, it would be desirable (although not necessary) for him to summon an advisory jury on this question.

We should not be taken as saying that a plagiarism case can never arise in which absence of similarities is so patent that a summary judgment for defen-

---

[19] Where plaintiff relies on similarities to prove copying (as distinguished from improper appropriation) paper comparisons and the opinions of experts may aid the court.

[22] It would, accordingly, be proper to exclude tone-deaf persons from the jury, cf. *Chatterton v. Cave*, 3 A.C. 483, 499-501, 502-504.

dant would be correct. Thus, suppose that Ravel's "Bolero" or Shostakovitch's "Fifth Symphony" were alleged to infringe "When Irish Eyes Are Smiling."[23] But this is not such a case. For, after listening to the playing of the respective compositions, we are, at this time, unable to conclude that the likenesses are so trifling that, on the issue of misappropriation, a trial judge could legitimately direct a verdict for defendant.

At the trial, plaintiff may play, or cause to be played, the pieces in such manner that they may seem to a jury to be inexcusably alike, in terms of the way in which lay listeners of such music would be likely to react. The plaintiff may call witnesses whose testimony may aid the jury in reaching its conclusion as to the responses of such audiences. Expert testimony of musicians may also be received, but it will in no way be controlling on the issue of illicit copying, and should be utilized only to assist in determining the reactions of lay auditors. The impression made on the refined ears of musical experts or their views as to the musical excellence of plaintiff's or defendant's works are utterly immaterial on the issue of misappropriation; for the views of such persons are caviar to the general — and plaintiff's and defendant's compositions are not caviar.

....

Modified in part; otherwise reversed and remanded.

....

CLARK, CIRCUIT JUDGE (dissenting). While the procedure followed below seems to me generally simple and appropriate, the defendant did make one fatal tactical error. In an endeavor to assist us, he caused to be prepared records of all the musical pieces here involved, and presented these transcriptions through the medium of the affidavit of his pianist.... [A]fter repeated hearings of the records, I could not find therein what my brothers found. The only thing definitely mentioned seemed to be the repetitive use of the note e^2 in certain places by both plaintiff and defendant, surely too simple and ordinary a device of composition to be significant. In our former musical plagiarism cases we have, naturally, relied on what seemed the total sound effect; but we have also analyzed the music enough to make sure of an intelligible and intellectual decision. Thus in *Arnstein v. Edward B. Marks Music Corp.*, 2 Cir., 82 F.2d 275, 277, Judge L. Hand made quite an extended comparison of the songs, concluding, inter alia: "... the seven notes available do not admit of so many agreeable permutations that we need be amazed at the re-appearance of old themes, even though the identity extend through a sequence of twelve notes."...

It is true that in *Arnstein v. Broadcast Music, Inc.*, 2 Cir., 137 F.2d 410, 412, we considered "dissection" or "technical analysis" not the proper approach to support a finding of plagiarism, and said that it must be "more ingenuous, more like that of a spectator, who would rely upon the complex of his impressions." But in its context that seems to me clearly sound and in accord with what I have in mind. Thus one may look to the total impression to repulse the charge of plagiarism where a minute "dissection" might dredge up some

---

[23] In such a case, the complete absence of similarity would negate both copying and improper appropriation.

points of similarity. Hence one cannot use a purely theoretical disquisition to supply a total resemblance which does not otherwise exist. Certainly, however, that does not suggest or compel the converse — that one must keep his brain in torpor for fear that otherwise it would make clear differences which do exist. Music is a matter of the intellect as well as the emotions; that is why eminent musical scholars insist upon the employment of the intellectual faculties for a just appreciation of music.

Consequently I do not think we should abolish the use of the intellect here even if we could. When, however, we start with an examination of the written and printed material supplied by the plaintiff in his complaint and exhibits, we find at once that he does not and cannot claim extensive copying, measure by measure, of his compositions. He therefore has resorted to a comparative analysis — the "dissection" found unpersuasive in the earlier cases — to support his claim of plagiarism of small detached portions here and there, the musical fillers between the better known parts of the melody. And plaintiff's compositions, as pointed out in the cases cited above, are of the simple and trite character where small repetitive sequences are not hard to discover. It is as though we found Shakespeare a plagiarist on the basis of his use of articles, pronouns, prepositions, and adjectives also used by others. The surprising thing, however, is to note the small amount of even this type of reproduction which plaintiff by dint of extreme dissection has been able to find.

... The usual claim seems to be rested upon a sequence of three, of four, or of five — never more than five — identical notes, usually of different rhythmical values. Nowhere is there anything approaching the twelve-note sequence of the *Marks* case, *supra*....

In the light of these utmost claims of the plaintiff, I do not see a legal basis for the claim of plagiarism. So far as I have been able to discover, no earlier case approaches the holding that a simple and trite sequence of this type, even if copying may seem indicated, constitutes proof either of access or of plagiarism....

[On remand, after jury trial, judgment was entered for the defendant. *See* 158 F.2d 795 (2d Cir. 1946), *cert. denied*, 330 U.S. 851 (1947).]

QUESTIONS

1. Given the limited tonal range that a popular song composer uses, the confinements of conventional harmony, and the frequency with which we observe that many pop songs sound alike, how likely is it that a defendant will ever be able to prevail on a motion for summary judgment after the *Arnstein* decision? Isn't that decision an invitation to litigate frivolous claims, which are almost certain to reach a jury or to force an unfair settlement? (At any time on the dockets of the federal courts in New York City and Los Angeles, one is likely to find a few song-infringement suits, typically brought by the affronted aspiring songwriter pro se.)

2. Wouldn't it be sensible to have some judicially recognized "rule of thumb" regarding the number of consecutive notes of an earlier copyrighted song that may be duplicated (consciously or not) without fear of liability for infringement? (Judge Clark appears to opt for twelve notes, more or less. Is that too many?) Would it be feasible to formulate such a rule? Would it have to take into account whether the notes were in the accompaniment or in the melody? In the verse (introduction) or chorus (main melody section)? In the main theme or in the "bridge"?

3. Is it relevant in determining infringement that the plaintiff's song ceased to be popular five years ago? Is it relevant that the plaintiff's work is an operatic aria and the defendant's is a jukebox hit with little or no overlapping audience?

4. What should be the role of experts in musical, artistic or literary infringement cases? On what issues can they make the greatest contribution? On what issues should the fact-finder rely primarily on personal observation or on intuition?

Dawson v. Hinshaw Music, Inc., 905 F.2d 731 (4th Cir.), *cert. denied,* 498 U.S. 981 (1990). The court held that the determination of "substantial similarity" as the second test under *Arnstein v. Porter* is to be made from the perspective of the audience that was intended by the author to constitute the commercial market. This will often be what *Arnstein* referred to as the "ordinary observer," but it need not be the lay person when the work is designed to appeal to an audience with specialized knowledge. One example is a computer program, which, when being compared with another program, must be scrutinized by an expert. Another example is a toy or a computer game made for children; there, substantial similarity between works should be assessed from a child's perspective. The "ordinary observer" test should be displaced, however, only when the intended audience has "specialized expertise" and not merely when its tastes might differ from those of the lay observer.

The work litigated in the instant case was a musical arrangement of a spiritual. The court of appeals therefore suggested that the trial court should be free (on remand) to determine whether the intended audience was a lay audience or rather choral directors having specialized knowledge of choral music. The court also suggested that if there were indeed a specialized audience for the parties' spirituals and if that audience (i.e., choral directors) would ordinarily compare the works of plaintiff and defendant by examining printed sheet music rather than by listening to recordings of the two arrangements, then it would not be reversible error for the district court to exclude recordings from the trial.

a. Proof of Copying

CIRCUMSTANTIAL PROOF OF COPYING

In *Arnstein v. Porter,* the Second Circuit stated that the similarities between "Begin the Beguine" and plaintiff's songs, and the sale of one million copies of plaintiff's "A Mother's Prayer" as well as the public performance of others of plaintiff's songs, raised a sufficient possibility that Cole Porter had access to and copied from the songs to permit a trial on the issue. In the "My Sweet Lord" case immediately below, George Harrison's access to plaintiff's song was inferred from the song's status as a top hit in England and the United States, when Harrison, then a Beatle, would have had ample opportunity to hear the song.

In other instances, however, access and copying may be less subject to inference. In *Heim v. Universal Pictures Co.,* 154 F.2d 480 (2d Cir. 1946), the Second Circuit declined to hold that the similarities between plaintiff's and defendant's songs resulted from access to and copying of plaintiff's song, even though plaintiff's song was included in a motion picture that was widely exhibited throughout the United States, had been publicly performed in major cities, and had been sold in sheet music. The court held that the similarities between the songs derived from their common reference to Dvořák's "Humoresque," and that plaintiff's variations on Dvořák were not sufficiently distinctive to permit a finding that defendant copied from plaintiff rather than from Dvořák.

In *Selle v. Gibb,* 567 F. Supp. 1173 (N.D. Ill. 1983), *aff'd,* 741 F.2d 896 (7th Cir. 1984), the court affirmed a judgment n.o.v. that defendants, the Bee Gees, did not copy from plaintiff's song in creating "How Deep Is Your Love." Although the two songs contained many similarities, the court held there was no credible evidence of access to plaintiff's song when defendants created their song in France, and plaintiff's song was unpublished and had only been performed by plaintiff at Chicago-area weddings and bar mitzvahs.

The Seventh Circuit stated that striking similarities, indeed even complete identity, between two works will not support a finding of infringement unless there is "at least some other evidence which would establish a reasonable possibility that the complaining work was *available* to the alleged infringer.... Thus, although proof of striking similarity may permit an inference of access, the plaintiff must still meet some minimum threshold of proof which demonstrates that the inference of access is reasonable." (Emphasis in original.) The court affirmed the ruling below that plaintiff had failed to produce evidence justifying an inference of access.

The appellate court went on to discuss the concept of "striking similarity." Striking similarity is a term of art connoting more than substantial similarity. Striking similarities are those that concern material so unique or appearing in so complex a context in plaintiff's work that defendant would be most unlikely to have produced the same material in the same context by coincidence, accident, or independent creation. Thus, for example, where the allegedly copied material is standard to the medium or derives from a prior source, the similarities which defendant's music manifests with regard to this material will not be deemed "striking."

Reviewing the evidence produced at trial, the appellate court observed that the musical themes plaintiff alleged had been copied were themselves quite similar to themes in several prior musical works, including a Beatles song, and Beethoven's Fifth Symphony. The court therefore held that plaintiff had not demonstrated that the allegedly copied portions of his work presented the kind of subject matter upon which a finding of striking similarity could be based.

By contrast, the Second Circuit has recently declared its adherence to the original *Arnstein* "striking similarity" rule. In *Gaste v. Kaiserman,* 863 F.2d

1061 (2d Cir. 1988), the court reaffirmed its willingness to find copying, even without evidence of access, when the two works are exceptionally close. The court upheld the verdict that defendant's work, the immensely popular song "Feelings," infringed the rather obscure French song "Pour Toi." To the lay ear, the songs were indeed quite similar. Evidence of access was somewhat skimpy: some twenty years before defendant composed his song, plaintiff had sent sheet music of his song to a Brazilian music publisher who ultimately became defendant's music publisher. It was therefore possible that defendant's publisher provided access to plaintiff's work. Even absent that possibility, the trial judge instructed the jury, access could be presumed from striking similarity. In affirming this instruction, the Second Circuit stated:

> Appellants contend that undue reliance on striking similarity to show access precludes protection for the author who independently creates a similar work. However, the jury is only *permitted* to infer access from striking similarity; it need not do so. Though striking similarity alone can raise an inference of copying, that inference must be reasonable in light of all the evidence. A plaintiff has not proved striking similarity sufficient to sustain a finding of copying if the evidence as a whole does not preclude any possibility of independent creation.

Although the Second Circuit's approach to striking similarity at first appears less stringent and therefore more favorable to plaintiffs, the Seventh Circuit's standard may in fact be the more lenient one. Under the Seventh Circuit's version of the striking similarity doctrine, plaintiff must prove extraordinary similarity of nonbanal music, plus some possibility of access. Under the Second Circuit's test, plaintiff must prove extraordinary similarity, plus no possibility of independent creation. How would plaintiff show that defendant (and particularly, a successful composer defendant) could not have independently created the disputed work?

BRIGHT TUNES MUSIC CORP. v. HARRISONGS MUSIC, LTD.

420 F. Supp. 177 (S.D.N.Y. 1976)

OWEN, DISTRICT JUDGE. This is an action in which it is claimed that a successful song, My Sweet Lord, listing George Harrison as the composer, is plagiarized from an earlier successful song, He's So Fine, composed by Ronald Mack, recorded by a singing group called the "Chiffons," the copyright of which is owned by plaintiff, Bright Tunes Music Corp.

He's So Fine, recorded in 1962, is a catchy tune consisting essentially of four repetitions of a very short basic musical phrase, "sol-mi-re," (hereinafter motif A),[1] altered as necessary to fit the words, followed by four repetitions of

---

[1]

another short basic musical phrase, "sol-la-do-la-do," (hereinafter motif B).[2] While neither motif is novel, the four repetitions of A, followed by four repetitions of B, is a highly unique pattern.[3] In addition, in the second use of the motif B series, there is a grace note inserted making the phrase go "sol-la-do-la-re-do." [4]

My Sweet Lord, recorded first in 1970, also uses the same motif A (modified to suit the words) four times, followed by motif B, repeated three times, not four. In place of He's So Fine's fourth repetition of motif B, My Sweet Lord has a transitional passage of musical attractiveness of the same approximate length, with the identical grace note in the identical second repetition.[5] The harmonies of both songs are identical.[6]

George Harrison, a former member of The Beatles, was aware of He's So Fine. In the United States, it was No. 1 on the billboard charts for five weeks; in England, Harrison's home country, it was No. 12 on the charts on June 1, 1963, a date upon which one of the Beatle songs was, in fact, in first position. For seven weeks in 1963, He's So Fine was one of the top hits in England.

According to Harrison, the circumstances of the composition of My Sweet Lord were as follows. Harrison and his group, which include[d] an American gospel singer named Billy Preston,[7] were in Copenhagen, Denmark, on a singing engagement. There was a press conference involving the group going on backstage. Harrison slipped away from the press conference and went to a room upstairs and began "vamping" some guitar chords, fitting on to the chords he was playing the words, "Hallelujah" and "Hare Krishna" in various

---

[2]

[3] All the experts agreed on this.
[4]

[5] This grace note, as will be seen *infra,* has a substantial significance in assessing the claims of the parties hereto.

[6] Expert witnesses for the defendants asserted crucial differences in the two songs. These claimed differences essentially stem, however, from the fact that different words and number of syllables were involved. This necessitated modest alterations in the repetitions or the places of beginning of a phrase, which, however, has nothing to do whatsoever with the essential musical kernel that is involved.

[7] Preston recorded the first Harrison copyrighted recording of My Sweet Lord, of which more *infra,* and from his musical background was necessarily equally aware of He's So Fine.

ways.[8] During the course of this vamping, he was alternating between what musicians call a Minor II chord and a Major V chord.

At some point, germinating started and he went down to meet with others of the group, asking them to listen, which they did, and everyone began to join in, taking first "Hallelujah" and then "Hare Krishna" and putting them into four part harmony. Harrison obviously started using the "Hallelujah," etc., as repeated sounds, and from there developed the lyrics, to wit, "My Sweet Lord," "Dear, Dear Lord," etc. In any event, from this very free-flowing exchange of ideas, with Harrison playing his two chords and everybody singing "Hallelujah" and "Hare Krishna," there began to emerge the My Sweet Lord text idea, which Harrison sought to develop a little bit further during the following week as he was playing it on his guitar. Thus developed motif A and its words interspersed with "Hallelujah" and "Hare Krishna."

Approximately one week after the idea first began to germinate, the entire group flew back to London because they had earlier booked time to go to a recording studio with Billy Preston to make an album. In the studio, Preston was the principal musician. Harrison did not play in the session. He had given Preston his basic motif A with the idea that it be turned into a song, and was back and forth from the studio to the engineer's recording booth, supervising the recording "takes." Under circumstances that Harrison was utterly unable to recall, while everybody was working toward a finished song, in the recording studio, somehow or other the essential three notes of motif A reached polished form.

> Q. [By the Court]: ... you feel that those three notes ... the motif A in the record, those three notes developed somewhere in that recording session?
>
> Mr. Harrison: I'd say those three there were finalized as beginning there.
>
> ....
>
> Q. [By the Court]: Is it possible that Billy Preston hit on those [notes comprising motif A]?
>
> Mr. Harrison: Yes, but it's possible also that I hit on that, too, as far back as the dressing room, just scat singing.

Similarly, it appears that motif B emerged in some fashion at the recording session as did motif A. This is also true of the unique grace note in the second repetition of motif B.

> Q. [By the Court]: All I am trying to get at, Mr. Harrison, is if you have a recollection when that [grace] note popped into existence as it ends up in the Billy Preston recording.
>
> ....

---

[8] These words ended up being a "responsive" interjection between the eventually copyrighted words of My Sweet Lord. In He's So Fine the Chiffons used the sound "dulang" in the same places to fill in and give rhythmic impetus to what would otherwise be somewhat dead spots in the music.

> Mr. Harrison: ... [Billy Preston] might have put that there on every take, but it just might have been on one take, or he might have varied it on different takes at different places.

The Billy Preston recording, listing George Harrison as the composer, was thereafter issued by Apple Records. The music was then reduced to paper by someone who prepared a "lead sheet" containing the melody, the words and the harmony for the United States copyright application.

Seeking the wellsprings of musical composition — why a composer chooses the succession of notes and the harmonies he does — whether it be George Harrison or Richard Wagner — is a fascinating inquiry. It is apparent from the extensive colloquy between the Court and Harrison covering forty pages in the transcript that neither Harrison nor Preston were conscious of the fact that they were utilizing the He's So Fine theme. However, they in fact were, for it is perfectly obvious to the listener that in musical terms, the two songs are virtually identical except for one phrase. There is motif A used four times, followed by motif B, four times in one case, and three times in the other, with the same grace note in the second repetition of motif B.

What happened? I conclude that the composer, in seeking musical materials to clothe his thoughts, was working with various possibilities. As he tried this possibility and that, there came to the surface of his mind a particular combination that pleased him as being one he felt would be appealing to a prospective listener; in other words, that this combination of sounds would work. Why? Because his subconscious knew it already had worked in a song his conscious mind did not remember. Having arrived at this pleasing combination of sounds, the recording was made, the lead sheet prepared for copyright and the song became an enormous success. Did Harrison deliberately use the music of He's So Fine? I do not believe he did so deliberately. Nevertheless, it is clear that My Sweet Lord is the very same song as He's So Fine with different words, and Harrison had access to He's So Fine. This is, under the law, infringement of copyright, and is no less so even though subconsciously accomplished. *Sheldon v. Metro-Goldwyn Pictures Corp.*, 81 F.2d 49, 54 (2d Cir. 1936); *Northern Music Corp. v. Pacemaker Music Co., Inc.*, 147 U.S.P.Q. 358, 359 (S.D.N.Y. 1965).

Given the foregoing, I find for the plaintiff on the issue of plagiarism, and set the action down for trial on November 8, 1976 on the issue of damages and other relief as to which the plaintiff may be entitled. The foregoing constitutes the Court's findings of fact and conclusions of law.

So ordered.

[The Court of Appeals for the Second Circuit affirmed the holding of infringement, stating that access could be inferred from the top-hit status of the plaintiff's song and explicitly endorsing the principle of subconscious infringement. *ABKCO Music, Inc. v. Harrisongs Music, Ltd.*, 722 F.2d 988 (2d Cir. 1983).

[Subsequently, District Judge Owen found Harrisongs liable for some $1.6 million in damages. Matters became complicated and nasty when ABKCO, formerly the Beatles' business manager, purchased from plaintiff Brite Tunes for some $587,000 all of Brite Tunes' rights in and revenues from "He's So Fine," including copyright infringement damages such as those payable by Harrisongs. It was later held by the District Judge that ABKCO's dealings with Brite Tunes violated its fiduciary duties to Harrison and that it should therefore hold any revenues from "He's So Fine" in a "constructive trust" for Harrisongs, once Harrisongs reimbursed ABKCO in the amount of $587,000; because of a number of contracts and settlements regarding foreign rights, however, the judge, who was affirmed by the Court of Appeals for the Second Circuit, concluded that Harrisongs need reimburse ABKCO in an amount only somewhat more than half of the $587,000. It was not, then, until 1991 that the saga that began with George Harrison's 1970 subconscious infringement finally came to an end. For the intricate and unhappy details, see ABKCO Music, Inc. v. Harrisongs Music, Ltd., 944 F.2d 971 (2d Cir. 1991).]

QUESTIONS

1. It is uniformly held that copyright is infringed when one intentionally makes copies of a copyrighted work, even though the person copying does not know (and has no reason to know) of the copyright. For example, if a book publisher publishes a manuscript that has been represented to be an original work but is in fact a copy of a copyrighted work, the book publisher infringes. *De Acosta v. Brown*, 146 F.2d 408 (2d Cir. 1944). Is this a sound rule? What are the arguments for and against this rule?

2. Even assuming the above rule to be sound and widely endorsed, is not the case for infringement much more difficult when the defendant does not intend to reproduce any work by another and is unaware that he is copying at all? Why should liability be imposed in such a case?

3. How do you think the court should have ruled had defendant Harrison copied only motif A or motif B?

4. What if Harrison, idly sitting at the piano, purposely played the notes of motifs A and B *backwards* and, finding the resulting tune to be pleasant, added lyrics, and published and performed the new song. Is this an infringement?

b. Infringing Copying

ON THE DIFFERENCE BETWEEN PROVING COPYING AND PROVING INFRINGEMENT

To prove copyright infringement, plaintiff must show not only that defendant copied the work but that the copying was illicit. To this end, plaintiff must demonstrate not only that similarities exist between the works but that these similarities are substantial. One may evaluate the substantiality of the similarities with regard either to their quantity or to their quality. In either event, the substantial similarity between plaintiff's and defendant's works must go to their expression, not merely to their facts or ideas.

The subject matter of substantial similarity illustrates a key difference between proving copying and proving infringement. Similarities of facts or ideas may be probative of the existence of copying. Indeed, publishers of compilations often introduce "false facts" as a way to trace copying. Discovery of plaintiff's invented entry in a third party's work will generally defeat the second comer's claim of independent generation of the same material or information. *See, e.g., Financial Information, Inc. v. Moody's Inv. Serv.,* 808 F.2d 204, 205 (2d Cir. 1986) (publisher of daily bond call reports, suspecting copying by a competitor, "planted" some false information in its daily bond cards; reappearance of this information in defendant's bond reports demonstrated defendant' s copying). Once plaintiff shows copying, however, its demonstration is not complete; the substantial similarity standard requires evaluation of the nature of the correspondence between the two works. If, for example, defendant is shown to have copied only uncopyrightable information, no infringement has occurred. *See, e.g., ibid.* (while defendant clearly copied from plaintiff, its copying embraced no copyrightable expression — primarily because the court judged that plaintiff's cards exhibited no such expression). The materials which follow illustrate methods of and problems in determining whether defendant copied plaintiff's expression.

In *Laureyssens v. Idea Group, Inc.,* 964 F.2d 131 (2d Cir. 1992), the court focused upon the element of "similarity" which appears to be utilized at two different stages of the analysis propounded in *Arnstein v. Porter.* The question in *Laureyssens* was whether the plaintiff's jigsaw-type puzzle, named HAPPY CUBE — which had the unusual feature of being assembleable either in a flat form in a rectangular frame or into a three-dimensional hollow cube — was infringed by the defendant's SNAFOOZ puzzle. Although there was no dispute about the plaintiff's valid copyright in the puzzle design, the district court denied a preliminary injunction based on its conclusion that no serious question of infringement existed. The court of appeals affirmed.

In parsing the *Arnstein* requirements of first finding copying (usually based on access and similarity) and then finding unlawful appropriation ("by demonstrating that substantial similarities relate to protectible material"), the court relied heavily upon an article by the late Professor Latman, titled "'Probative Similarity' as Proof of Copying: Toward Dispelling Some Myths in Copyright Infringement," and posthumously published at 90 Colum. L. Rev. 1187 (1990). The court stated:

> A common form of indirect proof of copying — but far from the only form — is a showing of defendant's opportunity to come into contact with plaintiff's work and such similarities between the works which, under all the circumstances, make independent creation unlikely. Such similarities may or may not be substantial. They are not, however, offered for their own sake in satisfaction of the requirement that defendant has taken a substantial amount of protected material from the plaintiff's work. Rather, they are offered as probative of the act of copying and may accordingly for the sake of clarity conveniently be called "probative similarity."

Similarity that may be probative of copying — and it may in fact be insubstantial — may properly be uncovered through dissection and expert testimony. The defendant admitted access to the plaintiff's HAPPY CUBE puzzle, and the court found similarities that "are probative of copying and which at least raise a question of actual copying."

In turning to whether there was "substantial similarity as to protectible material," the court invoked the "ordinary observer" standard articulated by Judge Learned Hand in the *Peter Pan Fabrics* case, see *infra,* and stated: "[W]here a design contains both protectible and unprotectible elements, we have held that the observer's inspection must be more 'discerning,' ignoring those aspects of a work that are unprotectible in making the comparison." The court agreed with the trial judge that the similarities in the parties' works were principally in their idea and not in their expressive configuration.

Most of the cases in this subchapter deal with the question whether the defendant has "substantially" copied from the plaintiff's originally authored expression. It is worth noting that when such copying is indeed substantial, it matters not what kind of technology was used in making the unauthorized reproduction. Photocopy machines have been used for such purposes for at least two decades, and computers have also become familiar devices for making electronic reproductions. More recently, telefax machines have become commonplace in using telephone lines to make what are in effect long-distance photocopies.

In what appears to be a case of first instance, the court in *Pasha Pubs. Inc. v. Enmark Gas Corp.,* 22 U.S.P.Q.2d 1076 (N.D. Tex. 1992), found an infringement of the plaintiff's newsletter by the defendant's photocopying it in its entirety for employees in the home office in Dallas and the "faxing" of the newsletter to offices in Houston and Durham for employees there.

PETER PAN FABRICS, INC. v. MARTIN WEINER CORP.

274 F.2d 487 (2d Cir. 1960)

[A copyrighted design, "Byzantium," was imprinted upon bolts of cloth sold to garment manufacturers who later cut them into dresses. In doing so, the manufacturers cut or sewed the cloth so that copyright notices printed into the border or "selvage" of the cloth were no longer visible. The litigation was important in the area of copyrightability (accepting the extension of *Mazer v. Stein* to textile prints) and copyright notice (routine removal of the notice by customers of copyright owners did not forfeit copyright). But the words of Judge Learned Hand on the issue of substantial similarity have often been quoted:]

The test for infringement of a copyright is of necessity vague. In the case of verbal "works" it is well settled that although the "proprietor's" monopoly extends beyond an exact reproduction of the words, there can be no copyright in the "ideas" disclosed but only in their "expression." Obviously, no principle can be stated as to when an imitator has gone beyond copying the "idea," and has borrowed its "expression." Decisions must therefore inevitably be *ad hoc.* In the case of designs, which are addressed to the aesthetic sensibilities of an observer, the test is, if possible, even more intangible. No one disputes that the copyright extends beyond a photographic reproduction of the design, but one cannot say how far an imitator must depart from an undeviating reproduction to escape infringement. In deciding that question one should consider the uses for which the design is intended, especially the scrutiny that observers will give to it as used. In the case at bar we must try to estimate how far its overall appearance will determine its aesthetic appeal when the cloth is made into a garment. Both designs have the same general color, and the arches, scrolls, rows of symbols, etc. on one resemble those on the other though they are not identical. Moreover, the patterns in which these figures are distributed to make up the design as a whole are not identical. However, the ordinary observer, unless he set out to detect the disparities, would be disposed to overlook them, and regard their aesthetic appeal as the same. That is enough; and indeed, it is all that can be said, unless protection against infringement is to be denied because of variants irrelevant to the purpose for which the design is intended.

HERBERT ROSENTHAL JEWELRY CORP. v. KALPAKIAN
446 F.2d 738 (9th Cir. 1971)

BROWNING, CIRCUIT JUDGE: Plaintiff and defendants are engaged in the design, manufacture, and sale of fine jewelry.

Plaintiff charged defendants with infringing plaintiff's copyright registration of a pin in the shape of a bee formed of gold encrusted with jewels.... [A consent decree was entered, including an injunction against infringing the plaintiff's copyright. The plaintiff later moved for an order holding defendants in contempt.] The district court, after an evidentiary hearing, found that while defendants had manufactured and sold a line of jeweled bee pins, they designed their pins themselves after a study of bees in nature and in published works and did not copy plaintiff's copyrighted bee. The court further found that defendant's jeweled bees were "not substantially similar" to plaintiff's bees, except that both "do look like bees." The court concluded that defendants had neither infringed plaintiff's copyright nor violated the consent decree, and entered a judgment order denying plaintiff's motion. We affirm.

. . . .

II

Plaintiff contends that its copyright registration of a jeweled bee entitles it to protection from the manufacture and sale by others of any object that to the ordinary observer is substantially similar in appearance. The breadth of this claim is evident. For example, while a photograph of the copyrighted bee pin attached to the complaint depicts a bee with nineteen small white jewels on its back, plaintiff argues that its copyright is infringed by defendants' entire line of a score or more jeweled bees in three sizes decorated with from nine to thirty jewels of various sizes, kinds, and colors.

Although plaintiff's counsel asserted that the originality of plaintiff's bee pin lay in a particular arrangement of jewels on the top of the pin, the elements of this arrangement were never identified. Defendants' witnesses testified that the "arrangement" was simply a function of the size and form of the bee pin and the size of the jewels used. Plaintiff's counsel, repeatedly pressed by the district judge, was unable to suggest how jewels might be placed on the back of a pin in the shape of a bee without infringing plaintiff's copyright. He eventually conceded, "not being a jeweler, I can't conceive of how he might rearrange the design so it is dissimilar."

If plaintiff's understanding of its rights were correct, its copyright would effectively prevent others from engaging in the business of manufacturing and selling jeweled bees. We think plaintiff confuses the balance Congress struck between protection and competition under the Patent Act and the Copyright Act.

. . . .

Obviously a copyright must not be treated as equivalent to a patent lest long continuing private monopolies be conferred over areas of gainful activity without first satisfying the substantive and procedural prerequisites to the grant of such privileges.

Because copyright bars only copying, perhaps this case could be disposed of on the district court's finding that defendants did not copy plaintiff's bee pin. It is true that defendants had access to the plaintiff's pin and that there is an obvious similarity between plaintiff's pin and those of defendants. These two facts constitute strong circumstantial evidence of copying. But they are not conclusive. *Overman v. Loesser,* 205 F.2d 521, 523 (9th Cir. 1953); Nimmer on Copyright §§ 139.4, 141.2, and there was substantial evidence to support the trial court's finding that defendants' pin was in fact an independent creation. Defendants testified to independent creation from identified sources other than plaintiff's pin. The evidence established defendants' standing as designers of fine jewelry and reflected that on earlier occasions they had designed jeweled pins in the form of living creatures other than bees, including spiders, dragonflies, and other insects, birds, turtles, and frogs. Any inference of copying based upon similar appearance lost much of its strength because both pins were lifelike representations of a natural creature. Moreover, there were differences between defendants' and plaintiff's bees — notably in the veining of the wings.

Although this evidence would support a finding that defendants' bees were their own work rather than copied from plaintiff's, this resolution of the problem is not entirely satisfactory, particularly in view of the principle that copying need not be conscious, but "may be the result of subconscious memory derived from hearing, seeing or reading the copyrighted work at some time in the past." Howell's Copyright Law 129 (4th ed. 1962). *See Sheldon v. Metro-Goldwyn Pictures Corp.,* 81 F.2d 49, 54 (2d Cir. 1936); *Harold Lloyd Corp. v. Witwer,* 65 F.2d 1, 16 (9th Cir. 1933). It seems unrealistic to suppose that defendants could have closed their minds to plaintiff's highly successful jeweled bee pin as they designed their own.

A finding that defendants "copied" plaintiff's pin in this sense, however, would not necessarily justify judgment against them. A copyright, we have seen, bars use of the particular "expression" of an idea in a copyrighted work but does not bar use of the "idea" itself. Others are free to utilize the "idea" so long as they do not plagiarize its "expression." As the court said in *Trifari, Krussman & Fishel, Inc. v. B. Steinberg-Kaslo Co.,* 144 F. Supp. 577, 580 (S.D.N.Y. 1956), where the copyrighted work was a jeweled pin representing a hansom cab, "though an alleged infringer gets the idea of a hansom cab pin from a copyrighted article there can be no infringement unless the article itself has been copied. The idea of a hansom cab cannot be copyrighted. Nevertheless plaintiff's expression of that idea, as embodied in its pin, can be copyrighted."...

The critical distinction between "idea" and "expression" is difficult to draw.... At least in close cases, one may suspect, the classification the court selects may simply state the result reached rather than the reason for it. In our view, the difference is really one of degree as Judge Hand suggested in his striking "abstraction" formulation in *Nichols v. Universal Pictures Corp.*, 45 F.2d 119, 121 (2d Cir. 1930). The guiding consideration in drawing the line is the preservation of the balance between competition and protection reflected in the patent and copyright laws.

What is basically at stake is the extent of the copyright owner's monopoly — from how large an area of activity did Congress intend to allow the copyright owner to exclude others? We think the production of jeweled bee pins is a larger private preserve than Congress intended to be set aside in the public market without a patent. A jeweled bee pin is therefore an "idea" that defendants were free to copy. Plaintiff seems to agree, for it disavows any claim that defendants cannot manufacture and sell jeweled bee pins and concedes that only plaintiff's particular design or "expression" of the jeweled bee pin "idea" is protected under its copyright. The difficulty, as we have noted, is that on this record the "idea" and its "expression" appear to be indistinguishable. There is no greater similarity between the pins of plaintiff and defendants than is inevitable from the use of jewel-encrusted bee forms in both.

When the "idea" and its "expression" are thus inseparable, copying the "expression" will not be barred, since protecting the "expression" in such circumstances would confer a monopoly of the "idea" upon the copyright owner free of the conditions and limitations imposed by the patent law. [*Citations to, inter alia, Baker v. Selden* and *Morrissey v. Procter & Gamble* omitted.]

Affirmed.

QUESTIONS

1. Did the judgment for the defendant rest on a conclusion that it had not infringed, or on a conclusion that the plaintiff's pin was not the subject of copyright? (Are any clues provided by the court's reference to such cases as *Baker v. Selden* and *Morrissey v. Procter & Gamble*, in Chapter 2B, *supra*?)

2. Is idea/expression "merger" a question of law, or a question of fact? The breadth of plaintiff's claim in the bee pin allowed the *Kalpakian* court to rule that the subject matter of bee pins admits of insufficient variation of expression. But did the court *know* that this was the case? (Recall that the district court found defendant's pins *not* "substantially similar.") Should a court hear evidence on the question whether an idea in fact permits a highly limited range of expressions? *See, e.g., Apple Computer, Inc. v. Franklin Computer Corp.*, 714 F.2d 1240 (3d Cir. 1983); *Higgins v. Baker*, 309 F. Supp. 653 (S.D.N.Y. 1970). *Cf. Eckes v. Card Prices Update*, 736 F.2d 859 (2d Cir. 1984).

3. The *Kalpakian* court offers an economic rationale for the idea/expression dichotomy: "ideas" are subject matter we wish to leave open to competition;

"expression" is subject matter we feel comfortable allowing the copyright owner to exclude others from copying. In that light, consider the following:

> In copyright law, an "idea" is not an epistemological concept, but a legal conclusion prompted by notions — often unarticulated and unproven — of appropriate competition. Thus, copyright doctrine attaches the label "idea" to aspects of works which, if protected, would (or, we fear, might) preclude, or render too expensive, subsequent authors' endeavors.

Ginsburg, *No "Sweat?" Copyright and Other Protection of Works of Information After Feist v. Rural Telephone,* 92 Colum. L. Rev. 338, 346 (1992). Do you agree? Does it/should it make a difference whether the idea/expression inquiry is conducted at the outset, to determine whether plaintiff's work is copyrightable at all, or at the infringement stage, to determine if what defendant copied was protectible?

NICHOLS v. UNIVERSAL PICTURES CORP.

45 F.2d 119 (2d Cir. 1930)

L. HAND, CIRCUIT JUDGE. The plaintiff is the author of a play, "Abie's Irish Rose," which it may be assumed was properly copyrighted under section five, subdivision (d), of the Copyright Act, 17 USCA § 5(d). The defendant produced publicly a motion picture play, "The Cohens and The Kellys," which the plaintiff alleges was taken from it. As we think the defendant's play too unlike the plaintiff's to be an infringement, we may assume, arguendo, that in some details the defendant used the plaintiff's play, as will subsequently appear, though we do not so decide. It therefore becomes necessary to give an outline of the two plays.

"Abie's Irish Rose" presents a Jewish family living in prosperous circumstances in New York. The father, a widower, is in business as a merchant, in which his son and only child helps him. The boy has philandered with young women, who to his father's great disgust have always been Gentiles, for he is obsessed with a passion that his daughter-in-law shall be an orthodox Jewess. When the play opens the son, who has been courting a young Irish Catholic girl, has already married her secretly before a Protestant minister, and is concerned to soften the blow for his father, by securing a favorable impression of his bride, while concealing her faith and race. To accomplish this he introduces her to his father at his home as a Jewess, and lets it appear that he is interested in her, though he conceals the marriage. The girl somewhat reluctantly falls in with the plan; the father takes the bait, becomes infatuated with the girl, concludes that they must marry, and assumes that of course they will, if he so decides. He calls in a rabbi, and prepares for the wedding according to the Jewish rite.

Meanwhile the girl's father, also a widower, who lives in California, and is as intense in his own religious antagonism as the Jew, has been called to New York, supposing that his daughter is to marry an Irishman and a Catholic. Accompanied by a priest, he arrives at the house at the moment when the marriage is being celebrated, but too late to prevent it, and the two fathers, each infuriated by the proposed union of his child to a heretic, fall into unseemly and grotesque antics. The priest and the rabbi become friendly, exchange trite sentiments about religion, and agree that the match is good. Apparently out of abundant caution, the priest celebrates the marriage for a third time, while the girl's father is inveigled away. The second act closes with each father, still outraged, seeking to find some way by which the union, thus trebly insured, may be dissolved.

The last act takes place about a year later, the young couple having meanwhile been abjured by each father, and left to their own resources. They have had twins, a boy and a girl, but their fathers know no more than that a child has been born. At Christmas, each, led by his craving to see his grandchild, goes separately to the young folks' home, where they encounter each other, each laden with gifts, one for a boy, the other for a girl. After some slapstick comedy, depending upon the insistence of each that he is right about the sex of the grandchild, they become reconciled when they learn the truth, and that each child is to bear the given name of a grandparent. The curtain falls as the fathers are exchanging amenities, and the Jew giving evidence of an abatement in the strictness of his orthodoxy.

"The Cohens and The Kellys" presents two families, Jewish and Irish, living side by side in the poorer quarters of New York in a state of perpetual enmity. The wives in both cases are still living, and share in the mutual animosity, as do two small sons, and even the respective dogs. The Jews have a daughter, the Irish a son; the Jewish father is in the clothing business; the Irishman is a policeman. The children are in love with each other, and secretly marry, apparently after the play opens. The Jew, being in great financial straits, learns from a lawyer that he has fallen heir to a large fortune from a great-aunt, and moves into a great house, fitted luxuriously. Here he and his family live in vulgar ostentation, and here the Irish boy seeks out his Jewish bride, and is chased away by the angry father. The Jew then abuses the Irishman over the telephone, and both become hysterically excited. The extremity of his feelings makes the Jew sick, so that he must go to Florida for a rest, just before which the daughter discloses her marriage to her mother.

On his return the Jew finds that his daughter has borne a child; at first he suspects the lawyer, but eventually learns the truth and is overcome with anger at such a low alliance. Meanwhile, the Irish family who have been forbidden to see the grandchild, go to the Jew's house, and after a violent scene between the two fathers in which the Jew disowns his daughter, who decides to go back with her husband, the Irishman takes her back with her baby to his own poor lodgings. The lawyer, who had hoped to marry the Jew's daughter, seeing his plan foiled, tells the Jew that his fortune really belongs to the Irishman, who was also related to the dead woman, but offers to conceal his knowledge, if the Jew will share the loot. This the Jew repudiates, and, leaving the astonished lawyer, walks through the rain to his enemy's house to surrender the property. He arrives in great dejection, tells the truth, and abjectly turns to leave. A reconciliation ensues, the Irishman agreeing to share with him equally. The Jew shows some interest in his grandchild, though this is at most a minor motive in the reconciliation, and the curtain falls while the two are in their cups, the Jew insisting that in the firm name for the business, which they are to carry on jointly, his name shall stand first.

It is of course essential to any protection of literary property, whether at common law or under the statute, that the right cannot be limited literally to the text, else a plagiarist would escape by immaterial variations. That has never been the law, but, as soon as literal appropriation ceases to be the test, the whole matter is necessarily at large, so that, as was recently well said by a distinguished judge, the decisions cannot help much in a new case. *Fendler v. Morosco,* 253 N.Y. 281, 292, 171 N.E. 56. When plays are concerned, the plagiarist may excise a separate scene [*Daly v. Webster,* 56 F. 483 (C.C.A.2); *Chappell v. Fields,* 210 F. 864 (C.C.A.2); *Chatterton v. Cave,* L.R. 3 App. Cas. 483]; or he may appropriate part of the dialogue (*Warne v. Seebohm,* L.R. 39 Ch. D. 73). Then the question is whether the part so taken is "substantial," and therefore not a "fair use" of the copyrighted work; it is the same question as arises in the case of any other copyrighted work. *Marks v. Feist,* 290 F. 959 (C.C.A.2); *Emerson v. Davies,* Fed. Cas. No. 4436, 3 Story, 768, 795-797. But when the plagiarist does not take out a block in situ, but an abstract of the whole, decision is more troublesome. Upon any work, and especially upon a play, a great number of patterns of increasing generality will fit equally well, as more and more of the incident is left out. The last may perhaps be no more than the most general statement of what the play is about, and at times might consist only of its title; but there is a point in this series of abstractions where they are no longer protected, since otherwise the playwright could prevent the use of his "ideas," to which, apart from their expression, his property is never extended. *Holmes v. Hurst,* 174 U.S. 82, 86; *Guthrie v. Curlett,* 36 F.(2d) 694 (C.C.A.2). Nobody has ever been able to fix that boundary, and nobody ever can. In some cases the question has been treated as though it were analogous to lifting a portion out of the copyrighted work (*Rees v. Melville,* Mac-Gillivray's Copyright Cases [1911-1916], 168); but the analogy is not a good one, because, though the skeleton is a part of the body, it pervades and supports the whole. In such cases we are rather concerned with the line between expression and what is expressed. As respects plays, the controversy chiefly centers upon the characters and sequence of incident, these being the substance.

We did not in *Dymow v. Bolton,* 11 F.(2d) 690, hold that a plagiarist was never liable for stealing a plot; that would have been flatly against our rulings in *Dam v. Kirk La Shelle Co.,* 175 F. 902, 41 L.R.A. (N.S.) 1002, 20 Ann. Cas. 1173, and *Stodart v. Mutual Film Co.,* 249 F. 513, affirming my decision in (D.C.) 249 F. 507; neither of which we meant to overrule. We found the plot of the second play was too different to infringe, because the most detailed pattern, common to both, eliminated so much from each that its content went into the public domain; and for this reason we said, "this mere subsection of a plot was not susceptible of copyright." But we do not doubt that two plays may correspond in plot closely enough for infringement. How far that correspondence must go is another matter. Nor need we hold that the same may not be true as to the characters, quite independently of the "plot" proper, though, as far as we know, such a case has never arisen. If Twelfth Night were copyrighted, it is quite possible that a second comer might so closely imitate Sir

Toby Belch or Malvolio as to infringe, but it would not be enough that for one of his characters he cast a riotous knight who kept wassail to the discomfort of the household, or a vain and foppish steward who became amorous of his mistress. These would be no more than Shakespeare's "ideas" in the play, as little capable of monopoly as Einstein's Doctrine of Relativity, or Darwin's theory of the Origin of Species. It follows that the less developed the characters, the less they can be copyrighted; that is the penalty an author must bear for marking them too indistinctly.

In the two plays at bar we think both as to incident and character, the defendant took no more — assuming that it took anything at all — than the law allowed. The stories are quite different. One is of a religious zealot who insists upon his child's marrying no one outside his faith; opposed by another who is in this respect just like him, and is his foil. Their difference in race is merely an obbligato to the main theme, religion. They sink their differences through grandparental pride and affection. In the other, zealotry is wholly absent; religion does not even appear. It is true that the parents are hostile to each other in part because they differ in race; but the marriage of their son to a Jew does not apparently offend the Irish family at all, and it exacerbates the existing animosity of the Jew, principally because he has become rich, when he learns it. They are reconciled through the honesty of the Jew and the generosity of the Irishman; the grandchild has nothing whatever to do with it. The only matter common to the two is a quarrel between a Jewish and an Irish father, the marriage of their children, the birth of grandchildren and a reconciliation.

If the defendant took so much from the plaintiff, it may well have been because her amazing success seemed to prove that this was a subject of enduring popularity. Even so, granting that the plaintiff's play was wholly original, and assuming that novelty is not essential to a copyright, there is no monopoly in such a background. Though the plaintiff discovered the vein, she could not keep it to herself; so defined, the theme was too generalized an abstraction from what she wrote. It was only a part of her "ideas."

Nor does she fare better as to her characters. It is indeed scarcely credible that she should not have been aware of those stock figures, the low comedy Jew and Irishman. The defendant has not taken from her more than their prototypes have contained for many decades. If so, obviously so to generalize her copyright, would allow her to cover what was not original with her. But we need not hold this as matter of fact, much as we might be justified. Even though we take it that she devised her figures out of her brain de novo, still the defendant was within its rights.

There are but four characters common to both plays, the lovers and the fathers. The lovers are so faintly indicated as to be no more than stage properties. They are loving and fertile; that is really all that can be said of them, and anyone else is quite within his rights if he puts loving and fertile lovers in a play of his own, wherever he gets the cue. The plaintiff's Jew is quite unlike the defendant's. His obsession is his religion, on which depends such racial animosity as he has. He is affectionate, warm and patriarchal. None of these fit the defendant's Jew, who shows affection for his daughter only once, and who has none but the most superficial interest in his grandchild. He is tricky, ostentatious and vulgar, only by misfortune redeemed into honesty. Both are grotesque, extravagant and quarrelsome; both are fond of display; but these common qualities make up only a small part of their simple pictures, no more than any one might lift if he chose. The Irish fathers are even more unlike; the plaintiff's a mere symbol for religious fanaticism and patriarchal pride, scarcely a character at all. Neither quality appears in the defendant's, for while he goes to get his grandchild, it is rather out of a truculent determination not to be forbidden, than from pride in his progeny. For the rest he is only a grotesque hobbledehoy, used for low comedy of the most conventional sort, which any one might borrow, if he chanced not to know the exemplar.

The defendant argues that the case is controlled by my decision in *Fisher v. Dillingham* (D.C.) 298 F. 145. Neither my brothers nor I wish to throw doubt upon the doctrine of that case, but it is not applicable here. We assume that the plaintiff's play is altogether original, even to an extent that in fact it is hard to believe. We assume further that, so far as it has been anticipated by earlier plays of which she knew nothing, that fact is immaterial. Still, as we have already said, her copyright did not cover everything that might be drawn from her play; its content went to some extent into the public domain. We have to decide how much, and while we are as aware as any one that the line, wherever it is drawn, will seem arbitrary, that is no excuse for not drawing it; it is a question such as courts must answer in nearly all cases. Whatever may be the difficulties a priori, we have no question on which side of the line this case falls. A comedy based upon conflicts between Irish and Jews, into which the marriage of their children enters, is no more susceptible of copyright than the outline of Romeo and Juliet.

The plaintiff has prepared an elaborate analysis of the two plays, showing a "quadrangle" of the common characters, in which each is represented by the emotions which he discovers. She presents the resulting parallelism as proof of infringement, but the adjectives employed are so general as to be quite useless. Take for example the attribute of "love" ascribed to both Jews. The plaintiff has depicted her father as deeply attached to his son, who is his hope and joy; not so, the defendant, whose father's conduct is throughout not actuated by any affection for his daughter, and who is merely once overcome for the moment by her distress when he has violently dismissed her lover. "Anger" covers emotions aroused by quite different occasions in each case; so do "anxiety," "despondency" and "disgust." It is unnecessary to go through the catalogue for emotions are too much colored by their causes to be a test when used so broadly. This is not the proper approach to a solution; it must be more ingenuous, more like that of a spectator, who would rely upon the complex of his impressions of each character.

We cannot approve the length of the record, which was due chiefly to the use of expert witnesses. Argument is argument whether in the box or at the bar, and its proper place is the last. The testimony of an expert upon such issues, especially his cross-examination, greatly extends the trial and contributes nothing which cannot be better heard after the evidence is all submitted. It ought not to be allowed at all; and while its admission is not a ground for reversal, it cumbers the case and tends to confusion, for the more the court is led into the intricacies of dramatic craftsmanship, the less likely it is to stand upon the firmer, if more naive, ground of its considered impressions upon its own perusal. We hope that in this class of cases such evidence may in the future be entirely excluded, and the case confined to the actual issues; that is, whether the copyrighted work was original, and whether the defendant copied it, so far as the supposed infringement is identical.

The defendant, "the prevailing party," was entitled to a reasonable attorney's fee (section 40 of the Copyright Act [17 USCA § 40]).

Decree affirmed.

QUESTIONS

1. The plaintiff had obviously discovered a vein of extremely appealing popular drama — first-generation ethnic combatants reconciled, in the "melting pot" that was early twentieth century America, by the love of the younger generation. Defendant was apparently seeking to "horn in" on that eminently successful (and remunerative) theme. Reasoning from first principles, should that be permitted?

2. In these cases of literary plagiarism, to what extent and for what purposes might a defendant bring to the court's attention dramatic works that preceded that of the plaintiff?

3. When Judge Hand discusses the literal copying of dialogue, he states that takings that are "insubstantial" are allowable. Is "substantiality" to be determined by a quantitative test alone?

SHELDON v. METRO-GOLDWYN PICTURES CORP.

81 F.2d 49 (2d Cir. 1936)

L. HAND, CIRCUIT JUDGE. The suit is to enjoin the performance of the picture play, "Letty Lynton," as an infringement of the plaintiffs' copyrighted play, "Dishonored Lady." The plaintiffs' title is conceded, so too the validity of the copyright; the only issue is infringement. The defendants say that they did not use the play in any way to produce the picture; the plaintiffs discredit this denial because of the negotiations between the parties for the purchase of rights in the play, and because the similarities between the two are too specific and detailed to have resulted from chance. The judge thought that, so far as the defendants had used the play, they had taken only what the law allowed, that is, those general themes, motives, or ideas in which there could be no copyright. Therefore he dismissed the bill.

An understanding of the issue involves some description of what was in the public demesne, as well as of the play and the picture. In 1857 a Scotch girl, named Madeleine Smith, living in Glasgow, was brought to trial upon an indictment in three counts; two for attempts to poison her lover, a third for poisoning him. The jury acquitted her on the first count, and brought in a verdict of "Not Proven" on the second and third. The circumstances of the prosecution aroused much interest at the time not only in Scotland but in England; so much indeed that it became a cause célèbre, and that as late as 1927 the whole proceedings were published in book form. An outline of the story so published, which became the original of the play here in suit, is as follows: The Smiths were a respectable middle-class family, able to send their daughter to a "young ladies' boarding school"; they supposed her protected not only from any waywardness of her own, but from the wiles of seducers. In both they were mistaken, for when at the age of twenty-one she met a young Jerseyman of French blood, Emile L'Angelier, ten years older, and already the hero of many amorous adventures, she quickly succumbed and poured out her feelings in letters of the utmost ardor and indiscretion, and at times of a candor beyond the standards then, and even yet, permissible for well-nurtured young women. They wrote each other as though already married, he assuming to dictate her conduct and even her feelings; both expected to marry, she on any terms, he with the approval of her family. Nevertheless she soon tired of him and engaged herself to a man some twenty years older who was a better match, but for whom she had no more than a friendly complaisance. L'Angelier was not, however, to be fobbed off so easily; he threatened to expose her to her father by showing her letters. She at first tried to dissuade him by appeals to their tender memories, but finding this useless and thinking herself otherwise undone, she affected a return of her former passion and invited him to visit her again. Whether he did, was the turning point of the trial; the evidence, though it really left the issue in no doubt, was too indirect to satisfy the jury, perhaps in part because of her advocate's argument that to kill him only insured the discovery of her letters. It was shown that she had several times bought or tried to buy poison, — prussic acid and arsenic, — and that twice before his death L'Angelier became violently ill, the second time on the day after her purchase. He died of arsenical poison, which the prosecution charged that she had given him in a cup of chocolate. At her trial, Madeleine being incompetent as a witness, her advocate proved an alibi by the testimony of her younger sister that early on the night of the murder as laid in the indictment, she had gone to bed with Madeleine, who had slept with her throughout the night. As to one of the attempts her betrothed swore that she had been with him at the theatre.

This was the story which the plaintiffs used to build their play. As will appear they took from it but the merest skeleton, the acquittal of a wanton young woman, who to extricate herself from an amour that stood in the way of a respectable marriage, poisoned her lover. The incidents, the characters, the mise-en-scène, the sequence of events, were all changed; nobody disputes that the plaintiffs were entitled to their copyright. All that they took from the story they might probably have taken, had it even been copyrighted. Their heroine is named Madeleine Cary; she lives in New York, brought up in affluence, if not in luxury; she is intelligent, voluptuous, ardent and corrupt; but, though she has had a succession of amours, she is capable of genuine affection. Her lover and victim is an Argentinian, named Moreno, who makes his living as a dancer in night-clubs. Madeleine has met him once in Europe before the play opens, has danced with him, has excited his concupiscence; he presses presents upon her. The play opens in his rooms, he and his dancing partner who is also his mistress, are together; Madeleine on the telephone recalls herself to him and says she wishes to visit him, though it is already past midnight. He disposes of his mistress by a device which does not deceive her and receives Madeleine; at once he falls to wooing her, luring her among other devices by singing a Gaucho song. He finds her facile and the curtain falls in season.

The second act is in her home, and introduces her father, a bibulous dotard, who has shot his wife's lover in the long past; Laurence Brennan, a self-made man in the fifties, untutored, self-reliant and reliable, who has had with Madeleine a relation, half paternal, half-amorous since she grew up; and Denis Farnborough, a young British labor peer, a mannikin to delight the heart of well ordered young women. Madeleine loves him; he loves Madeleine; she will give him no chance to declare himself, remembering her mottled past and his supposedly immaculate standards. She confides to Brennan, who makes clear to her the imbecility of her self-denial; she accepts this enlightenment and engages herself to her high-minded paragon after confessing vaguely her evil life and being assured that to post-war generations all such lapses are peccadillo.

In the next act Moreno, who has got wind of the engagement, comes to her house. Disposing of Farnborough, who chances to be there, she admits Moreno, acknowledges that she is to marry Farnborough, and asks him to accept the situation as the normal outcome of their intrigue. He refuses to be cast off, high words pass, he threatens to expose their relations, she raves at him, until finally he knocks her down and commands her to go to his apartment that morning as before. After he leaves full of swagger, her eye lights on a bottle of strychnine which her father uses as a drug; her fingers slowly close upon it; the audience understands that she will kill Moreno. Farnborough is at the telephone; this apparently stiffens her resolve, showing her the heights she may reach by its execution.

The scene then shifts again to Moreno's apartment; his mistress must again be put out, most unwillingly for she is aware of the situation; Madeleine comes in; she pretends once more to feel warmly, she must wheedle him for he is out of sorts after the quarrel. Meanwhile she prepares to poison him by putting the strychnine in coffee, which she asks him to make ready. But in the course of these preparations during which he sings her again his Gaucho song, what with their proximity, and this and that, her animal ardors are once more aroused and drag her, unwillingly and protesting, from her purpose. The play must therefore wait for an hour or more until, relieved of her passion, she appears from his bedroom and while breakfasting puts the strychnine in his coffee. He soon discovers what has happened and tries to telephone for help. He does succeed in getting a few words through, but she tears away the wire and fills his dying ears with her hatred and disgust. She then carefully wipes away all traces of her finger prints and manages to get away while the door is being pounded in by those who have come at his call.

The next act is again at her home on the following evening. Things are going well with her and Farnborough and her father, when a district attorney comes in, a familiar of the household, now in stern mood; Moreno's mistress and a waiter have incriminated Madeleine, and a cross has been found in Moreno's pocket, which he superstitiously took off her neck the night before. The district attorney cross-questions her, during which Farnborough several times fatuously intervenes; she is driven from point to point almost to an avowal when as a desperate plunge she says she spent the night with

Brennan. Brennan is brought to the house and, catching the situation after a moment's delay, bears her out. This puts off the district attorney until seeing strychnine brought to relieve the father, his suspicions spring up again and he arrests Madeleine. The rest of the play is of no consequence here, except that it appears in the last scene that at the trial where she is acquitted, her father on the witness stand accounts for the absence of the bottle of strychnine which had been used to poison Moreno.

At about the time that this play was being written an English woman named Lowndes wrote a book called Letty Lynton, also founded on the story of Madeleine Smith. Letty Lynton lives in England; she is eighteen years old, beautiful, well-reared and intelligent, but wayward. She has had a more or less equivocal love affair with a young Scot, named McLean, who worked in her father's chemical factory, but has discarded him, apparently before their love-making had gone very far. Then she chances upon a young Swede — half English — named Ekebon, and their acquaintance quickly becomes a standardized amour, kept secret from her parents, especially her mother, who is an uncompromising moralist, and somewhat estranged from Letty anyway. She and her lover use an old barn as their place of assignation; it had been fitted up as a play house for Letty when she was a child. Like Madeleine Smith she had written her lover a series of indiscreet letters which he has kept, for though he is on pleasure bent Ekebon has a frugal mind, and means to marry his sweetheart and set himself up for life. They are betrothed and he keeps pressing her to declare it to her parents, which she means never to do. While he is away in Sweden Letty meets an unmarried peer considerably older than she, poor, but intelligent and charming; he falls in love with her and she accepts him, more because it is a good match than for any other reason, though she likes him well enough, and will make him suppose that she loves him.

Thereupon Ekebon reappears, learns of Letty's new betrothal, and threatens to disclose his own to her father, backing up his story with her letters. She must at once disown her peer and resume her engagement with him. His motive, like L'Angelier's, is ambition rather than love, though conquest is a flattery and Letty a charming morsel. His threats naturally throw Letty into dismay; she has come to loathe him and at any cost must get free, but she has no one to turn to. In her plight she thinks of her old suitor, McLean, and goes to the factory only to find him gone. He has taught her how to get access to poisons in his office and has told of their effect on human beings. At first she thinks of jumping out the window, and when she winces at that, of poisoning herself; that would be easier. So she selects arsenic which is less painful and goes away with it; it is only when she gets home that she thinks of poisoning Ekebon. Her mind is soon made up, however, and she makes an appointment with him at the barn; she has told her father, she writes, and Ekebon is to see him on Monday, but meanwhile on Sunday they will meet secretly once more. She has prepared to go on a week-end party and conceals her car near the barn. He comes; she welcomes him with a pretense of her former ardors, and tries to get back her letters. Unsuccessful in this she persuades him to drink a cup of chocolate into which she puts the arsenic. After carefully washing the pans and cups, she leaves with him, dropping him from her car near his home; he being still unaffected. On her way to her party she pretends to have broken down and by asking the help of a passing cyclist establishes an alibi. Ekebon dies at his home attended by his mistress; the letters are discovered and Letty is brought before the coroner's inquest and acquitted chiefly through the alibi, for things look very bad for her until the cyclist appears.

The defendants, who are engaged in producing speaking films on a very large scale in Hollywood, California, had seen the play and wished to get the rights. They found, however, an obstacle in an association of motion picture producers presided over by Mr. Will Hays, who thought the play obscene; not being able to overcome his objections, they returned the copy of the manuscript which they had. That was in the spring of 1930, but in the autumn they induced the plaintiffs to get up a scenario, which they hoped might pass moral muster. Although this did not suit them after the plaintiffs prepared it, they must still have thought in the spring of 1931 that they could satisfy Mr. Hays, for they then procured an offer from the plaintiffs to sell their rights for $30,000. These negotiations also proved abortive because the play continued to be objectionable, and eventually they cried off on the bargain. Mrs. Lowndes' novel was suggested to Thalberg, one of the vice-presidents of the Metro-Goldwyn Company, in July, 1931, and again in the following November, and he bought the rights to it in December. At once he assigned the preparation of a play to Stromberg, who had read the novel in January, and thought it would make a suitable play for an actress named Crawford, just then not employed. Stromberg chose Meehan, Tuchock and Brown to help him, the first two with the scenario, the third with the dramatic production. All these four were examined by deposition; all denied that they had used the play in any way whatever; all agreed that they had based the picture on the story of Madeleine Smith and on the novel, "Letty Lynton." All had seen the play, and Tuchock had read the manuscript, as had Thalberg, but Stromberg, Meehan and Brown swore that they had not; Stromberg's denial being however worthless, for he had originally sworn the contrary in an affidavit. They all say that work began late in November or early in December, 1931, and the picture was finished by the end of March. To meet these denials, the plaintiffs appeal to the substantial identity between passages in the picture and those parts of the play which are original with them.

The picture opens in Montevideo where Letty Lynton is recovering from her fondness for Emile Renaul. She is rich, luxurious and fatherless, her father having been killed by his mistress's husband; her mother is seared, hard, selfish, unmotherly; and Letty has left home to escape her, wandering about in search of excitement. Apparently for the good part of a year she has been carrying on a love affair with Renaul; twice before she has tried to shake loose, has gone once to Rio where she lit another flame, but each time she has weakened and been drawn back. Though not fully declared as an amour, there can be no real question as to the character of her attachment. She at length determines really to break loose, but once again her senses are too much for her and it is indicated, if not declared, that she spends the night with Renaul. Though he is left a vague figure only indistinctly associated with South America somewhere or other, the part was cast for an actor with a marked foreign accent, and it is plain that he was meant to be understood, in origin anyway, as South American, like Moreno in the play. He is violent, possessive and sensual; his power over Letty lies in his strong animal attractions. However, she escapes in the morning while he is asleep, whether from his bed or not is perhaps uncertain; and with a wax figure in the form of a loyal maid — Letty in the novel had one — boards a steamer for New York. On board she meets Darrow, a young American, the son of a rich rubber manufacturer, who is coming back from a trip to Africa. They fall in love upon the faintest provocation and become betrothed before the ship docks, three weeks after she left Montevideo. At the pier she finds Renaul who has flown up to reclaim her. She must in some way keep her two suitors apart, and she manages to dismiss Darrow and then to escape Renaul by asking him to pay her customs duties, which he does. Arrived home her mother gives her a cold welcome and refuses to concern herself with the girl's betrothal. Renaul is announced; he has read of the betrothal in the papers and is furious. He tries again to stir her sensuality by the familiar gambit, but this time he fails; she slaps his face and declares that she hates him. He commands her to come to his apartment that evening; she begs him to part with her and let her have her life; he insists on renewing their affair. She threatens to call the police; he rejoins that if so her letters will be published, and then he leaves. Desperate, she chances on a bottle of strychnine, which we are to suppose is an accoutrement of every affluent household, and seizes it; the implication is of intended suicide, not murder. Then she calls Darrow, tells him that she will not leave with him that night for his parents' place in the Adirondacks as they had planned; she renews to him the pledge of her love, without him she cannot live, an intimation to the audience of her purpose to kill herself.

That evening she goes to Renaul's apartment in a hotel armed with her strychnine bottle, for use on the spot; she finds him cooling champagne, but in bad temper. His caresses which he bestows plentifully enough, again stir her disgust not her passions, but he does not believe it and assumes that she will spend the night with him. Finding that he will not return the letters, she believes herself lost and empties the strychnine into a wine glass. Again he embraces her; she vilifies him; he knocks her down; she vilifies him again. Ignorant of the poison he grasps her glass, and she, perceiving it, lets him drink. He woos her again, this time with more apparent success, for she is terrified; he sings a Gaucho song to her, the same one that has been heard at Montevideo. The poison begins to work and, at length supposing that she has meant to murder him, he reaches for the telephone; she forestalls him, but she does not tear out the wire. As he slowly dies, she stands over him and vituperates him. A waiter enters; she steps behind a curtain; he leaves thinking Renaul drunk; she comes out, wipes off all traces of her fingerprints and goes out, leaving however her rubbers which Renaul had taken from her when she entered.

Next she and Darrow are found at his parents' in the Adirondacks; while there a detective appears, arrests Letty and takes her to New York; she is charged with the murder of Renaul; Darrow goes back to New York with her. The finish is at the district attorney's office; Letty and Darrow, Letty's mother, the wax serving maid are all there. The letters appear incriminating to an elderly rather benevolent district attorney; also the customs slip and the rubbers. Letty begins to break down; she admits that she went to Renaul's room, not to kill him but to get him to release her. Darrow sees that story will not pass, and volunteers that she came to his room at a hotel and spent the night with him. Letty confirms this and her mother, till then silent, backs up their story; she had traced them to the hotel and saw the lights go out, having ineffectually tried to dissuade them. The maid still further confirms them and the district attorney, not sorry to be discomfited, though unbelieving, discharges Letty.

We are to remember that it makes no difference how far the play was anticipated by works in the public demesne which the plaintiffs did not use. The defendants appear not to recognize this, for they have filled the record with earlier instances of the same dramatic incidents and devices, as though, like a patent, a copyrighted work must be not only original, but new. That is not however the law as is obvious in the case of maps or compendia, where later works will necessarily be anticipated. At times, in discussing how much of the substance of a play the copyright protects, courts have indeed used language which seems to give countenance to the notion that, if a plot were old, it could not be copyrighted. *London v. Biograph Co.* (C.C.A.) 231 F. 696; *Eichel v. Marcin* (D.C.) 241 F. 404. But we understand by this no more than that in its broader outline a plot is never copyrightable, for it is plain beyond peradventure that anticipation as such cannot invalidate a copyright. Borrowed the work must indeed not be, for a plagiarist is not himself pro tanto an "author"; but if by some magic a man who had never known it were to compose anew Keats's Ode on a Grecian Urn, he would be an "author," and, if he copyrighted it, others might not copy that poem, though they might of course copy Keats's. *Bleistein v. Donaldson Lithographing Co.,* 188 U.S. 239, 249; *Gerlach-Barklow Co. v. Morris & Bendien, Inc.,* 23 F.(2d) 159, 161 (C.C.A.2); Weil, Copyright Law, p. 234. But though a copyright is for this reason less vulnerable than a patent, the owner's protection is more limited, for just as he is no less an "author" because others have preceded him, so another who follows him, is not a tort-feasor unless he pirates his work. *Jewelers' Circular Publishing Co. v. Keystone Co.,* 281 F. 83, 92, 26 A.L.R. 571 (C.C.A.2); *General Drafting Co. v. Andrews,* 37 F.(2d) 54, 56 (C.C.A.2); *Williams v. Smythe* (C.C.) 110 F. 961; *American, etc., Directory Co. v. Gehring Pub. Co.* (D.C.) 4 F.(2d) 415; *New Jersey, etc., Co. v. Barton Business Service* (D.C.) 57 F.(2d) 353. If the copyrighted work is therefore original, the public demesne is important only on the issue of infringement; that is, so far as it may break the force of the inference to be drawn from likenesses between the work and the putative piracy. If the defendant has had access to other material which would have served him as well, his disclaimer becomes more plausible.

In the case at bar there are then two questions: First, whether the defendants actually used the play; second, if so, whether theirs was a[n infringing] use. [I]t is convenient to define such a use by saying that others may "copy" the "theme," or "ideas," or the like, of a work, though not its "expression." At any rate so long as it is clear what is meant, no harm is done. In the case at bar the distinction is not so important as usual, because so much of the play was borrowed from the story of Madeleine Smith, and the plaintiffs' originality is necessarily limited to the variants they introduced. Nevertheless, it is still true that their whole contribution may not be protected; for the defendants were entitled to use, not only all that had gone before, but even the plaintiffs' contribution itself, if they drew from it only the more general patterns; that is, if they kept clear of its "expression." We must therefore state in detail those similarities which seem to us to pass the limits of [licit copying]. Finally, in concluding as we do that the defendants used the play pro tanto, we need not charge their witnesses with perjury. With so many sources before them they might quite honestly forget what they took; nobody knows the origin of his inventions; memory and fancy merge even in adults. Yet unconscious plagiarism is actionable quite as much as deliberate. *Buck v. Jewell-La Salle Realty Co.*, 283 U.S. 191, 198; *Harold Lloyd Corporation v. Witwer*, 65 F.(2d) 1, 16 (C.C.A.9); *Fred Fisher, Inc. v. Dillingham* (D.C.) 298 F. 145.

The defendants took for their mise-en-scène the same city and the same social class; and they chose a South American villain. The heroines had indeed to be wanton, but Letty Lynton "tracked" Madeleine Cary more closely than that. She is overcome by passion in the first part of the picture and yields after announcing that she hates Renaul and has made up her mind to leave him. This is the same weakness as in the murder scene of the play, though transposed. Each heroine's waywardness is suggested as an inherited disposition; each has had an errant parent involved in scandal; one killed, the other becoming an outcast. Each is redeemed by a higher love. Madeleine Cary must not be misread; it is true that her lust overcomes her at the critical moment, but it does not extinguish her love for Farnborough; her body, not her soul, consents to her lapse. Moreover, her later avowal, which she knew would finally lose her lover, is meant to show the basic rectitude of her nature. Though it does not need Darrow to cure Letty of her wanton ways, she too is redeemed by a nobler love. Neither Madeleine Smith, nor the Letty of the novel, were at all like that; they wished to shake off a clandestine intrigue to set themselves up in the world; their love as distinct from their lust, was pallid. So much for the similarity in character.

Coming to the parallelism of incident, the threat scene is carried out with almost exactly the same sequence of event and actuation; it has no prototype in either story or novel. Neither Ekebon nor L'Angelier went to his fatal interview to break up the new betrothal; he was beguiled by the pretense of a renewed affection. Moreno and Renaul each goes to his sweetheart's home to detach her from her new love; when he is there, she appeals to his better side, unsuccessfully; she abuses him, he returns the abuse and commands her to come to his rooms; she pretends to agree, expecting to finish with him one way or another. True, the assault is deferred in the picture from this scene to the next, but it is the same dramatic trick. Again, the poison in each case is found at home, and the girl talks with her betrothed just after the villain has left and again pledges him her faith. Surely the sequence of these details is pro tanto the very web of the authors' dramatic expression; and copying them is not "fair use."

The death scene follows the play even more closely; the girl goes to the villain's room as he directs; from the outset he is plainly to be poisoned while they are together. (The defendants deny that this is apparent in the picture, but we cannot agree. It would have been an impossible denouement on the screen for the heroine, just plighted to the hero, to kill herself in desperation, because the villain has successfully enmeshed her in their mutual past; yet the poison is surely to be used on some one.) Moreno and Renaul each tries to arouse the girl by the memory of their former love, using among other aphrodisiacs the Gaucho song; each dies while she is there, incidentally of strychnine not arsenic. In extremis each makes for the telephone and is thwarted by the girl; as he dies, she pours upon him her rage and loathing. When he is dead, she follows the same ritual to eradicate all traces of her presence, but forgets tell-tale bits of property. Again these details in the same sequence embody more than the "ideas" of the play; they are its very raiment.

Finally in both play and picture in place of a trial, as in the story and the novel, there is substituted an examination by a district attorney; and this examination is again in parallel almost step by step. A parent is present; so is the lover; the girl yields progressively as the evidence accumulates; in the picture, the customs slip, the rubbers and the letters; in the play, the cross and the witnesses, brought in to confront her. She is at the breaking point when she is saved by substantially the same most unexpected alibi; a man declares that she has spent the night with him. That alibi there introduced is the turning point in each drama and alone prevents its ending in accordance with the classic canon of tragedy; i.e., fate as an inevitable consequence of past conduct, itself not evil enough to quench pity. It is the essence of the authors' expression, the very voice with which they speak.

We have often decided that a play may be pirated without using the dialogue. Were it not so, there could be no piracy of a pantomime, where there cannot be any dialogue; yet nobody would deny to pantomime the name of drama. Speech is only a small part of a dramatist's means of expression; he draws on all the arts and compounds his play from words and gestures and scenery and costume and from the very looks of the actors themselves. The play is the sequence of the confluents of all these means, bound together in an inseparable unity; it may often be most effectively pirated by leaving out the speech, for which a substitute can be found, which keeps the whole dramatic meaning. That as it appears to us is exactly what the defendants have done here; the dramatic significance of the scenes we have recited is the same, almost to the letter. True, much of the picture owes nothing to the play; some of it is plainly drawn from the novel; but that is entirely immaterial; it is enough that substantial parts were lifted; no plagiarist can excuse the wrong by showing how much of his work he did not pirate. We cannot avoid the conviction that, if the picture was not an infringement of the play, there can be none short of taking the dialogue.

The decree will be reversed and an injunction will go against the picture together with a decree for damages and an accounting. The plaintiffs will be awarded an attorney's fee in this court and in the court below, both to be fixed by the District Court upon the final decree.

Decree reversed.

QUESTIONS

1. Was there any issue as to "access" in this case? How likely is it that the defendants were being honest in the claims that they did not copy from the plaintiff's play? How likely is it that this affected the decision in the case?

2. Did the court hold that the Letty of the defendant's motion picture so closely tracked the Madeleine Cary of the plaintiff's play as to infringe the copyright in the character?

3. When explaining his conclusion that the crucial scenes in the motion picture infringed the comparable scenes in the plaintiff's play, does Judge Hand closely analyze the literary similarities or does he simply state his result? Is it possible to do much better?

4. Plaintiff, a doctor, wrote an article for the Journal of the American Medical Association concerning nineteenth-century cocaine use, in which he referred to the evidence in the Sherlock Holmes stories that Holmes was a cocaine user. Plaintiff speculated that Holmes's belief that he was stalked by Professor Moriarty resulted from cocaine-induced paranoia. Plaintiff also ascribed Holmes's disappearance in *The Final Problem* to Holmes's treatment for cocaine addiction, under the care of Sigmund Freud. Defendant, an author, after reading plaintiff's article, writes a detective novel adopting and expanding on plaintiff's exposition of a Holmes-cocaine-Freud link. How would you analyze plaintiff's claim that substantial portions of the novel and a subsequent film based on the novel infringe the copyright in his article? *See Musto v. Meyer,* 434 F. Supp. 32 (S.D.N.Y. 1977).

5. Sigmund Freund is a well-known professor of psychology and author of a leading college treatise on the subject. Carl Young, also a psychology professor, has recently published a competing text. Freund was the first writer in the field to adopt a light and easily readable style, utilizing colloquialisms and "homey" examples; Young's treatise has adopted the same style. Psychological theories initially developed by Freund are recounted by Young. There are other similarities: topic selection, chapter headings and organization, "nomenclature" (terms of art and professional definitions), charts and tables, and some problems (although Young writes them in his own words and places them in different sections of his book). Freund has sued Young for copyright infringement. Has Freund, on the above facts, made out a case for the jury on the issue of copying? Has he made out such a case on the issue of infringing similarity? *See Morrison v. Solomons,* 494 F. Supp. 218 (S.D.N.Y. 1980); *McMahon v. Prentice-Hall, Inc.,* 486 F. Supp. 1296 (E.D. Mo. 1980).

6. The producers of the well-known television game show, *To Tell the Truth,* have brought an action for copyright infringement against the producers of a recent arrival on the game show scene, *Bamboozle. To Tell the Truth* is played with a four-person panel of questioners (all celebrities), a panel of three "liars," and a master of ceremonies. The "liars" all pretend to be the same person. For example, one show featured three young men all claiming to be the man who had saved a four-year-old girl from the subway tracks. Each celebrity panelist is given a short period of time to question any of the "liars" in order to determine the imposters. Each of the panelists then votes; every wrong vote generates money to be split among the "liars." At the end of each of the two sequences on the show, the master of ceremonies asks, "Will the real [contestant's name] please stand up?"

Bamboozle also utilizes a panel of questioners (three rather than four, two of whom are celebrities and one noncelebrity), three "bamboozlers," and a master of ceremonies. Each of the three "bamboozlers" tells a different fantastic story — e.g., owning a turkey that jogs, or a rabbit that surfs, or a dog that bowls; one of these stories is true, and the panel's job is to determine which. The panelists take turns asking the "bamboozlers" questions. Following this, the two celebrity panelists give advice to the noncelebrity, who announces which story he believes true. Depending on the vote, either the panelist or the "bamboozlers" can win money. At the end of the show, the truth teller is revealed and demonstrates the fantastic incident or occurrence. Two such sequences are performed on each *Bamboozle* program.

The producers of both game shows have moved for summary judgment. How would you rule on the motion? *See Barris/Fraser Enters. v. Goodson-Todman Enters.*, 5 U.S.P.Q.2d 1887 (S.D.N.Y. 1988).

7. Because there is copyright infringement only when there is substantial unauthorized copying of "original" material authored by the plaintiff, a case such as *Sheldon* is complicated by the fact that much that is recounted in the plaintiff's novel was derived from historical events that are properly in the public domain. The court concluded that the defendant's motion picture tracked too much of the altogether fictional elements contributed by the plaintiff from her imagination. Essentially the same conclusion was reached rather recently in *Burgess v. Chase-Riboud*, 765 F. Supp. 233 (E.D. Pa. 1991), which involved a play that was held to infringe a novel about Thomas Jefferson that vividly elaborated on what must be described as a most vague and unsubstantiated amorous relationship between Jefferson and his slave Sally Hemings. In the proceeding for a declaratory judgment of noninfringement, the court summarized a number of scenes in the novel that were altogether fictional and that were followed too closely in the play written by the plaintiff.

Given the importance of uninhibited access to historical fact, at least as much with regard to Thomas Jefferson as Madeleine Smith, should the later author be "given the benefit of the doubt" in determining literary infringement in such cases? Should a burden be placed upon the author of "docudramas" and works of "faction" somehow to delineate at the time of publication what is the author's contribution and what is public-domain historical information? Or should the burden of making the distinction fall upon the later borrower of material?

APPROACHES TO "SUBSTANTIAL SIMILARITY"

Some lack of uniformity prevails in judicial application of the substantial-similarity test. In essence, courts differ over the subject matter to which the test is applied. Under one view, the fact-finder judges substantial similarity with respect to the whole of the copied portions of the plaintiff's work, including portions that viewed in isolation might not be eligible for copyright. Under another view, the fact-finder first removes from consideration the uncopyrightable elements of the copied material. Such elements include facts, ideas, and "scenes a faire" — trite, stock scenes or treatments of facts and ideas. The application of one or the other approach will frequently affect the outcome of the case, for any copyrighted literary work is likely to contain some, if not all, of these individually unprotectible elements.

For example, in *Sheldon v. Metro-Goldwyn Pictures Corp., supra,* the episodes that were apparently copied from the plaintiff's play, "Dishonored Lady," included factual detail drawn from the life of the historical Madeleine Smith, such as incriminating letters and a poisoning; and featured a number of arguably "stock" dramatic devices, such as the heroine's vilification of the villain, wiping away fingerprints, and leaving behind tell-tale evidence. Judge Hand, however, declined the defendants' invitation to review these discrete elements against the backdrop of an alleged common repertory of dramatic scenes. *Accord Novelty Textile Mills, Inc. v. Joan Fabrics Corp.,* 558 F.2d 1090 (2d Cir. 1977) (existence of works similar to and created before plaintiff's work is irrelevant unless defendant alleges that plaintiff copied from those works). In effect, such an analysis treats the selection and sequencing of these elements, perhaps unprotectible in isolation, as though they were a copyrightable compilation. *Compare Roth Greeting Cards v. United Card Co., supra,* which found copyrightable a greeting card that combined a simple drawing and a trite saying, and which concluded that the "total concept and feel" of the defendant's card was the same as the plaintiff's. More recently, addressing a suit involving the television game show *To Tell the Truth,* Judge Weinfeld cautioned: "But even though a television game show is made up entirely of stock devices, an original selection, organization, and presentation of such devices can nevertheless be protected.... Copying of a television producer's selection, organization and presentation of stock devices would therefore be a misappropriation." *Barris/Fraser Enters. v. Goodson-Todman Enters.,* 5 U.S.P.Q.2d 1887, 1891 (S.D.N.Y. 1988).

In contrast to the approach in the *Sheldon* case is the analysis employed in a decision involving alleged infringement by Alex Haley's "Roots." There, the trial court held that most of the alleged similarities between the plaintiff's and the defendant's novels concerned scenes that were commonplace to depictions of slavery in the Old South. Once these scenes were eliminated from consideration, the works could not be deemed substantially similar. *See Alexander v. Haley,* 460 F. Supp. 40 (S.D.N.Y. 1978).

This dissection and disqualification of uncopyrightable elements from a plaintiff's work has gained favor among some courts, especially when the court is leery of a result that would suggest monopolization of a common theme, or when the work at issue is a nonfiction work. *See, e.g., Hoehling v. Universal City Studios, Inc.,* 618 F.2d 972 (2d Cir.), *cert. denied,* 449 U.S. 841 (1980), *supra.* Nonetheless, other decisions have recognized that extraction of uncopyrightable elements runs the risk of overlooking the particular treatment, or the "expressive aspect of the combination," which an author accords individually unprotectible elements. *See, e.g., Warner Bros. v. American Broadcasting Sys.,* 720 F.2d 231 (2d Cir. 1983). The latter case involved a suit claiming infringement of the Superman character by a clumsy comedic television character with many of the same physical capacities. The court was prepared to concede that there was substantial copying, but found no liability principally because of the striking difference in the "total concept and feel" of the two characters. Is the "total concept and feel" analysis more appealing when it is used, as here, to provide a defense to copying than when it is used, as in *Roth Greeting Cards,* to make out a cause of action in compilation-infringement cases?

Recently, another court has expressed dissatisfaction with the "dissection" approach. In a thoughtful opinion, the judge in *Apple Computer, Inc. v. Microsoft Corp.,* 779 F. Supp. 133 (N.D. Cal. 1991), discussed the "variations on the substantial similarity of expression test":

> Consideration of the present motion has reawakened the court's concern with the apparent state of the law (especially in the Ninth Circuit) suggesting that elements of an allegedly infringed work which are found to be "unprotectible" must be eliminated from consideration in the substantial similarity of expression analysis. The problem results from the oftimes metaphysical line drawing between idea and expression by which courts rationalize their decisions. *Shaw v. Lindheim,* 908 F.2d 531 (9th Cir. 1990); *Sid & Marty Krofft Television v. McDonald's Corp.,* 562 F.2d 1157 (9th Cir. 1977) and *Arnstein v. Porter,* 154 F.2d 464 (2d Cir. 1946), *cert. denied,* 330 U.S. 851 (1947), demonstrate the difficulties which this dichotomy poses for even the most thoughtful judges. Removing unprotectible elements prior to the substantial similarity of expression test would preclude copyright protection for factual compilations containing an innovative selection or arrangement of elements because each element would be eliminated and nothing would be left for purposes of determining substantial similarity.
>
> Some dissection of elements and the application of merger, functionality, scenes a faire, and unoriginality theories are necessary to determine which elements can be used freely by the public in creating new works, so long as those works do not incorporate the same selection or arrangement as that of the plaintiff's work. Because there ought to be copyright protection for an innovative melding of elements from preexisting works, elements which have been deemed "unprotectible" should not be eliminated prior to the substantial similarity of expression analysis. Suppose defendant copied plaintiff's abstract painting composed entirely of geometric forms arranged in an original pattern. The alleged infringer could argue that each expressive element (i.e., the geometric forms) is unprotectible under the functionality, merger, scenes a faire, and unoriginality theories and, thus, all elements should be excluded prior to the substantial similarity of expression analysis. Then, there would be nothing left for purposes of determining substantial similarity of expression.
>
> In this example, elimination of "unprotectible" elements would result in a finding of no copyright infringement, which would be clearly inconsistent with the copyright law's purpose of providing incentives to authors of original works.
>
> Accordingly, the court concludes that even if elements are found "unprotectible," they should not be eliminated from the substantial similarity of expression analysis. Instead, if it is determined that the defen-

dant used the unprotectible elements in an arrangement which is not substantially similar to the plaintiff's work, then no copyright infringement can be found. If, on the other hand, the works are deemed substantially similar, then copyright infringement will be established even though the copyrighted work is composed of unprotectible elements. There is simply no other logical way of protecting an innovative arrangement or "look and feel" of certain works.

For a contrary view see *Computer Assocs. Int'l v. Altai, Inc.*, 982 F.2d 693 (2d Cir. 1992), *infra* Chapter 7, in which the court adopted, in the context of computer software protection, a "filtration" analysis that separates out "unprotectible" elements before comparing plaintiff's and defendant's works.

PROBLEM: SAM SPADE

The Ninth Circuit's descriptions of the story line of Dashiell Hammett's *The Maltese Falcon* and the CBS radio play *The Kandy Tooth* are reprinted below. *Warner Bros. Pictures v. Columbia Broadcasting Sys.*, 216 F.2d 945, 951-52 nn.8 & 9 (9th Cir. 1954).

The Maltese Falcon Story

The theme of the story of The Maltese Falcon is a complicated search for a fabulously valuable bird figurine called The Maltese Falcon. The action of the story centers in San Francisco from elsewhere, with the leading actors, or characters gathering there intent upon the objective. An attractive, alluring woman of uncertain age and reputation, by name Brigid O'Shaughnessy, assuming a false name and great distress, in search of help, called upon private detective Sam Spade, a clever, laconic, rangy-looking man whose morals and practices are none too idyllic, and well if not too favorably known to the police. Brigid qualifies within the requisite of the proverbial monumental liar, but, though Spade is not deceived, she manages to withhold the truth from him. A dunderheaded policeman and his partner enter the tangled story. Effie Perine is Spade's secretary, one of those see-all, know-all, self effacing paragons of loyal efficiency. A mystical character of a man who apparently is cooperating with Brigid against three others of their search-party gets shot to death and Spade is under suspicion. The leader of the search-party is a fat man named Gutman, of infinite patience and possessed of untold money. He proposes to pay a large sum to Sam who represents that he can deliver the bird. An effeminate lackey of a man by the name of Cairo does Gutman's bidding. A young, boyish gunman is under Gutman's orders. The story runs on at accelerated tempo in mystery until the captain of a ship, just in from the Orient, appears at Spade's apartment with a package in hand and falls dead from the boy's bullets sent into him just before he entered Spade's place. All gather at Sam's for the delivery of the bird, supposed to be in the package, and for payment of the money. Sam gets the award and Gutman gets the bird, which is a worthless counterfeit of the genuine. Gutman maintains his sang-froid. Brigid and Sam have trespassed the conventions. Yet, as somehow it is revealed the lady herself was the author of the first fatality, she is delivered over by the benevolent Sam and is sent on her way to San Quentin prison. These characters are skillfully depicted in a running, attractive style and distinctly assume individualism as distinguished from mere other persons.

Warner claims ownership of all of this including the characterizations with the characters' names, and the story.

The Kandy Tooth Story

The script opens with Sam Spade telephoning from jail to his faithful secretary, Effie Perine, early in the morning. Effie hurries to Sam who dictates his story. Dundy, the police officer, is present. Spade has received a telegram from the fat Caspar Gutman who had been marked "dead" from the end of The Maltese Falcon caper. The telegram is a warning about "an invidious pair of rogues," a dentist, and a charming woman named Hope Laverne, who have something to do with a "hidden tooth." Spade is bailed out by a mystery man who deposits $20,000.00 with the law. Gutman will shortly arrive in San Francisco. The dentist, so Spade dictated, had been ushered into his office by Effie and entreats him to get someone's "bridge." The dentist leaves. Spade contemplates "Hm-m-m ... Beware the Hidden Tooth." In comes Hope Laverne, a character along the line of Brigid O'Shaughnessy, and she is, or claims to be, a sister of the dentist. Hope explains the brother's obsession about a dental bridge. She wants to find him. Spade goes to a hotel, gets information from a house detective, and finds the brother, badly beaten; the two walk on the street — the dentist collapses. Spade takes him into a newsreel theater. The show excites him — it's about white elephants and particularly Oriental in character. Spade and the dentist go back to Spade's room. There Laverne recites a story of a tooth having been extracted from the jaw of a sacred body long since the occupant of an Oriental tomb. The tooth was taken by international rogues and installed by the dentist in the bridgework of an innocent refugee. The rogues are now attempting to locate the refugee and regain the priceless tooth.

Hope calls Spade on the telephone for help, and he goes, but is attacked by a boy, brother of the gun-boy in The Maltese Falcon. They scuffle and Spade is felled by a gun butt. He comes to in the presence of the imperturbable Gutman and strange happenings ensue. Spade finally gets the tooth in the ashes of the cremated body of the refugee, Herman Julius. $20,000.00 is paid upon delivery of the package containing the ashes. The tooth, by reason of a religious significance, is worth untold wealth to Gutman if he can produce it. A murder is committed; Hope and Sam had been more than friends. A Russian was mixed up in the plot. When Gutman saw that he had been duped through the delivery to him of the cremation residue, he took it as philosophically as when the bird in The Maltese Falcon turned out to be spurious. It develops that $20,000.00 had been put up for Sam's bail, and Sam puts up the same money as bail for Hope who gets into and out of jail. In some not very clear manner it all ends with no money gained by Spade, but Hope telephones her love after leaving jail, and Effie is not sure that the whole affair will net her a new ribbon for her typewriter.

1. Would you say these stories share the same "total concept and feel"?

2. Identify the similarities between the two stories. Which similarities concern copyrightable expression? Which concern noncopyrightable elements?

3. If you were to disqualify similarities based on elements you do not find copyrightable, would you find the stories "substantially similar"? If so, what would be the basis for your finding of substantial similarity?

EDUCATIONAL TESTING SERVICES v. KATZMAN

793 F.2d 533 (3d Cir. 1986)

[Plaintiff ETS develops and administers standardized tests, such as the Scholastic Aptitude Test (SAT), which it attempts to keep secret. Defendant, Katzman, operates Princeton Review, which, for a fee, prepares test takers and devises sample questions. The court of appeals first found that the ETS exam questions that were allegedly copied by the Princeton Review in preparing and distributing its "facsimile examinations" were copyrightable: they were not merely "ideas," nor were there so few ways to formulate questions that there was a "merger" of idea and expression so as to destroy copyrightability. The court then turned to the question whether the plaintiff was likely to prevail on its allegation that defendants had copied the ETS questions. It pointed out that "the record shows only rare instances of technically verbatim copying. However, ETS relies on the substantial similarity between its questions and those used by defendant to show copying." The court's discussion of substantial similarity follows.]

A finding of substantial similarity is an ad hoc determination. *See Peter Pan Fabrics, Inc. v. Martin Weiner Corp.,* 274 F.2d 487, 489 (2d Cir. 1960). We apply the reasonable person standard, under which

> the test is whether the accused work is so similar to the plaintiff's work that an ordinary reasonable person would conclude that the defendant unlawfully appropriated the plaintiff's protectible expression by taking material of substance and value.

. . . .

This case does not present the exact duplication between copyrighted test questions for medical school admission and those used by a different coaching business that was before the court in *Association of American Medical Colleges v. Mikaelian,* 571 F. Supp. 144 (E.D. Pa. 1983). There, the defendant's "facsimile" was an exact image of plaintiff's examination down to typeface and errors, *id.* at 148, and the court found that such similarities could only be explained by copying. *Id.* at 151.

Nonetheless, our examination discloses that at least some of Review's questions are so strikingly similar to those prepared by ETS as to lead to no other conclusion than that they were copied. For example, several of Review's math questions duplicate ETS' except for a change in the variables used. One example from the Math Level I Achievement Test will suffice:

ETS Question	*Review Question*

$$\text{If } \underline{x} = 3, \text{ then } \frac{\sqrt{x}}{3} = \qquad \text{If } \underline{x} = 4, \text{ then } \frac{\sqrt{x}}{4} =$$

(A) ⅓ (B) 1 (C) 3   (A) ¼ (B) 1 (C) 4
(D) 9 (E) 27   (D) 16 (E) 64

Other math questions were similarly altered merely by substituting different values for the numbers in ETS' equations, or making other minor alterations.

It is also evident that the Review's "facsimile" used questions copied from the ETS' SAT questions:

SAT Question	*Princeton Review "Facsimile"*
9. REPROBATE: (A) predecessor (B) antagonist (C) virtuous person (D) temporary ruler (E) strict supervisor	9. REPROBATE: (A) antagonist (B) predecessor (C) virtuous person (D) temporary ruler (E) strict supervisor

* * *

17. CONVEYOR BELT: PACKAGES: (A) forklift:warehouse (B) crane:ships (C) escalator:people (D) elevator:penthouse (E) scaffold:ropes	17. CONVEYOR BELT: PACKAGES: (A) crane:ships (B) forklift: warehouse (C) escalator:people (D) parachute:airplane (E) scaffold:ropes

In some of the other questions used by defendants and identified by ETS as infringing, the copying is not apparent, at least without more explanation than appears on this record. For example, ETS claims infringement in the following pair of questions:

ETS Question	*Review Question*

Even though history does not   President Carter felt that,
     A   A
actually repeat itself, knowledge of   by announcing all his
                        B   B

ETS Question	*Review Question*
history <u>can give</u> current problems a C	decisions while wearing a

familiar, <u>less</u> formidable look.
     D
	cardigan sweater, he <u>would give</u>
	                     C

<u>No error</u>
  E
	his presidency a friendly, <u>less</u>
	                                D

	formidable image. <u>No error</u> E

The substantial similarity between Review's question and ETS' question, which was designed to test whether the applicant knew that there was no grammatical error, eludes us.

We recognize that even in the absence of closely similar language, courts have found copyright infringement on the basis of "recognizable paraphrases." In *Meredith Corp v. Harper & Row, Publishers, Inc.*, 378 F. Supp. 786 (S.D.N.Y. 1974), *aff'd*, 500 F.2d 1221 (2d Cir. 1974), the district court found the text of the infringing textbook to be a paraphrase of the other, and hence an infringement. *See also Consolidated Music Publishers, Inc. v. Hansen Publishers, Inc.*, 339 F. Supp. 1161 (S.D.N.Y. 1972).

ETS apparently believes the "recognizable paraphrasing" cases apply to the illustration set forth immediately above. However, in both of the cited cases, there was a striking similarity between the two works. Here, there is nothing comparable. ETS complains that some of defendants' questions copy both the structure and wording of its questions, testing the same points in the same order. We have already sustained its contention with regard to the use of the same wording or substantially similar wording. On the other hand, its claim with respect to the use of the same structure sweeps too broadly. We are not convinced that ETS' copyright in the text of a question precludes a coaching school from testing the same concept in the same order, as long as it does not use the same or substantially similar language. In any event, it is an issue on which more specific district court's findings, based on an adequate record, are essential. However, since the record adequately supports ETS' contention of copying based on nearly verbatim or substantially similar questions, the fact that some questions referred to by ETS may not be infringing does not affect its substantial likelihood of success on the merits.

   . . . .

QUESTIONS

1. In the *ETS* case, compare the ETS question featuring the fraction $^x/_3$ and the Princeton Review question featuring the fraction $^x/_4$; consider the multiple-choice answers for each question. Was the court correct in concluding that the similarities in the matched questions and answers were ones of "expression" rather than of "idea"? Does this not in fact come perilously close to granting ETS a monopoly over all questions about square roots and particular algebraic solutions?

2. In the *ETS* case, the district court issued an injunction against Katzman, Princeton Review, and their employees and agents from

> copying, duplicating, distributing, selling, adapting, publishing, reproducing, renting, leasing, offering or otherwise transferring or communicating in any manner, orally or in written, printed, photographic or other form, including any communication in any class or other presentation, any questions, or any other information obtained directly from any of ETS' copyrighted secure tests.

On appeal, the defendants claim that the injunction is overbroad, particularly its ban upon "adapting" the ETS questions and even "information" obtained therefrom. Should those challenged phrases be stricken from the preliminary injunction?

STEINBERG v. COLUMBIA PICTURES INDUSTRIES

663 F. Supp. 706 (S.D.N.Y. 1987)

STANTON, DISTRICT JUDGE.

In these actions for copyright infringement, plaintiff Saul Steinberg is suing the producers, promoters, distributors and advertisers of the movie "Moscow on the Hudson" ("Moscow"). Steinberg is an artist whose fame derives in part from cartoons and illustrations he has drawn for *The New Yorker* magazine. Defendant Columbia Pictures Industries, Inc. (Columbia) is in the business of producing, promoting and distributing motion pictures, including "Moscow." Defendant RCA Corporation (RCA) was involved with Columbia in promoting and distributing the home video version of "Moscow," and defendant Diener Hauser Bates Co. (DHB) acted as an advertising agent for "Moscow." The other defendants were added to the complaint pursuant to a memorandum decision of this court dated November 17, 1986. These defendants fall into two categories: (1) affiliates of Columbia and RCA that were involved in the distribution of "Moscow" here and/or abroad, and (2) owners of major newspapers that published the allegedly infringing advertisement.

....

Plaintiff alleges that defendants' promotional poster for "Moscow" infringes his copyright on an illustration that he drew for *The New Yorker* [see illustrations on pp. 436-37] and that appeared on the cover of the March 29, 1976 issue of the magazine, in violation of 17 U.S.C. §§ 101-810. Defendants deny this allegation and assert the affirmative defenses of fair use as a parody, estoppel and laches.

Defendants have moved, and plaintiff has cross-moved, for summary judgment. For the reasons set forth below, this court rejects defendants' asserted defenses and grants summary judgment on the issue of copying to plaintiff.

....

II

The essential facts are not disputed by the parties despite their disagreements on nonessential matters. On March 29, 1976, *The New Yorker* published as a cover illustration the work at issue in this suit, widely known as a parochial New Yorker's view of the world. The magazine registered this illustration with the United States Copyright Office and subsequently assigned the copyright to Steinberg. Approximately three months later, plaintiff and *The New Yorker.* entered into an agreement to print and sell a certain number of posters of the cover illustration.

....

Defendants' illustration was created to advertise the movie "Moscow on the Hudson," which recounts the adventures of a Muscovite who defects in New York. In designing this illustration, Columbia's executive art director, Kevin Nolan, has admitted that he specifically referred to Steinberg's poster, and indeed, that he purchased it and hung it, among others, in his office. Furthermore, Nolan explicitly directed the outside artist whom he retained to execute his design, Craig Nelson, to use Steinberg's poster to achieve a more recognizably New York look. Indeed, Nelson acknowledged having used the facade of one particular edifice, at Nolan's suggestion that it would render his drawing more "New York-ish." Curtis Affidavit ¶ 28(c). While the two buildings are not identical, they are so similar that it is impossible, especially in view of the artist's testimony, not to find that defendants' impermissibly copied plaintiff's.

To decide the issue of infringement, it is necessary to consider the posters themselves. Steinberg's illustration presents a bird's eye view across a portion of the western edge of Manhattan, past the Hudson River and a telescoped version of the rest of the United States and the Pacific Ocean, to a red strip of horizon, beneath which are three flat land masses labeled China, Japan and Russia. The name of the magazine, in *The New Yorker*'s usual typeface, occupies the top fifth of the poster, beneath a thin band of blue wash representing a stylized sky.

The parts of the poster beyond New York are minimalized, to symbolize a New Yorker's myopic view of the centrality of his city to the world. The entire United States west of the Hudson River, for example, is reduced to a brown strip labeled "Jersey," together with a light green trapezoid with a few rudimentary rock outcroppings and the names of only seven cities and two states scattered across it. The few blocks of Manhattan, by contrast, are depicted and colored in detail. The four square blocks of the city, which occupy the whole lower half of the poster, include numerous buildings, pedestrians and cars, as well as parking lots and lamp posts, with water towers atop a few of the buildings. The whimsical, sketchy style and spiky lettering are recognizable as Steinberg's.

The "Moscow" illustration depicts the three main characters of the film on the lower third of their poster, superimposed on a bird's eye view of New York City, and continues eastward across Manhattan and the Atlantic Ocean, past a rudimentary evocation of Europe, to a clump of recognizably Russian-styled buildings on the horizon, labeled "Moscow." The movie credits appear over the lower portion of the characters. The central part of the poster depicts approximately four New York City blocks, with fairly detailed buildings, pedestrians and vehicles, a parking lot, and some water towers and lamp posts. Columbia's artist added a few New York landmarks at apparently random places in his illustration, apparently to render the locale more easily recognizable. Beyond the blue strip labeled "Atlantic Ocean," Europe is represented by London, Paris and Rome, each anchored by a single landmark (although the landmark used for Rome is the Leaning Tower of Pisa).

The horizon behind Moscow is delineated by a red crayoned strip, above which are the title of the movie and a brief textual introduction to the plot. The poster is crowned by a thin strip of blue wash, apparently a stylization of the sky. This poster is executed in a blend of styles: the three characters, whose likenesses were copied from a photograph, have realistic faces and somewhat sketchy clothing, and the city blocks are drawn in a fairly detailed but sketchy style. The lettering on the drawing is spiky, in block-printed handwritten capital letters substantially identical to plaintiff's while the printed texts at the top and bottom of the poster are in the typeface commonly associated with *The New Yorker* magazine.[2]

III

....

Defendants' access to plaintiff's illustration is established beyond peradventure. Therefore, the sole issue remaining with respect to liability is whether there is such substantial similarity between the copyrighted and accused works as to establish a violation of plaintiff's copyright....

The definition of "substantial similarity" in this circuit is "whether an average lay observer would recognize the alleged copy as having been appropriated from the copyrighted work." *Ideal Toy Corp. v. Fab-Lu Ltd.*, 360 F.2d 1021, 1022 (2d Cir. 1966); *Silverman v. CBS, Inc.*, 632 F. Supp. at 1351-52....

Moreover, it is now recognized that "[t]he copying need not be of every detail so long as the copy is substantially similar to the copyrighted work." ...

There is no dispute that defendants cannot be held liable for using the *idea* of a map of the world from an egocentrically myopic perspective. No rigid principle has been developed, however, to ascertain when one has gone beyond the idea to the expression, and "[d]ecisions must therefore inevitably be ad hoc." *Peter Pan Fabrics, Inc. v. Martin Weiner Corp.*, 274 F.2d 487, 489 (2d Cir. 1960) (L. Hand, J.)....

Even at first glance, one can see the striking stylistic relationship between the posters, and since style is one ingredient of "expression," this relationship is significant. Defendants' illustration was executed in the sketchy, whimsical style that has become one of Steinberg's hallmarks. Both illustrations represent a bird's eye view across the edge of Manhattan and a river bordering New York City to the world beyond. Both depict approximately four city blocks in detail and become increasingly minimalist as the design recedes into the background. Both use the device of a narrow band of blue wash across the top of the poster to represent the sky, and both delineate the horizon with a band of primary red.[3]

---

[2]The typeface is not a subject of copyright, but the similarity reinforces the impression that defendants copied plaintiff's illustration.

[3]Defendants claim that since this use of thin bands of primary colors is a traditional Japanese technique, their adoption of it cannot infringe Steinberg's copyright. This argument ignores the principle that while "[o]thers are free to copy the original ...

Illustration 1 — Steinberg's cover illustration
for The New Yorker

Illustration 2 — Columbia Pictures' promotional poster

Reproduced with permission of Columbia Pictures

The strongest similarity is evident in the rendering of the New York City blocks. Both artists chose a vantage point that looks directly down a wide two-way cross street that intersects two avenues before reaching a river. Despite defendants' protestations, this is not an inevitable way of depicting blocks in a city with a grid-like street system, particularly since most New York City cross streets are one-way. Since even a photograph may be copyrighted because "no photograph, however simple, can be unaffected by the personal influence of the author," *Time Inc. v. Bernard Geis Assoc.*, 293 F. Supp. 130, 141 (S.D.N.Y. 1968), *quoting Bleistein, supra,* one can hardly gainsay the right of an artist to protect his choice of perspective and layout in a drawing, especially in conjunction with the overall concept and individual details. Indeed, the fact that defendants changed the names of the streets while retaining the same graphic depiction weakens their case: had they intended their illustration realistically to depict the streets labeled on the poster, their four city blocks would not so closely resemble plaintiff's four city blocks. Moreover, their argument that they intended the jumble of streets and landmarks and buildings to symbolize their Muscovite protagonist's confusion in a new city does not detract from the strong similarity between their poster and Steinberg's.

While not all of the details are identical, many of them could be mistaken for one another; for example, the depiction of the water towers, and the cars, and the red sign above a parking lot, and even many of the individual buildings. The shapes, windows, and configurations of various edifices are substantially similar. The ornaments, facades and details of Steinberg's buildings appear in defendants', although occasionally at other locations. In this context, it is significant that Steinberg did not depict any buildings actually erected in New York; rather, he was inspired by the general appearance of the structures on the West Side of Manhattan to create his own New York-ish structures. Thus, the similarity between the buildings depicted in the "Moscow" and Steinberg posters cannot be explained by an assertion that the artists happened to choose the same buildings to draw. The close similarity can be explained only by the defendants' artist having copied the plaintiff's work. Similarly, the locations and size, the errors and anomalies of Steinberg's shadows and streetlight, are meticulously imitated.

In addition, the Columbia artist's use of the childlike, spiky block print that has become one of Steinberg's hallmarks to letter the names of the streets in the "Moscow" poster can be explained only as copying. There is no inherent justification for using this style of lettering to label New York City streets as it is associated with New York only through Steinberg's poster.

While defendants' poster shows the city of Moscow on the horizon in far greater detail than anything is depicted in the background of plaintiff's illustration, this fact alone cannot alter the conclusion. "Substantial similarity" does not require identity, and "duplication or near identity is not necessary to

---

[t]hey are not free to copy the copy." *Bleistein v. Donaldson Lithographing Co.,* 188 U.S. 239, 250, 23 S. Ct. 298, 300, 47 L. Ed. 460 (1903) (Holmes, J.). *Cf. Dave Grossman Designs, Inc. v. Bortin,* 347 F. Supp. 1150, 1156-57 (N.D. Ill. 1972) (an artist may use the same subject and style as another "so long as the second artist does not *substantially copy* [the first artist's] specific expression of his idea.")

establish infringement." *Krofft,* 562 F.2d at 1167. Neither the depiction of Moscow, nor the eastward perspective, nor the presence of randomly scattered New York City landmarks in defendants' poster suffices to eliminate the substantial similarity between the posters. As Judge Learned Hand wrote, "no plagiarist can excuse the wrong by showing how much of his work he did not pirate." *Sheldon v. Metro-Goldwyn Pictures Corp.,* 81 F.2d 49, 56 (2d Cir.), *cert. denied,* 298 U.S. 669, 56 S. Ct. 835, 80 L. Ed. 1392 (1936).

Defendants argue that their poster could not infringe plaintiff's copyright because only a small proportion of its design could possibly be considered similar. This argument is both factually and legally without merit. "[A] copyright infringement may occur by reason of a substantial similarity that involves only a small portion of each work." *Burroughs v. Metro-Goldwyn-Mayer, Inc.,* 683 F.2d 610, 624 n. 14 (2d Cir. 1982). Moreover, this case involves the entire protected work and an iconographically, as well as proportionately, significant portion of the allegedly infringing work. *Cf. Mattel, Inc. v. Azrak-Hamway Intern., Inc.,* 724 F.2d 357, 360 (2d Cir. 1983); *Elsmere Music, Inc. v. National Broadcasting Co.,* 482 F. Supp. 741, 744 (S.D.N.Y.), *aff'd,* 623 F.2d 252 (2d Cir. 1980) (taking small part of protected work can violate copyright).

. . . .

I also reject defendants' argument that any similarities between the works are unprotectible *scenes a faire,* or "incidents, characters or settings which, as a practical matter, are indispensable or standard in the treatment of a given topic." *Walker,* 615 F. Supp. at 436. *See also Reyher,* 533 F.2d at 92. It is undeniable that a drawing of New York City blocks could be expected to include buildings, pedestrians, vehicles, lamp posts and water towers. Plaintiff, however, does not complain of defendants' mere use of these elements in their poster; rather, his complaint is that defendants copied his *expression* of those elements of a street scene.

[The defendant also asserted the defenses of fair use (parody), estoppel (failure to protest the use of the Steinberg poster by other artists), and laches. The court rejected them all.]

On the next page are some further variations on the theme of the *New Yorker* poster. Assuming neither was produced with Steinberg's permission, does either infringe his copyright? Why or why not?

KISCH v. AMMIRATI & PURIS, INC.

657 F. Supp. 380 (S.D.N.Y. 1987)

[Plaintiff had taken a photograph of a woman seated in the Village Vanguard, a Manhattan nightclub; the woman was holding a concertina, and behind her was a large mural on the wall. Defendants were two companies marketing beverages, an advertising agency and a photographer hired by the agency. The allegedly infringing photograph was taken at the Village Vanguard and showed a man, seated in front of the same mural, holding a saxophone, with a bottle of lime juice on a table nearby. Defendants moved for summary judgment, conceding for purposes of the motion that they had had access to plaintiff's photograph. The court denied the motion, finding that there was sufficient evidence from which a reasonable conclusion might be reached that the defendants had copied the plaintiff's photograph and that the works would be regarded as substantially similar by an ordinary observer. The operative passages from the court's opinion follow.]

The Court has found no precedent, and the parties have cited none, which is substantively and procedurally on all fours with the instant case. It has been recognized, however, that where a photographer "in choosing subject matter, camera angle, lighting, etc., copies and attempts to duplicate all of such elements as contained in a prior photograph," then even though "the second photographer is photographing a live subject rather than the first photograph ... [s]uch an act would constitute an infringement of the first photograph...." 1 Nimmer § 2.08[E][1] at 2-112. An old case in the Court of Appeals for the Second Circuit applied this rule where the Court discerned "many close identities of pose, light, and shade, etc." even though it acknowledged that the "eye of an artist or a connoisseur will, no doubt, find differences" between the two photographs. *Seligman*, 212 F. at 931. On the other hand, if the elements of an earlier photograph are "by chance" duplicated subsequently by another photographer, the new photograph will not be held to infringe the earlier one because others are "entirely free to form [their] own conception" of the subject matter. *Id. Cf.* 1 Nimmer § 2.08[E][1] at 2-112.

Turning to a comparison of the two photographs involved in this case, there are differences between the works, to be sure. For example, plaintiff's photograph is in black and white while defendants' is in color. Plaintiff's photograph is of an unidentified woman while defendants' is of musician John Lurie. The woman in plaintiff's photograph is holding a concertina while John Lurie is holding a saxophone. A bottle of lime juice and a portion of a table appear only in defendants' photograph. There are also many similarities. Most noticeably, the two photographs were taken in the same small corner of the Village Vanguard nightclub. The same striking mural appears as the background for each photograph. Both John Lurie and the woman in plaintiff's photograph are seated and holding a musical instrument. In addition, the lighting, camera angle, and camera position appear to be similar in each photograph. The Court concludes that a rational trier of fact could find sufficient similarities to prove "copying." *See Arnstein*, 154 F.2d at 468, *quoted in Walker*, 784 F.2d at 51.

A closer question is posed with respect to the issue of "illicit copying (unlaw-

Kisch photograph   Ammirati & Puris photograph
Reproduced with permission   Reproduced with permission

ful appropriation)" under the "ordinary observer" test. *See id.* Still, the Court is unable to conclude that a rational trier of fact would not be permitted to find substantial similarity relating to protectible material. *See Walker,* 784 F.2d at 48; *Durham Industries, Inc.,* 630 F.2d at 918. Significantly, a rational trier of fact would be permitted to find that the underlying tone or mood of defendants' photograph was similar to the original conception expressed in plaintiff's work. Accordingly, defendants' motion to dismiss plaintiff's claim for copyright infringement is denied.

    . . . .

QUESTIONS

1. The court in *Steinberg* stated that "substantial similarity" means that "an average lay observer would recognize the alleged copy as having been appropriated from the copyrighted work." Is this too lenient a standard? For example, would not most persons familiar with the Steinberg *New Yorker* cover affirm that the Paris and Florence renditions, *supra* had been "appropriated" from Steinberg? Does that alone warrant a finding of infringement? Would the same visual process, and conclusion about legality, obtain if the fact-finder were instead to use the formula announced by Learned Hand in *Peter Pan* for determining whether two works are substantially similar, i.e., whether the ordinary observer "unless he set out to detect the disparities, would be disposed to overlook them, and regard their aesthetic appeal as the same"?

2. The *Steinberg* court stated that although the plaintiff's graphic "style" was not protectible, it was a significant ingredient in determining whether "expression" was copied. It stated the same about such things as the "child-like, spiky block print" used in delineating the street names. Is it possible to separate out these unprotectible elements in determining whether the defendant has copied too much protectible detail from the plaintiff? Is it analytically proper to separate them out?

3. In *Steinberg* and *Kisch* — and in some of the cases discussed in the note on infringement, below — the defendant may well have "based" its work on that of the plaintiff, but it also made a purposeful effort to incorporate changes in order to distance itself from the expressive details of the plaintiff's work. Courts sometimes speak of that effort disparagingly, counting it against the defendant on the issues of copying and illicit similarity. Even if not counted against the defendant, such an effort is commonly said not to cut in the defendant's favor. For example, the late Professor Nimmer has stated: "It is entirely immaterial that in many respects plaintiff's and defendant's work are dissimilar if in other respects similarity as to a substantial element of plaintiff's work can be shown." 3 Nimmer on Copyright § 13.03[B]. On the other hand, Professor Nimmer also states: "A defendant may legitimately avoid infringement by intentionally making sufficient changes in a work which would otherwise be regarded as substantially similar to that of the plaintiff's." *Id.* How would you reconcile these principles?

4. Blore Advertising Agency has brought an infringement action against 20/20 Advertising Agency, claiming that the latter's television commercial for eyewear is a substantial copy of its own television commercial for a local newspaper. Blore's advertisement features Deborah Shelton, an actress best known for her work in the *Dallas* television series. The commercial lasts thirty seconds. It begins with a close-up of Ms. Shelton and the word "Deborah" in the lower left of the screen. Then follows a series of rapid-edits of twenty close-ups of Shelton's face; she wears a white shirt with blue stripes. With each line of text the camera cuts to a new close-up of Shelton in a different pose, with a different hairstyle and expression. The script is as follows:

> What do the Daily News and a hot bubble bath have in common? ... Me.... I just love them both.... Everybody knows about the Daily News' commitment to the Valley ... and its commitment to excellence.... There is another paper that says it covers the Valley.... But everybody knows.... They're over the hill.... Can you imagine living in the Valley and not reading the Daily News? ... That's like wearing all new underwear and not getting hit by a bus.... What a waste.... Daily ... News.... Daily ... And Sundays.... You ... Ought to look into that.

The 20/20 advertisement, prepared for Duling Optical Company, also uses the services of Ms. Shelton, who is captured in fourteen different poses over thirty seconds. It also begins with a close-up and the words "Deborah Shelton" on the lower right of the screen. There are a series of close-up and medium-range shots, in which Ms. Shelton wears a blue-striped blouse. In each shot, she is featured in a new pose with a different pair of glasses or no glasses at all as well as a different hairstyle. Her pose changes with each phrase of text:

> There are some things in life that should take ... more than an hour.... But making your glasses isn't one of them.... Duling Optical Super Store ... Has thousands of designer frames ... And contact lenses to choose from.... I can have my eyes examined ... And have my new glasses and ... Contact lenses in about an hour.... And they're guaranteed to be ... Prescription perfect.... The Duling Optical Super Store ... The one-stop shopping ... That allows me more time for ... Other things.

Blore claims that 20/20 has copied the expressive elements of the Blore commercials. 20/20 claims that the plaintiff cannot use the copyright law to monopolize the rapid-edit montage style involving close-ups of a particular celebrity (with whom 20/20 entered into a lawful contract). What supporting arguments should each party make? How should the court rule? *See Chuck Blore & Don Richman Inc. v. 20/20 Adv., Inc.,* 674 F. Supp. 671 (D. Minn. 1987).

INFRINGEMENT OF PICTORIAL, GRAPHIC AND SCULPTURAL WORKS

As the *Steinberg* and *Kalpakian* cases make clear, the "substantial similarity" that makes out a case of infringement must flow from a copying of protectible "expression" and not merely the unprotectible "idea." As Learned Hand pointed out in a variety of copyright cases — involving not only pictorial works, as in *Peter Pan,* but also literary works, as in the renowned *Nichols* and *Sheldon* opinions — the line between idea and expression is elusive. The difficulties can be illustrated by several cases.

In *Alt v. Morello,* 227 U.S.P.Q. 49 (S.D.N.Y. 1985), the plaintiff created a photograph depicting a Cross-brand pen and pencil positioned at an angle on a dark grid against a dark background, with the tips of the pen and pencil in a yellow-toned circle lit from below. Defendant allegedly saw this photograph in the plaintiff's portfolio, made a copy of it, and distributed it as part of his own portfolio and through promotional mailers; this ultimately led to several advertising agencies and art directors suggesting to the plaintiff (who was seeking to work for them) that his photograph was suspiciously similar to the defendant's. Viewing the two pen-and-pencil photographs, the court concluded that "they are virtually the same; and indeed, only after close examination can minor differences be observed. The composition, backgrounds, colors, lighting, objects photographed and cropping, are substantially similar." The court stated that the ordinary observer would overlook such facts as that the two photographed pens and pencils are of a different brand, their angle is slightly different, and the circles a different shade of yellow; these were said to be "minute variations," which the court found to "constitute further evidence of copying." The court found an infringement regardless whether the defendant had actually photographed the plaintiff's photo or set-up, or had

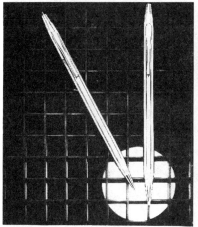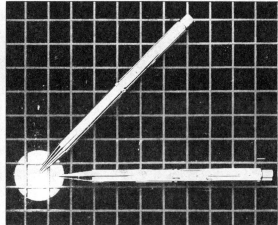

Plaintiff's photograph
Reproduced with permission

Defendant's photograph
Reproduced with permission

recreated the plaintiff's photograph from memory. The court rejected the defendant's claim that he had independently created his own photograph without copying, and found that there had been an unlawful appropriation. (Because the court found that the defendant had wilfully studied the plaintiff's work and deliberately duplicated it, while continuing to hold out his photograph as his own creative effort, the court, among other relief, doubled the usual measure of statutory damages, and ordered the delivery of all the defendant's transparencies and prints to the United States Marshal for destruction.)*

The *Alt* case involved the fairly straightforward depiction of familiar objects placed at angles. How difficult is it in these circumstances to draw an inference of copying? Is the defendant — assuming he has copied — appropriating "idea" or "expression"?

The same questions are raised in a pair of similar cases. In *Rachel v. Banana Republic, Inc.,* 228 U.S.P.Q. 416, 1986 CCH Copyright L. Dec. ¶ 25,889 (N.D. Cal. 1985), the plaintiff produced and sold synthetic animal heads (zebra, buffalo, gazelle, giraffe, rhino, and elephant) to the defendant for use in its stores in which it sells safari-type clothing and accessories. After the termination of their contract with the plaintiff, Banana Republic turned to another supplier of synthetic animal heads, whom plaintiff contended copied from them. The court, relying on *Kalpakian,* held that where an idea (i.e., synthetic decorative animal heads) is inseparable from the tangible expression of that idea "there will be protection against nothing other than identical

---

*After the defendant filed his appeal, a court-approved settlement was reached; it provided for a dismissal of the complaint with prejudice, vacating of the judgment, and a withdrawal of the court's findings, conclusions and opinions.

Plaintiff's Zebra Head   Defendant's Zebra Head
Reproduced with permission   Reproduced with permission

copying of the work." The plaintiff could not satisfy this standard:

> [T]he only similarities were that both sets of compared animal heads "are
> made of fiberglass, both have glass eyes, both have closed mouths, both
> have horns on the top of their heads, and both animals are made to look
> real. There the similarities stop. There is no question that defendants'
> animal forms are not exact replicas of plaintiff's. They are not "splash
> copies" such as would be produced if defendants used one of plaintiff's
> heads to make a mold from which to cast other identical heads.

Indeed, the plaintiff in his deposition testimony stated that all the defendant
had copied was the plaintiff's "concept" of "super-realistic animals made from
100 percent synthetic materials." The plaintiff also failed to offer proof to
rebut the defendant's claim of independent creation; the court concluded, on
the basis of depositions, that the defendant's animal forms "were made from
taxidermy head mounts or other sources completely independent from plaintiff's forms." Summary judgment was granted for the defendant.

The contrary result was reached in *Animal Fair, Inc. v. AMFESCO Indus.*,
620 F. Supp. 175 (D. Minn. 1985), *aff'd without opinion*, 794 F.2d 678 (8th Cir.
1986). There the dispute related not to animal heads but to animal feet, more
precisely a novelty bedroom slipper resembling a bear's foot. The court found
that the defendant had copied several features of the plaintiff's slipper, including the profile and shape, the number of toes, a colored animal print on
the slipper sole, and the textures and colors. The plaintiff offered testimony
from a wildlife zoologist and expert on bear anatomy to the effect that the
slipper's contours differed in several respects from those of a real bear's paw,

Plaintiff's Slipper
Reproduced with permission

Defendant's Slipper
Reproduced with permission

and the court found that the parties' slippers manifested all of those same fanciful features. Although the defendant emphasized certain differences from the plaintiff's slipper, the major one being the shape of the toe tips, the court concluded that the slippers "give the same overall impression to the casual observer," and that "the similarity is between the artistic or expressive aspects of the slipper design rather than simply the concept of a bear's paw type slipper." The minor differences "clearly do not alter the fact that defendant has captured the 'total concept and feel'" of the plaintiff's slipper.

The court in *Animal Fair* obviously understands that copyright cannot afford an exclusive right to manufacture slippers in the shape of animal feet, or even in the shape of a bear's foot. How many variations can there likely be in the contours and textures of a "cute" bear foot, given the additional fact that it must also be designed to slip over a human's foot for use as a slipper? Is the outcome of this case consistent with cases such as *Kalpakian* and *Banana Republic*? Might the outcome in *Animal Fair* be explainable by the fact that the year before the defendant designed the challenged slipper, it had manufactured and sold an indisputable "knock-off" of the plaintiff's design, had stopped doing so in response to a "cease and desist letter" from the plaintiff, and had then incorporated a number of changes in generating the slipper for which it was ultimately sued?

The *Animal Fair* decision is one of an increasing number that rely in making an infringement finding on the similarity in the "concept and feel" of the two works in litigation. The student may recall that the "concept and feel" formula was introduced by the Court of Appeals for the Ninth Circuit in the *Roth Greeting Cards* case, *supra*, involving simple greeting cards with simple drawings on the front and standard phrases inside. The *Kisch* decision uses something of the same approach when it states that a jury could reasonably find that the "underlying tone or mood" of the defendant's photograph was "similar to the original conception" expressed in the plaintiff's. By the same token, one might inquire whether the *Steinberg* decision, although not using the "concept and feel" formula, may not be extending protection to the plaintiff's conceptual ingenuity, rather than his expressive artistry.

If two works are similar only in "concept and feel" or "tone or mood," can it properly be said that there is an illicit copying of "expression" rather than "idea"? Indeed, is not the "concept and feel" standard facially inconsistent with the exclusion of "concepts" from the subject matter of copyright under § 102(b)? Or does the phrase, however unhappily worded, attempt to capture the point at which defendant has gone beyond mere mimicry of general style to capture elements of plaintiff's work which, however ill-defined, are particularly "expressive." Is there a better way to identify that point? (*Can* it be identified?)

The "concept and feel" standard seems to find its way more into cases of pictorial copyright than literary copyright, probably because the pictorial work can be viewed in a single glance as a totality. If applied to literary works, some might argue, the "concept and feel" approach could result in protecting plot ideas and stock devices. Does application of the standard to art works present a similar potential for overprotection?

QUESTION

The copyright owner of the top two posters on the facing page has brought an action against the distributors of the bottom two posters. The latter have filed a motion for summary judgment. They make the following arguments. (1) Each of the graphic elements in the plaintiff's posters — e.g., the rouged cheeks, the ruffled collar, the Mardi Gras masks — are in the public domain and should therefore be eliminated when applying the test of substantial similarity. (2) Even if those elements are regarded as copyrightable, and even if it is assumed that the defendants copied, they copied no more than the overall artistic style of the plaintiff's poster[s] rather than their detailed expression. How would you deal with these arguments, and how would you rule on the motion for summary judgment? *See Mistretta v. Curole*, 22 U.S.P.Q.2d 1707 (E.D. La. 1992).

AUTHORS REPRODUCING WORKS IN WHICH THEY NO LONGER OWN THE COPYRIGHT

In *Gross v. Seligman*, 212 F. 930 (2d Cir. 1914), a photographer posed a nude young woman for a photograph entitled "Grace of Youth." He then sold all rights in the photograph to plaintiff. Two years later he posed the same young woman for another photograph entitled "Cherry Ripe." Apart from a minor variation of background (and, the court noted, slight changes in the contours of the woman's figure resulting from the passage of two years), the sole difference between the two photographs was that the first showed her face in repose and the second had the woman smiling with a cherry stem between her teeth.

The court stressed that where the photographer, as well as the model, pose, light and shade were the same in both photographs, there is a very strong indication that the second photograph was merely a copy of the first. The exercise of artistic talent, the sine qua non of the first photograph's copyrightability, was used in the second photograph to create not a new independently copyrightable photograph, but a copy of the first photograph. Accordingly, infringement was found. By contrast, the court stated that another artist would be free to photograph the same young woman and create his own work, even though striking similarities might exist between this new photograph and the old, but that the original artist in this case had not created a new photograph, but copied the original.

More recently, in *Franklin Mint Corp. v. National Wildlife Art Exchange*, 575 F.2d 62 (3d Cir. 1978), a court was again faced with the situation whereby, in a later work, an artist had allegedly infringed the copyright that he no longer owned in one of his earlier works. This time the ruling was in favor of the artist, as the court resorted to the idea-expression distinction in finding that no infringement had occurred.

A nationally recognized wildlife artist was commissioned to paint a watercolor of cardinals for subsequent commercial exploitation by plaintiff National Wildlife Art Exchange. Using slides, photographs, sketches and two stuffed cardinals as source material, the artist completed "Cardinals on Apple Blossom" and, as previously agreed, sold it, along with all its attendant rights, to plaintiff. Three years later, as part of a series of bird life watercolors done for defendant Franklin Mint, the artist painted "The Cardinal," using some of the same source materials he had used to create "Cardinals on Apple Blossom." In addition, however, in painting "The Cardinal" he used new slides, photographs and sketches that had not been available to him earlier. The court held that an artist is free to use the same source material he has already used in creating a painting to create a different painting depicting the same subject matter.

In ruling for defendant, the court cited readily apparent dissimilarities between the two paintings in the area of color, body attitude and positioning of birds, linear effect, background, and composition. This "pattern of differences" was held sufficient to establish that the second painting represented "diversity of expression rather than only an echo."

Can these seemingly conflicting resolutions of similar problems be explained on the basis of the relative similarities and differences in the pair of works in each case? Can the complete identity of the source materials in *Gross* be contrasted with the lesser degree of overlap in *Franklin* to explain the different judgments? Or does the explanation for the opposite results reached in these two cases lie in the differences between the media of photography and watercolor painting? The *Franklin* court talked around this in a paragraph discussing the effect of the artist's style on the protectability of a copyright in an artistic work. (The *Gross* case is cited in a footnote to the discussion's conclusion.) The discussion concludes that a painting or drawing of photograph-like clarity and accuracy will be less protectable than a more abstract or impressionistic work where the expression is more personal and distinctive.

Both courts skirted an issue raised by cases of this kind: Does a lawsuit against an artist for infringement of a copyright in a work he has created possibly inhibit him from continuing to operate in his own style? In *Gross* the court ignored the possibility, and in *Franklin* the court merely noted that "an artist is free to consult the same source for another original painting." Compare the problems created when a songwriter transfers copyright and continues to write "reminiscent" music in his usual style, or when a novelist transfers copyright and continues to write in a comfortable genre using character types he has used before. *See Fantasy, Inc. v. Fogerty, supra* p. 304, and *Warner Bros. v. CBS, supra* p. 223.

On the above issues, consider the following observations by Judge Posner in *Schiller & Schmidt, Inc. v. Nordisco Corp.*, 969 F.2d 410, 414 (7th Cir. 1992):

> We might still suppose the evidence of copying of the layouts compelling were it not that the creator of the copyrighted work and the infringer were the same person. Although one can and often does copy one's own work (and so may be an infringer if one doesn't own the copyright on it), one is also more likely to duplicate one's own work without copying than another person would be likely to do. If Cezanne painted two pictures of Mont St. Victoire, we should expect them to look more alike than if Matisse had painted the second, even if Cezanne painted the second painting from life rather than from the first painting.

2. THE RIGHT TO MAKE PHONORECORDS

a. Musical Compositions: The Compulsory License Under § 115

The concept of a compulsory license was introduced into our copyright law in 1909. The Supreme Court had already decided in *White-Smith Music Pub'g Co. v. Apollo Co.*, 209 U.S. 1 (1908), that piano rolls (and by analogy phonograph records and the like) did not embody a system of notation that could be read and hence were not "copies" of the musical composition within the meaning of the law, but constituted merely parts of devices for mechanically performing the music. The exclusive right of the copyright owner to public performance already existed under the Act of 1897, and this undoubtedly included such *performance* by mechanical instruments. It was the right to *make* such devices that was lacking, and so Congress undertook to grant such right, but without intending to extend the right of copyright to the mechanical devices themselves. H.R. Rep. No. 2222, 60th Cong., 2d Sess. 9 (1909).

Because of what seemed at the time a well-grounded fear of monopolistic control of music for recording purposes, *id.,* Congress saw fit to qualify the right of mechanical control by providing in subsection (e) of § 1 that if the copyright proprietor himself used or sanctioned the use of his composition in this way, any other person was free to do so upon paying a royalty of two cents for each part (each roll or record) manufactured. A corresponding infringement provision was inserted in § 101(e). Mechanics were provided for the filing of notices by the compulsory licensor (notice of use) and licensee (notice of intention to use) and for payment.

These verbose and internally inconsistent provisions left many questions unanswered. However, the remarkable adjustment of the music industry to this unique provision resulted in its retention in 1976, but with changes designed to balance anew the competing interests and to answer some of these questions. *See generally* Rosenlund, *Compulsory Licensing of Musical Compositions for Phonorecords Under the Copyright Act of 1976,* 30 Hastings L.J. 683 (1979).

HOUSE REPORT

H.R. Rep. No. 94-1476, 94th Cong., 2d Sess. 107-09 (1976)

The provisions of sections 1(e) and 101(e) of the present law, establishing a system of compulsory licensing for the making and distribution of phonorecords of copyrighted music, are retained with a number of modifications in section 115 of the bill. Under these provisions, which represented a compromise of the most controversial issue of the 1909 act, a musical composition that has been reproduced in phonorecords with the permission of the copyright owner may generally be reproduced in phonorecords by another person, if that person notifies the copyright owner and pays a specified royalty....

Availability and scope of compulsory license

Subsection (a) of section 115 deals with three doubtful questions under the present law: (1) the nature of the original recording that will make the work available to others for recording under a compulsory license; (2) the nature of the sound recording that can be made under a compulsory license; and (3) the extent to which someone acting under a compulsory license can depart from the work as written or recorded without violating the copyright owner's right to make an "arrangement" or other derivative work. The first two of these questions are answered in clause (1) of section 115(a), and the third is the subject of clause (2).

The present law, though not altogether clear, apparently bases compulsory licensing on the making or licensing of the first recording, even if no authorized records are distributed to the public. The first sentence of section 115(a)(1) would change the basis for compulsory licensing to authorized public distribution of phonorecords (including disks and audio tapes but not the sound tracks or other sound records accompanying a motion picture or other audiovisual work). Under the clause, a compulsory license would be available to anyone as soon as "phonorecords of a nondramatic musical work have been distributed to the public in the United States under the authority of the copyright owner."

The second sentence of clause (1), which has been the subject of some debate, provides that "a person may obtain a compulsory license only if his or her primary purpose in making phonorecords is to distribute them to the public for private use." ... The committee concluded ... that the purpose of the compulsory license does not extend to manufacturers of phonorecords that are intended primarily for commercial use, including not only broadcasters and jukebox operators but also background music services.

... The basic intent of [the final sentence of clause (1)] is to make clear that a person is not entitled to a compulsory license of copyrighted musical works for the purpose of making an unauthorized duplication of a musical sound recording originally developed and produced by another. It is the view of the Committee that such was the original intent of the Congress in enacting the 1909 Copyright Act, and it has been so construed by the 3d, 5th, 9th and 10th Circuits ....

The second clause of subsection (a) is intended to recognize the practical need for a limited privilege to make arrangements of music being used under a compulsory license, but without allowing the music to be perverted, distorted, or travestied. Clause (2) permits arrangements of a work "to the extent necessary to conform it to the style or manner of interpretation of the performance involved," so long as it does not "change the basic melody or fundamental character of the work." The provision also prohibits the compulsory licensee from claiming an independent copyright in his arrangement as a "derivative work" without the express consent of the copyright owner.

THE ROYALTY RATE AND THE COPYRIGHT ROYALTY TRIBUNAL

Under § 115, a person wishing to obtain a compulsory license must file with the copyright owner a "notice of intention" to distribute phonorecords of the copyrighted work, and is to pay a royalty for each record of the work that is "made and distributed." One of the most heated issues in the revision process was the amount of the per-record royalty to be paid by record manufacturers (the compulsory licensees) to the owners of musical copyrights. The latter, although not arguing that the two-cent rate set in 1909 should mechanically be indexed to the increased cost-of-living in the subsequent sixty-five years, did urge that the royalty rate should be markedly increased beyond 2 cents. As stated in the 1975 Senate Report:

> They [the songwriters and publishers] maintain that 2 cents at the time of the 1965 House hearings was 6.1 percent of the list price per song on a typical album whereas today it is only 2.8 percent; and that, despite an aggregate increase in mechanical royalty payments, they represented almost 6 percent of industry sales in 1965 and less than 4 percent in 1975.

The recording companies, contending that no increase beyond the two-cent royalty was warranted, emphasized among other things the fact that the aggregate royalties paid to copyright owners in the preceding decade had doubled due to increased record sales and the introduction of the long-playing multi-song recording, and the fact that the two-cent royalty represented roughly the same percentage of the manufacturers' wholesale selling price in 1970 as it did in 1909. They also argued that an increase in the royalty rate even to 3 cents per song would have to be reflected in increased record prices to the public, a result opposed not only by consumers but also by recording artists, record distributors and retailers, and jukebox operators. If, on the other hand, record prices were not raised, the higher royalty would result in the demise of many marginal record companies as well as many wholesalers and retailers; this would lead to a reduction in the recording of new music and to greater concentration in the recording industry. The songwriters and publishing companies challenged the accuracy of the manufacturers' economic data, claimed that the recording industry was more than capable of absorbing a very minor increase in mechanical royalties without financial disasters, and asserted that (quoting again from the Senate Report) "they see no reason why an industry which has more than doubled the price per recorded selection over the last decade should be excused from paying fair compensation to those who created the music."

Weighing all of these arguments, the two Houses and ultimately the Conference Committee decided to increase the statutory royalty rate to 2.75 cents per recording. The legislative history made it explicit that the publishers and composers would be able to take their case, beginning in 1980, to a newly created agency, the Copyright Royalty Tribunal, for review of the statutory royalty rate in light of current economic evidence. Congress set forth, in § 801(b), several objectives that the Tribunal was to pursue in setting revised royalty rates; the student should peruse that section at this point.

In its 1980 proceedings, the Tribunal increased the royalty rate under § 115 from 2.75 cents (or .5 cent per minute, whichever is larger) to 4 cents for each recording of a copyrighted work (or .75 cent per minute, whichever is larger); the increase was made applicable to phonorecords made and distributed on or after July 1, 1981. Beyond that, the Tribunal provided for possible annual upward adjustments based on changes in record retail list prices, as determined by the Tribunal.

The Court of Appeals for the District of Columbia Circuit upheld the validity of the 4 cent per record royalty rate as within a reasonable range of possible rates that the Tribunal could establish using the criteria set forth in § 801(b)(1). However, the court struck down the Tribunal's arrangement for recurrent proceedings leading to regular increases in the statutory royalty rates. The court pointed to § 804(a) of the Copyright Act, which provides for a royalty adjustment in 1980 but not again until 1987 and each subsequent tenth year; the Tribunal had overstepped its statutory powers by scheduling annual proceedings in order to monitor the fairness of rates. Yet, were the Tribunal to conclude that no single rate could plausibly remain reasonable for the period 1980 to 1987, "we see nothing in the statute precluding the Tribunal from adopting a reasonable mechanism for automatic rate changes in interim years," provided that mechanism is "well-determined and beyond the Tribunal's discretion." *Recording Indus. Ass'n v. Copyright Royalty Tribunal,* 662 F.2d 1 (D.C. Cir. 1981).

Utilizing procedures that have complied with the court's decision, the Copyright Royalty Tribunal has since increased the per-recording royalty. Effective January 1, 1986, the rate to be paid by phonorecord manufacturers became 5 cents for each recording (made and distributed) of a song (or .95 cents per minute, whichever was larger). The Tribunal declared that thereafter the rate would increase biannually in automatic correspondence to changes in the Consumer Price Index. Based on those changes, the royalty rate has since consistently increased for successive two-year periods: to 5.25 cents (with a time equivalent for longer recordings) effective January 1, 1988; 5.7 cents in 1990; 6.25 cents in 1992; and, effective January 1, 1994, 6.60 cents. (Note the one-cent-per-recording increase between 1988 and 1992, and compare it with the ³/₄ cent increase between 1909 and 1978!) The pertinent regulation of the Tribunal is 37 C.F.R. § 307.3, which is set forth in Appendix D to the casebook.

In addition to its authority to adjust royalty rates under § 115 for phonorecords of nondramatic musical works, the Tribunal was also given by the 1976 Copyright Act comparable powers under the three other compulsory licenses that were introduced into our law for the first time: secondary transmissions by cable television systems (§ 111), public performance of musical compositions through jukebox plays (§ 116, since amended so as to displace temporarily the compulsory license with negotiated licenses between representatives of the music publishers and the jukebox operators), and the use of artworks and music on public radio and television broadcasting (§ 118). The Tribunal was to reassess the statutory rates in these four industries at different staggered times, so as to balance its workload and to take account of the varied speeds of economic change in those different industries. The Tribunal was also given the power, after collecting those various royalties, to distribute them among the pertinent copyright claimants, and to hold hearings in order to decide among disputed claims.

Bills introduced in Congress in 1993 would abolish the Copyright Royalty Tribunal, which a number of legislators thought was proving to be an unduly expensive standing administrative agency with only infrequent decisionmaking responsibilities; even some Tribunal members concurred in this assessment. The principal provisions of the bills would retain the compulsory licenses in §§ 111, 115 and 118, but would turn over to the Librarian of Congress the authority to change statutory rates and to distribute disputed royalties. The Librarian would in turn be empowered to appoint ad hoc arbitration panels (whose costs would be borne by the parties rather than through Government salaries). Royalty rate and distribution decisions by the arbitration panels would be subject to review by the Librarian for arbitrariness, and his or her decision would in turn be reviewable by the District of Columbia Circuit Court of Appeals. The § 116 compulsory license for jukeboxes would be eliminated from the statute altogether, and the negotiated licenses now contemplated in § 116A would be substituted (and that section renumbered as § 116). There is substantial expectation that this legislation will be enacted, with the life of the Copyright Royalty Tribunal having been limited to some fifteen years, but with most of its functions carried on through other persons. See S. 1346, H.R. 2840 (103rd Cong., 1st Sess.)

QUESTIONS

1. Is the compulsory license for recordings of musical compositions subject to attack under the copyright and patent clause of the Constitution?

2. It can probably be demonstrated that the fears of economic monopoly that justified the compulsory license in 1909 were unwarranted in 1976, when the new Copyright Act was passed. Given the control normally allowed by law to the copyright owner over the commercial exploitation of his or her work, is the fact that the recording industry is accustomed to operating under the compulsory license sufficient reason to preserve it in the current law?

3. Assume that a witty recording musician (whom we shall fancifully call Spike Jones) records his version of a recently successful love ballad, which incorporates speed-ups, hiccoughs, ambulance sirens, and the like; his version becomes quite popular, and many phonorecords are sold and considerable airtime given. If Jones tenders the statutory royalty for each record sold, has he infringed? If so, is that a sound result? If the infringement is not saved by § 115, is there some other section or principle on which Jones might rely? (Consider later whether the radio stations which play the Jones record are liable for infringement.)

THE "HARRY FOX LICENSE"

A large number of music publishers/copyright owners have authorized an organization called the Harry Fox Agency to grant licenses for the mechanical reproduction of music. Such reproduction includes synchronization with motion pictures and other audiovisual works, and recordings of dramatic-musical material, both of which involve a variety of contractual terms and conditions. But perhaps the greatest volume of transactions involves the recording of non-dramatic music under a document in the form of a letter from the Fox Agency, which identifies the copyrighted work and the publisher(s) for whom the Fox office is acting as agent, and contains substantially the following terms:

> You have advised us, in our capacity as Agent for the Publisher(s) referred to in (B) supra, that you wish to obtain a compulsory license to make and to distribute phonorecords of the copyrighted work referred to in (A) supra, under the compulsory license provision of Section 115 of the Copyright Act.
>
> Upon your doing so, you shall have all the rights which are granted to, and all the obligations which are imposed upon, users of said copyrighted work under the compulsory license provision of the Copyright Act, after phonorecords of the copyrighted work have been distributed to the public in the United States under the authority of the copyright owner by another person, except that with respect to phonorecords thereof made and distributed hereunder:

1. You shall pay royalties and account to us as Agent for and on behalf of said Publisher(s) quarterly, within forty-five days after the end of each calendar quarter, on the basis of phonorecords made and distributed;

2. For such phonorecords made and distributed, the royalty shall be the statutory rate in effect at the time the phonorecord is made, except as otherwise stated in (C) *supra*;

3. This compulsory license covers and is limited to one particular recording of said copyrighted work as performed by the artist and on the phonorecord number identified in (C) *supra* ...;

4. In the event you fail to account to us and pay royalties as herein provided for, said Publisher(s) or his Agent may give written notice to you that, unless the default is remedied within 30 days from the date of the notice, this compulsory license will be automatically terminated. Such termination shall render either the making or the distribution, or both, of all phonorecords for which royalties have not been paid, actionable as acts of infringement under, and fully subject to the remedies provided by, the Copyright Act;

5. You need not serve or file the notice of intention to obtain a compulsory license required by the Copyright Act....

Additional provisions:

The authority hereunder is limited to the manufacture and distribution of phonorecords solely in the United States, its territories and possessions and not elsewhere.

Credit: In regard to all phonorecords manufactured, distributed and/or sold hereunder, you shall include in the label copy of all such phonorecords, or on the permanent containers of all such phonorecords, printed writer/publisher credit in the form of the names of the writer(s) and the publisher(s) of the copyrighted work.

QUESTION

Identify the differences between the "Harry Fox license" and the strict terms of § 115 of the Copyright Act.

b. Sound Recordings Under § 114

The student must constantly be mindful of the distinction between a recorded composition (usually musical) and the recorded performance of such composition. It is the latter — called a "sound recording" — that is the subject of a set of specialized provisions in the 1976 Act, e.g., § 402 (notice), § 407 (deposit). Before noting the specific limitations on the exclusive rights in such works, we should recall their history. *See Goldstein v. California*, 412 U.S. 546, 178 U.S.P.Q. 129 (1973).

Until 1971, recorded performances were protected by state law, if they were protected at all. *See Capitol Records, Inc. v. Mercury Records Corp.*, 221 F.2d 657, 105 U.S.P.Q. 163 (2d Cir. 1955). It was such protection that was preserved by *Goldstein*. In 1971, Pub. L. 92-140 offered federal protection for the first time to sound recordings provided that they were "fixed" between February 15, 1972, and December 31, 1974. The latter deadline was later removed, Pub. L. 93-573, 88 Stat. 1873. The 1976 statute carries forward protection of these sound recordings under generally similar limitations.

Section 114 expressly limits the rights of the owner in such works to protection against recordings "that directly or indirectly recapture the actual sounds fixed in the [protected] recording." The provision does not prevent a recording "that consists entirely of an independent fixation of other sounds, even though such sounds imitate or simulate those in the copyrighted sound recording." Thus imitation through an independent recording is permitted, but capturing the fixed sounds by re-recording — even with some technical changes — can still amount to infringement.

A second limitation upon the rights of the copyright owner in a sound recording is the absence of a performance right, i.e., the right to control or be compensated for broadcast or other public performance of a genuine sound recording. Examine carefully the language of §§ 106 and 114 that makes it clear there is no public performance right in sound recordings. The 1976 Act expressly deferred resolving this issue and the debate surrounding it continues to be lively and is explored in greater detail *infra* at Chapter 6, Subchapter D5c.

A recent development, called sound sampling, has brought new attention to the scope of protection afforded by § 114. Sound sampling involves the exact duplication of portions (often very small portions, for example, a few beats of music played on a saxophone) of a sound recording for inclusion with other similarly acquired sounds into a new sound recording, or in a live performance. The resulting effect can be like an aural collage. Another form of sound sampling involves the reproduction through digital recording of small portions of a sound recording, followed by their analysis and reconstruction by computer. The computer synthesizer can extrapolate full musical or percussive lines from just a few sounds.

Although sound sampling techniques may subsequently alter the quality of the sounds recorded, this alone should not excuse the sound sampler from any copyright liability that would otherwise exist. Section 114 affords the sound recording copyright holder exclusive rights both over exact reproductions and over works "in which the actual sounds fixed are rearranged, remixed, or otherwise altered in sequence or quality." Moreover, although § 114 exempts from liability recordings which merely imitate, but do not actually reproduce, the sounds of an original sound recording — and thus generally makes the sound recording copyright weaker than copyrights for most other kinds of copyrighted works — the wording of that exemption may in fact favor sound recording copyright holders against sound samplers. Section 114(b) shelters "another sound recording that consists *entirely* of an independent fixation of other sounds" (emphasis supplied); it should follow that another sound recording which combines independently generated sounds with even a few reproduced sounds cannot enjoy the § 114 (b) exemption, and may be an infringement of the sound recording copyright. Of course, digital-sampling litigation — particularly when what is sampled is arguably *de minimis* — will likely raise such questions as whether the plaintiff has contributed original authorship and whether the defendant has made a fair use. One court has held that the repetition of three sampled words and their accompanying music constituted qualitatively significant copying and, therefore, infringement. *See Grand Upright Music Ltd. v. Warner Bros. Records, Inc.,* 780 F. Supp. 182 (S.D.N.Y. 1991) (sampling the phrase and tune "Alone Again, Naturally" as performed by Gilbert O'Sullivan.). *See generally* Bruce McGiverin, Note, *Digital Sound Sampling, Copyright and Publicity: Protecting Against the Electronic Appropriation of Sounds,* 87 Colum. L. Rev. 1723 (1987); James P. Allen, *Look What They've Done to My Song Ma — Digital Sampling in the '90s: A Legal Challenge for the Music Industry,* 9 U. Miami Ent. & Sports L. Rev. 179 (1992).

QUESTIONS

1. Articulate as precisely as you can what elements of authorship comprise a sound recording, and how they differ from the works (literary or musical) that are inscribed in the sound recording. Who contributes any such authorship?

2. Is a sound recording a "writing" subject to protection by Congress under the copyright clause of the Constitution? Is there an "author" of a sound recording, for purposes of the Constitution? Who is the owner of copyright in a sound recording? (This will determine such matters as whose name is placed in the notice of copyright. Review the appropriate sections of the Act.)

THE AUDIO HOME RECORDING ACT OF 1992

For the first time in U.S. copyright law, Congress in October 1992 enacted legislation specifically addressing the problem of private copying. The legislation is limited in scope, but may afford a first step toward broader regulation of unauthorized reproductions of copyrighted works by individuals for their private enjoyment. The legislation was spurred by the development of a new private copying medium, digital audiotape, whose superior recording capabilities prompted songwriters and sound-recording producers to fear that private copies would substantially displace sales of authorized recordings. Unlike analog tape, digital tape permits an apparently infinite number of "generations" of copies (copies from copies from copies), without loss of sound quality from copy to copy.

The legislation both adapts copyright law and imposes a "technological fix." It contains three main features: First, it expressly prohibits infringement actions for home audiotaping, whether digital or analog. Second, in return, it imposes royalty charges upon sales of digital audiotape recorders and recording media (i.e., blank tapes), to be paid by manufacturers and importers. (Note that there is no such surcharge on analog recording equipment or media.) Those royalties are then to be divided between two "Funds." One-third of the sums collected are marked for the "Musical Works Fund," for the benefit of "writers" (composers and lyricists) and music publishers; the remaining two-thirds for the "Sound Recordings Fund," for record producers and performers. Royalties in the Musical Works Fund are divided evenly between writers and publishers. Within the Sound Recordings Fund, an initial 4% of the revenues will go to nonfeatured musicians and vocalists; the remaining sums will be divided 40% to featured performers and 60% to record producers. The beneficiaries of the Funds receive the royalties not only for digital recordings, but for analog recordings as well.

Third, the law obliges manufacturers and importers to include in all consumer digital audiotape machines a "serial copy management system" (SCMS) that would disable the machines from recording a copy from a prior copy (but would permit unlimited "first generation" recordings from the original recorded source). The law also prohibits selling devices or offering services to override the SCMS.

The international implications of this change in our law are particularly worth noting. More than a dozen other nations already provide royalty systems for home recording, but by treating these systems as outside of the sphere of copyright — and thus not subject to the "national treatment" requirements of the Berne Convention — a number of those nations deny a share of such royalties to United States "authors" of songs and recordings. These nations invoke a "reciprocity" standard, and do for U.S. claimants only what the U.S. does for foreign claimants (i.e., before enactment of the audio home recording law, nothing). The Audio Home Recording Act is also formally outside the sphere of copyright, but the coverage of foreign claimants is in fact broader than the protection afforded under § 104 of the 1976 Copyright Act. (For a fuller discussion of § 104, see Chapter 10, *infra*.) While the Copyright Act protects foreign authors if they are the nationals of, or reside in, a country with which the U.S. has a copyright treaty, or if the work was first published in such a country, the Audio Home Recording Act provides for distribution of royalties to authors, performers and producers whose recordings are distributed in the U.S. No further point of attachment with the U.S. need be proved. Introduction here of a royalty system for home recording, accessible to foreign authors, performers and producers, may therefore give the United States the leverage to secure similar benefits for interested U.S. parties abroad.

B. THE RIGHT TO PREPARE DERIVATIVE WORKS UNDER § 106(2)

§ 106. Exclusive rights in copyrighted works

Subject to sections 107 through 118, the owner of copyright under this title has the exclusive rights to do and to authorize any of the following:

....

(2) to prepare derivative works based upon the copyrighted work: ....

HOUSE REPORT

H.R. Rep. No. 94-1476, 94th Cong., 2d Sess. 62 (1976)

Preparation of derivative works. — The exclusive right to prepare derivative works, specified separately in clause (2) of section 106, overlaps the exclusive right of reproduction to some extent. It is broader than that right, however, in the sense that reproduction requires fixation in copies or phonorecords, whereas the preparation of a derivative work, such as a ballet, pantomime, or improvised performance, may be an infringement even though nothing is ever fixed in tangible form.

To be an infringement the "derivative work" must be "based upon the copyrighted work," and the definition in section 101 refers to "a translation, musical arrangement, dramatization, fictionalization, motion picture version, sound recording, art reproduction, abridgment, condensation, or any other form in which a work may be recast, transformed, or adapted." Thus, to constitute a violation of section 106(2), the infringing work must incorporate a portion of the copyrighted work in some form; for example, a detailed commentary on a work or a programmatic musical composition inspired by a novel would not normally constitute infringements under this clause.

CHAFEE, REFLECTIONS ON COPYRIGHT LAW, 45 Columbia Law Review 503, 511 (1945)

The protection given the copyright-owner should not stifle independent creation by others. Nobody else should *market* the author's book, but we refuse to say nobody else should *use* it. The world goes ahead because each of us builds on the work of our predecessors. "A dwarf standing on the shoulders of a giant can see farther than the giant himself." Progress would be stifled if the author had a complete monopoly of everything in his book for fifty-six years or any other long period. Some use of its contents must be permitted in connection with the independent creation of other authors. The very policy which leads the law to encourage his creativeness also justifies it in facilitating the creativeness of others.

In the late eighteenth century, this ideal of the encouragement of independent creation was pushed so far as to allow translations and abridgments without the author's consent, on the ground that the new man had put in a great deal of his own work. Thus Lord Apsley, backed by Blackstone, gave immunity to an abridgment of Hawksworth's *Voyages,* calling it "a new and meritorious work," less expensive and more convenient to handle than the original; he said it could be read in a quarter of the time with all the substance preserved in language as good as Hawksworth's or better and in a more agreeable and useful manner.[16] This sort of reasoning made Dr. Johnson's blood boil. During the *Tour to the Hebrides,* Boswell mentioned Lord Monboddo's opinion, that if a man could get a work by heart, he might print it, as by such an act "the mind is exercised."

> Johnson: "No, sir, a man's repeating it no more makes it his property than a man may sell a cow which he drives home."
> I said printing an abridgment of a work was allowed, which was only cutting the horns and tail off the cow.
> Johnson: "No, sir, 'tis making the cow have a calf."

---

[16]*Anon.*, Loffit 775, 98 Eng. Rep. 913 (Ch. 1774). See also *Dodsley v. Kennersley,* Amb. 403, 27 Eng. Rep. 270 (Ch. 1761), refusing to enjoin abridgment of Johnson's *Rasselas;* this case may have influenced the Doctor's opinion of the iniquity of unauthorized abridgments.

Certainly this "exercise of the mind" test will not hold water. The author should not lose a large portion of his market so easily. Fortunately, our copyright law has abandoned its early tolerance of unauthorized abridgments and translations. They are ways for the author to reach the public and properly belong to him, as the 1909 Act expressly recognizes.[17]

Even when there is access, the precise boundaries of this defensive ideal of independent creation are hard to fix. Everybody agrees that the ideas in the copyrighted book are not protected. Another physicist can read Einstein's book and write about relativity. But he must not tell about it in Einstein's words. Should protection be limited to the precise words? If so, a translation, which uses entirely different words, would not infringe. Yet, if we protect more than precise words, where shall we stop? The line is sometimes drawn between an idea and its expression. This does not solve the problem, because "expression" has too wide a range. To some extent, the expression of an abstract idea should be free for use by others. No doubt, the line does lie somewhere between the author's idea and the precise form in which he wrote it down. I like to say that the protection covers the "pattern" of the work. This is not a solution, but I find it helpful as an imaginative description of what should not be imitated. For example, the idea of an Irish-Jewish marriage in a play may be borrowed. With this theme, some resemblance in characters and situations is inevitable, but the line of infringement may not yet be crossed. On the other hand, the pattern of the play — the sequence of events and the development of the interplay of the characters — must not be followed scene by scene. Such a correspondence of pattern would be an infringement although every word of the spoken dialogue was changed.

Even the first user of a plot or a human situation should not have a monopoly of it. The public should have the opportunity to see what other artists will do with the same plot or situation, after the fashion set by the Greek tragedians. Yet we want to encourage originality and not slavishness. There comes a point where the use of material is so close as not to give the public anything really new. At that point, the ideal of encouraging independent creation ceases to operate.

Mirage Editions, Inc. v. Albuquerque A.R.T. Co., 856 F.2d 1341 (9th Cir. 1988), *cert. denied,* 489 U.S. 1018 (1989). Mirage is the exclusive publisher of the graphic works of the late artist Patrick Nagel. Mirage and Nagel's widow own the copyright in his works, and have licensed the publication of a commemorative book compiling selected copyrighted individual Nagel art works. The defendant purchased copies of the book, cut out selected pages containing art prints, glued each print onto a black plastic material to provide a border, glued this product onto a rectangular white ceramic tile, and applied a transparent plastic film over the tile surface; the defendant then sold the tile, with artwork mounted thereon, to the public. The trial court

---

[17] 35 Stat. 1075 (1909), 17 U.S.C. § (b) (1940): "the exclusive right ... To translate ..., or make any other version thereof, if it be a literary work...." This last clause seems to comprise abridgments. The law before 1909 took the view condemned by Dr. Johnson. See 2 Ladas, § 368(5). The British law as to abridgments is also probably changed by the Act of 1911 ....

granted the plaintiff's motion for summary judgment of copyright infringement, and enjoined the removal, mounting and selling of the plaintiff's artwork. The court of appeals affirmed.

The court held that the defendant had prepared an infringing derivative work. It stated: "What appellant has clearly done here is to make another version of Nagel's art works ... and that amounts to preparation of a derivative work." Although the defendant argued that its product was not an "art reproduction" within the definition of "derivative work" in § 101, the court noted that the defendant "has ignored the disjunctive phrase 'or any other form in which a work may be recast, transformed or adapted.'" This language, said the court, "seems to encompass other alternatives besides simple art reproduction. By removing the individual images from the book and placing them on the tiles, perhaps the appellant has not accomplished reproduction. We conclude, though, that appellant has certainly recast or transformed the individual images by incorporating them into its tile-preparing process."

The court rejected the defendant's argument that as a lawful purchaser of the book, it could lawfully clip the pages and sell them to another, under the "first sale" doctrine incorporated in § 109(a) of the Copyright Act [to be discussed *infra* in this casebook]. The court held that the right of a purchaser to resell a work did not include the right also to prepare derivative works based on it.

[The Albuquerque Company tried again, by purchasing notecards bearing reproductions of artworks by Alaskan artist Rie Munoz, and then pasting them onto tiles in the same manner as in the *Mirage* case. The suit by Munoz was successful, with the Alaska federal district court holding the case governed squarely by the *Mirage* decision in its circuit. See *Munoz v. Albuquerque A.R.T. Co.*, 1993 WL 293804 (D. Alaska 1993).]

National Geographic Society v. Classified Geographic, Inc., 27 F. Supp. 655 (D. Mass. 1939). The well-known plaintiff, a nonprofit organization devoted to gathering and disseminating geographic knowledge, publishes the National Geographic Magazine. It also publishes books, such as "The Book of Birds," "The Book of Fishes," and "Horses of the World"; these books are formed by selecting and compiling articles published in the magazine. The defendant is in the business of arranging and compiling articles from the National Geographic Magazine (without the plaintiff's consent) and selling them in book form to the public; its books cover such topics as Birds, Fish, Domestic Animals, and Insects. The defendant does not reprint any of the plaintiff's copyrighted articles but obtains all of its material by purchasing copies of the National Geographic Magazine, tearing the magazines apart, bringing together articles of related subject matter, binding them in a substantial backing, and offering them for sale as original compilations of National Geographic articles.

The court held the defendant's activities to constitute copyright infringement. It began by holding that the defendant had violated the right to "publish" the plaintiff's articles, as provided under the 1909 Act, and held that this right to offer the work to the public by sale or distribution of copies should not necessarily be limited to the first publication, in light of other provisions of the act. The court went on to point out that the statute also gave the plaintiff the exclusive right to compile, adapt or arrange its copyrighted articles, and held that the defendant's use of lawfully purchased National Geographic Magazines constituted an unlawful compilation, adaptation or arrangement. Although the defendant was the owner of the physical material on which the copyrighted works were printed, it was not the owner of the right to make these kinds of unauthorized uses. The court distinguished cases holding that the purchaser of a second-hand book could, without the consent of the copyright owner, place it within a new cover and binding.

QUESTIONS

1. Is the court's decision in the *Mirage* case convincing? Consider a person who clips artwork from public domain books and magazines, affixes them to tiles and coats the tiles with a transparent surface — and then submits them to the Copyright Office for registration as derivative works. Should the Copyright Office find this to be a copyrightable derivative work? Consider both whether there is "original authorship" and whether the submitted work is a "derivative work" as defined in § 101. If the "tile art" fails to satisfy one or the other definition, then can comparable unauthorized use of copyrighted art work be an infringing derivative work under § 106(2)?

2. If an art collector purchases a copyrighted painting, can she freely place it within a frame of her own choosing without violating the Copyright Act? Are you infringing the copyright in this casebook by writing extensive notes in the margins and underlining the text?

3. Is the court's decision in the *National Geographic* case convincing? If the defendant there had purchased and then resold the back issues separately, or resold individual torn-out articles, presumably that would not have infringed the copyright (by virtue of the "first sale" doctrine soon to be discussed). Precisely what different economic interest of the plaintiff is implicated by the conduct in which the defendant actually engaged, and should that interest be protected by copyright?

4. The defendant in *National Geographic* was held to have engaged in the unauthorized act of "compiling" the plaintiff's articles. Is there a "compilation" right granted by § 106(2) of the Copyright Act?

HORGAN v. MACMILLAN, INC.

789 F.2d 157 (2d Cir. 1986)

[The plaintiff is executrix of the estate of George Balanchine, a giant in the field of twentieth-century choreography, who died in April 1983. Balanchine co-founded the New York City Ballet in 1948, and was its director, ballet master and chief choreographer. In 1954, he choreographed his version of the ballet, The Nutcracker, set to music by Tchaikovsky; the ballet is an adaptation of a nineteenth century folk tale and an earlier choreographic version by the Russian Ivanov. The "Balanchine Nutcracker" has been performed to great popular acclaim by the New York City Ballet Company and other ballet companies throughout the world; royalties were paid to Balanchine for these performances. The defendants in this action are the publisher Macmillan, two photographers, and an author (Switzer); all collaborated on a book titled "The Nutcracker: A Story and a Ballet." The book tells of the origins of The Nutcracker as a story and as a ballet, and devotes most of its pages to what is labeled "The Balanchine Ballet." It contains sixty color photographs of scenes from the Company's production of The Nutcracker, following the sequence of the ballet's story and dances; a text is interspersed providing the story including those portions not portrayed visually. The defendants were authorized by the New York City Ballet to create and publish the book. No consent, however, was secured from the Balanchine estate, which brought this action for copyright infringement, seeking preliminary and permanent injunctive relief.

From Switzer, The Nutcracker: A Story
and a Ballet (1985)

[The district judge ruled against the Balanchine estate. He found no infringement of the ballet because "choreography has to do with the flow of the steps in a ballet. The still photographs in the Nutcracker book, numerous though they are, catch dancers in various attitudes at specific instants of time; they do not, nor do they intend to, take or use the underlying choreography. The staged performance could not be recreated from them." The court drew an analogy to the inability to recreate a Beethoven symphony from a document containing only every twenty-fifth chord of the symphony.

[The court of appeals reversed and remanded. It reiterated the plaintiff's claim that the book was either a "copy" of the Balanchine choreographic work or a derivative work based thereon; and that in either case the test was whether there was "substantial similarity" and not whether the ballet could be reconstructed from the plaintiff's book. The defendants argued that the book could not possibly be substantially similar to the ballet because the essence of choreography is movement, which cannot be reproduced from pictures capturing only a fraction of an instant in time. Noting that this was a case of first impression, the court of appeals agreed with the plaintiff. The central part of its discussion follows.]

[T]he standard for determining copyright infringement is not whether the original could be recreated from the allegedly infringing copy, but whether the latter is "substantially similar" to the former. *Novelty Textile Mills, Inc. v. Joan Fabrics Corp.*, 558 F.2d 1090, 1092-93 (2d Cir. 1977); *Ideal Toy, supra,* 360 F.2d at 1022; *Peter Pan Fabrics, Inc. v. Martin Weiner Corp.*, 274 F.2d 487 (2d Cir. 1960). The test, as stated by Judge Learned Hand in *Peter Pan,* is whether "the ordinary observer, unless he set out to detect the disparities, would be disposed to overlook them, and regard their aesthetic appeal as the same." *Id.* at 489.

When the allegedly infringing material is in a different medium, as it is here, recreation of the original from the infringing material is unlikely if not impossible, but that is not a defense to infringement. See, e.g., *King Features Syndicate v. Fleischer,* 299 F. 533, 535 (2d Cir. 1924) (cartoon character infringed by toy doll); *Filmvideo Releasing Corp. v. Hastings,* 509 F. Supp. 60, 63-65, *aff'd in part, rev'd in part,* 668 F.2d 91 (2d Cir. 1981) (books infringed by movies). It surely would not be a defense to an infringement claim against the movie version of "Gone With The Wind" that a viewer of the movie could not recreate the book. Even a small amount of the original, if it is qualitatively significant, may be sufficient to be an infringement, although the full original could not be recreated from the excerpt. See, e.g., *Roy Export Co. Establishment v. Columbia Broadcasting System, Inc.,* 503 F. Supp. 1137, 1145 (S.D.N.Y. 1980), *aff'd,* 672 F.2d 1095 (2d Cir.), *cert. denied,* 459 U.S. 826, 103 S. Ct. 60, 74 L. Ed. 2d 63 (1982), and *Elsmere Music, Inc. v. National Broadcasting Co.,* 482 F. Supp. 741, 744 (S.D.N.Y.), aff'd, 623 F.2d 252 (2d Cir. 1980). In the former case, short film clips used in a film memorial to Charlie Chaplin were held to infringe full length films. In the latter, the use of four notes from a musical composition containing one hundred measures was held sufficient to infringe the copyrighted original.

Moreover, the district judge took a far too limited view of the extent to which choreographic material may be conveyed in the medium of still photography. A snapshot of a single moment in a dance sequence may communicate a great deal. It may, for example, capture a gesture, the composition of dancers' bodies or the placement of dancers on the stage. Such freezing of a choreographic moment is shown in a number of the photographs in the Switzer book, e.g., at pp. 30, 38, 42, 66-67, 68, 69, 74, 75, 78, 80, and 81. A photograph may also convey to the viewer's imagination the moments before and after the split second recorded. On page 76-77 of the Switzer book, for example, there is a two-page photograph of the "Sugar Canes," one of the troupes that perform in The Nutcracker. In this photograph, the Sugar Canes are a foot or more off the ground, holding large hoops above their heads. One member of the ensemble is jumping through a hoop, which is held extended in front of the dancer. The dancer's legs are thrust forward, parallel to the stage and several feet off the ground. The viewer understands instinctively, based simply on the laws of gravity, that the Sugar Canes jumped up from the floor only a moment earlier, and came down shortly after the photographed moment. An ordinary observer, who had only recently seen a performance of The Nutcracker, could probably perceive even more from this photograph. The single instant thus communicates far more than a single chord of a Beethoven symphony — the analogy suggested by the district judge.

It may be that all of the photographs mentioned above are of insufficient quantity or sequencing to constitute infringement; it may also be that they do copy but also are protected as fair use. But that is not what the district judge said in denying a preliminary injunction. The judge erroneously held that still photographs cannot infringe choreography. Since the judge applied the wrong test in evaluating appellant's likelihood of success on the preliminary injunction, we believe that a remand is appropriate....

Lewis Galoob Toys, Inc. v. Nintendo of America, Inc., 964 F.2d 965 (9th Cir. 1992), *cert. denied,* 113 S. Ct. 1582, 123 L. Ed. 2d 149 (1993). This controversy concerned the "Game Genie," a videogame "enhancer" — a computer program that, when used in conjunction with a Nintendo home video system and game cartridge, enables the player to alter up to three features of the game. For example, the Game Genie allows the player to increase the number of lives of the player's character, increase the speed at which the character moves, and allow the character to float above obstacles. The player controls the changes made by the Game Genie by entering codes provided by the Game Genie Programming Manual and Code Book. The Game Genie does not alter the data stored in the game cartridge. The Ninth Circuit rejected Nintendo's assertion that implementing these variations created unauthorized derivative works:

> A derivative work must have "form" or permanence.... The examples of derivative works provided by the Act all physically incorporate the underlying work or works. The Act's legislative history similarly indicates that "the infringing work must incorporate a portion of the copyrighted work in some form."
>
> The district court's finding that no independent work is created is supported by the record. The Game Genie merely enhances the audiovisual displays that originate in Nintendo game cartridges. The altered displays do not incorporate a portion of a copyrighted work in some form. Nintendo argues that the Game Genie's displays are as fixed in the hardware and software used to create them as Nintendo's original displays. Nintendo's argument ignores the fact that the Game Genie cannot produce an audiovisual display; the underlying display must be produced by a Nintendo Entertainment System and game cartridge. The Game Genie's display has no form. It cannot be a derivative work.
>
> Nintendo asserted at oral argument that the existence of a $150 million market for the Game Genie indicates that its audiovisual display must be fixed. We understand Nintendo's argument; consumers clearly would not purchase the Game Genie if its display was not "sufficiently permanent or stable to permit it to be perceived ... for a period of more than transitory

duration." 17 U.S.C. § 101. But, Nintendo's reliance on the Act's definition of "fixed" is misplaced. Nintendo's argument also proves too much; the existence of a market does not, and cannot, determine conclusively whether a work is an infringing derivative work. For example, although there is a market for kaleidoscopes, it does not necessarily follow that kaleidoscopes create unlawful derivative works when pointed at protected artwork. The same can be said of countless other products that enhance, but do not replace, copyrighted works.

Nintendo relies heavily on *Midway Mfg. Co. v. Artic Int'l, Inc.,* 704 F.2d 1009 (7th Cir.), *cert. denied,* 464 U.S. 823 (1983). *Midway* can be distinguished. The defendant in *Midway,* Artic International, marketed a computer chip that could be inserted in Galaxian video games to speed up the rate of play. The Seventh Circuit held that the speeded-up version of Galaxian was a derivative work. Artic's chip substantially copied and replaced the chip that was originally distributed by Midway. Purchasers of Artic's chip also benefitted economically by offering the altered game for use by the general public. The court acknowledged that the Copyright Act's definition of "derivative work" "must be stretched to accommodate speeded-up video games." Stretching that definition further would chill innovation and fail to protect "society's competing interest in the free flow of ideas, information, and commerce." *Sony Corp. of America v. Universal Studios, Inc.,* 464 U.S. 417, 429 (1984).

In holding that the audiovisual displays created by the Game Genie are not derivative works, we recognize that technology often advances by improvement rather than replacement. Some time ago, for example, computer companies began marketing spell-checkers that operate within existing word processors by signalling the writer when a word is misspelled. These applications, as well as countless others, could not be produced and marketed if courts were to conclude that the audiovisual display of a word processor and spell-checker combination is a derivative work based on the display of the word processor alone. The Game Genie is useless by itself; it can only enhance, and cannot duplicate, a Nintendo game's output. Such innovations rarely will constitute derivative works under the Copyright Act.

QUESTIONS

1. Are the following uses of a copyrighted work an infringement? If so, under what subsection of the 1976 Act?

(a) *X* secures a copy of the copyrighted motion picture film of the assassination of President Kennedy, taken at the scene by Abraham Zapruder, and makes a direct copy of the film.

(b) *X,* a few feet away from Mr. Zapruder at the time of the assassination, films exactly the same sequence of events with his own motion picture camera.

(c) *X* re-poses Oscar Wilde to match the Sarony photograph and takes his own still photograph, this one in color. (Assume for the purpose of the example that Wilde is alive and that the Sarony photograph is still in copyright.)

(d) *X*, seeing an attractive copyrighted photograph of the Golden Gate Bridge at sunset, positions himself at the same location and time and takes his own still photograph.

(e) An artist paints a cubistic version of the (copyrighted) Sarony photograph of Oscar Wilde.

(f) The defendant in the *Catalda* case reproduces the plaintiff's mezzotint engraving, but leaves out the deviations from the old master caused by the plaintiff's muscular tremor and poor eyesight.

(g) A sculptor makes a three-dimensional version of a copyrighted painting.

(h) A scholar makes a French translation of a copyrighted English-language novel.

(i) A novelist sees a copyrighted silent motion picture and writes a novel recounting all of the incidents in the film (and, obviously, supplying original dialogue).

(j) A journalist writing for a competing news weekly takes a news story from *Time* magazine and rewrites it for publication in his own words.

(k) An artist creates unauthorized illustrations for a book, giving visual form to, while closely following, the meticulous verbal descriptions of the characters and scenery.

(l) A writer creates a detailed verbal description of a painting.

2. Assume that a highly regarded teacher of high school physics prepares a book with text and problems which quickly becomes the bestselling work in the field. Another teacher publishes a pamphlet advertised as a book of solutions to the problems in the copyrighted text. In the pamphlet, the problems are not copied; the solutions consist of arithmetic equations, which show how the problem should be solved (utilizing, of course, the numbers used in the copyrighted textbook problems), and they are accompanied where possible with diagrams (also utilizing the same numbers). Do the solutions infringe the copyright on the problem book? *See Addison-Wesley Pub'g Co. v. Brown,* 223 F. Supp. 219 (E.D.N.Y. 1963).

3. Plaintiff Worlds of Wonder, Inc. manufactures the Teddy Ruxpin doll. The doll, shaped like a bear, has inside it a tape-playing mechanism attached to certain motors in the doll's eyes, nose and mouth. Audiotapes manufactured by W.O.W. and sold with Teddy have two tracks, one with sound and the other with digital information transmitted to the motors that move Teddy's face so that its movements are synchronized with the stories and songs emanating from the tape. The tape communicates a high-pitched male voice purporting to be that of Teddy Ruxpin. The doll has been enormously successful and in its first year has topped 1.5 million sales, or $93 million.

Defendant Veritel manufactures audiotapes for the exclusive purpose of utilization of the innards of Teddy Ruxpin. On the audio track, a high-pitched male voice tells stories (based on fairy tales) altogether different from those told on the W.O.W. tapes. Electromechanical impulses from the other track activate the Teddy Ruxpin bear in the same manner as do the W.O.W. tapes. When the Veritel tapes are inserted, Teddy's voice and movements are very much the same as when the W.O.W. tapes are used.

W.O.W. has placed proper copyright notice on its Teddy Ruxpin dolls and has registered them in the Copyright Office. (What category of work in § 102 is appropriate?) It has sued to enjoin Veritel from marketing tapes as described above. Who should prevail? *See Worlds of Wonder, Inc. v. Vector Intercontinental, Inc.*, 653 F. Supp. 135 (N.D. Ohio 1986); *Worlds of Wonder, Inc. v. Veritel Learning Sys.*, 658 F. Supp. 351 (N.D. Tex. 1986).

GILLIAM v. AMERICAN BROADCASTING COS.

538 F.2d 14 (2d Cir. 1976)

LUMBARD, CIRCUIT JUDGE: Plaintiffs, a group of British writers and performers known as "Monty Python," appeal from a denial by Judge Lasker in the Southern District of a preliminary injunction to restrain the American Broadcasting Company (ABC) from broadcasting edited versions of three separate programs originally written and performed by Monty Python for broadcast by the British Broadcasting Corporation (BBC). We agree with Judge Lasker that the appellants have demonstrated that the excising done for ABC impairs the integrity of the original work. We further find that the countervailing injuries that Judge Lasker found might have accrued to ABC as a result of an injunction at a prior date no longer exist. We therefore direct the issuance of a preliminary injunction by the district court.

Since its formation in 1969, the Monty Python group has gained popularity primarily through its thirty-minute television programs created for BBC as part of a comedy series entitled "Monty Python's Flying Circus." In accordance with an agreement between Monty Python and BBC, the group writes and delivers to BBC scripts for use in the television series. This scriptwriters' agreement recites in great detail the procedure to be followed when any alterations are to be made in the script prior to recording of the program. The essence of this section of the agreement is that, while BBC retains final authority to make changes, appellants or their representatives exercise optimum control over the scripts consistent with BBC's authority and only minor changes may be made without prior consultation with the writers. Nothing in the scriptwriters' agreement entitles BBC to alter a program once it has been recorded. The agreement further provides that, subject to the terms therein, the group retains all rights in the script.

Under the agreement, BBC may license the transmission of recordings of the television programs in any overseas territory. The series has been broadcast in this country primarily on non-commercial public broadcasting television stations, although several of the programs have been broadcast on commercial stations in Texas and Nevada. In each instance, the thirty-minute programs have been broadcast as originally recorded and broadcast in England in their entirety and without commercial interruption.

In October 1973, Time-Life Films acquired the right to distribute in the United States certain BBC television programs, including the Monty Python series. Time-Life was permitted to edit the programs only "for insertion of commercials, applicable censorship or governmental ... rules and regulations, and National Association of Broadcasters and time segment requirements." No similar clause was included in the scriptwriters' agreement between appellants and BBC. Prior to this time, ABC had sought to acquire the right to broadcast excerpts from various Monty Python programs in the spring of

1975, but the group rejected the proposal for such a disjointed format. Thereafter, in July 1975, ABC agreed with Time-Life to broadcast two ninety-minute specials each comprising three thirty-minute Monty Python programs that had not previously been shown in this country.

Correspondence between representatives of BBC and Monty Python reveals that these parties assumed that ABC would broadcast each of the Monty Python programs "in its entirety." On September 5, 1975, however, the group's British representative inquired of BBC how ABC planned to show the programs in their entirety if approximately 24 minutes of each 90 minute program were to be devoted to commercials. BBC replied on September 12, "we can only reassure you that ABC have decided to run the programmes 'back to back,' and that there is a firm undertaking not to segment them."

ABC broadcast the first of the specials on October 3, 1975. Appellants did not see a tape of the program until late November and were allegedly "appalled" at the discontinuity and "mutilation" that had resulted from the editing done by Time-Life for ABC. Twenty-four minutes of the original 90 minutes of recording had been omitted. Some of the editing had been done in order to make time for commercials; other material had been edited, according to ABC, because the original programs contained offensive or obscene matter.

In early December, Monty Python learned that ABC planned to broadcast the second special on December 26, 1975. [On December 15, the group filed this action for an injunction and damages. Although the district judge found that the damage caused to the plaintiffs by the "impairment of the integrity of their work" was irreparable, he declined to issue a preliminary injunction, in part because of the financial loss ABC would suffer by the cancellation of a program scheduled for a week later and Monty Python's "casualness" in pursuing the litigation.]...

Judge Lasker granted Monty Python's request for more limited relief by requiring ABC to broadcast a disclaimer during the December 26 special to the effect that the group dissociated itself from the program because of the editing. A panel of this court, however, granted a stay of that order until this appeal could be heard and permitted ABC to broadcast, at the beginning of the special, only the legend that the program had been edited by ABC. We heard argument on April 13 and, at that time, enjoined ABC from any further broadcast of edited Monty Python programs pending the decision of the court.

I

[The court concluded that the denial of injunctive relief would likely seriously injure the reputation of the plaintiffs, and that the grant of such relief against future ABC broadcasts (there having been no scheduling or advertising of such) would not harm defendant's relations with its affiliates or with the public.]

We then reach the question whether there is a likelihood that appellants will succeed on the merits. In concluding that there is a likelihood of infringement here, we rely especially on the fact that the editing was substantial, i.e., approximately 27 per cent of the original program was omitted, and the editing contravened contractual provisions that limited the right to edit Monty

Python material. It should be emphasized that our discussion of these matters refers only to such facts as have been developed upon the hearing for a preliminary injunction. Modified or contrary findings may become appropriate after a plenary trial.

Judge Lasker denied the preliminary injunction in part because he was unsure of the ownership of the copyright in the recorded program. Appellants first contend that the question of ownership is irrelevant because the recorded program was merely a derivative work taken from the script in which they hold the uncontested copyright. Thus, even if BBC owned the copyright in the recorded program, its use of that work would be limited by the license granted to BBC by Monty Python for use of the underlying script. We agree. [The court of appeals found the television program to be a "dramatization" (a term used in the 1909 Copyright Act) of the script, and thus independently copyrightable to the extent of its newly added material; but also held that this did not affect the force or validity of the copyright in the underlying script.]... Thus, any ownership by BBC of the copyright in the recorded program would not affect the scope or ownership of the copyright in the underlying script.

Since the copyright in the underlying script survives intact despite the incorporation of that work into a derivative work, one who uses the script, even with the permission of the proprietor of the derivative work, may infringe the underlying copyright. See *Davis v. E. I. DuPont deNemours & Co.*, 240 F. Supp. 612 (S.D.N.Y. 1965) (defendants held to have infringed when they obtained permission to use a screenplay in preparing a television script but did not obtain permission of the author of the play upon which the screenplay was based).

....

One who obtains permission to use a copyrighted script in the production of a derivative work ... may not exceed the specific purpose for which permission was granted. Most of the decisions that have reached this conclusion have dealt with the improper extension of the underlying work into media or time, i.e., duration of the license, not covered by the grant of permission to the derivative work proprietor. See *Bartsch v. Metro-Goldwyn-Mayer, Inc.*, 391 F.2d 150 (2d Cir.), *cert. denied*, 393 U.S. 826 (1968); *G. Ricordi & Co. v. Paramount Pictures Inc.*, 189 F.2d 469 (2d Cir.), *cert. denied*, 342 U.S. 849 (1951). Cf. *Rice v. American Program Bureau*, 446 F.2d 685 (2d Cir. 1971). Appellants herein do not claim that the broadcast by ABC violated media or time restrictions contained in the license of the script to BBC. Rather, they claim that revisions in the script, and ultimately in the program, could be made only after consultation with Monty Python, and that ABC's broadcast of a program edited after recording and without consultation with Monty Python exceeded the scope of any license that BBC was entitled to grant.

The rationale for finding infringement when a licensee exceeds time or media restrictions on his license — the need to allow the proprietor of the underlying copyright to control the method in which his work is presented to the public — applies equally to the situation in which a licensee makes an unauthorized use of the underlying work by publishing it in a truncated version. Whether intended to allow greater economic exploitation of the work, as in the media and time cases, or to ensure that the copyright proprietor retains a veto power over revisions desired for the derivative work, the ability of the copyright holder to control his work remains paramount in our copyright law. We find, therefore, that unauthorized editing of the underlying work, if proven, would constitute an infringement of the copyright in that work similar to any other use of a work that exceeded the license granted by the proprietor of the copyright.

If the broadcast of an edited version of the Monty Python program infringed the group's copyright in the script, ABC may obtain no solace from the fact that editing was permitted in the agreements between BBC and Time-Life or Time-Life and ABC. BBC was not entitled to make unilateral changes in the script and was not specifically empowered to alter the recordings once made; Monty Python, moreover, had reserved to itself any rights not granted to BBC. Since a grantor may not convey greater rights than it owns, BBC's permission to allow Time-Life, and hence ABC, to edit appears to have been a nullity. See *Hampton v. Paramount Pictures Corp.*, 279 F.2d 100 (9th Cir.), cert. denied, 364 U.S. 882 (1970); *Ilyin v. Avon Publications*, 144 F. Supp. 368, 372 (S.D.N.Y. 1956).

. . . .

Finally, ABC contends that appellants must have expected that deletions would be made in the recordings to conform them for use on commercial television in the United States. ABC argues that licensing in the United States implicitly grants a license to insert commercials in a program and to remove offensive or obscene material prior to broadcast. According to the network, appellants should have anticipated that most of the excised material contained scatological references inappropriate for American television and that these scenes would be replaced with commercials, which presumably are more palatable to the American public.

The proof adduced up to this point, however, provides no basis for finding any implied consent to edit. Prior to the ABC broadcasts, Monty Python programs had been broadcast on a regular basis by both commercial and public television stations in this country without interruption or deletion. Indeed, there is no evidence of any prior broadcast of edited Monty Python material in the United States. These facts, combined with the persistent requests for assurances by the group and its representatives that the programs would be shown intact belie the argument that the group knew or should have known that deletions and commercial interruptions were inevitable.

Several of the deletions made for ABC, such as elimination of the words "hell" and "damn," seem inexplicable given today's standard television fare.[8] If, however, ABC honestly determined that the programs were obscene in substantial part, it could have decided not to broadcast the specials at all, or it could have attempted to reconcile its differences with appellants. The network could not, however, free from a claim of infringement, broadcast in a substantially altered form a program incorporating the script over which the group had retained control.

---

[8] We also note that broadcast of the Monty Python specials was scheduled by ABC for an 11:30 p.m. to 1:00 a.m. time slot.

Our resolution of these technical arguments serves to reinforce our initial inclination that the copyright law should be used to recognize the important role of the artist in our society and the need to encourage production and dissemination of artistic works by providing adequate legal protection for one who submits his work to the public. See *Mazer v. Stein,* 347 U.S. 201 (1954). We therefore conclude that there is a substantial likelihood that, after a full trial, appellants will succeed in proving infringement of their copyright by ABC's broadcast of edited versions of Monty Python programs. In reaching this conclusion, however, we need not accept appellants' assertion that any editing whatsoever would constitute infringement. Courts have recognized that licensees are entitled to some small degree of latitude in arranging the licensed work for presentation to the public in a manner consistent with the licensee's style or standards.[9] See *Stratchborneo v. Arc Music Corp.,* 357 F. Supp. 1393, 1405 (S.D.N.Y. 1973); *Preminger v. Columbia Pictures Corp.,* 49 Misc. 2d 383, 267 N.Y.S.2d 594 (Sup. Ct.), *aff'd* 25 App. Div. 2d 830, 269 N.Y.S.2d 913 (1st Dept.), *aff'd* 18 N.Y.2d 659, 273 N.Y.S.2d 80, 219 N.E.2d 431 (1966). That privilege, however, does not extend to the degree of editing that occurred here especially in light of contractual provisions that limited the right to edit Monty Python material.

II

It also seems likely that appellants will succeed on the theory that, regardless of the right ABC had to broadcast an edited program, the cuts made constituted an actionable mutilation of Monty Python's work. This cause of action, which seeks redress for deformation of an artist's work, finds its roots in the continental concept of droit moral, or moral right, which may generally be summarized as including the right of the artist to have his work attributed to him in the form in which he created it. See 1 M. Nimmer, *supra,* at § 110.1.

American copyright law, as presently written, does not recognize moral rights or provide a cause of action for their violation, since the law seeks to vindicate the economic, rather than the personal, rights of authors. Nevertheless, the economic incentive for artistic and intellectual creation that serves as the foundation for American copyright law, *Goldstein v. California,* 412 U.S. 546 (1973); *Mazer v. Stein,* 347 U.S. 201 (1954), cannot be reconciled with the inability of artists to obtain relief for mutilation or misrepresentation of their work to the public on which the artists are financially dependent. Thus courts have long granted relief for misrepresentation of an artist's work by relying on theories outside the statutory law of copyright, such as contract law, *Granz v. Harris,* 198 F.2d 585 (2d Cir. 1952) (substantial cutting of original work constitutes misrepresentation), or the tort of unfair competition, *Prouty v. National Broadcasting Co.,* 26 F. Supp. 265 (D. Mass. 1939). See Strauss, *The Moral Right of the Author* 128-138, in Studies on Copyright (1963). Although such decisions are clothed in terms of proprietary right in one's creation, they also properly vindicate the author's personal right to prevent the presentation of his work to the public in a distorted form. See

---

[9] Indeed, the scriptwriters' agreement permitted BBC to make "minor" changes without consulting Monty Python. See note 2, *supra.*

Gardella v. Log Cabin Products Co., 89 F.2d 891, 895-96 (2d Cir. 1937); Roeder, *The Doctrine of Moral Right,* 53 Harv. L. Rev. 554, 568 (1940).

Here, the appellants claim that the editing done for ABC mutilated the original work and that consequently the broadcast of those programs as the creation of Monty Python violated the Lanham Act § 43(a), 15 U.S.C. § 1125(a).[10] This statute, the federal counterpart to state unfair competition laws, has been invoked to prevent misrepresentations that may injure plaintiff's business or personal reputation, even where no registered trademark is concerned. See *Mortellito v. Nina of California,* 335 F. Supp. 1238, 1294 (S.D.N.Y. 1972). It is sufficient to violate the Act that a representation of a product, although technically true, creates a false impression of the product's origin. See *Rich v. RCA Corp.,* 390 F. Supp. 530 (S.D.N.Y. 1975) (recent picture of plaintiff on cover of album containing songs recorded in distant past held to be a false representation that the songs were new); *Geisel v. Poynter Products, Inc.,* 283 F. Supp. 261, 267 (S.D.N.Y. 1968).

These cases cannot be distinguished from the situation in which a television network broadcasts a program properly designated as having been written and performed by a group, but which has been edited, without the writer's consent, into a form that departs substantially from the original work. "To deform his work is to present him to the public as the creator of a work not his own, and thus makes him subject to criticism for work he has not done." Roeder, *supra,* at 569. In such a case, it is the writer or performer, rather than the network, who suffers the consequences of the mutilation, for the public will have only the final product by which to evaluate the work.[11] Thus, an allegation that a defendant has presented to the public a "garbled," *Granz v. Harris, supra* (Frank, J., concurring), distorted version of plaintiff's work seeks to redress the very rights sought to be protected by the Lanham Act, 15 U.S.C. § 1125(a), and should be recognized as stating a cause of action under that statute. See *Autry v. Republic Productions, Inc.,* 213 F.2d 667 (9th Cir. 1954); *Jaeger v. American Intn'l Pictures, Inc.,* 330 F. Supp. 274 (S.D.N.Y. 1971), which suggest the violation of such a right if mutilation could be proven.

During the hearing on the preliminary injunction, Judge Lasker viewed the edited version of the Monty Python program broadcast on December 26 and the original, unedited version. After hearing argument of this appeal, this panel also viewed and compared the two versions. We find that the truncated version at times omitted the climax of the skits to which appellants' rare brand of humor was leading and at other times deleted essential elements in the schematic development of a story line.[12] We therefore agree with Judge

---

[10] That statute provides in part:

> Any person who shall affix, apply, or annex, or use in connection with any goods or services, ... a false designation of origin, or any false description or representation ... and shall cause such goods or services to enter into commerce ... shall be liable to a civil action by any person ... who believes that he is or is likely to be damaged by the use of any such false description or representation.

[11] This result is not changed by the fact that the network, as here, takes public responsibility for editing. See *Rich v. RCA Corp., supra.*

[12] A single example will illustrate the extent of distortion engendered by the editing. In one skit, an upper class English family is engaged in a discussion of the tonal

Lasker's conclusion that the edited version broadcast by ABC impaired the integrity of appellants' work and represented to the public as the product of appellants what was actually a mere caricature of their talents. We believe that a valid cause of action for such distortion exists and that therefore a preliminary injunction may issue to prevent repetition of the broadcast prior to final determination of the issues.[13]

[The court rejected ABC's claim that appellants were guilty of laches: "[W]e find no undue delay in the group's failure to institute this action until they were sufficiently advised regarding the facts necessary to support the action." It also held that the failure to name BBC and Time-Life as defendants was no bar to an injunction; they were not indispensable parties, since Monty Python rested its claim on its own copyright (not derived from the BBC's) and since it may secure complete relief by way of an injunction and damages against ABC alone.]

For these reasons we direct that the district court issue the preliminary injunction sought by the appellants.

QUESTIONS

1. What copyright was considered infringed in the "Monty Python" case? Under the court's analysis, is the BBC an infringer?

2. What contractual provision was violated? Was the existence of a contractual restriction crucial to the result? If copyright infringement could not have been found without a finding of breach of contract, shouldn't this case have been decided uniquely on state law grounds? Cf. *Bartsch v. Metro-Goldwyn-Mayer, Inc., supra.*

3. Some years ago, a computer-facilitated technique was developed to add color to motion picture films originally made in black-and-white. (The original films are in the public domain or, if they are still protected by copyright, permission to colorize has been given by the copyright owner, typically a production company or its assignee.) Certain frames of the film are identified for colorization; decisions are made about what colors to incorporate in the

---

quality of certain words as "woody" or "tinny." The father soon begins to suggest certain words with sexual connotations as either "woody" or "tinny," whereupon the mother fetches a bucket of water and pours it over his head. The skit continues from this point. The ABC edit eliminates this middle sequence so that the father is comfortably dressed at one moment and, in the next moment, is shown in a soaked condition without any explanation for the change in his appearance.

[13] Judge Gurfein's concurring opinion suggests that since the gravamen of a complaint under the Lanham Act is that the origin of goods has been falsely described, a legend disclaiming Monty Python's approval of the edited version would preclude violation of that Act. We are doubtful that a few words could erase the indelible impression that is made by a television broadcast, especially since the viewer has no means of comparing the truncated version with the complete work in order to determine for himself the talents of plaintiffs. Furthermore, a disclaimer such as the one originally suggested by Judge Lasker in the exigencies of an impending broadcast last December would go unnoticed by viewers who tuned into the broadcast a few minutes after it began.

We therefore conclude that Judge Gurfein's proposal that the district court could find some form of disclaimer would be sufficient might not provide appropriate relief.

frames, based upon research as to such matters as the color of an actor's hair or an adjacent building, and judgments are frequently made about appealing color combinations, about shading, etc.; and a computer is then used to "color" the remaining film frames in the pertinent scene sequences.

(a) Is the colorized version of the motion picture copyrightable as a derivative work?

(b) Does such colorization violate any rights of the director or other leading artistic contributors to the black-and-white original? (Recall that, in most instances, the motion picture will have been prepared as a work made for hire.)

4. Paramount Pictures Corporation produces motion pictures and distributes them by means that include videocassettes sold and rented by stores to retail customers. These videos contain several feet of tape as "lead-ins" to the featured film. Paramount places on those lead-ins warnings against use of the film in a manner that would violate the Copyright Act, as well as advertisements for others of its films and for commercial products. It has brought an action against Video Ads, a company that produces audiovisual advertising material for its clients and inserts that advertising onto the lead-ins of videocassettes supplied to Video Ads by local video stores; the client pays Video Ads, which in turn pays a smaller amount to the stores that turn over the videocassettes (which have been lawfully purchased by the stores). Paramount claims that the inserted commercials at the beginning of the tapes of its copyrighted motion pictures constitute a copyright infringement, as well as a form of unauthorized editing that violates the Lanham Act. How would you decide the case? *See Paramount Pictures Corp. v. Video Broadcasting Sys.,* 724 F. Supp. 808 (D. Kan. 1989).

MORAL RIGHTS

The *Gilliam* court alluded to the continental concept of moral rights, and to the author's prerogatives to secure proper attribution for her work and to preserve the work in the form in which it was created. These rights of attribution (also known as the right of "paternity") and of integrity are among the guarantees that nations party to the Berne Convention for the Protection of Literary and Artistic Works must afford authors from other member countries (Art. 6*bis*). The effective date of U.S. adherence to the Berne Convention was March 1, 1989.

The theory of moral rights holds that these rights inhere in and protect the personality of the author. While, according to the continental view, the author enjoys *both* moral and economic rights "by the sole fact of creating the work" (France, copyright law [law of March 11, 1957], art. 1), moral rights are conceptually separate from economic exploitation rights. Indeed, in many countries, moral rights are considered inalienable: the author retains them even after, or despite, transfer of economic rights. The Berne Convention, however, does not prohibit waiver or alienation of these rights, so long as a transfer of economic rights is not deemed of itself to effect a transfer of moral rights.

The extent to which U.S. copyright or other doctrines assimilate or simulate moral rights was hotly debated at the time of Berne adherence. *See generally Final Report of the Ad Hoc Working Group on U.S. Adherence to the Berne Convention,* 10 Colum.-VLA J.L. & Arts 513, 547-57 (1986) (concluding that, on the whole, U.S. law affords meaningful equivalents to moral rights). Since then, Congress has enacted explicit protections for the attribution and integrity interests of a limited class of visual artists. *See* Visual Artists Rights Act of 1990, P.L. 101-650, Title VI, 104 Stat. 5089 (1990). (This statute will be discussed more fully below.) However, artists not covered by this statute, as well as creators of literary, musical and audiovisual works, must continue to look to other sources of U.S. law to protect these interests. The Lanham Act has proven to be one resort. Indeed, the *Gilliam* decision signals some ability to accommodate the right of integrity both within the derivative works right under copyright, and under the federal trademarks law. Neither measure, however, offers a perfect substitute. Under U.S. copyright law, an author may assert the derivative works right against one who alters the work only if the author has retained that right, or has at least provided for a contractual right of approval of a grantee's changes. Although inalienability is not essential to moral rights as defined under the Berne Convention, it is an important feature of the rights of integrity and of attribution under many foreign legal systems.

Similarly, while claims derived from trademarks law may bolster the integrity interest, that law covers a range of activity narrower than the conduct that may give rise to a moral rights offense. For example, to the extent that attribution to the author of a work mutilated by another passes off as the author's a work no longer fully hers, the federal trademark law (and analogous state laws) may serve to protect the integrity interest. Indeed, attribution to the author of another's radical (or particularly inept) alterations may give rise to a defamation claim. But, if the changes to the work are clearly labeled as the product of someone other than the author, there is no deception in the presentation of the work; arguably, once the source of commercial falsehood is removed, the trademark and defamation claims vanish as well.

The right of attribution regarding a work neither altered nor mutilated seems more secure under current U.S. legal doctrines — at least when authorship is attributed to a third person — despite an early inhospitable reception in state common-law courts. The Copyright Act does not itself confer (or, for that matter, address) a right of attribution. The same provision of the Trademark Act of 1946 applied by the *Gilliam* court, however, has also been invoked in complaints by authors and other creative contributors that authorship or similar credit was improperly accorded to a third party. These plaintiffs asserted that attributing their work to another constituted a false representation or false designation of origin of goods in interstate commerce. Their claims have met a hospitable reception where defendant copied from plaintiff's work and cast himself as the author, *Marling v. Ellison,* 218 U.S.P.Q. 702 (S.D. Fla. 1982); where one co-author removed the names of his two co-authors, presenting a musical work as his alone, *Lamothe v. Atlantic Recording Corp.,* 847 F.2d 1403 (9th Cir. 1988); and where a book's editor failed to acknowledge the full extent of the contribution of one group of authors, conveying the impression that the work was almost entirely the product of a third party, *Dodd v. Ft. Smith School Dist.*, 666 F. Supp. 1278 (W.D. Ark. 1987). *Cf. Follett v. New Am. Library*, 497 F. Supp. 304 (S.D.N.Y. 1980) (upholding author's claim that he was improperly credited as the principal author rather than as one of several authors of the work).

Does a simple denial of authorship credit, without misattribution to a third party, or without misrepresenting the extent of a co-author's contribution, also constitute a false representation? One might argue that nonattribution inevitably entails falsehood; for example, it can falsely suggest that the author wished to remain anonymous. The Ninth Circuit has characterized nonattribution as "implied reverse passing off"; explicit misattribution or misrepresentation is "express reverse passing off." Both kinds of reverse passing off "involuntarily deprive [the creator] of the advertising value of its name and of the goodwill that otherwise would stem from public knowledge of the true source of the satisfactory product. The ultimate purchaser (or viewer) is also deprived of knowing the true source of the product ...." *Smith v. Montoro*, 648 F.2d 602 (9th Cir. 1981). *See also Lamothe, supra*, at n.2 ("defendants did not simply remove all trace of the source of the product, which might itself be actionable as implied reverse passing off"). Nonetheless, courts have not clearly enunciated an affirmative (noncontractual) right to compel attribution, in the absence of express misattribution. *But see Community for Creative Non-Violence v. Reid*, 846 F.2d 1485 (D.C. Cir. 1988), *aff'd on other grounds*, 490 U.S. 730 (1989) (joint owner of copyright in sculptural work, upon exercising right to reproduce the work, "might be obliged to credit [the sculptor of a portion of the work] as an author of the sculpture") (dictum).

VISUAL ARTISTS RIGHTS ACT OF 1990, §§ 101, 106A

17 U.S.C. §§ 101, 106A

§ 101. Definitions.

....

A "work of visual art" is —

(1) a painting, drawing, print, or sculpture, existing in a single copy, in a limited edition of 200 copies or fewer that are signed and consecutively numbered by the author, or in the case of a sculpture, in multiple cast, carved, or fabricated sculptures of two hundred or fewer that are consecutively numbered by the author and bear the signature or other identifying mark of the author; or

(2) a still photographic image produced for exhibition purposes only, existing in a single copy that is signed by the author, or in a limited edition of 200 copies or fewer that are signed and consecutively numbered by the author.

A work of visual art does not include —

(A)(i) any poster, map, globe, chart, technical drawing, diagram, model, applied art, motion picture or other audiovisual work, book, magazine, newspaper, periodical, data base, electronic information service, electronic publication, or similar publication;

(ii) any merchandising item or advertising, promotional, descriptive, covering, or packaging material or container;

(iii) any portion or part of any item described in clause (i) or (ii);

(B) any work made for hire; or

(C) any work not subject to copyright protection under this title.

....

§ 106A. Rights of certain authors to attribution and integrity

(a) RIGHTS OF ATTRIBUTION AND INTEGRITY. — Subject to section 107 and independent of the exclusive rights provided in section 106, the author of a work of visual art —

(1) shall have the right —

(A) to claim authorship of that work, and

(B) to prevent the use of his or her name as the author of any work of visual art which he or she did not create;

(2) shall have the right to prevent the use of his or her name as the author of the work of visual art in the event of a distortion, mutilation, or other modification of the work which would be prejudicial to his or her honor or reputation and

(3) subject to the limitations set forth in section 113(d), shall have the right—

(A) to prevent any intentional distortion, mutilation, or other modification of that work which would be prejudicial to his or her honor or reputation, and any intentional distortion, mutilation, or modification of that work is a violation of that right, and

(B) to prevent any destruction of a work of recognized stature, and any intentional or grossly negligent destruction of that work is a violation of that right.

(b) SCOPE AND EXERCISE OF RIGHTS. — Only the author of a work of visual art has the rights conferred by subsection (a) in that work, whether or not the author is the copyright owner. The authors of a joint work of visual art are coowners of the rights conferred by subsection (a) in that work.

(c) EXCEPTIONS. — (1) The modification of a work of visual art which is a result of the passage of time or the inherent nature of the materials is not a distortion, mutilation, or other modification described in subsection (a)(3)(A).

(2) The modification of a work of visual art which is the result of conservation, or of the public presentation, including lighting and placement, of the work is not a destruction, distortion, mutilation, or other modification described in subsection (a)(3) unless the modification is caused by gross negligence.

(3) The rights described in paragraph (1) and (2) of subsection(a) shall not apply to any reproduction, depiction, portrayal, or other use of a work in, upon, or in any connection with any item described in subparagraph (A) or (B) of the definition of "work of visual art" in section 101, and any such reproduction, depiction, portrayal, or other use of a work is not a destruction, distortion, mutilation, or other modification described in paragraph (3) of subsection (a)....

(d) TRANSFER AND WAIVER. — (1) The rights conferred by subsection (a) may not be transferred, but those rights may be waived if the author expressly agrees to such waiver in a written instrument signed by the author. Such instrument shall specifically identify the work, and uses of that work to which the waiver applies, and the waiver shall apply only to the work and uses so identified. In the case of a joint work prepared by two or more authors, a waiver of rights under this paragraph made by one such author waives such rights for all such authors....

The student should also consult §§ 113(d) and 301(f), also enacted in 1990 and set forth in Appendix A to the Casebook.

QUESTIONS

1. In addition to defining restrictively a "work of visual art," the federal Visual Artists Rights Act contains a long list of works *excluded* from the Act's coverage. Why do you suppose the statute contains such redundant and cumbersome language?

2. Among the works excluded from coverage are "works made for hire." If an artist hires assistants to work on a painting or sculpture — for example, welders for a large-scale steel sculpture — is the resulting work "for hire?" Do you suppose Congress intended to remove these kinds of works from the Act's protections? Can one resolve this anomaly by considering the work not "for hire" if the persons engaged by the artist would not be considered "authors"? Is this a sufficient solution?

3. In 1991 Phoebe Photographer created several fashion photographs which were published in magazines like *Vogue* and *GQ*. These photographs have since become prized as works of art. Responding to the popularity of her photos, Ms. Photographer, who has retained the original negatives of her work, creates limited editions of 200 of each of the fashion photographs, which she signs and numbers. Are these editions protected under the Visual Artists Rights Act?

4. Artemis Artist has displayed her recent canvasses and lithographs at the Gallery. Gallery has issued a catalogue depicting Artist's work. However, on the walls and in the catalogue, Gallery has failed to attribute any of the work to Artist. Which, if any, of Gallery's conduct violates the Visual Artists Rights Act?

5. Are works of architecture covered by VARA? Are works of literature or music? If not, should they be? Are motion pictures or other audiovisual works, as in the *Gilliam* case? Although Congress was urged to extend moral rights to film directors, it declined to do so, and instead simply enacted legislation requiring that any alterations of qualifying films made without the consent of the director must be labelled to disclose this fact. *See* 2 U.S.C. § 179 et seq. Why are creators of classic motion pictures accorded no moral rights (apart from accurate labelling)? Does it relate to the medium of film, or to the identity of those who would claim moral rights, or to the prevailing methods for commercially marketing (and editing and exhibiting) motion pictures?

STATE MORAL RIGHTS LEGISLATION

Before enactment of the federal Visual Artists Rights Act, several states, including California, New York, Massachusetts, New Jersey, Maine, Connecticut, Louisiana, New Mexico, Pennsylvania and Rhode Island, adopted laws protecting rights of integrity and of attribution in "works of fine art." These state law protections proved an important element in the argument advanced by some observers, and embraced by Congress in 1988, that the overall combination of federal and state laws together afforded sufficient coverage of moral rights to permit U.S. adherence to the Berne Convention without further specific federal legislation regarding moral rights.

Although the overall "fine arts" subject matter covered by the state laws is often similar, the rationales for and the terms of protection are not always identical. For example, the preamble to the California act, Cal. Civ. Code § 987(a), states:

> The Legislature hereby finds and declares that the physical alteration or destruction of fine art, which is an expression of the artist's personality, is detrimental to the artist's reputation, and artists therefore have an interest in protecting their works of fine art against such alteration or destruction; and that there is also a public interest in preserving the integrity of cultural and artistic creations.

The attribution and integrity rights (including the right not to have the work intentionally destroyed) are granted for the life of the artist plus fifty years; but the rights can be waived in an express writing signed by the artist.

The New York statute, N.Y. Arts & Cultural Affairs Law 14.03, is somewhat different. Its principal articulated concern is with the reasonable likelihood of "damage to the artist's reputation" resulting from an alteration, defacement, mutilation or other modified form. Accordingly, the New York statute does not outlaw this offensive conduct as such, but only the publishing or the public display of a work (or a reproduction of a work) in such altered form, when the work would reasonably be attributed to the artist and "damage to the artist's reputation is reasonably likely to result therefrom." There are several exceptions to the rights accorded to the artist:

(1) The act does not apply "to work prepared under contract for advertising or trade unless the contract so provides";

(2) the act expressly excludes motion pictures from its coverage;

(3) alteration or other modification of a work "resulting from the passage of time or the inherent nature of the materials" will not violate the act;

(4) a modification of a work in the course of reproducing it "that is an ordinary result of the medium of reproduction" will not violate the act; and

(5) destruction of a work is not expressly outlawed.

The New York statute is silent on the question whether the artist may waive the statutory rights in writing or otherwise. It is also silent as to the duration of those rights.

While the state laws and the federal statute now overlap to some extent, they are not completely congruent with respect to either subject matter covered or conduct prohibited. The following decision, applying the New York statute, illustrates some of the differences in purpose and scope between federal and state rights.

WOJNAROWICZ v. AMERICAN FAMILY ASS'N

745 F. Supp. 130 (S.D.N.Y. 1990)

CONNER, DISTRICT JUDGE.

Multimedia artist David Wojnarowicz brings this action to enjoin the publication of a pamphlet by defendants American Family Association ("AFA") and Donald E. Wildmon, Executive Director of AFA, and for damages based upon claims of copyright infringement, defamation, and violations of the Lanham Act and the New York Artists' Authorship Rights Act....

The expedited non-jury trial merged the evidentiary hearing on plaintiff's motion for preliminary injunction with the trial on the merits pursuant to Rule 65(a)(2), Fed. R. Civ. P.... Having reviewed the record and considered counsels' post-trial briefs, the Court concludes that plaintiff is entitled to judgment for defendants' violation of New York's Artists' Authorship Rights Act, but plaintiff's claims for copyright infringement, violation of the Lanham Act and defamation must be dismissed. This opinion incorporates the Court's findings of fact and conclusions of law pursuant to Rules 52(a) and 65(d), Fed. R. Civ. P.

Findings of Fact

Defendant AFA, formerly known as the National Federation For Decency, was founded in 1977 as a not-for-profit corporation by Donald E. Wildmon. Incorporated under the laws of the state of Mississippi, and headquartered in Tupelo, Mississippi, the AFA has over 60,000 members and approximately 500 local chapters nationwide, including a number in the state of New York. It is chartered for the declared purposes, inter alia, of promoting decency in the American society and advancing the Judeo-Christian ethic in America. Defendant Donald E. Wildmon, Executive Director of the AFA, is a citizen of the United States, residing in Tupelo, Mississippi. Since May 1989, the AFA has been actively campaigning against what it characterizes as the subsidization of "offensive" and "blasphemous" art by the National Endowment for the Arts (the "NEA"). Through contributions, it raised $5.2 million dollars in 1989.

Plaintiff, a citizen of the United States, residing in New York, New York, is a multi-media artist, whose work includes paintings, photographs, collages, sculptures, installations, video tapes, films, essays and public performances. A professional artist, plaintiff earns his living by selling his art works, many of which are assertedly directed at bringing attention to the devastation wrought upon the homosexual community by the AIDS epidemic. Plaintiff attempts through his work to expose what he views as the failure of the United States government and public to confront the AIDS epidemic in any meaningful way. To this end, plaintiff's art at times incorporates sexually explicit images for the avowed purpose of shaping community attitudes towards sexuality. As a result, his works have been the subject of controversy and public debate concerning government funding of non-traditional art.

Plaintiff's art works frequently employ groupings of images which are assertedly intended to convey composite messages. The works have received a measure of critical acclaim and have been featured in a number of museum and gallery exhibitions. Plaintiff earned approximately $15,000 from the sale of his art works in 1988, approximately $34,000 in 1989 and $17,000 to date this year.

From January 23, 1990 through March 4, 1990, the University Galleries at Illinois State University, Normal, Illinois, presented a comprehensive exhibition of plaintiff's work, entitled "Tongues of Flame" (the "exhibit"), and published a 128-page catalog (the "catalog") which contained reproductions of over sixty of plaintiff's works, as well as essays by plaintiff and others. The NEA awarded the University Galleries $15,000 to help pay for the exhibit and the catalog.

Plaintiff is the owner of the copyrights to all of the works displayed in the exhibit and of all of the reproductions of his work that appear in the catalog....

On or about April 12, 1990, the AFA and Wildmon published and distributed throughout the United States, including the Southern District of New York, the AFA pamphlet (the "pamphlet") in an effort to stop public funding by the NEA of art works such as plaintiff's. The pamphlet was mailed to 523 members of Congress, 3,230 Christian leaders, 947 Christian radio stations and 1,578 newspapers, at least twenty-eight of which were located in this district. Without plaintiff's authorization, Wildmon photographically copied fourteen fragments of plaintiff's works which he believed most offensive to the public and reproduced these fragments in the AFA pamphlet. These fourteen images, with three exceptions, explicitly depict sexual acts. The other three images portray Christ with a hypodermic needle inserted in his arm, and two ambiguous scenes which plaintiff represents as respectively depicting an African purification ritual and two men dancing together.

Wildmon wrote the text of the pamphlet, which is entitled "Your Tax Dollars Helped Pay For These 'Works of Art.'" It states in the introductory sentence that "the photographs appearing on this sheet were part of the David Wajnarowicz [sic] 'Tongues of Flame' exhibit catalog." The envelope in which the AFA pamphlet was mailed states that the "[p]hotos enclosed in this envelope were taken from the catalog of the 'Tongues of Flame' exhibit" and is marked "Caution — Contains Extremely Offensive Material."

Conclusions of Law

....

I. *New York's Artists' Authorship Rights Act*

New York's Artists' Authorship Rights Act, N.Y. Cultural Affairs Law Section 14.03 (McKinney's Supp. 1990), provides, in relevant part, that:

1. [N]o person other than the artist or a person acting with the artist's consent shall knowingly display in a place accessible to the public or publish a work of fine art or limited edition multiple of not more than three hundred copies by that artist or a reproduction thereof in an altered, defaced, mutilated or modified form if the work is displayed, published or reproduced as being the work of the artist, or under circumstances which would reasonable be regarded as being the work of the artist, and damage to the artist's reputation is reasonably likely to result therefrom ....

2. (b) The rights created by this subdivision shall exist in addition to any other rights and duties which may now or in the future be applicable.

3. (e) The provisions of this section shall apply only to works of fine art or limited edition multiples of not more than three hundred copies knowingly displayed in a place accessible to the public, published or reproduced in this state.

4. (a) An artist aggrieved under subdivision one or subdivision two of this section shall have a cause of action for legal and injunctive relief.

....

B. *Scope of Act*

Defendants next argue that the distribution of a photocopy of cropped images extracted from plaintiff's work is not a violation of the statute because it did not alter, deface, mutilate or modify plaintiff's original work. This Court does not agree. A literal reading of section 14.03(1) of the Authorship Rights Act clearly demonstrates that the statute guards against alterations of reproductions as well as of the original works:

1. [N]o person ... shall knowingly display in a place accessible to the public or publish a work of fine art ... *or a reproduction thereof* in an altered, defaced, mutilated or modified form if the work is displayed, published or *reproduced* as being the work of the artist.[3]

See Damich, *A Comparative Critique,* 84 Colum. L. Rev. at 1740 ("A more plausible interpretation of the reproduction provision — and one supported by statutory language — is that unfaithful reproductions activate the protection of the statute if publicly displayed so as to damage the reputation of the author of the original."). Moreover, section 14.03(3)(b) of the Act confirms its applicability to altered reproductions of artworks in which no physical change has been made in the original work. That subsection — by which 14.03 is expressly limited — states that:

---

[3] "'Reproduction' means a copy, in any medium, of a work of fine art, that is displayed or published under circumstances that, reasonably construed, evince an intent that it be taken as a representation of a work of fine art as created by the artist." N.Y. Arts & Cultural Affairs Law § 11.01(16) (McKinney's 1990).

In the case of a reproduction, a change that is an ordinary result of the medium of reproduction does not by itself create a violation of subdivision one of this section or a right to disclaim authorship under subdivision two of this section.

Sections 14.03(1) and 14.03(3)(b), read together, suggest that deliberate alterations (such as selective cropping), as distinguished from those that ordinarily result from the reproduction process (such as reduction in overall size or loss of detail), would constitute violations. See Damich, *A Comparative Critique*, 84 Colum. L. Rev. at 1740.

Defendants maintain that the statute's legislative history supports their contention that the display or publication envisioned is the altered original or limited edition multiple by a subsequent owner.... It is evident that the statute was intended to protect the integrity of the original artworks and the artist's limited edition multiples after they were sold or transferred to new owners. The statute prevents the new owner from displaying or publishing and attributing to the creator an altered version of that creator's work. However, nothing in the legislative history suggests that the New York legislature intended to limit the Act's protection to that scenario. To the contrary, because the intent of the bill was to protect not only the integrity of the artwork, but the reputation of the artist,[4] the spirit of the statute is best served by prohibiting the attribution to an artist of a published or publicly displayed altered reproduction of his original artwork. From a photographic reproduction, it cannot be seen whether the alteration was effected on the original or the copy, and both may cause the same harm to the artist's reputation when the altered version is published with attribution to him. In fact, the mass mailing of an altered photographic reproduction is likely to reach a far greater audience and cause greater harm to the artist than the display of an altered original, which may reach only a limited audience. While this situation may not have been expressly contemplated by the drafters, the wording of the statute literally covers it, and the spirit of the statute would be contravened by it.

Second, this Court rejects defendants' claim that the reproduction and publication of minor, unrepresentative segments of larger works, printed wholly without context, does not constitute an alteration, defacement, mutilation or modification of plaintiff's artworks. By excising and reproducing only small portions of plaintiff's work, defendants have largely reduced plaintiff's multi-imaged works of art to solely sexual images, devoid of any political and artistic context. Extracting fragmentary images from complex, multi-imaged collages clearly alters and modifies such work.

    ....

Defendants next claim that plaintiff has failed to demonstrate that the alteration, modification, defacement or mutilation has caused or is reasonably

---

[4]See Damich, *A Comparative Critique*, 84 Colum. L. Rev. at 1741 ("Clearly, the thrust of the New York statute is more toward protection of the artist's reputation than toward protection of the work.").

likely to result in damage to his reputation. Defendants urge that plaintiff's reputation has not been diminished in the eyes of his peers or gallery directors, dealers and potential buyers who determine his livelihood but, to the contrary, the increased exposure and publicity has enhanced his reputation. However, the trial testimony of Philip Yenawine, an expert on contemporary art, employed by the Modern Museum of Art in New York, established that there is a reasonable likelihood that defendants' actions have jeopardized the monetary value of plaintiff's works and impaired plaintiff's professional and personal reputation.

Yenawine testified that because the details in the pamphlet imply that plaintiff's work consists primarily of explicit images of homosexual sex activity, plaintiff's name will be "anathema" to museums. Museums unfamiliar with plaintiff's work, believing the pamphlet to be representative of his work, may fail to review his work, even though many of plaintiff's art works do not contain sexual images. Even museums familiar with plaintiff's work may be reluctant to show his work due to his perceived association with pornography.

Yenawine stated that this self-censorship will have an adverse impact on the value of plaintiff's work; individuals will be less likely to purchase plaintiff's art without the pedigree of museum shows and accompanying reviews. Similarly, defendants' misrepresentation of plaintiff's work may deter persons from attending his shows, which may, in turn, reduce the incentive for galleries and museums to include plaintiff's work in future shows. Additionally, the public may associate plaintiff with only the sexually explicit images which were taken out of his intended political and artistic context, resulting in a reasonable likelihood of harm to his reputation and to the market for his work. Yenawine further testified that although corporations would not have been likely to purchase those works of plaintiff's which contain sexual images, "a great number of [plaintiff's] images ... have no sexual representations whatsoever and deal with all sorts of other kinds of images...."

....

Defendants next assert that where the speech involves matters of public concern allegedly injuring the reputation of a public figure, actual malice must be proven to defeat First Amendment protection. While agreeing with the quotations submitted by defendants eloquently extolling the virtues of the First Amendment, this Court cannot agree that the alteration, defacement, mutilation or modification of artwork is protected speech, entitling defendants to immunity where they acted without actual malice. Clearly, the pamphlet contained protectable speech, namely, the protest against the subsidy of "obscene" art, which is entitled to the utmost First Amendment protection as the "unfettered interchange of ideas for the bringing about of political and social changes deserved by the people." See *New York Times Co. v. Sullivan*, 376 U.S. 254, 269 (1964). The public display of an altered artwork, falsely attributed to the original artist, however, is not the type of speech or activity that demands protection, because such deception serves no socially useful purpose. The New York Statute does not impede truthful speech, but rather prevents false attribution, requiring only accurate labeling to permit dissemination of

the desired message. Such labeling in no way diminishes the force of the
message. Defendants remain free to criticize and condemn plaintiff's work if
they so choose. They may present incomplete reproductions labeled as such or,
alternatively, without attribution of such images to plaintiff. However, they
may not present as complete works by plaintiff, selectively cropped versions of
his originals....

As to defendants' position that the statute is unconstitutionally vague and
overbroad, the Court again cannot agree. As explained above, the statute
encompasses altered reproductions as well as altered originals and altered
limited edition multiples. The statute is not impermissibly vague merely because it requires a determination as to whether damage to an artist's reputation is reasonably likely to result from an alteration and attribution.... Because the statute presently before the Court states that damage to the artist's
reputation must be "reasonably likely" to result, the test is clearly whether a
reasonable person would conclude that damage to the artist's reputation is
likely....

....

V. *Remedies*

A. *Prohibitive Injunction*

... Defendants' distribution of a pamphlet, suggesting that plaintiff's work
consists of sexually explicit images, has irreparably harmed plaintiff's professional and personal reputation and warrants injunctive relief. Accordingly,
defendants and all those in privity with them are hereby enjoined and restrained from further publication or distribution of the pamphlet in controversy. As stated in the Court's opinion and order dated June 28, 1990:

> This injunction shall not prohibit publication or distribution of other
> pamphlets or materials incorporating the photographic images contained
> in the pamphlet, or portions thereof, for the purpose of directly or indi-
> rectly influencing the National Endowment for the Arts or the United
> States Congress or other United States government officials to cease the
> direct or indirect subsidy or support of the creation, exhibition or publica-
> tion of such art with federal funds, provided that, such pamphlets or
> materials do not suggest to reasonable readers that a fragment of one of
> plaintiff's art works constitutes the complete work.

B. *Mandatory Injunction*

Plaintiff also seeks an order requiring defendants to undertake a corrective
mailing and to publish a corrective advertisement in a major daily newspaper.
New York's Artists' Authorship Rights Act specifically provides for a right of
"disattribution," N.Y. Arts & Cult. Aff. Law § 14.03(2)(a) (McKinney's Supp.
1990), and the Court believes it just to require defendants to distribute a
corrective communication to all those to whom they sent the original pamphlet. To minimize mailing costs, this corrective communication, to be, mailed
within ninety days from the date of this opinion and order, may be joined with

any other distribution by the defendants. The corrective communication should be submitted to the Court for approval after comment by all parties.

C. *Damages*

Under New York's Artists' Authorship Rights Act, an artist is also entitled to legal relief, i.e. damages, for a violation of the Act. N.Y. Art & Cult. Aff. Law § 14.03(4)(a) (McKinney's Supp. 1990). Even though plaintiff has established that defendants' actions were reasonably likely to result in damage to his reputation, he has proven no actual damages. So far as the record shows, not one gallery or museum currently scheduled to exhibit plaintiff's work has canceled; nor has one planned sale been cancelled. Plaintiff presented no evidence that he has been harmed in any other specific, quantifiable way. Accordingly, the Court hereby awards plaintiff nominal damages in the amount of $1.00.

....

QUESTION

Would defendant have escaped liability under the New York statute had his brochure not attributed the fragments to any particular artist, but had simply asserted that the fragments were illustrative of the kind of art that defendant's association deplored?

C. THE RIGHT TO DISTRIBUTE UNDER § 106(3)

HOUSE REPORT

H.R. Rep. No. 94-1476, 94th Cong., 2d Sess. 62 (1976)

Public distribution. — Clause (3) of section 106 establishes the exclusive right of publication: The right "to distribute copies or phonorecords of the copyrighted work to the public by sale or other transfer of ownership, or by rental, lease, or lending." Under this provision the copyright owner would have the right to control the first public distribution of an authorized copy or phonorecord of his work, whether by sale, gift, loan, or some rental or lease arrangement. Likewise, any unauthorized public distribution of copies or phonorecords that were unlawfully made would be an infringement. As section 109 makes clear, however, the copyright owner's rights under section 106(3) cease with respect to a particular copy or phonorecord once he has parted with ownership of it.

[Editors' Note. — Section 109(a) provides: "Notwithstanding the provisions of section 106(3), the owner of a particular copy or phonorecord lawfully made under this title, or any person authorized by such owner, is entitled, without authority of the copyright owner, to sell or otherwise dispose of the possession of that copy or phonorecord."]

FAWCETT PUBLICATIONS, INC. v. ELLIOT PUBLISHING CO.

46 F. Supp. 717 (S.D.N.Y. 1942)

CLANCY, DISTRICT JUDGE. This is a motion for summary judgment made by the plaintiff, the action being for an alleged infringement of a copyright. We note that the plaintiff states there is also involved a claim for unfair competition, but we find no such claim in the pleadings.

The plaintiff is engaged in the magazine publishing business as is the defendant. The plaintiff, on or about April 18, 1941, being then the author and proprietor of a publication known as "Wow Comics, No. 2 Summer Edition," copyrighted it and was, therefore, entitled to the exclusive right to print, reprint, publish, copy and vend it. Subsequent to this publication's issuance the defendant purchased secondhand copies of it and of another copyrighted publication of the plaintiff, which he makes the subject of the second cause of action, and bound them together with other comic publications not owned or copyrighted by the plaintiff within one copyrighted cover of its own with the words "Double Comics" thereon.

Section 1 of Title 17, U.S.C.A. grants to the copyright owner the exclusive right "to print, reprint, publish, copy, and vend the copyrighted work ...." The alleged infringement as set forth in the complaint is that the defendant published and placed upon the market said "Double Comics" containing the complete issue of plaintiff's publication, without its consent or approval, so that as thus limited, it must be determined whether the defendant violated the plaintiff's admitted exclusive right to publish and secondly to vend. The decisions appear to be uniform that the purpose and effect of the copyright statute is to secure to the owner thereof the exclusive right to multiply copies. *Bobbs-Merrill Co. v. Straus,* 210 U.S. 339; *Jeweler's Circular Pub. Co. v. Keystone Pub. Co.,* 281 F. 83 (C.C.A. 2d), *cert. denied,* 259 U.S. 581. It is conceded here that the defendant has not multiplied copies but merely resold the plaintiff's under a different cover. The exclusive right to vend is limited. It is confined to the first sale of any one copy and exerts no restriction on the future sale of that copy. *Bureau of National Literature v. Sells,* 211 F. 379; *Strauss v. American Publishers Ass'n* 231 U.S. 222; *Bentley v. Tibbals,* 223 F. 247 (C.C.A. 2d). The defendant is not charged with copying, reprinting or rearranging the copyrighted material of the plaintiff or any of its component parts nor has it removed the plaintiff's copyright notice.

The motion is denied.

QUESTIONS

1. If the defendant had in fact been charged with the acts enumerated in the court's last sentence, what would the outcome have been? Does the defendant in this case have a more, or less, sympathetic position than the defendant in the *National Geographic* case, *supra* at p. 463?

2. Suppose a bookstore receives from a publisher copyrighted prints picturing the mansion that is the setting of a novel. The bookstore is to distribute the print only as a premium with the purchase of copies of the novel, but instead it sells the prints. Does the publisher have a claim for copyright infringement, or for anything else? *Compare Burke & Van Heusen, Inc. v. Arrow Drug, Inc.,* 233 F. Supp. 881 (E.D. Pa. 1964) *with U.S. Naval Institute v. Charter Communications Inc.,* 936 F.2d 692 (2d Cir. 1991).

THE RECORD RENTAL AND COMPUTER-SOFTWARE RENTAL AMENDMENTS OF 1984 AND 1990

On October 4, 1984, Congress made a significant departure from the first-sale doctrine initially codified in the 1909 Act and endorsed in § 109(a). In the Record Rental Amendment of 1984, Pub. L. No. 98-450, Congress in a new § 109(b) declared:

> [U]nless authorized by the owners of copyright in the sound recording and in the musical works embodied therein, the owner of a particular phonorecord may not, for purposes of direct or indirect commercial advantage, dispose of, or authorize the disposal of, the possession of that phonorecord by rental, lease, or lending.

The obvious target of the new legislation was the record-rental store, which came upon the retail marketing scene in 1981 and by mid-1984 had grown to about 200 in number. These stores rented phonorecords to their customers for anywhere from 24 to 72 hours, at rates ranging from 99 cents to $2.50 per disc; most such stores also stocked blank cassette tapes, often sold at discount to customers renting albums. In the words of the Senate Report: "The Committee has no doubt that the purpose and result of record rentals is to enable and encourage customers to tape their rented albums at home.... Thus, a record rental and a blank tape purchase is now an alternative way of obtaining a record without having to buy one. The rental is a direct displacement of a sale." S. Rep. No. 98-162, 98th Cong., 1st Sess. 2 (1983). The Report referred to the proliferation of record-rental stores in Japan, numbering at the time approximately 1700, as well as the spread of the phenomenon to Canada and a number of countries in Western Europe. It also mentioned the recent development of the digital compact disc, scanned by a laser and nearly indestructible, thus permitting the record-rental shop to rent each disc hundreds of times. The Committee continued (at page 3):

> The Committee has concluded that record rentals pose a serious threat to America's record companies, music publishers, performers, songwriters, and record retailers.... Commercial record rentals in the United States hurt copyright owners when record rentals displace record sales. This is because record rentals are almost invariably followed by unauthorized home taping, thereby resulting in even fewer record sales. Yet copyright owners are not compensated either for the rental itself or for the unauthorized home recording. Thus, as record rentals become more widespread, they will undoubtedly add to the estimated $1 billion annual loss in record sales already caused by home taping....
>
> Ultimately, the Committee finds that uncompensated record rentals are contrary to the interests of consumers. As record sales drop because of the rental phenomenon, record companies will be forced to spread their production costs over the smaller number of records sold. This is likely to

cause the price of these records to increase — in effect forcing legitimate purchasers to subsidize those who tape rented records. In other words, consumers who honor the copyright laws will be penalized.

Just as significant, in the Committee's view, is the overall effect on musical creativity. Record companies have already retrenched as a result of home taping. The sales displacement caused by continued record rentals would require even greater cutbacks. The normal way in which record companies and music publishers have traditionally cut their costs has been to reduce risk. Record companies and music publishers will inevitably become less willing to take a chance on unknown artists and songwriters or to experiment with innovative musical forms. Again, the consumer is the ultimate loser.

The legislative reports made it clear that the new law would constitute only a minor modification of the first-sale doctrine. It would not restrict the right of the purchaser of a phonorecord to sell it or give it away. The amended § 109(b) explicitly provides that the record-renting ban is not to apply "to the rental, lease, or lending of a phonorecord for nonprofit purposes by a nonprofit library or nonprofit educational institution." Section 115(c) was amended so as to permit record rental or leasing for profit by a record manufacturer operating under that section's compulsory-license provision, so long as it shared its income from the rental or leasing with the copyright owner of the musical composition.

(Given the fact that the record-rental amendment was based upon congressional concern over the serious economic incursions resulting from wide-ranging home audiotaping, should the amendment be reconsidered and perhaps repealed now that further amendments in 1992 have expressly exempted home audiotaping and have given music copyright owners, record producers and performers a share in the sales proceeds from tape recorders and blank tapes?)

In 1990 Congress again modified the first-sale doctrine, this time by enacting the Computer Software Rental Amendments of 1990, Pub. L. No. 101-650, Title VII, 104 Stat. 5089 (1990). This amendment grants authors or producers of software the right to authorize or to prohibit the rental of copies, even after their initial sale. However, the scope of the right is more limited than that of the 1984 record rental amendment, for Congress included even more exceptions to the computer program rental right than it had imposed on the record rental right. The 1990 law excepts non-remunerative transfers of copies of programs within libraries, universities and schools. Moreover, software copyright owners may not prohibit the rental of copies contained within computer hardware when the programs are not normally susceptible to copying. As a result, the law does not hinder the rental of hardware, even when it contains chips or other fixations of programs. Thus, for example, this exemption permits untrammeled rental of cars containing computer voice programs that remind the driver that the seat belt is unbuckled or that "a door is ajar."

A very different exemption disables the program copyright owner from prohibiting the rental or the public performance or display of software intended to be used with or incorporated within a computer whose principal purpose is to permit the user to play video games (17 U.S.C. § 109(b) & (e)). This curious provision legislatively "overrules" the decision in *Red Baron-Franklin Park, Inc. v. Taito Corp.*, 883 F.2d 275 (4th Cir. 1989), *cert. denied*, 493 U.S. 1058 (1990), which had held that the first-sale doctrine permitted defendant's unauthorized importation of "grey market" circuit boards, but did not permit defendant publicly to perform the video games generated by the circuit boards. As a result, importers of grey market video game circuit boards may now exploit the games in arcades and by other means of public performance or display, without securing the copyright owner's permission. One may wonder whether this exemption was not intended to favor U.S. "mom and pop" video arcades to the detriment of (primarily Japanese) copyright owners of video games software.

Finally, the 1990 amendment allows noncommercial libraries to lend copies of computer programs to the public, so long as these copies bear a copyright notice. Aware that this exception could lead to abuse, Congress instructed the Copyright Office to prepare a study of the software lending practices of libraries and borrowers. 17 U.S.C. § 109(b)(2)(B).

The law was effective upon its enactment, and, like the record rental amendment, it contains a "sunset" clause; the law remains in effect until October 1, 1997 (the video games exemption terminates on October 1, 1995). However, the duration of the amendment may be extended by subsequent legislation.

Congress's purpose in enacting the software rental amendments recalls the purpose underlying the 1984 record rental amendment. Although both laws entitle the copyright owner to authorize rentals and thereby to participate in a rental market, the real purpose of both laws was not to derive revenue from rentals, but to stop the practice altogether. As with record rentals, computer program copyright owners feared, and demonstrated, that rentals led to unauthorized copying. *See, e.g.,* remarks of Senator Hatch, Cong. Rec. S17,577 (Oct. 27, 1990). However, the multiple exceptions to the software rental right cause concern that the law may not achieve its objective of forestalling copying by means of rentals. (Indeed, even were the rental right subject to fewer exceptions, one may wonder if private copying would be significantly curtailed.)

PUBLIC LENDING RIGHT

Because public libraries purchase only a few copies of a book and yet disseminate that work to a large number of people who might otherwise buy it, some countries (mostly European) have developed an alternative form of compensation to the author called a "public lending right." Generally, in these countries, an author receives a "royalty" based upon the circulation (actual or potential) of the work. In some countries, the royalty is correlated directly to the number of times the book is loaned to a library user. In others, the royalty is calculated on the basis of the library's holdings, regardless of how often a particular work is loaned to users. Finally, some countries provide for a one-time payment to the author at the time of acquisition, as a sort of "surcharge." Public lending right schemes are often enacted outside of the country's copyright laws. This is because many countries, the U.K., for example, consider the public lending right royalty as a kind of payment for services, rather than a traditional license for exploitation. *See* Brigid Brophy, A Guide to the Public Lending Right [U.K.] 53 (1983). It has been suggested, however, that countries choose to create the lending right separate from copyright in order to avoid application of the rule of national treatment, which requires that countries party to a copyright treaty accord the same copyright protections to foreign works from treaty countries as the protection granted to the signatory's own copyright owners. *See* Jennifer M. Schneck, Note, *Closing the Book on the Public Lending Right,* 63 N.Y.U. L. Rev. 878, 898 (1989).

DROIT DE SUITE

Another manifestation of the belief that authors should share in the subsequent profitable disposition of lawfully owned copies of their works is the so-called *droit de suite,* which provides that an artist shall share in the profits accruing to subsequent purchasers from the appreciation in value of the artist's works. Although the *droit de suite* exists in a number of European countries, California is the only state that has enacted a resale-royalties statute. It provides that:

> Whenever a work of fine art is sold and the seller resides in California or the sale takes place in California, the seller or his agent shall pay to the artist of such work of fine art or to such artist's agent 5 percent of the amount of such sale.

The artist's right is non-waivable and may be enforced by an action for damages with a three-year period of limitations; moneys payable to the artist will be paid to the state Arts Council if the seller cannot locate the artist within ninety days, and all moneys due the artist are exempt from attachment or execution of judgment by creditors of the seller. Among those sales exempted from the statute are resales for a gross price of less than $1,000, resales made more than twenty years after the death of the artist, and resales for a gross sales price less than the purchase price paid by the seller.

On the federal level, proponents of the *droit de suite* have made several attempts to incorporate the concept into the Copyright Act, most recently as a provision in the Visual Artists Rights Act of 1990, Pub. L. No. 101-650, Title VI, 104 Stat. 5089 (1990). Though the 1990 provision was ultimately deleted from the final bill, the effort was more successful than its predecessors: Congress did direct the Register of Copyrights to conduct a study examining the feasibility of adopting a resale-rights program in the United States.

On December 1, 1992, the Register reported that, based on the record developed through the inquiry, he had found insufficient justification for the adoption of the system in the U.S. copyright law. *See generally* U.S. Copyright Office, *Droit de Suite*: The Artists Resale Royalty (1992) [Report]. However, the Register's negative assessment was explicitly qualified by both the lack of conclusive data and the possibility that a harmonization of policy within the European Community countries might dictate a different conclusion. The Report concluded by proposing alternatives to *droit de suite,* such as creating a commercial rental right, and expanding the public display right (by amending

Section 109) to provide for an artist's right to license the work for public display even after the work has been sold. These alternatives might not in fact provide greater income for the artist, but would at least expand an artist's control over her work.

Ultimately, in the event that Congress were to override the Register's suggestion to reject *droit de suite*, the Report offered a model for the implementation of *droit de suite*. Drawing on several features from several sources, the Report suggested that the U.S. *droit de suite*: cover all works covered by the Visual Artists Rights Act (except those created in more than ten copies); endure as long as the copyright term; apply only to works sold at public auction; be calculated as three to five percent of the sale price with no minimum threshold; be collected by a private collecting society. Additionally, the right would extend prospectively, i.e., only to works created after passage of the law, and would cover foreign authors on the basis of reciprocity rather than national treatment. For a critical analysis of the Report, see Shira Perlmutter, *Resale Royalties for Artists: An Analysis of the Register of Copyrights' Report,* 16 Colum.-VLA J. L. & Arts 395 (1993).

QUESTIONS

1. Do you favor a general public lending right? How would you provide for such a right by amendment of the Copyright Act? For example, would it apply to all classes of works in § 102, or only to certain classes, such as literary works or audiovisual works? (Or only sound recordings?) Would it apply to all lending transactions (including public libraries) or only those for commercial purposes? Would your bill provide for an absolute ban on such lending or would it provide for a compulsory license? If the latter, how would the rates be established?

2. Do you favor a ban (or a compulsory license) regarding the subsequent sales of certain kinds of works, such as used textbooks? Doesn't the California resale royalties statute in effect create a compulsory license governing the resale of works of fine art? Is the statute an unconstitutional encumbrance upon the rights granted by the Copyright Act? *See Morseburg v. Balyon,* 621 F.2d 972 (9th Cir.), *cert. denied,* 449 U.S. 983 (1980). Should Congress amend the Act to provide for such resale royalties?

THE § 602(a) IMPORTATION RIGHT

§ 602. Infringing importation of copies or phonorecords

(a) Importation into the United States, without the authority of the owner of copyright under this title, of copies or phonorecords of a work that have been acquired outside the United States is an infringement of the exclusive right to distribute copies or phonorecords under Section 106, actionable under Section 501....

§ 501. Infringement of copyright

(a) Anyone who violates any of the exclusive rights of the copyright owner as provided by sections 106 through 119, or who imports copies or phonorecords into the United States in violation of section 602, is an infringer of the copyright.

The relationship among the § 106(3) distribution right, its limitation by § 109(a), and the § 602(a) importation right has provided the subject of several recent decisions. All have arisen in the context of the "grey market": the distribution in the United States of genuine goods (usually lawfully manufactured abroad, but sometimes manufactured in the U.S. for shipment overseas) imported into the United States without the authorization of the United States copyright holder. A strong dollar underlies the grey market; as a result of disparities in currency values, it can be cheaper for a distributor to purchase the goods abroad and import them to the United States (to undersell the authorized United States dealer) than to purchase the goods here.

Sebastian Int'l, Inc. v. Consumer Contacts (PTY) Ltd., 847 F.2d 1093 (3d Cir. 1988). Plaintiff manufactured shampoo in the U.S. for shipment to South Africa. Several cases of the goods made an unauthorized round trip, and were offered for sale in the U.S. by defendant. Plaintiff, claiming the shampoo bottle labels as a copyrighted work, invoked § 602(a) against the importation. The Third Circuit reversed the district court's holding for plaintiff. The Third Circuit reviewed prior decisions on the relationship of §§ 109(a) and 602(a);

> The appellate courts have had little occasion to analyze the interplay between the first sale doctrine of section 109(a) and the importation right of section 602(a), but the district courts have struggled with the problem in a number of situations. In *Columbia Broadcasting Sys. v. Scorpio Music Distrib.,* 569 F. Supp. 47 (E.D. Pa. 1983), *aff'd without opinion,* 738 F.2d 424 (3d Cir. 1984), the district court found infringement when copies, produced and sold exclusively in the Philippines under a license agreement, were imported into the United States — where the plaintiff owned the sole distribution rights. The district court concluded that the words "lawfully made under this title" in section 109(a) grant first sale protection only to copies legally made and sold in the United States. *Id.* at 49.
>
> In *T.B. Harms Co. v. Jem Records, Inc.,* 655 F. Supp. 1575 (D.N.J. 1987), the court also found infringement when phonorecords manufactured under license in New Zealand were imported into the United States. The court reached that conclusion despite the compulsory licensing provision applicable to phonorecords, commenting that the preliminary negotiations behind sections 602(a) and 115 did not furnish a reliable gauge of congressional intent. In particular, the court was wary of statements made by special interest groups and was reluctant to consider such views as expressions of the congressional intent shaping the Copyright Act.
>
> A similar problem arose in *Hearst Corp. v. Stark,* 639 F. Supp. 970 (N.D. Cal. 1986), when books lawfully made in England were imported

into the United States, where the plaintiff held the copyrights. The district court, finding an infringement, decided that the first sale doctrine did not modify the importation restraints of section 602(a). *Id.* at 976-77.

In *Nintendo of America, Inc. v. Elcon Indus.*, 564 F. Supp. 937 (E.D. Mich. 1982), the court enjoined the defendants from distributing electronic audio-visual games made in Japan under a license expressly limited to the territories of Japan. The agreement prohibited importation into the United States, where the plaintiff owned all the distribution rights under copyright. *But Cf. Neutrogena Corp. v. United States,* No. 2:88-0566-1, slip op. (D.S.C. Apr. 5, 1988) (first sale defense available where goods manufactured in United States and sold to defendant by third party); *Cosmair, Inc.,* slip op., (section 109 limits section 602 where products manufactured in the United States and re-imported).

But the court did not find those decisions persuasive:

> Under the first sale doctrine, when plaintiff made and then sold its copies, it relinquished all further rights "to sell or otherwise dispose of possession of that copy." Unquestionably that includes any right to claim infringement of the section 106(3) distributive rights for copies made and sold in the United States. With respect to future distribution of those copies in this country, clearly the copyright owner already has received its reward through the purchase price.
>
> Nothing in the wording of section 109(a), its history or philosophy, suggests that the owner of copies who sells them abroad does not receive a "reward for his work." Nor does the language of section 602(a) intimate that a copyright owner who elects to sell copies abroad should receive "a more adequate award" [sic] than those who sell domestically. That result would occur if the holder were to receive not only the purchase price, but a right to limit importation as well.
>
> Consequently, we agree with the district court that the place of sale is not the critical factor in determining whether section 602(a) governs. We differ, however, with the district court's finding of infringement because, in our view, a first sale by the copyright owner extinguishes any right later to control importation of those copies.
>
> Section 602(a) does not purport to create a right in addition to those conferred by section 106(3), but states that unauthorized importation is an infringement of "the exclusive [section 106(3)] right to distribute copies." Because that exclusive right is specifically limited by the first sale provisions of § 109(a), it necessarily follows that once transfer of ownership has cancelled the distribution right to a copy, the right does not survive so as to be infringed by importation.

BMG Music v. Perez, 952 F.2d 318 (9th Cir.), *cert. denied,* 112 S. Ct. 2997, 120 L. Ed. 2d 873 (1992). BMG Music, and other record companies, license the manufacture and sale of their recordings in foreign countries. They brought an infringement action against Perez, who purchased those recordings abroad and without authorization imported them to and sold them in the United States. The district court found that Perez had violated section 602(a) and issued a preliminary injunction, which Perez ignored, leading to a finding of contempt. On appeal, Perez contended — relying in part on the decision of the Third Circuit in *Sebastian* — that section 602(a) was in effect superseded by the first-sale doctrine under section 109(a).

The Court of Appeals for the Ninth Circuit disagreed. It held that the words "lawfully made under this title" in section 109(a) afforded first-sale protection only to copies legally made and sold in the United States, such that it did not shelter the importation of recordings manufactured and sold abroad. The court, relying on *CBS v. Scorpio Music Distrib.*, 569 F. Supp. 47 (E.D. Pa. 1983), *aff'd without opinion*, 738 F.2d 424 (3d Cir. 1984), concluded that any other reading would render section 602 "virtually meaningless." It distinguished *Sebastian* as a case in which the copyrighted material was initially manufactured in and exported from the United States, and then imported back.

Is this distinction, in both *Sebastian* and *BMG Music*, convincing?

QUESTIONS

1. Support from the text of the Copyright Act may be garnered either for application of § 602(a) only to foreign-made works, or for its application to any works imported without authorization regardless of their place of manufacture and initial sale. Which position makes more sense?

2. Does the use of § 602(a) to prohibit the importation of books published under license abroad and out-of-print in the United States violate the First Amendment? *See Hearst Corp. v. Stark,* 639 F. Supp. 970 (N.D. Cal. 1986).

D. RIGHTS OF PUBLIC PERFORMANCE AND DISPLAY UNDER § 106(4), (5)

1. PRE-1976 PERFORMING RIGHTS

Performing rights came relatively late in statutory copyright development. The right was first recognized as to dramatic compositions by the amendatory Act of 1856, 11 Stat. 138, and as to musical compositions by the Act of 1897, 29 Stat. 481. Neither was limited to performances "for profit," but where the performance of music was "willful, and for profit," the act constituted a misdemeanor punishable by imprisonment "for a period not exceeding one year." Rev. Stat. § 4966.

At the turn of the twentieth century, the main source of revenue for the composer had long been by way of royalties from the sale of copies of his or her work in the form of sheet music, and sometimes these ran into large sums. Before radio, an average hit song may have sold over a million copies of sheet music. (This was reportedly reduced to 50,000 by 1940.) *See* Shull, *Collecting Collectively: ASCAP's Perennial Dilemma,* 7 ASCAP Copyright Law Symposium 35 n.2 (1956).

Little thought was given to the performing right, notwithstanding that by the Act of 1897 damages for unlicensed performance were collectible "at such sum, not less than $100 for the first and $50 for every subsequent performance, as to the court shall appear to be just." Although copyrighted music was played for years in public places throughout the country, only a few reported cases are found dealing with infringement of this right under the pre-1909 law, and the outcome was not encouraging to the composer. But soon all this was to be changed. The increasing use of popular music, so vastly stimulated by the rise of the motion picture and radio industries, and the contemporaneous decline in revenue from the sale of copies, at last awakened composers to the possibilities inherent in the performing right.

In 1909, the Copyright Act was amended to give to the owner of copyright in a musical composition the exclusive right to perform it "publicly for profit."

a. "For Profit" Performances

In order to take full advantage of that new statutory right, a group of prominent popular composers — among them Victor Herbert and John Philip Sousa — in 1914 formed the American Society of Composers, Authors and Publishers, the first performing rights organization in the United States. The purpose of the organization was to serve as a clearinghouse for performing-rights licensing (thereby reducing the cost of individual licensing) and as an agency to monitor performances and police infringements. With the aid of their able and dedicated attorney, Nathan Burkan, ASCAP embarked on a litigation campaign to establish their statutory rights. First attempts were not promising; the Court of Appeals for the Second Circuit held that the term "for profit" in the 1909 Act meant a direct pecuniary charge to hear the performance, i.e. an admission fee. This view was, however, resoundingly overturned by the United States Supreme Court in a decision of major significance, *Herbert v. Shanley Co.*, 242 U.S. 591 (1917), written in characteristically insightful and pithy style by Justice Holmes.

The Shanley Company, in its restaurant on Broadway, used the services of professional singers, accompanied by an orchestra, to perform on its stage such songs as Victor Herbert's "Sweethearts," from an operetta of the same name. The Court found this kind of performance to be "for profit" in spite of the fact that no separate charge was made for the music. Justice Holmes stated:

> If the rights under the copyright are infringed only by a performance where money is taken at the door, they are very imperfectly protected.... The defendants' performances are not eleemosynary. They are part of a total for which the public pays, and the fact that the price of the whole is attributed to a particular item which those present are expected to order is not important. It is true that the music is not the sole object, but neither is the food, which probably could be got cheaper elsewhere. The object is a repast in surroundings that to people having limited powers of conversation, or disliking the rival noise, give a luxurious pleasure not to be had from eating a silent meal. If music did not pay, it would be given up. If it pays, it pays out of the public's pocket. Whether it pays or not, the purpose of employing it is profit, and that is enough.

A number of other decisions gave broad compass to the phrase "for profit." *M. Witmark & Sons v. Pastime Amusement Co.*, 298 F.2d 479 (E.D.S.C.), *aff'd*, 2 F.2d 1020 (4th Cir. 1924) (court rejected arguments that a movie-theater organist was an independent contractor and that her performance did not directly generate profit for the theater owner); *Associated Music Pub'rs, Inc. v. Debs Mem. Radio Fund, Inc.*, 141 F.2d 852 (2d Cir. 1944) (nonprofit broadcasting station, operated for educational and cultural purposes and paying for only one-third of its airtime by accepting commercial advertising, was held to have performed a song "for profit" even though it was played on a program that had no commercials.)

b. "Public" Performances

It will be seen that the statutory definition of public performance in § 101 of the 1976 Act recognizes that a performance can be public even though received in separate places and/or at different times. This is consistent with the earlier determination that a radio broadcast is "public." *See, e.g., Jerome H. Remick & Co. v. American Auto. Accessories Co.*, 5 F.2d 411 (6th Cir.), *cert. denied*, 269 U.S. 556 (1925). Under the 1909 law, a number of cases raising the question of what constitutes a "public" performance centered about face-to-face situations or exhibition of a motion picture at a single location, such as at a social club or summer camp. The question became less pressing as to motion pictures because of the ruling in *Patterson v. Century Prods., Inc.*, 93 F.2d 489, 35 U.S.P.Q. 471 (2d Cir. 1937), *cert. denied*, 303 U.S. 655, 37 USPQ 844 (1938), that the flashing upon the screen of a picture results in making an enlarged copy thereof, and therefore constitutes a violation of the right to copy granted in § 1(a) of the 1909 law, regardless of the public or private character of the performance.

c. The "Multiple Performance" Doctrine

As noted, most of the significant cases under the 1909 Act raising the issue of public performance of a musical composition for profit centered upon the concepts of "public" and "for profit." So long as the musical rendition took place in a face-to-face setting, with the performers and listeners in the same concert hall, or dance hall, or theater, or restaurant, there was no debate as to whether a "performance" was taking place. The development of radio and television broadcasting, however, undermined definitional simplicity, as performers and listeners became geographically remote and as intermediate retransmission agencies became necessary to bring sounds or sights from one to the other. Thus emerged the judge-made doctrine of "multiple performance" under the 1909 Act. Four Supreme Court decisions dominated this development.

(1) **Buck v. Jewell-LaSalle Realty Co.**, 283 U.S. 191 (1931). The act of a hotel proprietor of making available to its guests, by means of radio receivers and loudspeakers in public and private rooms, the *unauthorized* rendition of copyrighted music by a neighboring broadcasting station was here held to constitute *performance* of the original program. The Court held further that

foreknowledge of the selections to be played was immaterial, because intention to infringe is not essential under the Copyright Act, and that one who merely "tunes in" on his receiving set actually performs the work in the statutory sense of the term and therefore runs the risk of incurring a suit for infringement if he does so in public for the purpose of commercial profit. The court of appeals accordingly found on remand that the specific acts of the proprietor of the hotel constituted a "public performance for profit." 51 F.2d 726, 10 U.S.P.Q. 70 (8th Cir. 1931).

(2) **Fortnightly Corp. v. United Artists Television, Inc.**, 392 U.S. 390 (1968). The retransmission of local copyrighted television programs by community antenna television systems was held not to "perform" the programs. In a 5-to-1 decision, the Court drew a dichotomy between broadcasters and viewers and, after analysis of the functions of each, determined that a CATV system "falls on the viewer's side of the line," since it "no more than enhances the viewer's capacity to receive the broadcaster's signals." The Court treated *Jewell-LaSalle* as "a questionable 35-year-old decision that in actual practice has not been applied outside its own factual context," 392 U.S. at 401 n.30, 158 U.S.P.Q. at 6 n.30, namely, where the original broadcast had been unauthorized. *Id.* n.18. The dissenting opinion of Justice Fortas argued that "the interpretation of the term 'perform' cannot logically turn on the question whether the material that is used is licensed or not licensed." 392 U.S. at 406 n.5, 158 U.S.P.Q. at 8 n.5.

(3) **Teleprompter Corp. v. Columbia Broadcasting System**, 415 U.S. 394 (1974). It was soon argued that the *Fortnightly* case did not cover systems that originated certain programs; used microwave transmissions (rather than solely cable); included commercials in their transmissions; interconnected with other systems; or offered subscribers "distant signals," i.e., signals not ordinarily receivable by house-top antennas or both house-top and tower-mounted antennas. The Court of Appeals for the Second Circuit held in *Teleprompter* that this last characteristic did distinguish such a system from those involved in *Fortnightly,* because its "function in this regard is no longer merely to enhance the subscriber's ability to receive signals that are in the area; it is now acting to bring signals into the community that would not otherwise be receivable on an antenna, even a large community antenna erected in that area."

The Supreme Court reversed, rejecting all of the attempts to distinguish the *Fortnightly* case.

The importation of distant broadcast signals was deemed no different functionally from that of strengthening local signals blocked by buildings or topography. "The privilege of receiving the broadcast electronic signals and of converting them into the sights and sounds of the program inheres in all members of the public who have the means of doing so. The reception and rechanneling of these signals for simultaneous viewing is essentially a viewer function, irrespective of the distance between the broadcasting station and the ultimate viewer." Finally, the Court rejected the plaintiff's contention that cable retransmission of distant programs should infringe because of the deleterious impact upon the economics and market structure of copyright licensing.

When a copyright holder first licenses a copyrighted program to be shown on broadcast television, he typically cannot expect to recoup his entire investment from a single broadcast. Rather, after a program has had a "first run" on the major broadcasting networks, it is often later syndicated to affiliates and independent stations for "second run" propagation to secondary markets. The copyright holders argue that if CATV systems are allowed to import programs and rechannel them into secondary markets they will dilute the profitability of later syndications, since viewer appeal, as measured by various rating systems, diminishes with each successive showing in a given market.... Unlike propagators of other copyrighted material, such as those who sell books, perform live dramatic productions, or project motion pictures to live audiences, holders of copyrights for television programs or their licensees are not paid directly by those who ultimately enjoy the publication of the material — that is, the television viewers — but by advertisers who use the drawing power of the copyrighted material to promote their goods and services. Such advertisers typically pay the broadcasters a fee for each transmission of an advertisement based on an estimate of the expected number and characteristics of the viewers who will watch the program....

By extending the range of viewability of a broadcast program, CATV systems ... do not interfere in any traditional sense with the copyright holders' means of extracting recompense for their creativity or labor.... Instead of basing advertising fees on the number of viewers within the range of direct transmission plus those who may receive "local signals" via a CATV system, broadcasters whose reception ranges have been extended by means of "distant" signal CATV rechanneling will merely have a different and larger viewer market.... From the point of view of the copyright holders, such market changes will mean that the compensation a broadcaster will be willing to pay for the use of copyrighted material will be calculated on the basis of the size of the direct broadcast market augmented by the size of the CATV market.

These shifts in current business and commercial relationships, while of significance with respect to the organization and growth of the communications industry, simply cannot be controlled by means of litigation based on copyright legislation enacted more than half a century ago, when neither broadcast television nor CATV was yet conceived. Detailed regulation of these relationships, and any ultimate resolution of the many sensitive and important problems in this field, must be left to Congress.

(4) **Twentieth Century Music Corp. v. Aiken,** 422 U.S. 151 (1975). A divided Court held that the reception of copyrighted music from radio broadcasts and its transmission through four speakers installed in the ceiling of a fast-food shop did not constitute a "performance" on the part of the restaurant owner. The defendant had hooked up his radio to the four speakers, and throughout the day received the music, news, entertainment, and advertising

that was broadcast, for the enjoyment and edification of his employees and customers.

The Court majority reasoned that members of the audience in a concert hall, theater, or restaurant do not "perform" the musical works they hear (and also suggested that the same was true when one sang a copyrighted song in the shower).

> If, by analogy to a live performance in a concert hall or cabaret, a radio station "performs" a musical composition when it broadcasts it, the same analogy would seem to require the conclusion that those who listen to the broadcast through the use of radio receivers do not perform the composition. And that is exactly what the early federal cases held. "Certainly those who listen do not perform, and therefore do not infringe." *Jerome H. Remick & Co. v. General Electric Co.*... "One who manually or by human agency merely actuates electrical instrumentalities, whereby inaudible elements that are omnipresent in the air are made audible to persons who are within hearing, does not 'perform' within the meaning of the Copyright Law." *Buck v. Debaum*, 40 F.2d 734, 735 (S.D. Cal. 1929)

The Court stated that *Buck v. Jewell-LaSalle* was to be limited to its facts (i.e., an unauthorized broadcast by the radio station), and that *Fortnightly* and *Teleprompter* had "expressly disavowed the view that the reception of an electronic broadcast can constitute a performance, when the broadcaster himself is licensed to perform the copyrighted material that he broadcasts." The Court concluded that if the sophisticated technological and programming facilities of cable television did not warrant a finding of a "performance," then surely that would be true for one who "merely activated his restaurant radio."

The Court made some general observations about the reach of copyright protection in a time of technological innovation.

> The limited scope of the copyright holder's statutory monopoly, like the limited copyright duration required by the Constitution, reflects a balance of competing claims upon the public interest: Creative work is to be encouraged and rewarded, but private motivation must ultimately serve the cause of promoting broad public availability of literature, music, and the other arts.... When technological change has rendered its literal terms ambiguous, the Copyright Act must be construed in light of this basic purpose.

The Court buttressed its holding by noting that a finding of infringement would make it impracticable for ASCAP (the plaintiff's public-performance licensee) evenhandedly to collect royalties from the countless business establishments with radio or television sets on their premises; and also that such a finding would unfairly authorize ASCAP to extract "an untold number of licenses for what is basically a single public rendition of a copyrighted work."

QUESTIONS

1. In the absence of any explicit definition of the term "perform" in the 1909 Act, should the Court have been so confident in its conclusions that one does not "perform" a song when singing it in the shower or when turning a knob on the radio, or presumably also when placing a needle onto a phonograph record? Would all shower-Pavarottis be copyright infringers if the Court had concluded otherwise? (Put aside the question who would do the policing.)

2. What interpretive philosophy should properly actuate the Court in a period of technological change unanticipated by Congress? Can the *Fortnightly* and *Teleprompter* cases be usefully understood as manifesting the Court's reluctance to hamper the development of a new technology unantici-pated in 1909?

3. In deciding whether the owner of copyright of a song has rights that have been infringed through "performance," ought it to matter — as the *Aiken* Court believed — whether it is feasible for the copyright owner, or its licensee such as ASCAP or BMI, to police those rights, or whether it will do so even-handedly?

2. PERFORMING RIGHTS UNDER THE 1976 ACT

§ 106. Exclusive rights in copyrighted works

Subject to sections 107 through 120, the owner of copyright under this title has the exclusive rights to do and to authorize any of the following:

. . . .

(4) in the case of literary, musical, dramatic and choreographic works, pan-tomimes, and motion pictures and other audiovisual works, to perform the copyrighted work publicly;

. . . .

[*Editors' Note:* The 1976 Act has, subject to certain specified limitations, extended the copyright monopoly to public performances without regard to whether the performance is "for profit." In reviewing the cases and materials addressing the 1976 Act right of public performance, keep in mind the follow-ing questions: 1. Is the act at issue a "performance"? 2. Is the performance "public"? 3. Is there an applicable exemption from liability?]

a. The Meaning of "Perform" Under the 1976 Act

§ 101. Definitions

As used in this title, the following terms and their variant forms mean the following:

. . . .

To "perform" a work means to recite, render, play, dance, or act it, either directly or by means of any device or process or, in the case of a motion picture or other audiovisual work, to show its images in any sequence or to make the sounds accompanying it audible.

HOUSE REPORT

H.R. Rep. No. 94-1476, 94th Cong., 2d Sess. 64 (1976)

Definitions

Under the definitions of "perform," "display," "publicly," and "transmit" in section 101, the concepts of public performance and public display cover not only the initial rendition or showing, but also any further act by which that rendition or showing is transmitted or communicated to the public. Thus, for example: a singer is performing when he or she sings a song; a broadcasting network is performing when it transmits his or her performance (whether simultaneously or from records); a local broadcaster is performing when it transmits the network broadcast; a cable television system is performing when it retransmits the broadcast to its subscribers; and any individual is performing whenever he or she plays a phonorecord embodying the performance or communicates the performance by turning on a receiving set. Although any act by which the initial performance or display is transmitted, repeated, or made to recur would itself be a "performance" or "display" under the bill, it would not be actionable as an infringement unless it were done "publicly," as defined in section 101. Certain other performances and displays, in addition to those that are "private," are exempted or given qualified copyright control under sections 107 through 118.

To "perform" a work, under the definition in section 101, includes reading a literary work aloud, singing or playing music, dancing a ballet or other choreographic work, and acting out a dramatic work or pantomime. A performance may be accomplished "either directly or by means of any device or process," including all kinds of equipment for reproducing or amplifying sounds or visual images, any sort of transmitting apparatus, any type of electronic retrieval system, and any other techniques and systems not yet in use or even invented.

Congress's broadly sweeping definition of "perform" was intended, in part, to overrule the Supreme Court decisions in *Teleprompter, Fortnightly,* and *Aiken, supra.* It should now be clear that any means of rendering a copyrighted work, whether directly or indirectly through a chain of communicative devices, constitutes a performance. Note further that Congress emphasized that a performance may be accomplished by "techniques and systems not yet in use or even invented." Congress thus seems to have endeavored to ensure that, with respect to the scope of activities encompassed within the concept of performance, "technological change" would not render the Act's "literal terms ambiguous." *Cf. Aiken, supra.*

b. "Public" Performances Under the 1976 Act

§ 101. Definitions

....

To perform or display a work "publicly" means —

(1) to perform or display it at a place open to the public or at any place where a substantial number of persons outside of a normal circle of a family and its social acquaintances is gathered; or

(2) to transmit or otherwise communicate a performance or display of the work to a place specified by clause (1) or to the public, by means of any device or process, whether the members of the public capable of receiving the performance or display receive it in the same place or in separate places and at the same time or at different times.

To "transmit" a performance or display is to communicate it by any device or process whereby images or sounds are received beyond the place from which they are sent.

....

HOUSE REPORT

H.R. Rep. No. 94-1476, 94th Cong., 2d Sess. 64-65 (1976)

Under clause (1) of the definition of "publicly" in section 101, a performance or display is "public" if it takes place "at a place open to the public or at any place where a substantial number of persons outside of a normal circle of a family and its social acquaintances is gathered." One of the principal purposes of the definition was to make clear that, contrary to the decision in *Metro-Goldwyn-Mayer Distributing Corp. v. Wyatt*, 21 C.O. Bull. 203 (D. Md. 1932), performances in "semipublic" places such as clubs, lodges, factories, summer camps, and schools are "public performances" subject to copyright control. The term "a family" in this context would include an individual living alone, so that a gathering confined to the individual's social acquaintances would normally be regarded as private. Routine meetings of businesses [sic] and governmental personnel would be excluded because they do not represent the gathering of a "substantial number of persons."

Clause (2) of the definition of "publicly" in section 101 makes clear that the concepts of public performance and public display include not only performances and displays that occur initially in a public place, but also acts that transmit or otherwise communicate a performance or display of the work to the public by means of any device or process. The definition of "transmit" — to communicate a performance or display "by any device or process whereby images or sound are received beyond the place from which they are sent" — is broad enough to include all conceivable forms and combinations of wired or wireless communications media, including but by no means limited to radio and television broadcasting as we know them. Each and every method by which the images or sounds comprising a performance or display are picked up and conveyed is a "transmission," and if the transmission reaches the public in any form, the case comes within the scope of clauses (4) or (5) of section 106.

Under the bill, as under the present law, a performance made available by transmission to the public at large is "public" even though the recipients are not gathered in a single place, and even if there is no proof that any of the potential recipients was operating his receiving apparatus at the time of the transmission. The same principles apply whenever the potential recipients of the transmission represent a limited segment of the public, such as the occupants of hotel rooms or the subscribers of a cable television service. Clause (2) of the definition of "publicly" is applicable "whether the members of the public capable of receiving the performance or display receive it in the same place or in separate places and at the same time or at different times."

QUESTIONS

Which of the following is a "public" performance?

1. The performance of copyrighted music at a very large wedding in the home of the parents of the bride.

2. The performance of copyrighted music at a very small wedding in a hotel room.

3. Transmission of a copyrighted audiovisual work by closed circuit television to the many apartments in a cooperative apartment building the co-op board of which exercises a right of approval or veto over prospective apartment buyers and dwellers.

COLUMBIA PICTURES INDUSTRIES, INC. v. AVECO, INC.

800 F.2d 59 (3d Cir. 1986)

STAPLETON, CIRCUIT JUDGE.

Plaintiffs, appellees in this action, are producers of motion pictures ("Producers") and bring this copyright infringement action against the defendant, Aveco, Inc. Producers claim that Aveco's business, which includes renting video cassettes of motion pictures in conjunction with rooms in which they may be viewed, violates their exclusive rights under the Copyright Act of 1976, 17 U.S.C. § 101 et seq. The district court agreed and we affirm. Jurisdiction below was predicated on 28 U.S.C. §§ 1331 and 1338(a).

. . . .

I

Among their other operations, Producers distribute video cassette copies of motion pictures in which they own registered copyrights. They do so knowing that many retail purchasers of these video cassettes, including Aveco, rent them to others for profit. Aveco also makes available private rooms of various sizes in which its customers may view the video cassettes that they have chosen from Aveco's offerings. For example, at one location, Lock Haven, Aveco has thirty viewing rooms, each containing seating, a video cassette player, and television monitor. Aveco charges a rental fee for the viewing room that is separate from the charge for the video cassette rental.

Customers of Aveco may (1) rent a room and also rent a video cassette for viewing in that room, (2) rent a room and bring a video cassette obtained elsewhere to play in the room, or (3) rent a video cassette for out-of-store viewing.

Aveco has placed its video cassette players inside the individual viewing rooms and, subject to a time limitation, allows the customer complete control over the playing of the video cassettes. Customers operate the video cassette players in each viewing room and Aveco's employees assist only upon request. Each video cassette may be viewed only from inside the viewing room, and is not transmitted beyond the particular room in which it is being played. Aveco asserts that it rents its viewing rooms to individual customers who may be joined in the room only by members of their families and social acquaintances. Furthermore, Aveco's stated practice is not to permit unrelated groups of customers to share a viewing room while a video cassette is being played. For purposes of this appeal we assume the veracity of these assertions.

II

As the owners of copyrights in motion pictures, Producers possess statutory rights under the Copyright Act of 1976, 17 U.S.C. §§ 101-810. Among these are the exclusive rights set out in Section 106 .... Producers do not, in the present litigation, allege infringement of their exclusive rights "to do and to authorize [the distribution of] copies or phonorecords of the copyrighted work to the public by sale or other transfer of ownership, or by rental, lease, or lending." Thus, Aveco's rental of video cassettes for at-home viewing is not challenged.

Producers' claim in this litigation is based on the alleged infringement of their "exclusive right ... to perform the copyrighted work publicly" and to "authorize" such performances. Producers assert that Aveco, by renting its viewing rooms to the public for the purpose of watching Producers' video cassettes, is authorizing the public performance of copyrighted motion pictures.

Our analysis begins with the language of the Act. We first observe that there is no question that "performances" of copyrighted materials take place at Aveco's stores. "To perform" a work is defined in the Act as, "in the case of a motion picture or other audiovisual work, to show its images in any sequence or to make the sounds accompanying it audible." Section 101. As the House Report notes, this definition means that an individual is performing a work whenever he does anything by which the work is transmitted, repeated, or made to recur. H.R. Rep. No. 1476, 94th Cong., 2d Sess. 63, *reprinted in* 1976 U.S. Code Cong. & Ad. News 5659, 5676-77.

Producers do not argue that Aveco itself performs the video cassettes. They acknowledge that under the Act Aveco's *customers* are the ones performing the works, for it is they who actually place the video cassette in the video cassette player and operate the controls. As we said in *Columbia Pictures Industries v. Redd Horne*, 749 F.2d 154, 158 (3d Cir. 1984), "[p]laying a video cassette ... constitute[s] a performance under Section 101." However, if there is a public performance, Aveco may still be responsible as an infringer even though it does not actually operate the video cassette players. In granting copyright owners the exclusive rights to "authorize" public performances, Congress intended "to avoid any questions as to the liability of contributory infringers. For example, a person who lawfully acquires an authorized copy of a motion picture would be an infringer if he or she engages in the business of renting it to others for purposes of an unauthorized public performance." H.R. Rep. No. 1476, 94th Cong., 2d Sess. 61, *reprinted in* 1976 U.S. Code Cong. &

Ad. News at 5674; *see* S. Rep. No. 473, 94th Cong., 1st Sess. 57 (1975). In our opinion, this rationale applies equally to the person who knowingly makes available other requisites of a public performance. Accordingly, we agree with the district court that Aveco, by enabling its customers to perform the video cassettes in the viewing rooms, authorizes the performances.[3]

The performances of Producers' motion pictures at Aveco's stores infringe their copyrights, however, only if they are "public." The copyright owners' rights do not extend to control over private performances. The Act defines a public performance.

   ....

We recently parsed this definition in *Redd Horne,* a case similar to the one at bar. The principal factual distinction is that in Redd Horne's operation, known as Maxwell's Video Showcase, Ltd. ("Maxwell's"), the video cassette players were located in the stores' central areas, not in each individual screening room. Maxwell's customers would select a video cassette from Maxwell's stock and rent a room which they entered to watch the motion picture on a television monitor. A Maxwell's employee would play the video cassette for the customers in one of the centrally-located video cassette players and transmit the performance to the monitor located in the room. Thus, unlike Aveco's customers, Maxwell's clientele had no control over the video cassette players.

The *Redd Horne* court began its analysis with the observation that the two components of clause (1) of the definition of a public performance are disjunctive. 749 F.2d at 159. "The first category is self-evident; it is 'a place open to the public.' The second category, commonly referred to as a semi-public place, is determined by the size and composition of the audience." *Id.* The court then concluded that the performances were occurring at a place open to the public, which it found to be the entire store, including the viewing rooms.

> Any member of the public can view a motion picture by paying the appropriate fee. The services provided by Maxwell's are essentially the same as a movie theatre, with the additional feature of privacy. The relevant "place" within the meaning of Section 101 is each of Maxwell's two stores, not each individual booth within each store. Simply because the cassettes can be viewed in private does not mitigate the essential fact that Maxwell's is unquestionably open to the public.

749 F.2d at 159.

The *Redd Horne* court reached this conclusion despite the fact that when a customer watched a movie at Maxwell's, the viewing room was closed to other

---

[3] Aveco authorizes the performances that occur in the viewing rooms no less when the copyrighted video cassette is obtained from some other source. Aveco encourages the public to make use of its facilities for the purpose of viewing such tapes and makes available its rooms and equipment to customers who bring cassettes with them. By thus knowingly promoting and facilitating public performances of Producers' works, Aveco authorizes those performances even when it is not the source of Producers' copyrighted video cassettes. *RCA Records v. All-Fast Systems, Inc.,* 594 F. Supp. 335 (S.D.N.Y. 1984) (provision of facilities used for unlawful copying enjoined as an infringement); *Italian Book Corp. v. Palms Sheepshead Country Club, Inc.,* 186 U.S.P.Q. 326 (E.D.N.Y. 1975).

members of the public. Nevertheless, Aveco asserts that factual differences between Maxwell's stores and its own require a different result in this case.

Aveco first observes that when Maxwell's employees "performed" the video cassettes, they did so in a central location, the store's main area. This lobby was undeniably "open to the public." Aveco suggests that, in *Redd Horne*, the location of the customers in the private rooms was simply irrelevant, for the *performers* were in a public place, the lobby. In the case at bar, Aveco continues, its employees do not perform anything, the customers do. Unlike Maxwell's employees located in the public lobby, Aveco's customers are in private screening rooms. Aveco argues that while these viewing rooms are available to anyone for rent, they are private during each rental period, and therefore, not "open to the public." The performance — the playing of the video cassette — thus occurs not in the public lobby, but in the private viewing rooms.

We disagree. The necessary implication of Aveco's analysis is that *Redd Horne* would have been decided differently had Maxwell's located its video cassette players in a locked closet in the back of the stores. We do not read *Redd Horne* to adopt such an analysis. The Copyright Act speaks of performances at a place open to the public. It does not require that the public place be actually crowded with people. A telephone booth, a taxi cab, and even a pay toilet are commonly regarded as "open to the public," even though they are usually occupied only by one party at a time. Our opinion in *Redd Horne* turned not on the precise whereabouts of the video cassette players, but on the nature of Maxwell's stores. Maxwell's, like Aveco, was willing to make a viewing room and video cassettes available to any member of the public with the inclination to avail himself of this service. It is this availability that made Maxwell's stores public places, not the coincidence that the video cassette players were situated in the lobby. Because we find *Redd Horne* indistinguishable from the case at bar, we find that Aveco's operations constituted an authorization of public performances of Producers' copyrighted works.

Aveco's reliance on the first sale doctrine is likewise misplaced. The first sale doctrine, codified at 17 U.S.C. § 109(a), prevents the copyright owner from controlling future transfers of a particular copy of a copyrighted work after he has transferred its "material ownership" to another. *Redd Horne,* 749 F.2d at 159. When a copyright owner parts with title to a particular copy of his copyrighted work, he thereby divests himself of his exclusive right to vend that particular copy. *Id. See United States v. Powell,* 701 F.2d 70, 72 (8th Cir. 1983); *United States v. Moore,* 604 F.2d 1228, 1232 (9th Cir. 1979). Accordingly, under the first sale doctrine, Producers cannot claim that Aveco's rentals or sales of lawfully acquired video cassettes infringe on their exclusive rights to vend those cassettes.

However, in *Redd Horne,* we found that, because of the limited control the customer had over the video cassette, Maxwell's had not actually rented or transferred the ownership in the cassette to its customers. Because we found that there had not been a "future transfer," there was no opportunity to even apply the first sale doctrine.

In the case at bar, even assuming, *arguendo,* both a waiver by Producers of their Section 106(3) distribution rights and a valid transfer of ownership of the video cassette during the rental period, the first sale doctrine is nonetheless irrelevant. The rights protected by copyright are divisible and the waiver of one does not necessarily waive any of the others. *See* Section 202. In particular, the transfer of ownership in a particular copy of a work does not affect Producers' Section 106(4) exclusive rights to do and to authorize public performances. *Redd Horne,* 749 F.2d at 160; *Powell,* 701 F.2d at 72; *Moore,* 604 F.2d at 1232. It therefore cannot protect one who is infringing Producers' Section 106(4) rights by the public performance of the copyrighted work.

III

We therefore conclude that Aveco, by renting its rooms to members of the general public in which they may view performances of Producers' copyrighted video cassettes, obtained from any source, has authorized public performances of those cassettes. This is a violation of Producers' Section 106 rights and is appropriately enjoined. We therefore will affirm the order of the district court.

QUESTIONS

1. In the *Redd Horne* case, the Third Circuit placed weight on the definition of "public performance" by way of a "transmission" in § 101. It concluded that the showing of the videotapes by Maxwell's was a "transmission" which was public even though the viewers watched the films at different times, with one small group following another. Consider, first, whether Maxwell's was indeed "transmitting" the motion pictures. Consider, second, whether — assuming Maxwell's was the person "performing" the motion pictures — *Redd Horne's* conclusions are therefore inapplicable when the "performing" in the *Aveco* case is done by the small viewing groups rather than by the store owner.

2. Presumably, had Aveco's customers taken the rented videotapes home with them, and viewed them there the same evening, neither the rental nor the viewing would have constituted a copyright infringement. Why should there be any different result when the viewers, for their own convenience, remain on Aveco's premises, in separate rooms, and view the tapes there? *See Opinion of Ohio Att'y Gen. 87-108* (Dec. 29, 1987), 1988 CCH Copyright L. Dec. ¶ 26,240.

3. Was the court correct in finding Aveco to infringe with respect to the small-group viewing of videotapes that the group itself brings onto the premises, having purchased, rented, or borrowed them from elsewhere? Would the purchaser of the videotape brought to and performed in the Aveco store be an infringer?

4. Sleepwell Motel has television sets in all of its private guest rooms, and attached to each set is a videocassette recorder. Motel guests may rent, for $4 per night, any number of videocassettes that the motel has purchased from a local video store and stocks at the motel registration counter. These cassettes are then taken back to the guest rooms for viewing through the VCRs. Owners of copyrighted motion pictures have brought an action against Sleepwell Motel for copyright infringement. What should the result be? Is the *Aveco* decision distinguishable? *See Columbia Pictures Indus. v. Professional Real Estate Investors, Inc.,* 866 F.2d 278 (9th Cir. 1989). Does it make a

difference if the motion pictures are transmitted to private rooms, one customer at a time? *See On Command Video Corp. v. Columbia Pictures Indus.,*
777 F. Supp. 787 (N.D. Cal. 1991).

3. PERFORMING RIGHTS SOCIETIES

OCASEK v. HEGGLUND

116 F.R.D. 154 (D. Wyo. 1987)

BRIMMER, CHIEF JUDGE.

. . . .

This is an action for copyright infringement brought by four copyright
owners against the owner and operator of a dance hall in Douglas, Wyoming.
The plaintiffs allege that five (5) musical compositions owned by them were
publicly performed at the defendant's establishment on February 1, 1985
and/or February 2, 1985 without their authorization and thus in violation of
their copyrights....

[The defendant served notice on the plaintiff songwriters that she intended
to take their depositions some six weeks later in Cheyenne, Wyoming. Although the plaintiffs objected to the taking of depositions and sought a protective order, the Magistrate issued an order granting the motion to compel
depositions, concluding that anyone electing to sue in the District of Wyoming
is obligated to appear there to be deposed. He held that the defendant had an
absolute right to discovery on such issues as the identity or substantial similarity of the music at issue, the nature and extent of damages and of future
injury to the plaintiffs. On appeal, the court reversed the Magistrate's order.]

The plaintiffs are members of the American Society of Composers, Authors
and Publishers (ASCAP). As explained below, due to the difficult nature of
enforcing a copyright, copyright owners have ceded to ASCAP certain powers
of enforcement such that discovery which is considered reasonable and routine
in most situations is not so in copyright infringement actions involving
ASCAP or like organizations.[1]

The purpose of ASCAP is to enforce the copyright for the owner. In the area
of musical composition copyright, the need for this type of service is particularly acute. As the United States District Court for the Southern District of
New York has explained,

> Prior to ASCAP's formation in 1914 there was no effective method by
> which composers and publishers of music could secure payment for the
> performance for profit of their copyrighted works. The users of music,
> such as theaters, dance halls and bars, were so numerous and widespread,
> and each performance so fleeting an occurrence, that no individual copy-
> right owner could negotiate licenses with users of his music, or detect
> unauthorized uses. On the other side of the coin, those who wished to
> perform compositions without infringing the copyright were, as a practi-
> cal matter, unable to obtain licenses from the owners of the works they

---

[1]For example, Broadcast Music, Inc. (BMI) provides services similar to ASCAP....

wished to perform. ASCAP was organized as a "clearinghouse" for copyright owners and users to solve these problems.

Columbia Broad. Sys., Inc. v. American Soc. of Comp., 400 F. Supp. 737, 741 (S.D.N.Y. 1975). The Supreme Court has also recognized the copyright owner's need for some other party to enforce its copyright, stating that

> Because a musical composition can be "consumed" by many different people at the same time and without the creator's knowledge, the "owner" has no real way to demand reimbursement for the use of his property except through the copyright laws *and* an effective way to enforce those legal rights. *See Twentieth Century Music Corp. v. Aiken,* 422 U.S. 151, 162, 95 S. Ct. 2040, 2047, 45 L. Ed. 2d 84 (1975). It takes an organization of rather large size to monitor most or all uses and to deal with users on behalf of the composers. Moreover, it is inefficient to have too many such organizations duplicating each other's monitoring of use.

Broadcast Music, Inc. v. CBS, 441 U.S. 1, 19 n. 32, 99 S. Ct. 1551, 1562 n. 32, 60 L. Ed. 2d 1 (1978). Thus it is acknowledged by most, and taken for granted by some, that ASCAP, or some similar organization, will enforce a composer's or publisher's copyright.

Typically, composers enforce their copyright via membership in ASCAP. As part of the terms of the membership agreement, the copyright owner grants to ASCAP a non-exclusive right to license public performances of the member's copyrighted musical compositions. The membership agreement authorizes ASCAP to prevent the infringement of the copyright, to act as the member's attorney-in-fact and to litigate and take all necessary legal actions to prevent unauthorized public performances of the member's copyrighted musical works and to collect damages for infringements.

In order to accomplish this rather formidable task,

> ASCAP provides its members with a wide range of services. It maintains a surveillance system of radio and television broadcasts to detect unlicensed uses, institutes infringement actions, collects revenues from licensees and distributes royalties to copyright owners in accordance with a schedule which reflects the nature and amount of the use of their music and other factors.

Columbia Broad. Sys., Inc. v. American Soc. of Comp., 400 F. Supp. at 742. ASCAP also employs a number of field agents who monitor unlicensed, local entertainment establishments to check for unauthorized uses of its members' compositions. In short, ASCAP handles virtually every aspect of enforcing the member's copyright, from licensing users to litigating unauthorized uses, and the copyright owner is virtually uninvolved with the actual enforcement activities; ASCAP members typically have no personal knowledge of infringements on their copyrights, but are completely dependent on ASCAP to protect their rights.

Yet for all of ASCAP's broad power to enforce its members' copyrights, it cannot bring an infringement suit in its own name....

... The Copyright Act has always specified that only the copyright owner, or the owner of exclusive rights under the copyright, as of the time the acts of infringement occur, has standing to bring an action for infringement of such rights; a non-exclusive licensee does not have standing. 17 U.S.C. § 501(b)....

In this case, as is typical of most ASCAP-assisted infringement suits, two ASCAP investigators visited the defendant's establishment in Douglas, Wyoming, on February 1 and 2, 1985. *See, e.g., Stone City Music v. Thunderbird, Inc.,* 116 F.R.D. 473 (N.D. Miss. 1987). They noted which of their members' compositions were performed and subsequently submitted a written report to their regional director. Based on this report and ASCAP's own records that the defendant was not licensed by it, ASCAP initiated this lawsuit for copyright infringement on behalf of their members, the plaintiffs herein.... [Under Federal Rule of Civil Procedure 26(b) and (c), a court is to limit discovery — and may issue a protective order — when discovery is found to be unduly burdensome or expensive.]

[T]he Court finds that the plaintiffs are entitled to a protective order pursuant to Rule 26(c)(3). The reasons for which the magistrate and the defendant assert that the plaintiffs must be deposed constitute information that is either irrelevant, not known by the plaintiffs or discoverable via a less costly or burdensome method.

The magistrate ordered the plaintiffs be deposed to discover information about the identity and/or substantial similarity of the music at issue and the nature and extent of damages and injury. The defendant echoed these concerns at oral argument, contending that she needed to depose the plaintiffs to discover information in regard to damages, proof that the music played was that of the plaintiffs' and plaintiffs' present suffering as justification for an injunction.

In regard to the issue of identity or substantial similarity, the Court finds that it is irrelevant to this case for infringement.... [I]n order to make out their case for infringement, in addition to submitting documentation of their copyrights, the plaintiffs need only prove that their works were performed without authorization. "The degree of similarity to the original is irrelevant if the work is held out to be a performance of the copyrighted work." *George Simon, Inc. v. Spatz,* 492 F. Supp. 836, 838 (W.D. Wis. 1980). The Court finds, therefore, that the plaintiffs may not be deposed in order to establish similarity.

Information regarding damages is also irrelevant since the plaintiffs have requested statutory damages pursuant to 17 U.S.C. § 504(c)(1). Since the statute determines what factors should be considered and the exact amount is a matter of the court's discretion, the amount of damages is not a matter subject to proof....

It is also pointless to depose the plaintiffs as to the nature and extent of their claimed serious and continuing injuries and harms. These items presumably relate to the plaintiffs' request for a permanent injunction against future infringements pursuant to 17 U.S.C. § 502(a). However, in actions such as these, the plaintiff need not establish irreparable injury in order to obtain an injunction. Under § 502(a), "an injunction will issue when there is a 'substantial likelihood of further infringement of plaintiffs' copyrights.'" *Id.* at 634....

As to proof of the unauthorized public performance of the plaintiffs' songs, it is clear that the plaintiffs have no knowledge of these events. As in most infringement cases enforced by ASCAP, ASCAP investigators actually witness the unauthorized public performance of the plaintiffs' songs. These investigators write a report and submit it to their district manager who then submits it to the ASCAP national director. The Court notes that ASCAP followed this standard operating procedure in this case and that all of these ASCAP employees are available to be deposed in this forum. Significantly, the defendant does not argue that the plaintiffs have knowledge of the actual performance. We find, therefore, that the plaintiffs are not the proper or likely source for this admittedly relevant information and that discovery of this information does not justify deposing the plaintiffs. *See, Girlsongs v. J.N.S. Grand, Inc.,* No. 84-C-7890 (N.D. Ill. June 9, 1986).

In light of the foregoing, the Court finds that if there is, in fact, some relevant information which the defendant can discover from the plaintiffs, she may do so by way of written interrogatories. Deposing the plaintiffs in these types of cases is unduly burdensome and expensive.... The very purpose of ASCAP is to relieve the copyright owner of the time-consuming and expensive task of enforcing his rights; requiring that the owner be deposed defeats this purpose. Although this particular case, by itself, may not seem especially burdensome to the plaintiffs, this case must be viewed as part of the aggregate of all cases in which the plaintiffs must enforce their rights. As a general rule, to allow the defendants to depose the plaintiffs in these types of infringement suits would render the enforcement procedure so costly and burdensome as to preclude the vindication of the principle of copyright. Therefore, the Court must grant the plaintiffs' request for a protective order against the taking of their depositions.

....

Today public performance is the major source of revenue in the music industry. ASCAP and Broadcast Music Inc. (BMI), the two major performing rights organizations in the U.S., license the performance rights of their more than 100,000 members to hundreds of thousands of users — generating well over $600 million in royalties annually. SESAC (a much smaller, privately owned organization) performs similar functions. "As a practical matter virtually every domestic copyrighted composition is in the repertory of either ASCAP, which has over 3 million compositions in its pool, or BMI, which has over one million.... Almost all broadcasters hold blanket licenses from both ASCAP and BMI." *CBS v. ASCAP,* 400 F. Supp. 737, 742 (S.D.N.Y. 1975), *rev'd,* 562 F.2d 130 (2d Cir. 1977), *rev'd,* 441 U.S. 1 (1979), *on remand,* 205 U.S.P.Q. 880 (2d Cir. 1980).

Copyright holders — the composers, lyricists and publishers — become members of ASCAP or BMI by granting the non-exclusive right to license public performance of their musical compositions in a non-dramatic fashion.

These rights are in turn granted to networks, local television stations, radio stations, nightclubs, hotels, and other users in blanket licensing agreements that allow the licensee full use of any licensed works. Licensing fees vary from industry to industry (although similarly situated licensees must be treated equally). The networks pay a flat fee. Local television and radio stations pay a fee based on sponsorship receipts (less certain deductions). Fees for "general establishments" depend on a number of factors: drinking prices, seating capacity, frequency of music performances, type of rendition, admission charges, etc. Hotel and motel fees take into account total entertainment expenditures; concert rates depend on admission price and seating capacity; background music users such as Muzak pay a fee based primarily on the number and character of subscribers. Users who contend that a proposed ASCAP fee is unreasonable may have a reasonable fee determined by the United States District Court for the Southern District of New York. To resolve disputes with music users, BMI includes arbitration provisions in its license agreements.

Collecting the money from users, even with the variety of fee schedules, is relatively simple because of the nature of the blanket licensing, which permits licensees to use any and all music in the repertoire. But the very simplicity of collecting a single fee from a blanket licensee creates difficulties in the apportioning and distributing of the collected royalties. Surveys and logging of broadcasts are conducted by the performing rights organizations, which then apply formulas in order to distribute royalties. Dissatisfied members or affiliates have remedies under the ASCAP and BMI consent decrees. A closer look at the history and provisions of the ASCAP decree is in order.

The increasing importance of the broadcast industry in the late 1930's heightened the importance of performance rights licensing. With ASCAP operating almost alone in the field, a growing antagonism developed between the society and the broadcast users of copyrighted musical works. Finally, angered over what they considered exorbitant licensing fees and unacceptable ASCAP practices, the broadcasters refused to negotiate with ASCAP, forming their own performance rights organization (BMI) and boycotting ASCAP music. "This was the era when 'Jeanie With the Light Brown Hair' was burned in effigy on college campuses and the listening public was surfeited with Latin American rhythms." [Statement of March 13, 1958 of Victor Hansen before the House Select Comm. on Small Business, Subcomm. No. 5, Hearings, Policies of American Society of Composers, Authors, and Publishers 138-141 (March-April 1958)].

On February 25, 1941, the Antitrust Division of the Department of Justice filed a civil complaint against ASCAP, charging Sherman Act violations. A consent agreement was signed one week later. See 1940-43 Trade Cases ¶ 56,104 (S.D.N.Y. 1941). That decree was amended in significant respects in 1950, and again ten years later. See 1950-51 Trade Cas. ¶ 62,595 (S.D.N.Y. 1950); Timberg, *The Antitrust Aspects of Merchandising Modern Music: The ASCAP Consent Judgment of 1950*, 19 Law & Contemp. Probs. 294 (1954); Garner, *United States v. ASCAP: The Licensing Provisions of the Amended Final Judgment of 1950*, 23 Bull. Copyr. Soc'y 119 (1976). (For the BMI consent decree, see 1966 Trade Cas. ¶ 71,941 (S.D.N.Y. 1966).) The amended ASCAP consent decree has a number of important features: (1) ASCAP is prohibited from discriminating against similarly situated licensees. (2) ASCAP may not acquire exclusive rights to license members' performance rights; composers, authors and publishers also have the right to negotiate licenses on their own. (3) ASCAP is required to offer per-program licenses in addition to the blanket licenses. (4) Membership requirements (including withdrawal rights) and voting rights have been made more lenient than previously. (5) Movie theatre licensing is prohibited, i.e., the performance of music is cleared by the producer at the source (the result of the *Alden-Rochelle* case). (6) A procedure for determination of reasonable fees by the District Court for the Southern District of New York is established. (7) Internal governance regulations, such as those relating to Board elections (in order to eliminate what had been a self-perpetuating Board), are imposed. (8) Distribution of royalties is to be based on less subjective terms than dictated in the original 1941 accord and is to be based primarily on a more objective survey system.

Although this twenty-year history of antitrust consent decrees helped calm the government, certain users subject to ASCAP and BMI licensing — particularly the broadcasters — were still not satisfied. They simply could not accept blanket licensing, which exacted the same fee regardless of the level of use. A decade-long attack by a television network proved to be unsuccessful.

Under the blanket license, the licensee may use any music in the repertory of the licensor, as often as desired, for a single fee. Payment is either a flat sum or a percentage of the licensee's revenue and is therefore not related to the amount used or the particular works used. CBS claimed, in lawsuits against ASCAP and BMI, that the blanket license was an agreement unlawfully restraining trade (i.e., a price-fixing device that was per se unlawful) in violation of § 1 of the Sherman Act and sought to have both performing rights societies barred from using it, or, alternatively, to require them to charge predetermined amounts each time copyrighted music is used on the air.

Although the Second Circuit Court of Appeals agreed with CBS, its judgment was overturned by the Supreme Court. In *BMI v. CBS,* 441 U.S. 1 (1979), the Court ruled that the blanket license was not a per se violation, and remanded the case to have the licensing practice evaluated using rule-of-reason analysis.

In applying rule-of-reason standards, the Second Circuit held that CBS must first establish that the practice has a restraining effect in the industry. This issue was deemed to have been left unresolved by the Supreme Court's decision. The fact that there is no price competition among songs is not determinative on this question. However, it is crucial that there is the opportunity to obtain individual performing rights. "If the opportunity to purchase performing rights to individual songs is fully available, then it is customer preference for the blanket license, and not the license itself, that causes the lack of price competition among songs. *CBS v. ASCAP,* 620 F.2d 930, 935 (2d Cir. 1980), *cert. denied,* 450 U.S. 970 (1981). The issue then is whether direct licensing is feasible. The court of appeals, after reviewing the district court's findings, agreed that CBS had failed to prove the factual predicate of its claim — the nonavailability of alternatives to the blanket license. *See* Hartnick,

The Network Blanket License Triumphant — The Fourth Round of the ASCAP-BMI-CBS Litigation, 2 Com. & L. 49 (1980).

In a different series of proceedings, the challenge to blanket licensing moved from the network level down to the local broadcasting level. In *Buffalo Broadcasting Corp. v. ASCAP,* 546 F. Supp. 274 (S.D.N.Y. 1982), *rev'd,* 744 F.2d 917 (2d Cir. 1984), the district court held that requiring local television stations to purchase blanket licenses for the performance of copyrighted music in syndicated programs was an unreasonable restraint of trade in violation of the Sherman Act. The court distinguished *CBS v. ASCAP,* holding that local broadcasters lacked the market power of the networks to obtain licenses directly from the copyright owners. The Second Circuit, however, reversed, holding that the local broadcasters had not demonstrated a lack of power to obtain performance rights through a mechanism other than blanket licenses.

More recently, the attack upon the blanket license was taken up by a cable system, Showtime/The Movie Channel (SMC), which challenged not the overall validity of the blanket-license device but rather the reasonableness of the blanket-license rate charged by ASCAP for the soundtrack music in motion pictures performed on SMC's cable programs. In exercising its jurisdiction to determine the reasonableness of such rates, the District Court in the Southern District of New York (the "rate court") rejected ASCAP's request for a fee of 25 cents per SMC cable subscriber as well as SMC's suggested fee of 8 cents per subscriber, and settled instead on a rate of 15 cents. In the first appellate challenge to such a fee determination under the consent decree, the Court of Appeals for the Second Circuit affirmed the determination of the fee. Although ASCAP had pointed to its blanket-license fees with Home Box Office and the Disney Channel as most pertinent in determining a reasonable fee for its license with SMC, the District Court found that the HBO license fee was higher than fair value because of ASCAP's undue market power; the Court of Appeals agreed that ASCAP's market power was sufficiently great as to warrant consideration in setting a reasonable (and lower) fee for others, and it affirmed the lower court's factual findings and legal conclusions. *ASCAP v. Showtime/The Movie Channel, Inc.,* 912 F.2d 563 (2d Cir. 1990).

"GRAND" AND "SMALL" RIGHTS

The performing rights organizations license only nondramatic musical rights, the so-called "small" rights. The "grand" (dramatic) rights are licensed only by the copyright holders, who have traditionally felt capable of monitoring the more detectable dramatic performances. Little was it realized that this dramatic/non-dramatic distinction generated a definitional problem of increasing significance. Until some twenty years ago, there was a dearth of litigation on this issue. A 1955 case held that a medley of songs from *The Student Prince* performed as part of a ten-scene costumed extravaganza revue was not a dramatic presentation. *April Prods., Inc. v. Strand Enters., Inc.,* 221 F.2d 292 (2d Cir. 1955). Rather, the performance by Ben Yost and His Royal Guardsmen was an "entr' acte" and contributed nothing to the show's overall plot.

The problem was once again confronted — this time with a different result — in a series of cases involving performances of selections from the rock opera

Jesus Christ Superstar. In *Rice v. American Program Bureau,* 446 F.2d 685 (2d Cir. 1971), a booking agent who had secured an ASCAP license was enjoined from performing either the work in its entirety or even excerpts accompanied by words, pantomime, dance or visual representations of the opera as a whole. In *Robert Stigwood Group, Ltd. v. Sperber,* 457 F.2d 50 (2d Cir. 1972), another performance was enjoined. Here, the performance was without costume, but almost all of the songs were presented in identical sequence to the original and performers maintained specific characters throughout the performance. The court held that the performance was dramatic even without scenery, costumes and dialogue and despite the concert setting. The court's injunctive decree, arguably overbroad, forbade:

> (1) performing any song in such a way as to follow another song in the same order as in the original *Jesus Christ Superstar* opera;
> (2) performing any songs from the opera accompanied by dramatic action, scenic accessory or costumes.

There are differing points of view as to how best to distinguish between dramatic performances (not covered by the ASCAP license to the performer) and non-dramatic performances. One extreme, put forward by former ASCAP attorney Herman Finkelstein, defines non-dramatic performances as "renditions of a song ... without dialogue, scenery or costumes." Finkelstein, *The Composer and the Public Interest — Regulation of Performing Right Societies,* 19 Law & Contemp. Probs. 275, 283 n.32 (1954). This, however, would exclude from the ASCAP license, quite questionably, a song that is sung by a person wearing a pertinent costume or standing in front of a simply decorated flat. At the other extreme is the *April Productions* rule, that "the performance of a noninstrumental musical composition (i.e. lyrics and music) would be dramatic only if it were accompanied by material from the dramatico-musical work of which the composition was a part." Such a rule, however, would unwisely allow an ASCAP licensee to perform, for example, all of the songs from "South Pacific" in sequence with freshly written transition dialogue, so long as no dialogue is borrowed directly from the Hammerstein book.

Professor Nimmer suggests as more appropriate the language in the ASCAP blanket television license which defines a dramatic performance as "a performance of a musical composition on a television program in which there is a definite plot depicted by action and where the performance of the musical composition is woven into and carries forward the plot and its accompanying action. The use of dialogue to establish a mere program format or the use of any non-dramatic device merely to introduce a performance of a composition shall not be deemed to make such a performance dramatic." He continues: "A performance of a musical composition is dramatic if it aids in telling a story, otherwise it is not."

4. THE RIGHT OF PUBLIC DISPLAY

§ 106. Exclusive rights in copyrighted works

Subject to sections 107 through 120, the owner of copyright under this title has the exclusive rights to do and to authorize any of the following:

....

(5) in the case of literary, musical, dramatic, and choreographic works, pantomimes, and pictorial, graphic, or sculptural works, including the individual images of a motion picture or other audiovisual work, to display the copyrighted work publicly.

§ 101. Definitions

As used in this title, the following terms and their variant forms mean the following:

....

To "display" a work means to show a copy of it, either directly or by means of a film, slide, television image, or any other device or process or, in the case of a motion picture or other audiovisual work, to show individual images nonsequentially.

....

§ 109. Limitations on exclusive rights: Effect of transfer of particular copy or phonorecord

....

(c) Notwithstanding the provisions of section 106(5), the owner of a particular copy lawfully made under this title, or any person authorized by such owner, is entitled, without the authority of the copyright owner, to display that copy publicly, either directly or by the projection of no more than one image at a time, to viewers present at the place where the copy is located.

(d) The privileges prescribed by subsections (a) and (c) do not, unless authorized by the copyright owner, extend to any person who has acquired possession of the copy or phonorecord from the copyright owner, by rental, lease, loan, or otherwise, without acquiring ownership of it.

NOTE

"Clause (5) of section 106 represents the first explicit statutory recognition in United States copyright law of an exclusive right to show a copyrighted work, or an image of it, to the public. The existence or extent of this right under the present [1909] statute is uncertain and subject to challenge." S. Rep. No. 94-473, at 59; H.R. Rep. No. 94-1476, at 63. A particularly troubling issue was whether the showing of a pictorial work on a television broadcast was an infringing "copy" under the 1909 act; the evanescence of the image helped convince at least one court that it was not. *Mura v. Columbia Broadcasting Sys.*, 245 F. Supp. 587 (S.D.N.Y. 1965).

The newly created right of display is limited, in common with the performing right in § 106(4), to *public* presentation, and it applies only to specified types of works. (The student should consult the definition of "publicly" in § 101.) It will be noted that sound recordings are not afforded a statutory right of public display, and that audiovisual works are covered only to the extent of nonsequential presentation of individual images; sequential presentation would amount to a "performance." Moreover, the right to display published pictorial, graphic and sculptural works by public broadcasters on television is covered by a compulsory license granted in § 118. Finally, the right of public display is limited by the provisions of § 109(c), discussed in the passages from the House Report immediately below. (As originally enacted in 1976, this section was designated as 109(b).)

HOUSE REPORT

H.R. Rep. No. 94-1476, 94th Cong., 2d Sess. 64, 79-80 (1976)

... In addition to the direct showings of a copy of a work, "display" would include the projection of an image on a screen or other surface by any method, the transmission of an image by electronic or other means, and the showing of an image on a cathode ray tube, or similar viewing apparatus connected with any sort of information storage and retrieval system.

....

Effect of display of copy

Subsection [(c)] of section 109 deals with the scope of the copyright owner's exclusive right to control the public display of a particular "copy" of a work (including the original or prototype copy in which the work was first fixed). Assuming, for example, that a painter has sold the only copy of an original work of art without restrictions, would it be possible for him to restrain the new owner from displaying it publicly in galleries, shop windows, on a projector, or on television?

Section 109[(c)] adopts the general principle that the lawful owner of a copy of a work should be able to put his copy on public display without the consent of the copyright owner. As in cases arising under section 109(a), this does not mean that contractual restrictions on display between a buyer and seller would be unenforceable as a matter of contract law.

The exclusive right of public display granted by section 106(5) would not apply where the owner of a copy wishes to show it directly to the public, as in a gallery or display case, or indirectly, as through an opaque projector....

On the other hand, section 109[(c)] takes account of the potentialities of the new communications media, notably television, cable and optical transmission devices, and information storage and retrieval devices, for replacing printed copies with visual images. First of all, the public display of an image of a copyrighted work would not be exempted from copyright control if the copy from which the image was derived were outside the presence of the viewers. In other words, the display of a visual image of a copyrighted work would be an infringement if the image were transmitted by any method (by closed or open circuit television, for example, or by a computer system) from one place to members of the public located elsewhere.

Moreover, the exemption would extend only to public displays that are made "either directly or by the projection of no more than one image at a time." Thus, even where the copy and the viewers are located at the same place, the simultaneous projection of multiple images of the work would not be exempted. For example, where each person in a lecture hall is supplied with a separate viewing apparatus, the copyright owner's permission would generally be required in order to project an image of a work on each individual screen at the same time.

The committee's intention is to preserve the traditional privilege of the owner of a copy to display it directly, but to place reasonable restrictions on the ability to display it indirectly in such a way that the copyright owner's market for reproduction and distribution of copies would be affected. Unless it constitutes a fair use under section 107, or unless one of the special provisions of section 110 or 111 is applicable, projection of more than one image at a time, or transmission of an image to the public over television or other communication channels, would be an infringement for the same reasons that reproduction in copies would be. The concept of "the place where the copy is located" is generally intended to refer to a situation in which the viewers are present in the same physical surroundings as the copy, even though they cannot see the copy directly.

QUESTIONS

1. The House Report confirms that the copyright owner may not prevent a public display by the owner of a particular copy (including the original). What about other problems which may arise between the owner of rights under copyright and the owner of the chattel? For example, may the chattel owner frustrate the copyright owner's exercise of the reproduction right by denying him access to the only copy of the work? See Chapter 1F, *supra*.

2. Last year, Art Teest donated an abstract geometric canvas painted by him to the Institute of Very Contemporary Art at the Urban University. This year, as the University fell upon hard economic times, it decided to sell certain of its assets, including some paintings at the Institute, Teest's painting among them. When the auction was held at the Institute, it was also shown on a closed-circuit television system to audiences at five separate locations within the University and also at alumni clubs throughout the country. Persons in attendance at those locations could see the artworks being auctioned and could submit their bids. Teest's painting was auctioned off for a price that he regarded as embarrassingly low — and he was also distressed about how quickly the Institute got rid of his painting. He has consulted you and wishes to know whether he has any legal recourse against the Institute and the University. What will you tell him? Consider too, as you study the materials immediately below, whether any exemptions in the Copyright Act apply to the conduct challenged by Teest.

5. EXEMPTIONS FROM THE RIGHTS OF PUBLIC PERFORMANCE AND DISPLAY

a. Certain Nonprofit Performances and Displays

§ 110. Limitations on exclusive rights: Exemption of certain performances and displays

Notwithstanding the provisions of section 106, the following are not infringements of copyright:

(1) performance or display of a work by instructors or pupils in the course of face-to-face teaching activities of a nonprofit educational institution, in a classroom or similar place devoted to instruction, unless, in the case of a motion picture or other audiovisual work, the performance, or the display of individual images, is given by means of a copy that was not lawfully made under this title, and that the person responsible for the performance knew or had reason to believe was not lawfully made;

(2) performance of a nondramatic literary or musical work or display of a work, by or in the course of a transmission, if —

   (A) the performance or display is a regular part of the systematic instructional activities of a governmental body or a nonprofit educational institution; and

   (B) the performance or display is directly related and of material assistance to the teaching content of the transmission; and

   (C) the transmission is made primarily for —

      (i) reception in classrooms or similar places normally devoted to instruction, or

      (ii) reception by persons to whom the transmission is directed because their disabilities or other special circumstances prevent their attendance in classrooms or similar places normally devoted to instruction, or

      (iii) reception by officers or employees of governmental bodies as a part of their official duties or employment;

(3) performance of a nondramatic literary or musical work or of a dramatico-musical work of a religious nature, or display of a work, in the course of services at a place of worship or other religious assembly;

(4) performance of a nondramatic literary or musical work otherwise than in a transmission to the public, without any purpose of direct or indirect commercial advantage and without payment of any fee or other compensation for the performance to any of its performers, promoters, or organizers, if —

   (A) there is no direct or indirect admission charge; or

   (B) the proceeds, after deducting the reasonable costs of producing the performance, are used exclusively for educational, religious, or charitable purposes and not for private financial gain, except where the copyright owner has served notice of objection to the performance under the following conditions;

      (i) the notice shall be in writing and signed by the copyright owner or such owner's duly authorized agent; and

      (ii) the notice shall be served on the person responsible for the performance at least seven days before the date of the performance, and shall state the reasons for the objection; and

      (iii) the notice shall comply, in form, content, and manner of service, with requirements that the Register of Copyrights shall prescribe by regulation;

(5) communication of a transmission embodying a performance or display of a work by the public reception of the transmission on a single receiving apparatus of a kind commonly used in private homes, unless —

> (A) a direct charge is made to see or hear the transmission; or
> (B) the transmission thus received is further transmitted to the public[.]
>
>   ....

(7) performance of a nondramatic musical work by a vending establishment open to the public at large without any direct or indirect admission charge, where the sole purpose of the performance is to promote the retail sale of copies or phonorecords of the work, and the performance is not transmitted beyond the place where the establishment is located and is within the immediate area where the sale is occurring;

    ....

HOUSE REPORT

H.R. Rep. No. 94-1476, 94th Cong., 2d Sess. 81-86 (1976)

Face-to-face teaching activities

Clause (1) of section 110 is generally intended to set out the conditions under which performances or displays, in the course of instructional activities other than educational broadcasting, are to be exempted from copyright control. The clause covers all types of copyrighted works, and exempts their performance or display "by instructors or pupils in the course of face-to-face teaching activities of a nonprofit educational institution," where the activities take place "in a classroom or similar place devoted to instruction."

There appears to be no need for a statutory definition of "face-to-face" teaching activities to clarify the scope of the provision. "Face-to-face teaching activities" under clause (1) embrace instructional performances and displays that are not "transmitted." The concept does not require that the teacher and students be able to see each other, although it does require their simultaneous presence in the same general place. Use of the phrase "in the course of face-to-face teaching activities" is intended to exclude broadcasting or other transmissions from an outside location into classrooms, whether radio or television and whether open or closed circuit. However, as long as the instructor and pupils are in the same building or general area, the exemption would extend to the use of devices for amplifying or reproducing sound and for projecting visual images. The "teaching activities" exempted by the clause encompass systematic instruction of a very wide variety of subjects, but they do not include performances or displays, whatever their cultural value or intellectual appeal, that are given for the recreation or entertainment of any part of their audience.

Works affected. — Since there is no limitation on the types of works covered by the exemption, teachers or students would be free to perform or display anything in class as long as the other conditions of the clause are met. They could read aloud from copyrighted text material, act out a drama, play or sing a musical work, perform a motion picture or filmstrip, or display text or pictorial material to the class by means of a projector. However, nothing in this provision is intended to sanction the unauthorized reproduction of copies or phonorecords for the purpose of classroom performance or display, and the clause contains a special exception dealing with performances from unlawfully made copies of motion pictures and other audiovisual works, to be discussed below.

Instructors or pupils. — To come within clause (1), the performance or display must be "by instructors or pupils," thus ruling out performances by actors, singers, or instrumentalists brought in from outside the school to put on a program. However, the term "instructors" would be broad enough to include guest lecturers if their instructional activities remain confined to classroom situations. In general, the term "pupils" refers to the enrolled members of a class.

Nonprofit educational institution. — Clause (1) makes clear that it applies only to the teaching activities "of a nonprofit educational institution," thus excluding from the exemption performances or displays in profit-making institutions such as dance studios and language schools.

Classroom or similar place. — The teaching activities exempted by the clause must take place "in a classroom or similar place devoted to instruction." For example, performances in an auditorium or stadium during a school assembly, graduation ceremony, class play, or sporting event, where the audience is not confined to the members of a particular class, would fall outside the scope of clause (1), although in some cases they might be exempted by clause (4) of section 110....

....

Instructional broadcasting

Works affected. — The exemption for instructional broadcasting provided by section 110(2) would apply only to "performance of a non-dramatic literary or musical work or display of a work." Thus, the copyright owner's permission would be required for the performance on educational television or radio of a dramatic work, of a dramatico-musical work such as an opera or musical comedy, or of a motion picture....

....

Intended recipients. — ... [T]he instructional transmission need only be made "primarily" rather than "solely" to the specified recipients to be exempt. Thus, the transmission could still be exempt even though it is capable of reception by the public at large. Conversely, it would not be regarded as made "primarily" for one of the required groups of recipients if the principal purpose behind the transmission is reception by the public at large, even if it is cast in the form of instruction and is also received in classrooms. Factors to consider in determining the "primary" purpose of a program would include its subject matter, content, and the time of its transmission.

....

Certain other nonprofit performances

In addition to the educational and religious exemptions provided by clauses (1) through (3) of section 110, clause (4) contains a general exception to the exclusive right of public performance that would cover some, though not all, of the same ground as the present "for profit" limitation.

Scope of exemption. — The exemption in clause (4) applies to the same general activities and subject matter as those covered by the "for profit" limitation today: public performances of nondramatic literary and musical works. However, the exemption would be limited to public performances given directly in the presence of an audience whether by means of living performers, the playing of phonorecords, or the operation of a receiving apparatus, and would not include a "transmission to the public." Unlike the clauses (1) through (3) and (5) of section 110, but like clauses (6) through (8), clause (4) applies only to performing rights in certain works, and does not affect the exclusive right to display a work in public.

No profit motive. — In addition to the other conditions specified by the clause, the performance must be "without any purpose of direct or indirect commercial advantage." This provision expressly adopts the principle established by the court decisions construing the "for profit" limitation: that public performances given or sponsored in connection with any commercial or profit-making enterprises are subject to the exclusive rights of the copyright owner even though the public is not charged for seeing or hearing the performance.

No payment for performance. — An important condition for this exemption is that the performance be given "without payment of any fee or other compensation for the performance to any of its performers, promoters, or organizers." The basic purpose of this requirement is to prevent the free use of copyrighted material under the guise of charity where fees or percentages are paid to performers, promoters, producers, and the like. However, the exemption would not be lost if the performers, directors, or producers of the performance, instead of being paid directly "for the performance," are paid a salary for duties encompassing the performance. Examples are performances by a school orchestra conducted by a music teacher who receives an annual salary, or by a service band whose members and conductors perform as part of their assigned duties and who receive military pay. The committee believes that performances of this type should be exempt, assuming the other conditions in clause (4) are met, and has not adopted the suggestion that the word "salary" be added to the phrase referring to the "payment of any fee or other compensation."

Admission charge. — Assuming that the performance involves no profit motive and no one responsible for it gets paid a fee, it must still meet one of two alternative conditions to be exempt. As specified in subclauses (A) and (B) of section 110(4), these conditions are: (1) that no direct or indirect admission charge is made, or (2) that the net proceeds are "used exclusively for educational, religious, or charitable purposes and not for private financial gain."

Under the second of these conditions, a performance meeting the other conditions of clause (4) would be exempt even if an admission fee is charged, provided any amounts left "after deducting the reasonable costs of producing the performance" are used solely for bona fide educational, religious, or charitable purposes. In cases arising under this second condition and as provided in subclause (B), where there is an admission charge, the copyright owner is given an opportunity to decide whether and under what conditions the copyrighted work should be performed; otherwise, owners could be compelled to make involuntary donations to the fund-raising activities of causes to which they are opposed. The subclause would thus permit copyright owners to prevent public performances of their works under section 110(4)(B) by serving notice of objection, with the reasons therefor, at least seven days in advance.

QUESTIONS

1. By providing in § 110(4)(B) for the serving by the copyright owner of a "notice of objection" to certain nonprofit public performances, does Congress contemplate that advance word of all such performances must be communicated by the promoters or performers to the copyright owner? If not, how often will the copyright owner actually be aware of such performances? Should the copyright owner, in order to deal with this problem, serve a "blanket" notice of objection, covering all of his musical compositions, to all institutions where there is some chance of its performance (e.g., all colleges and all secondary schools)? (Obviously, ASCAP or BMI could much more effectively serve such notices than could individual composers.) Would such a blanket notice, served in futuro, be adequate under § 110(4) to remove the exemption? *See* 37 CFR § 201.13, at Appendix C of the casebook.

Are any of the following exempted under § 110?

2. Taking advantage of the first fine spring day, a high school English teacher conducts her class in the park, where she and her students read portions of a copyrighted play out loud.

3. A high school teacher makes an unauthorized slide of a copyrighted art work. He then displays the slide to his art appreciation class. The teacher knows that the slide was not lawfully made.

4. A high school teacher shows a video to her class. The video was rented, and bore the label "For Private Viewing Only."

5. During a special church service directed at the younger generation, a performance is given of substantial excerpts (in sequence) from the rock musical "Jesus Christ Superstar."

6. Members of a religious sect perform portions of "Jesus Christ Superstar" in Times Square to inattentive passers-by.

7. A law student sings popular copyrighted songs in Times Square, and, passing the hat, requests contributions toward his law school tuition.

8. A stereo store demonstrates its audio equipment through performance of sound recordings of copyrighted music.

EDISON BROS. STORES v. BROADCAST MUSIC, INC.

954 F.2d 1419 (8th Cir.), *cert. denied,* 112 S. Ct. 1995, 118 L. Ed. 2d 590 (1992)

BOWMAN, Circuit Judge.

Broadcast Music, Inc. (BMI), appeals the District Court's decision to grant summary judgment in favor of Edison Brothers Stores, Inc., in Edison's suit for a declaratory judgment that its stores qualify for an exemption from the vesting of exclusive rights of performance in the owners of copyrighted works. *See Edison Bros. Stores, Inc. v. Broadcast Music, Inc.,* 760 F. Supp. 767 (E.D. Mo. 1991). We affirm.

The relevant facts are not in dispute. BMI is a performing rights organization that collectively licenses, as assignee of the rights of its copyright-holding clients (primarily publishers and songwriters), the public performance of such clients' copyrighted works.

Edison owns a chain of approximately 2500 retail clothing and shoe stores doing business as Chandlers, Jeans West, Fashion Conspiracy, Size 5-7-9 Shops, J. Riggins, Bakers, The Wild Pair, and others. Most of Edison's stores operate a single radio receiver with two attached shelf speakers to play radio broadcasts in the stores for the enjoyment of employees and customers. The equipment is simple and inexpensive. Edison has promulgated a radio usage policy and requires the adherence of these stores to the rules therein. The District Court summarized the policy as follows:

1. Only simple, low grade radio-only receivers are to be used.
2. Only two speakers may be attached to a radio receiver.
3. The speakers must be placed within 15 feet of the receiver.
4. Speakers that are built into the walls or ceilings must not be used. Only portable box speakers are allowed.
5. [Edison will a]dvise each store manager that they are not to use tapes, cassettes, or any other type of recording equipment in their stores. They are to play the radio only.

Edison Bros. Stores, 760 F. Supp. at 769-70, *quoted in* Brief of Appellee at 7. BMI has submitted no evidence that any of the Edison stores to which the radio usage policy applies have failed to comply with it.

Approximately 220 of Edison's stores have more sophisticated audio and video systems or subscribe to commercial music services. Edison pays license fees to BMI or to commercial services licensed by BMI or other performing rights organizations for the music played in these stores. In recent years BMI approached Edison about licensing the remaining stores in its chain. Negotiations between the two parties evidently broke down, and Edison filed suit in District Court seeking declaratory relief. The court, agreeing with Edison's position, declared that the radio systems in use at Edison's unlicensed stores qualified for the so-called homestyle exemption to the exclusive performance rights that copyright owners enjoy under federal law. BMI appeals.

... BMI and Edison both filed motions for summary judgment and thus apparently agree there are no disputed issues of material fact. Therefore we are left with a purely legal question involving interpretation of the Copyright Act.

I

Under the Copyright Act, the owner of the copyright of a musical work has the exclusive right, among other rights, to perform the copyrighted work publicly. 17 U.S.C.A. § 106(4) (West Supp. 1991). The Act, however, provides exemptions for certain performances. 17 U.S.C. § 110 (1988). Among the acts that are not "infringements of copyright" is the following:

> [C]ommunication of a transmission embodying a performance or display of a work by the public reception of the transmission on a single receiving apparatus of a kind commonly used in private homes, unless —
>
> > (A) a direct charge is made to see or hear the transmission; or
> > (B) the transmission thus received is further transmitted to the public[.]

Id. § 110(5). The issue before the District Court, and now before us, is whether Edison's 2000-plus radio receivers, each with two attached speakers and each operated in a different store, qualify for this homestyle exemption. BMI insists that, for several reasons, the exemption is unavailable to Edison.

Clearly, each radio in an Edison store is a "single receiving apparatus" and is "communicat[ing] ... a transmission embodying a performance ... of a work by the public reception of the transmission." The receivers in the Edison stores are tuned to local radio stations and play anything and everything, including musical works, that the radio stations broadcast while the stores' receivers are on. No "direct charge is made to see or hear the transmission," and there is no contention that the broadcast is "further transmitted to the public" beyond the stores.

The sticking point for the parties, and the basis for BMI's first argument, is Edison's multiple locations, each employing a single receiver and two speakers in conformity with the company's radio usage policy. BMI argues that the statutory requirement that the transmission be received "on a single receiving apparatus of a kind commonly used in private homes" is not satisfied by this arrangement; although BMI concedes that an individual receiver and speaker set-up in one store may fit within the exemption, it takes the position that Edison lost section 110(5) protection as soon as it installed the second receiving apparatus in another of its stores. BMI contends that the statute requires that we consider the equipment of any one owner *in toto,* and not on a per-store basis, when we decide whether or not the exemption applies and find (as of course we would if we did as BMI suggests) that Edison is not in fact operating a "single receiving apparatus" within the meaning of the statute.

We cannot accept BMI's interpretation of section 110(5), as it defies the plain language of the statute. Section 110(5) does not say that a person, company, or other entity must own or operate only a single receiver to qualify for the exemption; it refers to "the communication of *a* transmission embodying *a* performance ... of a work" (emphasis added). We think it obvious that the language refers to a single location. "The statute does not ask how many receiving apparatuses were used to receive a number of different works. The language of the statute thus strongly suggests that the proper analysis should be limited to the area where a single work is performed." *Broadcast Music, Inc. v. Claire's Boutiques, Inc.,* 949 F.2d 1482, 1490 (7th Cir. 1991). If we were to embrace BMI's argument and reach the result it suggests, the equipment used in any Edison store, including those stores that have more sophisticated equipment, would be attributable to each of the other stores owned by Edison for purposes of the Copyright Act. Such a result does not comport with the statutory language.

We agree with the District Court "that it is not appropriate to focus on the number of stores involved, but rather on whether each store duplicates the requirements of the homestyle exception." *Edison Bros. Stores*, 760 F. Supp. at 770. There is no evidence in the record that any of Edison's unlicensed stores fail to meet the statutory criteria for entitlement to the section 110(5) exemption.

BMI claims that the legislative history of the exemption supports its multiple receiver argument. Our reading of the legislative history reveals nothing that convinces us that each store in a retail chain should not be considered for the homestyle exemption individually, as seems plain from the straightforward language of section 110(5). We certainly will not use the legislative history to which BMI directs our attention as a basis for reading into the statute limitations its language does not express. *See Union Bank v. Wolas*, __ U.S. __, __, 112 S. Ct. 527, 530, 116 L. Ed. 2d 514, 521 (1991) ("Given the clarity of the statutory text, respondent's burden of persuading us that Congress intended to create or to preserve a special rule [not expressed in the statutory language] is exceptionally heavy.").

II

BMI also bases its next argument on the legislative history of the enactment. BMI is not asking us to use legislative history to assist in clarifying an ambiguous statute; we are being asked to use legislative history to rewrite the section 110(5) exemption to add new requirements.

BMI contends that the physical size of Edison's stores removes the chain and its individual stores from the protection of the section 110(5) exemption.[4] In order to reach such a result, BMI would have us read into the exemption a requirement that total space in the stores must not exceed 1055 square feet, with the area open to the public not to exceed 620 square feet. Brief of Appellant at 9, 11. The basis for this argument is a Supreme Court decision in a copyright case antedating the enactment of section 110(5) and the Report of the House Judiciary Committee relating to that section.

In *Twentieth Century Music Corp. v. Aiken*, 422 U.S. 151, 95 S. Ct. 2040, 45 L. Ed. 2d 84 (1975), the Supreme Court had before it the issue of whether the proprietor of a food shop who installed and played a radio with four speakers on the premises of his business was required to pay licensing fees for the music thus provided for his patrons. The Court, holding that in so using a

---

[4]Edison asserts that the record on the size of its stores is inadequate for BMI to sustain this claim factually, regardless of its legal viability. *See* Brief of Appellee at 35 & n. 13. BMI, on the other hand, claims that the record demonstrates the average square footage of Edison's unlicensed stores is 2268 square feet, with 800 to 1200 square feet open to the public. Reply Brief of Appellant at 18 n. 11. Clearly this is a disputed question of fact, but in view of our holding that a store's physical size is not a factor that requires consideration under the statute, it is irrelevant and does not require resolution in order for us to affirm the District Court's entry of summary judgment in favor of Edison.

radio Aiken was not "performing" within the meaning of the Copyright Act, ruled that he was not. The House Report on the 1976 amendments to the Copyright Act suggests that the section 110(5) exemption was added to the Copyright Act in response to the Court's opinion in *Aiken*. H.R. Rep. No. 1476, 94th Cong., 2d Sess. 86-87 (1976), *reprinted in* 1976 U.S.C.C.A.N. 5659, 5700-01. The Report indicates that the new exemption was intended to supersede the Court's holding in *Aiken* that the playing of a radio in a commercial establishment open to the public is not a "performance," and thus not an infringing act. At the same time, the Report suggests that on the facts of *Aiken* the Court's decision exempting Aiken from the payment of licensing fees was appropriate and deserving of codification.

The language from the Report upon which BMI focuses is this: "the Committee considers this fact situation [in *Aiken*] to represent the outer limit of the [homestyle] exemption, and believes that the line should be drawn at that point." *Id.* at 87, *reprinted in* 1976 U.S.C.C.A.N. at 5701. Even accepting *arguendo* the untenable proposition that we would give greater weight to what a House Committee "considers" than to the text the entire Congress enacts and the President signs, BMI neglects to point out that the "fact situation" described in the Report, which immediately precedes the above-quoted language, makes no mention of square footage: "Under the particular fact situation in the *Aiken* case, assuming a small commercial establishment and the use of a home receiver with four ordinary loudspeakers grouped within a relatively narrow circumference from the set, it is intended that the performances would be exempt under clause (5)." *Id.* Further, the "fact situation" as described in *Aiken* makes no mention of the square footage of Aiken's shop:

> The respondent George Aiken owns and operates a small fast-service food shop in downtown Pittsburgh, Pa., known as "George Aiken's Chicken." Some customers carry out the food they purchase, while others remain and eat at counters or booths. Usually the "carry-out" customers are in the restaurant for less than five minutes, and those who eat there seldom remain longer than 10 or 15 minutes.
>
> A radio with outlets to four speakers in the ceiling receives broadcasts of music and other normal radio programming at the restaurant. Aiken usually turns on the radio each morning at the start of business. Music, news, entertainment, and commercial advertising broadcast by radio stations are thus heard by Aiken, his employees, and his customers during the hours that the establishment is open for business.

Aiken, 422 U.S. at 152, 95 S. Ct. at 2042.[5]

---

[5] Not only were square footage figures omitted from the Supreme Court's opinion in *Twentieth Century Music Corp. v. Aiken*, 422 U.S. 151, 95 S. Ct. 2040, 45 L. Ed. 2d 84 (1975), they also are nowhere to be found in either of the opinions from the courts below. *Twentieth Century Music Corp. v. Aiken*, 500 F.2d 127 (3d Cir. 1974) (subsequent history omitted); *Twentieth Century Music Corp. v. Aiken*, 356 F. Supp. 271 (W.D. Pa. 1973) (subsequent history omitted). Apparently, the dimensions of Aiken's shop first appeared in a published opinion in *Sailor Music v. Gap Stores, Inc.*, 516 F. Supp. 923, 924 (S.D.N.Y.), *aff'd*, 668 F.2d 84 (2d Cir. 1981), *cert. denied*, 456 U.S. 945, 102 S. Ct. 2012, 72 L. Ed. 2d 468 (1982), filed some five years after the enactment of

BMI directs our attention to several opinions where, BMI maintains, the square footage of the establishment attempting to qualify for the exemption was discussed. Having reviewed these cases, we reject as totally inaccurate BMI's assertion that "in virtually every case the excessive square footage of the defendant's store alone was found to disqualify the defendant from invoking the Section 110(5) exemption." Brief of Appellant at 27 n. 14. The fact is that in none of these cases did the court base its decision solely on the square footage of the stores without considering the nature of the equipment, i.e., whether it was "homestyle," nor did any of them declare that they would have reached the same result based only upon the square footage of the infringing stores. Moreover, none of the cases cited has any binding precedential force in this Circuit.

The closest we come to Eighth Circuit precedent on this issue is this Court's dicta in *National Football League v. McBee & Bruno's, Inc.*, 792 F.2d 726 (8th Cir. 1986), in which the challenged action was the receipt via satellite antenna of blacked-out NFL games and the playing of the broadcasts on television sets in bars. Although the Court noted that "[t]he factors listed in the legislative history do speak of the size of the area where the transmission will be played," *id.* at 731, the Court said nothing about a maximum square footage. Further, the Court stated that the 1976 legislative history indicates that "to decide whether an infringement had occurred, the critical question instead would be the type of equipment used by the putative infringer." *Id.* at 730. The Court also quoted this language from the legislative history of the exemption:

> [T]he clause would exempt small commercial establishments whose proprietors merely bring onto their premises standard radio or television equipment and turn it on for their customers' enjoyment, but it would impose liability where the proprietor has a commercial "sound system" installed or converts a standard home receiving apparatus ... into the equivalent of a commercial sound system.

Id. at 730-31 (quoting H.R. Rep. No. 1476, 94th Cong., 2d Sess. 87 (1976), *reprinted in* 1976 U.S.C.C.A.N. 5659, 5701). Clearly, this passage from the legislative history directs attention to the quality of the sound system used, and not to the square footage of the establishment using it.[7]

---

section 110(5). There is no indication of the source of the information in the *Sailor* opinion.

[7] If BMI wishes to base its argument here on language from the legislative history, it should also note the opening remarks of the portion of the House Report that discusses section 110(5):

> Unlike the first four clauses of section 110, clause (5) is not to any extent a counterpart of the "for profit" limitation of the present statute. It applies to performances and displays of all types of works, and *its purpose is to exempt from copyright liability anyone who merely turns on, in a public place, an ordinary radio or television receiving apparatus of a kind commonly sold to members of the public for private use.*

Although the legislative history is interesting, it is beside the point; we need only look to the statute itself. If Congress intended to impose a physical size limitation on the establishment qualifying for the exemption, it might easily have written it into the statute. But it did not; it did not even qualify the exemption by limiting its availability to a "small commercial establishment," the language of the legislative history. The statute focuses on the equipment being used, and so must we. This Court is not a legislative body, and it has no authority to rewrite the statute.

The same observation applies fully to BMI's next argument: that the legislative history supports its contention that a section 110(5) exemption is available only if "the business [does] not have the ability to pay for its use of music or [is not] of sufficient size to justify, as a practical matter, a subscription to a commercial background music service." Brief of Appellant at 11. The legislative history BMI relies upon is this:

> It is the intent of the conferees that a small commercial establishment of the type involved in *Twentieth Century Music Corp. v. Aiken,* which merely augmented a home-type receiver and which was not of sufficient size to justify, as a practical matter, a subscription to a commercial background music service, would be exempt.

H.R. Conf. Rep. No. 1733, 94th Cong., 2d Sess. 75 (1976) (citation omitted), *reprinted in* 1976 U.S.C.C.A.N. 5810, 5816.[8]

The intent expressed in the report of the House conferees is irrelevant when the statutory language does not say or even imply that the size or financial wherewithal of the establishment has a bearing on eligibility for the homestyle exemption. As with the square footage requirement that BMI would have us read into the exemption, the opinions of other courts that mention this language do not persuade us that, even though Congress enacted the law without any such requirement, it truly intended a size-and-financial-means test to be a part of the statute. *See Claire's Boutiques,* 949 F.2d at 1492 ("no case has relied solely on the financial size or ability of the defendant as a reason for denying the application of § 110(5)"). Moreover, we surmise that any such requirement would surely run into constitutional problems for

---

H.R. Rep. No. 1476, 94th Cong., 2d Sess. 86 (1976), *reprinted in* 1976 U.S.C.C.A.N. 5659, 5700 (emphasis added). That summary of the exemption makes no mention of any size or financial restrictions.

[8] BMI argues for expansion of this putative requirement and suggests that "of sufficient size to justify ... a subscription to a commercial background music service," the language found in the legislative history (and only in the legislative history), equates with "able to afford a commercial background music service or to pay the license fee to a performing rights organization." *See* Brief of Appellant at 29 ("it is beyond dispute that Edison has the ability to compensate the creators and publishers of the music that it uses in its stores"). This expansion would take us even further afield from the statutory language. The Eighth Circuit dicta BMI quotes as support for its argument says nothing about ability to pay: "[T]he question as a practical matter is whether the defendant establishment is of the size and kind that Congress would expect to obtain a license through a subscription music service." *Nat'l Football League v. McBee & Bruno's, Inc.,* 792 F.2d 726, 731 (8th Cir. 1986) (decision denying section 110(5) exemption based primarily on the type of equipment used).

vagueness: who would determine when an establishment is "of sufficient size to justify ... a subscription to a commercial background music service," and what criteria would they use?

We hold that 17 U.S.C. § 110(5) does not require that the square footage of a qualifying establishment be less than 1055, with fewer than 620 square feet open to the public; nor does it require that the entity's ability to pay for a commercial background music service be considered. The focus of the statute is on the equipment in use, and as each of Edison's unlicensed stores uses only homestyle equipment each qualifies for the homestyle exemption.

III

Finally, BMI argues that the District Court's decision defeats the purpose of the Copyright Act and conflicts with this country's international treaty obligations. We find no merit in BMI's contention that the District Court's interpretation of the statute expands the scope of the homestyle exemption beyond the intent of Congress. *See Aiken,* 422 U.S. at 163, 95 S. Ct. at 2047 ("exaction of such multiple tribute [by authorizing the sale of numerous licenses for a single broadcast of a copyrighted work] would go far beyond what is required for the economic protection of copyright owners, and would be wholly at odds with the balanced congressional purpose behind" the exclusive right of public performance) (footnote omitted). If Congress had intended the exemption to be limited so as to exclude large retail chain stores such as Edison, it might easily have shown that intention in the language of the statute. It did not and we will not assume that the omission was a mere oversight on the part of the legislators. We note there is here no contention, nor could there plausibly be, of a "'scrivener's error' producing an absurd result." *Union Bank,* __ U.S. at __, 112 S. Ct. at 534, 116 L. Ed. 2d at 525 (Scalia, J., concurring).

BMI's argument that this decision interferes with the international treaty obligations of the United States also fails. The treaty in question is the international copyright agreement known as the Berne Convention. Berne Convention for the Protection of Literary and Artistic Works, S. Treaty Doc. No. 27, 99th Cong., 2d Sess. (1986). The Convention, signed on September 9, 1886, as revised at Paris on July 24, 1971, entered into force for the United States on March 1, 1989. *See* Berne Convention Implementation Act of 1988, Pub. L. No. 100-568, § 13, 102 Stat. 2853, 2861 (1988). Congress then revised the Copyright Act (although section 110(5) was unaffected) and declared that the Act as amended "satisf[ies] the obligations of the United States in adhering to the Berne Convention and no further rights or interests shall be recognized or created for that purpose." *Id.* § 2(3), 102 Stat. 2853.

BMI asserts that the District Court's interpretation of section 110(5) to provide shelter for Edison under the homestyle exemption expands the scope of the exemption to such a degree that it renders section 110(5) in violation of the United States' treaty obligations under Article 11[bis] of the Berne Convention. Under that article, authors of artistic works have exclusive rights to authorize "the public communication by loudspeaker or any other analogous instrument transmitting, by signs, sounds or images, the broadcast of the work." Berne Convention, art. 11[bis](iii), S. Treaty Doc. No. 27, 99th Cong., 2d

Sess. 44 (1986). The flaw in BMI's argument is that the District Court's interpretation of section 110(5) does not expand the homestyle exemption, but merely declares that the statutory language means what it says. We cannot presume that Congress, in enacting this language, intended something else, and we know that Congress declared its handiwork to be consistent with the Berne Convention. Congress thus declared the public policy of the United States and, for us, that is the end of the matter.

Congress was emphatic that the United States' participation in the Berne Convention should not give rise to an expanded claim of copyright protection.

> No right or interest in a work eligible for protection under this title may be claimed by virtue of, or in reliance upon, the provisions of the Berne Convention, or the adherence of the United States thereto. Any rights in a work eligible for protection under this title that derive from this title, other Federal or State statutes, or the common law, shall not be expanded or reduced by virtue of, or in reliance upon, the provisions of the Berne Convention, or the adherence of the United States thereto.

17 U.S.C.A. § 104(c) (West Supp. 1991). In view of this unmistakably clear congressional directive, BMI's claim to a "right or interest ... by virtue of ... the adherence of the United States" to the Berne Convention cannot be sustained.

The judgment of the District Court is affirmed.

QUESTIONS

1. In an action brought by BMI at about the same time as the *Edison* case, infringement of 88 musical compositions was claimed against a chain of retail stores owned by Claire's Boutiques, Inc. On the following facts, how should the plaintiff distinguish the *Edison* decision, and how should the court rule? (Consider in particular BMI's assertion that the defendant is "further transmitting" the radio broadcasts and thus expressly outside of the exemption in section 110(5).)

Claire's owns and operates 719 stores under the name Claire's Boutiques and 30 stores under the name Arcadia. These retail establishments are located throughout the United States and are open to the public during normal business hours. Claire's stores range in size from 458 square feet to 2000 square feet. The average size of a Claire's Boutique store is 861 square feet, and 628 of the Boutique stores are less than 1055 square feet. The average size of each Arcadia store is 2022 square feet, and 27 out of the 30 Arcadia stores are greater than 1055 square feet.

During fiscal year 1990, Claire's had net sales of $168,674,000 and earned $13,402,000 in net income. The Claire's Boutiques stores accounted for the majority of these sales ($165,767,233).

Claire's has a policy to provide the following stereo components to each of its stores: a Radio Shack Optimus STA-20 5-watt stereo receiver, two Realistic Minimus 7 speakers, an indoor antenna, and speaker wire. As a general rule, Claire's ships a radio receiver to each new Claire's store. General contractors install the speakers and associated wiring pursuant to corporate specifications designed to conceal the wiring as much as possible. In the three-and-a-half-year period from 1987 to July 1990, Claire's purchased at least 527 receivers, 1240 speakers, FM antennas, and speaker wire at a total cost of $108,112.42. Claire's currently owns and operates at least 669 receivers and 1338 speakers.

The individual Claire's Boutiques and Arcadia stores use the receivers provided by corporate headquarters to receive and play radio broadcasts during regular business hours. The receivers are ordinarily kept in a small storage room at the back of Claire's stores. The door between this room and the selling area is typically closed during business hours. Two strands of speaker wire run from the speaker jacks in the back of the receiver to speakers in the store's selling area. Both strands run through a hole in the wall separating the storage room from the selling area. One strand is attached to a speaker that is hung from the ceiling in the rear corner of the selling area. The other strand of wire runs above the dropped ceiling and is connected to the second speaker which is also hung from the ceiling. The first speaker is an average of 5-15 feet from the receiver, and the second speaker is an average of 20-35 feet from the receiver. Both speakers are hidden by a decorative dropped ceiling. *See Broadcast Music, Inc. v. Claire's Boutiques, Inc.*, 949 F.2d 1482 (7th Cir. 1991), *cert. denied*, 112 S. Ct. 1942, 118 L. Ed. 2d 547 (1992).

2. Do any of the following qualify for the § 110(5) exemption?

(a) A small neighborhood bar has its patrons watch sports programs on a four-foot television screen.

(b) A television store tunes in all of its demonstration model television sets so that consumers can observe the quality of reception on the various sets.

(c) A television store places a tuned-in television set in the window so that passers by can see the television programs on the set.

(d) A teenager carries a suitcase-sized radio down the street, with the volume at full blast.

(e) An office graces its small reception area with a home-type radio, and also retransmits the radio signal to telephone callers whom the receptionist puts on "Hold." *See Prophet Music Inc. v. Shamla Oil Co.*, 26 U.S.P.Q.2d 1554 (D. Minn. 1993).

b. Secondary Transmissions, Including by Cable and Satellite — §§ 111, 119

Because of the broad definition of "public performance" in the 1976 Copyright Act, it is a violation of this § 106(4) right for a person, without the consent of the copyright owner, to receive a transmission of the copyrighted work and then to retransmit it to yet another location (where there are members of the public). Examples would be a hotel's retransmitting by electrical devices the sounds of a radio broadcast into its lobby, elevators or dining room; or the retransmission of a television broadcast by cable or satellite to persons well beyond the local viewing area of the broadcast station. Do any of these activities, facially infringements, warrant some sort of protected status — either through a statutory exemption or as the beneficiary of a compulsory license?

Section 111(a)(1) exempts such a "secondary transmission" that takes the form of "relaying, by the management of a hotel, apartment house, or similar establishment, of signals transmitted by a broadcast station licensed by the Federal Communications Commission, within the local service area of such station, to the private lodgings of guests or residents of such establishment, and no direct charge is made to see or hear the secondary transmission." The House Report (at p. 92) points out that the exemption does not extend to "dining rooms, meeting halls, theatres, ballrooms, or similar places that are outside of a normal circle of a family and its social acquaintances." In effect, the hotel is permitted to do what might be regarded as the functional equivalent of placing an ordinary radio or television set in its private rooms. Thus has Congress dealt with the issue so conspicuously addressed by the Supreme Court in *Buck v. Jewell-LaSalle, supra,* and its progeny.

The balance of § 111 of the Copyright Act focuses principally on secondary transmission of television broadcasts by cable services. The provisions attempt to dovetail copyright policy with the regulatory policies of the Federal Communications Commission. The major distinction to be drawn for both FCC and copyright regulation is between cable retransmission of "local" and "distant" broadcast signals. Local signals are those that reach the viewers in the area where the cable system is located; distant signals are those that are imported from broadcast stations at such a distance that they could not otherwise be received by viewers in the area in which the cable system is located. In general, a broadcast signal is "distant" if it is retransmitted by a cable system located more than 100 miles from the signal's point of origin.

The FCC regulations governing cable systems have changed significantly over the past two decades — reflecting in part the development of cable television from an infant industry to a most profitable one that rivals the popularity of over-the-air television broadcast networks and stations, and in part changes in the regulatory philosophy of the agency. For most of the period since the effective date of the 1976 Copyright Act, FCC regulations have provided that if a cable system is located in the "local service area" of a broadcast station, then the system *must* carry that station's programs to the cable subscribers; if a cable system wishes to retransmit distant signals, then it *may* do so, subject to conditions imposed by the Commission.

The compulsory-license provisions of § 111 of the Copyright Act are designed to advance the usual copyright policies — providing a fair market return to the copyright owner as an incentive for creative authorship — while accommodating the broadcasting regulatory policies of the FCC. A cable system will be entitled to re-transmit distant signals if, basically, such re-transmission is permitted by the FCC and if the cable system complies with the requirements of § 111(d) requiring the periodic filing of statements of account and payment of royalties (the usual obligations of compulsory licensees under the copyright law). The statute recognizes that — at least in the circumstances of the cable and broadcast industries in 1976 — although cable systems derive income from their re-transmissions and should be required to pay the creators of the copyrighted programs they carry, individual royalty negotiations with all copyright owners would be unduly burdensome.

The semi-annual accountings filed by the cable systems identify the broadcast stations whose signals were re-transmitted in the preceding six months, state the total number of subscribers to the cable system and the gross amounts paid for the system's "basic service" (as distinguished from installations and pay channels), and identify the non-network programs carried by the cable system beyond the local service area of the primary transmitter. The latter information is the basis for computing what is known as the "distant signal equivalent," a factor that plays an important role in calculating the royalties to be paid by the compulsory licensee; the other principal factor is the gross receipts from subscribers for the service of providing secondary transmissions. *See Cablevision Co. v. Motion Picture Ass'n of Am.*, 836 F.2d 599 (D.C. Cir. 1988) (interpretation of "gross receipts" and "basic service" in § 111(d)(2)(B)). Royalty payments must accompany the semi-annual statements of account that are filed with the Register of Copyrights.

The statutory provisions for the computation of royalties are among the lengthiest in the statute. No royalty is exacted for the re-transmission of local signals, because this is assumed not to threaten the existing market for owners of copyrighted programs (whose payment from the broadcast stations takes into account viewers in the "local service area" whether they receive the program off-the-air or by cable). Nor does the compulsory license recompense the copyright owner for re-transmission of network programming, including programs from distant markets; the network compensates the program owner based upon all of the markets served by the network. Copyright liability under § 111 is thus based upon the cable transmission of distant non-network programming, which carries the program to an area beyond which it has been licensed and which thus adversely affects the ability of the copyright owner to exploit the work in that distant market.

The royalty fee is determined by a two-step process. First, a value called a "distant signal equivalent" is assigned to all distant signals carried by the cable system, weighted according to the different amounts of non-network programming carried by the broadcast station. *See* § 111(f). These values are added up, and then a scale of percentages as set forth in § 111(d)(1) of the statute is determined by the cumulative total of DSEs and is then multiplied by the cable system's gross receipts. The Copyright Royalty Tribunal is given the power, by § 801(b)(2), to adjust the statutory percentages to be used in calculating royalty rates. The Tribunal exercised this power in 1980, to take account of inflation and increased subscriber charges, as well as changes in FCC regulations that expanded the right of cable systems to carry distant signals; these increases in the statutory percentages of gross receipts to be paid as royalties were sustained in *National Cable T.V. Ass'n v. Copyright Royalty Tribunal*, 724 F.2d 176 (D.C. Cir. 1983).

The Register of Copyrights receives all of these fees from all cable systems operating under the compulsory license, and then after the deduction of administrative costs, they are distributed by the Copyright Royalty Tribunal to copyright owners whose works were included in secondary transmissions of non-network television programs beyond the local service area of the primary transmitter. *See* § 111(d)(3). No royalty fees are to be distributed to copyright owners for the re-transmission of either "local" or "network" programs. The statute encourages claimants to agree among themselves regarding the division of the royalties, and if there is no controversy among the claimants, the Tribunal is to distribute the royalties; if there is a controversy, then the CRT will resolve it. (Bills pending in Congress in late 1993 would abolish the Tribunal and turn over its rate-setting and royalty-distribution authority to the Librarian of Congress, who can utilize ad hoc arbitration panels.)

When distribution decisions are to be made, the Tribunal divides its proceedings into two phases. In Phase I, the Tribunal allocates percentages of the fund to specific groups of claimants; for example, the general pattern has been nearly 70% to "program suppliers" (i.e., motion picture companies engaged in production and distribution of programs to television broadcasters, and syndicators of television programs), and some 15% to professional sports leagues. In Phase II of the cable-royalty distribution proceedings, the Tribunal makes allocations among the individual claimants within each category (e.g., within the "program supplier" group, the Motion Picture Association of America is entitled to roughly 97-98% of the royalties), although this allocation is usually worked out consensually among the respective claimants.

The overall size of the royalty fund for cable re-transmissions has grown dramatically since the $17 million distributed for the 1978 calendar year. The fund grew to $28 million in 1980, $113 million in 1985, and nearly $189 million in 1991 (the most recent year for which information is available).

Section 111, besides identifying the kinds of cable re-transmissions that are subject to a compulsory license, also identifies what re-transmissions will be infringements (subject to various conditions and limitations): when the primary transmission is not by a licensed broadcast station but is, for example, by closed-circuit television or a background music service or a pay-cable program; when signals are re-transmitted without taking the usual steps of filing accounts and paying royalties; when there is willful or repeated re-transmission of signals which a cable system is not permitted by the FCC to carry; when the cable system willfully alters the content of any program in the primary transmission or the advertising therein; or when, rather than re-transmitting a primary transmission simultaneously, the cable system first records it and then transmits the recorded program at a later time.

In 1988, Congress created a new, temporary, compulsory license for secondary transmissions by satellite carriers to certain "earth stations," i.e., household satellite "dishes" capturing signals for private home viewing. Home dishes make possible individuals' direct receipt not only of popular independent "superstations" (such as WTBS and WGN) but also of distant signals from network stations; they provide particular benefits for persons living in remote areas served neither by off-air signals nor by a cable system. Yet they dilute the economic return of copyright owners from transmitted public performances (e.g., by substituting for cable systems).

Inspired by the cable compulsory license under § 111, the satellite compulsory license has some distinctive features. During the initial four-year period of § 119's implementation, royalty rates were set at a flat fee of 12 cents a month per subscriber for each received superstation signal and 3 cents a month per subscriber for each received network signal; during a second period, of two years, rates are set by negotiation and binding arbitration. (The six-year "sunset" period has been extended by statutory amendment.) Section 119 rests on the assumption that Congress should impose a compulsory license only when the marketplace cannot suffice; thus, the six-year "sunset" provision. Some restrictions are placed upon re-transmission of the signals of certain network affiliates in order to prevent disruption of the networks' special exclusivity arrangements.

Bills presently being considered in Congress have taken two different approaches to the cable and satellite compulsory licenses. One would combine the two into a single comprehensive section that would cover all forms of retransmissions of copyrighted broadcast programs, regardless of the precise form of technology used for that purpose; this would allow the law to adapt to newly developing technologies without need for statutory change. Until that is accomplished, there is likely to be confusion about the respective areas of coverage of sections 111 and 119. Thus, in *National Broadcasting Co. v. Satellite Broadcast Networks Inc.*, 940 F.2d 1467 (11th Cir. 1991), the court of appeals held that the definition of "cable system" under Section 111 includes satellite rebroadcast facilities; nonetheless, the Copyright Office in January 1992 issued a regulation (effective January 1994) that neither satellite carriers nor the emerging wireless television systems qualify as cable systems for purposes of compulsory licensing; and most recently a district court within the Eleventh Circuit has held that the Copyright Office regulation must be set aside as in conflict with the court of appeals holding. *See Satellite Broadcasting & Communications Ass'n v. Oman*, __ F. Supp. __ (D. Ga. 1993).

A second and far more radical proposal would eliminate the compulsory license altogether as applied to such retransmissions; the proponents contend that whatever need there might have been for a compulsory license to shelter the emerging cable industry has now been eliminated by the great commercial success of re-transmission services, and that the establishment of terms and royalty rates should best be done through marketplace negotiations rather than by an agency of the federal government. It is very likely that some form of one or the other bill will be enacted into law in the not distant future.

c. Sound Recordings — § 114

Sections 106(4) and 114(a) make it clear that the owner of copyright in a sound recording — as distinguished from the musical or literary work embodied therein — is given by the statute the right to "dub" the recorded sounds onto another phonograph record or tape, but not the exclusive right to "perform" the sound recording. Thus, when a sound recording is played over the radio or in a jukebox, royalties are payable to the owner of copyright in the musical composition but not to the record manufacturer or to the performing artists.

In the more than ten years of congressional hearings and deliberations that preceded the enactment of the 1976 Copyright Act, one of the more hotly debated issues was whether "performers' rights" should be granted in connection with the public playing of sound recordings. Congress chose to delay disposition of the matter by providing, in § 114(d), that the Register of Copyrights, after consulting with the affected interests, "shall submit to the Congress a report setting forth recommendations as to whether this section should be amended to provide for performers and copyright owners of copyrighted material any performance rights in such material," along with specific legislative recommendations if appropriate. On the basis of extensive legal and economic surveys, as well as public hearings, the Register in March 1978 set forth her own recommendations to Congress. *See Performance Rights in Sound Recordings*, 95th Cong., 2d Sess. (June 1978) (House Jud. Comm. Print No. 15).

The Register first explored a number of issues bearing on the question of extending performing rights to performers and record manufacturers. She concluded, invoking the 1971 Record Piracy Act and its incorporation in the 1976 Copyright Act, that sound recordings are properly treated as "writings," and performers and record producers as "authors," for purposes of the constitutional Copyright Clause. On the basic economic issue, broadcasters and other users of sound recordings argued that the "free airplay" of sound recordings provided adequate compensation to performers and record producers in the form of increased record sales, increased attendance at live performances, and increased popularity of individual artists. The Register, however, concluded that these benefits were "hit or miss," that they also provided direct commercial advantage to the record user, and that performing rights should be accorded even to those not involved in the making of "hit" records. The broadcasters also argued that the imposition of performance royalties would create such a severe financial burden that marginal stations would be driven out of business, and other stations would be forced to curtail or abandon certain kinds of programming (public service, classical, etc.) in favor of high-income-producing programming in order to survive. Here, too, the Register found "no hard economic evidence" to support these arguments; an independent economic study commissioned by the Copyright Office concluded that the payment of royalties was unlikely to cause serious disruption within the broadcasting industry.

The Register therefore concluded that such performers' rights should be granted and that this should be done under the Copyright Act, in light of "considerations of national uniformity, equal treatment, and practical effectiveness." She summarized her reasons as follows:

> Broadcasters and other commercial users of recordings have performed them without permission or payment for generations. Users today look upon any requirement that they pay royalties as an unfair imposition in the nature of a "tax." However, any economic burden on the users of recordings for public performance is heavily outweighed, not only by the commercial benefits accruing directly from the use of copyrighted sound recordings, but also by the direct and indirect damage done to performers whenever recordings are used as a substitute for live performances. In all other areas the unauthorized use of a creative work is considered a copyright infringement if it results either in damage to the creator or in profits to the user. Sound recordings are creative works, and their unauthorized performance results in both damage and profits. To leave the

creators of sound recordings without any protection or compensation for their widespread commercial use can no longer be justified.

Pursuant to the mandate of § 114(d), the Register then proposed a bill that has served as a prototype of proposed legislation introduced in Congress in several subsequent years. The principal features of her proposal were as follows:

1. Section 106(4) would be amended to extend the right of public performance to sound recordings, and the definition of "perform" in § 101 would be amended to include the making audible of sounds in a sound recording.

2. The performance right in sound recordings would not, however, be exclusive but rather would be subject to a compulsory license — which would embrace the playing of the recording on radio and television, through cable retransmissions, and in jukeboxes.

3. The Copyright Royalty Tribunal would divide the collected royalty payments (less governmental administrative costs) among all claimants, either pursuant to the claimants' agreement regarding the size of their respective shares (such agreement to be exempted from the antitrust laws) or if there is a dispute regarding the division of the royalties, according to the Tribunal's own determination. The distribution would be divided between "owners of copyright" in the sound recording and all persons participating as performers on the recording. (This sort of division of royalties is very much like that endorsed by Congress in the 1992 Audio Home Recording Act, which creates a fund to be divided among record producers and performers as compensation for the at-home *reproduction* of recordings, as distinguished from their public *performance*. See Section A.2.b of this chapter, *supra*.)

Although the issue of performance rights in sound recordings became somewhat dormant in the latter 1980s, it has been revived again by the development of so-called digital audio broadcasting. This technology permits radio stations to deliver near-perfect digitized sound (from digital recording media such as compact discs) to the listener's home, by way of a transmission system (like cable television) whereby subscribers would have access to multichannel digital cable services playing, for example, all classical music on one channel, rock on another, and country-western on a third. The concern is that so many home subscribers, with digital radio transmission and with their digital tape recorders at home, will resort to personal-use taping that there will be a most serious incursion upon the market for phonorecords, to the obvious detriment of both record companies and recording artists. Giving such companies and artists rights to claim royalties when their recordings are broadcast or otherwise transmitted to homes would help to redress the resulting economic injury. Granting such performance rights would also bring U.S. law into greater harmony with the law of foreign jurisdictions and would thus make it easier to justify the claims of U.S. recording artists to royalties for the public performances of their records abroad. A recent report prepared by the U.S. Copyright Office once again endorses such performance rights, particularly in light of the digital audio technologies. H.R. 2576, pending in the 103rd Congress in late 1993, would amend § 106 to add a new exclusive right: "in the case of sound recordings, to perform the copyrighted work publicly by means of a digital transmission."

d. "Jukebox" Public Performances — §§ 116 and 116A

The 1909 Act contained an express exemption from liability for unauthorized performance of music by means of coin-operated machines where there was no admission fee to the place of performance. This so-called jukebox exemption, originally designed to insulate the "penny parlor," became a haven for an increasingly profitable jukebox industry. Legislative assaults on the exemption failed throughout most of this century. The elimination of the exemption in the 1976 Act, and the substitution of a compulsory-license arrangement — with a modest statutory royalty rate, subject to redetermination by the Copyright Royalty Tribunal — were most significant steps in protecting the copyright owner's exclusive right of public performance.

Not surprisingly, the precise amount of the statutory royalty was a subject of considerable debate throughout the revision process. As enacted, § 116(b)(1)(A) provided for a royalty fee of $8 per year per jukebox, which would cover all of the musical works placed in that box. Acting pursuant to statutory authorization in §§ 801(b) and 804(a), the Copyright Royalty Tribunal initiated proceedings in January 1980 to determine whether the statutory rates warranted adjustment; hearings were held, with appearances by the three performing rights societies representing copyright owners (ASCAP, BMI and SESAC) and by representatives of the jukebox industry (the Amusement and Music Operators Association). The Tribunal determined that jukebox operators should pay an increased royalty fee of $25 per jukebox in 1982 and 1983, and $50 in subsequent years, with a cost-of-living adjustment to be introduced in 1987. On judicial review, the Tribunal's action was upheld against claims by the performing rights societies that a more reasonable royalty would have been in the range of $70-$140, as well as against claims by AMOA that the $25/$50 fee was inconsistent with Congress's intent and would have a serious adverse impact upon many jukebox operators. *Amusement & Music Operators Ass'n v. Copyright Royalty Tribunal,* 676 F.2d 1144 (7th Cir.), *cert. denied,* 459 U.S. 907 (1982).

In its initial distribution of jukebox royalties in 1978, the Copyright Royalty Tribunal allocated 47.5% of the fund each to ASCAP and BMI, and 5% to SESAC (the three societies actually mentioned by name in § 116(c)(4)) — and since then, the societies have voluntarily settled their claims among themselves. The size of the distributable fund has mounted steadily, particularly as the per-box royalty fee has increased through the years (including a cost-of-living increase in 1987), from an initial distributable fund of $1.12 million in 1978 to $6.2 million in 1988.

In the latter year, Congress reviewed the compulsory-license provisions to determine whether modification was required in order to render United States law consistent with Berne Convention requirements. The jukebox licensing provisions were found to be inconsistent with Article 11(1) of the Convention. Accordingly, a newly enacted § 116A contemplates that the jukebox operators and the copyright owners will negotiate a voluntary license agreement on the terms and rate of royalty payments and division of fees; if negotiations founder, the parties may resort to arbitration. Licensing arrangements have been successfully negotiated and, pursuant to § 116A(d), they have displaced the compulsory-license provisions of the original § 116, which can be revived if private licensing terminates for any reason. The license arrangements voluntarily negotiated by AMOA and the performing rights societies provide for the payment of $275 for the year for the operator's first jukebox, $55 per box for the second through the tenth box, and $48 per year for the eleventh and each box beyond; this royalty structure clearly works to the disadvantage of the person who operates only a small number of jukeboxes. (Legislative amendments pending in 1993 would eliminate § 116 as originally enacted and replace it altogether with a renumbered § 116A, thus fully eliminating the jukebox compulsory license after what would be a fifteen-year trial period.)

e. Public Broadcasting — § 118

A limitation on performing rights that was adopted late in the development of the 1976 Act is the compulsory license for public broadcasting. Public broadcasters, while acknowledging that copyright holders should receive payments for their valuable contributions to high-quality programming, emphasized the "multitude of administratively cumbersome and very costly rights 'clearance' problems that cannot help but impair the vitality" of public broadcasting were there to be no compulsory license; the financial and administrative burdens of securing clearances would overwhelm the budgets of the public broadcasters, which are financed by public support and donations. The musical performing rights societies argued against the compulsory license, which it thought wrong in principle even if utilized in three other statutory situations for special historical reasons. Rebutting the argument regarding administrative burden, they emphasized that commercial broadcasters had for many years secured negotiated licenses that were working well, and that even public broadcasters had traditionally negotiated for synchronization (or recording) licenses in the past, for lack of a "for profit" limitation on such synchronization under the 1909 Act. A particularly strong argument against the compulsory license for public broadcasters was the increasing overlap in function between public and commercial broadcasting:

> Public broadcasting has grown and changed significantly in the past decade and will continue to do so. It now competes with commercial broadcasting as a national medium, and its programming contains much of the same types of entertainment and cultural material presented by commercial broadcasters. The revenues of public broadcasting have grown significantly....

Although § 118 as originally proposed included a compulsory license for public broadcasting of nondramatic literary works, this was eliminated in the revision process. The outcome was a compulsory license with respect to performing and display rights in published nondramatic musical, pictorial, graphic, and sculptural works performed or displayed on "a noncommercial educational broadcast station," § 118(d), by a "public broadcasting entity,"

§ 118(g). In addition, such entities may record and distribute programs embodying such works for broadcasts by other such stations. Section 118(d)(2). (They also enjoy under § 114(b) the right to reproduce sound recordings for educational broadcasting purposes.) Provision is made for public schools and other nonprofit institutions to tape the broadcast of the specified works for nonprofit face-to-face instructional use within seven days.

The fees and other terms concerning use under § 118 are not set forth in the statute; rather the immediate task of determining them was given to the Copyright Royalty Tribunal (soon possibly to be replaced by the Librarian of Congress, aided by ad hoc arbitration panels), in the absence of voluntary negotiation. The latter is also encouraged, *inter alia,* by antitrust exemptions. Section 118(b). Specific timetables are imposed by the statute for rate determinations. The prevailing rates can be found in Part 304 of the Tribunal's regulations, in Appendix D of this casebook.

f. Compatibility with the Berne Convention of Compulsory Licenses and Other Qualifications of the Performance and Display Rights

The previous materials addressed the many limitations that United States copyright law imposes on the exclusive exercise of the public performance and display rights. Some of these limitations are outright exemptions from liability; others, in the form of compulsory licenses, substitute government regulation for free selection of licensees and negotiation of royalty rates. Is this diverse collection of restraints upon the copyright holder's free and full exercise of copyright compatible with the Berne Convention's specification of composers' and dramatists' exclusive rights in "any communication to the public" and to "public performance by any means or process" (Art. 11)?

Although the Berne Convention generally sets a high level of minimum protection, it does tolerate some qualifications to the principle of exclusive right under copyright. Article 13.1 of the treaty explicitly permits member countries to provide for compulsory licenses for the making of sound recordings of musical works. Note that § 114 of the United States Copyright Act, precluding a performance right in sound recordings, does not contravene the Berne Convention because that treaty does not cover sound recordings. (Another treaty, the Geneva Phonograms Convention, secures international protection for sound recordings, but, like § 114, this convention is limited to reproduction rights.) Article 11, bis.2 of the Berne Convention allows member countries to qualify rights to broadcasts and secondary transmissions, subject to a guarantee of equitable remuneration "which, in the absence of agreement, shall be fixed by competent authority." This text appears consistent with the provisions in Title 17 for compulsory licenses for cable retransmissions and for public broadcasting. The remaining compulsory license, for jukeboxes, as set out in the 1976 Act, however, did not fit any exemption or limitation authorized in the Berne Convention. *See generally Final Report of the Ad Hoc Working Group on U.S. Adherence to the Berne Convention,* 10 Colum.-VLA J. L. & Arts 513, 533-40 (1986). The 1988 amendments, therefore, substituted an initial system of negotiated licenses for the current jukebox compulsory license (the compulsory license remains as a residual measure in the event that private negotiations fail). Finally, most, and perhaps all, of the § 110 exemptions to the performance and display rights may be accommodated within the Berne Convention's underlying authorization to member countries to maintain "minor reservations" to the general rights of public performance, broadcasting and retransmission. The drafters of the most recent version of the Berne Convention (Stockholm 1967/Paris 1971) anticipated that these reservations would extend to small-scale or publicly beneficial uses such as "religious ceremonies, performances by military bands and the requirements of education and popularization." *Id.* at 535; *see also* World Intellectual Property Organization, *Guide to the Berne Convention* ¶ 11.6 (1978).

GENERAL REVIEW QUESTIONS

What, if any, are the copyright infringements in the following cases?

1. *E* exhibits a copyrighted painting, which it owns, in an art gallery, without the consent of *A*, the artist and owner of copyright. *E* exhibits the same painting on a television program.

2. *H* Hotel hires a three-piece band to play copyrighted music at the hotel restaurant; there is no admission charge or entertainment charge. *E* (exclusive) membership social club has a band playing the same music at weekend dances.

3. Michael Jackson plays a copyrighted song in a television studio; ABC television network transmits the performance to its local television affiliates, which broadcast it; a viewer turns on the television set in a room filled with family friends; and a doctor does the same for the patients in her waiting room.

4. *H* Hotel pipes the sound from the Jackson television show into the hotel elevators and private guest rooms. It also plays a different rendition of that song through its Muzak background-music service system, into private guest rooms.

5. A jukebox operator places a phonorecord of *C*'s song in a coin-operated jukebox, and the record is frequently played; the performance of the song is by *P* and the record is made by the *R* Recording Company.

6. Arthur Miller's "Death of a Salesman" is performed by students in a 12th-grade classroom.

(a) Assume instead that one of the performers is a professional actor, an alumnus of the school.

(b) Assume instead that the student performance is in the school auditorium.

(c) Assume that the student classroom performance is transmitted by closed-circuit television to all high school English classes in the school district.

7. The high school glee club opens an assembly program in the school auditorium with a copyrighted hymn. It also sings the hymn at the beginning of a school football game; tickets are sold to the game, the proceeds being devoted to uniforms and other expenses of the school's athletic teams and musical organizations.

8. The high school glee club makes a recording of the copyrighted song, and publicly distributes the recording. Jolly Roger Records "dubs" the sounds onto its own phonorecords (without any consents) and sells them to the public. A disc jockey plays the glee club record over local radio station WDJ.

9. Officials within the California prison system have in the past year purchased at retail prices cassettes of copyrighted motion pictures, from stores lawfully selling videotapes and videodiscs. The videotapes bear a legend stating: "This tape is exclusively for viewing in private homes. Any duplication, or any public showing, is a violation of the law." They are kept in a central prison-system library, under the control of prison authorities, from which they are distributed to a number of state prison facilities. At these facilities (e.g., the California state penitentiary), the videotapes are taken to recreational areas containing television sets and are inserted into hooked-up videotape recorders so that the complete film can be viewed upon the television screen. Prison inmates are informed of the time and location of showing of particular films, and are invited to attend. A given prison facility will retain the film, and exhibit it, over a few days and will then return it to the central system library. Because the same tape is shown fairly often, the typical individual viewing is attended by some eight to ten inmates. Upon learning of this use, the copyright owners of the motion pictures in question bring an action against the California Commission of Prisons. Will the action be successful? Why? *Compare* Cal. Att'y Gen. No. 81-503 (Feb. 5, 1982), in 1982 Copyright L. Dec. (CCH) ¶ 25,368, *with* Louisiana Att'y Gen. No. 84-436 (Jan. 10, 1985), in 29 BNA P.T.C.J. 480.

10. Should persons confined to nursing homes for long-term health care be permitted — free of charge to the home — to view copyrighted motion pictures on videocassettes, just as they would have to pay no license fee had they been viewing the video in their homes? Bills were recently introduced to allow this, after some film distributors claimed that nursing homes were obliged to purchase a public performance license, which in some instances would have cost thousands of dollars. After hearings in 1990, congressional representatives urged that a private agreement be made between motion picture companies and nursing home representatives to allow such videocassette performances, in a manner that was uniform, binding and transaction-free. In the summer of 1990, such an agreement was reached. Under it a nursing home becomes a non-exclusive licensee as soon as the film distributor receives confirmation that the home has tendered a $10 contribution to a charitable organization designated by the distributor. The home may not make a direct charge for the performance of the copyrighted film, and the showing must take place in a common area or living room and may not be further transmitted by closed-circuit television or by any other means. Licenses will remain in effect until January 1, 2001. Do you believe the filmmakers (including Turner, Paramount, Warner, Columbia, MCA, Disney, MGM/UA, 20th Century Fox, and Orion) acquiesced in such an arrangement because their legal claims were weak, or because pressing such claims would have made for poor public relations? *See* BNA, 40 P.T.C.J. 309 (Aug. 9, 1990).

E. FAIR USE

1. THE TRADITIONAL UNDERSTANDING

Despite the constitutional authorization to Congress to secure to authors "the exclusive Right to their ... Writings," Art. 1, § 8, cl. 8, we have already encountered many statutory qualifications of the author's exclusivity. *See* Subchapter D, *supra,* of this chapter. The "fair use" exception to copyright protection constitutes perhaps the most significant, and the most venerable, limitation on an author's or copyright holder's prerogatives. Originally a judge-made doctrine, the exception is now codified at § 107 of the 1976 Act. In essence, the traditional concept of fair use excused reasonable unauthorized appropriations from a first work, when the use to which the second author put the appropriated material in some way advanced the public benefit, without substantially impairing the present or potential economic value of the first work.

Justice Story's decision in *Folsom v. Marsh,* 9 F. Cas. 342, 348 (C.C.D. Mass. 1841) (No. 4,901), appears to offer the first enunciation of the principles of the fair use doctrine in United States copyright law (although the appellation "fair use" is a later development, see *Lawrence v. Dana,* 15 F. Cas. 26 (C.C.D. Mass. 1869) (No. 8,136)). Justice Story sought to distinguish between an excusable unauthorized use and an infringing use. Quotation of portions of a work as part of an essay reviewing the work or as part of a biography of the writer might satisfy the former standard, but "if so much is taken, that the value of the original is sensibly diminished, or the labors of the original author are substantially to an injurious extent appropriated by another, that is sufficient, in point of law, to constitute a piracy pro tanto." *Accord, Story v. Holcombe,* 23 F. Cas. 171 (C.C.D. Ohio 1847) (No. 13,497) (suit by Story's executors against author of condensed version of Story's *Commentaries on Equity Jurisprudence*) ("sufficient may be taken to form a correct idea of the whole; but no one is allowed, under the pretense of quoting, to publish either the whole or the principal part of another man's composition; and therefore a review must not substitute for the book reviewed.") While Justice Story may primarily have emphasized "the degree in which the use may prejudice the sales, or diminish the profits, or supercede the objects of the original work," he also counselled consideration of "the nature and objects of the selections made," and "the quantity and value of the materials used." (*Cf.* 17 U.S.C. § 107(1), (3), (4), *infra*).

Subsequent fair use decisions developed a theory of fair use, and added further content to the classification of works which might be subject to or might benefit by the fair use exemption. In *Rosemont Enters. v. Random House, Inc.,* 366 F.2d 303 (2d Cir. 1966), *cert. denied,* 385 U.S. 1009 (1976), the Court of Appeals for the Second Circuit excused the copying, by the authors of an unauthorized biography of Howard Hughes, of portions of magazine articles about Hughes in which Hughes' agents had acquired the copyrights. The court announced a constitutional foundation for the fair use doctrine (366 F.2d at 307):

The fundamental justification for the [fair use] privilege lies in the constitutional purpose in granting copyright protection in the first instance, to wit, "To Promote the Progress of Science and the Useful Arts.".... To serve that purpose, "courts in passing upon particular claims of infringement must occasionally subordinate the copyright holder's interest in a maximum financial return to the greater public interest in the development of art, science and industry."... Whether the privilege may justifiably be applied to particular materials turns initially on the nature of the materials, e.g., whether their distribution would serve the public interest in the free dissemination of information and whether their preparation requires some use of prior materials dealing with the same subject matter.

The "public benefit" standard supplied in *Rosemont* seems to render information-based works, such as histories, biographies, and works of science the most likely fair use subject matter. This is a two-edged sword: the biographer may be able to invoke the fair use privilege in her own defense against copying from a prior fact-based work, but she may find herself equally susceptible to a subsequent biographer's borrowing from her.

In some respects, *Rosemont* and *Folsom v. Marsh* represent opposite poles of the traditional fair use doctrine. *Folsom* seems to concentrate most on the harm of the borrowing to the first author, while *Rosemont* seeks primarily to discern the advantages which the public may derive from the borrowing. Under either approach, however, to be "fair," defendant's use must have been "productive," i.e., defendant must have built upon the work of the plaintiff by way of criticism, elaboration, or the like. The "productive" use has special appeal under fair use analysis for the reasons articulated by Professor Chafee in his seminal article, *Reflections on the Law of Copyright,* 45 Colum. L. Rev. 503, 533: "The world goes ahead because each of us builds on the work of our predecessors. A dwarf standing on the shoulders of a giant can see farther than the giant himself." The more the second work incorporates and depends upon the first work, the less likely it was to be deemed a fair use, either because it tends to substitute for the first work (*Folsom* approach), or because its lack of a significant independent contribution to the prior work tends to diminish the credibility of a defense that the second work is adding to the corpus of art or knowledge (*Rosemont* approach).

2. SECTION 107 OF THE 1976 COPYRIGHT ACT

§ 107. Limitations on exclusive rights: Fair use

Notwithstanding the provisions of section 106, the fair use of a copyrighted work, including such use by reproduction in copies or phonorecords or by any other means specified by that section, for purposes such as criticism, comment, news reporting, teaching (including multiple copies for classroom use), scholarship, or research, is not an infringement of copyright. In determining whether the use made of a work in any particular case is a fair use the factors to be considered shall include —

(1) the purpose and character of the use, including whether such use is of a

commercial nature or is for nonprofit educational purposes;

(2) the nature of the copyrighted work;

(3) the amount and substantiality of the portion used in relation to the copyrighted work as a whole; and

(4) the effect of the use upon the potential market for or value of the copyrighted work.

The fact that a work is unpublished shall not itself bar a finding of fair use if such finding is made upon consideration of all the above factors.

HOUSE REPORT

H.R. Rep. No. 94-1476, 94th Cong., 2d Sess. 65-66 (1976)

General background of the problem

The judicial doctrine of fair use, one of the most important and well-established limitations on the exclusive right of copyright owners, would be given express statutory recognition for the first time in section 107. The claim that a defendant's acts constituted a fair use rather than an infringement has been raised as a defense in innumerable copyright actions over the years, and there is ample case law recognizing the existence of the doctrine and applying it. The examples enumerated at page 24 of the Register's 1961 Report, while by no means exhaustive, give some idea of the sort of activities the courts might regard as fair use under the circumstances: "quotation of excerpts in a review or criticism for purposes of illustration or comment; quotation of short passages in a scholarly or technical work, for illustration or clarification of the author's observations; use in a parody of some of the content of the work parodied; summary of an address or article, with brief quotations, in a news report; reproduction by a library of a portion of a work to replace part of a damaged copy; reproduction by a teacher or student of a small part of a work to illustrate a lesson; reproduction of a work in legislative or judicial proceedings or reports; incidental and fortuitous reproduction, in a newsreel or broadcast, of a work located in the scene of an event being reported."

Although the courts have considered and ruled upon the fair use doctrine over and over again, no real definition of the concept has ever emerged. Indeed, since the doctrine is an equitable rule of reason, no generally applicable definition is possible, and each case raising the question must be decided on its own facts. On the other hand, the courts have evolved a set of criteria which, though in no case definitive or determinative, provide some gauge for balancing the equities. These criteria have been stated in various ways, but essentially they can all be reduced to the four standards which have been adopted in section 107 ....

The specific wording of section 107 as it now stands is the result of a process of accretion, resulting from the long controversy over the related problems of fair use and the reproduction (mostly by photocopying) of copyrighted material for educational and scholarly purposes. For example, the reference to fair use "by reproduction in copies or phonorecords or by any other means" is mainly intended to make clear that the doctrine has as much application to photocopying and taping as to older forms of use; it is not intended to give these kinds of reproduction any special status under the fair use provision or to sanction any reproduction beyond the normal and reasonable limits of fair use. Similarly, the newly-added reference to "multiple copies for classroom use" is a recognition that, under the proper circumstances of fairness, the doctrine can be applied to reproductions of multiple copies for the members of a class.

The Committee has amended the first of the criteria to be considered — "the purpose and character of the use" — to state explicitly that this factor includes a consideration of "whether such use is of a commercial nature or is for non-profit educational purposes." This amendment is not intended to be interpreted as any sort of not-for-profit limitation on educational uses of copyrighted works. It is an express recognition that, as under the present law, the commercial or non-profit character of an activity, while not conclusive with respect to fair use, can and should be weighed along with other factors in fair use decisions.

General intention behind the provision

The statement of the fair use doctrine in section 107 offers some guidance to users in determining when the principles of the doctrine apply. However, the endless variety of situations and combinations of circumstances that can arise in particular cases precludes the formulation of exact rules in the statute. The bill endorses the purpose and general scope of the judicial doctrine of fair use, but there is no disposition to freeze the doctrine in the statute, especially during a period of rapid technological change. Beyond a very broad statutory explanation of what fair use is and some of the criteria applicable to it, the courts must be free to adapt the doctrine to particular situations on a case-by-case basis. Section 107 is intended to restate the present judicial doctrine of fair use, not to change, narrow, or enlarge it in any way.

THE CODIFICATION OF THE FAIR USE DOCTRINE

Decisions construing the new statutory text have confronted a variety of problems stemming from the structure and language of § 107.

First, how should the preamble, or opening sentence, be interpreted? The text lists a variety of illustrative uses which may constitute fair uses. Note the use of the phrase "such as," which is defined in § 101 (along with "including"). Does this mean that the listed purposes have been randomly selected as appealing examples, or does it mean that they share a particular characteristic that then serves as a limitation upon the availability of the fair use defense? If the listed purposes are meant to share a limiting characteristic, what is it? That they all advance knowledge? That they are all "productive" uses? Should one conclude that a use — for example, a nonproductive commercial use — which is neither mentioned in the list nor analogous to a listed use cannot qualify as a fair use?

This issue was directly addressed by the Court of Appeals for the Eleventh Circuit in *Pacific & S. Co. v. Duncan*, 744 F.2d 1490 (11th Cir. 1984), *cert. denied*, 471 U.S. 1004 (1985). There, the defendant videotaped segments from copyrighted television news programs and marketed them to the subject of the particular news clip. The lower court held that the preamble to § 107 in effect required that a defendant's use must be a "productive" one in order to be a fair use, and that in view of the defendant's failure to meet that requirement, it was inappropriate to weigh the four factors set forth in the second sentence of that section. The court of appeals disagreed (although it ultimately found no fair use):

> We agree with TV News Clips that the district court should have considered the four factors set out in the statute. The statute uses mandatory language to the effect that in a fair use determination, the "factors to be considered *shall* include" (emphasis added) the four listed. The preamble merely illustrates the sorts of uses likely to qualify as fair uses under the four listed factors.

Under the court's interpretation in the *Duncan* case, as reinforced by the approach taken by the Supreme Court in the *Sony* case, set out more fully below, the four factors delineated in the second sentence of § 107 should be considered in all cases in which fair use is asserted as a defense. But the language does not preclude consideration of other factors. Courts have, in fact, declined to assign an exclusive role to these factors, and have instead regularly introduced additional considerations.

Thus, courts have inquired into the "amount and substantiality of the portion used" not only "in relation to the copyrighted work as a whole," but in relation to *defendant*'s work as well. *See, e.g., Harper & Row v. Nation Enters.*, 105 S. Ct. 2218 (1985) (300 words copied from plaintiff's 450-page book constituted 13% of defendant's article). They have tended to be more lenient when the unauthorized use was "incidental," that is, when the plaintiff's work was captured as part of a larger permissible reproduction or performance. *See, e.g., Italian Book Co. v. ABC*, 458 F. Supp. 65 (S.D.N.Y. 1978) (portion of plaintiff's song performed in "Little Italy" street festival was included in defendant's television news coverage of festival). *But see Schumann v. Albuquerque Corp.*, 664 F. Supp. 473 (D.N.M. 1987) (broadcast of entire copyrighted songs played by band at local festival not fair use; because the broadcast had "entertainment value," it was held to be competitive with uses copyright owners would license).

The "incidental use" analysis was applied under the 1909 Act in a number of difficult cases. In *Mura v. Columbia Broadcasting Sys.*, 245 F. Supp. 587 (S.D.N.Y. 1965), the plaintiff's hand puppets were displayed and manipulated for some 35 seconds by Mr. Green Jeans and Captain Kangaroo in the course of a musical segment on the latter's television program. This was found to be a use that was brief, incidental and fair. In *Karll v. Curtis Pub. Co.*, 39 F. Supp. 836 (E.D. Wis. 1941), an article in the *Saturday Evening Post* about the Green Bay Packers football team reproduced the lyrics of the eight-line chorus of "Go! You Packers Go!," the copyrighted "official song" of the team. The court found that the lyrics were "relatively unimportant" in the context of the entire article. Pushing that point of view to an extreme, the court in *Broadway Music Corp. v. F.R. Pub. Corp.*, 31 F. Supp. 817 (S.D.N.Y. 1940), upheld as fair the quotation, in a short column in *The New Yorker* noting the death of silent-movie star Pearl White, of the lyrics of a song written many years before to describe her screen exploits; the lyrics ran some twelve lines, the *New Yorker*'s own text was about as long.

Do you agree with the result of these cases? In the *New Yorker* case, what should the result be if the lyrics had instead been incorporated in a twenty-page pamphlet entitled "Songs of the Twenties," sold for $2 in music stores? *Compare Johns & Johns Printing Co. v. Paull-Pioneer Music Corp.*, 102 F.2d 282 (8th Cir. 1939). Should an impersonator of, say, Louis Armstrong be advised that he may sing part or all of the song "Hello Dolly!" (or perhaps a song less distinctly identified with Armstrong) in a stage or television performance?

In applying the fair use doctrine, courts have tended to be far less lenient when defendant's conduct betrayed callous disregard for plaintiff's interests. Emphasizing the equitable nature of the defense, courts have cautioned, "the fair use doctrine is not a license for corporate theft, empowering a court to ignore a copyright whenever it determines the underlying work contains material of public importance." *Iowa State Univ. Research Found. v. ABC*, 621 F.2d 57, 61 (2d Cir. 1980). One court has observed: "Because fair use presupposes 'good faith' and 'fair dealing,' ... courts may weigh 'the propriety of the defendant's conduct' in the equitable balance of a fair use determination." *Fisher v. Dees*, 794 F.2d 432 (9th Cir. 1986). *See* L. Weinreb, *Fair's Fair: A Comment on the Fair Use Doctrine*, 103 Harv. L. Rev. 1137 (1990).

A similar message can be found in the Supreme Court's references in *Harper & Row Pub'rs, Inc. v. Nation Enterprises*, 471 U.S. 539 (1985), to the "purloined manuscript" of President Ford's memoirs that illicitly came into the hands of the publisher of *Nation Magazine*; and to the illicit photographing, through an illegal entry in the dark of night, of segments of a copyrighted motion picture of the assassination of President Kennedy, undertaken by an author in the course of preparing a serious book about that tragic event, *Time, Inc. v. Bernard Geis Assocs.*, 293 F. Supp. 130 (S.D.N.Y. 1968) (although the court found this misbehavior to have been counterbalanced by the author's proffer to the plaintiff of all royalties generated by the sale of his book). Forceful contrary arguments have been made, however, to the effect that any wrongdoing on the part of a defendant asserting fair use, even if constituting a private injury, should be discounted in assessing the more compelling public interests at stake in the fair use analysis. *See* P. Leval, *Toward a Fair Use Standard*, 103 Harv. L. Rev. 1105 (1990). Which of these positions is more compelling? (For consideration of the question whether it counts against fair use that the defendant has placed the borrowed copyrighted work in a pornographic or salacious setting, see the cases set forth below relating to parody.)

Related to the issue of improper conduct as a factor beyond the four listed in § 107 is whether or not the defendant requested permission of the copyright owner before making an unauthorized use. On the one hand, it can be argued that the making and denial of such a request counts against the defendant, who is thereby put on notice of the plaintiff's disapproval and establishes willful misbehavior. On the other hand, such requests should be encouraged, both as a courtesy and as a possible prelude to a negotiated arrangement for compensation — and it might be argued that in any event it is circular to impose on a user an obligation to seek permission, when the very question for the court to decide is whether the use is fair so that no permission need be sought. Which of these positions is more compelling? In some fair use contexts, such as parody of a copyrighted work, it is extremely unlikely that permission or license will be granted, and it is in precisely such a case that fair use can properly be regarded as indispensable to foster the defendant's work in the face of such predictable "market failure." *See Fisher v. Dees, supra*: "Parodists will seldom get permission from those whose works are parodied. Self-esteem is seldom strong enough to permit the granting of permission even in exchange for a reasonable fee.... The parody defense to copyright infringement exists precisely to make possible a use that generally cannot be bought."

The presence or absence of a convenient vehicle for securing licenses has indeed been taken into account among the "equitable" considerations that supplement the factors listed in the statute. Thus, in *American Geophysical Union v. Texaco*, 802 F. Supp. 1 (S.D.N.Y. 1992), involving the making of single photocopies of scientific journal articles by researchers working for a large petroleum company, the court concluded that — even if such photocopying might have been reasonable and fair in 1970, lest scientific progress be inhibited by the high transaction costs of securing publishers' permissions — the development of the Copyright Clearance Center since the late 1970s has provided a "convenient, reasonable licensing system" that can facilitate research-based photocopying for a single comprehensive fee, paid in advance and covering thousands of scientific journals.

Just as many courts have been disinclined to find fair use when they regard the defendant's activity as wrongful or immoral, by the same token, courts may be more inclined to deem defendant's use fair if it suspects the copyright owner of unreasonable conduct. *See, e.g., Rosemont, supra* (Howard Hughes appeared to be invoking copyrights in biographical articles in order to prevent others from writing about his life).

The development of additional fair use criteria does not, however, diminish the importance of the statutorily listed factors. Their itemization should not be treated as an invitation to perfunctory or mechanical application. The Second Circuit has castigated lower courts for treating the factors as mere impediments for defendants to "overcome":

> The four factors which the fair use statute identifies as relevant to a determination of whether the doctrine applies ... are equitable considerations to be assessed and weighed by the court; they are not simply hurdles over which an accused infringer may leap to safety from liability. Rather than a sequence of four rigid tests, the fair use analysis consists of a "sensitive balancing of interests."

Financial Information, Inc. v. Moody's Inv. Serv., 751 F.2d 501, 507-08 (2d Cir. 1984) (citation omitted).

a. Judicial Application of § 107

SONY CORP. OF AMERICA v. UNIVERSAL CITY STUDIOS, INC.

464 U.S. 417 (1984)

JUSTICE STEVENS delivered the opinion of the Court.

[Plaintiff-respondents own the copyrights on certain publicly broadcast television programs. The principal defendant-petitioner was Sony Corp., manufacturer of the Betamax video tape recorder (VTR), and other defendants were Sony's advertising agency, retail distributors of the Betamax, and a home user. Plaintiffs alleged that home videotaping of their programs constituted an infringement of copyright, and that Sony was liable as a contributory infringer. Plaintiffs sought damages and profits, as well as an injunction against the manufacture and marketing of the Betamax VTR. The record showed that the principal use of the VTR is for "time shifting," i.e. the recording of a program that the VTR owner cannot view as it is being televised and the watching of the taped program at a later time (followed by the erasing of the program). The district court found that time shifting was a fair use of the plaintiffs' copyrighted programs and that Sony was not liable as a contributory infringer. The court of appeals disagreed on both issues. A divided (5-4) Supreme Court reversed the decision of the court of appeals.

[After analyzing the pertinent law regarding contributory infringement (see Chapter 6, Subchapter F2, infra), the Court concluded that "the sale of copying equipment, like the sale of other articles of commerce, does not constitute contributory infringement if the product is widely used for legitimate, unobjectionable purposes. Indeed, it need merely be capable of substantial noninfringing uses." The Court concluded that there was a substantial number of television-program copyright owners (particularly of sports, religious, and educational programs) who have no objection to the videotape recording (and then erasure) of their programs for time-shifting purposes. It then turned to the question whether the unauthorized home taping of programs owned by persons such as the plaintiffs constituted fair use, for if it did then the manufacture of the Betamax VTR could not be deemed contributory copyright infringement. The Court began its analysis by considering § 107.]

That section identifies various factors that enable a Court to apply an "equitable rule of reason" analysis to particular claims of infringement. Although not conclusive, the first factor requires that "the commercial or nonprofit character of an activity" be weighed in any fair use decision. If the Betamax were used to make copies for a commercial or profit-making purpose, such use would presumptively be unfair. The contrary presumption is appropriate here, however, because the District Court's findings plainly establish that time-shifting for private home use must be characterized as a noncommercial, nonprofit activity. Moreover, when one considers the nature of a televised copyrighted audiovisual work, see 17 U.S.C. § 107(2), and that time-shifting merely enables a viewer to see such a work which he had been invited to witness in its entirety free of charge, the fact that the entire work is reproduced, see id., at § 107(3), does not have its ordinary effect of militating against a finding of fair use.

This is not, however, the end of the inquiry because Congress has also directed us to consider "the effect of the use upon the potential market for or value of the copyrighted work." *Id.*, at § 107(4). The purpose of copyright is to create incentives for creative effort. Even copying for noncommercial purposes may impair the copyright holder's ability to obtain the rewards that Congress intended him to have. But a use that has no demonstrable effect upon the potential market for, or the value of, the copyrighted work need not be prohibited in order to protect the author's incentive to create. The prohibition of such noncommercial uses would merely inhibit access to ideas without any countervailing benefit.

Thus, although every commercial use of copyrighted material is presumptively an unfair exploitation of the monopoly privilege that belongs to the owner of the copyright, noncommercial uses are a different matter. A challenge to a noncommercial use of a copyrighted work requires proof either that the particular use is harmful, or that if it should become widespread, it would adversely affect the potential market for the copyrighted work. Actual present harm need not be shown; such a requirement would leave the copyright holder with no defense against predictable damage. Nor is it necessary to show with certainty that future harm will result. What is necessary is a showing by a preponderance of the evidence that *some* meaningful likelihood of future harm exists. If the intended use is for commercial gain, that likelihood may be presumed. But if it is for a noncommercial purpose, the likelihood must be demonstrated.

In this case, respondents failed to carry their burden with regard to home time-shifting....

There was no need for the District Court to say much about past harm. "Plaintiffs have admitted that no actual harm to their copyrights has occurred to date." [480 F. Supp.], at 451.

On the question of potential future harm from time-shifting, the District Court offered a more detailed analysis of the evidence. It rejected respondents' "fear that persons 'watching' the original telecast of a program will not be measured in the live audience and the ratings and revenues will decrease," by observing that current measurement technology allows the Betamax audience to be reflected. *Id.*, at 466.[36] It rejected respondents' prediction "that live

---

[36] "There was testimony at trial, however, that Nielsen Ratings has already developed the ability to measure when a Betamax in a sample home is recording the program. Thus, the Betamax will be measured as a part of the live audience. The later diary can augment that measurement with information about subsequent viewing." 480 F. Supp., at 466.

In a separate section, the District Court rejected plaintiffs' suggestion that the commercial attractiveness of television broadcasts would be diminished because Betamax owners would use the pause button or fast-forward control to avoid viewing advertisements: "It must be remembered, however, that to omit commercials, Betamax owners must view the program, including the commercials, while recording. To avoid commercials during playback, the viewer must fast-forward and, for the most part, guess as to when the commercial has passed. For most recordings, either practice may be too tedious. As defendants' survey showed, 92% of the programs were recorded with commercials and only 25% of the owners fast-forward through them. Advertisers will have to make the same kinds of judgments they do now about whether persons viewing

television or movie audiences will decrease as more people watch Betamax tapes as an alternative," with the observation that "[t]here is no factual basis for [the underlying] assumption." *Ibid.* It rejected respondents' "fear that time-shifting will reduce audiences for telecast reruns," and concluded instead that "given current market practices, this should aid plaintiffs rather than harm them." *Ibid.* And it declared that respondents' suggestion "that theater or film rental exhibition of a program will suffer because of time-shift recording of that program" "lacks merit." 480 F. Supp., at 467.[37]

After completing that review, the District Court restated its overall conclusion several times, in several different ways. "Harm from time-shifting is speculative and, at best, minimal." *Ibid.* "The audience benefits from the time-shifting capability have already been discussed. It is not implausible that benefits could also accrue to plaintiffs, broadcasters, and advertisers, as the Betamax makes it possible for more persons to view their broadcasts." *Ibid.* "No likelihood of harm was shown at trial, and plaintiffs admitted that there had been no actual harm to date." *Id.,* at 468-469. "Testimony at trial suggested that Betamax may require adjustments in marketing strategy, but it did not establish even a likelihood of harm." *Id.,* at 469. "Television production by plaintiffs today is more profitable than it has ever been, and, in five weeks of trial, there was no concrete evidence to suggest that the Betamax will change the studios' financial picture." *Ibid.*

The District Court's conclusions are buttressed by the fact that to the extent time-shifting expands public access to freely broadcast television programs, it yields societal benefits. Earlier this year, in *Community Television of Southern California v. Gottfried,* 459 U.S. 498, n. 12, 103 S. Ct. 885, 891-892 (1983), we acknowledged the public interest in making television broadcasting more available. Concededly, that interest is not unlimited. But it supports an interpretation of the concept of "fair use" that requires the copyright holder to demonstrate some likelihood of harm before he may condemn a private act of time-shifting as a violation of federal law.

When these factors are all weighed in the "equitable rule of reason" balance, we must conclude that this record amply supports the District Court's conclusion that home time-shifting is fair use. In light of the findings of the District Court regarding the state of the empirical data, it is clear that the Court of Appeals erred in holding that the statute as presently written bars such conduct.[38]

---

televised programs actually watch the advertisements which interrupt them." *Id.,* at 468.

[37] "This suggestion lacks merit. By definition, time-shift recording entails viewing and erasing, so the program will no longer be on tape when the later theater run begins. Of course, plaintiffs may fear that the Betamax will keep the tapes long enough to satisfy all their interest in the program and will, therefore, not patronize later theater exhibitions. To the extent this practice involves librarying, it is addressed in section V.C., *infra.* It should also be noted that there is no evidence to suggest that the public interest in later theatrical exhibitions of motion pictures will be reduced any more by Betamax recording than it already is by the television broadcast of the film." 480 F. Supp., at 467.

[38] The Court of Appeals chose not to engage in any "equitable rule of reason" analysis in this case. Instead, it assumed that the category of "fair use" is rigidly circum-

....

JUSTICE BLACKMUN, with whom JUSTICE MARSHALL, JUSTICE POWELL, and JUSTICE REHNQUIST join, dissenting.

....

Despite [an] absence of clear standards, the fair use doctrine plays a crucial role in the law of copyright. The purpose of copyright protection, in the words of the Constitution, is to "promote the Progress of Science and useful Arts." Copyright is based on the belief that by granting authors the exclusive rights to reproduce their works, they are given an incentive to create, and that "encouragement of individual effort by personal gain is the best way to advance public welfare through the talents of authors and inventors in 'Science and the useful Arts.'" *Mazer v. Stein,* 347 U.S. 201, 219 (1954). The monopoly created by copyright thus rewards the individual author in order to benefit the public. *Twentieth Century Music Corp. v. Aiken,* 422 U.S. 151, 156 (1975); *Fox Film Corp. v. Doyal,* 286 U.S. 123, 127-128 (1932); see H.R. Rep. No. 2222, 60th Cong., 2d Sess., 7 (1909).

There are situations, nevertheless, in which strict enforcement of this monopoly would inhibit the very "Progress of Science and useful Arts" that copyright is intended to promote. An obvious example is the researcher or scholar whose own work depends on the ability to refer to and to quote the work of prior scholars. Obviously, no author could create a new work if he

---

scribed by a requirement that every such use must be "productive." It therefore concluded that copying a television program merely to enable the viewer to receive information or entertainment that he would otherwise miss because of a personal scheduling conflict could never be fair use. That understanding of "fair use" was erroneous.

Congress has plainly instructed us that fair use analysis calls for a sensitive balancing of interests. The distinction between "productive" and "unproductive" uses may be helpful in calibrating the balance, but it cannot be wholly determinative. Although copying to promote a scholarly endeavor certainly has a stronger claim to fair use than copying to avoid interrupting a poker game, the question is not simply two-dimensional. For one thing, it is not true that all copyrights are fungible. Some copyrights govern material with broad potential secondary markets. Such material may well have a broader claim to protection because of the greater potential for commercial harm. Copying a news broadcast may have a stronger claim to fair use than copying a motion picture. And, of course, not all uses are fungible. Copying for commercial gain has a much weaker claim to fair use than copying for personal enrichment. But the notion of social "productivity" cannot be a complete answer to this analysis. A teacher who copies to prepare lecture notes is clearly productive. But so is a teacher who copies for the sake of broadening his personal understanding of his specialty. Or a legislator who copies for the sake of broadening her understanding of what her constituents are watching; or a constituent who copies a news program to help make a decision on how to vote.

Making a copy of a copyrighted work for the convenience of a blind person is expressly identified by the House Committee Report as an example of fair use, with no suggestion that anything more than a purpose to entertain or to inform need motivate the copying. In a hospital setting, using a VTR to enable a patient to see programs he would otherwise miss has no productive purpose other than contributing to the psychological well-being of the patient. Virtually any time-shifting that increases viewer access to television programming may result in a comparable benefit. The statutory language does not identify any dichotomy between productive and nonproductive time-shifting, but does require consideration of the economic consequences of copying.

were first required to repeat the research of every author who had gone before him. The scholar, like the ordinary user, of course could be left to bargain with each copyright owner for permission to quote from or refer to prior works. But there is a crucial difference between the scholar and the ordinary user. When the ordinary user decides that the owner's price is too high, and forgoes use of the work, only the individual is the loser. When the scholar forgoes the use of a prior work, not only does his own work suffer, but the public is deprived of his contribution to knowledge. The scholar's work, in other words, produces external benefits from which everyone profits. In such a case, the fair use doctrine acts as a form of subsidy — albeit at the first author's expense — to permit the second author to make limited use of the first author's work for the public good. See Latman, Fair Use Study 31; Gordon, *Fair Use as Market Failure: A Structural Analysis of the Betamax Case and Its Predecessors*, 82 Colum. L. Rev. 1600, 1630 (1982).

A similar subsidy may be appropriate in a range of areas other than pure scholarship. The situations in which fair use is most commonly recognized are listed in § 107 itself; fair use may be found when a work is used "for purposes such as criticism, comment, news reporting, teaching, ... scholarship, or research." The House and Senate Reports expand on this list somewhat, and other examples may be found in the case law. Each of these uses, however, reflects a common theme: each is a *productive* use, resulting in some added benefit to the public beyond that produced by the first author's work.[31]

The fair use doctrine, in other words, permits works to be used for "socially laudable purposes." See Copyright Office, Briefing Papers on Current Issues, reprinted in 1975 House Hearings 2051, 2055. I am aware of no case in which the reproduction of a copyrighted work for the sole benefit of the user has been held to be fair use.[32]

I do not suggest, of course, that every productive use is a fair use.... But when a user reproduces an entire work and uses it for its original purpose,

---

[31] Professor Seltzer has characterized these lists of uses as "reflect[ing] what in fact the subject matter of fair use has in the history of its adjudication consisted in: it has always had to do with the use by a second author of a first author's work." L. Seltzer, Exemptions and Fair Use in Copyright 24 (1978) (emphasis removed). He distinguishes "the mere reproduction of a work in order to use it for its intrinsic purpose — to make what might be called the 'ordinary' use of it." When copies are made for "ordinary" use of the work, "ordinary *infringement* has customarily been triggered, not notions of fair use" (emphasis in original). *Ibid.* See also M. Nimmer, Copyright § 13.05[A][1] (1982) ("Use of a work in each of the foregoing contexts either necessarily or usually involves its use in a derivative work").

[32] *Williams & Wilkins Co. v. United States*, 203 Ct. Cl. 74, 487 F.2d 1345 (1973), *aff'd* by an equally divided Court, 420 U.S. 376 (1975), involved the photocopying of scientific journal articles; the Court of Claims stressed that the libraries performing the copying were "devoted solely to the advancement and dissemination of medical knowledge," 203 Ct. Cl., at 91, 487 F.2d, at 1354, and that "medical science would be seriously hurt if such library photocopying were stopped." *Id.*, at 95, 487 F.2d, at 1356.

The issue of library copying is now covered by § 108 of the 1976 Act. That section, which Congress regarded as "authoriz[ing] certain photocopying practices which may not qualify as a fair use," 1975 Senate Report 67; 1976 House Report 74, U.S. Code Cong. & Admin. News 1976, p. 5688, permits the making of copies only for "private study, scholarship, or research." §§ 108(d)(1) and (e)(1).

with no added benefit to the public, the doctrine of fair use usually does not apply. There is then no need whatsoever to provide the ordinary user with a fair use subsidy at the author's expense.

The making of a videotape recording for home viewing is an ordinary rather than a productive use of the Studios' copyrighted works. The District Court found that "Betamax owners use the copy for the same purpose as the original. They add nothing of their own." 480 F. Supp., at 453. Although applying the fair use doctrine to home VTR recording, as Sony argues, may increase public access to material broadcast free over the public airwaves, I think Sony's argument misconceives the nature of copyright. Copyright gives the author a right to limit or even to cut off access to his work. *Fox Film Corp. v. Doyal*, 286 U.S. 123, 127 (1932). A VTR recording creates no public benefit sufficient to justify limiting this right. Nor is this right extinguished by the copyright owner's choice to make the work available over the airwaves. Section 106 of the 1976 Act grants the copyright owner the exclusive right to control the performance and the reproduction of his work, and the fact that he has licensed a single television performance is really irrelevant to the existence of his right to control its reproduction. Although a television broadcast may be free to the viewer, this fact is equally irrelevant; a book borrowed from the public library may not be copied any more freely than a book that is purchased.

....

I recognize, nevertheless, that there are situations where permitting even an unproductive use would have no effect on the author's incentive to create, that is, where the use would not affect the value of, or the market for, the author's work. Photocopying an old newspaper clipping to send to a friend may be an example; pinning a quotation on one's bulletin board may be another. In each of these cases, the effect on the author is truly *de minimis*. Thus, even though these uses provide no benefit to the public at large, no purpose is served by preserving the author's monopoly, and the use may be regarded as fair.

Courts should move with caution, however, in depriving authors of protection from unproductive "ordinary" uses. As has been noted above, even in the case of a productive use, § 107(4) requires consideration of "the effect of the use upon the *potential* market for or value of the copyrighted work" (emphasis added). "[A] particular use which may seem to have little or no economic impact on the author's rights today can assume tremendous importance in times to come." Register's Supplementary Report 14. Although such a use may seem harmless when viewed in isolation, "[i]solated instances of minor infringements, when multiplied many times, become in the aggregate a major inroad on copyright that must be prevented." 1975 Senate Report 65.

I therefore conclude that, at least when the proposed use is an unproductive one, a copyright owner need prove only a *potential* for harm to the market for or the value of the copyrighted work....

The Studios have identified a number of ways in which VTR recording could damage their copyrights. VTR recording could reduce their ability to market their works in movie theaters and through the rental or sale of pre-recorded videotapes or videodiscs; it also could reduce their rerun audience, and consequently the license fees available to them for repeated showings. Moreover, advertisers may be willing to pay for only "live" viewing audiences, if they believe VTR viewers will delete commercials or if rating services are unable to measure VTR use; if this is the case, VTR recording could reduce the license fees the Studios are able to charge even for first-run showings. Library-building [i.e., taping copyrighted television programs for indefinite retention and repeated viewings] may raise the potential for each of the types of harm identified by the Studios, and time-shifting may raise the potential for substantial harm as well.

Although the District Court found no likelihood of harm from VTR use, 480 F. Supp., at 468, I conclude that it applied an incorrect substantive standard and misallocated the burden of proof....

The District Court's reluctance to engage in prediction in this area is understandable, but, in my view, the court was mistaken in concluding that the Studios should bear the risk created by this uncertainty. The Studios have demonstrated a potential for harm, which has not been, and could not be, refuted at this early stage of technological development....

[T]he Court ... purports to apply to time-shifting the four factors explicitly stated in the statute. The first is "the purpose and character of the use, including whether such use is of a commercial nature or is for nonprofit educational purposes." § 107(1). The Court confidently describes time-shifting as a noncommercial, nonprofit activity. It is clear, however, that personal use of programs that have been copied without permission is not what § 107(1) protects. The intent of the section is to encourage users to engage in activities the primary benefit of which accrues to others. Time-shifting involves no such humanitarian impulse. It is likewise something of a mischaracterization of time-shifting to describe it as noncommercial in the sense that that term is used in the statute. As one commentator has observed, time-shifting is noncommercial in the same sense that stealing jewelry and wearing it — instead of reselling it — is noncommercial. Purely consumptive uses are certainly not what the fair use doctrine was designed to protect, and the awkwardness of applying the statutory language to time-shifting only makes clearer that fair use was designed to protect only uses that are productive.

The next two statutory factors are all but ignored by the Court — though certainly not because they have no applicability. The second factor — "the nature of the copyrighted work" — strongly supports the view that time-shifting is an infringing use. The rationale guiding application of this factor is that certain types of works, typically those involving "more of diligence than of originality or inventiveness," *New York Times Co. v. Roxbury Data Interface, Inc.*, 434 F. Supp. 217, 221 (N.J. 1977), require less copyright protection that other original works. Thus, for example, informational works, such as news reports, that readily lend themselves to productive use by others, are less protected than creative works of entertainment. Sony's own surveys indicate that entertainment shows account for more than 80 percent of the programs recorded by Betamax owners.

The third statutory factor — "the amount and substantiality of the portion used" — is even more devastating to the Court's interpretation. It is undisputed that virtually all VTR owners record entire works, see 480 F. Supp., at

454, thereby creating an exact substitute for the copyrighted original. Fair use is intended to allow individuals engaged in productive uses to copy small portions of original works that will facilitate their own productive endeavors. Time-shifting bears no resemblance to such activity, and the complete duplication that it involves might alone be sufficient to preclude a finding of fair use. It is little wonder that the Court has chosen to ignore this statutory factor.

The fourth factor requires an evaluation of "the effect of the use upon the potential market for or value of the copyrighted work." This is the factor upon which the Court focuses, but once again, the Court has misread the statute. As mentioned above, the statute requires a court to consider the effect of the use on the *potential* market for the copyrighted work. The Court has struggled mightily to show that VTR use has not *reduced* the value of the Studios' copyrighted works in their *present* markets. Even if true, that showing only begins the proper inquiry. The development of the VTR has created a new market for the works produced by the Studios. That market consists of those persons who desire to view television programs at times other than when they are broadcast, and who therefore purchase VTR recorders to enable them to time-shift. Because time-shifting of the Studios' copyrighted works involves the copying of them, however, the Studios are entitled to share in the benefits of that new market. Those benefits currently go to Sony through Betamax sales. Respondents therefore can show harm from VTR use simply by showing that the value of their copyrights would *increase* if they were compensated for the copies that are used in the new market. The existence of this effect is self-evident.

    ....

QUESTIONS

1. Which opinion within the Court do you find the more convincing? Which opinion does a better job of discussing the four factors in § 107? Does the majority's refusal to require that all "fair" uses be productive uses suggest a new direction for fair use analysis?

2. Should "copying for personal enrichment" (*Sony* at n. 40) be a fair use? Does the difficulty in enforcing copyright interests against individual, private users play a role in your evaluation of the "fairness" of the use? *Compare American Geophysical Union v. Texaco, Inc., infra* this chapter.

3. How different would the Court's analysis be if the record showed that a significant proportion of home videotaping was done for the purpose of "librarying" rather than "time shifting"? (What are the proportions in *your* household, or the households of your friends?)

4. Congress has recently imposed a levy on the price of digital recording equipment and blank digital audiotape. *See* Audio Home Recording Act of 1992, *supra.* This law also forecloses the bringing of a copyright infringement action against manufacturers and sellers of recording machines and tape, whether digital or analog, even though no levy is collected from the analog machines and tape. On the other hand, the law provides for distribution of royalties from the levy to music copyright owners (i.e., songwriters and publishers) and to performing artists and record producers of both digital and analog audio recordings. If the *Sony* case had been brought today, how, if at all, would the enactment of this law affect your analysis of *Sony*'s fair use claim?

5. If a small college were about to be favorably featured on a television news program, and it asked you for advice about whether it is lawful to make a videotape of the segment of the program and to distribute the short tape to potential applicants, what advice would you give? Would your answer be different if it merely retained a few copies of the videotape in the college admissions office, to show to potential applicants?

Would it infringe for a "video newsclipping service" to tape entire news programs and then to attempt to sell the tapes to the persons or organizations featured in the various segments of the programs? Should this be treated as falling within the reference to "news reporting" (or some other mentioned use) in the first sentence of § 107? If not, does that conclusively (or presumptively) make the case against the newsclipping service, or is it necessary in all cases to consider and weigh each of the four factors in the second sentence? Would you advise the newsclipping service to refrain from its activities or, in the alternative, to seek a license from the broadcasting station? *See Pacific & Southern Co. v. Duncan,* 744 F.2d 1490 (11th Cir. 1984), *cert. denied,* 471 U.S. 1004 (1985).

HARPER & ROW PUBLISHERS, INC. v. NATION ENTERPRISES
471 U.S. 539 (1985)

JUSTICE O'CONNOR delivered the opinion of the Court.

This case requires us to consider to what extent the "fair use" provision of the Copyright Revision Act of 1976 (hereinafter the Copyright Act), 17 U.S.C. § 107, sanctions the unauthorized use of quotations from a public figure's unpublished manuscript. In March 1979, an undisclosed source provided The Nation Magazine with the unpublished manuscript of "A Time to Heal: The Autobiography of Gerald R. Ford." Working directly from the purloined manuscript, an editor of The Nation produced a short piece entitled "The Ford Memoirs — Behind the Nixon Pardon." The piece was timed to "scoop" an article scheduled shortly to appear in Time Magazine. Time had agreed to purchase the exclusive right to print prepublication excerpts from the copyright holders, Harper & Row Publishers, Inc. (hereinafter Harper & Row), and Reader's Digest Association, Inc. (hereinafter Reader's Digest). As a result of The Nation article, Time canceled its agreement. Petitioners brought a successful copyright action against The Nation. On appeal, the Second Circuit reversed the lower court's finding of infringement, holding that The Nation's act was sanctioned as a "fair use" of the copyrighted material. We granted certiorari, 467 U.S. 1214 (1984), and we now reverse.

I

In February 1977, shortly after leaving the White House, former President Gerald R. Ford contracted with petitioners Harper & Row and Reader's Digest, to publish his as yet unwritten memoirs. The memoirs were to contain "significant hitherto unpublished material" concerning the Watergate crisis, Mr. Ford's pardon of former President Nixon and "Mr. Ford's reflections on this period of history, and the morality and personalities involved." App. to Pet. for Cert. C-14—C-15. In addition to the right to publish the Ford memoirs in book form, the agreement gave petitioners the exclusive right to license prepublication excerpts, known in the trade as "first serial rights." Two years later, as the memoirs were nearing completion, petitioners negotiated a prepublication licensing agreement with Time, a weekly news magazine. Time agreed to pay $25,000, $12,500 in advance and an additional $12,500 at publication, in exchange for the right to excerpt 7,500 words from Mr. Ford's account of the Nixon pardon. The issue featuring the excerpts was timed to appear approximately one week before shipment of the full length book version to bookstores. Exclusivity was an important consideration; Harper & Row instituted procedures designed to maintain the confidentiality of the manuscript, and Time retained the right to renegotiate the second payment should the material appear in print prior to its release of the excerpts.

Two to three weeks before the Time article's scheduled release, an unidentified person secretly brought a copy of the Ford manuscript to Victor Navasky, editor of The Nation, a political commentary magazine. Mr. Navasky knew that his possession of the manuscript was not authorized and that the manuscript must be returned quickly to his "source" to avoid discovery. 557 F. Supp. 1067, 1069 (SDNY 1983). He hastily put together what he believed was "a real hot news story" composed of quotes, paraphrases, and facts drawn exclusively from the manuscript. *Ibid.* Mr. Navasky attempted no independent commentary, research or criticism, in part because of the need for speed if he was to "make news" by "publish[ing] in advance of publication of the Ford book." App. 416-417. The 2,250-word article, reprinted in the Appendix to this opinion, appeared on April 3, 1979. As a result of The Nation's article, Time canceled its piece and refused to pay the remaining $12,500.

Petitioners brought suit in the District Court for the Southern District of New York, alleging conversion, tortious interference with contract, and violations of the Copyright Act.... [Although the district judge held that The Nation's use of the Ford material was not a fair use, a divided court of appeals panel disagreed.] Examining the four factors enumerated in § 107, see *infra*, at 547, n. 2, the majority found the purpose of the article was "news reporting," the original work was essentially factual in nature, the 300 words appropriated were insubstantial in relation to the 2,250-word piece, and the impact on the market for the original was minimal as "the evidence [did] not support a finding that it was the very limited use of expression *per se* which led to Time's decision not to print the excerpt." The Nation's borrowing of verbatim quotations merely "len[t] authenticity to this politically significant material ... complementing the reporting of the facts." 723 F.2d, at 208. The Court of Appeals was especially influenced by the "politically significant" nature of the subject matter and its conviction that it is not "the purpose of the Copyright Act to impede that harvest of knowledge so necessary to a democratic state" or "chill the activities of the press by forbidding a circumscribed use of copyrighted words." *Id.*, at 197, 209.

II

We agree with the Court of Appeals that copyright is intended to increase and not to impede the harvest of knowledge. But we believe the Second Circuit gave insufficient deference to the scheme established by the Copyright Act for fostering the original works that provide the seed and substance of this harvest. The rights conferred by copyright are designed to assure contributors to the store of knowledge a fair return for their labors. *Twentieth Century Music Corp. v. Aiken,* 422 U.S. 151, 156 (1975).

Article I, § 8, of the Constitution provides:

> The Congress shall have Power ... to Promote the Progress of Science and useful Arts, by securing for limited Times to Authors and Inventors the exclusive Right to their respective Writings and Discoveries.

As we noted last Term: "[This] limited grant is a means by which an important public purpose may be achieved. It is intended to motivate the creative activity of authors and inventors by the provision of a special reward, and to allow the public access to the products of their genius after the limited period of exclusive control has expired." *Sony Corp. of America v. Universal City Studios, Inc.,* 464 U.S. 417, 429 (1984). "The monopoly created by copyright thus rewards the individual author in order to benefit the public." *Id.,* at 477 (dissenting opinion). This principle applies equally to works of fiction and nonfiction. The book at issue here, for example, was two years in the making, and began with a contract giving the author's copyright to the publishers in exchange for their services in producing and marketing the work. In preparing the book, Mr. Ford drafted essays and word portraits of public figures and participated in hundreds of taped interviews that were later distilled to chronicle his personal viewpoint. It is evident that the monopoly granted by copyright actively served its intended purpose of inducing the creation of new material of potential historical value.

... The copyright holders of "A Time to Heal" complied with the relevant statutory notice and registration procedures. See §§ 106, 401, 408; App. to Pet. for Cert. C-20. Thus there is no dispute that the unpublished manuscript of "A Time to Heal," as a whole, was protected by § 106 from unauthorized reproduction. Nor do respondents dispute that verbatim copying of excerpts of the manuscript's original form of expression would constitute infringement unless excused as fair use. See 1 M. Nimmer, Copyright § 2.11[B], p. 2-159 (1984) (hereinafter Nimmer). Yet copyright does not prevent subsequent users from copying from a prior author's work those constituent elements that are not original — for example, quotations borrowed under the rubric of fair use from other copyrighted works, facts, or materials in the public domain — as long as such use does not unfairly appropriate the author's original contributions. *Ibid.*; A. Latman, Fair Use of Copyrighted Works (1958), reprinted as Study No. 14 in Copyright Law Revision Studies Nos. 14-16, prepared for the Senate Committee on the Judiciary, 86th Cong., 2d Sess., 7 (1960) (hereinafter Latman). Perhaps the controversy between the lower courts in this case over copyrightability is more aptly styled a dispute over whether The Nation's appropriation of unoriginal and uncopyrightable elements encroached on the originality embodied in the work as a whole. Especially in the realm of factual narrative, the law is currently unsettled regarding the ways in which uncopyrightable elements combine with the author's original contributions to form protected expression. Compare *Wainwright Securities, Inc. v. Wall Street Transcript Corp.*, 558 F.2d 91 (CA2 1977) (protection accorded author's analysis, structuring of material and marshaling of facts), with *Hoehling v. Universal City Studios, Inc.*, 618 F.2d 972 (CA2 1980) (limiting protection to ordering and choice of words). See, *e.g.*, 1 Nimmer § 2.11[D], at 2-164 — 2-165.

We need not reach these issues, however, as The Nation has admitted to lifting verbatim quotes of the author's original language totaling between 300 and 400 words and constituting some 13% of The Nation article. In using generous verbatim excerpts of Mr. Ford's unpublished manuscript to lend authenticity to its account of the forthcoming memoirs, The Nation effectively arrogated to itself the right of first publication, an important marketable subsidiary right. For the reasons set forth below, we find that this use of the copyrighted manuscript, even stripped to the verbatim quotes conceded by The Nation to be copyrightable expression, was not a fair use within the meaning of the Copyright Act.

III

A

Fair use was traditionally defined as "a privilege in others than the owner of the copyright to use the copyrighted material in a reasonable manner without his consent." H. Ball, Law of Copyright and Literary Property 260 (1944) (hereinafter Ball). The statutory formulation of the defense of fair use in the Copyright Act reflects the intent of Congress to codify the common-law doctrine. 3 Nimmer § 13.05. Section 107 requires a case-by-case determination whether a particular use is fair, and the statute notes four nonexclusive factors to be considered. This approach was "intended to restate the [pre-existing] judicial doctrine of fair use, not to change, narrow, or enlarge it in any way." H. R. Rep. No. 94-1476, p. 66 (1976) (hereinafter House Report).

"[T]he author's consent to a reasonable use of his copyrighted works ha[d] always been implied by the courts as a necessary incident of the constitutional policy of promoting the progress of science and the useful arts, since a prohibition of such use would inhibit subsequent writers from attempting to improve upon prior works and thus ... frustrate the very ends sought to be attained." Ball 260. Professor Latman, in a study of the doctrine of fair use commissioned by Congress for the revision effort, see *Sony Corp. of America v. Universal City Studios, Inc.*, 464 U.S., at 462-463, n. 9 (dissenting opinion), summarized prior law as turning on the "importance of the material copied or performed from the point of view of the reasonable copyright owner. In other words, would the reasonable copyright owner have consented to the use?" Latman 15.[3]

---

[3] Professor Nimmer notes: "[Perhaps] no more precise guide can be stated than Joseph McDonald's clever paraphrase of the Golden Rule: 'Take not from others to such an extent and in such a manner that you would be resentful if they so took from you.'" 3 Nimmer § 13.05[A], at 13-66, quoting McDonald, *Non-infringing Uses*, 9 Bull. Copy-

As early as 1841, Justice Story gave judicial recognition to the doctrine in a case that concerned the letters of another former President, George Washington.

> [A] reviewer may fairly cite largely from the original work, if his design be really and truly to use the passages for the purposes of fair and reasonable criticism. On the other hand, it is as clear, that if he thus cites the most important parts of the work, with a view, not to criticise, but to supersede the use of the original work, and substitute the review for it, such a use will be deemed in law a piracy.

Folsom v. Marsh, 9 F. Cas. 342, 344-345 (No. 4,901) (CC Mass.) As Justice Story's hypothetical illustrates, the fair use doctrine has always precluded a use that "supersede[s] the use of the original." *Ibid.* Accord, S. Rep. No. 94-473, p. 65 (1975) (hereinafter Senate Report).

Perhaps because the fair use doctrine was predicated on the author's implied consent to "reasonable and customary" use when he released his work for public consumption, fair use traditionally was not recognized as a defense to charges of copying from an author's as yet unpublished works.[4] Under common-law copyright, "the property of the author ... in his intellectual creation [was] absolute until he voluntarily part[ed] with the same." *American Tobacco Co. v. Werckmeister,* 207 U.S. 284, 299 (1907); 2 Nimmer § 8.23, at 8-273. This absolute rule, however, was tempered in practice by the equitable nature of the fair use doctrine. In a given case, factors such as implied consent through *de facto* publication on performance or dissemination of a work may tip the balance of equities in favor of prepublication use.... But it has never been seriously disputed that "the fact that the plaintiff's work is unpublished ... is a factor tending to negate the defense of fair use." *Ibid.* Publication of an author's expression before he has authorized its dissemination seriously infringes the author's right to decide when and whether it will be made public, a factor not present in fair use of published works. Respondents contend, however, that Congress, in including first publication among the rights enumerated in § 106, which are expressly subject to fair use under § 107, intended that fair use would apply *in pari materia* to published and unpublished works. The Copyright Act does not support this proposition.

---

right Soc. 466, 467 (1962). This "equitable rule of reason," *Sony Corp. of America v. Universal City Studios, Inc.,* 464 U.S., at 448, "permits courts to avoid rigid application of the copyright statute when, on occasion, it would stifle the very creativity which that law is designed to foster." *Iowa State University Research Foundation, Inc. v. American Broadcasting Cos.,* 621 F.2d 57, 60 (CA2 1980). See generally L. Seltzer, Exemptions and Fair Use in Copyright 18-48 (1978).

[4] See Latman 7; Strauss, Protection of Unpublished Works (1957), reprinted as Study No. 29 in Copyright Law Revision Studies Nos. 29-31, prepared for the Senate Committee on the Judiciary, 86th Cong., 2d Sess., 4, n. 32 (1961) (citing cases); R. Shaw, Literary Property in the United States 67 (1950) ("[T]here can be no 'fair use' of unpublished material"); Ball 260, n. 5 ("[T]he doctrine of fair use does not apply to unpublished works"); A. Weil, American Copyright Law § 276, p. 115 (1917) (the author of an unpublished work "has, probably, the right to prevent even a 'fair use' of the work by others"). Cf. M. Flint, A User's Guide to Copyright ¶ 10.06 (1979) (United Kingdom) ("no fair dealing with unpublished works"); *Beloff v. Pressdram Ltd.,* [1973] All E.R. 241, 263 (Ch. 1972) (same).

The Copyright Act represents the culmination of a major legislative reexamination of copyright doctrine. See *Mills Music, Inc. v. Snyder,* 469 U.S. 153, 159-160 (1985); *Sony Corp. of America v. Universal City Studios, Inc.,* 464 U.S., at 462-463, n. 9 (dissenting opinion). Among its other innovations, it eliminated publication "as a dividing line between common law and statutory protection," House Report, at 129, extending statutory protection to all works from the time of their creation. It also recognized for the first time a distinct statutory right of first publication, which had previously been an element of the common-law protections afforded unpublished works. The Report of the House Committee on the Judiciary confirms that "Clause (3) of section 106, establishes the exclusive right of publication.... Under this provision the copyright owner would have the right to control the first public distribution of an authorized copy ... of his work." *Id.,* at 62.

Though the right of first publication, like the other rights enumerated in § 106, is expressly made subject to the fair use provision of § 107, fair use analysis must always be tailored to the individual case. *Id.,* at 65; 3 Nimmer § 13.05[A]. The nature of the interest at stake is highly relevant to whether a given use is fair. From the beginning, those entrusted with the task of revision recognized the "overbalancing reasons to preserve the common law protection of undisseminated works until the author or his successor chooses to disclose them." Copyright Law Revision, Report of the Register of Copyrights on the General Revision of the U.S. Copyright Law, 87th Cong., 1st Sess., 41 (Comm. Print 1961). The right of first publication implicates a threshold decision by the author whether and in what form to release his work. First publication is inherently different from other § 106 rights in that only one person can be the first publisher; as the contract with Time illustrates, the commercial value of the right lies primarily in exclusivity. Because the potential damage to the author from judicially enforced "sharing" of the first publication right with unauthorized users of his manuscript is substantial, the balance of equities in evaluating such a claim of fair use inevitably shifts.

The Senate Report confirms that Congress intended the unpublished nature of the work to figure prominently in fair use analysis. In discussing fair use of photocopied materials in the classroom the Committee Report states:

> A key, though not necessarily determinative, factor in fair use is whether or not the work is available to the potential user. If the work is "out of print" and unavailable for purchase through normal channels, the user may have more justification for reproducing it .... The applicability of the fair use doctrine to unpublished works is narrowly limited since, although the work is unavailable, this is the result of a deliberate choice on the part of the copyright owner. Under ordinary circumstances, the copyright owner's "right of first publication" would outweigh any needs of reproduction for classroom purposes.

Senate Report, at 64. Although the Committee selected photocopying of classroom materials to illustrate fair use, it emphasized that "the same general standards of fair use are applicable to all kinds of uses of copyrighted material." *Id.,* at 65....

Even if the legislative history were entirely silent, we would be bound to conclude from Congress' characterization of § 107 as a "restatement" that its effect was to preserve existing law concerning fair use of unpublished works as of other types of protected works and not to "change, narrow, or enlarge it." *Id.*, at 66. We conclude that the unpublished nature of a work is "[a] key, though not necessarily determinative, factor" tending to negate a defense of fair use. Senate Report, at 64. See 3 Nimmer § 13.05, at 13-62, n. 2; W. Patry, The Fair Use Privilege in Copyright Law 125 (1985) (hereinafter Patry).

We also find unpersuasive respondents' argument that fair use may be made of a soon-to-be-published manuscript on the ground that the author has demonstrated he has no interest in nonpublication. This argument assumes that the unpublished nature of copyrighted material is only relevant to letters or other confidential writings not intended for dissemination. It is true that common-law copyright was often enlisted in the service of personal privacy. See Brandeis & Warren, *The Right to Privacy,* 4 Harv. L. Rev. 193, 198-199 (1890). In its commercial guise, however, an author's right to choose when he will publish is no less deserving of protection. The period encompassing the work's initiation, its preparation, and its grooming for public dissemination is a crucial one for any literary endeavor. The Copyright Act, which accords the copyright owner the "right to control the first public distribution" of his work, House Report, at 62, echoes the common law's concern that the author or copyright owner retain control throughout this critical stage.... The author's control of first public distribution implicates not only his personal interest in creative control but his property interest in exploitation of prepublication rights, which are valuable in themselves and serve as a valuable adjunct to publicity and marketing.... Under ordinary circumstances, the author's right to control the first public appearance of his undisseminated expression will outweigh a claim of fair use.

B

Respondents, however, contend that First Amendment values require a different rule under the circumstances of this case. The thrust of the decision below is that "[t]he scope of [fair use] is undoubtedly wider when the information conveyed relates to matters of high public concern." *Consumers Union of the United States, Inc. v. General Signal Corp.,* 724 F.2d 1044, 1050 (CA2 1983) (construing 723 F.2d 195 (1983) (case below) as allowing advertiser to quote Consumer Reports), *cert. denied,* 469 U.S. 823 (1984). Respondents advance the substantial public import of the subject matter of the Ford memoirs as grounds for excusing a use that would ordinarily not pass muster as a fair use — the piracy of verbatim quotations for the purpose of "scooping" the authorized first serialization. Respondents explain their copying of Mr. Ford's expression as essential to reporting the news story it claims the book itself represents. In respondents' view, not only the facts contained in Mr. Ford's memoirs, but "the precise manner in which [he] expressed himself [were] as newsworthy as what he had to say." Brief for Respondents 38-39. Respondents argue that the public's interest in learning this news as fast as possible outweighs the right of the author to control its first publication.

The Second Circuit noted, correctly, that copyright's idea/expression dichotomy "strike[s] a definitional balance between the First Amendment and the Copyright Act by permitting free communication of facts while still protecting an author's expression." 723 F.2d, at 203. No author may copyright his ideas or the facts he narrates. 17 U.S.C. § 102(b). See, e.g., *New York Times Co. v. United States,* 403 U.S. 713, 726, n. (thus in U.S. Rpts.) (1971) (BRENNAN, J., concurring) (Copyright laws are not restrictions on freedom of speech as copyright protects only form of expression and not the ideas expressed); 1 Nimmer § 1.10[B][2]....

Respondents' theory, however, would expand fair use to effectively destroy any expectation of copyright protection in the work of a public figure. Absent such protection, there would be little incentive to create or profit in financing such memoirs, and the public would be denied an important source of significant historical information. The promise of copyright would be an empty one if it could be avoided merely by dubbing the infringement a fair use "news report" of the book. See *Wainwright Securities Inc. v. Wall Street Transcript Corp.,* 558 F.2d 91 (CA2 1977), *cert. denied,* 434 U.S. 1014 (1978).

Nor do respondents assert any actual necessity for circumventing the copyright scheme with respect to the types of works and users at issue here. Where an author and publisher have invested extensive resources in creating an original work and are poised to release it to the public, no legitimate aim is served by pre-empting the right of first publication. The fact that the words the author has chosen to clothe his narrative may of themselves be "newsworthy" is not an independent justification for unauthorized copying of the author's expression prior to publication....

In our haste to disseminate news, it should not be forgotten that the Framers intended copyright itself to be the engine of free expression. By establishing a marketable right to the use of one's expression, copyright supplies the economic incentive to create and disseminate ideas....

It is fundamentally at odds with the scheme of copyright to accord lesser rights in those works that are of greatest importance to the public. Such a notion ignores the major premise of copyright and injures author and public alike. "[T]o propose that fair use be imposed whenever the 'social value [of dissemination] ... outweighs any detriment to the artist,' would be to propose depriving copyright owners of their right in the property precisely when they encounter those users who could afford to pay for it." Gordon, *Fair Use as Market Failure: A Structural and Economic Analysis of the Betamax Case and Its Predecessors,* 82 Colum. L. Rev. 1600, 1615 (1982). And as one commentator has noted: "If every volume that was in the public interest could be pirated away by a competing publisher, ... the public [soon] would have nothing worth reading." Sobel, *Copyright and the First Amendment: A Gathering Storm?,* 19 ASCAP Copyright Law Symposium 43, 78 (1971). See generally Comment, *Copyright and the First Amendment: Where Lies the Public Interest?,* 59 Tulane L. Rev. 135 (1984).

Moreover, freedom of thought and expression "includes both the right to speak freely and the right to refrain from speaking at all." *Wooley v. Maynard,* 430 U.S. 705, 714 (1977) (BURGER, C. J.). We do not suggest this right not to speak would sanction abuse of the copyright owner's monopoly as an instrument to suppress facts. But in the words of New York's Chief Judge Fuld:

> The essential thrust of the First Amendment is to prohibit improper restraints on the *voluntary* public expression of ideas; it shields the man who wants to speak or publish when others wish him to be quiet. There is necessarily, and within suitably defined areas, a concomitant freedom *not* to speak publicly, one which serves the same ultimate end as freedom of speech in its affirmative aspect.

Estate of Hemingway v. Random House, Inc., 23 N.Y.2d 341, 348, 244 N.E.2d 250, 255 (1968). Courts and commentators have recognized that copyright, and the right of first publication in particular, serve this countervailing First Amendment value. See *Schnapper v. Foley,* 215 U.S. App. D.C. 59, 667 F.2d 102 (1981), *cert. denied,* 455 U.S. 948 (1982); 1 Nimmer § 1.10[B], at 1-70, n. 24; Patry 140-142.

In view of the First Amendment protections already embodied in the Copyright Act's distinction between copyrightable expression and uncopyrightable facts and ideas, and the latitude for scholarship and comment traditionally afforded by fair use, we see no warrant for expanding the doctrine of fair use to create what amounts to a public figure exception to copyright. Whether verbatim copying from a public figure's manuscript in a given case is or is not fair must be judged according to the traditional equities of fair use.

IV

Fair use is a mixed question of law and fact. *Pacific & Southern Co. v. Duncan,* 744 F.2d 1490, 1495, n. 8 (CA11 1984). Where the district court has found facts sufficient to evaluate each of the statutory factors, an appellate court "need not remand for further factfinding ... [but] may conclude as a matter of law that [the challenged use] do[es] not qualify as a fair use of the copyrighted work." *Id.,* at 1495. Thus whether The Nation article constitutes fair use under § 107 must be reviewed in light of the principles discussed above....

Purpose of the Use. The Second Circuit correctly identified news reporting as the general purpose of The Nation's use. News reporting is one of the examples enumerated in § 107 to "give some idea of the sort of activities the courts might regard as fair use under the circumstances." Senate Report, at 61. This listing was not intended to be exhaustive, see *ibid.*; § 101 (definition of "including" and "such as"), or to single out any particular use as presumptively a "fair" use. The drafters resisted pressures from special interest groups to create presumptive categories of fair use, but structured the provision as an affirmative defense requiring a case-by-case analysis. See H.R. Rep. No. 83, 90th Cong., 1st Sess., 37 (1967); Patry 477, n. 4. "[W]hether a use referred to in the first sentence of section 107 is a fair use in a particular case will depend upon the application of the determinative factors, including those mentioned in the second sentence." Senate Report, at 62. The fact that an article arguably is "news" and therefore a productive use is simply one factor in a fair use analysis.

We agree with the Second Circuit that the trial court erred in fixing on whether the information contained in the memoirs was actually new to the public.... The Nation has every right to seek to be the first to publish information. But The Nation went beyond simply reporting uncopyrightable information and actively sought to exploit the headline value of its infringement, making a "news event" out of its unauthorized first publication of a noted figure's copyrighted expression.

The fact that a publication was commercial as opposed to nonprofit is a separate factor that tends to weigh against a finding of fair use. "[E]very commercial use of copyrighted material is presumptively an unfair exploitation of the monopoly privilege that belongs to the owner of the copyright." *Sony Corp. of America v. Universal City Studios, Inc.*, 464 U.S., at 451. In arguing that the purpose of news reporting is not purely commercial, The Nation misses the point entirely. The crux of the profit/nonprofit distinction is not whether the sole motive of the use is monetary gain but whether the user stands to profit from exploitation of the copyrighted material without paying the customary price. See *Roy Export Co. Establishment v. Columbia Broadcasting System, Inc.*, 503 F. Supp., at 1144; 3 Nimmer § 13.05[A][1], at 13-71, n. 25.3.

In evaluating character and purpose we cannot ignore The Nation's stated purpose of scooping the forthcoming hardcover and Time abstracts. App. to Pet. for Cert. C-27. The Nation's use had not merely the incidental effect but the *intended purpose* of supplanting the copyright holder's commercially valuable right of first publication. See *Meredith Corp. v. Harper & Row, Publishers, Inc.*, 378 F. Supp. 686, 690 (SDNY) (purpose of text was to compete with original), *aff'd*, 500 F.2d 1221 (CA2 1974). Also relevant to the "character" of the use is "the propriety of the defendant's conduct." 3 Nimmer § 13.05[A], at 13-72. "Fair use presupposes 'good faith' and 'fair dealing.'" *Time Inc. v. Bernard Geis Associates*, 293 F. Supp. 130, 146 (SDNY 1968), quoting Schulman, *Fair Use and the Revision of the Copyright Act*, 53 Iowa L. Rev. 832 (1968). The trial court found that The Nation knowingly exploited a purloined manuscript. App. to Pet. for Cert. B-1, C-20 — C-21, C-28 — C-29. Unlike the typical claim of fair use, The Nation cannot offer up even the fiction of consent as justification. Like its competitor newsweekly, it was free to bid for the right of abstracting excerpts from "A Time to Heal." Fair use "distinguishes between 'a true scholar and a chiseler who infringes a work for personal profit.'" *Wainwright Securities Inc. v. Wall Street Transcript Corp.*, 558 F.2d, at 94, quoting from Hearings on Bills for the General Revision of the Copyright Law before the House Committee on the Judiciary, 89th Cong., 1st Sess., ser. 8, pt. 3, p. 1706 (1966) (statement of John Schulman).

Nature of the Copyrighted Work. Second, the Act directs attention to the nature of the copyrighted work. "A Time to Heal" may be characterized as an unpublished historical narrative or autobiography. The law generally recognizes a greater need to disseminate factual works than works of fiction or fantasy. See Gorman, *Fact or Fancy? The Implications for Copyright*, 29 J. Copyright Soc. 560, 561 (1982).

[E]ven within the field of fact works, there are gradations as to the relative proportion of fact and fancy. One may move from sparsely embellished maps and directories to elegantly written biography. The extent to which one must permit expressive language to be copied, in order to assure dissemination of the underlying facts, will thus vary from case to case.

Id., at 563. Some of the briefer quotes from the memoirs are arguably necessary adequately to convey the facts; for example, Mr. Ford's characterization of the White House tapes as the "smoking gun" is perhaps so integral to the idea expressed as to be inseparable from it. Cf. 1 Nimmer § 1.10[C]. But The Nation did not stop at isolated phrases and instead excerpted subjective descriptions and portraits of public figures whose power lies in the author's individualized expression. Such use, focusing on the most expressive elements of the work, exceeds that necessary to disseminate the facts.

The fact that a work is unpublished is a critical element of its "nature." 3 Nimmer § 13.05[A]; Comment, 58 St. John's L. Rev., at 613. Our prior discussion establishes that the scope of fair use is narrower with respect to unpublished works. While even substantial quotations might qualify as fair use in a review of a published work or a news account of a speech that had been delivered to the public or disseminated to the press, see House Report, at 65, the author's right to control the first public appearance of his expression weighs against such use of the work before its release. The right of first publication encompasses not only the choice whether to publish at all, but also the choices of when, where, and in what form first to publish a work.

In the case of Mr. Ford's manuscript, the copyright holders' interest in confidentiality is irrefutable; the copyright holders had entered into a contractual undertaking to "keep the manuscript confidential" and required that all those to whom the manuscript was shown also "sign an agreement to keep the manuscript confidential." App. to Pet. for Cert. C-19 — C-20. While the copyright holders' contract with Time required Time to submit its proposed article seven days before publication, The Nation's clandestine publication afforded no such opportunity for creative or quality control. *Id.*, at C-18. It was hastily patched together and contained "a number of inaccuracies." App. 300b-300c (testimony of Victor Navasky). A use that so clearly infringes the copyright holder's interests in confidentiality and creative control is difficult to characterize as "fair."

Amount and Substantiality of the Portion Used. Next, the Act directs us to examine the amount and substantiality of the portion used in relation to the copyrighted work as a whole. In absolute terms, the words actually quoted were an insubstantial portion of "A Time to Heal." The District Court, however, found that "[T]he Nation took what was essentially the heart of the book." 557 F. Supp., at 1072. We believe the Court of Appeals erred in overruling the District Judge's evaluation of the qualitative nature of the taking. See, *e.g.*, *Roy Export Co. Establishment v. Columbia Broadcasting System, Inc.*, 503 F. Supp., at 1145 (taking of 55 seconds out of 1 hour and 29-minute film deemed qualitatively substantial). A Time editor described the chapters on the pardon as "the most interesting and moving parts of the entire manuscript." Reply Brief for Petitioners 16, n. 8. The portions actually quoted were selected by Mr. Navasky as among the most powerful passages in those chapters. He testified that he used verbatim excerpts because simply reciting the information could not adequately convey the "absolute certainty with which [Ford] expressed himself," App. 303; or show that "this comes from President Ford," *id.*, at 305; or carry the "definitive quality" of the original, *id.*, at 306. In short, he quoted these passages precisely because they qualitatively embodied Ford's distinctive expression.

As the statutory language indicates, a taking may not be excused merely because it is insubstantial with respect to the *infringing* work. As Judge Learned Hand cogently remarked, "no plagiarist can excuse the wrong by showing how much of his work he did not pirate." *Sheldon v. Metro-Goldwyn Pictures Corp.*, 81 F.2d 49, 56 (CA2), *cert. denied*, 298 U.S. 669 (1936). Conversely, the fact that a substantial portion of the infringing work was copied verbatim is evidence of the qualitative value of the copied material, both to the originator and to the plagiarist who seeks to profit from marketing someone else's copyrighted expression.

Stripped to the verbatim quotes, the direct takings from the unpublished manuscript constitute at least 13% of the infringing article. See *Meeropol v. Nizer*, 560 F.2d 1061, 1071 (CA2 1977) (copyrighted letters constituted less than 1% of infringing work but were prominently featured). The Nation article is structured around the quoted excerpts which serve as its dramatic focal points. See Appendix to this opinion, *post*, p. 570. In view of the expressive value of the excerpts and their key role in the infringing work, we cannot agree with the Second Circuit that the "magazine took a meager, indeed an infinitesimal amount of Ford's original language." 723 F.2d, at 209.

Effect on the Market. Finally, the Act focuses on "the effect of the use upon the potential market for or value of the copyrighted work." This last factor is undoubtedly the single most important element of fair use.[9] See 3 Nimmer § 13.05[A], at 13-76, and cases cited therein. "Fair use, when properly applied, is limited to copying by others which does not materially impair the marketability of the work which is copied." 1 Nimmer § 1.10[D], at 1-87. The trial court found not merely a potential but an actual effect on the market. Time's cancellation of its projected serialization and its refusal to pay the $12,500 were the direct effect of the infringement. The Court of Appeals rejected this fact-finding as clearly erroneous, noting that the record did not establish a causal relation between Time's nonperformance and respondents' unautho-

---

[9] Economists who have addressed the issue believe the fair use exception should come into play only in those situations in which the market fails or the price the copyright holder would ask is near zero. See, e.g., T. Brennan, *Harper & Row v. The Nation*, Copyrightability and Fair Use, Dept. of Justice Economic Policy Office Discussion Paper 13-17 (1984); Gordon, *Fair Use as Market Failure: A Structural and Economic Analysis of the Betamax Case and Its Predecessors*, 82 Colum. L. Rev. 1600, 1615 (1982). As the facts here demonstrate, there is a fully functioning market that encourages the creation and dissemination of memoirs of public figures. In the economists' view, permitting "fair use" to displace normal copyright channels disrupts the copyright market without a commensurate public benefit.

rized publication of Mr. Ford's *expression* as opposed to the facts taken from the memoirs. We disagree. Rarely will a case of copyright infringement present such clear-cut evidence of actual damage. Petitioners assured Time that there would be no other authorized publication of *any* portion of the unpublished manuscript prior to April 23, 1979. *Any* publication of material from chapters 1 and 3 would permit Time to renegotiate its final payment. Time cited The Nation's article, which contained verbatim quotes from the unpublished manuscript, as a reason for its nonperformance.... [O]nce a copyright holder establishes with reasonable probability the existence of a causal connection between the infringement and a loss of revenue, the burden properly shifts to the infringer to show that this damage would have occurred had there been no taking of copyrighted expression. See 3 Nimmer § 14.02, at 14-7 — 14-8.1. Petitioners established a prima facie case of actual damage that respondents failed to rebut. See *Stevens Linen Associates, Inc. v. Mastercraft Corp.*, 656 F.2d 11, 15 (CA2 1981). The trial court properly awarded actual damages and accounting of profits. See 17 U.S.C. § 504(b).

More important, to negate fair use one need only show that if the challenged use "should become widespread, it would adversely affect the *potential* market for the copyrighted work." *Sony Corp. of America v. Universal City Studios, Inc.*, 464 U.S., at 451 (emphasis added); *id.*, at 484, and n. 36 (collecting cases) (dissenting opinion). This inquiry must take account not only of harm to the original but also of harm to the market for derivative works. See *Iowa State University Research Foundation, Inc. v. American Broadcasting Cos.*, 621 F.2d 57 (CA2 1980); *Meeropol v. Nizer, supra*, at 1070; *Roy Export v. Columbia Broadcasting System, Inc.*, 503 F. Supp., at 1146. "If the defendant's work adversely affects the value of any of the rights in the copyrighted work (in this case the adaptation [and serialization] right) the use is not fair." 3 Nimmer § 13.05[B], at 13-77 — 13-78 (footnote omitted).

It is undisputed that the factual material in the balance of The Nation's article, besides the verbatim quotes at issue here, was drawn exclusively from the chapters on the pardon. The excerpts were employed as featured episodes in a story about the Nixon pardon — precisely the use petitioners had licensed to Time. The borrowing of these verbatim quotes from the unpublished manuscript lent The Nation's piece a special air of authenticity — as Navasky expressed it, the reader would know it was Ford speaking and not The Nation. App. 300c. Thus it directly competed for a share of the market for prepublication excerpts....

V

... In sum, the traditional doctrine of fair use, as embodied in the Copyright Act, does not sanction the use made by The Nation of these copyrighted materials. Any copyright infringer may claim to benefit the public by increasing public access to the copyrighted work. See *Pacific & Southern Co. v. Duncan*, 744 F.2d, at 1499-1500. But Congress has not designed, and we see no warrant for judicially imposing, a "compulsory license" permitting unfettered access to the unpublished copyrighted expression of public figures.

The Nation conceded that its verbatim copying of some 300 words of direct quotation from the Ford manuscript would constitute an infringement unless excused as a fair use. Because we find that The Nation's use of these verbatim excerpts from the unpublished manuscript was not a fair use, the judgment of the Court of Appeals is reversed, and the case is remanded for further proceedings consistent with this opinion.

It is so ordered.

JUSTICE BRENNAN, with whom JUSTICE WHITE and JUSTICE MARSHALL join, dissenting.

The Court holds that The Nation's quotation of 300 words from the unpublished 200,000-word manuscript of President Gerald R. Ford infringed the copyright in that manuscript, even though the quotations related to a historical event of undoubted significance — the resignation and pardon of President Richard M. Nixon. Although the Court pursues the laudable goal of protecting "the economic incentive to create and disseminate ideas," *ante,* at 558, this zealous defense of the copyright owner's prerogative will, I fear, stifle the broad dissemination of ideas and information copyright is intended to nurture. Protection of the copyright owner's economic interest is achieved in this case through an exceedingly narrow definition of the scope of fair use. The progress of arts and sciences and the robust public debate essential to an enlightened citizenry are ill served by this constricted reading of the fair use doctrine. See 17 U.S.C. § 107. I therefore respectfully dissent.

. . . .

With respect to a work of history, particularly the memoirs of a public official, the statutorily prescribed analysis cannot properly be conducted without constant attention to copyright's crucial distinction between protected literary form and unprotected information or ideas. The question must always be: Was the subsequent author's use of *literary form* a fair use within the meaning of § 107, in light of the purpose for the use, the nature of the copyrighted work, the amount of literary form used, and the effect of this use of literary form on the value of or market for the original?

Limiting the inquiry to the propriety of a subsequent author's use of the copyright owner's literary form is not easy in the case of a work of history. Protection against only substantial appropriation of literary form does not ensure historians a return commensurate with the full value of their labors. The literary form contained in works like "A Time to Heal" reflects only a part of the labor that goes into the book. It is the labor of collecting, sifting, organizing, and reflecting that predominates in the creation of works of history such as this one. The value this labor produces lies primarily in the information and ideas revealed, and not in the particular collocation of words through which the information and ideas are expressed. Copyright thus does not protect that which is often of most value in a work of history, and courts must resist the tendency to reject the fair use defense on the basis of their feeling that an author of history has been deprived of the full value of his or her labor. A subsequent author's taking of information and ideas is in no sense piratical because copyright law simply does not create any property interest in information and ideas.

The urge to compensate for subsequent use of information and ideas is perhaps understandable. An inequity seems to lurk in the idea that much of the fruit of the historian's labor may be used without compensation. This, however, is not some unforeseen byproduct of a statutory scheme intended primarily to ensure a return for works of the imagination. Congress made the affirmative choice that the copyright laws should apply in this way: "Copyright does not preclude others from using the ideas or information revealed by the author's work. It pertains to the literary ... form in which the author expressed intellectual concepts." H.R. Rep. No. 94-1476, at 56-57. This distinction is at the essence of copyright. The copyright laws serve as the "engine of free expression," *ante,* at 558, only when the statutory monopoly does not choke off multifarious indirect uses and consequent broad dissemination of information and ideas. To ensure the progress of arts and sciences and the integrity of First Amendment values, ideas and information must not be freighted with claims of proprietary right.

In my judgment, the Court's fair use analysis has fallen to the temptation to find a copyright violation based on a minimal use of literary form in order to provide compensation for the appropriation of information from a work of history. The failure to distinguish between information and literary form permeates every aspect of the Court's fair use analysis and leads the Court to the wrong result in this case. Application of the statutorily prescribed analysis with attention to the distinction between information and literary form leads to a straightforward finding of fair use within the meaning of § 107.

. . . .

[T]he Court introduces into analysis of this case a categorical presumption against prepublication fair use. See *ante,* at 555 ("Under ordinary circumstances, the author's right to control the first public appearance of his undisseminated expression will outweigh a claim of fair use").

This categorical presumption is unwarranted on its own terms and unfaithful to congressional intent.[19] Whether a particular prepublication use will impair any interest the Court identifies as encompassed within the right

---

[19] The Court lays claim to specific congressional intent supporting the presumption against prepublication fair use. See *ante,* at 553, quoting S. Rep. No. 94-473, p. 64 (1975); *ante,* at 551, n. 4, 553-554. The argument based on congressional intent is unpersuasive ....

[T]he Court's reliance on congressional adoption of the common law is also unpersuasive. The common law did not set up the monolithic barrier to prepublication fair use that the Court wishes it did. See, e.g., *Estate of Hemingway v. Random House, Inc.,* 53 Misc. 2d 462, 279 N.Y.S.2d 51 (S. Ct. N.Y. Cty.), *aff'd,* 29 App. Div. 2d 633, 285 N.Y.S.2d 568 (1st Jud. Dept. 1967), *aff'd on other grounds,* 23 N.Y.2d 341, 244 N.E.2d 250 (1968). The statements of general principle the Court cites to support its contrary representation of the common law, see *ante,* at 551, n. 4, are themselves unsupported by reference to substantial judicial authority. Congressional endorsement of the common law of fair use should not be read as adoption of any rigid presumption against prepublication use. If read that way, the broad statement that the Copyright Act was intended to incorporate the common law would in effect be given the force of nullifying Congress' repeated methodological prescription that definite rules are inappropriate and fact-specific analysis is required. The broad language adopting the common-law approach to fair use is best understood as an endorsement of the essential fact-specificity and case-by-case methodology of the common law of fair use.

of first publication, see *ante,* at 552-555, will depend on the nature of the copyrighted work, the timing of prepublication use, the amount of expression used, and the medium in which the second author communicates....

....

Balancing the Interests. Once the distinction between information and literary form is made clear, the statutorily prescribed process of weighing the four statutory fair use factors discussed above leads naturally to a conclusion that The Nation's limited use of literary form was not an infringement. Both the purpose of the use and the nature of the copyrighted work strongly favor the fair use defense here. The Nation appropriated Mr. Ford's expression for a purpose Congress expressly authorized in § 107 and borrowed from a work whose nature justifies some appropriation to facilitate the spread of information. The factor that is perhaps least favorable to the claim of fair use is the amount and substantiality of the expression used. Without question, a portion of the expression appropriated was among the most poignant in the Ford manuscript. But it is difficult to conclude that this taking was excessive in relation to the news reporting purpose. In any event, because the appropriation of literary form — as opposed to the use of information — was not shown to injure Harper & Row's economic interest, any uncertainty with respect to the propriety of the amount of expression borrowed should be resolved in favor of a finding of fair use. In light of the circumscribed scope of the quotation in The Nation's article and the undoubted validity of the purpose motivating that quotation, I must conclude that the Court has simply adopted an exceedingly narrow view of fair use in order to impose liability for what was in essence a taking of unprotected information.

....

QUESTIONS

1. Much copyrighted material may be of public interest. Indeed, it may contain considerable news value. When the press's or other authors' claimed need for unfettered (and unpaid) access to copyrighted works encounters the first author's objections, does a copyright/First Amendment conflict arise? The Supreme Court in *Harper & Row* indicated that the assertion of such a conflict evokes a false dichotomy: copyright may in fact promote First Amendment goals.

Similarly, courts and commentators generally agree that the copyright law may accommodate First Amendment concerns by application of two established copyright doctrines: the idea/expression dichotomy, and the fair use doctrine. The idea/expression dichotomy preserves free access to an author's "ideas" and information; the fair use defense aids those second authors who can demonstrate a compelling justification for copying the first author's *expression.* If the use of the first author's expression is not "fair," then neither should it be shielded by the First Amendment. Are you convinced? Even if, for example in the case of excessive quotation of copyrighted materials in a serious critical biography, the court rejects the fair use defense, should First Amendment policies induce the court not to enjoin publication, but rather to limit recovery to money damages? *See New Era Pubs. v. Henry Holt & Co.,* 873

F.2d 576 (2d Cir.), *en banc rehearing denied by divided court*, 884 F.2d 659 (2d Cir. 1989).

Assuming a First Amendment defense were appropriate (independent of the fair use defense), should it merely excuse its beneficiary from obtaining permission, or should it also defeat the first author's claim to compensation for the unlicensed use? In other words, if there are situations in which the First Amendment requires unfettered access to copyrighted works, should that access also be unpaid?

2. Regarding the fourth fair use factor, the *Harper & Row* court held that once plaintiff has demonstrated adverse economic consequences flowing from defendant's use, the burden shifts to defendant to prove that the ill effects stemmed merely from defendant's publication of uncopyrightable *information,* rather than from defendant's publication of plaintiff's *expression.* How would defendant go about making such a showing?

3. Review the Court's analysis of the copyright holder's interests in being the one to publish first. Are these interests any less acute when the unpublished material is information, rather than expression?

4. *Harper & Row* concerned preemptive publication of an about-to-be-published work. Does the fair use analysis change if the author wishes *never* to publish the work from which defendant seeks to quote? *See Salinger v. Random House,* 811 F.2d 90 (2d Cir.), *cert. denied,* 108 S. Ct. 213 (1987).

In *Salinger,* defendant biographer had obtained access to Salinger's unpublished letters in libraries where the letters' recipients had deposited them. The libraries made the letters available to researchers on the condition that the letters would not be reproduced. The court quickly dismissed the argument that availability of the Salinger letters in publicly accessible libraries entitled the biographer to copy from the letters. Assuming the library had not imposed conditions on researchers' access to the letters, *should* their public availability affect the fair use analysis? Should a library's imposition of conditions of access make a difference?

FAIR USE OF UNPUBLISHED WORKS

The emphasis placed by the Supreme Court in the *Harper & Row* case upon the fact that President Ford's manuscript was unpublished set in motion a train of events that would lead seven years later, in 1992, to a brief but significant amendment to § 107. The Court had examined the narrow scope given, in common-law copyright, to fair use for unpublished works; the intention of the 1976 Congress not to alter the prevailing understanding of fair use; and the significant interests that the author of an unpublished work has in privacy and in the creative decision when and where a work is first to see the light of publication. The Court concluded "that the unpublished nature of a work is '[a] key, though not necessarily determinative, factor' tending to negate a defense of fair use."

In a series of decisions, the Court of Appeals for the Second Circuit, inspired by the Supreme Court in the *Harper & Row,* so limited the quotation of unpublished letters, diaries and journals in biographical writings that many authors and publishers of nonfiction works (who are almost always subject to suit in the Second Circuit) sounded the alarm and were ultimately successful in having the statute amended.

In **Salinger v. Random House, Inc.,** 811 F.2d 90 (2d Cir.), *cert. denied,* 484 U.S. 890 (1987), the court of appeals took the unusual step of reversing a trial court so as to direct the issuance of a preliminary injunction against the publication of a literary biography, because of the author's intended use of quotations from the letters of reclusive author J.D. Salinger. The 1986 galley proofs of the book by Ian Hamilton quoted from and closely paraphased language from 44 letters written by Salinger to friends (including Ernest Hemingway and Learned Hand) between 1939 and 1961 that were still protected by federal copyright; those letters had been donated by the recipients to research libraries at Harvard, Princeton and the University of Texas. The court found: "Of these 44 letters, the Hamilton biography copies (with some use of quotation or close paraphrase) protected sequences constituting at least one-third of 17 letters and at least 10 percent of 42 letters. These sequences are protected, notwithstanding that they include some reporting of facts and an occasional use of a commonplace word or expression.... The material closely paraphrased frequently exceeds ten lines from a single letter."

The court, stating that the common law "appears to have denied the defense of fair use to unpublished works," and conceding that § 107 now makes even the right of first publication subject to the fair use defense, viewed *Harper & Row* as controlling and read it to mean that "unpublished letters normally enjoy insulation from fair use copying." The court of appeals found that the first factor in § 107 favored Hamilton's "scholarly biography," but that a biographer's interests were amply protected by allowing the reference to facts found in earlier letters and did not require extended quotation of expression for purposes of "accuracy" or "vividness." "The copier is not at liberty to avoid 'pedestrian' reportage by appropriating his subject's literary devices." As for the second factor, the court looked only to the unpublished nature of the Salinger letters: "[W]e think that the tenor of the Court's entire discussion [in *Harper & Row*] of unpublished works conveys the idea that such works normally enjoy complete protection against copying any protected expression." This factor was found to "weigh heavily" in Salinger's favor, as did the third factor: "The taking is significant not only from a quantitative standpoint but from a qualitative one as well.... To a large extent, [the copied passages] make the book worth reading. The letters are quoted or paraphrased on approximately 40 percent of the book's 192 pages." The fourth factor was found to weigh "slightly" for Salinger, despite his disavowal of any intention to publish his letters; § 107 requires consideration of the copyright owner's "potential market" and Salinger has the right to change his mind and to protect his *opportunity* to sell his letters (which were said to have a current value in excess of $500,000). The biography — which "copies virtually all of the most interesting passages of the letters — would likely impair the market for their publication.

The court concluded by reflecting on the impact of its decision upon the writing of biography, history, and contemporary events, and concluded that there would be no interference. "The facts may be reported.... Hamilton is entirely free to fashion a biography that reports these facts. But Salinger has a right to protect the expressive content of his unpublished writings for the term of his copyright, and that right prevails over a claim of fair use under "ordinary circumstances."

Two cases soon reached the same court of appeals involving biographies of the controversial figure L. Ron Hubbard, the discoverer of the "science" of Dianetics and the founder of the Church of Scientology. The plaintiff in both cases was New Era Publishers, holder of Hubbard's copyrights by bequest; in both cases, the biographies were highly critical of Hubbard, and New Era sought injunctions. In **New Era Pubs. v. Henry Holt & Co.,** 873 F.2d 576 (2d Cir. 1989), *cert. denied,* 493 U.S. 1094 (1990), the biography quoted from Hubbard's unpublished diaries, journals and letters; the district judge distinguished *Salinger* (where he had also been the district judge) by finding that the use of Hubbard's words was for the most part not to "enliven" the text but was, rather, essential in order to buttress controversial assertions and conclusions about Hubbard's character. A divided court of appeals affirmed the denial of a preliminary injunction, but only because of the plaintiff's unduly long delay in seeking relief; on the merits, the court majority rejected the defense of fair use, emphasizing its narrow scope in the copying of unpublished works and rejecting the distinction between quotation to enliven the text and quotation needed to buttress a claim about an historical figure. The court also rejected the biographer's claim that the First Amendment could afford greater protection than copyright, and found that the First Amendment sheltered no more copying than would the doctrine of fair use.

In an unusual proceeding, the defendant publisher — which *prevailed* before the Second Circuit panel (because of laches) — petitioned for a rehearing *en banc*, seeking an overturning by the full court of the panel's fair use and First Amendment conclusions. The petition was denied, but again in a most unusual manner — with extended opinions by a split court. 884 F.2d 659 (2d Cir. 1989). The judge who had written the panel's majority opinion confirmed the basic points made there, but four judges dissented from the denial of the requested rehearing; the latter, in an effort to assuage possible concerns of publishers and biographers, attempted to narrow what were technically only *dicta* by the panel regarding fair use and concluded that the quotation of small amounts of unpublished material could be fair when used to report facts accurately.

The following year, in **New Era Pubs. v. Carol Pub'g Group**, 904 F.2d 152 (2d Cir.), *cert. denied,* 498 U.S. 921 (1990), which involved quotation from Hubbard's *published* writings, the court of appeals reversed the district judge for too narrowly applying *Salinger* and the first *New Era* decision. It emphasized that works of criticism, scholarship and research merit favorable treatment under the first factor in § 107, that quotations of copyrighted materials are often necessary to convey information and perceptions about historical figures, that published copyrighted material is not entitled to as much protection as unpublished material, and that the publication of the defendant's critical biography would not sate an audience inclined to read the Hubbard writings as incorporated in an authorized and favorable biography. (It is fair to say that much of the court's supportive references to history and biography, and much of its analysis — although dealing with unauthorized quotation of published materials — was directly inconsistent with corresponding analysis in the first *New Era* decision.)

In 1991, while bills were being considered in Congress to modify § 107 so as to make it more hospitable to the quotation, by biographers and historians, of unpublished materials, the Court of Appeals for the Second Circuit decided yet another pertinent case, **Wright v. Warner Books, Inc.,** 953 F.2d 731 (2d Cir. 1991). There the court affirmed a summary judgment for the author and publisher of a biography of the African-American author Richard Wright, which quoted and paraphrased a modest amount of material from Wright's journals and letters. Noting that "unpublished works are the favorite sons of factor two" in § 107, the court nonetheless found that the other three factors favored the defendant, and found fair use. The court read *Harper & Row* and *Salinger* to hold that unpublished materials are *ordinarily* not subject to fair use copying, but it concluded that no pertinent case has "erected a *per se* rule regarding unpublished works. The fair use test remains a totality inquiry, tailored to the particular facts of each case."

The hearings on a number of bills to amend § 107 were unusual in the respect that three of the judges who had written in the *Salinger* and *New Era* cases (including the district judge who had been reversed twice) presented testimony in Congress; they also published law review articles on the issue. Finally, after three years of deliberations, Congress approved amendatory language to § 107, and the President signed the bill on October 24, 1992, P.L. 102-492. Simply, the following sentence was added to the end of Section 107: "The fact that a work is unpublished shall not itself bar a finding of fair use if such finding is made upon consideration of all the above factors."

What exactly does this mean? That an unpublished work is not by virtue of that fact, and that alone, beyond the reach of quotation or close paraphrase? (Had the cases just discussed ever given such overpowering weight to the unpublished status of a copyrighted work?) Or, does it mean that a court is to assess all of the usual factors under § 107 and is not to give any weight at all to whether the plaintiff's work is published or unpublished? (Does that not give much too little weight to the unpublished nature of a work, contrary to the *Harper & Row* decision and to the second factor in § 107?) The authoritative Committee report, H. Rep. No. 102-836, 102d Cong., 2d Sess. 9 (1992) had this to say:

> [T]he word "itself" is designed to ensure that the courts do not erect a per se rule barring any fair use of unpublished works. Each claim of fair use of an unpublished work should involve a careful consideration of all four statutory factors as well as any other factors the court deems relevant.... At the same time, it is not the Committee's intention to alter the weight currently given by the courts to the unpublished nature of a work under the second fair use factor. The general principles regarding fair use of unpublished works set forth by the Supreme Court in *Harper & Row v. Nation Enterprises* still apply.

Craft v. Kobler, 667 F. Supp. 120 (S.D.N.Y. 1987). In this controversy concerning the plaintiff's *published* works, the district court looked to the distinction drawn in *Salinger* between copying to achieve literary vividness and copying material that is integral to the second author's argument or analysis. The decision rejected the fair use defense interposed by the author of a biography of composer Igor Stravinsky; the infringement action was brought by Robert Craft, who was Stravinsky's co-author, literary executor, and close colleague. The court determined that the defendant took more quotations and paraphrases from published works by Stravinsky and Craft than were necessary to the task of writing a critical biography. The Stravinsky sentences that the court found properly quoted or closely paraphrased were deemed by the court to be necessary to support analysis by the biographer that "depends on a perception of the style of writing and manner of expression" of Stravinsky, which "could not be made effectively without direct quotation." Most of Kobler's quotations and paraphrases did not fit within this category. "More common are takings of Stravinsky's radiant, startlingly expressive phrases to make a richer, better portrait of Stravinsky, and to make better reading than a drab paraphrase reduced to bare facts." The court attempted to articulate a standard that fell somewhere between the defendant's liberal proposal and an arguably quite narrow reading of the decision of the Court of Appeals in the then recently decided *Salinger* case.

In support of Kobler's quotation of such examples of Stravinsky's wit and power of description, the defendants argue that for a biography or critical study of an author, the doctrine of fair use gives latitude to quote protected matter for the purpose of illustrating and communicating the subject's powers of observation and expression.

Surely there is merit to the argument. Nor is it contradicted by the recent admonition of the Court of Appeals in *Salinger*: "This dilemma [of choosing between loss of accuracy and vividness and risking an injunction] is not faced by the biographer who elects to copy only the factual content of letters. The biographer who copies only facts incurs no risk of an injunction; ... [W]hen dealing with copyrighted expression, a biographer ... may frequently have to content himself with reporting only the fact of what the subject did, even if he thereby pens a 'pedestrian' sentence. The copier is not at liberty to avoid 'pedestrian' reportage by appropriating his subject's literary devices." 811 F.2d at 96-97. Taken out of context this passage appears to bar the biographer of an author from using any of his subject's protected expression whether done to achieve accuracy in the rendition of the subject's idea or to illustrate comments on the subject's writing style, skill and power. The biographer would be restricted to telling his readers, "This Mickey Spillane, boy, he sure can write." He would not be permitted to take examples of protected material to illustrate the point. A full reading of the Salinger opinion makes clear, however, that this discussion refers only to takings from unpublished copyrighted material, as to which the court ruled there is little opportunity for fair use.

I agree with the defendants that the fair use doctrine gives latitude to the biographer of an author to quote limited excerpts of published copyrighted work to illustrate the descriptive skill, wit, power, vividness, and originality of the author's writing.

But the license is not unlimited. In assessing claims of fair use, we must consider the number, size and importance of appropriated passages, as well as their individual justifications....

In my view, Kobler's takings are far too numerous and with too little instructional justification to support the conclusion of fair use. Kobler uses Stravinsky's colorful words without restraint throughout the book to describe and comment on the events and personages of Stravinsky's life. Most of these passages do not individually present a compelling justification of fair use. By a conservative count (that includes neither the doubtful rulings, cases of disputed ownership, nor claims based on translations), the appropriations constitute approximately 3% of the volume of Kobler's book. The importance of these passages to the book far exceeds that percentage. Stravinsky's colorful epigrams animate the narrative. I think Kobler might agree that they are the liveliest and most entertaining part of the biography.

QUESTIONS

1. The court seems to accord the second author little latitude to enhance his works by copying the first author's most evocative expressions. On the other hand, use of the first author's vivid language may be permissible to illustrate a second author's argument concerning the authorship or literary style of the prior work. Are you satisfied with a court's ability to discern when a second author is making a critical use of the prior work, as opposed to a merely decorative use? Is there any better alternative?

2. James Haberman is an artist and photographer. He creates surrealistic "assemblies" and sculptures, and then photographs them. He has won artistic awards and has had his works displayed in galleries and museums. His authorized agents license others to reproduce his photographs for sale in art stores, and a number of his photographs are marketed as postcards. Hustler Magazine, without Haberman's consent, has purchased and reproduced two of his postcards in separate issues of the magazine, in its "Bits and Pieces" column. That column consists of brief items concerning events, personalities, products and services that will interest and amuse Hustler readers. One of Haberman's photographic postcards appeared in a January issue; it was reproduced in full in color, at one-fifth the size of the original postcard, and occupied one-twentieth of the page. The second color postcard reproduction appeared in the June issue, reduced somewhat in size and occupying one-sixth of the page. Each photograph was accompanied by a few sentences of text, commenting on the odd elements of the work, and mentioned Haberman by name along with his business address. Each copy of Hustler sold one million copies. Since the publication of the photographs in Hustler, public purchases of the Haberman cards have increased slightly, and Haberman has continued to garner prizes and gallery and museum exhibitions. Haberman consults you regarding his rights against Hustler. Advise him. *See Haberman v. Hustler Magazine,* 626 F. Supp. 201 (D. Mass. 1986).

3. Plaintiff is the authorized manufacturer of the so-called "Ronbo" poster. The poster superimposes President Reagan's face on a muscular body (looking very much like that of motion picture actor Sylvester Stallone) which is firing a machine gun in a jungle setting. The body is intended to mimic the title

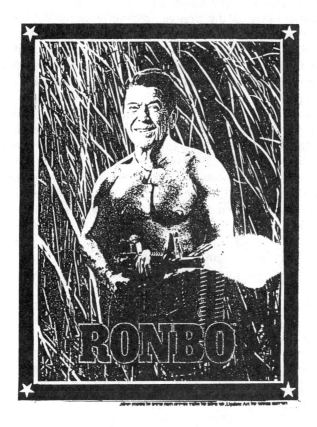

Reproduced with permission of Update Art, Inc.

character from the movie "Rambo." Defendant publishes an Israeli newspaper (Maariv) that is also distributed in the United States. In a recent weekend edition, Maariv carried a story discussing what it called the "Reaganization" of American motion picture films. The article noted that many recent films have military-related pro-American, anti-Soviet themes; it discussed such movies as Rambo and Rocky IV, and purported to relate them to the political climate in the Reagan years. The story was accompanied by a full-page (8½" × 11") reproduction of the "Ronbo" poster; other photographs in the story were half that size or smaller. The plaintiff's consent was not secured for the reproduction of the "Ronbo" poster. Evaluate the likely success of a lawsuit for copyright infringement. *See Update Art, Inc. v. Maariv Israel Newspaper, Inc.,* 635 F. Supp. 228 (S.D.N.Y. 1986).

4. Consumers Union (CU) publishes a copyrighted monthly magazine, Consumer Reports (CR), which reports at length on its evaluation, after rigorous testing, of a wide array of consumer products. Although a high rating from CU is of great commercial value to a manufacturer, CU — in an effort to maintain its objectivity and integrity — declines to run any outside advertising in CR and it has steadfastly refused to grant permission to others to use its name or copyrighted materials in advertisements. The July issue of CR contained an article evaluating and comparing eighteen different models of lightweight vacuum cleaners. Four models manufactured by Regina were discussed and rated; the Powerteam 6910 model was judged the best of all models tested by a good margin, while the other three were rated fair to poor.

Regina asked CU for permission to quote its favorable evaluation in an advertising campaign, but CU refused. Regina nonetheless proceeded to prepare and broadcast a television advertisement that featured a voice-over and simultaneous display of the text of several quotations from the CR article, such as: "Far ahead of the pack in cleaning ability.... Of all the lightweights tested, only one worked well.... The 6910 is the only cleaner tested that is an adequate substitute for a full-sized vacuum." While the announcer speaks, the screen notes a disclaimer: "Consumer Reports is not affiliated with Regina and does not endorse Regina products or any other products."

CU has brought an action for copyright infringement and Regina has raised the defense of fair use. Should that defense be sustained? *See Consumers Union of U.S., Inc. v. New Regina Corp.*, 664 F. Supp. 753 (S.D.N.Y. 1987). (Is it important to know how lengthy the CR article was? *See Henry Holt & Co. v. Liggett & Myers Tobacco Co.*, 23 F. Supp. 302 (E.D. Pa. 1938).)

5. A year ago, Hustler Magazine ran a parody advertisement based upon the "first time" advertisements of Campari liquor. The parody portrayed the Reverend Jerry Falwell, a nationally known fundamentalist minister, describing his "first time" as being incest with his mother in an outhouse. Falwell reproduced and distributed by mail the Hustler advertisement, along with a request for contributions to aid him in litigation against Hustler, to combat pornography, and to aid religious television stations to reinforce America's moral fiber. The Falwell campaign raised $700,000. Hustler Magazine has sued for copyright infringement, and Falwell has asserted fair use. How should the case be decided? *See Hustler Magazine, Inc. v. Moral Majority, Inc.*, 796 F.2d 1148 (9th Cir. 1986).

b. Particular Problems

(1) Parody

In addition to works of history, biography, and the like, the most fertile ground for fair-use analysis has been works of satire or parody. Of course, one can prepare a satirical comment on one's times in the form of an independently created literary, musical, or artistic work. It is not unusual, however, for a satirist or parodist to utilize the creative work of another, either for the purpose of poking fun at the borrowed work itself or for the purpose of poking fun at some altogether extrinsic social and political phenomenon. To the extent that parody can thus be viewed as a form of critical analysis, it serves the kind of social purpose that has traditionally justified a fair-use claim. (Do you find satire or parody among the listed categories or preferred uses in § 107 of the 1976 Copyright Act?)

Although it is arguable that satire or parody — particularly in the more scatological manifestations found in some of the cases — does not make quite the exalted claim of historical and scientific research works that borrow from earlier copyrighted materials, it is also arguable that these light-hearted efforts make a particularly appealing case for invocation of the fair-use doctrine. First, there is no "plagiarism" in the sense of a covert theft of copyrighted material; the satirist normally identifies the borrowed work and writes for an audience that is familiar with that work. Second, because of the typically large stylistic differences between the copyrighted work and the satire, the latter is not likely to substitute for the former in the marketplace. Third, it is not likely that the owner of copyright in the "serious" work will create, or license another to create, a derivative parody; at least, this is far less likely than his creation, or authorization, of a "serious" derivative work. Satire or parody might be threatened as an art form if courts were not rather generous in permitting it. Fourth, parody, in order to be at all effective, will in many instances *have* to reproduce parts of earlier copyrighted works. Do you find these arguments persuasive? Do they justify freer rein in using copyrighted material for satirical purposes than for serious purposes? Are there arguments that cut quite to the contrary?

Prominently featured in the parody cases that arose under the 1909 Act were three entertainment institutions of the 1950s and 1960s — Jack Benny, Sid Caesar, and Mad Magazine. The *Benny* and *Caesar* cases, decided by the same district judge, might be viewed as establishing the outer boundaries for application of the fair use doctrine in the area of parody. In *Benny v. Loew's, Inc.,* 239 F.2d 532 (9th Cir. 1956), *aff'd by an equally divided Court,* 356 U.S. 43 (1958), Jack Benny did a fifteen-minute take-off (in his half-hour television program) on the motion picture melodrama "Gaslight," which had starred Ingrid Bergman and Charles Boyer. Benny played the Boyer role of the husband trying deviously to drive his wife insane; the Bergman part was played by actress Barbara Stanwyck. The district judge found the following similarities between the film and the television parody: the locale and period; the main setting; the characters; the story points; the development of the story, i.e., the treatment (except that the defendants' was by way of burlesque), the incidents, the sequence of events, the points of suspense, the climax; and much of the dialogue, with minor variations. The court concluded that had the defendants' condensed teleplay been of a serious nature, "it would be crystal clear" that it would be a substantial taking and an infringement. The court asked whether such a taking ought nonetheless to be permitted when it is "by the use of burlesque." The court answered the question in the negative. The court of appeals agreed that "parodized or burlesque taking is to be treated no differently from any other appropriation," and affirmed. Although the same court later repudiated the latter proposition, see *Walt Disney Productions v. Air Pirates, infra,* the *Benny* case continues to be treated as a case in which the defendants' taking was so extensive in so many respects that the fair use defense was properly rejected, even though the use was for the purpose of parody.

At the other extreme was *Columbia Pictures Corp. v. NBC,* 137 F. Supp. 348 (S.D. Cal. 1955), decided while the *Benny* case was on appeal. Sid Caesar's television parody, "From Here to Obscurity," used some of the same general settings, incidents and character types as the copyrighted motion picture, "From Here to Eternity." But the character interaction and the story details were slapstick in the extreme. The court concluded that the defendants took only what was "sufficient to cause the viewer to recall and conjure up the original ... a necessary element of burlesque." It found the Caesar skit to be original and different from the film in its development, treatment and expression: "There is no substantial similarity between said burlesque and said motion picture as to theme, characterizations, general story line, detailed sequence of incidents, dialogue, points of suspense, subclimax or climax."

In effect, the *Caesar* court found that the taking of protectible expression from "From Here to Eternity" was insubstantial, and that all that defendants copied was the unprotectible "idea." The defendants' taking was thus merely to "conjure up" the original serious work being parodied. This "conjuring up" standard — or, more generally, the question how extensive quantitatively or qualitatively can be the material borrowed from the plaintiff's work — was also at the heart of the well-known *Berlin* case.

Berlin v. E.C. Publications, Inc., 329 F.2d 541 (2d Cir.), *cert. denied,* 379 U.S. 822 (1964). "Mad Comics" furnished parody lyrics to be "sung to the tune of" the popular songs of such well-known tunesmiths as plaintiff Irving Berlin. The comic book described its work as a "collection of parody lyrics to 57 old standards which reflect the idiotic world we live in today"; and the court of appeals stated that "the parodies were as diverse in their targets for satire as they were broad in their humor." The court furnished two examples, with the original lyrics (of "The Last Time I Saw Paris" and "Blue Skies") on the left-hand side, and the Mad parodies on the right.

The last time I saw Paris
Her heart was warm and gay,
I heard the laughter
   of her heart
in ev'ry street cafe.
	The first time I saw Maris
	He'd signed up with the A's!
	He slugged the ball but
	   never found
	How big league baseball pays!

The last time I saw Paris,
   Her trees were dressed for
   spring,
And lovers walked beneath
   those trees,
and birds found songs to sing.
	The next time I saw Maris
	A Yankee he'd become!
	And now endorsements earn
	   for him
	A most substantial sum!

I dodged the same old taxicabs that I had dodged for years;	He signed a contract with Gillette To plug their razor blades!

The chorus of their squeaky
horns
was music to my ears.

And when he found he cut himself,
He went and plugged Band-Aids!

The last time I saw Paris
Her heart was warm and gay.
No matter how they change her
I'll remember her that way.

The last time I saw Maris
He plugged six brands of beer!
The Democrats should pay him
To plug the New Frontier!

Blue Skies
smiling at me
Nothing but Blue Skies
do I see,

Blue Cross
Had me agree
To a new Blue Cross
Policy!

Bluebirds
singing a song
Nothing but Bluebirds
all day long,

Blue Cross
Said I would be
Happy that Blue Cross
Covered me!

Never saw the sun
shining so bright,
Never saw things
going so right,

Then I took a fall,
Leg in a splint;
They said that I
Should read the fine print!

Noticing the days
hurrying by,
When you're in love
my! how they fly,

When a very high
Fever I ran,
They told me I
Took out the wrong plan!

Blue days
all of them gone
Nothing but blue skies
from now on.

That's Blue Cross
There seems to be
Plenty for Blue Cross!
None for me!

The trial judge awarded summary judgment to the defendants as to twenty-three of the twenty-five songs in litigation, and the court of appeals affirmed.

It examined earlier parody cases, particularly the *Benny* and *Caesar* cases, which it summarized as turning upon the "relative significance or 'substantiality' — in terms of both quality and quantity — of the material taken from the original motion pictures." The court concluded that it was not necessary to determine whether a standard more lenient to the user than the "substantiality" test should be applied in parody cases, because

> [w]e believe in any event that the parody lyrics involved in this appeal would be permissible under the most rigorous application of the 'substantiality' requirement.

The disparities in theme, content and style between the original lyrics and the alleged infringements could hardly be greater. In the vast majority of cases, the rhyme scheme of the parodies bears no relationship whatsoever to that of the originals. While brief phrases of the original lyrics were occasionally injected into the parodies, this practice would seem necessary if the defendants' efforts were to "recall or conjure up" the originals; the humorous effect achieved when a familiar line is interposed in a totally incongruous setting, traditionally a tool of parodists, scarcely amounts to a "substantial" taking, if that standard is not to be woodenly applied. Similarly, the fact that defendants' parodies were written in the same meter as plaintiffs' compositions would seem inevitable if the original was to be recognized, but such a justification is not even necessary; we doubt that even so eminent a composer as plaintiff Irving Berlin should be permitted to claim a property interest in iambic pentameter.

[A]s a general proposition, we believe that parody and satire *are* deserving of substantial freedom — both as entertainment and as a form of social and literary criticism.... At the very least, where, as here, it is clear that the parody has neither the intent nor the effect of fulfilling the demand for the original, and where the parodist does not appropriate a greater amount of the original work than is necessary to "recall or conjure up" the object of his satire, a finding of infringement would be improper.

Although the general approach of courts to the decision of parody cases has remained the same after the effective date of the 1976 Copyright Act, judges have for the most part attempted to fit their analysis into the framework of § 107. Is satire or parody among the preferred purposes itemized in the preamble to § 107? Is it a use "such as" the itemized uses? Under § 107(1), the parodists' use is almost always in the context of commercial activity, but it is also commonly a "productive" use that on occasion has some edifying purpose. Should it matter, in applying this first factor, whether the defendant's parody is aimed at the plaintiff's work itself or rather satirizes some extrinsic social or political phenomenon? (Arguably, a greater amount of copying is necessary to pursue the former objective than to pursue the latter.) Under § 107(2), the targeted work is rarely scientific or informational; it is usually a well-known entertainment vehicle itself. The "amount and substantiality" will of course vary, both as to the plaintiff's work as a measuring rod and as to the defendant's work. And, under § 107(4), the impact of the parody upon the "potential market for or value of" the targeted work may be as difficult to determine as when fair use is claimed by creators of more serious works. But will not the adverse competitive impact likely be less when the defendant's use is for the purpose of parody? And even if the "value" of the targeted work is arguably diminished when the parody takes the form of a telling critique, is that what § 107(4) has in mind? What factors other than those listed in § 107 will likely come into play in parody cases?

These issues are explored in the following cases. Some were governed by § 107, while others were governed by the 1909 Act but were decided with an eye on the 1976 Act already in effect.

Walt Disney Productions v. Air Pirates, 581 F.2d 751 (9th Cir. 1978). The defendants published a bawdy cartoon magazine which pictorially depicted characters originated by the plaintiff (such as Mickey Mouse and Donald Duck) in sexual situations and using drugs and the like. The court rejected the defense of fair use. It stated that the two most significant factors in parody cases are whether the parody "fills the demand for the original" and how substantial is the copying. The court interpreted the *Benny* case as one in which the fair use defense was precluded because of "virtually complete or almost verbatim" copying. It was not necessary to determine whether the

defendants' cartoons met that standard, for they failed to pass muster under the "conjuring up" standard announced in the *Berlin* case; defendants took more than was necessary to recall the Disney characters to the reader. The court emphasized the "widespread public recognition" of such Disney characters, and stated that in a comic book a recognizable caricature is easy to draw without close copying (whereas more copying might be necessary in order to parody, say, a speech). It may not have been "fatal" that the Air Pirates cartoons "were parodying life and society in addition to parodying the Disney characters," but "to the extent that the Disney characters are not also an object of the parody ... the need to conjure them up would be reduced if not eliminated." The defendants argued that the humorous effect of parody is best achieved when the Disney characters are recognized at first glance, but the court rejoined that the law does not give the parodist the right to make the "best parody," and that courts must weigh into the equation the rights of the copyright owner.

> That balance has been struck at giving the parodist what is necessary to conjure up the original, and in the absence of a special need for accuracy ..., that standard was exceeded here. By copying the images in their entirety, defendants took more than was necessary to place firmly in the reader's mind the parodied work and those specific attributes that are to be satirized.

QUESTIONS

1. When courts permit the parodist to copy enough of the plaintiff's work to "conjure it up," does this mean merely that the parodist is free to copy the "idea" underlying a copyrighted work as opposed to its "expression" (as perhaps best illustrated by the *Sid Caesar* case)? Or does it mean that the parodist is free to copy an insubstantial quantitative amount (as in the *Berlin* case)? If either of those formulations is correct, is it necessary in parody cases even to reach the fair use question, as distinguished from the questions of copyrightability or infringement?

2. Is there not a special tolerance due defendants in art parody cases — such as *Air Pirates* — in comparison to literary parody cases, quite to the contrary of what the *Air Pirates* court held? Does not the *Air Pirates* requirement of a "caricature" rather than a close copy of the famous Disney characters run the risk that the public will be uncertain what character is being parodied? Does it make sense to require purposeful distortion of a well-known cartoon character in order to avoid an infringement finding?

3. Note the point brought out in the *Air Pirates* case to the effect that the parodist is not to be afforded the right to make the "best parody" and that this artistic preference by the parodist must be subordinated to the interest of the copyright owner in protecting its own creative expression. Is this not essentially the same as the point made in the *Salinger* and *Craft* cases about the biographer's obligation under the law to content himself with less than the most vivid recreation of the biographical subject? Do you find the point equally convincing in both contexts?

4. Do you share the view that the court ought not to consider the alleged pornographic or scatological nature of the defendant's work in analyzing the fair use question? Reexamine the court's opinion in the *Mitchell Brothers* case, Chapter 2, Subchapter H *supra,* regarding the copyrightability of an allegedly obscene motion picture film. Even assuming that the analysis there is sound, does it follow from the fact that the court should not hold an X-rated film to be uncopyrightable that it should also refrain from weighing the defendant's "X rating" in determining whether its use is "fair"?

5. Silly Singing Telegrams (SST) is in the business of franchising a singing telegram delivery service. It supplies to its franchisees costumes, props and skits to be used in rendering such service. It features delivery by persons dressed as cartoon characters, particularly Superman and Wonder Woman. The telegram delivery personnel are garbed in heroic tights patterned in color and decoration after those of the comic book prototypes. SST encourages the use of characteristic phrases to be "ad libbed" at the time of delivery, such as: "This looks like a job for Superman," "Able to leap tall buildings in a single bound," and the like. Delivery personnel also come armed with balloons depicting the cartoon characters; these balloons are manufactured by the copyright owner (DC Comics) of the Superman and Wonder Woman characters and are lawfully sold. DC Comics features those two cartoon heroes not only in books and films but also in all manner of merchandise, including school supplies, clothing, wallpaper and linens. It does not, however, engage in the singing telegram delivery business or in any business quite like it. DC Comics has brought an action against SST for copyright infringement, and both parties have stipulated to the above facts and have moved for summary judgment. How should the court rule? *See DC Comics, Inc. v. Unlimited Monkey Business, Inc.,* 598 F. Supp. 110 (N.D. Ga. 1984).

FISHER v. DEES

794 F.2d 432 (9th Cir. 1986)

SNEED, CIRCUIT JUDGE:

The plaintiffs-appellants, Marvin Fisher and Jack Segal, appeal the district court's grant of summary judgment disposing of their federal claim for copyright infringement and their state-law claims for unfair competition, defamation, and product disparagement. We affirm.

I. *Factual and Procedural Background*

The plaintiffs-appellants, Marvin Fisher and Jack Segal (the composers), composed and own the copyright to the '50s standard "When Sunny Gets Blue" (the song). In late 1984, a law firm representing the defendants-appellees — disc jockey Rick Dees, Atlantic Recording Corp., and Warner Communications, Inc.[1] — contacted Fisher and requested permission to use part or

---

[1] All the defendants-appellees occupy the same position in this suit. For purposes of convenience, we shall henceforth refer only to defendant-appellee Rick Dees. What is said with respect to him applies equally to the others.

all of the music to "When Sunny Gets Blue" in order to create a comedic and inoffensive version of the song. Fisher refused the request.

A few months later, Dees released a comedy record album (also issued in cassette form) called *Put It Where the Moon Don't Shine*. One cut on the album, entitled "When Sonny Sniffs Glue" (the parody), is an obvious take-off on the composer's song. The parody copies the first six of the song's thirty-eight bars of music — its recognizable main theme. In addition, it changes the original's opening lyrics — "When Sunny gets blue, her eyes get gray and cloudy, then the rain begins to fall" to "When Sonny sniffs glue, her eyes get red and bulgy, then her hair begins to fall." The parody runs for 29 seconds of the approximately forty minutes of material on Dees's album.

The composers brought an action in federal district court for copyright infringement, unfair competition, product disparagement, and defamation. The complaint included a proper demand for a jury trial. Before the commencement of discovery, both sides filed motions for summary judgment. The district court granted summary judgment in favor of Dees on all the composers' claims and the composers timely filed this appeal.

II. *Discussion*

....

A. *Copyright Infringement*

Dees urges affirmance of summary judgment on the claim for copyright infringement on the ground that the copying of the song for purposes of parody constituted a fair use.[2] We agree for the reasons discussed below.

---

[2] We reject out of hand the appellees' other two arguments for affirmance. The first one — that the first amendment gives parodists a blanket protection from copyright infringement actions — has previously been rejected by this circuit. *See Walt Disney Productions v. Air Pirates*, 581 F.2d 751, 758-59 (9th Cir. 1978) (holding that "the idea-expression line" separating infringement from non-infringement "'represents an acceptable definitional balance as between copyright and free speech interests'" (quoting *Sid & Marty Krofft Television Productions, Inc. v. McDonald's Corp.*, 562 F.2d 1157, 1170 (9th Cir. 1977))), *cert. denied*, 439 U.S. 1132, 99 S. Ct. 1054, 59 L. Ed. 2d 94 (1979). The second one — that the taking from the song was *de minimis* and thus not violative of the composers' copyright — is not supported by the facts. As a rule, a taking is considered *de minimis* only if it is so meager and fragmentary that the average audience would not recognize the appropriation. *See, e.g., Elsmere Music, Inc. v. National Broadcasting Co.*, 482 F. Supp. 741, 744 (S.D.N.Y.) (holding that a parodist's copying of four notes in a 100-measure composition was not merely a *de minimis* taking where that musical phrase was the heart of the composition), *aff'd per curiam*, 623 F.2d 252 (2d Cir. 1980). Here, the appropriation would be recognized instantly by anyone familiar with the original. As an analytical matter, moreover, it would seem contradictory to assert that copying for parodic purposes could be *de minimis*. A parody is successful only if the audience makes the connection between the original and its comic version. To "conjure up" the original work in the audience's mind, the parodist must appropriate a substantial enough portion of it to evoke recognition.

1. *Overview of the fair-use doctrine*

[I]n § 107, parody was not classified as a *presumptively* fair use. *See Harper & Row*, 105 S. Ct. at 2231. Each assertion of the "parody defense" must be considered individually, in light of the statutory factors, reason, experience, and, of course, the general principles developed in past cases.

There have been few cases in this circuit involving the parody branch of the fair-use doctrine.... [I]n *Walt Disney Productions v. Air Pirates*, 581 F.2d 751 (9th Cir. 1978), *cert. denied*, 439 U.S. 1132, 99 S. Ct. 1054, 59 L. Ed. 2d 94 (1979), we gave the *Benny* opinion a narrow interpretation and acknowledged that parody is a potential fair use subject to the multi-factor analysis codified in section 107. *See id.* at 756-58.

2. *Applying the fair-use test*

The composers advance five principal reasons why the parody before us is not a fair use: (1) the so-called parody is not actually a parody, or at least is not a parody of the composers' song; (2) Dees acted in bad faith; (3) Dees's use is commercial in nature; (4) the parody competes in the same market — record albums and tapes — as the song; and (5) the taking is more substantial than was reasonably necessary to "conjure up" the original in the mind of the audience.

In addition, the composers assert that the question of fair use is an issue for the jury....

. . . .

No material historical facts are at issue in this case. The parties dispute only the ultimate conclusions to be drawn from the admitted facts. Because, under *Harper & Row*, these judgments are legal in nature, we can make them without usurping the function of the jury.

(b) *Substantive fair-use issues*

We now turn to the composers' numerous substantive arguments as to why the fair-use defense is not available.

(1) *The subject of the parody*

The composers assert that the parody, although it borrows from the original work, was not "directed" at the original. That is, a humorous or satiric work deserves protection under the fair-use doctrine only if the copied work is at least partly the target of the work in question. *See Walt Disney Productions v. Air Pirates*, 581 F.2d 751, 758 n. 15 (9th Cir. 1978), *cert. denied*, 439 U.S. 1132, 99 S. Ct. 1054, 59 L. Ed. 2d 94 (1979). Otherwise, there is no need to "conjure up" the original in the audience's mind and no justification for borrowing from it. *Id.; accord MCA, Inc. v. Wilson*, 677 F.2d 180, 185 (2d Cir. 1981).

We requested counsel to provide us with tapes of both Dees's parody and the original (as sung by Johnny Mathis). Although we have no illusions of musical expertise, it was clear to us that Dees's version was intended to poke fun at the composers' song, and at Mr. Mathis's rather singular vocal range. We reject the notion that the song was used merely as a vehicle to achieve a comedic objective unrelated to the song, its place and time. *Cf. id.* at 183-85 (purpose of saving the effort of composing original music); *infra* note 5.

(2) *The propriety of Dees's conduct*

One theme running through the composers' briefs is that Dees's alleged bad conduct should bar his use of the equitable defense of fair use. The principle invoked is sound. Because "'[f]air use presupposes "good faith" and "fair dealing,"'" *Harper & Row,* 105 S. Ct. at 2232 (quoting *Time Inc. v. Bernard Geis Associates,* 293 F. Supp. 130, 146 (S.D.N.Y. 1968)), courts may weigh "the propriety of the defendant's conduct" in the equitable balance of a fair use determination, 3 M. Nimmer, Nimmer on Copyright § 13.05[A], at 13-72 to -73 (rev. ed. 1985).

Nonetheless, we conclude that the composers have failed to identify any conduct of Dees that is sufficiently blameworthy. For example, Fisher and Segal fault Dees for using the song after Fisher expressly refused him permission to do so. In their view, this shows bad faith on Dees's part. We cannot agree. Parodists will seldom get permission from those whose works are parodied. Self-esteem is seldom strong enough to permit the granting of permission even in exchange for a reasonable fee. *See* Note, *The Parody Defense to Copyright Infringement: Productive Fair Use After* Betamax, 97 Harv. L. Rev. 1395, 1397 n. 12 (1984) [hereinafter cited as *Parody Defense*]. The parody defense to copyright infringement exists precisely to make possible a use that generally cannot be bought. *See* 3 M. Nimmer, *supra,* § 13.05[C], at 13-89; Gordon, *Fair Use as Market Failure: A Structural and Economic Analysis of the* Betamax *Case and Its Predecessors,* 82 Colum. L. Rev. 1600, 1633 & n. 177. Moreover, to consider Dees blameworthy because he asked permission would penalize him for this modest show of consideration. Even though such gestures are predictably futile, we refuse to discourage them.

The composers also claim that the parody is immoral and thus unprotected by the fair-use doctrine. They cite the parody's irreverent references to drug addiction and its purported use of obscenities. Assuming without deciding that an obscene use is not a fair use, *but see Pillsbury Co. v. Milky Way Productions, Inc.,* 215 U.S.P.Q. 124, 131 & n. 10 (N.D. Ga. 1981), we conclude, after listening to it, that the parody is innocuous — silly perhaps, but surely not obscene or immoral.

(3) *The purpose and character of the use*

The first fair-use factor section 107 directs courts to consider is "the purpose and character of the use, including whether such use is of a commercial nature or is for nonprofit educational purposes." 17 U.S.C. § 107(1)(1982). The parties agree that the parody is a commercial use of the song. This fact "tends to weigh against a finding of fair use," *Harper & Row,* 105 S. Ct. at 2231, because "every commercial use of copyrighted material is presumptively an unfair exploitation of the monopoly privilege that belongs to the owner of the copyright." *Sony Corp. v. Universal City Studios, Inc.,* 464 U.S. 417, 451, 104 S. Ct. 774, 793, 78 L. Ed. 2d 574 (1984).

We recognize, however, that many parodies distributed commercially may be "more in the nature of an editorial or social commentary than ... an attempt to capitalize financially on the plaintiff's original work." *Milky Way Productions,* 215 U.S.P.Q. at 131 (footnote omitted). In such cases, of which this is one, the initial presumption need not be fatal to the defendant's cause. The defendant can rebut the presumption by convincing the court that the parody does not unfairly diminish the economic value of the original. *See id.* & n. 9.

(4) *The economic effect of the use*

Thus, we must turn our attention to the fourth factor in the fair-use analysis — "the effect of the use upon the potential market for or value of the copyrighted work," 17 U.S.C. § 107(4). This factor, not surprisingly, "is undoubtedly the single most important element of fair use." *Harper & Row,* 105 S. Ct. at 2234 (footnote omitted).

In assessing the economic effect of the parody, the parody's critical impact must be excluded. Through its critical function, a "parody may quite legitimately aim at garroting the original, destroying it commercially as well as artistically." B. Kaplan, An Unhurried View of Copyright 69 (1967). Copyright law is not designed to stifle critics. "'Destructive' parodies play an important role in social and literary criticism and thus merit protection even though they may discourage or discredit an original author." *Parody Defense,* 96 Harv. L. Rev. at 1411. Accordingly, the economic effect of a parody with which we are concerned is not its potential to destroy or diminish the market for the original — any bad review can have that effect — but rather whether it *fulfills the demand* for the original. Biting criticism suppresses demand; copyright infringement usurps it. Thus, infringement occurs when a parody supplants the original in markets the original is aimed at, or in which the original is, or has reasonable potential to become, commercially valuable. *See, e.g., Air Pirates,* 581 F.2d at 756; *Berlin v. E.C. Publications, Inc.,* 329 F.2d 541, 545 (2d Cir.), *cert. denied,* 379 U.S. 822, 85 S. Ct. 46, 13 L. Ed. 2d 33 (1964); *Parody Defense, supra,* at 1409-11.

This is not a case in which commercial substitution is likely. "When Sunny Gets Blue" is "a lyrical song concerning or relating to a woman's feelings about lost love and her chance for ... happiness again." Appellants' Opening Brief at 3. By contrast, the parody is a 29-second recording concerning a woman who sniffs glue, which "ends with noise and laughter mixed into the song." *Id.* at 7. We do not believe that consumers desirous of hearing a romantic and nostalgic ballad such as the composers' song would be satisfied to purchase the parody instead. Nor are those fond of parody likely to consider "When Sunny Gets Blue" a source of satisfaction. The two works do not fulfill the same demand. Consequently, the parody has no cognizable economic effect on the original.

(5) *The amount and substantiality of the taking*

This court has also consistently focused on the third fair-use factor — the amount and substantiality of the taking, 17 U.S.C. § 107(3). *See Air Pirates,*

581 F.2d at 756. Thus far, however, we have provided few concrete guidelines; we have merely sketched the outer boundaries of the inquiry. On the one hand, "substantial copying by a defendant, combined with the fact that the portion copied constituted a substantial part of the defendant's work," does not automatically preclude the fair use defense. *Id.* On the other hand, "copying that is virtually complete or almost verbatim" will not be protected. *Id.* In *Air Pirates*, we ultimately based our analysis on the so-called "conjure up" test. *See Air Pirates*, 581 F.2d at 757 (citing *Berlin v. E.C. Publications, Inc.*, 329 F.2d 541 (2d Cir.), *cert. denied*, 379 U.S. 822, 85 S. Ct. 46, 13 L. Ed. 2d 33 (1964), and *Columbia Pictures Corp. v. National Broadcasting Co.*, 137 F. Supp. 348 (S.D. Cal. 1955)). As the *Air Pirates* opinion articulated it, the test asks "whether the parodist has appropriated a greater amount of the original work than is necessary to 'recall or conjure up' the object of his satire." *Id.* The composers interpret this test to limit the amount of permissible copying to that amount necessary to evoke only *initial* recognition in the listener.

We disagree with this rigid view. As the Second Circuit stated in *Elsmere Music, Inc. v. National Broadcasting Co.*, 623 F.2d 252 (2d Cir. 1980) (per curiam):

> [T]he concept of "conjuring up" an original came into the copyright law not as a limitation on how much of an original may be used, but as a recognition that a parody frequently needs to be more than a fleeting evocation of an original in order to make its humorous point. A parody is entitled at least to "conjure up" the original.

Id. at 253 n. 1 (citation omitted). *Air Pirates* does not compel a different view. In that case — which concerned the near-verbatim copying of Disney characters in the defendants' underground comic book — we concluded that the defendants "took more than was necessary to place firmly in the reader's mind the parodied work and those specific attributes that [were] to be satirized," 581 F.2d at 758. We did not set a fixed limit on copying, but merely expressed our judgment that that particular parody could easily have been accomplished through more restricted means.

We singled out three considerations that we thought important in determining whether a taking is excessive under the circumstances — the degree of public recognition of the original work, the ease of conjuring up the original work in the chosen medium, and the focus of the parody. *See Air Pirates*, 581 F.2d at 757-58. Because the Disney characters were familiar and graphics was a relatively easy medium for parody, we concluded that close copying was impermissible. *See id.* But we expressly noted that media other than the graphic arts might justify greater leeway. We observed: "[W]hen the medium involved is a comic book, a recognizable caricature is not difficult to draw, so that an alternative that involves less copying is more likely to be available than if a speech, for instance, is parodied." *Id.* at 758.

The unavailability of viable alternatives is evident in the present case. Like a speech, a song is difficult to parody effectively without exact or near-exact copying. If the would-be parodist varies the music or meter of the original substantially, it simply will not be recognizable to the general audience. This "special need for accuracy," provides some license for "closer" parody. *See id.*

To be sure, that license is not limitless: the parodist's desire to make the best parody must be "balanced against the rights of the copyright owner in his original expressions." *Id.* We think the balance tips in the parodists' favor here. In view of the parody's medium, its purposes, and its brevity, it takes no more from the original than is necessary to accomplish reasonably its parodic purpose.

(6) *Summation*

We conclude that "When Sonny Sniffs Glue" is a parody deserving of fair-use protection as a matter of law. Thus, we affirm the district court's grant of summary judgment on the copyright claim. [The court also rejected the plaintiff's claims based on state unfair competition and defamation laws.]

Acuff-Rose v. Campbell, 972 F.2d 1429 (6th Cir. 1992), *cert. granted,* 113 S. Ct. 1642, 123 L. Ed. 2d 264 (1993). The publisher of Roy Orbison's song "Oh, Pretty Woman" alleged that the song "Pretty Woman" by the rap group 2 Live Crew infringed the copyright in the Orbison composition. The 2 Live Crew version adopted the melody and tracked the lyrics of Orbison's song, and reproduced (indeed, may have sampled) a guitar riff that recurs throughout the Orbison original. 2 Live Crew also altered the melody and lyrics: the music was deliberately distorted, and the group substituted lyrics denigrating the object of the singer's attentions. For example, where Orbison sang of a "Pretty Woman," 2 Live Crew recounted a "Pretty Woman" in their first verse, but a "big hairy woman," a "bald-headed woman," and a "two-timin' woman" in their second, third, and fourth verses. In contrast to Rick Dees' 29-second parody of "When Sunny Gets Blue," the 2 Live Crew version runs longer than the Orbison original.

A divided Sixth Circuit panel rejected 2 Live Crew's fair use defense. Although purporting to accept the district court's finding that the defendants' work was a parody, much of the majority's discussion challenges defendants' claim to be commenting on the Orbison original. The majority found defendant's commercial purpose to be the dominant consideration under the "purpose and character" factor. The extent of defendants' copying also weighed heavily against its fair use claim; the majority held that defendants had "purloin[ed] a substantial part of the essence of the original." Finally, the majority held that plaintiff's potential market was adversely affected because, even if plaintiff's and defendants' versions appealed to distinct audiences, defendants' version jeopardized plaintiff's potential market for *derivative* versions of its song.

The dissent objected that the majority was insufficiently sensitive to the parodic nature of defendants' version, and had overemphasized the commercial nature of the use. Nor, to the dissent, did defendants take more than necessary to accomplish their parodic objective. Regarding the final factor, the dissenting judge emphasized the lack of overlap of plaintiff's and defendants' audiences. Moreover, even admitting that there is a market for licensed parodies that defendant may have invaded, a finding of economic harm would tend to "turn[] copyright holders into censors of parody."

QUESTIONS

1. Who should determine if defendant's work takes only so much as is needed to accomplish its parodic aim? Are you comfortable with having judges make this determination? Are you comfortable with having judges accept defendants' assertions of necessity?

2. Those familiar with "When Sunny Gets Blue" will know that the song can surely be "conjured up" merely by singing the first five notes along with the defendant's matching words. Yet the court permitted the defendant to record what was in effect the entire melody of the plaintiff's song. (On the other hand, that melody was a half-minute long.) Was it proper for the court to conclude that copying the entire melody was necessary for "conjuring up" purposes? (Would you now advise Mad Comics that it may not merely publish parody lyrics to well-known songs but may also reproduce the musical notation so that people can accompany themselves on the piano?)

3. Recall the exclusion in § 115 from the compulsory license for making phonorecords of a song if the recorded arrangement changes the "basic melody or fundamental character of the work." Does this suggest that recorded musical parodies should not readily be tolerated through the "back door" of the fair use defense?

4. Are the parody cases going a bit overboard when they appear to take it for granted that parody is a significant form of artistic and/or social criticism worthy of extensive judicial protection at the expense of the copyright owner? Is that a convincing assumption in cases such as *Fisher v. Dees* and *Acuff-Rose v. Campbell*? On the other hand, can courts pass judgment as to which parodies are more or less culturally or socially useful? Are you troubled by the *Acuff-Rose* majority's expressions of doubt that 2 Live Crew's "Pretty Woman" was a parody of Roy Orbison's "Oh, Pretty Woman"?

5. How should the "potential market" factor of § 107(4) be applied in parody cases? Should parody be given no more "breathing room" than copying for more serious dramatic or musical purposes, because both the parody and the original can be characterized as competing forms of entertainment? Or, on the other hand, should parody normally be given far greater protection because it can be presumed not to "fulfill the demand for the original"? *See Metro-Goldwyn-Mayer, Inc. v. Showcase Atlanta Co-op. Prods.*, 479 F. Supp. 351 (N.D. Ga. 1979), and 216 U.S.P.Q. 685 (N.D. Ga. 1981).

Does the latter view, particularly as applied in *Fisher*, give parody far too great a range to benefit unfairly from the creative work of the plaintiff without payment? On the other hand, does the former view, particularly as applied in *Acuff-Rose*, give parody far too narrow a range in which to operate? Indeed, under that court's view, is there room for anything other than a (perhaps oxymoronic) licensed parody? How can one show the presence or absence of actual or potential adverse market impact resulting from a parody?

6. In *Fisher*, the court observed: "The parody defense to copyright infringement exists precisely to make possible a use that generally cannot be bought."

It is a corrective for "market failure." Is that an equally valid observation for other forms of fair use? *See* Gordon, *Fair Use as Market Failure: A Structural and Economic Analysis of the* Betamax *Case and Its Predecessors,* 82 Colum. L. Rev. 1600.

ROGERS v. KOONS

960 F.2d 301 (2d Cir.), *cert. denied,* 113
S. Ct. 365, 121 L. Ed. 2d 278 (1992)

CARDAMONE, CIRCUIT JUDGE:

The key to this copyright infringement suit, brought by a plaintiff photographer against a defendant sculptor and the gallery representing him, is defendants' borrowing of plaintiff's expression of a typical American scene — a smiling husband and wife holding a litter of charming puppies. The copying was so deliberate as to suggest that defendants resolved so long as they were significant players in the art business, and the copies they produced bettered the price of the copied work by a thousand to one, their piracy of a less well-known artist's work would escape being sullied by an accusation of plagiarism.

BACKGROUND FACTS

A. *Rogers*

We think it helpful to understanding this appeal to set forth the principals' professional backgrounds. Plaintiff, Art Rogers, a 43-year-old professional artist-photographer, has a studio and home at Point Reyes, California, where he makes his living by creating, exhibiting, publishing and otherwise making use of his rights in his photographic works. Exhibitions of his photographs have been held in California and as far away as Maine, Florida and New York. His work has been described in French ("Le Monde"), British ("The Photo") and numerous American publications, including the Journal of American Photography, Polaroid's Close-Up Magazine and the Popular Photography Annual. Rogers' photographs are part of the permanent collection of the San Francisco Museum of Modern Art, the Center for Creative Photography at the University of Arizona and Joseph E. Seagrams and Sons in New York City. He has taught photography at the San Francisco Museum of Modern Art.

B. *Creating The Photograph "Puppies"*

In 1980 an acquaintance, Jim Scanlon, commissioned Rogers to photograph his eight new German Shepherd puppies. When Rogers went to his home on September 21, 1980 he decided that taking a picture of the puppies alone would not work successfully, and chose instead to include Scanlon and his wife holding them. Substantial creative effort went into both the composition and production of "Puppies," a black and white photograph. At the photo session, and later in his lab, Rogers drew on his years of artistic development. He selected the light, the location, the bench on which the Scanlons are seated and the arrangement of the small dogs. He also made creative judgments concerning technical matters with his camera and the use of natural light. He prepared a set of "contact sheets," containing 50 different images, from which one was selected.

After the Scanlons purchased their prints for $200, "Puppies" became part of Rogers' catalogue of images available for further use, from which he, like many professional photographers, makes his living. "Puppies" has been used and exhibited a number of times. A signed print of it has been sold to a private collector, and in 1989 it was licensed for use in an anthology called "Dog Days." Rogers also planned to use the picture in a series of hand-tinted prints of his works. In 1984 Rogers had licensed "Puppies," along with other works, to Museum Graphics, a company that produces and sells notecards and post-cards with high quality reproductions of photographs by well-respected American photographers including, for example, Ansel Adams. Museum Graphics has produced and distributed the "Puppies" notecard since 1984. The first printing was of 5,000 copies and there has been a second similar size printing.

C. *Koons*

Defendant Jeff Koons is a 37-year-old artist and sculptor residing in New York City. After receiving a Bachelor of Fine Arts degree from Maryland Institute College of Art in 1976, he worked at a number of jobs, principally membership development at the Museum of Modern Art in New York. While pursuing his career as an artist, he also worked until 1984 as a mutual funds salesman, a registered commodities salesman and broker, and a commodities futures broker. In the ten years from 1980 to 1990 Koons has exhibited his works in approximately 100 Group Exhibitions and in eleven one-man shows. His bibliography is extensive. Koons is represented by Sonnabend Gallery, New York, Donald Young Gallery, Chicago, and Galerie Max Hetzler, Cologne, Germany. His works sell at very substantial prices, over $100,000. He is a controversial artist hailed by some as a "modern Michelangelo," while others find his art "truly offensive." A New York Times critic complained that "Koons is pushing the relationship between art and money so far that everyone involved comes out looking slightly absurd."

D. *Creating the Sculpture "String of Puppies"*

After a successful Sonnabend show in 1986, Koons began creating a group of 20 sculptures for a 1988 exhibition at the same gallery that he called the "Banality Show." He works in an art tradition dating back to the beginning of the twentieth century. This tradition defines its efforts as follows: when the artist finishes his work, the meaning of the original object has been extracted and an entirely new meaning set in its place. An example is Andy Warhol's reproduction of multiple images of Campbell's soup cans. Koons' most famous work in this genre is a stainless steel casting of an inflatable rabbit holding a carrot. During 1986 and 1987 the sculptor traveled widely in Europe looking at materials and workshops where he might fabricate materials for the Banality Show. He decided to use porcelain, mirrors and wood as mediums. Certain European studios were chosen to execute his porcelain works, other studios chosen for the mirror pieces, and the small Demetz Studio, located in the northern hill country town of Ortessi, Italy, was selected to carve the wood sculptures.

Koons acknowledges that the source for "String of Puppies" was a Museum Graphics notecard of "Puppies" which he purchased in a "very commercial, tourist-like card shop" in 1987. After buying the card, he tore off that portion showing Rogers' copyright of "Puppies." Koons saw certain criteria in the notecard that he thought made it a workable source. He believed it to be typical, commonplace and familiar. The notecard was also similar to other images of people holding animals that Koons had collected. Thus, he viewed the picture as part of the mass culture — "resting in the collective sub-consciousness of people regardless of whether the card had actually ever been seen by such people."

Appellant gave his artisans one of Rogers' notecards and told them to copy it. But in order to guide the creation of a three-dimensional sculptural piece from the two-dimensional photograph, Koons communicated extensively with the Demetz Studio. He visited it once a week during the period the piece was being carved by the workers and gave them written instructions. In his "production notes" Koons stressed that he wanted "Puppies" copied faithfully in the sculpture. For example, he told his artisans the *"work must be just like photo* — features of photo must be captured;" later, *"puppies need detail in fur. Details* — Just Like Photo!;" other notes instruct the artisans to *"keep man in angle of photo* — mild lean to side & mildly forward — same for woman," to "keep woman's big smile," and to "keep [the sculpture] very, very realistic;" others state, *"Girl's nose is too small. Please make larger as per photo*;" another reminds the artisans that "The puppies must have variation in fur *as per photo* — not just large area of paint — variation *as per photo*." (emphasis supplied).

To paint the polychromed wood "String of Puppies" sculptures, Koons provided a chart with an enlarged photocopy of "Puppies" in the center; painting directions were noted in the margin with arrows drawn to various areas of the photograph. The chart noted, "Puppies, painted in shades of blue. Variation of light-to-dark *as per photo*. Paint realistic *as per photo*, but in blues." and "Man's hair, white with shades of grey *as per black and white photo!*" (emphasis supplied).

When it was finished, "String of Puppies" was displayed at the Sonnabend Gallery, which opened the Banality Show on November 19, 1988. Three of the four copies made were sold to collectors for a total of $367,000; the fourth or artist's copy was kept by Koons. Defendant Koons' use of "Puppies" to create "String of Puppies" was not authorized by plaintiff. Rogers learned of Koons' unauthorized use of his work through Jim Scanlon, the man who had commissioned Rogers to create "Puppies." A friend of Scanlon's, who was familiar with the photograph, called to tell him that what she took to be a "colorized" version of "Puppies" was on the front page of the calendar section of the May 7, 1989 Sunday Los Angeles Times. In fact, as she and Scanlon later learned, the newspaper actually depicted Koons' "String of Puppies" in connection with an article about its exhibition at the Los Angeles Museum of Contemporary Art.

Rogers Photograph
1980 Art Rogers/Pt. Reyes. Reproduced with permission.

Koons Sculpture

DISCUSSION

....

II. *Unauthorized Copying by Defendant*

The trial court found original elements of creative expression in the copy-righted work were copied and that the copying was so blatantly apparent as not to require a trial. We agree that no reasonable juror could find that copying did not occur in this case. First, this case presents the rare scenario where there is direct evidence of copying. Koons admittedly gave a copy of the photograph to the Italian artisans with the explicit instruction that the work be copied. Moreover, the importance of copying the very details of the photograph that embodied plaintiff's original contribution — the poses, the shading, the expressions — was stressed by Koons throughout the creation of the sculpture. His instructions invariably implored that the creation must be designed "as per photo." This undisputed direct evidence of copying is sufficient to support the district court's granting of summary judgment.

Substantial similarity does not require literally identical copying of every detail. Such similarity is determined by the ordinary observer test. Thus, Koons' allegation that a trial judge uneducated in art is not an appropriate decision-maker misses the mark; the decision-maker, whether it be a judge or a jury, need not have any special skills other than to be a reasonable and average lay person....

[H]ad appellant simply used the idea presented by the photo, there would not have been infringing copying. But here Koons used the identical expression of the idea that Rogers created; the composition, the poses, and the expressions were all incorporated into the sculpture to the extent that, under the ordinary observer test, we conclude that no reasonable jury could have differed on the issue of substantial similarity. For this reason, the district court properly held that Koons "copied" the original.... Koons' additions, such as the flowers in the hair of the couple and the bulbous noses of the puppies, are insufficient to raise a genuine issue of material fact with regard to copying in light of the overwhelming similarity to the protected expression of the original work....

III. *The Fair Use Doctrine*

Defendant Koons further defends his use of Rogers' work "Puppies" to craft "String of Puppies" under a claim of a privilege of "fair use."...

1. *Purpose and Character of the Use*

The first factor, purpose and character of the use, asks whether the original was copied in good faith to benefit the public or primarily for the commercial interests of the infringer. Knowing exploitation of a copyrighted work for personal gain militates against a finding of fair use. And — because it is an equitable doctrine — wrongful denial of exploitative conduct towards the work of another may bar an otherwise legitimate fair use claim. Relevant to this issue is Koons' conduct, especially his action in tearing the copyright mark off of a Rogers notecard prior to sending it to the Italian artisans. This action suggests bad faith in defendant's use of plaintiff's work, and militates against a finding of fair use.

The Supreme Court has held that copies made for commercial or profit-making purposes are presumptively unfair. See *Sony Corp. of America.* The Court explained in a subsequent case that the "crux of the profit/nonprofit distinction is not whether the sole motive of the use is monetary gain but whether the user stands to profit from exploitation of the copyrighted material without paying the customary price." *Harper & Row, Publishers, Inc. v. Nation Enterprises.* We have stated that, though it is a significant factor, whether the profit element of the fair use calculus affects the ultimate determination of whether there is a fair use depends on the totality of the factors considered; it is not itself controlling. Thus, while we note that Koons' substantial profit from his intentionally exploitive use of Rogers' work also militates against the finding of fair use, we turn next to consider his contention that the primary purpose of the use was for social comment.

Parody or Satire as Fair Use: The Act expressly provides that comment on or criticism of a copyrighted work may be a valid use under the fair use doctrine. We must analyze therefore whether "String of Puppies" is properly considered a comment on or criticism of the photograph "Puppies." Koons argues that his sculpture is a satire or parody of society at large. He insists that "String of Puppies" is a fair social criticism and asserts to support that proposition that he belongs to the school of American artists who believe the mass production of commodities and media images has caused a deterioration in the quality of society, and this artistic tradition of which he is a member proposes through incorporating these images into works of art to comment critically both on the incorporated object and the political and economic system that created it. These themes, Koons states, draw upon the artistic movements of Cubism and Dadaism, with particular influence attributed to Marcel Duchamp, who in 1913 became the first to incorporate manufactured objects (readymades) into a work of art, directly influencing Koons' work and the work of other contemporary American artists. We accept this definition of the objective of this group of American artists.

To analyze Koons' parody defense, we must first define it. Parody or satire, as we understand it, is when one artist, for comic effect or social commentary, closely imitates the style of another artist and in so doing creates a new art work that makes ridiculous the style and expression of the original. Under our cases parody and satire are valued forms of criticism, encouraged because this sort of criticism itself fosters the creativity protected by the copyright law. We have consistently held that a parody entitles its creator under the fair use doctrine to more extensive use of the copied work than is ordinarily allowed under the substantial similarity test.

Hence, it must first be determined whether "String of Puppies" is a parody of Rogers' work for purposes of the fair use doctrine. We agree with the district court that it is not. It is the rule in this Circuit that though the satire need not be only of the copied work and may, as appellants urge of "String of Puppies," also be a parody of modern society, the copied work must be, at least in part, an object of the parody, otherwise there would be no need to conjure up the original work.

We think this is a necessary rule, as were it otherwise there would be no real limitation on the copier's use of another's copyrighted work to make a statement on some aspect of society at large. If an infringement of copyrightable expression could be justified as fair use solely on the basis of the infringer's claim to a higher or different artistic use — without insuring public awareness of the original work — there would be no practicable boundary to the fair use defense. Koons' claim that his infringement of Rogers' work is fair use solely because he is acting within an artistic tradition of commenting upon the commonplace thus cannot be accepted. The rule's function is to insure that credit is given where credit is due. By requiring that the copied work be an object of the parody, we merely insist that the audience be aware that underlying the parody there is an original and separate expression, attributable to a different artist. This awareness may come from the fact that the copied work is publicly known or because its existence is in some manner acknowledged by the parodist in connection with the parody. Of course, while our view of this matter does not necessarily prevent Koons' expression, although it may, it does recognize that any such exploitation must at least entail "paying the customary price." *Harper & Row Publishers, Inc.*, 471 U.S. at 562.

The problem in the instant case is that even given that "String of Puppies" is a satirical critique of our materialistic society, it is difficult to discern any parody of the photograph "Puppies" itself. We conclude therefore that this first factor of the fair use doctrine cuts against a finding of fair use. The circumstances of this case indicate that Koons' copying of the photograph "Puppies" was done in bad faith, primarily for profit-making motives, and did not constitute a parody of the original work.

2. *Nature of the Copyrighted Work*

The next fair use factor asks what is the nature of the work that has been copied. Where the original work is factual rather than fictional the scope of fair use is broader. Whether the original is creative, imaginative, or represents an investment of time in anticipation of a financial return also should be considered. Here "Puppies" was a published work of art. As an original expression it has more in common with fiction than with works based on facts, such as, for example, biographies or telephone directories. Since "Puppies" was creative and imaginative and Rogers, who makes his living as a photographer, hopes to gain a financial return for his efforts with this photograph, this factor militates against a finding of fair use.

3. *Amount and Substantiality of Work Used*

Where the amount of copying exceeds permissible levels, summary judgment has been upheld. To a large degree, this factor involves the same analysis as that used when determining if the copy is substantially similar to the original.... Appellants claim that under a parody defense their use of Rogers' work did not exceed the level permitted under the fair use doctrine. As discussed previously, this Circuit has traditionally afforded parodists significant leeway with respect to the extent and nature of their copying. Yet, even under such a defense there are limitations on what constitutes fair use. Here, the essence of Rogers' photograph was copied nearly in toto, much more than would have been necessary even if the sculpture had been a parody of plaintiff's work. In short, it is not really the parody flag that appellants are sailing under, but rather the flag of piracy. Moreover, because we have already determined that "String of Puppies" is not a parody of Rogers' work, appellants cannot avail themselves of this heightened tolerance under a parody defense.

... Koons' copying of Rogers' work was the essence of the photograph, and designedly done as the notes to the Italian artisans conclusively reveal. Koons went well beyond the factual subject matter of the photograph to incorporate the very expression of the work created by Rogers. We find that no reasonable jury could conclude that Koons did not exceed a permissible level of copying under the fair use doctrine.

4. *Effect of the Use on the Market Value of the Original*

The fourth factor looks at the effect of the use on the market value of the original. The Supreme Court in *Stewart* stated that the fourth factor "is the 'most important, and indeed, central fair use factor.'" See also *Harper & Row*. Under this factor a balance must be struck between the benefit gained by the copyright owner when the copying is found an unfair use and the benefit gained by the public when the use is held to be fair. The less adverse impact on the owner, the less public benefit need be shown to sustain non-commercial fair use. It is plain that where a use has no demonstrable impact on a copyright owner's potential market, the use need not be prohibited to protect the artist's incentive to pursue his inventive skills. Yet where the use is intended for commercial gain some meaningful likelihood of future harm is presumed.

A critical inquiry under this factor then is whether defendants Koons and Sonnabend planned to profit from their exploitation of "Puppies" without paying Rogers for their use of his photo — that is, whether Koons' work is primarily commercial in nature. We have already concluded that it is. In this case, of course, the copy was in a different medium than the original: one was a three-dimensional piece of sculpture, and the other a two-dimensional black and white photo. But the owner of a copyright with respect to this market-factor need only demonstrate that if the unauthorized use becomes "widespread" it would prejudice his potential market for his work. The reason for this rule relates to a central concern of copyright law that unfair copying undercuts demand for the original work and, as an inevitable consequence, chills creation of such works. Hence the inquiry considers not only harm to the market for the original photograph, but also harm to the market for derivative works. It is obviously not implausible that another artist, who would be willing to purchase the rights from Rogers, would want to produce a sculpture like Rogers' photo and, with Koons' work extant, such market is reduced. Similarly, defendants could take and sell photos of "String of Puppies," which would prejudice Rogers' potential market for the sale of the "Puppies" notecards, in addition to any other derivative use he might plan....

Here there is simply nothing in the record to support a view that Koons produced "String of Puppies" for anything other than sale as high-priced art. Hence, the likelihood of future harm to Rogers' photograph is presumed, and plaintiff's market for his work has been prejudiced.

. . . .

QUESTIONS

1. What weight should be given, if any, to whether the defendant is satirizing the plaintiff's work as such or is instead making a satirical comment upon some extrinsic social or political condition? How easy is the distinction to draw? Do any of the above cases clearly exemplify a distinction between these two types of parodies? Is the argument for permitting copying of a work in order to comment on something else stronger or weaker in the realm of "appropriation art"?

2. The following comments may help the student more fully to appreciate the artistic objectives of the defendant Koons. They are quoted from M. Buskirk, *Appropriation Under the Gun,* 80 Art in America 37 (1992):

> The appropriation of imagery from mass media and other sources is, of course, a strategy central to postmodern art. Koons is only one of a number of artists who have responded to an increasingly image-saturated society by taking pictures directly from the media, advertising or elsewhere and repositioning them within their own work. Still, despite the widespread practice of appropriation by artists over the last three decades [mentioning Andy Warhol, Robert Rauschenberg and David Salle], its legal standing has remained uncertain....
>
> In discussions of contemporary art, appropriation is generally understood as a method that uses recontextualization as a critical strategy. In theory, when an artist places a familiar image in a new context, the maneuver forces the viewer to reconsider how different contexts affect meaning and to understand that all meaning is socially constructed. In legal circles, however, the term 'appropriation' carries strong negative connotations, signifying essentially theft or piracy....
>
> [I]n dismissing the idea that Koons's work could function as an act of criticism, [the district court and the court of appeals] demonstrated an insistence on unambiguous and pointed criticism, suggesting that works based on nuance, multivalence or ambiguity are less likely to win the day in the legal arena.... [B]oth decisions gave primary emphasis to the overall similarity in the arrangement of the human and animal figures while deemphasizing the dramatic differences between the two works in terms of medium, scale, color, detail and context in which they would be appreciated....
>
> [If, in another pending case against Koons, involving his sculpture based on a cartoon dog in the Garfield comic strip] the judge rules that Koons's use of the familiar Odie also fails to function as a form of criticism or commentary, then the limitations on artists who wish to make works that respond to the contemporary world of existing, mass-media images will be very confining indeed.

Is there any way — for legislators or judges, at least — to resolve this seemingly irreconcilable, and culturally impoverishing, clash between copyright law and the art world? If, underlying the decision in the *Rogers* case are beliefs held by the court that Koons's claims were not to be taken seriously, and that a finding of no fair use would not really be culturally impoverishing, is it proper for federal judges to implement these beliefs in their decisionmaking?

(2) New Technologies of Copying for Research and Education

The advent and wide availability of the photocopy machine, and more recently, of personal computers, have posed important challenges to the enforcement of the copyright law. They have also compelled reconsideration of the role of the fair use doctrine in shielding personal and educational copying. While judicial attention to problems caused by new technologies of copying has so far focussed on the photocopier, the ever-expanding availability and storage capacity of digital media and copying devices promise to supplant the photocopier as the major means of private and institutional copying.

Historically, the advent of faster, more effective means of copying has obliged the copyright system to respond to the new technology. The photocopier affords one illustration. Copying by hand was sufficiently arduous to carry its own limitations as to both length of copied passages and the number of copies. The same was true of copying by typewriter and even by early forms of duplicating machines, such as the mimeograph (where the prototype had to be generated by typewriting and could be used only a limited number of times). Wide use of the photocopy machine brought the capacity to generate copies unlimited in length and in number. Copymaking became so widely dispersed throughout businesses, schools, libraries and even homes as to be largely beyond the reach of practicable monitoring. Of course, much of what was photocopied would have been unprotectible by copyright, such as eighteenth century poetry and federal court opinions. Just as obviously, much of what has been copied is material that is protected by the law of copyright.

When photocopying is done by profit-making enterprises in the course of promoting their commercial activities, copying — particularly in multiples — will normally be infringing and not protected by the fair use doctrine. In such cases, the major problem for the copyright owners is to police their copyright; as noted below, see Note, Collective Administration of the Reproduction Right, *infra* at p. 644, this can feasibly be done through organizations acting on behalf of large numbers of copyright owners for purposes of policing, licensing and royalty distribution. At the other extreme, the making of a single photocopy of a copyrighted work (particularly a short one) by a private individual for personal use would most likely be regarded as fair use and, even when not, could most probably not feasibly be monitored and prevented. (Videotape technology is, of course, a close cousin of photocopying devices, and the Supreme Court has employed the fair use doctrine rather generously in the case of home videotaping for purposes of "time shifting," in the *Sony* decision, already discussed.)

The most perplexing legal issues in the area of photocopying arise in institutions that lie in between the large commercial enterprise and the home copyist. The most prominent examples are schools and libraries. Their access to books, and their commitment to dissemination of knowledge, induce schools and libraries to use photocopying in aid of what they view as their fundamental and valuable social purposes. Their nonprofit status (for the most part) contributes to the plausibility of their reliance on the fair use defense. On the other hand, the volume of photocopying done by such institutions (particularly colleges and universities), the large potential adverse impact upon copyright owners, and the visibility and amenability to monitoring of many of these institutions, all contribute to a reasonable desire to curb photocopying excesses, at least when uncompensated.

During the process of revision of the 1909 Copyright Act, a great deal of attention was given to the proper scope of photocopying of copyrighted works on the part of schools and libraries. Congress eventually dealt with these two sets of institutions in very different ways: schools, under the more general rubric of fair use under § 107, and libraries, under the very specific and detailed exemptions in § 108. These will now be considered in that order.

One of the most controversial purposes touched upon in § 107 is "teaching." We have already examined a number of specific exemptions for educational uses sprinkled through the statute. *See, e.g.,* §§ 110(1), 110(2), and 112(b). In addition, teachers will continue to rely on the general principles of fair use as now embodied in § 107.

These partial limitations were enacted instead of the blanket exemption for teaching proposed by educational groups. An impetus for this proposal was a case that demonstrated that a teacher could be held liable for arranging and minimally duplicating and performing a musical work, despite the absence of profit and a number of other circumstances seemingly favoring the defendant. *Wihtol v. Crow,* 309 F.2d 777, 135 U.S.P.Q. 385 (8th Cir. 1962).

DRAFT, SECOND SUPPLEMENTARY REPORT OF THE REGISTER OF COPYRIGHTS, Chapter II, pp. 2-6, 25-28, 30 (1975)

No issue arising under the general revision bill has been hashed over more thoroughly than the extent to which educators can reproduce and distribute copyrighted works outside of copyright control. The 1973 hearings on this question in the Senate, and the 1975 hearings in the House, produced some changes in position but no new arguments on the substantive issues. These arguments can be summarized very briefly as follows:

Arguments of educational organizations:

1. It is important that the doctrine of fair use be recognized in the statute, and that its applicability to reproduction for educational and scholarly purposes be made as clear as possible in the statute and report.

2. A provision on fair use alone is not sufficient to answer the needs of education, since teachers need more certainty about what they can and cannot do than the unpredictable doctrine of fair use can provide.

3. Teachers actually create a market for authors and publishers, and are not interested in the kind of mass copying that damages copyright owners.

4. Teachers must be enabled to make creative use of all of the resources available to them in the classroom to supplement textbooks and to seize the "teachable moment," by reproducing a variety of copyrighted materials, such as contemporaneous reports and analyses, isolated poems, stories, essays, etc., for purposes of emphasis, illustration, or bringing a lesson up to date.

5. The "not-for-profit" principle of present law should be applied to restricted educational copying that will not hurt the publishing industry and that will further American education, which is the paramount public interest.

6. Subjecting the use of modern teaching tools to requirements for advance clearance and payment of fees will stifle originality in teaching and inhibit the use of the teacher's imagination and ingenuity.

7. Various proposals for voluntary or compulsory licensing are too complicated and burdensome to be acceptable to teachers, who would be deterred from using valuable works by the necessity for paperwork and payments. Any blanket scheme would imply payment for all uses, even those that would be considered free under the doctrine of fair use.

Arguments of authors and publishers:

1. The doctrine of fair use should be confirmed in the statute, but by its nature it is an equitable rule of reason that must be flexible to avoid a statutory freezing of unintended results. Authors and publishers have no desire to oppress teachers or to stop minor or incidental reproduction of the sort that is undoubtedly fair use under the present law; their concern is with the potential danger of massive, unreasonable abuse.

2. Arguments that, since reproductions for educational and scholarly purposes have become increasingly easy and cheap, they should be made legal, are unreasonable and untenable.

3. The present "for profit" limitation has nothing whatever to do with copying. The argument that education should be exempt because it does not make a profit overlooks the fact that uncompensated educational uses, particularly in the textbook, reference book, and scientific publishing areas, result in direct and serious loss to copyright owners, and destroy the incentives for authorship and publication. Education is the textbook publisher's only market, and the main source of income of many authors.

4. Reproducing devices in educational establishments have proliferated tremendously, and unit costs continue to decrease. It is becoming easier and cheaper to make a copy than to buy one. Uninhibited reproduction of copyrighted material by a single educator, taken alone, might not do measurable damage to a particular author or publisher, but uninhibited reproduction of copyrighted material by all educators and educational establishments will literally destroy some important forms of authorship and publishing....

5. Workable voluntary licensing systems that would place no unwarranted budgetary or administrative burdens on copyright owners, and that would fully recognize the doctrine of fair use, are already being worked out, and should be expanded and encouraged by all concerned....

General comments:

... Over the years, some of the educators have seemed to be arguing that, with respect to photocopying, they enjoy under the present law a "not-for-profit" limitation co-extensive with that applicable to certain performances, and that somehow this "right" is being taken away from them. This line of argument tended to produce a rather testy reaction, since plainly the only explicit "not-for-profit" limitations on the copyright owner's exclusive rights under the present law are with respect to public performances of nondramatic literary and musical works. On the other hand, although the commercial or nonprofit character of a use is not necessarily conclusive with respect to fair use, in combination with other factors it can and should weigh heavily in fair use decisions. It would certainly be appropriate to emphasize this point in the legislative commentary dealing with fair use and educational photo-copying....

Conclusion

... [T]here is a fact that must be faced. Right now, there are activities connected with teaching that constitute infringement, not fair use, and these are bound to increase. Everyone seems to assume that they will somehow be licensed and that royalties will somehow be paid, but as a practical matter this cannot and will not be done on an individual, item-by-item basis. We are entering an era when blanket licensing and collective payments are essential if the educator is not to be a scofflaw and the author's copyright is not to be a hollow shell. It is not going to be easy, but once the scope of fair use in this field of activity has been clarified by legislative action, immediate efforts to establish workable licensing or clearinghouse arrangements will have to begin.

Extended discussion of educational photocopying in House and Senate Committee Reports in 1967, 1975, and 1976 culminated in *Guidelines for Classroom Copying in Not-For-Profit Educational Institutions,* H.R. Rep. No. 94-1476, *supra,* at 68-71. These are reproduced immediately below. The House committee expressed the belief that these guidelines, agreed upon by certain interested groups, "are a reasonable interpretation of the minimum standards of fair use." *Id.* at 72. The conferees stated that they "accept as part of their understanding of fair use" the Guidelines, as corrected and amended. *See* 122 Cong. Rec. H10727 (Sept. 21, 1976), H10875 (Sept. 22, 1976). The Guidelines seem to offer for the first time what users have long sought — some numerical guide to how much can be taken. And indeed their very purpose is to fulfill "the need for greater certainty and protection for teachers." H.R. Rep. No. 94-1476, *supra,* at 72. The Report makes quite clear, however, that this "greater certainty" may be temporary because of changing conditions.

AGREEMENT ON GUIDELINES FOR CLASSROOM COPYING IN NOT-FOR-PROFIT EDUCATIONAL INSTITUTIONS

With Respect to Books and Periodicals*

The purpose of the following guidelines is to state the minimum standards of educational fair use under Section 107 of H.R. 2223. The parties agree that the conditions determining the extent of permissible copying for educational purposes may change in the future; that certain types of copying permitted under these guidelines may not be permissible in the future; and conversely that in the future other types of copying not permitted under these guidelines may be permissible under revised guidelines.

Moreover, the following statement of guidelines is not intended to limit the types of copying permitted under the standards of fair use under judicial decision and which are stated in Section 107 of the Copyright Revision Bill. There may be instances in which copying which does not fall within the guidelines stated below may nonetheless be permitted under the criteria of fair use.

I. Single Copying for Teachers

A single copy may be made of any of the following by or for a teacher at his or her individual request for his or her scholarly research or use in teaching or preparation to teach a class:

A. A chapter from a book;

B. An article from a periodical or newspaper;

C. A short story, short essay or short poem, whether or not from a collective work;

D. A chart, graph, diagram, drawing, cartoon or picture from a book, periodical, or newspaper;

II. Multiple Copies for Classroom Use

Multiple copies (not to exceed in any event more than one copy per pupil in a course) may be made by or for the teacher giving the course for classroom use or discussion; *provided that:*

A. The copying meets the tests of brevity and spontaneity as defined below; *and,*

B. Meets the cumulative effect test as defined below; *and,*

C. Each copy includes a notice of copyright.

Definitions

Brevity

(i) Poetry: (a) A complete poem if less than 250 words and if printed on not

---

*These guidelines were developed by three organizations: The Ad Hoc Committee of Educational Institutions and Organizations on Copyright Law Revision; the Authors League of America, Inc.; and the Association of American Publishers, Inc.

more than two pages or, (b) from a longer poem, an excerpt of not more than 250 words.

(ii) Prose: (a) Either a complete article, story or essay of less than 2,500 words, or (b) an excerpt from any prose work of not more than 1,000 words or 10% of the work, whichever is less, but in any event a minimum of 500 words.

(Each of the numerical limits stated in "i" and "ii" above may be expanded to permit the completion of an unfinished line of a poem or of an unfinished prose paragraph.)

(iii) Illustration: One chart, graph, diagram, drawing, cartoon or picture per book or per periodical issue.

(iv) "Special" works: Certain works in poetry, prose or in "poetic prose" which often combine language with illustrations and which are intended sometimes for children and at other times for a more general audience fall short of 2,500 words in their entirety. Paragraph "ii" above notwithstanding such "special works" may not be reproduced in their entirety; however, an excerpt comprising not more than two of the published pages of such special work and containing not more than 10% of the words found in the text thereof, may be reproduced.

Spontaneity

(i) The copying is at the instance and inspiration of the individual teacher, and

(ii) The inspiration and decision to use the work and the moment of its use for maximum teaching effectiveness are so close in time that it would be unreasonable to expect a timely reply to a request for permission.

Cumulative Effect

(i) The copying of the material is for only one course in the school in which the copies are made.

(ii) Not more than one short poem, article, story, essay or two excerpts may be copied from the same author, nor more than three from the same collective work or periodical volume during one class term.

(iii) There shall not be more than nine instances of such multiple copying for one course during one class term.

[The limitations stated in "ii" and "iii" above shall not apply to current news periodicals and newspapers and current news sections of other periodicals.]

III. *Prohibitions as to I and II Above*

Notwithstanding any of the above, the following shall be prohibited:

(A) Copying shall not be used to create or to replace or substitute for anthologies, compilations or collective works. Such replacement or substitution may occur whether copies of various works or excerpts therefrom are accumulated or reproduced and used separately.

(B) There shall be no copying of or from works intended to be "consumable" in the course of study or of teaching. These include workbooks, exercises, standardized tests and test booklets and answer sheets and like consumable material.

(C) Copying shall not:

(a) substitute for the purchase of books, publishers' reprints or periodicals;

(b) be directed by higher authority;

(c) be repeated with respect to the same item by the same teacher from term to term.

(D) No charge shall be made to the student beyond the actual cost of the photocopying.

QUESTION

As the above material suggests, the issue of educational photocopying was most contentious and explored in great detail in the committee deliberations and reports. Congress chose neither to grant a blanket educational exemption for such copying nor to write an elaborate legislative provision akin to § 108 on library photocopying. Instead, classroom photocopying was dealt with through the insertion of two specific phrases within the more general phraseology of § 107: the "body" of the section lists as a preferred purpose "teaching (including multiple copies for classroom use)," and the listed factors to be considered include whether there is use for "nonprofit educational purposes" rather than commercial purposes. Doesn't this rather clearly demonstrate a purposeful sheltering of educational copying, at least to a degree considerably greater than that which obtains in other fair-use situations (such as parody or history)?

BASIC BOOKS, INC. v. KINKO'S GRAPHICS CORP.

758 F. Supp. 1522 (S.D.N.Y. 1991)

MOTLEY, DISTRICT JUDGE.

Plaintiffs, all major publishing houses in New York City, brought this suit against Kinko's alleging copyright infringement pursuant to the Copyright Act of 1976. 17 U.S.C. § 101, et seq. More specifically, plaintiffs allege that Kinko's infringed their copyrights when Kinko's copied excerpts from books, whose rights are held by the plaintiffs, without permission and without payment of required fees and sold the copies for a profit....

This court finds and concludes that defendant did violate the Copyright Act, that plaintiffs did not misuse their copyrights nor are they estopped from asserting their rights under the copyrights. With regard to the copyrights that were not recorded before filing the complaint, this court finds them to be validly asserted. Finally, Kinko's has not convincingly shown that the excerpts it appropriated without seeking permission were a fair use of the works in question. This court hereby awards plaintiffs injunctive relief, as well as statutory damages in the amount of $510,000, attorneys fees and costs.

Findings of Fact

There are 12 instances of copyright infringement alleged in this case. The 12 excerpts, which vary in length from 14 to 110 pages, were copied from books previously published by the plaintiffs, compiled in five numbered packets ("anthologies") with excerpts from other books and distributed by Kinko's. Kinko's neither sought nor obtained permission to copy any of these works....

[The excerpts included in this suit were sold at two Kinko's stores, one of which serviced students at New York University and the New School for Social Research, and the other one, students at Columbia University. One packet included 388 pages of photocopied material taken from 25 books; it was sold to three students and was priced at $24.00. The excerpts in suit ran from 14 to 53 pages, which constituted between 5% and 24% of the copyrighted works; in each instance, at least one entire chapter was copied. A second packet included 383 pages taken from 43 books; it was sold to 10 students and was priced at $20.07. The two excerpts in suit contained 20 and 40 pages, or 6% and 8% of the copyrighted works — one chapter from one work, and half a chapter from the other. The third packet (324 pages from 23 sources) was sold for $21.50 to 33 students; it contained material from only one of the works in suit — 22 pages or 14% of the work, an entire chapter. The fourth packet (292 pages from 22 sources) was sold for $17.75 to 48 students; it contained material from two of the works in suit, in one instance three chapters totaling 100 pages (13-14% of the book), and in another instance 65 pages (17-18%), more than two chapters. The fifth packet (212 pages from 7 sources) was sold for $11.00 to 132 students; it contained material from only one of the works in suit — three chapters totaling 110 pages (25-28%) from a well-known 12-chapter biography of Lyndon Johnson. Some of the allegedly infringed books were in-print and others were out-of-print. In each instance, the court determined — considering the § 107 factor of "amount and substantiality" — that the amount copied either weighed against the defendant or weighed "heavily" against the defendant.]

Each packet has a cover page, printed with the Kinko's logo, "Kinko's Copies: Professor Publishing," the name of the course and professor, the designated packet number, and a price listing. There is a space on the price listing to designate the royalty charges included. Only one packet lists a charge for royalty fees. On the inside cover of three of the five packets is a sheet entitled "Education and Fair Use: The Federal Copyright Law." It lists the § 107 fair use factors and displays the Professor Publishing logo and course information. None of the excerpts carries a copyright creditline as required by copyright law.

It is undisputed that Kinko's markets and provides its copying services directly to university professors and students. At trial, Kinko's presented marketing brochures produced by the company which are distributed by their marketing representatives to university professors and used as the subject of follow-up visits. These brochures openly solicit from the professors lists of readings they plan to use in their courses. Kinko's then copies excerpts, some quite large, and sells them in bound form with excerpts copied from other books as well. Unaudited financial statements of Kinko's Graphics Corporation for the years 1988 and 1989 show revenue of $42 million and $54 million, respectively, and net profit of $200,000 and $3 million, respectively. Its assets totalled $12 million in 1988 and $15 million in 1989. (PX 25a.) Appropriately, plaintiffs refer to this bound packet as an "anthology." Plaintiffs derive a significant part of their income from textbook sales and permissions fees. Kinko's has conducted its Professor Publishing business at least since the mid-1980's.

Discussion

I. *Fair Use*

... This case is distinctive in many respects from those which have come before it. It involves multiple copying. The copying was conducted by a commercial enterprise which claims an educational purpose for the materials. The copying was just that — copying — and did not "transform" the works in suit, that is, interpret them or add any value to the material copied, as would a biographer's or critic's use of a copyrighted quotation or excerpt. Because plaintiffs specifically allege violation of both, this court has the task of evaluating the copying under fair use doctrine and the "Agreement on Guidelines for Classroom Copying in Not-For-Profit Educational Institutions" ("Classroom Guidelines").

A. *The 4 Factors of Fair Use*

1. *Purpose and Character of the Use*

Section 107 specifically provides that under this factor we consider "whether [the] use is of a commercial nature or is for *nonprofit* educational purposes." 17 U.S.C. § 107; see also *Marcus v. Rowley,* 695 F.2d 1171, 1175 (9th Cir. 1983). The Supreme Court has held that "commercial use of copyrighted material is presumptively an unfair exploitation of the monopoly privilege that belongs to the owner of the copyright." *Sony Corp.,* 464 U.S. at 451. Additionally, the Supreme Court has found that "the distinction between 'productive' and 'unproductive' uses may be helpful in calibrating the balance [of interests]." *Id.* at 455 n. 40. While both are significant considerations, neither of these is determinative.

Transformative use.

It has been argued that the essence of "character and purpose" is the transformative value, that is, productive use, of the secondary work compared to the original. District Court Judge Leval has noted that, "the use ... must employ the quoted matter in a different manner or for a different purpose from the original. A quotation of copyrighted material that merely repackages or republishes the original is unlikely to pass the test." Leval, *Toward a Fair*

Use Standard, 103 Harv. L. Rev. 1105, 1111 (1990) (suggesting a balancing between the justification for and the extent of the taking). Kinko's work cannot be categorized as anything other than a mere repackaging.

Most contested instances of copyright infringement are those in which the infringer has copied small portions, quotations or excerpts of works and represents them in another form, for example, a biography, criticism, news article or other commentary. [Citations omitted.] In this case, there was absolutely no literary effort made by Kinko's to expand upon or contextualize the materials copied.... The excerpts in suit were merely copied, bound into a new form, and sold. The plaintiffs refer to this process as "anthologizing." The copying in suit had productive value only to the extent that it put an entire semester's resources in one bound volume for students. It required the judgment of the professors to compile it, though none of Kinko's.

Commercial use.

The use of the Kinko's packets, in the hands of the students, was no doubt educational. However, the use in the hands of Kinko's employees is commercial. Kinko's claims that its copying was educational and, therefore, qualifies as a fair use. Kinko's fails to persuade us of this distinction.

Kinko's has not disputed that it receives a profit component from the revenue it collects for its anthologies. The amount of that profit is unclear; however, we need only find that Kinko's had the intention of making profits. Its Professor Publishing promotional materials clearly indicate that Kinko's recognized and sought a segment of a profitable market, admitting that "tremendous sales and profit potential arise from this program." Kinko's Policies and Procedures Manual, chapter 9, at 1 (PX 11) (further noting that "these orders can be the easiest to run, and the most profitable." *Id.*).

Although Kinko's tries to impress this court with its purportedly altruistic motives, the facts show that Kinko's copying had "the *intended purpose* of supplanting the copyright holder's commercially valuable right." See *Harper & Row,* 471 U.S. at 562 .... Kinko's shows that it is keenly aware of students' and professors' preoccupation with educational costs and provides additional services to get their business: offering campus pick-up and delivery and free copyright permission assistance. See "Campus Rep Marketing Materials 1988." The extent of its insistence that theirs are educational concerns and not profitmaking ones boggles the mind.

Kinko's has periodically asserted that it acted at the instruction of the educational institution, that is, as the agent of the colleges and is without responsibility. Yet, Kinko's promotional materials belie this contention particularly because Kinko's takes responsibility for obtaining copyright permission while touting the expertise of its copyright permissions staff (a "service [which] is provided at no charge to all Kinko's customers"). "Copyright Information Letter to Faculty Members," in Kinko's Copyright and Professor Publishing Handbook, at 40.

Kinko's is paid directly by students who come into its stores to purchase the packets. Professors do not pay a fee; in fact, Kinko's provides incentives to professors for choosing their copy center over others.

While financial gain "will not preclude [the] use from being a fair use," *New York Times Co. v. Roxbury Data Interface, Inc.*, 434 F. Supp. 217, 221 (D.N.J. 1977), consideration of the commercial use is an important one.

"The crux of the profit/nonprofit distinction is not whether the sole motive of the use is monetary gain but whether the user stands to profit from exploitation of the copyrighted material without paying the customary price." *Harper & Row*, 471 U.S. at 562. This is precisely the concern here and why this factor weighs so strongly in favor of plaintiffs....

2. *The Nature of the Copyrighted Work*

The second factor concerns the nature of the copyrighted work. Courts generally hold that "the scope of fair use is greater with respect to factual than non-factual works." *New Era Publications v. Carol Publishing Group*, 904 F.2d at 157. Factual works, such as biographies, reviews, criticism and commentary, are believed to have a greater public value and, therefore, uses of them may be better tolerated by the copyright law.... The books infringed in suit were factual in nature. This factor weighs in favor of defendant.

3. *The Amount and Substantiality of the Portion Used*

"There are no absolute rules as to how much of a copyrighted work may be copied and still be considered a fair use." *Maxtone-Graham v. Burtchaell*, 803 F.2d 1253 (2d Cir.), *cert. denied*, 481 U.S. 1059, 107 S. Ct. 2201, 95 L. Ed. 2d 856 (1987). This third factor considers not only the percentage of the original used but also the "substantiality" of that portion to the whole of the work; that is, courts must evaluate the qualitative aspects as well as the quantity of material copied....

Courts have found relatively small quantitative uses to be fair use. See, e.g., *New Era Publications*, 904 F.2d at 158 (court found as fair that defendant used a "minuscule" amount of 25 works: 5-6% of 12 works, 8% or more of 11 works "each of the 11 being only a few pages in length."); *Iowa State University Research Found., Inc. v. Am. Broadcasting Cos., Inc.*, 621 F.2d at 61-62 (court found unfair copying of 8% of videotape never before broadcast); *Maxtone-Graham*, 803 F.2d at 1263 (inclusion of 4.3% of work was fair); *Salinger*, 811 F.2d at 98-99 (finding this factor weighed "heavily" in favor of Salinger, the court found no fair use of quotation and paraphrasing totalling one-third of 17 letters, and 10% of 42 letters); *Harper & Row*, 471 U.S. at 564-65 (the 300 copyrighted words appropriated to the Times article were an insubstantial portion of the work but "'essentially the heart of the book.'").

Additionally, "reference to a work's availability is appropriate." *Wright v. Warner Books, Inc.*, 748 F. Supp. at 112. Therefore, longer portions copied from an out-of-print book may be fair use because the book is no longer available. (This has been thought to be true because, presumably, there is little market effect produced by the copying. However, plaintiffs in this case convincingly argue that damage to out-of-print works may in fact be greater since permissions fees may be the only income for authors and copyright owners.). This court finds and concludes that the portions copied were critical parts of the books copied, since that is the likely reason the college professors used them in their classes. Cf. *Harper & Row,* 471 U.S. at 565 ("the fact that a substantial portion of the infringing work was copied verbatim is evidence of the qualitative value of the copied material."). While it may be impossible to determine, as the Court did in *Harper & Row,* that the quoted material was "essentially the heart of" the copyrighted material, *id.* at 565, it may be inferred that they were important parts.

This factor, amount and substantiality of the portions appropriated, weighs against defendant. In this case, the passages copied ranged from 14 to 110 pages, representing 5.2% to 25.1% of the works. See Findings of Fact, *supra,* for discussion of amount copied. In one case Kinko's copied 110 pages of someone's work and sold it to 132 students. Even for an out-of-print book, this amount is grossly out of line with accepted fair use principles.

In almost every case, defendant copied at least an entire chapter of a plaintiff's book. This is substantial because they are obviously meant to stand alone, that is, as a complete representation of the concept explored in the chapter. This indicates that these excerpts are not material supplemental to the assigned course material but *the* assignment. Therefore, the excerpts, in addition to being quantitatively substantial, are qualitatively significant.

4. *The Effect of the Use on Potential Markets for or Value of the Copyrighted Work*

The fourth factor, market effect, also fails the defendant. This factor has been held to be "undoubtedly the single most important element of fair use." *Harper & Row,* 471 U.S. at 566. "To negate fair use one need only show that if the challenged use 'should become widespread, it would adversely affect the *potential* market for the copyrighted work.'" *Id.* at 568 (quoting *Sony Corp.,* 464 U.S. at 451, emphasis added).

Kinko's confirms that it has 200 stores nationwide, servicing hundreds of colleges and universities which enroll thousands of students. The potential for widespread copyright infringement by defendant and other commercial copiers is great. In this case, Kinko's has admitted that its market for these anthologies or packets is college students. The packets were compiled as a result of orders placed by professors at Columbia University, New York University and the New School for Social Research as to what readings they needed to supply their courses. In this case, the competition for "student dollars" is easily won by Kinko's which produced 300 to 400-page packets including substantial portions of copyrighted books at a cost of $24 to the student. Packet #34 contained excerpts from 20 different books, totalled 324 pages, and cost $21.50. While it is possible that reading the packets whets the appetite of students for more information from the authors, it is more likely that purchase of the packets obviates purchase of the full texts. This court has found that plaintiffs derive a significant part of their income from textbook sales and permissions. This court further finds that Kinko's copying unfavorably impacts upon plaintiffs' sales of their books and collections of permissions fees. This impact is more powerfully felt by authors and copyright owners of the out-of-print books, for whom permissions fees constitute a significant source of income. This factor weighs heavily against defendant.

5. *Other Factors*

In this case an important additional factor is the fact that defendant has effectively created a new nationwide business allied to the publishing industry by usurping plaintiffs' copyrights and profits. This cannot be sustained by this court as its result is complete frustration of the intent of the copyright law which has been the protection of intellectual property and, more importantly, the encouragement of creative expression. Because of the vastness and transitory nature of its business (Kinko's has 200 stores nationwide which are typically located near colleges), it has become difficult for plaintiffs to challenge defendant.

Additionally, the Classroom Guidelines express a specific prohibition of anthologies. The fact that these excerpts were compiled and sold in anthologies weighs against defendant.

Kinko's claims that "the evidence shows that course packets are of tremendous importance to teaching and learning, and are the subject of widespread and extensive use in schools throughout the country" and that "an injunction against the educational photocopying at issue would pose a serious threat to teaching and the welfare of education." Defendant's Proposed Conclusions of Law, at 23. This appears to be a "fair use by reason of necessity" argument. Kinko's has failed to prove this central contention which is that enjoining them from pirating plaintiffs' copyrights would halt the educational process.

Kinko's did not produce any professor to testify that he or she uses course packets and would be disabled from teaching effectively if Kinko's could not copy without paying permissions fees. Defendant did produce a witness, Dr. Bruce Johnson, who testified to the results of a survey he conducted which showed the widespread use of course packets by college professors and the reasons for this use. Notwithstanding professors' complaints of costly original materials, rapid change in course subject matter, and inadequate current offerings — which are all good reasons for desiring anthologies — defendant's witnesses did not produce evidence which would explain why they could not seek and pay for permission to create these anthologies. Dr. Johnson's survey fails to do so. This argument also fails.

B. *The Classroom Guidelines*

The Classroom Guidelines, entitled the "Agreement on Guidelines for Classroom Copying in Not-For-Profit Educational Institutions," are a part of the legislative history of the Copyright Act of 1976. H.R. Rep. No. 1476, 94th Cong., 2d Sess. 68 (1976). These Guidelines were the result of negotiation and agreement among the Ad Hoc Committee of Educational Institutions and Organizations on Copyright Law Revision, the Authors League of America, Inc., and the Association of American Publishers. *Id.* at 67....

For a proper analysis, there must be initial consideration given to the issue of what comprises educational copying and whether Kinko's status as a for-profit corporation, and its profitmaking intent, renders it outside of a Guidelines review. We believe that it does.

Kinko's contends that it serves an important function in the educational process — providing prompt, cost-effective service to educational institutions.

If they did not provide this service to colleges and universities, they claim, these institutions and their students would suffer educationally and financially. However, Kinko's is *in the business* of providing copying services for whomever is willing to pay for them and, as evidenced in this case, students of colleges and universities are willing to pay for them.

This commercial copying can be contrasted to library copying.... Classroom and library copying are viewed more sympathetically "since they generally involve no commercial exploitation and ... [have] socially useful objectives.... This is not true of photocopy shops, which reproduce for profit." Nimmer, § 13.05[E], at 13-93 — 13-94, & n. 69.

This court finds and concludes that even if Kinko's copying warranted review under the Classroom Guidelines, it is excessive and in violation of the Guidelines requirements.[11]

There is dispute as to whether the Guidelines represent a maximum or minimum of allowable copying. The Guidelines assert its intended meaning thusly: "the purpose of the following guidelines is to state the minimum and not the maximum standards of educational fair use under Section 107 of H.R. 2223." *Id.* at 68. The Guidelines clearly state that notwithstanding their promulgation, fair use standards may be more or less permissive — depending upon the circumstances and based upon equitable considerations.... This court finds that the copying in suit clearly deviates from the letter and spirit of the Guidelines.

Under the section "Multiple Copies for Classroom Use," the stated premise is that "multiple copies (not to exceed in any event more than one copy per pupil in a course) may be made by *or for* the teacher giving the course for classroom use or discussion...." H.R. Rep. No. 1476, at 68 (emphasis supplied). The Guidelines provide that a teacher may make multiple copies of copyrighted material if the copying meets the tests of brevity, spontaneity, and cumulative effect and so long as "each copy includes a notice of copyright." *Id.* at 68. It has already been found that Kinko's failed to include copyright notices on any of the works in suit.

Brevity, in prose, is defined as "a complete article, story or essay of less than 2,500 words," or an excerpt of "not more than 1,000 words or 10% of the work, whichever is less." *Id.* Defendant does not meet this requirement.

Spontaneity requires that "the inspiration and decision to use the work and the moment of its use for maximum teaching effectiveness [be] so close in time that it would be unreasonable to expect a timely reply to a request for permission." *Id.* at 69. Because Kinko's copying coincided with the start of each semester and was prompted by Kinko's obtaining a list of course materials from professors, we find that the copying in suit cannot be considered spontaneous. The anthologies were created to last the full semester, or at least for several weeks, since they averaged 200 to 400 pages per course packet.

---

[11] We have evaluated Kinko's acts pursuant to Guidelines requirements because we find the circumstance of copying for college students to be particularly compelling in this case, even though Kinko's is not a teacher or other educational institution and we have found no agency relationship between Kinko's and the college professors involved. See agency discussion *infra*.

Additionally, while it is true that modern teaching methods present copyright dilemmas by requiring frequent updating of information from varied sources, the excerpts in suit were not copied from current publications. The most recent publication date among the books in suit was 1985.

Cumulative effect proscribes any more than "nine instances of multiple copying for one course during one class term," limits the copied material to one course only, and to no more than one piece of work per author. House Report, at 69. Defendants fail this requirement. Of the five course packets containing 7, 22, 23, 25, and 43 instances of multiple copying, four of them clearly exceed the nine permissible instances.

Anthologies. In addition to these tests, most of which defendant has failed, Kinko's conduct appears to violate a specific mandate of the Classroom Guidelines:

> III. *Prohibitions as to I and II Above.* Notwithstanding any of the above, the following shall be prohibited:
>
> (A) *Copying shall not be used to create or to replace or substitute for anthologies, compilations or collective works....*
> (C) Copying shall not: (a) substitute for the purchase of books, publishers' reprints or periodicals.
> (D) No charge shall be made to the student beyond the actual cost of the photocopying.

Id. at 69-70 (emphasis added). Plaintiffs argue that, notwithstanding the "safe harbor" provided in the spontaneity, brevity and cumulative effect requirements of Parts I and II, Part III of the Guidelines "flatly and unequivocally prohibits" copying of the sort in suit. Plaintiffs' Post-Trial Memorandum of Law, at 21 ["Plaintiffs' Post-Trial Memo"]. Defendant urges the court to seek a less rigid view of the meaning of the Guidelines. We are convinced that this is the more prudent path than a bright line pronouncement and refuse to hold that all unconsented anthologies are prohibited without a fair use analysis. However, the fact that these excerpts were placed in anthologies weighs significantly against defendant.[14] ...

V. *Relief*

[The court enjoined infringements of the works in suit and also of "works which may not now be copyrighted or even in existence but, in the future, may be copied by defendant.... When liability has been determined, a history of continuing infringement and a significant threat of future infringement exists, a court must enjoin infringement of future copyrighted works." The court enjoined the defendant "from future anthologizing and copying of plaintiffs' works without permission and prepayment of fees in the manner shown violative of the concept of fair use as proved in this case, and including similar

[14]The 1966 House Report noted: "[E]ducation is the textbook publishers' only market, and ... many authors receive their main income from licensing reprints in anthologies and textbooks; if an unlimited number of teachers could prepare and reproduce their own anthologies, the cumulative effect would be disastrous." H.R. Rep. No. 2237, 89th Cong., 2d Sess. at 62 (1966).

works not currently existing but which may in the future be owned by plaintiffs and as to which plaintiffs have not consented." As to the statutory damages sought by the plaintiffs, the court stated that it should take a number of factors into consideration: fair market value of the rights infringed, revenue lost by the plaintiff and profits gained by the defendant, the infringer's state of mind, and deterrence of future infringement. The court noted that Kinko's had failed to instruct its employees in the pertinent aspects of copyright law, evidencing that Kinko's had "remained willfully blind to the consequences of their activity.... [S]ubstantial damages are necessary to deter Kinko's future infringements.... [T]his court will assess statutory damages in the amount of $50,000 for nine of the 12 infringements, and $20,000 for three of the infringements [where the copying was less] for a total of $510,000. Here we are not attempting to measure the financial loss to the plaintiff but to deter the defendant from future infringing copying." Moreover, because Kinko's copying was willful, the court awarded attorney's fees and costs to the plaintiffs.]

2. Agency

Defendant claims it acted as the agent of the educational institutions when it copied the excerpts in suit. Section 504(c) provides that the court "shall remit statutory damages ... where an infringer believed and had reasonable grounds for believing that his or her use of the copyrighted work was a fair use ..., *if* the infringer was (i) an employee or agent of a nonprofit educational institution ...." 17 U.S.C. § 504(c)(2). Kinko's claims to demonstrate its role as an agent through several factors: the professor selects the works to be copied, directs Kinko's to copy, and seeks permission to copy *on behalf of* the professor.... Defendant cites no caselaw in support of its position that this constitutes an agency relationship.

....

Plaintiffs assert that Kinko's presented no testimony at trial from the universities involved that there was any agency relationship to demonstrate the requisite element of direction and control. Because Kinko's has not shown that the professors exerted a sufficient level of control over the relationship, we agree with plaintiffs that this defense is not available to Kinko's.

Even if Kinko's could show an agency relationship, it has not shown that its behavior was the kind anticipated by Congress and excused under section 504(c).[15] Implicit in section 504(c) is some showing that the defendant was an innocent actor. The agency relationship requires that the defendant lack con-

---

[15] By analogy, Section 108 of the House Report, entitled "Reproduction by Libraries and Archives," provides that:

> [I]t would not be possible for a non-profit institution, by means of contractual arrangements with a commercial copying enterprise, to authorize the enterprise to carry out copying and distribution functions that would be exempt if conducted by the non-profit institution itself.

H.R. Rep. No. 94-1476, 94th Cong., 2d Sess. 74 (1976). This comes as close to approximating the present circumstance as anything plainly stated in the legislative history and supports persuasively plaintiffs' argument that Congress did not intend to permit Kinko's to act as an agent of the colleges to conduct the volume of copying shown in this suit.

trol over its actions. This kind of actor, understandably, should be protected. Kinko's was no such innocent party.

Kinko's had control over the permissions process: determination whether a passage required permission or was fair use; whether permission was sought after the fair use determination; and when and how permission was pursued. The professors merely handed in the signed form, claiming responsibility, but in actuality relinquished several key aspects of control to Kinko's. Therefore, Kinko's has failed to show that it should receive remitted damages....

QUESTIONS

1. If, following the *Kinko's* decision, your university were to bring all course-related photocopying "in house" through copy centers located in various schools and departments, would this copying constitute fair use under § 107? Would it fall within the Educational Guidelines?

2. Do you agree with Judge Motley's conclusions that the purpose and character of Kinko's use are something other than educational and that Kinko's should not be treated as if it were an agent of the university and the faculty?

3. If you were a professor, were aware of the *Kinko's* decision, and wished to have Kinko's or some other commercial copy store reproduce course materials from copyrighted books, what action would you take? Would you be inclined to give up such photocopying altogether, change your syllabus, and require your students to buy the books? Would you give your students a reading list and instruct them to make their own photocopies?

4. Judge Motley adopts the concept of "transformative use" urged by Judge Leval in a recent law review article. Partisans of the transformative use theory would disqualify from the fair use privilege any copying that adds nothing to the earlier work that is reproduced or that uses it for essentially decorative purposes. To what extent has the Court of Appeals for the Second Circuit adopted the standard of transformative use? To what extent has the Supreme Court? What do you think of it?

5. Do the materials photocopied for your courses appear to satisfy the requirements of the Educational Guidelines? If the "brevity" component of the Guidelines is satisfied, why should it be necessary to satisfy as well the "spontaneity" and "cumulative effect" criteria? Is the latter criterion, viewed in isolation, wise? Can it be practicably implemented in a university setting?

6. A public school district wishes to conduct a music-performance competition. A well-regarded panel of music educators has been selected to serve as judges. The school district wishes to know whether it is free to make photocopies of the complete piece of music to be performed by the students, so that each judge may have a copy of the piece to facilitate appraisal of the students' performances. Is such photocopying permissible? *See Kansas Attorney General's Opinion,* 1981 Copyright L. Dec. (CCH) ¶ 25,331 (Aug. 25, 1981).

AMERICAN GEOPHYSICAL UNION v. TEXACO, INC.

802 F. Supp. 1 (S.D.N.Y. 1992) (appeal pending)

LEVAL, J.

This class action tests the question whether it is lawful under the U.S. Copyright Act, 17 U.S.C. § 101 et seq., for a profit-seeking company to make unauthorized copies of copyrighted articles published in scientific and technical journals for use by the company's scientists employed in scientific research. The plaintiffs are publishers of scientific and technical journals that publish copyrighted material under assignment from the authors. The defendant is Texaco Inc., one of the largest corporations in the United States, which engages in all aspects of the petroleum business from exploration through transportation and refining to retail marketing. This opinion decides the limited issue whether the making of single copies from plaintiffs' journals by a Texaco scientist is fair use under Section 107 of the Copyright Act of 1976. 17 U.S.C. § 107.... Many of the facts are not seriously disputed.

Texaco's Scientific Research. Texaco engages in substantial scientific research directed toward improving Texaco's products and developing new products and processes. Texaco employs between 400 and 500 scientists and engineers at six research centers in the United States, including one in Beacon, New York. It spends in excess of $80 million annually in carrying on scientific and technical research, including an average of approximately $37 million a year from 1985 to 1987 at the Beacon facility.

To support its research activities, Texaco subscribes to numerous scientific and technical journals, some published by various of the plaintiffs, and maintains large libraries of such materials. Texaco scientists, on learning of an article that may be helpful or important to their research, regularly make (or cause to be made by Texaco's research libraries) a photocopy to be read, kept in their personal files and used in the laboratory in the course of their research work....

Plaintiffs contend that by this photocopying Texaco infringes the plaintiffs' copyrights. In answer to the complaint, Texaco raises the defense, among others, of "fair use." It contends that such photocopying by scientists in industry is a reasonable and customary practice, necessary to the conduct of scientific research, and that it does not infringe the publishers' copyrights. The parties have stipulated that, prior to the trial of any other issues, trial would be submitted to the Court on a written record limited to the question of fair use under § 107.

Donald Chickering, II, Ph.D. For convenience and to avoid untoward discovery expenses with respect to largely duplicative matters, the stipulation provides that the trial of the issue of fair use be conducted with respect to eight photocopies found in the files of an arbitrarily selected one of Texaco's several hundred scientific researchers. The lot fell on one Donald H. Chickering, II, Ph.D., employed at the Texaco research center at Beacon, New York. Chickering's files were found to contain a number of photocopies of numerous items from various scientific and technical journals. As the subject of this limited issue trial, plaintiffs selected eight copies of complete pieces that appeared in the Journal of Catalysis, a monthly publication of Academic Press, Inc., which is one of the plaintiffs in this action.... These included four "articles," two "notes" and two "letters to the editor." Each of them was published with a copyright notice showing Academic Press as the owner of the copyright and reserving all reproduction rights. It is assumed for purposes of the trial of the fair use issue that each was indeed copyrighted matter and that the copyright had been validly assigned by the authors to Academic Press.

In each case Chickering photocopied the entirety of the particular article, note or letter. He selected those pieces because the discussion was pertinent to research that he was conducting or expected to conduct in the future and because he expected that the discussion and the information conveyed would be helpful to him in conducting research for Texaco. Although Texaco's papers and the affidavits of its personnel repeatedly refer to Chickering's use of these materials as his "personal" use, it is clear that this refers to research pursuant to Chickering's employment for the benefit of his employer Texaco.

Academic Press and the Journal of Catalysis. Academic Press, the publisher of Catalysis, is a major publisher of scholarly scientific, technical and medical journals, monographs and books. Academic Press is a wholly-owned subsidiary of Harcourt Brace Jovanovich, Inc., the nation's largest scientific and medical book and journal publisher. Currently, Academic Press publishes 105 scientific, medical and technical journals covering a wide range of specialties in the physical, life and behavioral sciences.

Catalysis first appeared in 1962. It is published monthly. It includes three classes of items: articles, notes and letters to the editor. They vary in form and size, articles being the longest, letters to the editor the shortest. (Because there is no functional distinction between the three for purposes of this inquiry, they are all referred to here as "articles.") All articles in the journal are devoted to scientific and technical matters. Each monthly issue is around 200 pages long and contains approximately 20-25 articles.

Every article published in Catalysis is unsolicited; none is written by Academic Press employees. Academic Press does not pay authors for the right to publish an article. Authors interested in publishing in Catalysis are directed to submit their articles directly to one of the journal's two editors. Authors are informed that if their manuscript is accepted for publication, the copyright in the article, including the right to reproduce the article in all forms and media, shall be assigned to Academic Press....

Academic Press sells two types of subscriptions to Catalysis: an institutional rate, which is charged to both profit and nonprofit institutions, and an individual rate. In 1989, an institutional subscription to Catalysis cost $828. The individual rate is half the institutional rate. The subscription rates have increased since 1972 at a rate more than three times the increase in the Consumer Price Index. Texaco's Beacon facility, which pays the institutional rate, had purchased one subscription to Catalysis until 1983, when it doubled its subscriptions. In 1988, the Beacon facility increased its subscriptions to three, the number it continues to purchase to date.

In addition to yearly subscriptions, Academic Press offers back issues of Catalysis for sale. Back issues are available separately for three years following publication. Thereafter, they are bound together as annual volumes and are offered only in that form. In addition, reprints are available, with the author's prior approval, but only on a minimum order of 100 copies. Each order for reprints is printed separately and takes an average of three weeks to be filled.

The Copyright Clearance Center: Authorizations to Copy. Academic Press also offers users authorization to photocopy pieces from Catalysis through the mechanism of the Copyright Clearance Center Inc. ("CCC"). The CCC is a nonprofit, central clearing-house established in 1977 by publishers, authors and photocopy users which, as agent for publishers, grants blanket advance permission for a fee to photocopy copyrighted material registered with CCC, and forwards the fees collected to copyright owners, net of service charge. CCC was formed in response to a Congressional recommendation that an efficient mechanism be established to license photocopying.... CCC's Board of Directors is comprised of representatives from the publishing, author and photocopy-user communities. As of 1990, approximately 8,000 domestic and foreign publishers had registered approximately 1.5 million publications with CCC.

Currently, CCC offers two principal services for obtaining advance permission to photocopy copyrighted material that publishers have registered with the CCC. The first method, inaugurated in 1978, is called the Transactional Reporting Service ("TRS"). TRS provides photocopy users with blanket permission to photocopy from any CCC-registered publication, provided the user subsequently reports the making of the photocopy and pays the fees required by the copyright owner. The fee is printed on the first page of each article. The fee for each copy of an article in Catalysis has been $2 from 1978 through 1982 and $3 thereafter.... Since January 1, 1983, the information provided to CCC has been reduced to the journal's standard International Standard Serial Number ("ISSN"), publication year, and the photocopy permissions fee set by the publisher (multiplied by the number of copies made). (The necessary information is set forth at a lower corner of the first page of each article in the journal.)[5] To comply with TRS, a user company might place log sheets at photocopy machines. Whenever company personnel made copies of material covered by CCC, they would make a log entry noting the journal number and year, the numbers of pages and of copies, and the fees prescribed. Library personnel would collect these logs and submit them monthly to CCC with payment.

Some major corporate users objected to the administrative costs of training personnel and setting up recordkeeping necessary for full compliance with TRS. Jane C. Ginsburg, *Reproduction of Protected Works for University Research or Teaching,* 39 J. Copyright Soc'y 181, 209 (1992) (hereinafter

---

[5] Each issue of Catalysis also contains a masthead statement asserting:

No part of this publication may be reproduced or transmitted in any form or by any means, electronic or mechanical, including photocopy, recording, or any information storage and retrieval system, without permission in writing from the copyright owner.

The appearance of the code at the bottom of the first page of an article in this journal indicates the copyright owner's consent that copies of the article may be made for personal or internal use, or for the personal or internal use of specific clients. This consent is given on the condition, however, that the copier pay the stated, per copy fee through the Copyright Clearance Center, Inc. ..., for copying beyond that permitted by Sections 107 or 108 of the U.S. Copyright Law. This consent does not extend to other kinds of copying, such as copying for general distribution, for creating new collective works, or for resale. Copy fees for pre-1982 articles are the same as those shown for current articles.

"Ginsburg, Reproduction of Protected Works"). In response, in 1983, CCC inaugurated a second service for obtaining advance permission to photocopy that eliminated the TRS's reporting requirements. This was the Annual Authorization Service ("AAS"). AAS was designed by two econometricians working with the cooperation of major corporate users. Under the AAS, the corporate user is granted a blanket annual license to make photocopies for internal use of any copyrighted material contained in any of the journals and books registered with the CCC. The annual license fee is determined on the basis of a limited photocopying survey, factored by the licensee's employee population and the copying fees for the journals regularly copied by that user. Upon payment of an annual license fee, the AAS licensee is authorized to make unlimited numbers of photocopies from CCC registered publications for internal use. The license is for one year, renewable for an additional year at the licensee's option. At the end of a two-year period a new license can be obtained.

The revenue derived from the TRS and the AAS is allocated among the publishers that have registered publications with the CCC, net of CCC's service charges, in accordance with the users' photocopying of their material. The basic fee for photocopying per unit of material is not set by CCC but rather by the individual publishers.

As of January 1991, there were approximately 400 users reporting under the TRS method, and over 100 corporate licensees under the AAS method. The AAS licensees include eleven major petroleum companies (Exxon, Mobil Oil, Amoco, Ashland Oil, BP America, Chevron, Marathon Oil, Atlantic Richfield, Occidental Petroleum, Phillips Petroleum, and Sun Refining and Marketing) as well as other major research-oriented corporations including Allied Signal, Ciba-Geigy, AT&T and its Bell Labs Division, DuPont, Eastman Kodak, Dow Corning, General Electric, IBM, Monsanto, Olin, PPG, Polaroid, Texas Instruments, 3M, Union Carbide, United Technologies and USX. As of January 1991, total permission fees paid to CCC under the TRS program from its inception have amounted to approximately $9 million. Total fees paid by licensees under the AAS program from its inception to January 1985 have amounted to about $18 million. CCC's combined TRS and AAS revenue and distributions have increased each year.

Copyright Protection and the Doctrine of Fair Use

....

First Factor — The Purpose and Character of the Secondary Use

Throughout the development of the fair use doctrine, courts consistently expressed preference for secondary uses that did not merely copy and offer themselves as substitutes for the original copyrighted text, but that used the matter taken from the copyrighted work for some new objective or purpose.... Courts eventually generalize[d] that under the first factor "productive" uses were favored. *Sony,* 446 U.S. 417, 478-479 (Blackmun, J., dissenting). (The word "productive" was not necessarily an ideal description of the line of authorities because it risked the misconception that it encompassed any copying for a socially useful purpose. In fact, ... what the early authorities had meant was a secondary use that was productive in that it produced a new purpose or result, different from the original — in other words, a secondary use that transformed, rather than superseded, the original.)...

The *Sony* holding did not overturn the preexisting concept that productive or transformative uses were favored over non-productive, merely superseding copies. It ruled only that productivity was not determinative in the inquiry, and that equitable considerations could lead to a conclusion of fair use in spite of a non-productive copying....

What has emerged since the Supreme Court's *Sony* decision seems to be a two-track pattern of interpretation of the first factor: Secondary users have succeeded in winning the first factor by reason of either (1) transformative (or productive) non-superseding use of the original, or (2) noncommercial use, generally for a socially beneficial or widely accepted purpose.

Where courts have considered transformative, productive, non-superseding secondary uses of the type that were favored in the historical development of fair use, they have attached little importance to the presence of profit motivation. Courts have recognized that most instructive publishing activity involves profit motivation. Thus text books, newspapers, criticism, historical books, medical and scientific materials, are all published in major part by commercial publishers with a profit motive. Furthermore, authors and scientists, critics and journalists, all must earn their living and frequently receive payment for their writings. The ability to quote from written texts is extremely important for such writing. If the existence of a profit motive were virtually to disqualify writing from entitlement to fair use protection, its benefits would virtually disappear, and the categories of enterprise cited in the introductory language of Section 107 — criticism, comment, news reporting, teaching, scholarship and research — would be effectively barred use of quotation unless they were done as philanthropy. Thus courts have repeatedly found in favor of transformative secondary uses on the first factor, notwithstanding the presence of profit motivation. [Citations omitted.] Thus, although courts ritualistically proclaim, almost as a mantra, that every commercial use is "presumptively" unfair, that presumption is easily overcome by a transformative, non-superseding use. [Citations omitted.]

On the other hand, as to the second track, the *Sony* opinion makes clear that at least certain nonprofit uses can qualify as fair use, even though they may involve nonproductive superseding copies. The Court of Claims in *Williams & Wilkins v. National Institute of Health* [487 F.2d 1345 (Ct. Cl. 1973), *aff'd by an equally divided Court,* 420 U.S. 376 (1975)] had reached a similar conclusion.

Williams & Wilkins involved photocopying carried on by scientists at the National Institute of Health and the National Medical Library. In making its finding of fair use the court stressed that this copying was being done by governmental nonprofit organizations devoted exclusively to the advancement of science. 487 F.2d at 1354. The court made clear that the freedom from the "taint" of commercial gain was essential to the finding of fair use. The Court of Claims strongly implied that its conclusion would have been opposite had a motive of commercial gain been present.

I conclude that on either branch of the analysis plaintiffs win the first factor, as Texaco's copying is neither transformative nor noncommercial.... Texaco's copying is not of the transformative, non-superseding type that has historically been favored under the fair use doctrine. Texaco simply makes mechanical photocopies of the entirety of relevant articles. Nor is the copy of the original employed as part of a larger whole, for some new purpose. The dimensions of the original and of the copy are identical. The principal purpose of Texaco's copies is to supersede the original and permit duplication, indeed, multiplication. A scientist can make a copy, to be read subsequently and kept for future reference, without preventing the circulation of the journal among co-workers. This kind of copying contributes nothing new or different to the original copyrighted work. It multiplies the number of copies....

Texaco argues that this copying should be considered "productive" because its purpose is to advance scientific discovery.[6] The argument fails for several reasons. That is not the kind of productivity that was intended by the discussions and holdings. [W]hat was meant was that the copying should produce something new and different from the original, and not that a superseding copy would qualify, so long as it was made in pursuit of a beneficial cause. If the latter were the meaning of the doctrine, precious little would be left of the copyright protection as applied to scholarly or scientific writing. For scholarly and scientific writing has no readership except among those who use it in scholarly and productive or educational undertakings. If that fact alone were sufficient to justify the making of superseding copies, the authors and publishers of scholarly, scientific and educational materials could not protect their copyrights and could not survive as against inexpensive copier technology....

Texaco argues also that its copies should be considered transformative because it is important for scientists like Chickering to work with a photocopy and not with the original. It argues that the original is in many ways not useful to a scientist.... The most prominent feature of this copying is that the copies supersede the original and multiply its presence. Thus even if some transformative purpose was present in transferring the article from its jour-

---

[6]Texaco points out that "research" is one of the categories listed in the introductory portion of the statute as illustrative of activities in which fair use can be found ... and that there are Second Circuit opinions that ostensibly make these categories presumptively determinative of this first factor.

I do not believe the Circuit intended by those assertions to nullify or disregard the historical focus of fair use adjudication on whether the particular use is superseding or productive. For such a ruling would contradict the Supreme Court's instruction in *Nation* that "the examples enumerated in § 107 [are] to 'give some idea of the sort of activities the courts might regard as fair use under the circumstances'.... This listing *was not intended to be exhaustive ... or to single out any particular use as presumptively a 'fair' use.*" It would fly in the face of the legislative assertion to merely "restate [the doctrine] ... not to change, narrow or enlarge it in any way." Finally, it is incompatible with the oft-stated assertion under the first factor that commercial uses are presumptively unfair.

So, for example, in *Weissman* the Circuit gave no weight to the fact that the secondary use was for "teaching," "scholarship" and "research," and awarded the first factor to the copyright owner because the secondary use was superseding, nonproductive and motivated by professional advancement.

nal into a slender photocopy, that use is overshadowed by the primary aspect of the copying, which is to multiply copies.

Finally, Texaco argues its use of copies should be considered favorably under the first factor because the principal purpose of the copying is to state reported facts accurately. A number of courts and commentators have noted that quotation can be a favored secondary use (of the transformative type) when quotation is necessary to convey factual material (or ideas) accurately, or to demonstrate the validity of assertions of fact. [Citations omitted.]

Texaco argues that photocopying by its scientists should come within this principle. It contends that its scientists have little or no interest in copying the expressive portions of the originals, that what they need are primarily the formulas, graphs and tables that set forth the results of studies and experiments. Note taking would not only consume inordinate time, but carry a high risk of costly error.

Although the argument has some merit, it does not prevail on these facts. First, Chickering and his colleagues do not copy only the formulas, graphs and tables. The eight-item sample (as well as the other photocopies) taken from Chickering's files (and others) shows that the practice is to copy the entire article. Furthermore, his deposition showed that he often made the copies before reading the original. Neither the practice nor the purpose were limited to the accurate preservation of the facts contained in formulas, graphs and tables. The major purpose of such photocopying has been multiplication of copies. This permits the scientist to defer reading, and to keep possession of an additional copy without hoarding the original issue of the journal, so that the original can circulate without delay among colleagues (each of whom may do likewise), or return to the library where all colleagues will have access to it. Texaco's argument, although ingenious, simply does not fit the facts of the case.

Texaco's copying is for commercial gain. Nor does this come within the class of copying that has prevailed under the first factor because of its nonprofit educational or social value.

Texaco contends its copying should be considered comparable to that in *Williams & Wilkins* — copying done by scientists for the purpose of advancing science, rather than for commercial gain. Texaco emphasizes the social good to be derived from its research, including the development of cleaner burning, more efficient fuels to benefit the earth's ecology and resources.... Texaco contends it shares the results of its research with the scientific community at large by encouraging its scientists to write and publish articles and make presentations at scientific symposia.

Notwithstanding all this, I cannot accept Texaco's argument. Granted, the copiers are scientists, they are using their copies to assist in socially valuable scientific research, and they do not resell the copies. Nonetheless their research is being conducted for commercial gain. Its purpose is to create new products and processes for Texaco that will improve its competitiveness and profitability. Chickering testified that he selected articles to copy because they related to the research that he was doing in the course of his employment at Texaco. The purpose of this research was in each case to improve Texaco's commercial performance.

In sum, because the secondary use in question was copying of a superseding nature (done to create additional copies of the original) and was not transformative (or productive in the fair use sense), and because it was carried on in a commercial context for the purpose of producing profits, I find that plaintiffs easily prevail on the first factor inquiring into the purpose and character of the use.

Second Factor — The Nature of the Copyrighted Work

The second factor under § 107 looks to the "nature of the copyrighted work." Although there is an aspect of the facts that favors plaintiffs, I conclude that this factor favors Texaco.

The aspect that favors the plaintiffs is that the articles and materials published in Catalysis are created for publication with the purpose and intention of benefitting from the protection of the copyright law. These are the kinds of exercises of authorship that the copyright law was designed to protect in its objective "to promote the progress of science." In contrast, there are other types of writings that enjoy copyright protection although they are made for purposes incompatible with the public-benefit objective of the copyright law, such as functional communications intended to be kept secret. Examples might be an extortion note, or a bank robber's written instructions to confederates with diagrams assigning tasks for carrying out the robbery. Such writings in no way partake of the purpose to promote the advance of knowledge; they may enjoy a lower claim to protection from fair use than writing created for public dissemination with the intent to benefit from the protections of the copyright.

Copyright protection is vitally necessary to the dissemination of scientific articles of the sort that are at issue. This is not because the authors insist on being compensated. To the contrary, such articles are written and published without direct payment to the authors. But copyright protection is essential to finance the publications that distribute them. Circulation of such material is small, so that subscriptions must be sold at very high prices. If cheap photoduplications could be freely made and sold at a fraction of the subscription price, Catalysis would not sell many subscriptions; it could not sustain itself, and articles of this sort would simply not be published. And without publishers prepared to take the financial risk of publishing and disseminating such articles, there would be no reason for authors to write them; even if they did, the articles would fail to achieve distribution that promoted the progress of science. Being the type of authorship that the copyright laws were designed to protect, this type of publication has a stronger claim to protection from copying than secretive private functional communications. See discussion in Leval, *Toward a Fair Use Standard,* at 1116-1122.

On the other hand, courts have often observed that "the scope of fair use is greater with respect to factual than nonfactual works." [Citations omitted.]... The material here being copied by Texaco's scientists is "essentially factual in nature, *Maxtone-Graham,* 803 F.2d at 1263, consisting of reports on scientific experimental research. The texts describe procedures followed and characterize the results found. Results are expressed largely in tables and graphs. I therefore conclude that the second factor favors Texaco.

Third Factor — Amount and Substantiality of Portion Used

The third factor looks to "the amount and substantiality of the portion used in relation to the copyrighted work as a whole." This factor clearly favors the plaintiffs, as Chickering has copied the entirety of the copyrighted articles in question. The Supreme Court acknowledged in *Sony* that the reproduction of an entire copyrighted work ordinarily "militates against a finding of fair use." *Sony*, 464 U.S. at 450 ....

Texaco argues that its scientists should be found to have copied only a small fraction of the copyrighted work when they photocopy an entire article. Texaco points out that Academic Press registers entire issues of the Journal of Catalysis with the Copyright Office and does not register separately the individual articles. As an average issue of Catalysis is around 200 pages long while an average article is 8 to 10 pages long, Texaco argues that the photocopying of an article copies approximately 4% of the copyrighted work.

This argument constitutes imaginative lawyering, but it does not prevail. Each article, note or letter published in Catalysis is a separately authored work, protected by a copyright, which the authors have assigned to Academic Press. Because it would involve gigantic expense and inconvenience to register separately each of the 20 odd items that appear in an individual issue, Academic Press registers each issue with the Copyright Office. It does not follow from the manner of registration with the Copyright Office that the "copyrighted work" for the purposes of fair use analysis consists of the entire issue rather than the separate creations of the separate authors. Plaintiffs win the third factor.

Fourth Factor — Effect on the Market for the Copyrighted Work

The fourth factor looks at "the effect of the use upon the potential market for or value of the copyrighted work." Plaintiffs contend that were it not for the photocopying practiced by Texaco's scientists, Texaco would need to provide its scientists additional copies through any one or more of a number of different routes, all of which would substantially supplement the revenues of the copyright owning publishers.[14] Plaintiffs argue Texaco could purchase additional subscriptions; it could purchase back issues or back volumes; it could order tear sheets from document delivery services that purchase sub-

---

[14] In appraising the effect of Texaco's photocopying on the values of the publishers' copyrights, Chickering's eight copies are considered as representative, and not as the universe of alleged infringement. Chickering is one of 400-500 scientists employed by Texaco in research. His files contained numerous copies of items from Catalysis, as well as from other publications. This does not include additional copies Chickering may have made from time to time and later discarded. Texaco's own evidence is to the effect that such photocopying is "customary" among scientists employed in research. The evidence submitted, including the annual license fees established by CCC for similar large petroleum companies, supports the inference of voluminous photocopying in the aggregate by Texaco's scientists, that would justify very substantial license fees if such copying is not fair use.

scriptions; it could order photocopies from document services that make copies under license agreements with the plaintiff-publishers and pay royalties to the publishers for all copies made; it could negotiate a license directly with a particular publisher to pay a blanket fee for the right to make photocopies at will; or, alternatively, Texaco could photocopy articles as needed for its scientists by operating under the TRS or AAS license services offered by the CCC.

I find that plaintiffs have powerfully demonstrated entitlement to prevail as to the fourth factor.

Texaco does not seriously contest that its scientists need photocopies of pertinent scientific journal articles to use in conducting their research. Indeed, Texaco argues the need is so great that it should dictate a finding of fair use. (This argument is discussed below in the section on equitable factors.) It is clear that, if the making of unauthorized photocopies is found not to be a fair use, Texaco will nonetheless continue to provide its scientists with copies, so long as there exists a means of doing so that is not excessively expensive or burdensome. The publishers have persuasively shown that there exist convenient and reasonably priced procedures by which Texaco could obtain the necessary additional copies for its scientists. If court rulings established that the existing practice of making photocopies violates plaintiffs' copyright, Texaco would resort to one or more of these procedures to provide its scientists with copies that are necessary for their research, and Texaco's doing so would add significantly to the plaintiffs' revenues and the value of its copyrights.

... I accept as correct that Texaco would not ordinarily fill the need now being supplied by photocopies through the purchase of back issues or back volumes. I accept also that Texaco would not fill this need by enormously enlarging the number of its subscriptions. Nonetheless, this does not significantly undermine the plaintiffs' position.

The plaintiffs have shown that there are a variety of other avenues Texaco could and would follow to provide its scientists promptly and relatively inexpensively with working copies of articles for their files (which would produce revenues for the publishers). These include the ordering of photocopies from document delivery services that would pay royalties to the publishers, the negotiation of blanket licenses with individual publishers, and the use of a CCC license under either the TRS or the AAS.

Morever, although I accept Texaco's contention that it would not replace its scientists' individual copies by vastly increasing the number of subscriptions, the evidence supports the inference that, if Texaco stopped photocopying, it would increase the number of subscriptions somewhat. It is important that scientific and technical journals be promptly circulated so that research scientists are made promptly aware of new published studies in the areas of their work. Previously, Texaco has increased the number of its subscriptions to Catalysis (from one to two and later to three) in order to speed up the circulation process. The evidence shows that scientists will make a photocopy of an article in order not to slow down the circulation process. If that photocopying stopped, the circulation would slow down; scientists would hold onto an issue for a longer time before continuing its routing. To speed up the circulation, it seems likely that Texaco would add at least a modest number of subscriptions to Catalysis which would increase Academic Press' revenues. Nor does

Texaco's evidence contradict the probability that, if it stopped photocopying, its scientists would place orders for photocopies with document delivery services; such document services would promptly make and deliver photocopies, bill Texaco a modest fee, and pay royalties to the publisher under a private license agreement.

Finally, as noted above, the publishers have shown that the copying licenses offered by CCC would also satisfy the needs of Texaco's scientists for photocopies at a reasonable cost and burden to Texaco. This would provide significant additional revenue to the publishers and add value to their copyrights....

Texaco also argues that Academic Press' growing subscription revenues and glowing profitability disprove that it is being harmed by Texaco's photocopying practices.... The argument has no merit. Furthermore, it distorts the statutory standard. In order to prevail on the fourth factor, the copyright owner is not required to demonstrate that it has been reduced to poverty by the defendant's copying. Rather, "to negate fair use one need only show that if the challenged use 'should become widespread, it would adversely affect the *potential* market for the copyrighted work.'" *Nation,* 471 U.S. at 458 (*quoting Sony,* 464 U.S. at 451) (emphasis added). The fact that the copyright owner is realizing rich profits from the exploitation of its copyrights despite the unauthorized copying has no logical tendency to prove that the secondary user's copying is not diminishing those profits. If the copyright owner would be receiving significantly higher revenue but for the defendant's uncompensated copying, the standard is satisfied, regardless of revenues already being received....

Finally, Texaco argues that courts should not attach undue importance to the fourth factor of loss of copyright revenue.... Texaco is quite right in my view that to give dominant significance to loss of revenue under the fourth factor can result in denying protection to secondary uses that richly deserve it on the basis of other factors (primarily the first). Suppose, for example, a nonprofit foundation for the study of history produces a new history of the cold war, including fascinating insights into the motivations of Krushchev, substantiated by a few brief quotations from speeches and writings previously unknown in this country. Assume that examination of the first three factors would powerfully indicate a fair use, but the enormous sales of the new book would generate a substantial royalty if the quotations are not fair use. Will the loss of potential royalty income convert a fair use into an infringement — subject even to injunction — because of the asserted predominance of the fourth factor? The same question can be put as to a parody. If the fourth factor is by far the most important, this may mean a parody that flops is a fair use, but a commercially successful parody infringes.

There is considerable force in Texaco's argument that this should not be the law.... [The district judge hypothesized an important historical work, produced by a nonprofit foundation, which quoted briefly from previously unknown speeches and writings of a major foreign political figure. He concluded that any possibly substantial royalty income for such quotation ought not to outweigh all other factors pointing toward fair use.] The importance of the fourth factor should depend on the analysis produced by examination of all the factors. If the other factors clearly indicate that the secondary use should be considered fair use, then the copyright owner's deprivation of royalty revenue might play very little role in the analysis.

In short, Texaco argues that all four factors should play a role; that fair use inquiry is highly fact-specific, and that the degree to which one or another factor dominates in a particular analysis will change from instance to instance. I believe that Texaco's arguments express a correct understanding of the law of fair use. I do not think the Supreme Court would disagree with Texaco's argument. The statement in the *Nation* that the fourth factor "is the single most important element," 471 U.S. at 566, assumes a greater importance when quoted in isolation than it projected in the context of the *Nation* opinion as a whole. For, in going through the factors one by one, the Supreme Court ascribed importance to each of them.... Notwithstanding the oft-quoted assertion of the paramount importance of the fourth factor, I agree with Texaco that in an appropriate case the Supreme Court would give proper importance to the other statutory factors and would not allow the mere loss of hypothetical royalty revenue to convert a fair use into an infringement.

Nonetheless this argument does not help Texaco in this case. This is not a case where hypothetical loss of revenue arguably converts fair use to infringement. Here, without reaching the fourth factor, analysis of the other considerations strongly favors the plaintiffs' contention that Texaco's copying infringes the publishers' copyrights. The fourth factor merely confirms that conclusion. Thus, even if the Supreme Court would agree that the fourth factor is not always the most important, that would not help Texaco here.

In view of the fact that the publishers have demonstrated a substantial harm to the value of their copyrights through such copying, the fourth factor gives strong support to the conclusion that this copying is not a fair use.

Equitable Rule of Reason

The Supreme Court in *Sony* characterized the fair use doctrine as an "equitable rule of reason."... *Sony*, 464 U.S. at 448 & n.31 (quoting H. Rep. No. 94-1476, at 66-66, U.S. Code Cong. & Admin. News 1976 at 5680), and explained in *Stewart* that the fair use doctrine "'permits courts to avoid rigid application of the copyright statute when, on occasion, it would stifle the very creativity which that law is designed to foster.'" *Stewart*, 495 U.S. at 236 (quoting *Iowa State University Research Foundation, Inc. v. American Broadcasting Cos.*, 621 F.2d 57, 60 (2d Cir. 1980)); see generally, Lloyd L. Weinreb, *Fair's Fair: A Comment on the Fair Use Doctrine*, 103 Harv. L. Rev. 1137 (1990). The statute, furthermore, does not characterize the four listed factors as exclusive. Thus, although I find that analysis under the four enumerated factors strongly favors the plaintiffs, I go on to consider a number of equitable arguments proffered by Texaco that do not fit neatly into the four-factor analysis....

[The court assessed and rejected Texaco's claim that its fair use assertion was essentially parallel to those sustained in *Sony* and *Williams & Wilkins*. After reiterating the differences between *Sony* and the instant case, Judge Leval turned to *Williams & Wilkins*.] Some of the differences call for comment. Those are the Court of Claims' conclusion that medicine and medical research would be "seriously hurt" if NIH and NML were forbidden from engaging in the copying practice, see 487 F.2d at 1356; and that a solution to the problem was beyond the court's power. See 487 F.2d at 1359-1360. Since the time of that decision, circumstances have substantially changed; such findings are no longer justified.

A problem that has bedeviled the application of the copyright laws to the making of copies has been the transaction costs of arriving at a license agreement, when a small number of photocopies is made. An honest user, who would be happy to pay a reasonable royalty, faces the problem of the enormous administrative difficulty and expense of making an agreement with the copyright owner for a license to make a single copy. Notwithstanding that the transaction might ultimately involve a fee of no more than a few dollars, enormous time, expense and burden may be involved for both sides in reaching such an agreement. The would-be copier would need to write to the copyright owner (assuming the name and current address can be readily found in the publication), propose a license and ask what the fee would be. The copyright owner would need to set a fee for the proposed transaction (if it did not have standardized rates) and to write back to the copier, who might then accept the proposed royalty fee (or make a counter offer). Eventually, through an exchange of correspondence involving a minimum of three letters, agreement could be reached, the copier would send a check for a few dollars to cover the royalty, and proceed to make a copy. A two-dollar royalty might easily engender hundreds of dollars of transaction costs, consuming many wasted hours. It might also delay the making of the copy for weeks.

Because of the outlandishly wasteful delay, expense, and inconvenience involved in negotiating such a transaction, virtually no user has been willing to do it.[20] It therefore became a widespread practice that universities, foundations, research institutes and business companies simply photocopied without authorization. In *Williams & Wilkins* the court noted that during 1970 NIH's library made about 93,000 photocopies, aggregating nearly 1,000,000 pages. Since that time the volume of publications and the practice of photocopying have so proliferated, it is likely that today's numbers are vastly higher. It is clear that scientists at the NIH could not reasonably have entered into negotiations with medical publishers every time their work called for the making of a photocopy of a journal article. The *Williams & Wilkins* court therefore had considerable basis for concluding that medical research would have been substantially harmed by a ruling forbidding such unauthorized copying. Researchers might have been forced to do without photocopies, which would have been a substantial impediment to their research, or would have needed to engage in absurdly inefficient negotiations. The Court of Claims contemplated that the problem might conceivably be solved by the establishment of compulsory license fees, but concluded that this was beyond the court's power.

---

[20] Moreover, because hypothetical royalty payments at issue are so small for each copy, it was not practicable for copyright owners to seek to enforce their rights. See *Collectives That Collect* at 2-3.

The monumental change since the decision of *Williams & Wilkins* in 1973 has been the cooperation of users and publishers to create workable solutions to the problem. See generally *Collectives That Collect* at 45-53. Most notable has been the creation of the CCC, and its establishment of efficient licensing systems — the TRS, established in 1978, followed by the AAS, established in 1983. Because some large users found that the TRS imposed administrative and recordkeeping burdens more onerous than they were eager to assume, the TRS was less successful than had been hoped. In response to the request of users for a system that would free them from TRS' recordkeeping burdens, the CCC developed the Annual Authorization Service. Upon the payment of a single global fee based on an audit of the user's photocopying practice, AAS permits free copying without any administrative burden of recordkeeping or reporting. As noted above, many of the largest corporations involved in research have become licensees under a CCC Annual Authorization.[21]

In addition to the framework created by the CCC, publishers and individual users have also, since *Williams & Wilkins,* developed private annual licensing agreements. For example, AT&T Bell Labs, in addition to its membership in the CCC, has over 200 agreements with publishers covering photocopying with respect to some 350 journals that are not registered with the CCC. Furthermore, publishers have extended photocopying licenses to document delivery services.

In this manner, private cooperative ingenuity has found practical solutions to what had seemed unsurmountable problems. Texaco can no longer make the same claims as were successfully advanced by the NIH to the Court of Claims in 1973. A finding that such unauthorized copying is an infringement would no longer impede the progress of science. Texaco could conveniently, and without undue administrative burden, retain the benefits of photocopying at will, simply by complying with one of the CCC's licensing systems.

Texaco contends that the availability of CCC authorizations is irrelevant to this action. It contends this is so because it needs no authorization if the copying is a fair use. This is so, but it does not support the claim of irrelevance. Texaco's strongest arguments may be that photocopying has become "reasonable and customary," *Nation,* 471 U.S. at 550, and that failure to

---

[21]Two other CCC licensing programs are illustrative of the ways in which mechanisms have evolved in the age of photocopying to protect the copyrights of authors and publishers without imposing impracticable burdens on photocopy users. First, the CCC has established the Academic Pilot Licensing Program with several universities to develop a blanket licensing program modeled on the AAS for university photocopying. It is expected that the blanket license will cover individual and collective research or administrative reprography, but not "course packets," which are expected to continue to be licensed on a transactional basis. See Ginsburg, *Reproduction of Protected Works,* at 210 and Appendix C.

Second, following this court's decision in *Basic Books, Inc. v. Kinko's Graphics Corp.,* 758 F. Supp. 1522 (S.D.N.Y. 1991) (finding that photocopy business' unauthorized copying of excerpts from books for compilation into university course packets was not a fair use), the CCC received between 1200 to 2000 daily requests for permissions from photocopy businesses. In response, the CCC started the Academic Permissions Service ("APS"). APS is a transactional license program for the purpose of creating course packets and anthologies that is available to copy shops, as well as university copy centers and departments. See Ginsburg, *Reproduction of Protected Works* at 210-211.

permit it would substantially harm scientific research, as *Williams & Wilkins* found. Those arguments depend, however, on the absence of a convenient, reasonable licensing system. Now because of CCC's licensing arrangements (and the other parallel steps taken by the owner-user communities), those consequences no longer obtain. Reasonably priced, administratively tolerable licensing procedures are available that can protect the copyright owners' interests without harming research or imposing excessive burdens on users. To the extent such photocopying was "customary," it has become far less so as many giant corporate users have subscribed to the CCC systems. To the extent the copying practice was "reasonable" in 1973, it has ceased to be "reasonable" as the reasons that justified it before the CCC have ceased to exist....

The availability of a TRS or AAS license from the CCC renders moot the argument that so influenced *Williams & Wilkins* that a finding of infringement would harm science. The acceptance and use of CCC services by large research-oriented business corporations, including eleven major petroleum companies, undermines Texaco's reliance on the contention that unauthorized photocopying is customary and reasonable in private industrial research laboratories.

Exercising imaginative advocacy, Texaco musters a number of other equitable arguments that are superficially seductive but, in the end, unpersuasive. Pointing out that the authors (who are the intended beneficiaries of the copyright law) are not paid for their work and generally favor liberal photocopying rights, Texaco seeks to characterize the publishers as greedy abusers who obtain their merchandise for free, sell it at a high profit and finally seek to stifle scientific research by extorting tribute for photocopying. Virtually every segment of this construct is flawed, illogical and contrary to the principle on which the copyright law is founded.

First, it is misleading to characterize the authors as unpaid. Although it is true that Academic Press and similar publishers do not pay authors money to publish their articles, the authors derive benefit from the publication of their works far more important than any small royalty the traffic might bear. Authors of such scientific and technical material have a substantial economic motivation as well as other interests in having their studies published in prestigious journals. Such publication enhances their professional reputations in a manner that translates itself into remuneration. The remuneration is achieved through growth of prestige and a consequent ability to command greater salaries or more prestigious and powerful positions. Cf. *Weissmann*, 868 F.2d at 1324 ("In an academic setting, profit is ill-measured in dollars. Instead, what is valuable is recognition because it so often influences professional advancement and academic tenure"). It is by their choice that authors publish in such journals as Catalysis, notwithstanding absence of payment.

Secondly, the fact that many authors favor a liberal photocopy practice is completely irrelevant, by reason of the fact that these authors have assigned their copyright, and with it, their rights of authorship. It is true that the copyright law grants exclusive rights in their writings to the authors. See 17 U.S.C. § 201(a). But by the same token, it grants to authors the power to assign those rights, 17 U.S.C. § 201(d)(1), which they have done. Authors recognize that publishers have little incentive to assume the financial risks of publishing unless the publisher is protected from copying. Accordingly, it is commonplace for authors to assign their rights of authorship to publishers for at least some agreed time on whatever terms may be available. Having made such assignment, the author cannot continue to control the benefits of the copyright.

It is not surprising that authors favor liberal photocopying; generally such authors have a far greater interest in the wide dissemination of their work than in royalties — all the more so when they have assigned their royalties to the publisher. But the authors have not risked their capital to achieve dissemination. The publishers have. Once an author has assigned her copyright, her approval or disapproval of photocopying is of no further relevance.

Finally, Texaco's argument seeks to undermine the publishers' legitimacy in seeking compensation for photocopying by reason of their substantial profits. This argument is both unfounded in fact and wrong as a matter of copyright law. Notwithstanding the evidence of the current prosperity of Academic Press, Texaco has certainly not shown that the publication of scientific materials is a business that commands excessive profits. To the contrary, plaintiffs have shown that the publication of scientific journals requires a large investment and a long period of losses endured in the hope of reaching eventual profitability.

Furthermore, Texaco's attempt to deprecate the interest of the copyright owner by reason of profits it has realized through its copyrights is directly contrary to the theory on which the copyright law is premised. The copyright law *celebrates* the profit motive, recognizing that the incentive to profit from the exploitation of copyrights will redound to the public benefit by resulting in the proliferation of knowledge. Again quoting Madison, "The public good fully coincides ... with the claims of individuals." The Federalist, No. 43 at 186. The profit motive is the engine that ensures the progress of science. The principle is admirably demonstrated by the facts of this case. Through its ability to profit from its exclusive rights over the works assigned to it, Academic Press has expanded its range so that it publishes 105 scientific, medical and technical journals. The result is the progress of science; the means is the profit motive, which is underwritten by the law of copyright. Texaco's demagogic effort to undermine the publishers' rights by tarring them as wealthy profiteers carries no force in copyright analysis, which does not begrudge copyright profits....

QUESTIONS

1. Judge Leval's determination that large-scale photocopying is not fair use when a "convenient, reasonable licensing system" is available enjoys support in the international copyright community. The World Intellectual Property Organization has proposed a protocol to the Berne Convention that would permit member countries to impose a fair use-like exemption on photocopying (for noncommercial, educational purposes), but only if no collective licensing arrangement is available in the member country. *See* WIPO, Committee of Experts on a Possible Protocol to the Berne Convention for the Protection of Literary and Artistic Works, ¶¶ 76-103, BCP/CE/I/3 (September 20, 1991).

There is growing agreement that the photocopy machine, and analogous more recent technologies such as the optical scanner, have created a market for excerpts of copyrighted works. If copyright owners can administer that market, for example, through (in Judge Leval's words) "reasonably priced, administratively tolerable licensing procedures," then copying excerpts without payment unfairly undermines an important source of revenue.

Do you agree that the "fairness" of the copying should depend on its amenability to reasonable copyright enforcement? In other words, is it merely circular to conclude that a copyright owner can convert a "fair use" into an unfair one, simply by asserting a willingness to collect royalties and creating convenient measures for doing so?

2. Do you believe that the district court correctly decided the *Texaco* case? Do you agree, for example, that the first factor cuts against the defendant even though its copying was not for resale but rather for utilization in research? Do you agree, for example, with the court's conclusion that photocopying of the type done by Dr. Chickering was neither customary nor reasonable? (Even if it is customary and reasonable, should that affect the fair use analysis?)

3. How should the analysis and outcome of the *Texaco* case be affected under the following changed assumptions: (a) The defendant is a law firm, whose partners and associates make single copies of articles in law reviews and other periodicals for retention in their files or brief cases? (b) The defendant is a university, whose faculty members make single copies of articles in learned journals for retention in their research files? (c) The defendant is a state government, whose judges (and their law clerks) make single copies of journal articles to assist in the research and drafting of court opinions?

4. Assume that, following *Texaco,* the defendant company, or one like it, uses an optical scanner to digitize its entire current library of reference books and periodicals. It also digitizes all incoming books and periodicals. The material (assume all of it is under copyright) is now available to all of Texaco's researchers, simultaneously. As a result, Texaco eliminates its extra hardcopies of books and journals, and cuts back on the number of current subscriptions to journals, limiting itself to one hardcopy per work. Texaco's library software permits researchers not only to access reference books and periodicals on individual work stations, but to download all or part of the work to disk or paper. The software also allows the accessed material to be searched according to a variety of protocols (e.g., key words, or phrases). You are counsel to Texaco. Is all or any part of Texaco's new program fair use? If the program, in whole or in part, is not fair use, how would you advise satisfying the various copyright interests at stake?

Would your analysis be significantly altered if the corporate user were a nonprofit university, which employs the software to generate course materials, available to students on-line, on disk, or in hardcopy?

COLLECTIVE ADMINISTRATION OF THE REPRODUCTION RIGHT AND OTHER ISSUES OF MODERN COPYING TECHNOLOGY

As Judge Leval's *Texaco* opinion emphasizes, the advent of the Copyright Clearance Center, and its "administratively tolerable" program for licensing photocopy rights was crucial to the rejection of the copier's fair use claim. The student has already encountered collective licensing, in the materials on ASCAP's and BMI's enforcement of the public performance right in nondramatic musical compositions, *supra*. The impetus for an organization like the CCC parallels the concerns that prompted the creation and development of the music licensing societies. In both cases, many unauthorized exploitations escape the notice of individual rights holders. Just as monitoring and seeking compensation for small-scale, obscure music uses, such as performances in local bars or on telephone "hold," would be arduous and costly for any single copyright owner, so tracking and billing for copies made for individual or for intra-corporate use would be onerous, intrusive, and ill-adapted to individual enforcement. Yet ready availability of copying media, such as photocopiers, optical scanners, and computer printers, makes even massive and systematic, yet essentially hidden, copying not only possible but pervasive.

Photocopying and similar widely disseminated means of reproduction thus prompts copyright holders' to collective action. Collective action also benefits copyright users, for it enables a user seeking authorization to copy many different works to obtain permission from a single source. Hence the role of the Copyright Clearance Center (CCC), a consortium of publishers of scientific and technical books and journals, formed in 1977 to respond to these needs.

Publishers registered with the CCC authorize the granting of nonexclusive licenses for all their titles. The CCC then offers users — primarily for-profit corporations engaging in considerable photocopying for research and development — yearly licenses, authorizing photocopying for internal use of any or all of the works enrolled with the CCC. The publishers set the royalty rates for the registered titles. The CCC calculates each user's license fee by applying the publishers' royalty rates for each title to statistical surveys of users' copying activities.

While the CCC's current efforts focus primarily on photocopying of printed works, the consortium is also studying application of collective licensing techniques to computer software. The increasing availability of literary works in digital format, moreover, has posed other challenges to the enforcement of the reproduction right. It is now possible to obtain access through individual computer terminals to vast amounts of material stored on CD ROMs or in on-line data bases. (A CD ROM looks like a compact disk; each disk stores four to five thousand pages of digitally encoded literary works.) Recall that entry of a work into a computer's memory, even for subsequent erasure once the machine is shut off, constitutes the making of a copy. Each time an individual user obtains access to a copyrighted work through an on-line data base (for example, users of LEXIS or WESTLAW may access certain legal treatises), a compensable reproduction has occurred. To obtain compensation for this kind of use, several publishers of research and scientific periodicals have formed another consortium, called ADONIS, which delivers regularly updated CD ROMs containing the texts of the periodicals to on-line services to which users may subscribe. The user's access to these works may be easily discerned, and remunerated on a kind of pay-per-view basis.

But if the user does not avail himself of an on-line service, the reproduction may, at least at first impression, seem more difficult to trace. Suppose, for example, the user consults a CD ROM in a library. In this case, the data base is freestanding; using the CD ROM together with a terminal and printing out some or all of its contents can be like taking a hard copy book to a photocopier. The copyright owner of a work stored on CD ROM would not be likely to know when, where, or how often the work was being reproduced.

In this instance, however, technology may not only facilitate highly diffused reproduction of copyrighted works, it may also supply the means of ensuring effective compensation for the use. Several universities have participated in an experimental program with University Microfilms Incorporated, called BART (Billing and Royalty Tracking). Each page of material entered on the BART program's CD ROMs is encoded so that a record may be made each time a page is accessed and printed out. Access to printed versions of these works is made available by means of a debit card which end-users may buy from the library. The lump sum purchase price of the card covers the making of a certain number of copies. Each time the card is inserted into a computer printer and a copy is made from the CD ROM, the corresponding number of units is deducted from the available total on the card. Many university and other libraries already have such cards for photocopiers. A photocopier card system, however, does not keep track of what materials are copied. The BART system, by contrast, does record precisely what materials have been copied, and in what quantities. As a result, the copying, even from a freestanding source, is no longer hidden, and participating copyright owners may receive royalties commensurate with the actual copying of their works.

COPYING BY NONPROFIT LIBRARIES

Section 108 of the 1976 Act sets forth a special regime favoring certain acts of copying by (primarily) nonprofit libraries. Congress in the 1976 Act thus recognized the unique social and educational functions libraries perform. However, the special library copying provisions seem best adapted to photocopying; they may require reassessment when the copying is accomplished by computer. For example, several provisions of Section 108 limit the copying privilege to the making of "facsimile" copies. That term is not defined in the Act. It is not clear that the term would cover on-screen digital representations of the work or digital copies on disk, although it might extend to printouts, particularly if they reproduced screen images that in turn captured not only the text but the graphic elements of the digitized print work. Moreover, while Section 108 permits the making of single copies for certain user requests, a digital copy can be communicated simultaneously to as many users as can be accommodated at the library's work stations, or as are connected to the library via modem.

Recent events may hasten the reevaluation of the Copyright Act's library copying privileges. In 1993, the United States Library of Congress announced plans to scan into digital form large portions of its holdings to make them available to users on-line, potentially worldwide through information retrieval services. (This phenomenon is not confined to the U.S.: the Bibliothèque de France intends to scan 300,000 volumes in its collection for the same purpose.) The enormous quantity of these libraries' holdings, and the potentially limitless copying of works received on-line that could result, threaten to erode the copyrights underlying the works made available in this fashion.

In the meantime, it is important to understand the current contours of the statutory library copying exceptions. Although at least some of the copying in which nonprofit libraries engage might well qualify for the fair use exemption, section 108 explicitly requires library copying to be considered separately (though not necessarily exclusively) from the section 107 fair use factors. Therefore, when assessing the ability of a library to copy a protected work, the relationship between sections 107 and 108 should be properly understood. The statute seems to be clear in providing the § 108 exemption entirely apart from any fair use possibilities enjoyed by the library. Section 108(f)(4). This has led to the library position that section 108 "merely identifies certain copying situations which are conclusively presumed to be legal without affecting the right of fair use which continues as a general and flexible concept of law." Library Photocopying and the U.S. Copyright Law of 1976, p. vii (Special Libraries Association Pamphlet, Dec. 29, 1977). On the other hand, the author/publisher groups take the view that "[s]ection 108 authorizes certain kinds of library photocopying that could not qualify as 'fair use.'" Photocopying by Academic, Public and Nonprofit Research Libraries 5 (Association of American Publishers, Inc., and Authors League Pamphlet, May 1978). In any event, the library exemption in section 108 does not extend to the library patron, who therefore must still rely on the § 107 formulation of fair use. Section 108(f)(2).

The provisions of section 108 may be summarized as follows: (1) It defines the coverage of works negatively through partial exclusions set forth in section 108(h). The net result is that the section is most important with respect to books, periodicals, sound recordings, and television news programs (section 108(f)(3)). (2) It sets forth general preconditions for library photocopying in section 108(a) and (g). (3) It specifies in section 108(b), (c), (d), and (e) the situations in which, under limitations and conditions over and above those in (a) and (g), works may be reproduced. (4) It covers miscellaneous matters in section 108(f) and provides in section 108(i) for a report from the Register in 1983 and at five-year intervals thereafter "setting forth the extent to which this section has achieved the intended statutory balancing of the rights of creators, and the needs of users."

To qualify, a library or archives need not be nonprofit or open to the public. It must, however, make the reproduction and distribution of material "without any purpose of direct or indirect commercial advantage" and, if not open to the public, be open at least to persons doing research in a specialized field who are not necessarily affiliated with the institution in question. The legislative interpretation of these requirements finally permitted libraries in a for-profit organization potentially to qualify, but subject to all the conditions and prohibitions of the section. H.R. Rep. No. 94-1733, *supra,* at 73-74. *But cf.* Brennan, *Legislative History and Chapter 1 of S.22,* 22 N.Y.L.S. L. Rev. 193, 202 (1976); S. Rep. No. 94-473, *supra,* at 67. Thus it is the reproduction and distribution that must be nonprofit, not the enterprise.

Additionally, the reproduction must contain a copyright notice. Section 108(a)(3). It will be interesting to note whether a library must affirmatively add some kind of notice when it has been omitted (under the temporary umbrella of section 405) or whether a library need only repeat on the reproduction itself whatever notice is affixed anywhere on the copy of the work from which the reproduction is taken. The view of certain libraries thus far is even less expansive, i.e., that this subsection merely requires a warning or "notice" that the material may be copyrighted.

The privilege is to make "no more than one copy or phonorecord of a work." Section 108(a). This means no more than one *at a time,* as long as the reproduction is "isolated and unrelated" and not "the related or concerted reproduction or distribution of multiple copies or phonorecords of the same material...." Section 108(g)(1). The additional limitation against "systematic reproduction or distribution," which applies to periodical articles, is discussed below.

Two of the situations in which reproduction is permitted for a library's own use have never caused any controversy. One, originally introduced into the 1967 House-passed H.R. 2512, 90th Cong., 1st Sess., provides for facsimile reproduction of unpublished works for archival preservation. Section 108(b). (This privilege, as well as others provided in section 108, is subject to any contractual obligation undertaken by the library in connection with the deposit of a manuscript. Section 108(f)(4).) The other permits facsimile reproduction of a published work solely for the replacement of a copy or phonorecord "that is damaged, deteriorating, lost, or stolen," but only "if the library or archives has, after a reasonable effort, determined that an unused replacement cannot be obtained at a fair price." Section 108(c). *See* H.R. Rep. No. 94-1476, *supra,* at 75-76. This provision, as well as others in section 108, is analyzed against the background of fundamental copyright concepts in Seltzer, *Exemptions and Fair Use in Copyright: The "Exclusive Rights" Tensions in the New Copyright Act,* 24 Bull. Copyright Soc'y 215, 307 (1977).

Unavailability of copies at a fair price after reasonable investigation is also the standard for the slightly more controversial "out of print" provision in section 108(c). This permits the reproduction, under such circumstances, of an entire work for a user if the library has no notice that the material will be used for other than "private study, scholarship, or research" and it prominently posts a warning to be prescribed by regulation. Section 108(e). Such a regulation has already been issued. 37 C.F.R. § 201.14 (1988).

This provision was introduced in 1969 (S. 543, 91st Cong.) as librarians responded to the commencement of the *Williams & Wilkins* case. After the trial decision favorable to the publisher in 1972, efforts were redoubled to secure an exemption for journal articles even if not "out of print." The result was the special provision in section 108(d), subject to the limiting provisions in section 108(g)(2) and partially clarified by another set of guidelines. This complex structure dealing with a narrow question may be traced as follows:

A reproduction, directly or through interlibrary "loan," may be made of "no more than one article or other contribution to a copyrighted collection or periodical issue" or of a "small part of any other copyrighted work" under the same provisions as to good faith and posted warnings as in the "out of print" provision in section 108(e).

But such reproduction, as indicated above, must be "isolated and unrelated" and specifically must not be "systematic." Section 108(g)(2). Examples of "systematic" copying are furnished in the Senate Report.

SENATE REPORT

S. Rep. No. 94-473 at 70-71 (1975)

Multiple copies and systematic reproduction

Subsection (g) provides that the rights granted by this section extend only to the "isolated and unrelated reproduction of a single copy," but this section does not authorize the related or concerted reproduction of multiple copies of the same material whether made on one occasion or over a period of time, and whether intended for aggregate use by one individual or for separate use by the individual members of a group. For example, if a college professor instructs his class to read an article from a copyrighted journal, the school library would not be permitted, under subsection (g), to reproduce copies of the article for the members of the class.

Subsection (g) also provides that section 108 does not authorize the systematic reproduction or distribution of copies or phonorecords of articles or other contributions to copyrighted collections or periodicals or of small parts of other copyrighted works whether or not multiple copies are reproduced or distributed. Systematic reproduction or distribution occurs when a library makes copies of such materials available to other libraries or to groups of users under formal or informal arrangements whose purpose or effect is to have the reproducing library serve as their source of such material. Such systematic reproduction and distribution, as distinguished from isolated and unrelated reproduction or distribution, may substitute the copies reproduced by the source library for subscriptions or reprints or other copies which the receiving libraries or users might otherwise have purchased for themselves, from the publisher or the licensed reproducing agencies.

While it is not possible to formulate specific definitions of "systematic copying," the following examples serve to illustrate some of the copying prohibited by subsection (g).

(1) A library with a collection of journals in biology informs other libraries with similar collections that it will maintain and build its own collection and will make copies of articles from these journals available to them and their patrons on request. Accordingly, the other libraries discontinue or refrain from purchasing subscriptions to these journals and fulfill their patrons' requests for articles by obtaining photocopies from the source library.

(2) A research center employing a number of scientists and technicians subscribes to one or two copies of needed periodicals. By reproducing photo-

copies of articles the center is able to make the material in these periodicals available to its staff in the same manner which otherwise would have required multiple subscriptions.

(3) Several branches of a library system agree that one branch will subscribe to particular journals in lieu of each branch purchasing its own subscriptions, and the one subscribing branch will reproduce copies of articles from the publication for users of the other branches.

Because librarians contended that the "systematic" disqualification thus introduced in the Senate swallowed up the whole exemption, a proviso was inserted by the House committee in section 108(g)(2) as follows:

> That nothing in this clause prevents a library or archives from participating in interlibrary arrangements that do not have, as their purpose or effect, that the library or archives receiving such copies or phonorecords for distribution does so *in such aggregate quantities as to substitute for a subscription to or purchase of such work.* (Emphasis added.)

This proviso, which addresses itself only to the interlibrary situation and not reproduction by a library directly for its patrons, was accepted in the House-passed version of S. 22.

The question whether this proviso would be accepted by the Senate conferees was eased by the clarification of its scope. This was accomplished by the development of guidelines by the interested parties under the aegis of the National Commission on New Technological Uses of Copyrighted Works (CONTU), directed solely to the definition of "such aggregate quantities" in the proviso to section 108(g)(2). H.R. Rep. No. 94-1733, *supra,* at 72-73. For example, the basic formula deemed to warrant subscription to a given periodical is a group of requests "within any calendar year for a total of six or more copies of an article or articles published in such periodical within five years prior to the date of the request." *Id.*

The result of this particular development is as follows: A library whose requests exceed the number set forth in the guidelines is deemed to be substituting for subscription or purchase and is therefore engaging in "systematic reproduction" within the meaning of section 108(g)(2); it would therefore lose the exemption in section 108(d). Its only recourse, unless other parts of section 108 apply, is to argue that, despite the foregoing, it is still engaging in fair use within the meaning of section 107.

It is no wonder that some libraries, preferring to avoid the mine field described above, are removing themselves from photocopying activities. Some install coin-operated machines seeking to avail themselves of the provision in section 108(f)(1) that:

Nothing in this section —

(1) shall be construed to impose liability for copyright infringement upon a library or archives or its employees for the unsupervised use of reproducing equipment located on its premises: *Provided,* That such

equipment displays a notice that the making of a copy may be subject to the copyright law....

QUESTIONS

To what extent, if any, do sections 108 and 107 excuse the following acts:

(a) Seeking to fill in gaps in its collection of Jane Austen novels, Columbus University library secures by interlibrary loan from the Penn University library copies of the missing volumes, photocopies these, and returns the originals to Penn.

(b) Same as above, except that Columbus scans the volumes into its data-base.

(c) Same as (a), except that the copied works are unpublished letters of Jane Austen, none of them currently or previously in Columbus' collection.

(d) Same as (c), except that Columbus scans the letters.

(e) Same as (a), except that the library copies the volumes at the request of a member of the university faculty.

(f) Same as (e), except that the copies are requested by an editor employed by a for-profit textbook company.

(g) The Columbus University law school library, seeking to alleviate over-crowding on its shelves, and to save subscription costs, discards its three extra sets of the West federal reporters (retaining one complete hard-copy set), and makes the cases available to users via on-line services, such as WESTLAW and LEXIS.

(h) Same as (g), except that the Columbus library scans the West reporters, and makes the database thus generated available to users.

GENERAL REVIEW QUESTIONS

1. Consider the following uses of a short song written for four-part chorus and copyrighted by *C*. Copyright infringement or fair use? (Something else?)

(a) *S* (a scholar), for convenience in research, secures a copy of the song in a music library and hand-copies it onto blank musical notation sheets.

(b) *S* pays ten cents per page to photocopy the song on the library photocopy machine.

(c) *S* reproduces the song on an electromagnetic computer tape by which he accumulates data for a computer analysis of melodic, harmonic and rhythmic patterns.

(d) *S* reproduces the song in his textbook on musical form, 5000 copies of which are being used in university music courses throughout the United States.

(e) *T* (a teacher) holds up a copy of the song (which he purchased) in front of his classroom — and then circulates it among the students — in the course of a lesson in music history.

(f) *T* uses a projection machine and projects the purchased copy of the song onto a screen in front of the classroom.

(g) *T* makes thirty photocopies of the song for use in classroom instruction.

(h) *T* makes thirty photocopies of the song for use in his music mid-term examination.

(i) *D* (glee club director) purchased twenty copies of the song for a glee club performance but in spite of precautions five students lost their copies and *G*, on the eve of performance, supplied replacement copies on the photocopy machine.

(j) *D* leads the glee club in the song as background music to stage action by the college drama club, in a play designed to raise money for the school athletic program.

2. Tom Tilden is a teacher of high school English, who regularly has his students read some of the plays of Shakespeare. Last month, the copyrighted motion picture of *Hamlet* was shown on television. Tilden used his videotape machine to make a tape of the film as it was being shown on television, and last week he ran the tape through a classroom television set so that the film could be viewed by his students during the school day. Has the Copyright Act been violated? If so, what are the remedies?

3. The Encyclopaedia Britannica produces educational films and videotapes for sale, rental, and television exhibition. It permits, for a fee, educational television station WNED in Buffalo, New York, to broadcast certain of its copyrighted films and tapes. For several years, these works have been in turn taped off-the-air by a nonprofit organization established pursuant to the New York Education Law: BOCES (the Board of Educational Services for Erie County). BOCES provides educational services on a cooperative basis to the nineteen school districts within its geographic region, and is funded by those school districts (containing 100 affiliated public schools). The BOCES Videotape and Television Service has nine employees and an annual budget of some $300,000. It maintains a library of some 5,000 tapes, many of which have been made off-the-air from WNED broadcasts, and it sends a catalogue of all of its tapes to all school teachers in the district. A teacher may fill out and return to BOCES a written request form, and BOCES will make a copy of the requested tape (typically on videotape supplied by the teacher's school) and send it to the teacher. These tapes are normally shown six or seven times, to different classes, and are then erased or sent back to BOCES in connection with a new request form. BOCES regards this as a form of "time shifting," i.e., the taping for subsequent classroom showing of a broadcast that is not initially at an optimal time for instructional purposes. The videotapes made by BOCES in this manner number in the thousands each year.

Encyclopaedia Britannica has asked BOCES to cease its videotaping of the educational films and tapes in which the Encyclopaedia owns copyright, and has insisted that BOCES instead negotiate a license whereby it may make videotapes directly from the Encyclopaedia's films or from WNED broadcasts upon the payment of royalties (based upon the number of playback machines that are used to show the videotapes in the BOCES school districts). BOCES has refused to enter into such a royalty arrangement, and continues to make and distribute videotapes, for educational purposes, of copyrighted films and tapes. The Encyclopaedia Britannica has brought an action for damages and an injunction. BOCES claims fair use. How should the case be decided? *See Encyclopaedia Britannica Educational Corp. v. Crooks,* 542 F. Supp. 1156 (W.D.N.Y. 1982), and 558 F. Supp. 1247 (W.D.N.Y. 1983).

4. Assume that a cartographer explores a hitherto uncharted geographic area and that she prepares, publishes, and copyrights a painstakingly detailed map of that area. Another individual refers to that map and makes an unauthorized chart that lists the distances between all points on the map, as well as altitudes and population (also shown on the map for the first time). Has the copyright on the map been infringed? Does the answer rest upon an analysis of copyrightability? Of infringement? Of fair use? Is there any difference in the determining factors under these analyses?

F. REMEDIES

§ 501. Infringement of copyright

(a) Anyone who violates any of the exclusive rights of the copyright owner as provided by sections 106 through [120] or of the author as provided in section 106A, or who imports copies or phonorecords into the United States in violation of section 602, is an infringer of the copyright or right of the author, as the case may be. For purposes of this chapter (other than section 506), any reference to copyright shall be deemed to include the rights conferred by section 106A(a). As used in this subsection, the term "anyone" includes any State, any instrumentality of a State, and any officer or employee of a State or instrumentality of a State acting in his or her official capacity. Any State, and any such instrumentality, officer, or employee, shall be subject to the provisions of this title in the same manner and to the same extent as any nongovernmental entity.

(b) The legal or beneficial owner of an exclusive right under a copyright is entitled, subject to the requirements of section 411, to institute an action for any infringement of that particular right committed while he or she is the owner of it. The court may require such owner to serve written notice of the action with a copy of the complaint upon any person shown, by the records of the Copyright Office or otherwise, to have or claim an interest in the copyright, and shall require that such notice be served upon any person whose interest is likely to be affected by a decision in the case. The court may require the joinder, and shall permit the intervention, of any person having or claiming an interest in the copyright.

1. INJUNCTIONS

Injunctive relief is grounded on long-established principles of equity. Section 502(a) of the 1976 Act provides that (except as against the Government) a court "may … grant temporary and final injunctions on such terms as it may deem reasonable to prevent or restrain infringement of a copyright." The Act also provides, in § 502(b), for nationwide service of such injunctions and certain mechanics for out-of-district enforcement.

Whenever equity has jurisdiction to grant an injunction by final decree, it has the power to grant a preliminary injunction, generally for the purpose of maintaining the status quo. Preliminary injunctions have been very important in copyright cases, and it is generally acknowledged that courts issue them far more routinely in such cases than in other sorts of disputes. A long-held view has been that if the plaintiff establishes a prima facie case as to validity of copyright and its infringement, a temporary injunction will generally be issued. Recent appellate cases have concluded that irreparable injury may be presumed once the plaintiff satisfactorily proves that it will likely prevail on the merits. *See, e.g., Apple Computer, Inc. v. Formula International, Inc.,* 725 F.2d 521, 525 (9th Cir. 1984).

It is also true that a permanent injunction routinely issues when copyright validity and infringement are ultimately found. Again, it is normally assumed that compensatory relief will not adequately redress the injury, often because it is difficult to assess, and that the infringement will likely continue in the future unless enjoined. An interesting and difficult issue arises when the defendant's work, rather than being merely an exact or close reiteration of the plaintiff's, incorporates the plaintiff's protectible expression only in part but adds a significant measure of independent creative elements.

In *Stewart v. Abend,* 495 U.S. 207 (1990), for example, the defendant's well-known motion picture, Rear Window, was based upon a copyrighted short story, but added creative contributions of the screen writers, the director Alfred Hitchcock, the actors Jimmy Stewart and Grace Kelly and others, the cinematographer and the composer of the musical score. Once it was determined that the continued distribution of the film was a copyright infringement, after the renewal term of the underlying short story had vested in the successors of the story writer, should the court enjoin future distribution, exhibition, and other marketing of the motion picture? (See the opinion below, *Abend v. MCA, Inc.,* 863 F.2d 1465 (9th Cir. 1988).) When a serious critical biography of a public figure incorporates and infringes a number of passages from unpublished letters still protected by copyright, should publication of the biography be enjoined? See *New Era Pubs. v. Henry Holt & Co.,* 873 F.2d 576, *rehearing en banc denied with opinions,* 884 F.2d 659 (2d Cir. 1989). In the latter case, publication of the book can be allowed by the court, provided the infringing passages are expunged; but that cannot be done with the Hitchcock film. Would an injunction in the latter case unduly penalize the film makers and deprive the public of their valuable creative contributions, and might the plaintiff's interests be adequately protected through a judicial decree allowing continued distribution and exhibition upon the payment of a reasonable royalty — equivalent to a judicially created compulsory license? Is this within the power of a court of equity? *See* P. Goldstein, Copyright § 11.2.1.1 (1989).

A question sometimes arises whether an injunction against an infringing defendant should be limited to the precise work in issue in the case. Assume, for example, that a T-shirt distributor has been found liable for infringing the copyright on the Disney characters Mickey and Minnie Mouse, and the trial court has found that, absent an injunction, there is a likelihood of continued infringements. Disney asks the court to include in its injunctive order a direction to refrain from copying, as well, Donald Duck, Huey, Duey, Louie, Pluto, Goofy and Roger Rabbit — all characters in whom Disney owns the copyright. Should this broad injunction be issued? *See Walt Disney Co. v. Powell,* 897 F.2d 565 (D.C. Cir. 1990).

Somewhat more difficult is the question whether an injunction should extend so as to bar copying of works that the plaintiff will create in the future, and that the court concludes the defendant is likely to infringe unless directed otherwise. Suppose, for example, a "videoclip" service is in the business of making what the court finds to be infringing videotapes of copyrighted news broadcasts, and markets the clips to the persons or institutions depicted in the various news segments. Is it proper for the trial court to enjoin taping of the plaintiff's future news programs for such an illicit purpose? Or does this, as the defendant argues, undermine the requirement in § 411(a) of the Copyright Act that copyright in a work be registered before an infringement action may be brought? Is the answer to be found in the text of § 502(a)? *See ibid.*; *Basic Books v. Kinko's Graphics Corp.*, 758 F. Supp. 1522, 1542 (S.D.N.Y. 1991).

In addition to an injunction, other specific nonmonetary relief — such as impounding and destruction of the infringing articles — is available to a successful plaintiff under both the 1909 and 1976 statutes. For the mechanics to be utilized under the 1976 Act, see § 503 and the House Report at 160.

2. INDIVIDUAL, VICARIOUS, AND CONTRIBUTORY LIABILITY

HOUSE REPORT

H.R. Rep. No. 94-1476, 94th Cong., 2d Sess. 158-60 (1976)

Vicarious liability for infringing performances

The committee has considered and rejected an amendment to this section intended to exempt the proprietors of an establishment, such as a ballroom or night club, from liability for copyright infringement committed by an independent contractor, such as an orchestra leader. A well-established principle of copyright law is that a person who violates any of the exclusive rights of the copyright owner is an infringer, including persons who can be considered related or vicarious infringers. To be held a related or vicarious infringer in the case of performing rights, a defendant must either actively operate or supervise the operation of the place wherein the performances occur, or control the content of the infringing program, and expect commercial gain from the operation and either direct or indirect benefit from the infringing performance. The committee has decided that no justification exists for changing existing law, and causing a significant erosion of the public performance right.

It must always be remembered that copyright infringement is a tort. Accordingly all persons participating therein are liable. In a typical case, this may include the publisher, printer, and vendor. *See American Code Co. v. Bensinger*, 282 F. 829 (2d Cir. 1922). But the net of liability may extend much farther — to those having a less direct involvement in the infringement as well as to individuals perpetrating the infringing acts on behalf of a corporate employer. And although absence of knowledge or intention may affect the shaping of remedies, it is not a defense. *See* Latman & Tager, *Liability of Innocent Infringers of Copyrights,* 2 Studies on Copyright 1045 (Arthur Fisher mem. ed. 1963).

Infringers are not merely those subject to rules of vicarious liability exemplified by the agency principle of *respondeat superior*. For reconfirmation under the 1976 Act, see H.R. Rep. No. 94-1476. It has been aptly stated:

> When the right and ability to supervise coalesce with an obvious and direct financial interest in the exploitation of copyrighted materials — even in the absence of actual knowledge that the copyright monopoly is being impaired [citations omitted] — the purposes of copyright law may be best effectuated by the imposition of liability upon the beneficiary of that exploitation.

Shapiro, Bernstein & Co. v. H.L. Green Co., 316 F.2d 304, 307, 137 U.S.P.Q. 275, 277 (2d Cir. 1963).

In the *H.L. Green* case, the proprietor of a department store was held liable, along with its phonograph record concessionaire. This was consistent with a line of "ballroom cases," e.g., *Dreamland Ball Room, Inc. v. Shapiro, Bernstein & Co.,* 36 F.2d 354, 3 U.S.P.Q. 288 (7th Cir. 1929), as well as related contexts, e.g., *Buck v. Jewell-LaSalle Realty Co.,* 283 U.S. 191, 9 U.S.P.Q. 17 (1931), emphasizing that liability was not limited to intentional infringements or strict principal-agent situations.

In an effort to apply or extend this principle (often with a view toward finding more solvent defendants), plaintiffs have joined such entities as advertising agencies or radio stations on which allegedly piratical merchandise is advertised, *Screen Gems-Columbia Music, Inc. v. Mark-Fi Records, Inc.,* 256 F. Supp. 399 (S.D.N.Y. 1966), as well as sponsors of allegedly infringing broadcasts. *Davis v. E.I. du Pont De Nemours & Co.,* 240 F. Supp. 612 (S.D.N.Y. 1965). Cf. *Rohauer v. Killiam Shows, Inc.,* 379 F. Supp. 723, 183 (S.D.N.Y. 1974), *rev'd on other grounds,* 551 F.2d 484 (2d Cir. 1977), *cert. denied,* 431 U.S. 949 (1977).

In copyright cases, a corporate officer or employee personally involved in or directing the infringement is liable along with his or her corporation. *H.M. Kolbe Co. v. Shaff,* 240 F. Supp. 588 (S.D.N.Y. 1965), *aff'd,* 352 F.2d 285 (2d Cir. 1965). In an interesting, and arguably unsound, recent development, a number of courts have used the *H.L. Green* two-step test to impose personal liability on corporate officers for copyright infringements on the part of the corporation itself. For example, in closely held companies operating nightclubs or local radio stations, the top officers will typically have the right to supervise the activities of the company and will, either by way of salary or share ownership, have an interest in its financial success. Some courts, as a condition of imposing personal liability, require active participation on the part of the officer in the corporation's infringing activities, e.g., *BMI v. Behulak,* 1987 CCH Copyright L. Dec. ¶ 26,070 (M.D. Fla. 1986).

Many, however, impose vicarious liability, with joint and several responsibility for damages, even though the officer has no direct knowledge of the infringing activities. *E.g., Boz Scaggs Music v. KND Corp.,* 491 F. Supp. 908 (D. Conn. 1980) (dictum, later frequently cited to support holdings, that corporate officer who satisfies the *H.L. Green* tests may be liable "even in the absence of actual knowledge that the copyright monopoly is being impaired" and "even in the absence of any knowledge of the infringement"). In *Engel v.*

Wild Oats, Inc., 644 F. Supp. 1089 (S.D.N.Y. 1986), liability for statutory damages for the unauthorized imprinting of a photograph on T-shirts and sweatshirts was imposed on the officers and directors of both the shirt-designer company and the distributing company. *See also Mallven Music v. 2001 VIP of Lexington, Inc.,* 230 U.S.P.Q. 543 (E.D. Ky. 1986) (court notes that the corporate president, not actively involved in management, admitted "that he hopes to 'hide' behind the corporate shield and restrict personal liability"). Although almost all of the pertinent cases are at the district court level, the application of *H.L. Green* to impose personal liability on a corporate officer has recently been endorsed by the Court of Appeals for the Eighth Circuit, in *RCA/Ariola Int'l, Inc. v. Thomas & Grayston Co.,* 845 F.2d 773 (1988).

What is troubling about these cases is that they appear to be willing, without even adverting to the tension in the law, to rely on precedents that impose liability on one company for the copyright infringements of others, as a justification for "piercing the veil" that is ordinarily available under general principles of corporate law to shield against individual liability. Are there any special circumstances in copyright cases that warrant this apparent departure from such longstanding principles?

How should the court decide the following case? Songwriter *A* claims that his song "Blue of the Night" is infringed by the song "Gold of the Day," which was written and recorded by Rock Group *B* and published by *C* Corp. (which owns the copyright in the latter song). *A* brings an action against *B* and *C* for infringement. *A* also sues The Harry Fox Agency, Inc.; Fox, you will recall, licenses third persons to make recordings of "Gold of the Day" and collects recording royalties and pays them over to *C*. *A* can prove that Fox exercises some discretion in granting and monitoring recording licenses and that it receives commissions on the basis of the royalties it collects. Fox moves for summary judgment, claiming it is merely an agent for a fully disclosed principal, *C*. Should the case against Fox be dismissed? *See Dixon v. Atlantic Recording Corp.,* 227 U.S.P.Q. 559 (S.D.N.Y. 1985).

Besides the issue of vicarious liability, a defendant may be liable for contributory infringement. The Second Circuit defined that term in *Gershwin Pub'g Corp. v. Columbia Artists Mgt., Inc.,* 443 F.2d 1159, 1162 (2d Cir. 1971): "One who, with knowledge of the infringing activity, induces, causes or materially contributes to the infringing conduct of another, may be held liable as a 'contributory infringer.'" The major Supreme Court pronouncement on contributory infringement is to be found in the *Betamax* case, an action brought by copyright owners of television programs in which the principal defendant was the Sony Corporation of America, whose Betamax videotape recorder was being used by purchasers for home taping of television broadcasts (particularly to enable viewing at a later and more convenient time).

Sony Corp. of America v. Universal City Studios, Inc., 464 U.S. 417 (1984). Although the Copyright Act makes no specific reference to contributory infringement, the Supreme Court endorsed the possibility of imposing liability for copyright infringement on persons who have not themselves engaged in the infringing activities, because the concept "is merely a species of the broader problem of identifying the circumstances in which it is just to hold one individual accountable for the actions of another." The Court determined, however, that vicarious liability could not be imposed solely on the ground that defendants "have sold equipment with the constructive knowledge that their customers may use that equipment to make unauthorized copies of copyrighted material." Rather, analogizing from the patent law, which expressly recognizes contributory infringement, and which also affords an exemption for "staple article[s] or commodit[ies] of commerce suitable for substantial noninfringing uses," 35 U.S.C. § 271(a), (b), the Supreme Court held that the ability of a videocassette recorder to copy copyrighted motion pictures would not render the manufacturers of the machine liable for contributory infringement "if the product is widely used for legitimate, unobjectionable purposes. Indeed it need merely be capable of substantial noninfringing uses." The Court concluded — because many copyright owners of television programs do not object to home videotaping and because even unauthorized home videotaping, for time shifting purposes, is a fair use — that "the Betamax is, therefore, capable of substantial noninfringing uses. Sony's sale of such equipment to the general public does not constitute contributory infringement of respondent's copyrights."

Justice Blackmun, writing for four dissenters, concluded that unauthorized home videotaping of copyrighted television programs is not a fair use and that Sony should be found liable as a contributory infringer if it "has induced and materially contributed to the infringing conduct of Betamax owners." Unlike the Court majority, which would absolve the manufacturer or seller of a product (such as a videotape recorder, a photocopying machine, a typewriter, or a camera) whenever the product is merely capable of substantial noninfringing uses, Justice Blackmun would accord protection to the defendant only if a "significant portion of the product's use is noninfringing.... If virtually all of the product's use, however, is to infringe, contributory liability may be imposed; if no one would buy the product for noninfringing purposes alone, it is clear that the manufacturer is purposely profiting from the infringement, and that liability is appropriately imposed." The dissenting Justices would have remanded for findings as to the proportion of videotaping that is unauthorized by copyright owners and thus illegal.

Although the theories of vicarious liability and contributory liability are distinct, they are very frequently confused and the pertinent criteria muddled. The court in the following case makes a lucid and helpful effort at clarifying the distinction.

DEMETRIADES v. KAUFMANN

690 F. Supp. 289 (S.D.N.Y. 1988)

GOETTEL, J:

[Plaintiff Demetriades and his real estate development firm DDI arranged to have copyrighted architectural plans drawn up for a residence to be built in Scarsdale. Defendants Mr. and Mrs. Kaufmann purchased a lot down the street from another developer, Gallo Brothers, which agreed to construct a

home with a "substantially identical design" to the plaintiff's; Gallo retained
MCR Consulting Engineers, which simply secured a copy of the DDI plans and
traced them. The court found the Kaufmanns, Gallo and MCR to have infringed, and enjoined the use of the copied plans in constructing the
Kaufmann house. Demetriades also sought to impose liability upon the company that had served as real estate broker for the sale from Gallo to the
Kaufmanns.]

The Realtor's Liability

Defendants Dudley D. Doernberg Company and one of its employees, Judy
Koch (the "Doernberg defendants"), move for summary judgment on the copyright claim on grounds that they cannot be held liable for whatever infringement took place in this action. Their involvement in this case may be succinctly summarized.

Put simply, the Doernberg defendants sold the unimproved lot at 24 Cooper
Road to the Kaufmanns, a service for which they received a handsome fee.
The fee was negotiated and, although it was larger than the standard percentage for sale of an unimproved lot, it apparently was not pegged to the value of
the house ultimately to be constructed. Regardless, it is clear that Gallo
Brothers were not interested in simply selling the lot, a fact known to the
Doernberg defendants. Instead, Gallo Brothers required that purchase of the
lot be part and parcel of a deal in which Gallo Brothers would build a home on
that lot for the ultimate purchaser.

It also appears that at some point during negotiations between the
Kaufmanns and Gallo Brothers, the Doernberg defendants became aware that
the Kaufmanns sought construction of a house on the lot in question "of
'substantially identical design' to the Demetriades house at 12A Cooper
Road." *Demetriades I,* 680 F. Supp. at 660. In addition, there is a substantial
factual dispute as to whether the Doernberg defendants ultimately became
aware that the other defendants had obtained and/or were duplicating the
plaintiffs' architectural plans. Although it is conceded that the Doernberg
defendants had no hand in the direct copying of plaintiffs' plans, plaintiffs
argue that the Doernberg defendants may be held derivatively liable for the
direct copying engaged in by the other defendants. Plaintiffs contend that the
role played by the Doernberg defendants in getting the parties together, their
brokering of the real estate transaction, their knowledge that the deal was
dependent both on construction of a home (Gallo Brothers' demand) and construction of a home imitative of the Demetriades house (the Kaufmanns' desire), and their alleged knowledge of the ongoing copying of plaintiffs' plans
all combine to create sufficient involvement with the infringing activity to
warrant liability on their part.

Federal copyright law, unlike patent law, does not expressly create any
form of derivative, third-party liability. *Sony Corp. v. Universal City Studios,
Inc.,* 464 U.S. 417, 434, *reh'g denied,* 465 U.S. 1112 (1984). Courts have long
recognized, however, that one may be held liable for the infringing acts of
another, even if such a third party was in no way directly involved in the
actual copying and had no knowledge that the infringing acts in question

were illegal. *Gershwin Publishing Corp. v. Columbia Artists Management, Inc.*, 443 F.2d 1159, 1161-62 (2d Cir. 1971).

In delineating the contours of this third-party liability, and because copyright is analogous to a species of tort, "common law concepts of tort liability are relevant in fixing the scope of the statutory copyright remedy....'' *Screen Gems-Columbia Music Inc. v. Mark-Fi Records, Inc.*, 256 F. Supp. 399, 403 (S.D.N.Y. 1966) (Weinfeld, J.). Guided, therefore, by well established precepts of tort liability, it appears that two avenues of third-party liability in copyright have grown up in the law — "vicarious liability" (grounded in the tort concept of respondeat superior) and "contributory infringement" (founded on the tort concept of enterprise liability). Although the Supreme Court has noted that "'the lines between direct infringement, contributory infringement and vicarious liability are not clearly drawn,'" *Sony*, 464 U.S. at 435 n.17 (quoting the district court's opinion), a coherent body of rules seems ascertainable from the precedent of this circuit.

As to vicarious liability, the Second Circuit has noted that "(w)hen the right and ability to supervise (the infringer) coalesce with an obvious and direct financial interest in the exploitation of copyrighted materials," a third party may be held liable for the direct infringement by another. *Shapiro, Bernstein & Co. v. H.L. Green Co.*, 316 F.2d 304, 307 (2d Cir. 1963). Courts relying on this theory of third-party liability repeatedly have emphasized that some degree of control or supervision over the individual(s) directly responsible for the infringement is of crucial importance.[6]

The doctrine of "vicarious liability" is inapplicable in this case. We may assume that the Doernberg defendants derived some benefits from the infringement at issue; but that is of little avail to plaintiffs since there is no meaningful evidence (as one might expect) suggesting that the Doernberg defendants exercised any degree of control over the direct infringers. Compare *Shapiro, Bernstein*, 316 F.2d at 308 (holding defendant vicariously liable since it had "the power to police carefully" the infringer's conduct).

The theory of liability ostensibly propounded in the parties' papers is based on "contributory infringement," although the parties (particularly plaintiffs) seem somewhat unsure of the applicable legal standard. That standard, however, was clearly and succinctly set forth in *Gershwin*, which held that "(o)ne who, with knowledge of the infringing activity, induces, causes, or materially contributes to the infringing conduct of another, may be held liable as a 'contributory' infringer." *Gershwin*, 443 F.2d at 1162. In uncovering the doctrinal basis for this theory of liability, Judge Weinfeld noted that "the basic common law doctrine that one who knowingly participates in or furthers a tortious act is jointly and severally liable with the prime tortfeasor is applicable in suits arising under the Copyright Act." *Screen Gems*, 256 F. Supp. at 403, cited with approval in *Gershwin*, 443 F.2d at 1162. Thus, just as benefit

---

[6] It was this ability to supervise or control the direct infringers, coupled with profits reaped from the infringing acts, that served as the basis for liability in the famous "dance hall cases," collected at *Sony*, 464 U.S. at 437 n.18 and *Screen Gems*, 256 F. Supp. at 402 n.5. See also *Sygma Photo News, Inc. v. High Society Magazine, Inc.*, 778 F.2d 89, 92 (2d Cir. 1985) (finding corporation vicariously liable given its exercise of control over the shell corporation that engaged in the infringement).

and control are the signposts of vicarious liability, so are knowledge and participation the touchstones of contributory infringement.

The knowledge of the Doernberg defendants, either actual or constructive, of the direct infringing in this case is an issue in considerable dispute between the parties. Resolution of that matter is of no consequence, however, since, even assuming that these defendants possessed the requisite knowledge about the infringing activity, they cannot fairly be said to have participated in that infringement — i.e., "induce(d), cause(d), or materially contribute(d)" to the statutory violation. *Gershwin,* 443 F.2d at 1162.

The only evidence linking the Doernberg defendants to any participation in or furtherance of the infringement in this case are two telephone calls made by Ms. Koch to Rocco Circosta, an employee of MCR Consulting Engineers (the firm retained by Gallo Brothers to duplicate the plaintiffs' architectural plans). Those calls, each made at the insistence of defendant John Gallo, were initiated to (1) determine the status of the plans (production of a set of plans apparently had not proceeded at a pace the Kaufmanns desired) and (2) ensure that the completed plans would be delivered for the Kaufmanns' inspection to a specified location. There is no indication that the Doernberg defendants made these or any other contacts with the purpose of providing any direct assistance in expediting the copying process (if, indeed, they knew that copying was going on). Nor is there any evidence that the Doernberg defendants provided the means or facilities for the admitted copying. To the contrary, the extensive discovery conducted to date, including the depositions of all parties, makes clear that the real estate transaction in this matter was handled by the Doernberg defendants while the construction issues were matters largely between the Kaufmanns, Gallo Brothers, and MCR Consulting Engineers.

The Supreme Court has noted that "the concept of contributory infringement is merely a species of the broader problem of identifying the circumstances in which it is just to hold one individual accountable for the actions of another." *Sony,* 464 U.S. at 435. We are familiar with no concept of justice that would permit extension of third-party liability in this case on so attenuated a basis. Something more — deriving from one's substantial involvement — is needed. See Restatement (Second) of Torts § 876(b) (1977) (establishing third-party, enterprise liability when one knows of another's tortious conduct and substantially aids or encourages that endeavor); id. at comment d ("The assistance of or participation by the defendant may be so slight that he is not liable for the act of another."). To hold otherwise would, in our view, flatly contradict the plain law of this circuit. See especially *Gershwin,* 443 F.2d at 1163 (holding concert promoter liable as contributory infringer, for infringements by artists it was promoting, due to promoter's "pervasive participation" in creating an audience for the artists); *Screen Gems,* 256 F. Supp. at 404-05 (denying summary judgment to advertising agency, radio station, and shipper of bootleg records given evidence of their knowing participation in the promotion or sale of these infringing products). The mere fact that the Doernberg defendants brokered a real estate transaction that ultimately was connected to a copyright infringement is not enough. Simply put, that quantum of participation necessary to impart liability to third parties is lacking as to the realtor in this case.

Plaintiffs, relying on *Screen Gems,* argue that knowledge and benefits are enough to warrant third-party liability in this case (i.e., the Doernberg defendants knew of the infringing activity and benefitted therefrom). In essence, they rely on a hybrid form of liability, confusing and combining the knowledge prong of contributory infringement with the benefit prong of vicarious liability. This conclusion, we think, misunderstands both Judge Weinfeld's holding in *Screen Gems* and the intellectual foundations of vicarious and contributory infringement .... which serve to distinguish the two. A simple knowledge and benefit test would cast wide the net of third-party liability, ensnaring individuals far too remotely or only tangentially involved in the infringement. Such an approach would drain from the concept of liability its substantive meaning.

For all of these reasons, we grant summary judgment for the Doernberg defendants on the copyright claim.

....

QUESTIONS

1. Does the Supreme Court majority in the *Sony* case hold that so long as a machine is "merely capable of substantial noninfringing uses" its manufacturer will not be held a contributory copyright infringer even if the machine in fact is widely used for infringing purposes? Is that a tenable conclusion?

2. Defendant manufactures a machine called the "Prom Blaster," which makes duplicate, backup copies of videogame cassettes. Defendant also manufactures several videogame cassettes, and specifically authorizes purchasers of the "Prom Blaster" to make backup copies of defendant's videocassettes. Other videogame producers do not authorize reproduction of their cassettes via the "Prom Blaster." Defendant asserts that it is not a contributory infringer because (a) the machine may be put to the legitimate use of copying defendant's own videogame cassettes; and (b) the machine may be used to make noninfringing "archival" copies of other videogame producer's cassettes. Has defendant established its exemption from contributory liability under the *Betamax* test? Is defendant correct that "archival" copies of other videogames are noninfringing copies? *See Atari v. JS&A Group,* 597 F. Supp. 5 (N.D. Ill. 1983), *appellate jurisdiction sustained,* 747 F.2d 1422 (Ct. App. Fed. Cir. 1984).

3. DAMAGES

§ 504. Remedies for infringement: Damages and profits

(a) *In General* — Except as otherwise provided by this title, an infringer of copyright is liable for either —

(1) the copyright owner's actual damages and any additional profits of the infringer, as provided by subsection (b); or

(2) statutory damages, as provided by subsection (c).

(b) *Actual Damages and Profits* — The copyright owner is entitled to recover the actual damages suffered by him or her as a result of the infringement, and any profits of the infringer that are attributable to the infringement and are not taken into account in computing the actual damages. In establishing the infringer's profits, the copyright owner is required to present proof only of the infringer's gross revenue, and the infringer is required to prove his or her deductible expenses and the elements of profit attributable to factors other than the copyrighted work.

....

HOUSE REPORT

H.R. Rep. No. 94-1476, 94th Cong., 2d Sess. 162 (1976)

In allowing the plaintiff to recover "the actual damages suffered by him or her as a result of the infringement," plus any of the infringer's profits "that are attributable to the infringement and are not taken into account in computing the actual damages," section 504(b) recognizes the different purposes served by awards of damages and profits. Damages are awarded to compensate the copyright owner for losses from the infringement, and profits are awarded to prevent the infringer from unfairly benefiting from a wrongful act. Where the defendant's profits are nothing more than a measure of the damages suffered by the copyright owner, it would be inappropriate to award damages and profits cumulatively, since in effect they amount to the same thing. However, in cases where the copyright owner has suffered damages not reflected in the infringer's profits, or where there have been profits attributable to the copyrighted work but not used as a measure of damages, subsection (b) authorizes the award of both.

The language of the subsection makes clear that only those profits "attributable to the infringement" are recoverable; where some of the defendant's profits result from the infringement and other profits are caused by different factors, it will be necessary for the court to make an apportionment. However, the burden of proof is on the defendant in these cases; in establishing profits the plaintiff need prove only "the infringer's gross revenue," and the defendant must prove not only "his or her deductible expenses" but also "the elements of profit attributable to factors other than the copyrighted work."

FRANK MUSIC CORP. v. METRO-GOLDWYN-MAYER, INC.

772 F.2d 505 (9th Cir. 1985)

[The plaintiffs own the copyright in the 1953 Broadway musical *Kismet* and the songs from that show. Pursuant to a license from the plaintiffs, MGM produced and released in 1955 a motion picture version of *Kismet*. In April 1974, defendant MGM Grand Hotel staged a musical revue in its Ziegfield Theatre; the revue, titled *Hallelujah Hollywood,* was staged, produced and directed by defendant Arden, and contained ten acts of singing, dancing and variety performances. One of the acts was billed as a tribute to the musical film *Kismet*. The act was comprised of four scenes, featured persons in the costumes of ancient Baghdad, and featured five songs from the plaintiffs'

Kismet; of the eleven minutes consumed by this act in the hotel revue, approximately six minutes of music was taken from the plaintiffs' play. The total running time of *Hallelujah Hollywood* was approximately 100 minutes, except on Saturday evenings when it was shortened to 75 minutes (which included the full *Kismet* act) so that it could be performed three times rather than the usual two times per night. The revue continued to be performed with the *Kismet* act until July 1976 when, after protest from the plaintiffs, new music was substituted. In total, the *Kismet* sequence was used in approximately 1,700 performances of the hotel show.

[The defendants claimed that their performances of the *Kismet* songs were no infringement because they had been licensed by ASCAP on behalf of the plaintiffs. The court, however, construed the ASCAP license not to extend to the performances involved here because they were in the context of visual representations of the *Kismet* stage costumes and scenery. The court then turned to the question of remedies. Although the case was governed by the 1909 Act, all of the court's discussion would be pertinent to the application of the remedial provisions of the 1976 Act.]

1. *Actual Damages*

"Actual damages" are the extent to which the market value of a copyrighted work has been injured or destroyed by an infringement. 3 M. Nimmer, Nimmer on Copyright § 14.02, at 14-6 (1985). In this circuit, we have stated the test of market value as "what a willing buyer would have been reasonably required to pay to a willing seller for plaintiffs' work." *Krofft I*, 562 F.2d at 1174.

The district court declined to award actual damages. The court stated that it was "unconvinced that the market value of plaintiffs' work was in any way diminished as a result of defendant's infringement.".... Plaintiffs contend the district court's finding is clearly erroneous in light of the evidence they presented concerning the royalties *Kismet* could have earned in a full Las Vegas production. Plaintiffs did offer evidence of the royalties *Kismet* had earned in productions around the country. They also introduced opinion testimony, elicited from plaintiff Lester and from *Kismet*'s leasing agent, that a full production of *Kismet* could have been licensed in Las Vegas for $7,500 per week. And they introduced other opinion testimony to the effect that *Hallelujah Hollywood* had destroyed the Las Vegas market for a production of plaintiffs' *Kismet*.

In a copyright action, a trial court is entitled to reject a proffered measure of damages if it is too speculative. *See Peter Pan Fabrics, Inc. v. Jobella Fabrics, Inc.*, 329 F.2d 194, 196-97 (2d Cir. 1964). Although uncertainty as to the amount of damages will not preclude recovery, uncertainty as to the fact of damages may. *Universal Pictures Co. v. Harold Lloyd Corp.*, 162 F.2d at 369; *see also* 3 M. Nimmer, *supra*, § 14.02, at 14-8 to -9. It was the *fact* of damages that concerned the district court. The court found that plaintiffs "failed to establish *any* damages attributable to the infringement." (Emphasis in original.) This finding is not clearly erroneous.

Plaintiffs offered no disinterested testimony showing that *Hallelujah Holly-wood* precluded plaintiffs from presenting *Kismet* at some other hotel in Las Vegas. It is not implausible to conclude, as the court below apparently did, that a production presenting six minutes of music from *Kismet,* without telling any of the story of the play, would not significantly impair the prospects for presenting a full production of that play. Based on the record presented, the district court was not clearly erroneous in finding that plaintiffs' theory of damages was uncertain and speculative.

2. *Infringer's Profits*

[A] prevailing plaintiff in an infringement action is entitled to recover the infringer's profits to the extent they are attributable to the infringement. 17 U.S.C. § 101(b); *Krofft,* 562 F.2d at 1172. In establishing the infringer's profits, the plaintiff is required to prove only the defendant's sales; the burden then shifts to the defendant to prove the elements of costs to be deducted from sales in arriving at profit. 17 U.S.C. § 101(b). Any doubt as to the computation of costs or profits is to be resolved in favor of the plaintiff. *Shapiro, Bernstein & Co. v. Remington Records, Inc.,* 265 F.2d 263 (2d Cir. 1959). If the infringing defendant does not meet its burden of proving costs, the gross figure stands as the defendant's profits. *Russell v. Price,* 612 F.2d 1123, 1130-31 (9th Cir. 1979), *cert. denied,* 446 U.S. 952, 100 S. Ct. 2919, 64 L. Ed. 2d 809 (1980).

The district court, following this approach, found that the gross revenue MGM Grand earned from the presentation of *Hallelujah Hollywood* during the relevant time period was $24,191,690. From that figure, the court deducted direct costs of $18,060,084 and indirect costs (overhead) of $3,641,960, thus arriving at a net profit of $2,489,646.

Plaintiffs' challenge these computations on a number of grounds....

....

We find ... merit in plaintiffs' ... challenge to the deduction of overhead costs. They argue that defendants failed to show that each item of claimed overhead assisted in the production of the infringement. The evidence defendants introduced at trial segregated overhead expenses into general categories, such as general and administrative costs, sales and advertising, and engineering and maintenance. Defendants then allocated a portion of these costs to the production of *Hallelujah Hollywood* based on a ratio of the revenues from that production as compared to MGM Grand's total revenues. The district court adopted this approach.

We do not disagree with the district court's acceptance of the defendants' method of allocation, based on gross revenues. Because a theoretically perfect allocation is impossible, we require only a "reasonably acceptable formula." *Sammons v. Colonial Press, Inc.,* 126 F.2d at 349; *see Kamar International, Inc. v. Russ Berrie & Co.,* 752 F.2d at 1333. We find, as did the district court, that defendants' method of allocation is reasonably acceptable.

We disagree with the district court, however, to the extent it concluded the defendants adequately showed that the claimed overhead expenses actually contributed to the production of *Hallelujah Hollywood.* Recently, in *Kamar International,* we stated that a deduction for overhead should be allowed "only when the infringer can demonstrate that [the overhead expense] was of actual assistance in the production, distribution or sale of the infringing product." 752 F.2d at 1332 ....

We do not doubt that some of defendants' claimed overhead contributed to the production of *Hallelujah Hollywood.* The difficulty we have, however, is that defendants offered no evidence of what costs were included in general categories such as "general and administrative expenses," nor did they offer any evidence concerning how these costs contributed to the production of *Hallelujah Hollywood.* The defendants contend their burden was met when they introduced evidence of their total overhead costs allocated on a reasonable basis. The district court apparently agreed with this approach. That is not the law of this circuit. Under *Kamar International,* a defendant additionally must show that the categories of overhead actually contributed to sales of the infringing work. 752 F.2d at 1332. We can find no such showing in the record before us. Therefore, we conclude the district court's finding that "defendants have established that the items of general expense [the general categories of claimed overhead] contributed to the production of 'Hallelujah Hollywood'" was clearly erroneous.

Plaintiffs next challenge the district court's failure to consider MGM Grand's earnings on hotel and gaming operations in arriving at the amount of profits attributable to the infringement. The district court received evidence concerning MGM Grand's total net profit during the relevant time period, totaling approximately $395,000,000, but its memorandum decision does not mention these indirect profits and computes recovery based solely on the revenues and profits earned on the production of *Hallelujah Hollywood* (approximately $24,000,000 and $2,500,000 respectively). We surmise from this that the district court determined plaintiffs were not entitled to recover indirect profits, but we have no hint as to the district court's reasons.

Whether a copyright proprietor may recover "indirect profits" is one of first impression in this circuit. We conclude that under the 1909 Act indirect profits may be recovered.

The 1909 Act provided that a copyright proprietor is entitled to "all the profits which the infringer shall have made from such infringement...." 17 U.S.C. § 101(b). The language of the statute is broad enough to permit recovery of indirect as well as direct profits....

The allowance of indirect profits was considered in *Sid & Marty Krofft Television Productions, Inc. v. McDonald's Corp.,* 1983 Copyright L. Rep. (CCH) ¶ 25,572 at 18,381 (C.D. Cal. 1983) (*Krofft II*), *on remand from* 562 F.2d 1157 (9th Cir. 1977), a case involving facts analogous to those presented here. The plaintiffs, creators of the "H.R. Pufnstuf" children's television program, alleged that they were entitled to a portion of the profits McDonald's earned on its food sales as damages for the "McDonaldland" television commercials that infringed plaintiffs' copyright. The district court rejected as speculative the plaintiffs' formula for computing profits attributable to the infringement. However, the court's analysis and award of in lieu damages indicate that it considered indirect profits recoverable. The court stated, in awarding $1,044,000 in statutory damages, that "because a significant portion of defendants' profits made from the infringement are not ascertainable, a higher

award of [statutory] in lieu damages is warranted." *Id.*, at 18,384; see also
Cream Records Inc. v. Jos. Schlitz Brewing Co., 754 F.2d 826, 828-29 (9th Cir.
1985) (awarding profits from the sale of malt liquor for Schlitz's infringing use
of plaintiff's song in television commerical).

Like the television commercials in *Krofft II, Hallelujah Hollywood* had promotional value. Defendants maintain that they endeavor to earn profits on all
their operations and that *Hallelujah Hollywood* was a profit center. However,
that fact does not detract from the promotional purposes of the show — to
draw people to the hotel and the gaming tables. MGM's 1976 annual report
states that "[t]he hotel and gaming operations of the MGM Grand-Las Vegas
continued to be materially enhanced by the popularity of the hotel's entertainment[, including] 'Hallelujah Hollywood', the spectacularly successful production revue...." Given the promotional nature of *Hallelujah Hollywood,* we
conclude indirect profits from the hotel and gaming operations, as well as
direct profits from the show itself, are recoverable if ascertainable.

3. *Apportionment of Profits*

How to apportion profits between the infringers and the plaintiffs is a complex issue in this case. Apportionment of direct profits from the production as
well as indirect profits from the hotel and casino operations [is] involved here,
although the district court addressed only the former at the first trial.

When an infringer's profits are attributable to factors in addition to use of
plaintiff's work, an apportionment of profits is proper.... The burden of proving apportionment, (i.e., the contribution to profits of elements other than the
infringed property), is the defendant's.... We will not reverse a district court's
findings regarding apportionment unless they are clearly erroneous....

After finding that the net profit earned by *Hallelujah Hollywood* was approximately $2,500,000, the district court offered the following explanation of
apportionment:

> While no precise mathematical formula can be applied, the court con-
> cludes in light of the evidence presented at trial and the entire record in
> this case, a fair approximation of the profits of Act IV attributable to the
> infringement is $22,000.

The district court was correct that mathematical exactness is not required.
However, a reasonable and just apportionment of profits is required. *Sheldon
II,* 309 U.S. at 408, 60 S. Ct. at 688; *Universal Pictures Co. v. Harold Lloyd
Corp.,* 162 F.2d at 377.

Arriving at a proper method of apportionment and determining a specific
amount to award is largely a factual exercise. Defendants understandably
argue that the facts support the district court's award. They claim that the
infringing material, six minutes of music in Act IV, was an unimportant part
of the whole show, that the unique features of the Ziegfield Theater contributed more to the show's success than any other factor. This is proved, they
argue, by the fact that when the music from *Kismet* was removed from *Hallelujah Hollywood* in 1976, the show suffered no decline in attendance and the
hotel received no complaints.

Other evidence contradicts defendants' position. For instance, defendant Donn Arden testified that *Kismet* was "a very important part of the show" and "[he] hated to see it go." Moreover, while other acts were deleted from the shortened Saturday night versions of the show, Act IV "Kismet" never was.

We reject defendants' contention that the relative unimportance of the *Kismet* music was proved by its omission and the show's continued success thereafter. *Hallelujah Hollywood* was a revue, comprised of many different entertainment elements. Each element contributed significantly to the show's success, but no one element was the sole or overriding reason for that success. Just because one element could be omitted and the show goes on does not prove that the element was not important in the first instance and did not contribute to establishing the show's initial popularity.

The difficulty in this case is that the district court has not provided us with any reasoned explanation of or formula for its apportionment. We know only the district court's bottom line: that the plaintiffs are entitled to $22,000. Given the nature of the infringement, the character of the infringed property, the success of defendants' show, and the magnitude of the defendants' profits, the amount seems to be grossly inadequate. It amounts to less than one percent of MGM Grand's profits from the show, or roughly $13 for each of the 1700 infringing performances.[11]

On remand, the district court should reconsider its apportionment of profits, and should fully explain on the record its reasons and the resulting method of apportionment it uses. Apportionment of indirect profits may be a part of the calculus. If the court finds that a reasonable, nonspeculative formula cannot be derived, or that the amount of profits a reasonable formula yields is insufficient to serve the purposes underlying the statute, then the court should award statutory damages....

4. *Liability of Joint Infringers*

The district court granted judgment of $22,000 "against defendants" in the plural. Yet if the district court intended that each of the defendants be jointly and severally liable for the $22,000 award, this was error.

---

[11] The apportionment percentages in similar cases are markedly higher. See, e.g., *Universal Pictures Co. v. Harold Lloyd Corp.,* 162 F.2d at 377 (infringing use of one comedy sketch in motion picture; court affirmed award of 20% of the infringing movie's profits); *MCA, Inc. v. Wilson,* 677 F.2d 180, 181-82 (2d Cir. 1981) (defendants copied substantial portion of plaintiff's song, "Boogie Woogie Bugle Boy," substituted "dirty" lyrics, and performed the song as a portion of an erotic nude show; court affirmed special master's award of approximately $244,000 representing 5% of defendants' total profits from the show); *Lottie Joplin Thomas Trust v. Crown Publishers, Inc.,* 592 F.2d at 657 (infringing songs filled one side of five-record set; court affirmed award of 50% of profits because inclusion of infringing songs made record set the only "complete" collection of Scott Joplin's works); *Abkco Music, Inc. v. Harrisongs Music, Ltd.,* 508 F. Supp. 798, 800-801 (S.D.N.Y. 1981) (infringing song reproduced on one side of single record, "flip side" contained noninfringing song, court awarded 70% of profits from sales of the single because infringing song was more popular than noninfringing song; similarly, court awarded 50% of profits for reproduction of same song on album containing twenty-one other songs).

When a copyright is infringed, all infringers are jointly and severally liable for plaintiffs' *actual damages*, but each defendant is severally liable for his or its own illegal *profit*; one defendant is not liable for the profit made by another. *MCA, Inc. v. Wilson*, 677 F.2d 180, 186 (2d Cir. 1981); 3 M. Nimmer, *supra*, § 12.04[C][3], at 12-50; see *Cream Records, Inc. v. Jos. Schlitz Brewing Co.*, 754 F.2d at 829.

    ....

REINHARDT, CIRCUIT JUDGE, concurring:
    I concur fully in the majority opinion, except for Section B.1, I would hold that the district court clearly erred in finding that appellants "failed to establish *any* damage attributable to the infringement." It seems evident to me that the inclusion of "Kismet" as a part of 1,700 performances of *Hallelujah Hollywood* served to reduce the market value of appellant's property in the Las Vegas area. The testimony in the record amply supports this proposition. There is no evidence that would support the opposite conclusion. Under these circumstances, I believe the district court clearly erred in disregarding the testimony offered by appellants.

Cream Records, Inc. v. Jos. Schlitz Brewing Co., 754 F.2d 826 (9th Cir. 1985). Schlitz Brewing Co. used in one of its beer commercials some music from a copyrighted rhythm and blues composition, "The Theme From 'Shaft'." The trial court accepted the contention of the copyright owner, Cream, that the value of a license to use the entire song for a year was $80,000; and concluded that a reasonable license fee for the small part used by Schlitz would be some 15% of that amount, or $12,000. Because there was evidence that another manufacturer approached Cream for a license but withdrew when the Schlitz commercial was aired, and because there was no evidence that Cream was willing to grant a license for use of less than the entire copyrighted work, the court of appeals concluded that the full $80,000 was the proper measure of the extent to which Schlitz's "unauthorized use destroyed the value of the copyrighted work" for licensing purposes.
    Cream also claimed a percentage of Schlitz's profits on the sale of malt liquor for the period during which the infringing commercial was broadcast; total profits were $4.876 million, and Cream sought 1.37% of that amount, or $66,800, as the portion attributable to the infringement. It argued that the expenditure for the infringing commercial constituted 13.7% of Schlitz's advertising budget for the year, and that the infringing music was responsible for 10% of the commercial's advertising power. The trial court concluded that the infringement was "minimal," consisting principally of a repeated ten-note accompaniment pattern; that the infringing material did not add substantially to the value of the commercial; that while the commercial was successful and "sold some beer" and that the "music had a portion of it," the portion was "minuscule." He concluded: "I have interpolated as best I can. They made a profit of $5 million. One-tenth of 1 percent is $5,000," and he awarded that. Cream contended that it was entitled to all of its claimed allocable profits,

because Schlitz failed to introduce evidence of the portions of its profits not attributable to the infringement.

The court of appeals rejected this contention, and upheld the allocation made by the trial court. "[W]here it is clear, as it is in this case, that not all of the profits are attributable to the infringing material, the copyright owner is not entitled to recover all of those profits merely because the infringer fails to establish with certainty the portion attributable to the non-infringing elements. [In such cases, where] the evidence suggests some division which may rationally be used as a springboard it is the duty of the court to make some apportionment." The court quoted from a decision of Learned Hand: "[W]e are resolved to avoid the one certainly unjust course of giving the plaintiff everything, because the defendants cannot with certainty compute their own share. In cases where plaintiffs fail to prove their damages exactly, we often make the best estimate we can, even though it is really no more than a guess (*Pieczonka v. Pullman Co.*, 2 Cir., 102 F.2d 432, 434), and under the guise of resolving all doubts against the defendants we will not deny the one fact that stands undoubted." It then concluded —

> By claiming only 1.37% of Schlitz's malt liquor profits, Cream recognizes the impropriety of awarding Cream all of Schlitz's profits on a record that reflects beyond argument that most of these profits were attributable to elements other than the infringement. As to the amount of profits attributable to the infringing material, "what is required is ... only a reasonable approximation," *Sheldon v. Metro-Goldwyn Pictures Corp.*, 309 U.S. at 408, 60 S. Ct. at 688; see also *Twentieth Century-Fox Film Corp. v. Stonesifer*, 140 F.2d 579, 583-84 (9th Cir. 1944); *MCA, Inc. v. Wilson*, 677 F.2d 180, 186 (2d Cir. 1981), and Cream's calculation is in the end no less speculative than that of the court. The disparity between the amount sought by Cream and the amount awarded by the court appears to rest not so much upon a difference in methods of calculation as upon a disagreement as to the extent to which the commercial infringed upon the copyright and the importance of the copyrighted material to the effectiveness of the commercial. These were determinations for the district court to make....

QUESTIONS

1. On the issue of damages, more particularly the plaintiff's lost opportunity to license others after the infringing use of its music, are *Cream Records* and *Frank Music* reconcilable? In *Frank Music,* why could the court not have awarded damages based upon the reasonable value of a license from the copyright owners to perform the five songs used in the defendants' revue? Is that not the economic injury the copyright owner suffers when another publicly performs its music without authorization?

2. On the issue of profits, was it proper for the Ninth Circuit to require Schlitz to disgorge some of its beer profits; and if so, how should it be shown (and by which party) what portion of those profits are properly allocable to the use of a repeating ten-note bass pattern in one of its beer commercials? Was it proper for that court to require the MGM Grand to disgorge some of the profits from its hotel rooms and casinos; and if so, how should it be shown (and by which party) what portion of those profits are properly allocable to the use of five of plaintiffs' songs in an eleven-minute act in a musical revue in the hotel theater?

3. A jury found that the popular song "Feelings," written by Morris Albert, infringed the plaintiff's song "Pour Toi," and brought in a verdict in the amount of $500,000. Albert consults you on the question whether the jury award can be reduced by the trial judge so as to apportion them between the infringing music and the noninfringing lyrics. What kind of evidence might you present on this issue? What is the likelihood of success? *See Gaste v. Kaiserman,* 863 F.2d 1061 (2d Cir. 1988).

4. Recall the motion picture, "Letty Lynton" in *Sheldon v. Metro-Goldwyn Pictures Corp., supra.* Since not all of the defendants' motion picture was taken from the plaintiff's play, and a substantial part of its success was no doubt attributable to other elements (e.g., the public domain story itself, the cinematic contributions of the MGM studio, Joan Crawford as the star), what should the remedy be? Should MGM be enjoined from further exhibition? Should plaintiff be awarded damages measured by her lost opportunity to sell her play to Hollywood? If so, what is to be made of the fact that her play was apparently unsalable under the obscenity standards of the period? Should MGM disgorge its profits from the exhibition of the infringing film? How are "profits" to be calculated and, more obviously, should MGM be permitted to reduce the award by the profits attributable to the non-infringing components mentioned above? *See Sheldon v. Metro-Goldwyn Pictures Corp.,* 309 U.S. 390 (1940).

5. Suppose the defendant infringes the plaintiff's copyright by embodying the plaintiff's design for costume jewelry (selling for $8.00) into gold jewelry (selling for $800). How should the defendant's profits be apportioned so as to afford the plaintiff an appropriate recovery?

---

§ 504. Remedies for infringement: Damages and profits

. . . .

(c) *Statutory Damages —*

(1) Except as provided by clause (2) of this subsection, the copyright owner may elect, at any time before final judgment is rendered, to recover, instead of actual damages and profits, an award of statutory damages for all infringements involved in the action, with respect to any one work, for which any one infringer is liable individually, or for which any two or more infringers are liable jointly and severally, in a sum of not less than $250 or more than $10,000 as the court considers just. For the purposes of this subsection, all the parts of a compilation or derivative work constitute one work. [Editor's Note: The minimum figure was increased to $500 and the maximum to $20,000 in the Berne Convention Implementation Act of 1988.]

(2) In a case where the copyright owner sustains the burden of proving, and the court finds, that infringement was committed willfully, the court in its

discretion may increase the award of statutory damages to a sum of not more than $50,000 [increased to $100,000 by the 1988 amendments]. In a case where the infringer sustains the burden of proving, and the court finds, that such infringer was not aware and had no reason to believe that his or her acts constituted an infringement of copyright, the court in its discretion may reduce the award of statutory damages to a sum of not less than $100 [increased to $200 by the 1988 amendments]. The court shall remit statutory damages in any case where an infringer believed and had reasonable grounds for believing that his or her use of the copyrighted work was a fair use under section 107, if the infringer was: (i) an employee or agent of a nonprofit educational institution, library, or archives acting within the scope of his or her employment who, or such institution, library, or archives itself, which infringed by reproducing the work in copies or phonorecords; or (ii) a public broadcasting entity which or a person who, as a regular part of the nonprofit activities of a public broadcasting entity (as defined in subsection (g) of section 118) infringed by performing a published nondramatic literary work or by reproducing a transmission program embodying a performance of such a work.

HOUSE REPORT

H.R. Rep. No. 94-1476, 94th Cong., 2d Sess. 161-63 (1976)

... Recovery of actual damages and profits under section 504(b) or of statutory damages under section 504(c) is alternative and for the copyright owner to elect; as under the present law, the plaintiff in an infringement suit is not obliged to submit proof of damages and profits and may choose to rely on the provision for minimum statutory damages. However, there is nothing in section 504 to prevent a court from taking account of evidence concerning actual damages and profits in making an award of statutory damages within the range set out in subsection (c).

Statutory damages

Subsection (c) of section 504 makes clear that the plaintiff's election to recover statutory damages may take place at any time during the trial before the court has rendered its final judgment. The remainder of clause (1) of the subsection represents a statement of the general rates applicable to awards of statutory damages. Its principal provisions may be summarized as follows:

1. As a general rule, where the plaintiff elects to recover statutory damages, the court is obliged to award between $250 and $10,000. It can exercise discretion in awarding an amount within that range but, unless one of the exceptions provided by clause (2) is applicable, it cannot make an award of less than $250 or of more than $10,000 if the copyright owner has chosen recovery under section 504(c).

2. Although, as explained below, an award of minimum statutory damages may be multiplied if separate works and separately liable infringers are involved in the suit, a single award in the $250 to $10,000 range is to be made "for all infringements involved in the action." A single infringer of a single work is liable for a single amount between $250 and $10,000, no matter how

many acts of infringement are involved in the action and regardless of whether the acts were separate, isolated, or occurred in a related series.

3. Where the suit involves infringement of more than one separate and independent work, minimum statutory damages for each work must be awarded. For example, if one defendant has infringed three copyrighted works, the copyright owner is entitled to statutory damages of at least $750 and may be awarded up to $30,000. Subsection (c)(1) makes clear, however, that, although they are regarded as independent works for other purposes, "all the parts of a compilation or derivative work constitute one work" for this purpose. Moreover, although the minimum and maximum amounts are to be multiplied where multiple "works" are involved in the suit, the same is not true with respect to multiple copyrights, multiple owners, multiple exclusive rights, or multiple registrations. This point is especially important since, under a scheme of divisible copyright, it is possible to have the rights of a number of owners of separate "copyrights" in a single "work" infringed by one act of a defendant.

4. Where the infringements of one work were committed by a single infringer acting individually, a single award of statutory damages would be made. Similarly, where the work was infringed by two or more joint tortfeasors, the bill would make them jointly and severally liable for an amount in the $250 to $10,000 range. However, where separate infringements for which two or more defendants are not jointly liable are joined in the same action, separate awards of statutory damages would be appropriate.

Clause (2) of section 504(c) provides for exceptional cases in which the maximum award of statutory damages could be raised from $10,000 to $50,000, and in which the minimum recovery could be reduced from $250 to $100. The basic principle underlying this provision is that the courts should be given discretion to increase statutory damages in cases of willful infringement and to lower the minimum where the infringer is innocent. The language of the clause makes clear that in these situations the burden of proving willfulness rests on the copyright owner and that of proving innocence rests on the infringer, and that the court must make a finding of either willfulness or innocence in order to award the exceptional amounts....

Engel v. Wild Oats, Inc., 644 F. Supp. 1089 (S.D.N.Y. 1986). Plaintiff is the daughter and executrix of the late and renowned photographer Ruth Orkin Engel. Defendant Wild Oats manufactured T-shirts and sweatshirts bearing reproductions of one of Ms. Engel's still-life color photographs of Central Park, taken from a book of her photographs. These shirts were marketed by defendant New World Sales. Liability for infringement was conceded, and the only issue was damages. At the hearing, plaintiff Engel produced no evidence of either her damages or defendants' profits; she testified to her mother's reputation as a photographer, but stated that the damage to that reputation resulting from the copyright infringement was difficult to ascertain. Wild Oats, with 104 employees, produces 360,000 shirts per month; it produced some 2,500 shirts with the infringing design, on which its records showed net profits and sales commissions of $1,878.52. Plaintiff sought statutory damages ($50,000 for willful infringement), and defendants argued that such damages should be limited by defendants' profits.

The court invoked § 504(c) and stated that it was for the plaintiff to choose, at any time before final judgment, whether to elect actual damages and profits, or statutory damages; and that it was for the court, within a wide discretion, to determine a "just" award. Such flexibility accords with the goals of providing the copyright owner with "a potent arsenal of remedies against the infringer" and of discouraging further infringement. The court disagreed with the defendants' contention that their profits should "control" the determination of statutory damages; such profits are to be considered, but only along with other factors, including "the nature of the copyright, the difficulty of proving actual damages, the circumstances of the infringement, and in particular whether the infringement was willful." The latter factor may warrant increasing the ceiling for statutory damages to $50,000. The court continued:

> The court finds that the infringement by Wild Oats was willful. The preponderance of the evidence indicates that the art director at Wild Oats copied the late Ms. Engel's photograph from the copyrighted book *More Pictures from My Window*. The art director knew or should have known that the unauthorized reprinting of a photograph from the book was a copyright violation. See *Fallaci v. New Gazette Literary Corp., supra,* 568 F. Supp. at 1173. Although the Court finds no direct proof of the art director's actual knowledge of the copyright infringement, the compelling circumstantial evidence of his reckless disregard for, if not actual knowledge of, plaintiff's rights in the photograph is sufficient to establish willfulness. *Wow & Flutter Music v. Len's Tom Jones Tavern, Inc.,* 606 F. Supp. 554, 556 (W.D.N.Y. 1985); see *Lauratex Textile Corp. v. Allton Knitting Mills, Inc.,* 519 F. Supp. 730, 733 (S.D.N.Y. 1981).
>
> The court also takes note of circumstances apart from Wild Oats' willfulness surrounding the infringement in this case. The nature of plaintiff's copyright — ownership of a rarefied, artistic subject matter — is unusually susceptible to damage when reproduced on the rather less rarefied medium of a T-shirt or sweat shirt. The scale of the infringement was not slight as defendants have distributed approximately 2,500 shirts in the open market. At the same time, the extent of plaintiff's actual damage is virtually impossible to ascertain. The harm of the infringement to the late Ms. Engel's artistic reputation, in the form of lost revenues from her works, may become evident only over the years to come.
>
> In light of all of these circumstances, the court has determined that $20,000 is the proper award of damages in this case. The award is adequate both to compensate plaintiff for her losses and to remind defendants and other would-be infringers of the seriousness of copyright violations.

....

QUESTIONS

1. Under what circumstances should a plaintiff elect statutory damages? At what point in the proceeding? Can the court decide to award statutory damages under the 1976 Act or is the election solely the plaintiff's?

2. Suppose a Christmas line of six plush toys infringes copyright by depicting a comic strip character in different poses. A year later, the Christmas line of the same manufacturer includes four different versions of the character. If a successful copyright infringement suit for statutory damages is brought against all these items in the latter year, what is the maximum recovery? *See Walt Disney Co. v. Powell*, 897 F.2d 565 (D.C. Cir. 1990).

3. Author has written three one-act plays, one in 1989, one in 1991, and one in 1993. She publishes them under one cover in 1994. Zenith Drama Company, without authorization, performs the plays in a commercial playhouse in Chicago — the first play every night in April, the second play every night in May, and the third play every night in June. What is the maximum amount of statutory damages that Author can properly claim? *See Cormack v. Sunshine Food Stores, Inc.*, 675 F. Supp. 374 (E.D. Mich. 1987); *Robert Stigwood Group Ltd. v. O'Reilly*, 530 F.2d 1096 (2d Cir.), *cert. denied*, 429 U.S. 848 (1976).

4. Horty Culture has published a book about the planting and care of flowers; the book contains 132 color photographs of seedlings. Seeds Incorporated markets flower seeds in small packets, and each packet is adorned by a color photograph of the pertinent seedling, reproduced directly from the photographs in Culture's copyrighted book. Culture sues Seeds, and claims statutory damages, 132-times over. Seeds, claiming that its infringement was not willful, concedes liability in the maximum amount of only $20,000. Who has the stronger case? *See Stokes Seeds, Ltd. v. Geo. W. Park Seed Co.*, 783 F. Supp. 104 (W.D.N.Y. 1991).

5. In the *Krofft v. McDonald's* litigation discussed by the court in the *Frank Music* case, *supra*, there was a finding that the infringed Pufnstuf characters made their first appearance on a television cartoon show, and that they subsequently appeared in other such shows, in comic books, and in various merchandise items (such as masks, stickers and puzzles); and also that the McDonald's infringements were manifested in 114 different and frequently aired television commercials, 66 promotional items (such as McDonaldland cookies, puppets, glasses, posters), and 60 personal appearances by persons dressed as McDonaldland characters. Advise Krofft regarding the amount of statutory damages to which it would be entitled under § 504(c). How does your figure compare with that actually awarded by the *Krofft* court under the 1909 Act, after finding willful infringement — $1,044,000!

6. The student should recall that under § 412, timely registration of copyright is a condition to the award of statutory damages and attorney's fees; this is indeed probably the principal reason why most copyright owners register. The importance of doing so was brought home in a recent case in which a magazine, in order to capture the overly elaborate prose (and the egotism) of a well-known author and teacher, quoted 52 percent of the unpublished letter that he had circulated to prospective students. The trial court found infringement and no fair use, but held that it could not grant an award of statutory damages: the work was unpublished and was not registered when the infringement occurred. *See Lish v. Harper's Magazine Found.*, 807 F. Supp. 1090, 1109 (S.D.N.Y. 1993). In such a situation, are the statutory-damage policies favoring compensation and deterrence outweighed by the policies favoring prompt registration (particularly with respect to unpublished materials such as letters)? Should pre-infringement registration be discarded as a condition of entitlement to statutory damages?

A significant issue arising in some recent cases is whether the assessment of statutory damages under § 504(c) is to be made by the district judge or by the jury. That section refers to "a sum of not less than $500 or more than $20,000 as the court considers just." But it is not clear whether Congress intended "court" to mean a judge in all cases, or more loosely to include the jury as well in actions in which a jury would otherwise be appropriate. Nor is it clear whether, even assuming it is for the judge to assess statutory damages, a jury in such a case is also stripped of the power to rule on such non-monetary issues as copyright validity, copying, substantial similarity, and the like.

Actions "at law" may be tried to a jury; only judges rule on claims in "equity." A copyright infringement suit seeking actual damages clearly constitutes a "legal" action, for which a jury is available. What of a demand for statutory damages? The 1976 Act gives the judge considerable discretion in setting an award of statutory damages. Are these damages therefore to be deemed within the judge's general equitable powers, and thus outside the realm of a jury-triable action at law?

In *Educational Testing Servs. v. Katzman*, 670 F. Supp. 1237 (D.N.J. 1987), the court concluded in favor of jury trials. It cited several supportive arguments. As in an action at law, the remedy is monetary. Moreover, the judge's discretion is not complete: if liability is found, the court must enter judgment for at least the minimum statutory amount. The court found similarities between statutory damages and punitive damages (the latter are clearly "legal"); the amount of the award turns on the wilfulness of plaintiff's conduct. Most significantly, the court relied on the procedural aspects of the election of statutory damages:

> [T]he procedure whereby statutory damages are chosen strongly suggests a close connection between actual and statutory damages. As noted, plaintiff may elect the "in lieu of" [statutory] damages any time before final judgment.... [I]f statutory damages were equitable the possibility clearly exists that a plaintiff could seek actual damages up to a point at which a jury trial was proceeding badly and then effectively yank the question of damages from the jury by electing statutory damages.

(Although the court's concern that classifying statutory damages as "equitable" could provoke manipulation of the trial seems appealing, one may inquire, if the trial is going so badly that plaintiff fears too low an award of actual damages, why would he expect a significantly higher award of statutory damages?) Another court has ruled statutory damages to be equitable, on the principal ground that the remedy was "enacted for cases in which plaintiff can [not] prove actual damages and thus has no adequate remedy at law." *See Billy Steinberg Music v. Cagney's Pub'g,* 9 U.S.P.Q.2d 1749 (N.D. Ill. 1988), and decisions cited therein.

One federal appellate court has recently ruled that the right to a jury remains even when plaintiff has elected statutory damages. In *Video Views, Inc. v. Studio 21, Ltd.,* 925 F.2d 1010 (7th Cir.), *cert. denied,* 112 S. Ct. 181, 116 L. Ed. 2d 143 (1991), the court held: "We believe that the statutory damage provisions of the Copyright Act were intended to relieve the aggrieved copyright owner of the task of proving its actual damages, not to relieve the alleged infringer of its right to a jury trial on other factual issues."

The Eleventh Circuit, in *Cable/Home Commun. Corp. v. Network Prods., Inc.,* 902 F.2d 829 (11th Cir. 1990), rejected defendant's demand for a jury trial on the assessment of statutory damages. However, the Eleventh and Seventh Circuit decisions are not inconsistent. Both courts agreed that the judge is to determine the amount of statutory damages. The Seventh Circuit ruled on the availability of jury determination of other issues in the suit, most notably, whether there was liability for infringement. In the case before the Eleventh Circuit, the district judge had granted summary judgment to plaintiff on the question of liability, and thus jury trial on that question was not at issue.

On the availability of jury trials in suits for statutory damages, compare Note, *The Availability of Jury Trials in Copyright Infringement Cases: Limiting the Scope of the Seventh Amendment,* 83 Mich. L. Rev. 1950 (1985) with Patry, *The Right to a Jury in Copyright Cases,* 29 J. Copyright Soc'y 139 (1981).

4. COSTS AND ATTORNEY'S FEES

LIEB v. TOPSTONE INDUSTRIES, INC.

788 F.2d 151 (3d Cir. 1986)

WEIS, CIRCUIT JUDGE.

[Plaintiff produced an audiocassette tape of sounds associated with Halloween, and after registering it for copyright, he entered into an agreement to have defendant Topstone distribute it. Topstone thereafter terminated the contract and began marketing its own cassette with Halloween sounds; it did not pirate any sounds from the plaintiff's recording, but merely imitated its style and content. When the plaintiff so conceded in the course of discovery in this copyright infringement action, the defendant moved for summary judgment, invoking § 114(b) of the Copyright Act which bars only the unauthorized recapturing of the actual sounds fixed in another's recording, but not imitating those sounds in an independently fixed-recording. The trial court agreed with the defendant, granted summary judgment, and also dismissed the plaintiff's pendent claims under state law for contract breach and bad faith. However, the trial judge, without explanation, denied the defendant's motion for attorneys' fees, in support of which the defendant had argued that the plaintiff's copyright claim was frivolous and filed in bad faith.]

On appeal, defendants contend that the district court abused its discretion in failing to award counsel fees under the Copyright Act....

Section [505] of the Copyright Act, 17 U.S.C. § 505, states that "In any civil action under this title, the court in its discretion may allow the recovery of full costs by or against any party .... [T]he court may also award a reasonable attorney's fee to the prevailing party as part of the costs." This section was enacted in 1976 as a part of the revision of the Copyright Act, but the Act of 1909 similarly provided that "The court may award to the prevailing party a reasonable attorney's fee as part of the costs." 17 U.S.C. § 40.

....

The statutory language provides that the allowances of fees to the prevailing party is not mandated in every case but is entrusted to the evaluation of the district court. The proper limits within which that discretion must be exercised remain unclear despite more than three-quarters of a century of experience with the statute.

Cases in the Court of Appeals for the Ninth Circuit have established a finding of bad faith as a prerequisite for a grant of fees. *Cooling Systems and Flexible, Inc. v. Stuart Radiator, Inc.,* 777 F.2d 485, 493 (9th Cir. 1985); *Jartech, Inc. v. Clancy,* 666 F.2d 403, 407 (9th Cir. 1982). The Court of Appeals for the Eleventh Circuit has taken a less restrictive position. In *Original Appalachian Artworks, Inc. v. Toy Loft, Inc.,* 684 F.2d 821, 832 (11th Cir. 1982), the court concluded that "a showing of bad faith or frivolity" is not required for an award. The "only preconditions ... [are] that the party receiving the fee be the 'prevailing party' and that the fee be reasonable." *Id.* at 832.

The decisions of other courts of appeals fall somewhere between these two extremes. In *Eisenschiml v. Fawcett Publications, Inc.,* 246 F.2d 598, 604 (7th Cir. 1957), the court reversed an award in favor of the defendant where the plaintiff had presented "a very close question." More recently that court found no abuse of discretion in a fee assessment where "there was abundant evidence that the infringement was willful." *Taylor v. Meirick,* 712 F.2d 1112, 1122 (7th Cir. 1983).

The Court of Appeals for the Second Circuit appears to be shifting its standards....

The court adopted a double standard in *Diamond v. Am-Law Publishing Corp.,* 745 F.2d 142 (2d Cir. 1984), deciding that prevailing plaintiffs generally should receive attorney's fees, but a defendant should recover only if the plaintiff's claims are "objectively without arguable merit." *Id.* at 148. Subjective bad faith as a prerequisite was held to be unnecessary. The court based its newly found need for differentiation on a public policy to discourage infringement and to encourage plaintiffs to press "colorable" copyright claims. To the same effect, see *Grosset & Dunlap, Inc. v. Gulf & Western Corp.,* 534 F. Supp. 606 (S.D.N.Y. 1982).

The *Diamond* case was roundly criticized in *Cohen v. Virginia Electric & Power Co.,* 617 F. Supp. 619 (E.D. Va. 1985). That court found no support in the statutory language, legislative history, or policy considerations for anything other than an evenhanded approach. Finding no objective bad faith but noting that the "plaintiff lost and deserved to lose," the court awarded fees to the defendant, commenting however on the necessity for eliminating excessive charges. *Id.* at 623.

Precedents in this court are notable for their absence....

Given the lack of guidance from our earlier decisions, discussion of some of the relevant criteria may assist the district court on remand. We recognize at the outset that the statutory authorization is broad and evidences an intent to rely on the sound judgment of the district courts. Had Congress intended to condition the award of fees on the presence of bad faith, the statutory provision would have been surplusage. "[E]ven under the American common-law rule attorney's fees may be awarded against a party who has proceeded in bad faith." *Christiansburg Garment Co. v. EEOC,* 434 U.S. 412, 419, 98 S. Ct. 694, 699, 54 L. Ed. 2d 648 (1978). We think that limiting assessments to those cases where bad faith is shown unduly narrows the discretion granted to the district judges. Finding no indication either in statutory language or legislative history that bad faith should be a prerequisite to a fee award, we decline to so limit the conditions under which an assessment may be made.

Nor do we accept the double standard for plaintiffs and defendants. Like the *Cohen* court, we find no justification for such a departure from the law's presumed equality of treatment. Although *Diamond* divined an intent to encourage copyright holders to pursue infringers, we note that in many cases the defendants are holders. Similarly, we fail to see the virtue in encouraging an attempt to enlarge the scope of the copyright monopoly beyond that conferred by the statute.

....

Thus we do not require bad faith, nor do we mandate an allowance of fees as a concomitant of prevailing in every case, but we do favor an evenhanded approach. The district courts' discretion may be exercised within these boundaries. Factors which should play a part include frivolousness, motivation, objective unreasonableness (both in the factual and in the legal components of the case) and the need in particular circumstances to advance considerations of compensation and deterrence. We expressly do not limit the factors to those we have mentioned, realizing that others may present themselves in specific situations. Moreover, we may not usurp that broad area which Congress has reserved for the district judge.

Having decided that fees should be awarded, the district court must then determine what amount is reasonable under the circumstances. As we noted in *Chappell,* 334 F.2d at 306, the relative complexity of the litigation is relevant. Also, a sum greater than what the client has been charged may not be assessed, but the award need not be that large.... The relative financial strength of the parties is a valid consideration, ... as are the damages. Where bad faith is present that, too, may affect the size of the award. *Landsberg v. Scrabble Crossword Game Players, Inc.,* 736 F.2d 485 (9th Cir. 1984).

In this case, plaintiff had ample opportunity to justify the filing of a lawsuit that patently had no legal merit. The principal justification plaintiff has proffered to this court has been the absence of bad faith, which as we noted above is not a prerequisite for the award of counsel fees under the Copyright Act. Thus, under ordinary circumstances, an award of some counsel fees to defendants would be appropriate. However, the arguments before the district court may suggest some other reason why an award of counsel fees is inappropriate, and we do not preclude the district court from so concluding on remand.

If the district court concludes that fees are proper, it should then consider the relative simplicity of the defense, and whether the retention of out-of-town counsel with the accompanying increased expense was necessary. The sum requested is large, and we note that it may be both disproportionate to the amount at stake and excessive in light of the plaintiff's resources. We emphasize that the aims of the statute are compensation and deterrence where appropriate, but not ruination.

....

[Editor's Note: The Supreme Court has granted a petition for certiorari in *Fantasy, Inc. v. Fogerty*, 984 F.2d 1524 (9th Cir. 1993), to decide precisely the issue raised in *Lieb v. Topstone*. A decision is expected during the Court's 1993 term.]

As noted just above, § 412 has conditioned the award of statutory damages and attorney's fees upon timely registration. In the 1976 Act, Congress allowed a three-month grace period for registration with regard to published works, because Congress anticipated that "newsworthy or suddenly popular works may be infringed almost as soon as they are published, before the copyright owner has had a reasonable opportunity to register his claim." H.R. Rep. No. 1476, 94th Cong., 2d Sess. at 158 (1976). It has been stated that "Congress did not, however, apparently envision the even more unusual situation where *an author, who is about to publish and register,* has had a draft wrongfully copied." *Harper & Row v. Nation Enters.*, 557 F. Supp. 1067, 1073 (S.D.N.Y.) (emphasis in original), *rev'd on other grounds*, 723 F.2d 195 (2d Cir. 1983), *cert. granted*, 104 S. Ct. 2655 (1984). Thus so long as the work is both unpublished and unregistered at the time of the infringement, no attorney's fees may be awarded, even if defendant's conduct would otherwise give rise to an award.

It may thus be to the advantage of a copyright owner to contend that its work has been "published," in cases in which an infringement commences quickly thereafter. This can sometimes give rise to a dispute about whether the plaintiff's work was published at the time of the infringement. In *Aitken, Hazen, Hoffman, Miller, P.C. v. Empire Constr. Co.*, 542 F. Supp. 252 (D. Neb. 1982), an architect claimed that a builder infringed the copyright on the architect's plans for a residential complex by making copies of those plans for use in building the same complex nearby. In early 1978, the plaintiff filed copies of its architectural plans with a government department to obtain a building permit, and also gave copies to the builder of the project so that they might be used by subcontractors and suppliers. The defendant, without consent, copied the plans in 1979 and proceeded with its building into 1980. The architect did not register its copyright until April 1980. The court found that the defendant had infringed, but it declined to award attorney's fees to the plaintiff. It held that the public filing of the plans and their distribution to subcontractors and suppliers did not constitute "publication" as defined in

§ 101 of the 1976 Copyright Act. Because the plans were therefore unpublished and unregistered in 1979 when the defendant "commenced" infringing, attorney's fees (and statutory damages as well) were barred by virtue of section 412(1).

The moral for the practicing attorney is clear — if a work is likely to be of commercial value (and even sometimes if it is not and the author may well be concerned about litigation, as in the *Lish* case relating to a teacher's unpublished letter to prospective students), it is best to register the copyright, and to do it promptly. As already noted, it is the desire to preserve a potential claim to statutory damages and attorney's fees that is perhaps the principal reason why copyright owners are advised to secure prompt registration.

5. STATUTE OF LIMITATIONS

A significant limitation upon the rights of a copyright owner to sue for infringement is, of course, the statute of limitations. Under § 507, the period of limitations for both criminal and civil proceedings is three years. Statute of limitations questions are usually straightforward enough, but courts have had to grapple with some difficult issues of application.

First, is the running of the statute "tolled" until the plaintiff actually learns of the infringement, or does the statute begin to run as soon as acts of infringement occur? If the defendant "fraudulently conceals" the acts of infringement, the statute will be tolled. The prevailing rule is that even absent such concealment, the statute will be tolled during the period when a reasonable person in the plaintiff's shoes would not have discovered the infringement. *E.g., Taylor v. Meirick,* 712 F.2d 1112 (7th Cir. 1983).

A more troubling question is whether repeated acts of infringement constitute a single "continuing" wrong, so that the plaintiff may sue for all infringing acts if the last one falls within the three-year statutory period. Suppose, for example, that a book club in 1985 advertises and sells almost all of its 10,000 copies of a book that contains infringing material; the only sales after that year are in 1988, when it "remainders" its copies by selling its inventory of 100 copies at sharply reduced prices to discount book stores. The copyright owner sues in 1990.

The defendant book club claims that damages must be limited to the 100 copies sold within the previous three years; it claims that, otherwise, substantial and possibly ruinous liability might be extended forever, so long as there is one infringing act within the three years prior to suit. The copyright owner contends, however, that the infringing sales are all part of a single continuing transaction, which is not ended for purposes of starting the running of the statutory period until the last infringing act is committed; otherwise, the copyright owner to protect its rights would have to bring successive piecemeal lawsuits. Which is the sounder view? The courts are sharply divided. *Compare Tailor v. Meirick, id., with Gaste v. Kaiserman,* 669 F. Supp. 583 (S.D.N.Y. 1987).

6. CRIMINAL LIABILITY

Section 506 of the Copyright Act imposes federal criminal liability for various acts (not all of which would render the actor liable for civil remedies). Section 506(a) provides: "Any person who infringes a copyright willfully and for purposes of commercial advantage or private financial gain shall be punished as provided in section 2319 of title 18."

The named section of the criminal code was amended in significant respects in October 1992. Previously, the section declared to be a felony only the large-scale and willful reproduction and distribution of pirated or bootlegged motion pictures and musical records or tapes. As amended, the unauthorized reproduction or public distribution (but no other exclusive right of the copyright owner) of *any* kind of copyrighted work may be a felony, if the acts are willful (i.e., with knowledge that the conduct is prohibited by law), if they are for purposes of commercial advantage or private financial gain, and if at least ten copies with a retail value of more than $2,500 are reproduced or distributed within a 180-day period; this is punishable by up to five years' imprisonment. Up to ten years' imprisonment may be imposed for a second or subsequent offense. In all other cases, the defendant may be imprisoned for up to one year. Fines may be imposed up to $250,000 for individuals and $500,000 for organizations. When Congress amended the Copyright Act in 1990 so as to accord rights of integrity and attribution to visual artists (§ 106A(a)), it also provided, in § 506(f), that violations of those rights cannot give rise to criminal liability.

As the language of § 506(a) makes clear, although innocent intent is not a defense to civil copyright liability, in criminal prosecutions the government must prove that the accused intended to infringe (rather than merely to make or distribute copies). Section 506(b) requires that the court order the forfeiture and destruction of all copies or phonorecords, and manufacturing devices, in a criminal case — a remedy that is left to the court's discretion in civil cases.

Section 506(c) criminalizes the knowing placement of a false copyright notice or the knowing distribution or importation of any article bearing such notice; and § 506(d) penalizes the fraudulent removal of a copyright notice. The maximum fine under either of these two sections is $2,500. It should be noted that the acts condemned by these two subsections are not infringements of copyright for which civil remedies are available. *See Eden Toys, Inc. v. Florelee Undergarment Co.,* 697 F.2d 27, 37 n.10 (2d Cir. 1982); *Scarves by Vera, Inc. v. American Handbags, Inc.,* 188 F. Supp. 255 (S.D.N.Y. 1960). This may help to explain why they have apparently never been successfully invoked as a basis for a criminal prosecution. Finally, § 506(e) imposes criminal liability for false representations of material fact in applying for copyright registration.

In *Dowling v. United States,* 473 U.S. 207 (1985) (6-to-3 decision), the Supreme Court addressed the issue whether liability for copyright offenses could arise under federal criminal statutes aside from the relevant sections of the Copyright Act. After reviewing the language and legislative history of the National Stolen Property Act, 18 U.S.C. § 2314, which proscribes interstate and foreign transport of "goods" knowing the same to have been "stolen, converted, or taken by fraud," the Court determined that distributing "bootleg" phonorecords did not fall within the ambit of that Act. The rationale of *Dowling* is that given the very specific provisions of the amended Copyright Act of 1976, and in particular of 17 U.S.C. § 506(a), Congress did not intend broad criminal laws regarding stolen property — with punishments up to ten years in prison — to encompass copyright infringement. Justice Blackmun, writing for the Court, stated: "The copyright owner ... holds no ordinary chattel. A copyright, like other intellectual property, comprises a series of carefully defined and carefully delimited interests to which the law affords correspondingly exact protections." Thus it seems clear that without explicit congressional authorization, courts will not impose criminal penalties for conduct within the ban of the Copyright Act.

The interpretation in *Dowling* was applied in *United States v. Brown,* 925 F.2d 1301 (10th Cir. 1991). There, the defendant had been employed as a computer programmer and had made an unauthorized copy of a source code in which his employer held the copyright, although the hard computer disk onto which he copied the program did not belong to the employer. The court held that criminal convictions under the NSPA had always involved stolen physical goods, and it was not the intent of Congress that the NSPA was to function so as to criminalize copyright infringement. (The court observed that ambiguities in a criminal statute should be resolved in favor of the accused.)

With the exception of sound recordings made before 1972 (see § 301(c) of the Copyright Act), persons accused of conduct which creates criminal or civil liability under the federal Copyright Act are exempt from state criminal prosecution. *See, e.g., Crow v. Wainwright,* 720 F.2d 1224 (11th Cir. 1983), *cert. denied,* 469 U.S. 819 (1984) (preemption of state stolen-property crime, held equivalent to copyright infringement under the federal act). Even more clearly, actions that are lawful under the Copyright Act cannot be rendered criminal by state statutes.

Chapter 7

COPYRIGHT PROTECTION OF COMPUTER SOFTWARE

In copyright law, the category "literary works" now embraces newer technological expressions, notably computer programs. How well do the principles enunciated for plays, novels, and the like, translate to computer programs? Indeed, should these principles apply at all, or is some different, perhaps more computer-specific, mode of analysis more appropriate? As you read the materials that follow, think about whether the copyright law should approach problems of software protection differently, or whether maintenance of continuity best serves the respective interests in this area.

INTRODUCTION*

Noted Stanford University computer scientist Donald Knuth has declared:

> The process of preparing programs for a digital computer is especially attractive, not only because it can be economically and scientifically rewarding, but also because it can be an aesthetic experience much like composing poetry or music.[1]

With these same sentiments, possibly, the daughter of Lord Byron, Ada Augusta, Countess of Lovelace, became the first acknowledged programmer, in collaboration with British inventor Charles Babbage. With his "Analytical Engine" Babbage created in the 19th century a machine embodying many of the principles of the modern digital computer. With a series of mechanical gears and shafts for performing the calculations, and though lacking internal memory storage for program or data, the machine could implement a program, via the use of input cards: operation cards designating the required operations and variable cards for data.

Most digital computers have five functional components: (1) input; (2) storage of the input by memory; (3) a control unit that receives data from memory and gives instructions for the arithmetic; (4) an arithmetic unit that carries out the control's commands; and (5) an output capability. The computer program in a general sense instructs the computer regarding the things it is to do. In the industry, the physical machinery is referred to as hardware and the instructional material as software. A digital computer operates on data expressed in digits, solving a problem by doing arithmetic as a person would do it by head and hand, but at awesome speed. The digits are based on combinations of ones and zeros representing on and off positions of switches. Some of the digits are stored as components of the computer. Others are introduced

---

*The editors thank Ariel Reich, Columbia Law School class of 1993, for his assistance in revising these materials.

[1]Donald E. Knuth, The Art of Computer Programming v (2d ed. 1973).

into the computer in a form that it is designed to recognize. The computer operates then upon both new and previously stored data.

The first electronic automatic computer, ENIAC, was developed at the Moore School of the University of Pennsylvania over 1943-1946 and was a giant, in modern terms, in dimensions only: 18,000 vacuum tubes, weighing 30 tons and occupying a room 30' x 50'. Early computers were so expensive that only the government or the largest corporations could even consider owning them. In order to function, the typical early computer required an environment in which temperature and humidity were carefully monitored.

Since ENIAC, the actual components may have changed — the calculating elements evolving from vacuum tubes to transistors to integrated circuitry, memory from mercury-delay lines and electrostatic storage tubes to magnetic memory to random access memory (RAM), output devices from slow-moving line printers to high-resolution graphics monitors — but, the basic operating principles remain the same.

On the other hand, the accessibility of computers to users has changed radically. Initially, computers were used by a single programmer at a time; the computers were controlled by programs that were created by their manufacturers and that were used exclusively for that particular computer. When large mainframe computers emerged in the 1960's, their functions became available to multiple simultaneous users. The computer could interact with users with video terminals on a time-sharing basis, or could service batches of jobs in the background. The advent of the microcomputer in the late 1970's returned computer capabilities to the single user, albeit to far more people and with far greater capability. Though mainframe and even supercomputers have continued to evolve, the microcomputer is the one that has transformed the industry the most in the past decade.

A computer program starts out as a series of instructions in a computer language employed and understood by trained humans. Regardless of the computer language used, this human-intelligible ("higher level") version of the program is known as "source code." The source code is then translated into "binary language," i.e., a series of ones and zeros representing electric charges or the lack of such charges. This "lower level" language is called "object code." Very persevering, highly trained humans can understand certain forms of object code. As a final step, the object code is electronically or photochemically encoded onto a storage medium such as a tiny silicon chip or a diskette. Microcode embodied on a chip is known as a ROM (Read Only Memory), and the chip becomes part of the computer's circuitry, while a diskette may be inserted and removed.

The development of computer capabilities has been aided enormously by the evolution of computer languages. Programming in binary machine language is an arduous and meticulous enterprise. However, most programming is done in source code. The progression of high-level languages from FORTRAN to PL/I to "C" to ADA and beyond, has achieved serveral results. First, the higher level languages free the programmer from the idiosyncrasies of the hardware of particular computers. It thus becomes easier to adapt the program to different kinds of computers. (A program that can be compatible with different "hardware platforms" is "portable.") Second, the evolution of high level languages has promoted the development of a language structure that makes code-writing less error-prone; this in turn speeds creation of new programs. Finally, advances in programming languages facilitate "modularity," which enables programs to be separated by function; this makes large projects feasible. Thus, programs can be written for any purpose: from microcode — the programs wired into the hardware that run the computer processors — to the operating systems, with their unglamorous task of providing all the low-level operations and utilities that allow the application programs — those the user interacts with — to operate as easily and seamlessly as possible.

In due course, the Copyright Office was faced with the question of the registrability of computer programs. In 1964 the Office determined to make registration of such works under its "rule of doubt," but required deposit of a human-readable form of the program (e.g., a printout) if the program had been published in only machine-readable form. Furthermore, the computer industry was not then eagerly pressing for copyright protection of computer programs. Overall, the industry believed that trade secret protection afforded sufficient coverage. Customers were contractually bound to refrain from examining either the hardware (except for minor servicing) or the program code. This arrangement was feasible in an era of proprietary systems with vertically-integrated computer companies: the customer would buy an entire computer package, both the hardware and software, from the same manufacturer. One proprietor's package would operate together but its components would be incompatible with any other system. When these market conditions changed, the computer industry became very interested in copyright protection.

A. LEGISLATIVE POLICY

Although there were no judicial decisions under the 1909 Act validating the Copyright Office practice of registering claims to copyright in computer programs, the more controversial question during the 1960's seemed to be the issue of infringement by computer, i.e., "the impact of [copyright] on the use of copyrighted materials in computers and other forms of information storage and retrieval systems." H.R. Rep. No. 94-1476 at 48. The congressional response to the problem was twofold. First, Congress established a National Commission on New Technological Uses of Copyrighted Works ("CONTU") to study computers and copyright as well as photocopying and to make specific recommendations to Congress. Pub. L. No. 93-573, 93d Cong., 2d Sess. (1974). Second, a stop-gap provision (presumably pending the CONTU report) was inserted as § 117 of the revision bill that eventually became the 1976 Act. This section carried forward the law in effect on December 31, 1977, as to rights with respect to computer usage of copyrighted works. The House Report suggested quite clearly that § 102 of the Act was to be understood to provide protection not only for computer programs but computerized data bases as well.

CONTU, consisting of distinguished individuals selected, pursuant to congressional directive, from authors and other copyright owners, copyright users, and "the public," and assisted by an expert staff, produced a Final Report on July 31, 1978. A surprising consensus developed to consider copyright liability as potentially attaching to the unauthorized storage of a work in a computer memory. An equally surprising controversy arose as to whether computer programs should remain copyrightable. The majority was of the view that they should; Commissioners Hersey and Karpatkin disagreed; and Commissioner Nimmer filed a statement concurring with the majority.

1. THE CONTU REPORT

The following materials are excerpts from the majority statement in the Commission's report.

FINAL REPORT OF THE NATIONAL COMMISSION ON NEW TECHNOLOGICAL USES OF COPYRIGHTED WORKS (1978)

Computer Programs

Computer programs are a form of writing virtually unknown twenty-five years ago. They consist of sets of instructions which, when properly drafted, are used in an almost limitless number of ways to release human beings from such diverse mundane tasks as preparing payrolls, monitoring aircraft instruments, taking data readings, making calculations for research, setting type, operating assembly lines, and taking inventory. Computer programs are prepared by the careful fixation of words, phrases, numbers, and other symbols in various media. The instructions that make up a program may be read, understood, and followed by a human being. For both economic and humanitarian reasons, it is undesirable for people to carry out manually the process described in painstaking detail in a computer program. Machines, lacking human attributes, cannot object to carrying out repetitious, boring, and tedious tasks. Because machines can and do perform these tasks, people are free to do those other things which they alone can do or in which they find a more rewarding expenditure of their efforts.

Great changes have occurred in the construction of computers, as well as in the media in which programs are recorded. Periodic progress has seen the development, utilization, and, in some cases, passage into obsolescence of bulky plug boards, punched paper cards and tape, magnetic tapes and disks, and semiconductor chips. It should be emphasized that these developments reflect differences only in the media in which programs are stored and not in the nature of the programs themselves.

The evolution of these media is similar to that of devices for playing recorded music. Circuit boards may be compared to music boxes, and punched paper to piano rolls, while magnetic disks and tapes store music and programs in precisely the same manner. Both recorded music and computer programs are sets of information in a form which, when passed over a magnetized head, cause minute currents to flow in such a way that desired physical work is accomplished.

The need for protecting the form of expression chosen by the author of a computer program has grown proportionally with two related concurrent trends. Computers have become less cumbersome and expensive, so that individuals can and do own computers in their homes and offices with more power than the first commercial computers, while at the same time, programs have become less and less frequently written to comply with the requirements imposed by a single-purpose machine.

Just as there was little need to protect the ridged brass wheel in a nine-teenth-century music box, so too was there little reason to protect the wired circuit or plug boards of early computers. The cost of making the wheel was inseparable from the cost of producing the ridged final product. The cost of copying a reel of magnetic tape, whether it contains a Chopin étude or a computer program, is small. Thus, the following proposition seems sound: if the cost of duplicating information is small, then it is simple for a less than scrupulous person to duplicate it. This means that legal as well as physical protection for the information is a necessary incentive if such information is to be created and disseminated.

. . . .

As the number of computers has increased dramatically, so has the number of programs with which they may be used. While the first computers were designed and programmed to perform one or a few specific tasks, an ever increasing proportion of all computers are general-purpose machines which perform diverse tasks, depending in part upon the programs with which they are used. Early programs were designed by machine manufacturers to be used in conjunction with one model or even one individual computer. Today, many programs are designed to operate on any number of machines from one or more manufacturers. In addition, and perhaps even more importantly, there is a growing proportion of programs created by persons who do not make ma-chines. These people may be users or they may be — and increasingly are — programmers or small firms who market their wares for use by individual machine owners who are not in a position to write their own programs. Just as Victrola once made most of the first record players and records, so too did early machine manufacturers write most of the first programs. Victrola's suc-cessor, RCA, still produces sound recordings (but, interestingly enough, not phonographs), but so do hundreds of other firms. If present computer industry trends continue, it is all but certain that programs written by nonmachine manufacturers will gain an increasing share of the market, not only because writing programs and building machines are two very different skills that need not necessarily occur simultaneously, but also because program writing requires little capital investment.

The cost of developing computer programs is far greater than the cost of their duplication. Consequently, computer programs, as the previous discus-sion illustrates, are likely to be disseminated only if:

1. the creator may recover all of its costs plus a fair profit on the first sale of the work, thus leaving it unconcerned about the later publication of the work; or

2. the creator may spread its costs over multiple copies of the work with some form of protection against unauthorized duplication of the work; or

3. the creator's costs are borne by another, as, for example, when the gov-ernment or a foundation offers prizes or awards; or

4. the creator is indifferent to cost and donates the work to the public.

The consequence of the first possibility would be that the price of virtually any program would be so high that there would necessarily be a drastic reduction in the number of programs marketed. In this country, possibilities three and four occur, but rarely outside of academic and government-sponsored research. Computer programs are the product of great intellectual effort and their utility is unquestionable. The Commission is, therefore, satisfied that some form of protection is necessary to encourage the creation and broad distribution of computer programs in a competitive market.

The Commission's conclusion is that the continued availability of copyright protection for computer programs is desirable. This availability is in keeping with nearly two centuries' development of American copyright doctrine, during which the universe of works protectible by statutory copyright has expanded along with the imagination, communications media, and technical capabilities of society. Copyright, therefore, protects the program so long as it remains fixed in a tangible medium of expression but does not protect the electro-mechanical functioning of a machine. The way copyright affects games and game-playing is closely analogous: one may not adopt and republish or redistribute copyrighted game rules, but the copyright owner has no power to prevent others from playing the game.

. . . .

Copyright and Other Methods Compared

The purpose of copyright is to grant authors a limited property right in the form of expression of their ideas. The other methods used to protect property interests in computer programs have different conceptual bases and, not surprisingly, work in different ways. An appreciation of those differences has contributed to the Commission's recommendation that copyright protection not be withdrawn from programs. Patents are designed to give inventors a short-term, powerful monopoly in devices, processes, compositions of matter, and designs which embody their ideas. The doctrine of trade secrecy is intended to protect proprietors who use a "formula, pattern, device or compilation of information" in their business "which gives [them] an opportunity to obtain an advantage over competitors who do not know or use it." Unfair competition is a legal theory which, among other things, proscribes misrepresentation about the nature and origin of products in commerce. Each of these forms of protection may inhibit the dissemination of information and restrict competition to a greater extent than copyright.

In certain circumstances, proprietors may find patent protection more attractive than copyright, since it gives them the right not only to license and control the use of their patented devices or processes but also to prevent the use of such devices or processes when they are independently developed by third parties. Such rights last for seventeen years. The acquisition of a patent, however, is time consuming and expensive, primarily because a patentee's rights are great and the legal hurdles an applicant must overcome are high. A work must be useful, novel, and nonobvious to those familiar with the state of the art in which the patent is sought. The applicant must prove these conditions to the satisfaction of the Patent and Trademark Office or, failing that, to the Court of Customs and Patent Appeals or the Supreme Court.

Even if patents prove available in the United States, only the very few programs which survive the rigorous application and appeals procedure could be patented. Once such protection attached, of course, all others would be barred from using the patented process, even if independently developed.

Trade secrecy is a doctrine known in every American jurisdiction. As a creature of state statute or common law it differs somewhat from state to state. The premise on which trade secrecy is based is this: if a business maintains confidentiality concerning either the way in which it does something or some information that it has, then courts should protect the business against the misappropriation of that secret. Although many proprietors feel secure when using trade secrecy, there are several problems they must face with respect to its use in protecting programs. Because secrecy is paramount, it is inappropriate for protecting works that contain the secret and are designed to be widely distributed. Although this matters little in the case of unique programs prepared for large commercial customers, it substantially precludes the use of trade secrecy with respect to programs sold in multiple copies over the counter to small businesses, schools, consumers, and hobbyists. Protection is lost when the secret is disclosed, without regard to the circumstances surrounding the disclosure. The lack of uniform national law in this area may also be perceived by proprietors as reducing the utility of this method of protection.

From the user's standpoint, there are additional drawbacks. Users must cover the seller's expenses associated with maintaining a secure system through increased prices. Their freedom to do business in an unencumbered way is reduced, since they may need to enter into elaborate nondisclosure contracts with employees and third parties who have access to the secrets and to limit that access to a very small number of people. Since secrets are by definition known to only a few people, there is necessarily a reduced flow of information in the marketplace, which hinders the ability of potential buyers to make comparisons and hence leads to higher prices.

Experts in the computer industry state that a further problem with respect to trade secrecy is that there is much human effort wasted when people do for themselves that which others have already done but are keeping secret. This was emphasized in the reports to the Commission prepared by the Public Interest Economics Center and the New York University economists.

The availability of copyright for computer programs does not, of course, affect the availability of trade secrecy protection. Under the Act of 1976 only those state rights that are equivalent to the exclusive rights granted therein (generally, common law copyright) are preempted. Any decline in use of trade secrecy might be based not upon preemption but on the rapid increase in the number of widely distributed programs in which trade secret protection could not be successfully asserted.

The common law doctrine of unfair competition of the misappropriation variety is based upon the principle that one may not appropriate a competitor's skill, expenditure, and labor. It prohibits false advertising and the "passing off" of another's work as one's own. While there is a small body of federal unfair competition law, it is largely a state doctrine with the same lack of national uniformity that besets trade secrecy. Although unfair competition may provide relief ancillary to copyright in certain situations, its scope is not as broad, and it seems unlikely that it alone could provide sufficient protection against the misappropriation of programs. For example, the unauthorized copying of any work for any purpose could be a copyright infringement without amounting to unfair competition.

The answers to such economic questions as the effect of protection on the market and the opportunity it creates for an uncompetitive rate of return tend to show that, of the various potential modes of protection, copyright has the smallest negative impact.

Copyrightability of Data Bases

. . . .

Similar also to a telephone directory, copyright in a dynamic data base protects no individual datum, but only the systematized form in which the data are presented. The use of one item retrieved from such a work — be it an address, a chemical formula, or a citation to an article — would not under reasonable circumstances merit the attention of the copyright proprietor. Nor would it conceivably constitute infringement of copyright. The retrieval and reduplication of any substantial portion of a data base, whether or not the individual data are in the public domain, would likely constitute a duplication of the copyrighted element of a data base and would be an infringement. In any event, the issue of how much is enough to constitute a copyright violation would likely entail analysis on a case-by-case basis with considerations of fair use bearing on whether the unauthorized copying of a limited portion of a data base would be held noninfringing. Fair use should have very limited force when an unauthorized copy of a data base is made for primarily commercial use. Only if information of a substantial amount were extracted and duplicated for redistribution would serious problems exist, raising concerns about the enforcement of proprietary rights.

It appears that adequate legal protection for proprietary rights in extracts from data bases exists under traditional copyright principles as expressed in the new law, supplemented by still-available relief under common-law principles of unfair competition. The unauthorized taking of substantial segments of a copyrighted data base should be considered infringing, consistent with the case law developed from infringement of copyright in various forms of directories.[1117] In addition, common-law principles of misappropriation which, according to the legislative reports accompanying the new law, are not preempted with regard to computer data bases are available to enforce proprietary rights in these works.

[1117] See *Leon v. Pacific Tel. & Tel. Co.*, 91 F.2d 484 (9th Cir. 1937); *Jeweler's Circular Pub. Co. v. Keystone Pub. Co.*, 281 F. 83 (2d Cir. 1922), *cert. denied*, 259 U.S. 581 (1922), *aff'g* 274 F. 932 (S.D.N.Y. 1921); *New York Times Co. v. Roxbury Data Interface, Inc.*, 434 F. Supp. 217, 194 U.S.P.Q. 371 (D.N.J. 1977). [Eds.' note: the Supreme Court's ruling in *Feist v. Rural Telephone, supra*, calls into question the continued validity of these decisions.]

Computer-Authored Works

On the basis of its investigations and society's experience with the computer, the Commission believes that there is no reasonable basis for considering that a computer in any way contributes authorship to a work produced through its use. The computer, like a camera or a typewriter, is an inert instrument, capable of functioning only when activated either directly or indirectly by a human. When so activated it is capable of doing only what it is directed to do in the way it is directed to perform.

Computers may be employed in a variety of ways in creating works that may be protected by copyright. Works of graphic art may consist of designs, lines, intensities of color, and the like selected and organized with the assistance of a computer. A computer may be used to assist an artist in filling in numerous frames in an animation sequence, thus reducing the amount of time and effort otherwise needed to prepare an animated work.

In the case of computer music, a program may be designed to select a series of notes and arrange them into a musical composition, employing various tonal qualities and rhythmic patterns. The computer may also be used to simulate musical instruments and perform the music so composed.

In other instances, a computer may be used to manipulate statistical information to produce an analysis of that information. The resulting work may bear little similarity to the original form or arrangement of the work being analyzed, as in the case of an economic forecast produced by the manipulation of raw economic data. A computer may, on the other hand, be employed to extract and reproduce portions of a work. In every case, the work produced will result from the contents of the data base, the instructions indirectly provided in the program, and the direct discretionary intervention of a human involved in the process.

To be entitled to copyright, a work must be an original work of authorship. It must be a writing within the meaning of that term as used in the Copyright Clause of the Constitution. The Supreme Court has interpreted this requirement to include "any physical rendering of the fruits of creative intellectual or aesthetic labor." The history of the development of the concept of originality shows that only a modicum of effort is required. In *Alfred Bell & Co. Ltd. v. Catalda Fine Arts, Inc.*, a federal court of appeals, speaking through Judge Frank, observed:

> All that is needed to satisfy both the Constitution and the statute is that the "author" contributed something more than a "merely trivial" variation, something recognizably "his own." ... No matter how poor artistically the "author's" addition, it is enough if it be his own.

Thus, it may be seen that although the quantum of originality needed to support a claim of authorship in a work is small, it must nevertheless be present. If a work created through application of computer technology meets this minimal test of originality, it is copyrightable. The eligibility of any work for protection by copyright depends not upon the device or devices used in its creation, but rather upon the presence of at least minimal human creative effort at the time the work is produced.

Computers are enormously complex and powerful instruments which vastly extend human powers to calculate, select, rearrange, display, design, and do other things involved in the creation of works. However, it is a human power they extend. The computer may be analogized to or equated with, for example, a camera, and the computer affects the copyright status of a resultant work no more than the employment of a still or motion-picture camera, a tape recorder, or a typewriter. Hence, it seems clear that the copyright problems with respect to the authorship of new works produced with the assistance of a computer are not unlike those posed by the creation of more traditional works.

....

The Input Issue [Infringement by Computer]

The issue whether copyright liability should attach at the input or output stage of use in conjunction with a computer — i.e., at the time a work is placed in machine-readable form in a computer memory unit or when access is sought to the work existing in computer memory — has been the primary source of disagreement regarding copyright protection for works in computer-readable form. This issue provided the major impetus for the introduction of section 117 into the copyright revision bill.[163] It appears, nevertheless, that the provisions of the new copyright law offer appropriate and sufficient guidance to determine what acts create copyright liability in this area. The protection afforded by section 106 of the new law seemingly would prohibit the unauthorized storage of a work within a computer memory, which would be merely one form of reproduction, one of the exclusive rights granted by copyright.[164]

Considering the act of storing a computerized data base in the memory of a computer as an exclusive right of the copyright proprietor appears consistent both with accepted copyright principles and with considerations of fair treatment for potentially affected parties. Making a copy of an entire work would normally, subject to some possible exception for fair use, be considered exclu-

---

[163] 17 U.S.C. § 117 provides as follows: "Notwithstanding the provisions of sections 106 through 116 and 118, this title does not afford to the owner of copyright in a work any greater or lesser rights with respect to the use of the work in conjunction with automatic systems capable of storing, processing, retrieving, or transferring information, or in conjunction with any similar device, machine, or process, than those afforded to works under the law, whether title 17 or the common law or statutes of a State, in effect on December 31, 1977, as held applicable and construed by a court in an action brought under this title."

This section was first introduced in the copyright revision bill in 1969 (see 91st Cong., 1st Sess., December 10, 1969, S. 543 [Committee Print]), at which time the impact of the computer, and particularly the "input-output" question, was causing great concern on the part of copyright proprietors. Section 117 was agreed upon by interested parties as a means of permitting passage of the revision bill without committing Congress to a position on the computer-related issue until more study could be undertaken.

[164] It may be that the use of the term *input* to describe the act to which copyright liability attaches has been misleading. A more accurate description of the process by which a work may be stored in a computer memory would indicate that a reproduction is created within the computer memory to make the work accessible by means of the computer.

sively within the domain of the copyright proprietor. One would have to assume, however, that fair use would apply rarely to the reproduction in their entirety of such compendious works as data bases.[165] If a copy of the work is to be stored in a computer and subsequently made accessible to others, its creation would have to be properly authorized by the copyright proprietor. That only one copy is being made, or even that the owner of the computer system intends to exact no fee for providing access to the work, would no more insulate the copies from liability for copyright infringement than would similar circumstances insulate a public library which made unauthorized duplications of entire copyrighted works for its basic lending functions.[166]

Under normal circumstances, the transfer by sale or lease of a copyrighted work in computer-readable form, such as a data base, would be a meaningless transaction unless implicit in the transfer was the authorization to place or reproduce a copy in the memory unit of the transferee's computer. Any limitations on the use to be made of the copy would be a matter to be negotiated between private parties, guided by applicable public policy considerations. The proprietor of a work in computer-readable form would, under any foreseeable circumstances, be able to control by contract the future disposition of machine-readable copies of his proprietary work. The proprietor of copyright in such a work would always have a valid cause of action, arising either under copyright or contract, if a reproduction of the work were entered into a computer without the proprietor's authorization, or if a transferee authorized a third party to enter a copy into the memory unit of a computer in violation of the terms of a valid agreement with the proprietor. That copyright would not provide the sole right and remedy for unauthorized use of a protected work neither is unique to the protection of proprietary interests in computer-readable works nor is it a situation to be considered undesirable.

Accordingly, the Commission believes that the application of principles already embodied in the language of the new copyright law achieves the desired substantive legal protection for copyrighted works which exist in machine-readable form. The introduction of a work into a computer memory would, consistent with the new law, be a reproduction of the work, one of the exclusive rights of the copyright proprietor. The unauthorized transfer of an existing machine-readable embodiment of a work could subject the violators to remedies for breach of contract. Principles of fair use would be applicable in limited instances to excuse an unauthorized input of a work into computer memory. Exemplifying such fair uses could be the creation of a copy in a computer memory to prepare a concordance of a work or to perform a syntactical analysis of a work, which but for the use of a computer would require a prohibitive amount of human time and effort. To satisfy the criteria of fair use, any copies created for such research purposes should be destroyed

---

[165] See 17 U.S.C. § 107 for statutory criteria governing fair use.

[166] The example of a copyrighted work placed in a computer memory solely to facilitate an individual's scholarly research has been cited as a possible fair use. The Commission agrees that such a use, restricted to individual research, should be considered fair. To prevent abuse of fair use principles, any copy created in a machine memory should be erased after completion of the particular research project for which it was made.

upon completion of the research project for which they were created. Should the individual or institution carrying on this research desire to retain the copy for archival purposes or future use, it should be required to obtain permission to do so from the copyright proprietor.

Recommendations for Statutory Change

To make the law clear regarding both proprietors' and users' rights, the Commission suggests that the following changes to the Copyright Act of 1976 be made:

1. That section 117 as enacted be repealed.
2. That section 101 be amended to add the following definition:

> A "computer program" is a set of statements or instructions to be used directly or indirectly in a computer in order to bring about a certain result.

3. That a new section 117 be enacted as follows:

> *§ 117: Limitations on exclusive rights: computer programs*
>
> Notwithstanding the provisions of § 106, it is not an infringement for the rightful possessor of a copy of a computer program to make or authorize the making of another copy or adaptation of that computer program *provided:*
>
> (1) that such a new copy or adaptation is created as an essential step in the utilization of the computer program in conjunction with a machine and that it is used in no other manner, or
>
> (2) that such new copy or adaptation is for archival purposes only and that all archival copies are destroyed in the event that continued possession of the computer program should cease to be rightful.
>
> Any exact copies prepared in accordance with the provisions of this section may be leased, sold, or otherwise transferred, along with the copy from which such copies were prepared, only as part of the lease, sale, or other transfer of all rights in the program. Adaptations so prepared may be transferred only with the authorization of the copyright owner.

The 1976 Act, without change, makes it clear that the placement of any copyrighted work into a computer is the preparation of a copy and, therefore, a potential infringement of copyright. Section 117, designed to subject computer uses of copyrighted works to treatment under the old law, vitiates that proscription, at least insofar as machine-readable versions are not *copies* under the 1909 Act. Therefore, to prevent any question concerning the impropriety of program piracy and to assure that all works of authorship are treated comparably under the new law, section 117 should be repealed.

Because the placement of a work into a computer is the preparation of a copy, the law should provide that persons in rightful possession of copies of programs be able to use them freely without fear of exposure to copyright liability. Obviously, creators, lessors, licensors, and vendors of copies of programs intend that they be used by their customers, so that rightful users would but rarely need a legal shield against potential copyright problems. It is easy to imagine, however, a situation in which the copyright owner might desire, for good reason or none at all, to force a lawful owner or possessor of a copy to stop using a particular program. One who rightfully possesses a copy of a program, therefore, should be provided with a legal right to copy it to that extent which will permit its use by that possessor. This would include the right to load it into a computer and to prepare archival copies of it to guard against destruction or damage by mechanical or electrical failure. But this permission would not extend to other copies of the program. Thus, one could not, for example, make archival copies of a program and later sell some while retaining some for use. The sale of a copy of a program by a rightful possessor to another must be of all rights in the program, thus creating a new rightful possessor and destroying that status as regards the seller. This is in accord with the intent of that portion of the law which provides that owners of authorized copies of a copyrighted work may sell those copies without leave of the copyright proprietor.

2. CONGRESSIONAL ACTION

In 1980, Congress amended the Copyright Act, adding to § 101 the definition recommended by CONTU, deleting § 117, and replacing it with a provision virtually identical to the one recommended by CONTU. The one change Congress effected was to substitute the term "'owner' of a copy of a computer program" for CONTU's "'rightful possessor' of a copy of a computer program." In view of the dearth of legislative history accompanying the 1980 amendments, it has been stated that "it is fair to conclude, since Congress adopted [CONTU's] recommendations without alteration, that the CONTU report reflects the Congressional intent." *Midway Mfg. Co. v. Strohon,* 564 F. Supp. 741, 750 n.6 (N.D. Ill. 1983).

QUESTIONS

1. What is the significance of the change Congress did make in the CONTU recommended text from affording "rightful possessors" of software limited private copying and adaptation rights, to restricting the class of beneficiaries of these rights to computer program "owners"? Many software producers have endeavored to circumvent the grant of rights in § 117 by asserting retention of ownership of the physical copies of the programs. So-called "shrinkwrap licenses" printed on the outside covers of software packages typically notify the purchaser that the producer "retains title to and ownership of the program," and stress that "You may not decompile, disassemble, or otherwise reverse engineer the program. You may not modify the program in any way without the prior written consent of [the producer]." ("Terms and Conditions" appearing on outside wrapper of WordPerfect package.)

Are such "licenses" valid? *See Vault Corp. v. Quaid Software Ltd.,* 847 F.2d 255 (5th Cir. 1988); Maher, *The Shrink-Wrap License: Old Problems in a New Wrapper,* 34 J. Copyright Soc'y 292 (1987); Fischer, *Reserving All Rights Beyond Copyright: Nonstatutory Restrictive Notices,* 34 J. Copyright Soc'y 249 (1987).

2. A company employes 100 persons. Each of these employees has a desk and computer terminal workstation. The company has purchased one copy of a word processing program, and proposes to load it into the central computer, thereby making it available to all employees who log onto the company's "local area network." Absent a negotiated license to do so, would the company incur liability for copyright infringement were it to execute this plan? *See MAI Sys. Corp. v. Peak Computer Inc.*, 991 F.2d 511 (9th Cir. 1993).

3. Nibble is a monthly magazine aimed at users of Apple brand computers. Each issue contains some fifteen computer programs that readers may type into their Apple computers and then use. Copyright in the programs is owned by Nibble. For magazine purchasers who are reluctant to take the twenty to thirty hours necessary to type each program directly into their computer, Nibble sells (for $25) disks on which their programs are already encoded.

Compu-Type offers a "typing service" to purchasers of Nibble and other similar publications. For a fee of $7.50 it will put on a computer disk all of the programs that appear in an issue of Nibble; it sells such a disk only to persons who certify that they have purchased the pertinent issue of Nibble, and it does not supply any instructions with the disks it sells (so that its customers must use Nibble magazine to secure any such instructions). Compu-Type produces its disks for sale by first typing the Nibble programs into a computer and then transferring them to a "master disk," which is in turn used to transfer the programs to blank disks.

Nibble has brought an infringement action against Compu-Type. It claims that although purchasers of Nibble may, of course, type the Nibble programs into their own Apple computer, Compu-Type acts unlawfully when it types those programs onto a disk which is then sold to readers of Nibble magazine. Compu-Type relies on § 117. Both parties have moved for summary judgment. What judgment would you render? *See Micro-Sparc, Inc. v. Amtype Corp.*, 592 F. Supp. 33 (D. Mass. 1984).

4. The Atari Company manufactures and sells the 2600 home computer as well as accompanying cartridges of videogames, such as Pac-Man. The cartridges contain a computer program that causes the audiovisual aspects of the game to emanate from a connected television screen; the program is contained in a Read Only Memory (ROM) chip, which can neither be reprogrammed nor erased. The Prom Blaster Company manufactures and sells a device for making "back up" copies of videogames used in the Atari 2600 computer. The user places the Atari cartridge in one slot and a blank cartridge in another, and within three minutes an exact duplicate is made. Atari has brought an action against Prom Blaster for contributory copyright infringement, i.e., knowingly inducing, causing or materially contributing to another's infringement. Both parties stipulate that Prom Blaster will be liable should it be found that a purchaser's use of its duplicating machine is an infringement. Prom Blaster claims that the primary use of its device is the making of "archival copies" within the exception set forth in § 117. Do you agree? *See Atari, Inc. v. JS&A Group, Inc.*, 597 F. Supp. 5 (N.D. Ill. 1983).

B. THE DEVELOPMENT OF THE CASE LAW

1. SOURCE AND OBJECT CODE

APPLE COMPUTER, INC. v. FRANKLIN COMPUTER CORP.

714 F.2d 1240 (3d Cir. 1983)

SLOVITER, CIRCUIT JUDGE.

I. *Introduction*

Apple Computer, Inc. appeals from the district court's denial of a motion to preliminarily enjoin Franklin Computer Corp. from infringing the copyrights Apple holds on fourteen computer programs.... [T]he district court denied the preliminary injunction, *inter alia,* because it had "some doubt as to the copyrightability of the programs." *Apple Computer, Inc. v. Franklin Computer Corp.,* 545 F. Supp. 812, 812 (E.D. Pa. 1982). This legal ruling is fundamental to all future proceedings in this action and, as the parties and amici curiae seem to agree, has considerable significance to the computer services industry. Because we conclude that the district court proceeded under an erroneous view of the applicable law, we reverse the denial of the preliminary injunction and remand.

II. *Facts and Procedural History*

Apple, one of the computer industry leaders, manufactures and markets personal computers (microcomputers), related peripheral equipment such as disk drives (peripherals), and computer programs (software). It presently manufactures Apple II computers and distributes over 150 programs. Apple has sold over 400,000 Apple II computers, employs approximately 3,000 people, and had annual sales of $335,000,000 for fiscal year 1981. One of the byproducts of Apple's success is the independent development by third parties of numerous computer programs which are designed to run on the Apple II computer.

Franklin, the defendant below, manufactures and sells the ACE 100 personal computer and at the time of the hearing employed about 75 people and had sold fewer than 1,000 computers. The ACE 100 was designed to be "Apple compatible," so that peripheral equipment and software developed for use with the Apple II computer could be used in conjunction with the ACE 100. Franklin's copying of Apple's operating system computer programs in an effort to achieve such compatibility precipitated this suit.

Like all computers both the Apple II and ACE 100 have a central processing unit (CPU) which is the integrated circuit that executes programs. In lay terms, the CPU does the work it is instructed to do. Those instructions are contained on computer programs.

....

The CPU can only follow instructions written in object code. However, programs are usually written in source code which is more intelligible to humans. Programs written in source code can be converted or translated by a "compiler" program into object code for use by the computer. Programs are generally distributed only in their object code version stored on a memory device.

A computer program can be stored or fixed on a variety of memory devices, two of which are of particular relevance for this case. The ROM (Read Only Memory) is an internal permanent memory device consisting of a semi-conductor or "chip" which is incorporated into the circuitry of the computer. A program in object code is embedded on a ROM before it is incorporated in the computer. Information stored on a ROM can only be read, not erased or rewritten[3] .... The other device used for storing the programs at issue is a diskette or "floppy disk," an auxiliary memory device consisting of a flexible magnetic disk resembling a phonograph record, which can be inserted into the computer and from which data or instructions can be read.

Computer programs can be categorized by function as either application programs or operating system programs. Application programs usually perform a specific task for the computer user, such as word processing, checkbook balancing, or playing a game. In contrast, operating system programs generally manage the internal functions of the computer or facilitate use of application programs. The parties agree that the fourteen computer programs at issue in this suit are operating system programs.

Apple filed suit in the United States District Court for the Eastern District of Pennsylvania pursuant to 28 U.S.C. § 1338 on May 12, 1982, alleging that Franklin was liable for copyright infringement of the fourteen computer programs, patent infringement, unfair competition, and misappropriation. Franklin's answer in respect to the copyright counts included the affirmative defense that the programs contained no copyrightable subject matter. Franklin counterclaimed for declaratory judgment that the copyright registrations were invalid and unenforceable, and sought affirmative relief on the basis of Apple's alleged misuse....

After expedited discovery, Apple moved for a preliminary injunction to restrain Franklin from using, copying, selling, or infringing Apple's copyrights. The district court held a three day evidentiary hearing limited to the copyright infringement claims. Apple produced evidence at the hearing in the form of affidavits and testimony that programs sold by Franklin in conjunction with its ACE 100 computer were virtually identical with those covered by the fourteen Apple copyrights. The variations that did exist were minor, consisting merely of such things as deletion of reference to Apple or its copyright notice. ....

Franklin did not dispute that it copied the Apple programs. Its witness admitted copying each of the works in suit from the Apple programs. Its factual defense was directed to its contention that it was not feasible for Franklin to write its own operating system programs. David McWherter, now Franklin's vice-president of engineering, testified he spent 30-40 hours in November 1981 making a study to determine if it was feasible for Franklin to write its own Autostart ROM program and concluded it was not because

---

[3] In contrast to the permanent memory devices a RAM (Random Access Memory) is a chip on which volatile internal memory is stored which is erased when the computer's power is turned off.

"there were just too many entry points in relationship to the number of instructions in the program." Entry points at specific locations in the program can be used by programmers to mesh their application programs with the operating system program. McWherter concluded that use of the identical signals was necessary in order to ensure 100% compatibility with application programs created to run on the Apple computer. He admitted that he never attempted to rewrite Autostart ROM and conceded that some of the works in suit (*i.e.* Copy, Copy A, Master Create, and Hello) probably could have been rewritten by Franklin. Franklin made no attempt to rewrite any of the programs prior to the lawsuit except for Copy, although McWherter testified that Franklin was "in the process of redesigning" some of the Apple programs and that "[w]e had a fair degree of certainty that that would probably work." Apple introduced evidence that Franklin could have rewritten programs, including the Autostart ROM program, and that there are in existence operating programs written by third parties which are compatible with Apple II.

Franklin's principal defense at the preliminary injunction hearing and before us is primarily a legal one, directed to its contention that the Apple operating system programs are not capable of copyright protection.

....

IV. *Discussion*

A. *Copyrightability of a Computer Program Expressed in Object Code*

Certain statements by the district court suggest that programs expressed in object code, as distinguished from source code, may not be the proper subject of copyright. We find no basis in the statute for any such concern....

Although section 102(a) does not expressly list computer programs as works of authorship, the legislative history suggests that programs were considered copyrightable as literary works. *See* H.R.Rep. No. 1476, 94th Cong., 2d Sess. 54, *reprinted in* 1976 U.S. Code Cong. & Ad. News 5659, 5667 ("'literary works' ... includes ... computer programs")....

The 1980 amendments added a definition of a computer program:

> A "computer program" is a set of statements or instructions to be used directly or indirectly in a computer in order to bring about a certain result.

17 U.S.C. § 101. The amendments also substituted a new section 117 which provides that "it is not an infringement for the owner of a copy of a computer program to make or authorize the making of another copy or adaptation of that computer program" when necessary to "the utilization of the computer program" or "for archival purposes only." 17 U.S.C. § 117. The parties agree that this section is not implicated in the instant lawsuit. The language of the provision, however, by carving out an exception to the normal proscriptions against copying, clearly indicates that programs are copyrightable and are otherwise afforded copyright protection.

We considered the issue of copyright protection for a computer program in *Williams Electronics, Inc. v. Artic International, Inc.,* [685 F.2d 870 (3d Cir. 1982)] and concluded that "the copyrightability of computer programs is firmly established after the 1980 amendment to the Copyright Act." 685 F.2d at 875. At issue in *Williams* were not only two audiovisual copyrights to the "attract" and "play" modes of a video game, but also the computer program which was expressed in object code embodied in ROM and which controlled the sights and sounds of the game. Defendant there had argued "that when the issue is the copyright on a computer program, a distinction must be drawn between the 'source code' version of a computer program, which ... can be afforded copyright protection, and the 'object code' stage, which ... cannot be so protected," an argument we rejected. *Id.* at 876.

The district court here questioned whether copyright was to be limited to works "designed to be 'read' by a human reader [as distinguished from] read by an expert with a microscope and patience," 545 F. Supp. at 821. The suggestion that copyrightability depends on a communicative function to individuals stems from the early decision of *White-Smith Music Publishing Co. v. Apollo Co.,* 209 U.S. 1 (1908), which held a piano roll was not a copy of the musical composition because it was not in a form others, except perhaps for a very expert few, could perceive. See 1 Nimmer on Copyright § 2.03[B][1] (1983). However, it is clear from the language of the 1976 Act and its legislative history that it was intended to obliterate distinctions engendered by *White-Smith.* H.R. Rep. No. 1476, *supra,* at 52, *reprinted in* 1976 U.S. Code Cong. & Ad. News at 5665.

Under the statute, copyright extends to works in any tangible means of expression *"from which they can be perceived,* reproduced, or otherwise communicated, either directly or *with the aid of a machine or device."* 17 U.S.C. § 102(a) (emphasis added). Further, the definition of "computer program" adopted by Congress in the 1980 amendments is "sets of statements or instructions to be used *directly or indirectly* in a computer in order to bring about a certain result." 17 U.S.C. § 101 (emphasis added). As source code instructions must be translated into object code before the computer can act upon them, only instructions expressed in object code can be used "directly" by the computer. *See Midway Manufacturing Co. v. Strohon,* 564 F. Supp. 741 at 750-751 (N.D. Ill. 1983). This definition was adopted following the CONTU Report in which the majority clearly took the position that object codes are proper subjects of copyright. *See* CONTU Report at 21. The majority's conclusion was reached although confronted by a dissent based upon the theory that the "machine-control phase" of a program is not directed at a human audience. *See* CONTU Report at 28-30 (dissent of Commissioner Hersey).

The defendant in *Williams* had also argued that a copyrightable work "must be intelligible to human beings and must be intended as a medium of communication to human beings," *id.* at 876-77. We reiterate the statement we made in *Williams* when we rejected that argument: "[t]he answer to defendant's contention is in the words of the statute itself." 685 F.2d at 877.

The district court also expressed uncertainty as to whether a computer program in object code could be classified as a "literary work." However, the category of "literary works," one of the seven copyrightable categories, is not confined to literature in the nature of Hemingway's *For Whom the Bell Tolls.* The definition of "literary works" in section 101 includes expression not only in words but also "numbers, or other ... numerical symbols or indicia," thereby expanding the common usage of "literary works." *Cf. Harcourt, Brace & World, Inc. v. Graphic Controls Corp.,* 329 F. Supp. 517, 523-24 (S.D.N.Y. 1971) (the symbols designating questions or response spaces on exam answer sheets held to be copyrightable "writings" under 1909 Act); *Reiss v. National Quotation Bureau, Inc.,* 276 F. 717 (S.D.N.Y. 1921) (code book of coined words designed for cable use copyrightable). Thus a computer program, whether in object code or source code, is a "literary work" and is protected from unauthorized copying, whether from its object or source code version. *Accord Midway Mfg. Co. v. Strohon,* 564 F. Supp. at 750-751; *see also GCA Corp. v. Chance,* 217 U.S.P.Q. at 719-20.

B. *Copyrightability of a Computer Program Embedded on a ROM*

Just as the district court's suggestion of a distinction between source code and object code was rejected by our opinion in *Williams* issued three days after the district court opinion, so also was its suggestion that embodiment of a computer program on a ROM, as distinguished from in a traditional writing, detracts from its copyrightability. In *Williams* we rejected the argument that "a computer program is not infringed when the program is loaded into electronic memory devices (ROMs) and used to control the activity of machines." 685 F.2d at 876. Defendant there had argued that there can be no copyright protection for the ROMs because they are utilitarian objects or machine parts. We held that the statutory requirement of "fixation," the manner in which the issue arises, is satisfied through the embodiment of the expression in the ROM devices. *Id.* at 874, 876; *see also Midway Mfg. Co. v. Strohon,* 564 F. Supp. at 751-752; *Tandy Corp. v. Personal Micro Computers, Inc.,* 524 F. Supp. at 173. *cf. Stern Electronics, Inc. v. Kaufman,* 669 F.2d 852, 855-56 (2d Cir. 1982) (audiovisual display of video game "fixed" in ROM). Therefore we reaffirm that a computer program in object code embedded in a ROM chip is an appropriate subject of copyright. *See also* Note, *Copyright Protection of Computer Program Object Code,* 96 Harv. L. Rev. 1723 (1983); Note, *Copyright Protection for Computer Programs in Read Only Memory Chips,* 11 Hofstra L. Rev. 329 (1982).

C. *Copyrightability of Computer Operating System Programs*

We turn to the heart of Franklin's position on appeal which is that computer operating system programs, as distinguished from application programs, are not the proper subject of copyright "regardless of the language or medium in which they are fixed." Brief of Appellee at 15 (emphasis deleted).

....

Franklin contends that operating system programs are *per se* excluded from copyright protection under the express terms of section 102(b) of the Copyright Act, and under the precedent and underlying principles of *Baker v. Selden,* 101 U.S. 99 (1879). These separate grounds have substantial analytic overlap.

....

Franklin reads *Baker v. Selden* as "stand[ing] for several fundamental principles, each presenting ... an insuperable obstacle to the copyrightability of Apple's operating systems." It states:

> *First, Baker* teaches that use of a system itself does not infringe a copyright on the description of the system. *Second, Baker* enunciates the rule that copyright does not extend to purely utilitarian works. *Finally, Baker* emphasizes that the copyright laws may not be used to obtain and hold a monopoly over an idea. In so doing, *Baker* highlights the principal difference between the copyright and patent laws — a difference that is highly pertinent in this case.

Brief of Appellee at 22.

Section 102(b) of the Copyright Act, the other ground on which Franklin relies, appeared first in the 1976 version, long after the decision in *Baker v. Selden.* It provides:

> In no case does copyright protection for an original work of authorship extend to any idea, procedure, process, system, method of operation, concept, principle, or discovery, regardless of the form in which it is described, explained, illustrated, or embodied in such work.

It is apparent that section 102(b) codifies a substantial part of the holding and dictum of *Baker v. Selden. See* 1 Nimmer on Copyright § 2.18[D], at 2-207.

We turn to consider the two principal points of Franklin's argument.

1. *"Process," "System" or "Method of Operation"*

Franklin argues that an operating system program is either a "process," "system," or "method of operation" and hence uncopyrightable. Franklin correctly notes that underlying section 102(b) and many of the statements for which *Baker v. Selden* is cited is the distinction which must be made between property subject to the patent law, which protects discoveries, and that subject to copyright law, which protects the writings describing such discoveries. However, Franklin's argument misapplies that distinction in this case. Apple does not seek to copyright the method which instructs the computer to perform its operating functions but only the instructions themselves. The method would be protected, if at all, by the patent law, an issue as yet unresolved. *See Diamond v. Diehr,* 450 U.S. 175 (1981).

Franklin's attack on operating system programs as "methods" or "processes" seems inconsistent with its concession that application programs are an appropriate subject of copyright. Both types of programs instruct the computer to do something. Therefore, it should make no difference for purposes of section 102(b) whether these instructions tell the computer to help prepare an income tax return (the task of an application program) or to translate a high level language program from source code into its binary language object code form (the task of an operating system program such as "Applesoft"). Since it is only the instructions which are protected, a "process" is no more involved because the instructions in an operating system program may be used to activate the operation of the computer than it would be if instructions were written in ordinary English in a manual which described the necessary steps to activate an intricate complicated machine. There is, therefore, no reason to afford any less copyright protection to the instructions in an operating system program than to the instructions in an application program.

Franklin's argument, receptively treated by the district court, that an operating system program is part of a machine mistakenly focuses on the physical characteristics of the instructions. But the medium is not the message. We have already considered and rejected aspects of this contention in the discussion of object code and ROM. The mere fact that the operating system program may be etched on a ROM does not make the program either a machine, part of a machine or its equivalent. Furthermore, as one of Franklin's witnesses testified, an operating system does not have to be permanently in the machine in ROM, but it may be on some other medium, such as a diskette or magnetic tape, where it could be readily transferred into the temporary memory space of the computer. In fact, some of the operating systems at issue were on diskette. As the CONTU majority stated,

> Programs should no more be considered machine parts than videotapes should be considered parts of projectors or phonorecords parts of sound reproduction equipment.... That the words of a program are used ultimately in the implementation of a process should in no way affect their copyrightability.

CONTU Report at 21.

Franklin also argues that the operating systems cannot be copyrighted because they are "purely utilitarian works" and that Apple is seeking to block the use of the art embodied in its operating systems. This argument stems from the following dictum in *Baker v. Selden:*

> The very object of publishing a book on science or the useful arts is to communicate to the world the useful knowledge which it contains. But this object would be frustrated if the knowledge could not be used without incurring the guilt of piracy of the book. And where the art it teaches cannot be used without employing the methods and diagrams used to illustrate the book, or such as are similar to them, such methods and diagrams are to be considered as necessary incidents to the art, and given therewith to the public; not given for the purpose of publication in other works explanatory of the art, but for the purpose of practical application.

101 U.S. at 103. We cannot accept the expansive reading given to this language by some courts, *see, e.g., Taylor Instrument Companies v. Fawley-Brost Co.,* 139 F.2d 98 (7th Cir. 1943), *cert. denied,* 321 U.S. 785 (1944). In this respect we agree with the views expressed by Professor Nimmer in his treatise. *See* 1 Nimmer on Copyright § 2.18[C].

Although a literal construction of this language could support Franklin's reading that precludes copyrightability if the copyright work is put to a utilitarian use, that interpretation has been rejected by a later Supreme Court decision. In *Mazer v. Stein,* 347 U.S. 201, 218 (1954), the Court stated: "We find nothing in the copyright statute to support the argument that the intended use or use in industry of an article eligible for copyright bars or invalidates its registration. We do not read such a limitation into the copyright law." *Id.* at 218. The CONTU majority also rejected the expansive view some courts have given *Baker v. Selden,* and stated, "That the words of a program are used ultimately in the implementation of a process should in no way affect their copyrightability." *Id.* at 21. It referred to "copyright practice past and present, which recognizes copyright protection for a work of authorship regardless of the uses to which it may be put." *Id.* The Commission continued: "The copyright status of the written rules for a game *or a system for the operation of a machine* is unaffected by the fact that those rules direct the actions of those who play the game or *carry out the process.*" *Id.* (emphasis added). [W]e can consider the CONTU Report as accepted by Congress since Congress wrote into the law the majority's recommendations almost verbatim. *See* 18 Cong. Rec. H10767 (daily ed. Nov. 17, 1980) (Rep. Kastenmeier: Bill "eliminates confusion about the legal status of computer software by enacting the recommendations of [CONTU] clarifying the law of copyright of computer software"); 18 Cong. Rec. S14766 (daily ed. Nov. 20, 1980) (Sen. Bayh: "[t]his language reflects that proposed by [CONTU"]).

Perhaps the most convincing item leading us to reject Franklin's argument is that the statutory definition of a computer program as a set of instructions to be used in a computer in order to bring about a certain result, 17 U.S.C. § 101, makes no distinction between application programs and operating programs. Franklin can point to no decision which adopts the distinction it seeks to make. In the one other reported case to have considered it, *Apple Computer, Inc. v. Formula International, Inc.,* 562 F. Supp. 775 (C.D. Cal. 1983), the court reached the same conclusion which we do, *i.e.* that an operating system program is not *per se* precluded from copyright. It stated, "There is nothing in any of the statutory terms which suggest [sic] a different result for different types of computer programs based upon the function they serve within the machine." *Id.* at 780. Other courts have also upheld the copyrightability of operating programs without discussion of this issue. *See Tandy Corp. v. Personal Micro Computers, Inc.,* 524 F. Supp. at 173 (input-output routine stored in ROM which translated input into machine language in a similar fashion as Applesoft and Apple Integer Basic proper subject of copyright); *GCA Corp. v. Chance,* 217 U.S.P.Q. at 719-20 (object code version of registered source code version of operating programs is the same work and protected).

2. *Idea/Expression Dichotomy*

Franklin's other challenge to copyright of operating system programs relies on the line which is drawn between ideas and their expression. *Baker v. Selden* remains a benchmark in the law of copyright for the reading given it in *Mazer v. Stein, supra,* where the Court stated, "Unlike a patent, a copyright gives no exclusive right to the art disclosed; protection is given only to the expression of the idea — not the idea itself." 347 U.S. at 217 (footnote omitted).

The expression/idea dichotomy is now expressly recognized in section 102(b) which precludes copyright for "any idea." This provision was not intended to enlarge or contract the scope of copyright protection but "to restate ... that the basic dichotomy between expression and idea remains unchanged." H.R. Rep. No. 1476, *supra,* at 57, *reprinted in* 1976 U.S. Code Cong. & Ad. News at 5670.

The legislative history indicates that section 102(b) was intended "to make clear that the expression adopted by the programmer is the copyrightable element in a computer program, and that the actual processes or methods embodied in the program are not within the scope of the copyright law." *Id.*

Many of the courts which have sought to draw the line between an idea and expression have found difficulty in articulating where it falls. *See, e.g., Nichols v. Universal Pictures Corp.,* 45 F.2d 119, 121 (2d Cir. 1930) (L. Hand, J.); *see* discussion in 3 Nimmer on Copyright § 13.03[A]. We believe that in the context before us, a program for an operating system, the line must be a pragmatic one, which also keeps in consideration "the preservation of the balance between competition and protection reflected in the patent and copyright laws." *Herbert Rosenthal Jewelry Corp. v. Kalpakian,* 446 F.2d 738, 742 (9th Cir. 1971). As we stated in *Franklin Mint Corp. v. National Wildlife Art Exchange, Inc.,* 575 F.2d 62, 64 (3d Cir.), *cert. denied,* 439 U.S. 880 (1978), "Unlike a patent, a copyright protects originality rather than novelty or invention." In that opinion, we quoted approvingly the following passage from *Dymow v. Bolton,* 11 F.2d 690, 691 (2d Cir. 1926):

> Just as a patent affords protection only to the means of reducing an inventive idea to practice, so the copyright law protects the means of expressing an idea; and it is as near the whole truth as generalization can usually reach that, *if the same idea can be expressed in a plurality of totally different manners, a plurality of copyrights may result,* and no infringement will exist.

(emphasis added).

We adopt the suggestion in the above language and thus focus on whether the idea is capable of various modes of expression. If other programs can be written or created which perform the same function as an Apple's operating system program, then that program is an expression of the idea and hence copyrightable. In essence, this inquiry is no different than that made to determine whether the expression and idea have merged, which has been stated to occur where there are no or few other ways of expressing a particular idea. *See, e.g., Morrissey v. Procter & Gamble Co.,* 379 F.2d 675, 678-79 (1st Cir. 1967); *Freedman v. Grolier Enterprises, Inc.,* 179 U.S.P.Q. 476, 478 (S.D.N.Y. 1973) ("[c]opyright protection will not be given to a form of expression necessarily dictated by the underlying subject matter"); CONTU Report at 20.

The district court made no findings as to whether some or all of Apple's operating programs represent the only means of expression of the idea underlying them. Although there seems to be a concession by Franklin that at least some of the programs can be rewritten, we do not believe that the record on that issue is so clear that it can be decided at the appellate level. Therefore, if the issue is pressed on remand, the necessary finding can be made at that time.

Franklin claims that whether or not the programs can be rewritten, there are a limited "number of ways to arrange operating systems to enable a computer to run the vast body of Apple-compatible software," Brief of Appellee at 20. This claim has no pertinence to either the idea/expression dichotomy or merger. The idea which may merge with the expression, thus making the copyright unavailable, is the idea which is the subject of the expression. The idea of one of the operating system programs is, for example, how to translate source code into object code. If other methods of expressing that idea are not foreclosed as a practical matter, then there is no merger. Franklin may wish to achieve total compatibility with independently developed application programs written for the Apple II, but that is a commercial and competitive objective which does not enter into the somewhat metaphysical issue of whether particular ideas and expressions have merged.

In summary, Franklin's contentions that operating system programs are *per se* not copyrightable is unpersuasive. The other courts before whom this issue has been raised have rejected the distinction. Neither the CONTU majority nor Congress made a distinction between operating and application programs. We believe that the 1980 amendments reflect Congress' receptivity to new technology and its desire to encourage, through the copyright laws, continued imagination and creativity in computer programming. Since we believe that the district court's decision on the preliminary injunction was, to a large part, influenced by an erroneous view of the availability of copyright for operating system programs and unnecessary concerns about object code and ROMs, we must reverse the denial of the preliminary injunction and remand for reconsideration....

Data General Corp. v. Grumman Systems, 825 F. Supp. 340, 354-55 (D. Mass. 1993). Data General registered its computer programs with the Copyright Office in source code, and Grumman copied only their object-code versions. The court rejected Grumman's defense that it had therefore not copied protected material:

> Grumman argues that it is entitled to judgment in its favor because Data General failed to prove that the MV/ADEX computer programs admittedly copied and used by Grumman were the same works in which Data General held copyrights. More specifically, Grumman asserts that Data General was required to prove the *object code* programs copied by Grumman are the same as the *source code* programs registered with the Copyright Office. Since Data General did not produce the source code for any version of MV/ADEX, it is argued that Data General could not prove that Grumman's admitted use of the object code programs infringed the source code programs registered with the Copyright Office. As I explained in my October 9, 1992 ruling, Grumman's argument is flawed.
>
> Contrary to Grumman's understanding, the materials deposited with the Copyright Office do not define the substantive protection extended to the registered work. Indeed, the Copyright Act expressly provides that copyright "registration is not a condition of copyright protection," and may be obtained at any time during the subsistence of the copyright. 17 U.S.C.A. § 408(a). Since copyright protection exists without regard to copyright registration, it follows that the deposit that accompanies a registration cannot by itself define the copyrighted work. In this case, the source code deposits that were made with the Copyright Office were

merely symbols, rather than definitions, of the protected work. *See Midway Mfg. Co. v. Artic Int'l, Inc.,* 211 U.S.P.Q. (BNA) 1152, 1158 (N.D. Ill. 1981) ("It is the work that cannot be copied or incorporated and not the specific tangible expression on file in the Copyright Office."). Thus, Data General held copyrights on the various versions of the computer program MV/ADEX, not the source code version of MV/ADEX.

Similarly, Grumman misconceives as three separate programs the registered computer program, source code version of that program, and object code version of that program. Though Grumman has admittedly used MV/ADEX in its object code form, it claims there was no proof that it infringed the "registered source code program." The Copyright Office, however, "considers source code and object code as two representations of the same computer program. For registration purposes, the claim is in the *computer program* rather than in any particular representation of the program." Copyright Office, Compendium II of Copyright Office Practices § 321.03 (1984) (emphasis in original); *e.g., Apple Computer, Inc., v. Franklin Computer Corp.,* 714 F.2d 1240, 1249 (3rd Cir. 1983), *cert. dismissed,* 464 U.S. 1033, 104 S. Ct. 690, 79 L. Ed. 2d 158 (1984). Accordingly, while Data General had the burden of proving that Grumman copied MV/ADEX in one of its protected forms, Data General could meet that burden by showing infringement of either the source code or the object code version of the MV/ADEX.

QUESTIONS

1. Do you agree with the court in *Apple v. Franklin* that a copyrightable work need not be "intended as a medium of communication to human beings"? Should there be a distinction between computer programs that communicate directly to the computer, but that nonetheless also yield a communication to a human being, and programs that perform no function other than to instruct the computer to perform internal operations themselves and do not produce further communications to human beings?

2. Is there any distinction pertinent to copyright between a program that instructs a computer to perform a process (such as translating statements from source code to object code), and a literary work that instructs humans to perform a process (such as baking a cake)?

2. "STRUCTURE, SEQUENCE AND ORGANIZATION"

WHELAN ASSOCIATES v. JASLOW DENTAL LABORATORY, INC.

797 F.2d 1222 (3d Cir. 1986), *cert. denied,* 479 U.S. 1031 (1987)

BECKER, CIRCUIT JUDGE.

This appeal involves a computer program for the operation of a dental laboratory, and calls upon us to apply the principles underlying our venerable copyright laws to the relatively new field of computer technology to determine the scope of copyright protection of a computer program. More particularly, in this case of first impression in the courts of appeals, we must determine whether the structure (or sequence and organization)[1] of a computer program is protectible by copyright, or whether the protection of the copyright law extends only as far as the literal computer code. The district court found that the copyright law covered these non-literal elements of the program, and we agree. This conclusion in turn requires us to consider whether there was sufficient evidence of substantial similarity between the structures of the two programs at issue in this case to uphold the district court's finding of copyright infringement. Because we find that there was enough evidence, we affirm.

[Plaintiff Whelan Associates is engaged in the business of developing and marketing custom computer programs. Defendants Edward and Rand Jaslow operate Jaslow Dental Laboratory, Inc. (Jaslow Lab), which manufactures dental prosthetics and devices. Jaslow Lab has significant bookkeeping and administrative tasks, relating to equipment, inventory, customer lists, and billing. Rand Jaslow concluded that the business operations of Jaslow Lab could be made more efficient if they were computerized, and after unsuccessfully attempting to prepare a program for that purpose, he hired a company that developed custom-made software; that company (the predecessor of plaintiff Whelan Associates) wrote a program called Dentalab, which was written in a computer language known as EDL (Event Driven Language) to be used on Jaslow Lab's IBM computer. Whelan Associates purchased rights to the Dentalab program from the company that had developed it, and entered into an agreement with Jaslow Lab, whereby the latter agreed to serve as sales representative for the Dentalab program for marketing to other dental laboratories. This arrangement worked amicably from mid-1980 to mid-1982.

[At about the latter date, Rand Jaslow decided to devise a program that could serve essentially the same function as Dentalab but that could be used more widely by dental laboratories using simpler computer systems, and he in fact devised such a program in the BASIC language; it was called the Dentcom program, which Whelan Associates claims is an infringement of its own Dentalab program. The District Court sustained that claim, and the Court of Appeals affirmed.]

III. *Technological Background*

We begin with a brief description of computer programs and an explanation of how they are written. This introduction is necessary to our analysis of the issue in this case.

A computer program is a set of instructions to the computer. Most programs accept and process user-supplied data. The fundamental processes utilized by a program are called algorithms (mechanical computational procedures) and are at the heart of the program. *See* Keplinger, *Computer Software — Its Nature and Its Protection,* 30 Emory L.J. 483, 484-85 (1984). These algorithms must be developed by the human creativity of the programmer and the program therefore cannot contain any algorithms not already considered by

---

[1] We use the terms "structure," "sequence," and "organization" interchangeably when referring to computer programs, and we intend them to be synonymous in this opinion.

humans. Although a computer cannot think or develop algorithms, it can execute them faster and more accurately than any human possibly could. *See* R. Saltman, Copyright in Computer-Readable Works 59 (1977).

The creation of a program often takes place in several steps, moving from the general to the specific. Because programs are intended to accomplish particular tasks, the first step in creating the program is identifying the problem that the computer programmer is trying to solve. In this case, Rand Jaslow went to Strohl and stated that his problem was record-keeping for his business. Although this was an accurate statement of the problem, it was not specific enough to guide Elaine Whelan. Before she could write the Dentalab program, she needed to know more about Jaslow Lab's business — how orders were processed, what special billing problems might arise, how inventory might be correlated to orders, and other characteristics of the dental prosthetics trade.

As the programmer learns more about the problem, she or he may begin to outline a solution. The outline can take the form of a flowchart, which will break down the solution into a series of smaller units called "subroutines" or "modules," each of which deals with elements of the larger problem. *See* Note, *Defining the Scope of Copyright Protection for Computer Software,* 38 Stan. L. Rev. 497, 500-01 (1986). A program's efficiency depends in large part on the arrangements of its modules and subroutines; although two programs could produce the same result, one might be more efficient because of different internal arrangements of modules and subroutines. Because efficiency is a prime concern in computer programs (an efficient program being obviously more valuable than a comparatively inefficient one), the arrangement of modules and subroutines is a critical factor for any programmer. In the present case, the Dentalab program had numerous modules pertaining to inventory, accounts receivable, various dentist-patient matters, and payroll, among others. *See* App. at 1588-1698 (showing flowcharts of subroutines). Some of the modules were simple; others were quite complex and involved elaborate logical development.

As the program structure is refined, the programmer must make decisions about what data are needed, where along the program's operations the data should be introduced, how the data should be inputted, and how it should be combined with other data. The arrangement of the data is accomplished by means of data files, discussed *infra* at 1242-44, and is affected by the details of the program's subroutines and modules, for different arrangements of subroutines and modules may require data in different forms. Once again, there are numerous ways the programmer can solve the data-organization problems she or he faces. Each solution may have particular characteristics — efficiencies or inefficiencies, conveniences or quirks — that differentiate it from other solutions and make the overall program more or less desirable. Because the Dentalab program was intended to handle all of the business-related aspects of a dental laboratory, it had to accommodate and interrelate many different pieces and types of data including patients' names, dentists' names, inventory, accounts receivable, accounts payable, and payroll.

Once the detailed design of the program is completed, the coding begins. Each of the steps identified in the design must be turned into a language that the computer can understand. This translation process in itself requires two steps. The programmer first writes in a "source code," which may be in one of several languages, such as COBOL, BASIC, FORTRAN, or EDL. The choice of language depends upon which computers the programmer intends the program to be used by, for some computers can read only certain languages. Once the program is written in source code, it is translated into "object code," which is a binary code, simply a concatenation of "0"s and "1"s. In every program, it is the object code, not the source code, that directs the computer to perform functions. The object code is therefore the final instruction to the computer.

As this brief summary demonstrates, the coding process is a comparatively small part of programming. By far the larger portion of the expense and difficulty in creating computer programs is attributable to the development of the structure and logic of the program, and to debugging, documentation and maintenance, rather than to the coding. *See* Frank, Critical Issues in Software 22 (1983) (only 20% of the cost of program development goes into coding) .... The evidence in this case shows that Ms. Whelan spent a tremendous amount of time studying Jaslow Labs, organizing the modules and subroutines for the Dentalab program, and working out the data arrangements, and a comparatively small amount of time actually coding the Dentalab program.

IV. *Legal Background*

A. *The elements of a copyright infringement action* — To prove that its copyright has been infringed, Whelan Associates must show two things: that it owned the copyright on Dentalab, and that Rand Jaslow copied Dentalab in making the Dentcom program.... Although it was disputed below,... the district court determined, and it is not challenged here, that Whelan Associates owned the copyright to the Dentalab program. We are thus concerned only with whether it has been shown that Rand Jaslow copied the Dentalab program.

As it is rarely possible to prove copying through direct evidence, *Roth Greeting Cards v. United Card Co.*, 429 F.2d 1106, 1110 (9th Cir. 1970), copying may be proved inferentially by showing that the defendant had access to the allegedly infringed copyrighted work and that the allegedly infringing work is substantially similar to the copyrighted work.... The district court found, and here it is uncontested, that Rand Jaslow had access to the Dentalab program, both because Dentalab was the program used in Jaslow Labs and because Rand Jaslow acted as a sales representative for Whelan Associates. *See Whelan Associates v. Jaslow Dental Laboratory*, 609 F. Supp. at 1314. Thus, the sole question is whether there was substantial similarity between the Dentcom and Dentalab programs....

C. *The arguments on appeal* — On appeal, the defendants attack on two grounds the district court's holding that there was sufficient evidence of substantial similarity. First, the defendants argue that because the district court did not find any similarity between the "literal" elements (source and object code) of the programs, but only similarity in their overall structures, its finding of substantial similarity was incorrect, for the copyright covers only the literal elements of computer programs, not their overall structures. Defendants' second argument is that even if the protection of copyright law extends to "non-literal" elements such as the structure of computer programs, there was not sufficient evidence of substantial similarity to sustain the district court's holding in this case. We consider these arguments in turn.

V. *The Scope of Copyright Protection of Computer Programs*

It is well, though recently, established that copyright protection extends to a program's source and object codes.... The question [is] whether mere similarity in the overall structure of programs can be the basis for a copyright infringement, or, put differently, whether a program's copyright protection covers the structure of the program or only the program's literal elements, i.e., its source and object codes.

Title 17 U.S.C. § 102(a)(1) extends copyright protection to "literary works," and computer programs are classified as literary works for the purposes of copyright. *See* H.R. Rep. No. 1476, 94th Cong., 2d Sess. 54, *reprinted in* 1976 U.S. Code Cong. & Ad. News 5659, 5667. The copyrights of other literary works can be infringed even when there is no substantial similarity between the works' literal elements. One can violate the copyright of a play or book by copying its plot or plot devices.... By analogy to other literary works, it would thus appear that the copyrights of computer programs can be infringed even absent copying of the literal elements of the program. Defendants contend, however, that what is true of other literary works is not true of computer programs. They assert two principal reasons, which we consider in turn.

A. *Section 102(b) and the dichotomy between idea and expression* — It is axiomatic that copyright does not protect ideas, but only expressions of ideas....

1. *A rule for distinguishing idea from expression in computer programs* — It is frequently difficult to distinguish the idea from the expression thereof.... The Court's test in *Baker v. Selden* suggests a way to distinguish idea from expression. Just as *Baker v. Selden* focused on the end sought to be achieved by Selden's book, the line between idea and expression may be drawn with reference to the end sought to be achieved by the work in question. In other words, *the purpose or function of a utilitarian work would be the work's idea, and everything that is not necessary to that purpose or function would be part of the expression of the idea. Cf. Apple Computer, Inc. v. Formula Int'l, Inc.,* 562 F. Supp. 775, 783 (C.D. Ca. 1983) ("Apple seeks here not to protect *ideas* (i.e. making the machine perform particular functions) but rather to protect their particular *expressions ...*"), *aff'd,* 725 F.2d 521 (9th Cir. 1984). Where there are various means of achieving the desired purpose, then the particular means chosen is not necessary to the purpose; hence, there is expression, not idea.[28]

---

[28]... As will be seen, *see infra* at 1238-39, the idea of the Dentalab program was the efficient management of a dental laboratory (which presumably has significantly different requirements from those of other businesses). Because that idea could be accomplished in a number of different ways with a number of different structures, the structure of the Dentalab program is part of the program's expression, not its idea.

....

Although the economic implications of this rule are necessarily somewhat speculative, we nevertheless believe that the rule would advance the basic purpose underlying the idea/expression distinction, "the preservation of the balance between competition and protection reflected in the patent and copyright laws." *Herbert Rosenthal Jewelry Corp. v. Kalpakian*, 446 F.2d 738, 742 (9th Cir. 1971); *see also Apple Computer*, 714 F.2d at 1253 (quoting *Kalpakian*); *supra* n.27. As we stated above, *see supra* at 1231, among the more significant costs in computer programming are those attributable to developing the structure and logic of the program. The rule proposed here, which allows copyright protection beyond the literal computer code, would provide the proper incentive for programmers by protecting their most valuable efforts, while not giving them a stranglehold over the development of new computer devices that accomplish the same end.

....

Finally, one commentator argues that the process of development and progress in the field of computer programming is significantly different from that in other fields, and therefore requires a particularly restricted application of the copyright law. According to this argument, progress in the area of computer technology is achieved by means of "stepping-stones," a process that "requires plagiarizing in some manner the underlying copyrighted work." Note, 68 Minn. L. Rev. at 1292 (footnote omitted). As a consequence, this commentator argues, giving computer programs too much copyright protection will retard progress in the field.

We are not convinced that progress in computer technology or technique is qualitatively different from progress in other areas of science or the arts. In balancing protection and dissemination, *see supra* at 1235 & n.27, the copyright law has always recognized and tried to accommodate the fact that all intellectual pioneers build on the work of their predecessors.[33] Thus, copyright principles derived from other areas are applicable in the field of computer programs.

2. *Application of the general rule to this case* — The rule proposed here is certainly not problem-free.... [I]t is clear that the purpose of the utilitarian Dentalab program was to aid in the business operations of a dental laboratory.[34] *See supra* 1225. It is equally clear that the structure of the program was not essential to that task: there are other programs on the market, com-

---

[33]Long before the first computer, Sir Isaac Newton humbly explained that "if [he] had seen farther than other men, it was because [he] had stood on the shoulders of giants."

[34]We do not mean to imply that the idea or purpose behind *every* utilitarian or functional work will be precisely what it accomplishes, and that structure and organization will therefore always be part of the expression of such works. The idea or purpose behind a utilitarian work may be to accomplish a certain function *in a certain way, see, e.g., Baker v. Selden*, 101 U.S. at 100 (referring to Selden's book as explaining "a peculiar system of book-keeping"), and the structure or function of a program might be essential to that task. There is no suggestion in the record, however, that the purpose of the Dentalab program was anything so refined; it was simply to run a dental laboratory in an efficient way.

petitors of Dentalab and Dentcom, that perform the same functions but have different structures and designs.

This fact seems to have been dispositive for the district court:

> ... There are many ways that the same data may be organized, assembled, held, retrieved and utilized by a computer. *Different computer systems may functionally serve similar purposes without being copies of each other. There is evidence in the record that there are other software programs for the business management of dental laboratories in competition with plaintiff's program. There is no contention that any of them infringe although they may incorporate many of the same ideas and functions.* The "expression of the idea" in a software computer program is the manner in which the program operates, controls and regulates the computer in receiving, assembling, calculating, retaining, correlating, and producing useful information either on a screen, print-out or by audio communication.

Whelan Associates v. Jaslow Laboratory, 609 F. Supp. at 1320 (emphasis added). We agree. The conclusion is thus inescapable that the detailed structure of the Dentalab program is part of the expression, not the idea, of that program.

....

VI. *Evidence of Substantial Similarity*

Defendants' second argument is that even if copyright protection is not limited to computer programs' literal elements as a matter of law, there is insufficient evidence of substantial similarity presented in this case to support a finding of copyright infringement....

....

C. *The five subroutines* — With respect to the final piece of evidence, Dr. Moore's testimony about the five subroutines found in Dentalab and Dentcom, defendants state that they "fail to understand how a substantial similarity in *structure* can be established by a comparison of only a small fraction of the two works." Appellants' Brief at 43, *see also* Reply Br. at 12. The premise underlying this declaration is that one cannot prove substantial similarity of two works without comparing the entirety, or at least the greater part, of the works. We take this premise to be the defendants' argument.

The premise does not apply in other areas of copyright infringement. There is no general requirement that most of each of two works be compared before a court can conclude that they are substantially similar. In the cases of literary works — novels, movies, or plays, for example — it is often impossible to speak of "most" of the work. The substantial similarity inquiry cannot be simply quantified in such instances. Instead, the court must make a qualitative, not quantitative, judgment about the character of the work as a whole and the importance of the substantially similar portions of the work....

Computer programs are no different. Because all steps of a computer program are not of equal importance, the relevant inquiry cannot therefore be the purely mechanical one of whether most of the programs' steps are similar.

Rather, because we are concerned with the overall similarities between the programs, we must ask whether the most significant steps of the programs are similar.... Dr. Moore's testimony was thus in accord with general principles of copyright law. As we hold today that these principles apply as well to computer programs, we therefore reject the defendants' argument on this point.

....

VII. *Conclusion*

We hold that (1) copyright protection of computer programs may extend beyond the programs' literal code to their structure, sequence, and organization, and (2) the district court's finding of substantial similarity between the Dentalab and Dentcom programs was not clearly erroneous. The judgment of the district court will therefore be affirmed.

QUESTION

The court in *Whelan* presumably could have characterized any of the following as the function, or "idea," of the copyrighted Dentalab program: (1) the effecting of a useful outcome; (2) the operation of a dental laboratory; (3) the billing, accounting, recording of doctor and patient names and addresses, and tracking inventory in a dental laboratory; (4) the performance of those same functions in an efficient manner on specific-model computers; (5) the performance of those same functions in a specific manner and order, on specific-model computers. Which of these characterizations best reflects the court's? Which of these do you think best distinguishes "idea" from "expression"? Does the court provide any guidance as to how it formulates the distinction between idea and expression in this case?

COMPUTER ASSOCIATES INTERNATIONAL, INC. v. ALTAI, INC.

982 F.2d 693 (2d Cir. 1992)

WALKER, CIRCUIT JUDGE.

... [T]his case deals with the challenging question of whether and to what extent the "non-literal" aspects of a computer program, that is, those aspects that are not reduced to written code, are protected by copyright. While a few other courts have already grappled with this issue, this case is one of first impression in this circuit. As we shall discuss, we find the results reached by other courts to be less than satisfactory. Drawing upon long-standing doctrines of copyright law, we take an approach that we think better addresses the practical difficulties embedded in these types of cases. In so doing, we have kept in mind the necessary balance between creative incentive and industrial competition.

[The District] Judge found that defendant Altai, Inc.'s ("Altai"), OSCAR 3.4 computer program had infringed plaintiff Computer Associates' ("CA"), copyrighted computer program entitled CA-SCHEDULER. With respect to CA's second claim for copyright infringement, Judge Pratt found that Altai's OSCAR 3.5 program was not substantially similar to a portion of CA-SCHEDULER called ADAPTER, and thus denied relief....

Background

I. *Computer Program Design*

The first step in this procedure is to identify a program's ultimate function or purpose. An example of such an ultimate purpose might be the creation and maintenance of a business ledger. Once this goal has been achieved, a programmer breaks down or "decomposes" the program's ultimate function into "simpler constituent problems or 'subtasks,'" which are also known as subroutines or modules. In the context of a business ledger program, a module or subroutine might be responsible for the task of updating a list of outstanding accounts receivable. Sometimes, depending upon the complexity of its task, a subroutine may be broken down further into sub-subroutines.

Having sufficiently decomposed the program's ultimate function into its component elements, a programmer will then arrange the subroutines or modules into what are known as organizational or flow charts. Flow charts map the interactions between modules that achieve the program's end goal.

In order to accomplish these intra-program interactions, a programmer must carefully design each module's parameter list. A parameter list, according to the expert appointed and fully credited by the district court, Dr. Randall Davis, is "the information sent to and received from a subroutine." *See* Report of Dr. Randall Davis, at 12. The term "parameter list" refers to the form in which information is passed between modules (e.g. for accounts receivable, the designated time frame and particular customer identifying number) and the information's actual content (e.g. 8/91-7/92; customer No. 3). *Id.* With respect to form, interacting modules must share similar parameter lists so that they are capable of exchanging information.

"The functions of the modules in a program together with each module's relationships to other modules constitute the 'structure' of the program." Englund, at 871. Additionally, the term structure may include the category of modules referred to as "macros." A macro is a single instruction that initiates a sequence of operations or module interactions within the program. Very often the user will accompany a macro with an instruction from the parameter list to refine the instruction (e.g. current total of accounts receivable (macro), but limited to those for 8/91 to 7/92 from customer No. 3 (parameters)).

In fashioning the structure, a programmer will normally attempt to maximize the program's speed, efficiency, as well as simplicity for user operation, while taking into consideration certain externalities such as the memory constraints of the computer upon which the program will be run. "This stage of program design often requires the most time and investment."

Once each necessary module has been identified, designed, and its relationship to the other modules has been laid out conceptually, the resulting program structure must be embodied in a written language that the computer can read. This process is called "coding," and requires two steps. First, the programmer must transpose the program's structural blueprint into a source code. This step has been described as "comparable to the novelist fleshing out the broad outline of his plot by crafting from words and sentences the paragraphs that convey the ideas." The source code may be written in any one of several computer languages, such as COBAL, FORTRAN, BASIC, EDL, etc., depending upon the type of computer for which the program is intended. Once the source code has been completed, the second step is to translate or "compile" it into object code. Object code is the binary language comprised of zeros and ones through which the computer directly receives its instructions.

After the coding is finished, the programmer will run the program on the computer in order to find and correct any logical and syntactical errors. This is known as "debugging" and, once done, the program is complete.

II. *Facts*

CA is a Delaware corporation, with its principal place of business in Garden City, New York. Altai is a Texas corporation, doing business primarily in Arlington, Texas. Both companies are in the computer software industry — designing, developing and marketing various types of computer programs.

The subject of this litigation originates with one of CA's marketed programs entitled CA-SCHEDULER. CA-SCHEDULER is a job scheduling program designed for IBM mainframe computers. Its primary functions are straightforward: to create a schedule specifying when the computer should run various tasks, and then to control the computer as it executes the schedule. CA-SCHEDULER contains a sub-program entitled ADAPTER, also developed by CA. ADAPTER is not an independently marketed product of CA; it is a wholly integrated component of CA-SCHEDULER and has no capacity for independent use.

Nevertheless, ADAPTER plays an extremely important role. It is an "operating system compatibility component," which means, roughly speaking, it serves as a translator. An "operating system" is itself a program that manages the resources of the computer, allocating those resources to other programs as needed. The IBM's System 370 family of computers, for which CA-SCHEDULER was created, is, depending upon the computer's size, designed to contain one of three operating systems: DOS/VSE, MVS, or CMS. As the district court noted, the general rule is that "a program written for one operating system, e.g., DOS/VSE, will not, without modification, run under another operating system such as MVS." ADAPTER's function is to translate the language of a given program into the particular language that the computer's own operating system can understand.

The district court succinctly outlined the manner in which ADAPTER works within the context of the larger programs. In order to enable CA-SCHEDULER to function on different operating systems, CA divided the CA-SCHEDULER into two components:

> — a first component that contains only the task-specific portions of the program, independent of all operating system issues, and
> — a second component that contains all the interconnections between the first component and the operating system.

In a program constructed in this way, whenever the first, task-specific, component needs to ask the operating system for some resource through a "system call," it calls the second component instead of calling the operating system directly.

The second component serves as an "interface" or "compatibility component" between the task-specific portion of the program and the operating system. It receives the request from the first component and translates it into the appropriate system call that will be recognized by whatever operating system is installed on the computer, e.g., DOS/VSE, MVS, or CMS. Since the first, task-specific component calls the adapter component rather than the operating system, the first component need not be customized to use any specific operating system. The second interface component insures that all the system calls are performed properly for the particular operating system in use. ADAPTER serves as the second, "common system interface" component referred to above.

A program like ADAPTER, which allows a computer user to change or use multiple operating systems while maintaining the same software, is highly desirable. It saves the user the costs, both in time and money, that otherwise would be expended in purchasing new programs, modifying existing systems to run them, and gaining familiarity with their operation. The benefits run both ways. The increased compatibility afforded by an ADAPTER-like component, and its resulting popularity among consumers, makes whatever software in which it is incorporated significantly more marketable.

[In 1982, defendant Altai began marketing its own job scheduling program entitled ZEKE, which was designed for use in conjunction with a VSE operating system; later, Altai decided to rewrite ZEKE to run in an MVS operating system. An Altai employee, Williams (soon to become Altai president) induced a longtime friend, Arney, to leave CA and come to work for Altai. Williams knew of CA-SCHEDULER and ADAPTER, but did not know that the latter was a component of the former; nor had he seen the codes of either program. Arney, however, was fully familiar with various aspects of ADAPTER — and when he left CA for Altai in January 1984, Arney took with him copies of the source code for both the VSE and MVS versions of ADAPTER, in knowing violation of his employment agreement with CA. Arney convinced Williams that the best way to make ZEKE compatible with the MVS operating system was to introduce a "common system interface" component into ZEKE; this new component was to be named OSCAR. Arney quickly completed the OSCAR/VSE and OSCAR/MVS versions, in the process copying approximately 30% of OSCAR's code from CA's ADAPTER program — this was not known to anyone at Altai, including Williams.

[The first generation of OSCAR programs was known as OSCAR 3.4; it was used for some three years as a component of the ZEKE product, when CA first learned that Altai may have appropriated parts of ADAPTER and brought this action for copyright infringement and trade secret misappropriation. For the first time, Williams learned that Arney had copied much of the OSCAR code from ADAPTER, and he had Arney point out the tainted sections of the OSCAR code. Williams initiated OSCAR's rewrite; the goal was to excise all portions copied from ADAPTER and save as much of OSCAR 3.4 as legitimately could be used. None of the programmers had been involved in the initial development of OSCAR 3.4, and Arney was entirely excluded from the process. Williams gave the programmers a description of the ZEKE operating system, and the OSCAR rewrite project was completed after six months in

November 1989; the resulting program was entitled OSCAR 3.5. From then on, Altai shipped only OSCAR 3.5 to its customers. In the court's words, "While Altai and Williams acted responsibly to correct what Arney had wrought, the damage was done. CA's lawsuit remained."]

Discussion

We address only CA's appeal from the district court's rulings that: Altai was not liable for copyright infringement in developing OSCAR 3.5 ....

CA contends that the district court applied an erroneous method for determining whether there exists substantial similarity between computer programs, and thus, erred in determining that OSCAR 3.5 did not infringe the copyrights held on the different versions of its CA-SCHEDULER program. CA asserts that the test applied by the district court failed to account sufficiently for a computer program's non-literal elements.

I. Copyright Infringement

For the purpose of analysis, the district court assumed that Altai had access to the ADAPTER code when creating OSCAR 3.5. Thus, in determining whether Altai had unlawfully copied protected aspects of CA's ADAPTER, the district court narrowed its focus of inquiry to ascertaining whether Altai's OSCAR 3.5 was substantially similar to ADAPTER. Because we approve Judge Pratt's conclusions regarding substantial similarity, our analysis will proceed along the same assumption.

As a general matter, and to varying degrees, copyright protection extends beyond a literary work's strictly textual form to its non-literal components. As we have said, "it is of course essential to any protection of literary property ... that the right cannot be limited literally to the text, else a plagiarist would escape by immaterial variations." *Nichols v. Universal Pictures Co.,* 45 F.2d 119, 121 (2d Cir. 1930) (L. Hand, J.), *cert. denied,* 282 U.S. 902 (1931). Thus, where "the fundamental essence or structure of one work is duplicated in another," courts have found copyright infringement. [The court cited precedents involving ballet, motion pictures, television programs, and plays.] *Accord Stewart v. Abend,* 495 U.S. 207, 238 (1990) (recognizing that motion picture may infringe copyright in book by using its "unique setting, characters, plot, and sequence of events"). This black letter proposition is the springboard for our discussion.

A. Copyright Protection for the Non-literal Elements of Computer Programs

It is now well settled that the literal elements of computer programs, i.e., their source and object codes, are the subject of copyright protection. *See Whelan* (source and object code); *CMS Software Design Sys., Inc. v. Info Designs, Inc.,* 785 F.2d 1246, 1249 (5th Cir. 1986) (source code); *Apple Computer, Inc. v. Franklin Computer Corp.,* 714 F.2d 1240, 1249 (3d Cir. 1983), *cert. dismissed,* 464 U.S. 1033 (1984) (source and object code); *Williams Electronics, Inc. v. Artic Int'l, Inc.,* 685 F.2d 870, 876-77 (3d Cir. 1982) (object code). Here, as noted earlier, Altai admits having copied approximately 30% of the OSCAR

3.4 program from CA's ADAPTER source code, and does not challenge the district court's related finding of infringement.

In this case, the hotly contested issues surround OSCAR 3.5. As recounted above, OSCAR 3.5 is the product of Altai's carefully orchestrated rewrite of OSCAR 3.4. After the purge, none of the ADAPTER source code remained in the 3.5 version; thus, Altai made sure that the literal elements of its re-vamped OSCAR program were no longer substantially similar to the literal elements of CA's ADAPTER.

According to CA, the district court erroneously concluded that Altai's OSCAR 3.5 was not substantially similar to its own ADAPTER program. CA argues that this occurred because the district court "committed legal error in analyzing [its] claims of copyright infringement by failing to find that copy-right protects expression contained in the non-literal elements of computer software." We disagree.

CA argues that, despite Altai's rewrite of the OSCAR code, the resulting program remained substantially similar to the structure of its ADAPTER program. As discussed above, a program's structure includes its non-literal components such as general flow charts as well as the more specific organiza-tion of inter-modular relationships, parameter lists, and macros. In addition to these aspects, CA contends that OSCAR 3.5 is also substantially similar to ADAPTER with respect to the list of services that both ADAPTER and OSCAR obtain from their respective operating systems. We must decide whether and to what extent these elements of computer programs are pro-tected by copyright law.

The statutory terrain in this area has been well explored. *See Lotus Dev. Corp. v. Paperback Software Int'l,* 740 F. Supp. 37, 47-51 (D. Mass. 1990); *see also Whelan,* 797 F.2d at 1240-42. The Copyright Act affords protection to "original works of authorship fixed in any tangible medium of expression." 17 U.S.C. § 102(a). This broad category of protected "works" includes "literary works," *id.,* which are defined by the act as

> works, other than audiovisual works, expressed in words, numbers, or other verbal or numerical symbols or indicia, regardless of the nature of the material objects, such as books, periodicals, manuscripts, phonorec-ords, film tapes, disks, or cards, in which they are embodied.

17 U.S.C. § 101. While computer programs are not specifically listed as part of the above statutory definition, the legislative history leaves no doubt that Congress intended them to be considered literary works. *See* H.R. Rep. No. 1476, 94th Cong., 2d Sess. 54, *reprinted in* 1975 U.S.C.C.A.N. 5659, 5667 (hereinafter *"House Report"*); *Whelan,* 797 F.2d at 1234; *Apple Computer,* 714 F.2d at 1247.

The syllogism that follows from the foregoing premises is a powerful one: if the non-literal structures of literary works are protected by copyright; and if computer programs are literary works, as we are told by the legislature; then the non-literal structures of computer programs are protected by copyright. *See Whelan,* 797 F.2d at 1234 ("By analogy to other literary works, it would thus appear that the copyrights of computer programs can be infringed even absent copying of the literal elements of the program."). We have no reservation in joining the company of those courts that have already ascribed to this logic [citations omitted]. However, that conclusion does not end our analysis. We must determine the scope of copyright protection that extends to a computer program's non-literal structure.

As a caveat, we note that our decision here does not control infringement actions regarding categorically distinct works, such as certain types of screen displays. These items represent products of computer programs, rather than the programs themselves, and fall under the copyright rubric of audiovisual works. If a computer audiovisual display is copyrighted separately as an audiovisual work, apart from the literary work that generates it (i.e., the program), the display may be protectable regardless of the underlying program's copyright status. *See Stern Electronics, Inc. v. Kaufman,* 669 F.2d 852, 855 (2d Cir. 1982) (explaining that an audiovisual works copyright, rather than a copyright on the underlying program, extended greater protection to the sights and sounds generated by a computer video game because the same audiovisual display could be generated by different programs). Of course, the copyright protection that these displays enjoy extends only so far as their expression is predictable. *Data East USA, Inc. v. Epyx, Inc.,* 862 F.2d 204, 209 (9th Cir. 1988). In this case, however, we are concerned not with a program's display, but the program itself, and then with only its non-literal components. In considering the copyrightability of these components, we must refer to venerable doctrines of copyright law.

1) *Idea vs. Expression Dichotomy*

It is a fundamental principle of copyright law that a copyright does not protect an idea, but only the expression of the idea. *See Baker v. Selden,* 101 U.S. 99 (1879); *Mazer v. Stein,* 347 U.S. 201, 217 (1954). This axiom of common law has been incorporated into the governing statute.... Congress made no special exception for computer programs. To the contrary, the legislative history explicitly states that copyright protects computer programs only "to the extent that they incorporate authorship in programmer's expression of original ideas, as distinguished from the ideas themselves."

The essentially utilitarian nature of a computer program further complicates the task of distilling its idea from its expression. In order to describe both computational processes and abstract ideas, its content "combines creative and technical expression." The variations of expression found in purely creative compositions, as opposed to those contained in utilitarian works, are not directed towards practical application. For example, a narration of Humpty Dumpty's demise, which would clearly be a creative composition, does not serve the same ends as, say, a recipe for scrambled eggs — which is a more process oriented text. Thus, compared to aesthetic works, computer programs hover even more closely to the elusive boundary line described in § 102(b).

The doctrinal starting point in analyses of utilitarian works, is the seminal case of *Baker v. Selden,* 101 U.S. 99 (1879)....

To the extent that an accounting text and a computer program are both "a set of statements or instructions ... to bring about a certain result," 17 U.S.C.

§ 101, they are roughly analogous. In the former case, the processes are ultimately conducted by human agency; in the latter, by electronic means. In either case, as already stated, the processes themselves are not protectable. But the holding in *Baker* goes farther. The Court concluded that those aspects of a work, which "must necessarily be used as incident to" the idea, system or process that the work describes, are also not copyrightable. *Selden*'s ledger sheets, therefore, enjoyed no copyright protection because they were "necessary incidents to" the system of accounting that he described. From this reasoning, we conclude that those elements of a computer program that are necessarily incidental to its function are similarly unprotectable.

While *Baker v. Selden* provides a sound analytical foundation, it offers scant guidance on how to separate idea or process from expression, and moreover, on how to further distinguish protectable expression from that expression which "must necessarily be used as incident to" the work's underlying concept. In the context of computer programs, the Third Circuit's noted decision in *Whelan* has, thus far, been the most thoughtful attempt to accomplish these ends.

The court in *Whelan* faced substantially the same problem as presented by this case. There, the defendant was accused of making off with the non-literal structure of the plaintiff's copyrighted dental lab management program, and employing it to create its own competitive version. In assessing whether there had been an infringement, the court had to determine which aspects of the program involved were ideas, and which were expression.... The "idea" of the program at issue in *Whelan* was identified by the court as simply "the efficient management of a dental laboratory."

So far, in the courts, the *Whelan* rule has received a mixed reception. While some decisions have adopted its reasoning [citations omitted], others have rejected it [citations omitted].

Whelan has fared even more poorly in the academic community, where its standard for distinguishing idea from expression has been widely criticized for being conceptually overbroad [citations omitted]. The leading commentator in the field has stated that, "the crucial flaw in [*Whelan*'s] reasoning is that it assumes that only one 'idea,' in copyright law terms, underlies any computer program, and that once a separable idea can be identified, everything else must be expression." 3 Nimmer § 13.03[F], at 13-62.34. This criticism focuses not upon the program's ultimate purpose but upon the reality of its structural design. As we have already noted, a computer program's ultimate function or purpose is the composite result of interacting subroutines. Since each subroutine is itself a program, and thus, may be said to have its own "idea," *Whelan*'s general formulation that a program's overall purpose equates with the program's idea is descriptively inadequate.

....

2) *Substantial Similarity Test for Computer Program Structure: Abstraction-Filtration-Comparison*

We think that *Whelan*'s approach to separating idea from expression in computer programs relies too heavily on metaphysical distinctions and does not place enough emphasis on practical considerations. As the cases that we shall discuss demonstrate, a satisfactory answer to this problem cannot be reached by resorting, a priori, to philosophical first principles.

As discussed herein, we think that district courts would be well-advised to undertake a three-step procedure, based on the abstractions test utilized by the district court, in order to determine whether the non-literal elements of two or more computer programs are substantially similar. This approach breaks no new grounds; rather, it draws on such familiar copyright doctrines as merger, scenes a faire, and public domain. In taking this approach, however, we are cognizant that computer technology is a dynamic field which can quickly outpace judicial decisionmaking. Thus, in cases where the technology in question does not allow for a literal application of the procedure we outline below, our opinion should not be read to foreclose the district courts of our circuit from utilizing a modified version.

In ascertaining substantial similarity under this approach, a court would first break down the allegedly infringed program into its constituent structural parts. Then, by examining each of these parts for such things as incorporated ideas, expression that is necessarily incidental to those ideas, and elements that are taken from the public domain, a court would then be able to sift out all non-protectable material. Left with a kernel, or possibly kernels, of creative expression after following this process of elimination, the court's last step would be to compare this material with the structure of an allegedly infringing program. The result of this comparison will determine whether the protectable elements of the programs at issue are substantially similar so as to warrant a finding of infringement. It will be helpful to elaborate a bit further.

Step One: Abstraction

As the district court appreciated, the theoretic framework for analyzing substantial similarity expounded by Learned Hand in the *Nichols* case is helpful in the present context. In *Nichols,* we enunciated what has now become known as the "abstractions" test for separating idea from expression. While the abstractions test was originally applied in relation to literary works such as novels and plays, it is adaptable to computer programs. In contrast to the *Whelan* approach, the abstractions test "implicitly recognizes that any given work may consist of a mixture of numerous ideas and expressions."

As applied to computer programs, the abstractions test will comprise the first step in the examination for substantial similarity. Initially, in a manner that resembles reverse engineering on a theoretical plane, a court should dissect the allegedly copied program's structure and isolate each level of abstraction contained within it. This process begins with the code and ends with an articulation of the program's ultimate function. Along the way, it is necessary essentially to retrace and map each of the designer's steps — in the opposite order in which they were taken during the program's creation.

As an anatomical guide to this procedure, the following description is help-ful:

> At the lowest level of abstraction, a computer program may be thought of
> in its entirety as a set of individual instructions organized into a hierar-
> chy of modules. At a higher level of abstraction, the instructions in the
> lowest-level modules may be replaced conceptually by the functions of
> those modules. At progressively higher levels of abstraction, the functions
> of higher-level modules conceptually replace the implementations of
> those modules in terms of lower-level modules and instructions, until
> finally, one is left with nothing but the ultimate function of the pro-
> gram.... A program has structure at every level of abstraction at which it
> is viewed. At low levels of abstraction, a program's structure may be quite
> complex; at the highest level it is trivial.

Step Two: Filtration

Once the program's abstraction levels have been discovered, the substantial
similarity inquiry moves from the conceptual to the concrete. Professor
Nimmer suggests, and we endorse, a "successive filtering method" for separating protectable expression from non-protectable material. *See generally* 3
Nimmer § 13.03[F]. This process entails examining the structural components
at each level of abstraction to determine whether their particular inclusion at
that level was "idea" or was dictated by considerations of efficiency, so as to be
necessarily incidental to that idea; required by factors external to the program itself; or taken from the public domain and hence is non-protectable
expression. The structure of any given program may reflect some, all, or none
of these considerations. Each case requires its own fact specific investigation.

Strictly speaking, this filtration serves "the purpose of defining the scope of
plaintiff's copyright." *Brown Bag Software v. Symantec Corp.*, No. 89-16239,
slip op. 3719, 3738 (9th Cir. April 7, 1992) (endorsing "analytic dissection" of
computer programs in order to isolate protectable expression). By applying
well developed doctrines of copyright law, it may ultimately leave behind a
"core of protectable material." 3 Nimmer § 13.03[F][5], at 13-72. Further ex-
plication of this second step may be helpful.

(a) *Elements Dictated by Efficiency*

The portion of *Baker v. Selden,* discussed earlier, which denies copyright
protection to expression necessarily incidental to the idea being expressed,
appears to be the cornerstone for what has developed into the doctrine of
merger. *See Morrissey v. Procter & Gamble Co.*, 379 F.2d 675, 678-79 (1st Cir.
1967) (relying on *Baker* for the proposition that expression embodying the
rules of a sweepstakes contest was inseparable from the idea of the contest
itself, and therefore were not protectable by copyright); *see also Digital Communications,* 659 F. Supp. at 457. The doctrine's underlying principle is that
"when there is essentially only one way to express an idea, the idea and its
expression are inseparable and copyright is no bar to copying that expression." *Concrete Machinery Co. v. Classic Lawn Ornaments, Inc.,* 843 F.2d 600,

606 (1st Cir. 1988). Under these circumstances, the expression is said to have "merged" with the idea itself. In order not to confer a monopoly of the idea upon the copyright owner, such expression should not be protected. *See Herbert Rosenthal Jewelry Corp. v. Kalpakian,* 446 F.2d 738, 742 (9th Cir. 1971).

CONTU recognized the applicability of the merger doctrine to computer programs. In its report to Congress it stated that:

> Copyrighted language may be copied without infringing when there is but a limited number of ways to express a given idea.... In the computer context, this means that when specific instructions, even though previously copyrighted, are the only and essential means of accomplishing a given task, their later use by another will not amount to infringement.

CONTU Report at 20. While this statement directly concerns only the application of merger to program code, that is, the textual aspect of the program, it reasonably suggests that the doctrine fits comfortably within the general context of computer programs.

Furthermore, when one considers the fact that programmers generally strive to create programs "that meet the user's needs in the most efficient manner," the applicability of the merger doctrine to computer programs becomes compelling. In the context of computer programs design, the concept of efficiency is akin to deriving the most concise logical proof or formulating the most succinct mathematical computation. Thus, the more efficient a set of modules are, the more closely they approximate the idea or process embodied in that particular aspect of the program's structure.

While, hypothetically, there might be a myriad of ways in which a programmer may effectuate certain functions within a program, — i.e., express the idea embodied in a given subroutine — efficiency concerns may so narrow the practical range of choice as to make only one or two forms of expression workable options. *See also Whelan,* 797 F.2d at 1243 n.43 ("It is true that for certain tasks there are only a very limited number of file structures available, and in such cases the structures might not be copyrightable..."). Of course, not all program structure is informed by efficiency concerns. It follows that in order to determine whether the merger doctrine precludes copyright protection to an aspect of a program's structure that is so oriented, a court must inquire "whether the use of this particular set of modules is necessary efficiently to implement that part of the program's process" being implemented. If the answer is yes, then the expression represented by the programmer's choice of a specific module or group of modules has merged with their underlying idea and is unprotected.

Another justification for linking structural economy with the application of the merger doctrine stems from a program's essentially utilitarian nature and the competitive forces that exist in the software marketplace. Working in tandem, these factors give rise to a problem of proof which merger helps to eliminate.

Efficiency is an industry-wide goal. Since, as we have already noted, there may be only a limited number of efficient implementations for any given program task, it is quite possible that multiple programmers, working independently, will design the identical method employed in the allegedly infringed work. Of course, if this is the case, there is no copyright infringement.

Under these circumstances, the fact that two programs contain the same efficient structure may as likely lead to an inference of independent creation as it does to one of copying. Thus, since evidence of similarly efficient structure is not particularly probative of copying, it should be disregarded in the overall substantial similarity analysis.

We find support for applying the merger doctrine in cases that have already addressed the question of substantial similarity in the context of computer program structure. Most recently, in *Lotus Dev. Corp.*, 740 F. Supp. at 66, the district court had before it a claim of copyright infringement relating to the structure of a computer spreadsheet program. The court observed that "the basic spreadsheet screen display that resembles a rotated 'L'..., if not present in every expression of such a program, is present in most expressions." Similarly, the court found that "an essential detail present in most if not all expressions of an electronic spreadsheet — is the designation of a particular key that, when pressed, will invoke the menu command system." *Id.* Applying the merger doctrine, the court denied copyright protection to both program elements.

In *Manufacturers Technologies, Inc. v. Cams, Inc.*, 706 F. Supp. 984, 995-99 (D. Conn. 1989), the infringement claims stemmed from various alleged program similarities "as indicated in their screen displays." Stressing efficiency concerns in the context of a merger analysis, the court determined that the program's method of allowing the user to navigate within the screen displays was not protectable because, in part, "the process or manner of navigating internally on any specific screen displays ... is limited in the number of ways it may be simply achieved to facilitate user comfort."...

We agree with the approach taken in these decisions, and conclude that application of the merger doctrine in this setting is an effective way to eliminate non-protectable expression contained in computer programs.

(b) *Elements Dictated by External Factors*

We have stated that where "it is virtually impossible to write about a particular historical era or fictional theme without employing certain 'stock' or standard literary devices," such expression is not copyrightable. *Hoehling v. Universal City Studios, Inc.*, 618 F.2d 972, 979 (2d Cir.), *cert. denied*, 449 U.S. 841 (1980). For example, the *Hoehling* case was an infringement suit stemming from several works on the Hindenberg disaster. There we concluded that similarities in representations of German beer halls, scenes depicting German greetings such as "Heil Hitler," or the singing of certain German songs would not lead to a finding of infringement because they were "'indispensable, or at least standard, in the treatment of'" life in Nazi Germany. *Id.* (*quoting Alexander v. Haley*, 460 F. Supp. 40, 45 (S.D.N.Y. 1978)). This is known as the scenes a faire doctrine, and like "merger," it has its analogous application to computer programs. *Cf. Data East USA*, 862 F.2d at 208 (applying scenes a faire to a home computer video game).

Professor Nimmer points out that "in many instances it is virtually impossible to write a program to perform particular functions in a specific computing environment without employing standard techniques." This is a result of the fact that a programmer's freedom of design choice is often circumscribed by extrinsic considerations such as (1) the mechanical specifications of the computer on which a particular program is intended to run; (2) compatibility requirements of other programs with which a program is designed to operate in conjunction; (3) computer manufacturers' design standards; (4) demands of the industry being serviced; and (5) widely accepted programming practices within the computer industry.

Courts have already considered some of these factors in denying copyright protection to various elements of computer programs. In the *Plains Cotton* case, the Fifth Circuit refused to reverse the district court's denial of a preliminary injunction against an alleged program infringer because, in part, "many of the similarities between the ... programs [were] dictated by the externalities of the cotton market."

In *Manufacturers Technologies,* the district court noted that the program's method of screen navigation "is influenced by the type of hardware that the software is designed to be used on." Because, in part, "the functioning of the hardware package impacted and constrained the type of navigational tools used in plaintiff's screen displays," the court denied copyright protection to that aspect of the program. *Cf. Data East USA,* 862 F.2d at 209 (reversing a district court's finding of audio-visual work infringement because, inter alia, "the use of the Commodore computer for a karate game intended for home consumption is subject to various constraints inherent in the use of that computer").

Finally, the district court in *O-Co Industries* rested its holding on what, perhaps, most closely approximates a traditional scenes a faire rationale. There, the court denied copyright protection to four program modules employed in a teleprompter program. This decision was ultimately based upon the court's finding that "the same modules would be an inherent part of any prompting program."

Building upon this existing case law, we conclude that a court must also examine the structural content of an allegedly infringed program for elements that might have been dictated by external factors.

(c) *Elements Taken From the Public Domain*

Closely related to the non-protectability of scenes a faire, is material found in the public domain. Such material is free for the taking and cannot be appropriated by a single author even though it is included in a copyrighted work. *See E.F. Johnson Co. v. Uniden Corp. of America,* 623 F. Supp. 1485, 1499 (D. Minn. (1985); *see also Sheldon,* 81 F.2d at 54. We see no reason to make an exception to this rule for elements of a computer program that have entered the public domain by virtue of freely accessible program exchanges and the like. *See Brown Bag Software,* slip op. at 3732 (affirming the district court's finding that "'plaintiffs may not claim copyright protection of an ... expression that is, if not standard, then commonplace in the computer software industry.'"). Thus, a court must also filter out this material from the allegedly infringed program before it makes the final inquiry in its substantial similarity analysis.

Step Three: Comparison

The third and final step of the test for substantial similarity that we believe appropriate for non-literal program components entails a comparison. Once a court has sifted out all elements of the allegedly infringed program which are "ideas" or are dictated by efficiency or external factors, or taken from the public domain, there may remain a core of protectable expression. In terms of a work's copyright value, this is the golden nugget. At this point, the court's substantial similarity inquiry focuses on whether the defendant copied any aspect of this protected expression, as well as an assessment of the copied portion's relative importance with respect to the plaintiff's overall program. *See Data East USA,* 862 F.2d at 208 ("To determine whether similarities result from unprotectable expression, analytic dissection of similarities may be performed. If ... all similarities in expression arise from use of common ideas, then no substantial similarity can be found.")

3) *Policy Considerations*

....

CA and some amici argue against the type of approach that we have set forth on the grounds that it will be a disincentive for future computer program research and development. At bottom, they claim that if programmers are not guaranteed broad copyright protection for their work, they will not invest the extensive time, energy and funds required to design and improve program structures. While they have a point, their argument cannot carry the day. The interest of the copyright law is not in simply conferring a monopoly on industrious persons, but in advancing the public welfare through rewarding artistic creativity, in a manner that permits the free use and development of non-protectable ideas and processes.

Recently, the Supreme Court has emphatically reiterated that "the primary objective of copyright is not to reward the labor of authors...." *Feist Publications, Inc. v. Rural Telephone Service Co., Inc.,* 111 S. Ct. 1282, 1290 (1991) ....

Feist teaches that substantial effort alone cannot confer copyright status on an otherwise uncopyrightable work. As we have discussed, despite the fact that significant labor and expense often goes [sic] into computer program flow-charting and debugging, that process does not always result in inherently protectable expression. Thus, *Feist* implicitly undercuts the *Whelan* rationale, "which allowed copyright protection beyond the literal computer code ... [in order to] provide the proper incentive for programmers by protecting their most valuable efforts." We note that *Whelan* was decided prior to *Feist* when the "sweat of the brow" doctrine still had vitality. In view of the Supreme Court's recent holding, however, we must reject the legal basis of CA's disincentive argument.

Furthermore, we are unpersuaded that the test we approve today will lead to the dire consequences for the computer program industry that plaintiff and some amici predict. To the contrary, serious students of the industry have been highly critical of the sweeping scope of copyright protection engendered by the *Whelan* rule, in that it "enables first comers to 'lock up' basic programming techniques as implemented in programs to perform particular tasks."

To be frank, the exact contours of copyright protection for non-literal program structure are not completely clear. We trust that as future cases are decided, those limits will become better defined. Indeed, it may well be that the Copyright Act serves as a relatively weak barrier against public access to the theoretical interstices behind a program's source and object codes. This results from the hybrid nature of a computer program, which, while it is literary expression, is also a highly functional, utilitarian component in the larger process of computing.

Generally, we think that copyright registration — with its indiscriminating availability — is not ideally suited to deal with the highly dynamic technology of computer science. Thus far, many of the decisions in this area reflect the courts' attempt to fit the proverbial square peg in a round hole. The district court, and at least one commentator, has suggested that patent registration, with its exacting up-front novelty and non-obviousness requirements, might be the more appropriate rubric of protection for intellectual property of this kind. 1103, 1123-25 (1991); *see also Lotus Dev. Corp. v. Borland Int'l, Inc.,* (discussing the potentially supplemental relationship between patent and copyright protection in the context of computer programs). In any event, now that more than 12 years have passed since CONTU issued its final report, the resolution of this specific issue could benefit from further legislative investigation — perhaps a CONTU II.

In the meantime, Congress has made clear that computer programs are literary works entitled to copyright protection. Of course, we shall abide by these instructions, but in so doing we must not impair the overall integrity of copyright law. While incentive based arguments in favor of broad copyright protection are perhaps attractive from a pure policy perspective, ultimately, they have a corrosive effect on certain fundamental tenets of copyright doctrine. If the test we have outlined results in narrowing the scope of protection, as we expect it will, that result flows from applying, in accordance with Congressional intent, long-standing principles of copyright law to computer programs. Of course, our decision is also informed by our concern that these fundamental principles remain undistorted.

B. *The District Court Decision*

We turn now to our review of the district court's decision in this particular case.

The district court had to determine whether Altai's OSCAR 3.5 program was substantially similar to CA's ADAPTER. We note that Judge Pratt's method of analysis effectively served as a road map for our own, with one exception — Judge Pratt filtered out the non-copyrightable aspects of OSCAR 3.5 rather than those found in ADAPTER, the allegedly infringed program. We think that our approach — i.e., filtering out the unprotected aspects of an allegedly infringed program and then comparing the end product to the structure of the suspect program — is preferable, and therefore believe that district courts should proceed in this manner in future cases.

We opt for this strategy because, in some cases, the defendant's program structure might contain protectable expression and/or other elements that are not found in the plaintiff's program. Since it is extraneous to the allegedly copied work, this material would have no bearing on any potential substantial similarity between the two programs. Thus, its filtration would be wasteful and unnecessarily time consuming. Furthermore, by focusing the analysis on the infringing rather than on the infringed material, a court may mistakenly place too little emphasis on a quantitatively small misappropriation which is, in reality, a qualitatively vital aspect of the plaintiff's protectable expression.

The district court took the first step in the analysis set forth in this opinion when it separated the program by levels of abstraction. The district court stated:

> As applied to computer software programs, this abstractions test would progress in order of "increasing generality" from object code, to source code, to parameter lists, to services required, to general outline. In discussing the particular similarities, therefore, we shall focus on these levels.

While the facts of a different case might require that a district court draw a more particularized blueprint of a program's overall structure, this description is a workable one for the case at hand.

Moving to the district court's evaluation of OSCAR 3.5's structural components, we agree with Judge Pratt's systematic exclusion of non-protectable expression. With respect to code, the district court observed that after the rewrite of OSCAR 3.4 to OSCAR 3.5, "there remained virtually no lines of code that were identical to ADAPTER." Accordingly, the court found that the code "presented no similarity at all."

Next, Judge Pratt addressed the issue of similarity between the two programs' parameter lists and macros. He concluded that, viewing the conflicting evidence most favorably to CA, it demonstrated that "only a few of the lists and macros were similar to protected elements in ADAPTER; the others were either in the public domain or dictated by the functional demands of the program." As discussed above, functional elements and elements taken from the public domain do not qualify for copyright protection. With respect to the few remaining parameter lists and macros, the district court could reasonably conclude that they did not warrant a finding of infringement given their relative contribution to the overall program. In any event, the district court reasonably found that, for lack of persuasive evidence, CA failed to meet its burden of proof on whether the macros and parameter lists at issue were substantially similar.

The district court also found that the overlap exhibited between the list of services required for both ADAPTER and OSCAR 3.5 was "determined by the demands of the operating system and of the applications program to which it [was] to be linked through ADAPTER or OSCAR." *Id.* In other words, this aspect of the program's structure was dictated by the nature of other programs with which it was designed to interact and, thus, is not protected by copyright.

Finally, in his infringement analysis, Judge Pratt accorded no weight to the similarities between the two programs' organizational charts, "because [the charts were] so simple and obvious to anyone exposed to the operation of the program[s]." CA argues that the district court's action in this regard "is not consistent with copyright law" — that "obvious" expression is protected, and that the district court erroneously failed to realize this. However, to say that elements of a work are "obvious," in the manner in which the district court used the word, is to say that they "follow naturally from the work's theme rather than from the author's creativity." This is but one formulation of the scenes a faire doctrine, which we have already endorsed as a means of weeding out unprotectable expression.

Since we accept Judge Pratt's factual conclusions and the results of his legal analysis, we affirm his dismissal of CA's copyright infringement claim based upon OSCAR 3.5. We emphasize that, like all copyright infringement cases, those that involve computer programs are highly fact specific. The amount of protection due structural elements, in any given case, will vary according to the protectable expression found to exist within the program at issue.

QUESTIONS

1. Articulate the differences between the *Whelan* and *Altai* analyses of copyright infringement. Which is the more convincing analysis with respect to computer programs? Which is the more convincing analysis with respect to literary works more generally?

2. Evaluate in particular the approach of the *Altai* court toward what it calls "abstraction-filtration-comparison." Is that analytical process properly to be applied in assessing infringement of novels (or dramatic works or motion pictures) as well? For example, should a court "filter" out all material in a plaintiff's novel that is in the public domain because factual, and elements that are abstract enough to be considered "ideas," and elements that are routine in the genre so as to be considered "scenes a faire," and other elements that are thought insufficiently original — *before* making a comparison with the defendant's work as to substantial similarity? Does that approach comport with Judge Hand's decision in *Sheldon*? Does that approach not ignore the "authorship" reflected in selecting, coordinating and arranging these public domain elements? *See Gates Rubber Co. v. Bando American, Inc.*, 798 F. Supp. 1499, 1516 (D. Colo. 1992). Compare the note on Approaches to Substantial Similarity at p. 425 *supra*, and its reference to *Apple Computer, Inc., v. Microsoft Corp.*, 779 F. Supp. 133 (N.D. Cal. 1991).

3. If it can be said that the court's analysis in *Altai* is perhaps stricter on the plaintiff than is true in literary cases generally, is that justified by the "functionality" of the programs claimed by Computer Associates? Consider other functional works, and the application of the court's method of separating unprotectible idea from protectible expression, i.e., splitting the overall program into its component modules and subroutines. How would that analysis be applied to such "functional" works as cookbooks? Or manuals for the assembly of a machine or for the playing of a game? Or law school casebooks?

3. USER INTERFACE: SCREENS AND COMMAND SEQUENCES

[The following Note is drawn from a Report (pp. 11-16) prepared by a group of legal academics at a conference sponsored by the Center for the Study of Law, Science and Technology (LaST) at the Arizona State University College of Law, in February 1989. The Report was titled *Computer Software and Copyright Protection: The "Structure, Sequence and Organization," and "Look and Feel" Questions.*]

PROTECTION OF USER INTERFACES

User interfaces include all of the devices by which the human user can interact with the computer in order to accomplish the tasks the computer is programmed to perform. Screen displays of images and text are often important components of the user interface, but user interfaces may also include hardware extensions (such as keyboards, "mice", joysticks, or switches) and sounds, depending on how the programmed computer has been designed to interact with the user.

... [S]everal traditional copyright doctrines may limit the scope of protection in user interfaces, in addition to the basic idea/expression distinction. For example, copyright does not protect systems, processes, procedures, or methods, and aspects of user interfaces that fall into these categories would not be protected. Other aspects of user interfaces may lack sufficient expressive authorship to be eligible for copyright protection. In other cases, the number of ways to express a particular aspect may be so limited that idea and expression merge, in which case copyright protection would be unavailable. Even without merger, there are well-reasoned cases denying protection to generic or commonplace expression in videogames (scénes à faire), and these precedents seem especially applicable to user interfaces at the present time.

... [W]hat copyright law considers to be protectible expression varies with the nature of the work. Thus, software user interfaces displaying words or other symbols on screens range from the highly fanciful (such as certain videogame displays), which are afforded a broad scope of copyright protection, to the highly functional (such as a gasoline pump meter displaying the amount and cost of gasoline), which may be unprotectible by copyright due to lack of originality, because of the idea/expression distinction, or for other reasons.

... [C]opyright should not protect aspects of an interface that optimize, in a way for which there is no viable substitute, such design goals as rapid execution, accuracy of results, error reduction, number and/or speed of keystroke functions, or time, effort, or cost of becoming skilled at using the program. Such functionally optimal aspects of an interface should not be protected regardless of whether the original designer consciously employed systematic design analysis aimed at optimization or simply discovered an optimal interface aspect by intuition. Consequently, to the extent the competing programmer can demonstrate that aspects of the original interface are functionally optimal, and that there are few ways to devise alternative interface elements that will perform the function equally well, reproduction of those original interface elements by a competing program will not infringe. (It must be borne in mind that the copyright in the interface is distinct from the copyright in the program. A competitor who invokes this exception pertaining to the interface must still develop the program generating the interface in a legal manner.)

... [C]opyright protection in the user interface does not extend to any single, given function that is a member of that interface's command list, nor does it extend to any group of commands (functions) each of which is natural, normal, or obvious for a program of that type. Thus, any word processing program should be able to include commands (functions) for entering letters and words, moving phrases, setting margins, saving text, and so forth....

Even given that a particular command or set of commands (functions) might be unprotected by copyright, however, there remains the possibility that the manner by which the commands are portrayed on the screen and/or instruct the user on how to invoke them might be protected. In this case, putting the question of standardization of user methodology to one side, the issue is whether copyright protection in one means of portraying the command set (individually or collectively) and indicating the manner of their use would substantially restrict developers of competing programs designed to perform the same tasks as the original. In deciding the scope of copyright protection in these manners of portrayal, the court should consider such factors as constraints on representing commands on the screen that flow from the hardware as well as the natural or logical ways of portraying those commands and the methods for involving them on the screen. Where these constraints as a practical matter reduce the number of ways to portray commands to one or a very small number, copyright protection must be severely limited or even denied completely.

The case that follows — *Lotus v. Paperback Software* — and subsequent cases brought by *Lotus Development Corp.* against other software producers (see, e.g., *Lotus v. Borland, infra*), concerned competitors' development of rival spreadsheet programs that were "work alikes" to plaintiff's Lotus spreadsheet. A "work alike" program mimics many aspects of the initial program's user interface, thereby permitting the user to adopt the new program without having to become familiar with different screen layouts or command key placement and sequences.

LOTUS DEVELOPMENT CORP. v. PAPERBACK SOFTWARE INTERNATIONAL, INC.

740 F. Supp. 37 (D. Mass. 1990)

KEETON, DISTRICT JUDGE.

The expression of an idea is copyrightable. The idea itself is not. When applying these two settled rules of law, how can a decisionmaker distinguish between an idea and its expression?

Answering this riddle is the first step — but only the first — toward disposition of this case in which the court must decide, among other issues, (1) whether and to what extent plaintiff's computer spreadsheet program, Lotus 1-2-3, is copyrightable, (2) whether defendants' VP-Planner was, on undisputable facts, an infringing work containing elements substantially similar to copyrightable elements of 1-2-3, and (3) whether defendants' proffered juris-dictional and equitable defenses are meritorious....

The outcome of this case depends on how this court, and higher courts on appeal, should answer a central question about the scope of copyrightability of computer programs. For the reasons explained in this Opinion, I conclude that this question must be resolved in favor of the plaintiff, Lotus.

....

IV. *The Legal Test for Copyrightability Applicable to This Case*

A. *Functionality, Useful Articles, and the Useful-Expressive Distinction*

Defendants suggest that the user interface of Lotus 1-2-3 is a useful, "func-tional" object like the functional layout of gears in an "H" pattern on a stan-dard transmission, the functional assignment of letters to keys on a standard QWERTY keyboard, and the functional configuration of controls on a musical instrument (e.g., keys of a piano). Lewis Affdvt. paras. 52-54. These "func-tional" "useful articles," defendants contend, are not entitled to copyright protection.

....

Defendant's proposed analogy is ... similar to the analogy drawn by [CONTU] Commissioner Hersey between a computer program and an object that is designated to do work — for example, the cam of a drill. CONTU, Final Report at 58-60 (Hersey, C., dissenting). His view, however, was in dissent, and not a view advanced by CONTU. Because Congress adopted CONTU's recommendations practically verbatim, it is reasonable to infer that Congress did not adopt Commissioner Hersey's view. Moreover, I conclude that defen-dants' contentions ... are inconsistent with the legislative history and statu-tory mandates.... If, in a context such as that ... of this case, an idea and its expression were taken to be inseparable and the expression therefore not copyrightable, copyright law never would, as a practical matter, provide com-puter programs with protection as substantial as Congress has mandated — protection designed to extend to original elements of expression however em-bodied. I credit the testimony of expert witnesses that the bulk of the creative work is in the conceptualization of a computer program and its user interface, rather than in its encoding, and that creating a suitable user interface is a more difficult intellectual task, requiring greater creativity, originality, and insight, than converting the user interface design into instructions to the machine.... Defendants' contentions would attribute to the statute a purpose to protect only a narrowly defined segment of the creative development of computer programs, and to preclude from protection even more significant creative elements of the process. Such a result is fundamentally inconsistent with the statutory mandates....

... In effect, their proposed rule would work this way: Anything that is useful is a "useful article"; nothing about a "useful article" is ever copyrightable; because 1-2-3 is useful, and is an article, it is not copyrightable.

A more sensible interpretation of the statutory mandate is that the mere fact that an intellectual work is useful or functional — be it a dictionary, directory, map, book of meaningless code words, or computer program — does not mean that none of the elements of the work can be copyrightable. Also, the statute does not bar copyrightability merely because the originality of the expression becomes associated, in the marketplace, with usefulness of the work to a degree and in dimensions not previously achieved by other products on the market.... To hold otherwise would be to deny copyright protection to the most original and least obvious products of the creative mind merely because the marketplace accepts them as distinctively "functional." Such a rule would grant copyright protection for only those products that fall far short of being the best available. Rather than promoting and encouraging both the development and disclosure of the best, such a rule would offer incentives to market only the second, or third, or tenth best, and hold back the best for fear that it is too good for copyrightability. Copyrightability is not a synonym for imperfection.

Accordingly, I conclude that a court, in determining whether a particular element is copyrightable, must not allow one statutory mandate — that functionality or usefulness is not itself a basis for copyrightability — to absorb and destroy another statutory mandate — that elements of expression are copyrightable. Elements of expression, even if embodied in useful articles, are copyrightable if capable of identification and recognition independently of the functional ideas that make the article useful. This mandate may be viewed as a corollary of the central distinction of copyright law between idea and expression, which is explored further immediately below.

... [If] the expression of an idea has elements that go beyond all functional elements of the idea itself, and beyond the obvious, and if there are numerous other ways of expressing the non-copyrightable idea, then those elements of expression, if original and substantial, are copyrightable.

C. Elements of the Legal Test for Copyrightability

... [A] statement of the most significant elements of the legal test for copyrightability, consistent with precedents, begins:

> FIRST, in making the determination of "copyrightability," the decision-maker must focus upon alternatives that counsel may suggest, or the court may conceive, *along the scale from the most generalized conception to the most particularized,* and choose some formulation — some conception or definition of the "idea" — for the purpose of distinguishing between the idea and its expression.

As Learned Hand recognized in a 1930 case concerning the alleged infringement of the copyright of a play:

> Upon any work, and especially upon a play, a great number of patterns of increasing generality will fit equally well, as more and more of the incident is left out. The last may perhaps be no more than the most general statement of what the play is about, and at times might consist only of its title; but there is a point in this series of abstractions where they are no longer protected, since otherwise the playwright could prevent the use of his "ideas," to which, apart from their expression, his property is never ex-

tended. Nobody has ever been able to fix that boundary, and nobody ever can.

Nichols, 45 F.2d at 121 (citations omitted)....

In addition to taking account of the distinction between generality and specificity, to make use of Hand's abstraction scale for applying the idea-expression distinction we need to identify and distinguish between essential and nonessential details of expressing the idea. Some, but of course not all, details, are so essential that their omission would result in a failure to express *that* idea, or in the expression of only a different and *more general* idea. Accordingly, two more elements in the legal test for copyrightability are:

> SECOND, the decisionmaker must focus upon whether an alleged expression of the idea is limited to elements essential to expression of *that* idea (or is one of only a few ways of expressing the idea) or instead includes identifiable elements of expression not essential to every expression of that idea.
>
> THIRD, having identified elements of expression not essential to every expression of the idea, the decisionmaker must focus on whether those elements are a substantial part of the allegedly copyrightable "work."

In addressing this third element of the test for copyrightability, the decisionmaker is measuring "substantiality" not merely on a quantum scale but by a test that is qualitative as well. *SAS Institute,* 605 F. Supp. at 829-30 ("the piracy of even a quantitatively small fragment ('a rose by any other name would smell as sweet') may be qualitatively substantial").

....

V. *Application of the Legal Test to Lotus 1-2-3*

A. *"Look and Feel"*

In musical, dramatic, and motion picture works, and works of literature, nonliteral elements that are copyrightable have sometimes been described as the "total concept and feel" of a work, *Roth Greeting Cards,* 429 F.2d at 1110; *Krofft Television,* 562 F.2d at 1167, "the fundamental essence or structure" of a work, 3 M. Nimmer & D. Nimmer, Nimmer on Copyright § 13.03[A][1] (1989), or "the 'pattern' of the work," Chaffee, *Reflections on the Law of Copyright: Part I,* 45 Colum. L. Rev. 503, 513 (1945). In the context of computer programs, nonliteral elements have often been referred to as the "look and feel" of a program ....

Despite its widespread use in public discourse on the copyrightability of nonliteral elements of computer programs, I have not found the "look and feel" concept, standing alone, to be significantly helpful in distinguishing between nonliteral elements of a computer program that are copyrightable and those that are not....

B. *The User Interface*

Plaintiff in the present case, not now pressing any argument that the phrase "look and feel" is a satisfactory description of the copyrightable elements of Lotus 1-2-3, suggests that the copyrightable nonliteral elements are more appropriately described by the phrase "user interface." According to plaintiff, the "user interface" of 1-2-3 includes such elements as "the menus (and their structure and organization), the long prompts, the screens on which they appear, the function key assignments, [and] the macro commands and language," Plaintiff's Post-Trial Brief at 53 (Docket No. 319). I turn now to examining these elements more closely. Like manual spreadsheets, *Baker,* 101 U.S. at 100, the electronic spreadsheet presents a blank form on which numerical, statistical, financial or other data can be assimilated, organized, manipulated and calculated. Galler Decl. paras. 101-103; Lewis Affdvt. para. 92. In both Lotus 1-2-3 and VP-Planner, as in many other electronic spreadsheet programs, a highlighted element of the basic screen display resembles an "L" rotated ninety degrees clockwise with letters across the top to designate columns, and numbers down the left side to designate rows. See Appendices 1 (VisiCalc), 2 (1-2-3), and 3 (VP-Planner). Cf. Multiplan, which also has a rotated "L" screen display, but which uses numbers for both columns and rows (Tr. Ex. (Trial Exhibit) 132). The intersection of each column and row is a "cell" in which a value (e.g., 31,963), formula (e.g., one that adds a column of numbers), or label (e.g., "Cost of Goods") may be entered.

Both programs utilize a "two-line moving-cursor menu," which presents the user with a list of command choices (e.g., "file," "copy," "quit") and a moving cursor to use in communicating ("entering") the choice. The menu is called up to the screen by pressing the slash ("/") key, and is located either above the rotated "L" (as in 1-2-3, see Appendix 2) or below the rotated "L" (as in VP-Planner, see Appendix 3). Cf. Multiplan, which uses a three-line moving cursor menu (Tr. Ex. 132); Excel, which has "pull-down" bar menus (Tr. Ex. 79).

The top line of the two-line menu contains a series of words, each of which represents a different command. For example, the top line of the first, or main, menu in 1-2-3 reads: "Worksheet Range Copy Move File Graph Data Quit." See Appendix 2; cf. Appendix 3 (main menu in VP-Planner). The first word of the line is highlighted to signify the command that will be chosen if the "enter" key is pressed; the highlighting, or "cursor," moves to the right or left if the right or left cursor key is pressed.

The second line of the menu displays a "long prompt," which contains further information about the highlighted command. In some cases, the long prompt is a description of the highlighted command (e.g., for command "Copy," the long prompt reads: "Copy a cell or range of cells"); in other cases, the long prompt provides a list of the menu command subchoices that will be available if the highlighted command is chosen (e.g., for command "Worksheet," the long prompt reads: "Global, Insert, Delete, Column-Width, Erase, Titles, Window, Status"; see Appendix 2; cf. Appendix 3 (VP-Planner)). In the latter case, if the highlighted command is subsequently chosen, the words that appeared in the long prompt will now appear as second-level menu command choices on the top line of the menu, and a new long prompt will take its place on the second line.

In addition to having the option of selecting a command by moving the cursor to the command and pressing the "enter" key, a user may instead press the key representing the first letter of the command word (e.g., "C" for "Copy,"

"W" for "Worksheet"). For this reason, each word representing each command on a given menu line must start with a different letter. See Galler Affdvt. paras. 105-117; Lewis Decl. paras. 96-97.

Function keys present an additional way for the user to communicate with, and operate, the programmed computer. Each program assigns certain frequently-used commands to the various "function keys" (labelled "F1," "F2," "F3," etc.) on the keyboard. For example, in 1-2-3, "F1" corresponds to the command "Help," and "F2" to the command "Edit." Galler Decl. para. 125. VP-Planner, in contrast, assigns the function keys to the commands on the top line of the menu. Thus, for example, when VP-Planner is in its main menu mode, "F1" corresponds to the command "Help," "F2" to the command "Worksheet," "F3" to the command "Range," "F4" to the command "Copy," and so on. See Appendix 3 (function key numbers listed before command terms).

Typically, users adapt particular spreadsheets to their specific needs. Suppose, for example, that in order to achieve a desired result, a user must perform the same sequence of commands repeatedly in order to cause the computer to execute the same functions repeatedly (e.g., calculating depreciation based on certain financial data, or saving the spreadsheet and printing a copy of it). Rather than going step-by-step through the same sequence of commands each time there is a need to perform a particular function, the user may store a sequence of command terms as a "macroinstruction," commonly called a "macro," and then, with one command stroke that invokes the macro, cause the programmed computer to execute the entire sequence of commands....

C. *Elements of the User Interface as Expression*

Applying to 1-2-3 the legal test stated in Part IV(C), *supra,* I consider first where along the scale of abstraction to conceive the "idea" for the purpose of distinguishing between the idea and its expression.

At the most general level of Hand's abstractions scale, *Nichols,* 45 F.2d at 121 — the computer programs at issue in this case, and other computer programs that have been considered during the course of trial, are expressions of the idea of a computer program for an electronic spreadsheet. Defendants are quite correct, then, in asserting that the idea of developing an electronic spreadsheet is not copyrightable — that the core idea of such a spreadsheet is both functional and obvious, even to computer users who claim no technical competence. Thus, even though programs like VisiCalc, 1-2-3, Multiplan, SuperCalc4, and Excel are very different in their structure, appearance, and method of operation, each is, at the most basic level, just a different way of expressing the same idea: the electronic spreadsheet....

The idea for a two-line moving cursor menu is also functional and obvious, and, indeed, is used in a wide variety of computer programs including spreadsheet programs. Nevertheless, it does not follow that every possible method of designing a menu system that includes a two-line moving cursor is non-copyrightable.

Of course, if a particular expression of the idea of an electronic spreadsheet communicates no details beyond those essential to stating the idea itself, then that expression would not be copyrightable. The issue here is whether Lotus 1-2-3 does go beyond those details essential to any expression of the idea, and includes substantial elements of expression, distinctive and original, which are thus copyrightable.

The idea for an electronic spreadsheet was first rendered into commercial practice by Daniel Bricklin. As a student at Harvard Business School in the late 1970's, Bricklin envisioned a "magic blackboard" that would recalculate numbers automatically as changes were made in other parts of the spreadsheet. Eventually, aided by others, he transformed this idea into VisiCalc, the first commercial electronic spreadsheet. See Bricklin Affdvt. paras. 48-96 (Docket No. 217). Bricklin's idea for VisiCalc was a revolutionary advance in the field of computer programming. Dauphinais Affdvt. para. 98 (Docket No. 280).

Although VisiCalc was a commercial success, implementational characteristics limited the scope and duration of its marketability as a spreadsheet product. Most notably, VisiCalc was originally programmed for use on the Apple II computer, which had limited memory (32K of RAM), limited screen display capabilities (only 40 characters per line), and limited keys available on the keyboard (no function keys and no up and down cursor keys). When VisiCalc was later rewritten for use on the IBM PC (which was introduced in August 1981), it was transferred with minimal changes and without taking advantage of many of the PC's more extensive capabilities.

Mitchell Kapor and Jonathan Sachs, the original authors of 1-2-3, exploited this opportunity. Building on Bricklin's revolutionary idea for an electronic spreadsheet, Kapor and Sachs expressed that idea in a different, more powerful way. 1-2-3 took advantage of the IBM PC's more expansive memory and more versatile screen display capabilities and keyboard. 1-2-3, like many electronic spreadsheet programs since, could thus be thought of as an evolutionary product that was built upon the shoulders of VisiCalc.

Just as 1-2-3 expressed the idea of an electronic spreadsheet differently from VisiCalc, so did Microsoft's Excel. Originally written for the Apple Macintosh computer, it exploits the enhanced graphics capabilities of the Macintosh, as well as the mouse input device that is standard with the Macintosh. Excel has pull-down bar menus rather than a two-line moving-cursor menu, and a very different menu-command hierarchy. Tr. Ex. 79.

As already noted, these three products — VisiCalc, 1-2-3, and Excel — share the general idea of an electronic spreadsheet but have expressed the idea in substantially different ways. These products also share some elements, however, at a somewhat more detailed or specific point along the abstractions scale. One element shared by these and many other programs is the basic spreadsheet screen display that resembles a rotated "L." See Appendices 1 (VisiCalc), 2 (1-2-3), and 3 (VP-Planner). Although Excel uses a different basic spreadsheet screen display that more closely resembles a paper spreadsheet, there is a rather low limit, as a factual matter, on the number of ways of making a computer screen resemble a spreadsheet. Accordingly, this aspect of electronic spreadsheet computer programs, if not present in every expression of such a program, is present in most expressions. Thus the second element of the legal test weighs heavily against treating the rotated "L" screen display as a copyrightable element of a computer program. *Morrissey,* 379 F.2d at 678-79.

Another expressive element that merges with the idea of an electronic spreadsheet — that is an essential detail present in most if not all expressions of an electronic spreadsheet — is the designation of a particular key that, when pressed, will invoke the menu command system. The number of keys available for this designation is limited for two reasons. First, because most of the keys on the keyboard relate either to values (e.g., the number keys and mathematical operation keys) or labels (e.g., the letter keys), only a few keys are left that can be used, as a practical matter, to invoke the menu command system. Without something more, the programmed computer would interpret the activation of one of these keys as an attempt by the user to enter a value or label into a cell. Second, because users need to invoke the command system frequently, the key designated for this purpose must be easily accessible. For example, the user should not be required to press two keys at the same time (such as "Shift," "Alt," or "Ctrl" along with another key).

As just noted, when all the letter, number, and arithmetic keys are eliminated from consideration, the number of keys remaining that could be used to invoke the menu command system is quite limited. They include the slash key ("/") and the semi-colon key (";"). The choice of the creators of VisiCalc to designate the slash ("/") key to invoke the menu command system is not surprising. It is one of very few practical options. Thus the second element of the legal test weighs heavily against copyrightability of this aspect of VisiCalc — and of 1-2-3. This expression merges with the idea of having a readily available method of invoking the menu command system.

Other elements of expression a decisionmaker may regard as either essential to every expression of an electronic spreadsheet, or at least "obvious" if not essential, include the use of the " + " key to indicate addition, the "-" key to indicate subtraction, the "*" key to indicate multiplication, the "/" key within formulas to indicate division, and the "enter" key to place keystroke entries into the cells. See Dauphinais Affidavit, para. 78.

Each of the elements just described is present in, if not all, at least most expressions of an electronic spreadsheet computer program. Other aspects of these programs, however, need not be present in every expression of an electronic spreadsheet. An example of distinctive details of expression is the precise "structure, sequence, and organization," *Whelan,* 797 F.2d at 1248, of the menu command system.

Consider first the menu command system of VisiCalc. The main menu command line reads: "Command: BCDEFGIMPRSTVW-." See Appendix 1. Each of these letters (or, to use defendants' experts' preferred terminology, "symbolic tokens") stands for a different command — in this case: Blank, Clear, Delete, Edit, Format, Global, Insert, Move, Print, Replicate, Storage, Titles, Version Number, Window, and "-" for "Label Repeating." Many of these commands invoke submenus which also contain a series of letters, each of which represents a submenu command choice. See VisiCalc Command Structure Chart (Tr. Ex. 140, pp. 3-3 and 3-4).

This particular expression of a menu structure is not essential to the electronic spreadsheet idea, nor does it merge with the somewhat less abstract idea of a menu structure for an electronic spreadsheet. The idea of a menu structure — including the overall structure, the order of commands in each menu line, the choice of letters, words, or "symbolic tokens" to represent each command, the presentation of these symbolic tokens on the screen (i.e., first letter only, abbreviations, full words, full words with one or more letters capitalized or underlined), the type of menu system used (i.e., one-, two-, or three-line moving-cursor menus, pull-down menus, or command-driven interfaces), and the long prompts — could be expressed in a great many if not literally unlimited number of ways.

The fact that some of these specific command terms are quite obvious or merge with the idea of such a particular command term does not preclude copyrightability for the command structure taken as a whole. If particular characteristics not distinctive individually have been brought together in a way that makes the "whole" a distinctive expression of an idea — one of many possible ways of expressing it — then the "whole" may be copyrightable. The statutory provisions regarding "compilation," 17 U.S.C. §§ 101, 103, are not essential to this conclusion, but do reinforce it. A different total structure may be developed even from individual components that are quite similar and limited in number. To determine copyrightability, a court need not — and, indeed, should not — dissect every element of the allegedly protected work. Rather, the court need only identify those elements that are copyrightable, and then determine whether those elements, *considered as a whole,* have been impermissibly copied. *Atari Games Corp. v. Oman,* 888 F.2d 878, 882-83 (D.C. Cir. 1989) (rejecting "component-by-component analysis," and ruling instead that focus must ultimately be on "work as a whole").

It is plain that plaintiff did not impermissibly copy copyrighted elements of VisiCalc. Lotus 1-2-3 uses a very different menu structure. In contrast with VisiCalc's one-line main menu that reads "Command: BCDEFGIMPRSTVW-," the main menu of Lotus 1-2-3, which uses a two-line moving-cursor menu system, reads: "Worksheet Range Copy Move File Graph Data Quit." See Appendix 2. Most of the submenus similarly present a list of up to about ten full-word menu choices, presented in order of predicted frequency of use rather than alphabetically. See Lotus 1-2-3 Command Tree Chart (Tr. Ex. 176, pp. 3-2 and 3-3). Other spreadsheet programs have also expressed their command structures in completely different ways....

I conclude that a menu command structure is capable of being expressed in many if not an unlimited number of ways, and that the command structure of 1-2-3 is an original and nonobvious way of expressing a command structure. Emery Decl. para. 15. Accordingly, the menu structure, taken as a whole — including the choice of command terms, the structure and order of those terms, their presentation on the screen, and the long prompts — is an aspect of 1-2-3 that is not present in every expression of an electronic spreadsheet. It meets the requirements of the second element of the legal test for copyrightability.

Finally, I consider the third element of the legal test — whether the structure, sequence, and organization of the menu command system is a substantial part of the alleged copyrighted work — here Lotus 1-2-3. That the answer to this question is "yes" is incontrovertible. The user interface of 1-2-3 is its most unique element, and is the aspect that has made 1-2-3 so popular. That defendants went to such trouble to copy that element is a testament to its substantiality. Accordingly, evaluation of the third element of the legal test weighs heavily in favor of Lotus.

Taking account of all three elements of the legal test, I determine that copyrightability of the user interface of 1-2-3 is established.

VI. *Copying of Lotus 1-2-3*

... Not only is the copying in this case so "overwhelming and pervasive" as to preclude, as a matter of law, any assertion of independent creation, ... but also, defendants in this case have admitted that they copied these elements of protected expression.

Dr. James Stephenson, founder of defendant Stephenson Software, is the original developer of the program that was eventually released as VP-Planner....

... By December 1983, Stephenson entered into a letter of intent with Adam Osborne regarding publication of VP-Planner. Osborne thereafter organized defendant Paperback Software. Stephenson Affdvt. paras. 66-82.

Throughout 1984, defendants continued to improve VP-Planner. In the autumn, they recognized the success of 1-2-3 and reached the conclusion that spawned this litigation: VP-Planner, in order to be a commercial success, would have to be "compatible" with 1-2-3. "The only way to accomplish this result," defendants believed, "was to ensure that *the arrangement and names of commands and menus in VP-Planner conformed to that of Lotus 1-2-3*." Id. at para. 117 (emphasis added). See generally *id.* at paras. 99-130. Such compatibility would allow users to transfer spreadsheets created in 1-2-3 to VP-Planner without loss of functionality for any macros in the spreadsheet. Also, such compatibility would allow users to switch from 1-2-3 to VP-Planner without requiring retraining in the operation of VP-Planner.

To some degree at least, defendants' premises have proved incorrect in hindsight. That is, first, as Excel has proved, a spreadsheet program did not have to be exactly compatible with 1-2-3 in order to be a commercial success. Second, copying the menu structure was not the *only* way to achieve aspects of this desired compatibility. For example, defendants could have instead added a macro conversion capability as the creators of Excel have successfully done (the Microsoft Excel Macro Translation Assistant), and could have provided an on-line help function that would show users the VP-Planner equivalent for 1-2-3 commands.... These points do not weigh significantly in the present decision, however, because even if VP-Planner otherwise would have been a commercial failure, and even if no other technological ways of achieving macro and menu compatibility existed, the desire to achieve "compatibility" or "standardization" cannot override the rights of authors to a limited monopoly in the expression embodied in their intellectual "work."

Defendants admit that, once these fateful decisions were made by Stephenson and Osborne, defendants converted VP-Planner into a program more like

1-2-3 — indeed, a program that they have publicly advertised as a "workalike for 1-2-3."... [T]he VP-Planner manual could truthfully declare:

> VP-Planner is designed to work like Lotus 1-2-3, keystroke for keystroke.... VP-Planner's worksheet is a feature-for-feature workalike for 1-2-3. It does macros. It has the same command tree. It allows the same kind of calculations, the same kind of numerical information. Everything 1-2-3 does, VP-Planner does.

VP-Planner Manual at xi, 1.11.

The court's comparison of the 1-2-3 menu command hierarchy and the VP-Planner menu hierarchy confirms that VP-Planner "has the same command tree" as 1-2-3 — that is, that defendants copied the expression embodied in the 1-2-3 menu hierarchy. It is true that there are some differences between 1-2-3's menu structure and VP-Planner's menu structure.... The works are, nevertheless, substantially, indeed, strikingly, similar. As Judge Learned Hand held in a copyright case involving a pattern on a bolt of cloth that was used to make dresses, infringement may be found despite some differences between two works ....

From the perspective of both an expert and an ordinary viewer, the similarities overwhelm differences....

Moreover, even if some elements of VP-Planner were very different, it would not give defendants a license to copy other substantial elements of 1-2-3 verbatim. If one publishes a 1,000-page book of which only a 10-page segment is an unauthorized reproduction of copyrighted material, and if the 10-page segment is a qualitatively substantial part of the copyrighted work, it is not a defense to a claim of infringement that the book is 99% different from the copyrighted material. Thus, defendants' proof that VP-Planner has many features that are different from Lotus 1-2-3 is off point. The more relevant question is: does it have significant features that are substantially similar? I conclude, on the record before me, that there is no genuine dispute of material fact on this question. The answer to this question must be "yes."

VII. *A Postscript on the Nature of Decisionmaking in This Case*

....

D. *Opinion Evidence and Premises of Legal Rulings*

... [D]efendants offered the following opinion testimony of a witness qualified as an expert in computer software development:

> If the law is interpreted to say that a developer may not make a new program that can use the data files and inputs accepted by existing programs, then computer advancement as we know it will be slowed....
>
> I believe that such a decision would throw the entire software industry into confusion.... There would be a chilling effect on development and advancement in many areas....
>
> If aspects of screen displays that are governed by functionality (such as a command language like the 1-2-3 command structure) are held to be

within the scope of copyright protection, then progress in application and systems computer programs could be dramatically slowed in the United States.

Bricklin Affdvt. paras. 176-77, 179-80. See also Samuelson & Glushko, *Comparing the Views of Lawyers and User Interface Designers,* 30 Jurimetrics at 137 (concluding on basis of survey that leading user interface designers oppose strong copyright protection for elements of a user interface because such protection would be harmful, rather than helpful, to the industry)....

... [P]laintiff responded with sharply contrasting opinions in its post-trial brief:

> *First,* the tremendous growth and success of the U.S. software industry is the direct result of the creative and original efforts of its software developers, laboring under the protection of the copyright laws. Innovation has been the key to market success....
>
> *Second,* to the extent that defendants attempt to characterize this struggle as pitting large heartless corporate giants against lonely and defenseless developers working out of their dens and basements, the defendants do not understand what is at stake here. If the elements of a computer program at issue here were to lose their copyright protection, the biggest losers of all would be the small developers. The history of this industry has been one of creative designers who identify an unfilled need in the market and then design and build a superior product to fill that need.... The developers' ability to realize substantial rewards for their creative efforts has depended entirely upon the legal protection copyright has afforded their work.
>
> If the defendants could rewrite the law, however, those days would be over. The first time a developer demonstrated an attractive new product at Comdex or Softeach or some other industry gathering, hundreds of programmers in corporate research laboratories around the world would set to work creating their own versions of the program to compete with the original. A major firm, with a staff of talented programmers, could fairly promptly create a clone of almost any new program and, in so doing, rob the author of much of the value of his creative efforts. The original author might have a head start, but that would provide little comfort once the major firms hit the market with their "new" products.... If copying were legal, the creators would lose out. It is as simple as that.
>
> It is no accident that the world's strongest software industry is found in the United States, rather than in some other jurisdiction which provides weaker protection for computer programs. The system is working, and there is no reason to change it.

....

The opinion testimony offered in this case failed completely to focus on circumstances existing at any time Congress acted to enact or amend any part of the copyright law. For this reason, it has little, if any, value in illuminating issues of law presented in this case....

... In the 1976 Act, Congress manifested an intention to encourage innovation in the computer programming field, and to do so through copyright law that explicitly gives substantial protection to innovative *expression* in intellectual "works," including computer programs. Congress made this decision despite expert testimony that extending copyright protection to computer programs might have "disastrous consequences ... on standardization in electronic data processing," despite academic criticism of the decision to extend copyright protection to computer programs, and despite explicit proposals that copyright protect only "the instructions themselves" while leaving others free to otherwise "replicate [another's] program exactly."

When a court determines the meaning of the copyright statute in a new context, different from what could have been known to even the most prescient observer at the time Congress acted, the court must respect the congressional mandate — especially with respect to congressional determinations of premise facts — and is constrained to search not for what the court might now independently consider to be the best accommodation of competing interests but instead to determine an accommodation in this new context that is consistent with the accommodation that Congress enacted for the context to which it spoke....

... If anything, user interfaces have become more expressive and more communicative since 1976 and 1980. I thus conclude that I must disregard defendants' experts' predictions of doom for the computer programming industry if copyright is extended to the user interface and other nonliteral elements of computer programs that embody expression .... Rather, this legal issue must be resolved in such a way as to extend copyright protection, clearly and unequivocally, to those nonliteral elements of computer programs that embody original expression.

E. *Defendants' Policy Arguments Founded on the OTSOG Principle*

One more of defendants' policy arguments deserves attention. Despite statutory mandates supporting the conclusion that elements of the user interface of 1-2-3 are copyrightable, defendants argue that the need to achieve compatibility and standardization compels rejection of that conclusion on policy grounds. Copyrightability of a user interface, they argue, will frustrate the public interest in allowing programmers to achieve innovation by "borrowing" and improving upon ideas of other programmers, and will undermine attempts to achieve compatibility and standardization among different programs. Especially in the vital area of user interfaces, defendants contend, copyrightability will have adverse consequences on encouraging innovation and on the broader public welfare.

Defendants' general contention — that "Progress of Science and useful Arts" cannot occur unless authors and inventors are privileged to build upon earlier progress and earlier innovation — has long been a virtually unchallenged premise in all branches of the law of intellectual property. An early expression of the point is Newton's declaration: "If I have seen further it is by standing on ye sholders of Giants." Sir Isaac Newton, Letter to Robert Hooke,

February 5, 1675/1676, quoted in R. Merton, On the Shoulders of Giants: A Shandean Postscript 31 (1965).[3]

This principle, which Merton has referred to as "OTSOG" (based on the modernized "on the shoulders of giants"), *id.* at 270, is also firmly established in our case law:

> In truth, in literature, in science and in art, there are, and can be, few, if any, things, which in an abstract sense, are strictly new and original throughout. Every book in literature, science and art, borrows, and must necessarily borrow, and use much which was well known and used before.

Emerson v. Davies, 8 F. Cas. 615, 619 (C.C.D. Mass. 1845) (No. 4,436) (Story, J.). See also *Ecclesiastes* 1:9-10 ("There is no new thing under the sun. Men may say of something, 'Ah, this is new!' — but it existed long ago before our time."). Defendants, however, attempt to squeeze something from the OTSOG cornerstone that is not there.

Two possible applications of OTSOG in the field of computer programming are relevant to this case. First, innovation in computer programming is advanced as each programmer builds upon the ideas of previous programmers. Second, some of the innovative ideas may be expressed in a particular way that is so effective or efficient that the expression becomes standardized throughout the field even though the idea is capable of being expressed in other ways — that is, even though the particular expression is not an essential detail to every expression of the idea. Although both of these corollaries of OTSOG are important to the future of computer programming, neither was embraced by Congress ... in such a way as to override the public interest in conferring upon an author a right to a limited monopoly in the author's "work."

The metaphorical "shoulders of giants" on which successors may legally stand are not as broad as defendants contend. The legally relevant shoulders of programming giants are their ideas — and do not extend to all of their expressions. The encouragement of innovation requires no more. It is sufficient that programmers are privileged to borrow and improve upon previous ideas — such as the ideas for an electronic spreadsheet and a two-line moving cursor menu. Adequate room for innovation remains even though successors are barred from copying earlier authors' particular expressions — such as the particular structure, sequence, and organization of a menu command system. *Pearl Systems,* 8 U.S.P.Q.2d at 1525.

---

[3]Newton's now-famous phrase — "on ye sholders of Giants" — may have been copied, at least in its "total concept and feel," from Bernard of Chartres who, according to Merton, authored the OTSOG aphorism in the early twelfth century when he taught: "we are like dwarfs standing [or sitting, for those dwarfs who prefer safety to far-ranging vision] upon the shoulders of giants, and so able to see more and see farther than the ancients." Merton, OTSOG at 178-92. As Merton demonstrates, however, Bernard himself was standing on the shoulders of Priscian, a sixth-century grammarian, who wrote: "The younger [e.g., the more recent] the scholars, the more sharp-sighted." *Id.* at 194-95 (brackets added by Merton). Of course, Priscian's passage presents only the idea; it took Bernard to express that idea in the metaphor of giants and dwarfs.

The second corollary of the "OTSOG" principle relevant to this case concerns standardization. Defendants have argued that 1-2-3, and specifically, 1-2-3's menu structure and macro command facility, has set a *de facto* industry standard for all electronic spreadsheets. Thus, defendants had no choice, they argue, but to copy these expressive elements from 1-2-3. Had they not copied these elements (including the macro facility), users, who had been trained in 1-2-3 and had written elaborate macros to run on 1-2-3 spreadsheets, would be unwilling to switch to VP-Planner. VP-Planner would be a commercial failure. Neither the factual nor the legal predicate of the argument is supportable.

First, defendants' argument ignores the commercial success of Excel, an innovative spreadsheet program that is not compatible with 1-2-3, either in its menu structure or in its macro command facility. Also, defendants argument ignores the alternatives to direct copying that were legally available to them.

As already explained, to the extent that VP-Planner was concerned with compatibility for macros written originally for 1-2-3, VP-Planner could have provided for a translation device that could read 1-2-3 macros and convert them, automatically, into macros that could be run on VP-Planner. Microsoft Corporation successfully included such a capability in Excel and Lotus itself has written such a capability for translating macros among different-language versions of 1-2-3. Defendants have not offered persuasive evidence to show that they could not have done the same with VP-Planner. That "it would have been an extremely complicated task" and would have cost defendants more to do so, Dauphinais Affdvt. para. 163, is not a reason for denial of copyright protection to 1-2-3. Copyright protection always has consequences of this kind....

Defendants' standardization argument is flawed for another reason as well. As explained above, one object of copyright law is to protect expression in order to encourage innovation. It follows, then, that the more innovative the expression of an idea is, the more important is copyright protection for that expression. By arguing that 1-2-3 was so innovative that it occupied the field and set a *de facto* industry standard, and that, therefore, defendants were free to copy plaintiff's expression, defendants have flipped copyright on its head. Copyright protection would be perverse if it only protected mundane increments while leaving unprotected as part of the public domain those advancements that are more strikingly innovative.

Finally, the entire argument about standardization may be questioned on a more fundamental ground. Defendants have cited no statutory provision or precedent that has ever declared that standardization, when not achieved *de jure,* is necessarily in the public's best interest. The court is aware of no such precedent or legislative mandate. A moment's reflection is enough to disclose that the public interest in extensive standardization is a sharply debatable issue. See, e.g., Tarter Decl. paras. 34-45; cf. the QWERTY typewriter keyboard (discussed in Farrell, *Standardization and Intellectual Property,* 30 Jurimetrics 35, 36-38 (1989)). Decisive against defendants' contention, in any event, is that the particular way they propose that the court resolve this dispute would reduce copyright protection far below the mandate of the copyright act.

....

QUESTIONS

1. The *Lotus v. Paperback* court discusses an "obviousness" criterion for protection. Is this akin to the patent "non-obviousness" standard? Is the court applying patent criteria to plaintiff's user interface? If not, what *does* the court's "obviousness" criterion mean?

2. Judge Keeton observes that "the bulk of the creative work is in the conceptualization of a computer program and its user interface, rather than in its encoding, and ... creating a user interface is a more difficult intellectual task, requiring greater creativity, originality, and insight, than converting the user interface design into instructions to the machine." Assuming that this is true, and even persuasive as a matter of economics, does it also make a user interface an "original work of authorship" in the copyright sense?

3. The court appears to hold that the keystrokes on a computer keyboard and the manner in which commands are given to the computer user may be copyrightable — assuming some creativity and a significant range of possible choices. In what "subject matter" category in § 102(a) do these fall?

4. Did the court in *Lotus v. Paperback* do a good job in responding to the defendant's argument that the Lotus spreadsheet interface had become the "standard" in the field, such that copyright protection (and the attendant monopoly market position) should be minimized? Consider the QWERTY typewriter configuration, which was initially devised so as to maximize mechanical efficiency (by avoiding collisions among the internal elements of the typewriter responding to key strokes). If it were possible to secure copyright protection for such "subject matter" as keyboard configuration, how "thin" should such protection be if it could be shown that the QWERTY configuration had become the "standard," such that all typists had come instinctively to conform their finger (and thought) patterns to it? Should that configuration have been monopolized for 56 or 75 years? (Compare a copyrighted textbook, say in Economics, whose organizational structure becomes so dominant in the field that all later textbook writers feel compelled to adopt it in preparing their own books. Is the format thus copyrightable, and infringed?)

Lotus Development Corp. v. Borland International Inc., 799 F. Supp. 203 (D. Mass. 1992). In this case — representing only one phase of an ongoing litigation — the district court considered, first, whether Borland had in fact copied the menu commands and menu command structure of Lotus 1-2-3, and, second, whether what was copied was protected by copyright. On the first issue, Borland argued that it copied from third-party sources rather than from Lotus; but the court found that the third parties had not independently created the material (that Borland copied from them) but had themselves copied from Lotus, so that Borland's copying was a deliberate and unlawful imitation of the Lotus menu structure. The court then turned to the question whether the copied material was protectible by copyright, an issue that turned upon characterizing it as "idea" or "expression."

One may describe a number of conceptions of the 1-2-3 user interface. A non-exclusive list, commencing with the most abstract and moving toward the particular, includes:

(1) Lotus 1-2-3 is an electronic spreadsheet.

(2) It is a menu-driven electronic spreadsheet.

(3) Its user interface involves a system of menus, each menu consisting of less than a dozen commands, arranged hierarchically, forming a tree in which the main menu is the root/trunk of the tree and submenus branch off from higher menus, each submenu being linked to a higher menu by operation of a command.

(4) Its user interface involves a system of menus, each menu consisting of less than a dozen commands, arranged hierarchically, forming a tree in which the main menu is the root/trunk of the tree and submenus branch off from higher menus, each submenu being linked to a higher menu by operation of a command, so that all the specific spreadsheet operations available in Lotus 1-2-3 are accessible through the paths of the menu command hierarchy.

(5) Finally, one may conceive of the interface as that precise set of menu commands selected by Lotus, arranged hierarchically precisely as they appear in 1-2-3. Under this conception, the interface comprises the menu of commands "Worksheet," "Range," "Copy," "Move," "File," "Print," "Graph," "Data," "System," and "Quit," linked by operation of the command "Worksheet" to the menu of commands "Global," "Insert," "Delete," "Column," "Erase," "Titles," "Windows," "Status," and "Page," etc. (The completion of this proposed statement of the "idea," listing all of the more than 400 commands for which "etc." stands, would require several dozen more lines of text.)

Borland argues that the appropriate conception of the "idea" of the 1-2-3 interface is the fifth option. If that were the case, of course, there would be no elements of expression in the menu commands and menu command hierarchy and therefore no copyrightable aspects in them. The premise of Borland's argument is that an "idea" of Lotus 1-2-3 version 2.01 is complete compatibility with earlier versions of 1-2-3, and more precisely with macros generated for use with earlier versions. Borland argues that the precise menu commands and menu structure are necessary to such functional compatibility. Thus, the argument goes, the entire interface of version 2.01 is a functional system or "idea" and is not copyrightable. This argument is essentially tautological. As applied to any case involving a useful article, an argument of this kind would always define the idea to incorporate all the specifics of the particular expression of that idea in the allegedly copyrightable work. Nothing would be copyrightable under this methodology of analysis. The argument is an attempt to win by definition without focusing at any time on any substantive issue concerning the separation of idea and expression.

To select, at the opposite extreme, the very abstract statement of the idea of 1-2-3 as "an electronic spreadsheet" would be to draw an inappropriately abstract boundary between idea and expression.... I conclude that an appropriate conception of the "idea" or "system" of the 1-2-3 interface is the fourth of the five alternative conceptions stated above.

The second step in the court's analysis of copyrightability was, in effect, a determination whether the copied expressive material was subject to copying by virtue of the "merger" doctrine: "[T]he decisionmaker must focus upon whether an alleged expression of the idea, system, process, procedure, or method is limited to elements essential to expression of that idea, system, process, procedure, or method (or is one of only a few ways of expressing the idea, system, process, procedure, or method) or instead includes identifiable elements of expression not essential to every expression of that idea, system, process, procedure, or method."

A very satisfactory spreadsheet menu tree can be constructed using different commands and a different command structure from those of Lotus 1-2-3. In fact, Borland has constructed just such an alternate tree for use in Quattro Pro's native mode. Even if one holds the arrangement of menu commands constant, it is possible to generate literally millions of satisfactory menu trees by varying the menu commands employed.

This may be easily demonstrated. Recall the ten commands that appear in Lotus' main menu: "Worksheet," "Range," "Copy," "Move," "File," "Print," "Graph," "Data," "System," and "Quit." One can imagine an entirely plausible spreadsheet in which the "Worksheet" command has been named, quite naturally, "Spreadsheet." Of course, this might require changing the "System" command to avoid two commands abbreviated "S," perhaps to "DOS." The "Quit" command could be named "Exit" without any other modifications. The "Copy" command could be called "Clone," "Ditto," "Duplicate," "Imitate," "Mimic," "Replicate," and "Reproduce," among others (in some cases requiring modification of other commands in the menu). Additional possibilities include "Output" for "Print," "Draw" or "Chart" for "Graph," "Figures" or "Information" for "Data," "Scope" for "Range," and "Transfer" or "Relocate" for "Move."

Just these potential modifications of the main menu yield over 250 combinations of commands in the main menu with ten distinct first letters. Changes in submenus increase the number of possible menu hierarchies geometrically. Since there are dozens of independent submenus, the number of possible menu hierarchies is extremely large.... I conclude that it cannot be genuinely disputed that a large part of the structure and arrangement of the menu commands is not driven entirely by functional considerations. There are sufficient non-functional aspects that at least hundreds and perhaps thousands of different expressions of the function were possible when Lotus chose the particular structure of menu commands incorporated into Lotus 1-2-3.

The court also rejected Borland's claims that the sequencing of the Lotus menu-command terms was dictated by certain efficiencies, such as the frequency with which those terms were chosen by the user. Any number of arrangements could be equally efficient. "The arrangement of menu commands according to predicted frequency of use is not a major functional limitation on the number of arrangements of menu commands."

Finally, "having identified elements of expression not essential to every expression of the idea, system, process, procedure, or method, the decision-maker must focus on whether those expressive elements, taken together, are a substantial part of the allegedly copyrightable 'work.'" The court concluded that Borland had itself acknowledged that the Lotus menu commands, menu command hierarchy, macro language and keystroke sequences exhibited more than trivial creativity; no reasonable jury could find otherwise. "Lotus 1-2-3 was a dramatic change and improvement over what was available on the market at the time Lotus was created. Although a large portion of that improvement relates to the functional aspects of Lotus 1-2-3, the features that I have now concluded are expressive also played a substantial role."

Lotus Development Corp. v. Borland International, Inc., 1993 U.S. Dist. LEXIS 11688 (D. Mass. 1993):

> Relying on *Feist,* Borland contends that [its assertions] regarding functionality ... demonstrate that the form of the menu tree (including menu command names and structure) is not original. For the following reasons, I find that the menu tree is original....
>
> Borland contends that, because functional considerations played a role in formulating the 1-2-3 menu tree, the menu tree is not copyrightable. Borland's argument is susceptible of two interpretations, both lacking merit.
>
> First, one may interpret this argument as a contention that the functional considerations so permeate formulation of the menu tree that the menu tree is not separable from the "idea" of the program. This form of argument has nothing to do with the amount of creativity or originality involved. Derivation of a scientific formula may require a great deal of creativity and produce an original result. If the formula fails the copyrightability test, it is because the formula is not expressive — independently of creativity or originality. Casting the argument in terms of originality doctrine rather than separability does nothing to assist resolution of the issues in this case, and may lead to confusion. In any event, to the extent Borland raises the same separability argument that it has raised before, but dressed now in terms of originality, that argument was previously rejected by the court for good reason, and is now rejected again.
>
> Alternatively, Borland may be understood as contending that any work whose form is restricted to any material extent by functional considerations is not original. Without more, this contention is invalid on its face. Any original literary work is formulated according to functional considerations imposed by language, a desire for clarity, and a desire to express the ideas conveyed. As one of Borland's experts concedes, the first functional consideration (conveying the nature of executable operations) is not materially different from a functional consideration for selection of

words in any English writing. Accordingly, this type of "functional consideration" can remove a writing from copyright protection only if it restricts the forms of expression (that are separable from the idea or function of the work) to a limited number. Thus, cases referring to functional considerations and decided under originality doctrine, including those cited by Borland, uniformly refer to limits on the number of forms of expression given functional considerations. [Citations omitted.]

QUESTIONS

1. If all computer programs are to some extent "processes" — recall the § 101 definition of a "computer program" as "instructions ... to bring about a certain result" — how may one discern whether the program, or its elements, are "processes" in the forbidden § 102(b) sense?

2. To what extent should copyright protection be affected by the "functionality" of a work? The Copyright Act contains special provisions for pictorial, graphic and sculptural works that are functional or utilitarian, and provides for protection only for those elements of the work that can exist "separably" from the useful elements. Should a comparable standard be incorporated regarding nonpictorial works, such as computer programs and user interface (and cookbooks and machine-assembly instructions)?

COMPUTER SCREEN DISPLAYS*

The first computer screen displays were rather primitive affairs; in fact, the machines were referred to as "TTY" terminals because they emulated teletypes. These terminals would present lines of text which would each scroll up in turn as new lines were drawn. Eventually, special non-text characters were embedded amongst the text, which would be interpreted so as to permit characters to be drawn and remain anywhere on the screen. This technique is employed in programs like, for example, "Lotus 1-2-3." These displays were limited, however, on multi-user mainframe computers by the small time slices allotted individual users, and on the first microcomputers by sheer lack of computing power. Also, the perception that computers were the province of expert users militated against screen display development.

Though perhaps videogames led the way in introducing fanciful interfaces to casual users, it was precisely the notion that computers should be more accessible, as Apple Computer would say "a computer for the rest of us," that led various computer scientists, most notably at Xerox Palo Alto Research Center (PARC), to develop a series of visual metaphors making computer operation more intuitive. Referred to unaffectionately as WIMP's (Window, Interface, Mouse and Pull-down menu) or GUI's (graphical user interface), these systems have supplanted the earlier textor prompt-based systems. These displays demanded much more brute computing power and memory, as now the screen represented not an array of, say, 80 x 40 characters, but a

---

*The editors wish to thank Ariel Reich, Columbia Law School, class of 1993, for his assistance with these materials.

bitmap array of, say, 512 x 342 pixels (picture elements, the individual points on the screen), plus all the calculations that must be performed to animate those windows and menus.

The *Apple* case *infra* discusses the adaptation of the IBM-PC computer, running under MS-DOS, a prompt-based operating system, to a graphical user interface. The early versions of the IBM-PC lacked sufficient power to incorporate graphical features that Apple Computer would later find more than reminiscent of its own Macintosh computer. As the court there notes, the Macintosh, in turn, owes much to Xerox PARC's STAR computer.

The evolution of screen displays is certainly not at an end. If anything, the advent of multimedia, that is, the inclusion of audiovisual images into computer programs, and virtual reality, with three-dimensional imagery which literally projects the user into the computer world, promises to make screen displays even more engaging and more expressive.

Below are two screen displays of listings for Intellectual Property law firms. The first was generated by a Lotus program, and the second by Microsoft Windows. A version of the Microsoft Windows program was the target of a copyright infringement claim by Apple Computer, Inc., decided in the case that follows.

```
A4:"(G) [W34] 'Lyon & Lyon
              Range  Copy  Move  File  Print  Graph  Data  System  Quit
Global. Insert. Delete. Column. Erase. Titles. Window. Status. Page

  firmname                                address              city        state
  Bryan Cave McPheeters & McRoberts  3100 Crocker Center  Los Angeles  CA
  Irell & Manella                    1800 Ave. of the Star Los Angeles  CA
                                     611 W. Sixth St -- Suite  Los Angeles  CA
  Spensley Horn Jubas & Lubitz       1880 Century Park Eas Los Angeles  CA
  Abelman Frayne Recac & Schwab      708 Third Ave.           New York  NY
  Amster Rothstein & Ebenstein       90 Park Ave. - 21st F New York  NY
  Brumbaugh Graves Donohue & Raymond 30 Rockefeller Plaza  New York  NY
  Cooper & Dunham                    30 Rockefeller Plaza  New York  NY
  Cowan Liebowitz & Latman P.C.      605 Third Ave.           New York  NY
  Curtis Morris & Stafford P.C.      530 Fifth Ave.           New York  NY
  Davis Hoxie Faithfull & Hapgood    45 Rockefeller Plaza  New York  NY
  Felfe & Lynch                      805 Third Ave.           New York  NY
  Fish & Neave                       875 Third Ave.           New York  NY
  Fitzpatrick Cella Harper & Scinto  277 Park Ave.            New York  NY
  Grais & Phillips                   45 Broadway - 22nd Fl New York  NY
  Hopgood Calimafde Kalil Blaustein  60 E. 42nd St.           New York  NY
  Kenyon & Kenyon                    One Broadway             New York  NY
  Ladas & Parry                      26 W. 61st St.           New York  NY
  Levitt Greenberg Kaufman & Goldman 342 Madison Ave.         New York  NY
07-Jul-93  03:13 PM
```

Lotus

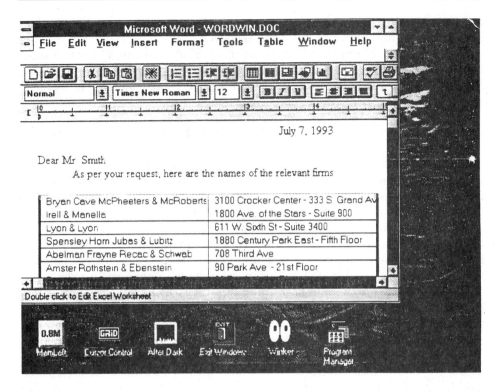

Microsoft

APPLE COMPUTER, INC. v. MICROSOFT CORP.

799 F. Supp. 1006 (N. D. Cal. 1992)

VAUGHN R. WALKER, DISTRICT JUDGE.

I

Apple Computer, Inc. ("Apple") filed this copyright infringement action on March 17, 1988, against Microsoft Corporation ("Microsoft") and Hewlett-Packard Company ("HP"), claiming that Microsoft's Windows 2.03 computer software and HP's NewWave computer software infringed seven copyrights held by Apple. The copyrights at issue protect the audiovisual works that Apple claims for the graphical user interface of its Macintosh computer. [The court went on to discuss previous rulings to be found at 709 F. Supp. 925, 717 F. Supp. 1428, and 759 F. Supp. 144. A non-exclusive license, granted by Apple in 1985 for Microsoft's Windows 1.0 software, was held not to be a complete defense for later versions of Windows, neither for Microsoft, nor for HP, which had obtained a license, in turn, for its NewWave software.]

To allow the court to determine which allegedly infringing Windows 2.03 and NewWave visual displays were not contained in Windows 1.0, to facilitate comparison of the works in suit and to give the court and the parties a means to determine the scope of copyright protection, Apple was asked to submit a list of alleged similarities between its works and the works of defendants. Apple filed this list on April 7, 1989. The list contained 189 alleged similarities between the Apple audiovisual works and Windows 2.03, and 147 similarities between the Apple works and NewWave.

The court then determined that under the 1985 Agreement 179 of the similarities claimed to be in Windows 2.03 were licensed, *Apple Computer, Inc. v Microsoft Corp.,* 717 F. Supp. 1428 (N.D. Cal. 1989), and that the agreement would cover all but 54 of the similarities alleged to be in NewWave, assuming of course that HP establishes that Microsoft in turn licensed these features to it, *Apple Computer, Inc. v Microsoft Corp.,* 759 F. Supp. 1444 (N.D. Cal. 1991).

. . . .

[Defendants' motions for summary judgment identified, analyzed and dissected the similarities between the interfaces, and asserted that none of the points of commonality gave rise to a viable copyright claim.] Apple refused to join the issues raised in defendants' motions. Apple contended that its own lists of similarities are not exact descriptions of any infringing features, but merely examples of the overall similarity of defendants' works. Sticking stubbornly to a "look and feel" or "gestalt" theory of this lawsuit, Apple was apparently of the belief that these passwords would automatically get its case around summary judgment motions and to a jury, regardless whether any of the visual displays that potentially comprise this "look and feel" are themselves protectible expression. Accordingly, Apple's response to the detailed arguments against protectibility that defendants made on an item-by-item basis was that, "we do not attempt here to chase every rabbit loosed by defendants' continuing focus on irrelevant detail." Unaided by any effective opposition from Apple to defendants' motions, the court on April 14, 1992, after analytically dissecting the works in suit as best it could under the circumstances, determined that the 10 remaining items alleged against Windows 2.03 were not protectible under copyright law, and that 53 of the 54 alleged similarities in NewWave were subject to no or little copyright protection. Apple promptly moved for reconsideration and, for the first time, addressed the merits of defendants' motions.

II

As noted in earlier orders, Apple's Macintosh microcomputer turned out to be one of the major commercial triumphs of the 1980s. Much of that success seemed to rest on the visual displays or images which the Macintosh generated on its computer screens. These proved highly intuitive, facilitated users' learning of how to operate the Macintosh and introduced millions to the wonderful capabilities for useful tasks which computers offer. [The court went on to discuss the nature of graphical user interfaces. The history of the Apple Macintosh was discussed in light of its origins in the Xerox Star computer running under the Smalltalk program. The advent of Microsoft's Windows 1.0 program and Hewlett-Packard's NewWave offered IBM-PC's comparable graphical capabilities.]

. . . .

IV

Apple contends that to "understand" the distinctive appearance of the Macintosh interface, "one needs to consider not only the individual elements that make up the appearance of the interface but also the way those elements are arranged and interact with one another to create the consistent and distinctive Macintosh interface." The claimed unifying idea of the Lisa and Macintosh works is "an interface suggestive of an office environment with a desktop background, implementing through animated graphical images and fanciful symbols what has been referred to as a 'desktop metaphor.'" Making the point literally, Apple's counsel has gone so far as to exhibit in the courtroom a chart purporting to show an alternative portrayal of this metaphor, a computer screen containing the image of a desk!

Apple's expert put such hyperbole aside and attempted to isolate the general concepts or ideas that make up the "desktop metaphor." Although the expert's descriptions are less than categorical, they principally include: multiple windows that serve as separate workspaces or mini-screens unto themselves; the ability to open and close these windows; icons that represent programs, files and documents; the use of a mouse to manipulate directly these visual displays; menu bars dedicated to an array of choices. These concepts arguably were used in the Macintosh because — to some degree — they emulate the familiar environment of the desktop and thus render the computer a somewhat less forbidding apparatus.

But Apple goes further than simply claiming that the Macintosh interface expresses these ideas. To the extent the individual features of the Macintosh interface are licensed or are unprotectible they are together, or in conjunction with the protectible features, claimed as a copyrightable arrangement — a "look and feel" which constitutes protectible expression apart from its individual elements....

The elements of such an arrangement serve a purely functional purpose in the same way that the visual displays and user commands of the dashboard, steering wheel, gear shift, brakes, clutch and accelerator serve as the user interface of an automobile. See *Synercom Technology, Inc. v. University Computing Co.*, 462 F. Supp. 1003, 1013 (N.D. Tex. 1978). Purely functional items or an arrangement of them for functional purposes are wholly beyond the realm of copyright as are other common examples of user interfaces or arrangements of their individual elements — the dials, knobs and remote control devices of a television or VCR, or the buttons and clocks of an oven or stove. Of course, the elements of these everyday user interfaces are seldom conflated into metaphoric images, but that does not mean that the user interface of a computer is less functional.

Under the law of this Circuit, an article which has "*any* intrinsic utilitarian function" can be denied copyright protection "except to the extent that its artistic features can be identified separately and are capable of existing independently as a work of art." *Fabrica Inc. v. El Dorado Corp.*, 697 F.2d 890, 893 (9th Cir. 1983) (emphasis in original). The very purpose of a computer user interface "lies in its ability to help people prepare and analyze their work quickly and flexibly." Comment, *Lotus Development Corp. v. Paperback Software International: Broad Copyright Protection for User Interfaces Ignores the Software Industry's Trend Toward Standardization*, 52 U. Pitt. L. Rev. 689, 705 n.65 (1991). Copyright protection can attach only to such a product's separate artistic features or can afford only such limited protection as appropriate when its features are the product of a compilation. See *Harper House, Inc. v. Thomas Nelson, Inc.*, 889 F.2d 197, 205 (9th Cir. 1989).

The similarity of such functional elements of a user interface or their arrangement in products of like kind does not suggest unlawful copying, but standardization across competing products for functional considerations. Standardization of the visual features in a computer's interface helps to achieve its purpose, a point which Apple learned early on when it insisted on interface uniformity for Macintosh applications and which has also been implicitly recognized by this court. *Ashton-Tate Corp. v. Ross,* 728 F. Supp. 597, 602 (N.D. Cal. 1989), *aff'd* 916 F.2d 516, 522 (9th Cir. 1990).

Some visual displays are or become so closely tied to the functional purpose of the article that they become standard. If "market factors play a significant factor in determining the sequence and organization" of a computer program, then those patterns may well be termed ideas beyond the ownership of any one seller. *Plains Cotton Co-Op v. Goodpasture Computer Serv.,* 807 F.2d 1256, 1262 (5th Cir. 1987). No better evidence of "market factors" (i.e., expectations of users) accounting for the features of computer user interfaces can be found than the almost invariable incorporation of those features in most graphical user interfaces. Microsoft's videotape Exhibits A and B, scénes à faire, establish that graphical user interfaces almost always incorporate the basic elements of the Macintosh interface; even some character-based interfaces possess some of these features.

To be sure, a few judges have said in relation to computer software that "the purpose or function of a utilitarian work would be the work's idea, and everything that is not necessary to the purpose or function would be part of the expression of the idea." See, e.g., *Whelan Associates v. Jaslow Dental Laboratory,* 797 F.2d 1222, 1236 (3d Cir. 1986); *Broderbund Software, Inc. v. Unison World,* 648 F. Supp. 1127 (N.D. Cal. 1986); *Digital Communications v. Softklone Distributing,* 659 F. Supp. 449, 462 (N.D. Ga. 1987). But this surely is too facile a distinction as it obscures rather than illuminates the first part of the analysis commanded by the Ninth Circuit, comparing the similarities of ideas.

The *Whelan* court dealt with claims that the defendant unlawfully copied plaintiff's dental laboratory record keeping program to create a competing program and determined that "the idea is the efficient organization of a dental laboratory." 797 F.2d at 1240. Apple relies heavily on Whelan's dichotomy to support its "desktop metaphor" line of attack and strenuously contends that it is consistent with Ninth Circuit authority.

As noted above, however, the Ninth Circuit has recognized that a single program may contain a number of nonprotectible ideas. See *Frybarger,* 812 F.2d 525. A single program need not limit its expression to one idea, a point that would seem particularly true in the case of software which controls a wide variety of computer functions. Furthermore, the parties' own understanding as shown by the negotiations leading to the 1985 Agreement demonstrates that Apple and Microsoft accepted specified visual displays as the protectible expression, not the entirety of the interface. 717 F. Supp. at 1431. Still further, the extensive criticism by courts and commentators of *Whelan* and kindred decisions has recognized that "*Whelan*'s general formulation that a program's overall purpose equates with the program's idea is descriptively inadequate," the product of "the opinion's somewhat outdated appreciation of computer science," and its heavy emphasis on "metaphysical distinctions" instead of "practical considerations." *Computer Assoc. Int'l, Inc. v. Altai, Inc,* [982 F.2d 693] (2d Cir. 1992). Most importantly, the *Whelan* rule distends copyright protection, placing off-limits alternative and improved means of expression and thereby upsetting the uneasy balance which copyright attempts to maintain by preventing free riders from ripping off creative expression while not stifling others from improving or extending that expression.

Copyright's purpose is to overcome the public goods externality resulting from the non-excludability of copier/free riders who do not pay the costs of creation. Peter S. Menell, *An Analysis of the Scope of Copyright Protection for Applications Programs,* 41. Stan. L. Rev. 1045, 1059 (1989). But overly inclusive copyright protection can produce its own negative effects by inhibiting the adoption of compatible standards (and reducing so-called "network externalities"). Such standards in a graphical user interface would enlarge the market for computers by making it easier to learn how to use them. *Id.* at 1067-70. Striking the balance between these considerations, especially in a new and rapidly changing medium such as computer screen displays, represents a most ambitious enterprise. Cf. *Lotus Dev. Corp. v. Paperback Software Int'l,* 740 F. Supp. 37 (D. Mass. 1990).

While the Macintosh interface may be the fruit of considerable effort by its designers, its success is the result of a host of factors, including the decision to use the Motorola 68000 microprocessor, the tactical decision to require uniform application interfaces, and the Macintosh's notable advertising. And even were Apple able to isolate that part of its interface's success owing to its design efforts, lengthy and concerted effort alone "does not always result in inherently protectible expression." *Computer Assoc. Int'l.*

By virtue of having been the first commercially successful programmer to put these generalized features together, Apple had several years of market dominance in graphical user interfaces until Microsoft introduced Windows 3.0, the first DOS-based windowing program to begin to rival the graphical capability of the Macintosh. The Macintosh still to this day offers graphical features that translate into competitive advantages. See Walter S. Mossberg, *PC Shoppers May Find It's Wise to Develop a Taste for Apples,* Wall St. Journal, Aug. 6, 1992, at B1. To accept Apple's "desktop metaphor"/"look and feel" arguments would allow it to sweep within its proprietary embrace not only Windows and NewWave but, at its option, also other desktop graphical user interfaces which employ the standardized features of such interfaces, and to do this without subjecting Apple's claims of copyright to the scrutiny which courts have historically employed. Apple's copyrights would hold for programs in existence now or in the future — for decades. One need not profess to know for sure where should lie the line between expression and idea, between protection and competition to sense with confidence that this would afford too much protection and yield too little competition.

The importance of such competition, and thus improvements or extensions of past expressions, should not be minimized. The Ninth Circuit has long shown concern about the uneasy balance which copyright seeks to strike: What is basically at stake is the extent of the copyright owner's monopoly — from how large an area of activity did Congress intend to allow the copyright owner to exclude others? *Herbert Rosenthal Jewelry Corp. v. Kalpakian,* 446 F.2d 738, 742 (9th Cir. 1971). The court declines Apple's invitation to use the advent of the microcomputer and its interface to abandon traditional standards which govern copyrights and invent some new law based on highly indefinite constructs such as "look and feel."[16] As a result, if "desktop metaphor" is to have any meaning in the context of a traditional copyright analysis, it should serve merely as a label for that group of "ideas" embodied in the Macintosh interface devoted to utilitarian uses of that computer, or as a shorthand way of describing the purpose or object of the panoply of ideas of multiple windows, iconic representation and manipulation, menus and object opening and closing functions to assist computer users in operation of their machines. "Desktop metaphor" does not describe the single unifying idea of the Macintosh interface, but is simply another name for the type of interface used on the Macintosh and is by no means exclusive to it.

V

The Apple lists of claimed similarities and the submissions of its own expert make evident the following groupings of standardized features or "ideas": (1) use of windows to display multiple images on a computer screen and facilitate interaction with the information contained in the windows; (2) use of icons to represent familiar objects from the office environment and facilitate organization of information stored in the computer's memory; (3) manipulation of icons to convey instructions and to control operation of the computer; (4) use of menus to store information or functions of the computers in a place that is convenient to reach, but saves screen space for other images; and (5) opening and closing of objects as a means of retrieving, transferring or storing information. For the reasons which follow in detail, these are common to all the works in suit, and must be deemed "ideas" and thus placed beyond the lone province of Apple or any other programmer. Having decided that a graphical user interface may be composed of many ideas, the court turns to deciding what elements of the Macintosh interface constitute protectible expression.

Microsoft moved for partial summary judgment that copyright protection does not extend to any of the 10 individual items on the first list that have not previously been deemed to be covered by the 1985 Agreement. The court granted the motion as to each of the items on three different grounds: merger; scénes à faire; due to limited number of ways to express idea. The court also ruled that 25 of the 54 items in the lists of similarities alleged against HP's NewWave products were not original to Apple, that 36 of the items were excluded from copyright protection under § 102(b), and that limited protection was afforded 17 items under scénes à faire and 20 items because of merger of idea and expression. Only [one] item, the use of a trash can to represent the discard folder, was determined not to be covered under any of the separate motions.

---

[16]Without dispute, a copier may not make "immaterial variations" and thereby escape copyright liability, *Nichols v. Universal Pictures Corp.*, 45 F.2d 119, 120 (2d Cir. 1930) (L. Hand, J.), and, to this limited extent, there is some legitimacy to a "look and feel" test, a point this court previously recognized. 779 F. Supp. at 135. But this test should be applied only after protectible expression has been identified, not before, as Apple would have this court do.

Apple in its motion for reconsideration has finally addressed the individual items on the lists. The court recognizes that the artistic expression that is associated with each item is the actual ground for the protection claimed, this being a suit over visual displays. The law of the Ninth Circuit makes plain, however, that when any of the various doctrines that limit the scope of protectibility are in operation, the affected expression may provide a basis for a claim of infringement only if the alleged copy is virtually identical to the plaintiff's version.

A. *Overlapping Windows*

The first and probably most notable idea associated with the Macintosh interface is the use of overlapping windows to display multiple images on a computer screen in order to facilitate organization of information and the user's interaction with it. Overlapping windows are central to Apple's claimed similarities and invariably present in graphical user interfaces.

> A1 The design and layout in Macintosh includes overlapping rectangular windows in front of a muted background pattern.

The court previously ruled that this item was not protectible (1) because the expression described is merged with the idea, (2) under the doctrine of scénes à faire, and (3) because of the limited number of ways to express the idea due to technical or design constraints....

Two parts of Apple's claim are easily decided. First, the rectangular shape of the windows is not a copyrightable feature in a computer graphical user interface or, indeed, any other medium of expression. 37 C.F.R. § 202.1(a). Second, the use of a muted background may arguably be a feature of the Macintosh interface not present in Windows 1.0, but there can be no serious contention of its protectibility. A muted background is a default image which appears on any portion of the screen not occupied by a window or menu bar and hardly can be said to represent the sort of creative achievement or expression which the law should exert itself to protect.[20] [The court went on to explain how the Macintosh approach, permitting windows to be expanded to any size and to overlap other windows, was less constrained than the screen switching and tiling modes of Windows 1.0. Tiling windows could, however, result in overlapping windows on a cluttered screen.]

Because a programmer must choose between switching images or splitting the screen, the means of expression are limited, and merger applies at least to the basic arrangements claimed in similarity A1.... [T]he Macintosh interface at most combines a possibly unlicensed switching technique, the only other means of expression, [with] that plainly licensed, splitting. Accordingly, the scénes à faire doctrine ought also to apply. Finally, use of overlapping windows in the Xerox, Lilith and Perq systems in the early 1980s shows beyond question that this concept is not original to Apple. The court's April ruling on A1 stands.

---

[20] Because this case involves visual display copyrights, the achievement at issue is the artistic decision to use a muted background, not the programming facility which makes it possible to generate that image.

[The court next considered Apple's claim that "The window design and layout in Macintosh includes windows which may appear partly on and partly off the screen"; and found this feature unprotectible. It concluded: "While the appearance of a window may represent protectible expression, the ability to move it part on or off the screen is indispensable to the convenient manipulation of information contained in these sub-screens and thus is unprotectible." For similar reasons, and also because it was an "obvious graphic" to express an unprotectible idea, the court declined to protect a Macintosh design animation that "drags a gray outline of the window along with the cursor when the mouse is pressed on a window's title bar."]

> B1 The design and layout in Macintosh includes the top-most overlapping window displayed as the active window.

This feature was previously found unprotectible by the court due to merger of idea and expression and as a standard industry feature, under scénes à faire. It appears that 17 of the 27 systems shown in Microsoft's videotape A have this feature. Indeed, it is hard to imagine the usefulness of an obscured window being the active window, under the so-called desktop metaphor or any other functional design, although apparently some systems have this option. The active top window idea was first used at Xerox PARC prior to its incorporation in the Lisa system by Apple. These reasons suggest that making the topmost window active is a standard industry feature.

Although Apple contends that the top window need not be the active window, citing the systems in the scénes à faire videotape in which other windows can be active, feature B1 clearly appears to be indispensable to the useful employment of the overlapping windows idea. Making the topmost window the sole active window serves the utilitarian function of helping to avoid the accidental input or output of information or manipulation of icons in a window for which this was not intended. This feature also overcomes the constraint imposed by the relatively fixed amount of screen space generally available in most monitors; operating memory has increased greatly in relation to the screen space able to accommodate it, making necessary sophisticated means to manage the information in memory. Furthermore, making the topmost window the active one is no more expression than reading the page to which a book is opened or working on the paper which is on the top of a stack. Instead, this is the description of a process that is inseparable from the idea of overlapping windows, and is thus but an unprotectible idea. Finally, the only expression that can be said to be involved, the graphics that indicate that a particular window is the active window, is feature A4, and covered by the 1985 license. 717 F. Supp. at 1433-34.

....

B. *Iconic Representation*

The Apple works in suit use icons that represent familiar objects from the office environment to facilitate the organization of information stored in the computer's memory. At the outset, iconic representation is not original to the Macintosh interface. In the context of computer graphics, the term appears to have originated with David Canfield Smith who, working at Xerox PARC in the mid-1970s, adopted the term as representing something more than a symbol, an embodiment of its properties. In the Macintosh interface, icons represent files, directories, and applications.

[The court reiterated its ruling that feature G5 — the design and layout of icons in Macintosh, which includes display of icons on the screen background behind any open windows — was unprotectible under merger and scénes à faire and was motivated primarily by space constraints; that scénes à faire and merger precluded protecting G6, the design and layout of icons in Macintosh which includes the icon's title (when displayed) centered beneath the icon; and, for similar reasons G14, the design and layout in Macintosh presenting the name of an object by displaying the name centered below the object's icon. Also, G12, the design and layout in Macintosh which presents icon images shaped like a page with a turned-down corner to indicate objects of type other than "directory," was deemed unoriginal. I1, the design and layout in Macintosh that presents the term "folder" to denote a disk directory, was excluded by § 102(b). The iconic system under G10, in which the design and layout in Macintosh associates a different icon image with each type of object and indicates the type of each object by presenting the object as the icon image corresponding to its type, was not deemed unique and separable from the ideas presented.]

> G11 The design and layout in Macintosh presents an icon image shaped like a file folder to indicate objects of type "directory."

Item G11 was previously found to lack originality. In its response to Apple's motion for reconsideration, HP urges the court to change its prior ruling denying HP's motions as to this item under § 102(b) and the various limiting doctrines, claiming that the use of an image of a file folder to represent a directory is but an unprotectible idea. The court disagrees. The idea behind this item is the use of a familiar object from the office environment that typically contains other objects, as the icon to represent a directory.

Merger, limited number of ways, and indispensable expression or scénes à faire do not limit the protection for the expression of this idea as a file folder. A file cabinet, a desk drawer, a bookshelf, a binder, an office safe, even a cardboard box could have served the same function. The court does not change this prior determination.

As to originality, given the idea as defined above, the expression is the use of an icon resembling a file folder.... All told, there is ample and uncontrovertible evidence in the record showing access to the prior works on the part of Apple employees.

The Star, Pictureworld, the Lisa and the Macintosh all used an icon shaped like a file folder as their expression of the idea of a container from the office to represent a directory. Comparing the artwork associated with the various renditions, all show common file folders with the tab on the top left. While they differ in slight details, these depictions could not but be found substantially similar in all material respects. Accordingly, the decision on lack of originality stands.

[As for G13, the design and layout in Macintosh presenting different images within the outline of a generic page icon to indicate objects of different non-directory type, the court reaffirmed its ruling that the actual icon images may be protectible. The court upheld its ruling that there was sufficient originality in H2, the design and layout in Macintosh displaying the special discard folder as an icon resembling a trash can.]

> H3 The design and layout of Macintosh presents the name "Trash" beneath the special discard folder. The name "Waste Basket" is presented in Lisa. NewWave displays the name "Waste Basket" beneath the special discard folder.

The court previously found H3, the name "Waste Basket," to be an unprotectible short phrase under 37 C.F.R. § 202.1(a), and to be subject to limited protection because inseparable or flowing naturally from its idea. Apple has not addressed the "short phrase" ground for decision, which in any event is upheld. A short phrase or name might have some relevance in determining the copyright in a literary work, but is merely an unprotectible aspect of a visual work. The court reverses the decision on the limited scope motion. The idea involved is the use of a common object to represent the place to discard objects, and is not limited to the use of an object from the office environment — witness Apple's use of an outdoor trash can rather than a waste paper basket. The name "Waste Basket" is not essential to this idea, for the icon could just as well have been a paper shredder, a toilet, a recycling bin, or perhaps, for the less environmentally fastidious, an open window. Thus, H3 is not subject to the merger or indispensable expression doctrines, but is unprotectible under 37 C.F.R. § 202.1(a).

....

C. *Object Opening/Closing*

The computer programs at bar utilize the opening and closing of objects as a means of retrieving, transferring or storing information....

> G28 Macintosh design animation displays a rapid sequence of expanding rectangles beginning at the icon's position and ending at the window's position when an icon is opened into a window.
> G29 Macintosh design animation displays a rapid sequence of [contracting] rectangles beginning at the window's position and ending at the icon's position when a window is closed into an icon.

Items G28 and G29 describe the sequence of expanding or contracting rectangles ("zooming rectangles") which signify that an icon has been opened into a window or a window closed into an icon. HP's motion that these features be given limited protection because of the limited number of ways to express the underlying idea was previously granted. The idea of providing to the user of a computer information connecting the open window to the icon from whence it came, upon reflection, does not seem to require the use of graphics such as "zooming rectangles." Even considering that rectangles may be easier for a computer to generate, see discussion of item A1, *supra,* it should not be hard to match an icon to an open window by instead showing, say, parallel lines growing in length until they reach the proximate size of the new window, and shrinking back into the icon when the window is closed, in a "slinky" effect.

The fact that only Lisa, Macintosh, GEM, and NewWave use a "zooming rectangles" feature convinces the court that any limit to the number of ways to match window and icon is not because of technical or design constraints so much as a lack of motivation on the part of software designers to provide a feature that performs this function. In the least, this is a triable issue of material fact. HP's motion for partial summary judgment on limited scope of protection is DENIED as to features G28 and G29....

D. *Menus*

Menus are employed in graphical user interfaces to store information or functions of the computers in a place that is convenient to reach, but saves screen space for other images.
[The court, applying to various menu features an analysis similar to that employed in the discussion of other program elements, found most of the menu features not protectible.]

E. *Icon Manipulation*

In the works at suit, icons are manipulated by the computer user to control operation of the computer, facilitating the organization of the information stored in the machine. [The court, applying an analysis similar to that employed in the discussion of other program elements, declined to revise its prior findings that the icon manipulation elements were not protectible.]
    ....

QUESTIONS

1. Reexamine the two computer screen displays reproduced between the *Lotus v. Paperback* and *Apple v. Microsoft* opinions, *supra*. The Lotus screen — as was true of the Lotus command menu in the *Paperback* case as well — is essentially a string of words using standard alphanumeric characters. The Microsoft screen, like the Apple graphical interface screen, utilizes icons, many of them quite fanciful, which were regarded as enormously imaginative when first introduced. Is it not rather odd to find the *Lotus* court being much more receptive to copyrightability claims than is the *Apple* court?

2. How do you think the *Apple v. Microsoft* court would have analyzed the similarities between Lotus 1-2-3 and V-P Planner, as compared with the court in *Lotus v. Paperback Software*? (Historically, one could certainly find programs with comparable or advanced features when Lotus 1-2-3 was first offered.) How do the two courts differ in their view of the role of functionalism?

3. Do you think the court in *Apple v. Microsoft* went too far in rejecting Apple's "desktop metaphor"/"look and feel" arguments? After all, many works, when broken down into their components, constitute simple or clichéd

elements. Does the court fail to account for expression that takes the form of "selection, coordination and arrangement"?

4. The court appears to find protectible expression in only a few elements, for example in zooming rectangles and icon design. Do you think the court's holding will result in different software designers producing very similar interfaces overall, but with idiosyncratic differences, as for example "black holes" (as on the NeXT computer) instead of "garbage cans," or windows expanding in a "slinky effect" (as the court suggests) instead of the telescoping expansion on the Macintosh? Is this to be regarded as a constructive aesthetic or economic outcome?

5. The district judges in the *Lotus* and *Microsoft* cases reach very different conclusions with respect to the "standardization" argument and the need to make freely available certain aspects of a computer's user interface that have become standard in the field. Which of the two positions is the more convincing?

4. REVERSE ENGINEERING AND COMPATIBILITY

SEGA ENTERPRISES v. ACCOLADE, INC.

977 F.2d 1510 (9th Cir. 1992)

REINHARDT, CIRCUIT JUDGE:

... We are asked to determine ... whether the Copyright Act permits persons who are neither copyright holders nor licensees to disassemble a copyrighted computer program in order to gain an understanding of the unprotected functional elements of the program. In light of the public policies underlying the Act, we conclude that, when the person seeking the understanding has a legitimate reason for doing so and when no other means of access to the unprotected elements exists, such disassembly is as a matter of law a fair use of the copyrighted work....

I. *Background*

Plaintiff-appellee Sega Enterprises, Ltd. ("Sega"), a Japanese corporation, and its subsidiary, Sega of America, develop and market video entertainment systems, including the "Genesis" console (distributed in Asia under the name "Mega-Drive") and video game cartridges. Defendant-appellant Accolade, Inc., is an independent developer, manufacturer, and marketer of computer entertainment software, including game cartridges that are compatible with the Genesis console, as well as game cartridges that are compatible with other computer systems.

Sega licenses its copyrighted computer code and its "SEGA" trademark to a number of independent developers of computer game software. Those licensees develop and sell Genesis-compatible video games in competition with Sega. Accolade is not and never has been a licensee of Sega. Prior to rendering its own games compatible with the Genesis console, Accolade explored the possibility of entering into a licensing agreement with Sega, but abandoned the effort because the agreement would have required that Sega be the exclusive manufacturer of all games produced by Accolade.

Accolade used a two-step process to render its video games compatible with the Genesis console. First, it "reverse engineered" Sega's video game programs in order to discover the requirements for compatibility with the Genesis console. As part of the reverse engineering process, Accolade transformed the machine-readable object code contained in commercially available copies of Sega's game cartridges into human-readable source code using a process called "disassembly" or "decompilation." Accolade purchased a Genesis console and three Sega game cartridges, wired a decompiler into the console circuitry, and generated printouts of the resulting source code. Accolade engineers studied and annotated the printouts in order to identify areas of commonality among the three game programs. They then loaded the disassembled code back into a computer, and experimented to discover the interface specifications for the Genesis console by modifying the programs and studying the results. At the end of the reverse engineering process, Accolade created a development manual that incorporated the information it had discovered about the requirements for a Genesis-compatible game. According to the Accolade employees who created the manual, the manual contained only functional descriptions of the interface requirements and did not include any of Sega's code.

In the second stage, Accolade created its own games for the Genesis. According to Accolade, at this stage it did not copy Sega's programs, but relied only on the information concerning interface specifications for the Genesis that was contained in its development manual. Accolade maintains that with the exception of the interface specifications, none of the code in its own games is derived in any way from its examination of Sega's code. In 1990, Accolade released "Ishido," a game which it had originally developed and released for use with the Macintosh and IBM personal computer systems, for use with the Genesis console....

With respect to Sega's copyright claim, the district court rejected Accolade's contention that intermediate copying of computer object code does not constitute infringement under the Copyright Act. It found that Accolade had disassembled Sega's code for a commercial purpose, and that Sega had likely lost sales of its games as a result of Accolade's copying. The court further found that there were alternatives to disassembly that Accolade could have used in order to study the functional requirements for Genesis compatibility. Accordingly, it also rejected Accolade's fair use defense to Sega's copyright infringement claim.

Based on its conclusion that Sega is likely to succeed on the merits of its claims for copyright and trademark infringement, on April 3, 1992, the district court enjoined Accolade from: (1) disassembling Sega's copyrighted code; (2) using or modifying Sega's copyrighted code; (3) developing, manufacturing, distributing, or selling Genesis-compatible games that were created in whole or in part by means that included disassembly ....

III. *Copyright Issues*

Accolade raises four arguments in support of its position that disassembly of the object code in a copyrighted computer program does not constitute copyright infringement. First, it maintains that intermediate copying does not infringe the exclusive rights granted to copyright owners in section 106 of the Copyright Act unless the end product of the copying is substantially similar to the copyrighted work. Second, it argues that disassembly of object code in order to gain an understanding of the ideas and functional concepts embodied in the code is lawful under section 102(b) of the Act, which exempts ideas and functional concepts from copyright protection. Third, it suggests that disassembly is authorized by section 117 of the Act, which entitles the lawful owner of a copy of a computer program to load the program into a computer. Finally, Accolade contends that disassembly of object code in order to gain an understanding of the ideas and functional concepts embodied in the code is a fair use that is privileged by section 107 of the Act.

Neither the language of the Act nor the law of this circuit supports Accolade's first three arguments. Accolade's fourth argument, however, has merit. Although the question is fairly debatable, we conclude based on the policies underlying the Copyright Act that disassembly of copyrighted object code is, as a matter of law, a fair use of the copyrighted work if such disassembly provides the only means of access to those elements of the code that are not protected by copyright and the copier has a legitimate reason for seeking such access. Accordingly, we hold that Sega has failed to demonstrate a likelihood of success on the merits of its copyright claim. Because on the record before us the hardships do not tip sharply (or at all) in Sega's favor, the preliminary injunction issued in its favor must be dissolved, at least with respect to that claim.

A. *Intermediate Copying*

We have previously held that the Copyright Act does not distinguish between unauthorized copies of a copyrighted work on the basis of what stage of the alleged infringer's work the unauthorized copies represent. *Walker v. University Books,* 602 F.2d 859, 864 (9th Cir. 1979) ("The fact that an allegedly infringing copy of a protected work may itself be only an inchoate representation of some final product to be marketed commercially does not in itself negate the possibility of infringement."). Our holding in Walker was based on the plain language of the Act. Section 106 grants to the copyright owner the exclusive rights "to reproduce the work in copies," "to prepare derivative works based upon the copyrighted work," and to authorize the preparation of copies and derivative works. 17 U.S.C. § 106 (1)-(2). Section 501 provides that "anyone who violates any of the exclusive rights of the copyright owner as provided by sections 106 through 118 ... is an infringer of the copyright." *Id.* § 501(a). On its face, that language unambiguously encompasses and proscribes "intermediate copying." *Walker,* 602 F.2d at 863-64; see also *Walt Disney Productions v. Filmation Associates,* 628 F. Supp. 871, 875-76 (C.D. Cal. 1986).

In order to constitute a "copy" for purposes of the Act, the allegedly infringing work must be fixed in some tangible form, "from which the work can be perceived, reproduced, or otherwise communicated, either directly or with the aid of a machine or device." 17 U.S.C. § 101. The computer file generated by the disassembly program, the printouts of the disassembled code, and the computer files containing Accolade's modifications of the code that were generated during the reverse engineering process all satisfy that requirement. The intermediate copying done by Accolade therefore falls squarely within the category of acts that are prohibited by the statute....

... [T]he question whether intermediate copying of computer object code infringes the exclusive rights granted to the copyright owner in section 106 of the Copyright Act is a question of first impression. In light of the unambiguous language of the Act, we decline to depart from the rule set forth in *Walker* for copyrighted works generally. Accordingly, we hold that intermediate copying of computer object code may infringe the exclusive rights granted to the copyright owner in section 106 of the Copyright Act regardless of whether the end product of the copying also infringes those rights. If intermediate copying is permissible under the Act, authority for such copying must be found in one of the statutory provisions to which the rights granted in section 106 are subject....

D. *Fair Use*

Accolade contends, finally, that its disassembly of copyrighted object code as a necessary step in its examination of the unprotected ideas and functional concepts embodied in the code is a fair use that is privileged by section 107 of the Act. Because, in the case before us, disassembly is the only means of gaining access to those unprotected aspects of the program, and because Accolade has a legitimate interest in gaining such access (in order to determine how to make its cartridges compatible with the Genesis console), we agree with Accolade. Where there is good reason for studying or examining the unprotected aspects of a copyrighted computer program, disassembly for purposes of such study or examination constitutes a fair use....

In determining that Accolade's disassembly of Sega's object code did not constitute a fair use, the district court treated the first and fourth statutory factors as dispositive, and ignored the second factor entirely. Given the nature and characteristics of Accolade's direct use of the copied works, the ultimate use to which Accolade put the functional information it obtained, and the nature of the market for home video entertainment systems, we conclude that neither the first nor the fourth factor weighs in Sega's favor. In fact, we conclude that both factors support Accolade's fair use defense, as does the second factor, a factor which is important to the resolution of cases such as the one before us.

(a)

With respect to the first statutory factor, we observe initially that the fact that copying is for a commercial purpose weighs against a finding of fair use. Harper & Row, 471 U.S. at 562. However, the presumption of unfairness that arises in such cases can be rebutted by the characteristics of a particular commercial use. *Hustler Magazine, Inc. v. Moral Majority, Inc.*, 796 F.2d 1148, 1152 (9th Cir. 1986); see also *Maxtone-Graham v. Burtchaell*, 803 F.2d 1253, 1262 (2d Cir. 1986), *cert. denied*, 481 U.S. 1059, 95 L. Ed. 2d 856, 107 S. Ct.

2201 (1987). Further "the commercial nature of a use is a matter of degree, not an absolute...." *Maxtone-Graham,* 803 F.2d at 1262.

Sega argues that because Accolade copied its object code in order to produce a competing product, the *Harper & Row* presumption applies and precludes a finding of fair use. That analysis is far too simple and ignores a number of important considerations. We must consider other aspects of "the purpose and character of the use" as well. As we have noted, the use at issue was an intermediate one only and thus any commercial "exploitation" was indirect or derivative.

The declarations of Accolade's employees indicate, and the district court found, that Accolade copied Sega's software solely in order to discover the functional requirements for compatibility with the Genesis console — aspects of Sega's programs that are not protected by copyright. 17 U.S.C. § 102(b). With respect to the video game programs contained in Accolade's game cartridges, there is no evidence in the record that Accolade sought to avoid performing its own creative work. Indeed, most of the games that Accolade released for use with the Genesis console were originally developed for other hardware systems. Moreover, with respect to the interface procedures for the Genesis console, Accolade did not seek to avoid paying a customarily charged fee for use of those procedures, nor did it simply copy Sega's code; rather, it wrote its own procedures based on what it had learned through disassembly. Taken together, these facts indicate that although Accolade's ultimate purpose was the release of Genesis-compatible games for sale, its direct purpose in copying Sega's code, and thus its direct use of the copyrighted material, was simply to study the functional requirements for Genesis compatibility so that it could modify existing games and make them usable with the Genesis console. Moreover, as we discuss below, no other method of studying those requirements was available to Accolade. On these facts, we conclude that Accolade copied Sega's code for a legitimate, essentially non-exploitative purpose, and that the commercial aspect of its use can best be described as of minimal significance.

We further note that we are free to consider the public benefit resulting from a particular use notwithstanding the fact that the alleged infringer may gain commercially. See *Hustler,* 796 F.2d at 1153 (quoting *MCA, Inc. v. Wilson,* 677 F.2d 180, 182 (2d Cir. 1981)). Public benefit need not be direct or tangible, but may arise because the challenged use serves a public interest. *Id.* In the case before us, Accolade's identification of the functional requirements for Genesis compatibility has led to an increase in the number of independently designed video game programs offered for use with the Genesis console. It is precisely this growth in creative expression, based on the dissemination of other creative works and the unprotected ideas contained in those works, that the Copyright Act was intended to promote. See *Feist Publications, Inc. v. Rural Tel. Serv. Co.,* __ U.S. __, 111 S. Ct. 1282, 1290, 113 L. Ed. 2d 358 (1991) (citing *Harper & Row,* 471 U.S. at 556-57). The fact that Genesis-compatible video games are not scholarly works, but works offered for sale on the market, does not alter our judgment in this regard. We conclude that given the purpose and character of Accolade's use of Sega's video game programs, the presumption of unfairness has been overcome and the first statutory factor weighs in favor of Accolade.

(b)

As applied, the fourth statutory factor, effect on the potential market for the copyrighted work, bears a close relationship to the "purpose and character" inquiry in that it, too, accommodates the distinction between the copying of works in order to make independent creative expression possible and the simple exploitation of another's creative efforts. We must, of course, inquire whether, "if [the challenged use] should become widespread, it would adversely affect the potential market for the copyrighted work," *Sony Corp. v. Universal City Studios,* 464 U.S. 417, 451, 78 L. Ed. 2d 574, 104 S. Ct. 774 (1984), by diminishing potential sales, interfering with marketability, or usurping the market, *Hustler,* 796 F.2d at 1155-56. If the copying resulted in the latter effect, all other considerations might be irrelevant. The *Harper & Row* Court found a use that effectively usurped the market for the copyrighted work by supplanting that work to be dispositive. 471 U.S. at 567-69. However, the same consequences do not and could not attach to a use which simply enables the copier to enter the market for works of the same type as the copied work.

Unlike the defendant in *Harper & Row,* which printed excerpts from President Ford's memoirs verbatim with the stated purpose of "scooping" a Time magazine review of the book, 471 U.S. at 562, Accolade did not attempt to "scoop" Sega's release of any particular game or games, but sought only to become a legitimate competitor in the field of Genesis-compatible video games. Within that market, it is the characteristics of the game program as experienced by the user that determine the program's commercial success. As we have noted, there is nothing in the record that suggests that Accolade copied any of those elements.

By facilitating the entry of a new competitor, the first lawful one that is not a Sega licensee, Accolade's disassembly of Sega's software undoubtedly "affected" the market for Genesis-compatible games in an indirect fashion. We note, however, that while no consumer except the most avid devotee of President Ford's regime might be expected to buy more than one version of the President's memoirs, video game users typically purchase more than one game. There is no basis for assuming that Accolade's "Ishido" has significantly affected the market for Sega's "Altered Beast," since a consumer might easily purchase both; nor does it seem unlikely that a consumer particularly interested in sports might purchase both Accolade's "Mike Ditka Power Football" and Sega's "Joe Montana Football," particularly if the games are, as Accolade contends, not substantially similar. In any event, an attempt to monopolize the market by making it impossible for others to compete runs counter to the statutory purpose of promoting creative expression and cannot constitute a strong equitable basis for resisting the invocation of the fair use doctrine. Thus, we conclude that the fourth statutory factor weighs in Accolade's, not Sega's, favor, notwithstanding the minor economic loss Sega may suffer.

(c)

The second statutory factor, the nature of the copyrighted work, reflects the fact that not all copyrighted works are entitled to the same level of protection. The protection established by the Copyright Act for original works of authorship does not extend to the ideas underlying a work or to the functional or factual aspects of the work. 17 U.S.C. § 102(b). To the extent that a work is functional or factual, it may be copied, *Baker v. Selden,* 101 U.S. 99, 102-04, 25 L. Ed. 841 (1879), as may those expressive elements of the work that "must necessarily be used as incident to" expression of the underlying ideas, functional concepts, or facts, *id.* at 104. Works of fiction receive greater protection than works that have strong factual elements, such as historical or biographical works, *Maxtone-Graham,* 803 F.2d at 1263 (citing *Rosemont Enterprises, Inc. v. Random House, Inc.,* 366 F.2d 303, 307 (2d Cir. 1966), *cert. denied,* 385 U.S. 1009, 17 L. Ed. 2d 546, 87 S. Ct. 714 (1967)), or works that have strong functional elements, such as accounting textbooks, *Baker,* 101 U.S. at 104. Works that are merely compilations of fact are copyrightable, but the copyright in such a work is "thin." *Feist Publications,* 111 S. Ct. at 1289.

Computer programs pose unique problems for the application of the "idea/expression distinction" that determines the extent of copyright protection. To the extent that there are many possible ways of accomplishing a given task or fulfilling a particular market demand, the programmer's choice of program structure and design may be highly creative and idiosyncratic. However, computer programs are, in essence, utilitarian articles — articles that accomplish tasks. As such, they contain many logical, structural, and visual display elements that are dictated by the function to be performed, by considerations of efficiency, or by external factors such as compatibility requirements and industry demands. *Computer Assoc. Int'l, Inc. v. Altai, Inc.,* 1992 U.S. App. LEXIS 14305, 23 U.S.P.Q.2D (BNA) 1241, 1253-56 (2d Cir. 1992) ("*CAI*"). In some circumstances, even the exact set of commands used by the programmer is deemed functional rather than creative for purposes of copyright. "When specific instructions, even though previously copyrighted, are the only and essential means of accomplishing a given task, their later use by another will not amount to infringement." CONTU Report at 20; see *CAI,* 23 U.S.P.Q.2d at 1254.

Because of the hybrid nature of computer programs, there is no settled standard for identifying what is protected expression and what is unprotected idea in a case involving the alleged infringement of a copyright in computer software. We are in wholehearted agreement with the Second Circuit's recent observation that "thus far, many of the decisions in this area reflect the courts' attempt to fit the proverbial square peg in a round hole." *CAI,* 23 U.S.P.Q.2d at 1257. In 1986, the Third Circuit attempted to resolve the dilemma by suggesting that the idea or function of a computer program is the idea of the program as a whole, and "everything that is not necessary to that purpose or function [is] part of the expression of that idea." *Whelan Assoc., Inc. v. Jaslow Dental Laboratory, Inc.,* 797 F.2d 1222, 1236 (3d Cir. 1986) (emphasis omitted). The *Whelan* rule, however, has been widely — and soundly — criticized as simplistic and overbroad. See *CAI,* 23 U.S.P.Q.2d at

1252 (citing cases, treatises, and articles). In reality, "a computer program's ultimate function or purpose is the composite result of interacting subroutines. Since each subroutine is itself a program, and thus, may be said to have its own 'idea,' Whelan's general formulation ... is descriptively inadequate." *Id.* For example, the computer program at issue in the case before us, a video game program, contains at least two such subroutines — the subroutine that allows the user to interact with the video game and the subroutine that allows the game cartridge to interact with the console. Under a test that breaks down a computer program into its component subroutines and sub-subroutines and then identifies the idea or core functional element of each, such as the test recently adopted by the Second Circuit in *CAI,* 23 U.S.P.Q.2D (BNA) at 1252-53, many aspects of the program are not protected by copyright. In our view, in light of the essentially utilitarian nature of computer programs, the Second Circuit's approach is an appropriate one.

Sega argues that even if many elements of its video game programs are properly characterized as functional and therefore not protected by copyright, Accolade copied protected expression. Sega is correct. The record makes clear that disassembly is wholesale copying. Because computer programs are also unique among copyrighted works in the form in which they are distributed for public use, however, Sega's observation does not bring us much closer to a resolution of the dispute.

The unprotected aspects of most functional works are readily accessible to the human eye. The systems described in accounting textbooks or the basic structural concepts embodied in architectural plans, to give two examples, can be easily copied without also copying any of the protected, expressive aspects of the original works. Computer programs, however, are typically distributed for public use in object code form, embedded in a silicon chip or on a floppy disk. For that reason, humans often cannot gain access to the unprotected ideas and functional concepts contained in object code without disassembling that code — i.e., making copies. *Atari Games Corp. v. Nintendo of America,* 975 F.2d 832 (Fed. Cir. 1992).

Sega argues that the record does not establish that disassembly of its object code is the only available method for gaining access to the interface specifications for the Genesis console, and the district court agreed. An independent examination of the record reveals that Sega misstates its contents, and demonstrates that the district court committed clear error in this respect.

[T]he record clearly establishes that humans cannot read object code. Sega makes much of Mike Lorenzen's statement that a reverse engineer can work directly from the zeros and ones of object code but "it's not as fun." In full, Lorenzen's statements establish only that the use of an electronic decompiler is not absolutely necessary. Trained programmers can disassemble object code by hand. Because even a trained programmer cannot possibly remember the millions of zeros and ones that make up a program, however, he must make a written or computerized copy of the disassembled code in order to keep track of his work. See generally Johnson-Laird, *Technical Demonstration of "Decompilation,"* reprinted in Reverse Engineering: Legal and Business Strategies for Competitive Design in the 1990's 102 (Prentice Hall Law & Business ed. 1992). The relevant fact for purposes of Sega's copyright infringement claim and Accolade's fair use defense is that translation of a program from object code into source code cannot be accomplished without making copies of the code....

... Those facts dictate our analysis of the second statutory fair use factor. If disassembly of copyrighted object code is per se an unfair use, the owner of the copyright gains a de facto monopoly over the functional aspects of his work — aspects that were expressly denied copyright protection by Congress. 17 U.S.C. § 102(b). In order to enjoy a lawful monopoly over the idea or functional principle underlying a work, the creator of the work must satisfy the more stringent standards imposed by the patent laws. *Bonito Boats, Inc. v. Thunder Craft Boats, Inc.*, 489 U.S. 141, 159-64, 103 L. Ed. 2d 118, 109 S. Ct. 971 (1989). Sega does not hold a patent on the Genesis console.

Because Sega's video game programs contain unprotected aspects that cannot be examined without copying, we afford them a lower degree of protection than more traditional literary works. See *CAI*, 23 U.S.P.Q.2d at 1257. In light of all the considerations discussed above, we conclude that the second statutory factor also weighs in favor of Accolade.

(d)

As to the third statutory factor, Accolade disassembled entire programs written by Sega. Accordingly, the third factor weighs against Accolade. The fact that an entire work was copied does not, however, preclude a finding [of] fair use. *Sony Corp.*, 464 U.S. at 449-50; *Hustler*, 795 F.2d at 1155 ("*Sony Corp.* teaches us that the copying of an entire work does not preclude fair use per se."). In fact, where the ultimate (as opposed to direct) use is as limited as it was here, the factor is of very little weight. Cf. *Wright v. Warner Books, Inc.*, 953 F.2d 731, 738 (2d Cir. 1991).

(e)

In summary, careful analysis of the purpose and characteristics of Accolade's use of Sega's video game programs, the nature of the computer programs involved, and the nature of the market for video game cartridges yields the conclusion that the first, second, and fourth statutory fair use factors weigh in favor of Accolade, while only the third weighs in favor of Sega, and even then only slightly. Accordingly, Accolade clearly has by far the better case on the fair use issue.

We are not unaware of the fact that to those used to considering copyright issues in more traditional contexts, our result may seem incongruous at first blush. To oversimplify, the record establishes that Accolade, a commercial competitor of Sega, engaged in wholesale copying of Sega's copyrighted code as a preliminary step in the development of a competing product. However, the key to this case is that we are dealing with computer software, a relatively unexplored area in the world of copyright law....

In determining whether a challenged use of copyrighted material is fair, a court must keep in mind the public policy underlying the Copyright Act....

[T]he fact that computer programs are distributed for public use in object code form often precludes public access to the ideas and functional concepts contained in those programs, and thus confers on the copyright owner a de facto monopoly over those ideas and functional concepts. That result defeats the fundamental purpose of the Copyright Act — to encourage the production of original works by protecting the expressive elements of those works while leaving the ideas, facts, and functional concepts in the public domain for others to build on. *Feist Publications,* 111 S. Ct. at 1290; see also *Atari Games Corp.,* slip op. at 18-20....

(f)

We conclude that where disassembly is the only way to gain access to the ideas and functional elements embodied in a copyrighted computer program and where there is a legitimate reason for seeking such access, disassembly is a fair use of the copyrighted work, as a matter of law. Our conclusion does not, of course, insulate Accolade from a claim of copyright infringement with respect to its finished products. Sega has reserved the right to raise such a claim, and it may do so on remand.

  ....

QUESTIONS

1. The *Sega* and *Altai* courts both characterize copyright protection for computer software as a "square peg in a round hole." Do you agree? Is this an appropriate position for the courts to take, given, as Judge Keeton emphasizes in *Lotus v. Paperback,* that Congress has chosen to protect computer software by copyright, and in so doing, has rejected the "square peg/round hole" argument? *See* Arthur R. Miller, *Computer Protection for Computer Programs, Databases, and Computer-Generated Works: Is Anything New Since CONTU,* 106 Harv. L. Rev. 978 (1993).

2. Can one fairly extract from the court's opinion in *Sega* a principle that "intermediate copying" of a copyrighted work will be strongly favored under fair use analysis when such copying is necessary (useful? convenient?) to extract unprotectible material from the copyrighted work, such as its ideas, facts, processes, etc.?

For example, can *Sega* be properly invoked by a scholar who, in preparing a concordance of all of the novels written by a twentieth century novelist, has the full text of those novels scanned into the memory bank of a computer, thus technically making a "reproduction" in the form of a copy? Can the Texaco Company properly invoke *Sega* to justify photocopying of individual journal articles for its researchers, because original journal issues cannot be safely taken into the laboratory (with exposure to chemicals), where the researchers wish to make use of the intricate mathematical formulas set forth by the journal authors?

REVERSE ENGINEERING/DECOMPILATION: A COMPARISON
OF EUROPEAN COMMUNITY AND U.S. COPYRIGHT LAW

The following is excerpted and adapted from Jérôme Huet and Jane C. Ginsburg, *Computer Programs in Europe: A Comparative Analysis of the 1991 EC Software Directive,* 30 Colum. J. Transnat'l L. 327 (1992):

The difficult and highly controversial question of decompilation is governed by Article 6 [of the European Council Directive on the Legal Protection of Computer Programs], which sets forth a compromise solution. [The Directive obliges all European Community member nations to adapt their domestic laws to the standards set forth in the Community texts. The Directive] provides in part:

> The authorization of the rightholder shall not be required where reproduction of the code and translation of its form ... are indispensable to obtain the information necessary to achieve the interoperability of an independently created computer program with other programs....

Decompilation may be defined as the rewriting, on the basis of the object code, of a pseudo-source code of the program — a version in humanly intelligible high-level language, such as the original programmer herself might have written to produce the machine-code version accessible to the user.

Article 6 permits reconstitution of the source code, but only for the purpose of achieving interoperability of programs, and only to the extent that reverse engineering enables the user to access information concerning the interfaces of the decompiled program. Article 9 provides that the decompilation right is imperative; the user may not contract this right away.[1]

Article 6 responds to two major problems that reverse engineering attempts to address: communication between systems on open networks (because to connect to the network one must learn the communications protocols of other programmers); and the creation of systems that are compatible with the standards imposed by the marketplace (an issue that arises most acutely in the domain of micro-computers). The Directive's Preamble repeatedly emphasizes the importance of these issues. Paragraph 9 declares that "the Community is fully committed to the promotion of international standardization" (and thus favors communication on open networks); paragraphs 10 and 11 stress that "the function of a computer program is to communicate and work together with other components of a computer system" and that "the parts of a program which provide for such interconnection and interaction between elements of software and hardware are generally known as 'interfaces,'" while paragraph 12 defines "interoperability" as "the ability to exchange information and mutually to use the information which has been exchanged."

This definition is crucial. It should engender a rather broad conception of lawful decompilation and exploitation of the results. This is because the Directive's goal is to achieve the exchange of information between programs and

---

[1] However, the supplier may be able to restrain decompilation by publishing information on interfaces. This is because Article 6.1(a) bars decompilation by the user if information necessary to achieve interoperability has already been made available by the supplier.

the use of one program together with another under the best technical conditions, that is, with full knowledge of the functional aspects of the interfaces of the studied program....

The Directive's real restrictions on decompilation pertain to the exploitation of information acquired by means of decompilation. The text makes clear that information may be used only to the extent necessary to achieve interoperability, and any program exploiting this information must be "independently created." Thus, one may not decompile a program for the purpose of creating a "knock-off" program that is substantially similar to the initial work. This is a classic principle of copyright law.

The phrase "independently created computer program" suggests that the program created by the person who performed the reverse engineering must be itself this person's own creation. Although this person may well be a potential competitor of the creator of the first program, the new program must not be a literal reproduction of the decompiled program, nor may it be too closely inspired by it. However, this rule simply recalls fundamental copyright principles. Hence, one may perceive something more in the Directive's phrase. Indeed, a widespread practice in the computer programming profession suggests that one can impose a more stringent standard regarding the manner of exploiting information derived from decompilation. The recommended method follows the so-called "clean-room technique," which involves two successive teams of programmers: the first team would decompile the program and identify information concerning interoperability; the second, never having encountered the decompiled program, then would create a competing program incorporating the information communicated by the first team. This method helps insure the independence of the creation of the second program.

However, whatever the method used, the prohibition on creating a program, or part of a program, similar to the decompiled program is not all-encompassing. Copying and exploitation nonetheless may occur when the decompiled program's instructions are banal or standard, or if the form of the program is dictated by the function it performs.

It may be too early to tell whether the decompiler enjoys broader prerogatives under the Directive or under U.S. copyright law. Two recent U.S. appellate court decisions have rejected copyright infringement claims challenging the establishment of unauthorized copies as an intermediate step in the creation of a potentially competing (albeit not necessarily substantially similar) end-product.

In a decision rendered shortly before the Ninth Circuit issued its opinion in *Sega v. Accolade, supra,* the Court of Appeals for the Federal Circuit, in *Atari Games Corp. v. Nintendo of America, Inc.,* 975 F.2d 832 (Fed. Cir. 1992), anticipating the jurisprudence of the Ninth Circuit, also held that intermediate copying could be a fair use.

Both the Federal and the Ninth Circuits' treatments of the reverse engineering issue recall the Directive's resolution: one may decompile a predecessor's program to understand its functions, but the knowledge thus acquired must be put to the creation, not of a reprise of the copied work, but of an independently authored, albeit potentially competing, program. Similarly, as both opinions stated, and as the Ninth Circuit particularly emphasized, decompilation will qualify as a fair use only where there is no other means of access to the unprotected programming information. However, the Federal and Ninth Circuits' approaches to decompilation appear more generous than the Directive's, for they are not limited to acquisition and exploitation of information regarding program interfaces. Under the Directive, the decompiler may not exploit information unrelated to "interoperability" between programs. By contrast, the Federal Circuit's analysis would permit the reverse engineer to use information pertaining to a variety of program elements that do not necessarily communicate with other programs. The Ninth Circuit, while emphasizing disassembly for purposes of promoting software-hardware compatibility, did not explicitly limit the scope of its fair use analysis to this context.[3]

The following example may illustrate the contrast between the EC and Federal/Ninth Circuits' delineation of permissible decompilation. A word processing program, such as WordPerfect, contains, in addition to the word processing elements with which the user interacts, elements that link the program to programs governing printer functions, and that connect the program to a variety of related programs, such as spell-checkers and thesauruses. Under the Directive, a programmer wishing to create a spell-checker that would work with WordPerfect would be permitted to exploit information derived from decompiling the WordPerfect program, but only insofar as that information relates to the interaction of the word processing and spell-checking programs. Under the Ninth and Federal Circuits' approaches, it appears that all information obtained from reverse engineering and making an intermediate high-level language copy of WordPerfect could be exploited to create not only a WordPerfect-compatible spell-checker, but a rival to WordPerfect itself. However, the resulting program could not reproduce the original copyrighted aspects of the decompiled work.

C. SEMICONDUCTOR CHIP PROTECTION

In the words of House Report No. 98-781, 98th Cong., 2d Sess. 2 (1984): "Integrated circuits, better known as semiconductor chips, have revolutionized our entire way of life. Semiconductor chips are used to operate microwave ovens, cash registers, personal and business computers, TV sets, refrigerators, hi-fi equipment, automobile engine controls, automatic machine tools, robots, printing presses, cardiac monitors and pacemakers, X-ray imaging and scanning equipment, blood testing equipment, word processors and printers, telephones, and many other medical, consumer, business, and industrial products.... More than perhaps any other invention, the semiconductor chip has brought us into the information age."

---

[3]The court stated: "The need to disassemble object code arises, if at all, only in connection with operations systems, system interface procedures, and other programs that are not visible to the user when operating — and then only when no alternative means of gaining an understanding of the ideas and functional concepts exists." Despite the caveat, the last category (programs invisible to users) may extend well beyond "interfaces."

"Chips" are collections of transistors formed on a single "integrated" structure; these transistors are etched into patterns on the chips' silicon base, and they work together (as minuscule switches) to perform assigned electronic functions. The configuration of transistors on the chip is achieved through a chemical "layering" process, and the ten or twelve layers on the typical chip are manufactured through the use of stencils or "masks." The design and manufacture of these chips can consume thousands of hours of engineer and technician time and cost millions of dollars. It is possible for a person seeking to reproduce the configuration of an existing semiconductor chip to make a photographic copy of the pattern of each transistor layer, i.e., to copy the "masks." This is far less costly and time-consuming than the design and manufacture of the chip by the innovating company.

Congress, concerned about the devastating economic effects on American industry of the unauthorized copying of "mask works," enacted legislation to outlaw such conduct in November 1984. Although the Senate bill (S. 1201, discussed in S. Rep. 98-425, 98th Cong., 2d Sess. (1984)) had assimilated mask works to copyrightable works under the 1976 Copyright Act, the House bill (H.R. 5525) opted for sui generis protection under an independent Chapter 9 of the Act, and it was this approach that prevailed.

The major hurdle to treating mask works as akin to other copyrightable subject matter was the application of § 113 and the definition of "pictorial, graphic and sculptural works" in § 101. Mask works are "two-dimensional and three-dimensional features of shapes, pattern and configuration of the surface of the layers of a semiconductor chip product" (H.R. Rep. No. 98-781 at 13), and are thus not protectible under conventional copyright analysis because their configuration is inseparable from a useful object. Another hurdle was our participation in the Universal Copyright Convention: "If the United States enacts copyright legislation to protect mask works, we would be required to give equivalent protection under the UCC; arguably we could stand thereafter alone in the obligation to protect works first published in UCC countries or created by UCC nationals. The United States could be required to protect, for example, the mask works of Japan, West Germany, and the Soviet Union [which do not protect mask works under the UCC], and receive no protection in return." (Id. at 7.)

It is instructive to set forth the discussion in the House Committee Report regarding the inaptness of conventional copyright protection. (Id. at 8-11.)

> In considering whether the copyright system could provide the best form of domestic protection for mask works, the Committee notes that the present copyright law does not protect useful articles, as such, and semiconductor chip products are useful articles, as defined in the Copyright Act. 17 U.S.C. 101 (definitions of "pictorial, graphic or sculptural works" and "useful article"). Moreover, while masks containing technical information and schematic drawings of chip layouts have been registered under the Copyright Act as technical drawings, the fundamental principle codified in 17 U.S.C. 113 has meant that any protection as a "technical drawing" does not protect the copyright owner of the drawing with respect to unauthorized duplication of the finished useful article repre-

sented by the drawing. No court has held that duplication of a semiconductor chip violates any rights in the registered technical drawing. Under
17 U.S.C. 113, no other conclusion seems likely.

... Photographs and audiovisual works are not useful articles under
copyright law, even if they are used for training or educational purposes,
for example. By contrast, mask works would be protected on the basis of
the technical and creative skill employed in laying out or designing electronic circuitry. Mask works have no intrinsic aesthetic purpose. Even if
the layouts convey information, that is not their sole or main purpose:
their primary purpose is to be used in the manufacture of a useful article
— semiconductor chip products.

The Committee decided that the formidable philosophical, constitutional, legal and technical problems associated with any attempt to place
protection for mask works or semiconductor chip designs under the copyright law could be avoided entirely by creating a sui generis form of
protection, apart from and independent of the copyright laws. This new
form of legal protection would avoid the possible distortion of the copyright law and would establish a more appropriate and efficacious form of
protection for mask works. Rather than risk confusion and uncertainty in,
and distortion of, existing copyright law as a result of attempting to
modify fundamental copyright principles to suit the unusual nature of
chip design, the Committee concludes that a new body of statutory and
decisional law should be developed. It should be specifically applicable to
mask works alone, and could be based on many copyright principles, and
other intellectual property concepts; it could draw by analogy on this
statutory and case law framework to the extent clearly applicable to
mask works and semiconductor chip protection, but should not be restricted by the limitations of existing copyright law.

The sui generis protection afforded by the new statute is a hybrid of patent
and copyright protection, although the resemblance to copyright is stronger.
Section 904 provides that protection under the Act begins on the date of
registration of the mask work or the date of "first commercial exploitation,"
whichever occurs earlier; protection ends ten years later. Section 902(b) provides that protection is not available for "a mask work that is not original"
(i.e., the work must be the independent creation of an author who did not copy
it), and it may not consist of "designs that are staple, commonplace, or familiar in the semiconductor industry, or variations of such designs, combined in a
way that, considered as a whole, is not original." The statutory rules regarding notice and registration are essentially the opposite of those under the 1976
Act as originally enacted: registration of the mask work within a reasonable
time is mandatory, upon pain of forfeiture if the work is not registered within
two years, § 908(a), but the M-in-a-circle notice is optional, § 909. Registration
is effected at the Copyright Office, which undertakes no search akin to that
for patents. Under § 905, the owner of the mask work enjoys the exclusive
rights of reproduction, importation, and distribution; and there is an explicit
provision for contributory infringement (unlike the 1976 Copyright Act).

Remedies, including "statutory damages," are limited in § 911 to damages; no criminal penalties are provided.

The close relationship with copyright protection is highlighted by two provisions concerning allowable unauthorized uses of protected mask works — despite the absence of an explicit "fair use" provision in Chapter 9. Section 902(c) employs familiar language: "In no case does protection under this chapter for a mask work extend to any idea, procedure, process, system, method of operation, concept, principle or discovery, regardless of the form in which it is described, explained, illustrated, or embodied in such work." Section 906 shelters so-called "reverse engineering," that is, the reproduction of a mask work "solely for the purpose of teaching, analyzing, or evaluating the concepts or techniques embodied" therein or the organization of components therein, even when that is done in order "to incorporate the results of such conduct in an original mask work which is made to be distributed." (Compare the judicial receptivity to certain types of "reverse engineering" of copyrighted computer programs, invoking the fair use doctrine. *E.g., Sega Enters. Ltd. v. Accolade, Inc., supra.*) The reasons for the latter provision are set forth in the House Report (at page 22):

> Based on testimony of industry representatives that it is an established industry practice to similarly make photo-reproductions of the mask work in order to analyze the existing chip so as to design a second chip with the same electrical and physical performance characteristics as the existing chip (so-called "form, fit and function" compatibility), and that this practice fosters fair competition and provides a frequently needed "second source" for chip products, it is the intent of the Committee to permit such reproduction by competitors where such reproduction is "solely for the purpose of teaching, analyzing, or evaluating" the concepts, techniques, etc. embodied in the work, rather than mere wholesale appropriation of the work and investment in the creation of the first chip.

Section 912 deals with the difficult issue of the relationship of the new statute to state and other federal laws. Most pertinently, the legislative history makes clear that ten-year protection for the design of mask works as useful objects is not meant in any way to displace whatever longer term copyright protection may be available for any works — such as computer programs or other literary works — that are stored in the semiconductor chip product.

Chapter 8

OTHER LEGAL PROTECTION FOR CREATIVITY

Although the law of copyright affords potentially broad protection for creative works, it by no means exhausts the theories providing support for claims of intellectual property. It is our intention to furnish a glimpse into four such theories reflected in state law — "passing off," misappropriation, idea protection, and the right of publicity. Each of them is a field unto itself and is frequently explored in detail in advanced courses. Nothing more is attempted here than to suggest the contours of these legal theories through representative cases. We will then be in a position to study the extent to which state rights and remedies may be preempted by federal copyright.

The student has already been introduced to the tort commonly known as "passing off," particularly as it relates to the copying of the titles of literary works or the names of characters. *See* Chapter 1, Subchapter E *supra*. A person is said to violate the law when he so promotes his goods or services as to create a likelihood that consumers will believe them to be (or be associated with) the goods or services of another. The purpose of the tort rule is to protect the reputation or goodwill of that other person and to protect the consuming public against confusion or deception. The application of the "passing off" theory to literary-property cases is rather straightforward.

It has been held, for example, that when a successful play entitled "The Gold Diggers" was made into a successful motion picture entitled "Gold Diggers of Broadway," it was unlawful for another to market a motion picture entitled "Gold Diggers of Paris" (at least without a conspicuous disclaimer that the picture was not based on the play or the earlier motion picture). *Warner Bros. Pictures, Inc. v. Majestic Pictures Corp.*, 70 F.2d 310 (2d Cir. 1934). It has also been held unlawful to draw popular comic-strip characters, using their names, in comic-strip settings unauthorized by the creator of the characters; the court concluded that "the figures and names have been so connected with the [artist] as their originator or author that the use by another of new cartoons exploiting the characters ... would be unfair to the public and to the plaintiff." *Fisher v. Star Co.*, 231 N.Y. 414, 132 N.E. 133, *cert. denied*, 257 U.S. 654 (1921) ("Mutt and Jeff").

In the other state claims of pertinence to copyright treated immediately below, the gist of the tort is something other than the "likelihood of confusion" which is essential to the tort of "passing off."

A. MISAPPROPRIATION

INTERNATIONAL NEWS SERVICE v. ASSOCIATED PRESS

248 U.S. 215 (1918)

MR. JUSTICE PITNEY delivered the opinion of the court.

The parties are competitors in the gathering and distribution of news and its publication for profit in newspapers throughout the United States. The Associated Press, which was complainant in the District Court, is a cooperative organization, incorporated under the Membership Corporations Law of the State of New York, its members being individuals who are either proprietors or representatives of about 950 daily newspapers published in all parts of the United States. That a corporation may be organized under that act for the purpose of gathering news for the use and benefit of its members and for publication in newspapers owned or represented by them, is recognized by an amendment enacted in 1901 (Laws N.Y. 1901, c. 436). Complainant gathers in all parts of the world, by means of various instrumentalities of its own, by exchange with its members, and by other appropriate means, news and intelligence of current and recent events of interest to newspaper readers and distributes it daily to its members for publication in their newspapers. The cost of the service, amounting approximately to $3,500,000 per annum, is assessed upon the members and becomes a part of their costs of operation, to be recouped, presumably with profit, through the publication of their several newspapers. Under complainant's by-laws each member agrees upon assuming membership that news received through complainant's service is received exclusively for publication in a particular newspaper, language, and place specified in the certificate of membership, that no other use of it shall be permitted, and that no member shall furnish or permit anyone in his employ or connected with his newspaper to furnish any of complainant's news in advance of publication to any person not a member. And each member is required to gather the local news of his district and supply it to the Associated Press and to no one else.

Defendant is a corporation organized under the laws of the State of New Jersey, whose business is the gathering and selling of news to its customers and clients, consisting of newspapers published throughout the United States, under contracts by which they pay certain amounts at stated times for defendant's service. It has wide-spread news-gathering agencies; the cost of its operations amounts, it is said, to more than $2,000,000 per annum; and it serves about 400 newspapers located in the various cities of the United States and abroad, a few of which are represented, also, in the membership of the Associated Press.

The parties are in the keenest competition between themselves in the distribution of news throughout the United States; and so, as a rule, are the newspapers that they serve, in their several districts....

....

The only matter that has been argued before us is whether defendant may lawfully be restrained from appropriating news taken from bulletins issued by complainant or any of its members, or from newspapers published by them, for the purpose of selling it to defendant's clients....

The federal jurisdiction was invoked because of diversity of citizenship, not upon the ground that the suit arose under the copyright or other laws of the United States. Complainant's news matter is not copyrighted. It is said that it could not, in practice, be copyrighted, because of the large number of dispatches that are sent daily; and, according to complainant's contention, news is not within the operation of the copyright act. Defendant, while apparently conceding this, nevertheless invokes the analogies of the law of literary property and copyright, insisting as its principal contention that, assuming complainant has a right of property in its news, it can be maintained (unless the copyright act be complied with) only by being kept secret and confidential, and that upon the publication with complainant's consent of uncopyrighted news by any of complainant's members in a newspaper or upon a bulletin board, the right of property is lost, and the subsequent use of the news by the public, or by defendant for any purpose whatever becomes lawful....

In considering the general question of property in news matter, it is necessary to recognize its dual character, distinguishing between the substance of the information and the particular form or collocation of words in which the writer has communicated it.

No doubt news articles often possess a literary quality, and are the subject of literary property at the common law; nor do we question that such an article, as a literary production, is the subject of copyright by the terms of the act as it now stands....

But the news element — the information respecting current events contained in the literary production — is not the creation of the writer, but is a report of matters that ordinarily are *publici juris;* it is the history of the day. It is not to be supposed that the framers of the Constitution, when they empowered Congress "to promote the progress of science and useful arts, by securing for limited times to authors and inventors the exclusive right to their respective writings and discoveries" (Const., Art. I, § 8, par. 8), intended to confer upon one who might happen to be the first to report a historic event the exclusive right for any period to spread the knowledge of it.

[E]xcept for matters improperly disclosed, or published in breach of trust or confidence, or in violation of law, none of which is involved in this branch of the case, the news of current events may be regarded as common property. What we are concerned with is the business of making it known to the world, in which both parties to the present suit are engaged.... The parties are competitors in this field; and, on fundamental principles, applicable here as elsewhere, when the rights or privileges of the one are liable to conflict with those of the other, each party is under a duty so to conduct its own business as not unnecessarily or unfairly to injure that of the other. *Hitchman Coal & Coke Co. v. Mitchell,* 245 U.S. 229, 254.

Obviously, the question of what is unfair competition in business must be determined with particular reference to the character and circumstances of the business. The question here is not so much the rights of either party as against the public but their rights as between themselves. See *Morison v. Moat,* 9 Hare, 241, 258. And although we may and do assume that neither party has any remaining property interest as against the public in uncopyrighted news matter after the moment of its first publication, it by no means follows that there is no remaining property interest in it as between themselves. For, to both of them alike, news matter, however little susceptible of ownership or dominion in the absolute sense, is stock in trade, to be gathered at the cost of enterprise, organization, skill, labor, and money, and to be distributed and sold to those who will pay money for it, as for any other merchandise. Regarding the news, therefore, as but the material out of which both parties are seeking to make profits at the same time and in the same field, we hardly can fail to recognize that for this purpose, and as between them, it must be regarded as *quasi* property, irrespective of the rights of either as against the public....

....

The peculiar features of the case arise from the fact that, while novelty and freshness form so important an element in the success of the business, the very processes of distribution and publication necessarily occupy a good deal of time. Complainant's service, as well as defendant's, is a daily service to daily newspapers; most of the foreign news reaches this country at the Atlantic seaboard, principally at the City of New York, and because of this, and of time differentials due to the earth's rotation, the distribution of news matter throughout the country is principally from east to west; and, since in speed the telegraph and telephone easily outstrip the rotation of the earth, it is a simple matter for defendant to take complainant's news from bulletins or early editions of complainant's members in the eastern cities and at the mere cost of telegraphic transmission cause it to be published in western papers issued at least as early as those served by complainant. Besides this, and irrespective of time differentials, irregularities in telegraphic transmission on different lines, and the normal consumption of time in printing and distributing the newspaper, result in permitting pirated news to be placed in the hands of defendant's readers sometimes simultaneously with the service of competing Associated Press papers, occasionally even earlier.

Defendant insists that when, with the sanction and approval of complainant, and as the result of the use of its news for the very purpose for which it is distributed, a portion of complainant's members communicate it to the general public by posting it upon bulletin boards so that all may read, or by issuing it to newspapers and distributing it indiscriminately, complainant no longer has the right to control the use to be made of it; that when it thus reaches the light of day it becomes the common possession of all to whom it is accessible; and that any purchaser of a newspaper has the right to communicate the intelligence which it contains to anybody and for any purpose, even for the purpose of selling it for profit to newspapers published for profit in competition with complainant's members.

The fault in the reasoning lies in applying as a test the right of the complainant as against the public, instead of considering the rights of complainant and defendant, competitors in business, as between themselves. The right of the purchaser of a single newspaper to spread knowledge of its contents gratuitously, for any legitimate purpose not unreasonably interfering with complainant's right to make merchandise of it, may be admitted; but to transmit that news for commercial use, in competition with complainant — which is what defendant has done and seeks to justify — is a very different matter. In doing this defendant, by its very act, admits that it is taking material that has been acquired by complainant as the result of organization and the expenditure of labor, skill, and money, and which is salable by complainant for money, and that defendant in appropriating it and selling it as its own is endeavoring to reap where it has not sown, and by disposing of it to newspapers that are competitors of complainant's members is appropriating to itself the harvest of those who have sown. Stripped of all disguises, the process amounts to an unauthorized interference with the normal operation of complainant' s legitimate business precisely at the point where the profit is to be reaped, in order to divert a material portion of the profit from those who have earned it to those who have not; with special advantage to defendant in the competition because of the fact that it is not burdened with any part of the expense of gathering the news. The transaction speaks for itself, and a court of equity ought not to hesitate long in characterizing it as unfair competition in business....

The contention that the news is abandoned to the public for all purposes when published in the first newspaper is untenable. Abandonment is a question of intent, and the entire organization of the Associated Press negatives such a purpose.... [P]ublication by each member must be deemed not by any means an abandonment of the news to the world for any and all purposes, but a publication for limited purposes; for the benefit of the readers of the bulletin or the newspaper as such; not for the purpose of making merchandise of it as news, with the result of depriving complainant's other members of their reasonable opportunity to obtain just returns for their expenditures.

It is to be observed that the view we adopt does not result in giving to complainant the right to monopolize either the gathering or the distribution of the news, or, without complying with the copyright act, to prevent the reproduction of its news articles; but only postpones participation by complainant's competitor in the processes of distribution and reproduction of news that it has not gathered, and only to the extent necessary to prevent that competitor from reaping the fruits of complainant's efforts and expenditure, to the partial exclusion of complainant, and in violation of the principle that underlies the maxim *sic utere tuo*, etc.

It is said that the elements of unfair competition are lacking because there is no attempt by defendant to palm off its goods as those of the complainant, characteristic of the most familiar, if not the most typical, cases of unfair competition. *Howe Scale Co. v. Wyckoff, Seamans & Benedict,* 198 U.S. 118, 140. But we cannot concede that the right to equitable relief is confined to that class of cases. In the present case the fraud upon complainant's rights is more direct and obvious. Regarding news matter as the mere material from which these two competing parties are endeavoring to make money, and treating it, therefore, as *quasi* property for the purposes of their business because they are both selling it as such, defendant's conduct differs from the ordinary case of unfair competition in trade principally in this that, instead of selling its own goods as those of complainant, it substitutes misappropriation in the place of misrepresentation, and sells complainant's goods as its own.

Besides the misappropriation, there are elements of imitation, of false pretense, in defendant's practices. The device of rewriting complainant's news articles, frequently resorted to, carries its own comment. The habitual failure to give credit to complainant for that which is taken is significant. Indeed, the entire system of appropriating complainant's news and transmitting it as a commercial product to defendant's clients and patrons amounts to a false representation to them and to their newspaper readers that the news transmitted is the result of defendant's own investigation in the field. But these elements, although accentuating the wrong, are not the essence of it. It is something more than the advantage of celebrity of which complainant is being deprived....

There is some criticism of the injunction that was directed by the District Court upon the going down of the mandate from the Circuit Court of Appeals. In brief, it restrains any taking or gainfully using of the complainant's news, either bodily or in substance, from bulletins issued by the complainant or any of its members, or from editions of their newspapers, *"until its commercial value as news to the complainant and all of its members has passed away."* The part complained of is the clause we have italicized; but if this be indefinite, it is no more so than the criticism. Perhaps it would be better that the terms of the injunction be made specific, and so framed as to confine the restraint to an extent consistent with the reasonable protection of complainant's newspapers, each in its own area and for a specified time after its publication, against the competitive use of pirated news by defendant's customers. But the case presents practical difficulties; and we have not the materials, either in the way of a definite suggestion of amendment, or in the way of proofs, upon which to frame a specific injunction; hence, while not expressing approval of the form adopted by the District Court, we decline to modify it at this preliminary stage of the case, and will leave that court to deal with the matter upon appropriate application made to it for the purpose.

The decree of the Circuit Court of Appeals will be

Affirmed.

Mr. Justice Clarke took no part in the consideration or decision of this case.

Mr. Justice Holmes:

When an uncopyrighted combination of words is published there is no general right to forbid other people repeating them — in other words there is no property in the combination or in the thoughts or facts that the words express. Property, a creation of law, does not arise from value, although exchangeable — a matter of fact. Many exchangeable values may be destroyed intentionally without compensation. Property depends upon exclusion by law from interference, and a person is not excluded from using any combination of words merely because someone has used it before, even if it took labor and genius to make it. If a given person is to be prohibited from making the use of words that his neighbors are free to make some other ground must be found. One such ground is vaguely expressed in the phrase unfair trade. This means that the words are repeated by a competitor in business in such a way as to convey a misrepresentation that materially injures the person who first used them, by appropriating credit of some kind which the first user has earned. The ordinary case is a representation by device, appearance, or other indirection that the defendant's goods come from the plaintiff. But the only reason why it is actionable to make such a representation is that it tends to give the defendant an advantage in his competition with the plaintiff and that it is thought undesirable that an advantage should be gained in that way. Apart from that the defendant may use such unpatented devices and uncopyrighted combinations of words as he likes. The ordinary case, I say, is palming off the defendant's product as the plaintiff's, but the same evil may follow from the opposite falsehood — from saying, whether in words or by implication, that the plaintiff's product is the defendant's, and that, it seems to me, is what has happened here.

... If the plaintiff is later in western cities it naturally will be supposed to have obtained its information from the defendant. The falsehood is a little more subtle, the injury a little more indirect, than in ordinary cases of unfair trade, but I think that the principle that condemns the one condemns the other. It is a question of how strong an infusion of fraud is necessary to turn a flavor into a poison. The dose seems to me strong enough here to need a remedy from the law. But as, in my view, the only ground of complaint that can be recognized without legislation is the implied misstatement, it can be corrected by stating the truth; and a suitable acknowledgment of the source is all that the plaintiff can require. I think that within the limits recognized by the decision of the Court the defendant should be enjoined from publishing news obtained from the Associated Press for __ hours after publication by the plaintiff unless it gives express credit to the Associated Press; the number of hours and the form of acknowledgment to be settled by the District Court.

MR. JUSTICE McKENNA concurs in this opinion.

MR. JUSTICE BRANDEIS dissenting....

[T]he fact that a product of the mind has cost its producer money and labor, and has a value for which others are willing to pay, is not sufficient to ensure to it this legal attribute of property. The general rule of law is, that the noblest of human productions — knowledge, truths ascertained, conceptions, and ideas — become, after voluntary communication to others, free as the air to common use. Upon these incorporeal productions the attribute of property is continued after such communication only in certain classes of cases where public policy has seemed to demand it. These exceptions are confined to productions which, in some degree, involve creation, invention, or discovery. But by no means all such are endowed with this attribute of property. The creations which are recognized as property by the common law are literary, dramatic, musical, and other artistic creations; and these have also protection under the copyright statutes. The inventions and discoveries upon which this attribute of property is conferred only by statute, are the few comprised within the patent law. There are also many other cases in which courts interfere to prevent curtailment of plaintiff's enjoyment of incorporeal productions; and in which the right to relief is often called a property right, but is such only in a special sense. In those cases, the plaintiff has no absolute right to the protection of his production; he has merely the qualified right to be protected

as against the defendant's acts, because of the special relation in which the
latter stands or the wrongful method or means employed in acquiring the
knowledge or the manner in which it is used. Protection of this character is
afforded where the suit is based upon breach of contract or of trust or upon
unfair competition.

The knowledge for which protection is sought in the case at bar is not of a
kind upon which the law has heretofore conferred the attributes of property;
nor is the manner of its acquisition or use nor the purpose to which it is
applied, such as has heretofore been recognized as entitling a plaintiff to
relief.

First: Plaintiff's principal reliance was upon the "ticker" cases; but they do
not support its contention. The leading cases on this subject rest the grant of
relief, not upon the existence of a general property right in news, but upon the
breach of a contract or trust concerning the use of news communicated; and
that element is lacking here....

... On the contrary it is conceded that both the bulletins and the papers
were issued in accordance with the regulations of the plaintiff. Under such
circumstances, for a reader of the papers purchased in the open market, or a
reader of the bulletins publicly posted, to procure and use gainfully, information therein contained, does not involve inducing anyone to commit a breach
either of contract or of trust, or committing or in any way abetting a breach of
confidence.

. . . .

Third: If news be treated as possessing the characteristics not of a trade
secret, but of literary property, then the earliest issue of a paper of general
circulation or the earliest public posting of a bulletin which embodies such
news would, under the established rules governing literary property, operate
as a publication, and all property in the news would then cease.... [W]here the
publication is in fact a general one, even express words of restriction upon use
are inoperative. In other words, a general publication is effective to dedicate
literary property to the public, regardless of the actual intent of its owner....

Fourth: Plaintiff further contended that defendant's practice constitutes
unfair competition, because there is "appropriation without cost to itself of
values created by" the plaintiff; and it is upon this ground that the decision of
this court appears to be based. To appropriate and use for profit, knowledge
and ideas produced by other men, without making compensation or even acknowledgment, may be inconsistent with a finer sense of propriety; but, with
the exceptions indicated above, the law has heretofore sanctioned the practice.
Thus it was held that one may ordinarily make and sell anything in any form,
may copy with exactness that which another has produced, or may otherwise
use his ideas without his consent and without the payment of compensation,
and yet not inflict a legal injury; and that ordinarily one is at perfect liberty to
find out, if he can by lawful means, trade secrets of another, however valuable, and then use the knowledge so acquired gainfully, although it cost the
original owner much in effort and in money to collect or produce.

Such taking and gainful use of a product of another which, for reasons of
public policy, the law has refused to endow with the attributes of property,
does not become unlawful because the product happens to have been taken

from a rival and is used in competition with him. The unfairness in competition which hitherto has been recognized by the law as a basis for relief, lay in the manner or means of conducting the business; and the manner or means held legally unfair, involves either fraud or force or the doing of acts otherwise prohibited by law....

That competition is not unfair in a legal sense, merely because the profits gained are unearned, even if made at the expense of a rival, is shown by many cases besides those referred to above. He who follows the pioneer into a new market, or who engages in the manufacture of an article newly introduced by another, seeks profits due largely to the labor and expense of the first adventurer; but the law sanctions, indeed encourages, the pursuit....

The means by which the International News Service obtains news gathered by the Associated Press is also clearly unobjectionable.... The manner of use is likewise unobjectionable. No reference is made by word or by act to the Associated Press, either in transmitting the news to subscribers or by them in publishing it in their papers. Neither the International News Service nor its subscribers is gaining or seeking to gain in its business a benefit from the reputation of the Associated Press. They are merely using its product without making compensation. See *Bamforth v. Douglass Post Card & Machine Co.*, 158 Fed. Rep. 355; *Tribune Co. of Chicago v. Associated Press*, 116 Fed. Rep. 126. That, they have a legal right to do; because the product is not property, and they do not stand in any relation to the Associated Press, either of contract or of trust, which otherwise precludes such use. The argument is not advanced by characterizing such taking and use a misappropriation.

It is also suggested, that the fact that defendant does not refer to the Associated Press as the source of the news may furnish a basis for the relief. But the defendant and its subscribers, unlike members of the Associated Press, were under no contractual obligation to disclose the source of the news; and there is no rule of law requiring acknowledgment to be made where uncopyrighted matter is reproduced....

Fifth: The great development of agencies now furnishing country-wide distribution of news, the vastness of our territory, and improvements in the means of transmitting intelligence, have made it possible for a news agency or newspapers to obtain, without paying compensation, the fruit of another's efforts and to use news so obtained gainfully in competition with the original collector. The injustice of such action is obvious. But to give relief against it would involve more than the application of existing rules of law to new facts. It would require the making of a new rule in analogy to existing ones. The unwritten law possesses capacity for growth; and has often satisfied new demands for justice by invoking analogies or by expanding a rule or principle. This process has been in the main wisely applied and should not be discontinued. Where the problem is relatively simple, as it is apt to be when private interests only are involved, it generally proves adequate. But with the increasing complexity of society, the public interest tends to become omnipresent; and the problems presented by new demands for justice cease to be simple. Then the creation or recognition by courts of a new private right may work serious injury to the general public, unless the boundaries of the right are definitely established and wisely guarded. In order to reconcile the new private right with the public interest, it may be necessary to prescribe limitations and rules for its enjoyment; and also to provide administrative machinery for enforcing the rules. It is largely for this reason that, in the effort to meet the many new demands for justice incident to a rapidly changing civilization, resort to legislation has latterly been had with increasing frequency....

Courts are ill-equipped to make the investigations which should precede a determination of the limitations which should be set upon any property right in news or of the circumstances under which news gathered by a private agency should be deemed affected with a public interest. Courts would be powerless to prescribe the detailed regulations essential to full enjoyment of the rights conferred or to introduce the machinery required for enforcement of such regulations. Considerations such as these should lead us to decline to establish a new rule of law in the effort to redress a newly-disclosed wrong, although the propriety of some remedy appears to be clear.

QUESTION

The Pottstown Mercury publishes a daily newspaper in Pottstown, Pennsylvania. It expends considerable money to develop its sources of local news, to train personnel, and accurately and concisely to compose local news items, which it protects by the insertion of a copyright notice on its masthead page and by registration with the Copyright Office. WPOT is a local radio station; many of its advertisers also advertise in the Pottstown Mercury. Its small staff of newswriters will frequently purchase the Mercury, among other newspapers, to become alerted to the news of the day, and will then utilize their own words in the preparation of copy for the radio news reports. The Pottstown Mercury has protested, but WPOT claims that by independently writing its own news-text, it is not engaging in copyright infringement. Apparently agreeing, the Mercury has commenced an action in a Pennsylvania state court, seeking an injunction against "any further appropriation of the plaintiff's local news without its permission or authorization."

Is the Supreme Court decision in the *International News Service* case technically controlling? Is its rationale persuasive on these facts? *See Pottstown Daily News Pub. Co. v. Pottstown Broadcasting Co.*, 411 Pa. 383, 192 A.2d 657 (1963).

The Supreme Court decided *INS* as a matter of federal common law. Twenty years later, in *Erie R.R. v. Tompkins*, 304 U.S. 64 (1938), the Court abolished federal common law of the *INS* variety. However, if *INS* is no longer good law at the federal level, many states have embraced, and even extended, its holding and rationale. *See generally* Douglas G. Baird, *Common Law Intellectual Property and the Legacy of International News Service v. Associated Press*, 50 U. Chi. L. Rev. 411 (1983). The following decision colorfully illustrates the reception of *INS* by state courts.

METROPOLITAN OPERA ASS'N v. WAGNER-NICHOLS RECORDER CORP.

199 Misc. 787, 101 N.Y.S.2d 483 (Sup. Ct. 1950), *aff'd,* 279 App. Div. 632, 107 N.Y.S.2d 795 (1st Dep't 1951)

GREENBERG, JUSTICE.

The plaintiffs Metropolitan Opera Association, Inc. (hereinafter referred to as "Metropolitan Opera"), and American Broadcasting Company, Inc. (hereinafter referred to as "American Broadcasting"), and the intervening plaintiff, Columbia Records, Inc. (hereinafter referred to as "Columbia Records"), move for a preliminary injunction to restrain the defendants from recording, advertising, selling or distributing musical performances of Metropolitan Opera broadcast over the air, and from using the name "Metropolitan Opera" or any similar name which is calculated to mislead the public into believing that the records sold by the defendants are records of performances made or sold under the control or supervision or with the consent of the plaintiffs....

The complaints of the plaintiffs allege in substance:

Metropolitan Opera is an educational membership corporation. Over a period of sixty years it has, by care, skill and great expenditure, maintained a position of pre-eminence in the field of music and grand opera. By reason of this skill and pre-eminence it has created a national and worldwide audience and thereby a large market for radio broadcasts and phonograph recordings of its performances. Metropolitan Opera has sold the exclusive right to broadcast its performances and the exclusive right to record its performances, as set forth below, and uses the proceeds to defray part of its operating expenses.

It has sold the exclusive right to make and sell phonograph records of its operatic performances and to use the names "Metropolitan Opera Orchestra," "Metropolitan Opera Chorus" and any other names identified with Metropolitan in connection with these phonograph records to Columbia Records, which has acquired a reputation and good will of great value. This contract is for a five-year period ending December 31, 1951. The exclusive nature of these rights is of the essence of the contract. In payment for these exclusive rights Metropolitan Opera receives royalties on records sold, with a guaranteed minimum of $125,000 during the five-year term of the contract. Columbia Records is required to pay the entire cost of each performance of an opera which it records. Metropolitan Opera has reserved to itself the right to approve all phonograph records of its performances before they may be offered for sale to the public.

Pursuant to this contract Metropolitan Opera's performances of three operas have been recorded and are now being offered for sale and sold. Columbia Records has incurred very substantial expenses in making these recordings and in preparing for the recording of additional operas, and it has extensively advertised the records and its exclusive right to record Metropolitan Opera performances.

Metropolitan Opera has sold the exclusive right to broadcast its opera performances during the 1949-50 season to American Broadcasting, for which Metropolitan Opera receives $100,000. Under this contract American Broadcasting is prohibited from making recordings of such performances except for certain limited purposes related to broadcasting. Negotiations for a similar contract for the 1950-51 and 1951-52 opera seasons are in progress. Under the contract for the 1949-50 season, American Broadcasting broadcast Metropolitan Opera performances of eighteen operas between November 26, 1949, and March 25, 1950.

Since November 26, 1949, the defendants have recorded these broadcast performances of Metropolitan Opera and have used their master recordings to make phonograph records of Metropolitan Opera performances. The defendants have advertised and sold these records as records of broadcast Metropolitan Opera performances. By reason of this publicity and the reputation of Metropolitan Opera, these records have aroused wide interest. Since the defendants, unlike Columbia Records, pay no part of the cost of the performance of the operas and are held to no standard of artistic or technical excellence, they incur only the very small cost of recording these performances "off the air." The quality of their recordings is inferior to that of Columbia Records and is so low that Metropolitan Opera would not have approved the sale and release of such records to the general public. By reason of their negligible costs, defendants are able in competition with Columbia Records to sell their records at considerably less than those of the latter, with a consequent loss of revenue to Columbia Records and Metropolitan Opera....

The defendants urge that the complaints fail to state a cause of action in that they do not allege the defendants are "palming off" their recordings as those of plaintiffs, or that plaintiffs are in competition with the defendants. They further urge that plaintiffs have no property right in the broadcast performances and that the defendants are therefore free to record these performances and sell their recordings.

The defendants' cross-motion attacking the complaints must necessarily be considered first.

In passing upon the question of the sufficiency of a complaint alleging unfair competition it is helpful to bear in mind the origin and evolution of this branch of law. It originated in the conscience, justice and equity of common-law judges. It developed within the framework of a society dedicated to freest competition, to deal with business malpractices offensive to the ethics of that society. The theoretic basis is obscure, but the birth and growth of this branch of law is clear. It is an outstanding example of the law's capacity for growth in response to the ethical as well as the economic needs of society. As a result of this background the legal concept of unfair competition has evolved as a broad and flexible doctrine with a capacity for further growth to meet changing conditions. There is no complete list of the activities which constitute unfair competition.

The statement of a sufficient cause of action in unfair competition, in the last analysis, is therefore dependent more upon the facts set forth and less upon technical requirements than in most causes of action. This may best be illustrated by a consideration of the objections raised by the defendants.

The defendants contend that no cause of action is stated due to the absence of an allegation of "palming off." One of the inferences which may fairly be drawn from the allegations of the complaint and the prayers for relief is that the activities of the defendants appropriate and trade on the name and reputation of Metropolitan Opera and tend to mislead the public into believing the recordings are made with the co-operation of Metropolitan Opera and under its supervision. However, even in the absence of such an inference the failure to allege "palming off" would not be a fatal defect. The early cases of unfair competition in which relief was granted were cases involving "palming off" — that is, the fraudulent representation of the goods of the seller as those of another. The early decisions condemning this practice were based on the two wrongs inflicted thereby: (1) The deceit and fraud on the public; and (2) the misappropriation to one person of the benefit of a name, reputation or business good will belonging to another. [Citations omitted.]

With the passage of those simple and halcyon days when the chief business malpractice was "palming off" and with the development of more complex business relationships and, unfortunately, malpractices, many courts, including the courts of this state, extended the doctrine of unfair competition beyond the cases of "palming off." The extension resulted in the granting of relief in cases where there was no fraud on the public, but only a misappropriation for the commercial advantage of one person of a benefit or "property right" belonging to another....

The defendants also raise the objection that the complaint does not include an allegation that the parties are actual competitors. This objection is rendered untenable by the intervention of Columbia Records. However, again, the existence of actual competition between the parties is no longer a prerequuisite....

The modern view as to the law of unfair competition does not rest solely on the ground of direct competitive injury, but on the broader principle that property rights of commercial value are to be and will be protected from any form of unfair invasion or infringement and from any form of commercial immorality, and a court of equity will penetrate and restrain every guise resorted to by the wrongdoer. The courts have thus recognized that in the complex pattern of modern business relationships, persons in theoretically non-competitive fields may, by unethical business practices, inflict as severe and reprehensible injuries upon others as can direct competitors. That defendants' piratical conduct and practices have injured and will continue to injure plaintiff admits of no serious challenge, and possible money damages furnishes no adequate remedy. That such practices constitute unfair competition both with Metropolitan Opera and Columbia Records is made abundantly clear by the record. Plaintiff Metropolitan Opera derives income from the performance of its operatic productions in the presence of an audience, from the broadcasting of those productions over the radio, and from the licensing to Columbia Records of the exclusive privilege of making and selling records of its own performances. Columbia Records derives income from the sale of the records which it makes pursuant to the license granted to it by Metropolitan Opera. Without any payment to Metropolitan Opera for the benefit of its extremely expensive performances, and without any cost comparable to that incurred by Columbia Records in making its records, defendants offer to the public recordings of Metropolitan Opera's broadcast performances. This constitutes unfair competition. *International News Service v. Associated Press,* 248 U.S. 215.

The New York courts have applied the rule in the International News Service case in such a wide variety of circumstances as to leave no doubt of their recognition that the effort to profit from the labor, skill, expenditures, name and reputation of others which appears in this case constitutes unfair competition which will be enjoined....

... The fostering and encouragement of fine performances of grand opera, and their preservation and dissemination to wide audiences by radio and recordings are in the public interest. The Metropolitan Opera, over a period of sixty years, has developed one of the finest, if not the finest, opera companies available to Americans. Through the media of recordings and broadcasts, an avenue of culture has been opened to vast numbers of Americans who have been able to enjoy the fruits of this great enterprise. To many, it is the only available source of grand opera. To refuse to the groups who expend time, effort, money and great skill in producing these artistic performances the protection of giving them a "property right" in the resulting artistic creation would be contrary to existing law, inequitable, and repugnant to the public interest. To hold that the broadcasts of these performances, making them available to a wider audience of Americans, deprives the Metropolitan Opera of all of its rights in this production and abandons the production to anyone to appropriate and exploit commercially, would indeed discourage the broadcasting of such operas and penalize not only the Metropolitan Opera but the public which now benefits from these broadcasts. Equity will not bear witness to such a travesty of justice; it will not countenance a state of moral and intellectual impotency. Equity will consider the interests of all parties coming within the arena of the dispute and admeasure the conflict in the scales of conscience and on the premise of honest commercial intercourse.

The complaints can also be sustained as stating a cause of action for unjustifiable interference with contractual rights of the plaintiffs. With full knowledge of the contract by which Metropolitan Opera has granted to Columbia Records the exclusive privilege of recording Metropolitan operas, the defendants have assumed the exercise of that privilege. Their action not only constitutes an attempt to secure the very benefit which the contract grants to Columbia Records, but also an interference with contractual relations which will be enjoined by a court of equity....

Defendants' cross-motion is therefore denied.

We come next to the original motion: The motion by the plaintiffs for a preliminary injunction.... Unless the defendants are enjoined before the season starts, Metropolitan Opera is likely to lose the major part of its royalties from the sale of the authorized records, and Columbia Records will similarly suffer a serious loss.

The continuance of defendants' activities during this coming season is also likely to cause to the Metropolitan Opera an irreparable harm far beyond even the damage to the present contracts for its broadcasting and recording rights. The release and sale of recordings of Metropolitan Opera performances unapproved as to quality and unlimited as to amount, yet clearly designated or known to be performances of Metropolitan Opera, may injure the reputation Metropolitan Opera has built up by so much travail and may seriously damage or glut the market for its works....

The conclusion here reached is not an onslaught on the currents of competition; it does not impose shackles on the arteries of enterprise. It simply quarantines business conduct which is abhorrent to good conscience and the most elementary principles of law and equity....

Carpenter v. United States, 484 U.S. 19 (1987). Petitioners Felis and Winans were convicted of violating several federal statutes, among them the mail and wire fraud statutes, 18 U.S.C. §§ 1341, 1343, and Carpenter was convicted of aiding and abetting. Those statutes provide that "[w]hoever, having devised or intending to devise any scheme or artifice to defraud, or for obtaining money or property by means of false or fraudulent pretenses, representations, or promises," uses (respectively) either the mails or wire, radio or television communication in interstate commerce, shall be fined or imprisoned or both. Winans, a reporter for the Wall Street Journal, was in 1982 one of two writers of a daily column, "Heard on the Street," which gave information and evaluations regarding specific stocks; the column was based largely on interviews of corporate executives. In the words of the Supreme Court: "Because of the 'Heard' column's perceived quality and integrity, it had the potential of affecting the price of the stocks which it examined." Under the official policy and practice at the Journal, known to Winans, information gained by Journal writers in the course of employment was to be the Journal's confidential information and was not to be revealed in advance of publication.

Despite this rule, Winans entered into a scheme in October 1983 in which he gave advance information as to the timing and contents of his "Heard" column to certain individuals connected with the Kidder Peabody brokerage firm in New York City. These individuals bought and sold stock on the basis of the probable impact of the column upon the market, and shared the profits. The contents of the column were not in any way altered to further the scheme. Over a four-month period, the brokers made a net profit of about $690,000 from prepublication trades based on information given by Winans about the contents of some twenty-seven "Heard" columns. The scheme was uncovered and criminal prosecutions and convictions followed.

The district court found that Winans had violated his duty of confidentiality to the Wall Street Journal, and had violated the mail and wire fraud statutes by appropriating confidential information. The court of appeals agreed that he had fraudulently misappropriated "property" within the statutes, in a manner that harmed the Journal. The Supreme Court affirmed, rejecting the petitioners' contentions that they did not obtain any "money or property" from the Journal and that the Journal's interest in prepublication confidentiality was no more than an "intangible consideration" beyond the reach of the statutes. The pertinent passages from the Court's opinion follow.

> The Journal, as Winans' employer, was defrauded of much more than its contractual right to his honest and faithful service, an interest too ethereal in itself to fall within the protection of the mail fraud statute, which "had its origin in the desire to protect individual property rights."
> [*McNally v. U.S.*, 483 U.S. __, __ n.8, 107 S. Ct. 2875, 97 L. Ed. 2d 292

(1987).] Here, the object of the scheme was to take the Journal's confidential business information — the publication schedule and contents of the "Heard" column — and its intangible nature does not make it any less "property" protected by the mail and wire fraud statutes. *McNally* did not limit the scope of § 1341 to tangible as distinguished from intangible property rights.

Both courts below expressly referred to the Journal's interest in the confidentiality of the contents and timing of the "Heard" column as a property right, 791 F.2d, at 1034-1035; 612 F. Supp., at 846, and we agree with that conclusion. Confidential business information has long been recognized as property. See *Ruckelshaus v. Monsanto Co.,* 467 U.S. 986, 1001-1004, 104 S. Ct. 2862, 2874, 81 L. Ed. 2d 815 (1984); *Dirks v. SEC,* 463 U.S. 646, 653, n.10, 103 S. Ct. 3255, 3260, n.10, 77 L. Ed. 2d 911 (1983); *Board of Trade of Chicago v. Christie Grain & Stock Co.,* 198 U.S. 236, 250-251, 25 S. Ct. 637, 639-40, 49 L. Ed. 1031 (1905); cf. 5 U.S.C. § 552(b)(4). "Confidential information acquired or compiled by a corporation in the course and conduct of its business is a species of property to which the corporation has the exclusive right and benefit, and which a court of equity will protect through the injunctive process or other appropriate remedy." 3 W. Fletcher, Cyclopedia of Law of Private Corporations § 857.1, p. 260 (rev. ed. 1986) (footnote omitted). The Journal had a property right in keeping confidential and making exclusive use, prior to publication, of the schedule and contents of the "Heard" columns. *Christie Grain, supra.* As the Court has observed before:

> "[N]ews matter, however little susceptible of ownership or dominion in the absolute sense, is stock in trade, to be gathered at the cost of enterprise, organization, skill, labor, and money, and to be distributed and sold to those who will pay money for it, as for any other merchandise." *International News Service v. Associated Press,* 248 U.S. 215, 236, 39 S. Ct. 68, 71, 63 L. Ed. 211 (1918).

Petitioners' arguments that they did not interfere with the Journal's use of the information or did not publicize it and deprive the Journal of the first public use of it, see Reply Brief for Petitioners 6, miss the point. The confidential information was generated from the business and the business had a right to decide how to use it prior to disclosing it to the public. Petitioners cannot successfully contend based on *Associated Press* that a scheme to defraud requires a monetary loss, such as giving the information to a competitor; it is sufficient that the Journal has been deprived of its right to exclusive use of the information, for exclusivity is an important aspect of confidential business information and most private property for that matter.

QUESTIONS

1. To what body of law did the Supreme Court turn in finding a "property right" in the Wall Street Journal's confidential prepublication business information?

2. Reflect on the copyright cases studied earlier, *Harper & Row v. Nation Enters.* and *Salinger v. Random House,* in light of the Supreme Court decision in *Carpenter v. United States.* Under what circumstances, if any, may an author who without authorization discloses unpublished or prepublication material written by others escape criminal liability?

B. IDEA PROTECTION: BREACH OF CONTRACT OR CONFIDENTIAL RELATIONSHIP

BLAUSTEIN v. BURTON

8 Cal. App. 3d 161, 88 Cal. Rptr. 319 (Dist. Ct. App. 1970)

[Plaintiff Blaustein was, in 1964, an experienced producer of motion pictures. In that year, he conceived an idea consisting of a number of elements: the starring of Richard Burton and Elizabeth Taylor (Mrs. Burton) in a motion picture based on Shakespeare's *The Taming of the Shrew,* to be directed by Franco Zeffirelli and filmed in Italy; the elimination of the so-called "frame" of the Shakespeare play, i.e., the play-within-a-play device, and beginning the film with the main body of the story; and the inclusion in the film of two key scenes (the wedding scene and the wedding-night scene) which in the Shakespeare play occur offstage and are merely described by a character on stage. Blaustein disclosed his idea first to Richard Burton's agent and then to the Burtons' Los Angeles attorney; the latter, through the Burtons' general counsel in New York and through their appointments secretary, arranged a meeting in June 1964 between Blaustein and the Burtons. Blaustein explained in full his idea to them, and Mr. Burton (speaking on behalf of his wife as well) expressed his enthusiasm for the idea, for Mr. Zeffirelli as director, and for Mr. Blaustein's involvement as producer. In March 1965, after a meeting in Ireland in which *The Taming of the Shrew* film project was discussed, an attorney for the Burtons telephoned Blaustein and informed him that he "might not be the producer if the film is ever made," but that "under any conditions ... there would be a reward for your contribution to the project." Mr. Blaustein was informed soon after that the Burtons and Zeffirelli acknowledged that Blaustein was the source of the idea for the motion picture. The motion picture was ultimately produced and exhibited beginning in or about March 1967, without Mr. Blaustein's participation. It was financed and distributed by Columbia Pictures Corporation. It starred the Burtons, was directed by Zeffirelli, was filmed in Italy, eliminated the play-within-a-play device, and included the two key scenes which in the play took place offstage. Blaustein received no money from the Burtons, and he was accorded no screen or advertising credit.

[Blaustein sued the Burtons for breach of express and implied-in-fact contracts. The trial court granted the defendants' motion for summary judgment, but the appellate court reversed.]

The rights of an idea discloser to recover damages from an idea recipient under an express or implied contract to pay for the idea in event the idea recipient uses such idea after disclosure is discussed in *Desny v. Wilder*, 46 Cal. 2d 715, 731-739 [299 P.2d 257], as follows: ...

An idea is usually not regarded as property, because all sentient beings may conceive and evolve ideas throughout the gamut of their powers of cerebration and because our concept of property implies something which may be owned and possessed to the exclusion of all other persons.... "The doctrine that an author has a property right in his ideas and is entitled to demand for them the same protection which the law accords to the proprietor of personal property generally finds no recognition either in the common law or in the statutes of any civilized country." (34 Am. Jur. 402-403, § 5; 18 C.J.S. 143, § 10e: cf. *Golding v. R.K.O. Pictures, Inc.* (1950), 35 Cal. 2d 690, 693-697, 702, 711-712 [221 P.2d 95]; *Burtis v. Universal Pictures Co., Inc.* (1953), 40 Cal. 2d 823, 831 [256 P.2d 933]; *Kurlan v. Columbia Broadcasting System* (1953), 40 Cal. 2d 799 [256 P.2d 962].) Whether the theory upon which this court sustained recovery in the *Golding* case may properly be classed as a property rights theory is not clear (see pp. 694-695 of 35 Cal. 2d and pp. 831, 836-837 of 40 Cal. 2d) but it is clear that California does not now accord individual property type protection to abstract ideas. (*Weitzenkorn v. Lesser* (1953), 40 Cal. 2d 778, 788-789 [256 P.2d 947].) This accords with the general weight of authority. (See generally, Nimmer, "*The Law of Ideas*," (1954) 27 So. Cal. L. Rev. 120 et seq. and cases cited.) "There may be literary property in a particular combination of ideas [and this must presuppose an expression thereof] or in the form in which ideas are embodied. There can be none in the ideas." *(Fendler v. Morosco* (1930) 253 N.Y. 281, 287 [171 N.E. 56, 58].) Neither common law nor statutory copyright extends protection to an idea as such. "[O]nly in the 'expression' of a copyrighted work does any monopoly inhere; the 'theme,' the 'plot,' the 'ideas' may always be freely borrowed." *(Dellar v. Samuel Goldwyn, Inc.* (1945, 2d C.C.A.), 150 F.2d 612.)

The principles above stated do not, however, lead to the conclusion that ideas cannot be a subject of contract. As Mr. Justice Traynor stated in his dissenting opinion in *Stanley v. Columbia Broadcasting System* (1950), *supra*, 35 Cal. 2d 653, 674 [221 P.2d 73, 23 A.L.R.2d 216]: "The policy that precludes protection of an abstract idea by copyright does not prevent its protection by contract. Even though an idea is not property subject to exclusive ownership, its disclosure may be of substantial benefit to the person to whom it is disclosed. That disclosure may therefore be consideration for a promise to pay .... Even though the idea disclosed may be 'widely known and generally understood' [citation], it may be protected by an express contract providing that it will be paid for regardless of its lack of novelty." (*Cf. Brunner v. Stix, Baer & Fuller Co.* (1944), 352 Mo. 1225 [181 S.W.2d 643, 646]; *Schonwald v. F. Burkart Mfg. Co.* (1947), 356 Mo. 435 [202 S.W.2d 7].) Amici supporting plaintiff add, "If a studio wishes to have an idea disclosed to it and finds that idea of sufficient value to make use of it, it is difficult to see how any hardship is involved in requiring payment of the reasonable value of the material submitted." The principles enunciated in the above quotation from Justice Traynor's dissent are accepted as the law of California (*Weitzenkorn v. Lesser* (1953), *supra,* 40 Cal. 2d 778, 791-792) and we have no quarrel with amici's postulation. This case, however, remains to be resolved.

The lawyer or doctor who applies specialized knowledge to a state of facts and gives advice for a fee is selling and conveying an idea. In doing that he is rendering a service. The lawyer and doctor have no property rights in their ideas, as such, but they do not ordinarily convey them without solicitation by client or patient. Usually the parties will expressly contract for the performance of and payment for such services, but, in the absence of an express contract, when the service is requested and rendered, the law does not hesitate to infer or imply a promise to compensate for it. (See *Buck v. City of Eureka* (1899), 124 Cal. 61, 66 [56 P. 612]; *Zumwalt v. Schwarz* (1931), 112 Cal. App. 734, 736 [297 P. 608]; *People's Nat. Bank v. Geisthardt* (1898), 55 Neb. 232, 237-238 [75 N.W. 582]; 6 Cal. Jur. 2d 378, § 181; 5 Am. Jur. 351, § 153; 41 Am. Jur. 256, § 142; 7 C.J.S. 1078, § 190(b); 70 C.J.S. 1023, § 68; see also *Long v. Rumsey* (1938), 12 Cal. 2d 334, 341-342 [84 P.2d 146].) In other words the recovery may be based on contract either express or implied. The person who can and does convey a valuable idea to a producer who commercially solicits the service or who voluntarily accepts it knowing that it is tendered for a price should likewise be entitled to recover....

An eminent writer says that "The elements requisite for an informal contract ... are identical whether they are expressly stated or implied in fact," citing e.g., *Lombard v. Rahilly* (1914), 127 Minn. 449 [149 N.W. 950], holding "A 'contract implied in fact' requires a meeting of the minds, an agreement, just as much as an 'express contract'; the difference between the two being largely in the character of the evidence by which they are established"; see also *Silva v. Providence Hospital of Oakland* (1939) 14 Cal. 2d 762, 773 [97 P.2d 798]. (Williston on Contracts, rev. ed., vol. 1, p. 8.) The same author describes quasi contracts by declaring that "as quasi contractual obligations are imposed by the law for the purpose of bringing about justice without reference to the intention of the parties, the only apparent restriction upon the power of the law to create such obligations is that they must be of such a sort as would have been appropriately enforced under common-law procedure by a contractual action. Indeed even this limitation is too narrow, for a bill in equity or a libel in admiralty might be the appropriate means of enforcing some quasi contractual obligations. As the law may impose any obligations that justice requires, the only limit in the last analysis to the category of quasi contracts is that the obligation in question more closely resembles those created by contract than those created by tort. On the other hand, a true contract cannot exist, however desirable it might be to have one, unless there is a manifestation of assent to the making of a promise. Furthermore, the measure of damages appropriate to contractual obligations differs from that applicable to quasi contracts.... It is also true that quasi contractual obligations are not so universally based on unjust enrichment or benefit as is sometimes supposed. There are many cases where the law enforces in a contractual action a duty to restore the plaintiff to a former status — not merely to surrender the benefit which the defendant has received."

....

From what has been shown respecting the law of ideas and of contracts we conclude that conveyance of an idea can constitute valuable consideration and can be bargained for before it is disclosed to the proposed purchaser, but once it is conveyed, i.e., disclosed to him and he has grasped it, it is henceforth his own and he may work with it and use it as he sees fit. In the field of entertainment the producer may properly and validly agree that he will pay for the service of conveying to him ideas which are valuable and which he can put to profitable use. Furthermore, where an idea has been conveyed with the expectation by the purveyor that compensation will be paid if the idea is used, there is no reason why the producer who has been the beneficiary of the conveyance of such an idea, and who finds it valuable and is profiting by it, may not then for the first time, although he is not at that time under any legal obligation so to do, promise to pay a reasonable compensation for that idea — that is, for the past service of furnishing it to him — and thus create a valid obligation.

... But, assuming legality of consideration, the idea purveyor cannot prevail in an action to recover compensation for an abstract idea unless (a) before or after disclosure he has obtained an express promise to pay, or (b) the circumstances preceding and attending disclosure, together with the conduct of the offeree acting with knowledge of the circumstances, show a promise of the type usually referred to as "implied" or "implied-in-fact." (See *Weitzenkorn v. Lesser* (1953), *supra,* 40 Cal. 2d 778, 794-795; *Elfenbein v. Luckenbach Terminals* (1933), 111 N.J.L. 67 [166 A. 91, 93].) That is, if the idea purveyor has clearly conditioned his offer to convey the idea upon an obligation to pay for it if it is used by the offeree and the offeree, knowing the condition before he knows the idea, voluntarily accepts its disclosure (necessarily on the specified basis) and finds it valuable and uses it, the law will either apply the objective test (discussed, *supra,* pp. 801-802) and hold that the parties have made an express (sometimes called implied-in-fact) contract, or under those circumstances, as some writers view it, the law itself, to prevent fraud and unjust enrichment, will imply a promise to compensate.

Such inferred or implied promise, if it is to be found at all, must be based on circumstances which were known to the producer at and preceding the time of disclosure of the idea to him and he must voluntarily accept the disclosure, knowing the conditions on which it is tendered. Section 1584 of the Civil Code ("[T]he acceptance of the consideration offered with a proposal, is an acceptance of the proposal") can have no application unless the offeree has an opportunity to reject the consideration — the proffered conveyance of the idea — before it is conveyed. Unless the offeree has opportunity to reject he cannot be said to accept. (Cf. *People v. Forbath* (1935), 5 Cal. App. 2d Supp. 767, 769-770 [42 P.2d 108]; *County of Ventura v. Southern Calif. Edison Co.* (1948), 85 Cal. App. 2d 529, 532 [193 P.2d 512]; *Krum v. Malloy* (1943), 22 Cal. 2d 132, 135

[137 P.2d 18].) The idea man who blurts out his idea without having first made his bargain has no one but himself to blame for the loss of his bargaining power. The law will not in any event, from demands stated subsequent to the unconditioned disclosure of an abstract idea, imply a promise to pay for the idea, for its use, or for its previous disclosure. The law will not imply a promise to pay for an idea from the mere facts that the idea has been conveyed, is valuable, and has been used for profit; this is true even though the conveyance has been made with the hope or expectation that some obligation will ensue. So, if the plaintiff here is claiming only for the conveyance of the idea of making a dramatic production out of the life of Floyd Collins he must fail unless in conformity with the above stated rules he can establish a contract to pay.

(*Desny v. Wilder, supra,* 46 Cal. 2d 715, 731-739.)

It is held that "... if a producer obligates himself to pay for the disclosure of an idea, whether it is for protectible or unprotectible material, in return for a disclosure thereof he should be compelled to hold to his promise. There is nothing unreasonable in the assumption that a producer would obligate himself to pay for the disclosure of an idea which he would otherwise be legally free to use, but which in fact, he would be unable to use but for the disclosure.

"The producer and the writer should be free to make any contract they desire to make with reference to the buying of the ideas of the writer; the fact that the producer may later determine, with a little thinking, that he could have had the same ideas and could thereby have saved considerable money for himself, is no defense against the claim of the writer. This is so even though the material to be purchased is abstract and unprotected material." (*Chandler v. Roach,* 156 Cal. App. 2d 435, 441-442 [319 P.2d 776].) An idea which can be the subject matter of a contract need not be novel or concrete. (*Donahue v. Ziv Television Programs, Inc.,* 245 Cal. App. 2d 593, 600 [54 Cal. Rptr. 130]; *Minniear v. Tors,* 266 Cal. App. 2d 495, 502 [72 Cal. Rptr. 287].)

. . . .

We are of the opinion that appellant's idea of the filming of Shakespeare's play "The Taming of the Shrew" is one which may be protected by contract.

Express or implied contracts both are based upon the intention of the parties and are distinguishable only in the manifestation of assent. The making of an agreement may be inferred by proof of conduct as well as by proof of the use of words. (12 Cal. Jur. 2d, Contracts, § 4, p. 186.) Whether or not the appellant and respondents here, by their oral declarations and conduct, as shown by the depositions and affidavits, entered into a contract whereby respondents agreed to compensate appellant in the event respondents used appellant's idea, is a question of fact which may not be properly resolved in a summary judgment proceeding, but must be resolved upon a trial of the issue. (Cf. *Silva v. Providence Hospital of Oakland,* 14 Cal. 2d 762, 774 [97 P.2d 798].) Even where a question of interpretation of contractual provisions is involved on a motion for summary judgment, it is settled that, if the opposing interpretations are both reasonable, a question of fact is raised which precludes summary judgment....

Confidential Relationship. Respondents urge that the record is devoid of any evidence tending to establish the fact that they breached a duty of confidence owed to appellant.

Appellant, in his affidavit, stated: "Because I knew Mr. French to be a highly reputable agent, had had prior dealings with him, had the same firm of attorneys as the Burtons and had been the recipient of an invitation, constantly renewed, to disclose my ideas and render services on the project, I reposed trust and confidence in the Burtons and their representatives and expected that my ideas would be kept in confidence by them. I did not expect or intend that defendants would go forward with production of 'Shrew' and make use of my ideas without my participation."

Under the rules governing the granting of a summary judgment, the foregoing declaration on the part of appellant, made in opposition to the motion for summary judgment, is sufficient to raise a triable issue of fact as to whether the disclosure of his idea to respondents was made in confidence, and was accepted by respondents upon the understanding that they would not use it without the consent of appellant. (Cf. *Thompson v. California Brewing Co.,* 150 Cal. App. 2d 469, 474 [310 P.2d 436].)

The judgment is reversed.

Davies v. Krasna, 54 Cal. Rptr. 37 (Cal. Ct. App. 1966). Davies, an author, alleged that he had submitted a script for a play to defendant producer, with the understanding that if the defendant used the script or its ideas, the plaintiff would be compensated. Defendant, however, wrote his own script, which allegedly copied the idea, central theme, and dramatic core of the plaintiff's work. Davies introduced evidence that, in the motion picture industry, "when stories and their central themes and dramatic cores were submitted to producers, there was an understanding and agreement that such submission was for a limited and confidential purpose and that use would not be made thereof unless there was appropriate payment by the producer." The court of appeals concluded that the plaintiff had raised an issue of fact as to whether Krasna breached a duty of confidence when he used Davies' idea for personal purposes. (It also found, however, that the judgment against the plaintiff on the implied-contract claim should be affirmed.)

> There appears to be no clear precedent by means of which the theory of breach of confidence can be readily applied to the evidence introduced by the plaintiff at the first trial. Some guidance, however, is found in the reasoning of Dean Havighurst: "Use by one to whom an idea has been disclosed in confidence is the usual basis of liability in the trade secret cases. It has perhaps less significance for the kinds of ideas with which we are here concerned. But breach of confidence is a possible theory of recovery in the case of unauthorized use of ideas other than trade secrets.... It must be made clear that a confidential disclosure cannot be predicated merely upon the statement of the originator that he is submitting his idea in confidence. Either there must be a preexisting relation of trust and

confidence, such as that of employer and employee, or the person to whom disclosure is made must agree to hold the idea in confidence and at least impliedly agree not to use it or disclose it to others. In this latter aspect the confidence is based upon contract, although it will be noted that it is not a contract to pay but rather a contract not to use." (Havighurst, *The Right to Compensation for an Idea* (1954) 49 Nw. U.L. Rev. 295, 311-312.)

Another legal writer has expressed his views as follows: "The courts will sometimes protect a plaintiff's idea on the theory of breach of confidential relationship. Such protection is akin to the traditional protection which equity will afford to a trade secret. However, an idea may not be wholly secret but only qualifiedly so and still command protection. The cases are by no means clear as to when a confidential relationship exists so as to render a defendant liable if he uses plaintiff's idea. Traditionally such a relationship exists between an employer and an employee with respect to secret ideas and processes. However, even where an employer-employee relationship does not exist courts will tend to find a confidential relationship when the parties deal on unequal terms resulting in one party reposing trust and confidence in the other's good faith.... Some courts regard a confidential relationship action as being based upon an express or implied agreement of the defendant to treat the idea disclosed in confidence. Certainly it is true that if a defendant expressly or impliedly agrees to treat plaintiff's idea in confidence, and then proceeds publicly to disclose the idea, he has acted in breach of contract. However, other courts go still further and regard the unauthorized disclosure of an idea submitted in confidence as justifying a remedy in equity entirely apart from any contract theory. Under this view a breach of confidential relationship action is usually equated to an action in quasi contract for unjust enrichment, even if under the given facts an express or an implied contract might also be upheld.... But the determination of whether a confidential relationship action sounds in contract or equity may be most significant with respect to the nature of the ideas which will be protected. Thus, if it is held that a relationship is confidential because of an express or implied agreement by the parties (and this includes an employment relationship) then there is no reason why a completely abstract idea should not be protected...." (Nimmer, *The Law of Ideas* (1954) 27 So. Cal. L. Rev. 119, 138-140.)...

In the present case the evidence was sufficient to support an inference that Mr. Davies, through his agent, submitted his idea to Jerry Wald with the reasonable expectation that he would be paid if his idea was used. The evidence was also sufficient to support the further inference that Mr. Wald, acting for Wald-Krasna Productions, Inc., accepted the submission of the idea with full awareness of the expectation of such payment in the event of use thereof. Consequently, there was a sufficient basis for a determination of the existence of a contract implied in fact for compensation upon use in accordance with Mr. Davies' expectation.

QUESTIONS

1. What are the elements of the following claims justifying idea protection? Which theories tend to favor the discloser of the idea and which tend to favor the recipient? Is it necessary, under any of these theories, that the idea disclosed be "concrete" or "novel"? What is the proper measure of liability under each theory?

    (a) Breach of express contract.
    (b) Breach of implied-in-fact contract.
    (c) Breach of implied-in-law contract.
    (d) Breach of confidential relationship.
    (e) Breach of fiduciary relationship.

2. Recall the observation of Justice Brandeis, dissenting in the *International News Service* case, *supra,* that "[t]he general rule of law is, that the noblest of human productions — knowledge, truths ascertained, conceptions, and ideas — become, after voluntary communication to others, free as the air to common use." Are the theories mentioned above, and the decided cases, consistent with this proposition?

3. Author has submitted a screen "treatment" to Studio. Author's three-page treatment outlines his ideas for a motion picture: an African prince comes to the U.S., loses his money and his title, and is reduced to working in a fast-food restaurant, where he finds true love. Author's contract with Studio provides that should Studio produce a motion picture "based on" Author's treatment, Author will receive a share of the profits. After a long series of meetings between Author and Studio, Studio informs Author that it will not follow through on his project. However, three years later, Studio releases a film whose plot includes all the treatment's elements mentioned above, plus many new elements. Author sues Studio for breach of contract. What result? *See Buchwald v. Paramount Pictures Corp.,* 13 U.S.P.Q.2d 1497 (Cal. Super. Ct. L.A. Cty. 1990).

C. RIGHT OF PUBLICITY

MARTIN LUTHER KING, JR., CENTER FOR SOCIAL CHANGE, INC. v. AMERICAN HERITAGE PRODUCTS, INC.

250 Ga. 135, 296 S.E.2d 697 (1982)

[The principal plaintiffs in this case are Coretta Scott King, as administratrix of the estate of Dr. Martin Luther King, and the Martin Luther King, Jr., Center for Social Change, a non-profit corporation that seeks to promote the ideals of Dr. King. The defendant company was engaged in the unauthorized manufacture and sale of plastic busts of Dr. King; the busts were advertised in magazines and newspapers, and were sold for $29.95. The defendant's efforts to secure the endorsement and participation of the plaintiff Center in marketing the bust were rejected. So too were moneys that were tendered by the defendant to the Center; the defendant had set aside 90 cents for the Center from the proceeds of each bust sold, and its advertising made reference to such a contribution. When the plaintiffs commenced their action for a preliminary injunction in a federal district court, more than 200 busts had already been sold. Although the court enjoined the use of the Center's name in the marketing of the busts, as well as copyright infringement by the defendant of certain speeches of Dr. King, it denied an injunction against the manufacture and sale of the busts. The plaintiffs appealed the partial denial of the injunction, and the Court of Appeals for the Eleventh Circuit certified the following questions to the state supreme court:]

(1) Is the "right of publicity" recognized in Georgia as a right distinct from the right of privacy?

(2) If the answer to question (1) is affirmative, does the "right to publicity" survive the death of its owner? Specifically, is the right inheritable and devisable?

(3) If the answer to question (2) is also affirmative, must the owner have commercially exploited the right before it can survive his death?

(4) Assuming the affirmative answers to questions (1), (2) and (3), what is the guideline to be followed in defining commercial exploitation and what are the evidentiary prerequisites to a showing of commercial exploitation?

The right of publicity may be defined as a celebrity's right to the exclusive use of his or her name and likeness. *Price v. Hal Roach Studios, Inc.,* 400 F. Supp. 836, 843 (S.D.N.Y. 1975); *Estate of Presley v. Russen,* 513 F. Supp. 1339, 1353 (D.N.J. 1981), and cases cited. The right is most often asserted by or on behalf of professional athletes, comedians, actors and actresses, and other entertainers. This case involves none of those occupations. As is known to all, from 1955 until he was assassinated on April 4, 1968, Dr. King, a Baptist minister by profession, was the foremost leader of the civil rights movement in the United States. He was awarded the Nobel Prize for Peace in 1964. Although not a public official, Dr. King was a public figure, and we deal in this opinion with public figures who are neither public officials nor entertainers. Within this framework, we turn to the questions posed.

1. Is the "right of publicity" recognized in Georgia as a right distinct from the right of privacy?

Georgia has long recognized the right of privacy. Following denial of the existence of the right of privacy in a controversial decision by the New York Court of Appeals in *Roberson v. Rochester Folding-Box Co.,* 171 N.Y. 538, 64 N.E. 442 (1902), the Georgia Supreme Court became the first such court to recognize the right of privacy in *Pavesich v. New England Life Ins. Co.,* 122 Ga. 190, 50 S.E. 68 (1905). See Prosser, Law of Torts, pp. 802-804 (1971).

In *Pavesich v. New England Life Ins. Co., supra,* the picture of an artist was used without his consent in a newspaper advertisement of the insurance company. Analyzing the right of privacy, this court held: "The publication of a picture of a person, without his consent, as a part of an advertisement, for the purpose of exploiting the publisher's business, is a violation of the right of privacy of the person whose picture is reproduced, and entitles him to recover without proof of special damage." 122 Ga. at 191(11), 50 S.E. at 68[11]. If the right to privacy had not been recognized, advertizers could use photographs of private citizens to promote sales and the professional modeling business would not be what it is today.

In the course of its opinion the *Pavesich* court said several things pertinent here. It noted that the commentators on ancient law recognized the right of personal liberty, including the right to exhibit oneself before the public at proper times and places and in a proper manner. As a corollary, the court recognized that the right of personal liberty included the right of a person not to be exhibited before the public, saying: "The right to withdraw from the public gaze at such times as a person may see fit, when his presence in public is not demanded by any rule of law is also embraced within the right of personal liberty. Publicity in one instance and privacy in the other is each guaranteed. If personal liberty embraces the *right of publicity,* it no less embraces the correlative right of privacy; and this is no new idea in Georgia law." 122 Ga. at 196, 50 S.E. at 70. (Emphasis supplied.)

Recognizing the possibility of a conflict between the right of privacy and the freedoms of speech and press, this court said: "There is in the publication of one's picture for advertising purposes not the slightest semblance of an expression of an idea, a thought, or an opinion, within the meaning of the constitutional provision which guarantees to a person the right to publish his sentiments on any subject." 122 Ga. at 219, 50 S.E. at 80. The defendants in the case now before us make no claim under these freedoms and we find no violation thereof.

Observing in dicta that the right of privacy in general does not survive the death of the person whose privacy is invaded, the *Pavesich* court said: "While the right of privacy is personal, and may die with the person, we do not desire to be understood as assenting to the proposition that the relatives of the deceased can not, in a proper case, protect the memory of their kinsman, not only from defamation, but also from an invasion into the affairs of his private life after his death. This question is not now involved, but we do not wish anything said to be understood as committing us in any way to the doctrine that against the consent of relatives the private affairs of a deceased person may be published and his picture or statue exhibited." 122 Ga. at 210, 50 S.E. at 76.

Finding that Pavesich, although an artist, was not recognized as a public figure, the court said: "It is not necessary in this case to hold, nor are we prepared to do so, that the mere fact that a man has become what is called a public character, either by aspiring to public office, or by holding public office, or by exercising a profession which places him before the public, or by engaging in a business which has necessarily a public nature, gives to every one the right to print and circulate his picture." 122 Ga. at 217-218, 50 S.E. at 79-80. Thus, although recognizing the right of privacy, the *Pavesich* court left open the question facing us involving the likeness of a public figure.[3]

---

[3] Following *Pavesich, supra,* this court has continued to recognize the right of privacy. In *Bazemore v. Savannah Hospital,* 171 Ga. 257, 155 S.E. 194 (1930), the court held that the parents of a child born with his heart outside his body, who died following surgery, could maintain a suit for invasion of their privacy against the hospital, a photographer and a newspaper which respectively allowed, photographed and published a nude post mortem picture of the child.

On the other hand, in *Waters v. Fleetwood,* 212 Ga. 161, 91 S.E.2d 344 (1956), it was held that the mother of a 14-year-old murder victim could not recover for invasion of

The "right of publicity" was first recognized in *Haelan Laboratories, Inc. v. Topps Chewing Gum, Inc.*, 202 F.2d 866 (2d Cir. 1953). There plaintiff had acquired by contract the exclusive right to use certain ball players' photographs in connection with the sales of plaintiff's chewing gum. An independent publishing company acquired similar rights from some of the same ball players. Defendant, a chewing gum manufacturer competing with plaintiff and knowing of plaintiff's contracts, acquired the contracts from the publishing company. As to these contracts the court found that the defendant had violated the ball players' "right of publicity" acquired by the plaintiff, saying (at 868):

> We think that, in addition to and independent of that right of privacy (which in New York derives from statute), a man has a right in the publicity value of his photograph, i.e., the right to grant the exclusive privilege of publishing his picture, and that such a grant may validly be made 'in gross,' i.e., without an accompanying transfer of a business or of anything else. Whether it be labelled a 'property' right is immaterial; for here, as often elsewhere, the tag 'property' simply symbolizes the fact that courts enforce a claim which has pecuniary worth.
>
> This right might be called a "right of publicity." For it is common knowledge that many prominent persons (especially actors and ballplayers), far from having their feelings bruised through public exposure of their likenesses, would feel sorely deprived if they no longer received money for authorizing advertisements, popularizing their countenances, displayed in newspapers, magazines, busses, trains and subways. This right of publicity would usually yield them no money unless it could be made the subject of an exclusive grant which barred any other advertiser from using their pictures.

In *Palmer v. Schonhorn Enterprises, Inc.*, 96 N.J. Super. 72, 232 A.2d 458 (1967), Arnold Palmer, Gary Player, Doug Sanders and Jack Nicklaus obtained summary judgment against the manufacturer of a golf game which used the golfers' names and short biographies without their consent. Although written as a right of privacy case, much of what was said is applicable to the right of publicity. In its opinion the court said (232 A.2d at 462):

> It would therefore seem, from a review of the authorities, that although the publication of biographical data of a well-known figure does not per se constitute an invasion of privacy, the use of that same data for the purpose of capitalizing upon the name by using it in connection with a commercial project other than the dissemination of news or articles or biographies does.

---

the mother's privacy from a newspaper which published and sold separately photographs of her daughter's body taken after it was removed from a river. There the court found that publication and reproduction for sale of a photograph incident to a matter of public interest or to a public investigation could not be a violation of anyone's right of privacy. See also *Georgia Gazette Publishing Co. v. Ramsey*, 248 Ga. 528, 284 S.E.2d 386 (1981). For other Georgia cases involving the right of privacy, see *Tanner-Brice Co. v. Sims*, 174 Ga. 13(4), 161 S.E. 819 (1931); *Goodyear Tire & Rubber Co. v. Vandergriff*, 52 Ga. App. 662, 184 S.E. 452 (1935).

The names of plaintiffs have become internationally famous, undoubtedly by reason of talent as well as hard work in perfecting it. This is probably true in the cases of most so-called celebrities, who have attained national or international recognition in a particular field of art, science, business or other extraordinary ability. They may not all desire to capitalize upon their names in the commercial field, beyond or apart from that in which they have reached their known excellence. However, because they presently do not should not be justification for others to do so because of the void. They may desire to do it later .... It is unfair that one should be permitted to commercialize or exploit or capitalize upon another's name, reputation or accomplishments merely because the owner's accomplishments have been highly publicized.

In *Haelan Laboratories, supra,* the court was concerned with whether a celebrity has the right to the exclusive use of his or her name and likeness. In *Palmer, supra,* the court was concerned with whether a person using the celebrity's name for the user's commercial benefit has the right to do so without authorization. At this point it should be emphasized that we deal here with the unauthorized use of a person's name and likeness for the commercial benefit of the user, not with a city's use of a celebrity's name to denominate a street or school.

The right to publicity is not absolute. In *Hicks v. Casablanca Records,* 464 F. Supp. 426 (S.D.N.Y. 1978), the court held that a fictional novel and movie concerning an unexplained eleven-day disappearance by Agatha Christie, author of numerous mystery novels, were permissible under the first amendment. On the other hand, in *Zacchini v. Scripps-Howard Broadcasting Co.,* 433 U.S. 562 (1977), a television station broadcast on its news program plaintiff's 15-second "human cannonball" flight filmed at a local fair. The Supreme Court held that freedom of the press does not authorize the media to broadcast a performer's entire act without his consent, just as the media could not televise a stage play, prize fight or baseball game without consent. Quoting from Kalven, *Privacy in Tort Law — Were Warren and Brandeis Wrong?,* 31 Law & Contemp. Prob. 326, 332 (1966), the Court said (433 U.S. at 576): "The rationale for [protecting the right of publicity] is the straight-forward one of preventing unjust enrichment by the theft of good will. No social purpose is served by having the defendant get free some aspect of the plaintiff that would have market value and for which he would normally pay."

The right of publicity was first recognized in Georgia by the Court of Appeals in *Cabaniss v. Hipsley,* 114 Ga. App. 367, 151 S.E.2d 496 (1966). There the court held that the plaintiff, an exotic dancer, could recover from the owner of the Atlanta Playboy Club for the unauthorized use of the dancer's misnamed photograph in an entertainment magazine advertising the Playboy Club. Although plaintiff had had her picture taken to promote her performances, she was not performing at the Playboy Club. The court used Dean William L. Prosser's four-pronged analysis of the right of privacy, saying: "... Dean Prosser has analyzed the many privacy cases in an article entitled 'Privacy,' published in 48 Calif. L. Rev. 383 (1960), and in reviewing the cases he suggests that the invasion of privacy is in reality a complex of four loosely related torts; that there are four distinct kinds of invasion of four different interests of plaintiff; that there are four disparate torts under a common name. These four torts may be described briefly as: (1) intrusion upon the plaintiff's seclusion or solitude, or into his private affairs; (2) public disclosure of embarrassing private facts about the plaintiff; (3) publicity which places the plaintiff in a false light in the public eye; (4) appropriation, for the defendant's advantage, of the plaintiff's name or likeness." 114 Ga. App. at 370, 151 S.E.2d at 499-500. Finding no violation of the first three rights of privacy, the court found a violation of the fourth, saying (114 Ga. App. at 377, 151 S.E.2d 496): "Unlike intrusion, disclosure, or false light, appropriation does not require the invasion of something secret, secluded or private pertaining to plaintiff, nor does it involve falsity. It consists of the appropriation, for the defendant's benefit, use or advantage, of the plaintiff's name or likeness.... 'The interest protected [in the "appropriation" cases] is not so much a mental as a proprietary one, in the exclusive use of the plaintiff's name and likeness as an aspect of his identity.' Prosser, *supra*, at 406." Although Ms. Hipsley was an entertainer (i.e., a public figure), the court found she was entitled to recover from the Playboy Club (but not from the magazine which published the Club's ad) for the unauthorized use of her photograph. However the court noted a difference in the damages recoverable in traditional right of privacy cases as opposed to right of publicity cases saying (114 Ga. App. at 378, 151 S.E.2d 496): "Recognizing, as we do, the fundamental distinction between causes of action involving injury to feelings, sensibilities or reputation and those involving an appropriation of rights in the nature of property rights for commercial exploitation, it must necessarily follow that there is a fundamental distinction between the two classes of cases in the measure of damages to be applied. In the former class (which we take to include the intrusion, disclosure, and false light aspects of the privacy tort), general damages are recoverable without proof of special damages. *Pavesich v. New England Life Ins. Co., supra*. In the latter class, the measure of damages is the value of the use of the appropriated publicity."

In *McQueen v. Wilson*, 117 Ga. App. 488, 161 S.E.2d 63, *reversed on other grounds*, 224 Ga. 420, 162 S.E.2d 313 (1968), the Court of Appeals upheld the right of an actress, Butterfly McQueen, who appeared as "Prissie" in the movie *Gone With the Wind*, to recover for the unauthorized use of her photograph, saying: "Both before and since *Pavesich* it has been recognized that the appropriation of another's identity, picture, papers, name or signature without consent and for financial gain might be a tort for which an action would lie...." 117 Ga. App. at 491, 161 S.E.2d at 65.

Thus, the courts in Georgia have recognized the rights of private citizens, *Pavesich, supra*, as well as entertainers, *Cabaniss* and *McQueen, supra*, not to have their names and photographs used for the financial gain of the user without their consent, where such use is not authorized as an exercise of freedom of the press. We know of no reason why a public figure prominent in religion and civil rights should be entitled to less protection than an exotic dancer or a movie actress. Therefore, we hold that the appropriation of another's name and likeness, whether such likeness be a photograph or sculpture, without consent and for the financial gain of the appropriator is a tort in

Georgia, whether the person whose name and likeness is used is a private citizen, entertainer, or as here a public figure who is not a public official.

In *Pavesich, supra,* 122 Ga. 190, 50 S.E. 68, this right not to have another appropriate one's photograph was denominated the right of privacy; in *Cabaniss v. Hipsley, supra,* 114 Ga. App. 367, 151 S.E.2d 496, it was the right of publicity. Mr. Pavesich was not a public figure; Ms. Hipsley was. We conclude that while private citizens have the right of privacy, public figures have a similar right of publicity, and that the measure of damages to a public figure for violation of his or her right of publicity is the value of the appropriation to the user. *Cabaniss v. Hipsley, supra*; see also *Uhlaender v. Henricksen,* 316 F. Supp. 1277, 1279-1280 (Minn. 1970). As thus understood the first certified question is answered in the affirmative.

2. Does the "right of publicity" survive the death of its owner (i.e., is the right inheritable and devisable)?

Although the *Pavesich* court expressly did not decide this question, the tenor of that opinion is that the right to privacy at least should be protectable after death. *Pavesich, supra,* 122 Ga. at 210, 50 S.E. at 76.

The right of publicity is assignable during the life of the celebrity, for without this characteristic, full commercial exploitation of one's name and likeness is practically impossible. *Haelan Laboratories v. Topps Chewing Gum, supra,* 202 F.2d at 868. That is, without assignability the right of publicity could hardly be called a "right." Recognizing its assignability, most commentators have urged that the right of publicity must also be inheritable....

The courts that have considered the problem are not as unanimous. In *Price v. Hal Roach Studios, Inc., supra,* 400 F. Supp. 836, the court reasoned that since the right of publicity was assignable, it survived the deaths of Stanley Laurel and Oliver Hardy. Other decisions from the Southern District of New York recognize the descendibility of the right of publicity, which has also been recognized by the Second Circuit Court of Appeals (*infra*).

In *Factors Etc., Inc. v. Pro Arts, Inc.,* 579 F.2d 215 (2d Cir. 1978), Elvis Presley had assigned his right of publicity to Boxcar Enterprises, which assigned that right to Factors after Presley's death. Defendant Pro Arts published a poster of Presley entitled "In Memory." In affirming the grant of injunction against Pro Arts, the Second Circuit Court of Appeals said (579 F.2d at 221): "The identification of this exclusive right belonging to Boxcar as a transferable property right compels the conclusion that the right survives Presley's death. The death of Presley, who was merely the beneficiary of an income interest in Boxcar's exclusive right, should not in itself extinguish Boxcar's property right. Instead, the income interest, continually produced from Boxcar's exclusive right of commercial exploitation, should inure to Presley's estate at death like any other intangible property right. To hold that the right did not survive Presley's death, would be to grant competitors of Factors, such as Pro Arts, a windfall in the form of profits from the use of Presley's name and likeness. At the same time, the exclusive right purchased by Factors and the financial benefits accruing to the celebrity's heirs would be rendered virtually worthless."

In *Lugosi v. Universal Pictures*, 25 Cal. 3d 813, 160 Cal. Rptr. 323, 603 P.2d 425 (1979), the Supreme Court of California, in a 4 to 3 decision, declared that the right of publicity expires upon the death of the celebrity and is not descendible. See *Guglielmi v. Spelling-Goldberg Productions*, 25 Cal. 3d 860, 160 Cal. Rptr. 352, 603 P.2d 454 (1979), decided two days after *Lugosi, supra*. Bela Lugosi appeared as Dracula in Universal Picture's movie by that name. Universal had acquired the movie rights to the novel by Bram Stoker. Lugosi's contract with Universal gave it the right to exploit Lugosi's name and likeness in connection with the movie. The majority of the court held that Lugosi's heirs could not prevent Universal's continued exploitation of Lugosi's portrayal of Count Dracula after his death. The court did not decide whether Universal could prevent unauthorized third parties from exploitation of Lugosi's appearance as Dracula after Lugosi's death.

In *Memphis Development Foundation v. Factors Etc., Inc.*, 616 F.2d 956 (6th Cir. 1980), Factors, which had won its case against Pro Arts in New York (see above), lost against the Memphis Development Foundation under the Court of Appeals for the Sixth Circuit's interpretation of Tennessee law. There, the Foundation, a non-profit corporation, planned to erect a statute [sic] of Elvis Presley in Memphis and solicited contributions to do so. Donors of $25 or more received a small replica of the proposed statue. The Sixth Circuit reversed the grant of an injunction favoring Factors, holding that a celebrity's right of publicity was not inheritable even where that right had been exploited during the celebrity's life.[4] The court reasoned that although recognition of the right of publicity during life serves to encourage effort and inspire creative endeavors, making the right inheritable would not. The court also was concerned with unanswered legal questions which recognizing inheritability would create. We note, however, that the court was dealing with a non-profit foundation attempting to promote Presley's adopted home place, the City of Memphis. The court was not dealing, as we do here, with a profit making endeavor.

In *Estate of Presley v. Russen, supra*, 513 F. Supp. 1339, the court found in favor of descendibility, quoting from Chief Justice Bird's dissent in *Lugosi v. Universal Pictures, supra*, 25 Cal. 3d 813, 160 Cal. Rptr. at 332, 603 P.2d at 434, and saying: "If the right is descendible, the individual is able to transfer the benefits of his labor to his immediate successors and is assured that control over the exercise of the right can be vested in a suitable beneficiary. 'There is no reason why, upon a celebrity's death, advertisers should receive a windfall in the form of freedom to use with impunity the name or likeness of the deceased celebrity who may have worked his or her entire life to attain celebrity status. The financial benefits of that labor should go to the celebrity's heirs....'" 513 F. Supp. at 1355.

For the reasons which follow we hold that the right of publicity survives the death of its owner and is inheritable and devisable. Recognition of the right of publicity rewards and thereby encourages effort and creativity. If the right of publicity dies with the celebrity, the economic value of the right of publicity

---

[4]The Second Circuit has now accepted the Sixth Circuit's interpretation of Tennessee law. *Factors Etc., Inc. v. Pro Arts, Inc.*, 652 F.2d 278 (2d Cir. 1981).

during life would be diminished because the celebrity's untimely death would seriously impair, if not destroy, the value of the right of continued commercial use. Conversely, those who would profit from the fame of a celebrity after his or her death for their own benefit and without authorization have failed to establish their claim that they should be the beneficiaries of the celebrity's death. Finally, the trend since the early common law has been to recognize survivability, notwithstanding the legal problems which may thereby arise. We therefore answer question 2 in the affirmative.

3. Must the owner of the right of publicity have commercially exploited that right before it can survive?

Exploitation is understood to mean commercial use by the celebrity other than the activity which made him or her famous, e.g., an inter vivos transfer of the right to the use of one's name and likeness.

... That we should single out for protection after death those entertainers and athletes who exploit their personae during life, and deny protection after death to those who enjoy public acclamation but did not exploit themselves during life, puts a premium on exploitation. Having found that there are valid reasons for recognizing the right of publicity during life, we find no reason to protect after death only those who took commercial advantage of their fame.

. . . .

Without doubt, Dr. King could have exploited his name and likeness during his lifetime. That this opportunity was not appealing to him does not mean that others have the right to use his name and likeness in ways he himself chose not to do. Nor does it strip his family and estate of the right to control, preserve and extend his status and memory and to prevent unauthorized exploitation thereof by others. Here, they seek to prevent the exploitation of his likeness in a manner they consider unflattering and unfitting. We cannot deny them this right merely because Dr. King chose not to exploit or commercialize himself during his lifetime.

Question 3 is answered in the negative, and therefore we need not answer question 4.

Certified questions 1 and 2 answered in the affirmative, question 3 answered in the negative, and question 4 not answered.

QUESTIONS

1. What exactly are the policies that underlie the rather recently developed "right of publicity"? For example, to what extent is the right based upon the same policies as the tort of "passing off"? (Consider a hypothetical case in which, during his lifetime, the image of Dr. King is displayed in connection with an advertisement for a soft drink?) To what extent is it based upon the policy, elaborated in the *INS* case, that one should not economically reap where one has not sown (by expense, time, effort and skill)? To what extent is it based upon the policy, similar to copyright, that such a right is necessary to provide an incentive to persons to use their talents to become highly visible in the entertainment world or elsewhere in the public eye? To what extent does it share other policies with the more traditional "rights of privacy" outlined by Dean Prosser?

2. The court in the principal case suggests that the result might have been different had the user of the King image sought to erect a public statue in his honor. How would the court justify such a distinction?

3. Would newspaper photographs of Dr. King during his lifetime violate his "right of privacy"? His "right of publicity"? Could Dr. King enjoin Sunday painters from painting his image, and hanging the painting in their home? Could he enjoin them from selling those paintings at local "flea markets"?

4. To what extent do public figures (even those not elected to public office) forego such publicity rights? Can an intelligible line be drawn between public officials, public heroes (e.g., Dr. King, an astronaut, the winner of an international piano competition), sports figures and entertainment figures?

5. The right of publicity is a state law right. While most states recognize some form of the right, not all agree as to the right's scope, nor as to its duration. Suppose you are a state court judge (or a federal judge exercising diversity jurisdiction) asked to rule on a claim involving the unauthorized nationwide sale of Dr. Martin Luther King T-Shirts. (a) Which state's law do you apply? (b) What should be the geographic scope of the remedy? *See, e.g., Carson v. Here's Johnny Portable Toilets, Inc.,* 810 F.2d 104 (6th Cir. 1987) (entry of fifty-state injunction for violation of Michigan right of publicity law, but with leave to defendant to seek modification of order if use of proposed tradename would prove licit in another state); Amend, *The Geographical Scope of Injunctions in Intellectual Property Cases,* 77 Trademark Rep. 49 (1987).

"NEIGHBORING RIGHTS"

Many foreign countries recognize copyright-like rights in performers, e.g., musicians and actors. These countries have upheld performers' interests in the reproduction and public communication of their creative contribution. Recognition of a performer's so-called "neighboring rights," however, may provoke conflicts with the copyright owner's rights. Suppose, for example, that the copyright owner authorizes the public performance of an audiovisual work, but an actor who appeared in the work does not wish to permit its public performance. Most countries adopting neighboring rights have devised a compromise: in most instances, performers are entitled to remuneration for the exploitation of their performances, but are not granted a right of control over the exploitation.

The United States has no formal system of neighboring rights. In general, performers enjoy no rights under copyright. An exception concerns performers whose aural contribution is captured on sound recordings. Under the Copyright Act's definition of a sound recording, its "authors" would appear to be the creators of the fixed sounds, i.e., the performers and the recording engineers. This variety of performers' copyright, however, may be of less value than might initially appear. First, the Copyright Act specifies that the exclusive rights in a sound recording extend to reproduction of the actual sounds, but not to imitation or to public performance. Second, and most practically, in many cases, the producer of the sound recordings may be the employer of the performers (in which case the work for hire rule would deny the performers the status of authors), or the producer will have obtained assignments of copyright from the performers. On the other hand, the Audio Home Recording Act of 1992, discussed *supra,* Chapter 6A.2.b, has extended to all performers (non-featured as well as featured) of recorded music the right to receive royalties for the private copying of their recorded performances.

In theory, the right of publicity may serve as a substitute for neighboring rights. In fact, particularly with respect to motion pictures, the contract between the performer and the producer may embrace an assignment of virtually all conceivable rights to exploit the performer's contribution. *See, e.g., Rooney v. Columbia Pictures Indus.,* 538 F. Supp. 211 (S.D.N.Y.), *aff'd mem.,* 714 F.2d 117 (2d Cir. 1982), *cert. denied,* 460 U.S. 1084 (1983) (rejecting actor Mickey Rooney's claim that film producer violated Rooney's right of publicity by authorizing sale of videocassettes of movies in which Rooney had performed; court held Rooney's contract covered the complained-of exploitation). On the other hand, collective action by performers' groups has occasionally offered something of a counterweight to producers' contractual power. *See* Gorman, *The Recording Musician and Union Power: A Case Study of the American Federation of Musicians,* 37 Sw. L.J. 697 (1983) (tracing the AFM bargaining strategy in the 1940s and 1950s to deal with the spread of recorded music in films and the broadcast media).

Zacchini v. Scripps-Howard Broadcasting Co., 433 U.S. 562 (1977). Plaintiff-petitioner Hugo Zacchini, a "human cannonball," sought damages against a local television station which had, without Zacchini's permission, filmed and broadcast his "entire act" on a local nightly news show. Zacchini had performed his cannonball act at a county fair. The act, as filmed, lasted approximately fifteen seconds. The Supreme Court of Ohio held that Zacchini had a state-law right to the publicity value of his performance, but that the performance was a matter of public interest, and the first amendment therefore shielded the television station from liability for the unauthorized appropriation of Zacchini's performance (absent an intention to appropriate it for some "private use" or an intention to injure the performer). The United States Supreme Court reversed, concluding that the First Amendment (as applied to the states by way of the Fourteenth Amendment) did not impede the application of state "right of publicity" law so as to impose liability upon the television station for money damages.

The Court distinguished *Time, Inc. v. Hill,* 385 U.S. 374 (1967), in which it found that the First Amendment required that there be proof of knowing falsity or reckless disregard for the truth in producing a play that showed the plaintiff family members in a "false light," one aspect of a state "right of privacy" law; the plaintiff's interest in such a case is reputational, akin to actions for defamation. In "right of publicity" cases, however, the state's interest "is in protecting the proprietary interest of the individual in his act in part to encourage such entertainment. [This interest] is closely analogous to the goals of patent and copyright law." Moreover, to protect the injured party in a "false light" case, it is necessary to minimize publication of information to the public, which clearly implicates constitutional concerns; whereas in "right of publicity" cases "an entertainer such as [Zacchini] usually has no objection to the widespread publication of his act as long as he gets the commercial benefit of such publication" (witness the fact that he did not seek injunctive relief but rather $25,000 to compensate him for lost revenues from his performance). In the *Time* case and others based on defamation, the plaintiffs claimed injury from the reporting of events, whereas here there was "an attempt to broadcast or publish an entire act for which the performer ordinarily gets paid" and the relief sought under the state's "right of publicity" law "would not serve to prevent [the broadcaster] from reporting the newsworthy facts" about Zacchini's act. "The Constitution no more prevents a State from requiring respondent to compensate petitioner for broadcasting his act on television than it would privilege respondent to film and broadcast a copyrighted dramatic work without liability to the copyright owner."

Justice Powell dissented, speaking for Justices Brennan and Marshall as well. He contended that the majority's quantitative standard — whether the defendant had broadcast "a performer's entire act" — was not clear, was not appropriately sensitive to First Amendment values, and could lead to an unfortunate degree of media self-censorship: a television news editor unsure whether certain film footage portrayed an "entire act" might decline coverage, even of clearly newsworthy events, or would instead confine the broadcast to merely verbal reporting. "The public is then the loser. This is hardly the kind of news reportage that the First Amendment is meant to foster." The dissenters proffered not a quantitative test but rather a test based upon the use that was made of the film footage: When used for a "routine portion of a regular news program, I would hold that the First Amendment protects the station from a 'right of publicity' or 'appropriation' suit, absent a strong showing by the plaintiff that the news broadcast was a subterfuge or cover for private or commercial exploitation." There was no such showing here. Unlike "right of privacy" cases, Zacchini welcomed publicity and made his act public, but sought to control the manner of its presentation to maximize the monetary benefits; under these circumstances he cannot, consistent with the First Amendment, complain of routine news reportage. (Justice Stevens filed a separate dissent.)

QUESTIONS

1. Having analogized the right of publicity to copyright, should not the Supreme Court in the *Zacchini* case have considered an analogous fair use limitation on the right of publicity which would have accommodated the television station's use? *See* Note, *Human Cannonballs and the First Amendment,* 30 Stan. L. Rev. 1185 (1978).

2. Starting from the assumption that state law could prevent the unauthorized televising on a news program of an entire nine-inning professional baseball game, for example the last game of the World Series, does it follow that the news coverage of the "entire" act of Mr. Zacchini must also be deemed tortious? Are there *any* circumstances in which First Amendment considerations would dictate a permission to televise the entire Zacchini performance? What, for example, if Mr. Zacchini, a local figure of some note, missed the target, and was severely injured?

MIDLER v. FORD MOTOR CO.

849 F.2d 460 (9th Cir. 1988)

NOONAN, J.

This case centers on the protectibility of the voice of a celebrated chanteuse from commercial exploitation without her consent. Ford Motor Company and its advertising agency, Young & Rubicam, Inc., in 1985 advertised the Ford Lincoln Mercury with a series of nineteen 30 or 60 second television commercials in what the agency called "The Yuppie Campaign." The aim was to make an emotional connection with Yuppies, bringing back memories of when they were in college. Different popular songs of the seventies were sung on each commercial. The agency tried to get "the original people," that is, the singers who had popularized the songs, to sing them. Failing in that endeavor in ten cases the agency had the songs sung by "sound-alikes." Bette Midler, the plaintiff and appellant here, was done by a sound-alike.

Midler is a nationally known actress and singer. She won a Grammy as early as 1973 as the Best New Artist of that year. Records made by her since then have gone Platinum and Gold. She was nominated in 1979 for an Academy award for Best Female Actress in *The Rose,* in which she portrayed a pop singer. Newsweek in its June 30, 1986 issue described her as an "outrageously original singer/comedian." Time hailed her in its March 2, 1987 issue as "a legend" and "the most dynamic and poignant singer-actress of her time."

When Young & Rubicam was preparing the Yuppie Campaign it presented the commercial to its client by playing an edited version of Midler singing "Do You Want To Dance," taken from the 1973 Midler album, "The Divine Miss M." After the client accepted the idea and form of the commercial, the agency contacted Midler's manager, Jerry Edelstein. The conversation went as follows: "Hello, I am Craig Hazen from Young and Rubicam. I am calling you to find out if Bette Midler would be interested in doing ...? Edelstein: "Is it a commercial?" "Yes." "We are not interested."

Undeterred, Young & Rubicam sought out Ula Hedwig whom it knew to have been as one of "the Harlettes" a backup singer for Midler for ten years. Hedwig was told by Young & Rubicam that "they wanted someone who could sound like Bette Midler's recording of [Do You Want To Dance]." She was asked to make a "demo" tape of the song if she was interested. She made an a capella demo and got the job.

At the direction of Young & Rubicam, Hedwig then made a record for the commercial. The Midler record of "Do You Want To Dance" was first played to her. She was told to "sound as much as possible like the Bette Midler record," leaving out only a few "aahs" unsuitable for the commercial. Hedwig imitated Midler to the best of her ability.

After the commercial was aired Midler was told by "a number of people" that it "sounded exactly" like her record of "Do You Want To Dance." Hedwig was told by "many personal friends" that they thought it was Midler singing the commercial. Ken Fritz, a personal manager in the entertainment business not associated with Midler, declares by affidavit that he heard the commercial on more than one occasion and thought Midler was doing the singing.

Neither the name nor the picture of Midler was used in the commercial; Young & Rubicam had a license from the copyright holder to use the song. At issue in this case is only the protection of Midler's voice. The district court described the defendants' conduct as that "of the average thief. They decided, 'If we can't buy it, we'll take it.'" The court nonetheless believed there was no legal principle preventing imitation of Midler's voice and so gave summary judgment for the defendants. Midler appeals.

The First Amendment protects much of what the media do in the reproduction of likenesses or sounds. A primary value is freedom of speech and press. *Time, Inc. v. Hill,* 385 U.S. 374, 388 (1967). The purpose of the media's use of a person's identity is central. If the purpose is "informative or cultural" the use is immune; "if it serves no such function but merely exploits the individual portrayed, immunity will not be granted." Felcher and Rubin, *Privacy, Publicity and the Portrayal of Real People by the Media,* 88 Yale L.J. 1577 1596 (1979). Moreover, federal copyright law preempts much of the area. "Mere imitation of a recorded performance would not constitute a copyright infringement even where one performer deliberately sets out to simulate another's performance as exactly as possible." Notes of Committee on the Judiciary, 17 U.S.C.A. § 114(b). It is in the context of these First Amendment and federal copyright distinctions that we address the present appeal.

Nancy Sinatra once sued Goodyear Tire and Rubber Company on the basis of an advertising campaign by Young & Rubicam featuring "These Boots Are Made For Walkin'," a song closely identified with her; the female singers of the commercial were alleged to have imitated her voice and style and to have dressed and looked like her. The basis of Nancy Sinatra's complaint was unfair competition; she claimed that the song and the arrangement had acquired "a secondary meaning" which, under California law, was protectible. This court noted that the defendants "had paid a very substantial sum to the copyright proprietor to obtain the license for the use of the song and all of its arrangements." To give Sinatra damages for their use of the song would clash with federal copyright law. Summary judgment for the defendants was affirmed. *Sinatra v. Goodyear Tire & Rubber Co.,* 435 F.2d 711, 717-718 (9th Cir. 1970), *cert. denied,* 402 U.S. 906 (1971). If Midler were claiming a secondary meaning to "Do You Want To Dance" or seeking to prevent the defendants from using that song, she would fail like Sinatra. But that is not this case. Midler does not seek damages for Ford's use of "Do You Want To Dance," and thus her claim is not preempted by federal copyright law. Copyright protects "original works of authorship fixed in any tangible medium of expression." 17 U.S.C. § 102(a). A voice is not copyrightable. The sounds are not "fixed." What is put forward as protectible here is more personal than any work of authorship.

Bert Lahr once sued Adell Chemical Co. for selling Lestoil by means of a commercial in which an imitation of Lahr's voice accompanied a cartoon of a duck. Lahr alleged that his style of vocal delivery was distinctive in pitch, accent, inflection, and sounds. The First Circuit held that Lahr had stated a cause of action for unfair competition, that it could be found "that defendant's conduct saturated plaintiff's audience, curtailing his market." *Lahr v. Adell Chemical Co.,* 300 F.2d 256, 259 (1st Cir. 1962). That case is more like this one. But we do not find unfair competition here. One-minute commercials of the sort the defendants put on would not have saturated Midler's audience and curtailed her market. Midler did not do television commercials. The defendants were not in competition with her. *See Halicki v. United Artists Communications, Inc.*, 812 F.2d 1213 (9th Cir. 1987).

California Civil Code section 3344 is also of no aid to Midler. The statute affords damages to a person injured by another who uses the person's "name, voice, signature, photograph or likeness, in any manner." The defendants did not use Midler's name or anything else whose use is prohibited by the statute. The voice they used was Hedwig's, not hers. The term "likeness" refers to a visual image not a vocal imitation. The statute, however, does not preclude Midler from pursuing any cause of action she may have at common law; the statute itself implies that such common law causes of action do exist because it says its remedies are merely "cumulative." *Id.* § 3344(g).

The companion statute protecting the use of a deceased person's name, voice, signature, photograph or likeness states that the rights it recognizes are "property rights." *Id.* § 990(b). By analogy the common law rights are also property rights. Appropriation of such common law rights is a tort in California. *Motschenbacher v. R.J. Reynolds Tobacco Co.*, 498 F.2d 821 (9th Cir. 1974). In that case what the defendants used in their television commercial for Winston cigarettes was a photograph of a famous professional racing driver's racing car. The number of the car was changed and a wing-like device known as a "spoiler" was attached to the car; the car's features of white pinpointing, an oval medallion, and solid red coloring were retained. The driver, Lothar Motschenbacher, was in the car but his features were not visible. Some persons, viewing the commercial, correctly inferred that the car was his and that he was in the car and was therefore endorsing the product. The defendants were held to have invaded a "proprietary interest" of Motschenbacher in his own identity. *Id.* at 825.

Midler's case is different from Motschenbacher's. He and his car were physically used by the tobacco company's ad; he made part of his living out of giving commercial endorsements. But as Judge Koelsch expressed it in *Motschenbacher,* California will recognize an injury from "an appropriation of the attributes of one's identity." *Id.* at 824. It was irrelevant that Motschenbacher could not be identified in the ad. The ad suggested that it was he. The ad did so by emphasizing signs or symbols associated with him. In the same way the defendants here used an imitation to convey the impression that Midler was singing for them.

Why did the defendants ask Midler to sing if her voice was not of value to them? Why did they studiously acquire the services of a sound-alike and instruct her to imitate Midler if Midler's voice was not of value to them? What they sought was an attribute of Midler's identity. Its value was what the market would have paid for Midler to have sung the commercial in person.

A voice is more distinctive and more personal than the automobile accouterments protected in *Motschenbacher*. A voice is as distinctive and personal as a face. The human voice is one of the most palpable ways identity is manifested. We are all aware that a friend is at once known by a few words on the phone. At a philosophical level it has been observed that with the sound of a voice, "the other stands before me." D. Ihde, Listening and Voice 77 (1976). *A forti-ori,* these observations hold true of singing, especially singing by a singer of renown. The singer manifests herself in the song. To impersonate her voice is to pirate her identity.

We need not and do not go so far as to hold that every imitation of a voice to advertise merchandise is actionable. We hold only that when a distinctive voice of a professional singer is widely known and is deliberately imitated in order to sell a product, the sellers have appropriated what is not theirs and have committed a tort in California. Midler has made a showing, sufficient to defeat summary judgment, that the defendants here for their own profit in selling their product did appropriate part of her identity.

Reversed and remanded for trial.

QUESTION

It is generally acknowledged that the first judicial recognition of the "right of publicity" was by Judge Frank in the *Haelan* case, discussed by the court in the *Martin Luther King* case. Presumably, the bubble gum cards that were the subject of controversy in *Haelan* bore some biographical and statistical information regarding the player pictured on the front. If a boardgame manufacturer were to market a baseball game in which the participants assume the role of one or another major league baseball team, and the play action is geared to the statistics of the team players — and those statistics are contained in a pamphlet appended to the rules of play — could the players, consistent with the First Amendment, enjoin the distribution of the board game?

Could they enjoin the marketing of a book that fully and accurately depicts the history of their team, their fellow players and themselves (on and off the field)? Where is the point, if any, at which the First Amendment concerns for the dissemination of accurate factual information conflicts with the "right of publicity"? *See Hicks v. Casablanca Records,* 464 F. Supp. 426 (S.D.N.Y. 1978).

D. TRADE DRESS

ROMM ART CREATIONS LTD. v. SIMCHA INTERNATIONAL, INC.

786 F. Supp. 1126 (E.D.N.Y. 1992)

SPATT, DISTRICT JUDGE.

Contrary to the well-known adage that "imitation is the sincerest form of flattery," in the instant case, imitation has resulted in a charge of trade dress infringement against the defendants. This case involves a rarely-visited area of the law — the interaction of the Lanham Act with the marketing and sale of limited editions and fine art posters based upon the work of an Israeli artist named Tarkay.

The plaintiffs are in the business of publishing and distributing such art works. In this action, they seek to enjoin, among other things, the manufacturing and selling of certain limited editions and fine art posters of an artist-competitor named Patricia Govezensky.

I. *Preliminary Statement*

The plaintiffs Romm Art Creations Ltd. ("Romm Art") and London Contemporary Art Limited ("Limited") move for a preliminary injunction, seeking to enjoin the defendants Simcha International, Inc. ("Simcha") from manufacturing, selling, advertising, or offering for sale in any manner posters, silk screens or limited editions of reproductions of certain paintings bearing the signature "Patricia."

II. *The Facts*

Plaintiff Romm Art Creations, Ltd. is a corporation organized under the laws of the State of New York and maintains offices in Glen Cove, New York. Plaintiff London Contemporary Art Ltd. is a corporation organized under the laws of Great Britain and maintains its offices in London, England. For several years prior to this suit, Romm Art has been engaged in the business of publishing and selling, on a wholesale basis, both fine art posters and limited edition paintings and sculptures. London is also engaged in the publication and sale of limited editions.

Romm Art was licensed by Givon Prints, an Israeli corporation, to be the exclusive world-wide distributor of Tarkay posters. Itzchak Tarkay is an Israeli artist of international renown. His works have been shown in Israel, the United States and various European countries. Tarkay gave to Givon Prints exclusive rights to reproduce various original art work as posters and/or limited editions. Givon, in turn, licensed Romm Art, whose customers include small poster shops, frame shops, art galleries, chain stores and distributors. Each of the limited editions and posters noted above is a reproduction of an original work from the artist's collection known as "Women and Cafes." According to the plaintiffs, the "Women and Cafes" series, as a result of widespread distribution and advertising, has "become recognized by the trade and by consumers as 'Tarkays.'" According to Piers Johnston, a principal of plaintiff London, Tarkay is the best selling of the thirty artists that London represents.

The defendant Simcha International, Inc. ("Simcha") maintains an office in Powder Springs, Georgia. Simcha buys and sells original works of art, limited editions and posters [and is] the distributor of the Patricia Govezensky limited editions and posters — the "Patricia" line at issue in this case.

The plaintiffs filed their complaint on October 23, 1991, alleging ... trade dress infringement under the Lanham Act; ... Romm Art alleges that the defendants' manufacture and sale of its reproductions of the Tarkay works and marks were for the "willful and calculated purpose of trading upon plaintiffs' goodwill" and "the secondary meaning created by Tarkay's unique and distinctive style and appearance." The plaintiffs further charge that:

23. The series of 'Patricia' paintings defendants have caused to be created are slavishly similar and entirely derivative of the works of Tarkay, and, more particularly, upon Tarkay's 'Women and Cafes' collection.
....
25. The 'Patricia' works are slavish imitations of Tarkay's artworks, prepared with the intention of causing potential customers and purchasers to confuse them with the already established and immensely popular 'Women and Cafes' works of Tarkay.
....
29. The publication of and advertising for the said Patricia reproductions has [sic] caused widespread consumer confusion due to the conscious and intentional similarity of the two bodies of work.
....

C. Lanham Act:

i. *Generally*

Section 43(a) of the Lanham Act, 15 U.S.C. § 1125(a), provides a statutory remedy for trademark or trade dress infringement and unfair competition to a party injured by a competitor's false designation of origin of its product, whether or not the aggrieved party has a registered trademark. Section 43(a) provides an additional remedy for the false or misleading or deceptive advertisement of facts. In short, the Lanham Act provides civil redress to one damaged by unfair competition through false or misleading advertising and/or trademark or trade dress infringement. Section 43(a), as amended, provides in relevant part as follows:

(a) Any person who, on or in connection with any goods or services, or any container for goods, uses in commerce any word, term, name, symbol, or device, or any combination thereof, or any ... false or misleading description of fact, or false or misleading representation of fact, which —

(1) is likely to cause confusion, or to cause mistake, or to deceive as to the affiliation, connection, or association of such person with another person, or as to the origin, sponsorship, or approval of his or her goods, services, or commercial activities by another person, or
(2) in commercial advertising or promotion, misrepresents the nature, characteristics, qualities ... of his ... goods, services or commercial activities,

shall be liable in a civil action by any person who believes that he or she is or is likely to be damaged by such act."

15 U.S.C. § 1125(a).

In order to succeed in this action, the plaintiffs must show that (1) the Tarkay trade dress has acquired secondary meaning, and (2) there is a likelihood of confusion as to the source of the product.

ii. *Trademark Infringement: Works of Aesthetic Art*

The Court finds that this suit falls within a rarely-tread area of the law, namely, the application of trade dress protection to works of art. Initially, the Court notes that the defendants have raised no objection to the Magistrate Judge's finding that 15 U.S.C. § 1125(a) provides relief for a claim of infringement of the trade dress of commercial reproductions of particular art works.

Courts have long recognized that recovery under § 43(a) is not restricted to federally registered trademarks, but extends to "words, symbols, collections of colors and designs, or advertising materials or techniques" that the purchasing public has come to associate with a single source.

To prevail on a trade dress infringement claim and prove unprivileged imitation — and ultimately to prevent copying of the appearance of a product — a plaintiff must establish that: "(1) the trade dress, whether a single feature or a combination of features, must be non-functional; (2) the trade dress must have acquired a secondary meaning; and (3) there must be a likelihood of confusion among consumers as to the source of the competing products."

This Court finds most persuasive the decision in *Hartford House Ltd. v. Hallmark Cards Inc.,* 647 F. Supp. 1533 (D. Colo. 1986), *aff'd,* 846 F.2d 1268 (10th Cir.), *cert. denied,* 488 U.S. 908 (1988). In *Hartford House,* a small commercial manufacturer of "non-occasion" greeting cards which conveyed emotional messages about personal relationships brought suit against Hallmark, alleging that its "Personal Touch" line of cards infringed the plaintiff's product. In finding that the Lanham Act was applicable in this type of situation, the district court stated the following:

> One salutary purpose of the Lanham Act in this context is to protect a creative artist's rights in his or her creation and thus provide incentive to be creative. By protecting and fostering creativity, a product with features different and perhaps preferable to the Blue Mountain product may well be developed. Offering consumers a choice in the non-occasion greeting card market stimulates, rather than stifles competition.

On appeal, the Tenth Circuit held that the district court was correct in determining preliminarily that the combination of the features comprising the trade dress (i.e., the overall appearance or look of Blue Mountain's "AireBrush Feelings" and "WaterColor Feelings" cards) is not functional and was thus protectable under § 43(a) of the Lanham Act.

In light of the foregoing, as well as the holdings in *Harlequin Enters. Ltd. v. Gulf & Western Corp.,* 644 F.2d 946 (2d Cir. 1981) (affirming preliminary injunction under § 1125[a] where overall features of book cover design of "Silhouette Romance" found likely to cause confusion with cover design of "Harlequin Presents" books) and *Hughes v. Design Look Inc.,* 693 F. Supp. 1500 (S.D.N.Y. 1988) (section 1125[a] applicable in case of fine art poster calendar), the Court [finds] that the Tarkay posters and limited editions are entitled to protection under § 1125(a) of the Lanham Act.

iii. *Trade Dress Infringement: Secondary Meaning*

Arbitrary or fanciful marks are eligible for protection without proof of secondary meaning. The degree of protection afforded under the Lanham Act is largely determined by the distinctiveness of the trade dress. An inherently distinctive trade dress is proof of secondary meaning.

Once the plaintiff has established that the trade dress has acquired secondary meaning in the marketplace, the burden shifts to the defendant to show that the trade dress sought to be protected is "functional," and therefore is not covered under section 43(a) of the Lanham Act. A combination of visual features that creates a distinctive visual impression is not functional and is protectable. The Court determines that the Tarkay posters and limited editions create just such a distinctive visual impression. Therefore, the Court finds that the Tarkay trade dress is not functional and is protected under the Lanham Act.

iv. *Trade Dress Infringement: "Likelihood of Confusion"*

Even though the plaintiff has established secondary meaning as to the source and is not defeated by the functionality defense, the plaintiff must also substantiate the second prong of "likelihood of confusion," which is a demonstration of "a likelihood that an appreciable number of ordinarily prudent purchasers are likely to be misled, or indeed simply confused, as to the source of the goods in question."

In assessing the likelihood of confusion, the Court must consider the 8 factors set forth in *Polaroid Corp. v. Polarad Electronics Corp.,* 287 F.2d 492, 495 (2d Cir.), *cert. denied,* 368 U.S. 820 (1961).

"The [*Polaroid*] factors are designed to help grapple with the 'vexing' problem of resolving the likelihood of confusion issue." Consequently, each factor is to be evaluated in the overall context of its impact on the essential question of likelihood of confusion. At the outset, however, the Court takes note of the fact that competing goods require less proof under the *Polaroid* factors than non-competitive items in establishing likelihood of confusion.

(1) *Strength of the Senior User's Mark:*

Strength of a mark has been defined as "its tendency to identify the goods sold under the mark as emanating from a particular ... source."

Having categorized the Tarkay trade dress as "arbitrary or fanciful," the Court [finds] that as imaginative, artistic portraits, the Tarkay images are strong marks. Other than aesthetic gratification, these images serve no other purpose than to identify their source/creator. This view is enhanced by the testimony of the plaintiffs' expert who stated that Tarkay is considered to be one of two of "the best selling artists in the poster market in the world." The Court therefore holds that the Tarkay trade dress is a strong mark warranting protection under the trademark laws.

(2) *Degree of Similarity Between the Two Marks:*

In determining similarity, "it is the combination of features as a whole rather than a difference in some of the details which must determine whether the competing product is likely to cause confusion in the mind of the public."

Having examined the color patterns and shading of the Tarkay works, the placement of figures in each of the pictures examined, the physical attributes of his women, the depiction of women sitting and reclining, their characteristic clothing vis-à-vis those portrayed by Patricia, the Court concludes that there is "sufficient similarity between the products to scrutinize the evidence for proof of confusion."

The test for determining similarity is whether the labels create the "same overall impression" when viewed separately. In light of the fact that the Tarkay and Patricia patterns are not dictated by function, and that a variety of patterns is possible, the similarity of the patterns is striking. When this striking similarity is factored into the likelihood of confusion analysis, in light of the strength of the Tarkay trade dress, consumer confusion is a likely result. The Court holds, therefore, that the trade dresses of Tarkay and Patricia create the "same overall impression" when viewed separately.

The Court finds the testimony of the defendants' expert, Dr. Robert Myron, to be significant on this point. Dr. Myron is chairman of the Art History Department at Hofstra University. Although Dr. Myron testified that the two trade dresses were dissimilar, he acknowledged that his ability to observe such dissimilarities was heightened by his expertise in art history. After initially indicating that he found no basis for likelihood of confusion among any particular segment of the purchasing public, Dr. Myron subsequently acknowledged that the level of sophistication of buyers of fine art posters was significantly different from that of art collectors. The general public's confusion is only increased when the name of the artist is eliminated or covered up in the matting and/or cropping process.

Having assessed the similarity of the marks under the *Polaroid* standard, the Court finds that the trade dresses are similar — the general impression conveyed to the public by these images does not differ significantly, and the similarities create an issue of fact on the likelihood of consumer confusion. The Court therefore finds the second factor of "similarity" in the plaintiffs' favor.

(3) *Competitive Proximity of the Two Products:*

Where the two products are in direct competition with each other, the likelihood of confusion increases. In the instant case, the same galleries carry and sell works by both Tarkay and Patricia. This fact was manifest in the statements of Steven Romm who testified that the works of both artists were exhibited at the 1991 Los Angeles Artexpo and who noted that the Artexpo catalog displayed the works of both artists as well as information about the plaintiffs and defendants as distributors of those works.

Such grouping in galleries and advertising materials favors a finding of "likelihood of confusion." Given this proximity, differences in methods of display do not eliminate "the likelihood that customers may be confused as to the source of the products, rather than as to the products themselves." The Court therefore [finds] that this close proximity between the images favors likelihood of confusion.

(4) *Likelihood Plaintiff Will "Bridge the Gap":*

This factor is normally addressed when the products being reviewed are not in direct competition with each other, and the question arises "is the plaintiff likely to enter this market?" Here, there is direction competition between Tarkay and Patricia, eliminating the need to consider this factor.

(5) *Evidence of Actual Confusion:*

"Evidence of actual confusion is a strong indication that there is a likelihood of confusion." The Court finds sufficient evidence of actual confusion based upon the following facts presented during the hearing: (1) Steven Romm's testimony regarding immediate concerns expressed by attendees at the Artexpo as well as by subsequent callers; (2) contact from Gallery owners such as Harriet Rinehart; (3) the testimony of defendants' expert Dr. Myron that there were only "slight differences" in the styles and print of the two artists and that the works were "quite similar in general appearances"; (4) Dr. Myron's enumeration of similar features, such as the use of two figures, the hats worn by the women, the patterned dresses, the background colors and the appearance of flora in each; and (5) the feedback from specific gallery owners distressed by the exact likenesses they perceived in Patricia. Consequently, the Court finds that this factor favors the plaintiffs.

(6) *Junior User's Good Faith:*

The Court turns now to the junior user's state of mind — i.e., whether he was aware of the plaintiff's mark when adopting his own. This consideration is relevant in determining likelihood of confusion as well as in balancing the equities.

In reviewing the exhibits, depositions, and testimony of the fact and expert witnesses on both sides, the court is disturbed with the similarity between Tarkay's 'On The Stage' and Patricia's 'Seated Women' leading the court to believe that at trial there might well be sufficiently serious questions going to the merits regarding the issue of good faith.

This "good faith" factor "looks to whether the defendant adopted its mark with the intention of capitalizing on the plaintiff's reputation and goodwill and any confusion between his and the senior user's product." Once the plaintiff has introduced evidence which, taken cumulatively, allows an inference of intentional copying, the burden of proof on the element of good faith is on the defendant. The defendants offered no such affirmative defense at the hearing nor have they raised any such argument in their Objections. In fact, the testimony of Dr. Myron, commenting on the two works noted above, clearly reflects his opinion that one artist copied from the other. The defendants did not refute this testimony.

The Second Circuit has held that evidence of intentional copying raises a presumption that the "second comer intended to create a confusing similarity." Although this factor alone is not dispositive, it bolsters a finding of consumer confusion. The Court finds the above evidence to be substantial on the issue of intentional copying. By failing to raise any reasonable defense to this inference, the defendants leave this Court with the strong perception that they have acted in bad faith. Consequently, the Court finds in favor of the plaintiffs on this factor of the "junior user's good faith."

(7) *Quality of the Junior User's Product:*

"If the quality of the junior user's product is of a low quality, the senior user's interest in avoiding any confusion is heightened." The Court finds the works of Tarkay and Patricia to be of very similar quality. However, the lack of marked difference in quality between goods supports the inference that they emanate from the same source. A senior user may sue to protect his reputation even where the infringer's goods are of top quality. Upon review of the testimony and relevant case law, the Court finds that this factor neither helps nor hinders the plaintiffs' case.

(8) *Sophistication of the Purchasers:*

The focus of this particular factor is whether consumers spend much time evaluating the product before making a purchase or whether it is considered a "grab off the shelf" product. According to Harriet Rinehart's testimony, "the average consumer, who is going into poster and commercial art galleries is not an educated customer. They are looking for the colors that they like, and they see an artist and they say this is a great look." On the basis of (1) the testimony of Ms. Rinehart and Dr. Myron about the level of consumer sophistication, (2) the testimony of Steven Romm concerning the average selling price of the respective posters, and (3) the defendants' price list reflecting an average price of thirty dollars for a poster, the Court finds that the inexpensive price per poster only adds to the likelihood of consumer confusion.

The Court is convinced that an ordinary buyer of fine art posters would not recognize the disparities. Therefore, the Court finds the evidence of "sophistication of the buyer" as support for a finding of likelihood of confusion to favor the plaintiffs.

V. *Assessment of the "Polaroid" Factors*

The determination of whether a likelihood of confusion has been established is a complex one, for there clearly are factors cutting both ways. However, the evidence, taken cumulatively, does allow an inference that there is some actual confusion as to source in the marketplace caused by the similarity of the competing trade dresses, and the Court draws such an inference.

The Court finds, after considering all of the *Polaroid* factors, that the defendants' trade dress does create a likelihood of confusion for an appreciable number of consumers. In reaching this decision, the Court places primary importance on the strength of the Tarkay trade dress, the similarity of the two trade dresses, the directly competitive nature of the products offered, the inference of intentional copying by the defendants, and the lack of "deliberate and measured product selection by consumers" in a gallery or poster shop.

Accordingly, the Court grants the plaintiff's motion for a preliminary injunction based upon the foregoing violations of the Lanham Act.

QUESTIONS

1. Recall the *Romm Art* court's approving quotation: "one salutary purpose of the Lanham Act in this context is to protect a creative artists' rights in his or her creation and thus provide incentive to be creative." Isn't that what copyright law is supposed to be about? Should trademark law be supplying the same incentives?

2. Isn't the court protecting the "Women and Cafés" concept and feel under the rubric of "trade dress"? Could the same result be achieved through the copyright law? Why do you suppose this case was not brought as a copyright infringement claim?

3. Given the fact that "Patricia's" name appeared prominently on her posters of women in cafés, how could the court find "likelihood of confusion" sufficient to make out a claim under the Lanham Act?

Chapter 9

FEDERAL PREEMPTION OF STATE LAW

THE SUPREMACY CLAUSE

The Supremacy Clause of the U.S. Constitution, Article VI, clause 2, provides:

> This Constitution, and the Laws of the United States which shall be made in Pursuance thereof; and all Treaties made, or which shall be made, under the Authority of the United States, shall be the supreme Law of the Land; and the Judges in every State shall be bound thereby, any Thing in the Constitution or Laws of any State to the contrary notwithstanding.

QUESTION

Note the potentially preemptive effect of: (a) the U.S. Constitution itself and (b) federal laws, and (c) treaties. Identify, within each of these sources, provisions dealing with patents and copyrights which might preempt state law on the same subject. Why were trademarks omitted from the previous sentence?

A. SUPREME COURT PREEMPTION DECISIONS IN INTELLECTUAL PROPERTY CASES

During the time when the 1909 Copyright Act was in effect, the Supreme Court dealt with several significant cases that raised the question whether some body of state law, such as unfair competition law, which banned copying of another's products was consistent with federal policy in the areas of patents and copyrights, as reflected both in the copyright and patent clause of the U.S. Constitution and in the terms of the respective federal statutes. Because neither the Patent Act nor the Copyright Act expressly dealt with the issue of preemption of related state laws (except for § 2 of the 1909 Copyright Act, which saved state-law protection of unpublished writings), the Court had to address this issue by deducing from the statutory terms and policies what the preemptive intention of Congress was. That interpretive process, and the Court's important conclusions, are evidenced in the cases that follow. These cases still represent the governing law in the patent area, for the Patent Act remains silent as to the continued vitality of pertinent state laws; but, although they continue to provide an important background in the area of copyright, the cases below have been largely superseded by the specific terms of § 301 of the 1976 Copyright Act, to be considered in the next section.

Sears, Roebuck & Co. v. Stiffel Co., 376 U.S. 225 (1964). Stiffel designed and secured design and mechanical patents on the "pole lamp," which proved to be a commercial success. Sears then began to sell a substantially identical

lamp, at a cheaper price. Stiffel brought a federal court action for infringement of its patents and for unfair competition under Illinois law (alleging
confusion in the trade as to the source of the lamps resulting from the identical shapes). The District Court found the patents to be invalid for want of
invention, but issued an injunction under state law against Sears' marketing
lamps identical to or confusingly similar to Stiffel's; the Court of Appeals
affirmed, holding (in the words of the Supreme Court) "Sears liable for doing
no more than copying and marketing an unpatented article." The Supreme
Court reversed.

The Court noted that the federal patent and copyright statutes since 1790
"are the supreme law of the land" and that "when state law touches upon the
area of these federal statutes, it is 'familiar doctrine' that the federal policy
'may not be set at naught, or its benefits denied' by the state law." The Court
noted that the privileges accorded to the patent holder are to be strictly construed; in particular, "[W]hen the patent expires the monopoly created by it
expires, too, and the right to make the article — including the right to make it
in precisely the shape it carried when patented — passes to the public." It
then continued:

> Thus the patent system is one in which uniform federal standards are
> carefully used to promote invention while at the same time preserving
> free competition. Obviously a State could not, consistently with the Su-
> premacy Clause of the Constitution, extend the life of a patent beyond its
> expiration date or give a patent on an article which lacked the level of
> invention required for federal patents. To do either would run counter to
> the policy of Congress of granting patents only to true inventions and
> then only for a limited time. Just as a State cannot encroach upon the
> federal patent laws directly, it cannot, under some other law, such as that
> forbidding unfair competition, give protection of a kind that clashes with
> the objectives of the federal patent laws.
>
> In the present case the "pole lamp" sold by Stiffel has been held not to
> be entitled to the protection of either a mechanical or a design patent. An
> unpatentable article, like an article on which the patent has expired, is in
> the public domain and may be made and sold by whoever chooses to do so.
> What Sears did was to copy Stiffel's design and to sell lamps almost
> identical to those sold by Stiffel. This it had every right to do under the
> federal patent laws. That Stiffel originated the pole lamp and made it
> popular is immaterial. "Sharing in the goodwill of an article unprotected
> by patent or trade-mark is the exercise of a right possessed by all — and
> in the free exercise of which the consuming public is deeply interested."
> *Kellogg Co. v. National Biscuit Co., supra*, 305 U.S., at 122. To allow a
> State by use of its law of unfair competition to prevent the copying of an
> article which represents too slight an advance to be patented would be to
> permit the State to block off from the public something which federal law
> has said belongs to the public. The result would be that while federal law
> grants only 14 or 17 years' protection to genuine inventions, see 35 U.S.C.
> §§ 154, 173, States could allow perpetual protection to articles too lacking
> in novelty to merit any patent at all under federal constitutional stan-

dards. This would be too great an encroachment on the federal patent system to be tolerated.

... [M]ere inability of the public to tell two identical articles apart is not enough to support an injunction against copying or an award of damages for copying that which the federal patent laws permit to be copied. Doubtless a State may, in appropriate circumstances, require that goods, whether patented or unpatented, be labeled or that other precautionary steps be taken to prevent customers from being misled as to the source, just as it may protect businesses in the use of their trademarks, labels, or distinctive dress in the packaging of goods so as to prevent others, by imitating such markings, from misleading purchasers as to the source of the goods. But because of the federal patent laws a State may not, when the article is unpatented and uncopyrighted, prohibit the copying of the article itself or award damages for such copying....

Compco Corp. v. Day-Brite Lighting, Inc., 376 U.S. 234 (1964). Plaintiff Day-Brite secured a design patent on a cross-ribbed reflector in its fluorescent lighting fixtures. Compco's predecessor copied it and marketed the copies, and Day-Brite brought this action for patent infringement and for unfair competition under Illinois law. Although the District Court held the design patent invalid and thus dismissed the patent infringement claim, it found that Compco had engaged in unfair competition by marketing a copied reflector having the same shape as Day-Brite's — a shape that identified Day-Brite in the trade — and thereby caused customer confusion. The Court of Appeals affirmed, and the Supreme Court granted certiorari. The Court, accepting the District Court's findings of fact regarding copying and confusion, nonetheless reversed.

The Court broadly interpreted the *Sears* decision to stand for the proposition that "when an article is unprotected by a patent or a copyright, state law may not forbid others to copy that article. To forbid copying would interfere with the federal policy, found in Art. I, § 8, cl. 8, of the Constitution and in the implementing federal statutes, of allowing free access to copy whatever the federal patent and copyright laws leave in the public domain." Because Day-Brite's design and mechanical patents were invalid, its fixture was thus "in the public domain and can be copied in every detail by whoever pleases."

Even though the ribbing pattern on the fixture identified Day-Brite to the trade and had thus acquired "secondary meaning," if the design "is not entitled to a design patent or other federal statutory protection, then it can be copied at will.... That an article copied from an unpatented article could be made in some other way, that the design is "nonfunctional" and not essential to the use of either article, that the configuration of the article copied may have a "secondary meaning" which identifies the maker to the trade, or that there may be "confusion" among purchasers as to which article is which or as to who is the maker, may be relevant evidence in applying a State's law requiring such precautions as labeling; however, and regardless of the copier's motives, neither these facts nor any others can furnish a basis for imposing liability for or prohibiting the actual acts of copying and selling." A state may, however, impose by law a requirement that those who make and sell copies must take precautions to label their products as their own.

QUESTIONS

1. Is the conflict articulated in *Sears* and *Compco* "constitutional" or "statutory," i.e., was state unfair competition law found to conflict with the patent and copyright clause of the U.S. Constitution or with the federal patent law? What is the obvious consequence of this distinction?

2. Would the *Sears-Compco* rule apply to subject matter outside the constitutional power of Congress? Within such power but outside the scope of subject matter covered by the patent statute? How does this latter category differ from the subject matter actually involved in *Sears* and *Compco*?

3. What evidence is there as to whether the sweep of these cases reaches copyright? As a matter of policy should copyright be distinguished?

Goldstein v. California, 412 U.S. 546 (1973). Petitioners made and marketed to the public through retail stores "pirated" tapes that copied the sounds of musical performances from commercially sold recordings, without the permission of or payment to the recording companies or performing artists. The pirated tapes were labeled with the name of the original recording and performers, but expressly disclaimed any relationship with those performers or with the original record company. The petitioners were convicted under § 653h of the California Penal Code, which declared such conduct a misdemeanor. (The petitioners activity had taken place in 1970 and 1971, before the U.S. Copyright Act was amended to accord for the first time copyright protection against record piracy; the federal statute expressly left to state law any rights with respect to sound recordings made before February 15, 1972.) The petitioners challenged the constitutionality of the California statute by virtue of the Supremacy Clause. They claimed, invoking the *Sears* and *Compco* cases, that Congress intended to allow individuals to copy any work which was not protected by a federal copyright. The Supreme Court disagreed, and affirmed the state convictions.

The Court turned first to the Copyright Clause of the Constitution to determine whether it reflected a relinquishing by the states of a copyright power that would otherwise be retained by them. The purpose of the constitutional provision authorizing Congress to enact copyright legislation was concededly to promote authorship through a single uniform system, without the need for multiple state registrations. But this "does not indicate that all writings are of national interest or that state legislation is, in all cases, unnecessary or precluded." Given the variety and diversity of the American population, and of its business and industry, "it is unlikely that all citizens in all parts of the country place the same importance on works relating to all subjects. Since the subject matter to which the Copyright Clause is addressed may thus be of purely local importance and not worthy of national attention or protection, we cannot discern such an unyielding national interest as to require an inference that state power to grant copyrights has been relinquished to *exclusive* federal control." A state granting copyright protection within its borders would not prejudice the interests of an adjacent state, which could permit persons within to copy; but "individuals who wish to purchase a copy of a work protected in their own State will be able to buy unauthorized copies in other States where no protection exists. However, this conflict is neither so inevitable nor so severe as to compel the conclusion, that state power has been relinquished to the exclusive jurisdiction of the Congress.... [E]xcept as to individuals willing to travel across state lines in order to purchase records or other writings protected in their own State, each State's copyrights will still serve to induce new artistic creations within that State — the very objective of the grant of protection."

Having determined that differences in copyright regulation among the states would not frustrate their respective interests, the Court considered whether it would frustrate national interests.

> ... [I]t is difficult to see how the concurrent exercise of the power to grant copyrights by Congress and the States will necessarily and inevitably lead to difficulty. At any time Congress determines that a particular category of "writing" is worthy of national protection and the incidental expenses of federal administration, federal copyright protection may be authorized. Where the need for free and unrestricted distribution of a writing is thought to be required by the national interest, the Copyright Clause and the Commerce Clause would allow Congress to eschew all protection. In such cases, a conflict would develop if a State attempted to protect that which Congress intended to be free from restraint or to free that which Congress had protected. However, where Congress determines that neither federal protection nor freedom from restraint is required by the national interest, it is at liberty to stay its hand entirely. Since state protection would not then conflict with federal action, total relinquishment of the State's power to grant copyright protection cannot be inferred.
>
> ... No reason exists why Congress must take affirmative action either to authorize protection of all categories of writings or to free them from all restraint. We therefore conclude that, under the Constitution, the States have not relinquished all power to grant to authors "the exclusive Right to their respective Writings."

The Court also rejected the petitioners' contention that the constitutional Copyright Clause, with its "limited times" provision, barred state copyright protection — such as California's against record piracy — that was indefinite in duration. The Court found the constitutional time limitation to speak only to congressional copyright legislation. Unlike an indefinite federal copyright, which would grant exclusive rights against all citizens and in all states, a state copyright, even unlimited in duration, "is confined to its borders.... [A]ny tendency to inhibit further progress in science or the arts is narrowly circumscribed. The challenged statute cannot be voided for lack of a durational limitation."

Even though California did not surrender its power to issue copyrights, its criminal statute could conceivably be invalidated under the Supremacy

Clause, if it were to stand "as an obstacle to the accomplishment and execution of the full purposes and objectives of Congress" reflected in the Copyright Act. The Court found that sound recordings were among the "writings" that the Constitution empowered Congress to regulate, but that Congress has the discretion to decide what specific classes of writings it will protect. Petitioners claimed that, by virtue of the congressional exclusion of sound recordings from the coverage of the 1909 Copyright Act (as distinguished from the musical compositions recorded), the states cannot bar their copying.

   ... [*Sears, Roebuck & Co. v. Stiffel Co.*, 376 U.S. 225 (1964), and *Compco Corp. v. Day-Brite Lighting*, 376 U.S. 234 (1964)], on which petitioners rely, do not support their position. In those cases, the question was whether a State could, under principles of a state unfair competition law, preclude the copying of mechanical configurations which did not possess the qualities required for the granting of a federal design or mechanical patent....

   In regard to mechanical configurations, Congress had balanced the need to encourage innovation and originality of invention against the need to insure competition in the sale of identical or substantially identical products. The standards established for granting federal patent protection to machines thus indicated not only which articles in this particular category Congress wished to protect, but which configurations it wished to remain free. The application of state law in these cases to prevent the copying of articles which did not meet the requirements for federal protection disturbed the careful balance which Congress had drawn and thereby necessarily gave way under the Supremacy Clause of the Constitution. No comparable conflict between state law and federal law arises in the case of recordings of musical performances. In regard to this category of "Writings," Congress has drawn no balance; rather, it has left the area unattended, and no reason exists why the State should not be free to act.... Congress has indicated neither that it wishes to protect, nor to free from protection, recordings of musical performances fixed prior to February 15, 1972.... Until and unless Congress takes further action with respect to recordings fixed prior to Feburary 15, 1972, the California statute may be enforced against acts of piracy such as those which occurred in the present case.

   There were two dissenting opinions filed, for a total of four Justices. Justice Douglas (for Justices Brennan and Blackmun as well) emphasized the concern expressed in the *Sears* and *Compco* decisions for national uniformity and competition in the areas of patent and copyright, and how inconsistent with those objectives were state copyright laws providing broad and unwarranted perpetual monopolies. Justice Marshall (also speaking for Justices Brennan and Blackmun) also supported preemption of the California statute. He concluded that Congress' listing of protected writings within the 1909 Act should be understood as mandating competition (i.e., the freedom to copy) with respect to other subject matter, such as pre-1972 sound recordings.

Ordinarily, the failure to enumerate "sound recordings" in § 5 would not be taken as an expression of Congress' desire to let free competition reign in the reproduction of such recordings, for, because of the realities of the legislative process, it is generally difficult to infer from a failure to act any affirmative conclusions.... But in *Sears* and its companion case, *Compco Corp. v. Day-Brite Lighting*, 376 U.S. 234 (1964), the Court determined that with respect to patents and copyrights, the ordinary practice was not to prevail. In view of the importance of not imposing unnecessary restraints on competition, the Court adopted in those cases a rule of construction that, unless the failure to provide patent or copyright protection for some class of works could clearly be shown to reflect a judgment that state regulation was permitted, the silence of Congress would be taken to reflect a judgment that free competition should prevail.... [I cannot find] in the course of legislation sufficient evidence to convince me that Congress determined to permit state regulation of the reproduction of sound recordings. For, whenever technological advances made extension of copyright protection seem wise, Congress has acted promptly.... This seems to me to reflect the same judgment that the Court found in *Sears* and *Compco:* Congress has decided that free competition should be the general rule, until it is convinced that the failure to provide copyright or patent protection is hindering "the Progress of Science and useful Arts."

The business of record piracy is not an attractive one; persons in the business capitalize on the talents of others without needing to assess independently the prospect of public acceptance of a performance. But the same might be said of persons who copy "mechanical configurations." Such people do provide low-cost reproductions that may well benefit the public. In light of the presumption of *Sears* and *Compco* that congressional silence betokens a determination that the benefits of competition outweigh the impediments placed on creativity by the lack of copyright protection, and in the absence of a congressional determination that the opposite is true, we should not let our distaste for "pirates" interfere with our interpretation of the copyright laws. I would therefore hold that, as to sound recordings fixed before February 15, 1972, the States may not enforce laws limiting reproduction.

QUESTIONS

1. Contrast the approach to preemption reflected in *Goldstein* on the one hand and *Sears-Compco* on the other. Did the Court in *Goldstein* satisfactorily distinguish *Sears* and *Compco*? Was the Court saying, simply, that the *Sears-Compco* philosophy applies only to potentially patentable subject matter and not to potentially copyrightable subject matter? Is this a tenable distinction?

2. Consider carefully the Court's statement that "the subject matter to which the Copyright Clause is addressed may thus be of purely local importance and not worthy of national attention or protection." On behalf of the Court — writing in an age of communications satellites, television, computers and telephone-transmissible photocopies — what constitutionally copyright-able subject matter would you give as examples? What is peculiarly "local" about an Elvis Presley recording as compared, for example, to a map of Phila-delphia (which the Founding Fathers promptly brought within the scope of the first Copyright Act in 1790)? How did the Court determine that sound recordings had been "left ... unattended" by Congress?

Kewanee Oil Co. v. Bicron Corp., 416 U.S. 470 (1974). Plaintiff-peti-tioner brought a diversity-of-citizenship action for misappropriation of trade secrets against certain former employees who had formed or joined the defen-dant company, a competing manufacturer of synthetic crystals. Petitioner alleged that the former employees, who had signed nondisclosure agreements while employed by Kewanee, had disclosed certain secret production processes to Bicron. The trial court, relying on Ohio trade-secret law, enjoined the dis-closure of the process; but the Court of Appeals for the Sixth Circuit reversed, finding that state law protection of the petitioner's trade secret, in commercial use for more than one year, was preempted by 35 U.S.C. § 101 of the federal patent law. Because four courts of appeals had held that state trade-secret law was not preempted, the Supreme Court granted certiorari; it reversed the judgment of the Sixth Circuit.

Ohio treats the petitioner's process as a protectible trade secret because, under the familiar definition in § 757 of the Restatement of Torts, it "is used in one's business, and ... gives him an opportunity to obtain an advantage over competitors who do not know or use it"; disclosure or unauthorized use "by those to whom the secret has been confided under the express or implied restriction of nondisclosure or nonuse" may be enjoined. Discovery of the trade secret is lawful, however, if achieved by independent invention, accidental disclosure, or by so-called reverse engineering. Novelty as required by the patent law is not required for trade secrets, although some novelty is required for otherwise the "secret" would be generally known.

The Supreme Court held, first, relying on *Goldstein,* that the Constitution does not oust the states from regulating discoveries that fall within the gen-eral subject matter of the patent and copyright clause. It then turned to whether there was a specific conflict with federally enacted patent law, incon-sistent with the Supremacy Clause of the Constitution. The Court stated that a central purpose of the patent laws, to provide "an incentive for inventors to risk the often enormous costs in terms of time, research, and development," was achieved by providing seventeen years of exclusive use, in exchange for which the inventor must disclose the invention by filing an application that fully and clearly describes the "manner and process of making and using" the invention, 35 U.S.C. § 112. The policies underlying trade-secret law are the maintenance of standards of commercial ethics and the encouragement of invention. The Court examined the interaction of these two systems of protec-tion of intellectual property, to determine whether state law presents "too great an encroachment on the federal patent system to be tolerated."

With regard to subject matter that trade-secret law can protect (e.g., customer lists or methods of doing business) but that are not within the subject matter of the patent laws (i.e., processes, machines, manufactures, compositions of matter), abolition of trade-secret protection would not result in increased disclosure of discoveries to the public; by hypothesis, patent protection is unavailable and disclosure through patent applications cannot be induced. As to patentable subject matter, there is no general conflict when the incentive to invent provided by the patent system is reinforced by the incentive to invent provided by trade-secret protection.

"The more difficult objective of the patent law to reconcile with trade secret law is that of disclosure, the *quid pro quo* of the right to exclude." The Court then separately considered three different categories of trade secrets to determine whether inventors will refrain from applying for patents because of the existence of trade-secret protection: "(1) The trade secret believed by its owner to constitute a validly patentable invention; (2) the trade secret known to its owner not to be so patentable; and (3) the trade secret whose valid patentability is considered dubious." The Court concluded that, with respect to all of these categories, the barring of state trade-secret protection would not advance the underlying policies of the patent laws, including disclosure; and that, indeed, the retention of trade-secret protection would in most situations reinforce patent policy.

The Court therefore concluded that state trade-secret law ought not be preempted by virtue of the Supremacy Clause.

> Trade secret law encourages the development and exploitation of those items of lesser or different invention than might be accorded protection under the patent laws, but which items still have an important part to play in the technological and scientific advancement of the Nation. Trade secret law promotes the sharing of knowledge, and the efficient operation of industry; it permits the individual inventor to reap the rewards of his labor by contracting with a company large enough to develop and exploit it. Congress, by its silence over these many years, has seen the wisdom of allowing the States to enforce trade secret protection. Until Congress takes affirmative action to the contrary, States should be free to grant protection to trade secrets.

Justice Marshall concurred. Contrary to the majority, he believed there was a significant possibility that inventors — particularly those who intend to use or sell the invention themselves rather than license it to others — would find trade-secret protection, indefinite in duration, preferable to patent protection, thus depriving society of public disclosure. Nonetheless, he inferred from the long coexistence of trade secrets and patent protection that Congress has not intended to exert pressure on inventors to use the patent system exclusively by withdrawing all other forms of legal protection. Justice Douglas (joined by Justice Brennan) dissented. He interpreted the *Sears* and *Compco* cases to stand for the proposition that "when an article is unprotected by a patent, state law may not forbid others to copy it, because every article not covered by a valid patent is in the public domain" so that free competition may prevail. Because the synthetic crystals produced by the petitioner are within the subject matter of the patent laws, Congress has adopted a policy of disclosure rather than secrecy, and has allowed a limited seventeen-year monopoly. Justice Douglas conceded that damages for theft of a trade secret might be a remedy within the power of the states, as a traditional measure redressing breach of contract or of a confidential relationship; but an injunction against use can properly be awarded only to enforce the patent laws and is thus preempted when grounded in state law.

QUESTIONS

1. Is not the *Kewanee* Court in effect upholding the power of the states to enact laws promoting a patent-like monopoly conditioned upon the maintenance of secrecy by the discoverer or inventor? Is the Court ignoring the extent to which such secrecy constitutes an inhibition upon competition, improvement in methods, cheaper products, and the like? If so, is there not a flat conflict with the basic policies of the patent laws?

2. Would the Court's logic justify a state's granting a patent monopoly of ten additional years after a seventeen-year federal patent had expired? Would it justify a state's making it a crime to infringe a patent granted by the United States Patent Office? If you would find these forms of state protection unpalatable under the federal patent scheme, how is state trade-secret protection different?

BONITO BOATS, INC. v. THUNDER CRAFT BOATS, INC.

489 U.S. 141 (1989)

[Plaintiff, a boat manufacturer, sought to enjoin defendant's use of a "direct molding process" to duplicate plaintiff's unpatented boat hulls. Plaintiff invoked a Florida statute that made "[i]t ... unlawful for any person to use the direct molding process to duplicate for the purpose of sale any manufactured vessel hull or component part of a vessel made by another without the written permission of that other person." Fla. Stat. § 559.94(2) (1987). The statute also made it unlawful for a person to "knowingly sell a vessel duplicated in violation of subsection (2)." The Florida Supreme Court held the statute conflicted with the federal patent law and was therefore invalid under the Supremacy Clause of the federal Constitution. The United States Supreme Court affirmed.]

JUSTICE O'CONNOR delivered the opinion of the [unanimous] Court.

[The federal patent law requires a] backdrop of free competition in the exploitation of unpatented designs and innovations. The novelty and nonobviousness requirements of patentability embody a congressional understanding, implicit in the Patent Clause itself, that free exploitation of ideas will be the rule, to which the protection of a federal patent is the exception.... The ultimate goal of the patent system is to bring new designs and technology into the public domain through disclosure. State law protection for techniques and designs whose disclosure has already been induced by market rewards may conflict with the very purpose of the patent laws by decreasing the range of ideas available as the building blocks of further innovation. The offer of federal protection from competitive exploitation of intellectual property would be rendered meaningless in a world where substantially similar state law protections were readily available. To a limited extent the federal patent laws must determine not only what is protected but also what is free for all to use....

Thus ... state regulation of intellectual property must yield to the extent that it clashes with the balance struck by Congress in our patent laws. The tension between the desire to freely exploit the full potential of our inventive resources and the need to create an incentive to deploy those resources is constant. Where it is clear how the patent laws strike that balance in a particular circumstance, that is not a judgment the states may second guess....

....

We believe that the Florida statute at issue in this case so substantially impedes the public use of the otherwise unprotected design and utilitarian ideas embodied in unpatented boat hulls as to run afoul of the teaching of our decisions in *Sears* and *Compco*. It is readily apparent that the Florida statute does not operate to prohibit "unfair competition" in the usual sense that the term is understood. The law of unfair competition has its roots in the common-law tort of deceit: its general concern is with protecting consumers from confusion as to source. While that concern may result in the creation of "quasiproperty rights" in communicative symbols, the focus is on the protection of consumers, not the protection of producers as an incentive to product innovation....

With some notable exceptions, including the interpretation of the Illinois law of unfair competition at issue in *Sears* and *Compco,* the common-law tort of unfair competition has been limited to protection against copying of non-functional aspects of consumer products which have acquired secondary meaning such that they operate as a designation of source.... The "protection" granted a particular design under the law of unfair competition is thus limited to one context where consumer confusion is likely to result; the design "idea" itself may be freely exploited in all other contexts.

In contrast to the operation of unfair competition law, the Florida statute is aimed directly at preventing the exploitation of the design and utilitarian conceptions embodied in the product itself.... Like the patentee, the beneficiary of the Florida statute may prevent a competitor from "making" the product in what is evidently the most efficient manner available and from "selling" the product when it is produced in that fashion. The Florida scheme offers this protection for an unlimited number of years to all boat hulls and their component parts, without regard to their ornamental or technological merit. Protection is available for subject matter for which patent protection has been denied or has expired, as well as for designs which have been freely revealed to the consuming public by their creators....

Our decisions since *Sears* and *Compco* have made it clear that the Patent and Copyright Clauses do not, by their own force or by negative implication, deprive the States of the power to adopt rules for the promotion of intellectual creation within their own jurisdictions. Thus, where "Congress determines that neither federal protection nor freedom from restraint is required by the national interest," *Goldstein [v. California]*, [412 U.S. 546], 559 [(1973)], States remain free to promote originality and creativity in their own domains.

Nor does the fact that a particular item lies within the subject matter of the federal patent laws necessarily preclude the States from offering limited protection which does not impermissibly interfere with the federal patent scheme. As Sears itself makes clear, States may place limited regulations on the use of unpatented designs in order to prevent consumer confusion as to source. In *Kewanee*, we found that state protection of trade secrets, as applied to both patentable and unpatentable subject matter, did not conflict with the federal patent laws. In both situations, state protection was not aimed exclusively at the promotion of invention itself, and the state restrictions on the use of unpatented ideas were limited to those necessary to promote goals outside the contemplation of the federal patent scheme. Both the law of unfair competition and state trade secret law have coexisted harmoniously with federal patent protection for almost 200 years, and Congress has given no indication that their operation is inconsistent with the operation of the federal patent laws.

Indeed, there are affirmative indications from Congress that both the law of unfair competition and trade secret protection are consistent with the balance struck by the patent laws. Section 43(a) of the Lanham Act, 60 Stat. 441, 15 U.S.C. § 1125(a), creates a federal remedy for making "a false designation of origin, or any false description or representation, including words or other symbols tending falsely to describe or represent the same ...." Congress has thus given federal recognition to many of the concerns that underlie the state tort of unfair competition, and the application of *Sears* and *Compco* to non-functional aspects of a product which have been shown to identify source must take account of competing federal policies in this regard. Similarly, as *Justice Marshall* noted in his concurring opinion in *Kewanee*: "State trade secret laws and the federal patent laws have co-existed for many, many, years. During this time, Congress has repeatedly demonstrated its full awareness of the existence of the trade secret system, without any indication of disapproval. Indeed, Congress has in a number of instances given explicit federal protection to trade secret information provided to federal agencies." *Kewanee, supra,* at 494 (concurring in result) (citation omitted). The case for federal preemption is particularly weak where Congress has indicated its awareness of the operation of state law in a field of federal interest, and has nonetheless decided to "stand by both concepts and to tolerate whatever tension there [is] between them." *Silkwood v. Kerr-McGee Corp.*, 464 U.S. 238, 256 (1984). The same cannot be said of the Florida statute at issue here, which offers protection beyond that available under the law of unfair competition or trade secret, without any showing of consumer confusion, or breach of trust or secrecy.

The Florida statute is aimed directly at the promotion of intellectual creation by substantially restricting the public's ability to exploit ideas that the patent system mandates shall be free for all to use. Like the interpretation of Illinois unfair competition law in *Sears* and *Compco*, the Florida statute represents a break with the tradition of peaceful coexistence between state market regulation and federal patent policy. The Florida law substantially restricts the public's ability to exploit an unpatented design in general circulation, raising the specter of state-created monopolies in a host of useful shapes and processes for which patent protection has been denied or is otherwise unobtainable. It thus enters a field of regulation which the patent laws have reserved to Congress. The patent statute's careful balance between public right and private monopoly to promote certain creative activity is a "scheme of federal regulation ... so pervasive as to make reasonable the inference that Congress left no room for the States to supplement it." *Rice v. Santa Fe Elevator Corp.,* 331 U.S. 218, 230 (1947).

Congress has considered extending various forms of limited protection to industrial design either through the copyright laws or by relaxing the restrictions on the availability of design patents. See generally Brown, *Design Protection: An Overview,* 34 UCLA L. Rev. 1341 (1987). Congress explicitly refused to take this step in the copyright laws, see 17 U.S.C. § 101; H. R. Rep. No. 94-1476, p. 55 (1976), and despite sustained criticism for a number of years, it has declined to alter the patent protections presently available for industrial design. See Report of the President's Commission on the Patent System, S. Doc. No. 5, 90th Cong., 1st Sess., 20-21 (1967). It is for Congress to determine if the present system of design and utility patents is ineffectual in promoting the useful arts in the context of industrial design. By offering patent-like protection for ideas deemed unprotected under the present federal scheme, the Florida statute conflicts with the "strong federal policy favoring free competition in ideas which do not merit patent protection." *Lear, Inc.,* 395 U.S., at 656. We therefore agree with the majority of the Florida Supreme Court that the Florida statute is preempted by the Supremacy Clause, and the judgment of that court is hereby affirmed.

B. COPYRIGHT PREEMPTION UNDER § 301 OF THE 1976 ACT

1. THE SAGA OF § 301

The preceding cases dealing with the preemption of state law show the Supreme Court attempting to divine the intention of Congress concerning the continuing vitality of state tort and trade-secret law — when Congress has not made its intention explicitly manifest. One would think that problems of federal preemption would be dispelled if Congress were specifically to address the matter in its legislation. Congress in fact did so in § 301 of the 1976 Act. In the words of the House Report (at p. 130), the preemption principles set forth in § 301 are "intended to be stated in the clearest and most unequivocal language possible, so as to foreclose any conceivable misinterpretation of its unqualified intention that Congress shall act preemptively, and to avoid the development of any vague borderline areas between State and Federal protection." In exploring the following materials, the student should consider whether this congressional objective has been achieved.

Section 301 reads as follows:

§ 301. Preemption with respect to other laws

(a) On and after January 1, 1978, all legal or equitable rights that are equivalent to any of the exclusive rights within the general scope of copyright as specified by section 106 in works of authorship that are fixed in a tangible medium of expression and come within the subject matter of copyright as specified by sections 102 and 103, whether created before or after that date and whether published or unpublished, are governed exclusively by this title. Thereafter, no person is entitled to any such right or equivalent right in any such work under the common law or statutes of any State.

(b) Nothing in this title annuls or limits any rights or remedies under the common law or statutes of any State with respect to —

(1) subject matter that does not come within the subject matter of copyright as specified by sections 102 and 103, including works of authorship not fixed in any tangible medium of expression; or

(2) any cause of action arising from undertakings commenced before January 1, 1978; or

(3) activities violating legal or equitable rights that are not equivalent to any of the exclusive rights within the general scope of copyright as specified by section 106; or

(4) State and local landmarks, historic preservation, zoning, or building codes, relating to architectural works protected under section 102(a)(8).

(c) With respect to sound recordings fixed before February 15, 1972, any rights or remedies under the common law or statutes of any State shall not be annulled or limited by this title until February 15, 2047....

(d) Nothing in this title annuls or limits any rights or remedies under any other Federal statute.

[Subsections (e) and (f), respectively, refer to the Berne Convention and provide for preemption of equivalent state laws regarding works of visual art that are covered by the Visual Artists Rights Act of 1990.]

There is hardly a more significant (and probably no more troublesome) question underlying the Act than the preemptive effect of this provision. Basically, this question is: How much of the common law (or state statutory law), particularly that of unfair competition, is left standing or is permitted to develop by the new copyright law?

In the analysis of this perhaps unanswerable question, several things at least are clear:

(1) The statute covers, as it must, only works "fixed in a tangible medium of expression." This is clearly intended to be most comprehensive and to cover not only things such as sound recordings, computer-readable material, and other known forms of fixation but also works fixed by any method "later developed." Moreover, it has already been seen that the limitation of preemption to "subject matter of copyright as specified by sections 102 and 103" still

covers a very broad area of material. Nevertheless oral works (such as improvised speeches), live jazz performances, and live demonstrations or displays by cathode rays are frequently never fixed in a tangible medium of expression. (As already noted, live broadcasts simultaneously taped are considered "fixed" under § 101.) Accordingly, copying and other copyright-type uses of such material are not regulated by the federal statute, and state regulation thereof is not preempted.

(2) Rights or remedies under other federal statutes are expressly saved from preemption by § 301(d). The patent statute, Title 35, U.S.C., is an example of such other (non-preempted) federal statute; and so too is the Federal Communications Act, 47 U.S.C. § 151 *et seq. See, e.g.,* § 111 of the Copyright Act. Perhaps the most intriguing statutory exception is offered by the Lanham Act, 15 U.S.C. § 1051 *et seq.,* not only in its provision for trademark registration of shapes which might otherwise be copyrightable, see, e.g., *In re Morton-Norwich Prods., Inc.,* 671 F.2d 1332 (C.C.P.A. 1982); *In re Mogen David Wine Corp.,* 328 F.2d 925 (C.C.P.A. 1964), 372 F.2d 539 (C.C.P.A. 1967), but also in its more open-ended "false representation" provision, § 43(a), 15 U.S.C. § 1125(a). *See, e.g., Coca Cola Co. v. Tropicana Prods., Inc.,* 690 F.2d 312 (2d Cir. 1982). *Cf. Gilliam v. American Broadcasting Co.,* 538 F.2d 14 (2d Cir. 1976), *supra.*

(3) Section 301 expressly obliterates "publication" as the dividing line between federal protection under the statute and common law protection (the new dividing line being "creation," i.e., "fixation"). Works are protected under the statute "whether published or unpublished" and indeed whether created before or after January 1, 1978. This means, at the very least, the abolition of common law literary property, often called "common law copyright," covering the copying of manuscripts, letters, diaries, private presentations, and other unpublished material fixed in a tangible medium of expression.

We turn now to aspects of § 301 that are not so clear. The statute sets forth two requirements for preemption under § 301: a "subject matter" test briefly discussed above (and whose more problematic features will be addressed in the next section), and an "equivalent rights" test. Just what Congress meant by state rights "that are not equivalent to any of the exclusive rights within the general scope of copyright as specified by Section 106" is not at all apparent — and was not even to the enacting Congress. Although Congress expressed a generally resounding preemptive intent, it vacillated on the question of what state rights are nonequivalent.

An earlier version of § 301(b)(3) included the following list of putatively nonequivalent state claims:

> [R]ights against misappropriation not equivalent to any of such exclusive rights, breaches of contract, breaches of trust, trespass, conversion, invasion of privacy, defamation, and deceptive trade practices such as passing off and false representation.

As you read the House Report accompanying this version of § 301, note the discussion of these state claims, and ask yourself whether preservation of such claims does not undermine the creation of a uniform federal copyright system.

HOUSE REPORT

H.R. Rep. No. 94-1476, 94th Cong., 2d Sess. 129-33 (1976)

Single Federal System

Section 301, one of the bedrock provisions of the bill, would accomplish a fundamental and significant change in the present law. Instead of a dual system of "common law copyright" for unpublished works and statutory copyright for published works, which has been the system in effect in the United States since the first copyright statute in 1790, the bill adopts a single system of Federal statutory copyright from creation. Under section 301 a work would obtain statutory protection as soon as it is "created" or, as that term is defined in section 101, when it is "fixed in a copy or phonorecord for the first time." Common law copyright protection for works coming within the scope of the statute would be abrogated, and the concept of publication would lose its all-embracing importance as a dividing line between common law and statutory protection and between both of these forms of legal protection and the public domain.

By substituting a single Federal system for the present anachronistic, uncertain, impractical, and highly complicated dual system, the bill would greatly improve the operation of the copyright law and would be much more effective in carrying out the basic constitutional aims of uniformity and the promotion of writing and scholarship. The main arguments in favor of a single Federal system can be summarized as follows:

1. One of the fundamental purposes behind the copyright clause of the Constitution, as shown in Madison's comments in The Federalist, was to promote national uniformity and to avoid the practical difficulties of determining and enforcing an author's rights under the differing laws and in the separate courts of the various States. Today, when the methods for dissemination of an author's work are incomparably broader and faster than they were in 1789, national uniformity in copyright protection is even more essential than it was then to carry out the constitutional intent.

2. "Publication," perhaps the most important single concept under the present law, also represents its most serious defect. Although at one time, when works were disseminated almost exclusively through printed copies, "publication" could serve as a practical dividing line between common law and statutory protection, this is no longer true. With the development of the 20th-century communications revolution, the concept of publication has become increasingly artificial and obscure. To cope with the legal consequences of an established concept that has lost much of its meaning and justification, the courts have given "publication" a number of diverse interpretations, some of them radically different. Not unexpectedly, the results in individual cases have become unpredictable and often unfair. A single Federal system would help to clear up this chaotic situation.

3. Enactment of section 301 would also implement the "limited times" provision of the Constitution, which has become distorted under the traditional concept of "publication." Common law protection in "unpublished" works is now perpetual, no matter how widely they may be disseminated by means other than "publication"; the bill would place a time limit on the duration of

exclusive rights in them. The provision would also aid scholarship and the dissemination of historical materials by making unpublished, undisseminated manuscripts available for publication after a reasonable period.

4. Adoption of a uniform national copyright system would greatly improve international dealings in copyrighted material. No other country has anything like our present dual system. In an era when copyrighted works can be disseminated instantaneously to every country on the globe, the need for effective international copyright relations, and the concomitant need for national uniformity, assume ever greater importance.

Under section 301, the statute would apply to all works created after its effective date, whether or not they are ever published or disseminated. With respect to works created before the effective date of the statute and still under common law protection, section 303 of the statute would provide protection from that date on, and would guarantee a minimum period of statutory copyright.

Preemption of State Law

The intention of section 301 is to preempt and abolish any rights under the common law or statutes of a State that are equivalent to copyright and that extend to works coming within the scope of the Federal copyright law. The declaration of this principle in section 301 is intended to be stated in the clearest and most unequivocal language possible, so as to foreclose any conceivable misinterpretation of its unqualified intention that Congress shall act preemptively, and to avoid the development of any vague borderline areas between State and Federal protection.

Under section 301(a) all "legal or equitable rights that are equivalent to any of the exclusive rights within the general scope of copyright as specified by section 106 ... are governed exclusively by" the Federal copyright statute if the works involved are "works of authorship that are fixed in a tangible medium of expression and come within the subject matter of copyright as specified by sections 102 and 103." All corresponding State laws, whether common law or statutory, are preempted and abrogated. Regardless of when the work was created and whether it is published or unpublished, disseminated or undisseminated, in the public domain or copyrighted under the Federal statute, the States cannot offer it protection equivalent to copyright. Section 1338 of title 28, United States Code, also makes clear that any action involving rights under the Federal copyright law would come within the exclusive jurisdiction of the Federal courts. The preemptive effect of section 301 is limited to State laws: as stated expressly in subsection (d) of section 301, there is no intention to deal with the question of whether Congress can or should offer the equivalent of copyright protection under some constitutional provision other than the patent-copyright clause of article 1, section 8.

As long as a work fits within one of the general subject matter categories of sections 102 and 103, the bill prevents the States from protecting it even if it fails to achieve Federal statutory copyright because it is too minimal or lacking in originality to qualify, or because it has fallen into the public domain. On the other hand, section 301(b) explicitly preserves common law copyright protection for one important class of works: works that have not been "fixed in any tangible medium of expression." Examples would include choreography that has never been filmed or notated, an extemporaneous speech, "original works of authorship" communicated solely through conversations or live broadcasts, and a dramatic sketch or musical composition improvised or developed from memory and without being recorded or written down. As mentioned above in connection with section 102, unfixed works are not included in the specified "subject matter of copyright." They are therefore not affected by the preemption of section 301, and would continue to be subject to protection under State statute or common law until fixed in tangible form.

The preemption of rights under State law is complete with respect to any work coming within the scope of the bill, even though the scope of exclusive rights given the work under the bill is narrower than the scope of common law rights in the work might have been.

....

In a general way subsection (b) of section 301 represents the obverse of subsection (a). It sets out in broad terms and without necessarily being exhaustive, some of the principal areas of protection that preemption would not prevent the States from protecting. Its purpose is to make clear, consistent with the 1964 Supreme Court decisions in *Sears Roebuck & Co. v. Stiffel Co.,* 376 U.S. 225, and *Compco Corp. v. Day-Brite Lighting, Inc.,* 376 U.S. 234, that preemption does not extend to causes of action, or subject matter outside the scope of the revised Federal copyright statute.

The numbered clauses of subsection (b) list three general areas left unaffected by the preemption: (1) subject matter that does not come within the subject matter of copyright; (2) causes of action arising under State law before the effective date of the statute; and (3) violations of rights that are not equivalent to any of the exclusive rights under copyright.

The examples in clause (3), while not exhaustive, are intended to illustrate rights and remedies that are different in nature from the rights comprised in a copyright and that may continue to be protected under State common law or statute. The evolving common law rights of "privacy," "publicity," and trade secrets, and the general laws of defamation and fraud, would remain unaffected as long as the causes of action contain elements, such as an invasion of personal rights or a breach of trust or confidentiality, that are different in kind from copyright infringement. Nothing in the bill derogates from the rights of parties to contract with each other and to sue for breaches of contract; however, to the extent that the unfair competition concept known as "interference with contract relations" is merely the equivalent of copyright protection, it would be preempted.

The last example listed in clause (3) — "deceptive trade practices such as passing off and false representation" — represents an effort to distinguish between those causes of action known as "unfair competition" that the copyright statute is not intended to preempt and those that it is. Section 301 is not intended to preempt common law protection in cases involving activities such as false labeling, fraudulent representation, and passing off even where the subject matter involved comes within the scope of the copyright statute.

"Misappropriation" is not necessarily synonymous with copyright infringement, and thus a cause of action labeled as "misappropriation" is not preempted if it is in fact based neither on a right within the general scope of copyright as specified by section 106 nor on a right equivalent thereto. For example, state law should have the flexibility to afford a remedy (under traditional principles of equity) against a consistent pattern of unauthorized appropriation by a competitor of the facts (i.e., not the literary expression) constituting "hot" news, whether in the traditional mold of *International News Service v. Associated Press,* 248 U.S. 215 (1918), or in the newer form of data updates from scientific, business, or financial data bases. Likewise, a person having no trust or other relationship with the proprietor of a computerized data base should not be immunized from sanctions against electronically or cryptographically breaching the proprietor's security arrangements and accessing the proprietor's data. The unauthorized data access which should be remediable might also be achieved by the intentional interception of data transmissions by wire, microwave or laser transmissions, or by the common unintentional means of "crossed" telephone lines occasioned by errors in switching.

The proprietor of data displayed on the cathode ray tube of a computer terminal should be afforded protection against unauthorized printouts by third parties (with or without improper access), even if the data are not copyrightable. For example, the data may not be copyrighted because they are not fixed in a tangible medium of expression (i.e., the data are not displayed for a period [of] not more than transitory duration).

Nothing contained in section 301 precludes the owner of a material embodiment of a copy or a phonorecord from enforcing a claim of conversion against one who takes possession of the copy or phonorecord without consent.

Section 301(b)(3)'s inclusion of a list of nonequivalent state claims provoked considerable controversy, and, at the last minute, when the bill came up for debate on the House floor on September 22, 1976, an amendment to delete the list was proposed. The following murky colloquy ensued:

> *Mr. Seiberling:* Mr. Chairman, I offer an amendment.
> The Clerk read as follows:
>
> [strike out the words "including rights against misappropriation not equivalent to any of such exclusive rights, breaches of contracts, breaches of trust, trespass, conversion, invasion of privacy, defamation, and deceptive trade practices such as passing off and false representation"]
>
> ....
>
> *Mr. Seiberling:* Mr. Chairman, my amendment is intended to save the "federal preemption" of State law section, which is section 301 of the bill, from being inadvertently nullified because of the inclusion of certain examples in the exemptions from preemption.
> This amendment would simply strike the examples listed in section 301(b)(3).

The amendment is strongly supported by the Justice Department, which believes that it would be a serious mistake to cite as an exemption from preemption the doctrine of "misappropriation." The doctrine was created by the Supreme Court in 1922 and it has generally been ignored by the Supreme Court itself and by the lower courts ever since.

Inclusion of a reference to the misappropriation doctrine in this bill, however, could easily be construed by the courts as authorizing the States to pass misappropriation laws. We should not approve such enabling legislation, because a misappropriation law could be so broad as to render the preemption section meaningless ....

Mr. Railsback: Mr. Chairman, may I ask the gentleman from Ohio, for the purpose of clarifying the amendment that by striking the word "misappropriation" the gentleman in no way is attempting to change the existing state of the law, that is as it may exist in certain States that have recognized the right of recovery relating to "misappropriation": is that correct?

Mr. Seiberling: That is correct. All I am trying to do is prevent the citing of them as examples in a statute. We are, in effect, adopting a rather amorphous body of State law and codifying it, in effect. Rather I am trying to have this bill leave the State law alone and make it clear we are merely dealing with copyright laws, laws applicable to copyrights.

Mr. Railsback: Mr. Chairman, I personally have no objection to the gentleman's amendment in view of that clarification and I know of no objections from this side.

....

Mr. Kastenmeier: Mr. Chairman, I too have examined the gentleman's amendment and was familiar with the position of the Department of Justice. Unfortunately, the Justice Department did not make its position known to the committee until the last day of markup.

Mr. Seiberling: I understand.

Mr. Kastenmeier: However, Mr. Chairman, I think that the amendment the gentleman is offering is consistent with the position of the Justice Department and accept it on this side as well.

122 Cong. Rec. H-10910 (daily ed. Sept. 22, 1976).

The Senate conferees acquiesced in the deletion of the list from § 301(b)(3); the Conference Report contains no comment on the intended effect of the deletion. For more detailed accounts of the tortuous legislative history of § 301, see, e.g., Brown, *Unification: A Cheerful Requiem for Common Law Copyright*, 24 UCLA L. Rev. 1070, 1089-1102 (1977); Diamond, *Preemption of State Law*, 25 Bull. Copyright Soc'y 204, 209-12 (1978); 1 Nimmer on Copyright § 1.01[B].

2. THE DEVELOPMENT OF THE CASE LAW

a. Works Coming Within the Subject Matter of Copyright

Baltimore Orioles, Inc. v. Major League Baseball Players Ass'n, 805 F.2d 663 (7th Cir. 1986), *cert. denied,* 107 S. Ct. 1593 (1987). In the midst of a dispute between major league baseball clubs and their players about the allocation of revenues from television broadcasts of games, the players wrote letters to the clubs and to television and cable companies asserting that game telecasts were unlawful. The players claimed that their consent to such telecasts had not been secured, and that the telecasts misappropriated their property rights in their athletic performances. Lawsuits were brought by the clubs and the players to secure a declaration regarding their respective rights in the game telecasts.

The court of appeals affirmed the judgment of the district court against the players. It held that telecasts of baseball games are copyrightable works, involving authorship regarding such matters as "camera angles, types of shots, the use of instant replays and split screens, and shot selection"; and that the clubs own the copyright, while the athletic performances of the players are contributed as employees to the televised "works made for hire." Despite this holding on the copyright issue, the players contended that broadcast of the games without their express consent "violates their rights to publicity in their performances." The clubs argued that any such publicity claim is preempted under § 301 of the Copyright Act, both because the players' athletic performances are within the subject matter of copyright and because the right of publicity is equivalent to a copyright claim.

On the former issue, the principal dispute concerned whether the players' performances are "fixed" so as to be covered by the Copyright Act. Although the game telecasts are recorded simultaneously with their transmission, and are therefore "fixed" within the definition in § 101 of the Act, the players contended that they were claiming rights in their performances, which are separate from the telecast and are not fixed. The court disagreed. Whatever might have been the case had the ballgames been played in a stadium without being broadcast or recorded,

> the Players' performances are embodied in a copy, *viz*, the videotape of the telecast, from which the performances can be perceived, reproduced, and otherwise communicated indefinitely. Hence, their performances are fixed in tangible form, and any property rights in the performances that are equivalent to any of the rights encompassed in a copyright are preempted.

The players also argued that their performances, "because they lack sufficient creativity," are not works of authorship within the subject matter of copyright under § 102. The court rejected this contention as well. It concluded that so long as a work falls within the listed categories in § 102, preemption of state claims equivalent to copyright will follow "even if [the work] fails to achieve Federal copyright because it is too minimal or lacking in originality to qualify." The court found, in any event, that the players' performances are brought within the scope of § 301 preemption by virtue of their incorporation in the recorded game telecasts, which *are* sufficiently creative.

The court then turned to the question whether the state-law right asserted by the players, the right of publicity, was equivalent to any of the rights included in § 106 of the Copyright Act. Because the players' right of publicity was allegedly violated merely by the telecasting of baseball games in which they played, the court found this alleged right to be equivalent to the right under § 106(4) publicly to perform an audiovisual work. Accordingly, § 301 compelled preemption of the state claim.

In preserving state law rights (including copyright-equivalent rights) regarding "Subject matter that does not come within the subject matter of copyright as specified by Sections 102 and 103, including works of authorship not fixed in any tangible medium of expression," what did Congress have in mind? The language of § 301(b)(1) suggests a congressional intent not to preempt state claims concerning a class of works or subject matter that extends beyond the class of unfixed works. What further uncopyrightable subject matter did Congress allow the states to regulate?

Note some problems arising out of Congress' reference in § 301(b)(1) to "*subject matter* that does not come within the subject matter of copyright..." (emphasis supplied). Section 301(b)(1) is not an exact mirror image of § 301(a), which refers to "*works of authorship* that are fixed in a tangible medium of expression and come within the subject matter of copyright ..." (emphasis supplied). Under a literal reading, emphasizing the nonparallelism of these two provisions, it may appear that works of authorship are as a whole governed exclusively by federal copyright law, but that noncopyrightable subject matter contained within a work of authorship may continue to receive state law protection. Thus, a state may forbid the copying of discrete ideas or facts contained within a copyrighted work, because such elements are excluded from copyright under § 102(b). Similarly, consider a compilation consisting of public domain poetry and new commentary. Under § 103, only the commentary and the organization of the compilation are within the subject matter of copyright. The preexisting poetry is excluded. Does the nonparallelism of §§ 301(a) and 301(b)(1) mean that state law may protect the public domain poetry? Or do not these anomalous results suggest that material which Congress specifically excluded from federal copyright protection in §§ 102 and 103 is to be protected under no legal regime, state or federal?

The literalist interpretation of § 301(b)(1) has found its adherents. For example, in *Bromhall v. Rorvik*, 478 F. Supp. 361 (E.D. Pa. 1979), the court rejected a preemption challenge to plaintiff's claim that defendant, who had read plaintiff's eight-page thesis abstract on the cloning of rabbits, had misappropriated plaintiff's rabbit cloning ideas in writing a book about the cloning of humans. Observing that under § 102(b) "copyright protection extends only to the *expression* of an idea, not the idea itself" (emphasis added), the court determined that claims relating to the idea itself were preserved under § 301(b)(1).

Another district court reached the same conclusion, in dictum, in *Past Pluto Prods. Corp. v. Dana*, 627 F. Supp. 1435 (S.D.N.Y. 1986). There the court dismissed an action for infringement of a plastic foam hat in the shape of the crown of the Statue of Liberty, finding that the plaintiff's work lacked original authorship in rendering the design of the public domain statue. In a footnote, however, the court expounded:

> Because plaintiff never asserted a claim for misappropriation, it is hardly necessary to decide whether such a claim would have been preempted by federal copyright law.... Nonetheless, it appears that a misappropriation claim by Past Pluto would not have been preempted, insofar as such a claim would have been based on defendants' misappropriation of plaintiff's idea, a subject matter beyond the scope of copyright law. See 17 U.S.C. § 102(b). It is clear that any state law action covering subject matter that does not come within the subject matter of federal copyright law as defined in 17 U.S.C. §§ 102 and 103 is not preempted.

Accord Goldstein, *Preempted State Doctrines, Involuntary Transfers and Compulsory Licenses: Testing the Limits of Copyright,* 24 UCLA L. Rev. 1107, 1119 (1977):

> The preferable interpretation of § 102(b) would leave the enumerated items open to protection by the states. This interpretation reads § 102(b) to specify that certain elements — ideas, procedures and the like — contained in original works of authorship are not protected. Since these elements are not the "works of authorship" to which § 102(b) refers, they are not within the subject matter of copyright [for purposes of § 301].

The prevailing view, however, holds that once the work at issue is a copyrightable "work of authorship," all claims concerning copying, whether of protected or unprotected material, are governed exclusively by federal law. Thus, in *Harper & Row v. Nation Enters.,* 723 F.2d 195 (2d Cir. 1983), *rev'd on other grounds,* 471 U.S. 539 (1985), the Second Circuit stated that state claims regarding the unauthorized advance publication of portions of the memoirs of Former President Gerald R. Ford concerned a "work of authorship" exclusively governed by federal law.

> The fact that portions of the Ford memoirs may consist of uncopyrightable material ... does not take the work as a whole outside the subject matter protected by the Act. Were this not so, states would be free to expand the perimeters of copyright protection to their own liking, on the theory that preemption would be no bar to state protection of material not meeting federal standards. That interpretation would run directly afoul of one of the Act's central purposes, to "avoid the development of any vague borderline areas between State and Federal protection."

Accord Gorman, *Fact or Fancy: The Implications for Copyright,* 29 J. Copyright Soc'y 560, 604 (1982):

> When Congress declares in section 102(b) that copyright in ... a literary work does not "extend to any idea" described, explained or embodied therein, it is not declaring such an idea outside of the subject matter of copyright so much as it is affirmatively declaring — as clearly as it can, and for the clearest of reasons — that ideas are free to be copied, adapted

and disseminated, and that no court is to construe the federal copyright monopoly as inhibiting that freedom. The implication for state law is equally clear: neither can the states. This is a compelling illustration of the kind of congressional declaration that the *Goldstein* Court had in mind when it said:

> Where the need for free and unrestricted distribution of a writing is thought to be required by the national interest, the Copyright Clause and the Commerce Clause would allow Congress to eschew all protection. In such cases, a conflict would develop if a State attempted to protect that which Congress intended to be free from restraint....

... The same can be said concerning the facts, principles, discoveries, and systems embodied in maps, directories, printed forms, and works of history or biography. All of these tangible works are either literary or graphic, and thus within the subject matter of copyright under section 102(a), such that the preemptive mandate of section 301 applies. A state may therefore not make it a tort to exercise rights equivalent to those in section 106, such as reproducing those works in copies, preparing adaptations or translations, making the first sale of copies to the public, or displaying them publicly. Nor may a state forbid the dissemination of the principles, discoveries, and systems embodied therein.

QUESTION

Which, if any, of the following state statutes address subject matter reserved under § 301(b)(1)?

(1) A proposed state statute protecting artistically designed buildings, furniture, refrigerators, food processors, automobiles, and other useful articles. *See Vermont Castings, Inc. v. Evans Prods. Co.,* 215 U.S.P.Q. 758 (D. Vt. 1981); *H₂O Swimwear Ltd. v. Lomas,* 164 A.D.2d 804, 560 N.Y.S.2d 19 (1st Dep't 1990).

(2) A proposed state statute protecting book design and typeface. *See Storch Enters. v. Mergenthaler Linotype,* 202 U.S.P.Q. 623 (E.D.N.Y. 1979).

(3) A proposed state statute protecting characters. *See Universal City Studios, Inc. v. T-Shirt Gallery, Ltd.,* 634 F. Supp. 1468 (S.D.N.Y. 1986).

(4) A proposed state statute protecting against the extraction of information from databases.

(5) A proposed state statute protecting works whose federal copyrights have expired.

(6) A proposed state statute protecting derivative works created without the authorization of the owner of copyright in the underlying work.

b. Rights Equivalent to Copyright

EHAT v. TANNER

780 F.2d 876 (10th Cir. 1985), *cert. denied,* 479 U.S. 820 (1986)

SEYMOUR, CIRCUIT JUDGE.

Andrew Ehat brought this action against Gerald and Sandra Tanner, dba Modern Microfilm Company (the Tanners), alleging injury from the Tanners' unauthorized reproduction and sale of literary material in which Ehat claimed a proprietary interest. Judgment was entered against the Tanners, and they appeal. We reverse.

Ehat was a scholar engaged in post-graduate research on the history of the Church of Jesus Christ of Latter-Day Saints (the LDS Church). The Tanners publish and distribute documents and works relevant to the LDS Church. In the course of his research, Ehat examined and took notes from a 350-page transcript of the William Clayton Journals at the LDS Church Archives.[1] Ehat gave to his colleague, Lyndon Cook, material consisting of quotations he and another researcher had taken from the Journals as well as his own notes and comments. This material was surreptitiously taken from Cook's office, copied, and replaced. One of these unauthorized copies found its way to the Tanners, who had no part in the original removal from Cook's office. They blacked out the material added by Ehat, printed the original extracts, and sold them to the public.

Ehat's complaint asserted claims under the federal copyright statutes, on which the judge granted summary judgment for the Tanners. In addition, the complaint alleged state common law claims for unfair competition and unjust enrichment. Following a bench trial on these claims, the Court entered judgment for Ehat. On appeal, the Tanners assert that the district court erred in awarding damages on Ehat's common law claims because those claims are preempted by the federal copyright statutes. We agree.

Federal copyright law was amended by the Copyright Act of 1976 to preempt state law ... Congress expressly stated that section 301 is intended to prevent "the States from protecting ... [a work] even if it fails to achieve Federal statutory copyright because it is too minimal or lacking in originality to qualify, or because it has fallen into the public domain." H.R. Rep. No. 1476, 94th Cong., 2d Sess. 131, *reprinted in* 1976 *U.S. Code Cong. & Ad. News* 5659, 5747. State law forbidding others to copy an article "unprotected by a patent or a copyright ... would interfere with the federal policy, found in Art. I, § 8, cl. 8, of the Constitution and in the implementing federal statutes, of allowing free access to copy whatever the federal patent and copyright laws leave in the public domain." *Compco Corp. v. Day-Brite Lighting, Inc.,* 376 U.S. 234, 237, 84 S. Ct. 779, 782, 11 L. Ed. 2d 669 (1964); *see also Suid v. Newsweek Magazine,* 503 F. Supp. 146, 148 (D.D.C. 1980).

Under section 301, a state common law or statutory claim is preempted if: (1) the work is within the scope of the "subject matter of copyright" as specified in 17 U.S.C. §§ 102, 103; and (2) the rights granted under state law are equivalent to any exclusive rights within the scope of federal copyright as set out in 17 U.S.C. § 106....

Literary works, including compilations and derivative works, are within the subject matter of copyright if they are original works of authorship fixed in any tangible medium of expression. *See* 17 U.S.C. §§ 102, 103. This is so

---

[1]William Clayton lived during the 1800's and was for a time the private secretary to Joseph Smith, the first president of the LDS Church. The Journals at issue were kept by Clayton from 1842 to 1846 while he and Joseph Smith lived in Nauvoo, Illinois.

notwithstanding the material could not be copyrighted. *See Harper & Row*, 723 F.2d at 200. The material at issue here clearly falls within the subject matter of copyright. The district court did not address this issue, and Ehat does not argue otherwise on appeal.

We now turn to whether the rights Ehat seeks to assert under state common law are equivalent to those exclusive rights within the scope of copyright. Under federal law, the owner of copyright has the exclusive right "to reproduce the copyrighted work" and "to distribute copies" to the public by sale. *See* 17 U.S.C. §§ 106(1), (3).

> When a right defined by state law may be abridged by an act which, in and of itself, would infringe one of the exclusive rights, the state law in question must be deemed preempted.... Conversely, when a state law violation is predicated upon an act incorporating elements beyond mere reproduction or the like, the rights involved are not equivalent and preemption will not occur.

Harper & Row, 723 F.2d at 200 (citations omitted).

In an effort to distinguish this case from a preempted claim, the district court granted Ehat relief based on its finding that, by printing and selling Ehat's notes, the Tanners "bodily appropriated the work product of plaintiff" and derived a profit from their misappropriation. Rec., vol. V, at 13-14. We need not decide whether this misappropriation of material states a claim for relief under Utah law. Assuming that it does, *see generally International News Service v. Associated Press*, 248 U.S. 215, 39 S. Ct. 68, 63 L. Ed. 211 (1918); Prosser & Keeton on Torts § 130 at 1020-22 (5th ed. 1984), we see no distinction between such a state right and those exclusive rights encompassed by the federal copyright laws. *See Warner Bros., Inc. v. American Broadcasting Cos.*, 720 F.2d 231, 247 (2d Cir. 1983) ("state law claims that rely on the misappropriation branch of unfair competition are preempted"); *Schuchart & Associates*, 540 F. Supp. at 943-44 (same). *See generally* 1 Nimmer § 1.01[B], at 1-16 to 1-22. We cannot agree with the district court that Ehat's state claim was not within the scope of copyright because it was based on his right in the notes "as a physical matter and property." Rec., vol. V, at 9. Ehat did not allege a state law claim of conversion to recover for the physical deprivation of his notes. Instead, he sought to recover for damage flowing from their reproduction and distribution. *See Harper & Row*, 723 F.2d at 200-01. Such reproduction interferes with an intangible literary or artistic property right equivalent to copyright. *See* 1 Nimmer § 1.01[B], at 1-14.4 n.51.

Our view of the nature of Ehat's claim is confirmed by the district court's award of damages. The court awarded $960, representing the Tanners' profits from the printing and sale of their publication, which is clearly an award for the reproduction of Ehat's work. The court also awarded $3,000 which it found Ehat suffered as a reduction in the market value of his master's thesis due to the misappropriation. This damage also flows from the reproduction of the material rather than from its physical taking. *See Harper & Row*, 723 F.2d at 201. Finally, the court awarded Ehat $12,000 for general damage to his reputation as a scholar resulting from "defendant's unlawful and improper publication." Rec., vol. V, at 15. Because the reputation injury arose out of the copying of Ehat's work, that claim is preempted as well. *See* 1 Nimmer § 1.10[B], at 1.14.2 n.49.

....

Ehat "cannot achieve by an unfair competition claim what [he] failed to achieve under [his] copyright claim." *See Durham Industries, Inc. v. Tomy Corp.*, 630 F.2d 905, 918 (2d Cir. 1980).

....

Accordingly, Ehat's state law claim is preempted. The case is reversed and remanded for further proceedings consistent with this opinion.

Harper & Row Publishers, Inc. v. Nation Enterprises, 723 F.2d 195 (2d Cir. 1983), *rev'd on other grounds,* 471 U.S. 539 (1985). The facts of the case are set forth *supra* p. 563. The manuscript of the Ford memoirs was improperly taken and turned over to The Nation magazine which, shortly before the publication of the Ford book, published an article borrowing substantial quotations from the manuscript. Time magazine, which had contracted to publish excerpts in conjunction with the publication of the Harper & Row book, decided not to do so and to withhold $12,500 payable to Harper & Row. Harper & Row and Reader's Digest brought an action for copyright infringement and for certain state law violations, including conversion and tortious interference with contractual relations. The district court found copyright infringement and no fair use, but dismissed the state-law claims as preempted. The court of appeals reversed on the copyright claim, finding fair use (this was reversed in turn by the Supreme Court), and it affirmed the dismissal of the state claims.

The court of appeals stated that a state-law claim is preempted if it can be established simply by proving acts, such as reproduction and the preparation of a derivative work, that violate § 106 of the Copyright Act. It found the plaintiffs' state claims to be of this kind.

The conversion claim was viewed by the court as ambiguous. To the extent it rested upon unauthorized publication of the Ford manuscript, it is "coextensive with an exclusive right already safeguarded by the Act — namely, control over reproduction and derivative use of copyrighted material," and is preempted. To the extent the plaintiffs complain about unauthorized possession of the papers themselves, such a theory would not be preempted: "Conversion, as thus described, is a tort involving acts — possession and control of chattels — which are qualitatively different from those proscribed by copyright law." However, a conversion claim was not adequately supported; "merely removing one of a number of copies of a manuscript (with or without permission) for a short time, copying parts of it, and returning it undamaged, constitutes far too insubstantial an interference with property rights to demonstrate conversion." (The lesser tort of trespass to chattels also would fail, for lack of actual damage to the property interfered with.)

The plaintiffs also asserted that The Nation had tortiously interfered with their contractual relations, "by destroying the exclusive right of an author and his licensed publishers to exercise and enjoy the benefit of the pre-book publication serialization rights." The court of appeals also found this claim to be preempted.

> If there is a qualitative difference between the asserted right and the exclusive right under the Act of preparing derivative works based on the copyrighted work, we are unable to discern it. In both cases, it is the act of unauthorized publication which causes the violation. The enjoyment of benefits from derivative use is so intimately bound up with the right itself that it could not possibly be deemed a separate element. *See* 1 Nimmer on Copyright § 1.01[B], at n. 46 (1983). As the trial court noted, the fact that cross-appellants pleaded additional elements of awareness and intentional interference, not part of a copyright infringement claim, goes merely to the scope of the right; it does not establish qualitatively different conduct on the part of the infringing party, nor a fundamental nonequivalence between the state and federal rights implicated.

Computer Associates International, Inc. v. Altai, Inc., 982 F.2d 693 (2d Cir. 1992) (For a fuller statement of the facts of this case, see Chapter 7). Defendant Altai created its OSCAR 3.5 program by a "clean room" examination of plaintiff CA's ADAPTER program, after learning that the OSCAR 3.4 program had been copied from ADAPTER by an Altai programmer who formerly worked for CA. The district court, affirmed by the Second Circuit, held that OSCAR 3.5 did not infringe the copyright in ADAPTER. Plaintiff also alleged that defendant's examination and reconstitution of the ideas of the ADAPTER program violated plaintiff's trade secret rights in the program. The court of appeals reversed the district court's finding of preemption, and held that trade secret claims have an "extra element" that changes the "nature of the action so that it is qualitatively different from a copyright infringement claim." The court explained its conclusion as follows:

> [M]any state law rights that can arise in connection with instances of copyright infringement satisfy the extra element test, and thus are not preempted by section 301. These include unfair competition claims based upon breaches of confidential relationships, breaches of fiduciary duties and trade secrets.... Trade secret protection, the branch of unfair competition law at issue in this case, remains a "uniquely valuable" weapon in the defensive arsenal of computer programmers. *See* 1 Milgrim on Trade Secrets § 2.06A[5] [c], at 2-172.4. Precisely because trade secret doctrine protects the discovery of ideas, processes, and systems which are explicitly precluded from coverage under copyright law, courts and commentators alike consider it a necessary and integral part of the intellectual property protection extended to computer programs....
>
> The legislative history of section 301 states that "[t]he evolving common law rights of ... trade secrets ... would remain unaffected as long as the causes of action contain elements, such as ... a breach of trust or confidentiality, that are different in kind from copyright infringement." House Report, at 5748.... Trade secret claims often are grounded upon a defendant's breach of a duty of trust or confidence to the plaintiff through improper disclosure of confidential material.... The defendant's breach of

duty is the gravamen of such trade secret claims, and supplies the "extra element" that qualitatively distinguishes such trade secret causes of action from claims for copyright infringement that are based solely upon copying.

The district court had read the plaintiff's trade secret claims to be based on no more than Altai's *use* of CA's program (which would in substance be merely a claim of illicit copying). But the court of appeals read those claims to include more pertinently an assertion that Altai had unlawfully *acquired* the program through its hiring of Arney, a former CA employee, who had violated his duty of loyalty and confidentiality. Proving CA's trade secret claims would turn upon whether Altai had actual or constructive notice of the fact that Arney was incorporating CA's trade secrets into the 3.4 and 3.5 programs that Altai developed. Because these latter issues had not been explored by the district court, the court remanded for further proceedings.

QUESTIONS

1. In *Ehat,* should the court have given greater weight to defendants' usurpation of plaintiff's interest in publishing the public domain documents *first*? (Should the court of appeals in the *Harper & Row* case have done so as well?) Are copyright or other public policies advanced by precluding all remedies against the unauthorized first publication of public domain materials laboriously gathered by another?

2. The *Ehat* court appears to hold that even a defamation claim is preempted if the reputation injury flows simply from the act of unauthorized publication. Do you agree? Is this conclusion consistent with the legislative history of § 301 of the Copyright Act? Must not closer attention be paid to the precise nature of the reputational injury? For example, is the preemption conclusion affected by whether the injury to a plaintiff's reputation stems from: (a) the appearance, as in *Ehat,* that a plaintiff-scholar was not the first to discover and publish, but was actually the "copycat"; (b) the poor grammar, spelling and organization in the plaintiff-scholar's draft, which would have assuredly been corrected in the editing process; or (c) the scurrilous comments made about a third person in the document published without authorization, when that third person sues?

3. Do you understand the difference, emphasized in *Altai,* between "wrongful acquisition" and "misappropriation by copying"? Why is the latter preempted, but not the former?

4. If, under state law, the misappropriation tort requires, as an element of the cause of action, proof of "commercial immorality," will that affect the question whether the tort is preempted by federal law? *See Mayer v. Josiah Wedgwood & Sons,* 601 F. Supp. 1523 (S.D.N.Y. 1985).

5. A tavern owner regularly uses his satellite dish to intercept cable television programs, which he exhibits through his wide-screen television set. The owner of the cable system brings an action under state law, charging "conversion" of the television signals. Should the action be dismissed by virtue of § 301 of the Copyright Act? *See Quincy Cablesystems, Inc. v. Sully's Bar, Inc.,* 650 F. Supp. 838 (D. Mass. 1986).

NATIONAL CAR RENTAL SYSTEM, INC. v. COMPUTER ASSOCIATES INTERNATIONAL, INC.

991 F.2d 426 (8th Cir. 1993)

MAGILL, CIRCUIT JUDGE.

We here deal with the difficult question of the extent to which the Copyright Act preempts state breach of contract actions alleging that the licensee of computer software exceeded limitations on the use of computer software contained in the license agreements. Computer Associates International, Inc., appeals from the district court's order resolving a motion for judgment on the pleadings and dismissing its breach of contract claim against National Car Rental as preempted under the Copyright Act. We conclude that the district court failed to grant Computer Associates all reasonable inferences from its pleadings, and hold that as properly construed, the cause of action as pled is not preempted. We reverse.

I. *Background*

Computer Associates International, Inc. (CA), creates and licenses computer software. CA licensed its programs to the appellee, National Car Rental Systems, Inc. (National), to process National's data on National's hardware in Bloomington, Minnesota. The 1990 license agreement between CA and National provided, as did earlier licenses, that National may use the licensed programs "only for the internal operations of Licensee and for the processing of its own data." A separate order form, incorporated into the license agreement, similarly provided that "use of the Licensed Program[s] is restricted to the internal operations of Licensee and for the processing of its own data."

Sometime in 1990, National decided to cease its internal computer operations and contract with an independent computer services vendor for computer related information services. Ultimately, National retained Electronic Data Systems Corporation (EDS) to provide these services. In connection with this transaction, National, EDS, and CA entered into a supplement addendum, which provided that EDS could use the licensed programs to process National's data. The supplement addendum provided that EDS would use the programs for the benefit of National subject to the terms and conditions of the 1990 license agreement, and solely "to process data of Licensee and in no event for the processing of data ... of any third party other than Licensee."

CA subsequently determined that National had been using the programs to process the data of third parties, including Lend Lease Trucks, Inc. (Lend Lease), and Tilden Car Rental, Inc. (Tilden), in violation of the license agreement, and that such use had continued through EDS under the supplement addendum. CA threatened to sue National if such use did not stop. National then brought a declaratory judgment action in the district court. National admitted in its complaint that it "has used the Licensed Software in its business activities ... including the activities relating to Tilden and Trucks [Lend Lease]," but requested a declaration that its use of the programs neither breached the license agreement nor infringed CA's copyright. CA asserted two counterclaims. In the first, it claimed that National's use of the programs, either individually or through EDS, for the benefit of Lend Lease and Tilden, breached the license agreement. In the second, CA claimed that National infringed its copyright by making an unauthorized copy of the software.

National moved for judgment on the pleadings under Rule 12(c), alleging that CA's first counterclaim was preempted under § 301(a) of the Copyright Act. In resolving the motion, the district court concluded that CA alleged a lease agreement between National and the third parties: National permitted them to use the software in exchange for payment. The district court concluded that this cause of action, as pled, was "equivalent" to the exclusive copyright right of distribution of copies of the work, and held it was preempted.

II. *Discussion*

A. *Standard of Review*

We review a motion for judgment on the pleadings de novo.... This court must accept as true all facts pled by the non-moving party, and grant all reasonable inferences from the pleadings in the non-moving party's favor. Thus, we must determine whether CA's first counterclaim, as pled, may reasonably be read only as a claim preempted by the Copyright Act....

B. *Characterization of CA's Pleadings*

... The district court noted that the computer software in question was within the subject matter of copyright, and thus focused on whether CA's breach of contract action sought to protect rights equivalent to the exclusive copyright rights. The court noted that National had not alleged which copyright right was equivalent to CA's action, but concluded that the distribution right was the only right potentially equivalent....

... Given our standard of review, we do not believe that CA's complaint may be read to allege that National actually distributed the program. The copyright holder's distribution right is the right to distribute copies. See 17 U.S.C. § 106(3).... CA does not specifically allege that National gave a copy of the program to Lend Lease or Tilden. CA alleges that "National has used and permitted the use of the Licensed Programs for the processing of data for the benefit of third parties." CA did not allege use by Lend Lease and Tilden, but instead alleged use for their benefit.... [W]e believe that such a pleading can be read, in context, to allege that National permitted EDS to use the programs for the benefit of Lend Lease and Tilden, with no copies ever going to Lend Lease and Tilden. EDS, however, was authorized under the supplement addendum to have a copy of the program. Thus, given our standard of review, we cannot read CA's pleadings to allege that National breached the contract by wrongfully distributing a copy of the program....

C. *Preemption of the Contractual Limitation on Use*

The question then becomes whether CA's allegation that National breached their contract by using the program in a fashion not allowed under the contract protects a right equivalent to one of the exclusive copyright rights. We believe it does not.

We agree with the district court that the computer program in question is within the subject matter of copyright. Thus we focus on the second preemption issue: whether the right sought under state law is equivalent to the exclusive rights under copyright. We must consider whether a limitation on the uses to which a licensee may put a licensed work is preempted even though those uses do not involve the exclusive copyright rights. As noted above, courts and commentators have framed this inquiry as whether the right in question is "infringed by the mere act of reproduction, performance, distribution or display." 1 Nimmer on Copyright § 1.01[B], at 1-13. Section 301 preempts only those state law rights that "'may be abridged by an act which, in and of itself, would infringe one of the exclusive rights' provided by federal copyright law." *Computer Assocs. Int'l, Inc. v. Altai, Inc.*, 982 F.2d 693, 716 (2d Cir. 1992) ....

We conclude that the alleged contractual restriction on National's use of the licensed programs constitutes an extra element in addition to the copyright rights making this cause of action qualitatively different from an action for copyright.

National initially contends that any complaint alleging use of a copyrighted work that exceeds the uses allowable under the license must be brought as a copyright infringement claim; contract claims containing such allegations are preempted. In support of this proposition, National cites several cases finding copyright infringement when the licensee's "use" of a copyrighted and licensed work exceeded the uses allowed under the license. See *S.O.S., Inc. v. Payday, Inc.*, 886 F.2d 1081, 1087 (9th Cir. 1989); *Cohen v. Paramount Pictures Corp.*, 845 F.2d 849, 853 (9th Cir. 1988); *Gilliam v. American Broadcasting Cos., Inc.*, 538 F.2d 14, 20 (2d Cir. 1976); *Frank Music Corp. v. Metro-Goldwyn-Mayer, Inc.*, 772 F.2d 505, 512 (9th Cir. 1985); *Wolff v. Institute of Elec. & Elecs. Eng'rs, Inc.*, 768 F. Supp. 66, 69 (S.D.N.Y. 1991); *National Bank of Commerce v. Shaklee Corp.*, 503 F. Supp. 533, 544 (W.D. Tex. 1980).

We believe that National reads these cases too broadly. First, only one of these cases involved preemption. See *Wolff*, 768 F.2d at 69. In *Wolff*, the plaintiff alleged that the defendant had both infringed his copyright and breached their contract by republishing a photograph licensed for only one publication. The court held that the breach of contract cause of action was preempted because, as the court construed it, the plaintiff merely alleged that the defendant breached their contract by infringing his copyright. *Wolff*, 768 F. Supp. at 69. None of the other cases involved preemption; however, in each, the conduct claimed as infringing involved one of the exclusive copyright rights. See *S.O.S.*, 886 F.2d at 1087 (licensee made a copy of the program and prepared a modified version without authorization); *Cohen*, 845 F.2d at 852 (company with a right to record musical composition for film and display film on television also sold and rented videocassettes to general public); *Gilliam*, 538 F.2d at 18 (defendant televised edited version of program without authorization); *Frank Music*, 772 F.2d at 512 (defendant staged musical revue in manner not allowed under the license); *Shaklee*, 503 F. Supp. at 544 (defendant inserted unauthorized advertising material into published work). Rather than stating a rule that any use exceeding the license is infringing, these cases establish that engaging in one of the acts reserved to the copyright holder under § 106, without a license to do so, is infringing. Moreover, the *Wolff* case stands at most for the proposition that a breach of contract claim alleging nothing more than an act of infringement is preempted. Given that we cannot read CA to allege that National engaged in one of the acts reserved to CA under § 106, these cases are inapposite.

Because we find no general rule holding breach of contract actions such as this one preempted, we examine specifically whether this cause of action seeks to protect rights equivalent to the exclusive copyright rights. We conclude that the contractual restriction on use of the programs constitutes an additional element making this cause of action not equivalent to a copyright action.

National disagrees with this characterization and attempts to read the term "use" in the license agreement as synonymous with the rights given to the copyright holder. We believe it is not ....

... CA does not claim that National is doing something that the copyright laws reserve exclusively to the copyright holder, or that the use restriction is breached "by the mere act of reproduction, performance, distribution or display." Instead, on this posture, CA must be read to claim that National's or EDS's processing of data for third parties is the prohibited act. None of the exclusive copyright rights grant CA that right of their own force. Absent the parties' agreement, this restriction would not exist. Thus, CA is alleging that the contract creates a right not existing under the copyright law, a right based upon National's promise, and that it is suing to protect that contractual right. The contractual restriction on use of the programs constitutes an extra element that makes this cause of action qualitatively different from one for copyright.

We believe that the legislative history of the Copyright Act supports this conclusion. In elaborating the meaning of the term "equivalent rights" the House committee report to the Copyright Act suggests that breaches of contract were not generally preempted: "nothing in the bill derogates from the rights of parties to contract with each other and to sue for breaches of contract." See H.R. Rep. No. 94-1476, 94th Cong., 2d Sess. 132, reprinted in 1976 U.S.C.C.A.N. 5659, 5748. This is not the end of the inquiry, however.

National contends that while the bill as initially drafted might have excluded breaches of contract from preemption, the bill as passed did not. National notes that § 301(b)(3) of the Copyright Act, as initially drafted and reported out of committee in the House, explicitly exempted breach of contract suits from preemption. This provision was then amended on the floor of the House to delete all the specific examples of non-preempted causes of action. National claims this action demonstrated congressional intent to remove the "safe harbor" from preemption for breach of contract actions. See, e.g., *Wolff v. Institute of Elec. & Elecs. Eng'rs, Inc.*, 768 F. Supp. 66 (S.D.N.Y. 1991) (deletion of safe harbor provision for breaches of contracts suggests that Congress did not intend generally to except them from preemption).

We disagree. Although the deletion of a provision from a final bill generally means that Congress intends to disavow what was formerly expressed, we believe in this case the facts surrounding the deletion of § 301(b)(3) suggest Congress did not intend to reverse the presumption of non-preemption for the examples initially included in § 301(b)(3). Instead, it appears that certain members of the House were concerned about the subsequent addition of the tort of misappropriation to the list of non-preempted causes of action, and suggested deletion of the specific examples in order to prevent confusion about the scope of preemption. We agree with Professor Nimmer that "[i]t seems clear that the amendment that caused such deletion was not intended substantively to alter Section 301(b)(3) as regards [those examples originally included]." 1 Nimmer on Copyright § 1.10[B], at 1-22; See also *Mayer v. Josiah Wedgwood & Sons, Ltd.*, 601 F. Supp. 1523, 1533 (S.D.N.Y 1985) (same); *Factors, Etc., Inc. v. Pro Arts, Inc.*, 496 F. Supp. 1090 (S.D.N.Y 1980) (same). Thus, we believe, the better view is that the legislative history suggests a congressional intent not to preempt breach of contract actions such as this one.[6] ...

Finally, National claims that CA's requested relief demonstrates its cause of action is equivalent to the exclusive rights under copyright. First, National notes that CA requested damages for unjust enrichment, damages National claims are preempted under § 301. National is correct in noting that certain courts have held claims for unjust enrichment preempted when based upon allegations that the defendant engaged in one of the acts reserved to the copyright holder under § 106. We do not read CA to allege that National was unjustly enriched as a result of a wrongful exercise of one of the § 106 rights. Rather, we read this allegation of damage as a further explanation of the damages CA intends to prove arising from the breach of contract. CA alleges generally that it has been damaged in an amount to be proved at trial, and it will have to prove those damages. In this context, we read its allegations of unjust enrichment as an attempt, albeit inartful, to allege that National received from Lend Lease and Tilden amounts that CA would have received had National not breached their contract. Second, National notes that CA requested return or destruction of any copies of its programs still in National's possession. It notes that the Copyright Act provides precisely that remedy, see

---

[6] We note that Nimmer has argued that the *Wolff* court was wrong to find preemption even though the act claimed to breach the contract involved one of the exclusive copyright rights. "Reverting to *Wolff*, the court could have required the plaintiff to adopt an election of remedies to the extent that the copyright and contract causes of action were deemed inconsistent. See § 10.15 [A] *infra*. Alternatively, it could have determined that any damage for contract breach was already subsumed in the copyright recovery. See § 14.02[B] & n.53.1 *infra*. Both those devices might have accomplished the same goal without reaching an erroneous preemption holding." 1 Nimmer on Copyright § 1.01[B], at 1-16.1. According to Nimmer, then, if a license agreement contains a provision prohibiting the licensee from copying the program, the licensor could sue for breach of contract rather than for copyright infringement. Other courts have concluded, however, that breach of contract actions in which the alleged breach consists of the exercise of one of the exclusive copyright rights are preempted. See *Wolff*, 768 F. Supp. at 69; *Howard v. Sterchi*, 725 F. Supp. 1572, 1579 (N.D. Ga. 1989); *Brignoli v. Balch, Hardy & Scheinman, Inc.*, 645 F. Supp. 1201, 1205 (S.D.N.Y 1986) (a breach of contract claim for "unauthorized use of copyrightable material falls squarely within § 301 and is thus preempted"). Because we decide that the specific contract right CA seeks to enforce is not equivalent to any of the copyright rights, we do not need to decide whether a breach of contract claim based on a wrongful exercise of one of the exclusive copyright rights is preempted.

17 U.S.C. § 504, and claims that the request for destruction shows the claim is equivalent to a copyright claim. We disagree. The parties' contract specifically provides for the return or destruction of the licensed programs upon any breach of the license agreement. This remedy would apply equally to this asserted breach (improper use) as to an action for breach of an agreement to pay royalties or license fees, which National admits would not be preempted. Furthermore, the copyright remedy of return or destruction applies even absent a preexisting relationship between the parties: it does not have to be stated in a contract or license agreement. We cannot conclude that this action is preempted simply because the parties' contract provides a remedy for breach identical to a remedy provided in copyright.

III. *Conclusion*

For all the foregoing reasons, we conclude that CA's cause of action, as pled, is not preempted by the Copyright Act. Therefore, we reverse the order of the district court dismissing CA's first counterclaim with prejudice and remand for further proceedings consistent with this opinion.

Smith v. Weinstein, 578 F. Supp. 1297 (S.D.N.Y.), *aff'd without opinion,* 738 F.2d 419 (2d Cir. 1984). Plaintiff, a professional comedy writer, came up with the idea of writing a screenplay about a prison rodeo in Texas. He discussed the idea with defendant Hannah Weinstein, a personal friend and sometime motion picture producer, and for a short period, they operated under a formal contract; various drafts of scripts submitted by Smith over time were rejected by Weinstein. She did, however, mention the prison rodeo concept to friends at Columbia Pictures, who engaged playwright Bruce Jay Friedman to prepare a screenplay; this resulted in the motion picture, "Stir Crazy" starring Richard Pryor. Friedman claimed that he never saw any of the plaintiff's drafts until he had completed the script for the film. Smith brought an action against Weinstein, Columbia and Friedman for copyright infringement and violation of state law.

The district court granted the defendants' summary judgment motion on the copyright claim, finding no substantial similarity between the plaintiff's and the defendants' screenplays. Smith also asserted against all of the defendants a claim for unfair competition, arguing that the defendants had profited by focusing on his prison rodeo idea and by confusing filmgoers. The court held that to the extent Smith claimed an unauthorized use of his ideas in "Stir Crazy," this was preempted as equivalent to copyright. To the extent Smith relied upon the defendants' marketing of their film so as to engender confusion as to source — a claim which the court found to be not equivalent to or preempted by copyright — he failed to create a triable issue of fact by offering evidence of confusion (especially in light of the industry custom of according conspicuous screen credit to the actual authors of films).

Plaintiff asserted against Ms. Weinstein alone claims for breach of contract and for breach of a confidential relationship, by virtue of her disclosure to Columbia of the prison-rodeo concept and certain elements of his script.

> [P]laintiff ... claims that Weinstein agreed, expressly or implicitly, to pay him for the value of his ideas if she decided to use them. A party may by contract agree to pay for ideas, even though such ideas could not be protected by copyright law. Rights under such an agreement are qualitatively different from copyright claims, and their recognition creates no monopoly in the ideas involved. Similarly, plaintiff's breach of confidence claim is nonequivalent to the rights one can acquire under copyright law; rather it rests on an obligation not to disclose to third parties ideas revealed in confidence, which obligation is judicially imposed only upon a party that accepts the relationship, and thus results in no monopoly. In short, these claims, narrowly read, focus on the relationship between individual parties and make actionable breaches of agreements between parties, or breaches of the trust they place in each other because of the nature of their relationship.

Although these claims were not preempted, the court — in view of its dismissal of the copyright claim — exercised its discretion to dismiss them without prejudice to their being raised in an appropriate state court.

QUESTIONS

1. Assume that the pleading by CA in the *National Car Rental* case had alleged that National had *distributed* copies of CA's software to Lend Lease Trucks and Tilden Car Rental for the latter companies to use in processing their business data — and assume that this distribution was in violation of an explicit provision in the CA-National license agreement. Would such distribution violate any of CA's exclusive rights under its software copyright? Would the court therefore conclude that CA cannot properly sue for breach of contract? Is that a tenable conclusion? Does it comport with the "extra element" theory of non-preemption? Does it comport with the legislative history of § 301(a)?

2. Assume that Publisher agrees to publish Author's book and to pay a $2.00 royalty for each copy of the book sold. After its first week of distributing the book to retail stores, Publisher repudiates the publishing contract and refuses to pay. Advise Author what tenable claims she has against Publisher, what court(s) she may sue in, and what remedies she can get. Are the *National Car Rental* and *Smith v. Weinstein* decisions consistent in their likely answers to these questions? If there is a difference, which is the sounder view?

A SUGGESTED PREEMPTION ANALYSIS

Some tentative steps might be taken here toward the formulation of a more constructive analysis for the implementation of § 301. State anti-copying claims might usefully be divided into three categories. The first category is of the kind about which Congress might say the following:

> "These state causes of action do contain elements which are not necessary in order to state a claim for copyright infringement. But those elements — loss of a contract with a third party, unjust enrichment, willful competitive injury — *can* be considered in the copyright action, and fitting remedies can be fashioned for redress."

If that is so, then copyright and its attendant rights and remedies should be treated as "occupying the field," and this category of state claim should be preempted.

As to a second category of state claim, Congress might say the following:

> "Here too, the state cause of action embraces elements which are not necessary in order to state a claim for copyright infringement. But here, these elements are of incidental concern or of no concern at all in determining appropriate remedies in the copyright action. Conversely, the fact that there has been copying is only incidental to the state claim, which is really designed to protect other and independent interests."

State causes of action for breach of contract, breach of a fiduciary or confidential relationship, trespass and conversion regarding tangible property, and privacy and defamation claims are of this kind. Because the Copyright Act focuses upon the economic injury resulting basically from copying itself, and is rather inattentive to the enforcement of promises, the protection of special relationships and physical property, and the personal hurt resulting from exposure or ridicule, preemption should not operate, and the state claims can survive.

The third category of state claim forces us to grapple with the fact that Congress' failure in the Copyright Act to embrace a particular interest within the statutory rights and remedies (as in the second category) may signal not hospitability toward state protection of that interest but rather congressional opposition. In this third category, there is once again an element in the state claim which is not of the kind which a federal court is invited to consider in a copyright action; but unlike the second category, the economic injury resulting from copying as such is not incidental to the state claim but is the essence of it. An example would be a state law barring phonorecord manufacturers from imitating the sounds on another's recording (as distinguished from "pirating" the actual sounds on that person's recording, which *is* a copyright infringement under §§ 106(1) and 114(b)). There would be no recovery for such imitation in a copyright action. When a state treats that particular form of copying, exempted from the copyright owner's monopoly, as at the core of its cause of action, it is likely to be affronting Congress' infringement (and exemption) policies and should thus be preempted.

QUESTIONS

1. Do you agree with the above analysis of nonequivalent state claims?

2. Which, if any, of the following state statutes or claims seek to protect rights equivalent to rights within the general scope of copyright?

(a) A New York statute which provides:

> Whenever a work of fine art is sold or otherwise transferred by or on behalf of the artist who created it, or his heirs or personal representatives, the right of reproduction thereof is reserved to the grantor until it passes into the public domain by act or operation of law unless such right is sooner expressly transferred by an instrument, note or memorandum in writing signed by the owner of the rights conveyed or his duly authorized agent. Nothing herein contained, however, shall be construed to prohibit the fair use of such work of art.

See *Ronald Litoff, Inc. v. American Express Co.*, 621 F. Supp. 981 (S.D.N.Y. 1985).

(b) A provision of the penal law which makes it a misdemeanor to distribute commercially a phonograph record, disc, tape or other article embodying an illegally recorded performance without the consent of the owner of such recorded performance. See *Crow v. Wainwright*, 720 F.2d 1224 (11th Cir. 1983).

(c) A state law "droit moral" statute, forbidding mutilation or distortion of works of art, literature, or music. What if the statute is limited to forbidding owners of works of the fine arts from mutilating or destroying them?

(d) A state statute forbidding forgery of works of art.

(e) A state statute granting a performance right to recording artists in their sound recordings.

(f) A state statute banning rentals of records, audiotapes, and videocassettes.

(g) A state statute mandating a resale royalty (i.e., a continuing royalty on subsequent sales) to creators of works of the fine arts. See *Morseburg v. Balyon*, 621 F.2d 972 (9th Cir.), *cert. denied*, 449 U.S. 983 (1980).

3. The song "Baby Love" was performed by the female singing trio "The Supremes" in the 1960s; their formal gowns and bouffant hairstyle were as familiar as their singing style. Recently, a television advertisement for "Dinty Moore" brand beef stew depicted, in part, three young black women, with bouffant hair, in sequined formal gowns singing "Dinty Moore, My Dinty Moore," to the tune of "Baby Love." The owner of copyright in the song, along with Motown Records (which owns the federally registered trademark "The Supremes"), and the singers who have comprised the trio through the years have brought an action against Dinty Moore in a state court. They assert a number of state-law claims. One claim is for unfair competition; the advertisement is said to convey the false impression that the copyright owner, Motown, and the singers have given their permission for the use of the song and the images of The Supremes. Another claim is for intentional and negligent interference with prospective business advantage; it is said that the advertisement impairs the copyright owner's ability to exploit the composition, and impairs the rights of The Supremes to exploit their recordings and other materials. A third claim is that the use of Supreme look-alikes and the performance of the song violate a state statute barring the "knowing use of another's name, voice or likeness for purposes of advertising or selling products without such person's prior consent." A fourth claim is that defendant's imitation of plaintiffs' vocal style and physical appearance for commercial purposes constitutes common-law misappropriation. Fifth, plaintiffs assert that defendant's conduct should be deemed to create a constructive trust for the payment of its profits to the plaintiffs. Finally, plaintiffs claim that they have a protected right in the likeness, style and image (the "persona") of The Supremes that is protectible under § 43(a) of the Lanham Act. How should the court rule on the defendant's motion for summary judgment? *See Motown Record Corp. v. Geo. A. Hormel & Co.,* 657 F. Supp. 1236 (C.D. Cal. 1987); *Universal City Studios, Inc. v. T-Shirt Gallery, Ltd.,* 634 F. Supp. 1468 (S.D.N.Y. 1986).

4. The Medical College Achievement Test (MCAT) is a copyrighted examination widely used by medical schools in their admissions process; the copyright covers the test forms, test questions and answer sheets. The Association of American Medical Colleges (AAMC) is the copyright owner of these materials, which it attempts to keep secret, and the Copyright Office has "secure test" regulations that permit registration while preserving secrecy. The State of New York has enacted a Truth in Testing Act that declares materials such as the MCAT to be "public records" that are subject to involuntary disclosure. The principal purpose of the statute is to permit citizens to confirm or challenge the validity and objectivity of the test questions and answers.

AAMC has brought an action in a federal court against the Governor and other officials of the State of New York. The Association claims that by forcing AAMC to disclose tests, answers and forms, the state is undermining AAMC's exclusive rights under the Copyright Act to reproduce and distribute these materials, and is facilitating infringement of those rights by others. AAMC claims that the New York statute must therefore be preempted and its enforcement enjoined.

The State of New York contends that, under the Supremacy Clause of the U.S. Constitution, the New York statute should be preempted only if its implementation "stands as an obstacle to the accomplishment and execution of the full purposes and objectives of Congress in proscribing copyright infringement." It also contends that its disclosure requirement should be understood to be a fair use of the copyrighted MCAT materials, such that the policies of the Copyright Act will not be frustrated by the New York statute.

Is this analytical framework, assuming it to be normally appropriate in the area of preemption of state law under the Supremacy Clause, appropriate under the Copyright Act? Should not § 301 be the exclusive text for determining the preemptive import of the Copyright Act? Under either § 301 or the broader Supremacy Clause analysis proffered by the defendant, should an injunction issue against the enforcement of the New York statute? *See Association of Am. Med. Colleges v. Cuomo,* 928 F.2d 519 (2d Cir.), *cert. denied,* 112 S. Ct. 184, 116 L. Ed. 2d 146 (1991).

5. The State of Georgia has enacted a law designed to protect artists against the unauthorized reproduction of their works. The statute defines a work of "fine art" as a painting, sculpture, drawing, photograph, craft work, fiber art, or work of graphic art. Its operative provision (Ga. Stat. Ann. § 10-1-510) states:

> No printer shall enter into any agreement with any customer to duplicate a work of fine art when that customer's aggregate paid and unpaid obligations to that printer for all such prior or current duplications of that work of fine art exceed $2,000.00 unless the printer obtains, at the time such aggregate obligation first exceeds $2,000.00, a signed statement from the customer that the customer has the legal right or license authorizing such duplication or that those rights have passed into the public domain pursuant to federal copyright laws.
>
> Any person who violates [this section] or who signs the statement provided for therein knowing it to be false shall be civilly liable therefor and the person damaged thereby may recover trebled actual damages, court costs, and attorney's fees.

Is this statute — which as originally enacted declared a violation to be a misdemeanor — preempted by the federal Copyright Act in whole or in part?

6. Is a contract claim to enforce the restrictive terms of a "shrink wrap license," that forbids the software purchaser from copying or adapting the program, preempted under § 301? Under other principles of preemption? In *Vault Corp. v. Quaid Software, Ltd.*, 847 F.2d 255 (5th Cir. 1988), the court held a state claim to enforce such a license preempted on the ground that it conflicted with § 117 of the Copyright Act, which permits owners of copies of computer programs to copy and adapt the programs in conjunction with the running of the machine, and to make backup copies. But, is it not always possible for an individual, by entering into a contract, to agree to forego the exercise of a statutory right? Is that not indeed the holding of such cases as *Smith v. Weinstein*? Consider the following language from the CONTU Report, at notes 167, 168:

> Outright sale by a copyright proprietor of a copy of a protected work, rather than a lease under which the proprietor retains ownership of a copy which the lessee may use in accord with negotiated terms and conditions, normally results in a complete loss of control over the copy which has been sold. This reflects the unwillingness of courts to enforce restrictions on the alienation of property once a complete transfer of ownership interest in any item of property has been accomplished.
>
> Remedies for breach of contract, if the right being protected is not equivalent to copyright, would not be preempted under the provisions of section 301 of the new law, and would accordingly be available to one who, on the strength of a copyright interest, granted permission to another to make certain uses of the copyrighted work only to have the terms of the authorization violated. There continues to be some scope for state enforcement of proprietary rights in intellectual property under the new copyright law. See House Report, *supra* note 1, pp. 130-33. That state law rather than federal would be involved presents few real problems. The existence of parallel but not equal rights under state and federal law reflects advantages as well as disadvantages inherent in a federal policy,

and generally both claims could be joined in the same federal cause of action under principles of pendent jurisdiction.

PREEMPTION POSTSCRIPT

In its precise terms, § 301 deals only with preemption of state laws that grant rights that are equivalent to reproduction, the preparation of derivative works, public distribution, and public performance and display. Technically, that section does not oust state law on matters such as copyright ownership. It is clear, however, that — for example — a state would be barred, by application of the Supremacy Clause, from fixing copyright ownership rights in an employee who had prepared a literary work within the scope of his employment. The allocation of rights between employer and employee is carefully treated in the Copyright Act, and the application of state law would be an obstacle to the policies reflected in the federal statute. The same would be true if a state, whether calling it a matter of contract or of property, were to purport to make the transfer of ownership in a physical object (a literary manuscript or an oil painting on canvas) conclusive evidence of the transfer of copyright ownership as well, in flat contradiction of § 202 of the Copyright Act. And, as evidenced by the decision in a recent case, state doctrines of agency law — such as an agent's "apparent authority" to make binding, albeit unauthorized, commitments on behalf of a property owner — must be subordinated to copyright doctrine such as that which makes innocence no defense to an infringement action. *See Pinkham v. Sara Lee Corp.*, 983 F.2d 824 (8th Cir. 1992).

In such instances, in which the terms and structure of § 301 appear not to apply, it becomes necessary to invoke more longstanding and generic approaches to preemption analysis, asking such questions as whether the federal policies reflected in one or another provision of the Copyright Act would be "set at naught, or its benefits denied" by the application of state law. To this extent, the pre-1978 Supreme Court cases dealing with preemption under the patent and copyright laws — including *Sears* and *Compco* — continue to provide useful sources for analysis.

Rano v. Sipa Press Inc., 987 F.2d 580 (9th Cir. 1993). Rano, a professional photographer, in 1978 entered into an oral license agreement of unspecified duration with Sipa Press, a photograph distribution syndicate; he gave Sipa a nonexclusive license to distribute his photographs, and Sipa agreed to pay him 50 percent of the net royalties. The relationship went smoothly for some eight years, but in 1986, Rano informed Sipa that he was changing agencies (claiming that Sipa, among other alleged delinquencies, had been failing to pay timely royalties); and in 1987 Rano wrote Sipa that he "did not authorize Sipa to sell any more of [his] photographs." Sipa, nonetheless, continued to do so and Rano sued for copyright infringement and also made a number of state-law claims. The principal question for decision was whether Rano had effectively terminated the 1978 license agreement, thus making later distributions of his photographs by Sipa a copyright infringement.

Rano's first contention was that he was entitled to terminate the license agreement at any time by virtue of California contract law, which allows either party to an agreement of nonspecified duration to terminate it at will. The Court of Appeals for the Ninth Circuit, however, rejected that contention and held that the California law on this issue was preempted.

> [A]pplication of this principle of California contract law here would directly conflict with federal copyright law. Under Section 203 of the Copyright Act, licensing agreements are not terminable at will from the moment of creation; instead, they are terminable at the will of the author only during a five year period beginning at the end of thirty-five years from the date of execution of the license unless they explicitly specify an earlier termination date. 17 U.S.C. § 203(a). Since California law and federal law are in direct conflict, federal law must control .... Section 203 applies to non-exclusive, as well as exclusive, licenses executed by the author on or after January 1, 1978....

The court went on, however, to agree with Rano that, under federal copyright law, Rano, as copyright owner, could properly claim infringement if Sipa had "exceeded the scope of the licensing agreement, breached a covenant or condition, or breached the agreement in such a substantial and material way as to justify rescission." Examining the facts of the case, the court concluded that any breach of the license agreement on the part of Sipa was minor, and did not entitle Rano to rescind it and sue for copyright infringement. The court found no material breach and granted summary judgment to Sipa. (It did, however, remand to the district court to rule upon Rano's state-law claim for breach of contract.)

QUESTION

Was this case correctly decided? Consider for example the following arguments that the court was wrong. (1) The court misconstrued § 203(a), which says nothing about the parties having to "explicitly specify" a shorter termination time in order to terminate in less than 35 years. (2) The purpose of § 203(a) being merely to protect the *author* against what would otherwise be the indefinite assignment (and loss) of his copyright, it is perverse to read that section so as to *disable* the author from terminating sooner, if allowed by state law. (3) Presumably the parties can always *negotiate* to allow the author to terminate before 35 years have passed; the California law should reasonably be viewed as having been incorporated by the parties into the 1978 license agreement by implication (although it should be mentioned that the agreement was made in France!).

Chapter 10

INTERNATIONAL DIMENSION OF COPYRIGHT

A. INTRODUCTION

Protection of exclusive rights in works of authorship has existed in some form since at least the dissemination of printing technology in the late fifteenth century. This protection, however, whether by way of royal privilege or of copyright, was exclusively territorial. Citizens of one nation or city-state might prevent unauthorized reproductions on their own soil, but rarely could they obtain recognition and enforcement of their rights abroad.

International protection of authors' rights developed during the nineteenth century. By the middle of that century, a few European nations had entered into bilateral treaties, or had passed legislation protecting foreign works on the basis of reciprocity.[1] Nonetheless, until the late 1800s, most authors had little recourse beyond endeavoring to secure protection outside their home countries through complex and cumbersome attempts to attribute multiple nationality status to their works. They sought to achieve this by publishing the work simultaneously in the countries whose protection they wished to obtain; under conflicts of law principles still recognized today, a work of authorship assumes the nationality (and hence, entitlement to local protection) of the country where it was first published.[2] *See, e.g., Routledge v. Low,* 3 H.L. 100 (1868) (works first published in Great Britain protected regardless of author's citizenship or domicile); S. Ricketson, *The Berne Convention for the Protection of Literary and Artistic Works 1886-1986,* at 22-23 (1987), listing countries protecting works on the basis of publication within the local territory.

By the mid-nineteenth century, authors' groups were calling for international agreements promoting formality-free protection for works of literature and art. These demands culminated in the adoption, in 1886, of the Berne Union for the Protection of Literary and Artistic Works (discussed *infra* Subchapter C.1 of this chapter). Original signatories included most of the Western European nations, as well as one African country, and some Carribean and Latin-American nations. The United States was not a party to the original Berne Convention. This treaty, revised at several instances from 1908 to

---

[1] See Abelman & Berkowitz, International Copyright Law, 22 N.Y.L.S. L. Rev. 619, 621-22 (1977). In 1852, however, France took the unusual step of according protection to all works of authorship, regardless of country of origin, and without reference to reciprocity. *See* S. Ricketson, The Berne Convention for the Protection of Literary and Artistic Works 1886-1986, 20-21 (1987).

[2] This procedure, however, did not always succeed; failure to achieve simultaneity of first publication, or inadequate compliance with local formalities, such as deposit and registration of the work, often frustrated authors' efforts.

1971, is one of two major international copyright agreements currently in force.

In this century, the international dimension of copyright law has assumed increasing importance, particularly to U.S. copyright holders and policy makers. There is now a worldwide market for U.S. copyrighted works, particularly computer software, audiovisual works, and popular music. There is also worldwide piracy of U.S. copyright works: survey results published by the United States International Trade Commission in 1988 indicated that overseas losses in the computer and entertainment industries to wilful infringement were over $7.2 billion.[3]

From the isolationist position which characterized U.S. international copyright relations until the middle of this century, the U.S. has become one of the leading proponents of adequate and effective transnational copyright protection. United States efforts in the last half-century to promote and secure international trade in copyrighted works have included sponsorship and membership in the other leading international copyright treaty, the Universal Copyright Convention. The U.S. has also entered into many bilateral agreements, and, more recently, has sought to encourage recognition of its copyrights by imposing trade-based sanctions on countries practicing or tolerating widespread piracy of U.S. works. Most recently, the U.S. has further signalled its commitment to international respect for copyright by joining the Berne Convention.

B. EARLY HISTORY OF U.S. INTERNATIONAL COPYRIGHT RELATIONS

SANDISON, THE BERNE CONVENTION AND THE UNIVERSAL COPYRIGHT CONVENTION: THE AMERICAN EXPERIENCE, 11 Colum.-V.L.A. J.L. & Arts 89, 90-95 (1986)

[Former Register of Copyrights Barbara Ringer has stated: "Until the Second World War the United States had little reason to take pride in its international copyright relations; in fact, it had a great deal to be ashamed of. With few exceptions its role in international copyright was marked by shortsightedness, political isolationism, and narrow economic self-interest."[4]]

---

[3] See U.S. International Trade Commission, *Foreign Protection of Intellectual Property Rights and the Effect on U.S. Industry and Trade* (Investigation No. 332-245 under § 332(g) of the Tariff Act of 1930) at 4-12, table 4-7 (February 1988). This figure marks a dramatic increase from the 1984 estimate of $1.5 billion for copyright industries generally. See Ladd, *To Secure Intellectual Property Rights in World Commerce* 1 (1984) in *Oversight on International Copyrights,* Hearing before the Subcommittee on Patents, Copyrights and Trademarks of the Senate Committee on the Judiciary 15, 98th Cong. 2d at 15 (1984). A 1987 General Accounting Office study labelled the following countries major infringers of U.S. copyrighted works, particularly books, audio and videocassettes, and computer software: Brazil, India, Indonesia, Malaysia, Philippines, Singapore, South Korea, Taiwan and Thailand. General Accounting Office, *International Trade: Strengthening Worldwide Protection of Intellectual Property Rights,* GAO/NSIAD-87-65, at 12-13, figure 1.2 (April 1987).

[4] Ringer, *The Role of the United States in International Copyright – Past, Present, and Future,* 56 Geo. L.J. 1050, 1051 (1968).

The grounds for this American self-criticism are twofold: in the first place, up to 1891, the United States denied copyright protection altogether to published works by nonresident foreigners; secondly, up to 1955 [when the United States joined the Universal Copyright Convention], the United States refused to enter into multilateral copyright relations outside the Western Hemisphere. Thus, for almost 200 years, it is fair to describe the American approach to international copyright relations as essentially isolationist.

The roots of American isolationism are clearly evident in the U.S. Copyright Act of 1790, which afforded protection to published works only if their authors were citizens or residents of the United States. In this respect, the first federal copyright statute merely mirrored antecedent state copyright statutes enacted by all but one of the 13 newly independent states between 1783 and 1786, which limited their protection to the works of U.S. residents. Of course, the United States was not alone in denying copyright protection to nonresident foreigners at that time: it was not until the first half of the 19th century that such protection was allowed, first by Denmark in 1828 and then by the other major nations of Europe. However, subsequent revisions of the U.S. copyright statute in 1802, 1831, 1856, 1865 and 1870, while greatly expanding the subject matter of protection, still left published works by nonresident foreigners unprotected.

In the absence of copyright protection under U.S. law, literary piracy of foreign — and particularly British — works grew dramatically in the 19th century. Not surprisingly, this produced great resentment among British authors, and none was more vociferous in his condemnation of U.S. law than Charles Dickens. Reporting on a visit to North America in 1842, Dickens wrote to his future biographer:

> I spoke, as you know, of international copyright, at Boston; and I spoke of it again at Hartford. My friends were paralysed with wonder at such audacious daring. The notion that I, a man alone by himself, in America, should venture to suggest to the Americans that there was one point on which they were neither just to their own countrymen nor to us, actually struck the boldest dumb! Washington Irving, Prescott, Hoffman, Bryant, Halleck, Dana, Washington Allston — every man who writes in this country is devoted to the question, and not one of them *dares* to raise his voice and complain of the atrocious state of the law. It is nothing that of all men living I am the greatest loser by it. It is nothing that I have a claim to speak and be heard. The wonder is that a breathing man can be found with temerity enough to suggest to the Americans the possibility of their having done wrong. I wish you could have seen the faces that I saw, down both sides of the table at Hartford, when I began to talk about Scott. I wish you could have heard how I gave it out. My blood so boiled as I thought of the monstrous injustice that I felt as if I were twelve feet high when I thrust it down their throats.

Unsuccessful attempts to establish copyright treaty relations with Great Britain were made in 1837, in 1853, and again in 1880-81, foundering each time on the opposition of American publishers who believed that their financial success depended upon being able to sell cheap reprints of British books....

Notwithstanding the opposition of the "book-selling leviathans" [as Anthony Trollope branded American publishers] and their friends in Congress, the movement for international copyright protection continued to gain ground in the United States in the second half of the 19th century, supported by a majority of American authors as well as a growing number of publishers. Most American authors favored copyright protection for foreign works, not only as a matter of principle, but also on economic grounds: without international copyright protection, they faced unfair competition from unauthorized reprints of British books which were cheaper because their British authors received no royalties. As Max Kampelman has noted, "American readers were less inclined to read the novels of Cooper or Hawthorne for a dollar when they could buy a novel of Scott or Dickens for a quarter." American authors were also hurt by the lack of reciprocal protection abroad. Longfellow, for example, complained that, although he had twenty-two publishers in England and Scotland, "only four of them took the slightest notice of my existence, even so far as to send me a copy of the book." American publishers, too, increasingly felt that action was needed to combat widespread literary piracy of foreign works, although they qualified their position by insisting that a foreign work should not be protected unless it was domestically manufactured.

Agitation for international copyright protection in the United States finally achieved success in the International Copyright Act of 1891. This legislation made copyright protection available to published works by nonresident foreigners on the basis of a proclamation by the President to the effect that their nation either afforded U.S. citizens copyright protection "on substantially the same basis as its own citizens" or was a party to an international agreement, to which the United States was also a party, providing for "reciprocity in the granting of copyright."[29] At the same time, however, the 1891 Act introduced a new requirement of domestic manufacture as a condition of copyright protection for every "book, photograph, chromo or lithograph."[30]

As Barbara Ringer has noted, this so-called "Manufacturing Clause" was the "compromise that made the Act of 1891 possible," since it effectively neutralized the opposition of American publishers. On the other hand, she points out that the requirements of the Manufacturing Clause "were so rigid that they made the extension of copyright protection to foreigners illusory."...

Under the authority of the 1891 Act, Presidential proclamations were issued in that year extending U.S. protection to the nationals of Great Britain and three other European nations. From 1891 to 1955, these and subsequent

---

[29] Act of March 3, 1891, ch. 565, § 13, 26 Stat. 1110 (1891). The Copyright Act of 1909 added a third basis for a presidential proclamation, namely, the granting by a foreign nation to American citizens of "copyright protection substantially equal to the protection secured" such foreign nation's nationals by American law or treaty. Copyright Act of 1909, § 8, 35 Stat. 1075 (1909).

[30] Acts of March 3, 1891, ch. 565, § 3, 26 Stat. 1106 (1891). The other formalities of domestic copyright protection — including registration and deposit of copies — were also made applicable to foreign works under the 1891 Act. See Ringer, *supra* note 1, at 1056-57.

Presidential proclamations were in fact the principal source of international copyright relations between the United States and the rest of the world. The United States stayed out of Berne, and although it entered into two multilateral copyright treaties prior to 1955 — the Mexico City Convention of 1902 and the Buenos Aires Convention of 1910 — these so-called "Pan American" Conventions were of limited application: their membership was confined to nations of the Western Hemisphere and they did not relieve the nationals of one member nation of the obligation of complying with the domestic formalities of another member nation.

. . . .

[Editors' Note: The United States finally joined a worldwide multilateral copyright treaty in 1955, when it ratified the Universal Copyright Convention [UCC]. As part of UCC adherence, the U.S. abandoned the requirement that foreign English-language works be printed in the U.S. The Manufacturing Clause, however, continued to apply to U.S. authors. As a result, a provision once intended to deprive foreigners of meaningful U.S. copyright protection now burdened U.S. authors, for it prevented U.S. parties from reducing production costs by importing authorized copies made more cheaply abroad. Nonetheless, the Manufacturing Clause remained in the 1976 act, despite increasing opposition from authors' groups. The 1976 compromise called for the clause's expiration in 1984. That year, however, Congress again voted, over the President's veto, to extend the clause until 1986. The Manufacturing Clause survived a first amendment challenge in *Authors League of America v. Oman*, 790 F.2d 220 (2d Cir. 1986), but finally expired at the end of 1986.]

C. INTERNATIONAL CONVENTIONS AND AGREEMENTS

The U.S. is now party to the two leading international copyright agreements, the Berne Convention and the Universal Copyright Convention. As of January 1993, the former convention had 95 members, and the latter had 89. The memberships are not completely overlapping, however. In 1993, 27 countries belonged only to the Berne Convention, and 21 adhered to the UCC but not to Berne. Adherents to the Berne Convention, but not the UCC, include Egypt, Romania, Thailand, Turkey, and many African nations (particularly the former French colonies). In many instances, the U.S. had no copyright relations with these countries before becoming a party to Berne. UCC members not party to Berne include Algeria, Nigeria, South Korea, the Russian Federation, and several Caribbean and Latin American nations.

In order to understand the U.S.'s treaty obligations and benefits, the student should first apprehend the general framework of these, and certain other copyright-related, treaties. Finally, it is also important to sketch U.S. bilateral copyright arrangements, not only because these afford our only copyright relationships with certain nations, but because bilaterals may be assuming increasing importance in the U.S.'s strategy for international copyright protection.

1. THE STRUCTURE OF THE LEADING MULTILATERAL COPYRIGHT TREATIES

Both the Berne Convention and the Universal Copyright Convention are essentially choice-of-law treaties. Rather than imposing a complete system of supranational substantive rules, these conventions, after setting forth the criteria under which works may come within the treaties' purview, primarily designate which law or laws apply to a protected copyright owner's claim. The criteria for a work's inclusion in the treaties' ambit are essentially the same in both the Berne and Universal Conventions. A work will qualify for protection under the treaties if its country of origin is a signatory. The notion of country of origin is generous: the Conventions set forth many points of contact, so as to increase the possibility of a work's inclusion. In general, country of origin is determined according to the author's citizenship or residence, or according to the country of first publication. A work will come within the treaties if, whether published or unpublished, its author is a national or resident of a member country. It will also be protected if it is first published in a member country. Under both conventions, moreover, "first" publication encompasses publication in a member country within thirty days of actual initial publication, if that act occurs in a nonsignatory country. (*See* Berne, art. 3; UCC, art. II.)

With regard to the legal regime of protection, in most instances, the treaties operate on the principle of National Treatment: they provide that a qualifying foreign work shall receive the same protection as would a local work. As a result, under these treaties, the law applicable to determine the scope of protection is the law of the country where protection is sought — generally, the law of the forum.

Designation of the forum's law to resolve most questions of infringement advances the theoretical principle of nondiscrimination against foreign authors. It also presents a practical advantage: local courts need not master a foreign copyright law. On the other hand, some anomalies result from the national treatment rule. If local laws substantively differ, a work may receive different degrees of protection depending on which side of an international border an infringement occurs. Indeed, the work may be protected in member countries even though it never qualified for protection in its country of origin. (*See* Berne, art. 5.2). The national treatment rule therefore does not necessarily enhance predictability of outcome in the international trade in copyrighted works. Two features of the treaties, however, temper the disruption that disparity of local laws might otherwise provoke. First, the treaties provide for certain substantive minima of protection, thus preventing a member country from refusing to accord effective protection to core classes of copyrighted works. Second, the treaties provide either explicitly, or implicitly, for some exceptions to applicability of the forum's law.

With respect to substantive minima, both the Berne Convention and the Universal Copyright Convention prescribe categories of works to be protected, minimum periods of protection, limitations on imposition of formalities, and forms of exploitation in which exclusive rights, or in some instances, at least equitable remuneration, must be assured. The categories of works encompass a broad range of literary and artistic works, including musical compositions and audiovisual works; sound recordings, however, do not come within the ambit of these categories. (Berne, art. 2; UCC, art. I). Regarding duration of copyright, the Berne Convention generally specifies a minimum period of life plus fifty years (or, for cinematographic, anonymous and pseudonymous works — when the author's identity is in fact unknown, fifty years) (art. 7), while the Universal Copyright Convention generally requires no less than twenty-five from publication (art. IV).

The Conventions diverge somewhat over the question of formalities. The Berne Convention categorically states: "The enjoyment and exercise of these rights [under copyright] shall not be subject to any formality" (art. 5.2). That treaty therefore prohibits not only formalities prerequisite to securing copyright protection (such as, under the U.S. 1909 Act, the notice requirement), but those necessary to its effective exercise and pursuit (such as, under the U.S. 1976 Act, the requirement of registration before initiation of a copyright infringment suit). The UCC allows member countries to impose compliance with formalities, but somewhat simplifies their array. Under UCC art. III, all of a member country's conditions on the initial existence of copyright shall be deemed satisfied if the foreign work was first and continuously published with an accompanying notice described in the Treaty. (UCC, art. III notice is essentially the same as the notice required by the U.S. 1976 Act before the 1988 amendments.) As a result of U.S. adherence to the Berne Convention, affixation of notice is no longer necessary to domestic protection, nor to protection in other Berne countries. It remains required, however, for coverage in those countries which are UCC, but not Berne, adherents, and which impose formalities. These include several Latin American nations, such as Colombia, Panama, and Venezuela.

The UCC also permits member countries to demand compliance with "procedural" formalities, such as registration and deposit prior to initiation of suit. (Art. III.3). Most interpretations of the Berne Convention, by contrast, deem such pre-suit conditions to be just as much proscribed as are formalities going to the initial existence of copyright.[5] Although the 1988 amendments to the U.S. copyright act eliminate the pre-suit registration prerequisite for foreign works from Berne countries, the requirement is retained for U.S. and other foreign works.

The primary forms of exploitation guaranteed by the Conventions are the rights of reproduction and public performance (including broadcasting). (Berne, arts. 9.1, 11 *bis*. 1, 11 *ter;* UCC, art. 4 *bis*. 1). Translations are another form of exploitation both treaties explicitly protect (subject to certain limita-

---

[5] Commentators of the 1908 Berlin revision of the Berne Convention (which eliminated all formalities; the original 1886 text eliminated all but those imposed by the country of origin) concurred that proscribed formalities included preconditions to suit. For example, P. Wauwermans, La Convention De Berne (Revisee a Berlin) Pour La Protection Des Oeuvres Litteraires Et Artistiques 72-73 (Brussels 1910), raises the question whether a deposit prior to suit rule (such as those then in force in France and in England) might be sustained on the ground that it is a condition to court action rather than a formality on which copyright validity depends. He responds, unequivocally, that such so-called "conditions" are just as much formalities, and are equally forbidden.

tions, some of which are available to all states, and others which specifically favor third-world nations). (Berne, arts. 8, 11.2, appendix; UCC, arts. V.1, V *bis, ter, quater*). The Berne Convention further specifies the protection of moral rights. (Art. 6 *bis*). Concerning limitations on copyright exclusivity, the Berne Convention permits imposition of certain compulsory licenses, particularly in the domains of mechanical reproduction, and broadcast-cable. (Arts. 13, 11 *bis*. 2). That treaty also authorizes a limited exemption from liability similar to U.S. copyright's fair use exception. (Art. 10). The most recent text of the Universal Copyright Convention tolerates any exception that does "not conflict with the spirit and provisions of" that treaty, so long as member countries "nevertheless accord a reasonable degree of effective protection to each of the rights to which exception has been made." (UCC, art. IV *bis*. 2).

The treaties further reduce the likelihood of highly disparate results in transnational protection by providing for certain exceptions to the rule of National Treatment. Most significantly, both documents state that where the duration of protection is shorter in the country of origin than in the forum country, the shorter period prevails. (Berne, art. 7.8; UCC, art IV.4).[6] Curiously, neither treaty clearly designates which law, that of the country of origin, or of the forum, governs the ownership and transfer of rights under copyright,[7] but these issues, at least in some instances, may also fall outside the national treatment rule. We will return to the topic of copyright ownership subsequently.

2. OTHER MAJOR MULTILATERAL TREATIES RELATED TO COPYRIGHT

As mentioned earlier, neither the Berne nor the Universal Conventions cover sound recordings. This is primarily because many countries other than the U.S. do not believe that the making of a sound recording comprehends sufficient originality of authorship, as opposed to technical expertise, to qualify for copyright protection. A separate treaty, the Geneva Phonograms Convention, protects rights of reproduction, public distribution, and importation interests in sound recordings. This treaty also operates on the principle of national treatment, leaving it to member countries to protect sound recordings either by means of copyright, of a specific right, of unfair competition, or by criminal sanctions.

The Brussels Satellite Convention obliges its members "to take adequate measures to prevent the distribution on or from its territory of any program-carrying signal by any distributor for whom the signal emitted to or passing

[6] The UCC provision, however, is not self-executing. Thus, an adherent must enact specific legislation to limit other member countries' works to their national copyright terms, otherwise the work will automatically receive the forum's term. The U.S. Congress has determined that the Berne Convention is not self-executing, Berne Convention Implementation Act of 1988, § 2, Pub. L. No. 100-568, 102 Stat. 2853 (1988), hence, absent specific legislation, the U.S. would not apply the Berne shorter term rule either.

[7] An exception is Berne, art. 14 *bis*, making the law of the forum the governing legislation regarding certain questions of ownership and transfer of rights in cinematographic works.

through the satellite is not intended." (Art. 2.1) The treaty does not specify the nature of these measures, leaving the degree and scope of protection, and means of enforcement to the signatory nations. This convention, moreover, addresses only point-to-point satellites, i.e., transmission of a signal to a satellite from which the signal is transmitted to an earth station which disseminates the signal to the ultimate recipients. At present no treaty clearly covers direct broadcast satellites (DBS), i.e., satellites whose signals may be captured directly by the ultimate recipient.[8]

Finally, the Rome Convention for the Protection of Performers, Producers of Phonograms, and Broadcasting Organizations, of which the U.S. is not a signatory, applies the principle of national treatment to protect a loose group of interests known as "neighboring rights." The rights adjoin copyright, and closely resemble copyright in organization, but are not subsumed within copyright. Most countries consider phonograms (sound recordings) and broadcast signals too lacking in originality to come within the scope of copyright. The copyright designation also eludes performers' rights because neighboring rights doctrine views the performer, however accomplished, as an adjunct to the creator (the playwright, the composer), rather than a creative contributor himself.

3. BILATERAL COPYRIGHT ARRANGEMENTS

Before the U.S. joined the Universal Copyright Convention in 1955, bilateral copyright agreements provided the predominant basis of overseas protection of U.S. works, and, correspondingly, of U.S. protection of foreign works. The 1909 Act authorized protection for alien authors if the foreign nation granted nondiscriminatory or reciprocal protection to U.S. authors; the President was to determine by proclamation that the foreign state was according such protection (a similar provision persists in the 1976 Act, 17 U.S.C. § 104, discussed *infra*). Bases for the proclamation included an exchange of diplomatic notes, or U.S. government officials' study of foreign laws, see Dixon, *Universal Copyright Convention and United States Bilateral Copyright Arrangements,* in T. Kupferman & M. Foner, Eds., Universal Copyright Convention Analyzed (1955). While the copyright act appears to make ascertainment of nondiscriminatory protection abroad the prerequisite to extension of U.S. protection to foreigners, the President's decision may not be judicially reviewable. Hence, the President may well have power to grant U.S. copyright to nationals of states which do not protect U.S. authors.

Following U.S. adherence to the UCC, bilateral arrangements receded from the U.S. international copyright scene. There were almost no states with

---

[8]Although language in the Rome Convention for the Protection of Performers, Producers of Phonograms, and Broadcasting Organizations, a treaty to which the U.S. does not adhere, arguably covers any form of satellite distribution, a leading commentator asserts that "The question whether transmission of a program by means of a space satellite with a view to it being seen by the public constitutes 'broadcasting' within [the treaty's] definition is a matter of controversy." C. Masouy/Ae, Guide to the Rome Convention and to the Phonograms Convention 54 (1981). There is general agreement that the Rome Convention does not cover cable redistributions of satellite signals.

whom the U.S. had had bilateral arrangements who were not also UCC members. More recently, however, bilaterals have again assumed significance. Many states, particularly in the Far East, with whom the U.S. had no previous multilateral or other copyright relations (indeed, several of these nations had no copyright law at all until recently), have begun to enact copyright laws affording a level of protection equalling or approaching international norms. At the same time, the U.S. and these nations have begun or concluded negotiations toward bilateral copyright arrangements. The bilateral route offers some attractions. First, it ensures protection for U.S. works prior to the foreign state's adherance to a multilateral treaty. Second, it may in fact secure a *greater* degree of protection than available under a multilateral treaty. More protection may be gained under a bilateral if the foreign nation agrees to retroactive copyright protection; that is, undertakes to protect U.S. works which would otherwise be in the public domain in the foreign state, because the works were created and disseminated before commencement of copyright relations with the U.S. By contrast, UCC article VII provides that the treaty affords no protection for works which are in the public domain in the country where protection is sought.

Retroactivity under the Berne Convention poses a more elusive issue, particularly for U.S. works. Berne, Art. 18, provides that a work still protected in its country of origin shall be protected by Berne members, unless the term of protection in the forum country has expired. That would appear to mean that the only reasons the treaty permits for not protecting a member country's work are the expiration of its copyright in either the country of origin or the forum country. Under this interpretation, a foreign country with which the U.S. had no copyright relations prior to Berne accession, for example, Thailand or Turkey, would be required to protect U.S. works created before Berne adherence, so long as the U.S. copyright term was still in force, even though those works would formerly have been in that country's public domain. (Since, prior to Berne accession, there was no copyright in these works in that forum, it would seem inaccurate to say that copyright in these works had expired in the forum.)

It may, however, appear somewhat incongruous for the U.S. to insist that foreign countries apply such an interpretation of the Berne Convention: the U.S. has itself determined that it has no Berne obligation to protect other Berne-country works which were unprotected in the U.S. pre-Berne, but were still copyrighted in their countries of origin. On the other hand, Art. 18 of the Berne Convention allows member countries to agree among themselves to afford more protection than the treaty might mandate. As a result, even among Berne members, bilateral arrangements affording retroactive protection of U.S. works may not only be consistent with the Convention, but, in view of U.S. application of the Convention at home, may be (if not necessary) particularly well-advised.

As of late 1988, the U.S. had entered into bilateral copyright arrangements with thirty-nine nations, and was close to concluding bilaterals with at least two more. The most recent bilateral arrangements have been made with Asian nations, including Taiwan and Singapore. In the future, bilateral negotiations may produce arrangements with another group of nations not party to either Berne or the UCC; this group includes many of the near eastern countries.

D. U.S.-BASED COPYRIGHT ACTIONS WITH AN INTERNATIONAL DIMENSION

1. PROTECTION OF ALIEN AUTHORS

The Register's Report on Revision of the U.S. Copyright Law recommended in 1961 that all foreign and domestic works be protected on the same basis, without regard to the nationality of the author (subject to restriction by presidential proclamation). *Report of the Register of Copyrights on the General Revision of the U.S. Copyright Law, Report to House Committee on the Judiciary,* 87th Cong., 1st Sess. 119 (1961). But this proposal never saw the light of legislative day; at least as to published works, the 1976 Act carries forward, though in liberalized form, the policy laid down in the Act of 1891, 26 Stat. 1106, and followed in the 1909 Act. Under this policy, the United States demands a quid pro quo for the extention of the copyright privilege to the nationals of any foreign state or nation who are not domiciled here.

Absent treaty obligations most foreign countries likewise condition copyright for nondomiciliary aliens on the existence of protection for their own nationals in the alien's country. Even France, which had long pursued a policy of protecting foreign authors regardless of the absence of reciprocal protection of French works in the author's country of origin, see generally H. Desbois, Le Droit D'Auteur en France 916-22 (3d ed. 1978), finally reserved the right to retaliate against nonprotection of its works. Decree of July 8, 1964.

The basic rule, both in the United States and abroad, is "national" rather than strictly "reciprocal" treatment; if an alien qualifies for local copyright protection, it is granted on the same terms as apply to a citizen and not on the terms of protection available in the alien's country.

In its coverage of all unpublished material (much of which had been protected by the common law), the 1976 Act adopts the common law rule of protection for unpublished works irrespective of the nationality or domicile of the author. (§ 104(a).) With respect to published works, however, protection is available under § 104(b) only if at least one of the following four conditions is satisfied:

> (1) one or more of the authors is, at the time of first publication, a national or domiciliary of:
>
> > (a) the United States, or
> > (b) a country with which we have a copyright treaty, including the Berne Convention and the Universal Copyright Convention (or the author is the sovereign authority of such a country), or
> > (c) no country, i.e., a stateless person. *Cf. Houghton-Mifflin Co. v. Stackpole Sons, Inc.,* 104 F.2d 306, 42 U.S.P.Q. 96 (2d Cir.), *cert. denied,* 308 U.S. 597, 43 U.S.P.Q. 521 (1939) (stateless persons protected under general grant of § 9 of 1909 law, since only citizens of foreign states must meet the specified nationality requirements);

(2) the work is first published in the United States or in a Berne or Universal Copyright Convention country;

(3) the work is first published by the United Nations (or any of its specialized agencies) or the Organization of American States; or

(4) the work comes within the scope of a presidential proclamation finding that the author's country accords nondiscriminatory or national treatment to works of United States authorship or first publication. (Pre-existing proclamations remain in force until further presidential action. Trans. & Suppl. § 104 (90 Stat. 2599).)

Domicile within the meaning of this section is no different from the ordinary usage of this legal term. To acquire domicile, there must be residence with intention to remain in the United States, which may be inferred from various circumstances such as declarations, marriage to an American, payment of taxes, voting, establishment of a home, etc. *See G. Ricordi & Co. v. Columbia Graphophone Co.*, 258 F. 72 (S.D.N.Y. 1919).

Of course, aside from these specific provisions, another basis of protection is any treaty supplementing Title 17 of the United States Code as the copyright "law of the land."

QUESTIONS

1. France is a member of the Berne Convention. Singapore has recently entered into a bilateral agreement with the United States that includes mutual obligations with respect to copyright. Saudi Arabia is one of the countries with which the United States has no copyright relations.

Which, if any, of the following works would be protected in the United States:

(a) A work by a Singaporean author, first published in Saudi Arabia.

(b) A work by a Saudi author, first published in Singapore.

(c) A work by a Saudi author, first published in France.

(d) A work by a Saudi author living in France.

(e) A work by a Saudi author employed by a French company.

2. A foreign nation is not a member of the Berne or Universal Copyright Convention or of a bilateral treaty with the United States. Indeed, that country has no domestic copyright law. You are counsel to an American company interested in becoming the United States distributor for dolls created and initially distributed in the foreign country by local creators. What problems do you see? What advice would you give your client?

3. Under § 104, first publication in the U.S. affords foreigners one means of protecting their works in the U.S. Whether the first publication occurred in the U.S., however, may not always be evident. Section 101 defines publication as public distribution of copies, or as the "offering to distribute copies or phonorecords to a group of persons for purposes of further distribution, public performance, or public display." Suppose a national of a country with whom the U.S. has no copyright relations seeks a U.S. distributor for the work. Assume further that the work has yet to be publicly distributed anywhere. Does an exchange of correspondence and/or telephone calls to and from the

U.S. and the foreign state regarding the proposed distribution constitute an offering in the U.S. for purposes of § 101? If the offeree-distributor is a single "person," natural or juridical, does the offering fail to meet § 101 criteria? Does § 101's reference to "further" distribution, public performance, or public display imply initial acts in the U.S.?

2. CLAIMS BEFORE U.S. COURTS ALLEGING VIOLATION OF RIGHTS ABROAD

a. Jurisdiction of U.S. Courts to Adjudicate Copyright Claims Presenting an Extraterritorial Element

It is important here to keep in mind the distinction between jurisdiction to adjudicate, and choice of law. The U.S. federal courts may have subject matter jurisdiction over an international copyright claim either by virtue of the grant of federal jurisdiction over copyright claims set forth in 28 U.S.C. § 1338(a) when the claim arises under the federal copyright act (see *infra*, part b), or by virtue of diversity of the parties' citizenship (and an amount in controversy of $50,000 or more) under 28 U.S.C. § 1332(a)(2). In the latter instance, a U.S. federal court has jurisdiction to adjudicate a claim of violation of a foreign copyright law, if the suit is between "citizens of a State and citizens or subjects of a foreign state." The following decision discusses the circumstances under which a U.S. court might retain jurisdiction over a copyright infringement action, even though U.S. law does not apply to the claim.

LONDON FILM PRODUCTIONS v. INTERCONTINENTAL COMMUNICATIONS

580 F. Supp. 47 (S.D.N.Y. 1984)

ROBERT L. CARTER, DISTRICT JUDGE.

This case presents a novel question of law. Plaintiff, London Film Productions, Ltd. ("London"), a British corporation, has sued Intercontinental Communications, Inc. ("ICI"), a New York corporation based in New York City, for infringements of plaintiff's British copyright. The alleged infringements occurred in Chile and other South American countries. In bringing the case before this Court, plaintiff has invoked the Court's diversity jurisdiction. 28 U.S.C. § 1332(a)(2). Defendant has moved to dismiss plaintiff's complaint, arguing that the Court should abstain from exercising jurisdiction over this action.

Background

London produces feature motion pictures in Great Britain, which it then distributes throughout the world. ICI specializes in the licensing of motion pictures, produced by others, that it believes are in the public domain. London's copyright infringement claim is based mainly on license agreements between ICI and Dilatsa S.A., a buying agent for Chilean television stations. The agreements apparently granted the latter the right to distribute and exhibit certain of plaintiff's motion pictures on television in Chile. London also alleges that ICI has marketed several of its motion pictures in Venezuela, Peru, Equador, Costa Rica and Panama, as well as in Chile.

Plaintiff alleges that the films that are the subjects of the arrangements between Dilatsa S.A. and defendant are protected by copyright in Great Britian as well as in Chile and most other countries (but not in the United States) by virtue of the terms and provisions of the Berne Convention.* The license agreements, it maintains, have unjustly enriched defendants and deprived plaintiff of the opportunity to market its motion pictures for television use.

Defendant questions this Court's jurisdiction because plaintiff has not alleged any acts of wrongdoing on defendant's part that constitute violations of United States law,[3] and, therefore, defendant claims that this Court lacks a vital interest in the suit. In addition, assuming jurisdiction, defendant argues that because the Court would have to construe "alien treaty rights," with which it has no familiarity, the suit would violate, in principle, the doctrine of *forum non conveniens*. In further support of this contention, defendant maintains that the law would not only be foreign, but complex, since plaintiff's claims would have to be determined with reference to each of the South American states in which the alleged copyright infringements occurred.

Determination

There seems to be no dispute that plaintiff has stated a valid cause of action under the copyright laws of a foreign country. Also clear is the fact that this Court has personal jurisdiction over defendant; in fact, there is no showing that defendant may be subject to personal jurisdiction in another forum. Under these circumstances, one authority on copyright law has presented an argument pursuant to which this Court has jurisdiction to hear the matter before it. M. Nimmer, 3 Nimmer on Copyright (1982). It is based on the theory that copyright infringement constitutes a transitory cause of action,[4] and hence may be adjudicated in the courts of a sovereign other than the one in which the cause of action arose. *Id.* at § 1703. That theory appears sound in the absence of convincing objections by defendant to the contrary.

Although plaintiff has not alleged the violation of any laws of this country by defendant, this Court is not bereft of interest in this case. The Court has an obvious interest in securing compliance with this nation's laws by citizens of foreign nations who have dealings within this jurisdiction. A concern with the conduct of American citizens in foreign countries is merely the reciprocal of that interest. An unwillingness by this Court to hear a complaint against its own citizens with regard to a violation of foreign law will engender, it would seem, a similar unwillingness on the part of a foreign jurisdiction when the question arises concerning a violation of our laws by one of its citizens who

---

*[Editors' Note: At the time of this decision the U.S. was not party to the Berne Convention.]

[3]The films named, although formerly subject to United States copyrights, are no longer so subject.

[4]*See* 3 Nimmer, *supra* at § 12.01[C] (copyright is intangible incorporeal right; it has no situs apart from domicile of proprietor).

has since left our jurisdiction. This Court's interest in adjudicating the controversy in this case may be indirect, but its importance is not thereby diminished.

Of course, not every violation of foreign law by a citizen of this country must be afforded a local tribunal, and defendants cite several cases in which, basically under general principles of comity, it would be inappropriate for this Court to exercise its jurisdiction. *Cf. Kalmich v. Bruno,* 404 F. Supp. 57, 61 (N.D. Ill. 1975), *rev'd on other grounds,* 553 F.2d 549 (7th Cir. 1977), *cert. denied,* 434 U.S. 940, 98 S. Ct. 432, 54 L. Ed. 2d 300 (1977). This is not one of those. The line of cases on which defendants rely can be distinguished on significant points. The Court in *Vanity Fair Mills, Inc. v. T. Eaton, Ltd.,* 234 F.2d 633 (2d Cir.), *cert. denied,* 352 U.S. 871, 77 S. Ct. 96, 1 L. Ed. 2d 76 (1956), the principal case of those cited, found that the district court had not abused its discretion in declining to assume jurisdiction over a claim for acts of alleged trademark infringement and unfair competition arising in Canada under Canadian law. As defendant here has acknowledged, the complaint raised a "crucial issue" as to the validity of Canadian trademark law. This factor weighed heavily in the Court's decision.

> We do not think it the province of United States district courts to determine the validity of trademarks which officials of foreign countries have seen fit to grant. To do so would be to welcome conflicts with the administrative and judicial officers of the Dominion of Canada.

Id. at 647. But as Nimmer has noted, "[i]n adjudicating an infringement action under a foreign copyright law there is ... no need to pass upon the validity of acts of foreign government officials," 3 Nimmer, *supra,* at § 1703, since foreign copyright laws, by and large, do not incorporate administrative formalities which must be satisfied to create or perfect a copyright. *Id.*

The facts in this case confirm the logic of Nimmer's observation. The British films at issue here received copyright protection in Great Britain simply by virtue of publication there. Copinger, Law of Copyright (9th ed. 1958), 21 et seq. Chile's adherence to the Berne Convention in 1970 automatically conferred copyright protection on these films in Chile. Therefore, no "act of state" is called into question here. Moreover, there is no danger that foreign courts will be forced to accept the inexpert determination of this Court, nor that this Court will create "an unseemly conflict with the judgment of another country." *See Packard Instrument Co. v. Beckman Instruments, Inc.,* 346 F. Supp. 408, 410 (N.D. Ill. 1972). The litigation will determine only whether an American corporation has acted in violation of a foreign copyright, not whether such copyright exists, nor whether such copyright is valid.

With respect to defendant's *forum non conveniens* arguments, it is true that this case will likely involve the construction of at least one, if not several foreign laws.[6] However, the need to apply foreign law is not in itself reason to

---

[6] Plaintiff has alleged infringements in Chile, Venezuela, Peru, Ecuador, Costa Rica and Panama. Since, under the Berne Convention, the applicable law is the copyright law of the state in which the infringement occurred, [sic] defendant seems correct in its

dismiss or transfer the case. *Manu Int'l S.A. v. Avon Products, Inc.*, 641 F.2d 62, 67-68 (2d Cir. 1981). Moreover, there is no foreign forum in which defendant is the subject of personal jurisdiction, and an available forum is necessary to validate dismissal of an action on the ground of *forum non conveniens*, for if there is no alternative forum "the plaintiff might find himself with a valid claim but nowhere to assert it." *Farmanfarmaian v. Gulf Oil Corp.*, 437 F. Supp. 910, 915 (S.D.N.Y. 1977) (Carter, J.), *aff'd*, 588 F.2d 880 (2d Cir. 1978).

While this Court might dismiss this action subject to conditions that would assure the plaintiff of a fair hearing, *Mizokami Bros. of Ariz. v. Mobay Chemical Corp.*, 660 F.2d 712, 719 (8th Cir. 1981), neither plaintiff nor defendant has demonstrated the relative advantage in convenience that another forum, compared to this one, would provide. *Overseas Programming Companies v. Cinematographische Commerz-Anstalt*, 684 F.2d 232, 235 (2d Cir. 1982). The selection of a South American country as an alternative forum, although it would afford greater expertise in applying relevant legal principles, would seem to involve considerable hardship and inconvenience for both parties. A British forum might similarly provide some advantages in the construction of relevant law, however, it would impose additional hardships upon defendant, and would raise questions, as would the South American forum, regarding enforceability of a resulting judgment. *See American Rice, Inc. v. Arkansas Rice Growers Co-op. Ass'n*, 701 F.2d 408, 417 (5th Cir. 1983). Where the balance does not tip strongly in favor of an alternative forum it is well-established that the plaintiff's choice of forum should not be disturbed.

For all of the above reasons, the Court finds it has jurisdiction over the instant case and defendant's motion to dismiss is denied, as is its motion to have the Court abstain from exercising its jurisdiction here....

QUESTIONS

1. Consider the likelihood that defendant in *London Films*, a U.S. citizen, would have been subject to personal jurisdiction, or would have consented to suit, in any of the foreign nations in which defendant was alleged to have distributed plaintiff's film. What relationship does that likelihood bear to the court's retention of jurisdiction?

2. Assume a reversal of the parties in *London Film*: plaintiff is a U.S. citizen, complaining of foreign citizen-defendant's exhibition abroad of films in violation of foreign copyright laws. Assume also that defendant is subject to general personal jurisdiction in the U.S. Analyze whether or not a U.S. court should retain jurisdiction.

3. The *London Films* court observed that the films at issue "although formerly subject to United States copyrights, are no longer so subject." Nonetheless, the films were still protected in Great Britain and in the relevant South American countries by virtue of the Berne Convention. Explain this disparity in duration.

---

assumption that the laws of several countries will be involved in the case. 3 Nimmer, *supra* at § 17.05.

b. Application of U.S. Copyright Law to Infringements Occurring, at Least in Part, Beyond U.S. Borders

PETER STARR PRODUCTION CO. v. TWIN CONTINENTAL FILMS, INC.

783 F.2d 1440 (9th Cir. 1986)

WIGGINS, CIRCUIT JUDGE.

Appellant Peter Starr Production Co. ("Starr") appeals from the judgment of the district court dismissing its copyright infringement action against Twin Continental Films, Inc. ("Twin") and Gautam Das, its manager, for lack of subject matter jurisdiction under 28 U.S.C. § 1338(a) (1982). Starr contends that the district court erred in concluding as a matter of law that Twin committed no act in the United States that violates United States copyright law and abused its discretion in dismissing the complaint without leave to amend. We reverse and remand.

Plaintiff's Allegation of Facts

Starr created an original motion picture entitled "Take It to the Limit" ("the motion picture"). The motion picture and its soundtrack were properly copyrighted on July 10, 1980, and Starr has since that time complied with the Copyright Act in preserving that copyright for itself.

In May of 1983, Starr authorized Roger Riddell, a business acquaintance and agent, to "explore the possibility" of finding European distributors for a number of films including "Take It to the Limit," but specifically told him that he had no authority to bind Starr. By late June, Riddell obtained several offers for the rights to the motion picture from Alpha Films Limited ("Alpha"), but Starr rejected all of them.

On or about June 10, 1983, without authority from Starr, Twin entered into a license agreement with Alpha purporting to grant to Alpha "the exclusive license to exhibit" the motion picture in certain areas outside the United States. The license agreement was negotiated in Cannes, France, but notes on its face that it was signed in Los Angeles, California.

On August 3, Starr was shown a copy of the Twin-Alpha license agreement by an agent of Star Media Sales (no relation to Starr). Starr told the agent that Starr was not interested in dealing with Alpha and the agent informed Alpha of this.

On August 16, 1983, Alpha ordered and received a print of the motion picture from Rank Film Laboratories ("Rank"), the custodian of the motion picture's negative, in London, England. Alpha's representative assured Rank that it had a contract authorizing access with Star Media Sales, acting as agent for Twin. Alpha subsequently reproduced the motion picture and distributed some 400 video cassettes of it in Sweden or the United Kingdom, or both.

Before February 17, 1984, through means not clear in the record, Alpha was told to and did stop distribution of the motion picture. As a result of the unauthorized distribution, however, another English distributor backed out of a pending distribution deal with Starr for the motion picture, causing a substantial loss to Starr.

On July 10, 1984, Starr filed the present action seeking damages and injunctive relief. Before answering the complaint, Twin moved for dismissal or in the alternative for summary judgment or for a more definite statement of facts. On February 7, 1985, the district court granted Twin's motion and dismissed the action for lack of subject matter jurisdiction. Starr timely appealed, and the case is properly before this court under 28 U.S.C. § 1291 (1982). *See also* 28 U.S.C. § 1295 (1982).

. . . .

In general, United States copyright laws do not have extraterritorial effect. *See Robert Stigwood Group, Ltd. v. O' Reilly,* 530 F.2d 1096, 1101 (2d Cir.), *cert. denied,* 429 U.S. 848, 97 S. Ct. 135, 50 L. Ed. 2d 121 (1976). As a result, infringing actions that take place entirely outside the United States are not actionable in United States federal courts. *Id.*

In the present case, Starr's complaint alleges that Twin infringed Starr's copyright by authorizing Alpha to exhibit the motion picture without Starr's consent. In effect, the complaint contends that Twin's execution of the contract purporting to license Alpha to exhibit the motion picture constitutes "authorization" under § 106.[2] This states a cause of action under the plain language of 17 U.S.C. §§ 106 and 501, quoted above. As the Supreme Court has noted:

> [A]n infringer is not merely one who uses a work without authorization by the copyright owner, but also one who authorizes the use of a copyrighted work without actual authority from the copyright owner.

Sony Corp. of America v. Universal City Studios, Inc., 464 U.S. 417, 104 S. Ct. 774, 785 n. 17, 78 L. Ed. 2d 574 (1984).

Starr's complaint also suggests that the illegal authorization occurred in the United States. Although the complaint does not specifically allege the place of authorization, a copy of the Twin-Alpha contract attached to the complaint states on its face that the contract was executed in Los Angeles on June 10, 1983.

. . . .

The district court therefore erred in concluding that "Plaintiff alleges only infringing acts which took place outside of the United States." Starr alleges that the execution of the contract illegally authorized use of the motion picture. That execution allegedly took place in the United States. The complaint therefore alleges an act of infringement within the United States. The cases prohibiting jurisdiction over extraterritorial infringements are inapposite, and the district court has subject matter jurisdiction under 28 U.S.C. § 1338(a).

. . . .

---

[2]Twin argues that the authorization, if any, actually occurred during the negotiation of the agreement in France, and not at the execution of the written document. This is logically a question of fact, however, and not at issue here. The contract attached to the complaint purports on its face to give a license "hereby," and the complaint thus alleges an infringement authorization under § 106.

Danjaq S.A. v. MGM/UA Communications Co., 773 F. Supp. 194 (C.D. Cal. 1991). Danjaq and MGM jointly owned copyrights to several "James Bond" motion pictures. MGM merged with Pathé, a major European motion picture producer and distributor. Before the merger, Pathé negotiated with television stations in France, Italy and Spain to license broadcast rights in the Bond films. At that time, Pathé was not a copyright owner of the Bond films. The licenses were contingent on Pathé's merger with MGM.

Complaining that Pathé had undersold the European broadcast rights, Danjaq alleged that Pathé's licenses constituted infringing "authorizations" of public performances in Europe. Because Pathé subsequently merged with MGM, and thereby became a co-owner of the Bond film copyrights, Pathé's conduct did not "culminate in a primary infringement of copyright." The court dismissed the infringement claim on two grounds. First, Pathé's authorizations were not infringing, because they were conditioned on Pathé's acquisition of copyright ownership. Second, the court held that the U.S. copyright law could not reach European television broadcasts.

> United States copyright laws do not operate extraterritorially. Even a public performance of a copyrighted film overseas does not violate the U.S. Copyright Act. It may, perhaps, violate the copyright protection laws of the country of performance, but not those of the United States. *Cf. Robert Stigwood Group v. O'Reilly,* 530 F.2d 1096, 1101 (2d Cir. 1976) ("The Canadian performances, while they may have been torts in Canada, were not torts here.").
>
> Taking as given that the performance of Bond films on European television would not infringe Danjaq's U.S. copyright, the court must conclude that Pathe's alleged authorization of such performances is not actionable under the U.S. Copyright Act, not any more than [would be an] authorization of nonpublic performances. The exclusive right of the copyright owner under Section 106 is not to authorize every performance of a motion picture, but only public performances and, because the section is enacted against a general background presumption of non-extraterritoriality, only in the United States.
>
> It is simply not possible to draw a principled distinction between a private performance of a motion picture in the United States and a public performance overseas. The copyright owner is not vested with the exclusive right either to do or to authorize private or overseas performances. Even as a matter of formal statutory construction, the exemptions from liability for both private and overseas performances arise as negative inferences from the text of Section 106. Private performances of motion pictures are not actionable because the Congress had failed to include such performances among the list of the copyright owner's exclusive rights. In the same manner, overseas performances are not actionable because the Congress has not chosen to enforce the U.S. copyright laws extraterritorially.
>
> To be sure, the complaint alleges that certain negotiations for foreign television rights were conducted in the United States and that such nego-

tiations constituted acts of authorization. These allegations, however, neglect the central lesson that an authorization of a noninfringing activity, such as a private or an overseas performance, is not actionable under the Copyright Act even if the authorization is made in the United States.

The strongest authority cited by Danjaq in contravention of this court's conclusion comes from *Peter Starr Prod. Co. v. Twin Continental Films, Inc.* In *Peter Starr,* the Ninth Circuit held that the district court had subject matter jurisdiction over a claim that the defendant authorized in the United States an overseas exhibition of a copyrighted film. It would be too facile, however, to conclude from this decision that the Ninth Circuit approved the imposition of liability in the circumstances described.

Peter Starr addressed itself entirely to the question of subject matter jurisdiction and not to the sufficiency of the claim. Indeed the Ninth Circuit only recently held that a copyright claim "arises under" federal law on the basis of a well-pleaded complaint. Hence, the complaint in *Peter Starr,* alleging authorization within the United States, may have been sufficiently well pleaded so as to arise under the U.S. Copyright Act; the Ninth Circuit has certainly so held. However, in that case the Ninth Circuit was neither presented with nor addressed the question, whether the complaint properly arising under federal law also stated a claim for relief under that law. This court concludes that the complaint in *Peter Starr* and Danjaq's instant complaint, while arising under the U.S. Copyright Act, failed to state a claim for relief under that Act.

BG Marketing USA Inc. v. Gerolsteiner Brunnen GmbH & Co., 782 F. Supp. 763 (W.D.N.Y. 1991). The court determined that the U.S. Copyright Act applied to defendant's sales in Germany to a German exporter of bottled water bearing allegedly infringing labels, when the bottles were destined for U.S. distribution. Defendant emphasized that its alleged infringing activities, including affixation of the labels, all occurred outside the United States. However, defendant knew, when it affixed the labels, that the bottles would be sold in the U.S.

The court held:

> Where copyright infringement occurs both inside and outside the United States, the district court has jurisdiction, but only over the U.S. infringement. An analysis of the copyright statute demonstrates that subject matter jurisdiction does exist in this case. Section 106 of Title 17 grants the owner of a copyright the exclusive rights "to do and to authorize" certain acts, among which are the reproduction and distribution of the copyrighted work. The distribution right includes the right to import copies of the work. Congress's use of the phrase "to authorize" was intended to establish the liability of a "contributory infringer," which is a person "who, with knowledge of the infringing activity, induces, causes, or materially contributes to the infringing conduct of another." H.R. Rep. No. 94-1476, 94th Cong., 2d Sess. 61 (1976).
>
> Infringement, then, may be either direct (e.g., actual distribution of the work), or contributory. Title 17 U.S.C. § 501 also makes this clear, since it defines a copyright "infringer" as "anyone who violates any of the exclu-

sive rights of the copyright owner ...." Since one of those rights is the right to authorize importation, then, one who knowingly induces, causes, or contributes to the importation of a copyrighted work may be liable as a contributory infringer.

In the case at bar, Gerolsteiner's alleged activities include both direct and contributory infringement. [Its] alleged labeling and sale of the bottles to the [U.S. distributor] would (assuming the copyright to be valid) constitute a direct infringement of [plaintiff's] reproduction and distribution rights. That act in itself would not confer subject matter jurisdiction over [defendant], however, because it occurred in Germany. However, the court cannot ignore the fact that Gerolsteiner is alleged to have sold the bottles to [the distributor] with the knowledge and intent that the water would then be exported to the United States and sold here. Gerolsteiner is also alleged to have specifically prepared the bottles for the American market in various ways, such as the manner in which they were packed for shipment. These allegations, if true, would support a claim of contributory infringement arising out of the importation of the water into this country.

I find that subject matter jurisdiction exists over Gerolsteiner. Although Gerolsteiner's acts concerning the label physically occurred in Germany, the policies underlying the non-extraterritoriality rule support upholding jurisdiction over Gerolsteiner.... The general principle expressed in the [antitrust extraterritoriality] cases, is that it is unfair to hold a person liable under the laws of this nation for acts done abroad, except when those acts are intended to, and do, have an effect within the United States. Applying this principle to copyright cases, the court holds that when a foreign corporation is alleged to have purposefully injected itself into the American market by shipping infringing goods here — regardless of whether it does so directly or through an importer — the defendant should not be allowed to use the principle of non-extraterritoriality to shield itself from the reach of American courts and American copyright law. See also *Danjaq, S.A. v. MGM/UA Communications Co.* (court looks to location of acts authorized by defendant, not to where authorization occurred, in determining whether authorization is actionable in United States court).

In deciding this issue, then, the court does not limit its inquiry to a purely mechanical examination of where Gerolsteiner's acts physically took place. In fact, it is precisely because the copyright statutes are aimed at infringement in the United States that the court must also consider the location of the effect of Gerolsteiner's alleged actions, i.e., the location of the ultimate direct infringement.

Update Art Inc. v. Modiin Publishers, 843 F.2d 67 (2d Cir. 1988). This action concerned an Israeli newspaper's unauthorized publication of a photograph of plaintiff U.S.-citizen's "Ronbo" poster, depicting Ronald Reagan's head atop Sylvester Stallone's gun-toting torso (See p. 585).

It is well established that copyright laws generally do not have extraterritorial application. There is an exception when the type of infringement permits further reproduction abroad — such as the unauthorized manufacture of copyrighted material in the United States. [citations omitted.]

Appellants [defendants] concede the magistrate's jurisdiction over the newspapers distributed in the United States. As the applicability of American copyright laws over the Israeli newspapers [distributed in Israel] depends on the occurrence of a predicate act in the United States, the geographic location of the illegal reproduction is crucial. If the illegal reproduction of the poster occurred in the United States and then was exported to Israel, the magistrate properly could include damages accruing from the Israeli newspapers. Since a large portion of the damage award accrued from the Israeli newspapers, our determination on this issue affects substantially the final judgment.

The court then held that in light of plaintiff's assertion that defendant made an initial copy of the Ronbo poster in the U.S., and of defendant's failure to produce contrary evidence (and its repeated failure to respond to discovery orders), "[d]amages accruing from the illegal infringement in the Israeli newspapers properly were awarded to Update [plaintiff]."

QUESTIONS

1. Is *BG Marketing* as consistent with *Danjaq* as the former court seems to think?

2. Are you persuaded that a wrongful copyright authorization occurring (at least in part) in the U.S. "arises under" the U.S. copyright law, but does not "state a claim for relief" under the U.S. copyright law?

3. Suppose a film distributor had authorized broadcast of the Bond films in a country in which U.S. copyrights are not protected (either because that country lacks a copyright law, or because it has no copyright relations with the U.S.). Assume that some of the acts of "authorization" had occurred in the U.S. Should the unavailability of protection in a foreign forum be dispositive in determining if there is liability under the U.S. Copyright Act? Should it make a difference if the distributor is a U.S. entity? *Cf. Ocean Garden, Inc. v. Marktrade Co.*, 953 F.2d 500, 21 U.S.P.Q.2d 1493 (9th Cir. 1991) (applying Lanham Trademarks Act to a U.S. defendant who allegedly, from its California headquarters, directed the affixation on cans of tuna, fished and packaged in Mexico and sold in the Far East, of labels confusingly similar to plaintiff's canned tuna labels).

4. Israel and the U.S. are both members of the Berne and Universal Copyright Conventions. The plaintiff in *Update Art* could have sought relief in Israel. The Israeli court, consistent with the treaties' choice of law directive, would have applied its own law. (Since the quantitatively predominant portion of the allegedly infringing activity occurred in Israel, the Israeli forum would also have corresponded to the, or a, place of the harm.) Assume that under Israeli copyright law, defendant's unauthorized reproduction would have been held an infringement, and would not have been excused under a local variant of the fair use defense. What, if any, difference does it make whether U.S. or Israeli law is applied to the claim? If the claim had been heard in an Israeli court, and the relief entered required defendant to perform acts in the U.S., would/should a U.S. court enforce the judgment?

5. Plaintiff, a Cayman Islands corporation, produces travel films. Defendant, a British cruise ship organization, does business in Florida; its liners leave from Miami for cruises in the Caribbean Sea. Plaintiff contends that defendant made an unauthorized copy of one of its films in Miami for the purpose of exhibiting it to cruise ship passengers during the voyage, and that defendant did so exhibit the film. Plaintiff has initiated an action in the U.S. District Court for the Southern District of Florida alleging infringement of its exclusive rights of reproduction and of public performance.

Does the court have subject-matter jurisdiction over the claim? Whose law applies? To what portions of the claim? What (if any) relief should the court afford? See *P&D Int'l v. Halsey Pub.*, 672 F. Supp. 1429 (S.D. Fla. 1987).

6. All of the following cases involved infringements straddling the U.S. and other nations. In which, if any, of them should the court award damages under U.S. law not only for conduct occurring in the U.S. but for subsequent infringing acts abroad?

> a. Defendant has produced and exhibited in the U.S. a motion picture held to infringe on plaintiff's literary work. Defendant has also shipped copies of the motion picture to Canada, where the film was publicly exhibited. *See Sheldon v. Metro Goldwyn Mayer Corp.*, 106 F.2d 45 (2d Cir. 1939), *cert. denied*, 309 U.S. 390 (1940).

> b. Defendant has given unauthorized public performances of plaintiff's theatrical work in the U.S. and Canada, but has not made or shipped any fixations of its infringing performances to Canada. *See Robert Stigwood Group, Ltd. v. O'Reilly*, 530 F.2d 1096 (2d Cir.), *cert. denied*, 419 U.S. 848 (1976).

> c. Defendant composed, reproduced, and publicly performed in the U.S. a musical composition held to infringe plaintiff's song. Defendant's work has been publicly performed throughout the world. *See Gaste v. Kaiserman*, 683 F. Supp. 63 (S.D.N.Y.), *aff'd*, 863 F.2d 1061 (2d Cir. 1988).

7. In providing for application of the law of the country where protection is sought, the treaties appear to anticipate that the forum country will be the country where the infringement occurs. The locus of the infringement, however, as the examples discussed above illustrate, may be difficult to determine, or may be multiple. Does designation of the forum's law satisfactorily respond to the problem of the multi-national infringement, or is there a better choice of law rule?

Zenger-Miller, Inc. v. Training Team GmbH, 757 F. Supp. 1062 (N.D. Ca. 1991). The court held it lacked subject matter jurisdiction over a California corporation's claim that its former licensee, a German corporation, infringed the copyright in plaintiff's training manuals. Although the parties' licensing agreement included choice of forum and choice of law provisions (both clauses designated California), the court held that the parties could not confer subject matter jurisdiction by contract. None of the alleged infringing activities occurred in the U.S. Moreover, none of the acts leading up to formation of the licensing agreement occurred in the U.S.

While it is true that the parties cannot confer subject matter jurisdiction on the court, it appears that the court overlooked an independent basis of judicial competence: diversity jurisdiction under 28 U.S.C. § 1332(a)(2), since plaintiff was a U.S. citizen, and defendant was a citizen of a foreign state. *Cf. London Film Prods. v. Intercontinental Comm., supra* (in claim asserting violation of foreign copyright law, subject matter jurisdiction based on diversity of citizenship between English plaintiff and U.S. defendant). Assuming that the court was competent to hear the claim, the next question is what law applies. Here, the parties chose the applicable law by contract. The court failed to consider whether, once an independent basis of adjudicatory authority has been established, the court should honor the parties' choice of law. Is there any reason why a court in these circumstances should not?

E. PROTECTION OF U.S. WORKS IN FOREIGN FORA

1. ISSUES LEFT OPEN BY THE BERNE AND UNIVERSAL COPYRIGHT CONVENTIONS

The major multilateral treaties specify application of the law of the country where protection is sought to determine the scope of protection and the nature of the relief available to qualifying works. We have seen that this designation does not always produce a clear choice of applicable law. The treaties present other lacunae, particularly regarding ownership of copyright interests. Consider the following problems which U.S. authors and copyright owners might encounter when seeking protection for their works overseas:

a. Authorship Status

While U.S. copyright law seems to equate the concept of authorship with initial ownership of rights of economic exploitation (hence, the work-for-hire doctrine denominates the employer the "author"), many other countries distinguish the two. Although these systems generally designate the creator the initial copyright holder (without regard to employment status), there are certain exceptions to this rule. Leading examples include cinematographic works and collective works such as a periodical or an encyclopedia. In these cases copyright devolves upon the employer-producer *ab initio,* or by presumption of transfer. Nonetheless, the rights at issue are those of economic exploitation, not "moral rights." These are independent of economic rights, and are personal to the actual creator of the work. As a result, even in those instances where a foreign law may denote a person or entity other than the creator the initial copyright owner, the creator continues to enjoy certain prerogatives of "authorship" with respect to the work. The question therefore may arise whether a U.S. employee-for-hire may claim authorship status in these countries, and thus avail herself of local moral rights protections.

Another example of the relevance of the initial title/author distinction concerns economic interests. An increasing number of foreign countries have inaugurated some variety of home taping royalty system. The collected sums are often divided among authors and producers of sound recordings and audiovisual works (and frequently also among performers). The authors' royalties accrue to them by virtue of their status as creators: the laws divide the sums into shares and specify royalty recipients by class description, rather than by reference to copyright ownership. Were royalties awarded on the latter basis, authors might be excluded: in general the authors (and performers) are not in fact economic rights holders in the sound recordings or audiovisual works, either because they have granted these rights by contract, or because local law has established a presumptive transfer of these rights to the producer.

A large proportion of the works reproduced by means of home taping are likely to be works of U.S. origin. Are U.S. authors, producers, and performers entitled to share in the local home taping royalties? If, under U.S. law, the producer is deemed the "author" (of a work for hire), will the royalty-distributing country respect the U.S.-law characterization, or will it award the author's share of the royalties only to the actual creators?

b. Initial Copyright Ownership

(1) Works Made for Hire

The copyright laws of many countries, primarily those of Anglo-American legal tradition, deem employers the initial owners of works created by employees pursuant to their employment. Many other nations, however, especially continental European countries and their former colonies, attribute initial ownership to the actual creator of the work, regardless of her employment situation. No rights pass to the employer without a contract of transfer from the employee. Assume an employee-created work of U.S. origin is exploited in one of these countries: who is/are the copyright owner/s in the country/ies of exploitation?

(2) Joint Works

Disparities in national laws exist both regarding the definition of a joint work, and concerning the rights of joint authors. Under U.S. law, given the prerequisite intent, the joint authors' contributions may comprise an inseparable or an interdependent whole. In certain other countries, however, only inseparable contributions form a joint work. Under U.S. law, any joint author may, subject to a duty to account, alienate rights in the work without securing permission from her co-author(s); in many other countries, all joint authors must agree to grant or license rights in the work. The following hypotheticals illustrate just a few of the questions to which the above discrepancies in domestic laws give rise, in the absence of a uniform choice of law principle:

— Varying definitions of a joint work can affect the work's duration. Assume that the work is a dramatico-musical composition, comprising the efforts of a composer and a lyricist. Under most countries' rules of duration of copyright, a joint work's copyright endures until a determined number of years (usually 50) from the death of the last surviving author. Assume a musical comedy is created in 1979. The composer dies in 1980; the lyricist in 2000. Assume further that the work is a U.S. work: under the law of the country of origin, the copyright will survive until 2050. If, however, the work is exploited in a country which requires inseparable contributions (and considers dramatico-musical works to be separable), does the local definition of joint work apply, with the result that the music will fall into the public domain not in 2050, but in 2030?

— The work is a book, first published in the U.S. Both authors are U.S. citizens. One author, without consulting the other, licenses publication rights for France. Under French law, all joint authors must agree to the transfer. Has the French grantee received a valid grant?

— Same as above, except that one co-author is French.

— The work is a book, first published in France. Both authors are French citizens. One author, without consulting the other, licenses publication rights for the U.S. Has the U.S. grantee received a valid grant?

— Same as above, except that one co-author is a U.S. citizen.

c. Grants of Rights

(1) Content of Contract

Normally, the law chosen by the parties is the applicable law. Nonetheless, courts may sometimes decline to give effect to certain contractual provisions deemed to offend strong local policy ("ordre public"). An example particularly pertinent to international copyright may be moral rights. Assume a U.S.-law contract between a U.S. author and a U.S. motion picture producer includes a waiver of any and all moral rights which the author might have. Under the domestic law of some nations, moral rights are inalienable. If a court in such a jurisdiction is asked to enforce the waiver, will it defer to the contract's designation of U.S. law? Would it make a difference if the author seeking the benefits of the local policy is a national of the forum?

Moral rights are not the only subject of strong local copyright policy. Many foreign copyright laws reveal rather more paternalistic assumptions than those which (with the notable exception of the termination provisions) underlie U.S. copyright law. Thus, for example, some foreign copyright laws state that the rights to new forms of exploitation, unknown at the time of contracting, accrue to the author, not to the grantee, even if the contract purported to transfer all the author's interest. Some countries impose a limit on the number of years during which a grant of rights in certain works may be valid. Others require the grantee to pay the author a percentage of the work's profits, rather than a flat, one-time payment. When a U.S. work is exploited in these nations, and the contract's terms are less favorable than those prescribed by the country of exploitation, is the U.S. creator entitled to claim the benefits of local law?

Note that the analysis may become more complicated (and manipulable) if the contract at issue fails to specify which law shall govern its content. In that instance, the forum may "localize" the contract, with reference to the nationality or domicile of the parties, the place of execution, and/or the place where performance is to be rendered. Localization within one country or another determines the applicable law (subject, again, to application of the forum's law if the otherwise applicable law strongly offends local public policy). Alternatively, the forum may simply apply the law of the grantee's nationality or domicile.

(2) Form of Contract

Normally, the law specified by the parties, or the law of the place of the contract's execution, governs questions going to the validity of the contract's form, i.e., whether certain provisions must be in writing, or how specific the grant must be. Local public policy may prove problematic here, too, however. Assume the forum country, seeking to protect authors from bad bargains, provides that the contract will be unenforceable by the grantee against the grantor unless it meets a very high level of specificity. Assume that a U.S.-made contract does not satisfy the forum's threshold. Can the grantor avoid the contract for failure to comply with local formal requirements?

(3) Choice of Law and Forum Selection Clauses

To what extent may copyright holders avoid the uncertainties of foreign law by including forum-selection and/or choice-of-law clauses in contracts with creators and with foreign grantees? The answer depends upon several considerations. Let us first examine choice-of-law clauses. Although the law chosen by the parties normally governs, there may be circumstances under which the court will decline to apply the law of the contract. Certain strongly held local public policies may require application of the forum's law without regard to the law chosen by the parties. In other instances, the court might initially apply the law of the contract, only to discover that a particular result thus generated contravenes local policy. For example, a foreign court construing a U.S. film production agreement might in general honor the contract's specification of United States law, but might refuse to give effect to waivers of the creative contributors' moral rights.

Uncertainties in the effectiveness of choice-of-law clauses suggest that the parties might resort to choice of judicial forum clauses. The premise would be that if the forum-selection clause is enforced, the preferred forum will enforce the parties' choice-of-law clause. But uncertainties will remain. Assuming the contract specifies a U.S. court, and the action is first brought in a foreign forum, will that forum consent to ouster of its jurisdiction? Some fora may deem forum-selection clauses contrary to public policy. Moreover, choice-of-forum clauses may be incomplete. For example, suppose the action is litigated in the U.S., but the judgment requires that defendant perform, or refrain from performing, acts abroad. Will a foreign court execute the U.S. judgment? (The enforceability of clauses specifying arbitration as a substitute for a judicial forum raises distinct issues.)

Even assuming that forum-selection and choice-of-law clauses would be honored abroad, are they effective only against parties to the contract, and against those in privity with the original contract parties? If the parties' specification of applicable law does not bind strangers, would the U.S. licensor or its foreign grantee be vulnerable to a third-party infringer's objection that, under local law, the U.S. party was not a copyright owner, or improperly transferred rights to the local grantee? As a general matter, it appears unseemly for a third party infringer to invoke local laws designed to protect *authors* against their *own* publishers or producers. The author is surely not benefiting from such appeals. Nonetheless, one should keep in mind the possibility that third-party interpositions of local law may defeat local claims.

2. TRADE-BASED MEASURES TO ENCOURAGE RESPECT OF U.S. COPYRIGHT INTERESTS ABROAD

Not all countries which trade in U.S. copyrighted works have formal copyright relations with the U.S. In general, these countries are significant consumers or reexporters of other countries' copyrighted works, but are not significant producers of their own copyrighted works. (More bluntly, these countries are often referred to as "pirate nations.") As a result, a U.S. threat of refusal to protect these countries' copyrighted works is not likely to prove very effective. Some other form of sanction is needed. Since the early 1980s, the U.S. has turned increasingly to trade-based measures to encourage certain countries to cease pirating U.S. works. The measures range from the denial of favorable (duty-free) treatment of a wide variety of imports from certain developing countries, to forbidding importation. The imports in question need not be copyrighted works nor related to copyrighted works; rather, for the sanctions to be effective, the affected goods usually are those forming an important sector of the offending nation's economy. *See generally* Trade Act of 1974, as amended in 1984, 19 U.S.C. § 2411, and as further strengthened by the Omnibus Trade and Competitiveness Act of 1988.

In addition, private parties may move under section 337 of the Tariff Act of 1930, 19 U.S.C. § 1337, as amended through 1988, to prevent importation of foreign-manufactured infringing copies. Section 337 authorizes the U.S. International Trade Commission, subject to the President's signature, to direct the Customs Service to exclude the copies at issue when the importation involves unfair methods of competition. The Commission has held that copyright infringement constitutes unfair competition. *See generally* Lupo, *International Trade Commission Section 337 Proceedings and their Applicability to Copyright Ownership,* 32 J. Copyright Soc'y 193 (1985).

Finally, the U.S. has pressed for negotiations within the General Agreement on Tariffs and Trade (GATT) to include an intellectual property protection code among the extant system of trade regulation codes. Were such a code adopted, GATT members, numbering over ninety nations,[9] would agree to guarantee copyrighted works Berne-level protection of economic rights. In addition, the current draft of the agreement would provide copyright owners rental rights in computer software and sound recordings, as well, under certain circumstances, as in audiovisual works. The draft would also establish that computer software is to be recognized as a literary work within the

---

[9] *See* J. Jackson & W. Davey, International Ecomomic Relations 311-12 n.39 (1986) for a list of GATT contracting members, and a list of nations applying GATT norms on a de facto basis.

meaning of the Berne Convention. If a member nation fails to afford such protection, the dispute would go to arbitration within the GATT. If the nonprotecting member did not prevail in the arbitration yet continued to pirate or tolerate piracy, the offended nation could subject the offender to certain forms of retaliation, including exclusion of goods and augmentation of tariffs. *See generally* Marshall Leaffer, *Protecting United States Intellectual Property Abroad: Toward a New Multilateralism,* 76 Iowa L. Rev. 273 (1991); Note, *Intellectual Property Rights and the GATT: United States Goals in the Uruguay Round,* 21 Vand. J. Transnat'l L. 367 (1988).

Addendum: General Review Problems

The following Problems cover a variety of issues in copyright law. They may afford the student a helpful means of review.

PROBLEM 1

The Museum of Moderately Modern Art (hereafter MOMMA) is planning a major show of twentieth-century American and European artists. Some of the works on display are part of MOMMA's permanent collection, some are on loan from other museums. Most of the works are well known to the public through their display in museums and their inclusion in scholarly and coffee table art books. But the highlights of the show will be several works by Picasso never previously exhibited, specially loaned by Picasso family members, as well as two new works by contemporary feminist political artist Barbara Kruger.

MOMMA anticipates many visitors to the show and hopes to recover its costs, and perhaps to defray general museum expenses, not only through ticket sales but through sales of postcards, catalogs, posters, and a variety of related merchandise, including calendars, note cards, shopping bags, scarves, placemats, decorative plates, board games, bed sheets, shower curtains, lunch boxes, kitchen canisters, and dish towels, all bearing full or partial reproductions of works in the show.

MOMMA has traditionally taken the position that it has the right to make and sell postcards, etc., of any work that it owns or exhibits. Recently, however, several artists have expressed disagreement with the museum's assertions and have threatened to initiate court action. Although MOMMA publicly adheres to its position, Curt Curator, the show's organizer, is concerned about what right the museum does in fact have to make and sell postcards and other merchandizing properties of the works to be included in the show. He further inquires whether, to the extent MOMMA may not have pertinent rights, they may be secured, and if so, how? You are counsel to MOMMA. Advise Mr. Curator.

PROBLEM 2

Your client has sent you the following draft advertisement detailing her plans for a new magazine:

Attention Wine Lovers!

Do you want to know the best wines and best values in America today?
Do you want the most recent reviews and vintage reports on the wines of Bordeaux, Burgundy, Germany, Italy, California and other important wine districts? Would you like to know the opinions of the world's leading wine writers, the ratings made by the top wine journals — all this in one convenient publication?

Announcing BACCH/ANNALS, America's first wine-review newspaper. It reports on the published wine reviews and opinions of every important wine columnist and wine writer printed in America today, plus the top wine authorities of England and France. It does so without their approval or involvement so it can objectively evaluate their reviews without bias or personal obligation.

BACCH/ANNALS is published mid-monthly so you can receive the latest wine news and reviews shortly after they appear in their original publications. BACCH/ANNALS is conveniently organized in a country-by-country, district-by-district, and wine-type by wine-type format that is a breeze to use. Each review is in a consistent style regardless of the newspaper or magazine it appeared in.

Retailers, Importers, Wine Producers and other members
of the wine trade, read this!

You get *all* the ratings from *all* the foremost wine writers from *all* the best wine reviews; you will save hundreds of dollars each year when you subscribe to BACCH/ANNALS. Best of all, BACCH/ANNALS is published on paper that is easy to reproduce in ads or catalogs or enlarge for in-store displays.

Based on the description set forth in the advertisement, advise your client concerning:

A. The risk of copyright liability she may incur if she publishes the magazine as it is described in the advertisement;

B. How she might modify the content of the magazine to diminish the risk of liability for copyright infringement.

PROBLEM 3

Seeking a publisher for his projected first detective novel, an aspiring young writer, Artiste Manqué, sends the following submission to Scrivener & Sons, Publishers:

"A strange case of poisoning pervaded Paris. Someone had unleashed a flock of infected bees in the Jardin de Luxembourg, with the design, successfully realized, of allowing the bees to mingle among the chestnut blossoms, poisoning the pollen, and asphyxiating all who might breathe the air through which the pollen wafted. The Sureté's crack detective, Commissaire Maldefoie, was dispatched to root out the evil-doer.

"Commissaire Maldefoie was the sort of robust *bon bourgeois* to be found at many a sidewalk cafe, but with a difference: he ate only the finest escargots, washed down with Sauternes — a combination to curdle the stomachs of his countrymen, but one which he maintained aided his famous mental acuity. When on a case, Maldefoie would often make notes while standing on his head in a yoga position and simultaneously barking orders to his hapless assistant, Inspecteur Vautrien.

"In unraveling the mystery of the poisoned pollen, Maldefoie meets up with a seductive part-time beekeeper who, during a break in a show at the Folies Bergeres (where she also works in the chorus line), discloses the names of the members of an international insect-raising gang, which may or may not be involved in the crime. From a disgruntled street sweeper, Maldefoie learns of CIA infiltration into the public gardeners' union. At a rendezvous with an informer in the Louvre, Maldefoie begins to suspect that Vautrien has been playing a double-game. These suspicions are confirmed when Maldefoie discovers his assistant hanged from the headless neck of the Winged Victory above the museum's monumental staircase.

"As the exciting denouement of a complicated plot, Maldefoie gathers all the suspects, including the beekeeper, the informant, the international insect raisers, and several CIA operatives, at the top of the Eiffel Tower, to reveal the name of the poisoner.

"If you want to know who did it and how Maldefoie found out, send me a publishing contract and a $100,000 advance."

Joyce Eliot, an enterprising editor in Scrivener's unsolicited manuscripts department, reads Manqué's submission and is enthusiastic about its possibilities. At first inclined to recommend a contract for Manqué, she then determines to send Manqué a rejection letter, and to work from his submission to write the novel herself. Eliot's finished novel incorporates and builds on the plot and characters as disclosed in Manqué's submission. It proves an enormous popular and financial success, and is optioned for a television series detailing the further adventures of Maldefoie.

Upon reading Eliot's novel, Manqué is enraged and commences an action alleging:

1. Co-ownership of copyright in the novel as a joint author;
2. Infringement of the copyright in the material submitted through Eliot's use of his plot and characters;
3. Misappropriation;
4. Misrepresentation.

Ms. Eliot has hired you to advise her about defending the suit. Set forth the factual and legal (including jurisdictional) bases of each claim; identify and elaborate on defenses you would raise with respect to each claim; and give your evaluation of the likelihood of success of these defenses. You may assume that all events transpired after January 1, 1978.

PROBLEM 4

Harold Hacker, a fifteen-year-old computer enthusiast, has developed an educational service for his high school classmates who have experienced difficulty in the Algebra course. Having correctly guessed the password to gaining access to the math department computer at Major University, Hacker has discovered that the computer includes in its data base the text of the Algebra textbook used in his high school, as well as the text of the Teacher's Manual with all of the solutions to the problems in the textbook. Hacker has stored the Teacher's Manual solutions on one of his computer disks. Hacker does not know much about copyright, but he suspects that printing out and distributing copies of the Manual from his disk may not be a good idea. Instead, therefore, Hacker invites his classmates, for a fee, to come over to his house to read the computer screen display of the Manual generated by Hacker's disk. As word spreads among high school students concerning Hacker's service, students from other schools contact Hacker about coming over to see the Manual. Unable to accommodate all the requests, Hacker agrees, for a fee, to go to a designated vacant lot to deliver a lecture disclosing the solutions contained in the Manual to students from other high schools.

You know more about copyright than Hacker does. Which of the following acts constitute infringement of what rights under copyright and why or why not?

1. Gaining access to Major University's computer.
2. Inputting the Teacher's Manual on a disk.
3. Inviting classmates over to read the screen display generated by the disk.
4. The lecture.

PROBLEM 5

Your client is Color Technology, Inc. (CTI), which has perfected a technique for adding realistic colors to black-and-white motion picture films. The process works as follows. A single film frame from each scene is selected by a CTI "colorist" who, with the use of a computer, codes the frame with a variety of colors chosen by the technician. In part, the colors chosen are intended to reproduce the actual colors of a person's hair, skin, etc., and of the scenic background, such as a flag or building; in part, the colors chosen are freely selected with a view toward an overall appealing color pattern. The computer is able to take account of movement from frame-to-frame within the scene, and can thus carry the selected colors onto any number of frames on the film.

CTI has recently acquired copies of several motion picture films that are in good enough condition to use for "colorizing." These films, upon their initial release, had all been commercially distributed and exhibited in the customary manner, i.e., the authorized distributor rented the film for a limited time to a motion picture theater for exhibition, and the theater promised to return the film to the distributor at the end of that period and not to give possession to anyone else or to make any copies. The oldest of the four films is from 1910; it bears a copyright notice with that date, and your research shows that its copyright was renewed in 1938. Another film in CTI's possession was released in 1970, and a third in 1980; neither, however, bears a copyright notice. A fourth film was just released in September 1989; it also has no copyright notice.

(a) CTI asks you whether it must secure anyone's permission before "colorizing" the four black-and-white films and then marketing the colorized versions for television broadcasting and videocassette sales and rentals. Give your advice, with reasons.

(b) CTI also asks you whether CTI will be able to stop others who would wish to make copies of the colorized CTI films, and whether any steps should be taken by CTI in order to protect its right. Give your advice, with reasons.

PROBLEM 6

Don's Supermarket decided to place an advertisement in one of the local newspapers at the time of the Thanksgiving holiday. Don went to the Daily Planet, and spoke to the head of the advertising staff, Paula Penn. Don gave Paula his business card, which contained a drawing of his supermarket and of some fruits and vegetables, and also the address and telephone number and business hours of the store. Don asked Paula to use the business card as the basis for the advertisement and to have the Daily Planet's advertising staff add some of the usual brief complimentary phrases about the freshness, quality and price of the products sold at Don's Supermarket.

Although Don did not see the finished advertisement prior to publication, he was pleased with it when it was printed prior to the Thanksgiving holiday, and he sent a check to the Daily Planet, to the attention of Paula Penn, in the amount of $300 as had been agreed upon. The check contained the legend on the back: "In full payment for the advertisement prepared by the Daily Planet as a work made for hire, and for the transfer of all other rights." Paula endorsed the check and the Daily Planet deposited it in the newspaper's bank account.

A few days ago, Don informed you of his intention to have the advertisement published in the other four local newspapers during the Christmas shopping season. Is he free to do so? Give your advice, with reasons.

PROBLEM 7

Paramount Pictures, Inc., produces and distributes motion pictures made for theatre and television exhibition. It owns the copyright in most of those films. You are its general counsel, and your specialty is intellectual property. Paramount's executives have formulated several questions, recounted below, on which they would like your advice in the form of a reasoned memorandum. Prepare that memorandum.

(a) Paramount has learned that airlines are considering making available to passengers flying in First Class a hand-held videotape player and a choice of videocassettes of motion picture films for personal viewing on long-distance flights. (This would be particularly attractive to the traveler who, for example, has already seen the film that is being shown to all of the passengers on the plane.) Paramount wants to know whether the airlines must secure its consent before making Paramount-owned films available in this fashion; if so, Paramount would consider requiring the payment of a reasonable royalty.

(b) Several members of the House and Senate have introduced identical bills to amend the Copyright Act so that the commercial rental of videotaped films would be an infringement. These bills are modeled on the Record Rental Amendment of 1984 and the Computer Software Rental Amendment of 1990. Paramount supports such legislation, which would afford it an opportunity to enter into negotiated royalty agreements with video store owners. Paramount wishes to know what the strongest arguments are that will likely be made against these bills, as well as whether there are any changes that Paramount might consider in order to improve them or to reduce legislative opposition.

(c) A few of Paramount's copyrighted films are musicals. Songs written under contract for use in those films are electronically fixed on the soundtrack so as to synchronize with the dramatic action on the film frames. Paramount has learned that a popular singer has just made a recording that includes several songs from one of Paramount's musical films and that this recording is selling very well in record stores across the country. Because Paramount believes that the singer's recorded performances are of very poor quality, it wishes to know whether it may prevent the continued sale of the records.

PROBLEM 8

An action has been brought for infringement of a statue. The statue, familiarly known as the Three Servicemen Statue, is part of the Vietnam Veterans Memorial in Washington. It was commissioned, and was selected after a juried competition. The defendant is manufacturing and selling small three-dimensional replicas of the statue. Neither the plaintiff's originality nor the defendant's copying is denied.

The defendant, however, has interposed several defenses. First, he claims that the artistic elements of the statue are not separable from its utilitarian function of honoring Vietnam veterans. Second, he claims that the statue, although sculpted by a civilian, was commissioned by the federal government and is therefore beyond the protection of copyright. Third, he claims that in any event the statue is a work made for hire, and the plaintiff has no standing to sue. Fourth, he claims that because the statue is open to view in a public place, the 1990 amendments to the Copyright Act permit the making of unauthorized reproductions.

How should the court dispose of these issues?

PROBLEM 9

Mellifluous Editions Inc., a commercial (albeit not very profitable) publisher specializing in works about music, wishes to compile and publish a catalogue of U.S. and European doctoral dissertations on modern music written during the last twenty years. No such listings are currently available from a single source. Mellifluous would acquire information for its listings from the following sources:

　　1. *Universal Dissertations Abstracts.* This CD ROM product lists all completed U.S. and Canadian doctoral dissertations in all academic fields. The listings are organized chronologically. Each academic discipline in which a thesis is written has a code number. The user can enter the code onto the CD ROM reader and thereby call up listings only for the dissertations in the field corresponding to the code. There is a code for Music and Music History, but no subcodes breaking the field down by period. The CD ROM contains two levels of information about each dissertation. At the first level, the CD ROM displays the title of the dissertation, the author's name, the school awarding the degree, and the year in which the doctoral degree was conferred. At the second level, the CD ROM offers abstracts of each listed dissertation. The abstracts are written

by the dissertation authors, and present a one-paragraph outline and summary of the dissertation.

   2. *MusiqueChronique.* The June issue of this French academic journal lists dissertations completed in Europe since publication of the prior year's listings. The listings are organized by field within Music History, for example, Renaissance, Baroque, Romantic, Modern. Within each field, the listings include the university conferring the degree, the title of the dissertation, and name of the author.

While *MusiqueChronique* is in conventional hard-copy format, *Universal Dissertation Abstracts* is available only on CD ROM. The CD ROM is made available to libraries subject to a "site license," through which the library agrees to permit patrons to access the information on the CD ROM only if they agree to the following terms and conditions:

   Any printing or downloading of information from *Universal Dissertation Abstracts* is permitted for personal use only and may not be used for other purposes.

Mellifluous is concerned that its project may pose copyright problems. In addition to identifying the problems, suggest how Mellifluous might go about working with the above sources in order to create listings, yet avoid liability to any of the publishers of the sources.

Bibliography

The following is a selective list of secondary materials, organized according to the chapters herein, that the casebook authors believe to be particularly useful background reading. Most of the references are to studies published since the enactment of the 1976 act, and since publication of the Third Edition of this casebook.

For general reference regarding domestic U.S. copyright law, M. & D. Nimmer, *Nimmer on Copyright* and Paul Goldstein, *Copyright: Principles, Law and Practice* (1989), are comprehensive treatises. W. Patry, *Latman's The Copyright Law* (6th ed. 1986), and Marshall Leaffer, *Understanding Copyright* (1990), are useful one-volume treatments. Also comprehensive are the studies prepared by a number of scholars in the late 1950's in connection with the Copyright Law Revision; these were initially published as Committee Prints by the Subcommittee on Patents, Trademarks, and Copyrights of the Committee on the Judiciary, U.S. Senate, 96th Cong., 2d Sess. (1960-61). They are currently available in bound form as *Studies on Copyright* (Arthur Fisher Memorial Edition, 1963). Leading journals in the field include the *Journal of the Copyright Society of the USA* and the *Columbia-VLA Journal of Law & the Arts.*

For general reference regarding international and comparative copyright law, the leading treatises are: Sam Ricketson, *The Berne Convention for the Protection of Literary and Artistic Works 1886-1986* (1987); Stephen M. Stewart, *International Copyright and Neighboring Rights* (2d ed. 1989); and Melville Nimmer and Paul Geller, *International Copyright Law and Practice* (1988). Leading international and comparative copyright journals publishing articles in English include: RIDA, the *Revue Internationale du Droit d'Auteur* (France); *IIC* [International Intellectual Property and Copyright] (Germany); and EIPR, the *European Intellectual Property Reporter* (UK).

CHAPTER 1. THE CONCEPT OF COPYRIGHT

Howard B. Abrams, *The Historic Foundation of American Copyright Law: Exploding the Myth of Common Law Copyright,* 29 Wayne L. Rev. 1119 (1983)

Stanley M. Besen & Leo Raskind, *An Introduction to the Law and Economics of Intellectual Property,* 5 J. Econ. Perspectives 3 (1991)

Ralph S. Brown, *Eligibility for Copyright Protection: A Search for Principled Standards,* 70 Minn. L. Rev. 579 (1985)

Zachariah Chafee, Jr., *Reflections on the Law of Copyright,* 45 Colum. L. Rev. 503, 719 (1945)

Francine Crawford, *Pre-Constitutional Copyright Statutes,* 23 Bull. Copyright Soc'y 11 (1975)

Paul Goldstein, *Copyright,* 38 J. Copyright Soc'y 109 (1991)

Wendy J. Gordon, *An Inquiry into the Merits of Copyright: The Challenges of Consistency, Consent, and "Encouragement" Theory*, 41 Stan. L. Rev. 1343 (1989)

Gary Kauffman, *Exposing the Suspicious Foundations of Society's Primacy in Copyright Law: Five Accidents*, 10 Colum.-VLA J.L. & Arts 381 (1986)

B. Kaplan, An Unhurried View of Copyright (1967)

Dennis S. Karjala, *Copyright and Misappropriation*, 17 U. Dayton L. Rev. 885 (1992)

David Ladd, *Securing the Future of Copyright: A Humanist Endeavor*, 9 Art & Law 413 (1985)

David Ladd, *The Harm of the Concept of Harm in Copyright*, 30 J. Copyright Soc'y 421 (1983)

William M. Landes & Richard A. Posner, *An Economic Analysis of Copyright Law*, XVIII J. Legal Stud. 325 (1989)

Jessica Litman, *Copyright and Information Policy*, 55 Law & Contemp. Probs. 185 (1992)

Jessica Litman, *The Public Domain*, 39 Emory L.J. 965 (1990)

L.R. Patterson, Copyright in Historical Perspective (1968)

Leo Raskind, *The Continuing Process of Refining and Adapting Copyright Principles*, 14 Colum.-VLA J.L. & Arts 125 (1990)

Barry J. Swanson, *The Role of Disclosure in Modern Copyright Law*, 70 J. Pat. & Trademark Off. Soc'y 217-36 (1988)

Russ VerSteeg, *Rethinking Originality*, 34 Wm. & Mary L. Rev. 801 (1993)

Alfred C. Yen, *The Interdisciplinary Future of Copyright Theory*, 10 Cardozo Arts & Ent. L.J. 423 (1992)

CHAPTER 2. COPYRIGHTABLE SUBJECT MATTER

A. IN GENERAL

Jessica Litman, *Copyright, Compromise and Legislative History*, 72 Cornell L. Rev. 857 (1987)

Jessica Litman, *Copyright and Technological Change*, 68 Or. L. Rev. 275 (1989)

Thomas P. Olson, *The Iron Law of Consensus: Congressional Responses to Proposed Copyright Reforms Since the 1909 Act*, 36 J. Copyright Soc'y 109 (1989)

B. FACTS AND IDEAS AS DISTINGUISHED FROM THEIR EXPRESSION

Amy B. Cohen, *Copyright Law and the Myth of Objectivity: The Idea-Expression Dichotomy and the Inevitability of Artistic Value Judgments*, 66 Ind. L. Rev. 175 (1990)

Robert C. Denicola, *Copyright in Collections of Facts: A Theory for the Protection of Nonfiction Literary Works*, 81 Colum. L. Rev. 516 (1981)

Jane C. Ginsburg, *Sabotaging and Reconstructing History: A Comment on the Scope of Copyright Protection in Works of History After Hoehling v. Universal City Studios*, 29 J. Copyright Soc'y 647 (1982)

Robert A. Gorman, *Fact or Fancy? The Implications for Copyright*, 29 J. Copyright Soc'y 560 (1982)

Robert A. Gorman, *Copyright Protection for the Collection and Representation of Facts*, 76 Harv. L. Rev. 1569 (1963)

Christopher Hill, *Copyright Protection for Historical Research: A Defense of the Minority View*, 31 ASCAP Copyright L. Symp. 45 (1984)

William Patry, *Copyright in Collections of Facts: A Reply*, 6 Comm. & L. 11 (1984)

Edward Samuels, *The Idea-Expression Dichotomy in Copyright Law*, 56 Tenn. L. Rev. 321 (1989)

David B. Wolf, *Is There Any Copyright Protection for Maps After* Feist, 39 J. Copyright Soc'y 224 (1992)

C. COMPILATIONS

Howard B. Abrams, *Originality and Creativity in Copyright Law*, 55 Law & Contemp. Probs. 3 (1992)

Jane C. Ginsburg, *Creation and Commercial Value: Copyright Protection for Works of Information*, 90 Colum. L. Rev. 1865 (1990)

Jane C. Ginsburg, *"No Sweat?" Copyright and Other Protection of Works of Information after* Feist v. Rural Telephone, 92 Colum. L. Rev. 338 (1992)

Robert A. Gorman, *The* Feist *Case: Reflections on a Path-Breaking Copyright Decision*, 18 Rutgers Computer & Tech. L.J. 731 (1992)

Marci A. Hamilton, *Justice O'Connor's Opinion in* Feist Publications Inc. v. Rural Telephone Service Co., *An Uncommon Though Characteristic Approach*, 38 J. Copyright Soc'y 83 (1990)

Paul J. Heald, *The Vices of Originality*, 1991 Sup. Ct. Rev. 143

L. Ray Patterson & Craig Joyce, *Monopolizing the Law: The Scope of Copyright Protection for Law Reports and Statutory Compilations*, 36 UCLA L. Rev. 719 (1989)

Shira Perlmutter, *The Scope of Copyright in Telephone Directories: Keeping Listing Information in the Public Domain*, 38 J. Copyright Soc'y 1 (1990)

Symposium, *Copyright Protection for Computer Databases, CD-ROMS and Factual Compilations* (pts. I,II), 17 U. Dayton L. Rev. 323, 731 (1992)

D. DERIVATIVE WORKS

Robert S. Brown, *The Widening Gyre: Are Derivative Works Getting Out of Hand?*, 3 Cardozo Arts & Ent. L.J. 1865 (1990)

Paul Goldstein, *Derivative Rights and Derivative Works in Copyright*, 30 J. Copyright Soc'y 209 (1982)

E. PICTORIAL, GRAPHIC AND SCULPTURAL WORKS

Ralph S. Brown, *Design Protection: An Overview*, 34 UCLA L. Rev. 1341 (1987)

Robert C. Denicola, *Applied Art and Industrial Design: A Suggested Approach to Copyright in Useful Articles*, 67 Minn. L. Rev. 707 (1983)

Michael J. Lynch, *Copyright in Utilitarian Objects: Beneath Metaphysics*, 16 Dayton L. Rev. 647 (1991)

Neal Milch, *Protection for Utilitarian Works of Art: The Design Patent/Copyright Conundrum*, 10 Colum.-VLA J.L. & Arts 211 (1986)

Shira Perlmutter, *Conceptual Separability and Copyright in the Designs of Useful Articles*, 37 J. Copyright Soc'y 339 (1990)

J. H. Reichman, *Design Protection After the Copyright Act of 1976: A Comparative View of the Emerging Interim Models*, 31 J. Copyright Soc'y 267 (1984)

J. H. Reichman, *Design Protection and the Legislative Agenda*, 55 Law & Contemp. Probs. 281 (1992)

J. H. Reichman, *Design Protection in Domestic and Foreign Copyright Law: From the Berne Revision of 1948 to the Copyright Act of 1976*, 1983 Duke L.J. 1143

F. ARCHITECTURAL WORKS

Jane C. Ginsburg, *Copyright in the 101st Congress: Commentary on the Visual Artists' Rights Act and the Architectural Works Copyright Protection Act of 1990*, 14 Colum.-VLA J.L. & Arts 477 (1990)

David E. Shipley, *Copyright Protection for Architectural Works*, 37 S.C. L. Rev. 393 (1986)

Raphael Winick, Note, *Copyright Protection for Architecture After the Architectural Works Copyright Protection Act of 1990*, 40 Duke L.J. 1598 (1992)

G. CHARACTERS

Stephen Clark, *Of Mice and Men, and Superman: The Copyrightability of Graphic and Literary Characters*, 28 St. Louis U. L.J. 959 (1984)

Michael Todd Helfand, Note, *When Mickey Mouse is as Strong as Superman: The Convergence of Intellectual Property Laws to Protect Fictional Literary and Pictorial Characters*, 44 Stan. L. Rev. 623 (1992)

Leslie A. Kurtz, *The Independent Legal Lives of Fictional Characters*, 1986 Wis. L. Rev. 429

Francis M. Nevins, *Copyright + Character = Catastrophe*, 39 J. Copyright Soc'y 303 (1992)

Dean D. Niro, *Protecting Characters Through Copyright Law: Paving a New Road Upon Which Literary, Graphic, and Motion Picture Characters Can All Travel*, 41 DePaul L. Rev. 359 (1992)

H. GOVERNMENT WORKS AND OTHER PUBLIC POLICY ISSUES

James M. Burcart, *No Title to Titles: An Analysis of the Lack of Copyright Protection for Literary Titles*, 32 ASCAP Copyright L. Symp. 75 (1986)

Kathleen Anne Fisher, *The Copyright in Choreographic Works: A Technical Analysis of the Copyright Act of 1976*, 31 ASCAP Copyright L. Symp. 145 (1984)

Leslie A. Kurtz, *Protection for Title of Literary Works in the Public Domain*, 37 Rutgers L. Rev. 53 (1984)

Marvin J. Nadiff, *Copyrightability of Works of the Federal and State Governments Under the 1976 Act,* 29 St. Louis U. L.J. 91 (1984)

Malla Pollack, *Intellectual Property Protection for the Creative Chef, or How to Copyright a Cake: A Modest Proposal,* 12 Cardozo L. Rev. 1477 (1991)

Andrea Simon, Note, *A Constitutional Analysis of Copyrighting Government-Commissioned Work,* 84 Colum. L. Rev. 425 (1984)

CHAPTER 3. OWNERSHIP

Amy B. Cohen, *"Arising Under" Jurisdiction and the Copyright Laws,* 44 Hasting L. Rev. 337 (1993)

Rochelle Cooper Dreyfuss, *The Creative Employee and the Copyright Act of 1976,* 54 U. Chi. L. Rev. 590 (1987)

Marci A. Hamilton, Note, *Commissioned Works as Works Made for Hire Under the 1976 Copyright Act: Misinterpretation and Injustice,* 135 U. Pa. L. Rev. 1281 (1987)

Julie Katzman, Note, *Joint Authorship of Commissioned Works,* 89 Colum L. Rev. 867 (1989)

Laura G. Lape, *Ownership of Copyrightable Works of University Professors: The Interplay Between the Copyright Act and University Copyright Policies,* 37 Vill. L. Rev. 223 (1992)

Note, *The Contribution Requirement to a Joint Work under the Copyright Act,* 12 Loy. L.A. Ent. L.J. 199 (1992)

Robert Penchina, Note, *The Creative Commissioner: Commissioned Works Under the Copyright Act of 1976,* 62 N.Y.U. L. Rev. 373 (1987)

Russ VerSteeg, *Copyright and the Educational Process: The Right of Teacher Inception,* 75 Iowa L. Rev. 381 (1990)

CHAPTER 4. DURATION AND RENEWAL AND TERMINATION OF TRANSFERS

Howard B. Abrams, *Who's Sorry Now? Termination Rights and the Derivative Works Exception,* 62 U. Det. L. Rev. 181 (1985)

Suzanne D. Anderson, Note, *Bleak House Revisited: An Appraisal of the Termination Provisions of the 1976 Copyright Act — Sections 203 and 304(c),* 65 Or. L. Rev. 829 (1986)

Peter Jaszi, *When Works Collide: Derivative Motion Pictures, Underlying Rights, and the Public Interest,* 28 UCLA L. Rev. 715 (1981)

Malcolm J. Mimms, Jr., *Reversion and Derivative Works Under the Copyright Acts of 1909 and 1976,* 28 ASCAP Copyright L. Symp. 1 (1982)

David Nimmer, *Nation, Duration, Violation, Harmonization: An International Copyright Proposal for the United States,* 55 Law & Contemp. Probs. 211 (1992)

Melville B. Nimmer, *Termination of Transfers Under the Copyright Act of 1976,* 125 U. Pa. L. Rev. 947 (1977)

Sam Ricketson, *The Copyright Term,* 23 IIC 753 (1992)

CHAPTER 5. FORMALITIES

Philip Abromats, *Nondisclosure of Preexisting Works in Software Copyright Registrations: Inequitable Conduct in Need of a Remedy,* 32 Jurimetrics J. 571 (1992)

Thomas P. Arden, *The Questionable Utility of Copyright Notice: Statutory and Non Legal Incentives in the Post-Berne Era,* 24 Loy. U. Chi. L.J. 259 (1993)

E. Fulton Brylawski, *Publication: Its Role in Copyright Matters, Both Past and Present,* 31 J. Copyright Soc'y 507 (1984)

Steven J. Metalitz, *Copyright Registration After* Feist: *New Rules and New Roles?,* 17 U. Dayton L. Rev. 763 (1992)

Nimmer, *Preface — The Old Copyright Act as a Part of the New Act,* 22 N.Y.L. Sch. L. Rev. 471 (1977)

CHAPTER 6. RIGHTS, LIMITATIONS AND REMEDIES

A. The Right to Reproduce the Work in Copies and Phonorecords Under § 106(1)

Henry V. Barry, *Toward a Model for Copyright Infringement,* 33 ASCAP Copyright L. Symp. 1 (1987)

Amy B. Cohen, *Masking Copyright Decisionmaking: The Meaninglessness of Substantial Similarity,* 20 U.C. Davis L. Rev. 719 (1987)

Stephen J. Jones, *Music Copyright in Theory and Practice: An Improved Approach for Determining Substantial Similarity,* 31 Duq. L. Rev. 277 (1993)

Alan Latman, *"Probative Similarity" as Proof of Copyright: Toward Dispelling Some Myths in Copyright Infringement,* 90 Colum. L. Rev. 1187 (1990)

Bruce J. McGiverin, Note, *Digital Sound Sampling, Copyright and Publicity: Protecting Against the Electronic Appropriation of Sounds,* 87 Colum. L. Rev. 1723 (1987)

Note, *A Cause of Action for Simulation of Sound Recordings? Yes! Reflections on the 1976 Copyright Act,* 38 Rutgers L. Rev. 139 (1985)

Note, *Toward a Unified Theory of Copyright Infringement for an Advanced Technological Era,* 96 Harv. L. Rev. 450 (1982)

Mitchell E. Radin, *The Significance of Intent to Copy in a Civil Action for Copyright Infringement,* 54 Temp. L.Q. 1 (1981)

Paul S. Rosenlund, *Compulsory Licensing of Musical Compositions for Phonorecords Under the Copyright Act of 1976,* 30 Hastings L.J. 683 (1979)

B. The Right to Prepare Derivative Works Under § 106(2) and Moral Rights

Stephen R. Barnett, *From New Technology to Moral Rights: Passive Carriers, Teletext, and Deletion as Copyright Infringement — The WGN Case,* 31 J. Copyright Soc'y 427 (1984)

Russell J. DaSilva, *Droit Moral and the Amoral Copyright: A Comparison of Artists' Rights in France and the U.S.,* 28 Bull. Copyright Soc'y 1 (1980)

Edward J. Damich, *State "Moral Rights" Statutes: An Analysis and Critique,* 13 Colum.-VLA J.L. & Arts 291 (1989)

Jane C. Ginsburg, *Copyright in the 101st Congress: Commentary on the Visual Artists' Rights Act and the Architectural Works Copyright Protection Act of 1990*, 14 Colum.-VLA J.L. & Arts 477 (1990)

Robert A. Gorman, *Federal Moral Rights Legislation: The Need for Caution*, 14 Nova L. Rev. 421 (1990)

Note, *An Author's Artistic Reputation Under the Copyright Act of 1976*, 92 Harv. L. Rev. 1490 (1979)

Russ VerSteeg, *Federal Moral Rights for Visual Artists: Contract Theory and Analysis*, 67 Wash. L. Rev. 827 (1992)

C. THE RIGHT TO DISTRIBUTE UNDER § 106(3)

Richard Colby, *The First Sale Doctrine: The Defense That Never Was?*, 32 J. Copyright Soc'y 77 (1984)

James P. Donohue, *The Use of Copyright Laws to Prevent the Importation of Genuine Goods*, 11 N.C. J. Int'l L. & Com. Reg. 183 (Spring 1986)

Paul D. Getzels, *Importation of Out-Of-Print Works Under the Copyright Act of 1976*, 10 Fordham Int'l L.J. 782 (Summer 1987)

Michael Kremen, *The Harms-Jem Case: One Court's Attempt to Reconcile the Compulsory Licensing Provision with the 1976 Copyright Act's Expanded Importation Protection*, 39 ASCAP Copyright L. Symp. 41 (1992)

Lee D. Neumann, *The Berne Convention and* Droit De Suite *Legislation in the United States: Domestic and International Consequences of Federal Incorporation of State Law for Treaty Implementation*, 16 Colum.-VLA J.L. & Arts 157 (1992)

Shira Perlmutter, *Resale Royalties for Artists: An Analysis of the Register of Copyrights' Report*, 16 Colum.-VLA J.L. & Arts 395 (1992)

Jennifer M. Schneck, Note, *Closing the Book on the Public Lending Right*, 63 N.Y.U. L. Rev. 878 (1989)

U.S. Copyright Office, *Droit de Suite: The Artists Resale Royalty* (1992) [Report], summarized at 16 Colum.-VLA J.L. & Arts 381 (1992)

D. RIGHTS OF PUBLIC PERFORMANCE AND DISPLAY UNDER § 106(4), (5)

Steven J. D'Onofrio, *In Support of Performance Rights in Sound Recordings*, 29 UCLA L. Rev. 168 (1981)

Thomas M. Goetzl & Stuart A. Sutton, *Copyright and the Visual Artist's Display Right: A New Doctrinal Analysis*, 9 Art & L. 15 (1984)

Robert A. Gorman, *The Recording Musician and Union Power: A Case Study of the American Federation of Musicians*, 37 Sw. L.J. 697 (1983)

John M. Kernochan, *Music Performing Rights Organizations in the United States of America: Special Characteristics, Restraints, and Public Attitudes*, 10 Colum.-VLA J.L. & Arts 333 (1986)

Judy A. Kim, *The Performers' Plight in Sound Recordings — Unique to the U.S.: A Comparative Study of the Development of Performers' Rights in the United States, England and France*, 10 Colum.-VLA J.L. & Arts 453 (1986)

U.S. Copyright Office, *Performance Rights in Sound Recordings*, Serial No. 15, Report to the House Subcommittee on Courts, Civil Liberties of the House Judiciary Comm. (June 1978)

E. Fair Use

Douglas Baird, *Changing Technology and Unchanging Doctrine: Sony Corporation v. Universal Studios, Inc.,* 1984 Sup. Ct. Rev. 237

Michael A. Chagaves, *Parody or Piracy: The Protective Scope of the Fair Use Defense to Copyright Infringement Actions Regarding Parodies,* 12 Colum.-VLA J.L. & Arts 229 (1988)

Robert C. Denicola, *Copyright and Free Speech: Constitutional Limitations on the Protection of Expression,* 67 Cal. L. Rev. 283 (1979)

William A. Fisher, *Reconstructing the Fair Use Doctrine,* 101 Harv. L. Rev. 1659 (1988)

Jane C. Ginsburg, *Reproduction of Protected Works for University Research or Teaching,* 39 J. Copyright Soc'y 181 (1992)

Paul Goldstein, *Copyright and the First Amendment,* 70 Colum. L. Rev. 983 (1970)

Wendy J. Gordon, *Fair Use as Market Failure: A Structural and Economic Analysis of the Betamax Case and Its Predecessors,* 82 Colum. L. Rev. (1982)

Karen Burke LeFevre, *The Tell-Tale "Heart": Determining "Fair" Use of Unpublished Texts,* 55 Law & Contemp. Probs. 153 (1992)

Pierre N. Leval, *Toward a Fair Use Standard,* 103 Harv. L. Rev. 1105 (1990)

Scott M. Martin, *Photocopying and the Doctrine of Fair Use: The Duplication of Error,* 39 J. Copyright Soc'y 345 (1992)

Melville B. Nimmer, *Does Copyright Abridge the First Amendment Guarantees of Free Speech and Press?,* 17 UCLA L. Rev. 1180 (1970)

James L. Oakes, *Copyrights and Copyremedies: Unfair Use and Injunctions,* 38 J. Copyright Soc'y 63 (1990)

L. Ray Patterson, *Free Speech, Copyright, and Fair Use,* 40 Vand. L. Rev. 1 (1987)

L. Ray Patterson, *Private Copyright and Public Communication: Free Speech Endangered,* 28 Vand. L. Rev. 1161 (1975)

Richard Posner, *When Is Parody Fair Use?,* 21 J. Legal Stud. 67 (1992)

Leo Raskind, *A Functional Interpretation of Fair Use: The Fourteenth Donald C. Brace Memorial Lecture,* 31 J. Copyright Soc'y 601 (1984)

Leon E. Seltzer, *Exemptions and Fair Use in Copyright: The "Exclusive Rights" Tensions in the New Copyright Act,* 24 Bull. Copyright Soc'y 215 (1977)

Lloyd L. Weinreb, *Fair's Fair: A Comment on the Fair Use Doctrine,* 103 Harv. L. Rev. 1137 (1990)

Alfred C. Yen, *When Authors Won't Sell: Parody, Fair Use and Efficiency in Copyright Law,* 62 U. Colo. L. Rev. 79 (1991)

Joseph E. Young, *Copyright and the New Technologies — The Case of Library Photocopying,* 28 ASCAP Copyright L. Symp. 51 (1982)

F. Remedies

Ralph S. Brown, *Civil Remedies for Intellectual Property Invasions: Themes and Variations,* 55 Law & Contemp. Probs. 45 (1992)

Wendy J. Gordon, *Of Harms and Benefits: Torts, Restitution and Intellectual Property,* 21 J. Legal Stud. 449 (1992)

Daniel M. Jochnowitz, Note, *Proof of Harm: A Dangerous Prerequisite for Copyright Protection,* 10 Colum.-VLA J.L. & Arts 153 (1985)

Peter Jaszi, *505 and All That — The Defendant's Dilemma,* 55 Law & Contemp. Probs. 107 (1992)

John M. Kernochan, *Imperatives for Enforcing Author's Rights,* 11 Colum.-VLA J.L. & Arts 587 (1987)

Timothy J. McClimon, Note, *Denial of the Preliminary Injunction in Copyright Infringement Cases: An Emerging Judicially Crafted Compulsory License,* 10 Colum.-VLA J.L. & Arts 277 (1986)

Nancy J. Niemeier, Note, *The Right to Trial by Jury in Copyright Infringement Suits Seeking Statutory Damages,* 17 S. Ill. U. L.J. 135 (1992)

William Patry, *The Right to a Jury in Copyright Cases,* 29 J. Copyright Soc'y 139 (1981)

Andrew W. Stumpff, Note, *The Availability of Jury Trials in Copyright Infringement Cases: Limiting the Scope of the Seventh Amendment,* 83 Mich. L. Rev. 1950 (1985)

Tiffany D. Trunko, Note, *Remedies for Copyright Infringement: Respecting the First Amendment,* 89 Colum. L. Rev. 1940 (1989)

CHAPTER 7. COPYRIGHT PROTECTION OF COMPUTER SOFTWARE

Philip Abromats, *Nondisclosure of Preexisting Works in Software Copyright Registrations: Inequitable Conduct in Need of a Remedy,* 32 Jurimetrics J. 571 (1992)

Ellen M. Bierman, Note, *It Walks Like a Duck, Talks Like a Duck, ... But Is It a Duck? Making Sense of Substantial Similarity Law as It Applies to User Interfaces,* 16 U. Puget Sound L. Rev. 319 (1992)

Anthony L. Clapes, Patrick Lynch & Mark R. Steinberg, *Silicon Epics and Binary Bards: Determining the Proper Scope of Copyright Protection for Computer Programs,* 34 UCLA L. Rev. 1495 (1987)

Randall Davis, *The Nature of Software and Its Consequences for Establishing and Evaluating Similarity,* 5 Software L.J. 299 (1992)

Walter A. Effross, *Assaying* Computer Associates v. Altai: *How Will the "Golden Nugget" Test Pan Out?,* 19 Rutgers Computer & Tech. L.J. 1 (1993)

Gary R. Ignatin, Comment, *Let the Hackers Hack: Allowing the Reverse Engineering of Copyrighted Computer Programs to Achieve Compatibility,* 140 U. Pa. L. Rev. 1999 (1992)

David W. Maher, *The Shrink-Wrap License: Old Problems in a New Wrapper,* 34 J. Copyright Soc'y 292 (1987)

Peter S. Menell, *An Analysis of the Scope of Copyright Protection for Application Programs,* 42 Stan. L. Rev. 1045 (1989)

Peter S. Menell, *Tailoring Legal Protection for Computer Software,* 39 Stan. L. Rev. 1329 (1987)

Arthur R. Miller, *Copyright Protection for Computer Programs, Databases, and Computer-Generated Works: Is Anything New Since CONTU?,* 106 Harv. L. Rev. 977 (1993)

Raymond T. Nimmer and Patricia A. Krauthaus, *Copyright and Software Technology Infringement: Defining Third Party Development Rights*, 62 Ind. L.J. 13 (1986)

Note, *Archival Backup Copying of Software: How Broad a Right?*, 14 Rutgers Computer & Tech. L.J. 391-412 (1988)

John W.L. Ogilvie, Note, *Defining Computer Program Parts Under Learned Hand's Abstractions Test in Software Copyright Infringement Cases*, 91 Mich. L. Rev. 526 (1992)

Leo Raskind, *The Uncertain Case for Special Legislation Protecting Computer Software*, 47 U. Pitt. L. Rev. 1131 (1986)

David A. Rice, *Public Goods, Private Contract and Public Policy: Federal Preemption of Software License Prohibitions Against Reverse Engineering*, 53 U. Pitt. L. Rev. 543 (1992)

Pamela Samuelson, *Allocating Ownership Rights in Computer-Generated Works*, 47 U. Pitt. L. Rev. 1185 (1986)

Pamela Samuelson, *Computer Programs, User Interfaces, and Section 102(b) of the Copyright Act of 1976: A Critique of* Lotus v. Paperback, 6 High Tech. L.J. 209 (1992)

Pamela Samuelson, *Modifying Copyrighted Software: Adjusting Copyright Doctrine to Accommodate a Technology*, 28 Jurimetrics J. 179 (1986)

Pamela Samuelson, *Some New Kinds of Authorship Made Possible by Computers and Some Intellectual Property Questions They Raise*, 53 U. Pitt. L. Rev. 685 (1992)

Peter G. Spivack, Note, *Does Form Follow Function? The Idea/Expression Dichotomy in Copyright Protection of Computer Software*, 38 UCLA L. Rev. 723 (1988)

Richard H. Stern, *Legal Protection of Screen Displays and Other User Interfaces for Computers: A Problem in Balancing Incentives for Creation Against Need for Free Access to the Utilitarian*, 14 Colum.-VLA J.L. & Arts 283 (1990)

Stephen Kyle Tapp & Daniel E. Wanat, *Computer Software Copyright Issues: Section 117 and Fair Use*, 22 Mem. St. U. L. Rev. 197 (1992)

Timothy S. Teter, Note, *Merger and the Machines: An Analysis of the Pro-Compatibility Trend in Computer Software Copyright Cases*, 45 Stan. L. Rev. 1061 (1993)

Charles Walter, *Defining the Scope of Software Copyright Protection for Maximum Public Benefit*, 14 Rutgers Computer & Tech. L.J. 1 (1988)

CHAPTER 8. OTHER LEGAL PROTECTION FOR CREATIVITY

Craig Y. Allison, Note, *Does a Copyright Coowner's Duty to Account Arise Under Federal Law?*, 90 Mich. L. Rev. 1998 (1992)

James M. Amend, *The Geographical Scope of Injunctions in Intellectual Property Cases*, 77 Trademark Rep. 49 (1987)

Marc J. Apfelbaum, Note, *Copyright and the Right of Publicity: One Pea in Two Pods?*, 71 Geo. L.J. 1567 (1983)

Douglas G. Baird, *Common Law Intellectual Property and the Legacy of International News Service v. Associated Press*, 50 U. Chi. L. Rev. 411 (1983)

Douglas G. Baird, Note, *Human Cannonballs and the First Amendment: Zacchini v. Scripps-Howard Broadcasting Co.*, 30 Stan. L. Rev. 1185 (1978)

Ralph S. Brown, *Copyright and Its Upstart Cousins: Privacy, Publicity, Unfair Competition: The Sixteenth Donald C. Brace Memorial Lecture*, 33 J. Copyright Soc'y 301 (1986)

Mark A. Fischer, *Reserving All Rights Beyond Copyright: Non-Statutory Restrictive Notices*, 34 J. Copyright Soc'y 249 (1987)

Ted D. Lee & Ann Livingston, *The Road Less Traveled: State Court Resolution of Patent, Trademarks or Copyright Disputes*, 19 St. Mary's L.J. 703 (1988)

L. Ray Patterson, *Copyright Overextended: A Preliminary Inquiry into the Need for a Federal Statute of Unfair Competition*, 17 U. Dayton L. Rev. 385 (1992)

Pamela Samuelson, *Information as Property: Do* Ruckelshaus *and* Carpenter *Signal a Changing Direction in Intellectual Property Law?*, 38 Cath. U. L. Rev. 365 (1989)

Pamela Samuelson, *Reviving* Zacchini: *Analyzing First Amendment Defenses in Right of Publicity and Copyright Cases*, 57 Tul. L. Rev. 836 (1983)

Peter Shapiro, *The Validity of Registered Trademarks for Titles and Characters after the Expiration of Copyright on the Underlying Work*, 31 ASCAP Copyright L. Symp. 69 (1984)

David E. Shipley & Jeffrey S. Hay, *Protecting Research: Copyright, Common-Law Alternatives and Federal Pre-Emption*, 63 N.C. L. Rev. 125 (1984)

CHAPTER 9. FEDERAL PREEMPTION OF STATE LAW

Howard B. Abrams, *Copyright, Misappropriation, and Preemption: Constitutional and Statutory Limits of State Protection*, 1983 Sup. Ct. Rev. 509

Ralph S. Brown, *Unification: A Cheerful Requiem for Common Law Copyright*, 24 UCLA L. Rev. 1070 (1977)

Jennifer R. Clarke, Note, *The California Resale Royalties Act as a Test Case for Preemption Under the 1976 Copyright Law*, 81 Colum. L. Rev. 1315 (1981)

Sidney A. Diamond, *Preemption of State Law*, 25 Bull. Copyright Soc'y 204 (1978)

Henry David Fetter, *Copyright Revision and the Preemption of State "Misappropriation" Law: A Study in Judicial and Congressional Interaction*, 27 ASCAP Copyright L. Symp. 1 (1982)

G.L. Francione, *The California Art Preservation Act and Federal Preemption by the 1976 Act — Equivalence and Actual Conflict*, 31 ASCAP Copyright L. Symp. 105 (1984)

Paul Goldstein, *Preempted State Doctrines, Involuntary Transfers and Compulsory Licenses: Testing the Limits of Copyright*, 24 UCLA L. Rev. 1107 (1977)

Jonathan Ellis Moskin, *Make Room for the Stars: Copyright Preemption and the Right of Publicity*, 33 ASCAP Copyright L. Symp. 159 (1987)

David E. Shipley, *Refusing to Rock the Boat, The* Sears/Compco *Preemption Doctrine Applied to* Bonito Boats v. Thundercraft, 25 Wake Forest L. Rev. 385 (1990)

CHAPTER 10. INTERNATIONAL DIMENSION OF COPYRIGHT

Gyorgy Boytha, *Some Private International Law Aspects of the Protection of Authors' Rights,* Copyright 399 (Oct. 1988)

Christine L. Chinni, *Droit D'Auteur Versus the Economics of Copyright: Implications for American Law of Accession to the Berne Convention,* 14 W. New Eng. L. Rev. 145 (1992)

Marc L. Damschroder, Note, *Intellectual Property Rights and the GATT: United States Goals in the Uruguay Round,* 21 Vand. J. Transnat'l L. 367 (1988)

R. Michael Gadbaw & T. Richards, Intellectual Property Rights: Global Consensus, Global Conflict? (1988)

Paul Edward Geller, *Copyright Protection in the Berne Union: Analyzing the Issues,* 13 Colum.-VLA J.L. & Arts 435 (1989)

General Accounting Office, *International Trade: Strengthening Worldwide Protection of Intellectual Property Rights,* GAO/NSIAD-87-65 (April 1987)

Jane C. Ginsburg & John M. Kernochan, *One Hundred and Two Years Later: The United States Adheres to the Berne Convention,* 13 Colum.-VLA J.L. & Arts 1 (1988)

Jane C. Ginsburg, *Colors in Conflicts: Moral Rights and the Foreign Exploitation of Colorized U.S. Motion Pictures,* 36 J. Copyright Soc'y 81 (1988)

Jerome Huet & Jane C. Ginsburg, *Computer Programs in Europe: A Comparative Analysis of the 1991 EC Software Directive,* 30 Colum. J. Transnat'l L. 327 (1992)

Robert A. Jacobs, *Work-for-Hire and the Moral Right Dilemma in the European Community: A U.S. Perspective,* 16 B.C. Int'l & Comp. L. Rev. 29 (1993)

Beryl R. Jones, *An Introduction to the European Economic Community and Intellectual Property,* 18 Brooklyn J. Int'l L. 665 (1992)

Georges Koumantos, *Private International Law and the Berne Convention,* Copyright 415 (Oct. 1988)

Marshall A. Leaffer, *Protecting U.S. Intellectual Property Abroad: Toward a New Multilateralism,* 76 Iowa L. Rev. 273 (1991)

Carol Motyka, *U.S. Participation in the Berne Convention and High Technology,* 39 ASCAP Copyright L. Symp. 107 (1992)

David Nimmer, *Nation, Duration, Violation, Harmonization: An International Copyright Proposal for the United States,* 55 Law & Contemp. Probs. 211 (1992)

Leo Raskind, *Protecting Computer Software in the European Economic Community: The Innovative New Directive,* 18 Brooklyn J. Int'l L. 729 (1992)

Alfred L. Rinaldo, Jr., *The Scope of Copyright Protection in the Unites States Under Existing Inter-American Relations,* 22 Bull. Copyright Soc'y 417 (1984)

Hamish R. Sandison, *The Berne Convention and the Universal Copyright Convention: The American Experience,* 11 Colum.-VLA J.L. & Arts 89 (1986)

Symposium, *Trade-Related Aspects of Intellectual Property,* 22 Vand. J. Transnat'l L. 689 (1989)

U.S. International Trade Commission, *Foreign Protection of Intellectual Property Rights and the Effect on U.S. Industry and Trade* (Investigation No. 332-245 under Section 332(g) of the Tariff Act of 1930) (Feb. 1988)
Edward Slavko Yambrusic, Trade-Based Approaches to the Protection of Intellectual Property (1992)

Table of Cases

References are to pages. Principal cases and the pages
where they appear are in italics.

Index

___

A

933

G

INTELLECTUAL PROPERTY—Cont'd
Right of publicity.
  Legal protection for creativity, pp. 804 to 819.
State law.
  Preemption of state law.
    Copyright act of 1976.
      Section 301 preemptions, pp. 843 to 872.
    Supreme court preemption decisions, pp. 831 to 843.

INTERNATIONAL DIMENSION OF COPYRIGHT, pp. 873 to 901.
Authorship.
  Protection of alien authors.
    U. S. based copyright actions with international dimension, pp. 883 to 885.
  Protection of U. S. works in foreign fora.
    Issues left open by Berne and Universal Copyright Conventions, pp. 896, 897.
Berne Convention, pp. 874 to 877.
  Protection of U. S. works in foreign fora.
    Issues left open by, pp. 896 to 900.
  Structure of leading multilateral copyright treaties, pp. 878 to 880.
Bilateral copyright arrangements, pp. 881 to 883.
Brussels Satellite Convention.
  Other major multilateral treaties related to copyrights, pp. 880, 881.
Extraterritorial elements.
  Jurisdiction of U. S. courts to adjudicate copyright claims presenting, pp. 885 to
    896.
Geneva Phonograms Convention.
  Other major multilateral treaties related to copyrights, pp. 880, 881.
Grants of right.
  Protection of U. S. works in foreign fora.
    Issues left open by Berne and Universal Copyright Convention, pp. 896 to 900.
Historical perspective.
  Early history of U. S. international copyright relations, pp. 874 to 877.
Infringement.
  Application of U. S. copyright law to infringements carrying beyond U. S. borders,
    pp. 889 to 896.
Jurisdiction.
  Claims before U. S. courts alleging violation of rights abroad.
    Jurisdiction of U. S. courts to adjudicate copyright claims presenting
      extraterritorial element, pp. 885 to 888.
Trade-based measures to encourage respect of U. S. copyright interests, pp. 900, 901.
Universal Copyright Convention.
  Protection of U. S. works in foreign fora.
    Issues left open by, pp. 896 to 900.
  Structure of leading multilateral copyright treaties, pp. 878 to 880.

J

JOINT WORKS.
Duration of copyright, p. 41.
Ownership.
  Initial ownership, pp. 271 to 281.

JUKEBOXES.
Jukebox exemption.
  Public performance and display.
    Copyright act of 1976.
      Sections 116, 116A, pp. 543, 544.

O

P

PREEMPTION OF STATE LAW, pp. 831 to 872.
Case law.
  Copyright act of 1976.
    Section 301.
      Development of case law, pp. 850 to 872.
    Intellectual property cases.
      Supreme court preemption decisions, pp. 831 to 843.
Copyright act of 1976.
  Section 301.
    Development of case law, pp. 850 to 872.
    Saga of section 301, pp. 843 to 850.
Intellectual property.
  Supreme court preemption decisions in intellectual property cases, pp. 831 to 843.
Rights equivalent to copyright.
  Copyright act of 1976.
    Section 301.
      Development of case law, pp. 854 to 872.
Supremacy clause, p. 831.
Works coming within subject matter.
  Copyright law.
    Copyright act of 1976.
      Section 301.
        Development of case law, pp. 850 to 854.

PROGRAMS.
Computers.
  See COMPUTERS.

PUBLICATION.
Notice of copyright.
  See FORMALITIES.

PUBLIC BROADCASTING.
Public performance and display.
  Exemptions from rights of public performance and display.
    Copyright act of 1976.
      Section 118, pp. 544, 545.

PUBLIC DISTRIBUTION.
Computers.
  Copyright act of 1976.
    Section 109(c).
      Computer-software rental amendments of 1990, pp. 492, 493.
Droit de Suite, pp. 494, 495.
Imports.
  Copyright act of 1976.
    Section 501(a).
      Infringement of copyright.
        Imports of copies or phonorecords, p. 495.
    Section 602(a).
      Infringing importation of copies or phonorecords, p. 495.
  Right of importation, pp. 495 to 498.
Phonorecords, pp. 489 to 498.
  Importation right, pp. 495 to 498.
  Record rental amendment of 1984, pp. 491 to 493.
Public lending right, pp. 493, 494.
Right to distribute.
  Copyright act of 1976.
    Section 106(3), pp. 489 to 498.

ROYALTIES.
Phonorecords.
  Right to make phonorecords.
    Royalty rate and copyright royalty tribunal, pp. 453 to 456.

S

SCULPTURAL WORKS.
Copies.
  Infringement generally, pp. 444 to 448.
Subject matter of copyright, pp. 179 to 216.
  Copyright act of 1976.
    Section 101.
      Definitions, p. 186.

SECONDARY TRANSMISSIONS.
Public performance and display.
  Exemptions from rights of public performance and display, pp. 536 to 540.

SEMICONDUCTOR CHIPS.
Computers, pp. 776 to 779.

SOFTWARE.
Computers.
  See COMPUTERS.

SOUND RECORDINGS.
Audio home recording act of 1992, pp. 459, 460.
Formalities.
  Notice.
    P-notice for sound recordings, pp. 374, 375.
Phonorecords.
  General provisions.
    See PHONORECORDS.
Public distribution.
  Copyright act of 1976.
    Section 109(b).
      Record rental amendment of 1984, pp. 491 to 493.
Public performance and display.
  Exemptions from rights of public performance and display.
    Copyright act of 1976.
      Section 114, pp. 540 to 543.
Record rental amendment of 1984.
  Copyright act of 1976.
    Section 109(b), pp. 491 to 493.
Reproduction of works.
  Copyright act of 1976.
    Section 114.
      Sound recordings under, pp. 457 to 460.

STATE LAW.
Preemption of state law, pp. 831 to 872.

STATUTE OF ANNE, pp. 1 to 4.

STATUTE OF LIMITATIONS.
Infringement, p. 680.

SUBJECT MATTER OF COPYRIGHT.
Architectural works, pp. 216 to 221.
Authorship.
  Copyright act of 1976.
    Section 102(a) in general, p. 85.

SUBJECT MATTER OF COPYRIGHT—Cont'd
Sculptural works—Cont'd
  Copyright act of 1976—Cont'd
    Section 113.
      Scope of exclusive rights, pp. 186, 187.
Typeface designs.
  Copyrightability, p. 210.
Useful articles, pp. 187 to 216.

SUBSISTING COPYRIGHTS.
Duration of copyright.
  Copyright act of 1976.
    Section 304, pp. 328, 329.

SUPREMACY CLAUSE.
Preemption of state, p. 831.

T

TEACHER EXCEPTION.
Works made for hire.
  Work for hire under 1976 act and teacher exception, pp. 267 to 270.

TELEVISION.
Cable transmissions.
  Public performance and display.
    Exemptions from rights of public performance and display.
      Secondary transmissions, pp. 536 to 540.
Public performance and display.
  Cable transmissions.
    Exemptions from rights of public performance and display, pp. 536 to 540.
  General provisions.
    See PUBLIC PERFORMANCE AND DISPLAY.

TRADE DRESS.
Infringement of copyrights, pp. 819 to 830.

TRADEMARKS.
Distinctions between copyrights and trademarks, pp. 62 to 77.

TRANSFERS OF OWNERSHIP, pp. 282 to 306.
Beneficial ownership, pp. 304 to 306.
By operation of law, pp. 302, 303.
Collective works.
  Contributions to collective works, p. 303.
Divisibility, pp. 282 to 289.
Recordation, pp. 289 to 291.
Scope of grant, pp. 291 to 304.
Termination of transfers, pp. 345 to 357.
  Copyright act of 1976.
    Section 203.
      Distinctions between termination rights under section 304(c) and section 203,
        pp. 353, 354.
      Summary of termination provisions, pp. 351, 352.
    Section 304(c).
      Summary of termination provisions under, pp. 351 to 353.

TREATIES.
Berne Convention.
  General provisions.
    See BERNE CONVENTION.
Bilateral copyright arrangements, pp. 881, 882.